MW00713222

For a complete discussion of the stock photo industry from both the stock agency's and the photographer's points of view, read the "Stock Photography Spotlight" on page 5.

1991 Photographer's Market

Managing Editor, Market Books Department:
Constance J. Achabal

International Standard Serial Number
0147-247X
International Standard Book Number
0-89879-424-2

1991
Photographer's Market

Where & How to Sell Your Photographs

Edited by
Sam A. Marshall

Assisted by
Veronica Gliatti

Cincinnati, Ohio

Contents

1 **From the Editor**

3 **How to Use Your Photographer's Market**

5 **Stock Photography Spotlight,** *by Sam A. Marshall*

14 **The Business of Photography**

14 *Copyrights/rights*
16 *Pricing and negotiating*
17 *Financial recordkeeping*
18 *Taxes*
20 *Insurance — business and personal*
21 *Model/property releases*

22 *Filing prints and transparencies*
22 *Marketing and self-promotion*
22 *Cover letters/queries/resumes*
23 *Mailing photo submissions*
24 *Portfolios*
24 *Advertising*
25 *Agents and reps*

Special Business Feature

26 **Copyright and Work for Hire: What Every Photographer Needs to Know,** *by M. C. Valada*

The Markets

33 **Advertising, Public Relations and Audiovisual Firms**

66 *Close-up: Nick Vedros, Vedros & Associates*
As this veteran advertising photographer points out, focusing your vision and career is a matter of "asking the right questions."

110 *Close-up: Bob Lukeman and Gordon Blocker, Lukeman-Blocker Productions, Inc.*
There's a high-tech revolution underway in AV, film and video — and plenty of room for photographers who just "get in and learn it," says this successful production team.

120 **Book Publishers**

153 **Businesses and Organizations**

170 *Close-up: Neal Slavin, Photographer*
Making a visual statement — and building client relationships — grows out of commitment to one's standards and ideas and to the client's message, says this celebrated commercial and fine art photographer.

174 **Galleries**

178 *Close-up: Herbert Ascherman, Jr., The Ascherman Gallery*
To further your career, become a better judge of your own work, this gallery owner recommends.

201 Newspapers and Newsletters

218 *Close-up: Bob Sacha, News/Magazine Photographer*
For both the accomplished news "stringer" and the ambitious beginner, self-assignments are a great way to show photo editors you can handle the assignment, advises this former UPI freelancer.

227 Paper Products

236 *Close-up: Carol Gibson, Hallmark Cards, Inc.*
This greeting card photo buyer suggests some methods that will give you the competitive edge in the multi-billion-dollar-a-year paper products industry.

245 Publications

246 **Consumer Publications**

294 *Close-up: D. Gorton, Photographer*
"Everything you see you can sell," says this experienced editorial photographer who tells how you can find multiple marketing opportunities in every shoot.

332 *Close-up: M.C. Marden, People Magazine*
The photo editor of People *outlines the qualities photographers need to be more successful in the "people" market.*

377 **Special Interest Publications**

380 *Close-up: Doug Damerst, AAA World*
When shooting for the special needs of some special interest magazines, some of your best work may very well go on off-camera, as this association publication's editor points out.

433 **Trade Publications**

457 *Close-up: Mike Delia, Firehouse*
Sometimes the best pictures for trade publications come from inside — "where the action is," this trade journal art director suggests.

500 Record Companies

510 *Close-up: Dave Bett, Relativity Records*
This record industry art director predicts independent record companies are the wave of the future for musicians — and photographers.

518 Stock Photo Agencies

561 *Close-up: Richard Steedman, The Stock Market, Inc.*
Success in the stock photo industry and related markets can be found, this stock agency president recommends, by reading the "signs of the times."

Services & Opportunities

573 **Contests**

578 **Workshops**

582 *Close-up: Roger Fremier and Gail Pierce, The Photographic Center of Monterey Peninsula*
According to this team of workshop professionals, participating in a photographic workshop can bring you many unexpected joys and insights.

586 **Recommended Books & Publications**

589 **Professional Organizations**

590 **Glossary**

594 **First Markets Index**

596 **Index**

From the Editor

Photography editor—and sometimes photographer—Sam Marshall, is seen here in the field—in the deforested vicinity of the volcano, Mt. St. Helens, in the state of Washington.

As one professional photographer recently observed, "Anyone who owns a camera can be a photographer . . . and almost everyone owns a camera." However, as we all know, not every photographer who attempts to sell his pictures is successful. He may have abundant creativity and technical ability, yet lack practical knowledge of photo-buying markets or fail to follow accepted business practices. *Photographer's Market* helps every photographer in overcoming these problems with its detailed listings of photo buyers' needs, insightful interviews with working professionals and continually upgraded business guidelines.

Since it is intended as a working reference, *Photographer's Market* contains many useful features. The market listings, for instance, are grouped into 13 different categories all looking to buy freelance photos or to assign work to freelancers. This year's edition contains some 450 new markets marked with an asterisk (*) for easy locating. A good introduction to the format of the listings is the section titled, How to Use Your Photographer's Market, on page 3.

There are also a number of practical new features. For instance, companies with a need for audiovisual, film and video materials have been marked with a special AV symbol (∎) for easier recognition. There are more than 300 such companies throughout the book. Most can be found in the first section which now incorporates the previously separate section, Audiovisual, Film and Video Firms, under the heading, Advertising, Public Relations and Audiovisual Firms. Other sections with AV listings include Businesses and Organizations, Galleries, Stock Photo Agencies, Contests and Workshops. Some listings, especially in the first section, also have more detailed information under the subheading, Audiovisual Needs.

In the Publications section, two markets with similar, specialized needs—Association

Publications and Company Publications—have been combined under the new heading, Special Interest Publications.

Another new feature in this edition is the First Markets Index. This index lists some 200 markets which are especially good for freelancers breaking into photography. Typically, these markets provide little or no payment for photos but do offer exposure, photocredits, and tearsheets or extra contributor's copies as compensation.

In addition to these features, this edition includes articles and interviews dealing with professionalism in photography. The first article is the Stock Photography Spotlight, which explores the expansive growth and opportunity for photographers in the stock photography field. Immediately following is the section titled, The Business of Photography, which reviews business practices and considerations essential to success of any freelance business. Also, this segment includes a special feature, Copyright and Work for Hire: What Every Photographer Needs to Know. This article explores legal issues of copyright ownership in light of the 1989 Supreme Court decision which has reaffirmed creators' rights.

Interviews with the experts

Once again, the popular Close-up interviews with guest experts are featured throughout the book. Each of the 13 articles in this edition addresses specific market conditions and needs. However, by reading all of them you can gain insight into many of the trends and business practices that play a role in today's photography industry.

Among this year's Close-ups are advertising photographer Nick Vedros, who discusses the process of developing a photographic vision and the value of mentoring; audiovisual producers Bob Lukeman and Gordon Blocker, who point out the high-tech revolution underway in the AV, film and video fields and strategies for breaking into those areas; news/magazine photographer Bob Sacha, who points out that good business skills and career success go hand-in-hand; editorial photographer D. Gorton, who comments on planning multi-market strategies and how to set one's work apart from others in today's highly competitive marketplace; photo editor M.C. Marden, who shares her views on the emergence of "people news" as a mainstay in consumer magazines; trade publication art director Mike Delia, who advises good action shots and strong photojournalistic treatment of subjects for sophisticated trade readerships; and art director Dave Bett, who recommends working with "indies" as "the best bet" in breaking into record company work.

As always, there are examples of successful freelance images throughout the book. With many interesting tips and comments from both photographers and photo buyers, these examples are especially helpful in showing what photo buyers are looking for. Also, greatly improved in this edition is the number of listings which include facsimile transmission (fax) numbers.

Freelance photography can be an exciting and profitable pursuit for every talented photographer who studies the always-changing marketplace and prepares himself to compete successfully. Accordingly, this new edition of *Photographer's Market* is dedicated to helping further your success in the coming year. I am confident that you will benefit from it time and again.

Sam A. Marshall

How to Use Your Photographer's Market

Before studying the listings and outlining your marketing strategies, read this section carefully for suggestions on how to make the most of your 1991 *Photographer's Market*. Pay special attention to the sample listing and the explanations of terms and abbreviations.

There are 13 market sections in the 1991 edition and each begins with a brief overview or introduction. The various markets differ in their practices, terms and requirements and it's important that you clearly understand the factors affecting how you do business with each market. Read this information in the introduction before singling out the listings you want to submit work to or query.

Keep in mind that the information you are reading in the listings came directly from key people with the firms listed. It is reported exactly as it was given to us. Accordingly, follow instructions and advice in the listings closely and provide the company or publication only with what it has requested.

The Glossary in the back of this book will explain unfamiliar terms you might discover while reading the listings.

For an explanation of the information given in the listings, match the numbered phrases in the hypothetical sample listing with the corresponding numbers in the copy that follows the listing.

> **(1)*RARE BIRD MAGAZINE**, 9999 Pennsylvania Ave. NW, Washington DC 22222. (202)999-9999. **(2)** Director: Thomas Finch. **(3)** Monthly magazine for birdwatchers, naturalists and general readership. **(4)** Estab. 1989. **(5)** Sample copy free with 8½×11 SAE, with approx. 65¢ postage.
> **Photo Needs: (6)** Uses 18-25 freelance photos per issue; majority purchased as part of photo/text packages. Interested in some stock photos. **(7)** Needs "photos of all species of wild birds, especially endangered species." Especially would like to see birds in their natural habitats, interacting with each other, in flight, in aquatic environments and so on. No strictly scenic shots; birds must be included in the shots. Special section on migratory birds in fall and spring each year; work is purchased six months in advance. **(8)** Model release required with any rare species of birds in captivity; captions required on all photos.
> **Making Contact & Terms: (9)** Query with story proposals or list of stock photo subjects. Submit finished manuscript with dupes of color slides for consideration. Do not send original transparencies. Provide resume, business card, flyer or brochure to be kept on file for possible future assignments. **(10)** Prefers to use 4×5 or larger format transparencies. Will consider 35mm transparencies; uses b&w only occasionally. **(11)** SASE. **(12)** Reports in 6-8 weeks. **(13)** Pays $200-350/color cover photo; $100-175/color inside photo; payment on b&w "depends on photo and how it's used." Pays on acceptance. Credit line given. **(14)** Buys one-time and promotional rights. **(15)** Previously published work and simultaneous submissions OK.
> **Tips: (16)** "Photographers should be highly selective in choosing their samples. We are currently saturated with North American species; we'd like to see more shots of varieties from the Southern Hemisphere. Get a copy of our publication and study it thoroughly for topics, story angles and styles of photo compositions. We need good action shots and would also like to have good close-ups of nesting as well as detailed plumage and facial shots."

(1) Asterisk. The (*) in front of a listing means that it's new to this edition.

(2) Contact person. The name and title of the person you should contact are given in most listings. If not, address your submission to the title listed after "Contact:".

(3) Descriptive information. Editorial descriptions and client lists appear in listings to help you slant your photography toward that specific publication or business.

(4) Established dates. The year in which a company or publication went into business is listed in this position if we have been given that information. Listings established in 1989 or 1990 are new businesses and possibly more open to freelance contributions.

(5) Available materials. Most listings will specify whether a sample copy of the publication, photo guidelines or client list are available. If there's a charge for providing these, that will be indicated also. When a listing mentions "SAE," it means to send a self-addressed envelope of the specified size along with the amount of postage required for having the sample mailed to you.

(6) Volume of work. The number or percentage of jobs assigned to freelancers or the number of photos bought gives you an idea of the size of the market.

(7) Photo needs. Specific photo needs for the year are included.

(8) Releases and captions. When a market states that it requires model releases for identifiable people, animals or property, you must have them available. A photo may meet a photo editor's needs exactly, but without the appropriate release it would be useless to him. Even if a market states that releases are optional or preferred, it's always a good idea to have them in hand when you submit photos.

(9) Method of contact. This specifies the recommended method of initial contact. If a listing requests samples, we have tried to clarify what types of samples it prefers. If the listing states it will keep material on file for possible future assignments, make sure your samples easily fit the average 8½ × 11" file.

(10) Image formats. This segment gives details about the preferred format of images to be submitted.

(11) Corresponding and submitting. If a market does not return submissions, especially unsolicited material, that is indicated in this area. Whenever corresponding with a listing, it is always professionally wise to include a business-size (#10), self-addressed, stamped envelope (SASE) to ensure a reply. If you are submitting material which you expect to have returned, you will also want to include a SASE of sufficient size and postage.

(12) Reporting time. "Reports in . . ." tells you how soon after a photo submission is sent you may expect to hear about your photo's status.

(13) Payment. This section breaks down the pay scale for the types of photo usage that are purchased.

(14) Rights. Note what types of rights the listing prefers to purchase. If several types are listed, it usually means the firm will negotiate. But not always. Be certain you and the photo buyer understand exactly what rights you are selling.

(15) Simultaneous submissions or previously published work. Markets (especially publications) which do not require exclusive submissions indicate this with an "OK" in this area of their listings. If it is not included, they will not accept such submissions.

(16) Tips. Be sure to read the tips in many of the listings. They can provide further insights into the photo buyer's needs.

Stock Photography Spotlight

by Sam A. Marshall

Stock photography — the selling and reselling of existing images — has been with us in some form virtually as long as photography has been in existence. One early would-be stock photographer, Mathew Brady, attempted to document the Civil War and resell images of that tragic historical moment — unsuccessfully — to an indifferent public. Another photography pioneer, Edward Steichen, later followed, recognizing the value of selling multiple reprint rights over single framed prints. However, stock photography as we know it today — a diverse, highly active agency-driven industry within an industry — is still quite a relatively recent phenomenon, having only come into its own within the last 10 to 20 years.

A recent industry estimate places the total number of stock photo agencies at close to 300, and newer agencies are being formed everyday. Some of the largest and most established firms have regional offices in various cities as well as overseas. Others are limited to regional markets, and some are even just single proprietor operations set up by photographers to market their own work. It is apparent that as more photo buyers discover the economic and practical benefits of stock over assignment photography more agencies will likely appear in response to accelerating demand.

In light of the tremendous growth and opportunity for photographers in today's stock industry, *Photographer's Market* believes that the key to your success in this complex market is a thorough understanding of it. Accordingly, we will share information and insights about this vast subject with you from a number of sources in this Spotlight report.

After a brief overview of the industry and trends in the marketplace, we will first look at stock photography from the stock agency's point of view — how agencies market stock photography, who their clients are, what they look for from photographers and so on. In the second part, we will look at stock in terms of the photographer's interests — how to approach and evaluate stock agencies, how to shoot for them, how to negotiate terms, and how to protect images and copyrights.

The how's and why's of the stock boom

The explosion in stock photography is quite like a chemical reaction: it's the result of several potent ingredients coming together. Photography certainly lends to the reaction, but the real catalysts are the economic pressures building in the larger marketplace (see the introduction to Advertising, Public Relations and Audiovisual Firms on page 33).

For these various economic and competitive reasons, more and more photo buyers have been seeking alternatives to buying photos which offer them the flexibility of maintaining a certain level of commercial activity while controlling costs. As photographers have also been looking to expand into new markets, more accomplished pros have been shooting primarily for stock and have helped to raise the standards of quality a great deal in the process. This has made stock photography all the more attractive to photo buyers.

In the not so distant past, stock photo agencies had labored under a reputation for typically offering bland, predictable, generic images, roughly the equivalent of "clip art" illustrations. Now that clients are finding that they can expect a high degree of style,

Sam A. Marshall is editor of Photographer's Market.

technique and uniqueness in stock images as well as a break on prices, they are turning to stock immediately instead of as a last resort.

The stock agency's point of view

Meeting client needs

Whether the "agent" is a corporate agency or an individual marketing his own existing images, the motive of stock photography is basically the same: to rent reprint rights to photos on a limited basis. An agency explores a client's needs, recommends specific images—or has them shot—according to the client's budget, and offers the rights for a set period of time, all in exchange for a fee. The agency will usually set up a contract with the photographer, who is typically paid royalties on sales on a quarterly schedule.

According to Richard Steedman, president of the New York-based stock agency, Stock Market, Inc. (also see interview on page 561, in Stock Photo Agencies), there are widespread misconceptions among freelance photographers about the functions of stock agencies. Initially, he notes, they think of stock as a way of unloading their "seconds" or making a quick sale of a handful of images.

"The modern agency is not an archives of photographs waiting for someone to come along and use. Instead, it's a marketing machine which is very active—even globally—in both the production of high-quality work and the pursuit of clients to make use of the work," says Steedman. "The agency works as a phantom client, assigning work to photographers, and then photographers craft pictures for the widest possible client needs."

Expecting high standards

Not only have photographers been helping to improve the quality of stock photos, but also, most stock agencies have been quick to upgrade their inventories since they seek to do business with top clients and expect high multiple resales of a given image. As Bob Roberts, of the H. Armstrong Roberts agency and immediate past president of the Picture Agency Council of America (PACA), points out, there is little or no room for amateurish work, "leftovers" or images that otherwise lack a strong ability to communicate visually.

"Technically, you've got to be at the top level," says Roberts. "The quality of images is improving so fast that it's even beyond the 'advanced amateur' level. It takes a lot of discipline and planning to learn to shoot for stock and anticipate what clients will buy." Accordingly, successful stock photographers work every week on the business of stock. Though not necessarily shooting stock every week, they are at the very least planning, propping, location scouting, casting, improving on technique or otherwise preparing for more stock business.

In a similar vein, Steedman says photographers must realize that stock is not a specialty but an industry unto itself. "We are not in the picture business . . . we are in the communications business," he remarks. "The finest photography is of little value if it does not help move the consumer toward a positive attitude regarding the client point of view, product or service. That is what the client pays for, and there is no escaping this fact."

Counting on originality

Steedman also points out that some photographers approach stock out of the desire to circumvent or cut out the assignment part of their industry and just sell pictures. They seem to chafe under the control of art directors or clients, and think that stock offers them the freedom to "do their own thing," he says.

"This is an unfortunate attitude because working within the system is precisely where one learns what this business is all about," he observes, noting that a great deal of stock work is geared toward advertising. "There *is* a lot of room for personal expression in our industry. We count on it from our photographers and encourage them to come up with new visual expressions to stay ahead of the competition. How to tell the same tale in fresh terms is an ongoing creative pursuit of all talented, intellectually active photographers. But let the amateur photographer dare to push weak, sloppy work over on a creative director of a major ad agency and he will fall flat."

As Steedman goes on to explain, a successful stock photographer typically "is very self-critical of his work and highly motivated to achieve high standards—just the kind of photographer every stock agency loves to have on board. So, the seasoning one gets in commercial work is essential if one is to succeed in a major way in this business. If a photographer cannot cut it commercially, there is little or no chance the result will be different in stock."

While agencies often advise aspiring stock photographers to review agency catalogs and industry references for insight into trends and quality, they are also quick to discourage imitation. Just now, the industry is shaking off its longstanding reputation for predictable, unimaginative images, and so many agencies have little patience for shopworn visual formulas. Also, there is a fine line between imitation and outright plagiarism, which most agencies strive to avoid at all costs. One of the industry's largest and most respected agencies, Comstock, Inc., has taken to running full-page ads against this practice in trade publications such as *Photo District News*. In these ads, the stock agency offers $1,000 rewards to anyone who reports on photographers who have plagiarized its images.

Looking for creativity

Agencies who are considering hiring a photographer vary in their requirements for an initial submission. Usually, after delivering a large quantity of photos—200, 500 or 1,000 images—photographers who sign on with an agency are expected to submit similar quantities on a regular basis. This can be either to fill in gaps in certain subject categories or to help build a file of specific images under that photographer's name, especially if he demonstrates a unique style.

It practically goes without saying that the images in the initial submission must be the photographer's best work, and tightly edited. According to Richard Steedman, the images should demonstrate the kind of work the photographer likes to do as well as reflect favorably on the photographer's professional status in the industry. Also, he adds, the submission should be prepared with the same care that one would give to preparing a portfolio for a major client in an assignment situation.

Once the photographer signs on and starts to produce for the agency, Steedman notes, aspects of the composition of images such as space for headlines, vertical or horizontal format, etc., are covered. "The submission will tell us all we need to know about the photographer," he says, explaining that the submission will reveal the degree of a photographer's creativity. "If it's there at all, it's there for all to see. We will not take on a photographer if we feel that we cannot make money with him."

Selling uniqueness

Though most agencies expect photographers to generate large quantities of photos, some will occasionally buy a few images outright. This is still rare and happens only when the images are of unusual subject matter and meet a certain client's needs. For instance, an agency may be looking for hard-to-duplicate setup shots or for unique editorial images of events or public figures. Some agencies specialize either in one subject, such as children, animals, science, sports, fashion or nature/travel, or a limited range of subject matter. Whether they have a few photos or an inventory of specialized images, photographers may find they have more to offer such an agency or one of the smaller regional firms.

Because agencies are placing much greater emphasis on quality over quantity, they are now limiting both the number of photographers they hire and the total amount of images in their files. They frequently purge lower-selling images—and photographers—to cut handling costs as well as to reinforce the client's perception of their images as fresh and unique. Another important way that agencies also stress uniqueness to clients is to hire and represent photographers exclusively.

Moving toward exclusivity

One benefit of exclusivity to agencies is, of course, that they can charge higher fees to clients. This is especially true when the agency represents a "name" photographer. However, competition among agency clients certainly plays the larger role in this trend. It's simply not good business to have the same image turn up in competing uses, such as ads or magazine covers in the same market. This is becoming even more crucial with the international market as more agencies do business with overseas firms.

Major agencies such as The Stock Market will most often not permit a photographer to work through other agencies. However, they will sometimes allow the photographer to continue selling his own work as long as it's not in conflict with the agency's stable of clients. Photographers who do desire to market different types of images to various agencies will usually contract with several regional or special subject agencies which have fewer problems with conflicting clients.

Marketing with newest methods

As several stock agency professionals have observed, stock has definitely become a "buyer's market." So agencies, just like photographers, have been scrambling to stake out a larger share of the market. This competition has spawned new ways of reaching and keeping customers.

Tried and true methods, such as trade advertising, mailings to prospects and trade show promotions, are how most agencies have built their client bases. Recently, however, a more targeted form of advertising—color catalogs which show a cross-section of an agency's available images—has practically become a staple of marketing to potential photo buyers. In particular, agencies which are developing inventories of top photographers are able to show off their roster of photographers much more effectively than in simple trade ads or brochures.

Some of the larger agencies publish several versions and sizes of their catalogs, and most publish periodic supplements which show new images. There are also industry directories such as the two-year-old *Stock Workbook* which include representative examples of images being offered by a wide cross-section of agencies. This 470-page directory, which features the images of more than 60 agencies and lists contact information for some 285 in all, is the largest of these.

Many art and creative directors, photo editors, corporate communications specialists, public relations staffers and other photo buyers either subscribe to or request catalogs and directories so they can research images to meet their needs. Henry Scanlon, whose agency, Comstock, Inc., published the first major stock catalog 10 years ago, has noted that cynics predicted art directors would shun catalogs, but now "they're the norm."[1]

One development that some in the industry predict will lead to "the stock photo agency of the future" is the use of computer and video technology in marketing and selling stock images. Some agencies are already sending out videotapes of stock stills and video footage as promotion pieces to clients. In particular, Comstock now has a computerized stock photo disk which holds about 450 images and can be used with various compatible desktop publishing systems. Clients who purchase the disk can call images off the disk and merge them right into their artwork. As videodisc technology is perfected and priced more affordably, it will likely become the primary vehicle of marketing for most agencies.

[1] Taken from "Stock Agencies Fighting for Bigger Market Shares," *Photo District News*, pg. 62, Sept. 1989.

Stock from the photographer's point of view

Is stock for you?

According to several stock agency owners, photographers must first "take stock" of themselves before getting into stock. After assessing their skills, their portfolio and their career objectives, photographers need to be very honest about whether stock helps them fulfill their ambitions as well as whether they are up to the challenges, these experts note.

"Stock gives you more control over your work," says Richard Steedman. "You can take charge of many additional opportunities for gaining exposure and generating sales, but a big factor is that you must know the ground rules."

Comstock's Henry Scanlon, while basically optimistic about career opportunities for photographers in stock, cautions photographers to consider realistically the current competitive climate. "There's always room for innovation, but [aspiring stock photographers] should realize that the level of work is very high. Being good isn't good enough. Study what different agencies do, look at what is selling and then do it better."

Finding the right agency

When looking for a first prospective agency, a photographer can ask himself lots of questions. Here are a few starters: What is the agency's specialty? Who are the agency's clients? How does my work help their clients? Am I a good match for them in terms of style, skill, experience and subject coverage? Do I have enough material to demonstrate my abilities? How much internal competition between photographers is there in this agency, and will my work be unique? Does the agency require an exclusive contract, and do I want to work exclusively or with several stock outlets? Does the contract specify transfer of copyrights? Does the agency provide timely reports of sales and royalties? How will working with this agency help me with sales and with my career objectives? Before even contacting a prospective agency, asking questions such as these can help a photographer to know whether he's ready to work in stock, or at least with this agency. Also, a photographer can avoid much wasted effort by realizing in advance if he's not a good fit for the agency.

There are also several key reasons why an agency might not be a good fit for the photographer. Primarily, it may simply be a difference between the needs of the agency and those of the photographer. However, it may also be a case of the agency's indifference to the needs of the photographer. Because the stock industry has been expanding so rapidly, a certain number of new firms have not yet acquired adequate organization or knowledge of ethical practices. Others simply choose to ignore them. Lawsuits often arise from abuse of photographer's rights, loss or theft of original images, late royalties and unshared profits. Being alert to such areas of potential problems is ultimately to the photographer's benefit.

Photographers should check how a prospective agency measures up. For instance, a good first step is to request copies of the agency's catalogs, contracts and various promotional materials. This can provide a great deal of insight about the agency's overall professionalism as well as specifics about terms, policies and payment schedules. Another method is to ask the agency for a list of its clients and some names and numbers of photographers on their roster. Both clients and photographers can be very instructive about an agency's practices, and a reputable firm should be willing to let a photographer contact them.

In particular, visiting an agency to meet its staff and see its facilities can be especially revealing. If after doing any or all of these things a photographer learns of anything suspicious or wants to confirm otherwise positive impressions, he can also make a point of talking to the Picture Agency Council of America. General inquiries are handled out of Philadelphia, at (215)386-8681. Complaints, on the other hand, should be directed to the Seattle branch, at (206)282-8116.

Reviewing the contract

The area of contracts is the one which determines in large part the relationship between the agency and the photographer, and as such, it is not one to be taken lightly. Photographers should look closely at *all* terms in a contract with a cautious eye. Ideally, an attorney should also study the contract for obscure, complicating clauses. Generally, it's better to work with agencies whose contracts are straightforward, rather than confusing or even deceptive.

Signing an exclusive contract offers many advantages to photographers, but can also limit their marketability and sales. On the plus side, agencies will often work more closely with photographers in developing a stylized inventory for specific client needs, and photographers may gain more insight into inside marketing strategies. However, some agencies are reluctant to guarantee a reliable level of income, so photographers need to think long and hard about their personal, long-term sales and marketing goals before locking into an exclusive contract. Regional agencies often require only limited exclusivity and so can offer more flexibility to photographers wanting exposure and sales in different markets.

Photographers especially need a thorough understanding of contract language in regard to copyright ownership and what rights the agency will offer to clients on their images. Typically, agencies will offer a wide variety of rights for limited periods according to a client's needs, i.e., exclusive rights to an image for three years or one-time reprint rights with no time designation. However, photographers must be very alert to any clauses that specify or suggest surrender of copyrights (see Copyright article on page 26). Some of the more common terms of this type include all rights, all reproduction rights, work for hire, in perpetuity (forever), assignment or transfer of rights, no right of reversion and exclusive property rights. Unless the opportunity and compensation are exceptionally good, photographers should never sign contracts containing such language.

One device that agencies have recently been using in the attempt to gain control of long-term rights is the automatic renewal clause. Basically, the clause works on the concept that every time the photographer delivers an image, the contract is automatically renewed for a specified number of years. A photographer may first approach an agency with the plan to work with it for a limited time period. So he signs a contract with these terms, and then finds he can't get out of it and resume his normal sales activity. Because these clauses, in effect, keep the photographer bound by the contract for much longer than he intended, photographers must also be careful not to sign such contracts. As current PACA President Marty Loken has noted, it is a common and not unreasonable practice for agencies to have marketing rights for a few years beyond the life of the contract. However, Loken speculates that a five-year limit will likely become standard.[2]

Clarifying fees and other costs

Stock contracts also commonly contain clauses about duping fees. Agencies often preserve original transparencies by making high-quality dupes which they then use for marketing purposes. Contracts will specify whether the agency will share the cost with the photographer, or pass on the entire cost to him. Also, some contracts allow the photographer upon termination of the contract to reclaim all dupes for which he has paid. However, in some cases, photographers must pay an additional charge to have them all returned.

Some of the major agencies have introduced a new charge: the filing fee. A typical fee is $2-per-slide, which reportedly goes to cover handling costs. Consider that a 200-slide submission would cost the photographer $400 and it's easy to see that this is a point to be weighed carefully. If a photographer is working for an agency which charges this fee, he generally should become more careful in editing his submissions in order to keep his costs down.

Marketing costs are another aspect of the terms covered in agency contracts. Generally,

[2] Taken from "A Closer Look at Stock," *Photo District News*, pg. 44, Sept. 1989.

Ethical guidelines for stock:

Before a photographer signs a contract with a stock photo agency, he needs some guarantee of fair treatment. The Picture Agency Council of America (PACA) has established a set of ethical guidelines to which all members in the council must adhere in order to retain their memberships. These guidelines are a good check list for the photographer to use when prospecting for an agency or negotiating his contract.

PACA members will openly and freely discuss with photographers:
- *Ownership of agency, and/or change thereof.*
- *Editing, inventory, and refiling procedures.*
- *Disposition of any suit or settlement pertaining to a specific photographer's work, including documentation if requested.*
- *International representation policies.*
- *Policies regarding free or reduced rate usages for charitable organizations.*
- *Sub agency or franchise representation policies.*

Member agencies should also offer photographers a fair and straightforward written contract, which should address such items as:
- *Payment schedule.*
- *Right to inspect agency records as they pertain to the individual photographer.*
- *Contract period and renewal.*
- *Charges, deductions or assessments related to the photographer's account.*
- *Procedure and schedule for return of photographs upon termination of contract.*

Also royalty statements should include:
- *An adequate photo description.*
- *A description or code for the usage.*
- *The amount of the photographer's share.*
- *An itemization of any deductions that are made.*

agencies will charge photographers for each image placed in their catalogs. Since approximately 20 percent of an agency's sales are spent on advertising and marketing, many agencies who charge photographers for this service feel quite justified in passing on that cost. The contract should specify exactly which of these costs and in what amounts the photographer is expected to cover.

When inspecting a contract, it's essential to realize that the overall profitability is more important than the percentage quoted. Commissions on sales typically range between 40 and 50 percent. However, photographers need to be aware that it's almost never straight profit. These various costs—plus taxes—can quickly strip away earnings on sales, and so photographers must read *and* understand the fine print which establishes the amounts and conditions of these various fees. Remember: real profit, or "net," is what is left after all the deductions are taken out.

Auditing the agency

One more area that is vital to a photographer's financial success with a stock agency is accountability. Primarily, a reputable agency should have a system of reporting regularly on all sales, fees charged and commissions to be paid. Also, payment should be made on a regular, timely basis. When agencies deviate from these practices, and especially from their own stated policies, photographers will often make an effort to monitor the agency or audit their sales records.

Most often, it is the smaller, more marginal stock agencies which are lax or unscrupulous in their accounting practices. However, as experts in the industry have noted, some larger agencies can be abusive, too. For their own protection, photographers should ask an agency directly about its accounting and payment policies, and look to see that such policies are spelled out in the contract.

Though it is not yet industry-wide, an organized agency will usually produce a monthly, itemized statement of sales and miscellaneous charges. Information that's also good to have on statements includes the names of clients who purchased usage of the pictures, clear identification of the images and quantities sold, and expected date of payment. Many agencies will typically pay photographers quarterly. On the other hand, some will pay upon receipt of payment from the client or in the next period if the client delays making payment for any good reason.

Unless a contract specifies that a photographer has the right to request an audit, a photographer who suspects he is being abused in this way may find the agency uncooperative in opening its books. Sometimes, the only recourse which a photographer has in such a case is legal action. However, an audit request can be more effective if several photographers working for the agency make a group request, and the accounting costs can be shared by the photographers. One accountant who specializes in the photography industry, Lou Biscotti, has pointed out that a fair, honest and organized agency takes this into its own hands, conducting annual audits with a Certified Public Accountant and reporting the findings to all contracted photographers.[3]

Shooting for stock

Though the clients of stock agencies are many of the same photo buyers as in the advertising, editorial and corporate markets, stock has its own particular nuances and needs which take some time to learn. As Richard Steedman has noted earlier, a photographer needs to have experience and creativity but the best way to learn stock is by actually working within the industry.

One of the primary methods of researching the needs of the market and learning what goes into highly marketable stock images is to study agency catalogs and stock industry references such as the *Stock Workbook*. Though it does not contain the visual information of catalogs and other stock directories, *Photographer's Market* can also be an excellent source of information about the subject and format needs of stock agencies (see listings in Stock Photo Agencies section, page 561). Other helpful resources include the *Stock Photography Handbook*, edited by Michal Heron and published by the American Society of Magazine Photographers; *Negotiating Stock Photo Prices*, by stock photographer, Jim Pickerell; and the monthly trade magazine, *Photo District News*.

In particular, if a photographer is not accustomed to obtaining model and property releases, he will find that they are practically indispensable when shooting for stock. Some agencies which specialize in news photography for editorial markets usually do not require such releases, but with the increase of legal retaliation in the general public more of these agencies are requiring them also.

For any work that is likely to be used as a magazine or book cover, releases are a "must." This also goes for all subjects which are of a sensational nature. Other subject matter that must also be authorized in writing include private property, homes, pets, boats, and government facilities and equipment. As Richard Steedman notes, getting the release is one more aspect of the photographer's professionalism vital to success in stock.

"Photographers have to stop trying to get around the issue of obtaining a proper model release," he says. "People are very litigious and will sue with no warning. For the most part

[3] Taken from "How to Audit Your Stock Agency," *Photo District News*, pg. 50, Sept. 1989.

stock agencies are not in the business of news gathering but of advertising and making profit. So, consequently agencies and photographers cannot hide behind the First Amendment to avoid the wrath of private individuals who feel that they have been commercially exploited."

Researching market trends

In regard to the content of stock images, Steedman points out (also see interview on page 561 in Stock Photo Agencies section) that stock photography reflects numerous trends in various other markets such as advertising and photojournalism. Many of these trends, he notes, have to do with style, technique, theme and subject matter. Much of this may already be apparent to photographers who work in these other major market areas. However, for the photographer unfamiliar with shifts in the social terrain, the reemergence of photojournalistic realism and the importance of symbolic content in photos, a great deal of market study is necessary.

"The best source of information of what is going on in the advertising world regarding content, trends, style and so on can be discovered by spending money and time in any large magazine store on a weekly basis," says Steedman, noting that research is a process that continually changes in response to the market. "Photographers cannot work in a vacuum. They must create images that speak to people's values." Accordingly, he adds, such research gives photographers a good window on trends in the stock world. "What is self-taught often sticks while spoonfed stuff is soon forgotten."

Real success stories

Success in stock photography is not acquired casually but comes through commitment to quality, professionalism and protecting one's interests. It's also vital to understand that success in stock will not happen overnight but is a process which may take three to five years to realize fully. As Craig Aurness, owner of the Los Angeles-based West Light agency notes in his special publication on the stock industry, *The Stock Report*, openness to learning and good business sense are becoming more valuable to photographers than mere creativity. "The real success stories," he observes, "are the businesslike photographers who listen to their agencies and produce, produce, produce."

The Business of Photography

While success in photography certainly requires creative and technical skills, a photographer who fails to see his work as a business and manage it effectively will not be able to survive and grow creatively.

For photographers who have not yet acquired a business sensibility, it's helpful to see things through the eyes of the people whose concerns are more financial than creative: the photo buyers. Many on the "other" side of the desk continually remind photographers that while photographers take pictures, they are not in the picture business. Instead, photographers and photo buyers are in one business together . . . communication. And in this business, professionalism and profit go hand-in-hand.

Photographers who see this distinction clearly function quite differently from strictly picture-oriented photographers. They approach their work with clients in terms of problem solving, i.e., What is the client trying to accomplish, and how can my images help him? Their creativity becomes collaborative and focused toward a clear objective. Most important, they learn to assign a value, or cost, to every service they provide to a client and conduct their business accordingly.

This section in *Photographer's Market* summarizes the many aspects of managing the business end of your photographic activities. There is valuable new information for all photographers in the always changing areas of taxes and insurance, revised guidelines on pricing and negotiating, and tips on numerous areas from organization and recordkeeping to self-promotion. In addition, we are featuring a special segment on copyright issues at the end of this section. This new information plus the standard practices which we review each year provide you with a reliable reference to the business of photography.

Prior to setting up your business, take the time to talk with other photographers about their business practices. What system of financial recordkeeping have they adopted? What types of insurance do they carry? What type of photo filing system have they found works best? Search out any professional photography associations in your town or look into taking a small business course at the local community college. The more knowledge you are armed with beforehand, the more business-related problems you'll be able to trouble-shoot effectively. There may come a time when you will want to consult a professional—whether it is a lawyer for contract counseling, or an accountant to help with your finances—take advantage of their expertise. Such guidance can be invaluable in preventing disaster caused by ignorance in some important aspect of your business.

Copyright/rights

Since your future livelihood as a photographer depends heavily upon the resale potential of your images, it is essential to know your rights under the law, how to negotiate terms and how to protect copyrights. Accordingly, this year's Business of Photography special segment is devoted to copyright issues. This article, titled Copyright and Work for Hire: What Every Photographer Needs to Know, begins on page 26.

Here are also a few basic practices you can implement to ensure protection of your copyright. Primarily, you should mark each of your images with a copyright symbol—copyright, copr. or ©—plus the year of creation as well as your name. Since the © symbol is universally accepted in most European countries and it is becoming more common for photographers to work with clients overseas, it is best to settle on this designation as you establish your routine practices. According to the Buenos Aires Convention, which covers many Western Hemisphere countries, copyright notices should also include the notation "All rights reserved" beneath the symbol, to provide extra protection. For convenience, you can have rubber stamps made or use a computer software package to create labels for your images. Such labeling is preferable to handmarking, since handwritten notices—especially those in ink—can sometimes become unreadable or bleed through into printed images.

In the event that you have to file suit against copyright infringement, you will receive more consideration and ultimately a fairer settlement if your copyright is registered with the federal government. To do this, you should write to the Copyright Office of the Library of Congress, Washington DC 20559. Request the form titled Form VA (works of visual arts). There is a $10 charge to register each photo and works can be registered as a group, though each image must bear its own copyright notice.

Obviously, registering photos can be expensive if you have a large number of images. So you may wish to decide which images are most valuable to you in terms of future resale value—as well as those most likely to be infringed—and register only those to keep down costs. Keep in mind, too, that images can be registered either before or within five years of their use.

Here is a list of image rights typically sold in the marketplace:
- One-time rights. These photos are "leased" on a one-time basis; one fee is paid for one use.
- First rights. This is generally the same as purchase of one-time rights though the photo-buyer is paying a bit more for the privilege of being the first to use the image. He may use it only once unless other rights are negotiated.
- Serial rights. The photographer has sold the right to use the photo in a periodical. It shouldn't be confused with using the photo in "installments." Most magazines will want to be sure the photo won't be running in a competing publication.
- Exclusive rights. Exclusive rights guarantee the buyers' exclusive right to use the photo in his particular market or for a particular product. A greeting card company, for example, may purchase these rights to an image with the stipulation that it not be sold to a competing company for a certain time period. The photographer, however, may retain rights to sell the image to other markets. Conditions should always be in writing to avoid any misunderstandings.
- Promotion rights. Such rights allow a publisher to use the photographer's photo for promotion of a publication in which the photo appeared. The photographer should be paid for promotional use in addition to the rights first sold to reproduce the image.
- All rights. This involves selling or assigning all rights to a photo for a specified period of time. This differs from work for hire, which always means the photographer permanently surrenders all rights to a photo and any claims to royalties or other future compensation. Terms for all rights—including time period of usage and compensation—should only be negotiated and confirmed in a written agreement with the client.

A valuable tool for any photographer trying to deal with all the copyright language and various forms of the photography business is the *SPAR* Do-It-Yourself Kit*. This survival package includes sample forms, explanations and checklists of all terms and questions a photographer should ask himself when negotiating a job and pricing it. It's available from SPAR, the Society of Photographer and Artist Representatives, Inc., Room 914, 1123 Broadway, New York, NY 10010. Phone: (212)924-6023. Price: Approximately $40.

As a quick reference, here are several areas that are helpful to remember when dealing with questions of copyright and rights:
- contracts
- licensing

- setting value and prices for images
- keeping records of all correspondence and submissions
- enforcement of rights

Pricing and negotiating

Pricing follows closely on the heels of usage and rights as these areas are intimately related for photographers. As one formula promoted by industry professionals has proclaimed, "Copyright is the key to usage, and usage is the key to pricing."

Many of the markets listed in *Photographer's Market* quote specific dollar amounts for buying single stock images or paying on assigned work. Whether the payment you are offered compensates you fairly for the work you have done, your overhead and the type of rights the client wants to purchase are important questions to ask yourself before you agree to do business with the client. Asking this question is especially critical when a client asks you to do work for hire or to transfer all rights to an image.

Some photographers—at least in the area of assignment work—work on a day rate, or sometimes a half-day rate. They will also bill the client for the number of finished pictures and for the type of rights the client wishes to purchase, as well as additional expenses such as equipment rental or hiring assistants. Typically, the photographer's strategy in such a case is to hold to the fee for the shoot as a basic, guaranteed rate. All other charges are negotiable, but the shoot fee remains fixed or the photographer does not do the work. When the client suggests a lower price, the photographer can then review the costs with the client and make adjustments in the complexity of the shoot's elements, the number of final shots or the usage. But the photographer does not just unconditionally lower his price. Accordingly, the photographer helps the client to get most if not all of what he wants at the price he wants, while ensuring that he will still get his base rate—which should include some profit.

An important advantage to breaking down the price for the client in this way is that it heads off the client coming back later and saying "Can you throw in one more print?" or trying to use the image in other ways not discussed. When negotiating the shoot, terms and price, it's a good idea to talk through all of the client's possible uses for the image. Then, you can either quote a higher price upfront if more usage is involved, or charge an extra fee later if the client requests additional usage or more images down the road.

In terms of selling images from your stock to various companies or publications, it's best to study a cross-section of prices that other businesses of these types are paying for photos as well as the rights they are buying. Then, before contacting any of these prospects, you will already be screening out some markets that do not meet your requirements for sales potential. Whether you decide to accept lower payment rates for your stock will have a great deal to do with other motives you may have, such as getting published, gathering photo credits or getting your foot in the door with a client. However, it is generally best for your long-term career strategy if you avoid underpricing too much in the beginning and try to establish a more consistent, accurate system for arriving at a fair value for your work.

Special markets, such as galleries and stock photo agencies, typically charge photographers a commission—from 20 to 50 percent—for displaying or representing their images. In these markets, payment on sales comes from the purchase of prints by gallery patrons, or from royalties on the rental of photos by clients of stock photo agencies. Accordingly, pricing formulas should be developed depending on your costs and current price levels in those markets, as well as on the basis of submission fees, commissions and other administrative costs charged to the photographer.

In general, photographers should be aware of a stagnation in the economy which is currently putting downward pressure on photo fees. (For more on this, read the section introduction for Advertising, Public Relations and Audiovisual Firms, on page 33.) Depending on whether photographers hold firm on their prices or give in to this client pressure to work for less, the market for photography may rebound more quickly or continue to wind down for the foreseeable future.

Financial recordkeeping

You won't know whether your business is making a profit unless you keep accurate financial records that allow you to determine profits and losses quickly. Browse around office supply stores to determine the type of ledger you feel can suit your business needs. Ideally, a ledger should include spaces for information such as job number, date of assignment, client name, expenses incurred, sales taxes and payments due. For tax purposes, be sure to retain all business receipts, invoices and cancelled checks to support ledger entries. For convenience, file these records in an envelope by month — it will be less time consuming when filling out income-tax forms each year. Using computer software which performs electronic spreadsheet functions is also a good way to organize your accounting records. If you set up basic ledgers on computer, then you can input sales, expenses and tax information daily, weekly or monthly, as needed.

Another business necessity you will want to look into is designing and printing business forms. These forms are useful when selling stock photography as well as shooting on assignment. For assignment work such forms should include columns for estimating services, assignment confirmation, and delivery of photos and invoicing. Photographers selling from stock will be concerned with delivery of photos and invoicing. When sending photos out in the marketplace be sure to itemize what images are being sent so the photo buyer and you will have a record. Business forms can be reproduced quickly and inexpensively at most quick-print services.

Also, either by purchasing or having access to a desktop publishing system and laser printer, you can design and produce forms specifically for your needs. With this kind of system, you can produce master forms to be duplicated or print them out for each client or sale. Not only does use of a business form help you keep track of your work, it presents a more professional appearance to the photo buyer who will perceive you as being organized and dependable.

Depending upon the size of your business and your sales volume, you may find professional assistance valuable when it comes to accounting and preparing taxes. Many photographers do their own bookkeeping in the beginning and delegate these tasks as they become more successful and involved in other aspects of their business. However, some photographers will — right from the beginning — at least have their records reviewed periodically by experts to ensure their accuracy. Whenever possible, try to find someone who works primarily with creative people or similar small business operators. Such specialists are often more familiar with the needs and problems of business people such as photographers, as well as any laws governing them.

Such review — whether done by you or by an expert — is important, too, for the overall financial health of your business. Looking closely at your costs and cash flow helps you to identify both profitable and unprofitable areas of your business. In particular, a good rule of thumb is that earnings should be in the range of 25 to 40 percent of your billings. If not, then it would be helpful to go back and study your records to see where you may need to cut costs or raise prices.

For any specific questions about starting up or maintaining your business, contact the Service Corps of Retired Executives Association (SCORE) at Suite 503, 1825 Connecticut Ave. NW, Washington, DC 20009. SCORE is a 12,000-member group of business men and women who provide free management assistance to those requiring expert advice. The phone number is (202)653-6279.

Taxes

Whether you're a freelance photographer or a fulltime studio owner, taxes are an inevitable part of the territory for you as an operator of a small business. The various types of taxes—income, payroll, social security and sales tax—all have a great deal of impact on your costs of doing business, and so must be considered as you are developing your pricing formulas. Accordingly, to keep your business profitable in both the short and the long term, it's best to learn what taxes are in effect in the area where you market your work and how to keep track of all tax-related information.

In general, current tax rates have decreased somewhat over the last few years. However, as changes in the economy begin to take hold in the 90s, these rates are likely to rise again. Also, there have been a number of changes in tax law which affect the amount and type of recordkeeping you have to do.

Once again, we want to remind you of one such change in federal tax law which is favorable to photographers and other creative people. This is the revision of the 1986 tax reform bill, the Technical Corrections Act. Under this revision, which just became effective on 1988 returns, photographers can now deduct any expenses accumulated in the production of images, within the same calendar year as they were produced. Previously, these expenses had to be spread out over a number of years until the image logged a profit. Without this revision, bookkeeping would have become unmanageable beyond a point for most photographers. The revision also relieved stock photographers, in particular, of the burden of projecting what the sales for certain images would be in the current year.

Another important related change under the 1986 Act has been a confusing new classification for individuals who incorporate as businesses. This is the Personal Service Corporation, or PSC classification. In most cases, individuals who incorporate their businesses in a number of professional areas automatically become classified as PSC's, and they are taxed at a very high rate of 34 percent. Though photography is not one of the professions that come under this category and is exempt from this tax rate, many individual photographers who incorporate have still been led to think that they must file as PSC's. As a result, the IRS has had to review claims by photographers and set some clearer guidelines.

Even though incorporated photographers were considered exempt from the PSC rate, they apparently qualified for another high tax rate. The catch was that according to UNICAP rules—the guidelines established under the original 1986 Act—incorporated photographers had been classified as manufacturers, and as such, were required to assign higher value to their inventories. Of course, this would often result in these photographers having to pay higher taxes. Lobbying efforts which led to the 1988 repeal of the UNICAP rules as they apply to photographers also made photographers effectively exempt from taxes on verifiable creative expenses. In other words, incorporated photographers are free of the obligation to both taxes. Nonetheless, all photographers are still subject to a number of taxes of which they must have a clear understanding and plan for accordingly.

If you are a freelancer—whether you have a primary source of income and photography serves as a sideline or photography is your fulltime pursuit—it's important to beware of higher tax rates on self-employment income. All income you receive without taxes being taken out by an employer qualifies as self-employment income. Normally, when you are employed by someone else, your income is taxed at a lower rate and the employer shares responsibility for the taxes due. However, when you are self-employed, even if only part-time, you are taxed at a higher rate on that income, and you must pay the entire amount yourself. This also applies to social security tax.

Freelancers frequently overlook self-employment and social security taxes and fail to set aside a sufficient amount of money. They also tend to forget state and local taxes are payable. If the volume of your photo sales reaches a point where it becomes a substantial percentage of your income, then you are required to pay estimated tax on a quarterly basis. This requires you to project what amount sales you expect to generate in a three-month period. However burdensome this may be in the short run, it works to your advantage in that you plan for and stay current with the various taxes you are expected to pay.

Many other deductions can be claimed by self-employed photographers. It's in your best interest to be aware of them. Examples of 100 percent deductible claims include production costs of resumes, business cards and brochures; photographer's rep commissions; membership dues; costs of purchasing portfolios and educational/business-related magazines and books; insurance, legal and professional services; and office expenses. Be aware that if you take a client out to dinner or treat him to some form of entertainment as a business investment, you may only deduct 80 percent of the costs. Making the photographer pay more out-of-pocket for meals and entertainment is the IRS's way of reducing abuses which have occurred.

Additional deductions may be taken if your office or studio is home-based. The catch here is that your work area can be used only on a professional basis; your office can't double as a family room after hours. The IRS also wants to see evidence that you use the work space on a regular basis via established business hours and proof of actively marketing your work. If you can satisfy these criteria then a percentage of mortgage interests, real estate taxes, rent, maintenance costs, utilities, and homeowner's insurance, plus office furniture and equipment, can be claimed on your tax form at year's end. (Furniture and equipment can be depreciated over a seven-year period.) To figure the percentage of your home or apartment that is used for business, divide the total floor space of your home or apartment (e.g., 4,000 sq. ft.) by the percentage used for business (e.g., 400) to get your answer (10 percent). Next, divide your total home expenses (e.g., $1,000) by 10 percent, and you've got your deductible total of $100.

Be aware that the above-mentioned deductions are only available to "professional" photographers, not hobbyists. The burden of proof will be on you if the IRS questions any deductions claimed. To maintain professional status in the eyes of the IRS you will need to show a profit for three years out of a five-year period. It also helps to maintain a professional image through use of business stationery containing your company name and logo, maintaining complete and accurate ledgers, actively marketing your photography, and joining professional or trade organizations related to your specialty. If you are working out of your home, be sure to keep separate records and bank accounts for personal and business finances, as well as a separate business phone.

Since the IRS can audit tax records as far back as seven years, it's vital to keep all paperwork related to your business. This includes invoices, vouchers, expenditures and sales receipts, canceled checks, deposit slips, register tapes and business ledger entries for this period.

Fulltime photographers—especially those who have a high sales volume—may be interested in investments as a tax shelter for their income. However, as experts in the industry have noted, you should avoid deferring income in this way for the foreseeable future since tax rates are quite likely to rise. In the long run, such tax deferments would result in higher business taxes. So, it's advisable that if you are already doing this, or have considered it, you should consult with a tax advisor or investment counselor to get complete, accurate information about such shelters.

In general, to plan properly for your taxes—especially when the size of your business and volume of sales increase—, you should seek out the advice of an accountant or a tax expert. As suggested before, it's best to work with someone familiar with the needs and concerns of small business people, particularly photographers. You can also obtain more background information about federal taxes and any recent changes in tax law for small business operators by contacting a local branch of the IRS. You can request a number of booklets which provide specific information on allowable deductions and rate structures. These include: 334—Tax Guide for Small Business; 463—Travel, Entertainment and Gift Expense; 505—Tax Withholding and Estimated Tax; 525—Taxable and Nontaxable Income; 533—Self-Employment Tax; 535—Business Expenses; 538—Accounting Periods and Methods; 587—Business Use of Your Home; 910—Guide to Free Tax Services; 917—Business Use of Car.

Insurance—business and personal

Taxes are not the only responsibility that self-employed photographers must take for themselves. Setting up proper insurance coverage on their business and themselves is also an important task. When deciding on the types of insurance—liability, property, health, disability and life—and the amounts of coverage, it's best to look carefully at your needs and at which companies can provide you with the best policies.

Generally, it's a good strategy to set up your business coverage with two main areas in mind. One area is liability to other people and protection of business property. This comes under business liability and office coverage. The second area is specifically for protection of your photo equipment. You must pay close attention to the policy terms because coverage varies. Some business policies offer protection for your office and equipment in case of damage from catastrophes such as fire, water damage and so on, but not theft. Besides your photographic equipment, certain office equipment such as computers or phone and fax machines is more likely to be stolen. So even though these items would be covered on some policies for damage, they would not be for theft. Since the policy for your photo gear already has a theft rider, you can often add other equipment to that policy.

Any photographer who works with people (this doesn't apply to assistants) on a regular basis in his studio, should carry liability coverage in case of an accident. Many times we're more concerned with property and equipment insurance, but if an injured client brings a lawsuit against you—and a jury rules in his favor—the settlement could easily skyrocket into hundreds of thousands of dollars. Liability settlements—as opposed to property damage—offer no finite monetary compensation limits to the victim. This uncertainty makes liability coverage crucial.

Worker's compensation, which applies to anyone whom you hire, is another form of insurance that is indispensable if you grow beyond being your only employee. This is available through most state governments or private insurance companies. In general, liability insurance covers members of the general public; worker's compensation insures employees. "Grey" areas come into the picture in many states because it's sometimes hard to determine according to labor and tax laws whether models, set builders or any other subcontractors are "employees." Therefore, a blend of liability coverage and worker's compensation should protect you in most cases.

Health and disability insurance are important to freelance photographers as well. With the high cost of hospitalization, health coverage is vital. Many professional or trade organizations such as the American Society of Magazine Photographers (ASMP) or Advertising Photographers of America (APA) offer health/disability packages to members. But, in order to qualify for disability coverage, you will need to accumulate a track record of sales so the insurance agent can calculate an income-average measure to determine the appropriate amount of coverage for you.

When you select a disability plan, first consider how long you could survive on your income—should a long-term injury occur—before you would need to rely on disability payments. Self-employed photographers will ideally want to have three to four months worth of "liquid" income accrued, such as cash-value life insurance, money-market accounts or savings accounts that can be dipped into in an emergency.

Since you don't want to go bankrupt paying insurance premiums for every potential disaster, you will want to first determine what misfortunes you can afford to pay out-of-pocket. In other words, protect yourself from losses that would be "catastrophic" to you.

It's important to "shop around" until you find an agent with whom you're comfortable, and one who is well versed in the professional needs of photographers. Check with other photographers, or call some photography trade groups for recommendations of agents in your area. Also, take the time to carefully read all policy clauses to be certain you get the insurance coverage you need. Finally, when you're researching companies to do business with, select those licensed to do business in your state.

Model and property releases

Photographers should be attuned to the need for obtaining model and property releases. Such a release gives the photographer the right to use, sell and publish the photo in editorial or advertising matter without fear of legal reprisals. In this age of stock photo sales, it is unknown whether the photo buyer will use the image for editorial or advertising use. It is wise to have model releases on file; their existence may gain you additional sales from buyers who prefer the work they use to be model released. The images can't ever be used in such a way as to embarrass or insult the subject, however.

Sample Model Release

In consideration for value received, I, _____, do hereby give (the photographer), and parties designated by the photographer, including clients, licensees, purchasers, agencies, and periodicals, the irrevocable right to use my name (and any fictional name) and photograph for sale to and reproduction in any medium for purposes of advertising, trade, display, exhibition or editorial use. I have read this release and fully understand its contents.

I affirm that I am more than 18 (21) years of age.

Witness: _____ Signed: _____
Address: _____ Address:_____
Date:_____

Guardian's Consent

I am the parent or legal guardian of the above-named minor and hereby approve the foregoing and consent to the photograph's use subject to the terms mentioned above.

I affirm that I have the legal right to issue such consent.

Witness: _____ Signed: _____
Address: _____ Address: _____
Date: _____

Usually photo rights purchased for editorial use (i.e., public education purposes) are free from the need for a model release. Such markets include newspapers, textbooks, filmstrips, encyclopedias or magazines. Photos used for advertising purposes always need model releases. If photographing children, remember that the guardian also must sign before the release is legally binding.

Lawyers also are advising photographers to obtain property releases, especially if recognizable property—including pets—will be used for advertising purposes. Since it is unclear exactly when property releases are needed, it would be wise to obtain one every time you shoot, for your own protection.

Additional samples of release forms can be found in ASMP's *Professional Business Practices in Photography*.

Filing prints and transparencies

Each photographer must work out his own system of coding and filing images according to what is best for his needs. You will want to talk to different photographers, first, to see what method of photo filing and retrieval works for them. Transparencies can be coded by a letter that would stand for a general topic, such as "A" for aviation subjects, "B" for medical shots, "C" for children, and so on. Within these areas, simply assign a numerical code to each transparency. Rohn Engh, author of *Sell & Re-Sell Your Photos*, says the key to easy retrieval also lies in setting up a good 3×5 index card system that catalogs cross-over subjects, such as pediatric shots of medical personnel and children interacting. When you receive a photo request, it will be much easier to find the requested photo when you simply have to refer to your catalog system rather than rifle through large numbers of images. For easy storage, invest in some 20-slide capacity 35mm transparency sleeves (or whatever size image sleeve your work requires), then store those in a notebook by subject letter, and within the sleeve itself by image number.

A slight variation of this coding can be used for black-and-white prints. You would still use the letter code "A", for instance to represent aviation subjects. The next number, however, would denote how many rolls of film have been shot in that subject heading, and the third number would represent which frame on a given roll of film was exposed. Such a coding system would read as A-35-26: "A" for aviation, "35" meaning this was the 35th roll of film shot, and "26" denoting the image to be pulled from the file is on the 26th frame. Black-and-white prints can be stored in a manila folder marked with this coding number, and a photocopy of that picture taken from the contact sheet. This latter step will help to more quickly identify the print in the folder, and if the folder is empty, will let you know at a glance what image to make more copies of. Cross referencing via 3×5 cards is important, too.

If you want to adapt the coding system previously described, you can adapt a numerical coding system in which "1" stands for negatives, "2" for transparencies, "3" for prints, etc. In this case 2-A-24 would stand for an aviation transparency assigned the number 24 for filing purposes. Don't forget the 3×5 card system here either. Many photographers are finding that use of a computer to store their image codes and captions is very helpful. If you are interested in going this route you will want to refer to Engh's book, which contains a chapter on use of the computer in a photography business. You will also want to watch photography publications for information they carry about the best computers for photography-related business uses, as well as talk to other photographers about their good—or not-so-good—experiences with different computer models.

Use of a computer can also help you track images submitted to photo buyers for consideration, and record which ones have been purchased and how much was paid for them. The process of tracking photos also can be accomplished manually by maintaining separate 'project' folders that let you review the status of submissions easily. Your payment ledger can be a useful tool here as well. All you need to note is the date photo submissions were sent out, when they were returned, and when payment was made. The photo's code can be entered in the ledger, thereby providing handy information about the status of a specific image.

Once you get a system of photo filing and retrieving adapted to your special needs, the time investment needed to maintain and add to the system can be done easily and with a limited time expenditure.

Marketing and self-promotion

Cover letters/queries/resumes

The cover letter and query letter are slightly different approaches to the same goal—making a photo sale. You, as the photographer, use either of these "vehicles" as a means to convince the photo buyer that your photography will enhance his product or service. Be sure to have the point you wish to make firmly in mind before you begin writing.

A proper cover letter should include an itemization of what photos you are submitting and caption information pertinent to each image. Photo captions should explain who, what, where, why and how. Try to avoid offering "when" information so you don't date your image(s). Also, be sure to make clear what rights you are offering for sale, and where you can be reached during the day if the photo buyer wishes to reach you via phone or mail. Keep your cover letter brief and concise.

If you want to send a query letter, try to limit it to one page. In publishing, the purpose of the query letter is to propose a photo story idea or a photo/text package. Make the story idea sound exciting, yet maintain an overall business tone in the proposal. This is also an excellent time to provide a bit more information about your photographic specialty; such material will establish credibility prior to your requesting an assignment from the photo-buyer. In the query letter you can either request the photo buyer's permission to shoot the assignment for his consideration, submit stock photos, or ask to be considered for an upcoming assignment.

Quite a few of the listings in *Photographer's Market* will be looking to buy stock photos for their future use, and will ask that photographers submit a stock photo list. A stock list is simply a summary of all the photos you have available on different subject matter or regions, whether black and white or color, in print or transparency form, and so on. You can either submit a stock list with your query letter to a market or send one when it is specifically recommended in a listing as the main method of contact.

Some photo buyers may ask you to shoot on speculation. Though this implies some interest on their part, if the material isn't used, you aren't compensated for your time and materials. If, however, you are hired on assignment and the material isn't used, you will be paid a "kill fee." Such a fee generally amounts to one-fourth to one-third of the agreed upon assignment fee. Be sure to negotiate the kill fee prior to taking an assignment.

Resumes also may be sent with your query letter to give the photo buyer more indepth information about your skills and previous experience. The resume should be attractive, and as complete as possible. Be sure to highlight past accomplishments beginning with photo experience (specify whether it's industrial, advertising, editorial, etc.) If you have any staff photo experience, include it, plus any photography-related education (including workshops attended), shows or exhibitions held, or awards and achievements earned in the photographic field. Professional memberships also are good to list.

Mailing photo submissions

Before sending photo submissions out into the marketplace, be sure to stamp each print or transparency with your copyright notice, and a "Return to: (your name, address, phone number) and an identifying number" (see the section "Filing prints and transparencies" for more information). The address and identifying number will assist both you and the photobuyer in locating any images which may be misplaced.

To ensure your images' safe arrival—and return—pay attention to the way you package them. Insert 8×10 black-and-white photos into an $8\frac{1}{2} \times 11$ plastic jacket; transparencies should be stored in protective vinyl pages. Most camera stores carry these in a variety of format sizes. Never submit photos or transparencies in mounted glass—the glass can break.

Be sure to include a return mailing label, adequate postage and an envelope with your submission. If you include a manila envelope, also pack two cardboard sheets to stiffen the envelope so your images aren't damaged. You can also buy heavy-weight cardboard envelopes that are reusable. These can be purchased at most office-supply or stationery stores.

Send your submissions via first class mail. The service is quicker and handling tends to be less rough. Many photographers also use certified mail. Though a certified package travels a bit slower than first class mail because it is logged in at each enroute destination, it is much easier to trace in the event of a mishap. To be sure that your photo submission is received by the photo buyer, include a self-addressed, stamped postcard so the editor can acknowledge that your photos did arrive safely. Be sure to specify on the postcard an itemization of what photos were included, so the editor or art director merely has to sign the card—it shouldn't be a time-consuming process for him.

There are other ways to safeguard against losing an irreplaceable image; some involve a little pre-planning. When submitting black-and-white prints, never send out the negatives. If a photo buyer is interested in purchasing your image, but doesn't like a technical flaw such as contrast, offer to send a reprint. Transparencies are a bit trickier. It is ideal to send out dupes with an offer to send the original if the other party is interested in purchasing rights to the image. Some labs can produce high-quality dupes, though you may want to decide which are your most valuable (marketable) images since this can become costly. If you're shooting an image that you feel is going to be marketable, expose multiple images (if this is possible) at the time you shoot your original. Using this method, you retain other "original" images should one be lost.

As more businesses and publications start to use facsimile transmission (fax) machines, more photographers have begun to submit trial images or proofs of assignments to clients by fax. We have added fax numbers to many of the listings in the various sections. However, since faxes are more or less considered a priority form of communication, it's advisable in terms of business etiquette not to use a fax to contact a listing until you have established a working relationship with them.

Portfolios

A time-honored promotional tool for photographers to demonstrate their abilities to prospective clients is the portfolio. And a well-prepared and well-presented portfolio is more vital than ever to succeed in today's competitive photographic markets.

An effective portfolio reflects not only the photographer's technical mastery but also his insight of and solutions to a client's communication problems. Selection of photos is therefore critical. Not all clients have the same problems, and so you should become familiar with the client's needs and select examples of your work--or shoot new work--showing your grasp of those needs.

One particular professional photographer has remarked that "What you show is what you get." This touches on a primary element in developing your portfolio--and in turn, your career--that you must first settle on what you want to shoot. For the beginning photographer, self-assignments are essential in building a portfolio that is targeted toward specific markets, not just a collection of random images. Also, for the established pro who is seeking a new market focus or who wants to cultivate a certain client with very select needs, shooting self-assignments is a key process in fine-tuning his portfolio.

Advertising

As photographers advance in their careers, especially when they're fulltime or have opened their own studios, they often turn to advertising as a means of promoting their business and visibility. Photographers usually develop a self-promotion card or a more elaborate piece with one or more of their pictures to send out to prospects and established clients on a periodic basis. As with the portfolio, the selection of photos is critical, as they should demonstrate your problem-solving skills rather than mere technical quality. Also, the first impression you make can make all the difference. So the piece must show your best work and it must look sharp, with a professional design and high-quality printing.

The advertising method currently becoming most standard among photographers is the mailing list and the direct mail campaign. Leads for the mailing list come from any contacts the photographers make or from listings in *Photographer's Market* and other industry references. In particular, listings in this book will sometimes ask for a photographer to send his self-promotion piece to introduce himself.

Photographers will also sometimes take out trade ads in industry publications and creative directories such as *Black Book*. These ads can be quite expensive and likely to reach only very specific types of clients such as art directors. Whether or not you decide to use trade ads will depend primarily upon your budget, the type of market you want to reach and the regions in which you plan to market your work.

Agents and reps

Another avenue that some photographers take in promoting themselves as they become more established is to work through an agent or photographer's representative, or "rep." This can be especially valuable for photographers who are involved in highly competitive markets such as advertising or who want to branch out to regional or national markets. The primary value of having a rep is that it frees the photographer to spend as much of his time as possible shooting or planning for work.

Since some photographers are less comfortable with the marketing and negotiating aspects of their business, using a rep can be very attractive. However, many photographers either like to rep themselves, or split the repping duties with another person. It's quite common with husband and wife photography teams that either or both of them will handle repping for their business. Of course, one big plus to keeping it "in the family" is that you don't have to pay out the rep's commission every time you make a sale.

Copyright and Work for Hire: What Every Photographer Needs to Know

by M.C. Valada

Since 1978, the words "work for hire" have been used by publishers and other buyers of photographic images to claim copyrights to work properly owned by photographers. If you've ever been an employee, as most of us have, then you know what work for hire is: it's what you do for your employer to earn a weekly paycheck and employment benefits. But if you are self-employed or a freelancer, work for hire is a legal fallacy which can make the company that gave you an assignment both your employer and owner of your copyrights. This can be even in spite of the fact that you receive no regular salary, employment benefits or other forms of financial security.

Work for hire benefits the client, not the photographer

Horror stories of work for hire abound in the creative fields, largely because a creator often has no idea how successful a particular work might become. For example, a photographer may take a picture of a child and a doctor for a magazine. If the photographer were to do it as a work for hire, all he would ever see as payment would be the day rate, let's say $350, plus expenses. Yet the photo could have great possibilities beyond that one use: to be used as a book or magazine cover elsewhere, to illustrate a brochure, to be used for a print ad, or to be included in a package design. Those usages could total many thousands of dollars worth of fees, which would go to the client who initially acquired the photographer's claim to copyright.

Far more likely for many photographers would be the case when they go to a publisher with photos which they have taken over the years (stock photography). The publisher reviews the photographer's stock images and, being interested in printing some of them, offers a nominal payment and photo credit. But then, when the check for payment arrives: surprise! It's imprinted with the words: "Personal endorsement required. Check void if this endorsement altered. This check is accepted as payment in full for rights to material described on face of check as work made for hire." Even though work for hire was originally intended under copyright law to apply only to assigned work, photographers are often faced with such wording on their stock sales, too.

M.C. Valada, a 16-year veteran of professional photography in Washington DC, is currently a student in arts/entertainment law at Case Western Reserve University School of Law. She has previously served on the National Board of Directors for the American Society of Magazine Photographers (ASMP), and as chairman of the Society's Rights Committee. In particular, she has been a participant in lobbying efforts in the copyright arena and was active with ASMP in the CCNV vs. Reid case.

Ruining the marketplace

Photographers who fall into either scenario are likely to find their images being brokered away by the client, and this has both short- and long-term consequences. By allowing the client to dictate terms and acquire the copyright in either way, the individual photographer narrows the marketplace not only for himself but eventually for all photographers.

Since photography is for the most part a "buyer's market," some clients assume that if a photographer will not do work for hire, they can find another who will. There are photographers who eventually cave in to this client pressure while others, eager to work, immediately jump at the job another photographer has refused to take. But photographers who do not resist this pressure create a ripple effect: prices for *all* photographers are pushed down; the individual photographer's potential for future income is seriously undermined with the loss of his copyright; and ultimately, the quality of work produced for clients is seriously lowered. Even the client ends up losing in the long run.

Abuse of copyright law

Under the original copyright laws, "work for hire" referred to work done by what we would all recognize as an employee. However, the drafters of the Copyright Act of 1976 expanded the scope of work for hire to include freelancers in nine limited areas (see sidebar on page 30). Even with this expansion, a written agreement between the client and the freelancer remained a central factor in determining the claim to copyright. In practice, however, written agreements were not executed as often as the drafters of the law thought they would be. This was because freelancers were not aware of using such agreements, plus some clients had found that it worked to their advantage not to suggest them or at least not to do so in a timely manner.

There is nothing in copyright law which *requires* that a designated commissioned work be a work made for hire. However, magazine publishers—whose products fall within the category of collective works—have been notorious for misquoting the law to unsuspecting photographers. During the time I served as Chair of the Rights Committee of the American Society of Magazine Photographers (ASMP), I had heard stories of photographers who were told that until the Copyright Act was changed they would have to sign a work-for-hire agreement "because that's the law." Also, some magazines have been reported to use three or four different contracts for different photographers. At times, magazines calling to offer me assignments would say they require work-for-hire terms. However, when I would refuse such terms, they would compromise and agree to pay me for one-time rights. In all such cases, photographers who are not aware of their rights and do not carefully negotiate them are most likely to lose them.

In the same way, other commissioning parties or clients have created paperwork which erroneously categorizes their projects (such as advertising photographs) as works for hire. Although the nine categories outlined in the copyright law seem clear and straightforward, it took 12 years and a Supreme Court decision to reign in the liberties which such parties had taken with the language.

Supreme Court's decision

In 1989, the Supreme Court made a key ruling on copyright law, and work for hire in particular, when it reached a decision in the case of *Community for Creative Non-Violence (CCNV) vs. James Earl Reid*. The Court's decision, which indirectly favored defendant Reid but was actually *against* work for hire, greatly clarified the intent of the existing copyright law to the benefit of all creative people, photographers included. In particular, the case redefined the concept of independent contracting and the rights vested to creative people under the Copyright Act of 1976.

Though not a photographer, sculptor Reid faced all of the challenges of the work-for-hire issue in CCNV's dispute with him. This Washington-based nonprofit organization, which is primarily involved in fighting homelessness, invited Reid to create a sculpture depicting homeless people. Reid agreed to donate his time and materials while CCNV supplied direction as well as the pedestal and steam grating on which the three sculpted characters huddled. While on the surface it may seem that Reid was "hired" and the sculpture was to some extent a joint creation, the question of terms or copyright never came up while the project was being negotiated. Reid registered the copyright in his name only after CCNV insisted on taking the sculpture on a national fundraising tour. Believing the statue would not survive being moved frequently from city to city, Reid took this step and refused to grant CCNV permission to use the sculpture in this way. Then, CCNV filed a counter-registration and a suit to establish copyright ownership in its name. In the end, the Court unanimously concluded that Reid was not an employee of CCNV and the sculpture was not work made for hire under the Act.

One major result of the decision in *CCNV vs. Reid* was that independent contractors (freelancers) now cannot unknowingly lose claim to their copyrights. A second result was a reaffirmation of the Copyright Act's 35-year time limit on the transfer of rights. As specified in the Act, even when a freelancer does knowingly sell all rights to his work, the claim to copyright reverts to the creator after 35 years.

In addition, the decision raised the question of whether or not creators who worked on assignment between 1978 and 1989 without written contracts and for clients who insisted the works be done as works for hire can reclaim their rights to their works. The question of reclaiming copyright applies to works done under a written agreement but in categories of works which are not covered under the work-for-hire section. Also, as amended, the copyright law now offers immediate protection for all works published since March 1, 1989, and works registered with the Copyright Office can be awarded double the damages available to unregistered works.

Value of written agreements

"After *Reid*, the only way that freelance photographers will lose their copyright rights is by signing a work-for-hire contract or making a written assignment of rights," says Charles D. Ossola, a partner in the Washington DC law firm of Hunton & Williams. Ossola represented the interests of two groups, the American Society of Magazine Photographers and the Copyright Justice Coalition, as *amicus curiae* (friends of the court) in support of the case defendant, Reid. "The Supreme Court determined that the categories are exclusive and that photography, not being one of the nine categories, is not eligible to be a work for hire unless a photographer is on staff. One of the most desirable effects of *Reid*, too, is that all parties are recognizing that some sort of written agreement is appropriate. Clients can still get all the rights they need by outlining them clearly in writing."

Before the *Reid* decision, a photographer who agreed to a written assignment of "all rights" to a client might believe that he was losing all rights, forever. However, the Copyright Act allows a creator to reclaim all rights 35 years after licensing, and so the rights in such cases are no longer given up forever. This allows the return of valuable images to photographers or their heirs, since the duration of a copyright is the life of the author plus fifty years—in most cases a considerably longer time than 35 years.

This illustrates one of the biggest differences between "work for hire" and a written assignment of rights. A freelancer can *never* reclaim the copyright of a work made for hire. But by executing a written assignment—even one of all rights—the law provides a way of returning the copyright to the creator. A photographer should consider these factors when negotiating fees.

Price based on usage

When a photograph is being used many times rather than only once, the photographer's fee should be higher. Similarly, if a client wants to restrict the use of a photograph for a long period, the photographer needs to be compensated differently than when he is free to license the same image to other clients during the same period.

According to Ossola, advertising agencies now appear to be eliminating work-for-hire language from purchase orders. It is being replaced, he notes, by language which indicates the purchase of all rights or exclusive usage, for limited periods. However, thanks to this change of terms, creators such as photographers now have a negotiating position.

"Work for hire" in many disguises

There are many words and phrases which might arise in negotiations with a client, or appear in a contract or on a check, which should alert the photographer that the client is trying to gain control of the work. These include: all rights or all reproduction rights, any and all subsidiary rights, assignment of copyright, assignment of rights, buyout, exclusive rights or full and exclusive property rights, unlimited use, world rights or worldwide exclusive rights, in perpetuity, and no right of reversion. Also, beware of the language in which the photographer "sells and/or assigns" to "client, its affiliated operations and licensees" or to "client, its successors and assigns (designated recipients)." Finally, be on guard for any language which makes the contract self-renewing, i.e., "agreement automatically renewable," or for any blanket statement covering all future work, i.e., "this agreement covers all future assignments." In such cases, photographers should not accept the terms unless they are spelled out in writing and signed by both parties for that assignment only. From one particular contract collected for presentation to Congress comes this gem:

> "You sell, assign, transfer and set over into Client, its successors and assigns (designated recipients) . . . all negatives, transparencies and film, together with the worldwide copyright thereof, and the right to so secure copyright therein of the entire world, with all your right, title and interest, both legal and equitable therein, and all other rights now known or hereafter to come into existence."

Photography in copyright categories

Three of the nine enumerated categories of work for hire (see sidebar on page 30) encompass photography: (1) contributions to collective works, (2) motion pictures or other audiovisual works and (3) supplementary works. An attempt to make "photographic or other portraits" a tenth category under "work for hire" failed during the original legislative process in 1976. Barbara Ringer, who was Registrar of Copyrights when the Copyright Act of 1976 was written, voiced her opposition to the attempt. Interestingly, she is quoted in a footnote in the *Reid* decision:

> "[Freelance] artists and photographers are among the most vulnerable and poorly protected of all beneficiaries of the copyright law, and it seems clear that, like serious composers and choreographers, they were not intended to be treated as 'employees' under the carefully negotiated definition [of work for hire] in section 101."

This footnote adds weight to the argument that photography simply cannot be treated as a work for hire when the photographer is a freelancer. Therefore, a photographer should insist on executing a written transfer of specific rights and refuse to sign a work for hire agreement (or check including such language), even when the work falls into the three categories mentioned. Since, for example, magazines are a major kind of collective work, and most magazines only need one-time rights to a photograph, it should be fairly easy for most photographers and clients to negotiate those terms.

Conditions and terms up front

Photographers should continue to protect themselves by using written agreements which preserve their copyrights. So everyone will know what is expected and misunderstandings can be avoided, photographers should discuss terms and conditions up front with their clients. They should also preserve copyright and authorship of images for themselves to avoid the pitfall of having a client claim to be a "joint author" in a work. The following example is the type of language which photographers can use on assignment confirmations and invoices to protect their work:

This agreement is for the licensing of commissioned photography, and the work created is not made work for hire, nor is it a joint work. Copyright rights and all other property rights in the photographs, except as otherwise specifically provided on the front of this agreement, belong to [photographer's name here], Photographer, and [his/her] heirs. Any additional uses of the photographs require the prior written agreement of Photographer on terms to be negotiated. Unless otherwise provided on the front of this agreement, any grant of rights is limited to one year from the date hereof for the territory of the United States of America.

Because the *Reid* decision prevents a client from going to court and claiming the work was made for hire, the photographer needs to protect himself from the other avenue remaining open to clients to claim ownership. The joint work argument which some clients have used says that the art direction, layouts, comps or hands-on arrangement of a photograph makes them joint authors with the photographer for copyright purposes. In such a case, the photographer shares the copyright with the other joint author, and both parties can exploit the photograph financially. Each party has to share the proceeds from any licensing as well, which can lead to tremendous bookkeeping headaches. In the long run, it's better for the photographer to make clear who is the sole owner of the work in writing before the shooting begins.

Work for hire definition:

Under the Copyright Act of 1976, section 101, a "work for hire" is defined as:
"(1) a work prepared by an employee within the scope of his or her employment; or
(2) a work . . .
- *specially ordered or commissioned for use as a contribution to a collective work**
- *as part of a motion picture or audiovisual work**
- *as a translation*
- *as a supplementary work**
- *as a compilation*
- *as an instructional text*
- *as a test*
- *as answer material for a test*
- *or as an atlas*

. . . if the parties expressly agree in a written instrument signed by them that the work shall be considered a work made for hire."

NOTE: The asterisk (*) denotes categories within the Copyright Law which apply to photography.

The real value of photography

As photographers learn to hold out for their rights and to resist surrendering their copyrights unless they are fairly compensated, another major spinoff will be that clients will learn the real value of photography. Buyers of photography who are used to having eager photographers gladly do work for hire when others turn it down will find fewer and fewer photographers to take advantage of. In the long run, these buyers will have to hire the best photographer for the money anyway rather than cut corners on price and settle for a trade-off on quality just to acquire the copyrights. However, this will happen *only* if photographers stand firm against such terms and treatment.

Work-for-hire not completely resolved

The decision in *Reid* has not settled all of the problems with the work-for-hire language in the Copyright Act. But it has helped to get Congress to pay attention to them. In June, 1989, Senator Thad Cochran introduced a bill, S. 1253, to amend the work-for-hire provisions of the Copyright Act, and to amend the language regarding joint authorship under the act. This bill was a revision of several others Senator Cochran has introduced since the early 1980s to revise the work-for-hire rules. It recognizes that the Supreme Court only addressed a few of the creators' concerns.

In September, 1989, the U.S. Senate's Judiciary Subcommittee on Patents, Copyrights and Trademarks held a hearing to discuss work-for-hire abuses under the Copyright Act. At that hearing, Senator Cochran said:

"Work for hire strikes at the heart of the relationship between creators and publishers, and it has been abused and now disrupts that relationship to the detriment of the public. The creative artists of America are being robbed of their incentive to work and of their rewards for working. We are all the poorer because of it."

Copyright is the key

Another important Supreme Court decision regarding copyright which came down in Spring, 1990 will benefit photographers. The case, which involved royalty claims for the Alfred Hitchcock film, *Rear Window*, arose out of the 1909 Copyright Act but the 1976 Act played a prominent role. Justice Sandra Day O'Connor wrote these words, which every photographer should not forget when negotiating:

"When a [creator] produces a work which later commands a higher price in the market than the original bargain provided, the copyright statute is designed to provide the [creator] the power to negotiate for the realized value of the work."

Finally, photography professional Richard Weisgrau, who represented ASMP before the Senate during the copyright hearings, summarizes both the timeliness and timelessness of the work-for-hire/copyright issue for photographers. "Progress in technology has greatly enhanced the value of copyright rights," he says. "Photographic images, for example, can easily be manipulated by computer and adapted for innumerable uses. Whoever owns the copyright will be able to control and profit from these multiple uses, many of which cannot be anticipated at the time the photographer clicks the shutter."

Key to Symbols and Abbreviations

■ *Audiovisual Markets*
*New Listings
SASE self-addressed stamped envelope
SAE self-addressed envelope
IRC International Reply Coupon, for use on reply mail in Canada and foreign markets
Ms, Mss manuscript(s)
© copyright
FAX facsimile transmission
(for definitions and abbreviations relating specifically to the photographic industry, see the glossary in the back of the book.)

Important Information on Market Listings

● *The markets listed in this book are those which are actively seeking new freelance contributors. Those companies not interested in hearing from new photographers are not included. If a particular magazine or other market is missing, it is probably not listed for that reason, or because 1) it has gone out of business; 2) it did not respond to our questionnaire requesting listing information; 3) it did not verify its listing from last year's edition; 4) it has failed to respond adequately to photographers' complaints against it; or 5) it requested that its listing be deleted.*
● *Market listings new to this edition are marked with an asterisk. These new markets are often the most receptive to new freelance talent.*
● *Although every buyer is given the opportunity to update his listing information prior to publication, the photography marketplace changes constantly throughout the year and between editions. Therefore it is possible that some of the market information will be out of date by the time you make use of it.*
● *Market listings are published free of charge to photography buyers and are not advertisements. While every measure is taken to ensure that the listing information is as accurate as possible, we cannot guarantee or endorse any listing.*
● Photographer's Market *reserves the right to exclude any listing which does not meet its requirements.*

The Markets

Advertising, Public Relations and Audio-visual Firms

Photography, because of its visual nature, plays a vital role in commerce of communicating information and value to consumers and encouraging commercial transactions. Products, services, publications ... all have come to depend upon visual communication for their success. Advertising and public relations agencies, of course, play a significant role in initiating such communication, and have traditionally worked closely with photographers as allies in this task. However, as the economy in the current cycle is cooling down from the relative fever pitch of the 80s, so is the demand for many products and services, and in turn, photography.

Mirroring larger trends

The advertising and PR markets are a mirror of the economic pressures building in the larger marketplace. For instance, creeping inflation, a continuing trend of corporate acquisitions and mergers, the tightening of government regulation on certain industries and increased rates of bankruptcy among heavy advertisers such as retail corporations have all put a chill on corporate communications budgets. As a result, advertising and public relations firms—as well as photographers—have been feeling the freeze.

In light of these trends, photographers with the ambition, skills and experience to work in the areas of advertising or PR should realize that the markets are getting leaner and meaner. As the competitive spiral has put downward pressure on photographic fees, i.e., photographers who charge less get more work, photographers everywhere have been scrambling to find new markets to supplement their income. Others have chosen to enter a new fulltime concentration, such as stock photography (see Stock Photography Spotlight, on page 5). Some veteran advertising photographers have checked out all together.

Transcend the ordinary

Though on the surface this sounds quite bleak, this is not to say that opportunity no longer exists in these markets. More than ever, advertising and PR agencies are placing a premium on top-notch skills, creativity and professionalism. In fact, these markets are already full of photographers who possess these qualities. But always in demand is the photographer who is not just good and does not just imitate but can take an ordinary subject or message and communicate it in a fresh, attention-getting way.

Indicating specific needs

All of these changes are reflected in this new edition of *Photographer's Market*. Some listings which have been in the book for several editions may now be absent because of any of a number of the financial or competitive reasons described above. For instance, they may have been driven out of business or snapped up in a corporate takeover. Others have chosen not to renew their listings because of being flooded with inappropriate or unprofessional submissions. However, many of the listings which have returned, as well as the numerous new listings, have taken more time to point out their very specific needs. So it pays you, the photographer, to pay close attention to those guidelines and needs and provide them only with what they indicate.

A number of factors go into how advertising and PR firms determine their rates of payment for photography. For instance, it may depend upon the client's budget, the type of shoot (studio or location), the type of usage and rights being purchased, and how talented or experienced the photographer is. We have made the attempt to obtain more specific information from listings about the rates of payment. However, some firms will still only discuss those terms with the photographer as a sale or assignment is being negotiated.

Also, we have included more detail about the rights a firm usually purchases. Advertising agencies, in particular, have tended to purchase all rights or assign work only on a "work-for-hire" basis. Since work for hire is a serious issue for all photographers to consider (see Copyright and Work for Hire article, on page 26), it is important that you look closely for this information in the listings.

Streamlined format and helpful articles

Some changes in the format and organization of this section appear in this edition. One major change is the inclusion of audiovisual markets, which were previously listed in the section Audiovisual, Film and Video Firms. These include a number of production houses as well as advertising or PR agencies with in-house production units. For easier recognition, any listing with various kinds of audiovisual, film or video needs has been marked with a special AV symbol—a black square—before the listing's name. Also, listings with these symbols may also include detailed descriptions under the subheading, "Audiovisual Needs."

In the two Close-up interviews in this section, the guest experts both stress that success in these markets depends greatly upon the qualities of professionalism, creativity and commitment. Advertising photographer Nick Vedros, owner of Nick Vedros & Associates in Kansas City, Missouri, explains how he has developed his photographic vision specifically for advertising and acquired an impressive stable of clients. Describing their experience in the audiovisual field are Bob Lukeman and Gordon Blocker of the Ft. Worth, Texas-based production firm, Lukeman-Blocker. In particular, they emphasize the abundant opportunities for photographers in AV, film and video and how the freelancer can make the transition.

Given the rapidly changing state of the advertising and PR markets today, you may find other articles in this book will shed some additional light on how to stay competitive and profitable. These include the Stock Photography Spotlight on page 5, the Copyright and Work for Hire article on page 26 and the Close-up interview with Richard Steedman on page 561, in the Stock Photo Agencies section.

Many ad agencies, PR firms and AV production companies hire locally- or regionally-based freelancers, and this information is included in listings where it applies. Accordingly, the listings are organized by state for easy reference.

Alabama

■**BARNEY & PATRICK INC.**, 300 St. Francis St., Mobile AL 36602. (205)433-0401. Ad agency. Vice President/Associate Creative Director: George Yurcisin. Types of clients: industrial, financial, medical, retail, fashion, fast food, tourism and food services.
Needs: Works with 1-3 freelance photographers/month. Uses photographers for consumer magazines, trade magazines, direct mail, brochures, P-O-P displays, audiovisuals, posters and newspapers.
Audiovisual Needs: Works with freelance filmmakers to produce TV and audiovisuals.
Specs: Uses 8×10 and 11×17 glossy b&w prints; 35mm, 2¼×2¼, 4×5 and 8×10 transparencies; 35mm film and videotape.
First Contact & Terms: Arrange a personal interview to show portfolio or query with samples and list of stock photo subjects. Provide resume, business card, brochure, flyer or tearsheets to be kept on file for possible future assignments. Does not return unsolicited material. Reports as needed. Payment "varies according to budget." Pays on receipt of invoice. Buys all rights. Model release required.
Tips: Prefers to see "slides and prints of top quality work, on time and within budget."

■**BARRY HUEY, BULLOCK & COOK, ADVERTISING, INC.**, 530 Beacon Parkway West, Birmingham AL 35209. (205)945-4974. FAX: (205)945-7414. Ad agency. Art Directors: Mike Macon/Melanie Townsend. Estab. 1972. Types of clients: retail, food and sporting goods. Client list provided on request.
Needs: Works with 6-10 freelance photographers/month. Uses photographers for consumer magazines, trade magazines, P-O-P displays, catalogs, posters and audiovisuals. Subjects include fishing industry and water sports.
Audiovisual Needs: Uses AV for product introductions, seminars and various presentations.
Specs: Uses 5×7 b&w; 35mm, 4×5 and 8×10 transparencies.
First Contact & Terms: Submit portfolio for review. Provide resume, business card, brochure, flyer or tearsheets to be kept on file for possible future assignments. Works on assignment basis only. Pays $50-400/b&w photo; $85-3000/color photo; $500-1600/day; $150-20,000/job. Payment is made on acceptance plus 31 days. Buys all rights. Model release and captions preferred.
Tips: Prefers to see "table top product with new exciting lighting."

■**J.H. LEWIS ADVERTISING, INC.**, 1668 Government St., Mobile AL 36604. (205)476-2507. President: Larry Norris. Creative Director: Spencer Till. Ad agency. Uses billboards, consumer and trade magazines, direct mail, foreign media, newspapers, P-O-P displays, radio and TV. Serves industrial, entertainment, financial, agricultural, medical and consumer clients. Commissions 25 photographers/year. Pays/job. Buys all rights. Model release preferred. Arrange a personal interview to show portfolio; submit portfolio for review; or send material, "preferably slides we can keep on file," by mail for consideration. SASE. Reports in 1 week.
B&W: Uses contact sheet and glossy 8×10 prints.
Color: Uses 8×10 prints and 4×5 transparencies.
Film: Produces 16mm documentaries. Pays royalties.

■**SPOTTSWOOD VIDEO/FILM STUDIO**, 2520 Old Shell Rd., Mobile AL 36607. (205)478-9387. Co-Owner: M. W. Spottswood. Estab. 1952. Types of clients: business, industry and government agencies.
Needs: Uses freelance photographers for films and videotapes.
Specs: Uses 16mm, 35mm film; U-matic ¾", 1" videotape and Beta System..
First Contact & Terms: "We just need the name and location of good photographers—we only use 4 or 5 a year, but when we need them we need them badly and quickly." Works with freelancers by assignment only; interested in stock photos/footage. Pay negotiable. Pays "50% up front and balance on acceptance." Buys all rights. Credit line sometimes given.

■ *The solid, black square before a listing indicates that the market uses various types of audiovisual materials, such as slides, film or videotape.*

Alaska

EVANS/KRAFT ADVERTISING, ALASKA DIVISION, 800 F St., Anchorage AK 99501. (907)258-2626. Ad agency. Art Director: Stephanie Russell. Types of clients: retail, hotel, restaurant, fitness, healthcare. Client list free with SASE.
Needs: Works with 1 freelance photographer/month. Uses photographers for consumer magazines, trade magazines, direct mail and brochures and collateral pieces. Subjects include Alaskan scenic shots.
Specs: Uses 11 × 14 matte b&w prints; 35mm, 2¼ × 2¼ and 4 × 5 transparencies.
First Contact & Terms: Query with samples. Provide resume, business card, brochure, flyer or tearsheets to be kept on file for possible future assignments. Does not return unsolicited material. Pays $500-700/day or minimum $100/job (depends on job). Pays on receipt. Buys all rights or one-time rights. Model release and captions preferred.
Tips: Prefers to see "high technical quality (sharpness, lighting, etc). All photos should capture a mood. Simplicity of subject matter. Keep sending updated samples of work you are doing (monthly). We are demanding higher technical quality and looking for more 'feeling' photos than still life of product."

Arizona

CHARLES DUFF ADVERTISING AGENCY, Box 34820, Phoenix AZ 85067-4820. (602)285-1660. Ad agency. Creative Director: Trish Spencer. Client list provided on request with SASE.
Needs: Works with 2-3 freelance photographers/month. Uses photographers for consumer and trade magazines, direct mail, P-O-P displays, catalogs. Subjects include: horses, dogs, cats and livestock.
Specs: Uses 8 × 10 b&w and color prints; 35mm, 4 × 5 transparencies. "Would prefer 4 × 5 but can accept any size transparency."
First Contact & Terms: Send unsolicited photos by mail for consideration; provide resume, business card, brochure, flyer or tearsheets to be kept on file for possible future assignments. SASE. Reports in 1 month. Pays $25-50/b&w photo; $100-300/color photo. Pays on receipt of invoice. Buys one-time rights. Model release preferred.
Tips: Prefers to see horses. Send samples of work for review.

■**FARNAM COMPANIES, INC.**, 2nd Fl., 301 W. Osborn, Phoenix AZ 85013-3928. (602)285-1660. Inhouse ad agency. Creative Director: Trish Spencer. Types of clients: animal health products, primarily for horses and dogs; some cattle.
Needs: Works with 2 freelance photographers/month. Uses photographers for direct mail, catalogs, consumer magazines, P-O-P displays, posters, AV presentations, trade magazines and brochures. Subject matter includes horses, dogs, cats, farm scenes, ranch scenes, cowboys, cattle and horse shows. Occasionally works with freelance filmmakers to produce educational horse health films and demonstrations of product use.
Specs: Uses 8½ × 10 glossy b&w and color prints; 35mm, 2¼ × 2¼ and 4 × 5 transparencies; 16mm and 35mm film and videotape.
First Contact & Terms: Arrange a personal interview to show portfolio; query with samples; send unsolicited photos by mail for consideration; provide resume, business card, brochure, flyer or tearsheets to be kept on file for possible future assignments. Works with freelance photographers on assignment basis only. SASE. Reports in 2 weeks or per photographer's request. Pays $25-75/b&w photo; $50-300/color photo. Pays on publication. Buys one-time rights. Model release required. Credit line given whenever possible.
Tips: "Send me a number of good, reasonably priced for one-time use photos of dogs, horses or farm scenes. Better yet, send me good quality dupes I can keep on file for *rush* use. When the dupes are in the file and I see them regularly, the ones I like stick in my mind and I find myself planning ways to use them. We are looking for original, dramatic work. We especially like to see horses, dogs, cats and cattle captured in artistic scenes or poses. All shots should show off quality animals with good conformation. We rarely use shots if people are shown and prefer animals in natural settings or in barns/stalls."

JOANIE L. FLATT AND ASSOC. LTD, Suite 2, 623 W. Southern Ave, Mesa AZ 85210. (602)835-9139. PR firm. CEO: Debbie Melcher. Types of clients: service, educational, insurance companies, developers, builders and finance.

Needs: Works with 2-3 photographers/month. Uses photographers for consumer magazines, brochures and group presentations. Subject matter varies.

Specs: Vary depending on client and job.

First Contact & Terms: Query with list of stock photo subjects. Provide resume, business card, brochure, flyer or tearsheets to be kept on file for possible future assignments. Works with local freelance photographers only. Does not return unsolicited material. Reports in 3 weeks. Photographer bids a job in writing. Payment is made 30 days after invoice. Buys all rights and sometimes one-time rights. Model release required. Captions preferred. Credit line given if warranted depending on job.

■**PAUL S. KARR PRODUCTIONS,** 2945 W. Indian School Rd., Phoenix AZ 85017. (602)266-4198. Contact: Paul Karr. Film & tape firm. Types of clients: industrial, business and education. Works with freelancers on assignment only.

Needs: Uses filmmakers for motion pictures. "You must be an experienced filmmaker with your own location equipment, and understand editing and negative cutting to be considered for any assignment." Primarily produces industrial films for training, marketing, public relations and government contracts. Does high-speed photo instrumentation. Also produces business promotional tapes, recruiting tapes and instructional and entertainment tapes for VCR and cable. "We are also interested in funded co-production ventures with other video and film producers."

Specs: Uses 16mm films and videotapes. Provides production services, including inhouse 16mm processing, printing and sound transfers, scoring and mixing and video production, post production, and film-to-tape services.

First Contact & Terms: Query with resume of credits and advise if sample reel is available. Pays/job; negotiates payment based on client's budget and photographer's ability to handle the work. Pays on production. Buys all rights. Model release required.

Tips: Branch office in Utah: Karr Productions, 1045 N. 300 East, Orem, Utah 84057. (801)226-8209. Contact: Mike Karr.

NELSON/RALSTON/ROBB COMMUNICATIONS, INC., Suite 1800, 3003 N. Central Ave., Phoenix AZ 85012. (602)264-2930. Creative Director: Paul John. Public relations, advertising, marketing, public affairs firm. Types of clients: financial, real estate developers/homebuilders, consumer products, utilities, health care, emergency services, industrial, electronics, political, legal, architectural, recreation/leisure and sports.

Needs: Works with 3-4 freelance photographers/month on assignment only basis. Provide flyer, rate sheets and business card to be kept on file for possible future assignments. Uses freelancers for consumer and trade magazines, newspapers, TV.

First Contact & Terms: Call for personal appointment to show portfolio. Prefers to see tearsheets, 8×10 or larger prints, and most important, b&w contact sheets of assignment samples in a portfolio. Freelancers selected according to needs, cost, quality and ability to meet deadlines. Negotiates payment based on client's budget, amount of creativity required from photographer, where the work will appear, complexity of assignment, and photographer's previous experience/reputation. Pays within 30 days of completed assignment.

Tips: "When interviewing a new photographer we like to see samples of work done on other assignments—including contact sheets of representative b&w assignments." Southern California office: Suite 180, 125 E. Baker St., Costa Mesa CA 92626. (714)957-1010. Senior Art Director: Dave Bryant.

WALKER AGENCY, Suite 102, 7950 E. Acoma, Scottsdale AZ 85260. (602)483-0185. Ad agency, PR firm. President: Mike Walker. Types of clients: banking, marine industry and outdoor recreation products, e.g., Yamaha Marine Group, Shimano Tackle, Impulse Fish Finders. Client list free with SASE.

Needs: Works with 2 photographers/month. Uses photographers for consumer magazines, trade magazines, posters and newspapers. Subjects include outdoor recreation scenes: fishing, camping, etc. "We also publish a newspaper supplement 'Escape to the Outdoors' which goes to 11,000 papers."

Specs: Uses 8×10 glossy b&w print with borders; 35mm, 2¼×2¼, 4×5 and 8×10 transparencies.

First Contact & Terms: Query with resume of credits; query with list of stock photo subjects; provide resume, business card, brochure, flyer or tearsheets to be kept on file for possible future assignments. Reports in 1 week. Pay rates vary with job. Pays on receipt of invoice. Buys all rights, or negotiates. Model releases required.

Tips: In portfolio/samples, prefers to see a completely propped scene. "There is now more opportunity for photographers within the Ad/PR industry."

Arkansas

BLACKWOOD, MARTIN, AND ASSOCIATES, Box 1968, 300 First Pl., Fayetteville AR 72702. (501)442-9803. Ad agency. Creative Dircctor: Gary Weidner. Types of clients: food, financial, medical, insurance, some retail. Client list provided on request.

Needs: Works with 3 freelance photographers/month. Uses photographers for direct mail, catalogs, consumer magazines, P-O-P displays, trade magazines and brochures. Subject matter includes "food shots—fried foods, industrial."

Specs: Uses 8×10 high contrast b&w prints; 35mm, 4×5 and 8×10 transparencies.

First Contact & Terms: Arrange a personal interview to show portfolio; query with samples; provide resume, business card, brochure, flyer or tearsheets to be kept on file for possible future assignments. Works with freelance photographers on assignment basis only. Does not return unsolicited material. Reports in 1 month. Payment depends on budget—"whatever the market will bear." Buys all rights. Model release preferred.

Tips: Prefers to see "good, professional work, b&w and color" in a portfolio of samples. "Be willing to travel and willing to work within our budget. We are using less b&w photography because of newspaper reproduction in our area. We're using a lot of color for printing."

■**FRAZIER IRBY SNYDER, INC.**, 1901 Broadway, Box 164858, Little Rock AR 72216. (501)372-4350. Ad agency. Senior Vice President/Creative Director: Pat Snyder. Types of clients: industrial, fashion, finance, entertainment.

Needs: Works with 3 freelance photographers/month. Uses photographers for consumer and trade magazines, direct mail, P-O-P displays, brochures, catalogs, posters and newspapers. Subjects include tourism, industrial and home entertainment.

Audiovisual Needs: Works with freelance filmmakers to produce TV commercials and training films. "We have our own inhouse production company named Ricky Recordo Productions with complete 16mm equipment."

Specs: Uses 8×10 b&w prints; $2\frac{1}{4} \times 2\frac{1}{4}$ and 4×5 transparencies; 16mm film and videotape.

First Contact & Terms: Query with list of stock photo subjects; provide resume, business card, brochure, flyer or tearsheets to be kept on file for possible future assignments. Works with freelance photographers on assignment basis only. Does not return unsolicited material. Reports in 3 weeks. Pays $100-350/b&w and color stock photo; $45-90/hour; $300-900/day. Pays on acceptance. Buys all rights if possible; one-time rights on stock photos. Model release required. Credit line "sometimes given, if requested."

Tips: "We look for something different—someone who can offer creative input to a project."

■**WILLIAMS/MCINTOSH & ASSOCIATES, INC.**, Box 789, Ft. Smith AR 72901. (501)782-5230. FAX: (501)782-6970. Creative Director: Jim Perry. Estab. 1983. Types of clients: financial, healthcare, manufacturing, tourism. Examples of ad campaigns: Touche-Ross, 401K and Employee Benefits (videos); Cummins Diesel engines (print campaigns); and Freightliner Trucks (sales promotion and training videos).

Needs: Works with 2-3 freelance photographers—filmmakers—videographers/month. Uses photographers for consumer magazines, trade magazines, direct mail, P-O-P displays, catalogs, posters, newspapers and audiovisual uses. Subject include: people, products and architecture. Reviews stock photos, film or video of healthcare and financial.

Audiovisual Needs: Uses photos/film/video for 30-second video and film TV spots, 5-10-minute video sales, training and educational.

Specs: Uses 5×7, 8×10 b&w prints; 35mm, $2\frac{1}{4} \times 2\frac{1}{4}$ and 4×5 transparencies.

First Contact & Terms: Query with samples, provide resume, business card, brochure, flyer or tearsheets to be kept on file for possible future assignments. Works with freelancers on assignment basis only. Cannot return material. Reports in 1-2 weeks. Pays $500-1,200/day. Pays on receipt of invoice and client approval. Buys all rights (work-for-hire). Model release required; photo captions preferred. Credit line given sometimes, depending on client's attitude (payment arrangement with photographer).

Tips: In freelancer's samples, wants to see "quality and unique approaches to common problems." There is "a demand to separate themselves with the use of fresh graphics and design solutions." Freelancers should "expect to be pushed to their creative limits, to work hard and be able to input ideas into the process, not just be directed."

California

■**AIRLINE FILM & TV PROMOTIONS**, 13246 Weidner, Pacoima CA 91331. (818)899-1151. President: Byron Schmidt. Types of clients: major film companies.
Audiovisual Needs: Works with 4-5 freelance photographers/month. Uses freelance photographers for films and videotapes. Subjects include publicity and advertising.
Specs: "Specifications vary with each production." Uses 8×10 color prints; 35mm transparencies; VHS videotape.
First Contact & Terms: Provide resume, business card, self-promotion piece or tearsheets to be kept on file for possible future assignments. Works on assignment only. Does not return unsolicited material. Payment varies per assignment and production: pays $250-500/b&w photo; $500-1,000/job. Pays on acceptance. Buys all rights. Model release required. Credit line sometimes given. Looks for work that shows "imagination."

AUSTIN ASSOCIATES, Suite 600, 2055 Gateway Pl., Santa Jose CA 95111. (408)453-7776. Ad agency. Art Director: Stuart Morgan. Serves high technology clients.
Needs: Works with 3 photographers/month. Uses work for billboards, consumer magazines, trade magazines, direct mail, P-O-P displays, newspapers. Subject matter of photography purchased includes: table top (tight shots of electronics products).
Specs: Uses 8×10 matte b&w and color prints; 35mm, 2¼×2¼, 4×5 or 8×10 transparencies.
First Contact & Terms: Arrange a personal interview to show portfolio, send unsolicited photos by mail for consideration; provide resume, business card, brochure, flyer or tearsheets to be kept on file for possible future assignments. Works on assignment basis only. Does not return unsolicited material. Reports in 3 weeks. Pays $500-2,500/job. Pays on receipt of invoice. Buys all rights (work-for-hire). Model release required, captions preferred.
Tips: Prefers to see "originality, creativity, uniqueness, technical expertise" in work submitted. There is more use of "photo composites, dramatic lighting, and more attention to detail" in photography.

AVISO, INC., Suite 104, 1150 Marina Village Pkwy., Alameda CA 94501. (415)865-5100. Ad agency, PR and marketing firm. Production Manager: Barbara Pacini. Estab. 1977. Types of clients: real estate, travel, business to business, food and wine.
Needs: Works with 3 freelance photographers/month. Uses photographers for consumer magazines, trade magazines, direct mail, newspapers, brochures and newsletters. Subjects include: interior and exterior buildings, people.
Specs: Uses b&w prints; 35mm, 2¼×2¼ and 4×5 transparencies. Specifications depend on the assignment.
First Contact & Terms: Query with resume of credits, business card, brochure, flyer or tearsheets to be kept on file for possible future assignments. Works with freelancers on an assignment basis only. SASE. Reports in 2 weeks. Pays $600-1,200/day. Pays 30 days after receipt of invoice. Buys all rights. Model release required. Credit lines given where feasible.
Tips: Looking for people, editorial and buildings. Looking especially for creative exposures and angles of buildings. "Send samples, we'll call if we have an assignment that seems appropriate." Trend is toward more slide shows, more black and white, candids of people.

BENNETT, ALEON, AND ASSOCIATES, Suite 212, 13455 Ventura Blvd., Sherman Oaks CA 91423. (818)990-8070. President: Aleon Bennett. Types of clients: finance, industrial.
Needs: Works with varied number of freelance photographers/month. Uses photographers for trade magazines and newspapers.
Specs: Uses b&w prints.
First Contact & Terms: Query with resume of credits. Does not return material. Pays per photo. Pays on acceptance. Buys all rights. Model release required; captions preferred.

■**RALPH BING ADVERTISING**, 16109 Selva Dr., San Diego CA 92128. Production Manager: Ralph Bing. Ad agency. Serves industrial (specializing in ferrous and nonferrous metals, warehousing, stamping, and smelting) and consumer (automotive, political, building and real estate development, food and restaurant) clients. Commissions 3 or 4 freelancers per year. Provide flyer to be kept on file for possible future assignments. Buys 2-15 photos/year. Pays $10-250/photo; $10-50/hour; $75-250/day; $10-250/project. Pays within 30 days of receipt of invoice and delivery of prints. Buys all rights. Model release required. Arrange personal interview to show portfolio; does not view unsolicited material.
Audiovisual Needs: Occasionally produces film for AV presentations and TV commercials. Does not pay royalties.
Specs: Uses 5×7 prints, b&w and color; also 35mm transparencies.
Tips: "Portfolio should be conveniently sized to be presented on desk or, possibly, lap."

■**BOSUSTOW VIDEO**, 3000 Olympic Blvd., Santa Monica CA 90404-9998. (213)315-4888. Director: Tee Bosustow. Production Manager: Amanda Foulger. Types of clients: broadcast, commercial, promotional, industrial, institutional, corporate and home video.
Needs: Uses photographers for videotape productions. Subjects include documentary, news, interviews and informational.
Specs: Uses one-inch Betacam-SP and ¼" U-matic videotape. Owns Sony BVW 300 and edit bays.
First Contact & Terms: "Please, no phone calls. We'll contact you from resume and sample reel, when job comes up." Works with local freelancers usually—limited out-of-town and out-of-country. Reports when job comes up. Pays $450-1,250/day. Payment based on payment schedule of client. Usually licenses for one project—camera person holds other rights.
Tips: "Usually use videographers with documentary style experience; production experience is preferable. Send one-page resume. List your best documentary and production experience, your rate, the gear you are proficient with and any awards. Short demo tapes are helpful, if you don't need them back."

■**THE CAPENER COMPANY**, Suite 300, 5830 Oberlin Dr., San Diego CA 92121. (619)238-8500. Ad agency. Creative Director: Mark Albertazzi. Types of clients: industrial, retail, finance.
Needs: Works with 3 freelance photographers/month. Uses photographers for billboards, consumer magazines, trade magazines, direct mail, P-O-P displays, catalogs, posters, newspapers and videos. Provide resume, business card, brochure, flyer or tearsheets to be kept on file for possible future assignments. Works on assignment basis only. Does not return unsolicited material. Pays by the job. Payment by client, 30-60 days. Buys all rights. Model release required.

■**DOCUMENTARY FILMS**, Box 97, Aptos CA 95001. (408)688-6632. Producer: M.T. Hollingsworth. AV firm. Estab. 1966. Serves clients in schools, colleges, universities, foreign governments and service organizations. Produces motion pictures.
Subject Needs: Language arts, nature, marine science, physical education, anthropology, dance and special education; 16 mm film material at all stages of production. Film length requirements: 10, 15 and 20 minutes. Prefers 16mm color prints and camera originals.
Audiovisual Needs: Produces 16mm originals, color print work, color internegative and release prints. Interested in stock footage. Film scripts considered.
Payment & Terms: Pays royalties by mutual agreement depending on production stage at which film is submitted. "Royalties for a film treatment. If the concepts are good, and the resulting film successful, the royalties will pay much more than single use rates." Buys all film distribution rights. Model release and captions required.
Making Contact: Send material by mail for consideration. "On first submission, send prints, NOT ORIGINALS, unless requested." SASE. Reports in 2 weeks.
Tips: "For films: have a specific market in mind. Send enough footage to show continuity, significant high points of action and content, personalities. Film should be clearly identified head and tails. Any accompanying sound samples should be in cassettes or ¼ inch reels clearly identified including proposed background music. We look for originality of concept, technical quality of craftmanship, creative and artistic elements, meticulous attention to detail. We do not use isolated single photos. Photos must tell a story which might become the basis or the idea on which to hang a film."

FRANSON & ASSOCIATES, INC., Suite 300, 181 Metro Dr., San Jose CA 95110. (408)453-5220. PR firm. President: Paul Franson. Types of clients: high tech.
Needs: Works with 2-4 freelance photographers/month. Uses freelance photographers for trade magazines, newspapers, press photos. Subjects include: application photography.
Specs: Uses 5×7, 8×10 glossy b&w prints; 35mm, 2¼×2¼, 4×5 transparencies.
First Contact & Terms: Query with resume of credits, send unsolicited photos by mail for consideration, query with samples, provide resume, business card, brochure, flyer or tearsheets to be kept on file for possible future assignments. Works with freelance photographers on assignment basis only. Does not return unsolicited material. Reports in 3 weeks. Pay negotiated. Pays within 30 days. Buys all rights. Model release required. Credit line given "when possible."
Tips: Prefers to see people, product, application. Out of area freelancers are needed when an assignment comes up out of town.

THE HITCHINS COMPANY, 22756 Hartland St., Canoga Park CA 91307. (818)715-0510. Ad agency. President: W.E. Hitchins. Types of clients: industrial, retail (food) and auctioneers.
Needs: Uses photographers for trade magazines, direct mail and newspapers.
Specs: Uses b&w and color prints. "Copy should be flexible for scanning."
First Contact & Terms: Provide resume, business card, brochure, flyer or tearsheets to be kept on file for possible future assignments. Works with freelancers on an assignment basis only. Cannot return material. Pays on receipt of invoice (30 days). Rights purchased "varies as to project." Model release required.

■**BERNARD HODES ADVERTISING**, 16027 Ventura Blvd., Encino CA 91436. (818)501-4613. Ad agency. Creative Director: Steve Mitchell. Produces "recruitment advertising for all types of clients." **Needs:** Works with 1 freelance photographer/month. Uses photographers for billboards, trade magazines, direct mail, P-O-P displays, brochures, catalogs, posters, newspapers, AV presentations and internal promotion. Also works with freelance filmmakers to produce TV commercials, training films (mostly stills).
First Contact & Terms: Query with samples "to be followed by personal interview if interested." Does not return unsolicited material. Reporting time "depends upon jobs in house; I try to arrange appointments within 3 weeks-1 month." Payment "depends upon established budget and subject." Pays on acceptance for assignments; on publication per photo. Buys all rights. Model release required.
Tips: Prefers to see "samples from a wide variety of subjects. No fashion. People-oriented location shots. Nonproduct. Photos of people and/or objects telling a story—a message. Eye-catching." Photographers should have "flexible day and ½ day rates. Must work fast. Ability to get a full day's (or ½) work from a model or models. Excellent sense of lighting. Awareness of the photographic problems with newspaper reproduction."

■**DEKE HOULGATE ENTERPRISES**, Box 7000-371, Redondo Beach CA 90277. (213)540-5001. PR firm. Contact: Deke Houlgate. Types of clients: industrial, automotive, sports. Client list free with SASE.
Needs: Works with 1-3 freelance photographers/month. Uses photographers for consumer and trade magazines, direct mail, brochures, posters, newspapers, and AV presentations. Works with freelance filmmakers to produce a videotape/film newsclip for news and sports TV feature coverage. Occasionally works with producers of barter and free TV 30-60 minute features.
Specs: Uses 8×10 b&w ("mostly") glossy prints; 35mm and 2¼×2¼ color transparencies; 16mm and ¾" (news) film; and 1" or 2" (feature) videotape.
First Contact & Terms: Query with list of stock photo subjects. SASE. Reporting time "depends on situation—as soon as client concurs, but early enough not to inconvenience photographer." Pay "variable but conforming to standard the photographer states. We don't ordinarily haggle, but we buy only what the client can afford." Payment by client, "immediately." Buys all rights. Model release and captions required. Credit line "usually not given, but not a hard and fast rule."
Tips: Prefers to see "photographer's grasp of story-telling with a photo; ability to take direction; ideas he/she can illustrate; understanding of the needs of editors. Take an outstanding photograph and submit, relating to one of our clients. If it's a good buy, we buy. If we buy, we strongly consider making assignments for otherwise unknown freelancers. Our company would rather service a photograph than a story, depending on quality. We'd rather pass on a photo than service a mediocre one. With cost-price squeeze, more PR firms will adopt this attitude."

■**INTERNATIONAL VIDEO NETWORK**, 2242 Camino Ramon, San Ramon CA 94583. (415)866-1121. FAX: (415)866-1121. Director of Marketing Communications: Gail Joerger. Estab. 1985. "Looking for transparencies on travel destinations; also freelance producers wishing to make travel videos for our company."
Needs: "Releasing 10-15 new titles a year." Uses photographers for videotapes and video jacket photos.
Specs: Uses transparencies and videotape. Contact for video needs.
First Contact & Terms: Provide query with stock photo list; provide resume, business card, self-promotion piece or tearsheets to be kept on file for possible future assignments. "I am interested in stock photos of travel destinations." Reports in 1 month. Pays $350-400/color photo. Pays on acceptance. Buys one-time rights. Captions and model releases preferred.

THE JONES AGENCY, 303 N. Indian Ave., Palm Springs CA 92262. (619)325-1437. Ad agency. Senior Art Director: John B. Thompson. Types of clients: retail, fashion, finance, hotels.
Needs: Works with 3-5 freelance photographers/month. Uses freelance photographers for consumer magazines, posters, newspapers, hotel brochures, interior design ads. Subjects include product, hotels, PR, interior design.
Specs: Uses 8×10 glossy b&w prints; 35mm, 2¼×2¼, 4×5, 8×10 transparencies.
First Contact & Terms: Arrange a personal interview to show portfolio; provide resume, business card, brochure, flyer or tearsheets to be kept on file for possible future assignments. Works with freelance photographers on assignment basis only. SASE. Reports in 2 weeks. Pay negotiated. Pays on receipt of invoice. Buys all rights. Model release required. Credit line "depends on job."
Tips: Prefers to see professional capabilities.

■**LE DUC VIDEO**, Suite A, 2002-21st St., Santa Monica CA 90404. (213)450-8275. Vice President: Dennis Gould. Types of clients: cable, home video market, corporate/industrial and music videos.
Needs: Works with 3-10 freelance photographers/month. Uses freelance photographers for slide sets, multimedia productions, videotapes and prints. Subjects vary.
Specs: "Video must meet broadcast specs." Uses 8×10 and horizontal matte-finish b&w and color prints; 35mm, 2¼×2¼ transparencies; Super 8, 16mm, 35mm film; U-matic ¾", 1", and Betacam videotape SVH5.
First Contact & Terms: Provide resume, business card, self-promotion piece or tearsheets to be kept on file for possible future assignments. Works on assignment only. SASE. Reports in 1 month. Pays $25-up/b&w photo; $35-up/color photo; $20-up/hour; $100-up/day; per job negotiated. Pays on acceptance. Buys one-time rights, all rights; "all rights for specific product." Model release required. Credit line given.
Tips: Have good work to show, have it organized and limited to 5 minutes in length. Have credits and references that can be verified. Looks for "both technical quality and the ability to deal with people, since most of our work involves either talking heads or people in action."

*****RICHARD BOND LEWIS & ASSOCIATES**, 1112 W. Cameron Ave., West Covina CA 91790. (818)962-7727. Ad agency. Creative Director: Dick Lewis. Estab. 1971. Types of clients: industrial, consumer products manufacturer, real estate, autos. Client list free with SASE.
Needs: Works with 1-2 freelance photographers/month. Uses photographers for billboards, consumer magazines, trade magazines, direct mail, catalogs and newspapers. Subjects include product photos.
Specs: Uses 4×5 color prints and 4×5 transparencies.
First Contact & Terms: Arrange a personal interview to show portfolio; provide resume, business card, brochure, flyer or tearsheets to be kept on file for possible future assignmnts. Works with freelance photographers on assignment basis only. Does not return unsolicited material. "Will return upon request." Payment negotiable. Pays "usually 10 days from receipt of invoice—no later than 30 days." Buys all rights; "we request negatives on completion of job." Model release required; captions preferred. Credit line given "if client approves."
Tips: Prefers to see a variety—people, industrial, product, landscape, some fashion. "Bring in portfolio and leave some samples which best describe your capabilities."

■**LODESTAR PRODUCTIONS**, 1330 Monument St., Pacific Palisades CA 90272. (213)454-0234. President: Dr. Edward D. Hurley. AV firm. Types of clients: business, industrial, finance, retail, nonprofit and educational. Examples of productions: Air France and RCA.
Needs: Uses photographers for AV presentations.
First Contact & Terms: Provide resume, business card, brochure, flyer or tearsheets to be kept on file for possible future assignments. Works with local freelancers on assignment only. Does not return unsolicited material. Reports as soon as possible. Payment negotiable. Buys one-time rights, exclusive product rights or all rights. or one-time rights. Model release required. Credit line sometimes given.
Tips: "Don't phone, but do send data."

MCMULLEN DESIGN & MARKETING, 15305 S. Normandie Ave., Gardena CA 90247. (213)515-1701. Creative/Art Director: Jim Krogel.
Specs: Uses 8×10 matte b&w prints; 35mm, 2¼×2¼, 4×5 transparencies.
First Contact & Terms: Arrange a personal interview to show portfolio, query with resume of credits; business card, brochure, flyer or tearsheets to be kept on file for possible future assignmnts. Works with local freelancers only. Does not return unsolicited material. Reports in 1 month. Pays $750-1,500/day or pays by the job. Pays 30 days from receipt of invoice. Buys all rights. Model release required.
Tips: Prefers to see industrial, automotive, general product. "Show good quality technical work, be a problem solver, no prima donnas."

■**MARKEN COMMUNICATIONS**, 1245 Oakmead Pkwy., Sunnyvale CA 94086. (408)738-1115. FAX: (408)738-1060. Ad agency and PR firm. Estab. 1977. Production Manager: Leslie Posada. Types of clients: furnishings, electronics and computers. Examples of recent ad campaigns include: Burke Industries (resilient flooring, carpet); Boole and Babbage (mainframe software); Maxar (PCs).
Needs: Works with 3-4 freelance photographers/month. Uses photographers for trade magazine, direct mail and catalogs. Subject matter includes product/applications.
Audiovisual Needs: Slide presentations and sales/demo videos.
Specs: Uses color and b&w prints; 35mm, 2¼×2¼ and 4×5 transparencies.
First Contact & Terms: Arrange a personal interview to show portfolio, query with samples or submit portfolio for review. "Call." Works with freelancers on an assignment basis only. SASE. Reports in 1 month. Pays $50-1,000/b&w photo; $100-1800/color photo; $50-100/hour; $500-1,000/day; $200-2,500/job. Pays 30 days after receipt of invoice. Model release required. Credit line given "sometimes."

■WARREN MILLER FILMS, 505 Pier Ave., Box 536, Hermosa Beach CA 90254. (213)376-2494. Production Manager: Don Brolin. Motion picture production house. Buys 5 films/year.
Subject Needs: Works with 5-20 freelance photographers/month. Uses photographers for outdoor cinematography of skiing (snow) and other sports. Also travel, documentary, promotional, educational and indoor studio filming. "We do everything from TV commercials to industrial films to feature length sports films."
Audiovisual Needs: Uses 16mm film. "We purchase exceptional sport footage not available to us."
Payment & Terms: Pays $150-200/day. Also pays by the job. Pays on receipt of invoice. Buys all rights. Credit line given.
Making Contact: Filmmakers may query with resume of credits and sample reel. "We are only interested in motion picture-oriented individuals who have practical experience in the production of 16mm motion pictures." Works on assignment only. SASE. Reports in 1 week.
Tips: Looks for technical mastering of the craft and equipment—decisive shot selection. "Make a hot demo reel and be a hot skier; be willing to travel."

■MORRIS MEDIA, #105, 2730 Monterey St., Torrance CA 90503. (213)533-4800. Contact: Operations Manager.
Needs: Uses 4-6 freelancers per month to produce slide sets and videotapes. Subjects vary according to projects.
Specs: Uses b&w and color prints, any size and format; 35mm and 2¼×2¼ transparencies; and ¾" and 1" NTSC videotape.
First Contact & Terms: Submit portfolio/demo tape by mail; query with samples; provide resume and list of stock photo subjects with business card, self-promotion piece or tearsheets to be kept on file for possible future assignments. Work with local freelancers on assignment only. Interested in stock photos; subjects vary. Cannot return materials. Reports in 1 week. Payment negotiable. Pays on publication/delivery. Buys all rights (work-for-hire). Captions preferred; model release required. Credit line given.
Tips: "Submit enough material initially to get acquainted." In samples/demos, wants to see creativity and fee range indicated.

■NATIONAL TELEVISION NEWS, INC., Suite 201A, 23480 Park Sorrento, Calabasas Park CA 91302. (818)883-6121. President: Howard Back.
Audiovisual Needs: Works with one freelancer per month to produce videotapes. Usually needed to shoot location video or news/feature coverage. Examples of types of clients: Sears (employee news magazine); Detroit Diesel Corp. (sales video); and Smith Kline Beckman (video news releases).
Specs: Uses ¾", Beta and M-l videotapes.
First Contact & Terms: Provide resume, business card, self-promotion piece, demo tape or tearsheets to be kept on file for possible future assignments. Works with freelancers on assignment only. Cannot return materials. Payment negotiable. Pays on acceptance. Buys all rights (work-for-hire). Captions and model release required.

NORTON-WOOD PR SERVICES, 1430 Tropical Ave., Pasadena CA 91107. (818)351-9216. PR firm. Partner-owner: Nat Wood. Types of clients: industrial.
Needs: Works with 1 freelance photographer/month. Uses freelance photographers for trade magazines, catalogs and brochures.
First Contact & Terms: Query with resume of credits, query with list of stock photo subjects. Works with local freelancers only. Reports in 2 weeks. Pays $50/hour; $500-750/day; $10/b&w photo. Pays on receipt of invoice. Buys all rights. Captions required. Credit line sometimes given.
Tips: Prefer to see industrial products, in-plant shots, personnel, machinery in use. "Be available for Western states assignments primarily. Use other than 35mm equipment."

■ON-Q PRODUCTIONS INC., 618 E. Gutierrez St., Santa Barbara CA 93103. (805)963-1331. President: Vincent Quaranta. Estab. 1984. Producers of multi-projector slide presentations and computer graphics. Buys 100 freelance photos/year; offers 50 assignments/year. Uses photos for brochures, posters, audiovisual presentations, annual reports, catalogs and magazines. Types of clients: industrial, fashion and finance.
Subject Needs: Scenic, people and general stock.
Specs: Uses 35mm, 2¼×2¼ and 4×5 transparencies.
Payment & Terms: Pays $100 minimum/job. Buys rights according to client's needs. Model releases and captions required.
Making Contact: Provide resume, business card, brochure, flyer or tearsheets to be kept on file for possible future assignments. SASE. Reports in 3 weeks.
Tips: Looks for stock slides for AV uses.

ORLIE, HILL & CUNDALL, INC., 20 Liberty Ship Way, Sausalito CA 94965. (415)332-3625. Vice President and Creative Director: Alan W. Cundall. Ad agency. Estab. 1987. Uses all media except foreign. Types of clients: industrial, retail, fashion, finance, computer and hi-tech, travel, healthcare, insurance and real estate. Examples of recent campaigns: West Coast Life (trade ads to insurance agents); Ross Hospital (seminars on drugs and alcohol); Lincoln Property Co. (direct mail campaign to building tenants). Works with 1 freelance photographer/month on assignment only basis. Provide resume, business card and brochure to be kept on file for future assignments. Pays on a per-photo basis; negotiates payment based on client's budget, amount of creativity required and where work will appear. Usually buys one-time rights. "Don't send anything unless it's a brochure of your work or company. We keep a file of talent—we then contact photographers as jobs come up."
Tips: "Most books are alike. I look for creative and technical excellence, then how close to our offices; cheap vs. costly; personal rapport; references from friends in agencies who've used him/her. Call first. Send samples and resume if I'm not 'granting' interviews due to work pressure. Keep in touch with new samples."

■**JONATHAN PARKER'S GATEWAYS INST.**, Box 1778, Ojai CA 93023. (805)646-0267. Executive Vice President: Sylvia Thompson.
Needs: Uses photographers for catalog work.
Specs: Uses color prints; 35mm and 2¼ × 2¼ transparencies.
First Contact & Terms: Submit portfolio by mail, query with samples. Works with local freelancers only. Interested in stock photos/footage. SASE. Reports in 2-3 weeks. Pays $200 + /color photo. Pays on publication. Buys one-time or all rights. Credit line given.
Tips: Looks for "landscapes, silhouettes and seascapes" in photos submitted.

PHOTEC, P.O. Box 20328, Long Beach CA 90801. Ad agency and stock photo agency. Manager/Owner: Steve Potter. Types of clients: industrial, commercial, marine, maritime, public services, retail, high-tech R&D, manufacturing, training and licensing agencies. Recent ad campaigns: Alquist Marine Services, Inc. (print ads, PR); Hobie Catamarans (brochures, sales PR materials); Pub Cruises, Inc. (brochures, ads, decor materials); Polymerics, Inc. (QA training materials, print ads, PR and annual reports).
Needs: Uses photography for consumer magazines, trade magazines, direct mail, catalogs, posters, signage, newspapers, brochures, annual reports and manuals. Subjects: (QC-QA) marine living (people live-aboards); boats in design, manufacture and use; high-tech/AC-AB technology and training manuals. Interested in reviewing photos of marine living and cruising, boats in design, manufacture and use; training, operating and maintenance photos, mainly R&D and manufacturing technology.
Specs: Uses 8 × 10 glossy b&w and color prints; 35mm, and 4 × 5, transparencies. VHS videotape.
First Contact & Terms: Query with resume of credits, list of photo subjects, samples; provide resume, business card, brochure, flyer/tearsheets to be kept on file with SASE. Pays via contract only. Model release where required. Photo captions preferred. Credit line usually given, depending on uses.
Tips: "Technical photographic capabilities, knowledge of boats and operating uses and an artistic sense are essential, but you should be more technical than 'arty.' Also, you should know graphics methods/limitations and printing technology; 'state-of-the-art photo technology, films and materials."

■**BILL RASE PRODUCTIONS, INC.**, 955 Venture Court, Sacramento CA 95825. (916)929-9181. Manager/Owner: Bill Rase. AV firm. Types of clients: industry, business, government, publishing and education. Produces filmstrips, slide sets, multimedia kits, motion pictures, sound-slide sets, videotapes, mass cassette, reel and video duplication. Photo and film purchases vary. Payment depends on job, by bid. Pays 30 days after acceptance. Buys one-time rights or all rights; varies according to clients needs. Model release required. Query with samples and resume of credits. Freelancers within 100 miles only. Does not return samples. SASE. Reports "according to the type of project. Sometimes it takes a couple of months to get the proper bid info."
Subject Needs: "Script recording for educational clients is our largest need, followed by industrial training, state and government work, motivational, etc." Freelance photos used in filmstrips and slides; sometimes motion pictures. No nudes. Color only for filmstrips and slides. Vertical format for TV cutoff only. Sound for TV public service announcements, commercials, and industrial films. Uses stock footage of hard-to-find scenes, landmarks in other cities, shots from the 1920s to 1980s, etc. Special subject needs include 35 mm and ¾-inch video shot of California landmark locations, espcially San Francisco, Napa Valley Wine Country, Gold Country, Lake Tahoe area, Delta area and Sacramento area. "We buy out the footage—so much for so much," or ¾-inch video or 35 mm slides. Uses 8 × 10 prints and 35mm transparencies.
Tips: "Video footage of the popular areas of this country and others is becoming more and more useful. Have price list, equipment list and a few slide samples in a folder or package available to send."

*■SARVER & WITZERMAN ADVERTISING, 3300 Industry, Long Beach CA 90806. (213)832-5863. Ad agency. President: Joe Witzerman. Estab. 1954. Types of clients: industrial and financial. Client list free with SASE.

Needs: Works with 3 freelance photographers/month. Uses photographers for billboards, consumer and trade magazines, direct mail, P-O-P displays, brochures, catalogs, posters, and newspapers. Subject needs: "from food to trucks." Works with freelance filmmakers to produce TV commercials.

Specs: Uses 8×10 to 16×20 b&w glossy prints; 35mm and 4×5 transparencies; 16mm film and videotape.

First Contact & Terms: Arrange a personal interview to show portfolio; send unsolicited material by mail for consideration. Works with freelance photographers on assignment basis only. SASE. Reports in 2 weeks. Pays \$\$100-500/b&w photo; \$300-600/color photo; \$50-125/hour; \$300-500/day and \$1,000-5,000/job. Pays on completion. Buys one-time and exclusive product rights. Model release required. Credit line given "when requested."

Tips: Second address: 2031 Daladier Dr., Rancho Paolos Verdes CA 90274.

■TAMARA SCOTT PRODUCTIONS, 19062 Two Bar Rd., Boulder Creek CA 95006. (408)338-9683.

Needs: Uses freelance photographers for filmstrips, slide sets, multimedia productions, films and videotapes.

First Contact & Terms: Submit portfolio by mail; query with samples, resume and photo stock list; provide resume, business card, self-promotion piece or tearsheets to be kept on file for possible future assignments. Works on assignment only; interested in stock photos/footage. Does not return unsolicited material. Reports "as needed." Pays \$25-75/hour; \$25-2,500/b&w photo; \$25-2,500/color photo; \$25-500/hour; \$200-2,500/day. Pays upon payment from client. Buys one-time rights, exclusive product rights or all rights. Model release required. Credit line given.

Tips: Looks for special effects, business portraiture, poster, greeting card and postcard imagery. "Submit samples to keep on file."

■RON TANSKY ADVERTISING CO., Suite 111, 14852 Ventura Blvd., #111, Sherman Oaks CA 91403. (818)990-9370. FAX: (818)990-0456. Ad agency and PR firm. Consulting Art Directors: Van Valencia, Norm Galston. Estab. 1976. Serves all types of clients.

Needs: Works with 2 freelance photographers/month. Uses photographers for billboards, consumer and trade magazines, direct mail, P-O-P displays, brochures, catalogs, signage, newspapers and AV presentations. Subjects include "mostly product—but some without product as well." Special subject needs include consumer electronics, nutrition products and over-the-counter drugs.

Audiovisual Needs: Works with freelance filmmakers to produce TV commercials.

Specs: Uses b&w or color prints; 2¼×2¼, 4×5 transparencies; 16mm and videotape film.

First Contact & Terms: Query with resume of credits; provide resume, business card, brochure, flyer or tearsheets to be kept on file for possible future assignments. SASE. Payment "depends on subject and client's budget." General payment range: Pays \$50-250/b&w photo; \$100-1,500/color photo; \$500-1,500/day; \$100-1,500/complete job. Pays in 30 days. Buys all rights. Model release required.

Tips: Prefers to see "product photos, originality of position and lighting" in a portfolio. "We look for creativity and general competence, i.e., focus and lighting as well as ability to work with models." Photographers should provide "rate structure and ideas of how they would handle product shots." Also, "Don't use fax unless we make request."

*■VIDEO IMAGERY, 204 Calle De Anza, San Clemente CA 92672. (714)492-5082. General Manager: Bob Fisher. Types of clients: industrial-manufacturing.

Needs: Works with 2 photographers/month. Uses photographers for videotapes. Subjects include training in the manufacturing concept, in light and heavy industrial.

Specs: Uses VHS, U-matic ¾" videotape.

First Contact & Terms: Query with resume. Works with freelancers by assignment only. Reports in 3 weeks. Buys all rights. Captions and model release required. Credit line given if requested.

The asterisk before a listing indicates that the market is new in this edition. New markets are often the most receptive to freelance submissions.

*∎DANA WHITE PRODUCTIONS, INC., 2623 29th St., Santa Monica CA 90405. (213)450-9101. FAX: (213)450-9101. AV firm. President: Dana White. Estab. 1977. Types of clients: corporate and educational. Examples of recent productions: 16-part AV "World of Work" program (shows career opportunities to high school students), Glencoe/McGraw-Hill; "Natural Gas" Clean Air Program, Southern California Gas Co.; Firescope, Emergency Training (8-part AV for firefighters).
Needs: Works with 2-3 freelance photographers/month. Uses photographers for catalogs, audiovisual and books. Subjects include: people, products and architecture. Interested in reviewing 35mm stock photos.
Audiovisual Needs: Uses all AV formats; also slides for multi-image slide shows using 1-9 projectors.
Specs: Uses b&w prints; 35mm, 2¼ × 2¼ transparencies.
First Contact & Terms: Arrange a personal interview to show portfolio; query with samples. Works with freelancers on assignment basis only. Cannot return material. Report time depends on schedule. Pays $10-100/hour; $50-350/day; $20-10,000/job; $20/color or b&w photo. Pays on acceptance and receipt of invoice. Buys all rights. Credit line given sometimes.
Tips: In freelancer's portfolio or demos, wants to see "quality of composition, lighting, saturation, degree of difficulty and importance of assignment." The trend is toward "more video, less AV." To break in, freelancer should "diversify, negotiate, get the job, don't get stuck in a fixed way of doing things. Work flexibly with producers."

Los Angeles

N.W. AYER, INC., 888 S. Figueroa St., Los Angeles CA 90017. (213)486-7400. Contact: VP/Creative Director. Ad agency.
Needs: Works with freelance photographers on assignment only basis. Uses photographers for billboards, consumer magazines, direct mail, brochures, flyers, newspapers, P-O-P displays, TV, trade magazines and AV.
First Contact & Terms: Call for personal appointment to show portfolio. Pays 30 days after receipt of approved invoice in N.Y. office.
Tips: Wants to see "quality not quantity."

BEAR ADVERTISING, 1424 N. Highland, Los Angeles CA 90028. (213)466-6464. Vice President: Bruce Bear. Ad agency. Uses consumer magazines, direct mail, foreign media, P-O-P displays and trade magazines. Serves sporting goods, fast foods and industrial clients. Works with 4 freelance photographers/month on assignment only basis. Provide business card and tearsheets to be kept on file for possible future assignments.
Payment & Terms: Pays $150-250/b&w photo; $200-350/color photo. Pays 30 days after billing to client. Buys all rights.
Making Contact: Call to arrange interview to show portfolio. Prefers to see samples of sporting goods, fishing equipment, outdoor scenes, product shots with rustic atmosphere of guns, rifles, fishing reels, lures, camping equipment, etc. SASE. Reports in 1 week.
Specs: Uses b&w and color photos.

BUTLER ADVERTISING, (formerly Butler Kosh Brooks), 940 N. Highland, Los Angeles CA 90038. (213)469-8128. Design firm. Account Executive: Michael Masterson. Estab 1987. Types of clients: fashion, entertainment, medical, home video distributors. Client list on request with SASE.
Needs: Works with 2 photographers/month. Uses photographers for a wide variety of work.
Specs: Uses b&w and color prints, transparencies.
First Contact & Terms: Query with resume of credits. Provide resume, business card, brochure, flyer or tearsheets to be kept on file for possible future assignments. Works with freelance photographers on assignment basis only. Does not return unsolicited material. Reports in 1 week.
Tips: "Submit resume and self promo—call to check if they've been received."

GORDON GELFOND ASSOCIATES, INC., 11500 Olympic Blvd., #377, Los Angeles CA 90048. (213)478-3600. FAX: (213)477-4825.Ad agency. Art Director: Barry Brenner. Types of clients: retail, financial, hospitals and consumer eletronic.
Needs: Works with 1-2 photographers/month. Uses freelance photographers for billboards, consumer magazines, trade magazines, direct mail and newspapers. Subject matter varies.
Specs: Uses b&w and color prints; 35mm, 2¼ × 2¼ and 4 × 5 transparencies.
First Contact & Terms: Arrange a personal interview to show portfolio, send unsolicited photos by mail for consideration, submit portfolio for review. Provide resume, business card, brochure, flyer or tearsheets to be kept on file for posssible future assignments. Works with local freelance photographers on assignment basis only. Does not return unsolicited material. Reports ASAP. Pays

by the job. Payment is made 30 days after receipt of invoice. Buys all rights. Model release required. Credit line sometimes given.
Tips: Preferred subjects, styles in portfolio or samples depends on assignment. "Works within a budget."

■**MYRIAD PRODUCTIONS,** Suite 402, 1314 N. Hayworth Ave., Los Angeles CA 90046. (213)851-1400. President: Ed Harris. Primarily involved with sports productions and events. Photographers used for portraits, live-action and studio shots, special effects photos, advertising, illustrations, brochures, TV and film graphics, theatrical and production stills. Works with freelance photographers on assignment only basis. Provide brochure, resume and samples to be kept on file for possible future assignments. Payment varies with assignment. Credit line sometimes given. Buys all rights. Send material by mail for consideration. Does not return unsolicited material. Reporting time "depends on urgency of job or production."
B&W: Uses 8×10 glossy prints.
Color: Uses 8×10 prints and 2×2 transparencies.
Tips: "We look for an imaginative photographer, one who captures all the subtle nuances, as the photographer is as much a part of the creative process as the artist or scene being shot. Working with us depends almost entirely on the photographer's skill and creative sensitivity with the subject. All materials submitted will be placed on file and not returned, pending future assignments. Photographers should not send us their only prints, transparencies, etc. for this reason."

ROGERS & COWAN, INC., Suite 400, 10,000 Santa Monica Blvd., Los Angeles CA 90067. (213)201-8800. FAX: (213)552-0412. Contact: Carol Renteria. PR firm. Estab. 1945. Types of clients: entertainment.
Needs: Works with qualified freelance photographers on assignment only basis. Uses photographers for consumer and trade magazines, posters, newspapers and feature films.
First Contact & Terms: Works with local freelancers only. Phone for appointment. Payment "depends on the job; usually pays $150-350/day."
Tips: In photographer's portfolio, wants to see "Clarity, composition, sensitivity to the eye contact. The way the portfolio is assembled will give me an idea of what I can expect of that photographer. I also like to see b&w contact sheets." To break in with this firm, "act like a professional—no one wants to hire a photographer who is constantly apologizing for lack of material in the portfolio. Just put the best in it—it's quality, not quantity that counts."

San Francisco

*■**ANDERSON/ROTHSTEIN, INC.,** 139 Townsend St., San Francisco CA 94107. (415)495-6420. FAX: (415)495-0319. Ad agency. Senior Art Director: Dean Narahara. Estab. 1982. Types of clients: food service and banking.
Needs: Works with 5-6 freelance photographers/filmmakers/videographers/month. Uses photographers for consumer, trade magazines, direct mail, P-O-P displays, catalogs, posters, newspapers, signage and audiovisual. Subjects include: food.
Audiovisual Needs: Occasionally uses 35mm slides for slide shows; infrequent need for film and videotape.
Specs: Uses b&w prints, any format or size. Uses 2¼×2¼, 4×5 and 8×10 transparencies.
First Contact & Terms: Arrange personal interview to show portfolio. Provide resume, business card, brochure, flyer or tearsheets to be kept on file for possible future assignments. Cannot return material. Reports in 1-2 weeks. Usually pays $1,000-2,000/day; specific terms negotiable. Buys all rights (work-for-hire) and one-time rights. Credit line sometimes given.

■**ARNOLD & ASSOCIATES PRODUCTIONS, INC.,** 2159 Powell St., San Francisco CA 94133. (415)989-3490. President: John Arnold. Types of clients: Fortune 500.
Needs: Works with 4 freelance photographers/month. Uses photographers for multimedia productions. Subjects include: national trade shows, permanent exhibits and national TV commercials.
Specs: Uses 35mm transparencies; 35mm film; U-matic ¾" and 1" videotape.
First Contact & Terms: Query with resume. Works with freelancers by assignment only. Does not return unsolicited material. Reports in 2 weeks. Pays $300-1,200/day. Pays net 20 days. Buys all rights. Model release and captions required.
Tips: "We produce top-quality, award winning productions working with top professionals able to provide highest quality work." Wants to see dramatic lighting, creative composition and sense of style in photos submitted.

PINNE/HERBERS ADVERTISING INC., (formerly Pinne Garvin Herbers & Hock, Inc.), 200 Vallejo St., San Francisco CA 94111. (415)956-4210. Creative Director: Robert Pinne. Art Directors: Pierre Jacot, Floyd Yost. Ad agency. Uses all media including radio and TV. Serves clients in electronics, finance, banking, software and hardware and transportation. Buys all rights. Call to arrange an appointment or submit portfolio by mail if out of town. Reports in 5 days. SASE.
Color: Uses transparencies and prints; contact sheet OK. "Do not send originals unsolicited." Model release required.
Tips: "Out of town talent should not send original material unless requested." Photographers should "be realistic as to whether his/her style would be applicable to our client list. If so, call for an appointment. It's a waste of both our time for me to say, 'that's beautiful work, but we can't use that type.' "

PURDOM PUBLIC RELATIONS, 395 Oyster Point, San Francisco CA 94080. (415)588-5700. PR firm. Estab. 1965. President: Paul Purdom. Types of clients: industrial and financial. Examples of recent PR campaigns: Sun Microsystems, Varian Associates, Calma Co. (all showing computers and instruments systems in use).
Needs: Works with 4-6 freelance photographers/month. Uses photographers for trade magazines, direct mail and newspapers. Subjects include industrial and scientific topics.
Specs: Uses 35mm and 2¼×2¼ transparencies; film: contact for specs.
First Contact & Terms: Query with resume of credits, list of stock photo subjects. Provide resume, business card, brochure, flyer or tearsheets to be kept on file for possible future assignments. Works with freelancers photographers on an assignment basis only. Does not return unsolicited material. Reports "as needed." Pays $50-150/hour, $400-1,500/day. Pays on receipt of invoice. Buys all rights. Model release preferred.

EDGAR S. SPIZEL ADVERTISING AND PUBLIC RELATIONS, 1782 Pacific Ave., San Francisco CA 94109. (415)474-5735. Ad agency and PR firm. President: Edgar S. Spizel. Types of clients: retail, finance, hotels, developers, arts, TV and radio.
Needs: Works with 2 freelance photographers/month. Uses photographers for consumer and trade magazines, direct mail, P-O-P displays, posters, signage and newspapers. Subjects include people, buildings, hotels, apartments, interiors.
Specs: Uses 8×10 glossy b&w and color prints; 35mm, 2¼×2¼, 4×5 transparencies.
First Contact & Terms: Send unsolicited photos by mail for consideration; provide resume, business card, brochure, flyer or tearsheets to be kept on file for possible future assignments. Works with freelance photographers on an assignment basis only. Does not return unsolicited material. Pays by the hour, day, or job. Pays on acceptance. Buys all rights. Model release required. Credit line sometimes given.

■**VARITEL VIDEO**, 350 Townsend St., San Francisco CA 94107. (415)495-3328. Vice President of Marketing and Sales: Lori Anderson. Production Manager: Mary Ann Fabian. Types of clients: advertising agencies.
Needs: Works with 10 freelance photographers/month. Uses freelance photographers for filmstrips, slide sets and videotapes. Also works with freelance filmmakers for CD Rom, Paint Box.
Specs: Uses color prints; 35mm transparencies; 16mm, 35mm film; VHS, Beta, U-matic ¾" or 1" videotape. Also, D2.
First Contact & Terms: Provide resume, business card, self-promotion piece or tearsheets to be kept on file for possible future assignments. Does not return unsolicited material. Reports in 1 week. Pays $50-100/hour; $200-500/day. Pays on acceptance. Rights vary.
Tips: Apply by resume and examples of work to Ed Grandlund and Allison Smith.

Colorado

*■**ART DIRECTION**, 2005 Broadway, Boulder CO 80302. (303)443-7603. FAX: (303)443-7605. Advertising and design firm. President: Bob Truemper. Types of clients: industrial, musical equipment and medical. Examples of ad campaigns: Ultimate Support, Inc. (musical equipment support, ie keyboard stands, etc.), introduced new keyboard stand—Ads, direct mail, and Product Flyer; Art Director's Club of Denver, produced and directed; awards show on video; Ivion (medical equipment co.), promotion on new portable IV pump for home use, direct mail series, 3-part to 3 different markets.

Needs: Works with 3 freelance photographers/—filmmakers—videographers/month. Uses photographers for consumer magazines, trade magazines, direct mail, P-O-P displays, catalogs and audiovisual. Subjects include: produce and/or image. Reviews stock photos/film or video footage depending on the current project in the studio.

Audiovisual Needs: Uses photos/film/video for corporate video/sales promotion video, occasional slide shows and TV commercials (film, usually).

Specs: Uses 8×10 matte b&w prints; 2¼×2¼ and 4×5 transparencies; 16 and 35mm film; Betacam videotape, usually.

First Contact & Terms: Query with samples; provide resume, business card, brochure, flyer or tearsheets to be kept on file for possible future assignments. Works with local freelancers only. SASE. Reports in 1-2 weeks. Pays $500-1,200/day. Pays 30 days after invoice. Buys one-time rights. Model release required. Credit line not given.

Tips: In freelancer's demos, wants to see "distinct style." Sees trend toward more video. If interested in breaking in, "keep trying." Photographers can make the transition into these media through "hard work, study, and being in the right place at the right time."

■**BULLOCH & HAGGART ADVERTISING INC.**, 226 E. Monument, Colorado Springs CO 80903. (719)635-7576. Ad agency. Estab. 1979. Art Director: Rick Specht. Types of clients: industrial, real estate, finance, high-tech.

Needs: Works with 2 freelance photographers/month. Uses photographers for consumer and trade magazines, direct mail, brochures, catalogs, newspapers, and AV presentations. Subjects include studio setups, location, some stock material.

Audiovisual Needs: Works with freelance filmmakers to produce commercials.

Specs: Uses b&w prints; 35mm, 2¼×2¼, 4×5 and 8×10 transparencies; 16mm and 35mm film and videotape.

First Contact & Terms: Arrange a personal interview to show portfolio, query with list of stock photo subjects; provide resume, business card, brochure, flyer or tearsheets to be kept on file for possible future assignments. Works with freelance photographers on assignment basis only. Does not return unsolicited material. Reports in 2 weeks. Pays $35-50/hour; $350-500/day. Pays 30 days after billing. Buys all rights or one-time rights. Model release required. Credit line "not usually given."

Tips: Prefers to see "professional (commercial only) work" in a portfolio. "We have little need for portraits and/or photojournalism. Photographers should be able to complete an assignment with minimal supervision. Our photographers solve problems for us. They need to understand deadlines and budgets, and should be able to take an assignment and add their creative input."

FOX, SWEENEY & TRUE, 707 Sherman, Denver CO 80203. (303)837-0510. Creative Director: Fran Scannell. Art Director: Chuck Norris. Ad agency. Serves clients in industry, finance and housing.

Needs: Works with 1-2 freelance photographers/month. Uses photographers for consumer and trade magazines, brochures/flyers and newspapers. Provide business card, brochure or flyer to be kept on file for possible future assignments.

First Contact & Terms: Negotiates payment based on nature of job. Pays in 30 days.

Tips: Prefers to see samples of best work; b&w, color transparencies and prints. "Be patient."

■**FRIEDENTAG PHOTOGRAPHICS**, 356 Grape St., Denver CO 80220. (303)333-7096. Manager: Harvey Friedentag. AV firm. Estab. 1957. Serves clients in business, industry, government, trade and union organizations. Produces slide sets, motion pictures and videotape. Works with 5-10 freelancers/month on assignment only. Provide flyer, business card and brochure and nonreturnable samples to show to clients. Buys 1,000 photos and 25 films/year.

Subject Needs: Business, training, public relations and industrial plants showing people and equipment or products in use.

Audiovisual Needs: Uses freelance photos in color slide sets and motion pictures. No posed looks. Also produces mostly 16mm Ektachrome and some 16mm b&w; ¾" and VHS videotape. Length requirement: 3-30 minutes. Interested in stock footage on business, industry, education, recreation and unusual information.

Specs: Uses 8×10 glossy b&w prints; 8×10 glossy color prints; transparencies; 35mm or 2¼×2¼ or 4×5 color transparencies.

First Contact & Terms: Send material by mail for consideration. SASE. Reports in 3 weeks. Pays $300/day for still; $500/day for motion picture plus expenses, or $25/b&w photo or $50/color photo. Pays on acceptance. Buys rights as required by clients. Model release required.

Tips: "More imagination needed, be different and above all, technical quality is a must. There are more opportunities now than ever, especially for new people. We are looking to strengthen our file of talent across the nation."

■**MERIWETHER PUBLISHING LTD.**, 885 Elkton Dr., Colorado Springs CO 80907. (719)594-4422. Editor: Arthur Zapel. "We create our own products—books, filmstrips or videotapes."
Needs: "Use very few—most is done in house. Uses photographers for slide sets and videotapes. We specialize in subjects relating to theater arts. We would consider any how-to photos or videotapes on acting, stage lighting or set design."
Specs: Uses 35mm transparencies; also "standard VCR videotapes."
First Contact & Terms: Query with resume; provide, business card, self-promotion piece or tearsheets to be kept on file for possible future assignments. Works with freelancers on assingment only. SASE. Reports in 3 weeks. Payment negotiable." Pays on acceptance. Buys one-time rights. Captions preferred; model releases required. Credit line given.
Tips: "Provide a marketable concept relating to our product line. We look for how-to photography about theater arts. Videotapes will be as important as books for publishers."

■**TRANSTAR PRODUCTIONS, INC.**, Suite C, 9520 E. Jewell Ave., Denver CO 80231. Contact: Doug Hanes. Motion picture and videotape production. Serves clients in business and industry. Produces 16mm films, ¾", Betacam and 1" video-tapes, multiprojector slide shows and sound tracks. Also offers ¾" video editing suite and ¼" multi-track sound studio.
Audiovisual Needs: Looking for freelance photographers, writers and film production personnel experienced in a variety of film and video areas.
Payment & Terms: Pays by the job, or per day. Pays negotiable rates; 50% of expenses up front; balance upon delivery of approved product.
Making Contact: Send resume and/or material before phone contact. Previous sales experience very helpful. "Know the business of film production."

Connecticut

■**AV DESIGN**, 1823 Silas Deane, P.O. Box 588, Rocky Hill CT 06067. (203)529-2581. FAX: (203)529-5480. Contact: Deborah Almeida. Types of clients: Industrial, finance, manufacturers, insurance and lecturers. Examples of ad campaigns: Pirelli Armstrong and Stanley Hardware, (multi-image presentations); also, Heublein, (product photography).
Audiovisual Needs: Works with 3 freelance photographers/month. Uses photographers for slide sets, multimedia productions and videotapes. Subjects include industrial—manufacturing.
Specs: Uses 8×10 b&w and color prints; 35mm, 2¼×2¼ and 4×5 transparencies.
First Contact & Terms: Query with samples, resume or stock photo list. Works with local freelancers on assignment basis only; interested in stock photos/footage. Reports in 1 month. Payment varies according to client's budget. Pays on acceptance. Buys all rights. Captions and model release preferred.

■**CORP VIDEO CENTER**, 250 Harbor Dr., Stamford CT 06904. (203)965-6666. Operations/Facilities Manager: Susan Haran. Examples of recent productions: "GE Monogram Kitchen", (still photography and video); "Electronic Information Systems (still photography).
Needs: Uses photographers for videotapes. Subjects include: corporate, industrial and live-action videos.
Specs: Uses ¾" Beta or 1" videotape.
First Contact & Terms: Provide resume, business card, self-promotion piece or tearsheets to be kept on file for possible future assignments; provide demo reel. Works with freelancers on assignment only. Pays $250-400/day or by project. Pays on booking—within 2-4 weeks of acceptance. Buys "unlimited" rights. Model releases required. Credit lines sometimes given depending on client and project.
Tips: "Since our freelancers represent us when doing a job, appearance, timeliness, and flexibility are important."

■**CURRENT AFFAIRS**, 346 Ethan Allen Hwy., Ridgefield CT 06877. (203)431-0421. Types of clients: educational and corporate.
Needs: Uses photographers for filmstrips, multimedia productions and videotapes.
Specs: Uses 35mm transparencies; VHS videotape.
First Contact & Terms: Provide resume, business card, self-promotion piece or tearsheets to be kept on file for possible future assignments. Works with local freelancers on assignment only; interested in stock photos/footage. Reports in 1 month. Pay individually negotiated. Buys one-time and all rights. Captions and model release required. Credit line sometimes given.

■**DISCOVERY PRODUCTIONS**, 1415 King St., Greenwich CT 06831. (203)531-6288. Proprietor: David Epstein. PR/AV firm. Serves educational and social action agencies. Produces 16mm and 35mm films. Works with up to 2 freelance photographers/month on assignment only basis. Provide resume to be kept on file for possible future assignments. Buys 2 films annually. Pays on use and 30 days. Buys all rights, but may reassign to filmmaker. Query first with resume of credits.
Film: 16mm and 35mm documentary, educational and industrial films. Possible assignments include research, writing, camera work or editing. "We would collaborate on a production of an attractive and practical idea." Model release required. Pays 25-60% royalty.

■**EAGLEVISION, INC.**, 800 Canal St., Stamford CT 06902. (203)359-8777. President: Michael Macari, Jr. Types of clients: corporate/industrial.
Needs: Works with 6 freelance photographers/month. Uses photographers for slide sets, films and videotapes. Subjects include industrial stills.
Specs: Uses b&w and color prints; 8mm, Super 8, 16mm and 35mm film.
First Contact & Terms: Submit portfolio by mail. Works with freelancers on assignment only; interested in stock photos/footage. Does not return unsolicited material. Reports in 1 month. Pays/job. Pays on completion. Buys all rights. Captions preferred; model releases required. Credit line given, depends on project.

■**GOODWICK ASSOCIATES, INC.**, 117 S. Main St., Newtown CT 06470. (203)426-1267. Ad agency. Creative Director: Nathalie Lutz. Types of clients: business-to-business and industrial. Examples of ad campaigns: Jovil Manufacturing (10 Reasons Why); Logix Computer (Hungry . . .); GE (When the Heat's On).
Needs: Works with 1 freelance photographer/month. Subjects include: location photos.
Audiovisual Needs: Interested in reviewing stock film/video footage.
Specs: Uses 5×7 color prints, b&w prints; 35mm, 2¼×2¼, 4×5 and 8×10 transparencies; ½″ videotape; film. Provide resume, business card, brochure, flyer or tearsheets to be kept on file for possible future assignments. Works with freelancers on an assignment basis only. Cannot return material. Reports in 2 weeks. Pays $50-100/hour, $500-700/day. Pays in 30 days. Buys all rights. Model release required. Credit line given sometimes, depending on client.

■**JACOBY/STORM PRODUCTIONS, INC.**, 22 Crescent Rd., Westport CT 06880. (203)227-2220. President: Doris Storm. Vice President: Frank Jacoby. AV firm. Types of clients: include industry and educational institutions. Produces filmstrips, slide shows, motion pictures and videotapes. Needs occasional photos of people (all ages and ethnic mixtures), urban/suburban life, school/classroom situations, and scenery. Buys one-time rights. "Pays on a per day or per job basis." Call to arrange an appointment or query with resume of credits. SASE.
Film: 16mm documentary, industrial and educational films in color and b&w. Possible assignments include only freelance crew assignments: assistant cameraman, gaffers, sound, editing, etc.
Color: Uses 35mm transparencies.
Tips: "We suggest that you design your portfolio to suit potential client—in our case, emphasize photojournalism techniques in 35mm color slides."

THE MORETON AGENCY, Box 749, East Windsor CT 06088. (203)627-0326. Ad agency. Art Director: Roy Kimball. Types of clients: industrial, sporting goods, corporate and consumer.
Needs: Works with 3-4 photographers/month. Uses photographers for consumer and trade magazines, direct mail, catalogs, newspapers and literature. Subject matter includes people, sports, industrial, product, sports and fashion.
Specs: Uses b&w prints; 35mm, 2¼×2¼, 4×5 and 8×10 transparencies.
First Contact & Terms: Provide business card, brochure, flyer or tearsheets to be kept on file for possible future assignments. Works with freelance photographers on assignment only. Does not return unsolicited material. Pays $800-1,500/day; other payment negotiable. Buys all rights. Model release required. Credit line negotiable.

■**PRAXIS MEDIA, INC.**, 18 Marshall St., South Norwalk CT 06854. (203)866-6666. FAX: (203)853-8299. Vice President and General Manager: Ron Nicodemus. Estab. 1981. Serves corporate/industrial clients. Produces children's and other home video products. Examples of recent clients: American Express, Random House and NFL Properties.
Needs: Works with 1-2 freelance photographers/month. Uses photographers for slide sets, multimedia productions and videotapes. Subjects include corporate primarily, some entertainment/music.
Audiovisual Needs: Uses slides, video and computer graphics.
First Contact & Terms: Provide resume, business card, self-promotion piece or tearsheets to be kept on file for possible future assignments. Works with local freelancers only; works with freelancers by assignment only. SASE. Reports in 2-3 weeks. Pays $250-1,000/day; $250-2,500/job. Pays via 45 day payment policy. Buys all rights.

Tips: Looks for a "creative eye," with good composition and lighting. "Follow up on calls—we normally hire local photographers/videographers."

■**SAVE THE CHILDREN,** Communications Center, 54 Wilton Rd., Westport CT 06880. (203)221-4165. Photo Resources Coordinator: Jerry Lang. Nonprofit organization. Produces slide presentations, 16mm film, videotapes, publications, and displays. Subjects and photo needs relate to children in poverty areas both in the US and overseas, as well as "examples of self-help and development projects, sponsored by Save the Children." Works with 0-5 freelance photographers/month on assignment only basis. Provide letter of inquiry, flyer and tearsheets to be kept on file for possible future assignments. Buys 25-200 photos and 3,000-4,000 feet of film annually. Buys all rights, but may reassign to photographer. Pays $75-300 minimum/day; negotiates payment based on client's budget and photographer's previous experience/reputation. Pays on receipt of materials. Query first with resume of credits. Reports in 1 month. SASE.
Video: Used in documentaries, fund raising films, public service films and TV commercials. Possible assignments include filming 1,500-2,500 feet of a Save the Children project on location, which will be submitted to Save the Children for processing and editing. "When catastrophe or natural disaster strikes a country in which we have programs, footage is needed immediately," but only on assignment. Model release required for US subjects.
B&W: Send contact sheet or negatives. Uses 5×7 glossy prints. Captions and model release required for US subjects.
Color: Send 35mm transparencies. Captions and model release required for US subjects.
Tips: "We need to communicate, as powerfully as possible, the desperate needs of the poor (have-not) people of the world—especially the children."

Delaware

■**LYONS MARKETING COMMUNICATIONS,** 715 Orange St., Wilmington DE 19801. (302)654-6146. Ad agency. Design Director: Erik Vaughn. Types of clients: consumer, corporate and industrial.
Needs: Works with 10 freelance photographers/month. Uses photographers for consumer and trade magazine ads, direct mail, P-O-P displays, catalogs, posters and newspaper ads. Subjects vary greatly. Some fashion, many "outdoor-sport" type of things. Also, high-tech business-to-business.
Specs: Format varies by use.
First Contact & Terms: Query with resume of credits and list of stock photo subjects. Provide resume, business card, brochure, flyer or tearsheets to be kept on file for possible future assignments. SASE. Reports in 3 weeks. Pays $1,000/day. Payment varies based on scope of job, abilities of the photographer. Pays on publication. Rights purchased vary. Model release required; captions preferred. Credit line given depending on job.
Tips: "We consider the subjects, styles, and capabilities of the photographer. Rather than guess at what we're looking for, show us what you're good at and enjoy doing. Be available on a tight and changing schedule; show an ability to pull together the logistics of a complicated shoot."

District of Columbia

■**SUSAN DAVIS ADVERTISING GROUP,** Suite 700, 1146 19th St. NW, Washington DC 20036. (202)775-8881. Ad agency, PR firm. Specialties: Events planning, international lobbying and consulting. Art Director: Jill Goldstein. Estab. 1973. Types of clients: hotel, finance, resort, home improvement, industrial and retail.
Needs: Works with 1 freelance photographer/month. Uses photographers for billboards, consumer magazines, catalogs and newspapers. Reviews stock photos, and film and video, as needed.
Specs: Uses color and b&w prints, all sizes; 4×5 transparencies.
First Contact & Terms: Send unsolicited photos by mail for consideration. Provide resume, business card, brochure, flyer or tearsheets to be kept on file for possible future assignments. Works with freelancers on an assignment basis only. SASE. Reports in 3 weeks. Payment terms vary. Buys all rights. Model release required, photo captions preferred. Credit line given sometimes, depending on photographer's request, and/or usage.
Tips: Looking for mostly resort, architecture, and everyday living with models, and studio set-ups. Also, interesting portraits and animals. "Since we have such a diversified company our needs are the same and I need to see a variety to file away in my bag of tricks." Trend in company is toward "larger variety of subject matter and needs." As for the industry, "shots must be creative!"

■HILLMANN & CARR INC., 2121 Wisconsin Ave. N.W., Washington DC 20007. (202)342-0001. Art Director: Michal Carr. Types of clients: corporations, government, associations and museums.
Audiovisual Needs: Uses photographers for filmstrips, slide sets, multimedia productions, films and videotapes. "Subjects are extremely varied and range from the historical to current events. We do not specialize in any one subject area. Style also varies greatly depending upon subject matter."
Specs: Uses 35mm transparencies; 16mm and 35mm film.
First Contact & Terms: Provide resume, business card, self-promotion pieces or tearsheets to be kept on file for possible future assignments. Works on assignment basis only. Does not return unsolicited material. "If material has been unsolicited and we do not have immediate need, material will be filed for future reference." Payment and rights negotiable. Captions preferred; model releases required.
Tips: *"Quality reproduction* of work which can be kept on file is extremely important."

KROLOFF, MARSHALL & ASSOCIATES, LTD., Suite 900, 1350 Connecticut Ave. NW, Washington DC 20036 (202)429-8877. Vice President: Maura Marshall. PR/management consulting firm. Types of clients: major corporate, public interest, international.
Needs: Needs photographers in the DC area with 24-hour development capabilities. Uses photographers for coverage of events, news photos and documentation.
First Contact & Terms: Query with resume of credits "and a Rolodex card with your name and phone number" to be kept on file. Pays $8 minimum/b&w photo; $10 minimum/color photo; $50 minimum/hour; $500 minimum/day; going rate. Buys "unlimited reprint" rights—photographer owns negatives. Credit line given.
Tips: "Find a specialty—if you cover an event on spec be sure to let organizers know what you have."

■JACK MORTON PRODUCTIONS, INC., 1825 Eye St. NW, Washington DC 20006. (202)296-9300. Production Manager: Kathleen McRoberts. Types of clients: corporations and associations.
Needs: Works with 4 freelance photographers/month. Uses photographers for multimedia productions, films and videotapes. Needs photographers, designers and coordinators for multi-image projects.
Specs: Uses 35mm transparencies; 16mm and 35mm film.
First Contact & Terms: Query with resume; provide resume, business card, self-promotion piece or tearsheets to be kept on file for possible future assignments. Works with freelancers by assignment only; interested in stock photos/footage. SASE. Reports in 3 weeks. Pays $300-500/day. Pays 3 weeks after invoice submitted. Buys one-time rights. Captions and model releases preferred. Credit line sometimes given.
Tips: "Submit as much as you can on first mailing to catch producer's interest and try to show as much as you can about your knowledge of AV."

■WORLDWIDE TELEVISION NEWS (WTN), Suite 300, 1705 DeSales St. NW, Washington DC 20036. (202)835-0750. FAX: (202)887-7978. Bureau Manager, Washington: Paul C. Sisco. AV firm. Estab. 1952. "We basically supply TV news on tape, for TV networks and stations. At this time, most of our business is with foreign nets and stations." Buys dozens of "news stories per year, especially sports."
Subject Needs: Generally hard news material, sometimes of documentary nature and sports.
Audiovisual Needs: Produces motion pictures and videotape. Works with 6 freelance photographers/month on assignment only.
Payment & Terms: Pays $100 minimum/job. Pays on receipt of material; nothing on speculation. Video rates about $400/half day, $750/full day or so. Negotiates payment based on amount of creativity required from photographer. Buys all video rights. Dupe sheets for film required.
Making Contact: Send name, phone number, equipment available and rates with material by mail for consideration. Provide business card to be kept on file for possible future assignments. Fast news material generally sent counter-to-air shipment; slower material by air freight. SASE. Reports in 2 weeks.

Florida

■AVID, INC., 130 E. Marks St., Orlando FL 32803. (407)423-9535. Production Mgr.: John Melkrantz.
Needs: Works with 5 freelance photographers/month. Uses photographers for films and videotapes. Uses 35mm film and Betacam SP in commercials—TV. Also uses Betacam SP for corporate video work.
Specs: Uses Betacam SP videotape.
First Contact & Terms: Provide resume, business card, self-promotion piece or tearsheets to be kept on file for possible future assignments. Also send demo reel. Works with freelancers on assignment only. SASE. Reports in 2 weeks. Pays $100-850/day. Pays on acceptance; prefers to pay on net 30

basis when possible. Buys all rights (work-for-hire). Credit line given depending on nature of project. Sometimes credits are rolled, but frequently not. Credits are included in press releases on projects to trade journals.

Tips: Give detailed description of your experience as a photographer whether in news, TV production or other. Looks especially for "good lighting in a variety of conditions." Also seeking "smooth moves, innovative angles." Advises still photographers interested in making the transition into film or video work to start bygripping shoots. Also suggests trying entry level positions at post-production facilities.

COLEE SARTORY, (formerly Colee & Co.), Suite 405, 631 US Hwy. #1, North Palm Beach FL 33408. (407)844-7000. Ad agency. Art Director: Cira Cosentino. Types of clients: industrial, finance, residential.
Needs: Works with 2-3 photographers/month. Uses photographers for trade magazines, newspapers, brochures. Subjects include residential, pertaining to client.
Specs: Uses b&w and color prints; 35mm, 2¼×2¼ and 4×5 transparencies.
First Contact & Terms: Arrange a personal interview to show portfolio, submit portfolio for review; provide resume, business card, brochure, flyer or tearsheets to be kept on file for possible future assignments. Works with local freelance photographers on an assignment basis only. Pays $50-100/ hour and $250-1,000/day. Pays on receipt of invoice. Buys all rights. Model release required.

WM. COOK ADVERTISING, Suite 1600, 225 Water St., Jacksonville FL 32202. (904)353-3911. Ad agency. Studio Manager: Michele Akra. Art Buyer: Susan Miller. Types of clients: corporate, retail, finance and transportation.
Needs: Works with 4-5 freelance photographers/month. Uses photographers for consumer and trade magazines, direct mail, P-O-P displays, and newspapers. Subjects vary: food, location—real estate and industrial, table top or model in studio. Examples of campaigns: First Union, (Performance Banking); Resorts International, (Imagine); Winn-Dixie, (You're Gonna See The Difference).
Specs: Uses 8×10 matte b&w prints; 35mm, 2¼×2¼, 4×5 transparencies.
First Contact & Terms: Query with samples; submit portfolio for review. Works with freelance photographers on assignment basis only. Does not return unsolicited material. Reports in 2 weeks. Pays $12-40/b&w photo, $150-250/hour, $800-2,000/day and $250-20,000/job. Pays on receipt of invoice. Buys one-time rights, and all rights "when possible." Model release required. Credit line given "only usually on public service type jobs when work is done free or for a nominal fee."
Tips: Prefers to see a mixture of table top and locations—limited number of pieces—only the best—judgment will be on worst pieces. "Contact us with a letter, with a follow-up phone call and/or color reproductions of work."

COVALT ADVERTISING AGENCY, 12907 N.E. 7th Ave., P.O. Box 610578, North Miami FL 33161. (305)891-1543. Ad agency. Creative Director: Fernando Vasquez. Types of clients: industrial, retail, finance.
Needs: Works with 2 freelance photographers/month. Uses photographers for billboards, consumer and trade magazines, direct mail, P-O-P displays and posters. Subjects include product/still life.
Specs: Uses b&w and color prints and 35mm transparencies.
First Contact & Terms: Arrange a personal interview to show portfolio. Provide resume, business card, brochure, flyer or tearsheets to be kept on file for possible future assignments. Works with local freelance photographers on assignment only. Does not return unsolicited material. Reports in 2 weeks. Pays $150 minimum/job. Pays on receipt of invoice. Buys all rights. Model release required.

CREATIVE RESOURCES, INC., 2000 S. Dixie Highway, Miami FL 33133. (305)856-3474. FAX: (305)856-3151. Chairman and CEO: Mac Seligman. Estab. 1970. PR firm. Handles clients in travel (hotels, resorts and airlines). Photos used in PR releases. Works with 1-2 freelance photographers/ month on assignment only basis. Provide resume to be kept on file for possible future assignments. Buys 10-20 photos/year. Pays $50 minimum/hour or $200 minimum/day. Negotiates payment based on client's budget. For assignments involving travel, pays $60-200/day plus expenses. Pays on acceptance. Buys all rights. Model release preferred. Query with resume of credits. No unsolicited material. SASE. Reports in 2 weeks. Most interested in activity shots in locations near clients.
B&W: Uses 8×10 glossy prints; contact sheet OK.
Color: Uses 35mm or 2¼×2¼ transparencies and prints.

*RICH FIELD ADVERTISING AGENCY, 2050 Spectrum Blvd., Ft. Lauderdale FL 33309. (305)938-7600. FAX: (305)938-7775. Inhouse ad agency for Personnel Pool of Americas, Inc. Advertising Supervisor: Daniel Cooper. Estab. 1946. Types of clients: temporary services.
Needs: Works with 2 photographers/month. Uses photographers for consumer magazines, trade magazines, direct mail, posters, newspapers and signage. Subjects include "People Helping People®." Reviews stock photos of people.

Specs: Uses color prints; 35mm, 2¼ × 2¼, 4 × 5 transparencies.
First Contact & Terms: Query with resume of credits; send unsolicited photos by mail for consideration. Works with local freelancers only. Cannot return material. Reports in 3 weeks or "as needed." Pays $1,000-1,500/day; other payment "depends on what service I'm going after." Pays on receipt of invoice. Buys all rights; "total buy-out only." Model release and photo captions required. Credit line given sometimes, "depending on usage."

HACKMEISTER ADVERTISING & PUBLIC RELATIONS, INC., Suite 205, 2727 E. Oakland Park Blvd., Ft. Lauderdale FL 33306. (805)568-2511. Ad agency and PR firm. President: Dick Hackmeister. Serves industrial, electronics manufacturers who sell to other businesses.
Needs: Works with 1 freelance photographer/month. Uses photographers for trade magazines, direct mail, catalogs. Subject needs include electronic products.
Specs: Uses 8 × 10 glossy b&w and color prints and 4 × 5 transparencies.
First Contact & Terms: "Call on telephone first." Does not return unsolicited material. Pays by the day and by the job. Buys all rights. Model release and captions required.
Tips: Looks for "good lighting on highly technical products—creativity."

RONALD LEVITT ASSOC. INC., 141 Sevilla, Coral Gables FL 33134. (305)443-3223. PR firm. President: Ron Levitt. Types of clients: corporate, fashion, finance.
Needs: Works with 3-4 freelance photographers/month. Uses photographers for consumer and trade magazines, direct mail, newspapers and brochures.
Specs: Uses b&w and color prints; 35mm transparencies.
First Contact & Terms: Arrange a personal interview to show a portfolio. Provide resume, business card, brochure, flyer or tearsheets to be kept on file for possible future assignments. Works with freelance photographers on assignment basis only. Reports immediately. Pays $75 minimum/hour; $600 minimum/day. Pays on receipt of invoice. Buys all rights. Model release required; captions preferred. Credit line sometimes given.

*■MYERS, MYERS & ADAMS ADVERTISING, INC., 938 N. Victoria Park Rd., Ft. Lauderdale FL 33304. (305)523-0202. Ad agency. Creative Director: Virginia Sours-Myers. Estab. 1986. Types of Clients: industrial, retail, fashion, finance, marine, restaurant, and medical and real estate.
Needs: Works with 3-5 photographers, filmmakers and/or videographers/month. Uses photographers for billboards, consumer magazines, trade magazines, direct mail, P-O-P displays, catalogs, newspapers and audiovisual. Subjects include: marine, food, real estate, medical and fashion. Wants to see "all subjects" in stock images and footage.
Audiovisual Needs: Uses photos/film/video for slide shows, film and videotape.
Specs: Uses all sizes b&w/color prints; 35mm, 2¼ × 2¼, 4 × 5 transparencies; 35mm film; 1", ¾, but to review need ½".
First Contact & Terms: Provide resume, business card, brochure, flyer or tearsheets to be kept on file for possible future assignments. Works with freelancers on assignment basis only. Cannot return material. Reports as needed. Pays $50-200/hour; $800-2,500/day; $50-10,000/job. Buys all rights (work-for-hire) and 1 years usage. Credit line given sometimes, depending on usage.
Tips: "We're not looking for arty-type photos or journalism. We need photographers that understand an advertising sense of photography: good solid images that sell the product." Sees trend in advertising toward "computer-enhanced impact and color effects. Send samples, tearsheets and be patient. Please don't call us. If your work is good we keep on file and as a style is needed we will contact the photographer. Keep us updated with new work." Advertising is using a fair amount of audiovisual work. "We use a lot of stills within our commercials. Make portfolio available to production houses."

PRUITT, HUMPHRESS, POWERS & MUNROE ADVERTISING AGENCY, INC., Suite B., 805 N. Gadsden, Tallahassee FL 32303. (904)222-1212. Creative Director: G.B. Powers. Ad Agency. Types of clients: industrial, consumer.
Needs: Works with 3-4 freelance photographers/month. Uses freelancers for consumer and trade magazines, direct mail, newspapers, P-O-P displays.
First Contact & Terms: Send portfolio for review. Pays 30 days after production.

■HACK SWAIN PRODUCTIONS, INC., 1185 Cattlemen Rd., Sarasota FL 34232. (813)371-2360. President: Tony Swain. Types of clients: corporate and educational.
Needs: "We have our own staff and use freelancers occasionally for special photo needs." Uses photographers for filmstrips, slide sets, multimedia productions, films and videotapes.
Specs: Uses 35mm and 2¼ × 2¼ transparencies; 16mm film; VHS, 1", U-matic ¾" videotapes.
First Contact & Terms: Query with stock photo list. Interested in stock photos/footage. SASE. Reporting time varies with complexity of project. Payment individually negotiated. Pays sometimes on acceptance; sometimes on completion of project. Buys all rights. Model release required. Credit line given whenever practical.

Tips: "We usually do our own photography, but seek freelance help for hard to find or hard to recreate historical photo materials. We like to have on file sources for such materials."

■**TEL—AIR INTERESTS, INC.**, 1755 NE 149th St., Miami FL 33181. (305)944-3268. Office Manager: Maria Vorsindo. AV firm. Serves clients in business, industry and government. Produces filmstrips, slide sets, multimedia kits, motion pictures, sound-slide sets and videotape. Buys 10 filmstrips and 50 films/year. Pays $100 minimum/job. Pays on production. Buys all rights. Model release required, captions preferred. Arrange a personal interview to show portfolio or submit portfolio for review. SASE. Reports in 1 month.
Specs: Uses b&w prints and 8 × 10 matte color prints; also 35mm transparencies.

Georgia

ANDERSON COMMUNICATIONS, 2245 Godby Rd., Atlanta GA 30349. (404)766-8000. Ad agency and PR firm. Account Executive: William Butler.
Needs: Uses photographers for billboards, posters, signage and newspapers.
First Contact & Terms: Provide resume, business card, brochure, flyer or tearsheets to be kept on file for possible future assignments. Works with local freelancers on assignment only. Does not return unsolicited material. Pays by the job; on acceptance. Model release preferred.

■**FRASER ADVERTISING**, Suite 110, 2531 Center West Pkwy., Augusta GA 30901. (404)737-6219. Ad agency. President: Jerry Fraser. Contact: Lynn Pace, operations manager. Types of clients: automotive, industrial, manufacturing, residential.
Needs: Works with "possibly one freelance photographer every two or three months." Uses photographers for consumer and trade magazines, catalogs, posters, and AV presentations. Subject matter: "product and location shots." Also works with freelance filmmakers to produce TV commercials on videotape.
Specs: Uses glossy b&w and color prints; 35mm, 2¼ × 2¼ and 4 × 5 transparencies; videotape and film. "Specifications vary according to the job."
First Contact & Terms: Provide resume, business card, brochure, flyer or tearsheets to be kept on file for possible future assignments. Works with freelance photographers on assignment only. Does not return unsolicited material. Reports in 1 month. Rates vary from job to job. Pays on publication. Buys all rights. Model release preferred.
Tips: Prefers to see "samples of finished work—the actual ad, for example, not the photography alone. Send us materials to keep on file and quote favorably when rate is requested."

■**PAUL FRENCH & PARTNERS, INC.**, 503, Gabbettville Rd., LaGrange GA 30240. (404)882-5581. Contact: Gene Ballard. AV firm. Estab. 1969. Types of clients: industrial, corporate.
Needs: Works with freelance photographers on assignment only basis. Uses photographers for filmstrips, slide sets, multimedia. Subjects include: industrial marketing, employee training and orientation, public and community relations.
Specs: Uses 35mm and 4 × 5 color transparencies.
First Contact & Terms: Query with resume of credits; provide resume to be kept on file for possible future assignments. Pays $75-150 minimum/hour; $600-1,200/day; $150 up/job, plus travel and expenses. Payment on acceptance. Buys all rights, but may reassign to photographer after use.
Tips: "We buy photojournalism . . . journalistic treatments of our clients' subjects. Portfolio: industrial process, people at work, interior furnishings product, fashion. We seldom buy single photos."

■**GARRETT COMMUNICATIONS**, Box 53, Atlanta GA 30301. (404)755-2513. Ad agency. President/Owner: Ms. Ruby Grant Garrett. Estab. 1979. Types of clients: technical. Examples of ad campaigns: Simons (help wanted); CIS Telecom (equipment); Anderson Communication (business-to-business).
Needs: Uses photographers for trade magazines, direct mail and newspapers. Interested in reviewing stock photos/video footage of people at work.
Audiovisual Needs: Uses stock video footage.
Specs: Uses 4 × 5 b&w prints; VHS videotape.
First Contact & Terms: Query with resume of credits, query with list or stock photo subjects; provide resume, business card, brochure, flyer or tearsheets to be kept on file for possible future assignments. Works with freelancers on an assignment basis only. SASE. Reports in 1 week. Pays per job. Pays on receipt of invoice. Buys one-time rights. Model release required; photo captions preferred. Credit line sometimes given, depending on client.

J. WALTER THOMPSON USA, 1 Atlanta Plaza, 950 E. Paces Ferry Rd., Atlanta GA 30026. (404)365-7300. Ad agency. Executive Vice President/Executive Creative Director: Michael Lollis. Vice President/Ass't Creative Directors: Monty Wyne and Norman Gray. Types of clients: varied.
Needs: Works with 4-6 studios or photographers/month. Uses photographers for billboards, consumer and trade magazines, direct mail and newspapers. Uses experienced professional photographers only.
First Contact & Terms: Send resume and samples. Payment negotiable by photo, day or project.

TUCKER WAYNE/LUCKIE & CO., Suite 2700, 230 Peachtree St. NW, Atlanta GA 30303. (404)521-7600. Contact: Business Manager/Creative. Ad agency. Serves a variety of clients including packaged products, food, utilities, transportation, agriculture and pesticide manufacturing.
Needs: Uses photographers for consumer and trade magazines, TV and newspapers.
First Contact & Terms: Call for appointment to show portfolio. Negotiates payment based on many factors such as where work will appear, travel requirements, budget, etc.

Idaho

BITTON ADVERTISING AGENCY, 1387 Cambridge, Idaho Falls ID 83401. (208)523-7300. Ad agency. "We publish a magazine and a newspaper of flyfishing." Owner: Dennis Bitton. Types of clients: retail, light industrial, agricultural, recreational lodges, etc.
Needs: Works with 1-2 freelance photographers/month. Uses photographers for trade magazines, direct mail, catalogs and newspapers. Subjects include flyfishing pictures.
First Contact & Terms: Send unsolicited photos by mail for consideration. SASE. Reports in 2 weeks. Pays $25-150/b&w photo, $35-175/color photo. Pays on publication. Buys one-time rights. Model release and captions preferred. Credit line given.
Tips: Prefers to see "anything to do with flyfishing." Send in pictures with SASE and deadline for their return.

Illinois

AMERICAN ADVERTISING, 850 N. Grove, Elgin IL 60120. (708)741-2400. Manager: Janice Melahn. Ad Agency. Uses freelance photographers for consumer and trade magazines, direct mail, newspapers and P-O-P displays. Serves clients in publishing and nonprofit foundations. Works with 2-3 freelance photographers/month on assignment only basis. Provide resume, flyer, business card and brochure to be kept on file for possible future assignments. Buys 100 photos/year. Local freelancers preferred. Interested in stock photos of families, groups of children, schools and teachers. Negotiates payment based on client's budget and amount of creativity required from photographer. Pays on production. Buys all rights. Model release required. Query with resume of credits. Does not return unsolicited material. Reports in 3 weeks.
B&W: Prefers contact sheet; print size depends on project. Pays $100-$150 minimum/photo.
Color: Prefers 2¼ × 2¼ or 4 × 5 transparencies; 35mm semigloss prints OK. Pays $100-400/photo.

THE BASINGER COMPANY, 5300 Gulf Rd., Skokie IL 60077. (708)966-8660. Ad agency. President: David Basinger. Types of clients: industrial, finance.
Needs: Uses photographers for consumer and trade magazines, direct mail and P-O-P displays. Subject material diverse—table top, location, figures.
Specs: Uses b&w and color prints; 35mm, 2¼ × 2¼, 4 × 5 and 8 × 10 transparencies.
First Contact & Terms: Arrange a personal interview to show portfolio; provide resume, business card, brochure, flyer or tearsheets to be kept on file for possible future assignments. Works with local freelance photographers on assignment basis only. Does not return unsolicited material. Pays on receipt of invoice. Buys all rights. Model release required.

BRAGAW PUBLIC RELATIONS SERVICES, Suite 807, 800 E. Northwest Highway, Palantine IL 60067. (312)934-5580. Contact: Richard S. Bragaw. PR firm. Estab. 1981. Types of clients: professional service firms, high tech entrepreneurs.
Needs: Works with 1 freelance photographer/month. Uses photographers for trade magazines, direct mail, brochures, newspapers, newsletters/news releases. Subject matter "products and people."
Specs: Uses 3 × 5, 5 × 7 and 8 × 10 glossy prints.
First Contact & Terms: Provide resume, business card, brochure, flyer or tearsheets to be kept on file for possible future assignments. Works with freelance photographers on assignment basis only. SASE. Pays $25-100/b&w photo; $50-200/color photo; $35-100/hour; $200-500/day; $100-1,000/job.

Pays on receipt of invoice. Buys all rights. Model release preferred. Credit line "possible."
Tips: "Execute an assignment well, at reasonable costs, with speedy delivery. Would like to use more photography."

ROBERT BRANDT AND ASSOCIATES, 806 York Rd., Hinsdale IL 60521. (708)325-2000. Ad agency. Art Director: Mary Picton. Types of clients: industrial, retail and finance.
Needs: Works with 2-3 freelance photographers/month. Uses photographers for consumer magazines, trade magazines, direct mail and P-O-P displays.
Specs: Uses 16×20 glossy prints.
First Contact & Terms: Query with samples. Works on assignment basis only. SASE. Reports in 2 weeks. Payment depends on subject matter and client. Pays on receipt. Buys all rights. Model release required; captions preferred.
Tips: Prefers to see creativity with subject matter, lighting, table top and people. "Start with a small project first to establish a good working relationship. Our clients vary from industrial to consumer."

JOHN CROW ADVERTISING AGENCY, 1104 S. 2nd St., Springfield IL 62704. (217)528-1076. President: Bryan J. Crowe. Ad agency. Uses photos for billboards, consumer and trade magazines, direct mail, newspapers, radio and TV. Serves clients in industry, commerce, aviation, banking, state and federal government, retail stores, publishing and institutes. Works with 1 freelance photographer/month on assignment only basis. Provide letter of inquiry, flyer, brochure and tearsheet to be kept on file for future assignments. Pays $50 minimum/job or $18 minimum/hour. Negotiates payment based on client's budget. Buys all rights. Model release required. Send material by mail for consideration. SASE. Reports in 2 weeks.
B&W: Uses glossy 8×10 prints.
Color: Uses glossy 8×10 prints and 2¼×2¼ transparencies.

CS&A ADVERTISING, 207 Landmark Dr., Normal IL 61761. (309)452-0707. Ad agency. Senior Art Director: David Schenck. Types of clients: industrial, finance, most often business-to-business type.
Needs: "We have an in-house photo studio. We freelance hard to get locations—off season—metro locations." Uses photographers for trade magazines, direct mail and P-O-P displays. Particular metro buildings and skylines, people shots and situations.
Specs: Uses 4×5 transparencies.
First Contact & Terms: Provide resume, business card, brochure, flyer or tearsheets to be kept on file for possible future assignments. "We will freelance if we can't get what we want from stock or if pricing is similar." Does not return unsolicited material. Reports in 2 weeks. Pays per b&w photo $25-450; per color photo $250-850; by the hour $40-85; by the day, $500-1,000. "Payment is made after all invoices are returned." Model release required; captions preferred.
Tips: Prefers to see buildings and people, construction, seasonal; unique angles and styles, no special effects industrial.

■DATA COMMAND INC., 329 E. Court, P.O. Box 548, Kankakee IL 60901. (815)933-7735. FAX: (815)935-8577. Director, Product Development: Aggie Posthumus. Estab. 1981. Types of clients: educational market (early childhood, K-12).
Needs: Works with 3-4 freelance photographers/year. Uses photographers for multimedia productions. Subjects: product shots; photos also used for packaging/teachers' manuals..
Specs: Uses 5×7 glossy b&w prints, various sizes glossy color prints; also 35mm color transparencies; 35mm film.
First Contact & Terms: Provide resume, business card, self-promotion piece or tearsheets to be kept on file for possible future assignments. Works with freelancers by assignment only; interested in stock photos/footage. SASE. Reports in 2 weeks. Pays by the job or by royalty; also pays $25-150/b&w photo; $50-250/color photo. Pays on acceptance. Buys all rights and exclusive rights in intended market. Captions preferred; model release required. Credit line sometimes given.
Tips: There is an increasing interest in educational use of computer graphics and computer-enhanced illustrations. Call and establish relationship. "The most recent photographer I spoke with usually comes to mind first."

*■EGD & ASSOCIATES, INC., 1801 H Hicks Rd., Rolling Meadow IL 60008. (708)991-1270. FAX: (708)991-1519. Ad agency. Vice President: Kathleen Dorn. Estab. 1970. Types of clients: industrial, retail, finance. Example of ad campaigns: Gould, Bostick and Jiffy Print.
Needs: Works with 7-8 freelance photographers—videographers/month. Uses photographers for billboards, consumer magazines, trade magazines, direct mail, P-O-P displays, catalogs and audiovisual. Subjects include: industrial products and facilities. Reviews stock photos/video footage of 'creative firsts.'

Audiovidual Needs: Uses photos/video for slide shows and videotape.

Specs: Uses 4×5, 8×10 b&w/color prints; 35mm, 2¼×2¼, 4×5, 8×10 transparencies; videotape.

First Contact & Terms: Arrange personal interview to show portfolio; provide resume, business card, brochure, flyer or tearsheets to be kept on file for possible future assignments. Works with local freelancers on assignment basis only. Cannot return material. Reports in 1-2 weeks. Pays according to "clients budget." Pays on 30 days of invoice. Model release required. Credit line sometimes given; credit line offered in lieu of payment.

Tips: Sees trend toward "larger budget for exclusive rights and creative firsts. Contact us every six months."

*■GANNON COMMUNICATIONS, 15 Salt Creek Lake, Hinsdale IL 60521. (708)325-3030. FAX: (708)850-7024. Ad agency, PR firm. Also handles marketing communications. President: Terrence S. Gannon. Estab. 1985. Types of clients: Corporate, industrial, financial, consumer products and service. Examples of ad campaigns: "Enjoy Summer All Year Long" for Duraco Products, Inc.; "Your Off-Site Personnel Department" for Employee Leasing of America; "When First Impressions Count" for RotaDyne Corporation. All three are ad/PR campaigns which are still active.

Needs: Works with 2-3 freelance photographers–filmmakers–videographers/month. Uses photographers for consumer magazine, trade magazine, direct mail, newspapers and audiovisual uses.

Audiovisual Needs: Uses slide shows and videotape for presentations, trade shows, sales meetings and seminars.

Specs: Uses 5×7, 8×10 color and b&w prints; 4×5 transparencies; videotape. Video specs depend on assignment.

First Contact & Terms: Arrange personal interview to show portfolio; provide resume, business card, brochure, flyer or tearsheets to be kept on file for possible future assignments. Works with local freelancers on assignment only. SASE. Reports on queries in 1-2 weeks; sometimes longer "depending on client whims." Pays $150-500/day; $150/color photo; $50/b&w photo; also pays based on assignment, type of job, time, etc. "We're competitive." Pays on receipt of invoice. Buys all rights (work-for-hire). Model release required; photo captions preferred. Credit line given sometimes, depending on use. For photos used with editorial placement, credits are up to the publication running the photo.

Tips: In portfolio or demos, looks for "an ability to comprehend the subject matter, the heart of the client's business. Tight, interesting shots. A photographer who knows how to take a vertical as well as horizontal shot." Sees trend toward more photography for PR clients, but "ad side about the same. And, of course, there's more use of video, especially VNRs (video news releases). B&W photography is especially important to newspaper business sections (editorial and trade magazine." Freelancers who want to work with this company should "Listen, learn. This is *our* client and we understand them. Take the best photos possible within the guidelines we set up, and no problem. If it's glitz, it won't fly–and you won't get paid." Generally, "the still photo, for corporate, financial and product material is still the most effective. The other media are as important, but each has its place in the communications mix."

■GOLDSHOLL DESIGN AND FILM, 420 Frontage Rd., Northfield IL 60093. (708)446-8300. Contact: Deborah Goldsholl. AV firm. Serves clients in industry and advertising agencies. Produces filmstrips, slide sets, multimedia kits, corporate brochures, merchandising material, and motion pictures. Works with 2-3 freelance photographers/month on assignment only basis. Provide letter of inquiry and brochure to be kept on file for future assignments. Buys 100 photos, 5 filmstrips and 25 films/year.

Subject Needs: Anything. No industrial equipment. Length requirement: 30 seconds to 30 minutes.

Film: Uses 16 and 35mm industrial, educational, TV, documentaries and animation. Interested in stock footage.

Photos: Uses contact sheet or 35mm, 2¼×2¼, 4×5 or 8×10 color transparencies.

Payment/Terms: Pays by the job or by the hour; negotiates payment based on client's budget, amount of creativity required from photographer, photographer's previous experience/reputation. Pays in 30 days. Buys all rights. Model release required.

Making Contact: Query with resume. SASE. Reports in 1 week.

*■KATZ, INC., Box 2827, Carbondale IL 62902-282. (618)687-3515. Ad agency, PR firm and AV firm. Production Manager: R. Borowy. Estab. 1980. Types of clients: industrial, retail, trade and show-business. Types of clients: industrial-commercial. Example of recent project: United Sales Corporation, Inc., various TV spots.

Needs: Uses varying number of freelancers per month. Uses photographers for trade magazines, direct mail, P-O-P displays, catalogs and audiovisual. Reviews stock photos, film or video of news material; other materials based on project needs.

Audiovisual Needs: Typically uses slides and videotape for slide presentations and non-broadcast elements. Uses film/videotape footage of 'stock' subjects; primarily on-location elements such as 'event' programs. Uses 8×10 b&w or color prints; 35mm or 8×10 transparencies; 16mm/35mm film;

¾"-1½ VHS videotape. "All film videotape material used/needed must be or 'broadcast' quality."
First Contact & Terms: Query with resume of credits; query with list of stock photo subjects; send unsolicited photos by mail for consideration; submit portfolio for review; send videotape demo reels (for AV assignments). Works with freelancers on an assignment basis only. Cannot return material. Reports in 1-3 months. Pays $35-60/b&w photo; $50-75/color photo; $5-35/hour; $100-300/day; $200-600 per job; will also pay union scale; other forms of payment to be arranged. Pays on acceptance; other payment schedules to be arranged. Buys all rights. Model release required; photo captions preferred. Credit line given sometimes, depending on assignments.
Tips: In freelancer's samples, "looking for 'candid'-type photos, color or b&w." For AV work, "film/video demo reels must have all elements that freelancer specializes in (i.e. commercials, news material, etc.)" More demand for film/video material, for broadcast and home video. Professionalism strongly advised: "no amateurs!" Still photographers interested in AV work "can use their photos for AV slides. Stills can be used for selected film/video elements."

■**ARTHUR MERIWETHER, INC.**, 1529 Brook Dr., Downers Grove IL 60515. (312)495-0600. Production Coordinator: Lori Ouska. Types of clients: corporations, ad agencies, associations.
Needs: Uses photographers for films, videotapes, PR photos. Subjects include documentation for PR releases, scientific photography.
Specs: Uses b&w negatives; 35mm, 2¼×2½ and 4×5 transparencies; 16mm film; U-matic ¾" videotape.
First Contact & Terms: Provide resume, business card, self-promotion piece or tearsheets to be kept on file for possible future assignments. Works with freelancers by assignment only; interested in stock photos/footage. Does not return unsolicited material. Payment individually negotiated. Pays within 30 days. Buys all rights. Model release required. Credit line sometimes given.

■**MOTIVATION MEDIA, INC.**, 1245 Milwaukee Ave., Glenview IL 60025. (312)297-4740. Production Manager: Glen Peterson. Manager/Creative Graphics Division: Perry Anderson. AV firm. Types of clients: manufacturers of consumer and capital goods, business associations, service industries. Produces multimedia/multiscreen productions, sound slide shows, video productions, filmstrips, 16mm film.
Subject Needs: Uses "a very wide variety" of photos obtained through assignment only. New product announcements, sales promotion, and sales training programs and public relations programs—"all on a variety of products and services, everything from jewelry, food, consumer products—autos, etc."
Audiovisual Needs: Uses 35mm, 2¼×2¼, 4×5 and 8×10 transparencies. Produces 16mm and videotape industrials. Possible assignments include serving as producer, responsible for all phases of production; serving as director, involved in studio and location photography and supervises editing; serving as film editor with "creative and conforming" duties; and serving as cinematographer.
First Contact & Terms: Provide resume to be kept on file for possible future assignments. Pays $350-750/day, or per job "as negotiated." Buys one-time rights normally. Query first with resume of credits. Reports in 2 weeks. SASE.
Tips: "All freelancers must show evidence of professional experience, versatility, and ability to adapt to different situations and formats. Still photographers should have examples of product and location photography in their portfolios. Contact Stan Kotecki, director of still photography, for appointment to show portfolio."

OMNI ENTERPRISES, 430 W. Roosevelt Rd., Wheaton IL 60187. (708)653-8200. FAX: (708)653-8218. Contact: Steve Jacobs. Ad agency. Estab. 1962. Uses photos for consumer and trade magazines, direct mail, newspapers and P-O-P displays. Types of clients: business, industrial, area development and financial. Needs photos of "all varieties—industrial and machine products and human interest." Works with an average of 3 freelance photographers/month on assignment only basis. Provide resume, flyer, business card, brochure, composites and list of equipment to be kept on file for possible future assignments. Buys 100 photos annually. Buys one-time, second (reprint) rights or all rights. Pays $50-500/b&w photo; $100-750/color photo; 50-150/hour; $400-1,500/day. Call for an appointment. Prefers to see composites in b&w and color. SASE.
B&W: Uses 5×7 and 8×10 glossy prints. Model release required.
Color: Uses 8×10 glossy prints, 2¼×2¼, 4×5 and 8×10 transparencies. Model release required.
Tips: In portfolio or samples, wants to see "creative composition; technical abilities, i.e., lighting, color balance, focus and consistency of quality. We need to see samples and have an idea of rates. Because we are loyal to present suppliers, it sometimes takes up to 6 months or longer before we begin working with a new photographer."

■**UNIVERSAL TRAINING SYSTEMS CO.**, 255 Revere Dr., Northbrook IL 60062. (708)498-9700. Vice President/Executive Producer: Richard Thorne. AV producers. Serves financial institutions, electronics manufacturers, producers of farm equipment, food processors, sales organizations, data processing firms, etc. Produces filmstrips, sound slide sets, multimedia kits, 16mm and videotape. Subjects include training, product education, personnel motivation, etc. Needs documentary and location photos. Works with freelance photographers on assignment only basis. Provide resume, business card and brochure to be kept on file for possible future assignments. Produces 20-25 films and videotapes annually. Buys "the right to use pix in one film or publication (for as long as the film or publication is used by clients). Exclusivity is not required. The right to sell pix to others is always the seller's prerogative." Pays per job or on a per-photo basis. Negotiates payment based on client's budget. Query with resume of credits. Reports in 2 weeks. SASE.

Film: Video for documentary, industrial and sales training. "We handle all casting and direction. We hire crews, photographers, etc." Model release required.

B&W: Uses 8×10 prints. Model release required.

Color: Uses transparencies or prints. Model release required.

Tips: Prefers to see "work of which the photographer is especially proud plus work which the photographer feels represents capability under pressure." There is a "massive move to video training, especially in the area of interactive video."

■**VIDEO I-D, INC.**, 105 Muller Rd., Washington IL 61571. (309)444-4323. President: Sam B. Wagner. Types of clients: health, education, industry, cable and broadcast.

Needs: Works with 5 freelance photographers/month to shoot slide sets, multimedia productions, films amd videotapes. Subjects "vary from commercial to industrial—always high quality."

Specs: Uses 35mm transparencies; 16mm film; U-matic ¾" and 1" videotape.

First Contact & Terms: Provide resume, business card, self-promotion piece or tearsheets to be kept on file for possible future assignments; "also send video sample reel." Works with freelancers by assignment only, "somewhat" interested in stock photos/footage. SASE. Reports in 3 weeks. Pays $8-25/hour; $65-250/day. Pays on acceptance. Buys all rights. Model release required. Credit line sometimes given.

Tips: Sample reel—indicate goal for specific pieces. "Show good lighting and visualization skills. Be willing to learn. Show me you can communicate what I need to hear — and willingness to put out effort to get top quality."

Chicago

■**AGS & R COMMUNICATIONS**, 314 W. Superior, Chicago IL 60010. (312)649-4500. Senior Vice President: Gary J. Ballenger. Types of clients: advertising, Fortune 1000 and Fortune 500 corporate and industrial companies.

Needs: Works with freelance photographers monthly depending on work load. Uses photographers for original slide and multimedia productions. Subjects include: portrait, table top, talent, 35mm pin-registered photo sequences and 4×5 and 8×10 color transparencies, and product shots.

Specs: Uses 5×7 and 8×10 b&w and color prints; 35mm, 2¼×2¼, 4×5 or 8×10 transparencies; 16mm or 35mm film; VHS, Beta, U-matic ¾", 1" videotape.

First Contact & Terms: Provide resume, business card, self-promotion piece or tearsheets to be kept on file for possible future assignments. "Do not call, please." Works with freelancers by assignment only; interested in stock photos/footage. SASE. Reports in 1-2 weeks. Pays 30 days after completion from invoice. Pay negotiated; $275-600/day. Model release required. Credit line sometimes given.

Tips: "You must have good people skills, be dependable and have strong skills in slide market."

BRITT & BRITT CREATIVE SERVICES, 2239 Michigan Ave. South, Chicago IL 60616. (312)225-9700. FAX: ((312)225-3760. Ad agency. Creative Director: Kaye Britt. Estab. 1985. Types of clients: retail, jewelry (wholesale and retail), healthcare and business-to-business.

Needs: Works with 1 freelance photographer/month. Uses photographers for consumer and trade magazines, direct mail, P-O-P displays, brochures, newspapers, and TV. Subjects include model and product photography. Also works with freelance filmmakers to produce TV commercials.

Specs: Uses 5×7 and 8×10 b&w or color glossy prints; 35mm, 4×5 and 8×10 transparencies; 16mm film and videotape.

First Contact & Terms: Arrange a personal interview to show portfolio (if local). Provide resume, business card, brochure, flyer or tearsheets to be kept on file for possible future assignments. Works with freelance photographers on assignment basis only. SASE. Reports immediately in person or on phone. Pays $50-200/b&w photo; $50-300/color photo; $30-90/hour; $200-800/day; and $40-1,000/job. Pays 30 days after acceptance. Buys exclusive product rights. Model release required. Credit line given "in some cases."

Tips: "Be flexible to do 'bread & butter' work without offense. There's a lot of latitude for creativity—the more, the better. Be capable of it as necessary."

E.H. BROWN ADVERTISING AGENCY, 20 N. Wacker Dr., Chicago IL 60606. (312)372-9494. Art Director: Arnold Pirsoul. Ad agency. Types of clients: primarily industrial, financial and consumer products.

Needs: Works with 3 photographers/month. Uses photographers for consumer and trade magazines and table-top.

First Contact & Terms: Call for appointment to show portfolio. Pays $300-1,200/b&w photo; $400-2,200/color photo; $400-2,000/day. Buys one-time rights, exclusive product rights or all rights.

Tips: Not interested in seeing high fashion photography. Looks for "good uniformity of work, excellent color work or b&w, dramatic photos, good creative ability of photographer."

■**CLEARVUE, INC.,** 6465 Avondale., Chicago IL 60631. (312)775-9433. Chief OP Officer: W. O. McDermed.

Audiovisual Needs: Works with 4-5 photographers/year. Uses photographers for filmstrips and video.

Specs: Uses 35mm transparencies.

First Contact & Terms: Query with resume. Works with freelancers by assignment only. SASE. Reports in 3 weeks. Pays $10-75/b&w photo; $10-75/color photo; $500-2,500/complete program. Pays on acceptance. Buys all rights. Captions required.

DANIEL J. EDELMAN, INC., 211 E. Ontario St., Chicago IL 60611. (312)280-7000. PR firm. AV Director: Roul Perez. Other offices: New York (212)757-9100; Dallas (214)696-6446; Houston (713)623-2666; Los Angeles (213)553-1560; San Francisco (415)433-538; St Louis (314)421-6460; Washington DC (202)393-1300. Types of clients: industrial, fashion, finance, consumer products, legal, real estate, toiletries, medical, high tech — "we handle the full spectrum of public relations areas in all types of industries."

Needs: Number of freelancers used per month "varies according to public relations programs underway but it could run approximately 3-5." Uses photos for consumer magazines, trade magazines, brochures, newspapers and AV presentations. Subjects include: products, on-site shots for case histories, special events such as groundbreaking, etc.

First Contact and Terms: Arrange a personal interview to show portfolio; provide resume, business card, flyer or tearsheets to be kept on file for possible future assignments. Works with freelancers on an assignment basis only. SASE. Reporting time "depends on the assignment." Freelancer charges are negotiated based on the type and length of assignment." Pays $35-100/hour; $300-1,000/day; $75 minimum/job (including film, processing); $4-8/b&w photo; $8.50-13/color photo. Pays on acceptance. Buys all rights. Model release required.

GARFIELD-LINN & COMPANY, 142 E. Ontario Ave., Chicago IL 60611. (312)943-1900. Art Director: Ralph Woods. Creative Director: David Mitchell. Ad agency. Types of clients: Serves a "wide variety" of accounts; client list provided upon request.

Needs: Number of freelance photographers used varies. Works on assignment only basis. Uses photographers for billboards, consumer and trade magazines, direct mail, brochures, catalogs and posters.

First Contact & Terms: Arrange interview to show portfolio and query with samples. Payment is by the project; negotiates according to client's budget.

DRUCILLA HANDY CO., #505, 333 N. Michigan Ave., Chicago IL 60601. (312)704-0040. PR firm. Executive Vice President: Barbara Jacobs. Handles public relations campaigns for home furnishings and products, retail, building products, other consumer products and services.

Needs: Works with one freelancer every two months. Uses photos for newspapers.

Specs: Uses 2¼ × 2¼ and 4 × 5 transparencies.

First Contact and Terms: Query with resume of credits. Works on assignment only. Does not return unsolicited material. Reports in 2 weeks. Pays $500-1,200/day "depending on assignment from client." Pays on receipt of invoice. Buys all rights. Model release and photo captions preferred. Credit line given sometimes, depending on magazine.

Tips: "Query first; mention other public relations firms and clients that you have worked with."

KEROFF & ROSENBERG ADVERTISING, 444 N. Wabash Ave., Chicago IL 60611. (312)321-9000. Ad agency. Art Directors: Bernie Kanuza and Norbert Shimkus. Estab. 1972. Types of clients: fashion, consumer products, banking, real estate, hotels. Examples of ad campaigns: Prudential (corporate campaign for real estate division); Marriott Hotels (ad and collateral); Centel Cellular (car phone ad campaign); Urban Shopping Centers (fashion ads for major centers in Chicago and Boston).

Needs: Uses 5 freelance photographers/month. Uses photographers for consumer magazines, trade magazines, posters and newspapers. Interested in reviewing stock photos/film or video footage (nothing specific at this time).

Specs: Uses b&w and color prints; 2¼ × 2¼, 4 × 5 transparencies.
First Contact & Terms: Query with resume of credits, or list of stock photo subjects; send unsolicited photos by mail for consideration; provide resume, business card, brochure, flyer or tearsheets to be kept on file for possible future assignments. Works with freelancers on assignment basis only. Reports in 1 month. Pays $200-1,000/day; pays by the project (including model, film etc.). Pays 30 to 60 days after invoice. Buys all rights. Model release required; photo captions preferred. Credit line given sometimes, depending on uniqueness of material.
Tips: Looks for "fashion (people, models and clothes), real estate (interiors and exteriors), table-top product shots." Freelancers wanting to break in with the company should "start with one project on a project basis, if work is good we would continue to use. We tend to work with same sources to provide consistency for quality, we work with different people at different budget levels." Trends in ad photography include "more lifestyle, less posed shots for fashion but with good attitude. All photography must be simple and graphic."

NOBLE & ASSOCIATES, (formerly Don Tennant Company), 500 N. Michigan Ave., Chicago IL 60611. (312)644-4600. Art Director: Mike Havel. Ad agency. Types of clients: all consumer firms; client list provided upon request.
First Contact & Terms: Works primarily with local freelancers, but considers others. Query with resume of credits. Payment is by the project; negotiates according to client's budget. "Occasionally works with freelance photographers on assignment basis."

QUALLY & COMPANY, INC., Suite 2502, 30 E. Huron, Chicago IL 60611. (312)944-0237. Ad agency and graphic design firm. Creative Director: Robert Qually. Types of clients: finance, package goods and business-to-business.
Needs: Uses 4-5 freelance photographers/month. Uses photographers for billboards, consumer and trade magazines, direct mail, P-O-P displays, posters and newspapers. "Subject matter varies, but is always a 'quality image' regardless of what it portrays."
Specs: Uses b&w and color prints; 35mm, 2¼ × 2¼, 4 × 5 and 8 × 10 transparencies.
First Contact & Terms: Query with samples or submit portfolio for review. Provide resume, business card, brochure, flyer or tearsheets to be kept on file for possible future assignments. Works only with local freelance photographers on assignment basis. Does not return unsolicited material. Reports in 2 weeks. Payment depends on circumstances. Pays on acceptance or net 45 days. Rights purchased depend on circumstances. Model release required. Credit lines sometimes given, depending on client's attitude.

RUDER FINN , (formerly Ruder Finn & Rotman), 444 N. Michigan Ave., Chicago IL 60611. (312)644-8600. President: Jim McAvoy. PR firm. Handles accounts for corporations, trade and professional associations, institutions and other organizations. Photos used in publicity, AV presentations, annual stockholder reports, brochures, books, feature articles, and industrial ads. Uses industrial photos to illustrate case histories; commercial photos for ads; and consumer photos—food, fashion, personal care products. Works with 4-8 freelance photographers/month nationally on assignment only basis. Provide resume, flyer, business card, tearsheets and brochure to be kept on file for possible future assignments. Buys over 100 photos/year. Present model release on acceptance of photo. Pays $25 minimum/hour, or $200 minimum/day. Negotiates payment based on client's budget and photographer's previous experience/reputation. Query with resume of credits or call to arrange an appointment. Prefers to see publicity photos in a portfolio. Will not view unsolicited material.

SANDER ALLEN ADVERTISING, INC., Suite 1020, 230 N. Michigan Ave., Chicago IL 60601. (312)444-1771. Art Director: Georgia Condon. Ad agency. Types of clients: mostly industrial.
Needs: Works with 2-3 freelance photographers/month. Uses photographers for P-O-P displays, consumer and trade magazines, direct mail, brochures/flyers and newspapers.
First Contact & Terms: Call for appointment to show portfolio. Negotiates payment based on client's budget and where work will appear.
Tips: Likes to see a broad range. Black and white, color transparencies and color prints.

■**SOCIETY FOR VISUAL EDUCATION, INC.**, 1345 W. Diversey Pkwy., Chicago IL 60614. (312)525-1500. Graphic Arts Manager: Cathy Mijou. Produces work inhouse for SVE products and services; no outside clients.
Audiovisual Needs: Uses photographers for filmstrips, multimedia productions and video. Subjects vary—for education market—preschool to Jr. High; every subject area (math, geography, etc.).
Specs: Uses b&w and color prints and 35mm transparencies and film.
First Contact & Terms: No phone calls. Query with samples; provide resume, business card, self-promotion piece or tearsheets to be kept on file for possible future assignments. Samples should be non-returnable—will be kept on file. Works with freelancers by assignment only, interested in stock

photos/footage. Returns material for review if requested with SASE, would prefer to keep as file samples. Reports if interested in using materials submitted. Pay varies according to scope and requirements of project. Pay specified at time of contract. Buys all rights.

Tips: "You should know about the company—products produced and markets sold to. We always look for technical expertise, composition, etc."

STONE & ADLER, INC., 1 East Wacker Dr., Chicago IL 60601. (312)329-1105. Senior VP/Executive Creative Director: David Moore. Senior Art Director: Gail Stoltz. Senior Art Director: Steve Wheeler. Ad agency. Types of clients: consumer, business-to-business, retail, industry, travel, etc.

Needs: Works with 5-8 freelance photographers/month. Uses photographers for direct mail, brochures, consumer and trade print, sales promotion and TV.

First Contact & Terms: Call for appointment to show portfolio. Negotiates payment based on client's budget and the job.

Tips: Looks for b&w prints, transparencies and printed samples; show style.

MORTON B. STONE AND ASSOCIATES, Suite 405, 1201 N. Clark St., Chicago IL 60610. (312)664-9780. PR firm. Art Director: Ken Vensel. Types of clients: medical and pharmaceutical.

Needs: Uses freelance photographers for consumer magazines. Subject matter includes medical tech, food, exercise shots.

Specs: Uses color transparencies.

First Contact & Terms: Provide resume, business card, brochure, flyer or tearsheets to be kept on file for possible future assignments. Works with freelance photographers on an assignment basis only. SASE. Reports in 1 month. Pays on receipt of invoice. Model release required. Credit line given.

DAVID H. STREMMEL & CO., 20 N. Wacker Dr., Chicago IL 60606. (312)726-4450. Ad agency and PR firm. President: David Stremmel. Types of clients: industrial.

Needs: Works with 3-4 freelance photographers/month. Uses photographers for trade magazines, brochures, catalogs. Subject matter: "in-plant scenes, machinery photos, table-top, some in-office scenes." Also works with freelance filmmakers to produce sales films.

Specs: Uses 4×5 and 8×10 b&w glossy prints; 35mm, 2¼×2¼, and 8×10 transparencies; Super 8mm film and videotape.

First Contact & Terms: Provide resume, business card, brochure, flyer or tearsheets to be kept on file for possible future assignments. Works with freelance photographers on assignment basis only. Does not return unsolicited material. Reports in 1 week. Pay negotiable. Buys all rights or one-time rights. Model release required.

Tips: Artists should "know manufacturing processes: set up and shoot quickly with minimum disruption." Business-to-business advertising is using a great deal of video.

■**UNIMAR**, (formerly O.M.A.R. Inc.) US Hispanic Communication, Suite 888, 980 N. Michigan Ave., Chicago IL 60611. (312)988-9490. Creative Director: Carolina Maya. Ad agency. Types of clients: consumer, food, TV and utilities.

Needs: Number of freelancers used varies. Works on assignment basis only. Uses photos for consumer magazines, posters, newspapers and TV.

First Contact & Terms: Local freelancers only. Query with resume of credits and samples, then follow up by phone. Pays per project; negotiates according to client's budget, but generally $150-500/b&w photo; $500-750/color photo; $150-250/hour; or $750-1,000/day.

Tips: "More women should go into photography."

■**G.W. VAN LEER & ASSOCIATES INTERNATIONAL**, 1850 N. Fremont, Chicago IL 60614. (312)751-2926. President: G.W. Van Leer. AV firm. Serves schools, manufacturers, associations, stores, mail order catalog houses. Produces filmstrips, motion pictures, multimedia kits, overhead transparencies, slide and sound-slide sets, nature photobooks and videotapes. Offers 3 freelance assignments/year; purchases 300 illustrations/year. "We are looking for complete photo stories on wildflowers in full color." Query with resume and samples. Reports in 3 weeks. SASE.

■**THE JOHN VOLK COMPANY**, Suite 2000, 676 N. St. Clair, Chicago IL 60611. (312)787-7117. Ad agency. Creative Director: Bill Block. Art Directors: Kathleen Pascoe and Caroline Adrian-Marchionna. Types of clients: agricultural. Free client list on request.

Needs: Works with 2-3 freelance photographers/month. Uses photographers for trade magazines, direct mail, P-O-P displays, brochures, posters, newspapers and AV presentations. Subjects include: "farm related products—tractors, chemicals."

Specs: Uses 35mm, 2¼×2¼ and 4×5 transparencies.

First Contact & Terms: Arrange a personal interview to show portfolio; provide resume, business card, brochure, flyer or tearsheets to be kept on file for possible future assignments. Works with freelance photographers on assignment basis only. Does not return unsolicited material. Pays $500-1,500/job (sometimes more). Rights purchased "depend on price and arrangement." Model release required.

Tips: "I would like to see examples of problem solving—something that would show that the photographer did more than just record what was there. I work with people who are always willing to shoot 'one more shot.' Farm ads are becoming more sophisticated and the quality of the photography is on a par with consumer ads. I'd like to see some new approaches to large equipment shooting (tractors, combines)."

Indiana

■**CALDWELL-VAN RIPER**, 1314 N. Meridian, Indianapolis IN 46202. (317)632-6501. Executive Creative Director: Jeffrey Leiendecker. Ad agency. Uses photos for billboards, consumer and trade magazines, direct mail, foreign media, newspapers, P-O-P displays, radio and TV. Serves all types of clients. Works with 2-5 freelance photographers/month on assignment only basis. Provide brochure or samples to be kept on file for future assignments.

Specs: Uses b&w photos and color transparencies. Uses filmmakers for TV spots, corporate films and documentary films.

Payment & Terms: Pays $200-2,000/hour, day and job. Negotiates payment based on client's budget. Model release required. Buys all rights.

Making Contact: Arrange a personal interview to show portfolio or submit portfolio for review. SASE. Reports in 1 week.

HEMINGER ADVERTISING, 318 Westwood Dr., Michigan City IN 46360. (219)879-6739. Ad agency. President: Jack Heminger. Types of clients: industrial, finance, transportation, hardware, electronics, healthcare.

Needs: Works with 1-2 freelance photographers every 6 weeks. Uses photographers for trade magazines, direct mail, P-O-P displays, catalogs and newspapers. Subjects include people, truck, hardline products.

Specs: Uses 5×7 and 8×10 b&w and color prints; 35mm, 2¼×2¼ and 4×5 transparencies.

First Contact & Terms: Provide resume, business card, flyer or tearsheets to be kept on file for possible future assignments. Works with freelancers on assignment basis only. Does not return unsolicited material. Reports in 2 weeks. Pays $150-250/photo. Pays on acceptance. Buy all rights. Model release required.

Tips: "We're looking for freelancers for location shots around the country, shooting client trucks and trailers in photographer's area."

■**KELLER CRESCENT COMPANY**, 1100 E. Louisiana, Evansville IN 47701. (812)426-7551 or (812)464-2461. Manager Still Photography: Cal Barrett. Ad agency, PR and AV firm. Uses billboards, consumer and trade magazines, direct mail, newspapers, P-O-P displays, radio and TV. Serves industrial, consumer, finance, food, auto parts, dairy products clients. Types of clients: Old National Bank, Community Coffee and Eureka Vac's. Works with 2-3 freelance photographers/month on assignment only basis. Provide business card, tearsheets and brochure to be kept on file for possible future assignments.

Specs: Uses 8×10 b&w prints; 35mm, 4×5 and 8×10 transparencies.

Payment & Terms: Pays $200-2,500/job; negotiates payment based on client's budget, amount of creativity required from photographer and photographer's previous experience/reputation. Buys all rights. Model release required.

Making Contact: Query with resume of credits, list of stock photo subjects; send material by mail for consideration. Prefers to see printed samples, transparencies and prints. Does not return unsolicited material.

METRO MARKETING GROUP, Suite 580, 8500 Keystone Crossing, Indianapolis IN 46240. (317)253-1851. Advertising agency. Art Director: Greg Pergal. Serves industrial, retail and fast food clients.

Needs: Works with 2-3 freelance photographers/month. Uses photographers for billboards, consumer and trade magazines, direct mail, P-O-P displays, catalogs, posters, signage and newspapers.

First Contact & Terms: Query with resume of credits or list of stock photo subjects. Provide resume, business card, brochure, flyer or tearsheets to be kept on file for possible future assignments. Works with local freelancers only. Does not return unsolicited material. Pays by the job. Buys all rights or one-time rights. Model release and captions preferred.

Close-up

Nick Vedros
Advertising Photographer
Vedros & Associates
Kansas City, Missouri

In the early days of his career, advertising photographer Nick Vedros looked to his heroes and mentors for inspiration and encouragement. Along the way he developed an appreciation for a variety of images and styles by "picking up bits and pieces" from photographers as diverse as Aaron Jones, Ernst Haas and Irving Penn. Now, nearly 13 years after launching his career, Vedros has become a mentor himself, known for his own distinct style of simple but dramatic black-and-white images.

Working both in the field and in his converted firehouse studio in Kansas City, Missouri, Vedros has defined himself with a penchant for experimentation and versatility. "From the beginning, I refused to specialize," he says, noting his desire for variety in his assignments. He adds that keeping himself flexible has paid him back handsomely by winning such clients as Apple Computers, Eastman Kodak, Sprint and Nissan.

Since 1987, Vedros has shared his commercial photography and business expertise in 21 cities through Eastman Kodak's Professional Photographer Forum. His segment, titled "Asking the Right Questions," is based on his own formula for success in this highly competitive field.

" 'Asking the Right Questions' has a multiple ring to it," Vedros says. The phrase, he explains, encompasses both the questions a photographer needs to ask art directors, as well as the questions he must constantly ask himself. Vedros says that at the beginning of a project he seeks answers to the most basic questions—everything from the type of reproduction requested to budget limitations to the style a director ultimately envisions. In the initial meeting with a client, "whoever has the better ideas gets more control," says Vedros. "I'm glad to go with an art director's decision if it's right on."

The portfolio, says Vedros, is the manifestation of one's career focus. When presenting his own work to those unfamiliar with it, Vedros presents a varied collection of commercial photos peppered with assignment work as well as personal projects for himself. However, Vedros admits, when an agency seeks specific qualities for a particular job, it's imperative to gear your portfolio to the project. In addition, he urges photographers to keep portfolios clean and to avoid mixing photo sizes and mats. "Don't discuss all the shutter speeds and f-stop information—no one cares." Most important, he adds, "show only the work you want to do for a living."

During the day-to-day routine, it is easy to fall into an unhealthy pattern of adapting a style or doing work you do not enjoy, says Vedros. So, as he stresses, it's important to monitor career progress and make changes accordingly. "Careers should be designed like a fine photograph," he says, noting the necessity of attention to detail. One way to focus your attention, he recommends, is with another question: Are you doing the type of photography you want to practice forever?

Vedros says that once he accepts a commercial project, he strives to obtain "a balance between moment and technique," which he notes as his key to taking quality photographs.

He developed this early in his career when he did extensive editorial and portrait work. Aside from helping him to hone his communication skills, editorial work taught him the element of "moment," or the ability to capture an instant on film. This ability aided him in his transition to commercial work, he says with conviction. "I wasn't ready for all the complex, technical information," he says. "I needed to break into photography gradually to absorb it all." Once he internalized the process, he was then able to handle the "very deliberate and planned" nature of advertising photography—where the emphasis is on technique, lighting and interpretation.

While Vedros, like most photographers, prefers to concentrate on creativity, he recognizes the need for maintaining a proper business outlook. "The shift from creative to business back to creative is exhausting," he says, noting that he handles business matters during the early part of his day, then moves into "creative gear and stays there." In addition, pointing out his belief that certain necessities of business are best left to professionals, he says he hires agents and designers to handle his marketing efforts.

Although designers have put together some slick direct mail packages for him, Vedros prefers "to advertise rather than sell," so he rarely solicits an agency for work. He has found his most rewarding marketing effort to be advertising in trade publications such as the *Black Book* and *Archive*.

There is no question, says Vedros, that the market is swimming with photographers seeking advertising work. But in his own opinion, he says "there is always room at the top." And you *can* get there, he stresses. Continue to learn from the experts through professional photography organizations, have a sense of purpose, and most important, "look different and market it."

—Jennifer Hogan

This pair of images, created by advertising photographer Nick Vedros, was originally used to illustrate a new products brochure being published by Eastman Kodak. The photos not only dramatize the metamorphosis of coal into diamonds, but also Vedros's strong command of the black-and-white medium.

■**OMNI COMMUNICATIONS**, Suite 103, 655 W. Carmel Dr., Carmel IN 46032. (317)844-6664. Senior President: Winston Long. AV firm. Types of clients: industrial, corporate, educational, governmental and medical.

Needs: Works with 6-12 freelance photographers/month. Uses photographers for AV presentations. Subject matter varies. Also works with freelance filmmakers to produce training films and commercials.

Specs: Uses b&w and color prints; 35mm transparencies; 16mm and 35mm film and videotape.

First Contact & Terms: Provide resume, business card, brochure, flyer or tearsheets to be kept on file for possible future assignments. Works with freelance photographers on assignment basis only. Does not return unsolicited material. Payment varies. Pays on acceptance. Buys all rights "on most work; will purchase one-time use on some projects." Model release required. Credit line given "sometimes, as specified in production agreement with client."

Kansas

MARKETAIDE, INC., Box 500, Salina KS 67402. (913)825-7161. Production Manager: Eric Lamer. Art Director: Rusty Nelson. Ad agency. Uses all media. Serves industrial, retail, financial, agribusiness and manufacturing clients. Needs photos of banks, agricultural equipment, agricultural dealers, custom applicators and general agricultural subjects. Buys all rights. "We generally work on a day rate ranging from $200-1,000/day." Pays within 30 days of invoice. Call to arrange an appointment. Provide resume and tearsheets to be kept on file for possible future assignments. Reports in 3 weeks. SASE.

Tips: Photographers should have "a good range of equipment and lighting, good light equipment portability, high quality darkroom work for b&w, a wide range of subjects in portfolio with examples of processing capabilities." Prefers to see "set-up shots, lighting, people, heavy equipment, interiors, industrial and manufacturing" in a portfolio. Prefers to see "8 × 10 minimum size on prints, or 35mm transparencies, preferably unretouched" as samples.

PATON PUBLIC RELATIONS, (formerly Paton & Associates), Box 7350, Leawood KS 66207. (913)491-4000. Contact: N.E. (Pat) Paton, Jr. Ad agency. Estab. 1956. Clients: medical, financial, home furnishing, professional associations, vacations resorts.

Needs: Works with freelance photographers on assignment only basis. Uses freelancers for billboards, consumer and trade magazines, direct mail, newspapers, P-O-P displays and TV.

First Contact & Terms: Call for personal appointment to show portfolio. Payment negotiable according to amoung of creativity required from photographer.

■**STEPHAN ADVERTISING AGENCY, INC.**, 247 N. Market, Wichita KS 67202. (316)265-0021. Art Director: Barb Branda. Ad agency. Uses billboards, consumer and trade magazines, direct mail, newspapers, P-O-P displays, radio and TV. Serves clients in retail, industry, finance and fashion. Works with approximately 5 freelance photographers/month on assignment only basis. Provide business card, tearsheets, brochure and rates (hourly, day, etc.).

Specs: Uses b&w and color prints and color transparencies. Also does a lot of videotape and film production. "Filmmakers should contact Nancy Rodriguez."

Payment & Terms: Negotiates payment based on client's budget and where the work will appear. Buys all rights. Model release required, captions preferred.

Making Contact: Arrange a personal interview to show portfolio or query with list of stock photo subjects. Prefers to see samples of product (food, industrial, people, fashion). SASE. Prefers local freelancers. Reports in 1 month.

Tips: "Have solid experience working with agencies and art directors. Be very comfortable with models—both professional and nonprofessional, i.e., employees of our clients, etc."

Kentucky

■**BARNEY MILLERS INC.**, 232 E. Main St., Lexington KY 40507. (606)252-2216. Chairman: Harry Miller.

Needs: Works with 3-4 freelance photographers/month. Uses photographers for video transfer, editing and titling. Subjects include weddings and special events.

Specs: Uses b&w and color prints; 35mm transparencies; 8mm, super 8, 16mm and 35mm film.

First Contact & Terms: Arrange a personal interview to show portfolio or submit portfolio by mail. Provide resume, business card, self-promotion piece or tearsheets to be kept on file for possible future assignments. Works with local freelancers only; interested in stock photos/footage. SASE. Reports in 1 week. Pays $35-200/hour. Pays on acceptance. Captions preferred. Credit line given if desired.

Louisiana

■**DUKE UNLIMITED**, Suite 1709, 1 Gallaria Blvd., Metairie LA 70001. (504)836-5150. Ad agency/PR firm. Art Director: Robert O Hair. Types of clients: hospitals, industrial, hotel, restaurant, financial, real estate development.
Needs: Works with 1-2 freelance photographers/month. Uses photographers for billboards, consumer and trade magazines, P-O-P displays, brochures, catalogs, signage, newspapers and AV presentations. Subjects include: people, industrial, housing, food. Also works with freelance filmmakers to produce TV commercials.
Specs: Uses 8 × 10 glossy b&w and color prints; 35mm, 2¼ × 2¼ and 4 × 5 transparencies; 16mm and 35mm film and videotape.
First Contact & Terms: Arrange a personal interview to show portfolio or send unsolicited photos by mail for consideration; provide resume, business card, brochure, flyer or tearsheets to be kept on file for possible future assignments. Works with freelance photographers on individual assignment, hourly or daily. SASE. Reports in 2 weeks. Pays/job. Pays on publication. Buys all rights. Model release required.
Tips: Prefers to see "a neat, concise package including a list of credits and resume. If possible, a basic price sheet. It is important that it all be in one neat package." Looks for work that will reproduce well and photographers who do consistently good work; ability and desire to work with art director; ability to light so that work looks uniform (especially when several shots will be used together in a brochure or ad).

RICHARD SACKETT EXECUTIVE CONSULTANTS, Suite 404, 8600 Pontchartrain Blvd., New Orleans LA 70124. (504)282-2568. Ad agency. Art Director: Stacey Richard. Types of clients: industrial, optical, retail, real estate, hotel, shopping center management, marine. Client list free with SASE.
Needs: Works with 3 photographers/month. Uses photographers for billboards, consumer and trade magazines, direct mail, P-O-P displays, posters, newspapers. Subject matter includes merchandise, places, scenery of the city, scenery of the sites of construction, mood photos and food.
Specs: Uses 35mm, 4 × 5 and 8 × 10 transparencies.
First Contact & Terms: Arrange a personal interview to show portfolio; send unsolicited photos by mail for consideration. Works with freelance photographers on an assignment basis only. SASE. Reports in 1 week. Pays $600-1,000/day and $3,000-40,000/job. Pays on publication or on receipt of invoice. Buys all rights. Model release required. Credit line given when appropriate.

Maryland

■**BARRETT ADVERTISING**, 1122 Kenilworth Dr., Baltimore MD 21204. (301)828-8686. FAX: (301)296-9359. Ad agency. President: Rich Barrett. Estab. 1969. Types of clients: business-to-business for high-tech and industrial clients. Example of ad campaign: The Racal Corporation, (Reaching Beyond Today's Standards).
Needs: Uses approximately 5-8 freelance photographers/month for billboards, trade magazines, direct mail, P-O-P displays, catalogs, posters, newspapers and trade shows. Interested in reviewing stock photos of industrial subjects.
Specs: Uses b&w and color prints, any size or format; 35mm, 2¼ × 2¼, 4 × 5 and 8 × 10 transparencies; also film. "Call for specs on film and videotape."
First Contact & Terms: Arrange a personal interview to show portfolio, query with list of stock photo subjects; provide resume, business card, brochure, flyer or tearsheets to be kept on file for possible future assignments. Works with freelancers on an assignment basis only. Does not return unsolicited material. Reports in 3 weeks. Pays on receipt of invoice. Buys one-time rights. Model release required. Credit line given "depending on price."
Tips: Trend is toward almost exclusively color work.

■**SAMUEL R. BLATE ASSOCIATES**, 10331 Watkins Mill Dr., Gaithersburg MD 20879-2935. (301)840-2248. AV and stock photo firm. President: Samuel R. Blate. Types of clients: business/professional, US government and private.

Needs: Works with 1 local freelance photographer/month. Uses photographers for editorial, direct mail, catalogs, consumer and trade magazines, posters, audiovisual presentations, brochures and signage. Subjects vary widely, but especially needs "people in office situations, with or without the use of a computer; people playing sports of all sorts."
Specs: Uses 8×10 b&w glossy prints; 35mm, 2¼×2¼ and 4×5 transparencies.
First Contact & Terms: Query with list of stock photo subjects; provide resume, business card, brochure, flyer, tearsheets or sample 35mm slide duplicates to be kept on file for possible future assignments. "Also send a categorical list of images available for stock use; we'll contact you as requirements dictate. We work with freelancers on assignment only." SASE. Reports in 3 weeks. Pays $50-1,500/b&w or color stock photos; $45/hour and $360/day; "price depends on media and circulation, as well as rarity, danger in taking the shot, etc." Pays on acceptance. "We try for one-time rights except when the client makes other demands, in which case we negotiate an upward adjustment." Model release and captions required. Credit line given "whenever possible."
Tips: "Submit work that shows technical and aesthetic excellence. We prefer shots which have the viewer inside subject—involved with it, in other words. We are slowly expanding our use of freelancers as conditions warrant."

THE COMMUNICATORS, INC., Suite 14, 966 Hungerford Dr., Rockville MD 20850. (301)279-0204. PR firm. Administrative Services Manager: Janet Ford. Types of clients: national trade and professional associations.
Needs: Uses variable number of freelancers per month. Uses photographers for consumer and trade magazines, direct mail, posters and newspapers. Subject matter varies—international youth activities to testimony on Capitol Hill.
Specs: Uses 8×10 b&w and color prints and 35mm transparencies.
First Contact & Terms: Query with resume of credits, query with list of stock photo subjects. Provide resume, business card, brochure, flyer or tearsheets to be kept on file for possible future assignments. Works with freelance photographers on assignment basis only. SASE. Reports in 1 month. Pays $200-10,000/job. Pays on receipt of invoice. Buys all or one-time rights. Model release and captions required. Credit line given.
Tips: In reviewing a photographer's portfolio or samples, looks for "story-telling ability." Query.

*CROSBY COMMUNICATIONS, 647 Ridgely Ave., Annapolis MD 21401. (301)266-1474. FAX: (301)266-1425. Ad agency. Art Director: Margy McArdle. Type of clients: finance, real estate and hospitals and misc.
Needs: Occasionally uses photographers for billboards, consumer magazines, trade magazines, direct mail, P-O-P displays, catalogs, posters, newspapers and signage. Subject matter is primarily architecture and industrial. Reviews stock photos.
Specs: Uses all sizes and formats.
First Contact & Terms: Query with list of stock photo subjects. Provide resume, business card, brochure, flyer or tearsheets to be kept on file for possible future assignments. Works on assignment only. SASE. Reports only if interested. Payment varies depending on job. Pays after clients pay, usually 30-90 days. Rights purchased vary. Model release preferred. Credit line given sometimes, depending on client or project.
Tips: In a freelancer's samples, wants to see "b&w: very few photographers show b&w studio. Timing is the key."

MARC SMITH COMPANY, INC., P.O. Box 5005, Severna Park MD 21146. (301)647-2606. Ad agency. Art Director: Ed Smith. Types of clients: industrial. Client list on request with SASE.
Needs: Uses photographers for trade magazines, direct mail, catalogs and trade show booths. Subjects include products, sales literature (still life), commercial buildings (interiors and exteriors).
Specs: Vary: b&w and color prints and transparencies.
First Contact & Terms: Provide resume, business card, brochure, flyer or tearsheets to be kept on file for possible future assignments. Works with freelance photographers on assignment basis only. Does not return unsolicited material. Reporting time varies from 1 week to 1 month. Pays by the job. Pays when client pays agency, usually 30-60 days. Buys all rights. Model release required; captions preferred.

■VAN SANT, DUGDALE & COMPANY, INC., The World Trade Center, Baltimore MD 21202. (301)539-5400. Executive Creative Director: J. Stanley Paulus. Creative Director: Richard Smith. Ad agency. Types of clients: corporations, consumer products and services, associations and industrial firms; "very wide range" of accounts; client list provided upon request.
Needs: Works on assignment only basis. Negotiates with photographers on each assignment based on the individual job and requirements. Uses photographers for consumer and trade magazines, brochures, catalogs, newspapers and AV presentations.

First Contact & Terms: Local freelancers only. Query with resume and follow up with personal appointment. Payment negotiated depending upon job.
Tips: "The freelancer should make a showing of his/her work to all our art directors and continue to keep us reminded of his/her work from time to time. Interviews and personal appointments not necessary."

Massachusetts

ELBERT ADVERTISING AGENCY, INC., Box 399, Zero Walpole St., Norwood MA 02062-0004. (617)769-7666. Production Manager: Gary Taitz. Ad agency. Uses all media. Serves clients in fashion and industry. Needs photos of food, fashion and industry; and candid photos. Buys up to 600 photos/year. Pays $25 minimum/hour. Call to arrange an appointment, submit portfolio, or send mailer. Reports in 1 week. SASE.
Specs: Uses 5×7, 8×10 semigloss b&w prints; contact sheet OK. Also uses color prints; and 35mm, $2\frac{1}{4} \times 2\frac{1}{4}$, 4×5 and 11×14 transparencies.

■**FILM I**, 990 Washington St., Dedham MA 02026. (617)329-3470. Account Executives: Robert Gilmore, Holly Haas. AV firm. Serves clients in schools and business. Produces filmstrips, slide sets, multimedia kits, motion pictures, sound-slide sets and videotape. Produces programs for inhouse presentations and commercial spots for TV. Works with 3-10 freelance photographers/month on assignment only basis. Provide resume, flyer and tearsheets to be kept on file for possible future assignments.
Film: Produces 35mm slides, super slides and 4×5; Super 8 and 16mm movies.
Photos: Uses 8×10 prints and 35mm transparencies.

MDK ALLIED, (formerly Allied Advertising Agency, Inc.), 800 Statler Bldg., Boston MA 02116. (617)482-4100. Ad agency. Production Manager: Chris McCloy.
Needs: Works with 2-4 freelance photographers/month. Uses photographers for billboards, consumer and trade magazines, direct mail, P-O-P displays, brochures, catalogs, posters, signage, newspapers, AV presentations, packaging, and press releases. Subject needs "too varied to list one particular type. About 70% industrial, 25% consumer/retail, 5% PR." Also works with freelance filmmakers to produce TV commercials, industrial films, P-O-P film loops.
Specs: Uses 8×10 RC and glossy b&w prints; 4×5, 8×10 color transparencies for studio work; 16mm, 35mm and videotape film.
First Contact & Terms: Arrange a personal interview to show portfolio. Works with freelance photographers on assignment basis only. Pays $60-150/hour, $600-3,000/day or $100-2,500/photo. Pays on acceptance. Buys all rights. Model release required. Credit line "usually not" given.
Tips: In a portfolio, prefers to see "cross section of types of photography that the photographer feels he/she handles most easily. Photographers are matched by their strong points to each assignment. Keep agency updated as to new projects."

MILLER COMMUNICATIONS, INC., 607 Boylston, Copley Sq., Boston MA 02116. (617)536-0470. Supervisor: Nancy Milka. PR firm. Handles high technology/computer accounts, computer communication. Photos used in press kits, consumer and trade magazines. Commissions 10 photographers/year. Pays $75 minimum/half day. Buys all rights. Model release preferred. Most interested in editorial type: photographs, head shots, creative product shots, user shots, equipment, and press conference coverage.
B&W: Uses contact sheet.
Color: Uses $2\frac{1}{4} \times 2\frac{1}{4}$ transparencies or contact sheet and negatives.
Tips: "Select a product the agency is representing and make up a portfolio showing this particular product from the simplest photography to the most sophisticated image-builder. Photographers we need must be thinkers, philosophers, not impulsive types who take 600 slides from which we can select 1 or 2 good pictures."

■**TR PRODUCTIONS**, 1031 Commonwealth Ave., Boston MA 02215. (617)783-0200. Executive Vice President: Ross P. Benjamin. Types of clients: industrial, commercial and educational.
Needs: Works with 1-2 freelance photographers/month. Uses photographers for slide sets and multimedia productions. Subjects include: people shots, manufacturing/sales and facilities.
Specs: Uses 35mm transparencies.
First Contact & Terms: Provide resume, business card, self-promotion piece or tearsheets to be kept on file for possible future assignments. Works with local freelancers by assignment only; interested in stock photos/footage. Does not return unsolicited material. Reports "when needed." Pays $300-1,000/day. Pays "14 days after acceptance." Buys all rights.

Michigan

■**CREATIVE HOUSE ADVERTISING, INC.**, Suite 301, 30777 Northwestern Hwy., Farmington Hills MI 48018. (313)737-7077. Sr. Vice President/Executive Creative Director: Robert G. Washburn. Ad agency. Uses photos for brochures, catalogs, annual reports, billboards, consumer and trade magazines, direct mail, newspapers, P-O-P displays, radio and TV. Serves clients in retailing, industry, finance and commercial products. Works with 4-5 freelance photographers/year on assignment only.
Needs: Uses b&w and color prints, and transparencies. Also produces TV commercials (35mm and 16mm) and demo film to industry. Does not pay royalties.
First Contact & Terms: Provide resume, business card, brochure, flyer and anything to indicate the type and quality of photos to be kept on file for future assignments. Pays $100-200/hour or $800-1,600/day; negotiates payment based on client's budget and photographer's previous experience/reputation. Pays in 1-3 months, depending on the job. Buys all rights. Model release required. Arrange personal interview to show portfolio; query with resume of credits, samples, or list of stock photo subjects; submit portfolio for review ("Include your specialty and show your range of versatility"); or send material by mail for consideration. Local freelancers preferred. SASE. Reports in 2 weeks.

*****DALLAS C. DORT AND CO.**, 900 Northbank Center, Flint MI 48502. (313)238-4677. FAX: (313)238-5671. President/Creative Director: Dallas C. Dort. Estab. 1972. Ad agency. Uses all media except foreign. Serves food, health care, retail, healthcare, government and travel clients. Works with freelance photographers on assignment only, approximately 10 times/year.
Needs: Uses b&w prints. Also uses color prints and film. Specifications for each per assignment.
First Contact & Terms: Send resume and samples to be kept on file for possible future assignments. Buys all rights. "We outline the job to the photographer, he quotes on the job and it is billed accordingly." Submit portfolio. SASE. Reports in 2 weeks.

*****EXPOTACULAR DISPLAYS DIVISION**, Compufax Corporation, 23077 Greenfield Rd., Suite 153, Southfield MI 48075. (313)557-8440. FAX: (313)557-2318. Display builder. President: Bob Molner. Types of Clients: Industrial, community service, charitable, environmental, institutional, religious and political. Recent clients include: Enterprise Auto Rental, Dynamic Temporary Services, and National Garages.
Needs: Uses up to 3 freelancers per month. Uses photographers for displays for trade-shows, expositions, etc. Subjects include human interest, industrial processing.
Specs: Uses 16×20 and larger matte b&w or color prints; 35mm, 2¼×2¼, 4×5 and 8×10 transparencies.
First Contact & Terms: Query with list of available suject matter. Works with freelancers on an assignment basis only. SASE. Reports in 1-2 weeks. Pays $100/color photo; $50/b&w photo; other rates subject to negotiation. Pays on acceptance or upon approval by exhibitor. Usually buys all rights, but other rights or usage fees negotiable. Model release required; photo captions preferred. Credit line given sometimes, depending on negotiation.
Tips: In freelancer's samples, looks for "human interest and involvement, dramatic, eye-catching potential, and pertinence to exhibitors display and selling needs." To contact, "send name, address, phone, and subjects specialty/specialties with non-returnable printed sample if available. Otherwise hold sample for our request."

■**LIGHT PRODUCTIONS**, 1915 Webster, Birmingham MI 48009. (313)642-3502. Producer: Terry Luke. Estab. 1972. Types of clients: corporations, industrial, businesses, training institutions and fashion magazines. Examples of productions: Rockwell International, "Heavytruck Computer Stories"; Arcade Machine, "What Can It Do?"
Needs: Works with 2-3 freelance photographers/month. Subjects include city people in activities, business activities, industrial, scenics landscapes, animals, travel sites and activities, models (glamour and nude). Reviews stock photos, film or video.
Audiovisual Needs: Uses freelance photographers for slide sets, multimedia productions and videotapes.
Specs: Uses 8×10 b&w prints, 5×7 and 8×10 glossy color prints, 35mm color slides; VHS, U-matic ¾" and SVHS videotape.
First Contact & Terms: Query with resume; query with stock photo list; provide resume, slides, business card, self-promotion piece or tearsheets to be kept on file for possible future assignments. Works with freelancers by assignment only; interested in stock photos/footage. May not return unsolicited material. Reports in 2 weeks. Pays $5-100/hour; $50-750/day; $10-1,000/job; $10+/color photo; $10+/b&w photo; sometimes also pays in "trades." Pays on publication. Buys one-time rights and all rights; depends on use. Model release and captions preferred. Credit line sometimes given.

Tips: In portfolios or demos, looks for "positive creative viewpoint fun, playful, active, sense of design—the unusual in the usual." Sees trend toward "more use of video, and manipulated computer images." To break into AV work, "join AV organizations, shoot stills of productions, volunteer your help, etc.".

■**PHOTO COMMUNICATION SERVICES, INC.**, 6410 Knapp N.E., Ada MI 49301. (616)676-1499. Commercial/Illustrative and AV firm. President: M.L. Jackson. Estab. 1970. Types of clients: commercial/industrial, fashion, food, general, human interest. Examples of recent clients: Harper & Row, internal corporate AV communications; Zondervan Family Bookstores, a semi-annual AV production for vendor recruitment/sales promotion.
Needs: Works with variable number of freelance photographers/month. Uses photographers for catalogs, P-O-P displays, AV presentations, trade magazines and brochures. Photographers used for a "large variety of subjects." Sometimes works with freelance filmmakers.
Audiovisual Needs: Primarily needs 35mm slides for industrial multi-image; also video and some film.
Specs: Uses 8×10 gloss and semigloss b&w and color prints (or larger); 35mm, 2¼×2¼, 4×5 and 8×10 transparencies; 16mm film; VHS/SVHS and ¾″ videotape.
First Contact & Terms: Query with resume of credits, samples or list of stock photo subjects. Works with freelance photographers on assignment basis only. SASE. Reports in 1 month. Pays $25-150/hour, $200-1,500/day, or private negotiation. Pays 30 days from acceptance. Rights negotiated. Model release required. Credit line given "whenever possible."
Tips: "Looks for professionalism in portfolio or demos. I'm not interested in people starting out looking for their first job. Be professional and to the point. If I see something I can use I will make an appointment to discuss the project in detail. We also have a library of stock photography and can be reached on the (Compuserve 76360, 113) or MCI mail (ID 247-7996) via your computer or Western Union Easylink (62909611) or (616)676-2429, BBS Electronic Mail System. Foresees growth of video, especially 'video walls,' but slowdown of multi-image."

PR ASSOCIATES, INC., 1600 Penobscot Bldg., Detroit MI 48226. (313)963-3396. PR firm. Manager, Advertising/Production: Conni Brown.
Needs: Works with 10 freelance photographers/month. Uses photographers for newspapers, newsletters, brochures and annual reports.
Specs: Uses 8×10 color and b&w prints; 35mm, 2¼×2¼, 4×5 and 8×10 transparencies.
First Contact & Terms: Arrange a personal interview to show portfolio. Works on assignment only. Reports in 1 week. Pays $60-85/hour; $400-600/day; or $7-15/photo. Pays 30-60 days after receipt of invoice. Buys all rights. Model release and captions required.
Tips: Prefers to see press conferences, b&w, architectural, and head and shoulder shots. "Be on time, be prepared and take some initiative."

ROSS ROY, INC., 100 Bloomfield Hills Parkway, Bloomfield Hills MI 48013. (313)433-6000. Ad agency. Contact: Art Director. Types of clients: Chrysler, K-Mart, FTD, Ameritech, La-Z-Boy, State of Michigan.
Needs: Uses freelance photographers for billboards, consumer and trade magazines, P-O-P displays, catalogs, posters, and newspapers. Subjects include retail, corporate, fashion, automotive, product.
Specs: Uses 8×10, 11×14 matte b&w prints; "all formats" transparencies.
First Contact & Terms: Arrange a personal interview to show portfolio; provide resume, business card, brochure, flyer or tearsheets to be kept on file for possible future assignments. Works with freelance photographers on assignment only. Does not return unsolicited material. Pays $250-1,500/b&w photo; $300-2,500/color photo; $750-2,000/day. Pays on receipt of invoice. Buys all rights. Model release required.
Tips: Prefers to see lighting, design and a sense of style and individuality. Contact Jean Oliveri for list of art directors; contact art directors individually for interview, or send tearsheets, flyers, etc. if out-of-town. "We use photography extensively, but tend to use mostly local for advertising; out-of-town (location) for automotive. Be persistent in calling to set up the initial contact, but don't be pesky. Work looks best as a combination of laminated tearsheets and mounted transparencies."

■**WALLER, COOK & MISAMORE ADVERTISING & PUBLIC RELATIONS**, Suite 100, 3001 Orchard Vista Dr. SE, Grand Rapids MI 49456. (616)940-0900. Ad agency. Art Director: Scott Scheerhorn. Types of clients: industrial, business-to-business. Client list free with SASE.
Needs: Works with 4-5 freelance photographers/month. Uses photographers for trade magazines, direct mail, P-O-P displays, catalogs, posters, AV presentations, case history articles. Subjects include products, illustrative, facilities, etc.

Specs: Uses all sizes b&w and color prints; 35mm, 2¼×2¼, 4×5, 8×10 transparencies, "all depending on situation."

First Contact & Terms: Query with resume of credits and samples; provide resume, business card, brochure, flyer or tearsheets to be kept on file for possible future assignments. Works with freelance photographers on an assignment basis only. Does not return unsolicited material. Reports in 1 week. Pays $50-200/hour; $300-1,500/day; $150/b&w photo; $600/color photo. Pays within 30 days. Buys all rights. Model release required.

Tips: Prefers to see industrial, products. "Please send letter, credentials, and samples printed if available."

Minnesota

■**BUTWIN & ASSOCIATES ADVERTISING, INC.**, 8700 Westmoreland Ln., Minneapolis MN 55426. (612)546-0203. Ad agency. President: Ron Butwin. Types of clients: industrial, retail, corporate.

Needs: Works with 1-2 freelance photographers/month. Uses photographers for billboards, direct mail, catalogs, newspapers, consumer magazines, P-O-P displays, posters, AV presentations, trade magazines, brochures and signage. Uses "a wide variety" of subjects and styles.

Audiovisual Needs: Works with freelance filmmakers to produce TV commercials and training films.

Specs: Uses all sizes b&w or color prints; 35mm and 2¼×2¼, 4×5 and 8×10 transparencies; 16mm film and videotape.

First Contact & Terms: Provide resume, business card, brochure, flyer or tearsheets to be kept on file for possible future assignments. Does not return unsolicited material. Usually buy all rights. Model release required. Credit line sometimes given.

■**CARMICHAEL-LYNCH, INC.**, 800 Hennepin Ave., Minneapolis MN 55403. (612)334-6000. Ad agency. Executive Creative Director: Jack Supple. Creative Directors: Frank Haggerty and Jud Smith. Send info to: Cathy Stroncek, creative coordinator. Types of clients: recreational vehicles, food, finance, wide variety. Client list provided on request.

Needs: Uses "maybe 8" freelance photographers/month. Uses photographers for billboards, consumer and trade magazines, direct mail, P-O-P displays, brochures, posters, newspapers, and other media as needs arise. Also works with freelance filmmakers to produce TV commercials.

Specs: Uses b&w and color prints; 35mm, 2¼×2¼, 4×5 and 8×10 transparencies; 16mm and 35mm film and videotape.

First Contact & Terms: Provide resume, business card, brochure, flyer or tearsheets to be kept on file for possible future assignments; submit portfolio for review; arrange a personal interview to show portfolio; works with freelance photographers on assignment basis only. Reports in 1 week. Pay depends on contract; $400-2,500/day; $200-2,500/job. Pays on acceptance. Buys all rights or one-time rights, "depending on agreement." Model release required.

Tips: "Be close at hand (Minneapolis, Detroit, Chicago). In a portfolio, we prefer to see the photographer's most creative work—not necessarily ads. Show only your most technically, artistically satisfying work."

MARTIN-WILLIAMS ADVERTISING INC., 10 S. 5th St., Minneapolis MN 55402. (612)340-0800. FAX: (612)342-9716. Ad agency. Production Coordinator: Lyle Studt. Estab. 1947. Types of clients: industrial, retail, fashion, finance, agricultural, business-to-business and food. Client list free with SASE.

Needs: Works with 6-12 photographers/month. Uses photographers for billboards, consumer and trade magazines, direct mail, catalogs, posters and newspapers. Subject matter varies.

Specs: Uses 8×10 and larger b&w and color prints, 35mm, 2¼×2¼, 4×5 and 8×10 transparencies.

First Contact & Terms: Arrange a personal interview to show portfolio; provide resume, business card, flyer or tearsheets to be kept on file for possible future assignments. Works with freelance photographers on an assignment basis only. SASE. Reports in 2 weeks. Payment individually negotiated. Pays $500-1,800/b&w photo; $600-1,800/color photo; $100-250/hour; $1,200-2,000/day; $600-$10,000/complete job. Pays on receipt of invoice. Buys one-time rights, exculsive product rights or all rights. Model release required.

Tips: Looks for "high quality work, imagination."

MEDIAWERKS, 1400 Hower Rd., Winona MN 55987. (507)454-1400. Ad agency. Art Director: David Spies. Estab. 1975. Types of clients: industrial, retail, fashion, finance and landscape.

Needs: Works with 4 freelance photographers/month for billboards, consumer and trade magazines, direct mail, P-O-P displays, catalogs, posters, signage and newspapers. Subjects include fashion, tabletop, and industrial.

Specs: Uses b&w and color prints, and transparencies; all sizes.

First Contact & Terms: Send unsolicited photos by mail for consideration. Provide resume, business card, brochure, flyer or tearsheets to be kept on file for possible future assignments. Works with freelance photographers on assignment basis only. Does not return unsolicited material. Pays $200-400/b&w photo; $400-700/color photo; $50-100/hour; $500-1,000/day. Pays on receipt of invoice. Buys exclusive product rights and one-time rights. Model release required.

Tips: Prefers to see fashion, tabletop photos, stock, industrial, outdoor environment, archival. "Submit samples of best work which includes approximate costs and type of involvement."

*■EDWIN NEUGER & ASSOCIATES, 1221 Nicollet Mall #320, Minneapolis MN 55403. (612)333-6621. FAX: (612)344-1809. PR firm. President: Ed Neuger. Types of clients: General, including industrial, retail and finance. Examples of projects: Washington Scientific Industries, Sheldahl, Inc. and Barrett Moving & Storage.

Needs: Works with 10 photographers—filmmakers—videographers/year. Uses photographers for trade magazines, direct mail, catalogs and audiovisual. Subjects include: people.

Audiovisual Needs: Slide shows, (single projector and multi-image) and videotape.

Specs: Uses color prints and transparencies.

First Contact & Terms: Query with samples. Works with local freelancers on assignment only. Reports in 6 weeks. Usually pays $1,000-2,000/day. Pays on receipt of invoice. Buys all rights (work-for-hire); sometimes negotiable. Model release preferred. Credit line given.

PIERCE THOMPSON & ASSOCIATES, INC., 6356 Smithtown Bay Rd., Excelsior MN 55331. (612)474-5502. President: R.P. Thompson. Types of clients: industrial, retail, financial, construction, medical, communications and insurance.

Needs: Works with 1-2 freelance photographers/month. Uses photographers for trade magazines, annual reports and publicity. Subject matter includes people, events, buildings and offices.

Specs: Uses 4×5 and 8×10 glossy b&w prints.

First Contact & Terms: Provide resume, business card, brochure, flyer or tearsheets to be kept on file for possible future assignments. Works with local freelancers on assignment basis only. Does not return unsolicited material. Payment is negotiable by the hour, day, job or per photo. Buys all rights. Model release required; captions preferred. Credit line given "at times."

Tips: "Send me information and rates on your company."

■THT INC. MARKETING & ADVERTISING, (formerly Vanguard Associates, Inc.), 1925 First Ave. South, Minneapolis MN 55403. (612)871-1998. President: Tom Pipton. Ad agency. Types of clients: government, consumer, fashion, food.

Needs: Uses photographers for billboards, consumer and trade magazines, direct mail, P-O-P displays, brochures, posters, newspapers, multimedia campaigns and AV presentations. Payment is by the project; negotiates according to client's budget.

*■WORLD WIDE PICTURES, 1201 Hennepin Ave., P.O. Box 59235, Minneapolis MN 55459. (612)338-3335. FAX: (612)338-3029. Film and video firm. Acting Director: Ken Engstrom. Estab. 1952. We serve the religious community and many others through advertising. Example of recent production: "The Crusade Story," Billy Graham Evangelistic Association.

Needs: Works with 5-10 photographers/filmmakers/videographers/month. Uses photographers for consumer magazines, trade magazines, direct mail, P-O-P displays, catalogs, posters, newspapers and audiovisual uses. Subjects include: evangelism and pubicity shots of film actors/actresses. Reviews stock photos, film or video.

Audiovisual Needs: Slides/videotape. Uses 8×10 b&w and color prints; 35mm transparencies; ½″, ¾″ and 1″ videotape.

First Contact & Terms: Query with resume of credits; provide resume, business card, brochure, flyer or tearsheets to be kept on file for possible future assignments. Works with freelancers on an assignment basis only. SASE. Reports in 3 weeks. Payment varies depending on job. Buys all rights and one-time rights. Model release preferred. Credit line given depending on project.

Tips: Sees trend toward computer graphics.

Missouri

*■ADAMSON ADVERTISING, 222 S. Central Ave., St. Louis MO 63105. (314)727-9500. FAX: (314)727-0561. Ad agency. Creative Director: Carl Schlanger. Estab. 1981. Types of clients: industrial, professional, consumer. Previous/current clients include: ITT Commercial Finance, Anheuser-Busch, Cooper Industries, Southwestern Bell and J.B. Lippincott.

Needs: Works with 4-6 freelance photographers/filmmakers/videographers each month. Uses photographers for trade magazines, newspapers and audiovisual. Subjects include: people and products (mostly still, some video).
Audiovisual Needs: Uses photos/film/video for various needs.
Specs: Uses b&w/color prints; transparencies; 1", Betacam, SVHS videotape.
First Contact & Terms: Arrange personal interview to show portfolio. Works with freelancers on an assignment basis only. SASE. Pays $500-2,000/day. Buys all rights (work-for-hire), and one-time rights. Model release required. Credit line not given.
Tips: "Moving away from slides toward using video almost exclusively. Sales tapes, video walls, etc."

*■BORGMEYER & MUSEN ADVERTISING, INC., Suite 103, 1850 Craigshire Rd., St. Louis MO 63146-4006. (314)275-8055. FAX: (314)275-7069. Ad agency. Art Director: Mary Margreiter. Estab. 1988. Types of clients: Finance, retail, industrial, business-to-business.
Needs: Uses 1-3 photographer/month for billboards, consumer magazines, trade magazines, direct mail, P-O-P displays, catalogs, newspapers, signage and brochures. Reviews stock photos/film or video footage geared toward client-type. "We shoot commercials for clients on both film and videotape."
Specs: Uses 8×10, b&w or color prints; 4×5 and 8×10 transparencies.
First Contact & Terms: Query with list of stock photo subjects. Provide resume, business card, brochure, flyer or tearsheets to kept on file for possible future assignments. Works mainly with freelancers on assignment only. SASE. Reports in 1 month. Pay "Depends on budgetary considerations of clients and projects." Buys all rights. Also, buys one-time rights if purchasing stock photos/film. Model release preferred; photo captions preferred. Credit line sometimes given, depending on clients and projects.
Tips: In freelancer's samples demos, wants to see "techniques in capturing feeling/mood aspect of client objectives or products." Sees trend toward "lots of b&w with splashes of spot color or hand tinting in certain key areas." To break in, "be willing to be flexible with budgets and client mandatories."

AARON D. CUSHMAN AND ASSOCIATES, INC., Suite 900, 7777 Bonhomme, St. Louis MO 63105. (314)725-6400. Executive Vice President/General Manager: Thomas L. Amberg. PR, marketing and sales promotion firm. Types of clients: real estate, manufacturing, travel and tourism, telecommunications, consumer products, corporate counseling.
Needs: Works with 3-5 freelance photographers/month. Uses photographers for news releases, special events photography, and various printed pieces. More news than art oriented.
First Contact & Terms: Call for appointment to show portfolio. Pays $50-100/b&w photo; $50-250/color photo; $50-100/hour; $350-750/day.
Tips: "We are using increasing amounts of architecturally oriented and consumer product-related stills."

EVERETT, BRANDT & BERNAUER, INC., 1805 Grand Ave., Kansas City MO 64108. (816)421-0000. Contact: James A. Everett. Ad agency. Types of clients: construction, finance, auto dealership, agribusiness, insurance accounts. Photos used in brochures, newsletters, annual reports, PR releases, AV presentations, sales literature, consumer and trade magazines. Usually works with 1-2 freelance photographers/month on assignment only basis. Provide resume and business card to be kept on file for possible future assignments. Buys 25 photos/year. Negotiates payment based on client's budget and amount of creativity required from photographer. Buys all rights. Model release required. Arrange a personal interview to show portfolio. Local freelancers preferred. SASE. Reports in 1 week.
B&W: Uses 5×7 prints.
Color: Uses prints and transparencies.
Tips: "We have a good working relationship with three local photographers and would rarely go outside of their expertise unless work load or other factors change the picture."

GEORGE JOHNSON ADVERTISING, 763 New Ballas Rd. S., St. Louis MO 63141. (314)569-3440. President: George Johnson. Art Director: Kathy Marcum. Ad agency. Uses all media except foreign. Types of clients: real estate, financial and social agencies. Works with 2 freelance photographers/month on assignment only basis.
First Contact and Terms: Provide resume and flyer to be kept on file for possible future assignments. Buys 50 photos/year. Pays $10-50/hour; negotiates payment based on client's budget and amount of creativity required. Pays in 60 days. Prefers to see working prints of typical assignments and tearsheets (application). Submit material by mail for consideration.

PARKER GROUP, INC., 6900 Delmar, St. Louis MO 63139. (314)727-4000. (314)727-3034. Ad agency and PR firm. Manager of Creative Services: Mary Tuttle. Estab. 1979. Types of clients: industrial, retail, fashion, healthcare, consumer and finance.

Needs: Works with 2-3 freelance photographers/month. Uses photographers for billboards, consumer magazines, trade magazines, direct mail, P-O-P displays, catalogs, posters, signage and newspapers.
First Contact & Terms: Query with resume of credits or with list of stock photo subjects. Provide resume, business card, brochure, flyer or tearsheets to be kept on file for possible future assignments. Works on assignment basis only. Does not return unsolicited material. Reports in 2 weeks. Pays $50-2,500/b&w photo; $250-5,000/color photo; $50-300/hour; $400-2,500/day; $150-10,000/complete job. Pays in 30 days. Model release required; captions preferred.

■**PREMIER FILM, VIDEO AND RECORDING,** 3033 Locust, St. Louis MO 63103. (314)531-3555. Secretary/Treasurer: Grace Dalzell. Types of clients: educational, social service and religious organizations.
Audiovisual Needs: Works with various number of freelance photographers/month. Uses photographers for filmstrips, slide sets, multimedia productions, films and videotapes.
Specs: Uses any size color prints; 35mm transparencies; reduction prints Super 8, 16mm, 35mm film; VHS, Beta, U-matic ¾" videotapes.
First Contact & Terms: Provide resume, business card, self-promotion piece or tearsheets to be kept on file for possible future assignments, "include letter with name, address and phone number." Works on assignment only. SASE. Reports "ASAP." Pays $2.50-250/b&w photo, $5-300/color photo, $5-16.50/hour, $40 minimum/day and $150-1,600/job. Pays on acceptance. Buys one-time, exclusive product and all rights; flexible. Credit line sometimes given.
Tips: "Nearly 100% of our freelance photographers are St. Louis residents." Looks for clean, traditional work with "integrity of reproduction, artistry, simplicity and especially beauty. To make best impression, be clean-cut in all presentations."

Montana

■**VIDEO INTERNATIONAL PUBLISHERS, INC.,** 118 Sixth St. S., Great Falls MT 59405. (406)727-7133. Administrative Director: Penny L. Adkins (Ms.). Types of clients: industrial, educational, retail and broadcast.
Needs: Works with 3-15 photographers/month. Uses photographers for films and videotapes. Subjects include television commercials, educational/informational programs. All video is shot "film-style" (lighted for film, etc.).
Specs: Uses U-matic ¾", prefers 1" C-format or high-speed, half-inch tape.
First Contact & Terms: Provide resume, business card, self-promotion piece or tearsheets to be kept on file for possible future assignments. Works with freelancers by assignment only; interested in stock photos/footage. SASE. Reports in 1 month. Pays upon completion of final edit. Buys all rights. Model release required. Credit line given.
Tips: "Send the best copy of your work on ¾" cassette. Describe your involvement with each piece of video shown."

Nebraska

■**SIGHT & SOUND, INC.,** 6969 Grover, Omaha NE 68106. (402)393-0999. President: Joel Knutson. Types of clients: medical, financial, business, government, agricultural.
Needs: Works with 2 photographers/month. Uses photographers for filmstrips, multimedia productions and videotapes. Subjects include promotional, motivational and instructive.
Specs: Uses 2¼×2¼ transparencies, U-matic ¾" videotape.
First Contact & Terms: Provide resume, business card, self-promotion piece or tearsheets to be kept on file for possible future assignments. Works with local freelancers only; interested in stock photos/footage. Reports as need arises. Buys all rights.

■**J. GREG SMITH,** Suite 102, 1004 Farnam, Burlington on the Mall, Omaha NE 68102. (402)444-1600. Art Director: Jane Yowell. Ad agency. Types of clients: finance, banking institutions, national and state associations, agriculture, insurance, retail, travel.
Needs: Works with 10 freelance photographers/year on assignment only basis. Uses photographers for consumer and trade magazines, brochures, catalogs and AV presentations. Special subject needs include outer space, science and forest scenes.

First Contact & Terms: Arrange interview to show portfolio. Pays $500/color photo; $60/hour; $800/day; varies/job. Buys all rights, one-time rights or others, depending on use. Looks for "people shots (with expression), scenics (well known, bright colors)."
Tips: Considers "composition, color, interest, subject and special effects when reviewing a portfolio or samples."

■**SWANSON, RUSSELL AND ASSOCIATES**, 1222 P St., Lincoln NE 68508. (402)475-5191. Executive Vice President/Creative Services: Brian Boesche. Ad agency. Types of clients: primarily industrial, financial and agricultural; client list provided on request.
Needs: Works with 10 freelance photographers/year on assignment only basis. Uses photographers for consumer and trade magazines, direct mail, brochures, catalogs, newspapers and AV presentations.
First Contact & Terms: Query first with small brochure or samples along with list of clients freelancer has done work for. Negotiates payment according to client's budget. Rights are negotiable.

Nevada

■**DAVIDSON & ASSOCIATES**, (formerly Davidson Advertising), 3940 Mohigan Way, Las Vegas NV 89119. (702)871-7172. President: George Davidson. Full-service ad agency. Types of clients: beauty, construction, finance, entertainment, retailing, publishing, travel. Photos used in brochures, newsletters, annual reports, PR releases, AV presentations, sales literature, consumer magazines and trade magazines. Arrange a personal interview to show portfolio, query with samples, or submit portfolio for review; provide resume, brochure and tearsheets to be kept on file for possible future assignments. Gives 150-200 assignments/year. Pays $15-50/b&w photo; $25-100/color photo; $15-50/hour; $100-400/day; $25-1,000 by the project. Pays on production. Buys all rights. Model release required.

■**NORMAN BEERGER PRODUCTIONS**, 3217 S. Arville St., Las Vegas NV 89102. (702)876-2328. Owner: Norman Beerger. Estab. 1984. Types of clients: consumers, catalog companies and video distributors/dealers.
Needs: Works with one freelance photographer/month. Uses photographers for videotapes, posters, video case covers and magazine ads. Subjects include wilderness scenes and weather, such as storms. Special subject needs include pictures of national parks in Utah—Zion, Bryce, Arches, Capitol Reef, Glen Canyon, etc.—used for video program covers.
Specs: Uses 35mm, $2\frac{1}{4} \times 2\frac{1}{4}$, 4×5 and 8×10 transparencies.
First Contact & Terms: Provide sample pictures of wilderness scenes. We are interested in stock photos/footage. SASE. Reports in 2 weeks. Pays $25-100/color photo. Pays on acceptance. Buys non-exclusive rights. Captions preferred. Credit line given.
Tips: "Samples of work are the best reference. When reviewing a specific picture we look for an impressive presence with a hint of unrevealed magnitude, yet to be seen, and the photographer's vision of not only the subject matter, but also the depth used to put the background in perspective. Still photographers interested in making the transition into film and video photography should prepare a portfolio of stock shots covering a cross section of the entire market needs."

■**TRI VIDEO TELEPRODUCTION—LAKE TAHOE**, Box 8822, Incline Village NV 89450. (702)323-6868. California Office: Suite C, 1615 5th St., Davis CA 95616. (916)758-5335. Director: Jon Paul Davidson. Types of clients: corporate.
Needs: Uses 3-4 freelance photographers/month. Uses photographers and videographers for publicity photography on the set. Subjects include video documentary, educational, motivational; b&w publicity photos.
Specs: Uses 5×7 SWG finish b&w prints; 16mm film; $\frac{3}{4}$" U-matic videotape; 1" and Betacam.
First Contact & Terms: Provide resume, business card, self-promotion piece or tearsheets to be kept on file for possible future assignments. Works with freelancers by assignment only. Does not return unsolicited material. Reports in 1 week. Pays by the hour and day. Pays on acceptance. Buys one-time rights. Model releases required. Credit line given.
Tips: "We work in several cities—mostly western. We would like to know competent poeple for production assistance. In reviewing samples, we look for good clean composition, proper exposure—nothing exotic. We are seeing much greater video use by corporate clients. Publicity photos are always needed. Photographers interested in making the transition from film to videography should proceed with care. Composition is the same, electronics aren't."

New Hampshire

LEGASSE ASSOCIATES, Box 99, Westminster St., Walpole NH 03608-0099. (603)756-4781. Advertising agency. Art Director: Tina Hoppock & Phil Thomsen. Types of clients: industrial, real estate, business-to-business. Clients list free for SASE.
Needs: Uses photographers for consumer magazines, trade magazines, direct mail, P-O-P displays, catalogs and newspapers. Subjects include studio still life of product; location shots of real estate; stock photo/location of outdoor scenes.
Specs: Uses 8×10 and 11×14 matte or glossy finish b&w prints; 35mm, 2¼×2¼, 4×5 and 8×10 transparencies.
First Contact & Terms: Arrange a personal interview to show portfolio query with resume of credits, list of stock photo subjects or samples; provide resume, business card, brochure, flyer or tearsheets to be kept on file for possible future assignments. SASE. Pays $350-750/day or /job. Pays on receipt of invoice. Buys all rights. Model release required.
Tips: Prefers to see "studio still life; dramatic lighting; metal; architectural."

*■STILLPOINT INTERNATIONAL, Box 640, Walpole NH 03608. (603)756-4225. Publisher. Promotion Director: Joy Hayes Puerto. Types of Clients: environmental, health and self-development.
Needs: Uses photographers for direct mail, catalogs, bookcovers, newsletter and posters. Subjects include: nature. Interested in reviewing stock photos/on nature and environment.
Specs: Uses 3×5 or larger b&w prints.
First Contact & Terms: Query with list of stock photo subjects; query with samples; provide resume, business card, brochure, flyer or tearsheets to be kept on file for possible future assignments. Works with freelancers on an assignment basis only. Reports in 1-2 weeks. Pays on per job basis. Contact for payment figures. Model release required. Credit line given.
Tips: In freelancer's color samples, wants to see "book covers, effective use of color and subject matter to translate essense of book"; 1″ b&w samples for "newsletter, scenes depicting both the beauty and devastation of the planet (especially forest related)." To break in, "keep trying and price work within range of small publisher."

New Jersey

ADLER, SCHWARTZ, INC., 14 Pine St., Morristown NJ 07960. (201)267-0400. Vice President: Peter Adler. Ad agency. Uses all media. Types of clients: automotive, electronic and industrial.
Needs: Works with freelance photographers on assignment only basis. Uses photographers for cars, people, fashion and still life.
First Contact & Terms: Provide business card and tearsheets to be kept on file for possible future assignments. Model release required. Buys all rights, but may reassign to photographer. Negotiates payment based on client's budget, amount of creativity required, where the work will appear and photographer's previous experience and reputation. Pays $1,000/b&w photo; $2,000/color photo; or $2,000/day. Call to arrange an appointment. "Show samples of your work and printed samples." Reports in 2 weeks.
Specs: Uses semigloss prints and transparencies. Model release required.
Tips: "Interested in cars (location/studio), still life (studio), location, editorial and illustration."

■AM CORP VIDEO PRODUCTIONS, 326 High St., Burlington NJ 08046. (609)387-3636. Owner: E. Burro. Nonprofit division, Legacy Productions; provides cultural, historic and public service video projects. Types of clients: mostly industrial.
Needs: Uses freelance camera men. Works with 2-4 freelance photographers/month. Subjects: on location, free-style video coverage.
Specs: Primarily U-matic ¾″ videotape, some VHS and Beta.
First Contact & Terms: Provide resume, business card, self-promotion piece or tearsheets to be kept on file for possible future assignments. Works with freelancers by assignment only. Does not return unsolicited material. Pays $5-10/hour; $50-100/day. Pays on completion of assignment. Buys all rights. Credit line given "when we deem appropriate."
Tips: Looks for point of view, visual interpretation of subject, technical ability of cameraman. "Rethink the process of image-making. Big difference is in visual storytelling."

ARDREY INC., Suite 314, 100 Menlo Park, Edison NJ 08837. (201)549-1300. PR firm. Office Manager: Lisa Fania. Types of clients: industrial. Client list provided on request.

Needs: Works with 10-15 freelance photographers/month throughout US. Uses photographers for trade magazines, direct mail, brochures, catalogs, newspapers. Subjects include trade photojournalism.

Specs: Uses 4×5 and 8×10 b&w glossy prints; 35mm, 2¼×2¼ and 4×5 transparencies.

First Contact & Terms: Provide resume, business card, brochure, flyer or tearsheets to be kept on file for possible future assignments. Works with freelance photographers on assignment basis only. SASE. Pays $150-450/day; "travel distance of location work—time and travel considered." Pays 30-45 days after acceptance. Buys all rights and negatives. Model release required.

Tips: Prefers to see "imaginative industrial photojournalism. Identify self, define territory you can cover from home base, define industries you've shot for industrial photojournalism; give relevant references and samples. Regard yourself as a business communication tool. That's how we regard ourselves, as well as photographers and other creative suppliers."

THE BECKERMAN GROUP, 35 Mill St., Bernardsville NJ 07924. (201)766-9238. Ad agency. Contact: Ilene Beckerman. Types of clients: industrial. Client list free with SASE.

Needs: Works with 3 photographers/month. Uses photographers for catalogs, posters, corporate internal organs and brochures. Subject matter includes table top.

Specs: Uses b&w prints and 2¼×2¼ transparencies.

First Contact & Terms: Arrange a personal interview to show portfolio; provide resume, business card, brochure, flyer or tearsheets to be kept on file for possible future assignments. Works with freelance photographers on an assignment basis only. Does not return unsolicited material. Payment individually negotiated; maximum $1,500/day. Pays on receipt of invoice. Buys all rights. Model release required.

Tips: Looks for "the ability to think conceptually and solve a problem in a strong fresh way."

■**CREATIVE ASSOCIATES**, 626 Bloomfield Ave., Verona NJ 07044. (201)857-3444. AV firm. Producer: Harrison Feather. Estab. 1975. Types of clients: industrial, cosmetic and pharmaceutical.

Needs: Works with 1-2 photographers—filmmakers—videographers/month. Uses photographers for trade magazines and audiovisual uses. Subjects include product and general environment. Reviews stock photos or videotape.

Audiovisual Needs: Uses photos/video for slides and videotape.

Specs: 35mm, 4×5 and 8×10 transparencies; Betacam videotape.

First Contact & Terms: Provide resume, business card, brochure, flyer or tearsheets to be kept on file for possible future assignments. Works with freelancers on an assignment basis only. SASE. Reports as needed. Pays $500-1,000/day; $1,500-3,000/job. Pays on publication. Buys all rights. Model release required. Photo captions preferred. Credit line sometimes given, depending on assignment.

■**CREATIVE PRODUCTIONS, INC.**, 200 Main St., Orange NJ 07050. (201)676-4422. Contact: William E. Griffing. AV producer. Types of clients: industry, advertising, pharmaceuticals and business. Produces film, video, slide presentations, multimedia, multiscreen programs and training programs. Works with freelance photographers on assignment only basis. Provide resume and letter of inquiry to be kept on file for future assignments.

Subject Needs: Subjects include sales promotion, sales training, industrial and medical topics. No typical school portfolios that contain mostly artistic or journalistic subject matter. Must be 3:4 horizontal ratio for film, video and filmstrips; 2:3 horizontal ratio for slides.

Specs: Uses b&w and color prints and transparencies. Produces video and 16mm industrial, training, medical and sales promotion films. Possible assignments include shooting "almost anything that comes along—industrial sites, hospitals, etc." Interested in some stock footage.

Payment & Terms: Negotiates payment based on photographer's previous experience/reputation and client's budget. Pays on acceptance. Buys all rights. Model release required.

Making Contact: Query first with resume of credits and rates. SASE. Reports in 1 week.

Tips: "We would use freelancers out-of-state for part of a production when it isn't feasible for us to travel, or locally to supplement our people on overload basis."

DIEGNAN & ASSOCIATES, Box 343 Martens, Lebanon NJ 08833. President: N. Diegnan. Ad agency/PR firm. Types of clients: industrial, consumer. Commissions 15 photographers/year; buys 20 photos/year from each. Local freelancers preferred. Uses billboards, trade magazines, and newspapers. Negotiates payment based on client's budget and amount of creativity required from photographer. Pays by the job. Buys all rights. Model release preferred. Arrange a personal interview to show portfolio. SASE. Reports in 1 week.

Specs: Uses b&w contact sheet or glossy 8×10 prints. For color, uses 5×7 or 8×10 prints; also 2¼×2¼ transparencies.

■**H.T. FENTON ASSOCIATES, INC.**, 308 Rt. 206, Somerville NJ 08876. (201)359-1100. Senior Art Director: Russ Jamison. Types of clients: agricultural, agri-chemical, industrial, business-to-business and heavy equipment (pavers, etc.).

Needs: Works with 3-5 freelance photographers/month. Uses photographers for billboards, direct mail, posters, P-O-P displays, newspapers, trade magazines, catalogs and salesmen's slide presentations. Subjects include: specific breeds of farm crops/animals, farm location situations, industrial locations, studio product and studio foods. "Call first or end printed sample(s) of best work."

Specs: Uses 4×5 and larger b&w prints; 35mm transparencies; 4×5 transparencies and 16mm sound or silent film, and video.

First Contact & Terms: Arrange a personal interview to show portfolio, query with resume of credits, list of stock photo subjects and samples, provide, business card, brochure, flyer or tearsheets to be kept on file for possible future assignments. "Call first for appointment—when you plan to be in our area." Pays $50-100/hour; $1,000/day; varies/job; varies/b&w photo. Pays on receipt of invoice up to 60 days after invoicing. Buys one-time and all rights; varies with job. Model release, if applicable, and captions required on stock shots of animal breeds, etc.

■**IMAGE INNOVATIONS, INC.**, Suite 201, 29 Clyde Rd., Somerset NJ 08873. (201)873-0700. President: Mark A. Else. AV firm. Types of clients: business, industry and government. Examples of productions: Warner-Lambert Co. and Johnson & Johnson-ARC.

Audiovisual Needs: Uses photographers for videotapes, multi-image and slide/sound.

Specs: Produces 35mm slides and video.

First Contact & Terms: Query with resume of credits. Works on assignment only. Provide resume and tearsheets to be kept on file for future assignments. Pays $300-600/day; $300 minimum/job. Pays 30 days after billing. Buys one-time rights. Model release required; captions optional. Works with talent in New York metropolitan area only.

Tips: "Uses photographers who are conceptually creative and can execute their ideas into a clear, concise, and interesting visual. We like to see samples that will reflect the photographers technical as well as creative abilities, regardless of the medium (b&w/color etc.)" Likes to see "true sense of professionalism and good work. Experience in the field is not always a deciding factor in determining freelance work."

■**INSIGHT ASSOCIATES**, 373 Rt 46 West, Fairfield NJ 07006. (201)575-5521. President: Raymond Valente. Types of clients: major industrial companies.

Needs: Works with 4 freelancers/month. Uses freelancers for filmstrips, slide sets, multimedia productions, videotapes and print material—catalogs. Subjects include: industrial productions. Examples of production: Matheson (safety), Witco Corp. (corporate image) and Volvo (sales training) P.S.E.&G..

Specs: Uses 35mm, 2¼×2¼ and 4×5 transparencies.

First Contact & Terms: Arrange a personal interview to show portfolio. Interested in stock photos/ footage. SASE. Reports in 1 week. Pays $450-750/day. on acceptance. Buys all rights. Model releases preferred. Credit line given.

Tips: "Freelance photographers should have knowledge of business needs and video formats. Also,versatility with video or location work. In reviewing a freelancer's portfolio or samples we look for content appropriate to our clients' objectives. We are seeing a heavy swing from slides to video production. Still photographers interested in making the transition into film and video photography should learn the importance of understanding a script."

■**INTERNATIONAL MEDIA SERVICES, INC.**, 718 Sherman Ave., Plainfield NJ 07060. (201)756-4060. AV firm/independant film and tape production company/media consulting firm. President/General Manager: Stuart Allen. Types of clients: industrial, advertising, print, fashion, broadcast and CATV.

Needs: Works with 0-25 freelance photographers/month; "depending on inhouse production at the time." Uses photographers for billboards, direct mail, catalogs, newspapers, consumer magazines, P-O-P displays, posters, AV presentations, trade magazines, brochures, film and tape. Subjects range "from scenics to studio shots and assignments"—varies with production requirements. Also works with freelance filmmakers to produce documentaries, commercials and training films.

Specs: Uses 8×10 glossy or matted b&w and color prints; 35mm, 2¼×2¼ and 8×10 transparencies; 16mm, 35mm film and ¾-1" videotape.

First Contact & Terms: Provide resume, business card, brochure, flyer or tearsheets to be kept on file for possible future assignments; query with resume of credits; or list of stock photo subjects; arrange a personal interview to show portfolio. SASE. Reporting time "depends on situation and requirements. We are not responsible for unsolicited material and do not recommend sending same. Negotiated rates based on type of work and job requirements." Usually pays $100-750/day, $25-2,500/

job. Rights negotiable, generally purchases all rights. Model release required; captions preferred. Credit line given.

Tips: "Wants to see a brief book containing the best work of the photographer, representative of the type of assignment sought. Tearsheets are preferred but must have either the original or a copy of the original photo used, or applicable photo credit. Send resume and sample for active resource file. Maintain periodic contact and update file."

■JANUARY PRODUCTIONS, P.O. Box 66, 210 6th Ave., Hawthorne NJ 07507. (201)423-4666. FAX: (201)423-5569. President: Allan W. Peller. Estab. 1973. AV firm. Types of clients: schools and public libraries. Audience consists of primary, elementary and intermediate-grade school students. Produces filmstrips. Subjects are concerned with elementary education—science, social studies, math and conceptual development. Payment amounts "depend on job." Buys all rights. Call to arrange an appointment or query with resume of credits and samples of work. SASE.
Audiovisual Needs: Uses 35mm transparencies for filmstrips.
Tips: Wants to see "clarity, effective use of space, design, etc."

■ROGER MALER, INC., Box 435, Mt. Arlington NJ 07856. (201)770-1500. Ad agency. President: Roger Maler. Types of clients: industrial, pharmaceutical and real estate.
Needs: Works with 3 freelance photographers/month. Uses photographers for billboards, trade magazines, direct mail, P-O-P displays, brochures, catalogs, newspapers and AV presentations.
Audiovisual Needs: Works with freelance filmmakers.
First Contact & Terms: Send resume, business card, brochure, flyer or tearsheets to be kept on file for possible future assignments. Works with freelance photographers on assignment only. Does not return unsolicited material. Payment varies. Pays on publication. Model release required. Credit line sometimes given.

*■R.J. MARTIN CO., INC., 315 Rt. 17, Paramus NJ 07652. (201)592-0952. Manager: Kurt von Seekamm. Types of clients: Fortune 500.
Needs: Works with 2-4 freelance photographers/month. Uses photographers for multimedia productions and videotapes. Subjects are various.
Specs: Uses 35mm, 2¼ × 2¼, 4 × 5, 8 × 10 transparencies; ½" Betacam and 1" videotape.
First Contact & Terms: Submit portfolio by mail; provide resume, business card, self-promotion piece or tearsheets to be kept on file for possible future assignments. Works on assignment only. Does not return unsolicited material. Reports in 2 weeks. Pays on per day or job basis. Pays by purchase order 30 days after work completed. Buys all rights. Model release required. Credit line given "when applicable."
Tips: "Be specific about your best work (what areas), be flexible to budget on project—represent our company when on business."

■SORIN PRODUCTIONS, INC., 4400 Rt. 9 South, Freehold NJ 07728. (201)462-1785. President: David Sorin. Type of client: corporate.
Needs: Works with 2 freelance photographers/month. Uses photographers for slide sets, multimedia productions, films and videotapes. Subjects include people and products.
Specs: Uses b&w and color prints; 35mm and 2¼ × 2¼ transparencies; 16mm film.
First Contact & Terms: Query with stock photo list. Provide resume, business card, self-promotion piece or tearsheets to be kept on file for possible future assignments. Works with freelancers by assignment only; interested in stock photos/footage. Does not return unsolicited material. Reports in 2 weeks. Pays by piece or job. Pays on acceptance. Buys all rights. Captions and model releases preferred. Credit line given by project.

New Mexico

MEDIAWORKS, 4002 Silver Avenue SE, Albuquerque NM 87108. (505)266-7795. President: Marcia Mazria. Ad agency. Types of clients: retail, industry, politics, government, law. Produces overhead transparencies, slide sets, motion pictures, sound-slide sets, videotape, print ads and brochures. Works with 1-2 freelance photographers/month on assignment only basis; provide resume, flyer and brochure to be kept on file for possible future assignments. Buys 70 photos and 5-8 films/year.

Subject Needs: Health, business, environment and products. No animals or flowers. Length requirements: 80 slides or 15-20 minutes, or 60 frames, 20 minutes.
Film: Produces ½" and ¾" video for broadcasts.
Photos: Uses b&w or color prints and 35mm transparencies, "and a lot of 2¼ transparencies and some 4×5 transparencies."
Payment/Terms: Pays $40-60/hour, $350-500/day, $40-800/job. Negotiates payment based on client's budget and photographer's previous experience/reputation. Pays on job completion. Buys all rights. Model release required.
Making Contact: Arrange personal interview or query with resume. Prefers to see a variety of subject matter and styles in portfolio. Does not return unsolicited material.

New York

ANNUAL REPORT GROUP, INC., 317 Middle Country Rd., Smithtown NY 11707. Ad agency. President: Hesso Bellem.
Needs: Uses photographers for brochures, trade magazine ads, catalogs and annual reports. Subjects include: personnel and facilities. Interested in reviewing stock photos of a technical nature.
Specs: Uses 35mm, 4×5 transparencies.
First Contact & Terms: Arrange a personal interview to show portfolio, submit portfolio for review; provide resume, business card, brochure, flyer or tearsheets to be kept on file for possible future assignments. Works with freelancers on an assignment basis only. Cannot return material. Reports in 1 week, "depends on job." Pays $75-80/hour; $600-700/day. Pays on acceptance. Buys all rights. Model release, photo captions required. Credit lines "sometimes" given.
Tips: Looks for "low-level lighting, close-ups, tight cropping" in samples. "Send work samples. Charge reasonable rates, so both of us can benefit."

C. L. & B. ADVERTISING, INC., 5790 Widewaters Pkwy. Syracuse NY 13214. (315)446-2280. Advertising, public relations and research. President: Richard Labs. Types of clients: industrial, fashion, finance.
Needs: Works with 4-6 freelance photographers/month. Uses photographers for billboards, consumer and trade magazines, P-O-P displays, catalogs and newspapers. Subject matter includes industrial, consumer, models, location and/or studio.
Specs: Uses all formats.
First Contact & Terms: "Send bio and proof sheet (if available) first; we will contact you if interested." Works with freelance photographers on an assignment basis only. Also uses stock photos. Does not return unsolicited material. Pays in 30 days. Buys all rights. Model release required. Credit line seldom given.
Tips: "We review your work and will call if we think a particular job is applicable to your talents. Renew every 6 months or earlier with an outstanding piece of work to offer."

WALTER F. CAMERON ADVERTISING, 50 Jericho Turnpike, Jericho, Long Island NY 11753. (516)333-2074. Ad agency. Art Director: Steve Levine. Types of clients: retail, trade and corporate. Client list free with SASE.
Needs: Uses photographers for consumer magazines, trade magazines, catalogs and newspapers. Subject matter varies from time to time; furniture settings, cars, product shots, on-location shots.
Specs: Uses 4×5 or 8×10 b&w and color glossy prints.
First Contact & Terms: Arrange a personal interview to show portfolio; submit portfolio for review; provide resume, business card, brochure, flyer or tearsheets to be kept on file for possible future assignments. Works with freelance photographers on an assignment basis only. Pays per hour or $300-400/day. Pays on receipt of invoice. Buys all rights. Model release required; captions preferred.

■**STEVEN COHEN,** 21 Fireplace Dr., Kings Park NY 11754. (516)269-4550. Contact: Steven Cohen. Examples of productions: TV commercials, documentaries, 2nd unit feature films and TV series - 2nd unit.
Needs: Uses photographers for film and videotapes.
Specs: Uses 16mm, 35mm film; 1", ¾" "U-matic and ½" VHS, Beta videotape.
First Contact & Terms: Query with resume, provide business card, self-promotion piece or tearsheets to be kept on file for possible future assignments. Works with freelancers on assignment only. Cannot return material. Reports in 1 week. Pays on acceptance or publication. Buys all rights (work-for-hire). Model releases required. Credit line given.

DE PALMA & HOGAN ADVERTISING, 50 Sawmill River Rd., Hawthorne NY 10532. (914)345-3030. Ad agency. Art Director: Art Glazer. Types of clients: food, drug, publishing. Client list free with SASE.
Needs: Works with 4 photographers/month. Uses photographers for consumer and trade magazines, direct mail, newspapers and TV.
Specs: Uses b&w and color prints; 35mm, 2¼×2¼, 4×5 and 8×10 transparencies.
First Contact & Terms: Arrange a personal interview to show portfolio; query with resume of credits or a list of stock photo subjects; provide resume, business card, brochure, flyer or tearsheets to be kept on file for possible future assignments. Pays $500-1,500/color photo. Pays on receipt of invoice. Buys all rights. Model release required; captions preferred.

*■EDUCATIONAL AUDIO VISUAL INC., 17 Marble Ave., Pleasantville NY 10570. (914)769-6332. FAX: (914)769-6350. AV firm. Executive Producer: Stephen C. Galleher. Estab. 1954. Types of clients: high schools. Examples of recent projects: Myths and Legends of Ancient Greece, The Grapes of Wrath and the 1930s, The French Revolution.
Needs: Works with 1 freelance photographer/month. Uses photographers for audiovisual uses. Subjects include: educational/historical material. Reviews stock photos.
Audiovisual Needs: Uses slides (copy camera chiefly).
Specs: Uses 35mm transparencies.
First Contact & Terms: Query with resume of credits; provide resume, business card, brochure, flyer or tearsheets to be kept on file for possible future assignments. Works with freelancers on assignment basis only. Prefers local freelancers. Cannot return material. Pays $15-20/hour. Pays on receipt of invoice. Buys all rights (work-for-hire) and one-time rights sometimes. Credit line given sometimes, depending on whether providing original images or just converting images to slides.

■EDUCATIONAL IMAGES LTD., Box 3456, West Side Station, Elmira NY 14905. (607)732-1090. Executive Director: Dr. Charles R. Belinky. AV publisher. Types of clients: educational market, grades 6-12 and college; also serves public libraries, parks and nature centers. Produces filmstrips, slide sets, and multimedia kits. Subjects include a heavy emphasis on natural history, ecology, anthropology, conservation, life sciences. Also is interested in other subjects especially chemistry, physics, astronomy, math. "We are happy to consider any good color photo series on any topic that tells a coherent story. We need pictures and text." Works with 12 freelance photographers/year. Buys 200-400 photos/year; film and video are "open." Buys all rights, but may reassign to photographer. Pays $150 minimum/ job, or on a per-photo basis. Query with resume of credits; submit material by mail for consideration. Prefers to see 35mm or larger transparencies and outline of related text in portfolio. Reports in 1 month. SASE.
Film/Video: "We are looking for good video material." Query first.
Color: Buys any size transparencies, but 35mm preferred. Will consider buying photo collections, any subject, to expand files. Will also look at prints, "if transparencies are available." Captions required; prefers model release.
Tips: "Write for our catalog. Write first with a small sample. We want complete or nearly complete AV programs—not isolated pictures usually. Be reliable. Follow up commitments on time and provide only sharp, well-exposed, well-composed pictures. Send by registered mail."

ALAN G. EISEN PUBLIC RELATIONS CO., INC., R.D. #2 Box 310, Narrowsburg NY 12764. (914)557-8651. PR Firm. President: Alan G. Eisen. Types of clients: consumer products and services.
Needs: Works with 1-2 photographers/month. Uses photographers for consumer and trade magazines, catalogs and newspapers. Subjects include: people with products.
Specs: Uses 5×7 matte b&w prints; 4×5 transparencies.
First Contact & Terms: Send resume, business card, brochure, flyer or tearsheets to be kept on file for possible future assignments. Works on assignment only. SASE. Reports back when photos needed. Payment rates per b&w and color photos are negotiable. Pays $200-5,000+/job. Buys all rights. Model release required.
Tips: Trends include "more natural people and settings for consumer photography, and more eye-catching glitz in trade photography. We look for the ability to draw the viewer into the photo situation—the quality of real, breathing life."

■ *The solid, black square before a listing indicates that the market uses various types of audiovisual materials, such as slides, film or videotape.*

HARRINGTON ASSOCIATES INC., 57 Fairmont Ave., Kingston NY 12401-5221. (914)331-7136. PR firm. President: Gerard Harrington. Estab. 1988. Types of clients: industrial, retail, fashion, finance, transportation, artistic and publishing.
Needs: Number of photographers used on a monthly basis varies. Uses photographers for consumer magazines, trade magazines, P-O-P displays, catalogs and newspapers. Subjects include: general publicity including head shots and candids. Also still lifes.
Specs: Uses b&w prints, any size and format. Also uses 4×5 color transparencies; and ¾ inch videotape.
First Contact & Terms: Provide resume, business card, brochure, flyer or tearsheets to be kept on file for possible future assignments. Works with freelancers on an assignment basis only. Does not return unsolicited material. Reports only when interested. Payment negotiated. Pays on receipt of invoice. Buys all rights. Model release and photo captions required. Credit line given whenever possible, depending on use.

■**HART/CONWAY CO., INC.**, 300 Triangle Building, Rochester NY 14604. (716) 232-2930. Ad agency. Estab. 1924. Executive Art Director: Edward Hettig. Types of clients: automotive, industrial, retail, public transit, finance, recreational.
Needs: Works with 2-3 freelance photographers/month. Uses photographers for consumer magazines, trade magazines, direct mail, newspapers and audiovisual. Subjects include: people and props (table top).
Audiovisual Needs: Uses freelance filmmakers to produce industrial productions, (5-15 minutes) and television spots (15- and 30-second).
Specs: Uses b&w and color prints; 2¼×2¼, 4×5 transparencies.
First Contact & Terms: Query with list of stock photo subjects; provide resume, business card, brochure, flyer or tearsheets to be kept on file for possible future assignments. Works with freelancers on an assignment basis only. Cannot return material. Reports in 1 week. Pays $40-2,500/b&w photo; $100-5,000/color photo; $25-250/hour; $400-1,800/day; $50-10,000/complete job. Buys one-time rights. Model release required; photo captions preferred. Credit line sometimes given, depending on usage/money.

KOPF, ZIMMERMANN, SCHULTHEIS, (formerly Kopf & Isaacson), 35 Pinelawn Rd., Melville NY 11747. (516)293-6115. Ad agency. Art Directors: Evelyn C. Rysdyk and Art Zimmermann. Types of clients: industrial (high tech, telephones, computers, software, etc.).
Needs: Works with 4 freelance photographers/month. Uses photographers for billboards, consumer and trade magazines, catalogs, posters, newspapers. Subjects include: still life (technical products), office situations with models. Examples of ad campaigns: PMI Motors (famous inventors), AMS (software born in the hospital).
Specs: Uses 35mm, 2¼×2¼, 4×5, 8×10 transparencies.
First Contact & Terms: Send unsolicited photos by mail for consideration, query with samples; provide resume, business card, brochure, flyer or tearsheets to be kept on file for possible future assignments. Works with freelance photographers on assignment only. Does not return unsolicited material. Reports in 3-4 weeks. Pays $100-700/b&w photo; $200-2,000/color photo; $600-2,500/day; and $250-2,500/job. Pays on receipt of invoice. Buys all rights. Model release required.
Tips: Prefers to see creative still life work and good people shots (annual report type); printed samples. Looks for good technical skills. Special note: "Show us something innovative. No grids, glows, or "rip-off styles."

S.R. LEON COMPANY, INC., 132 South St., Oyster Bay NY 11710. (516)922-0031. Creative Director: Max Firetog. Ad agency. Types of clients: food, retailing, construction materials, cosmetics, drugs. Provide business card and "any material that indicates the photographer's creative ability" to be kept on file for possible future assignments.
Needs: Works with 3-4 freelance photographers/month. Uses photographers for consumer and trade magazines, TV, brochures/flyers and newspapers.
First Contact & Terms: Call for appointment to show portfolio. Reports in 2 weeks. Pays $75-1,000/b&w photo; $150-3,000/color photo; $650-2,500/day.

McANDREW ADVERTISING CO., Box 254, 2125 St. Raymond Ave., Bronx NY 10462. (212)892-8660. Ad agency, PR firm. Contact: Robert McAndrew. Estab. 1961. Types of clients: industrial and technical.

Needs: Works with 1 freelance photographer/month. Uses photographers for trade magazines, direct mail, brochures, catalogs, newspapers. Subjects include industrial products.

Specs: Uses 8×10 glossy b&w or color prints; 4×5 or 8×10 transparencies.

First Contact & Terms: Provide resume, business card, brochure, flyer, tearsheets or non-returnable samples to be kept on file for possible future assignments. Works with local freelancers only. Pays $45-100/b&w photo; $85-200/color photo; $500-700/day. Pays in 60 days. Buys all rights. Model release required; captions preferred.

Tips: Photographers should "let us know how close they are, and what their prices are. We look for photographers who have experience in industrial photography." In samples, wants to see "sharp, well-lighted" work.

MCCUE ADVERTISING & PR INC., 91 Riverside Dr., Binghamton NY 13905. (607)723-9226. Ad agency and PR firm. President: Donna McCue. Types of clients: industrial, retail, all types.

Needs: Works with 5 freelance photographers/month. Uses photographers for consumer and trade magazines, direct mail, P-O-P displays, catalogs, signage and newspapers.

Specs: Uses 8×10 prints; 35mm, 4×5 transparencies.

First Contact & Terms: Provide resume, business card, brochure, flyer or tearsheets to be kept on file for possible future assignments. Does not return unsolicited material. Reports when assignment comes up. Payment negotiable. Pays in 30 days. Buys all rights. Model release required. Credit line sometimes given.

PRO/CREATIVES, 25 W. Burda Pl., Spring Valley NY 10977. President: David Rapp. Ad agency. Uses all media except billboards and foreign. Types of clients: package goods, fashion, men's entertainment and leisure magazines, sports and entertainment. Negotiates payment based on client's budget. Submit material by mail for consideration. Reports in 2 weeks. SASE.

Specs: Send any size b&w prints. For color, send 35mm transparencies or any size prints.

■**RONAN, HOWARD, ASSOCIATES, INC.**, 11 Buena Vista Ave., Spring Valley NY 10977-3040. (914)356-6668. Contact: Howard A. Ronan. Ad agency and PR firm. Uses direct mail, foreign media, newspapers and trade magazines. Serves clients in audiovisual media, motion picture services, video support equipment, portable power units, motion picture cameras, electronic components. Works with 1-2 freelance photographers/month on assignment only basis. Buys 50-100 photos/year. Pays per photo, $25-40/hour in photographer's studio or $250-400/"shoot" on location plus travel expenses. Negotiates payment based on client's budget. Query first with resume of credits.

B&W: Uses glossy prints. Model release required.

Color: Uses transparencies and paper prints. Model release required. Pays $100-500.

Tips: *Extra sharp details on products* are always the assignment. "Photographers must have new, or rebuilt to 'new' performance-ability cameras, high-powered (not the average strobe) strobes and other lights for location shooting, a full range of lenses including lenses suitable for macro, and must understand how to shoot color under fluorescents without going green. Be able to shoot client executives and have them show up with good 'head and shoulders' detail when reproduced in printed media."

JACK SCHECTERSON ASSOCIATES, 5316 251 Place, Little Neck NY 11362. (718)225-3536. Ad agency. President: Jack Schecterson. Estab. 1967. Types of clients: industrial and consumer.

Needs: Uses photographers for consumer and trade magazines, packaging, product, design, direct mail, P-O-P displays, brochures, catalogs, etc.

Specs: Uses b&w or color prints; 35mm, 2¼×2¼, 4×5 and 8×10 transparencies.

First Contact & Terms: Send resume, business card, brochure, flyer or tearsheets to be kept on file for possible future assignments. Does not return unsolicited material. Works on assignment only. Reporting time "subject to job time requirements." Pays according to client's budget. Buys all rights. Model release and captions required.

*■**TOBOL GROUP, INC.**, 33 Great Neck Rd., Great Neck NY 11021. (516)466-0414. FAX: (516)466-0776. Ad agency/design studio. Art Director: John Napolitano. Estab. 1981. High-tech, industrial, business-to-business and consumer. Examples of ad campaigns: Weight Watchers, (in-store promotion); British Ulecom, (consumer and trade ads); and Mainco, (trade ad).

Needs: Works with up to 4 photographers—videographers/month. Uses photographers for billboards, consumer magazines, trade magazines, direct mail, P-O-P displays, catalogs, posters, newspapers and audiovisual. Subjects are: varied; mostly still-life photography. Reviews business-to-business and commercials' video footage.

Audiovisual Needs: Uses videotape.
Specs: Uses 4×5, 8×10, 11×14 b&w prints; 35mm, $2\frac{1}{4} \times 2\frac{1}{4}$ and 4×5 transparencies; and $\frac{1}{2}"$ videotape.
First Contact & Terms: Send unsolicited photos by mail for consideration. Query with samples. Provide resume, business car, brochure, flyer or tearsheets to be kept on file for possible future assignments: follow-up with phone call. Works on assignment only. SASE. Reports in 3 weeks. Pays $100-10,000/job. Pays net 30. Rights purchased depends on client. Model release required. Credit line sometimes given, depending on client and price.
Tips: In freelancer's samples or demos, wants to see "the best they do—any style or subject as long as it is done well. Trend is photos or videos to be multi-functional. Show me your *best* and what you enjoy shooting. Get experience with existing company to make the transition from still photography to audiovisual."

■**UNISOURCE**, (formerly Leslie Aaron Associates), 363 DeGraw St., Brooklyn NY 11231. (718)643-2800. FAX: (718)643-2804. Ad agency, PR firm. Vice Pres./Client Services: Val Reisig. Vice Pres./Art Director: Don James. Estab. 1970. Types of clients: industrial, technical.
Needs: Works with 6-10 freelance photographers/month. Uses photographers for trade magazines, direct mail, catalogs, signage, literature and PR. Subjects include: machinery.
Audiovisual Needs: Uses freelancers to produce slides, film and videotape.
Specs: Uses 8×10 b&w prints; 4×5, 8×10 transparencies; film and videotape.
First Contact & Terms: Arrange a personal interview to show portfolio query with resume of credits submit portfolio for review; provide resume, business card, brochure, flyer or tearsheets to be kept on file for possible future assignments. Works with freelance photographers on assignment basis only. Does not return unsolicited material. Pays/photo; job. Pays on receipt of invoice. Buys all rights. Model release required.
Tips: Prefers to see industrial, plant photography, studio work—all subjects. Amateurism is discouraged. "Impress us with talent, experience and offer value."

■**VISUAL HORIZONS**, 180 Metro Park, Rochester NY 14623. (716)424-5300 FAX: (716)424-5313. AV firm. President: Stanley Feingold. Types of clients: industrial.
Audiovisual Needs: Works with 2 freelance photographers/month. Uses photographers for AV presentations. Also works with freelance filmmakers to produce training films.
Specs: Uses 35mm transparencies and videotape.
First Contact & Terms: Provide resume, business card, brochure, flyer or tearsheets to be kept on file for possible future assignments. Works with freelance photographers on assignment basis only. Pays on publication. Buys all rights. Model release and captions required.

WALLACK & WALLACK ADVERTISING INC., 33 Great Neck Rd., Great Neck NY 11021. (516)487-3974. VP/Creative: John Napolitano. Types of clients: fashion, industrial.
Needs: Works with 5-6 freelance photographers/year. Uses photographers for direct mail, catalogs, P-O-P displays, posters, trade and consumer magazines and brochures. Subject needs "very clean, graphic look. Black and white important."
Specs: Uses $2\frac{1}{4} \times 2\frac{1}{4}$, 4×5 and 8×10 transparencies; also 11×14 b&w prints.
First Contact & Terms: Provide resume, business card, brochure, flyer or tearsheets to be kept on file for possible future assignments. Works with freelancers on assignment only. SASE. Pays $75-750/b&w photo; $150-750/color photo; $350-1,800/day. Buys all rights. Written release required.
Tips: Prefers to see "what the photographer wants to shoot—his specialty, not a little of everything" in a portfolio.

*****HAROLD WARNER ADVERTISING, INC.**, 370 Franklin St., Buffalo NY 14202. (716)852-4410. FAX: (716)852-4725. Ad agency. Art Director: William Walsh. Estab. 1945. Types of clients: industrial. Previous/current clients: "We are the agency for 40 clients—all industrial."
Needs: Works with 3-4 photographers/month. Uses photographers for trade magazines, direct mail and catalogs. Subjects are varied—but all industrial. Reviews stock photos.
Specs: Uses 4×5 to 20×24, glossy and matte, b&w and color prints; 35mm, $2\frac{1}{4} \times 2\frac{1}{4}$, 4×5 and 8×10 transparencies.
First Contact & Terms: Arrange personal interview to show portfolio. Query with resume of credits. Query with list of stock photo subject. Provide resume, business card, brochure, flyer or tearsheets to be kept on file for possible future assignments. Works with freelancers on assignment only. Reports "as needed." Pays $500-800/day; specific rates negotiable. Pays on acceptance. Buys all rights. Model release required; photo captions preferred. No credit line given.
Tips: "Freelancers are few and far between who can deal with mundane, industrial topics such as machines and machine parts. Our work is largely industrial advertising, so we look for freelancers who can show experience and ability to shoot industrial subjects imaginatively."

ROGER WHITE ADVERTISING, 69 Main St., Binghamton NY 13905. (607)724-4356. Ad agency. Art Director: Robert Egan. Types of clients: industrial and retail. Examples of ad campaigns: Masonite Corp. (new product intro) Ward Manufacturing (new markets campaign) Tremco Inc. (corporate identity campaign).
Needs: Works with 1 freelance photographer/month. Uses photographers for trade magazines, direct mail, P-O-P displays, catalogs, posters, signage. Subject matter includes product shots, room sets and building exteriors. "Room interiors are our major line of work for photographers."
Specs: Uses 8 × 10 glossy b&w and color prints; 4 × 5 and 8 × 10 transparencies.
First Contact & Terms: Query with resume of credits or samples. Provide resume, business card, brochure, flyer or tearsheets to be kept on file for possible future assignments. Works on assignment only. Does not return unsolicited material. Reports in 2 weeks. Pays $5-35/8 × 10 b&w photo; $16-50/8 × 10 color photo; $30/hour; $240-1,600/day. Pays on acceptance or on receipt. Buys all rights or one-time rights (depends on the specific job). Model release required.
Tips: "Any professional presentation with quality work will be considered, along with pricing."

WOLF MANSFIELD BOLLING ADVERTISING INC., 506 Delware Ave., Buffalo NY 14202. (716)886-4000. Ad agency. Executive Art Director: Tod Martin. Types of clients: Consumer.
Needs: Works with 2 freelance photographers/month. Uses photographers for direct mail, catalogs, newspapers, consumer magazines, P-O-P displays, posters, AV presentations, trade magazines and brochures. Needs product, situation and location photos. Also works with freelance filmmakers for TV commercials and training films.
Specs: Uses 11 × 14 b&w and color prints; 35mm, 2¼ × 2¼, 4 × 5 and 8 × 10 transparencies; 16mm film and videotape.
First Contact & Terms: Arrange a personal interview to show portfolio or query with resume of credits. Works with freelance photographers on assignment basis only. Does not return unsolicited material. Reports in 2 weeks. Pays $50-150/hour; $450-1,500/day. Pays 1 month after acceptance. Buys all rights. Model release required.
Tips: In a portfolio, prefers to see transparencies and printed materials.

■**WOLFF ASSOCIATES**, 500 East Ave., Rochester NY 14607. (716)461-8300. Ad agency. Associate Creative Director/Art: David Reece. Types of clients: industrial, fashion.
Needs: Works with 3-4 freelance photographers/month. Uses photographers for billboards, consumer magazines, direct mail, P-O-P displays, brochures, catalogs, posters, newspapers, AV presentations. Also works with freelance filmmakers to produce TV commercials.
First Contact & Terms: Provide resume, business card, brochure, flyer or tearsheets to be kept on file for possible future assignments. Does not return unsolicited material. Pays $400-3,000/day.

■**ZELMAN STUDIOS, LTD.**, 623 Cortelyou Rd., Brooklyn NY 11218. (718)941-5500. General Manager: Jerry Krone. AV firm. Types of clients: industrial, education, publishing, business and government.
Needs: Works with freelancers on assignment only. Uses photographers for slide sets, filmstrips, motion pictures and videotape. Subjects include: people, machines and aerial.
Specs: Produces Super 8, 16mm and 35mm documentary, educational and industrial films and slide/sound shows. Uses 8 × 10 color prints; 35mm transparencies.
First Contact & Terms: Query with samples; send material by mail for consideration; submit portfolio for review; provide resume, samples and calling card to be kept on file for possible future assignments. Pays $50-100/color photo. Pays $250-800/job. Pays on acceptance. Buys all rights. Model release required; captions preferred.

New York City

■**ALDEN GROUP-PUBLIC RELATIONS DIVISION**, (formerly J.S. Alden Public Relations, Inc.), 535 5th Ave., New York NY 10017. (212)867-6400. Public Relations Director: Jeff Davis. Estab. 1955. PR firm. Photos used in newspapers, trade publications and general media. Types of clients: chemicals, health care, manufacturing and travel/resorts. Examples of ad campaigns: Gucci Eyewear (fashion), Sharp Watches (popular priced value). Most interested in product publicity by assignment; event/area coverage by assignment; portraits for publicity use; occasional use of models/props.

Audiovisual Needs: Assigns AV projects to filmmakers for industrial and commercial films.
Specs Uses glossy b&w prints. For color, uses glossy prints and transparencies; contact sheet and negatives OK.
First Contact & Terms: "Write first; describe your area of specialization and general abilities; access to models, props, studio; area/event/people coverage; equipment used; time and fee information; agency/commercial experience; and location and availability." SASE. Reports in 1 month or less. Buys all rights. Model release required.
Tips: "Work through our director." Also, "be able to respond quickly."

■**A.V. MEDIA CRAFTSMAN, INC.**, Suite 600, 110 E. 23rd St., New York NY 10010. (212)228-6644. President: Carolyn Clark. AV firm. Types of clients: corporate, internal communications, public relations, publishing and ad agencies.
Needs: Works with local AV specialists only. Uses photographers for filmstrips, slide shows, slide to video transfers, multimedia kits, and location work. No studio shots. Subjects include training and education.
Specs: Requires extensive AV experience which should be evident in portfolio. Others need not apply. Do not send slides or prints in the mail.
First Contact & Terms: Call and send brochure/flyer or samples to be kept on file for future assignments. Unsolicited material will not be returned. Pays $250-500/day; usually includes 3 locations and about 100 photographs. Payment made on agreed terms. Buys all rights. "Advance appointments are never made; call when you're in the area. If we're not busy, you are welcome."
Tips: Prefers to see samples illustrating various lighting conditions (factory, office, supermarket), ability to conceptualize, people working in corporations and active instructional sequences. When you call, refer to *Photographer's Market*. No scenics, food or studio shots.

■**ANITA HELEN BROOKS ASSOCIATES**, 155 E. 55th St., New York NY 10022. (212)755-4498. Contact: Anita Helen Brooks. PR firm. Types of clients: beauty, entertainment, fashion, food, publishing, travel, society, art, politics, exhibits and charity events.
Needs: Photos used in PR releases, AV presentations, consumer magazines and trade magazines. Works with photographers on assignment only. Provide resume and brochure to be kept on file for possible future assignments. Buys "several hundred" photos/year. Pays $50 minimum/job; negotiates payment based on client's budget. Credit line given. Model release preferred. Query with resume of credits. No unsolicited material; does not return unsolicited material. Most interested in fashion shots, society, entertainment and literary celebrity/personality shots.
Specs: Uses 8×10 glossy b&w prints; contact sheet OK. For color uses 8×10 glossy prints; contact sheet OK.

*■**COX ADVERTISING**, 379 W. Broadway, New York NY 10012. (212)334-9141. FAX: (212)334-9179. Ad agency. Associate Creative Directors: Marc Rubin and Beth Anderson. Types of clients: industrial, retail, fashion and travel.
Needs: Works with 2 freelance photographers—/videographers/month. Uses photographers for billboards, consumer magazines, trade magazines, direct mail, P-O-P displays, catalogs, posters, newspapers, signage and audiovisual. Reviews stock photos or video.
Audiovisual Needs: Uses photos for slide shows; also uses videotapes.
Specs: Uses 16×20 b&w prints; 35mm, 2¼×2¼, 4×5 and 8×10 transparencies.
First Contact & Terms: Arrange personal interview to show portfolio. Work with freelancers on assignment only. Cannot return material. Reports in 1-2 weeks. Pays minimum of $1,500/job; higher amounts negotiable according to needs of client. Pays within 30-60 days of receipt of invoice. Buys all rights when possible. Model release required. Credit line sometimes given.

■**DISCOVERY PRODUCTIONS**, 315 Central Park W 8E, New York NY 10025. (212)752-7575. Proprietor: David Epstein. PR/AV firm. Serves educational and social action agencies. Produces 16mm and 35mm films. Works with up to 2 freelance photographers/month on assignment only basis. Provide resume to be kept on file for possible future assignments. Buys 2 films annually. Pays on use and 30 days. Buys all rights, but may reassign to filmmaker. Query first with resume of credits.

The asterisk before a listing indicates that the market is new in this edition. New markets are often the most receptive to freelance submissions.

Film: 16mm and 35mm documentary, educational and industrial films. Possible assignments include research, writing, camera work or editing. "We would collaborate on a production of an attractive and practical idea." Model release required. Pays 25-60% royalty.

JODY DONOHUE ASSOCIATES, INC., 32 E. 57th St., New York NY 10022. (212)688-8653. PR firm. Art Production Manager: Elena Roman. Types of clients: fashion and beauty.
Needs: Uses freelancers for press kits, direct mail and P-O-P displays.
First Contact & Terms: Call for personal appointment to show portfolio. Selection based on "interview, review of portfolio, and strength in a particular area (i.e., still life, children, etc.)." Negotiates payment based on client's budget, amount of creativity required from photographer and where the work will appear. Pays freelancers on receipt of client's payment.
Tips: Wants to see "recent work and that which has been used (printed piece, etc.)."

■**RICHARD L. DOYLE ASSOC., INC.**, 15 Maiden Lane, New York NY 10038. (212)349-2828. FAX: (212)619-5350. Ad agency. President: R.L. Stewart, Sr. Estab. 1979. Types of clients: primarily in insurance/financial services and publishers. Client list free with SASE.
Needs: Works with 5-6 freelance photographers/month. Uses photographers for consumer and trade magazines, direct mail, newspapers, audiovisual, sales promotion and annual reports. Subjects include people—portrait and candid.
Audiovisual Needs: Typically uses prepared slides—in presentation formats, video promotions and video editorials.
Specs: Uses b&w and color prints; 35mm and 2¼ × 2¼ transparencies.
First Contact & Terms: Query with resume of credits and samples. Prefers resume, business card, brochure, flyer or tearsheets to be kept on file for possible future assignments. SASE. Reports in 2 weeks. Payment variable. Pays on acceptance or receipt of invoice. Buys all rights. Model release required; captions required.
Tips: Prefers to see photos of people; "good coverage/creativity in presentation. Be perfectly honest as to capabilities; be reasonable in cost and let us know you'll work *with us* to satisfy the client. Trends include more imaginative settings and composition in normally mundane situations."

*****EPSTEIN & WALKER ASSOCIATES**, #5A, 65 West 55 St., New York NY 10019. (212)246-0565. Ad agency. President/Creative Director: Lee Epstein. Types of clients: retail, publication, consumer and fashion. Examples of ad campaigns: *Woman's World Magazine*, (trade campaign to media buyers); Northville Gas, (radio/TV campaign to drivers); and Bermuda Shop, (woman's retail-image/fashion).
Needs: Works with 6-8 freelance photographers/year. Uses photographers for consumer magazines, trade magazines, direct mail and newspapers. Subjects include still life, people, fashion, etc.; "depends on concept of ads."
Specs: Any size of format b&w prints; also 35mm, 2¼ × 2¼ transparencies.
First Contact & Terms: Arrange personal interview to show portfolio. Provide resume, business card, brochure, flyer of tearsheets to be kept on file for possible future assignments. Works with local freelancers on assignment only. Cannot return material. Reports "as needed." Pays minimum of $300/b&w photo or negotiates day rate for multiple images. Pays within 30-60 days after receipt of invoice. Usually buys rights for "1 year usage across the board." Model release required. No credit line given.
Tips: Trend within agency is "to solve problems with illustration more because of budget restraints regarding models and location expenses." Is receptive to working with new talent. To break in, show "intelligent conceptual photography with exciting ideas and great composition."

RICHARD FALK ASSOCIATES, 1472 Broadway, New York NY 10036. (212)221-0043. President: Richard Falk. Estab. 1940. PR firm. Types of clients: industrial, entertainment. Examples of ad campaign: Barker Greeting-Cincinnati.
Needs: Works with about 4 freelance photographers/month. Uses photographers for newspapers and TV.
First Contact & Terms: Send resume. Provide business card and flyer to be kept on file for possible future assignments. Selection of freelancers based on "short letters or flyers, chance visits, promo pieces and contact at events." Also hires by contract. Does not return unsolicited material. Reports in 1 week. Pays $25-50/b&w photo; $35-50/color photo; $50-100/hour; and $100-300/job on negotiable basis. Buys one-time rights.
Tips: "Interested in people shots." Wants to see sharpness in images.

THE JOHNSTON GROUP, (formerly Jim Johnston Advertising, Inc.), 49 West 27th Penthouse, New York NY 10176. (212)779-1257. Creative Director: Doug Johnston. Ad agency. Uses consumer and trade magazines, direct mail, foreign media, newspapers, TV and radio. Serves clients in publishing and broadcasting, financial services, fashion, travel and high technology. Buys 25-50 photos/year. Local freelancers preferred. Pays $150-2,000/b&w or color photo; $20-250/hour; $150-2,000/day; $150-5,000/

job. Buys all rights. Model release required. Query with resume of credits, query with samples or list of stock photo subjects, or submit portfolio for review. SASE. Reports in 2 weeks.

B&W: Uses 8 × 10 or larger matte prints; contact sheet OK.

Color: Uses 8 × 10 or larger glossy prints and 2¼ × 2¼ or larger transparencies.

Film: Produces 16mm, 35mm documentary and sales film. Does not pay royalties.

Tips: Looks for "finish"—the ability to execute someone else's idea *flawlessly*. Also the ability to *compose* elements interestingly and the ability to *edit* a portfolio to leave out ugly work! Drop off a portfolio or send a promotional sample. "Please do not send reps."

*JORDAN, McGRATH, CASE AND TAYLOR, (formerly Jordan, Manning, Case, Taylor and McGrath), 445 Park Ave., New York NY 10022. (212)326-9100. Studio Manager: Jim Griffin. "There's a separate TV department which views TV reels." Ad agency. Uses all media. Clients include insurance companies, pharmaceutical, frozen foods, liquor and wine, hosiery manufacturers, banks, theater, facial cleanser, food products and Milton Bradley games. Needs still lifes and product photos. Buys 25-50 annually. Pays on a per-job or a per-photo basis. Call to arrange an appointment.

B&W: Uses contact sheets for selection, then double-weight glossy or matte prints. Will determine specifications at time of assignment. Pays $100 minimum.

Color: Uses transparencies. Will determine specifications at time of assignment. Pays $100 minimum.

KOEHLER IVERSEN ADVERTISING, 71 W. 23rd St., New York NY 10010. Ad agency. Creative Director: W. Peter Koehler. Types of clients: industrial, commercial and financial.

Needs: Works with 2 photographers/month. Uses freelance photographers for trade magazines, direct mail, catalogs and newspapers. Subjects include people/corporate.

Specs: Uses b&w and color prints; 35 mm, 2¼ × 2¼ transparencies.

First Contact & Terms: Query with samples, submit portfolio for review. Provide resume, business card, brochure, flyer or tearsheets to be kept on file for possible future assignments. Works with freelance photographers on assignment only. Does not return unsolicited material. Pays by the job or per photo. Payment made "30 days from receipt of invoice." Buys all rights. Model release required.

Tips: Looks for "originality, good composition."

▪DON LANE PICTURES, INC., 545 Eighth Ave., 7th Fl. S., New York NY 10018. (212)268-0101. Producer/Director: Don Lane. Types of clients: industrial.

Needs: Buys 10-1,000 photos, 1-5 filmstrips and 5-15 films/year. Uses photographers for filmstrips, slide sets, 16mm documentary style industrial films and videotape. Subjects include agriculture, medicine and industrial chemicals.

First Contact & Terms: Arrange a personal interview to show portfolio. Provide calling card and tearsheets to be kept on file for possible future assignments. Pays $150-500/day. Payment on acceptance. Buys all rights, but may reassign to photographer after use. Model release required.

Tips: Wants to see "location work, preferably using available light, in 'documentary' style. Include information on nature and purpose of assignment, technical problems solved, etc.".

▪MANHATTAN VIDEO PRODUCTIONS, INC., 12 W. 27th St., New York NY 10001. (212)683-6565. Production Manager: Alison McBryde.

Needs: Works with approximately 10 freelance personnel/month. Uses services of freelance cameramen and lighting director/cameramen. Subjects include talking heads to elaborate sets for video dramas. Interested in original videos suitable for the home video market.

First Contact & Terms: Query with resume followed by submission of demo reel. Works with freelancers by assignment only. SASE. Reports in 2 weeks. Payment made within 30 days. Rights purchased depend on project. Credit line given.

Tips: "Send resume listing experience and client list for reference. Follow with demo tape of work done with selections of commercial or corporate work. Work is judged by the quality of lighting, camera moves and selection of perspective and variation. We are seeing greater use of location footage in our industry. Still photographers interested in making the transition into film and video photography could volunteer service to production company initially on ground level and gain experience (hands-on) with facilities' equipment."

▪MARSDEN, 30 E. 33 St., New York NY 10016. (212)725-9220. Vice President/Creative Director: Stephen Flores. Types of clients: corporate, nonprofit, Fortune 500.

Needs: Works with 2-3 photographers/month. Uses photographers for filmstrips, slide sets, multimedia productions, films and videotapes. Subjects include industrial, technical, office, faces, scenics, special effects, etc.

Specs: Uses 35mm, 2¼×2¼, 4×5 and 8×10 transparencies; 16mm film; U-matic ¾″, 1″ and 2″ videotapes.
First Contact & Terms: Query with samples or a stock photo list; provide resume, business card, self-promotion piece or tearsheets to be kept on file for possible future assignments. Works with local freelancers only; interested in stock photos/footage. "We call when we have a need—no response is made on unsolicited material." Pays $25-1,000/color photo; $150-600/day. Pays on acceptance. Buys one-time rights. Model release preferred. Credit line rarely given.

■PETER MARTIN ASSOC. INC., 770 Lexington Ave., New York NY 10021. (212)838-3050. FAX: (212)838-4416. Ad agency, PR firm and AV firm. Vice President: Jai Imbrey. Types of clients: travel, food and wine, and products.
Needs: Uses photographers for consumer magazines, trade magazines, newspapers, signage, audiovisual and publicity. Subjects include: travel. Reviews stock photos or videos on Jamaica and tourism.
Audivisual Needs: Uses any size or format b&w prints; 35mm, 2¼×2¼, 4×5 tranparencies; also videotape.
First Contact & Terms: Query with list of stock photo subjects. Works on assignment only. Reports in 1-2 weeks. Pays $75-100/hour "for local event shoots." Pays $350-1,200/day "for product photography or travel shoots." Specific amounts negotiable. Buys all rights. Model release required. Credit line given.

*■MATTHEW-LAWRENCE ADVERTISING & SALES PROMOTION INC., 127 West 24th St., New York NY 10011. (212)620-7301. FAX: (212)463-0726. Ad agency. President: Larry Danziger. Types of clients: industrial, fashion and finance. Examples of ad campaigns: Monsanto (ads and promotion programs); Dupont (collateral material and videos); and Federal Express (collateral materials).
Needs: Works with 2-3 freelance photographers/filmmakers/videographers per month. Uses photographers for consumer magazines, trade magazines, direct mail, P-O-P displays and audiovisual. Reviews stock photos and video.
Audiovisual Needs: Video.
Specs: Uses any size of format b&w prints; 35mm, 2¼×2¼, 4×5 and 8×10 transparencies; also VHS videotape.
First Contact & Terms: Arrange personal interview to show portfolio. Provide resume, business card, brochure, flyer or tearsheets to be kept on file for possible future assignments. Work with freelancers on assignment only. Reports in 1-2 weeks. Pays $250-1,000/day. Pays on receipt of invoice. Buys all rights (work-for-hire). Model release required. Credit line sometimes given.
Tips: In freelancer's portfolio or demos, wants to see fashion and reportage.

*■RUTH MORRISON ASSOCIATES, 19 West 44th St., New York NY 10036. (212)302-8886. FAX: (212)302-5512. PR firm. Account Executive: Maggie Minarich. Estab. 1972. Types of clients: specialty foods, housewares, home furnishings.
Needs: Works with 1-2 freelance photographers—videographers/month. Uses photographers for consumer magazines, trade magazines, P-O-P displays, posters, newspapers, signage and audiovisual.
Audiovisual Needs: Uses photos and videotape.
Specs: Specifications vary according to clients' needs. Typically uses b&w and transparencies.
First Contact & Terms: Arrange personal interview to show portfolio; provide resume, business card, brochure, flyer or tearsheets to be kept on file for possible future assignments. Works with freelancers on assignment basis only. Reprots "as needed." Pays $50-1,000 depending upon client's budget. Rights negotiable. Credit line given sometimes, depending on use.

MOSS & COMPANY, INC., 49 W. 38th St., New York NY 10018. (212)575-0808. Art Directors: Sam Ferraro and Seymour Baluner. Ad agency. Serves clients in consumer products, manufacturing, utilities, insurance and packaged goods. Annual billing: $10,000,000.
Needs: Works with 2-3 freelance photographers/month. Uses photographers for billboards, consumer and trade magazines, direct mail, TV, brochures/flyers and newspapers.
First Contact & Terms: Call for appointment to show portfolio. Negotiates payment based on client's budget: $300-3,000/job; $600/b&w photo; $2,000/color photo. Prefers to see samples of still life and people.
Tips: "Photographer must be technically perfect with regard to shooting still life and people. *Then talented!*" \

MUIR CORNELIUS MOORE, 79 5th Ave., New York NY 10003. (212)463-7715. Chief Creative Officer: Richard Moore. Ad agency/design firm. Types of clients: banking, manufacturing, systems, computers, communications, other industries. Commissions photographers for specific assignments. Pays $750/day minimum. Query first with resume of credits.

Tips: Wants to see originality, good technique, versatility. "Only include best work in portfolio. Tailor presentation, as much as possible, to needs of the Agency. Send promotional material to Sue Moseson, Art Buyer. We need good advertising and corporate photographers."

MULLER, JORDAN, WEISS, INC., 666 5th Ave., New York NY 10103. (212)399-2700. Creative Director: Jerry Colman. Ad agency. Types of clients: fashion, agricultural, industrial/corporate, plastics, food firms, window and ceiling products.
Needs: Works with 50+ freelance photographers/year on assignment only basis. Uses photographers for consumer and trade magazines, direct mail, P-O-P displays, brochures, posters, newspapers and AV presentations.
First Contact & Terms: Phone for appointment. Pays $300 and up/b&w photo; $500 and up/color photo; $300-3,500/day.

NEWMARKS ADVERTISING AGENCY, 255 W. 26 St., New York NY 10001. (212)620-7600. Ad agency. Creative Director: Al Wasserman. Estab. 1893. Types of clients: industrial, finance, business-to-business, real estate, recruitment and fitness.
Needs: Uses photographers for consumer and trade magazines, direct mail, catalogs, posters and newspapers. Subjects include fitness and sports.
Specs: Uses 8×10 glossy b&w prints; 35mm, 2¼×2¼, 4×5, 8×10 transparencies.
First Contact & Terms: Query with photocopies of samples; provide resume, business card, brochure, flyer or tearsheets to be kept on file for possible future assignments. Works with freelance photographers on assignment only. Does not return unsolicited material. Reports in 1 week. Pays $350-900/b&w photo; $350-900/color photo; $500-1,500/day; and $750-5,000/job. Pays on acceptance and receipt of invoice. Buys one-time rights or all rights. Model release required; captions preferred. Credit line sometimes given.
Tips: Looks for originality. Send nonreturnable samples such as Xerox prints or shots.

*NOSTRADAMUS ADVERTISING, #1128A, 250 W. 57th, New York NY 10107. (212)581-1362. Ad agency. President: Barry Sher. Estab. 1974. Types of clients: politicians, nonprofit organizations and small businesses.
Needs: Uses freelancers occasionally for consumer magazines, trade magazines, direct mail, catalogs and posters. Subjects include: people and products.
Specs: Uses 8×10 glossy b&w and color prints; 8×10 transparencies.
First Contact & Terms: Provide resume, business car, brochure. Works with local freelancers only. Cannot return material. Pays $50-100/hour. Pays 30 days from invoice. Buys all rights (work-for-hire). Model release required. Credit line sometimes given.

RICHARD H. ROFFMAN ASSOCIATES, Suite 6A, 697 West End Ave., New York NY 10025. (212)749-3647. Contact: Vice President. Estab. 1960. PR firm. Types of clients: all types of accounts, "everything from A to Z." Free client list available with SASE. Photos used in public relations, publicity and promotion. Works with about 3 freelance photographers/month on assignment only.
First Contact & Terms: Provide resume, flyer, business card or brochure to be kept on file for possible future assignments. Buys about 40 photos annually. Negotiates payment based on client's budget, amount of creativity required, where work will appear and photographer's previous experience/reputation. Pays $10-20/hour; $50-100/day; $50-100/job; $35/b&w photo; $85/color photo. Pays on delivery. Submit model release with photo.
Tips: "Nothing should be sent except a business card or general sales presentation or brochure. Nothing should be sent that requires sending back, as we unfortunately don't have the staff or time. We have assignments from time to time for freelancers."

*■PETER ROGERS ASSOCIATES, 355 Lexington Ave., New York NY 10017. (212)599-0055. FAX:(212)682-4309. Ad agency. Art Directors: Laura and Tracy. Estab. 1977. Types of clients: retail, fashion and package goods. Examples of ad campaigns: "Images," Judith Leiber, spreads (magazine); "International Salons," Vidal Sassoon, TV and print; and "La Prairie," La Prairie, ads and PR.
Needs: Works with 10-20 freelancers/month. Uses photographers for trade magazines, consumer magazines, P-O-P displays, posters, signage and audiovisual. Subjects include: people and still life photos. Reviews video footage; beauty and fashion subject matter.
Audiovisual Needs: Uses film and videotape.
Specs: Uses b&w prints; 35mm and 8×10 transparencies; 35mm and 16mm film and ¾" videotape. Corporate images.
First Contact & Terms: Arrange personal interview to show portfolio; send unsolicited photos by mail for consideration; query with samples; submit portfolio for review; provide resume, business card, brochure, flyer or tearsheets to be kept on file for possible future assignments. Works with freelancers on assignment only. SASE. Reports in 2 weeks. Payment depends on artist and job. Pays on receipt

of invoice. Buys one-time rights and all rights; one-year buyout. Model release required. Credit line sometimes given.

Tips: In freelancer's work, wants to see "high style, editorial style, best quality, unique and well done technically. Trend is toward more informality, more dynamic. Be persistent, be cooperative, have a concept behind your work, and show intelligence. Also note, videotapes are made with stills all the time."

■**PETER ROTHHOLZ ASSOCIATES, INC.**, 380 Lexington Ave., New York NY 10168. (212)687-6565. Contact: Peter Rothholz. PR firm. Types of clients: pharmaceuticals (health and beauty), government, travel. Photos used in brochures, newsletters, PR releases, AV presentations and sales literature. Works with 2 freelance photographers/year, each with approximately 8 assignments. Provide letter of inquiry to be kept on file for possible future assignments. Negotiates payment based on client's budget. Credit line given on request. Buys one-time rights. Model release preferred. Query with resume of credits or list of stock photo subjects. Local freelancers preferred. SASE. Reports in 2 weeks.

B&W: Uses 8 × 10 glossy prints; contact sheet OK.

Tips: "We use mostly standard publicity shots and have some 'regulars' we deal with. If one of those is unavailable we might begin with someone new—and he/she will then become a regular."

SCHORR AND HOWARD COMPANY, 770 Lexington Ave., New York NY 10021. (212)935-5555. Account Executive: Martha Megill. Types of clients: industrial.

Needs: Works with 1-3 freelance photographers/month. Uses photographers for trade magazines. Subject matter includes manufacturing operations.

Specs: Uses b&w prints, 35mm and 2¼ × 2¼ transparencies (film and contact sheets).

First Contact & Terms: Provide resume, business card, brochure, flyer or tearsheets to be kept on file for possible future assignments. Works on assignment basis only. Does not return unsolicited material. Reports in 1 week. Pays $500-1,500/day. Pays on receipt of invoice. Buys all rights. Model release required.

Tips: Wants to see in portfolio or samples "solid industrial photography experience, particularly in manufacturing processes and operations." To break in, "send b&w and color samples of industrial work. Send brochure, flyer, tearsheets; follow up with call."

■**SHADOW LIGHT PRODUCTIONS**, 163 W 23 St., 5th Fl., New York NY 10011. (212)924-0015. Producer: Marc Chelnik. Estab. 1981. Types of clients: advertising, broadcast.

Needs: Uses photographers for films and videotapes. Subjects include special effects, commercials and film graphics.

Specs: Uses b&w prints; transparencies and 35mm film.

First Contact & Terms: Provide resume, business card, self-promotion piece or tearsheets to be kept on file for possible future assignments. Works with freelancers by assignment only. Does not return unsolicited material. Buys all rights. Credit line given.

■**SPENCER PRODUCTIONS, INC.**, 234 5th Ave., New York NY 10001. General Manager: Bruce Spencer. PR firm. Types of clients: business, industry. Produces motion pictures and videotape. Works with 1-2 freelance photographers/month on assignment only basis. Provide resume and letter of inquiry to be kept on file for possible future assignments. Buys 2-6 films/year. Pays $5-15/hour; $500-5,000/job; negotiates payment based on client's budget. Pays a royalty of 5-10%. Pays on acceptance. Buys all rights. Model release required. Query with resume of credits. "Be brief and pertinent!" SASE. Reports in 3 weeks.

Subject Needs: Satirical approach to business and industry problems. Freelance photos used on special projects. Length: "Films vary—from a 1-minute commercial to a 90-minute feature."

Film: 16mm color commercials, documentaries and features.

Tips: "Almost all of our talent was unknown in the field when hired by us. For a sample of our satirical philosophy, see paperback edition of *Don't Get Mad . . . Get Even* (W.W. Norton), by Alan Abel which we promoted, or *How to Thrive on Rejection* (Dembner Books, Inc.) or rent the home video "Is There Sex After Death?", an R-rated comedy featuring Buck Henry."

■**TALCO PRODUCTIONS**, 279 E. 44th St., New York NY 10017. (212)697-4015. President: Alan Lawrence. Vice President: Marty Holberton. Estab. 1964. PR and AV firm. Types of clients: industrial, education, fashion, labor, political and nonprofit organizations. Produces motion pictures and videotape. Works with freelancers on assignment only. Provide resume, flyer or brochure to be kept on file for possible future assignments. Prefers to see general work or "sample applicable to a specific project we are working on." Buys "a few" photos/year; does subcontract short sequences at distant locations. Payment negotiable according to client's budget and where the work will appear. Pays on acceptance. Buys all rights. Model release required.

Audiovisual Needs: 16mm and 35mm film, all professional videotape formats; documentaries, industrials, public relations. Filmmaker might be assigned "second unit or pick-up shots."
Tips: Filmmaker "must be experienced—union member is preferred. We do not frequently use freelancers except outside the New York City area when it is less expensive than sending a crew." Query with resume of credits only—don't send samples. "We will ask for specifics when an assignment calls for particular experience or talent." Returns unsolicited material if SASE included. Reports in 3 weeks.

TELE-PRESS ASSOCIATES, INC., 321 E. 53rd., New York NY 10022. (212)688-5580. President: Alan Macnow. Project Director: Devin Macnow. PR firm. Uses brochures, annual reports, PR releases, AV presentations, consumer and trade magazines. Serves beauty, fashion, jewelry, food, finance, industrial and government clients. Works with 3 freelance photographers/month on assignment only basis. Provide resume, business card and brochure to be kept on file for possible future assignments.
Specs: Uses 8×10 glossy b&w prints; 35mm, 2¼×2¼, 4×5 or 8×10 color transparencies. Works with freelance filmmakers in production of 16mm documentary, industrial and educational films.
Payment & Terms: Pays $100-200/b&w photo; $100-200/color photo; $800-1,500/day; negotiates payment based on client's budget. Buys all rights. Model release and captions required.
Making Contact: Query with resume of credits or list of stock photo subjects. SASE. Reports in 2 weeks.
Tips: In portfolio or samples, wants to see still life, and fashion and beauty, shown in dramatic lighting. "Send intro letter, do either fashion and beauty or food and jewelry still life."

North Carolina

BOB BOEBERITZ DESIGN, 247 Charlotte St., Asheville NC 28801. (704)258-0316. Graphic design studio. Owner: Bob Boeberitz. Estab. 1984. Types of clients: realtors, developers, retail, recording artists, mail-order firms, industrial, restaurants, hotels, book publishers.
Needs: Works with 1 freelance photographer every 2 or 3 months. Uses photographers for consumer and trade magazines, direct mail, brochures, catalogs, posters. Subjects include studio product shots; some location; some stock photos.
Specs: Uses 8×10 b&w glossy prints; 4×5 transparencies, 35mm slides.
First Contact & Terms: Provide resume, business card, brochure, flyer or tearsheets to be kept on file for possible future assignments. Does not return unsolicited material. Reports "when there is a need." Pays $50-200/b&w photo; $100-500/color photo; $50-100/hour; $350-1,000/day. Payment made on a per-job basis. Buys one-time and all rights. Model release preferred.
Tips: "I usually look for a specific specialty. No photographer is good at everything. I also consider studio space and equipment. Show me something different, unusual, something that sets them apart from any average local photographer. If I'm going out of town for something it has to be for something I can't get done locally."

CLELAND, WARD, SMITH & ASSOCIATES, Suite 520, Tobacco Square Bldg., 836 Oak St., Winston-Salem NC 27101. (919)723-5551. Ad agency. Production Manager: James K. Ward. Types of clients: primarily industrial and business-to-business.
Needs: Uses photographers for trade magazines, direct mail, brochures and catalogs. Subjects include: "product shots or location shots of plants, offices, workers and production flow; also technical equipment detail shots."
Specs: Uses 8×10 b&w and color prints and transparencies.
First Contact & Terms: Arrange a personal interview to show portfolio. Works on assignment only. Does not return unsolicited material. Payment varies; prefers to negotiate. Pays on acceptance. Buys all rights. Model release required.
Tips: Prefers to see "innovation—not just execution. We are not dazzled by pretty color. How the shot tells the story of the product is the important part."

*■IMAGE ASSOCIATES, 4314 Bland Rd., Raleigh NC 27609. (919)876-6400. FAX: (919)876-7064. AV firm. Creative Director: John Wigmore. Types of clients: industrial and corporate. Examples of ad campaigns: United Telespectrum Systems, Exide Electronics and Organon Teknika.
Needs: Works with 3 freelance photographers/month for audiovisual uses. Interested in reviewing stock photos.
Audiovisual Needs: Uses photos for slide shows.
First Contact & Terms: Provide resume, business card, brochure, flyer or tearsheets to be kept on file for possible future assignments. Works with freelancers on assignment basis only. Cannot return material. Reports in 1 month. Pays $50/color photo. Pays within 30 days of invoice. Buys all rights

(work-for-hire). Model release and photo captions required. Credit line given sometimes; negotiable.

SMITH & ASSOCIATES, INC., 5509 Monroe Rd., Charoltte NC 28212. (704)536-1275. Ad agency. Art Director: David Palmer. Types of clients: industrial, financial.
Needs: Works with 3-5 freelance photographers/month. Uses photographers for consumer and trade magazines, direct mail and catalogs. Subjects include product, people and locations.
Specs: Uses b&w and color prints; 35mm, 2¼ × 2¼ and 4 × 5 transparencies.
First Contact & Terms: Query with samples. Provide resume, business card, brochure, flyer or tearsheets to be kept on file for possible future assignments. Works with freelance photographers on assignment basis only. Does not return unsolicited material. Report time varies; "depends on how busy I am." Pays $750-1,000/day; by the job depending on the props, models, set construction, etc. Pays 30 days after invoice. Rights purchased depend on situation. Model release required; captions preferred. Credit lines given depending on situation.
Tips: Looks for "versatility, dramatic lighting, unusual angles or perspectives. Send printed samples to keep on file. Trends include more b&w, less special effects."

North Dakota

KRANZLER, KINGSLEY COMMUNICATIONS LTD., (formerly Kranzler, Saueressig Inc.), Box 693, Bismarck ND 58502. (701)255-3067. Ad agency. Art Director: Jayne Dement. Types of clients: industrial, financial, etc.
Needs: Works with 1 freelance photographer/month. Uses photographers for consumer and trade magazines, direct mail, P-O-P displays, catalogs, posters and newspapers. Subjects include local and regional.
Specs: Uses 8 × 10 glossy b&w/color prints; 35mm, 2¼ × 2¼ and 4 × 5 transparencies.
First Contact & Terms: Query with list of stock photo subjects. Provide resume, business card, brochure, flyer or tearsheets to be kept on file for possible future assignments. Works with freelance photographers on assignment basis only; local freelancers 90% of time. SASE. Reports in 2 weeks. Pays $15-75/b&w photo; $25-200/color photo; hour and day rates are negotiable depending on location and travel. Pays on publication. Buys all and one-time rights. Model release required; captions preferred. Credit line sometimes given.
Tips: In reviewing a photographer's portfolio or samples, prefers to see "people—working, playing—various views of each shot."

Ohio

■**BARON ADVERTISING, INC.,** 645 Hanna Bldg., Cleveland OH 44115. (216)621-6800. Ad agency. President: Selma Baron. Types of clients: food, industrial and financial. In particular, serves various manufacturers of tabletop and food service equipment.
Needs: Uses 20-25 freelance photographers/month. Uses photographers for direct mail, catalogs, newspapers, consumer magazines, P-O-P displays, posters, trade magazines, brochures and signage. Subject matter "diverse."
Audiovisual Needs: Works with freelance filmmakers for AV presentations.
First Contact & Terms: Arrange a personal interview to show portfolio. Query with list of stock photo subjects; provide resume, business card, brochure, flyer or tearsheets to be kept on file for possible future assignments. Works with freelancers on assignment basis only. Does not return unsolicited material. Payment "depends on the photographer." Pays on completion. Buys all rights. Model release required.
Tips: Prefers to see "food and equipment" photos in the photographer's samples. "Samples not to be returned other than regional photographers."

■**BRIGHT LIGHT PRODUCTIONS,** Suite 810, 602 Main St., Cincinnati OH 45202. (513)721-2574. President: Linda Spalazzi. Film and videotape firm. Types of clients: national, regional and local companies in the governmental, educational, industrial and commercial categories. Examples of productions: Perry & Derrick (TV spots), Jergen's (Eversoft Introduction) and Surf Cincinnati Waterpark (TV spots). Produces 16mm and 35mm films and videotape including Betacam. Works with freelancers on assignment only basis. Provide resume, flyer and brochure to be kept on file for possible future assignments. Pays $100 minimum/day for grip; negotiates payment based on photographer's previous experience/reputation and day rate (10 hrs). Pays within 30 days of

completion of job. Call to arrange appointment or query with resume of credits. Wants to see sample reels or samples of still work. Looking for "sensitivity to subject matter and lighting."
Film: 16mm and 35mm documentary, industrial, educational and commercial films. Sample assignments include camera assistant, gaffer or grip.

DAVID K. BURNAP ADVERTISING AGENCY, INC., 7106 Corporate Way, Dayton OH 45459. (513)439-4800. Ad agency. Senior Art Director: David Shurte. Types of clients: industrial, retail and finance.
Needs: Works with 2 freelance photographers/month. Uses photographers for trade magazines, direct mail, P-O-P displays, catalogs, newspapers.
First Contact & Terms: Arrange a personal interview to show portfolio or send unsolicited photos by mail for consideration. Works on assignment basis only. Does not return unsolicited material. Pays by the job; on receipt. Buys all rights or one-time rights. Model release required; captions preferred.

■**WILLIAM DITZEL PRODUCTIONS**, 933 Shroyer, Dayton OH 45419. (513)298-5381. Owner: William Ditzel. Types of clients: business/industrial.
Needs: Uses photographers for filmstrips, multimedia productions, films and videotapes. Subjects vary.
Specs: Uses b&w prints; 35mm and 2¼×2¼ transparencies; 16mm, 35mm film and video tape.
First Contact & Terms: Query with stock photo list. Provide resume, business card, self-promotion piece or tearsheets to be kept on file for possible future assignments. Works with freelancers on assignment only; interested in stock photos/footage. Does not return unsolicited material. Reports immediately when the material has been requested. Payment depends upon the level of expertise and equipment provided for a specific job. Generally, our freelancers work as a member of a location crew. Pays within 30 days. Buys one-time rights, all rights or as the project dictates. Credit line given depending upon usage.
Tips: Looks for "technical capabilities, willingness to take direction and to work as a member of a crew. Have a portfolio which represents your best professional efforts, and displays an honest example of what you enjoy doing the most. In video, offer a sample reel that defines *your* abilities, rather than the composite efforts of many craftsmen."

GRISWOLD INC., 101 Prospect Ave. W., Cleveland OH 44115. (216)696-3400. Executive Art Director: Tom Gilday. Ad agency. Types of clients: Consumer and industrial firms; client list provided upon request. Provide brochure to be kept on file for possible future assignments.
Needs: Works with freelance photographers on assignment only basis. Uses photographers for billboards, consumer and trade magazines, direct mail, P-O-P displays, brochures, catalogs, posters, newspapers and AV presentations.
First Contact & Terms: Works primarily with local freelancers but occasionally uses others. Arrange interview to show portfolio. Payment is by the day or by the project; negotiates according to client's budget. Pays on production.

■**HARDING PRODUCTIONS**, 4782 Unity Line Rd., New Waterford OH 44445. (216)457-7352. Owner: William R. Harding. Estab. Estab. 1983. Types of clients: industrial and corporate accounts, retail and television commercials.
Audiovisual Needs: Works with 5 freelancers/month for videotapes, audio and lighting, plus writing. Also looking for new ideas for the home VCR market, possibly 'how-to' data.
First Contact & Terms: Arrange a personal interview to show video demo reel; provide resume, business card, self-promotion piece or tearsheets to be kept on file for possible future assignments. Works with freelancers on assignment only. SASE. Reports in 2 weeks. Payment "very dependent on needs and skills"; $5-10/hour and $50-300/day. Pay is "negotiated at time of hiring." Buys all rights. May negotiate for use on certain projects. Credit line given.
Tips: "Call first and we will set up an appointment to see your work. We are interested only in self-starters who are motivated to get into this business and are willing to do what it takes to make it. Be prepared to show work you have actually done and not work of a crew you just happened to be on. If on a crew, tell us what you did yourself. Video is starting to dominate the industrial and corporate field. Clients are finding more and more ways to use it. We now do video exclusively."

■**HAYES PUBLISHING CO., INC.**, 6304 Hamilton Ave., Cincinnati OH 45224. (513)681-7559. Office Manager: Marge Lammers. AV producer. Types of clients: school, civic and right-to-life groups. Produces filmstrips and slide/cassette sets. Subjects include "miscellaneous baby, child and adult scenes." Needs photos of prenatal development of the human body and shots relating to abortion. Buys all rights. Contact by mail first. Reports in 2 weeks. SASE.
Specs: Contact by mail about specifications and needs for b&w first. For color, uses 35mm transparencies, or negatives with 5×7 glossy prints. Captions and model release required. Pays $50 minimum.

Tips: "We are always looking for excellent, thoroughly documented and authenticated photographs of early developing babies and of any and all types of abortions."

■**HOLLAND ADVERTISING**, 252 Ludlow Ave., Cincinnati OH 45220. (513)221-1252. Ad agency. Creative Director: Pat Reeves. Types of clients: retail, industrial and finance. Examples of ad campaigns: Astromet (trade magazines ad for ceramic furnace filters); Hilton Davis (brochure and ads for food colorings); Cincinnati Time (brochure for time clock systems).
Needs: Uses 2 freelance photographers/month. Uses photographers for billboards, consumer magazines, trade magazines, direct mail, P-O-P displays, catalogs, posters and newspapers. Subjects vary. Reviews stock photos, film or video.
Specs: Vary according to clients needs.
First Contact & Terms: Query with list of stock photo subjects, query with samples; provide resume, business card, brochure, flyer or tearsheets to be kept on file for possible future assignments. Works with freelancers on an assignment basis only. SASE. Reports in 2 weeks. Pays $20-35/hour; $500-1,000/day, $75-150/color photo; and $50-100/b&w photo. Also pays on estimate basis. Pays on publication. Buys all rights. Model release preferred. Credit line given "depending on assignment and price."
Tips: Trend toward "more stock photography being solicited and used."

■**JONES, ANASTASI, LENNON ADVERTISING, INC.**, 665 Frantz Rd., Dublin OH 43017. (614)764-1274. Creative Director/VP: Joe Anastasi. Ad agency. Types of clients: hospitals, insurance, colleges, food and restaurants and industrial.
Needs: Works on assignment basis only. Uses photographers for billboards, consumer and trade magazines, brochures, posters, newspapers and AV presentations.
First Contact & Terms: Arrange interview to show portfolio. Payment is by the hour, by the day, and by the project; negotiates according to client's budget.

*■**LIGGETT STASHOWER ADVERTISING, INC.**, 1228 Euclid Ave., Cleveland OH 44115. (216)348-8500. FAX: (216)861-1284. Ad agency. Contact: Linda M. Barberic. Estab. 1932. Types of clients: full service agency. Examples of recent clients: Ameritrust Bank, Sears Optical (Eyelab/cole) and Babcock and Wilcox.
Needs: Works with 50+ freelance photographers—filmmakers—videographers/month. Uses photographers for billboards, consumer magazines, trade magazines, direct mail, P-O-P displays, catalogs, posters, newspapers, signage and audiovisual uses. Interested in reviewing stock photos/film or video footage.
Audiovisual Needs: Uses photos/film/videos for trade show/commercials.
Specs: Uses b&w/color prints (size and finish varies); 35mm, 2¼×2¼, 4×5, 8×10 (rarely) transparencies; 16mm film; ¼-¾″ videotape.
First Contact & Terms: Send unsolicited photos by mail for consideration; query with samples; provide resume, business card, brochure, flyer or tearsheets to be kept on file for possible future assignments. Works with local freelancers only. SASE. Reports in 1-2 weeks. Pays $100 minimum/b&w photo; $100/hour; $1,200/day maximum. Pays within 30 days of acceptance. Rights purchased depends on jobs. Model release required. Credit line given sometimes, depending on usage.

LOHRE & ASSOCIATES INC., Suite 101, 2330 Victory Pkwy., Cincinnati OH 45206. (513)961-1174. Ad agency. President: Charles R. Lohre. Types of clients: industrial.
Needs: Works with 1 photographer/month. Uses photographers for trade magazines, direct mail, catalogs and prints. Subjects include: machine-industrial themes and various eye-catchers.
Specs: Uses 8×10 glossy b&w and color prints; 4×5 transparencies.
First Contact & Terms: Query with resume of credits; provide resume, business card, brochure, flyer or tearsheets to be kept on file for possible future assignments. Works with local freelancers only. SASE. Reports in 1 week. Pays $60/b&w photo; $250/color photo; $60/hour; $275/day. Pays on publication. Buys all rights.
Tips: Prefers to see eye-catching and thought-provoking images/non-human. Need someone to take 35mm photos on short notice in Cincinnati plants.

■**MIDWEST TALENT/CREATIVE TALENT**, 1102 Neil Ave., Columbus OH 43201. (614)294-7827. FAX: (614)294-3396. Talent Developer: Gary Aggas. Types of clients: talent and advertising agencies; production companies.
Needs: Works with 2-3 freelance photographers/month. Uses photographers for slide sets and videotapes. Subjects include portfolios and promotional shots of models and actors.
Specs: Uses 5×7 and 11×14 b&w prints; 35mm transparencies; and U-matic ¾″ videotape.
First Contact & Terms: Query with samples or resume. Works with freelancers by assignment only. SASE. Reports in 2-3 weeks. Pays $4-10/b&w photo, $4-25/color photo, $25-65/hour and $100-275/job. Pays on acceptance. Buys all rights. Credit line given.

Photographer Eric Hanson landed the assignment to shoot this photo by making a cold call to Cleveland-based Nationwide Advertising. James Herringshaw of Nationwide, who assigned the work to Hanson for $1,000, says it was used in a medical journal trade ad for nursing recruitment. As Hanson explains, the photo, which was shot and run in color, communicates "a warm feeling with dappled sunlight."

Tips: "Be concise, to the point and have good promotional package. We like to see well lit subjects with good faces."

NATIONWIDE ADVERTISING, INC., The Halle Bldg., 1228 Euclid Ave./Sixth Floor, Cleveland OH 44115. (216)579-0300. Creative Director: Jim Herringshaw. Ad agency. "This is a recruitment agency which is utilized by a wide variety of clientele, really indiscriminate."
Needs: Works with "very few freelancers but this could change." Uses freelancers for billboards, consumer and trade magazines, newspapers and TV.
First Contact & Terms: Send samples, but "does not want actual portfolio." Selects freelancers "by how easily accessible they are and the characteristics of their work." Negotiates payment based on client's budget. Does not return unsolicited material.

■**NORTHLICH, STOLLEY, LA WARRE,** (formerly Northlich, Stolley, Inc.), 200 W. 4th St., Cincinnati OH 45202. (513)421-8840. Creative Director: Don Perkins. Ad agency. Types of clients: financial, industrial, food service, package goods, durables; client list provided on request.
Needs: Works with 5-6 freelance photographers/month on assignment only basis. Uses photographers for consumer and trade magazines, direct mail, P-O-P displays, brochures, posters, signage, newspapers and AV presentations.
First Contact & Terms: Query with list of stock photo subjects; provide brochure, flyer and tearsheets to be kept on file for possible future assignments. Does not return unsolicited material. Reports in 1 week. Negotiates payment according to client's budget; $500-3,000/b&w photo; $400-6,000/color photo. Pays on production. Buys exclusive rights; all rights.

SMILEY/HANCHULAK, INC., 47 N. Cleveland-Massillon Rd., Akron OH 44313. (216)666-0868. Ad agency. Executive Art Director: Dominick Sorrent, Jr. Clients: all types.
Needs: Works with 1-2 photographers/month. Uses freelance photographers for consumer magazines, trade magazines, direct mail, P-O-P displays, catalogs, posters and sales promotion.
Specs: Uses 11 × 14 b&w and color prints, finish depends on job; 35mm or 2¼ × 2¼ (location) or 4 × 5 or 8 × 10 (usually studio) transparencies, depends on job.
First Contact & Terms: Arrange a personal interview to show portfolio; query with resume of credits, list of stock photo subjects or samples; send unsolicited photos by mail for consideration; or submit portfolio for review. Provide resume, business card, brochure, flyer or tearsheets to be kept on file for possible future assignments. If a personal interview cannot be arranged, a letter would be acceptable. Works with freelance photographers on assignment basis only. SASE. Report depends on work schedule. Pays by the day, or by the job. Buys all rights unless requested otherwise. Model release required. Captions preferred.
Tips: Prefers to see studio product photos. "Jobs vary—we need to see all types with the exception of fashion. We would like to get more contemporary but photo should still do the job."

*****WATT, ROOP & CO.,** 1100 Superior Ave., Cleveland OH 44114. (216)566-7019. PR firm. Manager of Design Operations: Thomas Federico. Estab. 1981. Types of clients: industrial and finance.
Needs: Works with 4 freelance photographers/month. Uses photographers for trade magazines and corporate/capabilities brochures. Subjects include: corporate.
First Contact & Terms: Provide resume, business card, brochure, flyer or tearsheets to be kept on file for possible future assignments. Works with local freelancers on assignment only. Reports "as needed." Pays $400-1,000/day. Pays on receipt of invoice. Buys all rights (work-for-hire). Model release and photo captions preferred. Credit line sometimes given.
Tips: Wants to see work that is "clean, professional with eye for interesting angles, etc."

■**WOLF, BLUMBERG, KRODY,** 2368 Victory Pkwy., Cincinnati OH 45206. (513)751-0258. Ad agency. Contact: Art Directors. Types of clients: industrial, retail, financial.
Needs: Works with 8 freelance photographers/month. Uses photographers for billboards, consumer and trade magazines, direct mail, P-O-P displays, catalogs, posters, signage, newspapers and videos. Subject matter varies.
Specs: Uses all sizes b&w and color prints; 35mm, 2¼ × 2¼, 4 × 5 and 8 × 10 transparencies.
First Contact & Terms: Arrange a personal interview to show portfolio. Works with freelance photographers on assignment basis only. Does not return unsolicited material. Reports in 1 week. Pays $200-1,000/day, other rates vary. Pays within 30 days. Buys all rights. Model release required.

WYSE ADVERTISING, 24 Public Square, Cleveland OH 44113. (216)696-2424. Art Director: Tom Smith. Ad agency. Uses billboards, consumer and trade magazines, direct mail, newspapers, P-O-P displays and TV. Serves clients in a variety of industries. Deals with 20 photographers/year.

Specs: Uses b&w photos and color transparencies. Works with freelance filmmakers in production of TV commercials.
Payment/Terms: Pays by hour, day and job. Buys all rights. Model release required.
Making Contact: Arrange a personal interview to show portfolio.

Oklahoma

BEALS ADVERTISING AGENCY, #200, 5005 Pennsylvania, Oklahoma City OK 73110. (405)848-8513. Ad agency. Account Executive: Jon Lundeen. Types of clients: industrial. Client list free with SASE.
Needs: Works with 10 freelance photographers/month. Uses photographers for trade magazines, direct mail, catalogs and posters. Subjects include mostly industrial.
Specs: Specifications vary.
First Contact & Terms: Provide resume, business card, brochure, flyer or tearsheets to be kept on file for possible future assignments. SASE. Reports in 2 weeks. Payment varies. Pays on receipt of invoice. Buys all rights. Model release preferred.

■**DPR COMPANY,** Suite 303, 2828 N.W. 57th St., Oklahoma City OK 73112. (405)848-6407. Owner: B. Carl Gadd. Estab. 1978. Industrial PR firm. Photos used in brochures and press releases. Buys 15-30 photos/year. Works on assignment only. Pays $75 minimum/hour, $400 minimum/day. Pays on production. Query with resume of credits or call to arrange an appointment; provide business card and flyer to be kept on file for possible future assignments. Reports in 1 week. Does not return unsolicited material.
Audiovisual Needs: Produces all types of film. Buys all rights.
B&W: Uses 5 × 7 glossy prints.
Color: Uses any size transparencies and prints.
Tips: "All material should be dated and the location noted. Videotape is now 65% of my product needs."

■**JORDAN ASSOCIATES ADVERTISING & COMMUNICATIONS,** 1000 W. Wilshire, Box 14005, Oklahoma City OK 73113. (405)840-3201. Director of Photography: John Williamson. Ad agency. Uses photographers for billboards, consumer and trade magazines, direct mail, foreign media, newspapers, P-O-P displays and TV, annual reports and public relations. Types of clients: banking, manufacturing, food, clothing. Generally works with 2-3 freelance photographers/month on assignment only.
Specs: Uses b&w prints and color transparencies. Works with freelance filmmakers in production of 16mm industrial and videotape, TV spots; short films in 35mm.
Payment & Terms: Pays $25-55 minimum/hour for b&w, $200-400 minimum/day for b&w or color (plus materials). Negotiates payment based on client's budget and where the work will appear. Buys all rights. Model release required.
Making Contact: Arrange a personal interview to show portfolio (prefers to see a complete assortment of work in a portfolio); provide flyer and business card to be kept on file for possible future assignments. SASE. Reports in 2 weeks.

Oregon

BEAR CREEK DIRECT , Box 906, Medford OR 97501. (503)776-2121, ext 3402. In-house ad agency for mail order companies. Executive Art Director: Chris Rose-Merkle. Types of clients: mail order fruit, bakery, floral and plants.
Needs: Works with 3 freelance photographers/month. Uses photographers for direct mail, catalogs and brochures.
Specs: Uses 35mm, 120mm and 4 × 5 transparencies.
First Contact & Terms: Provide resume, business card, brochure, flyer or tearsheets to be kept on file for possible future assignments. Does not return unsolicited material. Reports in 2 weeks. Pays $800-1,800/day; or $300-500/color photo. Pays on receipt. Buys all rights. Model release required.
Tips: "Show me *fantastic* food photography—beautiful flowers, plants, roses, gardens."

*■**CREATIVE COMPANY,** 3276 Commercial St. SE, Salem OR 97302. (503)363-4433. FAX: (503)363-6817. Ad agency. President/Creative Director: Jennifer L. Morrow. Estab. 1978. Types of clients: food products, health care, tourism, miscellaneous. Examples of recent clients: Kerr Concentrates, Smoke Craft and Cherriots.

Needs: Works with 1-2 freelancers/month. Uses photographers for direct mail, P-O-P displays, catalogs, posters, audiovisual and sales promotion packages.

Specs: Uses 5×7 and larger glossy color or b&w prints; 2¼×2¼, 4×5 transparencies.

First Contact & Terms: Arrange personal interiew to show portfolio; provide resume, business card, brochure, flyer or tearsheets to be kept on file for possible future assignments. Works with local freelancers only. SASE. Reports "when needed." Pays $50-300/b&w photo; $100-400/color photo; $20-75/hour; $400-1,200/day. Pays on publciation or "when client pays." Buys all rights (work-for-hire). Model release preferred. Credit line not given.

Tips: In freelancer's porfolio, looks for "product shots, lighting, creative approach, understanding of sales message and reproduction." Sees trend toward "more special effect photography, manipulation of photos in computers." To break in with this firm, "do good work, be responsive and understand what color separations and printing will do to photos."

RYAN COMMUNICATIONS, Suite 400, Century Tower Bldg., 1201 SW 12th, Portland OR 97201. (503)227-5547. Creative Director: Mike Arthur. Art Directors: Leslie Herzfeld, Patty Delenikos and Laurie Schultz. Ad agency and PR firm. Uses billboards, direct mail, foreign media, newspapers, promotions, P-O-P displays, TV, trade and consumer magazines, brochures, annual reports and slide/tape presentations. Serves industrial, corporate, retail and financial clients.

Needs: Deals with 5-10 photographers/year. Special subject needs include: corporate portraits, light industry, medical and some food—all both location and studio.

Specs: Uses 8×10 glossy b&w photos, RC prints for retouching and 35mm and 4×5 transparencies. Also uses freelance filmmakers in production on 16mm and tape industrial, training films and commercial production.

First Contact & Terms: Send material by mail for consideration. Provide business card, brochure, and flyer to be kept on file for possible future assignments. SASE. Prefers local freelancers. Reports in 2 weeks. "All projects quoted in advance. Payment depends entirely on client budget and goals." Rights purchased depend on job. Model release required.

Tips: Prefers to see "industrial, financial, business, promotional, humorous, special effects and product shots" in a portfolio. Prefers to see "prints, tearsheets to support transparencies" as samples. "We like to know the format used and why—also what equipment, studios, etc. are available. We look for something 'extra' in lighting and composition; good rapport with people for portraits and candids on location. Keep in touch, show us new projects. Send us sample postcards of mailings; we keep 'em on file and it really helps in selecting photographers!"

Pennsylvania

■**TED BARKUS COMPANY, INC.**, Suite 100, 1512 Spruce St., Philadelphia PA 19102. (215)545-0616. Ad agency and PR firm. President: Allen E. Barkus. Types of clients: industrial, finance, appliances, home furnishings, publishers, fashion and food.

Needs: Uses 1 freelance photographer/month. Uses photographers for direct mail, catalogs, newspapers, consumer magazines, P-O-P displays, posters, AV presentations, trade magazines and brochures. Subjects include "products, office scenes, etc." Uses freelance filmmakers to produce TV commercials and AV films.

Specs: Uses 4×5 and 8×10 b&w and color prints; 35mm transparencies; film and videotape.

First Contact & Terms: Arrange a personal interview to show portfolio. Works with local and New York freelancers only. SASE. Reports in 3 weeks. Payment varies. Pays on acceptance. Buys all rights. Model release required. Credit line sometimes given.

*****CHARLES EDELSTEIN ADVERTISING**, 92 Austin Dr., Holland PA 18966. (215)355-5015. Ad agency. President: Charles Edelstein. Types of clients: industrial and finance.

Needs: Works with 3 freelance photographers/month. Uses photographers for trade magazines, direct mail, catalogs and newspapers. Subjects include: management personnel, machinery, equipment, buildings and products.

First Contact & Terms: Provide resume, business card, brochure, flyer or tearsheets to be kept on file for possible future assignments. Usually works with freelancers on assignment. Reports only as needed. Pays $50-70/hour; $50/b&w photo. Pays on receipt of invoice. Buys all rights (work-for-hire). Model release required. Credit line not given.

Tips: Looks for freelancers with industrial or business-to-business experience.

HAWBAKER COMMUNICATIONS, INC., 1 Oliver Plaza, Pittsburgh PA 15222. (412)261-6519. Head Art Director: Ron Larson. Ad agency. Uses direct mail, newspapers, trade magazines, radio and TV. Serves primarily industrial clients. Commissions 10 photographers/year. Pays $100-500/b&w or color

photo; $400-1,200/day. Buys all rights. Model release required. Query with resume of credits. SASE. Reports in 2 weeks.
B&W: Uses 8×10 glossy prints; contact sheet and negatives OK.
Color: Uses 8×10 glossy prints, 35mm and 4×5 transparencies.

HELRIEGEL-KEENAN ADVERTISING, 546 Hamilton St., Allentown PA 18105. (215)435-9687. Ad agency. Art Director: Judith Nentwig. Types of clients: industrial, retail, fashion, finance, health care and high-tech.
Needs: Works with 7-8 freelance photographers/month. Uses photographers for billboards, consumer magazines, trade magazines, direct mail, posters, signage and newspapers.
Specs: Uses b&w and color prints; 35mm, 2¼×2¼, 4×5 and 8×10 transparencies.
First Contact & Terms: Query with samples. Provide resume, business card, brochure, flyer or tearsheets to be kept on file for possible future assignments. Does not return unsolicited material. Pays on receipt. Model release required. Credit line sometimes given.

■JERRYEND COMMUNCATIONS INC., Box 356H, RD #2, Birdsboro PA 19508. (215)689-9118. PR firm. Vice President: Jerry End. Types of clients: industrial, automotive aftermarket, financial, heavy equipment, nonprofit and public service. Examples of projects: Ingersoll-Rand Co./Motorsports (The Real Winners); Willson Safety Products (VIP/Very Important Products); Goodwill Industries (Projects With Industry).
Needs: Works with 2 freelance photographers/month. Uses photographers for consumer and trade magazines, catalogs, newspapers and AV presentations. Subjects include case histories/product applications.
Audiovisual Needs: Works with freelance filmmakers to produce training films, etc.
Specs: Uses 8×10 b&w repro-quality prints and color negatives.
First Contact & Terms: Provide resume, business card, brochure, flyer or tearsheets to be kept on file for possible future assignments. "Specify charges and terms." Works with freelance photographers on assignment basis only. SASE. Reports in 1 week. Pays "by estimate for project, $350 maximum." Pays on receipt of photos. Buys all rights. Model release required; captions preferred.
Tips: "We look for technical expertise in photo technique; clear reproducible photos for publicity use; and product photos reflecting scale of product to an identifiable subject."

■KENNEDY/LEE, INC., RD 12, York PA 17406. (717)757-4666. President: Don Kennedy. AV firm. "We are a fully staffed AV studio, primarily shooting broadcast-quality video and 16mm film. We seldom buy from freelancers. We do maintain a file of video/cinematographers with a professional track record, for specific assignments. On occasion, we buy still stock-shots (color only), to meet specific program requirements."
Needs: "Business communications is our business and that covers a broad spectrum of visual needs."
First Contact & Terms: "Do not send any work on spec. On first contact, send a letter, business card or brochure. Tell us what you do; what equipment you use. If you have samples we may keep, fine. We will return demo videotapes." On assignment generally pays $150/half-day, $250/full day, per person, plus going rates for equipment used and cost of film/video stock used. "We then own the footage. For stock shots or footage, we'll pay your price, based upon our use."
Tips: "Capturing light on an emulsion is what this business is all about. On occasion we might accept one-light-at-camera shooting, but generally demand more sophisticated techniques and results. We're not producing home movies."

LINDHULT & JONES, INC., ADVERTISING, 501 Office Center Dr., Ft. Washington PA 19034. (215)643-3115. Ad agency. Art Director: Russell Risko. Types of clients: industrial.
Needs: Works with 5 freelance photographers/month. Uses photographers for trade magazines, direct mail, P-O-P displays and catalogs. Subjects include table-top product photography.
Specs: Uses 8×10 matte or glossy b&w and color prints.
First Contact & Terms: Arrange a personal interview to show portfolio; submit portfolio for review. Provide resume, business card, brochure, flyer or tearsheets to be kept on file for possible future assignments. Now works with local freelancers only—may consider working with out-of-area photographers. Does not return unsolicited material. Reports when assignment is present. Pays $100-500/job. Pays on receipt of invoice. Buys all rights. Model release preferred.
Tips: Looks for "good crisp b&w and color tonal balance, lighting, contemporary photo backgrounds. Contact us showing samples of photo images/actually buy—have prices for each sample available."

THE NEIMAN GROUP, Harrisburg Transportation Center, 4th and Chestnut, Harrisburg PA 17101. (717)232-5554. Ad agency. Contact: Art Director. Types of clients: industrial, finance, health care.
Needs: Works with 4 freelance photographers/month. Uses photogaphers for trade magazines, direct mail, P-O-P displays, posters and newspapers. Subject matter includes health care and retail.
Specs: Uses 4×5 transparencies.
First Contact & Terms: Query with samples or submit portfolio for review. Works on assignment only. SASE. Reports in 2 weeks. Payment is made on 30 day terms. Model release required.

PERCEPTIVE MARKETERS AGENCY, LTD., Suite 185, 1100 E. Hector St., Conshohocken PA 19428. (215)825-8710. Ad agency. Art Director: William Middleton. Types of clients: retail furniture, contract furniture, lighting distribution companies, freight forwarding company, nonprofit organizations for the arts and publishers. Examples of recent ad campaigns: Pilot Air Freight (Quality Campaign), Sierra Group (Innovative Office Seating Campaign); Best Leibco (Aritsan Line Paintbrush Campaign). Client list free with SASE.
Needs: Buys 100 freelance photographs and makes 10-15 assignments/year. Uses photographers for consumer and trade magazines, direct mail, catalogs, posters and newspapers. Subjects include product, people and industrial (on location). No fashion.
Specs: Uses 8×10 b&w prints and 35mm, 2¼×2¼, 4×5 and 8×10 transparencies.
First Contact & Terms: Query with resume of credits and list of stock photo subjects; send unsolicited photos by mail for consideration; provide resume, business card, brochure, flyer or tearsheets to be kept on file for possible future assignments. Works only with local freelance photographers; works on assignment only. Reports after contract. Payment negotiable; typically pays $25/b&w photo; $50/color photo; $50/hour; $600/day. Pays on receipt of invoice, 30 day net. Buys all rights. Model release required. Credit line negotiable, depending on photo's use.

ROSEN-COREN AGENCY INC., 902 Fox Pavilion, Juketon PA 19046. (215)572-8131. PR firm. Office Administrator: Ellen R. Coren. Types of clients: industrial, retail, fashion, finance, entertainment.
Needs: Works with 4 freelance photographers/month. Uses photographers for PR shots.
Specs: Uses b&w prints.
First Contact & Terms: "Follow up with phone call." Works with local freelancers only. Reports when in need of service. Pays $50-65/hour; or /b&w and color photo. Pays when "assignment completed and invoice sent – 30 days."

*ROSKA DIRECT MARKETING, 1364 Welsh Rd., North Wales PA 19454. (215)643-9100. FAX: (215)643-2562. Art Director: Nancy M. Erb. Estab. 1981. Types of clients: retail, resort, finance, service and publishers.
Needs: Works with 1 freelance photographer/month. Uses photographers for direct mail. Subject matter includes mostly people.
Specs: Uses 8×10 prints and 2¼×2¼, 4×5 and 8×10 transparencies. Arrange a personal interview to show portfolio. Provide resume, business card, brochure, flyer or tearsheets to be kept on file for possible future assignments. SASE. Works on assignment only. Reports in 2 weeks. Pays $50-125/b&w photo; $110-450/color photo; $50-125/hour; $350-750/day; $100-1,500/complete job.. Pays on receipt. Buys all rights. Model release required; captions preferred.
Tips: Prefers to see creativity, lighting, clean shots. "Be competitive with rates, experience, studio size and location." To break in with firm, be "willing to try all aspects and angles."

SCEPTER GROUP, INC., Box 265, Morgantown PA 19543. (215)286-6020. Ad agency. Art Director: Bruce Becker. Types of clients: industrial, retail, financial.
Needs: Works with 3-5 freelance photographers/month. Uses photographers for consumer and trade magazines, P-O-P displays, catalogs and newspapers. Subjects include people and product.
Specs: Uses 8×10 glossy prints; 2¼×2¼ and 4×5 transparencies.
First Contact & Terms: Arrange a personal interview to show portfolio; send unsolicited photos by mail for consideration. Does not return unsolicited material. Pays $500-2,000/day. Pays on receipt of invoice. Rights flexible. Model release required.
Tips: Looks for "creativity, good product, situation, flair. Send samples, contact by phone."

LIZ SCOTT ENTERPRISES, Box 7138 Pittsburgh PA 15213. (412)661-5429. Contact: Liz Scott. Ad agency and PR firm. Types of clients: community organizations, publishing and private enterprise. Photos used in brochures, newsletters and PR releases. Works with 1 freelance photographer/month on assignment only basis. Provide resume and letter of inquiry to be kept on file for possible future assignments. Buys 5-10 photos/year. "We often receive our photos from our clients and rarely use freelancers. Photos are usually purchased by the client separately." Credit line given. Negotiates payment based on client's budget and where the work will appear. Buys all rights. Query with resume of credits. Local freelancers preferred. SASE. "Photographer must follow up queries unless SASE is

included." Interested in photos of persons involved in industrial, community or client projects. No art photos.
B&W: Uses 5×7 prints; contact sheet OK. Pays $10 minimum/photo.
Color: "There is little demand at this time for color."

■**THE SLIDEING BOARD**, 322 Blvd. of Allies, Pittsburgh PA 15222. (412)261-6006. General Manager: Rob Dillon. Types of clients: consumer, industrial, financial and business-to-business.
Needs: Works with 5-6 photographers/month. Uses freelance photographers for slide sets, multimedia productions and videotapes. Prefers to work with local freelancers, works with national freelancers for stock, location and some video work. Subjects vary by assignment.
Specs: Uses 35mm, 4×5, 8×10 transparencies; also Beta Cam SP videotape.
First Contact & Terms: Local freelancers call to arrange personal interview to show portfolio, slides or demo materials. All others provide resume, business card, self promotion piece or tearsheets to be kept on file for possible future assignments. SASE. Reports in 2 weeks. Payment varies by assignment. Payment made upon acceptance. Buys one-time rights or all rights. Captions and model releases preferred. Credit line sometimes given.
Tips: Photographers must have knowledge of how to shoot for multi-image, be able to understand objectives of assignment and have ability to work unsupervised.

■**RON SMILEY VISUAL PRODUCTIONS, INC. (RSVP)**, 58 N. 2nd. St., Philadelphia PA 19106. (215)829-9000. Manager: Brian Connor. Types of clients: broadcast, corporate, industrial.
Needs: Works with 2-4 freelance video photographers/month. Uses freelance photographers for films and videotapes. Subjects include EFP/ENG.
Specs: Uses Beta, U-matic ¼", 1" videotape, Beta SP and ¾" SP.
First Contact & Terms: Arrange a personal interview to show demo tape. Works with local freelancers only. Does not return unsolicited material. Pays $150-275/day. Pays net: 30 days. Buys all rights.
Tips: Show a tape of hand held, lighting, motion techniques, and high-and-low budget work.

■**E.J. STEWART INC.**, 525 Mildred Ave., Primos PA 19018. (215)626-6500. FAX: (215)626-2638. Studio and video facility. Director of Sales: Eric Bentley. Estab. 1970. Types of clients: coporate, commercial, industrial, retail.
Audiovisual Needs: Uses 15-25 freelancers per month for film and videotape productions.
Specs: Reviews film or video of industrial and commercial subjects. Uses various film and videotape (specs).
First Contact & Terms: Provide resume, business card, brochure, to be kept on file for possible future assignments. Work with freelancers on assignment basis only. Reports as needed. Pays $250-800/day; also pays "per job as market allows and per client specs." Photo captions preferred.
Tips: "The industry is really exploding with all types of new applications for film/video production." In freelancer's demos, "looks for a broad background with particular attention paid to strong lighting and technical ability." To break in with this firm, "be patient. We work with a lot of freelancers and have to establish a rapport with any new ones that we might be interested in before we will hire them." Also, "get involved on smaller productions as a 'grip' or assistant, learn the basics and meet the players."

■**VIDEOSMITH, INC.**, 100 Spring Garden, Philadelphia PA 19123. (215)398-5070. Production Manager: Matt Mussari. Types of clients: corporate, broadcast, institutional.
Needs: Works with 10-20 freelance photographers/month. Uses photographers for films and videotapes.
First Contact & Terms: Contact production manager directly. Works with local freelancers on assignment basis only. SASE. Reports in 1 month. Pays by the day, $150-350.
Tips: "Know *all* the basics of *all* aspects of film and video production—we don't do on-the-job training."

■**DUDLEY ZOETROPE PRODUCTIONS**, 19 E Central Ave., Paoli PA 19301. (215)644-4991. Producer: David Speace. Types of clients: corporate.
Needs: Works with 1-2 photographers/month. Uses freelance photographers for slide sets, multi-image productions, films and videotapes. Subject depends on client.
Specs: Uses 35 mm transparencies; videotape; 16mm and 35mm film.
First Contact & Terms: Arrange a personal interview to show portfolio. Provide resume, business card, self-promotion piece or tearsheets to be kept on file for possible future assignments. Works with freelancers by assignment only. Does not return unsolicited material. Reports in 1 week. Pays by the day. Payment made on acceptance. Buys all rights. Credit line sometimes given.

Tips: "Make your approach straight forward. Don't expect an assignment because someone looked at your portfolio. We are interested in photographers who can shoot for AV. They must be able to shoot from varied angles and present sequences that can tell a story."

Rhode Island

MARTIN THOMAS, INC., Advertising & Public Relations, 293 South Main St., Providence RI 02903. (401)331-8850. Ad agency and PR firm. Vice President: Thomas R. Rankin. Estab. 1987. Types of clients: industrial and business-to-business. Examples of ad campaigns: include Gloucester Engineering (New England Craftsmanship); Index, Inc. (cost savings with materials reduction); Geo. Mann & Co. (reduced labor, maintenance).
Needs: Works with 3-5 freelance photographers/month. Uses photographers for trade magazines. Subjects include: location shots of equipment in plants.
Specs: Uses 8×10 color and b&w prints; 35mm and 4×5 transparencies.
First Contact & Terms: Query with list of stock photo subjects. Provide resume, business card, brochure, flyer or tearsheets to be kept on file for possible future assignments. Send materials on pricing, experience. Works with local freelancers; works with freelancers on an assignment basis. Does not return unsolicited material. Pays $1,000/day. Pays on receipt of invoice. Buys all rights. Model release required; photo captions preferred.
Tips: To break in, demonstrate you "can be aggressive, innovative, realistic and can work within our parameters and budgets."

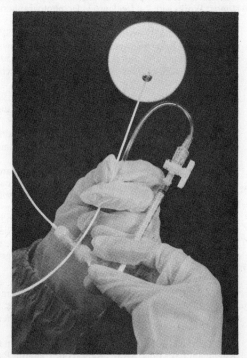

Rhode Island-based advertising agency Martin Thomas Inc. challenged photographer George Lavoie to "take an interesting photo of a catheter with drama." And, says agency principal Martin Pottle, Lavoie didn't let them down. The resulting 4×5 chrome, for which the agency bought all rights, has since been used in numerous applications for the client, Concept Polymer Technologies. As in this case, the agency typically pays a day rate of $1,000 and buys all rights for multiple uses.

South Carolina

LESLIE ADVERTISING AGENCY, 874 S. Pleasantburg Dr., Greenville SC 29607. (803)271-8340. Ad agency. Creative Coordinator: Marilyn Neves. Types of clients: industrial, retail, finance, food, resort.
Needs: Works with 1-2 freelance photographers/month. Uses photographers for consumer and trade magazines and newspapers.
Specs: Varied.
First Contact & Terms: Query with resume of credits, list of stock photo subjects and samples; submit portfolio for review "only on request"; provide resume, business card, brochure, flyer or tearsheets to be kept on file for possible future assignments. Occasionally works with freelance photographers on

assignment basis only. SASE. Reports ASAP. Pays $150-3,000/b&w photo; $150-3,000/color photo; $500-3,000/day. Pays on receipt of invoice. Buys all rights or one-time rights. Model release preferred.
Tips: "We always want to see sensitive lighting and compositional skills, conceptual stengths, a demonstration of technical proficiency and proven performance. Send printed promotional samples for our files. Call or have rep call for appointment with creative coordinator. Ensure that samples are well-presented and that they demonstrate professional skills."

■**SOUTH CAROLINA FILM OFFICE**, State Development Board, Box 927, Columbia SC 29202. (803)737-0400. Director: Isabel Hill. Types of clients: motion picture and television producers.
Needs: Works with 8 freelance photographers/month. Uses photographers to recruit feature films/ TV productions. Subjects include: location photos for feature films, TV projects, and national commercials.
Specs: Uses 3 × 5 color prints; 35mm transparencies; 35mm film; VHS, U-matic ¾" videotape.
First Contact & Terms: Submit portfolio by mail; provide resume, business card, self-promotion piece or tearsheets to be kept on file for possible future assignments. Works with local freelancers by assignment only. Does not return unsolicited material. Pays/yearly contract. Pays upon completion of assignment. Buys all rights.
Tips: "Experience working in the film/video industry is essential. Ability needed to identify and photograph suitable structures or settings to work as a movie location."

South Dakota

LAWRENCE & SCHILLER, 3932 S. Willow Ave., Sioux Falls SD 57106. (605)338-8000. Ad agency. Senior Art Director: Kirby Schultz. Types of clients: industrial, financial, manufacturing, medical.
Needs: Works with 3-4 freelance photographers/month. Uses photographers for consumer and trade magazines, direct mail, P-O-P displays, catalogs, posters and newspapers.
Specs: Uses 8 × 10 b&w prints; 35mm, 2¼ × 2¼ and 4 × 5 transparencies.
First Contact & Terms: Arrange a personal interview to show portfolio; submit portfolio for review. Provide resume, business card, brochure, flyer or tearsheets to be kept on file for possible future assignments. Works with freelance photographers on assignment basis only. Does not return unsolicited material. Reports as needed. Pays $500 maximum/day plus film and processing. Pays on acceptance. Buys all rights. Model release required; captions preferred.
Tips: In reviewing photographer's portfolios wants to see a "good selection of location, model, tabletop/studio examples—heavily emphasizing their forté. The best way for freelancers to begin working with us is to fill a void in an area in which we have either underqualified or overpriced talent—then handle as many details of production as they can. We see a trend in using photography as a unique showcase for products—not just a product (or idea) display."

Tennessee

■**CARDEN & CHERRY ADVERTISING AGENCY**, 1220 McGavock St., Nashville TN 37203. (615)255-6694. Ad agency. Art Director: Patricia Johnson. Types of clients: TV stations, dairies, savings and loans, car dealers (40%), industrial (40%), all others (20%).
Needs: Works with 2 freelance photographers/month. Uses photographers for direct mail, trade magazines and brochures. Subject needs vary.
Specs: Uses 8 × 10 b&w prints; 35mm and 4 × 5 transparencies and 16mm film.
First Contact & Terms: Provide resume, business card, brochure, flyer or tearsheets to be kept on file for possible future assignments. Works with local freelancers. Does not return unsolicited material. Reports in 3 weeks. Pays $40-120/hour; $300-1,000/day. Pays on acceptance. Buys all rights. Model release preferred.

*■**LAVIDGE AND ASSOCIATES**, 409 Bearden Park Circ., Knoxville TN 37919. (615)584-6121. FAX: (615)584-6756. Ad agency. Estab. 1950. Types of Clients: tourism, finance, food, apparel and sports. Examples of ad campaigns: Great Smoky Mountains, tourist brochure; Kerns Break, TV spot.
Needs: Works with freelancers "when need applies." Subjects include scenics and people. Interested in reviewing stock photos/video footage of people.
Audiovisual Needs: Uses slides and videotape.
Specs: Uses 35mm transparencies; videotape.
First Contact & Terms: Provide resume, business card, brochure, flyer or tearsheets to be kept on file for possible future assignments. Works with freelancers on assignment only. Cannot return material. Reports in 1-2 weeks. Pays according to job and client's budget. Pays on publication or receipt of

invoice. Buys all rights (work-for-hire). Model release required; photo captions preferred. Credit line given sometimes, depending on client.

Tips: Wants to see "clear, sharp, realistic photos, and of course the beauty of the shot." Sees trend where "photos replace illustration more each day." Advises freelancers to be patient. "I work on a very busy schedule, but I'm always wanting to find new work, fresh ideas."

Texas

ALAMO AD CENTER, INC., 217 Arden Grove, San Antonio TX 78215. (512)225-6294. Ad agency, PR and AV firm. President: Carl Mertens. Types of clients: industrial, fashion, finance.

Needs: Uses 3 freelance photographers/month. Uses photographers for billboards, direct mail, catalogs, newspapers, consumer magazines, P-O-P displays, trade magazines and brochures. Subject matter varies. Uses freelance filmmakers to produce TV commercials.

First Contact & Terms: Provide resume, business card, brochure, flyer or tearsheets to be kept on file for possible future assignments. Works with freelance photographers on assignment basis only. Does not return unsolicited material. Reporting time varies. Pays $25-75/hour; $50-200/day; payment by job varies. Pays on acceptance. Buys all rights. Model release required.

■**AVW AUDIO VISUAL, INC.,** 2241 Irving Blvd., Dallas TX 75207. (214)634-9060. Production Manager: Lynn Leuck. Types of clients: corporate, association.

Needs: Works with 3 freelance photographers/month. Uses photographers for multimedia productions, films and videotapes. Subjects include location photos, bold, descriptive looks, large quantities for multi-image.

Specs: Uses 35mm, 2¼ × 2¼ and 4 × 5 transparencies; and 16mm film.

First Contact & Terms: Provide resume, business card, self-promotion piece or tearsheets to be kept on file for possible future assignments. Works with freelancers by assignment only. Does not return unsolicited material. Reports in 2 weeks. Pays $50/hour; $500/day or by the job. Pays on acceptance. Buys all rights.

Tips: "Be familiar with special requirements of A/V photography—sequences, same subject using variety of angles; bold, graphic shots. Industry trends include more avant-garde usage, higher communications value. Still photographers interested in making the transition into film and video photography should assist, grip, create a show of their own using existing visuals, etc."

*****DORSEY ADVERTISING/PR.,** % Texas Affiliated Publishing Company, P.O. Box 270942, Dallas TX 75227-0942. Ad agency, newspaper publisher. Publisher: Lon G. Dorsey, Jr.. Types of clients: retail.

Needs: Uses photographers for newspapers. Subjects include: photojournalists on articles about homeless or street people.

First Contact & Terms: Send unsolicited photos by mail for consideration with SASE for return of all materials. SASE. Reports promptly. Pays $5-10/b&w photo; $7-20/color photo; $20-500/job. Pays on acceptance or publication. Buys all rights. Model release and photo captions required. Credit line sometime given.

Tips: In freelancer's demos, wants to see "Professionalism, clarity of purpose, without sex or negative atmosphere which could harm purpose of paper." The trend is toward "kinder, gentler situations, the 'let's help our fellows' attitude." To break in, "find out what we're about so we don't waste time with exhausting explanations. The name of our publication in question is "Streetpeople's Weekly News." We're interested in all homeless situations. Person(s) may send for a copy of paper by sending $2 to cover immediate handling (same day as received) and postage."

■**DYKEMAN ASSOCIATES, INC.,** 4415 Rawlins, Dallas TX 75219. (214)528-2991. Contact: Alice Dykeman or Cinda Nordgren. PR firm. Types of clients: health, finance, real estate, arts and leisure. Photos used in brochures, AV presentations, catalogs, news releases and magazines. Gives 100 assignments/year. Model release required. Arrange a personal interview to show portfolio. Photos purchased on assignment only. Provide business card and tearsheets to be kept on file for possible future assignments. Some interest in stock photos: industrial, construction, nature, recreation, architectural. "Whatever is needed to help tell the story in brochures, news releases or documentation of an event." Negotiates payment based on client's budget and photographer's previous experience/reputation. Does not return unsolicited material.

B&W: Uses glossy prints; contact sheet OK.

Color: Uses prints and transparencies.

Film: 35mm transparencies for AV presentations; 16mm and videotape for educational, training or fundraising films.

Tips: "In Dallas, we build a good group of photographers that we like working with, but for out-of-town assignments it's a little more difficult to find someone we know will perform right, follow through on time and can be easy to work with." Finds most out-of-town photographers by references of PR firms in other cities.

■**EDUCATIONAL FILMSTRIPS**, 1401 19th St., Huntsville TX 77340. (409)295-5767. CEO: George H. Russell. Types of clients: Jr. high through college (education only).

Needs: Subjects include various educational topics. Uses freelance photographers for filmstrips and videos.

Specs: Uses 35mm transparencies and videotape.

First Contact & Terms: Submit camera-ready 35mm slides in carousel tray with script or video tape. SASE. Reports in 1 month. Pays per filmstrip or video, royalty or purchase. Pays on acceptance or December of each year. Royalty. Buys exclusive product rights. Credit line given.

Tips: Visit local schools and ask to see most popular recent 35mm filmstrips and videos. Looks for "ability to produce a clear, concise curriculum-oriented educational product."

***EDUCATIONAL VIDEO NETWORK**, 1401 19th St., Huntsville TX 77340. (409)295-5767. FAX: (409)295-0233. AV firm. Chief Executive Officer: George H. Russell. Estab. 1954. Types of Clients: educational.

Needs: Works with 2 freelancers/month. Reviews stock video footage of any secondary educational subjects.

Audiovisual Needs: Uses videotape for all projects.

Specs: Uses super VHS or ¾" videotape.

First Contact & Terms: Query with samples. send copy of work on ½" VHS. SASE. Reports in 3 weeks. Pays in royalties or flat fee based on length, amount of post-production work, and marketability; royalties annually. Credit line given.

Tips: In freelancer's demos, looks for "compatibility with curriculum-oriented educational subjects." To break in with this firm, "review most popular curriculum-oriented subjects in your local high school media library. Shoot and review your work until you perfect your technique."

GROUP 400 ADVERTISING, Suite 301, 8480 Fredericksburg, San Antonio TX 78229. (512)697-8055. Ad agency. General Manager: Gary T. Young. Types of clients: industrial.

Needs: Works with 2-3 freelance photographers/month. Uses photographers for trade magazines, direct mail and special projects (special effects photography). Subjects include auction activity/equipment.

Specs: Uses 3x5 color prints; 35mm, 2¼ × 2¼ and 4 × 5 transparencies.

First Contact & Terms: Query with resume of credits and list of stock photo subjects. Provide resume, business card, brochure, flyer or tearsheets to be kept on file for possible future assignments. Works with freelance photographers on assignment basis only. SASE. Reports in 3 weeks. Payment individually negotiated. Pays on receipt of invoice, usually 30 days, net. Buys all rights. Model release required. Credit line sometimes given.

Tips: "Location is important for specific photo assignments. We use a substantial amount of photography for main auction company client—much internal production—freelance for special projects."

■**HEPWORTH ADVERTISING CO.**, 3403 McKinney Ave., Dallas TX 75204. (214)220-2415. President: S.W. Hepworth. Ad agency. Estab. 1952. Uses all media except P-O-P displays. Types of clients: industrial, consumer and financial. Examples of recent clients: Houston General Insurance, Holman Boiler, Hillcrest State Bank.

Needs: Uses photographers for trade magazines, direct mail, P-O-P displays, newspapers and audiovisual.

Specs: Uses 8 × 10 glossy color prints, 35mm transparencies.

First Contact & Terms: Cannot return material. Reports in 1-2 weeks. Pays $350 minimum/job; negotiates payment based on client's budget and photographer's previous experience/reputation. Submit portoflio by mail; solicits photos by assignment only. SASE. Pays on acceptance. Buys all rights (work-for-hire). Model release preferred. Sometimes gives credit line.

Tips: "For best relations with the supplier, we prefer to seek out a photographer in the area of the job location." Sees trend toward machinery shots. "Contact us by letter or phone."

Close-up

Bob Lukeman and Gordon Blocker
Lukeman-Blocker Productions
Dallas, Texas

As audiovisual producers Bob Lukeman and Gordon Blocker will tell you, anyone willing to jump into AV work with both feet will find opportunities are there for the taking. But, as they will also remind you, it takes the same degree of talent and passion as they have applied in their own careers to make the most of them.

"There's a whole range of opportunity for visual professionals, whether they're photographers, filmmakers or videographers," says Lukeman, of the Dallas, Texas-based AV firm, Lukeman-Blocker Productions. However, as he explains, talent is a given and self-motivation is crucial. "You get in and learn it. You can come from any background—editorial or advertising—and find ways to use your experience. Studio techniques are not an absolute. It's more important to have an 'eye' for the subject, move fast and get it all down."

Lukeman came into the business this way, shooting still work for print and advertising clients. And Blocker, whose domain has always been film and video, worked with a Houston television station after graduating from the University of Texas and opened his own production company by 1970. When the two met in the late 1970s, they began working together from time to time as freelancers, complementing each other's considerable strengths.

About four years ago, after this long, informal association, Lukeman and Blocker decided to join forces as a production team. "We realized we had a like-minded chemistry," says Blocker, noting that they look for the same quality in the talent they hire. "We share ideals and backgrounds, and our artistic abilities are interchangeable." As he notes, someone who is flexible and able "to fall in love with a project" will feel quite at home with them.

Throughout their collaboration, the partners have consistently produced award-winning work in documentaries, multi-image slide productions and video installations, better known as "video walls." Their clients have included ad agencies, banks and data processing companies, and nonprofit organizations. At this point, they are devoting increasing amounts of time to productions which incorporate computer imaging. Even with the increased use of high-tech tools, Blocker notes, the "basic creative processes remain constant." Not only is this happening with his company but also elsewhere in the industry, he adds. So there is growing demand for "someone who can grasp good production concepts and techniques."

Because of the high-tech revolution in AV, one might assume that the more formal education and visual training one has, the better. However, from their own experience, Lukeman and Blocker have found that little of what schools teach has application in the business world. For this reason, they will seldom hire someone straight out of school, but will opt for a freelancer with a track record.

According to Lukeman, familiarity with trends in production and client needs as well as with prospective AV firms, such as theirs, are vital to success. "A freelancer will get to first base with us if he has done his homework," he says. "Come to us offering ideas and be able to discuss some of our past projects. Once that initial contact is made, we look for multi-disciplinary expertise and decision-making ability. Ninety percent of what we do is business and the other ten is creative, so we look for someone who understands client relations and has a good philosophical grasp of the business, too."

One favorable trend for aspiring AV freelancers, says Lukeman, is an emphasis upon a gritty, grainy, photojournalistic look in AV stills and videos. "Even though an overall production might be very glitzy, the contributing elements often need to be rough, raw, realistic," he says, pointing out the wide range of production values currently being used. "The newer pro video cameras allow you to shoot low-light video of hard-to-shoot subjects. The newer film emulsions too are great. Freelancers can shoot high-speed stock of ambulances, helicopters, sporting events and so on, even with long lenses. In the finished production, they give the viewer a real good 'seat of the pants' feel for the subject."

Stressing the need for realistic expectations, both partners remind the aspiring AV freelancer that it takes "guts to make the transition" from print to the AV field. "There are some big differences," they observe, "but if the commitment is there, it's possible to get up to speed quickly."

— Suzanne Kay Pittman & Sam A. Marshall

Gordon Blocker and Bob Lukeman, (l-r), who are partners in the Texas-based production company, Lukeman-Blocker, encourage all photographers with ambitions in AV, film and video to "get in and learn it." As they realistically point out, it takes "guts to make the transition" from other markets, "but if the commitment's there, it's possible to get up to speed quickly."

LEVENSON & HILL, Box 619507, Dallas/Fort Worth Airport TX 75261. (214)556-0944. Ad agency. Creative Director: Fred Randall. Types of clients: retail products and service related.

Needs: Works with 2 photographers/month. Uses photographers for consumer and trade magazines, and newspapers.

Specs: Uses 35mm, 4×5 and 8×10 transparencies.

First Contact & Terms: Send unsolicited photos by mail for consideration; provide resume, business card, brochure, flyer or tearsheets to be kept on file for possible future assignments. Works with freelance photographers on an assignment basis only. Does not return unsolicited material. Pays $500-3,500/day; rates depend on usage and budget. Pays on receipt of invoice. Rights purchased with photos vary. Model release preferred. Credit lines may be given.

Tips: Prefers to see "fashion, dramatic lighting and new clean looks in samples submitted. Send brochures and tearsheets, call in a few weeks. We tend to shoot a lot at one time then have a lot of dead time."

*■LUKEMAN-BLOCKER PRODUCTIONS, Suite 103, 3003 Carlisle, Dallas TX 75204. (214)220-2034. FAX: (214)880-0325. AV firm. Contact: Bob Lukeman. Estab. 1984. Types of clients: corporate, nonprofit organizations and advertising/PR agencies. Examples of recent productions: Corporate Visitation Project for EDS Financial Services—videowall installation with interactive AV stations to provide information globally in headquarters facilities; Texas Seaport Museum Multi-Image Theater—consulting and installation of multi-image theater (15-projector, 6-channel stereo).

Audiovisual Needs: Works with 2-4 freelancers/month. Uses photographers for various corporate films and AV productions/installations, and self-promotion. Subjects depend on project. Reviews stock photos/film or video footage. Also, "requests are made for specific projects."

Specs: Uses b&w 8×10 prints; 35mm, 2¼×2¼, 4×5 and 8×10 transparencies; 16mm and 35mm motion picture film; BetaCam SP videotape.

First Contact & Terms: Query with resume of credits; provide resume, business card, brochure, flyer or tearsheets to be kept on file for possible future assignments. Works with freelancers on assignment only. SASE. Reports in one month. Pays $15-20/hour; pays $50-200/day. Each project has payments budgeted. Buys all rights and one-time rights. Model release preferred. Credit lines sometimes given.

Tips: Looks for freelancer's "artistic vision." Trend is towards more computer-enhanced imagery. "Get totally involved. Do self-assignments and lots of hard work" to make the transition into AV.

*■MARTINEZ & ASSOCIATES, 3500 Maple Ave #1070, Dallas TX 75219. (214)521-6060. FAX: (214)521-6066. Ad agency. Creative Coordinator: Debbie Diaz. Estab. 1985. Types of clients: snack food, beverage and transportation. Examples of ad campaigns: point-of-sale campaigns produced for Frito-Lay, Nestle and Tabasco.

Needs: Uses photographers for billboards, trade magazines, P-O-P displays, posters, newspapers and audiovisual. Reviews stock photos, film or video.

Audiovisual Needs: Uses videotape.

Specs: Uses 8×10 b&w prints; 2¼×2¼ transparencies; ½" and ¾" videotape.

First Contact & Terms: Send unsolicited photos by mail for consideration; provide resume, business card, brochure, flyer or tearsheets to be kept on file for possible future assignments. SASE. Reports in 1 month. Pays $750-1,500/day. Pays on receipt of invoice. Buys all rights (work-for-hire). Model release required. Credit line not given.

*■POLLARO MEDIA ADVERTISING & PRODUCTIONS, 400 West Main, Denison TX 75020. (214)463-2294. FAX: (214)465-2372. Ad agency. Art Director: Greg Mack. Estab. 1972. Types of clients: retail. Examples of ad campaigns: country music video for Atlantic Records; "Bored with Ford," TV/print campaign for Regional Oldsmobile; and Jessie White Series, TV ads for Tri State Acura Dealers.

Needs: Works with 10 freelance photographers—videographers/month. Uses photographers for billboards, consumer magazines, trade magazines, direct mail, P-O-P displays, catalogs, posters, newspapers, signage and audiovisual uses. Subjects include: retail automotive and miscellaneous retail. Interested in reviewing stock photos/video footage of various retail subjects.

Audiovisual Needs: Uses film and videotape.

First Contact & Terms: Query with samples; provide resume, business card, brochure, flyer or tearsheets to be kept on file for possible future assignments. Works with freelancers on assignment basis only. Cannot return material. Reports as needed. Payment varies according to project. Pays within 30 days. Buys one-time rights. Model release required; photo captions preferred. Credit line given sometimes, depending on project.

■**CARL RAGSDALE ASSOC., INC.**, 4725 Stillbrooke, Houston TX 77035. (713)729-6530. President: Carl Ragsdale. Types of clients: industrial and documentary film users.
Needs: Uses photographers for multimedia productions, films, still photography for brochures. Subjects include: industrial subjects—with live sound—interiors and exteriors.
Specs: Uses 35mm, 2¼ × 2¼, 4 × 5 transparencies; 16mm, 35mm film.
First Contact & Terms: Provide resume to be kept on file for possible future assignments. Works with freelancers by assignment only. Does not return unsolicited material. Pays $350-800/day; negotiable. Pays upon delivery of film. Buys all rights.
Tips: "Do not call. We refer to our freelance file of resumes when looking for personnel. Swing from film to video is major change—most companies are now hiring in-house personnel to operate video equipment. Resurgence of oil industry should improve the overall use of visuals down here." Photographer should have "ability to operate without supervision on location. Send samples of coverage of the same type of assignment for which they are being hired."

TED ROGGEN ADVERTISING AND PUBLIC RELATIONS, Suite 224, 1800 Augusta Dr. James Place, Houston TX 77057. (713)789-6216. Contact: Ted Roggen. Ad agency and PR firm. Handles clients in construction, entertainment, food, finance, publishing, and travel. Photos used in billboards, direct mail, radio, TV, P-O-P displays, brochures, annual reports, PR releases, sales literature and trade magazines. Buys 25-50 photos/year; gives 50-75 assignments/year. Pays $25-35/b&w photo; $50-275/ color photo. Pays on acceptance. Model release required; captions preferred. Arrange a personal interview to show portfolio or query with samples. "Contact me personally." Local freelancers preferred. SASE. Reports in 2 weeks. Provide resume to be kept on file for possible future assignments.
B&W: Uses 5 × 7 glossy or matte prints; contact sheet OK.
Color: Uses 4 × 5 transparencies and 5 × 7 prints.

■**SANDERS, WINGO, GALVIN & MORTON ADVERTISING**, Suite 100, 4110 Rio Bravo, El Paso TX 79902. (915)533-9583. Creative Director: Roy Morton. Ad agency. Uses billboards, consumer and trade magazines, direct mail, foreign media, newspapers, P-O-P displays, radio and TV. Types of clients: retailing and apparel industries. Free client list. Deals with 5 photographers/year.
Specs: Uses b&w photos and color transparencies. Works with freelance filmmakers in production of slide presentations and TV commercials.
Payment & Terms: Pays $65-500/hour, $600-3,500/day, negotiates pay on photos. Buys all rights. Model release required.
Making Contact: Query with samples, list of stock photo subjects; send material by mail for consideration; or submit portfolio for review. SASE. Reports in 1 week.

*■**EVANS WYATT ADVERTISING & PUBLIC RELATIONS**, Suite 624, The Atrium Bldg., 5151 Flynn Pkwy., Corpus Christi TX 78411. (512)854-1661. Ad agency, PR firm. Owner: E. Wyatt. Estab. 1975. Types of clients: industrial, financial, healthcare, automotive, educational and retail.
Needs: Works with 3-5 freelance photographers—videographers/month. Uses photographers for consumer magazines, trade magazines, direct mail, catalogs, posters and newspapers. Subjects include people and industrial. Interested in reviewing stock photos/video footage of any subject matter.
Audiovisual Needs: Uses slide shows and videos.
Specs: Uses 5 × 7 glossy b&w/color prints; 35mm, 2¼ × 2¼ transparencies; ½" videotape.
First Contact & Terms: Query with resume of credits; query with list of stock photo subjects; query with samples; submit portfolio for review; provide resume, business card, brochure, flyer or tearsheets to be kept on file for possible future assignments. Works with freelancers on assignment basis only. Reports in 1 month. Pays $400-1,000/day; $50-500/job; negotiated in advance of assignment. Pays on receipt of invoice. Buys all rights (work-for-hire). Model release required; photo captions preferred. Credit line given sometimes, depending on client's wishes.
Tips: Resolution and contrast are expected. Wants to see "sharpness, clarity and reproduction possibilities." Also, creative imagery (mood, aspect, view and lighting). Advises freelancers to "do professional work with an eye to marketability. Pure art is used only rarely." Video demo tape should be ½" format.

■**ZACHRY ASSOCIATES, INC.**, 709 North 2nd, Box 1739, Abilene TX 79604. (915)677-1342. Vice President/Production: Marvin Kirkham. Types of clients: industrial, institutional, religious service.
Needs: Works with 2 photographers/month. Uses photographers for slide sets, videotapes and print. Subjects include industrial location, product, model groups.
Specs: Uses 5 × 7, 8 × 10 b&w prints; 8 × 10 color prints; 35mm, 2¼ × 2¼ transparencies; VHS videotape.
First Contact & Terms: Query with samples and stock photo list; provide resume, business card, self-promotion piece or tearsheets to be kept on file for possible future assignments. Works with freelancers by assignment only; interested in stock photos/footage. SASE. Reports as requested. Pay

negotiable. Pays on acceptance. Buys one-time and all rights. Model release required. Credit line usually given.

Utah

EVANS/SALT LAKE, 110 Social Hall Ave., Salt Lake City UT 84111. (801)364-7452. Ad agency. Art Director: Michael Cullis. Types of clients: industrial, finance.
Needs: Works with 2-3 photographers/month. Uses photographers for billboards, consumer and trade magazines, direct mail, P-O-P displays, posters and newspapers. Subject matter includes scenic and people.
Specs: Uses color prints and 35mm, 2¼×2¼ and 4×5 transparencies.
First Contact & Terms: Query with list of stock photo subjects; submit portfolio for review; provide resume, business card, brochure, flyer or tearsheets to be kept on file for possible future assignments. Works with freelance photographers on an assignment basis only. SASE. Reports in 1-2 weeks. Payment negotiable. Pays on receipt of invoice. Buys one-time rights. Model release required; captions preferred. Credit live given when possible.

FOTHERINGHAM & ASSOCIATES, Suite 300, 215 S. State St., Salt Lake UT 84111. (801)521-2903. Ad agency. Art Directors: Randy Stroman and Paul Christensen. Types of clients: industrial, financial, development, resort, retail, commercial, automotive, high-tech.
Needs: Works with 6 photographers/month. Uses photographers for trade magazines, direct mail, P-O-P displays, catalogs and newspapers. Purchases all subjects. "We're growing."
Specs: Uses 8×10 b&w and color prints; 35mm, 2¼×2¼ and 4×5 transparencies.
First Contact & Terms: Arrange a personal interview to show portfolio; query with samples; provide resume, business card, brochure, flyer or tearsheets to be kept on file for possible future assignments. Works with freelance photographers on an assignment basis only. Does not return unsolicited material. Reports in 2 weeks. Payment negotiated individually. Pays on receipt of invoice. Buys all rights or one-time rights. Model release required. Credit line sometimes given.

*■HARRIS & LOVE, INC., Suite 1800, 136 E. So. Temple, Salt Lake City UT 84111. (801)532-7333. FAX: (801)532-6029. Art Directors: Dan Bianchi and Preston Wood. Estab. 1938. Types of clients: industrial, retail and finance.
Needs: Works with 4 freelance photographers—filmmakers—videographers/month. Uses photographers for billboards, consumer magazines, trade magazines, newspapers and audiovisual. Needs mostly images of food and people. Interested in reviewing stock photos/film or video footage on people, science, health-care and industrial.
Audiovisual Needs: Contact Creative Directors, Bob Wassone and Mike Froster by phone or mail.
Specs: Uses 35mm, 2¼×2¼, 4×5 transparencies.
First Contact & Terms: Send unsolicited photos by mail for consideration; submit portfolio for review; provide resume, business card, brochure, flyer or tearsheets to be kept on file for possible future assignments. Works with freelancers on assignment basis only. SASE. Reports in 1-2 weeks. Pays $85-100/hour; $850-1,000/day; $350-400/job; $350/color photo; $300/b&w photo. Pays on receipt of invoice. Buys all rights (work-for-hire). Model release required. Credit line given sometimes, depending on client, outlet or usage.
Tips: In freelancer's portfolio or demos, wants to see "craftsmenship, mood of photography and creativity." Sees trend toward "more abstract" images in advertising. "Most of our photography is a total buy out (work for hire). Photographer can only reuse images in his promotional material."

■PAUL S. KARR PRODUCTIONS, UTAH DIVISION, 1024 N. 250 East, Orem UT 84057. (801)226-8209. Vice President & Manager: Michael Karr. Types of clients: education, business, industry, TV-spot and theatrical spot advertising. Provides inhouse production services of sound recording, looping, printing & processing, high-speed photo instrumentation as well as production capabilities in 35mm and 16mm.
Subject Needs: Same as Arizona office but additionally interested in motivational human interest material—film stories that would lead people to a better way of life, build better character, improve situations, strengthen families.
First Contact & Terms: Query with resume of credits and advise if sample reel is available. Pays by the job, negotiates payment based on client's budget and ability to handle the work. Pays on production. Buys all rights. Model release required.

Vermont

■**MEDIA FORUM INTERNATIONAL, LTD.**, RFD 1, Box 107, West Danville, VT 05873. Contact: Editor, "Media Forum Books."
Needs: "We do international (multi-lingual) work: publish, translate and produce film/video, photo work. We use limited outsiders—by assignment only."
First Contact & Terms: Works with freelance photographers by assignment only. Pays per photo or by the job. Pays on acceptance. Buys one-time rights or all rights (work-for-hire). Captions preferred; model releases required. Credit line given.

Virginia

*■**CARLTON COMMUNICATIONS INC.**, 300 W. Franklin St., Richmond VA 23220. (804)780-1701. FAX: (804)225-8036. Ad agency and PR firm. Vice President/Creative Director: Dan Chamberlain. Types of clients: tourism, hi-tech, retirement, financial, and economic development. Examples of ad campaigns: safety belt campaign for State of Virginia; West Coast Campaign for Lawyers Title; and repeat work for Pioneer Federal Savings Bank.
Needs: Works with 2-3 freelancers/month. Uses photographers for billboards, consumer magazines, trade magazines, direct mail, P-O-P displays, catalogs, posters, newspapers, signage and audiovisual.
Audiovisual Needs: Uses film and videotape.
Specs: Uses b&w print; 35mm, 2¼×2¼, 4×5, 8×10 transparencies; 35mm or 16mm film; Betacam videotape.
First Contact & Terms: Provide resume, business card, brochure, flyer or tearsheets to be kept on file for possible future assignments. Works with freelancers on assignment basis only. SASE. Reports in 1 month. Pays $1,200/day; by project or day rate. Pays on receipt of invoice. Buys all rights (work-for-hire). Model release required. Credit line sometimes given.
Tips: In freelancer's portfolio or demos, looks for "high level of quality." Sees trend back toward black-and-white work. "Persistence" is best for breaking in with this firm.

Washington

***G.R. GOOD AND ASSOCIATES**, 24014 57th Ave. S.E., Woodinville WA 98072. (206)486-4446. Ad agency and PR firm. President: Gary Good. Estab. 1988. Types of clients: high-technology and industrial.
Needs: Works with 1 photographer/month. Uses photographers for trade magazines. Subjects include product photography.
Specs: Uses 8×10 glossy b&w/color prints; 4×5 transparencies.
First Contact & Terms: Query with list of stock photo subjects; provide resume, business card, brochure, flyer or tearsheets to be kept on file for possible future assignments. Works with local freelancers only. Cannot return material. Reports in 1 month. Pays $1,000-2,500/assignment. Pays on receipt of invoice. Buys all rights (work-for-hire); negotiable. Other rights sometimes purchased. Model release preferred. Credit line usually not given; negotiable.

■**KOSTOV AND ASSOCIATES**, 221 First Ave. W. #120, Seattle WA 98119. (206)285-2797. President: Michael Kostov. Full service audiovisual production studio.
Needs: Uses freelance photographers for audiovisual presentations; gives 6-12 assignments/year.
Specs: Uses 35mm transparencies.
First Contact & Terms: Provide resume, business card, brochure, flyer or tearsheets to be kept on file for possible future assignments. Deals with local freelancers only. Interested in stock photos. Does not return unsolicited material. Pays $250-400/day. Buys all rights, but will negotiate. Model releases preferred. Credit line sometimes given. Report time varies.
Tips: Interested in photographer's best work in slide format. "There is more need for stock usage for slide shows at a rate specific for AV."

MATTHEWS ASSOC. INC., Suite 1018, 603 Stewart St., Seattle WA 98101. (206)340-0680. PR firm. President: Dean Matthews. Types of clients: industrial.
Needs: Works with 0-3 freelance photographers/month. Uses photographers for trade magazines, direct mail, P-O-P displays, catalogs and public relations. Frequently uses architectural photography; other subjects include building products.

Specs: Uses 8×10 b&w and color prints; 35mm, 2¼×2¼ and 4×5 transparencies.
First Contact & Terms: Arrange a personal interview to show portfolio if local. If not, provide resume, business card, brochure, flyer or tearsheets to be kept on file for possible future assignments. Works with freelance photographers on assignment basis only. SASE. Pays by the hour, day or job. Pays on receipt of invoice. Buys all rights. Model release preferred.
Tips: Samples preferred depends on client or job needs. "Be good at industrial photography."

West Virginia

■**CAMBRIDGE CAREER PRODUCTS**, One Players Club Dr., Charleston WV 25311. (800)468-4227. FAX: (304)344-5583. President: E.T. Gardner, Ph.D.. Managing Director: Amy Pauley.
Needs: Works with 2 still photographers and 3 videographers per month. Uses photographers for multimedia productions, videotapes and catalog still photography. "We buy b&w prints and color transparencies for use in our 9 catalogs."
Specs: 5×7 or 8×10 b&w prints; 35mm, 2¼×2¼, 4×5, and 8×10 transparencies and videotape.
First Contact & Terms: Video producers arrange a personal interview to show portfolio. Still photographers should submit portfolio by mail. Interested in stock photos/footage on sports, hi-tech, young people, parenting, general interest topics and other. SASE. Reports in 2 weeks. Pays $20-80/b&w photo, $250-850/color photo and $8,000-45,000 per video production. Buys one-time and all rights (work-for-hire). Credit line given. "Cover color transparencies used for catalog covers and video production, but not for b&w catalog shots."
Tips: Still photographers should call our customer service department and get a copy of *all* our educational catalogs. Review the covers and inside shots, then send us appropriate high-quality material. Video production firms should visit our headquarters with examples of work. For still color photographs we look for high-quality, colorful, eye catching transparencies. B&w photographs should be on sports, home economics (cooking, sewing, dating, child rearing, parenting, food, etc.), and guidance (dating, sex, drugs, alcohol, careers, etc.) We have stopped producing educational filmstrips and now produce only full-motion video. Always need good b&w or color still photography for catalogs."

Wisconsin

BIRDSALL-VOSS & ASSOCIATES, INC., 1355 W. Towne Square Rd., Mequon WI 53209. (414)241-4890. Ad agency. Art Directors: Scotti Larson. Estab. 1984. Types of clients: travel, healthcare, financial, industrial and fashion clients such as Musebeck Shoes, Piedmont Vacations, Continental Vacations, WFSI-Milwaukee and Lavelle Industries.
Needs: Uses 5 freelance photographers/month. Works with billboards, consumer magazines, trade magazines, direct mail, catalogs, posters and newspapers. Subjects include: travel and healthcare. Interested in reviewing stock photos of travel scenes in Caribbean, California, Nevada, Mexico and Florida.
Specs: Uses 35mm, 2¼×2¼, 4×5, 8×10 transparencies.
First Contact & Terms: Arrange a personal interview to show portfolio or query with resume of credits or list of stock photo subjects; provide resume, business card, brochure, flyer or tearsheets to be kept on file for possible future assignments. Cannot return material. Pays 30 days on receipt of invoice. Buys all rights. Model release required.
Tips: Looks for "primarily cover shots for travel brochures; ads selling Florida, the Caribbean, Mexico, California and Nevada destinations."

MCDONALD DAVIS & ASSOCIATES, 250 W. Coventry Ct., Glendale WI 53217. (414)228-1990. Ad agency, PR firm, marketing consultants, all phases. Senior Art Directors: Laura Manthey, Bob Shriner, Carrie Nygen and Chuck Schiller. Types of clients: healthcare—"we are major leaders in this throughout the country;" also, Wisconsin Lottery. Client list free with SASE.
Needs: Works with 10 photographers/month; staff of 4 art directors. Uses freelance directors for billboards, consumer and trade magazines, direct mail, P-O-P displays, catalogs, posters, signage and newspapers. Subjects include healthcare, medical.

Specs: Uses 16×20 glossy b&w and color prints; 2¼×2¼ transparencies.
First Contact & Terms: Arrange a personal interview to show portfolio; query with list of stock photo subjects; submit portfolio for review; provide resume, business card, brochure, flyer or tearsheets to be kept on file for possible future assignments. Works with local freelance photographers on assignment basis only. SASE. Reports in 3 weeks. Pays $600-1,200/day; per photo, depends on usage. Pays on receipt of invoice. Buys all rights. Model release required.
Tips: Prefers to see medical, in color and b&w.

■**NELSON PRODUCTIONS, INC.,** 1533 N. Jackson St., Milwaukee WI 53202. (414)271-5211. President: David Nelson. Typse of Clients: industry, advertising. Produces motion pictures, videotapes, and slide shows.
Subject Needs: Industrial, people, graphic art and titles.
Specs: Uses transparencies.
Payment & Terms: Pays by the project. Buys one-time rights. Model release required.
Making Contact: Query with resume of credits or send material by mail for consideration. "We're looking for high quality photos with an interesting viewpoint."

WALDBILLIG & BESTEMAN, INC., 6225 University Ave., Madison WI 53705. (608)238-4767. Vice President/Senior Art Director: Gary Hutchins. Manager, Art Department: Tom Senatori. Types of clients: industrial, financial and health care.
Needs: Works with 4-8 freelance photographers/month. Uses photographers for consumer and trade magazines, direct mail, P-O-P displays, catalogs, posters, newspapers, brochures and annual reports. Subject matter varies.
Specs: Uses 8x9 glossy b&w and color prints; 35mm, 2¼×2¼, 4×5 transparencies.
First Contact & Terms: Provide resume, business card, brochure, flyer or tearsheets to be kept on file for possible future assignments. Works with freelance photographers on assignment basis only. Reports in 2 weeks. $100-200/b&w photo; $200-400/color photo. Pays on receipt of invoice. Buys all rights. Model release and captions required.
Tips: "Send unsolicited samples that do *not* have to be returned. Indicate willingness to do *any* type job. Indicate he/she has access to full line of equipment."

Canada

■**JACK CHISHOLM FILM PRODUCTIONS LTD.,** 229 Niagara St., Toronto, ON M6J 2L5 Canada. (416)366-4933. FAX: (416)366-2142. Production house and stock shot film and video library. President: Mary Di Tursi. Estab. 1956. Types of clients: finance and industrial, government, corporate and advertising agencies.
Needs: Uses stock film and video footage.
First Contact & Terms: Works with freelancers on an assignment basis only.

EVANS ADVERTISING AGENCY INC., Suite 10, 2395 Cawthra Rd., Mississauga, ON L5A 2W8 Canada. (416)848-1818. Ad agency. President: Robert Evans. Types of clients: industrial, fashion.
Needs: Works with 3-5 freelance photographers/month. Uses photographers for consumer and trade magazines, direct mail, catalogs and newspapers. Subject matter varies.
First Contact & Terms: Provide resume, business card, brochure, flyer or tearsheets to be kept on file for possible future assignments. Works with freelance photographers on assignment basis only. SAE and IRCs. Reports in 2 weeks. Pays per day or job. Pays on receipt of invoice. Buys all rights. Model release required.
Tips: Prefers to see variety, adaptability, technique.

■**WARNE MARKETING & COMMUNICATIONS,** Suite 810, 111 Avenue Rd., Toronto, ON M5R 3MI Canada. (416)927-0881. FAX: (416)927-1676. Ad agency. President: Keith Warne. Estab. 1979. Types of clients: business-to-business.
Needs: Works with 5 photographers/month. Uses photographers for trade magazines, direct mail, P-O-P displays, catalogs and posters. Subjects include: in-plant photography, studio set-ups and product shots. Special subject needs include in-plant shots for background use.
Audiovisual Needs: Uses both videotape and slides for product promotion.
Specs: Uses 8×10 glossy b&w and color prints; also 4×5 transparencies.
First Contact & Terms: Send letter citing related experience plus 2 or 3 samples. Works with freelance photographers on an assignment basis only. Does not return unsolicited material. Reports in 2 weeks. Pays $1,000-2,000/day. Pays within 30 days. Buys all rights. Model release required.

Tips: In portfolio/samples, prefers to see industrial subjects and creative styles. "We look for lighting knowledge, composition and imagination." Send letter and 3 samples, and wait for trial assignment.

Foreign

INTER-IMAGE, INC., No. 28, Mori Building, 4-16-13, Nishi Azabu, Minato-Ku, Tokyo 106 Japan. Tel (03)407-8691. Ad agency. Management Supervisor: Mark Homchick. Estab. 1975. Largest clients are Kawasaki (motorcycle and Jet Ski® watercraft consumer products plus industrial) and Canada Tourism/Canadian Airlines.
Needs: Works with 4 freelance photographers/month. Uses photographers for billboards, consumer magazines, trade magazines, direct mail, P-O-P displays, catalogs, posters, signage, newspapers and ads in dealer kits. Subjects include motorcycles and Jet Ski® watercraft.
Specs: Uses 35mm, 2¼×2¼, 4×5 and 8×10 transparencies.
First Contact & Terms: Provide resume, business card, brochure, flyer or tearsheets to be kept on file for possible future assignments. SASE. Reports ASAP; 2 months maximum. Buys all rights. Payment varies greatly, depending on job/usage. Standard rates. Payment made within 30 days of invoice assuming photos are acceptable. Model release required.
Tips: Prefers to see for Kawasaki: great action and/or special studio effects; for Canada accounts: unique nature photography.

Advertising, Public Relations and Audiovisual Firms/'90-'91 changes

The following advertising, public relations and audiovisual firms do not appear in the 1991 edition of *Photographer's Market* for a number of reasons. Primarily, they may be listings which appeared in the 1990 edition but did not respond to our request for an update of their information, have gone out of business or are overstocked with submissions. Also listed here are a number of firms which photographers have frequently asked us to have in the book but which did not return information to us.

AC&R Advertising (did not respond)
Ackerman, Hood & McQueen, Inc. (did not respond)
Ad Hoc Marketing Resources, Inc. (did not respond)
Aetna Life & Casualty (did not respond)
Alonso Y Asociados, S.A. (did not respond)
American List Counsel (did not respond)
Arnold & Co. (did not respond)
Aurelio & Friends, Inc. (did not respond)
Authenticated News International (did not respond)
Bafetti Communications (no longer in market)
Barr Films (did not respond)
Bauerlein Inc. (did not respond)
BBDO Worldwide Inc. (did not respond)
Bennett Lab (did not respond)
Bernstein-Rein Advertising Inc. (did not respond)
Board of Jewish Education (did not respond)
Brower, Lowe & Hall Advertising (did not respond)
Broyles Allebaugh & Davis, Inc. (did not respond)

Bryan/Donald Inc. (did not respond)
Burnett Company Inc., Leo (did not respond)
Burrell Communications Group (did not respond)
Buser & Assoc., Joe (not reviewing work)
Cabscott Broadcast Productions (did not respond)
Campbell-Mithun-Esty (did not respond)
Carter Advertising (did not respond)
Charter Marketing Group (did not respond)
Chevalier Advertising (no longer in market)
Chiat/Day, San Francisco, CA (did not respond)
Chiat/Day, Venice, CA (did not respond)
Cinema East Corp. (did not respond)
Cole & Webster (did not respond)
Corporate Media Communications, Inc. (did not respond)
Cramer-Krasselt Co. (did not respond)
Darby Media Group (did not respond)
DDB Needham Retail (did not

respond)
DDB Needham Worldwide, Inc. (did not respond)
Della Femina, McNamee W.C.R.S. (did not respond)
Diamond & Assoc. (did not respond)
Doyle & Partners Inc. (did not respond)
Eisner & Assoc. (did not respond)
Elms Productions, Charles (did not respond)
EMC Publishing (did not respond)
ENT/Gates Productions (did not respond)
Estey-Hoover Inc. (did not respond)
Fahlgren & Swink, Inc. (did not respond)
FCB/Leber Katz Partners (did not respond)
Fellers Fellers & Gaddis (did not respond)
Ferguson Associates, Inc., Thomas G. (did not respond)
Fire Prevention Through Films Inc. (did not respond)
Foote, Cone & Belding Communications Inc. (did not respond)

Furman Advertising Co., Inc. (did not respond)

Galloway-Wallace Advertising (did not respond)

Gardner Advertising (no longer in market)

Garner & Assoc. (did not respond)

Gerding Productions (did not respond)

GGH & M Advertising (did not respond)

Goodman & Associates (not reviewing work)

Graphic Workshop Inc. (did not respond)

Griffin Bacal, Inc. (did not respond)

Group Two Advertising Inc./ Florida (did not respond)

Gulf State Advertising (did not respond)

Gumpertz, Bentley, Fried (did not respond)

Guymark Studios (did not respond)

Handley & Miller Inc. (did not respond)

HDM (did not respond)

Hill, Holliday, Connors, Cosmopulos Inc. (did not respond)

Image Producers Inc., The (did not respond)

Interand Corp. (did not respond)

Izen Enterprises (did not respond)

JEF Films Inc. (did not respond)

JRB Advertising (did not respond)

Ketchum Communications Inc. (did not respond)

Key Advertising (did not respond)

Keystone Press Agency (did not respond)

King Public Relations, Lis (did not respond)

Kobs & Draft Advertising Inc. (did not respond)

Lardas Advertising, Christopher (did not respond)

Lefton Company Inc., Al Paul (did not respond)

Lewis Advertising (did not respond)

Lewis, Gilman & Kynett Inc. (did not respond)

Lipman, Richmond, & Greene (did not respond)

Long, Haymes & Carr, Inc. (did not respond)

Lyons Graphics, Inc. (not reviewing work)

Madden & Goodrum (did not respond)

Marshfilm Inc. (did not respond

Martin/Williams Advertising, Inc. (did not respond)

Masto, Dagastine & Assoc. (did not respond)

McCann-Erickson Worldwide (did not respond)

McKinney & Silver (did not respond)

Meier Advertising (did not respond)

Mekler/Ansell Assoc. (did not respond)

Meriweather Inc., Arthur (did not respond)

Muchnick Co., Paul (did not respond)

National Teaching Aids Inc. (did not respond)

Oglivy & Mather Inc. (did not respond)

Organization Management (did not respond)

Park Place Group (did not respond)

Philadelphia Music Works (did not respond)

Proconsul (did not respond)

Raymond, Kowal & Wicks (did not respond)

Ross Roy Group (did not respond)

Royal Communications Inc. (did not respond)

Ruhr/Paragon Inc. (did not respond)

Spelman Public Relations (not reviewing work)

Stern Communications, Lee Edward (did not respond)

Sullivan Co., Daniel F. (did not respond)

Tarragano Co. (did not respond)

Technical Educational Consultants (did not respond)

Texas Pacific Film Video (did not respond)

Thompson Advertising, Donohue (did not respond)

Tulchin Studios (did not respond)

Video Vision (did not respond)

Walt Disney Home Video (did not respond)

Waring & Larosa (did not respond)

Weston Woods Studio (did not respond)

Windsor Total Video (did not respond)

Looking at the multitude of books which use photographic illustration, one can see that book publishers depend heavily upon the work of photographers. However, as the book publishing market responds to the same economic pressures affecting other major markets, photographers may find sales and assignments with book publishers more scarce and the income less rewarding. The good news for freelancers, though, is that publishers tend to purchase limited rights to photos, such as book rights or one-time reprint rights. While the payment from one sale may be less than desired, it's possible to make up for it with multiple sales to different markets.

In spite of a generally more cautious and conservative attitude among book publishers, freelance photographers will find that the market is not suddenly in an "all or none" condition. For instance, there are more than 130 markets in this edition of *Photographer's Market*. In these markets, there is still a variety of opportunities open to the freelancer — some that will pay well — provided that the photographer can deliver images that help meet the publisher's special needs. Stock agencies fill these needs to a certain extent (see Stock Photography Spotlight, on page 5), but dealing with these agencies can often take a publisher a great deal of research time. Freelancers can sometimes save the publisher from spending this time by finding out their exact needs and then getting the right picture to the photo buyer at the right time — and at the right price.

Since many of the images purchased from freelancers are from the photographer's stock, it is often appropriate for the photographer to query the art director, photo editor or other photo buyer with a stock photo list — plus samples or tearsheets if requested — as the initial contact.

Aside from photos that are good- to top-quality and that are up-to-date in terms of styles and themes, book publishers look for various qualities when dealing with freelancers. Some publishers will want photos that speak to a very specific audience, such as a strong regional readership or one concerned with a shared special interest. Some publishers will have a need for a large quantity of photos from which to make selections or to develop an internal stock file, while others will specify only a few very select photos that will possibly meet their needs. Most place a great deal of importance on the overall professionalism of the freelancer, in everything from presentations or portfolios to pricing. In particular, one need quickly becoming common to all book publishers is to keep down their costs. Accordingly, they expect a photographer to "be flexible" on his pricing, or they turn to one who *is* flexible or to stock photo agencies.

Payment rates in the book publishing market vary a great deal, from the low end to above average. Publishers typically pay on either a per-image basis or by time, such as an hour or day rate. Many times the method of determining payment will depend upon whether it's for one or a few images, for a large bulk purchase of stock, or for assigned work.

Remember that much of your success in this market can come from multiple sales. However, unless a market indicates an "OK" in regard to simultaneous submissions or previously published work, you may be limited in reselling an image, at least for the duration of the first usage. So, read the listings closely for related information and plan your marketing strategy carefully to maximize your sales.

*A.D. BOOK CO., 10E. 39 St., 6th Floor, New York NY 10016. (212)889-6500. Art Director: Van Aaron. Estab. 1949. Publishes trade books for advertising visual professionals. Photos used for text illustration, book covers and dust jackets. Buys 20 freelance photos annually and gives 5-10 assignments annually.

Subject Needs: Current advertising. Model release and photo captions required.
Specs: Uses 8×11 b&w prints; 35mm transparencies.
Payment & Terms: Pays $100-350/color photo; $50-100/b&w photo. Credit line given sometimes. Buys book rights.
Making Contact: Provide resume, business card, brochure, flyer or tearsheets to be kept on file for possible future use. Interested in stock photos. SASE. Reports in 1 month. Photo guidelines free with SASE.

AMERICAN ARBITRATION ASSOCIATION, 140 West 51st St., New York NY 10020-1203. (212)484-4000. Editorial Director: Linda Miller. Publishes law-related materials on all facets of resolving disputes in the labor, commercial, construction and insurance areas. Photos used for text illustration. Buys 100 photos annually; assigns 15 freelance projects annually. Examples of recently published titles: *The Arbitration Journal,* cover and text; *Arbitration Times,* text; and *AAA Annual Report,* text.
Subject Needs: General business and industry-specific photos. Model release and photo captions preferred.
Specs: Uses 8×10 glossy b&w prints; 35mm transparencies.
Payment & Terms: Pays $250-400/color photo, $75-100/b&w photo, $75-100/hour. Credit lines given "depending on usage." Buys one-time rights. Also buys all rights "if we hire the photographer for a shoot." Simultaneous submissions and previously published work OK.
Making Contact: Provide resume, business card, brochure, flyer or tearsheets to be kept on file for possible future assignments. Interested in stock photos. SASE. Reports "as time permits."
Tips: In samples, looks especially for "good business and meeting photos." Over time, company is using less "photography because of scarcity of good photos in our area."

AND BOOKS, 702 S. Michigan, South Bend IN 46618. (219)232-3134. Senior Editor/Visuals: Emil Krause. Publishes nonfiction, adult and general. Photos used for text illustration and book covers. Buys 5-10 photos annually; gives 2-5 freelance assignments annually.
Subject Needs: Variable. Model release required; captions preferred.
Specs: Open.
Payment & Terms: Variable. Credit line given. Buys all rights. Simultaneous submissions and previously published work OK.
Making Contact: Provide resume, business card, brochure, flyer or tearsheets to be kept on file for possible future assignments. Interested in stock photos. SASE. Reports in 1 month.

ARCsoft PUBLISHERS, Box 132, Woodsboro MD 21798. (301)845-8856. President: Anthony R. Curtis. Publishes "books in personal computing and electronics trade paperbacks, space science, and journalism." Photos used for book covers. Buys 10 photos annually; gives 10 freelance assignments annually.
Subject Needs: Action shots of personal computer/human interaction action shots and electronics and space science close-up. Captions required.
Specs: Uses 35mm, 2¼×2¼ and 4×5 slides.
Payment & Terms: Payment per color photo or by the job; varies. Credit line given. Buys one-time rights and book rights. Simultaneous submissions and previously published work OK.
Making Contact: Query with resume of credits, samples or with list of stock photo subjects; provide business card, brochure, flyer, tearsheets to be kept on file for possible future assignments. SASE. Reports in 1 month.
Tips: "Send query and limit lists or samples to subjects in which we have an interest. We also publish the monthly news magazine *Space Today* and the annual *Space Almanac.*"

ARJUNA LIBRARY PRESS, 1025 Garner St., D, Space 18,Colorado Springs CO 80905. Director: Joseph A. Uphoff, Jr. Estab. 1979. Publishes research monographs, theory, biography, commentary in fine arts, surrealism and visual poetics with associated developments in mathematics. Photos used for text illustration and book covers. Example of Recently Published Title: *A Message From the Ruins,* metaphorical illustration.

The asterisk before a listing indicates that the market is new in this edition. New markets are often the most receptive to freelance submissions.

Subject Needs: Surrealist (imagist, static drama, cinematic expressionism) suitable for a general audience including children. Model release, photo captions preferred.

Specs: Uses 5 × 7 glossy (maximum size) b&w and color prints.

Payment & Terms: Payment is one copy of published pamphlet. Credit line given. Rights dependent on additional use. Simultaneous submissions and previously published work OK.

Making Contact: Query with samples, send unsolicited photos by mail for consideration, submit portfolio for review; provide resume, business card, brochure, flyer or tearsheets to be kept on file for possible future assignments. Cannot return material. Reports in "one year."

Tips: Looks for "surrealist strangeness, chiaroscuro, closed composition, conservative metaphor and image, relevant contemporary and historical symbolism" in photos reviewed. "This is the ground floor, we are making a significant reputation for ourselves but profitability is slow in arriving. We do provide a showcase for the avant garde. This effort is good advertising for the artist who wants to associate with current theoretical matters and the struggle progress in the arts demands."

ART DIRECTION BOOK CO., 10 E. 39th St., 6th Floor, New York NY 10016. (212)889-6500. Art Director: Ann Rutledge. Publishes advertising art, design, photography. Photos used for dust jackets. Buys 10 photos annually.

Subject Needs: Advertising. Model release and captions required.

Payment & Terms: Pays $200 minimum/b&w photo; $500 minimum/color photo. Buys one-time rights. Simultaneous submissions OK.

Making Contact: Submit portfolio for review. Uses photos by assignment only. SASE. Reports in 1 month.

ASHLEY BOOKS, INC., 4600 W. Commercial Blvd., Ft. Lauderdale FL 33319. (305)739-2221. Vice President: Joan Calder. Publishes cookbooks and other books. Sometimes needs photos for text illustration. Number of freelance photos bought annually varies; assigns about 25 freelance projects annually.

Subject Needs: Food, wines and the like.

Specs: Uses 5½ × 8½, 6 × 9 b&w and color prints.

Payment and Terms: Payment depends on quality of work and needs at time of job. Credit line given. Buys book rights. Simultaneous and previously published submissions OK.

Making Contact: Query with resume of credits; query with samples (do not send samples that need to be returned); provide resume, business card, brochure, flyer or tearsheets to be kept on file for possible future assignments. Always send query first. Deals with local freelancers only. Reports in 3 weeks; may be a little longer if work is seriously considered.

Tips: "We are only looking for photographers for our cookbooks or book jackets. Don't send valuable material. If you take exceptional photos your work should generally speak for itself. If your work is rejected, don't be discouraged, different jobs require different needs."

AUGSBURG FORTRESS, PUBLISHERS, Publication Services, Box 1209, Minneapolis MN 55440. (612)330-3300. Publishes Protestant/Lutheran books (mostly adult trade), religious education materials, audiovisual resources and periodicals. Photos used for text illustration, book covers, periodical covers and church bulletins. Buys 150 color photos and 1,000 b&w photos annually; very little work assigned annually.

Subject Needs: People of all ages, variety of races, activities, moods and unposed. In color, wants to see nature, seasonal, church year and mood.

Specs: Uses 8 × 10 glossy or semiglossy b&w prints, 35mm and 2¼ × 2¼ color transparencies.

Payment & Terms: Pays $25-75/b&w photo; $40-125/color photo and occasional assignments (fee negotiated). Credit line nearly always given. Buys one-time rights. Simultaneous submissions and previously published work OK.

Making Contact: Send material by mail for consideration. "We are interested in stock photos." Provide tearsheets to be kept on file for possible future assignments. SASE. Reports in 6-8 weeks. Guidelines free with SASE. "Write for guidelines, then submit on a regular basis."

AVE MARIA PRESS, University Campus, Notre Dame IN 46556. (219)287-2831. Production Manager: Paul J. Waddy. "We are primarily publishers of Catholic/Christian religious materials with emphasis on religious education, the sacraments, prayer, devotional books, the liturgy, children's books, etc." Photos used for text illustrations, promotional materials, book covers, dust jackets and audio cassette boxcards. Recent titles include "Journey Without End," "Prayer and Remembrance," "Woman To Woman." In all cases, photos used for covers. Buys 20-40 freelance photos annually.

Subject Needs: "Individuals, couples, families and groups—meaningful, real-life situations, not obviously posed or overly dramatic; also scenic, still life and nature." Model release preferred.
Specs: Uses b&w prints, 8×10 preferred, glossy finish.
Payment & Terms: Book jackets and paperback covers $50; inside book illustrations $30; miscellaneous use in catalogs, ads, etc. $10; cassette boxcards and slip cases $20. "Rates listed are subject to increase for an exceptional piece of work or to meet an exceptional need." Credit line given on copyright page. Buys one-time rights. Simultaneous submissions and previously published work OK. SASE. Reports in 1 month.
Making Contact: Send SASE for photo guidelines and rate card (1 page). In particular, wants to see "imaginative, new presentations of familiar subjects . . . photos that *suggest* a strong spiritual sense, or lack of it." Interested in stock photos. "Provide up to 10 samples of best work for us to maintain in our 'permanent' file."

AVON BOOKS, 105 Madison Ave., New York NY 10016. (212)481-5662. Art Director: Tom Egner. Publishes adult and juvenile fiction and non-fiction in mass market and soft-cover trade. Photos used for book covers. Gives several assignments monthly.
Subject Needs: Hand-tinted photographs, "mood shots"; food still lifes and stock photography.
Specs: Uses 35mm, 4×5 and 8×10 color transparencies.
Payment & Terms: Generally pays $600-1,200 for shots already taken; $1,000 and up for shoots, though seldom done; depends on job. Buys one time reproduction rights for the book, plus all advertising and promotional rights.
Making Contact: Drop off portfolio on Thursdays; provide business card, flyer, brochure and tearsheets to be kept on file for possible future assignments. SASE. "Our photo needs vary with each assignment. Send in samples or drop off a portfolio."

BEAUTIFUL AMERICA PUBLISHING COMPANY, 9725 SW Commerce Circle, PO Box 646, Wilsonville OR 97070. (503)682-0173. FAX: (503)682-0175. Librarian: Beverly A. Paul. Estab. 1986. Publishes nature, scenic, pictorial and history. Photos used for text illustration, pictorial. Buys 400-500 freelance photos annually, and assigns 10 freelance projects annually. Examples of recently published titles: *East Coast Victorians*, *U.S. 101 A Highway Adventure* and *Beautiful America's Idaho*.
Subject Needs: Nature and scenic. Model release and captions required.
Specs: Uses 35mm, 2¼×2¼, 4×5, and 8×10 transparencies.
Payment & Terms: Payment varies based on project; $100 min./color photo. Credit line given. Buys one-time rights. Simultaneous submissions and previously published work OK.
Making Contact: Provide resume, business card, brochure, flyer or tearsheets to be kept on file for possible future assignments. "Do NOT send unsolicited photos!!" Interested in stock photos. Reports in 1 month.

*BEHRMAN HOUSE INC., 235 Watchung Ave., West Orange NJ 07052. (201)669-0447. Editor: Ms. Ruby G. Strauss. Estab. 1921. Publishes Judaica textbooks. Photos used for text illustration, promotional materials and book covers. Recently published title: *My Jewish World*.
Subject Needs: Model release preferred.
Specs: No specific specifications for photography submitted/used.
Payment & Terms: Pays $50-500/color photo, $20-250/b&w photo. Credit line given.
Making Contact: Query with resume of credits. Query with samples. Provide resume, business card, brochure, flyer or tearsheets to be kept on file for possible future assignments. Interested in stock photos. SASE. Reports in 3 weeks. No photo guidelines.
Tips: Company trend is increasing use of photography.

*BLUE BIRD PUBLISHING, 1713 E. Broadway #306, Tempe AZ 85282. (602)968-4088. Owner: Cheryl Gorder. Estab. 1985. Publishes adult trade books on home education, home business, social issues (homelessness), etc. Photos used for text illustration. Buys 40 photos annually; offers 3 freelance assignments annually. Examples of recently published titles: *Homeless: Without Addresses in America* and *Home Business Resource Guide*. In both, photos used for text illustration.
Subject Needs: Types of photos "depends on subject matter of forthcoming books. We would like to see more freelance photos on the homeless in 1990." Model release required; photo captions preferred.
Specs: Uses b&w and color prints.
Payment & Terms: Pays $25-150/color photo, $25-150/b&w photo; also pays flat fee for bulk purchase of stock photos. Buys book rights. Simultaneous submissions and previously published work OK.
Making Contact: Query with list of stock photo subjects; provide resume, business card, brochure, flyer or tearsheets to be kept on file for possible future assignments. Interested in stock photos. SASE. Reports in 1 month. No photo guidelines available.

Tips: "We will continue to grow rapidly in the coming years and will have a growing need for stock photos and freelance work. Send a list of stock photos for our file. If a freelance assignment comes up in your area, we will call."

BONUS BOOK, INC., 160 E. Illinois St., Chicago IL 60611. (312)467-0580. Production Manager: Berry Gustafson. Publishes adult trade: sports, consumer, self-help, how-to and biography. Photos used for text illustration and book covers. Buys 30 freelance photos annually; gives 5 assignments annually.
Subject Needs: Model release and captions required.
Specs: Uses 8×10 matte b&w prints and 35mm transparencies. Pays in contributor's copies and $250 maximum for color transparency. Credit line given if requested. Buys book rights.
Making Contact: Query with resume of credits, query with samples; provide resume, business card, brochure, flyer or tearsheets to be kept on file for possible future assignments. Solicits photos by assignment only. Does not return unsolicited material. Reports in one month.
Tips: "Don't call. Send written query. In reviewing a portfolio, we look for composition, detail, high quality prints; well-lit studio work. We are not interested in nature photography or greeting card type photography."

R.R. BOWKER, 245 W. 17th, New York NY 10011. (212)337-7015. Art Director: June Evers. Publishes reference books. Photos used for promotional materials and book covers. Buys 10 photos annually; offers 1,000 freelance assignments annually. Used photos for direct mail campaign for "Who's Who in American Art."
Subject Needs: Uses book shots, i.e., people in library, children reading and so on.
Specs: Uses 8×10 matte b&w prints; 4×5 and 8×10 transparencies.
Payment & Terms: Pays $75-150/b&w photo, $300-500/color chrome. Buys all rights.
Making Contact: Arrange a personal interview to show portfolio; provide resume, business card, brochure, flyer or tearsheets to be kept on file for possible future assignments. Deals with local freelancers only. Interested in stock photos, but "cannot afford over $300 for stock." SASE.
Tips: Wants to see "good crisp b&w 8×10's."

BROOKS/COLE PUBLISHING COMPANY, 511 Forest Lodge Rd., Pacific Grove CA 93950. (408)373-0728. Photo Coordinator: Ruth Minerva. Publishes college textbooks only—political science, child development, social psychology, family, marriages, chemistry, computers, criminal justice, etc. Photos used for text illustration, book covers and dust jackets.
Subject Needs: Model release preferred.
Specs: Uses glossy b&w prints, 8×10; also transparencies, any format. Pays $25-100/b&w photo; $250-850/color photo. Credit line given. Buys one-time rights.
Making Contact: Query with list of stock photo subjects; submit portfolio for review; provide resume, business card, brochure, flyer or tearsheets to be kept on file for possible future assignments. Interested in stock photos. SASE. Reports in 2-3 weeks.

WILLIAM C. BROWN CO. PUBLISHERS, 2460 Kerper Blvd., Dubuque IA 52001. (319)588-1451. Director, Production and Design: Beverly Kolz. Manager of Design: Faye Schilling. Supervisor, Photo Research: Shirley Charley. Estab. 1944. Publishes college textbooks for most disciplines (music, computer and data processing, education, natural sciences, psychology, sociology, physical education, health, biology, art). In all cases, photos used for covers and/or interiors. Provide business card, brochure or stock list to be kept on file for possible future use. Submit material by mail for consideration. Pays up to $90/b&w interior photo; up to $135/color interior photo. Buys one-time rights; also all editions and derivative works. Reports in 1-2 months. SASE. Previously published work OK. Direct material to Photo Research. Pays on acceptance.
B&W: Send 8×10 glossy or matte prints.
Color: Send transparencies.
Book Cover: Send glossy or matte b&w prints or color transparencies. Payment negotiable.
Tips: We prefer to note your areas of specialties for future reference. We need *top quality* photography. To break in, be open to negotiate prices *below* ASMP rates."

CAMBRIDGE UNIVERSITY PRESS, 40 W. 20th St., New York NY 10011. (212)924-3900. FAX: (212)691-3239. Contact: Marjan A. Van Schaik. Publishes textbooks for people learning English as a second language (ESL). Uses photos for text illustration and book covers. Buys 100 freelance photos annually; offers 10 freelance assignments annually.
Subject Needs: See "Tips." Model release required.
Specs: Uses 5×7 or 8×10 glossy b&w, and color transparencies or slides.
Payment & Terms: Payment depends on job; $40-65 for a stock photo (not a photo assignment), varies with number of photos used. Credit line given. Buys nonexclusive world English-language rights for first edition and reprints. Simultaneous submissions and previously published work OK.

Making Contact: Query with samples; send unsolicited photos by mail for consideration. Provide resume, business card, brochure, flyer or tearsheets to be kept on file for possible future assignments. "Since we cannot be responsible for loss and/or damage, we do not accept transparencies and/or slides as sample material, but b&w and color photographs only, unless we can keep the material for our files." Interested in stock photos. Does not return unsolicited material. Reports as needed.

Tips: "Although our ESL textbooks span the entire gamut, some specialized subjects occur in almost every book: travel shots, especially big cities worldwide (overviews and famous landmarks), interesting people shots showing people from various nationalities and ethnic backgrounds in typical (but not stereotypical) communication situations, people on their jobs, famous people and celebrities. We use few historical subjects and we can always use humorous situations. Since our textbooks are geared towards the adult learner, we prefer photographs that feature adults."

CASSANDRA PRESS, Box 868, San Rafael CA 94915. (415)382-8507. President: Gurudas. Publishes New Age, metaphysical, holistic health, astrology, psychological and self help books. Photos used for text illustration and book covers. Examples of recently published titles: *The Magic and Science of Jewels and Stones*, Vol. I & II, and *Awakening to the Animal Kingdom*.
Subject Needs: Model release, photo captions preferred.
Specs: Uses b&w and color prints.
Payment & Terms: Pays $200-300/b&w photo; $200-500/color photo. Credit line given. Buys one-time and book rights.
Making Contact: Query with resume of credits and samples for review; send unsolicited photos by mail for consideration; provide business card, brochure, flyer or tearsheets to be kept on file for possible future assignments. Solicits photos by assignment only; interested in stock photos. SASE. Reports in 1 month.

CHRONICLE GUIDANCE PUBLICATIONS, INC., Aurora Street, Box 1190, Moravia NY 13118. (315)497-0330. Photo Editor: Charles DeMotte. Publishes occupational monographs of four, six, or eight pages in length. Photos used for text illustration. Buys 130+ freelance photos annually and offers 30+ assignments annually.
Subject Needs: People on the job, "not posed but actually working." Model release required.
Specs: Uses 8×10 glossy b&w prints.
Payment & Terms: Pays $55-125/b&w photo. Credit line given. Buys one-time rights. Simultaneous submissions and previously published work OK.
Making Contact: Provide resume, business card, brochure, flyer or tearsheets to be kept on file for possible future assignments. Interested in stock photos. SASE. Reports in 2 weeks. Photo guidelines, 'needs' list and sample brief free with legal size 9×12 SASE. Include 65¢ postage.
Tips: "Have a well-rounded sample of occupational photographs. We are looking for the unusual, but at the same time we want a photo that gives a feeling of what the job under discussion is all about. Require photos of women and minorities in nonstereotypical situations. Request a list of our needs, new titles are revised every year. We will also supply suspense dates. Photographers are free to submit work. We prefer they send contact sheets. Selections can be made on that basis. We are using more photography than ever; quality with more attention to details is the key, however."

CLEANING CONSULTANT SERVICES, 1512 Western Ave., Box 1273, Seattle WA 98111. (206)682-9748. Publisher: William R. Griffin. "We publish books on cleaning, maintenance and self-employment. Examples are related to janitorial, housekeeping, maid services, window washing, carpet cleaning, etc." Photos are used for text illustration, promotional materials, books covers and all uses related to production and marketing of our books. Buys 20-50 freelance photos annually; offers 5-15 freelance assignments annually.
Subject Needs: Photos of people doing cleaning work. Model release and captions preferred.
Specs: Uses 5×7 and 8×10 glossy b&w and color prints.
Payment & Terms: Pays $5-50/b&w photo; $5/color photo; $10-30/hour; $40-250/job; negotiable depending on specific project. Credit lines generally given. Buys all rights; depends on need and project; will negotiate rights purchased. Simultaneous submissions and previously published work OK.
Making Contact: Query with resume of credits, samples, list of stock photos subjects or send unsolicited photos by mail for consideration; provide resume, business card, brochure, flyer or tearsheets to be kept on file for possible future assignments. Interested in stock photos. SASE. Reports in 3 weeks.
Tips: "Photos of specific cleaning situations, people doing the work, before and after shots, unique work sites. Be willing to work at reasonable rates, selling two or three photos does not qualify you to earn top of the line rates. We expect to use more photos, but they must be specific to our market, which is quite select. Don't send stock sample sheets. Send photos that fit our specific needs."

CONSERVATORY OF AMERICAN LETTERS, Box 88, Thomaston ME 04861. (207)354-6550. President: Robert Olmstad. Publishes "all types of books except porn and evangelical." Photos used for promotional materials, book covers, and dust jackets. Buys 2-3 photos annually.

Book publisher Chronicle Guidance, Inc. had a hard time finding a photo of a woman electroplater to run in a publication covering occupational opportunities for women. But photographer Ernie Larsen, who had just finished an assignment in a plating lab for another client, made it easy for them. He queried the publisher about its photo needs, and "lo and behold," says Larsen, he had just what they needed. Chronicle Guidance paid Larsen $125 for one-time rights on this shot. As he notes, the publisher was very prompt in contacting him and making payment. "I have also sold two more photos to them, and seeing their want list, I think I can supply a lot more."

Subject Needs: Model release required if identifiable.
Specs: Uses 3×5 to 8×10 glossy b&w prints, also 5×7 or 6×9 color prints.
Payment & Terms: Pays $5-40/b&w photo; $35-150/color photo; per job payment negotiable. Credit line given. Buys one-time or book rights.
Making Contact: Query with list of stock photo subjects. Send unsolicited photos by mail for consideration. SASE. Reports in 1 week.

CONTEMPORARY PERSPECTIVES, INC., 145 E. 49th St., New York NY 10017. (212)753-3800. Art/ Design Coordinator: Tatiana Sayig. Publishes science, english and math textbooks. Photos are used for text illustration and book covers. Buys 4,500 photos annually. Recently published *The Wonders of Science*, 6 science workbooks for remedial high school students, published by Steck-Vaughn, created by us. Used color photos for covers and b&w for ⅛ of page (text illustration).
Subject Needs: Uses Earth Science, people and scientific. Model release, photo captions preferred.
Specs: Uses b&w prints; 35mm transparencies.
Payment & Terms: Pays $65-120/color photo; $50-75/b&w photo. Credit line given. Buys one-time rights. Previously published work OK.
Making Contact: Provide resume, business card, brochure, flyer or tearsheets to be kept on file for possible future assignments. SASE. Reports in 1 month.
Tips: "Send samples for our files. In samples, doesn't want to see anything too slick and no advertising. Wants to see educational shots (scientific and/or technical) and people of all ages doing specific things."

DAVID C. COOK PUBLISHING CO., 850 N. Grove, Elgin IL 60120. (708)741-2400. Director of Design Services: Randy Maid. Photo Acquisition Coordinator: Brenda Fox. Publishes books and Sunday school material for readers, pre-school through adult. Photos used primarily in Sunday school material for text illustration and covers, particularly in *Sunday Digest* (for adults), *Christian Living* (for senior high) and *Sprint* (for junior high). Younger age groups used, but not as much. Buys 200 photos minimum/year; offers 20 assignments/year. Pays $50-250/job or on a per-photo basis. Credit line given. Usually buys one-time rights. Model release preferred.
Subject Needs: Prefers to see Sunday school, church activities, social activities, family shots, people, action and sports. SASE. Previously published work OK. Mostly photos of junior and senior high age youth of all races and ethnic backgrounds; also adults and children under junior high age, and some preschool.
B&W: Uses glossy b&w and semigloss prints. Pays $30-50/photo. 8 × 10 prints are copied and kept on file for ordering at a later date.
Color: Uses 35mm and larger transparencies; contact sheet OK. Pays $75-200/photo.
Jacket/Cover: Uses glossy b&w prints and 35mm and larger color transparencies. Pays $50-250/photo.
Tips: "Make sure your material is identified as yours. Send material to the attention of Brenda Fox, Photo Acquisitions Coordinator."

CPI, 145 E. 49th St., New York NY 10017. (212)753-3800. Vice President: Sherry Olan. Publishes textbooks. Photos used for text illustrations. Buys 500 freelance photos annually and gives 30 freelance assignments annually.
Subject Needs: Children, families and science/nature. Model release required; captions preferred.
Specs: Uses 35mm transparencies.
Payment & Terms: Payment negotiated. Credit line given "usually on acknowledgement page." Rights vary. Simultaneous submissions and previously published work OK if details of other uses are provided.
Making Contact: Query with list of stock photo subjects; provide resume, business card, brochure, flyer or tearsheets to be kept on file for possible future assignments. Solicits photos by assignment; interested in stock photos. SASE. Reports in 1 month. Do not submit unsolicited originals, or any unsolicited photos without SASE.

CRAFTSMAN BOOK COMPANY, 6058 Corte Del Cedro, Carlsbad CA 92008. (619)438-7828. Art Director: Bill Grote. Publishes construction books. Photos used for text illustration, promotional materials, and book covers. Buys 60 freelance photos annually, and offers 10 freelance assignments annually.
Subject Needs: Photos of construction contractors at work, and carpenters at work. Model release required.
Specs: Uses 5 × 7 b&w prints and 35mm transparencies.
Payment & Terms: Pays $25/b&w photo; and $100/color photo. Buys all rights. Simultaneous submissions and previously published work OK.
Making Contact: Query with samples; provide resume, business card, brochure, flyer or tearsheets to be kept on file for possible future assignments. Interested in stock photos. SASE. Reports in 2 weeks.
Tips: "We especially need shots of construction workers on rooftops with lots of sky visible."

DELMAR PUBLISHERS INC., 2 Computer Drive W, Box 15-015, Albany NY 12212. Contact: Design Supervisor. Publishes vocational/technical and college textbooks. Examples of recently published titles: *Working: Skills for a New Age*, *Communication Technology*, *The World of Child Development* and *Auto Technology*. In all cases, photos used for cover and text illustrations.
Subject Needs: Agriculture, air conditioning/heating/refrigeration, automotive/power technology, blueprint reading, business, computer/data processing, construction, drafting/CAD, early childhood education, electrical trades, electronics technology, graphic arts, health occupations/nursing, hospitality/food/travel/tourism, machine trades, mathematics, metalworking, physics/mechanical technology, technical communication, technology/industrial arts and welding.
Specs: 8 × 10 or 5 × 7 glossy b&w prints; also transparencies.
Making Contact & Terms: Works with freelance photographers on assignment basis only. "We prefer to buy all rights to material used in interiors." Also buys one-time rights, all rights, and "rights for all editions of that particular book." Pays $25-50/b&w or color photo for internal use; $50-100/b&w cover and $50-350/color photo used for covers. Provide flyer to be kept on file for future assignments. "When writing please mention areas of expertise."
Tips: "Quality and deadlines are most important."

DELTA DESIGN GROUP, INC., 409 Washington Ave., Box 112, Greenville MS 38702. (601)335-6148. FAX(601)378-2826. President: Noel Workman. Publishes magazines dealing with cotton marketing, dentistry, gardening, health care, travel and southern agriculture. Photos used for text illustration, promotional materials and slide presentations. Buys 25 photos/year; offers 10 assignments/year. Pays $25 minimum/job. Credit line given, except for photos used in ads or slide shows. Rights negotiable. Model release required; captions preferred. Query with samples or list of stock photo subjects or send material by mail for consideration. SASE. Reports in 1 week. Simultaneous submissions and previously published work OK.

Subject Needs: Southern agriculture (cotton, rice, soybeans, sorghum, forages, beef and dairy, and catfish); all aspects of life and labor on the lower Mississippi River; Southern historical (old photos or new photos of old subjects); recreation (boating, water skiing, fishing, canoeing, camping).

Tips: "Wide selections of a given subject often deliver a shot that we will buy, rather than just one landscape, one portrait, one product shot, etc."

*DILLON PRESS, INC., 242 Portland Ave. S., Minneapolis MN 55415. (612)333-2691. Senior Editor: Tom Schneider. Estab. 1966. Publishes juvenile educational books. Photos used for text illustration, book covers, dust jackets. Buys 300-500 photos annually; offers 5-10 freelance assignments annually. Examples of recently published titles: *The Miniature Horse*, Gail LaBonte, photos on cover, back cover and inside text; Cheryl Halton, *Those Amazing Leeches*, photos on cover, back cover and inside text; and Catherine Reef, *Washington, D.C.*, photos on cover, back cover and inside text.

Subject Needs: Foreign countries and cities, U.S. cities and states, animals and biography subjects. Model release preferred; photo captions required.

Specs: Uses 8×10 glossy color/b&w prints; 35mm, 2¼×2¼, 4×5, 8×10 transparencies.

Payment & Terms: Pays $40-150/color photo, $25-75/b&w photo, $10-25/hour, $100-1,000/job. Credit line given. Buys one-time rights. Silumtaneous submissions and previously published work OK.

Making Contact: Query with list of stock photo subjects. Interested in stock photos. SASE. Reports in 1 month. No photo guidelines.

Tips: "Send a stock list with a complete breakdown of subject matter, and be flexible in negotiating rates for one-time use of photos in our books. We are using more and more color photography, and place increasing emphasis on the quality of the images used (clarity, composition, lighting, etc.)."

THE DONNING CO./PUBLISHERS, INC., 5659 Virginia Beach Blvd., Norfolk VA 23502. (804)461-8090. President: Stan Hainer. Publishes "pictorial histories of American cities, counties and states, coffee table volumes, carefully researched with fully descriptive photo captions and complementary narrative text, 300-350 photos/book."

Making Contact & Terms: Query with resume of credits and outline/synopsis for proposed book. Buys first rights or second (reprint) rights. Pays standard royalty contract. Permission from sources of nonoriginal work required. Reports in 2 months. SASE. Simultaneous submissions and previously published work OK. Free author guidelines.

Tips: Suggests that "photographers work with an author to research the history of an area and provide a suitable photographic collection with accompanying ms. In some cases the photographer is also the author."

EMC PUBLISHING, 300 York Ave., St. Paul MN 55101. (612)771-1555. Design and Production Manager: David K. Slater. Publishes educational textbooks. Photos used for text illustration and book covers.

Subject Needs: Subjects vary.

Specs: Uses 35 mm and 4×5 transparencies.

Payment & Terms: Payment varies. Credit line given. Rights purchased vary.

Making Contact: Query with resume of credits; provide resume, business card, brochure, flyer or tearsheets to be kept on file. Interested in stock photos. Does not return unsolicited material. Reports only as needed.

ENSLOW PUBLISHERS, INC, Box 777, Hillside NJ 07205. Production Manager: Mark Enslow. Photos used for text illustration, promotional materials, book covers, dust jackets. Buys 15-20 freelance photos annually and offers 1-2 assignments annually.

Subject Needs: Science and social issues.

Specs: Uses b&w prints.

Payment & Terms: Payment negotiated. Credit line given. Buys book rights. Simultaneous submissions OK.

Making Contact: "Send a few b&w photocopies of prints for us to keep for reference." Does not return unsolicited material.

ENTRY PUBLISHING, INC., 27 W. 96th St., New York NY 10025. (212)662-9703. President: Lynne Glasner. Publishes education/textbooks, secondary market. Photos used for text illustrations. Number of freelance photos bought and freelance assignments given vary.
Subject Needs: "Currently working on geography text, may need specific places." Model release required. Captions preferred.
Specs: Uses b&w prints.
Payment & Terms: Payment depends on job requirements. Credit line given if requested. Buys book rights. Simultaneous submissions and previously published work OK.
Making Contact: Query with list of stock photo subjects. Provide resume, business card, brochure, flyer or tearsheets to be kept on file for possible future assignments. Solicits photos by assignment only; interested in stock photos. SASE. Reports in 3 weeks.
Tips: "Have wide range of subject areas for review and use. Stock photos are most accessible and can be available quickly during production of book."

*EXPOSITION PHOENIX PRESS, INC., 6721 NW, 16th Terr., Ft. Lauderdale FL 33309. (305)975-9603. Contact: President. Estab. 1939. Publishes juvenile, how-to, cooking, fiction. Photos used for text illustration, promotional, book covers, dust jackets. Offers 5 freelance assignments annually. Examples of recently published titles: *Side Tracked, A Summer Song* and *It's Yours for the Asking*.
Specs: Uses 5×7 glossy b&w prints; 5×7 matte color prints. Model release required.
Payment & Terms: Credit line given. Buys one-time rights. Will consider previously published work.
Making Contact: Provide resume, business card, brochure, flyer or tearsheets to be kept on file for possible future assignments. SASE. Reports in 1 month. Photo guidelines available.
Tips: "Write to us for our projected needs."

FELL PUBLISHERS, INC., 2131 Hollywood Blvd., Hollywood FL 33020. (305)925-5242. Publisher: Don Cessne. Publishes magazines, hard-cover and paperback books. Categories include: Health and fitness, food and cooking, business/finance, self help, New Age and inspirational. Photos used for text illustration, book covers, dust jackets and magazine covers. Buys 20 freelance photos annually, and offers 20 freelance assignments annually. Examples of recently published titles: *Diet & Exercise Made Easy, America's Best Recipes* and *Diet Cuisine*. In all cases, photos used for magazine covers.
Subject Needs: Looking for small format, tabletop food shots. Also needs studio shots and outdoor shots of people. Model release required.
Specs: Uses 35mm and 2¼×2¼ transparencies.
Payment & Terms: Pays $200-325/color photo; day rates negotiable. Credit line not given. Buys all rights; will negotiate. Simultaneous submissions and previously published work OK.
Making Contact: Query with list of stock photo subjects. Provide resume, business card, brochure, flyer or tearsheets to be kept on file for possible future assignments. Interested in stock photos. SASE. Reports in 2 weeks.
Tips: Company is looking for: "a variety of well-executed photos with 'clean' design and styling. We are a small company, with a limited budget, trying to build up a file of stock photos. Please contact if interested." Submit samples that show originality; is not interested in typical shots. Trend is toward larger, full-bleed photos on covers and more photos that make use of natural lighting.

J.G. FERGUSON PUBLISHING CO., 200 West Monroe, Chicago IL 60606. Editorial: Carol Summerfield. Publishes vocational guidance works for high schools and college, subscriptions, reference books and corporate histories. Photos used for text illustration, promotional materials, book covers and dust jackets. Buys several hundred freelance photos bi-annually. Recently published titles: *Career Discovery Encyclopedia*, elementary school 6 volume set with jobs explained and illustrated by b&w photos and *Encyclopedia of Career and Vocational Guidance*, high school/college level.
Subject Needs: Persons at work in various occupational settings only. Model release and captions preferred.
Specs: Uses 8×10 b&w glossy prints; 35 mm transparencies.
Payment & Terms: Payment varies. Credit line given. Buys book rights. Simultaneous submissions and previously published work OK.
Making Contact: Interested in stock photos. Send stock list and resumé.
Tips: Wants to see "encyclopedia style black and white photos of people in their jobs with good caption information. We mainly search for specific career images, so a list indicating what a photographer has that may fulfill our needs is the single best method of getting work with us."

J. FLORES PUBLICATIONS, Box 163001, Miami FL 33116. Editor: Eli Flores. Publishes adult trade, nonfiction only: military, firearms and current events. Uses photos for text illustation, promotional materials and book covers.

Subject Needs: Action oriented, on the spot photographs. Model release required; captions preferred.

Specs: Uses any size glossy b&w prints, also color transparencies. Payment negotiable. Credit line given. Buys all rights; will negotiate. Simultaneous submissions and previously published work OK.

Making Contact: Query with samples and list of stock photo subjects. Interested in stock photos. SASE. Reports in 1 month.

Tips: "We look for stock that matches our need for a particular book or ad. The photographer should study the subject matter of books published by a particular publisher and submit photos that match. Photos are being used more than ever by book publishers. There are many books in which photographs play a more important role than the text."

MICHAEL FRIEDMAN PUBLISHING GROUP, INC., 15 W. 26th St., New York NY 10010. (212)685-6610. Photography Editor: Christopher Bain. Estab. 1979. Publishes adult trade: science and nature series; sports series; food and entertainment series; design series; gardening series; garden series; others. Photos used for text illustration, promotional materials, book covers and dust jackets. Buys 3,500 freelance photos annually; gives 20-30 freelance assignments annually.

Subject Needs: Captions preferred.

Specs: Uses 35mm, 2¼×2¼, 4×5 and 8×10 transparencies.

Payment & Terms: Payment upon publication of book for stock photos; within 30-45 days for assignment. Pays $50-100/color stock photo; by the job, $350-500 per day. Credit line given 95% of time, on page. Buys one-time rights (all editions of book). Simultaneous submissions and previously published work OK. No photo guidelines available.

Making Contact: Query with list of stock photo subjects. Interested in stock photos.

FRIENDSHIP PRESS, National Council of the Churches of Christ in the U.S.A., Room 552, 475 Riverside Dr., New York NY 10115. (212)870-2280. Art Director: E. Paul Lansdale. Publishes adult and juvenile textbooks on social consciousness, especially of US and Third World. Photos used for text illustration, promotional material, book covers, dust jackets and PR work. Buys 10+ freelance photos annually. Examples of recently published titles: *Breach Of Promise*, *South Africa's Moment Of Truth* and *A New View Of The World (Map Book)*." Photos used for covers and/or text.

Subject Needs: Social consciousness, people and places. Model release required; captions preferred.

Specs: Uses 8×10 glossy b&w and color prints; 2¼×2¼, 4×5 and 8×10 transparencies.

Payment & Terms: Pays $25-300/b&w photo and $75-450/color photo. Credit line given. Buys one-time rights or all rights; will negotiate with photographer unwilling to sell all rights. Simultaneous submissions and previously published work OK.

Making Contact: Arrange personal interview to show portfolio; query with resume of credits, samples or list of stock photo subjects; submit portfolio for review; provide resume, business card, brochure, flyer or tearsheets to be kept on file for possible future assignments. Solicits photos by assignment only. Interested in stock photos. Does not return unsolicited material.

Tips: "I like photocopies for my files with names, address and phone number."

GLENCOE PUBLISHING, Peoria Office, 809 W. Detweiller, Peoria IL 61615. (309)691-4454. Vice President: Donna M. Faull. Specializes in vocational education textbooks and related materials, industrial arts, home economics and career education. Uses candid, staged, cover quality photos.

Specs: Uses more color versus black & white photography.

Payment & Terms: Pays $30 minimum/b&w photo; $40 minimum/color photo; $15 minimum/hour; and $200/day. Buys all rights, some exclusive rights.

Making Contact: Send samples, resume. No drop-ins.

GLENCOE/MCGRAW HILL, (formerly Glencoe Publishing Co.), 15319 Chatsworth St., Mission Hills CA 91345. Attention: Photo Editor. Publishes elementary and high school textbooks, religion, careers, business, office automation, social studies and fine arts. Photos used for text illustration and book covers. Buys 500 photos annually. Occasionally offers assignments. Recently published titles: *Art Talk*, *Career Skills* and *Marketing Essentials*.

Subject Needs: Children and teens at leisure, in school, in Catholic church; inter with others: parents, siblings, friends, teachers; Catholic church rituals; young people (teens, early 20s) working, especially in jobs that go against sex-role stereotypes. Model release preferred.

Specs: Uses 8×10 glossy b&w prints and 35mm slides.

Payment & Terms: Pays $50/b&w photo, $100/color photo (¼ page). Usually buys one-time rights, but prefers to buy all rights on assignment photography with some out-takes available to photographer. Simultaneous submissions and previously published work OK.

Making Contact: Query with stock photo list. List kept on file for future assignments."

Tips: A good ethnic mix for models is important. We look for a contemporary unposed look."

GOOSE LANE EDITIONS LTD., 248 Brunswick St., Fredericton NB E3B 1C9 Canada. (506)450-4251. Production Manager: Julie Scriver. Estab. 1957. Publishes poetry, fiction, regional history and guide books. Photos are used for text illustration and on book covers and dust jackets. Buys 1-3 freelance photos/year; offers 2-5 assignments/year. Examples of recently published titles: *No Hay Fever and A Railway* (archival photos); *Killers, Thieves, Tramps & Sinners* (archival); and Spring 1990 catalogue (cover and interior illustration enlarged for display).

Subject Needs: Interested in non-figure images, landscapes and still life. Model release and photo captions preferred.

Specs: Uses 5×7 glossy b&w and color prints; 2¼×2¼ transparencies.

Payment & Terms: Pays $100-400/color photo; $50-200/b&w photo, and by contract/royalty. Credit line given. Buys book rights. Simultaneous submissions OK.

Making Contact: Provide resume, business card, brochure, flyer or tearsheets to be kept on file for possible future assignments. Deals with local freelancers only; interested in stock photos. SASE. Reports in 4-5 weeks.

Tips: "We are a small company and have a bias toward Candian sources; likely to access Canadian sources first."

*GRAND CANYON NATURAL HISTORY ASSOCIATION, P.O. Box 399, Grand Canyon AZ 86023. (602)638-2481. FAX: (602)638-2484. Publications Manager: Pamela Frazier. Estab. 1932. Publishes for juvenile to adult audience: books and other media such as posters and maps covering the human history, natural history, geology of the Grand Canyon and the Colorado Plateau. Scientific monograph series. Photos used for text illustration, book covers, dust jackets, brochures, posters, maps. Buys 10-150 photos annually; offers 1-4 freelance assignments annually. Examples of recently published titles: Lake Powell Boater's Guide, illustrate text & cover; Guides to Havasu & Hermit Trails, illustrate text, Exploring the Grand Canyon, illustrate text.

Subject Needs: Grand Canyon—specific natural & human history subjects; plants and animals, people using trails/facilities, geology, scenics. Wildlife, scenics, both b&w and color, representational/realism. Model release and photo captions required.

Specs: Uses 8×10 glossy b&w prints; 35mm, 2¼×2¼, 4×5, 8×10 transparencies.

Payment & Terms: Pays $15-500/color photo, $10-150/b&w photo, $50-3,000/job, royalty and/or assorted merchandise premiums. Buys one-time rights, book rights, all rights. Will negotiate with a photographer not willing to sell all rights. Simultaneous submissions and previously published work OK.

Making Contact: Arrange a personal interview to show portfolio. Query with resume of credits. Provide resume, business card, brochure, flyer or tearsheets to be kept on file for possible future assignments. Interested in stock photos. Cannot return material. Do not send unsolicited work. Reports in 1 month. No photo guidelines.

Tips: In photographer's portfolio "technical excellence assumed." Wants to see "fresh views of oft-photographed subjects and black & white images (for publications) with dramatic lighting, etc." Freelance photographer trying to break in should "present classic (not time-dated) images which capture dramatic lighting and color. Grand Canyon or Colorado Plateau-related only."

GRAPHIC ARTS CENTER PUBLISHING COMPANY, Box 10306, Portland OR 97210. (503)226-2402. Editorial Director: Douglas A. Pfeiffer. Publishes adult trade photographic essay books. Photos used for photo essays. Offers 5 freelance assignments annually.

Subject Needs: Landscape, nature, people, historic architecture and other topics pertinent to the essay. Captions preferred.

Specs: Uses 35mm, 2¼×2¼ and 4×5 (35mm as Kodachrome 25 or 64) slides.

Payment & Terms: Pays by royalty—amount varies based on project; minimum, but advances against royalty are given. Credit line given. Buys book rights. Simultaneous submissions OK.

Making Contact: "Photographers must be previously published in book form, and have a minimum of five years full-time professional experience to be considered for assignment."

Tips: "Prepare an original idea as a book proposal. Full color essays are expensive to publish, so select topics with strong market potential. We see color essays as being popular compared to b&w in most cases."

*GREENHAVEN PRESS, INC., P.O. Box 289009, San Diego CA 92128-9009. (619)485-7424. Contact: Photo Editor. Publishes educational books with school and library distribution only. Photos used for text illustration. Buys 1,500 photos annually. All inside photos used. Photo needs depend on topic. Model release required.

Specs: Uses 8 × 10 b&w prints; 35mm, 2¼ × 2¼ transparencies (can convert).
Payment & Terms: Pays $40-75/b&w photo. Credit line given. Buys one-time rights. Will consider previously published work.
Making Contact: Query with list of stock photo subjects. Provide resume, business card, brochure, flyer or tearsheets to be kept on file. Interested in stock photos. No guidelines.
Tips: In photographer's promo materials want to see "variety, wide enough selection to make me think of you even if I've not seen specific subject in your promo list. Get with one (or more) of the networks, there are several. Buyers submit needs to network, it is FAXED to our members same night."

H. P. BOOKS, Imprint of Price/Stern/Sloan, Ste. 304, 4742 N. Oracle Rd., Tucson AZ 85705. (602)292-9205. Editor: Vernon Gorter. Publishes 5 photo titles average/year. Publishes books on photography; how-to and camera manuals related to 35mm SLR photography, and lab work.
Specs: Uses 8½ × 11 format, 160 pages, liberal use of color; requires 200-400 illustrations. Pays royalty on entire book.
Making Contacts: Query first. SASE. Contracts entire book, not photos only. Accepts simultaneous or photocopied submissions. Reports in 4 weeks. Free catalog.
Recent Titles: *Pro Techniques of Glamour Photography*, by Gary Bernstein.
Tips: "Learn to write."

HARMONY HOUSE PUBLISHERS, 1008 Kent Rd., Goshen KY 40026. (502)228-4446. Owners: William Strode and William Butler. Estab. 1984. Publishes photographic books on specific subjects. Photos used for text illustration, promotion materials, book covers and dust jackets. Number of freelance photos purchased varies. Assigns 30 shoots each year. Photography books—*Virginia Military Institute The Spirit, Kentucky Crafts* and *Chariots of Iron—50 Years of U.S. Armor*.
Subject Needs: Captions required.
Specs: Uses 35mm, 2¼ × 2¼, 4 × 5 or 8 × 10 transparencies.
Payment & Terms: Rates of payment vary. Credit line given. Buys one-time rights and book rights. Simultaneous submissions and previously published work OK.
Making Contact: Query with resume of credits along with business card, brochure, flyer or tearsheets to be kept on file for possible future assignments. Query with samples or with list of stock photo subjects, or submit portfolio for review. Solicits photos by assignment mostly.
Tips: In portfolios, looking for "photography that is of the quality we use." To break in, "send in book ideas to William Strode, with a good tray of slides to show work." Freelancers are advised to send submissions to street address and queries or other correspondence to PO Box 90, Prospect, KY 40059.

*HARRISON HOUSE PUBLISHERS, 1029 N. Utica, Tulsa OK 74110. (918)582-2126. Art Director: Doug Belew. Estab. 1975. Publishes Christian trade books (paperbacks & hardbounds), Christian fiction and Christian videos. Photos used for text illustration, book covers, dust jackets. Buys 3 or 4 photos annually; offers 10 freelance assignments annually.
Subject Needs: Model release required; photo captions preferred.
Payment & Terms: Pays $150-500/color cover photo. Credit line given sometimes. Buys book rights.
Making Contact: Query with resume of credits. Query with list of stock photo subjects. Send unsolicited photos by mail for consideration. Provide resume, business card, brochure, flyer or tearsheets to be kept on file for possible future assignments. Solicits photos by assignment only. SASE. Reports in 1 month. No photo guidelines.

HERE'S LIFE PUBLISHERS, #F, 2700 Little Mountain Dr., San Bernardino CA 92405. (714)886-7981. (714)886-7985. Cover Development: Michelle Treiber. Photos used for promotional materials, book cover and dust jackets. Buys 20-30 photos annually; majority of photos shot on assignment. Examples of recently published titles: *When Your Dreams Die, Pathway Through Pain, Genesis, What Makes a Marriage Last* and *When Victims Marry*. All used as cover art.
Subject Needs: People, tabletop stills and landscape. Model release required.
Specs: Uses 8 × 10 glossy color prints; 2¼ × 2¼ and 4 × 5 transparencies.
Payment & Terms: Pays $300-500/color photo. Credit lines "sometimes" given. Buys all rights.
Making Contact: Query with resume of credits and samples; provide resume, business card, brochure, flyer or tearsheets to be kept on file for possible future assignments. Solicits photos by assignment only; interested in stock photos. SASE. Reports in 2 weeks.

HOLT, RINEHART AND WINSTON, 1627 Woodland Ave., Austin TX 78741. (512)440-5700. Manager of Photo Research: Debra Saleny. "The Photo Research Department in Austin obtains photographs for the School Division of HRW. We publish textbooks in all subject areas for kindergarten through grade 12 students." Photos used for text illustration, promotional materials and book covers. Buys

3,000 photos annually. Examples of recently published titles: *Modern Chemistry*, *Our World* (history) and *Et Vous* (French language).

Subject Needs: Photos to illustrate mathematics, the sciences—life, earth and physical, chemistry, history, foreign languages, art and the humanities. Model release and captions required.

Specs: Uses any size glossy b&w and color transparencies.

Payment & Terms: Pays $75-135/b&w photo; $100-160/color photo; $50-100/hour and $400-800/day. Credit line given. Buys one-time rights.

Making Contact: Query with resume of credits, stock photo list or samples. Interested in stock photos. Does not return unsolicited material. Reports "as soon as project allows."

Tips: "We use all types of photos, from portraits to setups to scenics. We like to see slides displayed in sheets or by carousel projector. We especially like photographers who have specialties . . . limit themselves to one/two subjects." Send a letter and printed flyer with a sample of work and a list of subjects in stock. Do not call. Looks for "natural looking, uncluttered photographs, labeled with exact descriptions, technically correct, and including no evidence of liquor, drugs, cigarettes or brand names."

HOME PLANNERS, INC., 3275 W. Ina Road, Suite 110, Tucson, AZ 85741. (602)297-8200. FAX: (602)297-6219. Art Director: Karin Lotarski. Estab. 1940. Publishes material on home building and planning and landscape design. Photos used for text illustration, promotional materials and book covers. Buys 50 freelance photos and offers 5 freelance assignments annually. Examples of recently published titles: *Tudor Homes, The Home Landscaper* and *Country Houses*. In all three, photos used for cover and text illustrations.

Subject Needs: Homes/houses—"but for the most part, it must be a specified house built by one of our plans." Model release preferred.

Specs: Uses 4×5 transparencies.

Payment & Terms: Pays $25-100/color photo; $500-750/day; maximum $500/4-color cover shots. Credit line given. Buys all rights; non-negotiable. Simultaneous submissions and previously published work OK.

Making Contact: Send unsolicited photos by mail for consideration. Provide resume, business card, brochure, flyer or tearsheets to be kept on file for possible future assignments. We solicit photos by assignment only. SASE. Reports in 1 month.

Tips: Looks for "ability to shoot architectural settings and convey a mood."

*HOMESTEAD PUBLISHING, Box 193, Moose WY 83012. Editor: Carl Schreier. Publishes 3-7 titles per year in adult and children's trade, Natural History, Western American and art. Photos used for text illustration, promotional, book covers and dust jackets. Buys 100-200 photos annually; offers 3-4 freelance assignments annually. Recently published titles: *Yellowstone: Selected Photographs*, *Field Guide to Yellowstone's Geysers, Hot Springs and Fumaroles*, and *Field Guide to Wildflowers of the Rocky Mountains*.

Subject Needs: Natural history. Model release preferred. Photo captions required; accuracy very important.

Specs: Uses 8×10 glossy b&w prints; 35mm, 2¼×2¼, 4×5 and 6×7 transparencies.

Payment & Terms: Pays $70-300/color photo, $50-300/b&w photo. Credit line given. Buys one-time rights; will negotiate with photographer not willing to sell all rights. Simultaneous submissions and previously published work OK.

Making Contact: Query with samples; provide resume, business card, brochure, flyer or tearsheets to be kept on file for possible future assignments. Interested in stock photos. SASE. Reports in 3-4 weeks.

Tips: In freelancer's samples, wants to see "top quality—must contain the basics of composition, clarity, sharp, in focus, etc. We discourage photographers from sending material if it is not of the highest quality."

HUMAN KINETICS PUB., 1607 N. Market St., Champaign IL 61820. (217)351-5076. Art Director: Keith Blomberg. Publishes sports, education for PE and wellness. Photos used for text illustration, book covers and dust jackets. Buys 20-30 freelance photos annually; gives 10 freelance assignments annually.

Markets which offer lower payment amounts, or photo credits and extra copies or tearsheets as payment are often receptive to the work of newcomers. For a list of such markets, see the First Markets Index preceding the General Index in the back of this book.

Subject Needs: Sports, education for PE and wellness. Model release preferred.
Specs: Uses 6×9, 8½×11 b&w and color prints; 35mm, 2½×2½, 4×5, 8×10 transparencies.
Payment & Terms: Pays $15/b&w photo; $20-200/color photo. Buys book rights.
Making Contact: Query with list of stock photo subjects; provide resume, business card, brochure, flyer or tearsheets to be kept on file for possible future assignments. Interested in stock photos. Does not return unsolicited material. Reports in 1 month or longer.

IGNATIUS PRESS, 2515 McAllister, San Francisco CA 94118. Art Assistant Production Editor: Roxanne Mei Lum. Publishes Catholic theology and devotional books (popular and scholarly).
Subject Needs: Photos of the Pope, priests and religions, sacraments, stained glass; religious subjects and symbols; families, parents and children; Catholic churches.
Specs: Uses various size b&w and color, glossy prints.
Payment & Terms: Credit lines given, usually in separate section. Buys all rights.
Making Contact: Provide resume, business card, brochure, flyer or tearsheets to be kept on file for possible future assignments; "we will make contact if interested." Send a few samples. Does not return unsolicited material.

*ILR PRESS, NY State School of Industrial and Labor Relations, Cornell University, Ithaca NY 14851-0952. (607)255-3061. Marketing and Promotion Manager: Andrea Fleck Clardy. Publishes books about all aspects of work and labor relations for academics, practitioners and the general public. Photos are used for book covers and catalog of publications. Buys 5 freelance photos annually.
Subject Needs: People at work in a wide variety of contexts, with high human interest and excellence in photo design. Model release required in most areas (for use on covers).
Specs: Uses b&w prints.
Payment & Terms: Pays $25-100/b&w photo. Credit line given. Buys one-time rights or book rights. Simultaneous submissions and previously published work OK.
Making Contact: Query with samples. Interested in stock photos. SASE. Reports in 1 month.
Tips: Prefers to see "b&w prints of high human interest images of people in the workforce. Particularly interested in photos that include women and people of color, high tech professions and worker/manager groups."

INTERNATIONAL MARINE PUBLISHING COMPANY, Box 220, Camden ME 04843. (207)236-6046. Production Director: Molly Mulhern. Publishes how-to books on nautical subjects. Photos used for text illustration, book covers and dust jackets. Buys 100 freelance photos and gives 5 freelance assignments annually. Examples of recently published titles: *A Cruising Guide to the Maine Coast*, photos used for cover and text; *Water Shots*; photos used for cover and text; *Fiberglass Boat Repair Manual*, photos used for cover and inside.
Subject Needs: Any nautically related photos. Model release preferred; captions required.
Specs: Uses b&w and color; any size.
Payment & Terms: Pays $30-100/color photo, $10-50/b&w photo and $15-30/hour. Credit line given. Buys book rights. Previously published work OK.
Making Contact: Query with samples. Sometimes interested in stock photos. Cannot guarantee return of unsolicited material. Reports in 1 month.

JAMESTOWN PUBLISHERS, Box 9168, Providence RI 02940. Courier Delivery: 544 Douglas Ave., Providence RI 02908. (401)351-1915. Production Supervisor: Diane Varone. Estab. 1969. Publishes reading developmental textbooks. "We need photos to illustrate covers and text material, covering a wide range of photo matter." Buys 20-40 photographs annually, and assigns 3 projects annually. Examples of recently published titles: *Reading Drills, Skimming & Scanning* and *Selections from the Black*; all photos used for text illustrations.
Subject Needs: "We use a wide variety of photos: biographical subjects, illustrative photos for covers, historical photos, nature, science, people, etc."
Specs: Uses 8×10 glossy b&w prints, 4×5 transparencies and 35 mm color slides.
Payment & Terms: Payment negotiated. Pays $75-125/b&w photo; $105-300/color photo. Credit line given. Buys one-time rights. Previously published work OK.
Making Contact: Query with list of stock photo subjects; provide resume, business card, brochure, flyer or tearsheets to be kept on file for possible future assignments. Interested in stock photos. Does not return unsolicited material. Reports in 1 month. Will work with U.S. photographers only.
Tips: Looks for "creativity, high contrast (for our b&w texts), plus diversity. Send stock lists. I keep all stock sources on a computer file. Keep sending updated lists."

*JUST US BOOKS, INC., 301 Main Street, #22-24, Orange NJ 07050. (201)672-7701. Design Director: Cheryl Willis Hudson. Estab. 1987. Publishes juvenile and picture books for children. Photos used for text illustration and book covers. Buys 30-40 photos annually. Examples of recently published titles:

Afro-Bets First Book About Africa, Afro-Bets Book of Black Heroes, and *Harambec*, a newspaper for young readers. All three titles are nonfiction.
Subject Needs: Needs photos of African-American children, their parents, their interests, and their communities both urban and suburban. Stock photos are often used. Model release and photo captions preferred.
Specs: Uses 8×10 b&w prints; 35mm and 4×5 transparencies.
Payment & Terms: Pays $25-150/color photo, $25-75/b&w photo. Pays on publication. Credit line given. Buys one-time rights and book rights. Simultaneous submissions and previously published work OK.
Making Contact: Arrange a personal interview to show portfolio. Query with list of stock photo subjects. Provide resume, business card, brochure, flyer or tearsheets to be kept on file for possible future assignments. SASE. No unsolicited photos accepted.
Tips: In photographer's portfolio, wants to see "fresh, positive, realistic depictions of African-American children in various situations." To break in, have "a positive, open attitude, a high degree of professionalism and a creative approach to illustrating children's materials with photos."

GEORGE KURIAN REFERENCE BOOKS, Box 519, Baldwin Place NY 10505-0519. (914)962-3287. President: George Kurian. Publishes trade reference. Photos used for text illustration, promotional materials, book covers and dust jackets. Buys 100 photos annually; offers 12 assignments annually. Examples of recently published titles: *Discovering America*, *Discovering Europe*, and *Album of Education*.
Subject Needs: Model release, photo captions preferred.
Specs: Uses glossy b&w and color prints.
Payment & Terms: Credit line given. Buys one-time rights. Simultaneous submissions and previously published work OK.
Making Contact: Query with samples, query with list of stock photo subjects. Interested in stock photos. Cannot return material. Reports in 1 month.

*LAYLA PRODUCTION INC., 310 E. 44, New York NY 10017. (212)697-6285. Manager: Lori Stein. Estab. 1980. Publishes adult trade, how-to and cooking books. Photos used for text illustration and book covers. Buys 150+ photos annually; offers 6 freelance assignments annually. Examples of recently published titles: *Golf's Magnificent Challenge*, used stock photos of courses as text; *That's All Folks*, assigned shooting of documents for illustration; and *Children of Bellevue Journal*, assigned shoot of kids in hospital.
Subject Needs: Sports and cooking. Model release required; photo captions preferred.
Specs: Specifications for submissions are very flexible .
Payment & Terms: Pays $50-200/color photo, $10-100/b&w photo, $25-100/hour, other methods of pay depends on job, budget and quality needed. Buys all rights. Will negotiate with a photographer not willing to sell all rights. Simultaneous submissions and previously published work OK.
Making Contact: Provide resume, business card, brochure, flyer or tearsheets to be kept on file for possible future assignments. SASE. Reports in 1 month if SASE; prefers no unsolicited material.
Tips: "We *do* keep all resumes/brochures sent on file—but our needs are few, and we don't often use unsolicited material."

LEBHAR-FRIEDMAN, 425 Park Ave., New York NY 10022. (212)371-9400. Senior Art Director: Milton Berwin. Publishes trade books, magazines and advertising supplements for the entire retailing industry. Photos used for text illustration, book covers and ad supplements. Pays $250/day and on a per-photo basis. Buys all rights. Model release required. Send material by mail for consideration. SASE. Reports in 2 weeks.
Subject Needs: In-store location and related subject matter.
B&W: Uses 8×10 prints. Pays $50-100/photo or less, according to size and use.
Color: Uses transparencies. Pays $150-300/photo.
Covers: Uses b&w prints and 2¼×2¼ color transparencies. Pays $50-300/photo.

LIBERTY PUBLISHING COMPANY, INC., Suite 202, 440 S. Federal Hwy., Deerfield Beach FL 33441. (305)360-9000. President: Jeffrey B. Little. Publishes adult trade paperbacks, software and videos. Subjects: how-to, cooking and general interest. Photos used for book covers. Buys 4-6 freelance photos annually.
Subject Needs: Still lifes, horseracing/gambling scenes, nature scenes. Model release required.
Specs: Uses any size or finish color prints; 35mm and 2¼×2¼ transparencies. "Chance of our paying attention to a submitted print is greater than with transparencies."
Payment & Terms: Pays $350 maximum/color photo; and $350 maximum/job. Credit line given. Buys all rights. Simultaneous submissions and previously published work OK.
Making Contact: Query with resume of credits and list of stock photo subjects. Provide resume, business card, brochure, flyer or tearsheets to be kept on file for possible future assignments. Interested in stock photos. SASE; 85¢ postage. Reports in 1 month.

Tips: "We only want to see samples if we have solicited photos for use as a book cover with a specific subject in mind. In that case, we evaluate balance of photo: Is there empty space in the proper place for book title and author's name to appear? Sharpness of image and pleasing combination of colors is also important. Subject matter would determine specifics. Often we are open to suggestions for subject matter of book cover photo. Photographer should be creative with cover ideas and suggest different photos for any book cover that could be appropriate with subject of book; he/she may request catalog of our current books to get ideas. We are becoming more interested in using color photographs on bookcovers. However, we are also willing to use other styles of covers. Availability and applicability of photo, as well as price, would determine whether or not we went with the photo."

LION PUBLISHING, Peter's Way, Sandy Lane W., Oxford OX4 5HG England. Phone: (0865)747550. FAX: (0865)747568. Picture Editor: Jo Egerton. Publishes children's, educational, general interest books, Bible handbooks and religious history. Photos used for text illustration, book covers and dust jackets. Examples of recently published titles: *A Way with Pain*, (color photos); *Jesus 2000,* cover, text illustrations (color and b&w); and *The Human Difference,* text illustration (color and b&w).
Subject Needs: General and religious. Model release preferred; photo captions required.
Specs: Uses b&w glossy prints; transparencies, all formats.
Payment & Terms: Pays £85/full page, £75/half page, £60/quarter page for general projects (transparencies). All other fees negotiable. Credit line given in a general acknowledgements list at beginning or end of book. Previously published work OK.
Making Contact: Arrange a personal interview to show portfolio. Query with list of stock photo subjects; provide resume, business card, brochure, flyer or tearsheets to be kept on file for possible future assignments. Interested in stock photos. SASE. Reports in 2 weeks.

LITTLE, BROWN & CO., 41 Mt. Vernon St., Boston MA 02108. (617)227-0730. Jacket Art Coordinator: Andrea Gove. Publishes adult trade. Photos used for book covers and dust jackets. Buys 20 photos annually; gives 5 freelance assignments annually.
Subject Needs: Model release required.
Payment and Terms: Credit line given. Buys one-time rights.
Making Contact: Query or arrange a personal portfolio viewing; provide resume, business card, brochure, flyer or tearsheets to be kept on file for possible future assignments. Interested in stock photos. SASE. Reporting time varies.

LLEWELLYN PUBLICATIONS, Box 64383, St. Paul MN 55164. (612)291-1970. Art Director: Terry Buske. Publishes consumer books (mostly adult trade paperback) with astrology and New Age subjects, geared toward a young, high-tech minded audience, and book catalogs. Uses photos for book covers. Buys 5-10 freelance photos annually.
Subject Needs: Science/fantasy, space photos, high tech and special effects. Model release preferred.
Specs: Uses 8×10 glossy color prints; 35mm or 4×5 transparencies.
Terms: Query with samples; provide slides, brochure, flyer or tearsheets to be kept on file for possible future assignments. Interested in stock photos. SASE. Reports in 3 weeks. Pays $125-600/color cover photo. Pays on publication. Credit line given. Buys one-time rights.
Tips: "Always send SASE. Send slides that can be kept on file. We are using more high-tech special effects."

*LUCENT BOOKS, P.O. Box 289011, San Diego CA 92128-9011. (619)485-7424. Contact: Photo Editor. Publishes educational—school and library distribution only. Photos used for text illustration, book covers. Example of recently published titles: *UFOs*, (Overview Series) inside and *Drugs & Sports* (Overview Series).
Subject Needs: Photo needs vary with topic. Model release required.
Specs: Uses 8×10 b&w prints; 35mm, 2¼×2¼ transparencies (can convert).
Payment & Terms: Pays $250/cover photo, $40-60/b&w photo. Credit line given. Buys one-time rights.
Making Contact: Query with list of stock photo subjects. Interested in stock photos. No photo guidelines.
Tips: In photographer's promo materials prefers "a variety of subject mattter." To break in "get with one of the stock networks. Buyers submit needs, network Faxes to members overnight."

MCDOUGAL, LITTELL AND COMPANY, 1560 Sherman Ave., Evanston IL 60201. (312)869-2300. Picture Editor: Carmine Fantasia. Textbooks, grades K-12. Photos used for text illustration and book covers. "We usually purchase from stock submissions of existing photos from freelance photographers or stock agencies."

Subject Needs: "We use photos to illustrate nonfiction literature selections and illustrate history books with historic sites—therefore we need nature scenes, news events, children age 4-18 and many different things based on which book is being prepared. We always need fine art photographers who shoot paintings." Model release and captions preferred.

Specs: Uses 35mm and 4×5 transparencies. "Prefer 4×5 but use a lot of 35mm. Black-and-whites used normally only for historic pictures shot when only b&w was available."

Payment & Terms: Pays $100-150/b&w photo; $135-210/color photo; follows ASMP rates. Credit line given. Buys one-time rights. Simultaneous submissions and previously published work OK.

Making Contact: Query with list of stock photo subjects. Provide resume, business card, brochure, flyer or tearsheets to be kept on file for possible future assignments. Interested in stock photos. SASE. Reports in 1 month.

Tips: "We are very open to seeing sophisticated computerized images or very new concepts combining art. Please do not send unsolicited original work."

MCGRAW-HILL, (formerly Random House), College Division, 27 Fl., 1221 Ave. of the Americas, New York NY 10020. Manager: Safra Nimrod. Estab. 1889. Recent titles include: *Cultural Anthropology, 3rd edition,* Bates/Plog (text illustrations, cover art); *Broadcasting,* Dominick (text illustrations); and *Social Experience 2nd edition* Vander-Zanden (text illustrations, cover art).

Needs: Uses photographers for college textbooks. Subjects include editorial, reportage, news, sociology, psychology, special effects, natural history, science, micrography—all college subjects.

Specs: Uses 8×10 repro quality b&w prints; color transparencies or repro-quality dupes.

First Contact & Terms: Provide resume, business card, self-promotion piece or tearsheets to be kept on file for possible future assignment. Do not send unsolicited photos. Interested in stock photos. Pay varies: $75-125/b&w photo; $100-160/color photo; $250-1,000/day. Pays on acceptance after sizes are determined. Buys one-time rights. Captions and model releases preferred. Credit line given.

Tips: "We look for professionalism in presentation, well edited work, consistent high quality—if there's one bad shot, we question the photographer's judgment." Looks for "editorial approach, clean, sharp images, unposed people and an interesting angle on a familiar subject. Send tearsheets or xeroxes. Be willing to negotiate prices."

MBKA, 65 1st Ave., Atlantic Highlands NJ 07716. (201)291-7992. Art Director: Ann M. Nelsen. Publishes adult and children's sports and fitness books. Photos used for text illustration, book covers and dust jackets. Buys 200 photos annually; gives 5-10 freelance assignments annually. Examples of recently published titles: *Red Foley's Best Baseball Book* (photos used on cover, in text, as stickers); *The Professional Baseball Trainers Book* (photos used on cover, as text illustration); *Topps Baseball Card Team Books* (cover photo only).

Subject Needs: Needs sports action shots and posed shots of athletes or models. Model release and photo captions required.

Specs: Uses glossy b&w prints; 4×5 transparencies.

Payment & Terms: Payment "depends on project." Credit line given. Buys book rights. Simultaneous submissions and previously published work OK.

Making Contact: Arrange a personal interview to show portfolio. Solicits photos by assignment only; interested in stock photos. Cannot return material. Reports in 2 weeks.

MERRILL PUBLISHING COMPANY, Box 508, Columbus OH 43216-0508. (614)759-6600. Photo Editor: Gail Meese. Cover Photo Editor: Brian Deet. Publishes college textbooks with emphasis in education, special ed., computer science, business, marketing, psychology, criminal justice, management and personnel, geography, geology and physics. Photos used for text illustration, promotional materials and book covers. Buys 1,000 text photos, 100 cover photos and offers 10-15 freelance assignments annually.

Subject Needs: Professionally lighted cover quality color and b&w photos of lively and unique general education activities with racial mix; special education students, mainstreamed students; computer usage in K-12, business and home; world geography with/out people; paleontology; and oceanography, including surface and underwater shots. All photos should be model released.

Specs: 8×10 glossy b&w prints with minimum ¼" border, 35mm or larger transparencies.

Payment & Terms: Competitive textbook prices paid on publication. Pays $50-120/b&w photo; $80-200/color photo; $50-70/hour; $350-500/day. Credit line given. Buys one-time, limited exclusive rights. Previously published work not in competing college textbooks acceptable.

Making Contact: Inquire by sending a list of stock photo subjects, business card, brochure, flyer or tearsheets. "Send 6 of your best shots to Gail Meese for consideration." Interested in stock photos only after inquiry and authorization to submit material with SASE and phone number. Averages 1-3 months return time for rejected or considered work, 3-9 months return time for published work. All photos for cover should be in color and addressed to Brian Deet.

Tips: If you don't have a promo piece, prefers to receive duplicate slides or extra prints and contact sheets to hold until needed. Keep promotional package small and quick to review. "The more of your work we have in our files, the more likely we will select you for publication."

METAMORPHOUS PRESS, Box 10616, Portland OR 97210. (503)228-4972. Editor: Lori Stephens. "We publish books and tapes in the subject areas of communication, health and fitness, education, business and sales, psychology, women and children. Photos used for text illustration, promotional materials, book covers and dust jackets. Examples of recently published titles: *Recreating Yourself*, used for cover; *Fitness Without Stress*, used for cover; *Power to the Dancers*. Photos used for cover and/or text illustration.
Payment & Terms: Payment negotiable. Credit line given. Buys one-time and book rights. Also buys all rights, but willing to negotiate. Simultaneous submissions and previously published work OK.
Making Contact: Query with samples list of stock photo subjects; provide resume, business card, brochure, flyer or tearsheets to be kept on file for possible future assignments. Solicits photos by assignment only. Interested in stock photos. Cannot return material. Reports as soon as possible.
Tips: "Let us have samples of specialties so we can match contents and styles to particular projects."

MILADY PUBLISHING CORPORATION, 4th Floor, 220 White Plains Rd., Tarrytown NY 10591. (914)332-4800. Contact: Editorial Director. Publishes textbooks for vocational education in areas of cosmetology, business education and personal development. Photos used for text illustration and trade magazine illustration.
Subject Needs: Hair styling, business education, manicuring, aesthetics and modeling. Model release and captions preferred.
Specs: Black and white glossy prints.
Payment & Terms: Payment negotiated. Credit line given. Rights purchased vary per usage. Simultaneous submissions and previously published work OK.
Making Contact: Provide resume, business card, brochure, flyer or tearsheets to be kept on file for possible future assignments. Solicits photos by assignment only. SASE. Reports in 2 weeks.

MILKWEED EDITIONS, Box 3226, Minneapolis MN 55403. (612)332-3192. FAX: (612)332-6248. Art Director: R.W. Scholes. Publishes fiction, nonfiction, poetry, visual arts books and collaborative text/photo books. Photos used for text illustration, book covers and dust jackets. Examples of recently published titles: *Village Without Mirrors*; photos used for text and cover. *Twin Sons of Different Mirrors*; b&w photos used for text illustration. *The Freedom of History*; color photo used for cover art.
Subject Needs: Most interested in high-quality photos, able to stand on own; should not be journalistic. Model release required; photo captions preferred.
Specs: Uses 10 × 12 b&w gloss prints and 35mm transparencies.
Payment & Terms: Pays $10-100/color or b&w photo. Credit line given. Buys one-time rights. Simultaneous submissions and previously published work OK.
Making Contact: Arrange a personal interview to show portfolio. Query with samples. Provide resume, business card, brochure, flyer or tearsheets to be kept on file. SASE. Reports in 1 month.
Tips: Would like to see series works, usually b&w. "Look at our books for use. Then send in a fairly good copy (or original) to keep on file, plus a slide sheet with address and SASE." Sees trend in company toward "an increased use (of photos) compared to past graphic works." The same is generally true among book publishers.

MILLIKEN PUBLISHING COMPANY, 1100 Research Blvd., St. Louis MO 63132. (314)991-4220. Managing Editor: Kathy Hilmes. Clients: teachers.
Needs: Works with very few photographers. Uses photographers for slide sets. Photos are needed now and then for covers. Needs vary widely from shots of children to landscapes, folkdance, other countries, monuments, etc.
Specs: Uses 8 × 10 glossy b&w and color prints; 35mm and 4 × 5 transparencies.
First Contact & Terms: Arrange a personal interview to show portfolio; query with stock photo list; provide resume, business card, self-promotion piece or tearsheets to be kept on file for possible future assignments. Works with local freelancers. SASE. Reports in 1 month. Pays on acceptance. Pays $25-100/b&w photo, $50-250/color photo, and $500-1,000/job. Buys all rights. Captions preferred; model release required. Credit line given.
Tips: In portfolios or samples, looks for "clarity and interest of subject."

MOON PUBLICATIONS, INC., 722 Wall St., Chico CA 95928. (916)895-3789. Creative Director: David Hurst. Estab. 1974. Publishes trade paper, travel guides and pictorial travel guides. Photos used for text illustration, promotional materials and book covers. Buys "a few" photos annually. Examples of recently published titles: *Bali Handbook*, cover; *Nevada Handbook*, cover; and *New Mexico Handbook*, cover.

Subject Needs: Travel—all 50 states. Photo captions preferred.
Specs: Uses 3×5, 5×7 b&w prints; 35mm, 2¼×2¼, 4×5, 8×10 transparencies.
Payment & Terms: Pays $50-300/color photo, $20-70/b&w photo. Credit line given. Buys one-time rights and rights for all editions (life of book). Simultaneous submissions and previously published work OK.
Making Contact: Query with list of stock photo subjects; provide resume, business card, brochure, flyer or tearsheets to be kept on file for possible future assignments. Interested in stock photos. SASE. Reports in 2 weeks.
Tips: Looks for unusual travel shots; people, places, things; entire US, the Pacific and Asia. "Be sure to query with list of stock photo subjects and tearsheets."

MOTORBOOKS INTERNATIONAL, 275 South Third St., Stillwater MN 55082. (612)439-6001. FAX: (612)439-5627. Publisher: Tim Parker. Publishes trade and specialist and how-to, automotive, aerospace and hobby. Photos used for text illustration, book covers and dust jackets. Buys 30 freelance photos and offers 12 assignments annually.
Subject Needs: Anything to do with transportation (not sailboats), tractors, cycles, airplane—U-2's. Model release and captions preferred.
Specs: Any size prints or transparencies.
Payment & Terms: Pay negotiated. Credit line given. Rights negotiable. Simultaneous submissions and previously published work OK.
Making Contact: Works mostly on assignment; interested in stock photos. SASE. Reports in 2 weeks.

MUSIC SALES CORP., 225 Park Ave. S., New York NY 10003. (212)254-2100. Contact: Daniel Earley. Publishes instructional music books, song collections and books on music. Recent titles include: *Judy Collins Anthology*, *Tom Waits* and *Rock Chord Guide*. Photos used for cover and/or interiors.
Needs: Buys 200 photos annually. Query first with resume of credits. Provide business card, brochure, flyer or tearsheet to be kept on file for possible future assignments. Buys one-time rights. Present model release on acceptance of photo. Reports in 2 months. SASE. Simultaneous submissions and previously published work OK.
B&W: Uses 8×10 glossy prints. Captions required. Pays $35-50.
Color: Uses 35mm, 2×2 or 5×7 transparencies. Captions required. Pays $100-500.
Jacket: Uses 8×10 glossy b&w prints; 35mm, 2×2 and 5×7 color transparencies. Captions required. Pays $50-150.
Tips: In samples, wants to see "the ability to capture the artist in motion with a sharp eye for framing the shot well. Portraits must reveal what makes the artist unique. We need rock, jazz, classical—on stage and impromptu shots. Please send us an inventory list of available stock photos of musicians. We rarely send photographers on assignment and buy mostly from material on hand." Send "business card and tear sheets or prints stamped 'proof' across them. Due to the nature of record releases and concert events, we never know exactly when we may need a photo. We keep photos on permanent file for possible future use."

THE NAIAD PRESS, INC., Box 10543, Tallahassee FL 32302. (904)539-9322. Editor: Barbara Grier. "We are the oldest and largest of the lesbian and lesbian/feminist publishing houses. We publish trade size paperback books, fiction, poetry, autobiography, biography, mysteries, adventure, self-help, sexuality, history, etc." Photos used for text illustration and book covers. Buys 3-5 photos annually from lesbian cover artists.
Subject Needs: Inquire. Model release required.
Specs: Uses 5×7 glossy b&w prints.
Payment & Terms: Credit line given. Buys all rights. Previously published work OK.
Making Contact: "Drop a note outlining work area." SASE. Reports in 3 weeks.
Tips: "We are interested in submissions from lesbian photographers particularly, and lesbian feminist photographers even more so. Very interested in having a location file of photographers for assigning author pictures (i.e., where the photographer is asked to photograph a local author for publicity purposes)."

NELSON-HALL PUBLISHERS, 111 N. Canal St., Chicago IL 60606. Editor: Stephen Ferrara. Publishes educational books for libraries and colleges. Heavy emphasis in social sciences. Photos used for text illustration, promotional materials, book covers and dust jackets. Model release required; captions preferred.
Payment & Terms: Pays $35 minimum/b&w photo; $75 minimum/color photo. Gives credit line. Buys one-time rights. Previously published work OK.
Making Contact: Query with resume of credits and list of stock photo subjects. Provide resume, flyer and business card to be kept on file for possible future assignments. Does not return unsolicited material.

NEW LEAF PRESS, INC., Box 311, Green Forest AR 72638. (501)438-5288. President: Tim Dudley. Publishes adult trade, cooking, fiction of religious nature and catalogs ads. Photos used for book covers and dust jackets. Buys 20 freelance photos annually. Does not assign freelance work. Example of recently published title: *The Kingdom*.
Subject Needs: Landscapes, people and flowers. Model release required; captions preferred.
Specs: Uses 6×8 gloss color prints.
Payment & Terms: Pays $100-250/color photo and $50-100/b&w photo. Credit line given. Buys one-time and book rights. Simultaneous submissions and previously published work OK.
Making Contact: Query with samples and list of stock photo subjects. Interested in stock photos. SASE. Reports in 2 weeks.
Tips: In order to contribute to the company, send "quality, crisp photos." Trend in book publishing is toward much greater use of photography.

NITECH RESEARCH CORPORATION, Box 638, Warrington PA 18976. President: Dr. William White, Jr. Publishes adult books on the Bible and ancient world and scientific and laboratory photography. Photos used for text illustration, book covers and dust jackets. Buys 100-300 photos annually.
Subject Needs: Needs "expert 35mm transparencies of ancient sites in Greece, Turkey, Lebanon, Israel, Egypt, Jordan, Syria, particularly ancient inscriptions, texts, papyri, scrolls, etc., also high grade laboratory and engineering. Special needs include architectural and archaeological sites, Eastern Mediterranean, First to Fourth Century, A.D."
Specs: 35mm, 2¼×2¼ and 4×5 slides.
Payment & Terms: Pays $15-75/b&w photo; $25-100/color photo. Credit line given. Buys one-time and all rights, book rights or all rights, but may reassign to the photographer after publication. Simultaneous submissions and previously published work OK.
Making Contact: Query with list of stock photo subjects or send unsolicited photos by mail for consideration. SASE. Reports in 1 month.
Tips: "We still need good subminiature and pinhole photos with complete data also microphotography. See our publication: *Kodak Workshop Series Close-Up Photography*; *Photomacrography: An Introduction (Focal)*, or our monthly column in *Shutterbug Ads*."

W.W. NORTON AND COMPANY, 500 Fifth Ave., New York NY 10110. (212)354-5500. College Department: Ms. Ruth Mandel. Publishes college textbooks. Photos used for text illustration, book covers and dust jackets. Examples of recently published titles: *Physics*, second ed.; *The American Age*; and *Fathers & Sons*, Norton critical ed. Photos used for cover and/or text.
Subject Needs: Vary.
Specs: Depend on use.
Payment & Terms: Credit line given. Buys one-time rights. Simultaneous submissions and previously published work OK.
Making Contact: Query with list of stock photo subjects. Do not enclose SASE. Reports in up to 3 months.
Tips: "Offer to send photocopies or negatives of possible photos. Be able to respond quickly to requests for deadlines."

NTC PUBLISHING GROUP, 4255 W. Touhy Ave., Lincolnwood IL 60646. (708)679-5500. VGM Career Books Editor: Mike Urban. Publishes career books. Uses photos for text illustration and book covers. Buys 5-10 freelance photos annually. Examples of recently published titles: *Opportunities in Biotechnology Careers*, *Opportunities in International Business Careers* and *Opportunities in Plumbing Careers*. In all cases photos used for covers and/or text.
Subject Needs: Black and white photos of persons working. Action photos of people in the fields of computer science, health and medical, aerospace, performing arts, microelectronics, forestry, photography, music, modeling, sports, business management, environmental, secretarial, food service, word processing, financial, printing and plastics. Model release and captions required.
Specs: Uses 5×7 and 8×10 glossy b&w prints.
Payment & Terms: Pays $25 maximum/b&w photo. Credit line given. Buys all rights. Simultaneous submissions and previously published work OK.
Making Contact: Query with list of stock photo subjects and photocopies of photos. Interested in stock photos. SASE. Reports in 1 month. Photo guidelines free with SASE.
Tips: "Send photocopies of b&w photos that could be used in career books."

*C. OLSON & CO., (formerly The Plan), Box 5100-PM, Santa Cruz CA 95063. (408)458-3365. Editor: C.L. Olson. Estab. 1977.
Photo Needs: Uses 10-20 photos/year b&w or color; all supplied by freelance photographers. "Looking for color photos of glaciers—from land, sea and air. Photos of well-known natural-hygienists. Also, photos of fruit and nut trees in public-access locations like parks, schools, churchs, streets, businesses, etc. in blossom, in fruit." Model release and captions preferred.

Making Contact & Terms: Send unsolicited photos by mail for consideration. SASE, plus #10 window envelope. Reports in 2 weeks. "All rates negotiable." Pays on either acceptance or publication. Credit line given on request. Negotiates rights purchased. Simultaneous submissions and previously published work OK.

Tips: Open to both amateur and professional photographers. "To ensure that we buy your work, be open to payment based on a royalty for each copy of a book we sell."

OUTDOOR EMPIRE PUBLISHING, INC., Box C-19000, Seattle WA 98109. (206)624-3845. General Manager: Dan Langdon. Publishes how-to, outdoor recreation and large-sized paperbacks. Photos used for text illustration, promotional materials, book covers and newspapers. Buys 6 photos annually; offers 2 freelance assignments annually.

Subject Needs: Wildlife, hunting, fishing, boating, outdoor recreation. Model release and captions preferred.

Specs: Uses 8×10 glossy b&w and color prints; 35mm, 2¼×2¼ and 4×5 transparencies.

Payment & Terms: Credit line given. Buys all rights; payment "depends on situation/publication." Simultaneous submissions and previously published work OK.

Making Contact: Query with samples or send unsolicited photos by mail for consideration; provide resume, business card, brochure, flyer or tearsheets to be kept on file for possible future assignments. Solicits photos by assignment only. SASE. Reports in 3 weeks.

Tips: Prefers to see slides or contact sheets as samples. "Be persistent; submit good quality work. Since we publish how-to books, clear, informative photos that tell a story are very important."

OXFORD UNIVERSITY PRESS, 200 Madison Ave., New York NY 10016. (212)679-7300, ext. 7274. Photo Researcher: Holland Mills. Publishes adult academic and trade books and college textbooks. Photos used for text illustration, promotional materials, book covers and dust jackets. Examples of recently published titles: *Putnam's Geology* by Birkeland & Larson; *North America: A Geography of the U.S. and Canada*; and *America by Design* by Kostof. In all cases, photos used for cover and text.

Subject Needs: Portraits, historical photos, art and architecture and miscellaneous.

Specs: Uses 8×10 glossy b&w prints; 4×5 transparencies.

Payment & Terms: Pays maximum $350/b&w photo; $400/color photo. Credit line given. Buys one-time rights. Previously published work OK.

Making Contact: Query with list of stock photo subjects. Provide resume, business card, brochure, flyer or tearsheets to be kept on file for possible future assignments. Solicits photos by assignment only; interested in stock photos. Does not return unsolicited material. No calls, please.

PADRE PRODUCTIONS, Box 840, Arroyo Grande CA 93421-0840. (805)473-1947. Editor: Lachlan P. MacDonald. Publishes general nonfiction books, children's books, nature, Western history and travel, and antiques and collectibles. Photos used for illustrating art and travel books. Example of a recently published title: *More Back Roads of the Central Coast* by Ron Stob, cover and text illustrations. "We're interested in California travel books dealing with a single area or destination." Buys 30-100 photos and 1-2 photo books annually. Query with resume of credits. Provide flyer, tearsheets, letter of inquiry and brochure to be kept on file for possible future assignments. Does not notify photographer when future assignments can be expected. Buys book rights only. Present model release on acceptance of photo. Reports in 4 weeks. SASE. Previously published work OK.

B&W: Send contact sheet. Captions required. Pays $5-100.

Color: Send transparencies. Captions required. Pays $10-150.

Jacket: Send glossy prints for b&w, glossy prints or transparencies for color. "We're interested in Western photographers available to do travel books and covers. Author jacket photos are supplied by authors when used." Pays $10-150.

Tips: "Return postage must accompany everything. Book ideas that include the text as well as photographs are most welcome. We would like to work with a photographer who knows the subject or area well, will work with us on layout, and can prepare camera-ready book for manufacture. Photographers who can do that can expect author credit and a standard royalty contract rather than a flat fee. We are particularly interested in photographers who are capable naturalists and interpret the environment as well as record it."

PARKER & SON PUBLICATIONS, INC., 2041 Davie Ave., City of Commerce CA 90040. (619)931-5979. Marketing Director: Beth Doll. Law book publishers. Uses photos for promotional materials. Buys about 15 freelance photos annually.

Subject Needs: Book photos for reproduction in promotional materials, some with surrounding desk accompaniments.

Specs: Uses 8×10 and 3×5 glossy b&w and color prints.

Payment & Terms: Pays $100-125/b&w photo and $175-200/color photo. Buys all rights.

Making Contact: Query with samples. Provide resume, business card, brochure, flyer or tearsheets to be kept on file for possible future assignments. SASE.

Tips: Looks for sharp, clean, professional photos of appeal to the legal profession. Uses "shots of product by itself . . . clean, straight lines, true color, bright whites, and clear copy. We publish law books that must be attractively depicted in photo form for reproduction in direct mail brochures that market our products. Brochures vary from glossy, coated stock, to uncoated."

PEANUT BUTTER PUBLISHING, 200 2nd. West Ave., Seattle WA 98119. (206)281-5965. Publisher: Elliott Wolf. Estab. 1971. Publishes cookbooks (primarily gourmet); restaurant guides; assorted adult trade books. Photos used for promotional materials and book covers. Buys 24-36 photos/year; offers up 5 freelance assignments/year. Recently published title: *Lynwood: The People, The Land, The City*, (text & cover photos).

Subject Needs: "We are primarily interested in shots displaying a variety of foods in an appealing table or buffet setting. Good depth of field and harmonious color are important. We are also interested in cityscapes that capture one or another of a city's more pleasant aspects. No models."

Specs: Uses 2¼×2¼ or 4×5 slides.

Payment & Terms: Pays $50-300/color photo. Credit line given. Buys one-time , exclusive product and all rights. Simultaneous submissions and previously published work OK.

Making Contact: Arrange a personal interview to show portfolio; query with samples or send unsolicited photos by mail for consideration. Interested in stock photos. SASE. Reports in 2 weeks.

Tips: "We need to see photos — samples or stocks — that meet our needs."

PELICAN PUBLISHING CO., INC., 1101 Monroe St., Gretna LA 70053. (504)368-1175. Production Manager: Dana Bilbray. Publishes general trade books. Photos used for book jackets. Query first with resume of credits. Buys all rights. Present model release on acceptance of photo. Pays $30-125/job. Reports in 6 weeks. Previously published photos OK. Photos purchased with accompanying ms.

Jacket: Uses glossy b&w prints or color "as specified." Captions required.

*THE PHOTOGRAPHIC ARTS CENTER, LTD., 163 Amsterdam Ave. #201, New York NY 10023. (212)838-8640. FAX: (212)873-7065. Publisher: Robert S. Persky. Estab. 1980. Publishes books on photography and art, emphasizing the business aspects of being a photographer, artist and/or dealer. Photos used for book covers. Examples of recently published titles: *Publishing Your Posters and Cards* (cover illustration); and *The Photographer's Complete Guide To Exhibition & Sales Spaces* (text illustration).

Subject Needs: Business of photography and art. Model release required.

Specs: Uses 5×7 glossy b&w print; 5×7 glossy color prints; 35mm transparencies.

Payment & Terms: Pays $25-100/color photo, $25-100/b&w photo. Credit line given. Buys one time rights.

Making Contact: Query with samples and text. Interested in stock photos. SASE. Reports in 3 weeks. No photo guidelines available.

Tips: Sees trend in book publishing toward "more use of computer manipulated images." In freelancer's submissions, looks for "manuscript or detailed outline of manuscript with submission." This is "most likely to receive favorable consideration." To break into book publishing, "Submit your personal best."

PLAYERS PRESS INC., Box 1132, Studio City CA 91604. (818)789-4980. Vice President: David Cole. Publishes entertainment books including theater, film and television. Photos used for text illustration, promotional materials book covers and dust jackets. Buys 50-1,000 photos annually.

Subject Needs: Entertainers, actors, directors, theatres, productions, actors in period costumes, scenic designs and clowns. Model release required; photo captions preferred.

Specs: Uses 8×10 glossy or matte b&w prints; 5×7 glossy color prints; 35mm, 2¼×2¼ transparencies.

Payment & Terms: Pays $5-500/color photo, $1-200/b&w photo. Credit line sometimes given, depending on book. Buys book and all rights; negotiates in case of all rights. Simultaneous submissions and previously published work OK.

Making Contact: Query with list of stock photo subjects, send unsolicited photos by mail for consideration. Interested in stock photos. SASE. Reports in 3 weeks.

Tips: "Do not telephone; submit only what we ask for."

POCKET BOOKS, 1230 Avenue of the Americas, New York NY 10020. (212)698-7000. VP/Exec. Art Director: Barbara Buck. Estab. 1939. Publishes hard covermass market and trade paperbacks. Photos used for book covers, uses mostly people and still life.
Payment & Terms: Payment varies with each project, negotiable. Buys one-time rights. Model release required.
Making Contact: Submit portfolio for review any day but Friday; provide tearsheets to be kept on file for possible future assignments. Interested in stock photos. SASE. Previously published work OK.
Tips: "I look for people who are conceptual as well as technically skilled. Do not call art directors! Drop off portfolio with us regularly with a variety of tearsheets to show us new work."

PUBLICATIONS INTERNATIONAL, LTD., 7373 N. Cicero Ave., Lincolnwood IL 60646. (708)676-3470. Contact: Carol Bezark. "We publish a wide variety of books and magazines aimed at the general audience and educational markets. We publish magazines, hard-cover originals, trade paperback originals, mass-market paperback originals in cookbooks, automotive, juvenile pop culture/non-fiction, investments, health, medical, calendars, hobbies, computer, animals, gardening, science, military and sports." Photos used for text illustration, book covers, dust jackets, editorial use, plus calendars. Buys over 500 photos annually.
Subject Needs: Animals, sports, baseball cards, personalities, wrestling, jets and aircraft, calendar subjects, teddy bears, quilts, microphotography. Model release and captions preferred.
Specs: Uses 4×6 minimum, glossy b&w and color prints; 35mm, 2¼×2¼, 4×5 and 8×10 transparencies.
Payment & Terms: Pays $25-50/b&w photo, $35-300/color photo. "We look for discounts on bulk purchases." Credit lines "usually noted in a photo credit block in the publication." Buys one-time rights. Simultaneous submissions and previously published work OK.
Making Contact: Query with resume of credits, query with list of stock photo subjects; provide resume, business card, brochure, flyer or tearsheets to be kept on file for possible future assignments (would prefer some tearsheets or non-returnable samples to keep on file for reference). Solicits photos by project needs; interested in stock photos. "Prefer to speak with photographer first to discuss our needs before material is sent." Reports in 1 to 3 months depending on project.
Tips: Do not send any original slides that need to be returned; send only tearsheets/samples. "For our company, photographers should be flexible on pricing and budgets. A working relationship can lead to repeat business. Also, we appreciate clearly labeled photos with photographer's name and cover letter on submission form indicating quantity of photos sent. Our company is using more calendar images and images aimed at a young elementary school audience. We are also moving toward high-quality 'coffee-table book' type images. Subjects are wide ranging."

RAINTREE PUBLISHERS, 310 W. Wisconsin Ave., Milwaukee WI 53203. (414)273-0873. Art Director: Suzanne Beck. Publishes juvenile (K-12) educational/text books. Photos used for book covers and text illustration.
Subject Needs: Science, nature, city/state and foreign country scenics, sport and recreation, historical and nostalgia, and industrial. Model release and captions preferred.
Specs: Uses 35mm, 2¼×2¼ and 4×5 transparencies.
Payment & Terms: "Each project is budgeted for overall product, each purchase is negotiable." Credit line given. Buys one-time rights.
Making Contact: Provide resume, business card, brochure, flyer or tearsheets to be kept on file for possible future assignments. No calls, please. Interested in stock photos. SASE. Reports in 1 month.
Tips: "As our books are geared toward children, we look for good color, recognizable subjects and people."

RESOURCE PUBLICATIONS, INC., Suite 290, 160 E. Virginia St., San Jose CA 95112. Editorial Director: Kenneth Guentert. Publishes religious books, magazines and books dealing with celebration resources. Photos used for text illustration and promotional materials. Buys 6 photos/year. Pays $15-35/hour. Credit line given. Buys all rights, but may reassign rights to photographer after publication. Model release required. Send material by mail for consideration. SASE. Reports in 6 weeks.
B&W: Uses 8×10 prints. Pays $5-25/photo.
Color: Uses 8×10 prints. Pays $5-25/photo.
Jacket/Cover: Uses b&w prints and color transparencies. Pays $5-25/photo.
Tips: "Book authors tend to work with their own photographers. However, we will talk with anyone dedicated to taking photos of liturgical space or situations."

RUNNING HEADS INC., 55 West 21 Street, New York NY 10010. (212)727-3434. Photo Editor: Ellie Watson. Estab. 1984. Publishes adult trade books specializing in interior design, architecture, gardening and nature. Photos used for text illustration, promotional materials, book covers and dust jackets. Buys 1,500 photos annually; offers 4-6 freelance assignments annually. Examples of recently published titles: *Gardening America*, (published by Viking) *Berries* (published by Bantam) and *Victorian Details;* text illustrations, cover art, etc.

Subject Needs: Interested in interior design, gardening and lifestyle photos. Model release required; photo captions preferred.

Specs: Uses 35mm, 2¼×2¼, 4×5 and 8×10 transparencies.

Payment & Terms: Pays $50/b&w or color photo; "pays freelancer according to budget." Photo credits given in back of book. Rights vary according to project. Simultaneous submissions and previously published work OK.

Making Contact: Arrange a personal interview to show portfolio. Query with resume of credits, samples, and list of stock photo subjects. Provide business card, brochure, flyer or tearsheets to be kept on file for possible future assignments. Works on assignment only; interested in stock photos. Reports in 1 month.

Tips: "You may send resume, tearsheets, list of credits and I will get back to you." Looks for "high-quality color work to be used in beautiful, very high-quality reproduction for heavily illustrated books."

This photo of "a loving father/daughter relationship" has helped photographer Sally Weigand both "financially and with more credits." Initially, book publisher William H. Sadlier, Inc. paid Weigand $115 for use in a textbook. After having filed the image with the stock photo agency, Picture Cube, Inc, the photographer was also able to sell one-time rights through the agency to West Publishing for another $60.

WILLIAM H. SADLIER, INC., 11 Park Place, New York NY 10007. (212)227-2120. Director of Photo Research, Editorial: Jim Saylor. Publishes religious education materials for all ages; academic textbooks, kindergarten-adult. Photos used for text illustration, promotional materials, book covers and posters. Buys 500 photos annually.

Subject Needs: Children interacting with families, friends, members of the opposite sex (all ethnic groups); nature; religious artwork. Model release required.

Specs: Uses 35mm, 2¼×2¼ and 4×5 transparencies, occasionally b&w prints.

Payment & Terms: Pays $25-100/b&w photo; $50-350/color photo. "Assignments are negotiated individually." Credit line given. Buys one-time rights, book rights or all rights. Simultaneous submissions OK.

Making Contact: Query with list of stock photo subjects and provide brochure, flyer or tearsheets to be kept on file for possible future assignments. Interested in stock photos. SASE.

Tips: Looks for colorful photos with good interaction and ethnic mix.

*ST. REMY PRESS, 417 St. Pierre, Suite 300, Montreal, PQ H24 2M4 Canada. (514)288-9250. Picture Editor: Michelle Turbide. Estab. 1984. Publishes adult trade. "We are a packager for Time-Life Books, Alexandria, VA." Photos used for text illustraton and book covers. Recently published titles include:

Fix It Yourself (series), *Time-Life's WWII Book*, and *Art of Our Century*.
Subject Needs: Travel and technology. Model release preferred; photo captions required.
Specs: Uses 35mm, 2¼ × 2¼, 4 × 5 transparencies.
Payment & Terms: Payment negotiable. Credit line given. Buys one-time rights. Previously published work OK.
Making Contact: Arrange a personal interview to show portfolio; provide resume, business card, brochure, flyer or tearsheets to be kept on file for possible future assignments. Interested in stock photo. SASE. Reports in 1 month. No photo guidelines available.
Tips: "We are not starting on a science and technology series for Time-Life called 'How Things Work' – first title is *Flight*. We will need exciting photos showing the difference between new science vs. nature."

SANDHILL CRANE PRESS, INC., 2406 NW 47th Terrace, Gainesville FL 32606. (904)371-9858. Acquisitions Editor: Ross H. Arnett. Publishes nature books (natural history, conservation, etc.). Photos used for text illustration, book covers and dust jackets. Examples of recently published titles: *Florida Butterflies*; *In Search of Reptiles and Amphibians*; and *Frogs, Toads, and Tree Toads*.
Specs: Uses 8 × 10 glossy b&w prints; 35mm transparencies.
Payment & Terms: Pays $50-100/color photo, $10-25/b&w photo. Also gives citation in publication as payment. Credit line given. Buys one-time rights. Simultaneous submissions and previously published work OK.
Making Contact: Query with resume of credits. Provide business card, brochure, flyer or tearsheets to be kept on file for possible future assignments. SASE. Reports in 2 weeks. Photo guidelines free with SASE.
Tips: "Fill frame with subject." Trend toward most photos being supplied by authors.

SCHUETTGE & CARLETON, 458 Gravatt, Berkeley CA 94705. (415)649-9271. Manager: Dick Schuettge. Estab. 1978. Publishes picture books for children, cook books and calendars (various subjects). Photos used for text illustration and calendars. Buys 200 photos and offers 3-4 freelance assignments annually. Recenlty published 20 Calendars: folk art, fine art, yachts, animals, nature landscape, architecture, sports, flowers, food and trains. Also, garden and food books (inside photos, cover etc.).
Subject Needs: Calendars – folk art, food, Americana, trains and boats, fine art; books for children – how to do it, what is it like. Calendar pictures should not be generic. Model release required; photo captions preferred.
Specs: Uses 8 × 10 b&w prints; 2¼ × 2¼, 4 × 5 and 8 × 10 transparencies.
Payment & Terms: Pays in royalty. Credit line given. Buys one-time and book rights. Also buys one-time and exclusive product rights. Simultaneous submissions and previously published work OK.
Making Contact: Arrange a personal interview to show portfolio, query with resume of credits, samples and list of stock photo subjects. Provide business card, brochure, flyer or tearsheets to be kept on file for possible future assignments. Interested in stock photos. SASE. Reports in 3 weeks.
Tips: Looks for "sharp well-balanced color. Doesn't want to see ordinary subjects but wants the usual top quality technique. Explain the file or stock characterstics carefully."

SELF-COUNSEL PRESS, 1481 Charlotte Rd., Vancouver BC V7J 1H1 Canada. (604)986-3366. Designer: Janette Lush. Publishes: adult trade, self-help books; legal, business, reference, financial, retirement, psychology and travel series. Photos used for promotional materials (book dummies, blurbs, posters) and book covers. Buys 6 photos and offers 6 freelance assignments annually. Examples of recently published titles: *Good Ethics Good Business, Margo Oliver's Cookbook for Seniors, The Business Guide to Profitable Customer Relations, Start and Run a Profitable Home-Based Business* and *Preparing a Successful Business Plan*. All photography used as cover art.
Subject Needs: Needs photos of business and people (business, seniors). Model release required.
Specs: Uses color prints; 35mm and 2¼ × 2¼ transparencies.
Payment & Terms: Pays $75-200/color photo, $100-250/job. Credit line sometimes given depending on agreed price, other circumstances. Buys book rights. Simultaneous submissions and previously published work OK, depending on circumstances.
Making Contact: Arrange a personal interview to show portfolio if possible. Query with samples or with list of stock photo subjects. Provide resume, business card, brochure, flyer or tearsheets to be kept on file for possible future assignments. Interested in stock photos; send catalog of stock photos. Cannot return material.
Tips: "Send samples but not originals. Generally unsolicited phone calls are not well-received since product is visual." "Catalogues are well-received."

*SIERRA PRESS, INC., P.O. Box 25, El Portal CA 95318. (209)379-2330. General Manager: Jim Wilson. Estab. 1984. Publishes color gift books, postcard books, postcards, posters and prints of national parks and monuments. Photos used for text illustration and book covers. Uses 100 photos annually; offers

4-5 freelance assignments annually. Example of recently published titles: *Wildflowers of Yosemite,* wildflower field guide; *Wish You Were Here®,* Yellowstone gift book (landscapes); and *Wish You Were Here® Postcard Books,* Grand Canyon, postcards.
Subject Needs: Brilliant and colorful landscapes utilizing dramatic lighting and intimate details of nature. Photo captions required.
Specs: Uses 35mm, 2¼ × 2¼, 4 × 5, 8 × 10 transparencies; they must be sharp, clear and concise.
Payment & Terms: Pays $50-250/color photo. Credit line given. Buys one-time rights. Simultaneous submissions and previously published work OK.
Making Contact: Query with list of stock photo subjects. SASE. Reports in 1 month. No photo guidelines sheet available.

*R. SIRKIS PUBLISHERS LTD., Box 22027, Tel Aviv 61220 Israel. (972)-3-751-0792. FAX: (972)-3-751-1628. Chairman: Rafael Sirkis. Publishes adult trade, juvenile, how-to and cooking. Photos used for text illustration, book covers and dust jackets. Buys 100 photos annually; offers 6 freelance assignments annually. Examples of recently published titles: "Pasta Diet," "Cocktails" and "Garnishes." All three titles are Hebrew language cooking and food-oriented books; photos used for text illustration.
Subject Needs: Food; buys only photos from stock. Model release required; photo captions preferred.
Specs: "All formats are accepted, if quality is excellent."
Payment & Terms: Pays $10-50/color photo, $5-25/b&w photo. Credit line given. Buys book rights. simultaneous submissions and previously published work OK.
Making Contact: Query with list of stock photo subjects; provide resume, business card, brochure, flyer or tearsheets to be kept on file for possible future assignments. Interested in stock photos. SASE. Reports in 1 month. Photo guidelines not available.

*SMITHSONIAN (BOOKS) INSTITUTION, 470 L Enfant Plaza SW #7100, Washington DC 20560. (202)287-3738. Senior Picture Editor: Frances C. Rowsell. Publishes adult trade. Fully illustrated coffee-table type books. Photos used for text illustration, promotional and book covers. Examples of recently published titles: *Lords of the Air,* picture with 320 text photos; *Images of America,* picture book with 320 images, mostly black and white.
Subject Needs: Subject needs vary. Model release preferred.
Specs: Uses 35mm, 2¼ × 2¼, 4 × 5, 8 × 10 transparencies.
Payment & Terms: Payment varies; negotiable. Credit line given. Buys one-time rights. Simultaneous submissions and previously published work OK.
Making Contact: Query with resume of credits; provide resume, business card, brochure, flyer or tearsheets to be kept on file for possible future assignments. Solicits photos by assignment only. Interested in stock photos. SASE. Reports only as needed.
Tips: "If photographer is top quality, we are pleased to see them."

SOUTH-WESTERN PUBLISHING COMPANY, 5101 Madison Rd., Cincinnati OH 45227. Assistant Director of Photographic Services, College Division: Diana Fears. South-Western publishes texts for the college market that include business-related as well as some vocational materials.
Needs: Uses photographers and photo researchers for textbook publishing. Subjects include occupational shots, human relations, work environment, high-tech, particularly in the field of computer technology.
Specs: Uses 8 × 10 b&w prints and 35mm, 2¼ × 2¼, 4 × 5 and 8 × 10 color transparencies.
First Contact & Terms: Provide business card, self-promotion piece or tearsheets to be kept on file for possible future assignments. Interested in stock photos. No response unless or until images are needed. Pay negotiated by use. Buys one-time rights usually. Model release required. Credit line given.

THE SPEECH BIN INC., 1766 Twentieth Avenue, Vero Beach, FL 32960. (407)770-0007. FAX: (407)770-0006. Senior Editor: J. Binney. Publishes textbooks and instructional materials for speech/language pathologists, audiologists and special educators. Photos used for book covers, instructional materials and catalogs..
Subject Needs: Children. Model release required.
Specs: Uses 8 × 10 glossy b&w prints.
Payment & Terms: Credit line "sometimes" given. Buys all rights; will negotiate with a photographer not willing to sell all rights. Previously published work OK.
Making Contact: Provide resume, business card, brochure, flyer or tearsheets to be kept on file for possible future assignments. Works on assignment only. SASE. Reports in 3 weeks.

STANDARD EDUCATIONAL CORP., 200 W. Monroe St., Chicago IL 60606. (312)346-7440. FAX: (312)580-7215. Picture Editor: Irene L. Ferguson. Publishes the New Standard Encyclopedia. Photos used for text illustration. Buys stock photos only; about 300 photos/year. Credit line given. Buys one-time rights. Model release preferred; captions required. Query with list of stock photo subjects. SASE.

Do not send unsolicited photos. Simultaneous submissions and previously published work OK. Reports in 1 month. To see style/themes used, look at encyclopedias in library, especially New Standard Encyclopedia.
Subject Needs: Major cities and countries, points of interest, agricultural and industrial scenes, plants and animals. Photos are used to illustrate specific articles in encyclopedia — the subject range is from A-Z.
B&W: Uses 8×10 glossy prints; contact sheet OK. Pays $75-125/photo.
Color: Uses transparencies. Pays $100-300/photo.

STAR PUBLISHING COMPANY, 940 Emmett Ave., Belmont CA 94002. (415)591-3505. Managing Editor: Stuart Hoffman. Publishes textbooks, regional history, professional reference books. Photos used for text illustration, promotional materials and book covers.
Subject Needs: Biological illustrations and microphotography. Model release and captions required.
Specs: Uses 5×7 minimum b&w and color prints, 35mm transparencies.
Payment & Terms: Payment variable "depending on publication and placement." Credit line given. Buys book rights or all rights. Previously published submissions OK.
Making Contact: Query with samples and list of stock photo subjects. Provide resume, business card, brochure, flyer or tearsheets to be kept on file for possible future assignments. Interested in stock photos. SASE.

STEWART, TABORI & CHANG, 740 Broadway, New York NY 10003. (212)460-5000. FAX: (212)995-0582. Photo Editor: Sarah Longacre. Associate Photo Editor: Jose Pouso. Estab. 1981. Publishes quality illustrated trade books on cooking, gardening, travel, style and art. Photos used for text illustration, promotional materials, book cover and dust jackets. Buys 1,000 photos and offers 15 freelance assignments annually. Examples of recently published titles: *Power Behind the Wheel* (196 photos; cover and text); *Social Gardens* (250 photos; cover and text); *Smithsonian Guide to Historic America* (South New England, Mid-Atlantic States, Virginia & Capital Region; 200 or more photos in each; cover & text).
Subject Needs: Deeply saturated colors, graphically beautiful, no people in pictures as a general rule. Model release "not usually an issue"; photo captions required.
Specs: Uses 8×10 b&w glossy prints; 35mm, 2¼×2¼, 4×5 and 8×10 transparencies.
Payment & Terms: Pays $75-150/color or b&w photo; $5,000-15,000/complete book. "If photographer gets contract for entire book, he receives project fee." Buys all rights, but will negotiate. Simultaneous submissions and previously published work OK.
Making Contact: Query with samples, query with list of stock photo subjects; provide resume, business card, brochure, flyer or tearsheets to be kept on file for possible future assignments. Works on assignment only; interested in stock photos. SASE. Reports in 2 months. Photo guidelines free with SASE.
Tips: "We like to have seen a representative sample of work so that when we have a specific subject we are working on for a book we know whether or not the photographer's work is appropriate for our company."

STONE WALL PRESS, 1241 30th St. NW, Washington DC 20007. President: Henry Wheelwright. Publishes national outdoor books and nonfiction. Photos used for text illustration, book covers and dust jackets.
Subject Needs: Dramatic color cover shots; very occasionally representative text illustrations. Model release required; captions preferred.
Specs: Uses 7×9 glossy color prints.
Payment & Terms: Credit line given. Buys book rights. Simultaneous submissions and previously published work OK.
Making Contact: Provide resume, business card, brochure, flyer or tearsheets to be kept on file for possible future assignments. Interested in stock photos. Does not return unsolicited material.

SYMMES SYSTEMS, Box 8101, Atlanta GA 30306. (404)876-7260. Photography Director: Ed Symmes. Publishes books about bonsai, the art of growing miniature plants.
Subject Needs: Needs pictures relating to bonsai; adding titles on other Japanese Arts — Netsuke, Ikebana, Scholar's desk, scrolls, etc. Photos used for text illustration and for book jackets.
Making Contact: Query first with resume of credits; provide tearsheets, brochure and dupe slides to be kept on file for possible future assignments. Notifies photographer if future assignments can be expected. Buys first rights or all rights. Present model release on acceptance of photo. Reports in 2 weeks. SASE. Simultaneous submissions and previously published work OK.
Specs: For b&w, send negatives with 8×10 glossy prints. Captions required; include location and species of subject. Pays $10 minimum. For color, send transparencies. Captions required; include location and species of subject. Pays $25 minimum to several hundred depending on usage.

Tips: "We're looking for super sharp images with uncluttered backgrounds."

THEOSOPHICAL PUBLISHING HOUSE, (Quest Books Imprint), 306 W. Geneva Rd., P.O. Box 270, Wheaton IL 60189-0270. (708)665-0130. Production Manager: Michael King. Estab. 1875. Publishes adult trade books on metaphysics, comparative religions, oriental philosophies, theosophy, astrology, transpersonal psychology, and New Age topics. Photos used for text illustration, promotional materials, book covers and dust jackets. Buys 5-10 photos annually. Examples of recently published titles: *The Wholeness Principle* (cover), *Intelligence Came First* (cover) and *Goddess Re-Awakening*, (cover & text).
Subject Needs: Subjects that might evoke a spiritual experience. Top quality nature scenes. Model release required; photo captions preferred.
Specs: Uses 5×7 glossy or matte b&w prints; 2¼×2¼ transparencies.
Payment & Terms: Pays $50-275/color photo, $25-150/b&w photo, pays in copies of books. Buys all rights, will negotiate with a photographer not willing to sell all rights. Previously published work OK.
Making Contact: Query with samples; provide resume, business card, brochure, flyer or tearsheets to be kept on file for possible future assignments. Interested in stock photos. SASE. Reports in 1 month.
Tips: "Send for our book catalog. Our text photo needs are limited. However, we are always seeking good color photos (transparencies) for covers. Ten to twelve new titles are published yearly." To break into publishing in general "examine closely each houses' catalogs to determine if their needs might be met by your specialty."

THORNDIKE PRESS, Box 159, Thorndike ME 04986. (207)948-2962. Art Director: Michael Anderson. Publishes adult trade in large print. Photos used for book covers and dust jackets. Buys 20 photos annually; gives no freelance assignments.
Subject Needs: "Types of photos depend on the particular project." Model release required; captions preferred.
Specs: Uses 5×7 or larger b&w matte prints; 35mm, 2¼×2¼ and 4×5 transparencies.
Payment & Terms: Pays $20-300/b&w photo and $20-300/color photo. Credit line given. Buys one-time rights. Simultaneous submissions and previously published work OK.
Making Contact: Query with non-returnable samples of work; interested in New England locales. SASE. Reports in 1 month.

TRANSPORTATION TRAILS, 9698 W. Judson, Polo IL 61064. FAX: (815)946-2347. Editor: Larry Plachmo. Estab. 1977. Publishes historical transportation titles. Photos used for text illustration, promotional materials, book covers, dust jackets and condensed articles in magazines. Buys over 500 photos annually. Examples of recently published titles: *The Longest Interurban Charter* text and cover; *Sunset Lines — The Story of The Chicago Aurora & Elgin Railroad* text; *The Steam Locomotive Directory of North America* text.
Subject Needs: Transportation, mainly bus or interurban, mainly historical. Model release preferred. "Company name, date and location are expected on photo or slides."
Specs: Uses glossy b&w prints; 35mm transparencies.
Payment & Terms: Rates vary depending on needs; $2.50-150/b&w photo. Credit line given. Buys one-time, book and all rights. Will negotiate with a photographer not willing to sell all rights. Simultaneous submissions and previously published work OK.
Making Contact: Query with samples of historical transportation photos. Interested in stock photos. SASE. Reports in 1 week.
Tips: In photographer's samples, "quality is not as important as location and date." Looks for "historical photos of buses and interurbans. Don't bother us with photos less than 30 years old."

THE TRINITY FOUNDATION, Box 169, Jefferson MD 21755. (301)371-7155. FAX: (806)372-6806. President: John Robbins. Estab. 1948. Publishes religion and philosophy and adult trade paperbacks. Photos used for book covers.
Subject Needs: Model release, photo captions preferred.
Specs: Uses any size color transparencies.
Payment & Terms: Credit line given. Buys book rights. Simultaneous submissions and previously published work OK.
Making Contact: Query with samples. Interested in stock photos. SASE. Reports in 1 month.
Tips: Looks for "sharp, clear pictures related to Christianity and philosophy."

THE TRUMPET CLUB/BANTAM/DOUBLEDAY/DELL, 666 Fifth Ave., New York NY 10103. (212)492-9595. Contact: Assistant Promotion Manager. "We are a student book club for middle and primary grades featuring juvenile fiction and nonfiction." Photos used as promotional materials and juvenile posters (paid and giveaway). Buys 10-15 freelance photos annually. "We have used only photo stock houses in the past and would like to use more freelance services."

Subject Needs: Very cute animal photos, preferably young animals with a strong emphasis on kittens and puppies in fun or cuddly poses. Model release required.

Specs: Uses color prints; 35 mm, 2¼ × 2¼, 4 × 5 and 8 × 10 transparencies.

Payment & Terms: Payment variable. Credit line given. Buys one-year exclusivity rights in the school book club market. Previously published work OK if not used as a poster for another student book club.

Making Contact: Arrange a personal interview to show portfolio. Query with list of stock photo subjects. Provide resume, business card, brochure, flyer or tearsheets to be kept on file for possible future assignments. Interested in stock photos. SASE. Reports in 2 weeks to 1 month.

Tips: "We are looking for adorable shots of animals, especially kittens and puppies. We have also used pandas, penguins, bunnies, koalas, owls and bears. We are also interested in educational and historical subjects like Mount Rushmore, presidents and famous human rights activists. Also, subjects of particular interest to boys, ages 8-12: racing cars, air force jets, celebrity sports stars, etc. A familiarity with these subjects and a strong background in animal photography is important."

2M COMMUNICATIONS LTD., 121 W. 27 St., New York NY 10001. (212)741-1509. FAX: (212)691-4460. President: Madeleine Morel. Estab. 1982. Publishes adult trade biographies. Photos used for text illustration. Buys approximately 200 photos annually. Examples of recently published titles: *Diane Keaton, Magic and the Bird* and *The Princess and the Duchess;* all for text illustration.

Subject Needs: Candids and publicity. Model release required; photo captions preferred.

Specs: Uses b&w prints; 35mm transparencies.

Payment & Terms: Pays $100-200/color photo, $50-100/b&w photo. Credit line given. Buys one-time book and world English language rights. Simultaneous submissions OK.

Making Contact: Query with list of stock photo subjects. Works on assignment only; interested in stock photos. Reports in 1 month.

TYNDALE HOUSE PUBLISHERS, 351 Executive Dr., Wheaton IL 60189. (708)668-8300. Photo Editor: A. Marlene Muddell. Publishes books "on a wide variety of subjects from a Christian perspective." Photos used for book jackets and text illustration and for the magazine, *The Christian Reader.* Buys 100 photos annually.

Subject Needs: Nature, people, especially the family and teenagers of mixed ages and backgrounds.

Making Contact & Terms: Call before sending photos. Does not return unsolicited submissions. We send guidelines if SASE is sent with request. Buys one-time rights. Pays $50-150/b&w inside photo and $75-150/color photo. Previously published work OK "if in non-competitive books."

Specs: Uses 8 × 10 glossy b&w prints, for text and cover; transparencies for cover.

Tips: "The best photos for our use usually tell a story. We want to see only your best work. We are looking only for unique, fresh images."

UNIVELT, INC., Box 28130, San Diego CA 92128. (619)746-4005. Manager: H. Jacobs. Publishes technical books on astronautics. Photos used for text illustration and dust jackets.

Subject Needs: Uses astronautics; most interested in photographer's concept of space, and photos depicting space flight and related areas. Model release preferred; captions required.

Specs: Uses 6 × 9 or 4½ × 6 b&w photos.

Payment & Terms: Pays $25 minimum/b&w photo. Credit line given, if desired. Buys one-time rights. Simultaneous submissions and previously published work OK.

Making Contact: Query with resume of credits; provide business card and letter of inquiry to be kept on file for possible future assignments. Interested in stock photos. SASE. Reports in 1 month.

Tips: "Photos should be suitable for front cover or frontispiece of space books."

VICTIMOLOGY, INC., 2333 N. Vernon St., Arlington VA 22207. (703)536-1750. Photography Director: Sherry Icenhower. Publishes books about victimology focusing on the victims not only of crime but also of occupational and environmental hazards. Recent titles include: *Spouse Abuse, Child Abuse,, Fear of Crime* and *Self-defense.* Photos used for text illustration. Buys 20-30 photos/year. Query with a resume of credits or submit material by mail for consideration. Buys all rights, but may reassign to photographer after publication. Submit model release with photo. Reports in 6 weeks. SASE. Simultaneous submissions and previously published work OK.

B&W: Send contact sheet or 8 × 10 glossy prints. Captions required. Payment depending on subject matter and use.

Color: Send 35mm transparencies, contact sheet or 5 × 7 or 8 × 10 glossy prints. "We will look at color photos only if part of an essay with text." Captions required. Pays $30 minimum.

Jacket: Send contact sheet or glossy prints for b&w; contact sheet, glossy prints or 35mm transparencies for color. Captions required. Pays $100-150 minimum.

WARNER BOOKS, 666 5th Ave., New York NY 10103. (212)484-3073. Creative Director: Jackie Merri Meyer. Publishes "everything but text books." Photos used for book covers and dust jackets. Buys approximately 20 freelance photos and offers approximately 30 assignments annually.
Subject Needs: People, food still life, glamourous women and couples. Model release required; captions preferred.
Specs: Uses color prints/transparencies; also some black & white and hand-tinting.
Payment & Terms: Pays $800/color photo; $650-1,200/job. Credit line given. Buys one-time rights. Simultaneous submissions and previously published work OK.
Making Contact: Submit portfolio for review; also send brochure, flyer or tearsheets to be kept on file for possible future assignments. Works on assignment only; interested in stock photos. Does not return unsolicited material.
Tips: Printed and published work (Color Xeroxes are OK, too.) are very helpful. Do not call, we do not remember names—we remember samples—be persistent.

SAMUEL WEISER, INC., Box 612, York Beach ME 03910. (207)363-4393. Production Manager: Betty Lundsted. Publishes adult trade—specializing in New Age, occult, etc. Uses photos for book covers and dust jackets. Buys 3-4 freelance photos annually.
Subject Needs: Nature—a photo of Tibet, a photo of health food, etc. Captions preferred "so we can credit properly on copyright page as to what subject is."
Specs: Uses any size color prints and 4×5 (open to other sizes) transparencies.
Payment & Terms: Pays $200-350/color photo. Credit line given on book cover and copyright page. Buys non-exclusive book rights. Simultaneous submissions and previously published work OK.
Making Contact: Query with resume of credits, samples and list of stock photo subjects; send unsolicited photos by mail for consideration. Provide resume, business card, brochure, flyer or tearsheets to be kept on file for possible future assignments. Interested in stock photos. SASE. Reports in 1 month.
Tips: "We are looking at what the photographer has to offer, especially in terms of book covers. We do not want an exclusive on a photo, but for the life of the book so we do not have to renegotiate if we reprint it. We are willing to give a photographer a few samples of the book, extra covers, and a credit line in order to help him/her get established. We don't mind using something that has been used before on a different product or in a different field. People think that the 'occult' is weird, so we get to see a lot of monsters and 'weird' art through the mail. However, anyone looking at our catalog, or our books, will see that our covers are pretty, lots of four-color photos and designs."

WESTERN PRODUCER PRAIRIE BOOKS, Box 2500, Saskatoon SK S7K 2C4 Canada. (306)665-3548. Editorial Director: Jane McHughen. Publishes natural history material. Photos used for text illustration, book cover and dust jackets. Buys 100 photos and offers 2 book projects annually. Examples of recently published titles: *The Wonder of Canadian Birds*, by Candace Savage (text and cover); and *Eagles of North America*, by Candace Savage (text).
Subject Needs: Natural history.
Specs: Uses 35mm transparencies.
Payment & Terms: Payment "negotiable," $150/b&w photo. Credit line given. Buys book rights. Simultaneous submissions and previously published work OK.
Making Contact: Query with list of stock photo subjects. Works on assignment only. Interested in stock photos. Cannot return material. Reports in 1 month.
Tips: "We solicit photos of particular subjects. If we have stock photo lists on file, we will mail out a call for submissions to holders of appropriate subject matter."

THE WHEETLEY COMPANY, INC., Suite 1100, 4709 Golf Rd., Skokie IL 60076. (312)675-4443. Art Director: Janet Sullentrup. Estab. 1986. Produces elementary and high school textbooks in all subjects. Photos used for text illustration and book covers. Examples of recently produced books: *Parenting and Teaching Young Children* (photos used for text and cover illustration, McGraw-Hill); *Guide to Modern Meals* (photos used for text and cover illustration, McGraw-Hill); *Possibilities in Reading* (photos used for text illustration, Graphic Learning); *The Living Constitution* (photos used for text and cover illustration, Glencoe).
Subject Needs: Subject matter depends upon the book being produced. Most photos used are "unposed" and/or include minority people. Model releases/photo captions preferred.
Specs: Uses glossy b&w prints; 35mm, $2\frac{1}{4} \times 2\frac{1}{4}$, 4×5 transparencies.
Payment & Terms: Pays $135-165/quarter page of color photos; $60-120/quarter page of b&w photos. Credit line sometimes given depending on the "style established for the book." Buys one-time or North American rights. Simultaneous submissions and previously published work OK.
Making Contact: Query with list of stock photo subjects; provide resume, business card, brochure, flyer or tearsheets to be kept on file for possible future assignments. Deals with local freelancers only; interested in stock photos. Cannot return unsolicited material. Reports in 1 month.

WIESER & WIESER, INC., 118 E. 25th St., New York NY 10010. (212)260-0860. FAX: (212) 505-7186. Editor: George J. Wieser. Estab. 1975. Publishes adult trade—how-to, cooking, travel and history. Photos used for text illustration and book covers. Serves industrial clients. Buys 1,000 photos and offers 12 freelance assignments annually.
Subject Needs: Model release required; photo captions preferred.
Specs: Uses 35mm and 4×5 transparencies.
Payment & Terms: Pays $20-100/color photo, $15-50/b&w photo; $2,500-4,000/job. Buys all rights; but will negotiate.
Making Contact: Query with resume of credits and samples. Works on assignment only. SASE. Reports in 3 weeks.

JOHN WILEY & SONS, INC., 605 3rd Ave., New York NY 10158. (212)850-6731. Photo Research Manager: Stella Kupferberg. Estab. 1806. Publishes college texts in all fields. Photos used for text illustration. Buys 4,000/year. Examples of recently published titles: *Vivo* (Spanish language) by Wilkins; *Chemistry* by Brady; and *Psychology* by Costin. In all three titles, 200+ photos used for text and cover illustration.
Subject Needs: Uses b&w and color photos for textbooks in psychology, business, computer science, biology, chemistry, geography, geology and foreign languages. Captions required.
Specs: Uses 8×10 glossy and semigloss b&w prints and 35mm color transparencies.
Payment & Terms: Pays $75-125/b&w print and $100-175/color transparency. Credit line given. Buys one-time rights. Simultaneous submissions and previously published work OK.
Making Contact: Query with list of stock photo subjects. SASE. "We return all photos securely wrapped between double cardboard by registered mail."
Tips: "Initial contact should spell out the material photographer specializes in, rather than a general inquiry about our photo needs. Tearsheets and flyers welcome."

WISCONSIN TRAILS BOOKS, Box 5650, Madison WI 53705. (608)231-2444. Production Manager: Nancy Mead. Estab. 1960. Publishes adult nonfiction, guide books and photo essays. Photos used for text illustration and book covers. Buys many photos and gives large number of freelance assignments annually. Recently published: *Oh Wisconsin*, all photographs and *Best Wisconsin Bike Trips*, cover and ⅓ inside-photos.
Subject Needs: Wisconsin nature and historic scenes and activities. Location information for captions preferred.
Specs: Uses 5×7 or 8×10 b&w prints and any size transparencies.
Payment & Terms: Pays $25-75/b&w photo; $50-175/color photo. Credit line given. Buys one-time rights. Simultaneous submissions and previously published work OK.
Making Contact: Query with samples or list of stock photo subjects, or send unsolicited photos by mail for consideration. SASE. Reports in 1 month. Provide resume to be kept on file for possible future assignments. Photo guidelines free on request with SASE.
Tips: "See our products and know the types of photos we use." Also see listing under Consumer Magazines.

WOODALL PUBLISHING, COMPANY, 28167 North Keith Drive, Lake Forest IL 60045. FAX: (708)362-8776. Editor: Ray Ives. Publishes consumer camping and recreational vehicle travel guides. Photos used for book covers. Buys 10-15 photos annually. Examples of recently published titles: *Woodall's 1989 Campground Directory*; *Woodall's 1989 Tent Camping Guide*; *Woodall's 1989 RV Buyer's Guide*. In all three, photos used for cover art.
Subject Needs: Scenics, camping and RVs. Model release required; photo captions preferred.
Specs: Uses 35mm, 2¼×2¼, 4×5 and 8×10 transparencies.
Payment & Terms: Payment "depends on circulation of title." Buys book rights. Previously published work OK.
Making Contact: Provide resume, business card, brochure, flyer or tearsheets to be kept on file for possible future assignments. Interested in stock photos. Cannot return material. Reports in 1 month.
Tips: "Write and request to be added to mailing list. Send brochure. Do not send original materials. Respond promptly when contacted." We use "more stock purchases through smaller agencies and through unrepresented photographers."

WORD PUBLISHING, 5221 N. O'Connor, Irving TX 75239. (214)556-1900. Design Director: Tom Williams. Publishes Christian books. Photos used for book covers, publicity, brochures, posters, product advertising and stock photos.
Subject Needs: Nature, portraits, studio shots and special effects.
Payment & Terms: Pays for stock $350-550. Credit line given. Buys all rights "for the life of the product, not negotiable."
Making Contact: Provide resume, business card, brochure, flyer or tearsheets to be kept on file for possible future assignments. SASE. Reports in 1 month.

WRITERS PUBLISHING SERVICE CO., 1512 Western Ave., Seattle WA 98101. (206)284-9954. Publisher: William R. Griffin. "We publish all types of books for independent authors, plus 10 to 15 books under our own imprint." Photos used for text illustration, promotional materials, book covers and dust jackets. Uses 80-100 freelance photos and offers 50 freelance assignments annually.

Subject Needs: Open to all types of material. Model release preferred; captions required. Separate division of company especially interested in photos of cleaning- and maintenance-related duties.

Specs: Uses 5×7 and 8×10 glossy b&w and color prints.

Payment & Terms: Pays $5-50 per b&w photo. Credit line given. Buys one-time, book or all rights. Will negotiate with a photographer not willing to sell all rights. Simultaneous submissions and previously published work OK.

Making Contact: Query with samples, list of stock photo subjects. Submit portfolio for review. Contact regarding ideas. Deals with local freelancers only; works on assignment only; interested in stock photos. SASE. Reports within 30 days.

Book Publishers/'90-'91 changes

The following book publishers appeared in the 1990 edition of *Photographer's Market* but are not in the 1991 edition. Those firms whose art directors or photo editors did not respond to our request for an update of their listings may not have done so for a variety of reasons—they may be out of business, for example, or they may be overstocked with submissions.

Aglow Publications (not reviewing work)
Agora (not reviewing work)
Allyn & Bacon (did not respond)
American References Publishing Corp. (no longer in market)
Bauhan Publisher, William L. (did not respond)
Benjamin Co., The (did not respond)
Benjamin/Cummings Publishing Company (not reviewing work)
Betterway (did not respond)
Canadian Arctic Resources Committee (did not respond)
Carol Publishing (did not respond)
Child's World (not reviewing work)
Eastview Editions (did not respond)
Elysium Growth Press (did not respond)
Farrar, Straus & Giroux, Inc. (not reviewing work)
Focal Press (not reviewing work)
Franciscan Communication (not reviewing work)
Franciscan Communication (not reviewing work)
Franklin Library (did not respond)
Godine, Publisher, David R. (not reviewing work)
Good News Publishers/Cross-

way Books (not reviewing work)
Grolier, Inc. (not reviewing work)
Heinle & Heinle Publishers, Inc. (not reviewing work)
Liturgy Training Publications (did not respond)
Living Flame Press (did not respond)
Livres Commoner's Books (not reviewing work)
Lodestar Books (did not respond)
M.M. Cole Publishing (did not respond)
McMillan McGraw Hill (did not respond)
Modern Handcraft (did not respond)
Morgan & Morgan (did not respond)
Natural Heritage/Natural History Inc. (did not respond)
Newbury House Publishers (did not respond)
Orchard Books (did not respond)
Pantheon Books (did not respond)
Parenting Press (no longer in market)
Penguin USA (did not respond)
Personal Selling Power Inc. (did not respond)
Prentice Hall (did not respond)
Quinlan Press (out-of-business)
Read N' Run Books (did not re-

spond)
Shapolsky Publishers (did not respond)
Simon & Schuster Inc. (did not respond)
St. Bede's Publications (no longer in market)
Standard Publishing (did not respond)
Steck-Vaughn Co. (did not respond)
T.F.H. Publications (did not respond)
Tapley, Publisher, Lance (did not respond)
Texas Monthly Press (did not respond)
Time Life Books (not reviewing work)
Travel Keys (no longer in market)
Troll Assoc. (did not respond)
Twenty-Third Publications (did not respond)
United Black Resource Press (did not respond)
University Publications of America (did not respond)
Walker & Co. (no longer in market)
Waterfront Books (did not respond)
White Cliffs Media Co. (did not respond)
Windsor Publications (did not respond)
Yee Wen Publishing Co. (did not respond)

Businesses and Organizations

According to experts in the photography industry, corporate photography has become the most radical of all the major photographic markets — radical in the sense of a photographer being more free to follow his own vision, not an art director's. Such freedom, however, is typically not free to all who seek it but a privilege earned — at least with the more prestigious clients.

As the internationally known commercial/fine arts photographer Neal Slavin, has noted, you must first distinguish yourself with a unique, identifiable style and market yourself constantly to demonstrate that this style is the kind of work you want to do. Eventually, as he explains, clients who identify with and understand your style will come to you for your "look." Educating clients in your visual vocabulary, of course, can be an extended process but one that does gather momentum — and clients — over time.

With more than 3 million businesses and many more organizations of various types in this country, freelance photographers interested in working directly with clients have many potential prospects. This market section in *Photographer's Market* offers just a sampling of many different types of both for-profit businesses and nonprofit associations or institutions. While many companies and organizations may already be working with advertising or public relations firms for promoting their products and activities, the listings in this section, in particular, also welcome direct contact from freelancers.

You will find a wide range of markets, from major corporations such as insurance companies to public interest and trade associations to universities and arts organizations. The types of photography which these listings usually require overlap somewhat with advertising and markets. However, unlike that work which is largely directed toward external media or audiences, the photography for these markets tends to be more for specialized applications. Among these are employee or membership commmunications, annual reports, and documentary purposes such as recording meetings and other group functions or theatrical presentations.

A fair number of these listings are receptive to stock images, while many have rather specific needs for which they assign photographers. These projects will sometimes require studio-type skills (again similar to the advertising/PR market), particularly in shooting corporate interiors and portraits of executives for annual reports. However, much of the coverage of meetings, events and performances calls for a different set of skills involving use of available light and fill flash. In particular, coverage of sporting events or theatrical performances may require agility with extreme or rapidly changing light conditions.

Unless these businesses and organizations are active at the national level, they typically prefer to work with local freelancers. Rates will vary widely depending upon the individual client's budget. We have tried to list current rates of payment where possible, but some listings have still only indicated "negotiable terms," or a per-shot, per-hour or per-day basis. When quoting a price, especially for assigned work, remember to start with a basic day rate plus expenses and negotiate for final number of images, types of usage and time period for usage.

In particular, many of these clients wish to buy all rights to the images since they are often assigned for specific needs. In such cases, be sure to negotiate your terms in such a way that these clients get all the rights they need but that you also ultimately retain the copyrights. (For more on this, see the article, Copyright and Work for Hire, on page 26).

Another tendency which this market has in common with advertising and PR is the occasional to regular need for audiovisual materials. Listings in this section with any kind of audiovisual, film or video needs have been marked with special AV symbol—a solid, black square—before the listing's name for easier recognition. Some of the listings also include more detailed descriptions under the subheading, Audiovisual Needs.

Of special interest to photographers who wish to exercise more artistic control over their images when dealing with clients is the Close-up interview with photographer Neal Slavin, on page 170. In this article, Slavin expands on some of the ways in which photographers can develop their personal vision while building a solid roster of clients.

THE ACTING COMPANY, Box 898, Times Square Station, New York NY 10108. (212)564-3510. Promotions Coordinator: John Miller. Produces an average of three shows per season as a touring repertory theater. Buys 30 freelance photos annually. Assigns 4 freelance projects annually. Uses photos for brochures, newsletters, posters and press releases.
Subject Needs: Most often uses freelancers to shoot photos of productions.
Specs: Uses 8×10 b&w prints; 35mm transparencies; b&w contact sheet or negatives.
Payment & Terms: Payment made on per job basis, up to $500 plus expenses. Credit line given. Buys all rights, but will negotiate. Captions required.
Making Contact: Provide resume, business card, brochure, flyer or tearsheets to be kept on file for possible future assignments. Accepts queries from anywhere, but solicits photos by assignment only. Cannot return unsolicited material.
Tips: Recommends that photographers have past theatrical experience, especially production photocall work. "We are a nonprofit theater, so prices must be low. A good working relationship with our theater could result in many future assignments." Trend is toward more photography in posters.

■**AGA GAS, INC.**, 6225 Oaktree Blvd., Box 94737, Cleveland OH 44101-4737. Advertising: Pamela A. Miles. Manufacturer of industrial gas and welding products, gas application technology. Buys 10-12 freelance photos annually; gives 30 freelance assignments annually. Photos used in brochures, newsletters, audiovisual presentations, annual reports, catalogs, magazines and PR releases.
Specs: Uses b&w and color prints; 35mm transparencies; b&w and color contact sheets; b&w and color negatives.
Payment & Terms: Payment negotiable. Credit line given. Buys all rights. Model release required; captions preferred.
Making Contact: Provide resume, business card, brochure, flyer or tearsheets to be kept on file for possible future assignments. Open to solicitations from anywhere; interested in stock photos. SASE.

ALLRIGHT CORPORATION, (formerly Allright Auto Parks, Inc.)1111 Fannin St., Floor 13, 1919 Smith St., Houston TX 77002. (713)222-2505. National Director of Public Relations: H. M. Sinclair. Company operates in 85 cities in the US and Canada. Uses photos of parking facilities, openings, before and after shots, unusual parking situations, and Allright facilities. Photos used in brochures, newsletters, newspapers, audiovisual presentations and catalogs. Pays $25 minimum/hour or on a per-photo basis. Buys all rights. Model release preferred. Arrange a personal interview to show portfolio; provide resume, brochure, flyer and tearsheets to be kept on file for future assignments. Does not notify photographer if future assignments can be expected. SASE. Reports in 2 weeks.
B&W: Uses 8×10 glossy prints.
Color: Uses 35mm transparencies or 8×10 glossy prints.
Tips: "We hire local photographers in our individual operating cities through the local manager, or directly by phone with photographers listed at national headquarters, or by prints, etc. sent in with prices from local cities to national headquarters or through local city headquarters."

AMATEUR SOFTBALL ASSOCIATION, 2801 NE 50th St., Oklahoma City OK 73111. (405)424-5266. Director of Communications: Bill Plummer, III. Promotion of amateur softball. Buys 3-4 photos year; gives 2-3 assignments annually. Photos used in newsletter, newspapers.
Subject Needs: Subjects include action sports shots.
Specs: Uses 8½×11 prints.
Payment & Terms: Pays $20/b&w photo; $50/color photo. Credit line given. Buys all rights. Model release preferred; captions required. SASE. Reports in 2 weeks.
Tips: Contact ASA National office first before doing any work.

AMERICAN DENTAL HYGIENISTS' ASSOCIATION, 444 N. Michigan Ave., Chicago IL 60611. (312)440-8900. Publishes journal 9 times/year.Buys 4 photos/year; gives 6 assignments/year. Photos used in posters and magazines.

Subject Needs: Photos of dental hygienists; young, professional women; children with good smiles; older citizens. Special subject needs include hazards in the workplace, sexual harassment, AIDS.
Specs: Uses 35mm, 2¼×2¼, 4×5 transparencies; b&w and color contact sheets.
Payment & Terms: Pays $35-200/b&w photo; $300-500/color photo. Credit line given. Buys one-time rights. Model release preferred.
Making Contact: Query with resume of credits and with samples. Solicits photos by assignment only. Does not return unsolicited material. Reports in 1 week.
Tips: Prefers to see clarity, quality, good graphic potential and creativity—the ability to illustrate a subject in a fresh way. "Work closely with a dental professional when shooting a technical shot. Members of our association are extremely particular about the popular depiction of dental hygienists."

AMERICAN HOCKEY MAGAZINE/U.S.A. HOCKEY, (formerly American Hockey Magazine/Amateur Hockey Association of U.S.), 2997 Broadmoor Valley Rd., Colorado Springs CO 80906. (719)576-4990. FAX: (719) 576-4975. Managing Editor/PR Director: Mike Schroeder. Estab. 1937. Provides national governing body for amateur hockey. Photos used in brochures and magazines for audience with hockey related interest.
Subject Needs: Hockey related action; human interest (hockey).
Specs: Uses 5×7 glossy b&w prints, 35mm transparencies.
Payment & Terms: Pays $25/b&w photo; $25/color photo; $200/job. Credit line given. Buys one-time rights or all rights, "usually one-time; may be limited all." Captions preferred.
Making Contact: Query with resume of credits, samples and list of stock photo subjects; provide resume, business card, brochure, flyer or tearsheets to be kept on file for possible future assignments. Solicits photos by assignment only. SASE. Reports in 3 weeks.
Tips: Prefers to see functional hockey action. "A person who can shoot *good* hockey action impresses me. Query me first by telephone. Send samples, if query is a go. Don't bother if you can't shoot good hockey action."

AMERICAN MUSEUM OF NATURAL HISTORY LIBRARY, PHOTOGRAPHIC COLLECTION, Library Services Department, Central Park West, 79th St., New York NY 10024. (212)769-5419. FAX: (212) 769-5233. Manager, Special Collections: Andrea LaSala. Estab. 1869. Provides services for advertisers, authors, film and TV producers, general public, government agencies, picture researchers, publishers, scholars, students and teachers who use photos for brochures, newsletters, posters, newspapers, annual reports, catalogs, magazines, books and exhibits.
Payment & Terms: Use fee schedule on request.
Making Contact: "We accept only donations with full rights (non-exclusive) to use; we offer visibility through credits. Credit line given. Model release and captions required.
Tips: "We do not review portfolios. Unless the photographer is willing to give up rights and provide images for donation with full rights (credit lines are given), the museum is not willing to accept work."

■**AMERICAN POWER BOAT ASSOCIATION,** 17640 E. Nine Mile Rd., Box 377, East Detroit MI 48021. (313)773-9700. Executive Editor: Renee Mahn Olejnik. Managing Editor: Marie Masters. Publications Editor: Renee Mahn. Sanctioning body for US power boat racing; monthly magazine. Majority of assignments made on annual basis. Photos used in monthly magazine, brochures, audiovisual presentations, PR releases, and programs.
Subject Needs: Power boat racing—action and candid.
Specs: Uses 5×7 and up b&w prints and b&w contact sheets. 35mm slides for cover.
Payment & Terms: Payment varies. Standard is $50 for cover; $15 for inside. Credit line given. Buys one-time rights. Captions preferred; I.D. required. Photo usage must be invoiced by photographer within the month incurred.
Making Contact: Initial personal contact preferred. Send unsolicited photos by mail for consideration; provide resume, business card, brochure, flyer or tearsheets to be kept on file for possible future assignments. SASE. Reports in 2 weeks when needed.
Tips: Prefers to see selection of shots of power boats in action or pit shots, candids, etc., (all ID'd).

AMERICAN RED CROSS, Photographic Services, 431 18th St. NW, Washington DC 20006. Photographic Manager: Joseph Matthews.
Subject Needs: Photos used to illustrate annual reports, articles, slide shows, ads and brochures. Model release must accompany photo. "We need pictures of Red Cross volunteers working to provide the range of service to the public that the organization does, especially dramatic scenes at disasters.

■ *The solid, black square before a listing indicates that the market uses various types of audiovisual materials, such as slides, film or videotape.*

The ability to capture a 'moment' or the interaction between people is important. Query by mail to describe material available. Do not send unsolicited photographs. Because of small staff size we can only respond to picture specific queries, no general mailings will be answered. Never present yourself as shooting for the Red Cross unless you are currently under contract to do so." "Needs" list not available.

Specs: Send b&w contact sheet or 8×10 glossy prints. For color, send 35mm or larger transparencies.

Payment & Terms: Per photo $15-200; assignment varies according to type and length of assignment and rights purchased; payment depends on applications to Red Cross and rights purchased. Buys all rights.

Tips: "We have photographers on staff, so we use freelancers infrequently. We are interested in knowing photographers in the Washington, D.C. area who can handle our extra work and photographers and photojournalists in other areas of the U.S. who could provide coverage there if the need should arise. If in the Washington, D.C. area, call for an interview; if in other areas, send an introductory letter stating the type of work you do best and some samples of your published work. Technically, the photographs in your portfolio should be flawless. We have the same needs for quality photography as any large corporation or organization. Take the time to research the type of work the Red Cross does; if you have the skill and the interest to help us support the goals of the Red Cross, contact me. Please also contact your local chapter. Many need newsletter and annual report photography, although this is best for 'new' photographers since many chapters have little or no budget for pictures. Volunteering time and work can sometimes get you published. Edit yourself more critically. Also, get opinion of someone whom you trust about your portfolio *before* you show it around."

AMERICAN SOCIETY FOR THE PREVENTION OF CRUELTY TO ANIMALS (ASPCA), 441 E. 92nd St., New York NY 10128. (212)876-7700. FAX: (212) 348-3031. Photo Editor: Nancy Bell. Estab.1866. Publishes quarterly newsletter, pamphlets, booklets. Examples: *Traveling With Your Pet* and ASPCA *Report*.

Subject Needs: Needs photos of animals (domestic and wild). Special subjects: farm, lab, and stray animals. Injured, endangered, trapped, marine wildlife caught in nets or impeded by plastics. Also, rain forest scenes and wildlife.

Payment & Terms: Pays $25-50/b&w photo (inside use); $25-50/color photo (inside use); $100 for cover use. Buys one-time rights. Credit line given. Captions required. Provide brochure and resume to be kept on file for possible future assignments. SASE. Reports when needed.

Tips: "I'm looking for good clear slides and sharp black and white prints. Of course, I look for mainly animal-related photos. it's nice to see unique work, with a different look to it. Photos that tell the story. A description of each photo is helpful. And, it's helpful to provide dupes that I can keep on file." Freelancers should "realize that the ASPCA is a nonprofit organization, so it has small budget for photos."

AMERICAN STAGE FESTIVAL, Box 225, Milford NH 03055. (603)673-4005. Producing Director: Richard Rose. Theater/performing arts. No estimate or number of photos purchased. Gives 15-20 freelance assignments annually. Photos used for brochures, newsletters, posters, newspapers, annual reports, magazines and PR releases.

Subject Needs: Theater.

Payment & Terms: Pays $40-150/job. Credit line given. Buys all rights. Model release required.; captions preferred.

Making Contact: Arrange a personal interview to show portfolio or query with samples. Provide resume, business card, brochure, flyer or tearsheets to be kept on file for possible future assignments. We deal with local freelancers only. SASE. Reports in 3 weeks.

Tips: Looking for experience at theatrical photography.

■**BANKERS LIFE & CASUALTY CO.**, 1000 Sunset Ridge Rd., Northbrook IL 60062. (708)498-1500. FAX: (708)205-1742. Graphics Manager: Chuck Pusateri. Estab. 1879. Buys freelance photos occasionally; offers 3-4 freelance assignments annually. Photos used in brochures, newsletters, posters and audiovisual.

Specs: Uses 35mm, 4×5, 8×10 transparencies; "some 1-inch videotape."

Payment & Terms: Pays $50/b&w or color photo. Pays on acceptance. Buys one-time rights; sometimes buys other rights. Model release preferred.

Making Contact: Provide resume, business card, self-promotion piece or tearsheets to be kept on file for possible future assignments. Interested in stock photos. Reports in 1-2 weeks.

Tips: After initial query, "follow up a week or so later with a call or letter." In freelancer's samples looks mostly for good composition. Sees trend toward "less outside usage of freelance" photos in insurance industry.

■**THE BERKSHIRE PUBLIC THEATRE**, 30 Union St., P.O. Box 860, Pittsfield MA 01202. (413)445-4631. Managing Director: Iris Bessell. Estab. 1976. "We provide year round productions of plays, musicals, cabarets and children's theater in our 298-seat theater." Buys contact sheets/30 freelance photos/year; gives 3 assignments/year. Photos used in brochures, newsletters, posters, PR releases and lobby displays.

Subject Needs: "We are looking for dramatic production shots that capture the essence of the particular piece of work we are exploring."

Audiovisual Needs: "Slides have been used in a number of productions. We are interested in video, but to date have only recorded our productions on videotape, and have not solicited freelance videography."

Specs: Uses 5×7 glossy or studio b&w prints, b&w contact sheets and negatives.

Payment & Terms: Credit line given. Buys all rights—"we often reprint photos for promos and list credits."

Making Contact: Query with resume of credits; provide resume, business card, brochure, flyer or tearsheets to be kept on file for possible future assignments. Solicits photos by assignment only. SASE. Reports in 1 month or sooner.

Tips: "We are a small but growing regional repertory theater in the Berkshires. Our capital is often limited and *strictly* budgeted. Patience and understanding goes a long way. We look for compelling photos that 'jump out' at us—photos that evoke a visceral response, are theatrically 'trendy'—and work. We look for clear, clean, focused prints. The ability to capture an actor's fleeting emotion. The quality of translating this to a solid print." Send SASE, samples, resumé and refer to listing for more specifics.

■**BLOUNT, INC.**, Box 949, Montgomery AL 36101-0949. (205)244-4200. FAX: (205)271-8150. Director of Corporate Communications: David Rickey. "An international company with manufacturing and construction operations: saw chain, hydraulic materials handling equipment, gun care products; and construction of non-residential, industrial and waste-to-energy projects." Buys less than 50 freelance photos annually; offers less than 20 freelance assignments annually. Photos used for audiovisual presentations, annual reports and magazines.

Subject Needs: Photos of our operations.

Specs: Uses 35mm, 2¼×2¼ and 4×5 transparencies. Works with freelance filmmakers for promotional videos.

Payment & Terms: Pays by the hour or by the day. Buys all rights; will negotiate with photographers not willing to sell all rights. Model release preferred.

Making Contact: Provide resume, business card, brochure, flyer or tearsheets to be kept on file for possible future assignments. Solicits photos by assignment only. SASE. Reports as needed.

CALIFORNIA REDWOOD ASSOCIATION, Suite 200, 405 Enfrente Dr., Novato CA 94949. (415)382-0662. FAX: (415)382-8531. Contact: Pamela Allsebrook. Estab. 1916. "We publish a variety of literature, a small black and white periodical, run color advertisements and constantly use photos for magazine and newspaper publicity. We use new, well-designed redwood applications—residential, commercial, exteriors, interiors and especially good remodels and outdoor decks, fences, shelters. Color of wood must look fresh and natural." Gives 40 assignments/year. "We can review scout shots and commission a job or pick up existing photos on a per piece basis. Payment based on previous use and other factors." Credit line given whenever possible. Usually buys all but national advertising rights. Model release required. Send query material by mail for consideration for assignment or send finished speculation shots for possible purchase. Prefers photographers with architectural specialization. Reports in 1 month. Simultaneous submissions and previously published work OK if other uses are made very clear.

Specs: Uses b&w prints, usually 35mm. For color, uses 2¼×2¼ and 4×5 transparencies; contact sheet OK.

Tips: "We like to see any new redwood projects showing outstanding design and use of redwood. We don't have a staff photographer and work only with freelancers. We do, however, tend to use people who are specialized in architectural photography. We generally look for justified lines, true color quality, projects with style and architectural design, and tasteful props. Find and take 'scout' shots or finished pictures of good redwood projects and send them to us."

*****CAROLINA BIOLOGICAL SUPPLY COMPANY**, 2700 York Rd., Burlington NC 27215. (919)226-6000. Stock Photo Manager: Cindy Bright. Estab. 1927. Produces educational materials in the biological, earth science, chemistry, physics and computer fields. Gives 10 or less assignments/year. Buys 50 or less freelance photos annually. Photos used in text illustration, promotional materials and filmstrips.

Subject Needs: Nature scenes, natural history, geological, etc., for use on specific projects.
Specs: Uses 35mm and 2¼×2¼ transparencies.
Payment & Terms: Pays $25-125/b&w photo; $30-125/color photo. Will also work on royalty basis. Pays within 30 days of acceptance. Credit line given. Buys one-time rights. Model release required; captions preferred.
Making Contact: Query with resume of credits or with list of stock photo subjects. Reports in 1 month.
Tips: "As the oldest and largest supplier of biological materials in the USA, we are contacted by authors in the sciences who need photographs. The chances of a science author requesting a photo from us are excellent. Label lists with genus and species if applicable."

*CHICAGO COMPUTER & LIGHT, INC., 5001 N. Lowell Ave., Chicago IL 60630. (312)283-2749. President: Larry Feit. Estab. 1976. Buys 24 photos annually; offers 4 freelance assignments annually. Photos used in newsletters, magazines, catalogs, press releases.
Subject Needs: New computer products for special sections and ads in trade journals.
Specs: Uses 35mm transparencies.
Payment & Terms: Pays $2,000/job. Pays on acceptance. Credit line sometimes given. Buys all rights; will negotiate with photographer not willing to sell all rights. Model release required; photo captions preferred.
Making Contact: Provide resume, business card, self-promotion piece or tearsheets to be kept on file for possible future assignments. SASE. Reports in 1-2 weeks.
Tips: In freelancer's samples, looks for "nice quality."

CHILD AND FAMILY SERVICES OF NEW HAMPSHIRE, 99 Hanover St., Box 448, Manchester NH 03105. (603)668-1920. Development Director: Ruth Zax. Statewide social service agency providing counseling to children and families. Uses photos of children, teenagers and families; "pictures depicting our services, such as an unwed mother, teenager on drugs or emotionally upset, couples and/or families—possibly indicating stress or conflict. Also looking for photos depicting healthy, happy children and families." Photos used in brochures, newspapers, posters, annual reports, news releases, and displays and exhibits. Buys 3-4 photos/year; gives 1-2 assignments/year. Pays $10 minimum/hour and on a per-photo basis. Credit line given on request. Buys all rights. Model release required. Send material by mail for consideration. Stock photos OK. Provide business card and tearsheets to be kept on file for future assignments. Notifies photographer if future assignments can be expected. SASE. Reports in 1 month.
B&W: Uses 5×7 glossy prints. Pays $10-50/photo.
Color: Uses 5×7 glossy prints. Pays $10-50/photo.
Tips: "Submit a few copies of applicable photos in which we might be interested rather than just a letter or form telling us what you have done or can do." Looks for "someone who can compose a photo that achieves an expression of feeling, emotion. Because we are primarily a service agency we want our artwork to reflect the clients we serve—people working on problems or solving them. We are looking for a range of emotions."

■COVENANT COLLEGE, Scenic Hwy., Lookout Mountain TN 37350. (404)820-1560, ext. 235. Director of Publications and Public Relations. Provides all in-house and out-of-house materials for departments at the college, especially Admissions, Development, Annual Support and PR, etc. Photos used in brochures, newsletters, posters, newspapers, audiovisual presentations, annual reports, catalogs, magazines, and PR releases. Buys $600 worth of photos annually; gives 1-2 major assignments/year and 10-20 small jobs/year.

The asterisk before a listing indicates that the market is new in this edition. New markets are often the most receptive to freelance submissions.

Subject Needs: The college, the faculty, administrators, students, etc. Interested in developing high quality, low budget slide presentation and/or video for admissions-recruitment.
Specs: Uses 4×5, 5×7 and 8×10 b&w and color prints; b&w contact sheets; b&w and color negatives.
Payment & Terms: Payment negotiated per photo, hour, job. $250/day. Credit line negotiable. Buys all rights.
Making Contact: Provide resume, business card, brochure, flyer or tearsheets to be kept on file for possible future assignments. Deals with local freelancers only.
Tips: "Soft sell us, please."

CUSTOM STUDIOS, INC., 1333-37 W. Devon, Chicago IL 60660. (312)761-1150. FAX: (312)761-7477. President: Gary Wing. Estab. 1966. Manufactures custom imprinted products such as T-shirts, jackets, caps, custom printed cups, key tags, ashtrays. Buys 10 freelance photos/year; offers 10 freelance assignments/year. Photos used in brochures, posters, newspapers, catalogs and magazines.
Subject Needs: Product shots and models wearing custom imprinted products.
Specs: Uses 4×5 to 8×10 matte or glossy b&w and color prints; b&w and color contact sheets.
Payment & Terms: Pays $20-60/b&w photo; $36-76/color photo; $20-30/hour; $100-200/day; $20-60/job. Credit line given. Buys one-time rights. Model release required.
Making Contact: Send unsolicited photos by mail, preferably with models for consideration; provide resume, business card, brochure, flyer or tearsheets to be kept on file for possible future assignments. Does not return unsolicited material. Reports in 3 weeks.
Tips: "Looking for models that have very attractive and sexy looks. Mostly fashion-type photos."

DAYTON BALLET, 140 N. Main St., Dayton OH 45402. (513)449-5060. FAX: (513)461-8353. Public Relations/Marketing Director: Elizabeth Reynolds. Estab. 1937. Schedules performances yearly. Offers 2-3 freelance assignments/year. Photos used in publicity materials and newspapers.
Subject Needs: "We're looking for photographers in our region who can capture fast movement in a low-light theater situation."
Specs: Uses b&w and color contact sheets; also transparencies.
Payment & Terms: Pays $3-6/b&w photo; $5-10/color photo. "We do not pay hourly fees—basically photographers can receive exposure if they are good and their photos are used for publication. We will negotiate if someone is exceptional and we want them to continue shooting for us." Credit line given. Buys all rights.
Making Contact: Send resume, business card, brochure, flyer or tearsheets to be kept on file for possible future assignments. SASE. "Also, make an appointment to come and shoot a dress rehearsal (no fee) and submit your contact sheets. If you're good, we'll order from the sheet and we'll invite you to shoot in the future and negotiate a fee."
Tips: To be successful for this type of market, have "a background in dance and a knowledge of shooting dance. Be quick and able to anticipate fast movement. Send samples of past dance photography work. Specifically ballet. Pictures should show dance movement captured with good lighting effects. Also they should be clear and sharp and show expression."

DREXEL UNIVERSITY, 32nd & Chestnut St., Philadelphia PA 19104. (215)895-2613. Assistant Vice President of Public Relations: Philip Terranova. Director of Publication: Deborah Perloe. Provides publications for both internal and external use, as well as press releases. Buys 250+ photos/year; gives 60+ assignments/year. Photos used in brochures, newsletters, posters, newspapers, annual reports, and PR releases.
Subject Needs: Events on campus, portraits and building shots.
Specs: Uses 8×10 glossy b&w prints and b&w contact sheets.
Payment & Terms: Pays $25-50/hour; $150-250/day. Credit line given. Buys all rights. Model release required.
Making Contact: Arrange a personal interview to show portfolio. Deals with local freelancers only and solicits photos by assignment only. Does not return unsolicited material.

■E&B MARINE INC., 201 Meadow Rd., Edison NJ 08818. (201)819-7400. FAX: (201)819-4771. Manager of Creative Services: Barbara Weinstein. Mail order catalog of boating equipment. Estab. 1950. Buys 650 freelance photos annually; offers 30 freelance assignments annually. Photos used for newsletters, newspapers, annual reports, catalogs, PR releases and store signage.
Subject Needs: Uses 4×5+ b&w prints; 35mm, 2¼×2¼ and 4×5 transparencies; b&w contact sheets. Works with freelance filmmakers on educational/promotional films.
Payment & Terms: Pays $50-250/color photo; $600-800/day. Buys one-time or all rights. Model release required. Captions preferred.
Making Contact: Query with resume of credits, samples or list of stock photo subjects; provide resume, business card, brochure, flyer or tearsheets to be kept on file for possible future assignments. SASE.

Tips: Always looking for lifestyle and mood shots of boaters. "Be flexible, familiar with boating. Understand layouts and how to 'shoot-to-size' for assembled separations."

FELLOWSHIP OF CHRISTIAN ATHLETES, 8701 Leeds Rd., Kansas City MO 64129. Editor, Sharing the Victory: John Dodderidge. Provides year-round outreach to athletes and coaches. Buys 12-15 photos/year. Photos used in magazines.
Subject Needs: Close-up and thoughtful or dramatic sports-related shots: "lots of high quality 35mm transparencies and color prints depicting the gamut of action and emotion in high-school-age team and individual sports; shots depicting camaraderie, sportsmanship, loyalty, humor etc., among both male and female athletes will be favorably considered."
Specs: Uses b&w and color prints, 35mm transparencies, b&w contact sheets.
Payment & Terms: Pays $50-100/b&w photo and $75-350/color photo. Credit line given alongside photo. Buys one-time rights. Model release preferred with close-ups but not necessary. Payment upon publication.
Making Contact: Query with samples. SASE. Reports in 1 week. "Best to study sample copy first. Send $1 plus 9×12 SASE."
Tips: In reviewing samples looks for "technical excellence (clarity, density, etc.); creativity (freshness of angle, mood, etc); and applications to magazine's target audience (in this case high school male/female athletes). "Wants to see 35mm color slides of *Sports Illustrated* quality" in samples.

GARY PLASTIC PACKAGING CORP., 530 Old Post Rd., No. 3, Greenwich CT 06830. (203)629-1480. Director, Marketing: Marilyn Hellinger. Manufacturers of custom injection molding; thermoforming; and stock rigid plastic packaging. Buys 10 freelance photos/year; gives 10 assignments/year. Photos used in brochures, catalogs and flyers.
Subject Needs: Product photography.
Specs: Uses 8×10 b&w and color prints; 2¼×2¼ slides; and b&w or color negatives.
Payment & Terms: Pays by the job and the number of photographs required. Buys all rights. Model release required.
Making Contact: Query with resume of credits or with samples. Follow-up with a call to set up an appointment to show portfolio. Prefers to see b&w and color product photography. Deals with local freelancers only. Solicits photos by assignment only. Provide resume to be kept on file for possible future assignments. Notifies photographer if future assignments can be expected. Does not return unsolicited material. Reports in 2 weeks.
Tips: The photographer "has to be willing to work with our designers."

*GREEN MOUNTAIN POWER, Box 850, Burlington VT 05402. (802)864-5731. FAX: (802)865-9129. Communications Manager: Dorothy Schnure. Estab. 1928. Provides electric utility. Buys 5 photos/year; offers 20 freelance assignments/year. Photos used in brochures and annual reports.
Subject Needs: Vermont scenics, company events, portraits, dramatic use of electricity, or electrical equipment.
Specs: Uses transparencies, all formats.
Payment & Terms: Payment negotiable according to project. Pays on acceptance. Credit line not given. Buys one-time rights, and all rights (work-for-hire); will negotiate with photographer not willing to sell all rights. Model release and photo captions required.
Making Contact: Provide resume, business card, self-promotion piece or tearsheets to be kept on file for possible future assignments. Interested in stock photos of Vermont scenics, dramatic electrical equipment. SASE. Reports in 1-2 weeks.
Tips: "Most photos must be of Vermont subjects, if showing a recognizable location." In freelancers' portfolio and samples, looks for "sense of drama, personal connection with subject."

■HAMPDEN-SYDNEY COLLEGE, Box 637, Hampden-Sydney VA 23943-0637. (804)223-4382. Director of Publications: Richard McClintock. 4-year Liberal Arts College. Buys 200 photos/year; gives 25 assignments/year. Photos used in brochures, newsletters, newspapers, audiovisual presentations, magazines, PR releases, and admissions marketing materials.
Subject Needs: Campus life.
Specs: Uses b&w and color prints; 35mm and 2¼×2¼ transparencies; b&w contact sheets.
Payment & Terms: Pays $5-15/b&w photo; $25-30/color photo; $250-1,000/job. Credit line given. Buys all rights "but can be arranged with photographer." Model release required; captions preferred.
Making Contact: Query with samples, business card, brochure, flyer or tearsheet to be kept on file for possible future assignments. Usually deals with local freelancers only. SASE. Reports in 2 weeks.

HILLSDALE COLLEGE, 33 College St., Hillsdale MI 49242. (517)437-7341. FAX: (517)437-3923. Director of Public Affairs: Bill Koshelnyk. Publishes alumni magazine, political/social action newsletter, brochures, books, etc. Photos used for text illustration, promotional materials, book covers and dust jackets. Buys 20-30 photos annually; assigns 5-10 shoots per year. Recently published *Hillsdale Magazine* and assorted brochures.

Subject Needs: Looking for photos "that deal with the college's national outreach programs, athletics or alumni." Model release preferred; photo captions required.

Specs: Uses 5×7 glossy b&w prints; 35mm, 2¼×2¼ transparencies.

Payment & Terms: Pays $50-100/color or b&w photo. Additional rates vary according to assignment. Credit lines given where possible. Buys all rights; will negotiate. Simultaneous submissions and previously published work OK.

Making Contact: Send unsolicited photos by mail for consideration. Interested in stock photos. SASE. Reports in 2 weeks.

Tips: "Photos must have something to do with the activities of Hillsdale College or prominent figures who participate in our programs. Our needs are rapidly growing."

■**HUBBARD MILLING COMPANY**, 424 N. Riverfront Dr., P.O. Box 8500, Mankato MN 56001. (507)625-1882. Supervisor, Marketing Communications: Debra L. Milbrandt. Estab. 1878. The Hubbard Feed Division manufactures animal feeds and animal health products. Buys 20 freelance photos annually; gives 10 freelance assignments annually. Photos used in brochures, newsletters, posters and audiovisual presentations.

Subject Needs: Livestock—beef cattle, dairy cattle, pigs, horses, sheep, dogs, cats.

Specs: Uses 3×5 and 5×7 matte b&w and color prints; 2¼×2¼ and 4×5 transparencies; and b&w and color negatives.

Payment & Terms: Pays $50-100/b&w photo; $200/color photo; $50-300/job. Buys one-time rights; all rights. Will negotiate with a photographer not willing to sell all rights. Model release required.

Making Contact: Query with samples; query with list of stock photo subjects; submit portfolio for review; provide resume, business card, brochure, flyer or tearsheets to be kept on file for possible future assignments. Solicits photos by assignment only. SASE. Reports in 2 weeks.

Tips: Prefers "to see the types of work the photographer does and what types of subjects she has done. We look for lots of agricultural photos in a more serious setting. Keep up with modern farming methods, use confinement shots when deemed necessary. Stay away from 'cutesy' shots."

ICART VENDOR GRAPHICS, 8568 W. Pico Blvd., Los Angeles CA 90035. (213)653-3190. Owner/President: Sandy Verin Brunton. Manufactures art deco and contemporary decorative art posters. Buys 2 freelance photos annually; give 2-4 freelance assignments annually. Photos used in brochures, posters, catalogs and magazines.

Subject Needs: Art deco and contemporary subjects with universal appeal.

Specs: Uses color prints.

Payment & Terms: Credit line given. Buys one-time rights.

Making Contact: Send unsolicited photos by mail for consideration; provide resume, business card, brochure, flyer or tearsheets to be kept on file for possible future assignments. Open to solicitations from anywhere. SASE. Reports in 1 month.

INNOVATIVE DESIGN & GRAPHICS, Suite 214, 1234 Sherman Ave., Evanston IL 60202. Art Director: Maret Thorpe. Photos used in magazines, brochures, newsletters and catalogs.

Subject Needs: Product shots, people shots, and topical shots for magazines.

Specs: Uses 8×10 glossy b&w prints, 35mm, 2¼×2¼, and 4×5 transparencies, b&w contact sheets, and b&w negatives.

Payment & Terms: Payment per job negotiated individually. Credit line given. Buys one-time rights or all rights. Model release required; captions preferred.

Making Contact: Provide resume, business card, brochure, flyer or tearsheets to be kept on file for possible future assignments. Solicits photos by assignment only. Interested in stock photos. SASE. "Reports when applicable assignment is available."

Tips: "We look for crisp photos to illustrate ideas, clear photos of products and products in use, and relaxed photos of business people at work. We prefer that freelancers submit work produced on larger-format equipment. Do no phone us to arrange to show your book. Send samples instead."

■**INTERNATIONAL RESEARCH & EDUCATION (IRE)**, 21098 IRE Control Center, Eagan MN 55121. (612)888-9635. IP Director: George Franklin, Jr. IRE conducts in-depth research probes, surveys, and studies to improve the decision support process. Company conducts market research, taste testing, brand image/usage studies, premium testing, and design and development of product/service marketing campaigns. Buys 75-110 photos/year; gives 50-60 assignments/year. Photos used in brochures, newsletters, posters, audiovisual presentations, annual reports, catalogs, PR releases, and as support material for specific project/survey/reports.

Subject Needs: "Subjects and topics cover a vast spectrum of possibilities and needs."

Audiovisual Needs: Uses freelance filmmakers to produce promotional pieces for 16mm or video-tape.

Specs: Uses prints (15% b&w, 85% color), transparencies and negatives.

Payment & Terms: Pays on a bid, per job basis. Credit line given. Buys all rights. Model release required.

Making Contact: Provide resume, business card, brochure, flyer or tearsheets to be kept on file for possible future assignments; "materials sent are put on optic disk for options to pursue by project managers responsible for a program or job." Solicits photos by assignment only. Does not return unsolicited material. Reports when a job is available.

Tips: "We look for creativity, innovation, and ability to relate to the given job and carry-out the mission accordingly."

AL KAHN GROUP, 221 W. 82 St., #PH-N, New York NY 10024. FAX: (212)877-4642. President: Al Kahn. Estab. 1976. Produces corporate I.D., brochures, annual reports and advertising. Buys 100 photos/year; offers 20 assignments/year. Photos used in brochures, posters, annual reports and magazines. Examples of recent projects: March of Dimes, "Don't smoke, drink, take drugs," (print and TV); and Medic Alert, corporate campaign, (print).

Subject Needs: Conceptual designs.

Specs: Uses prints, transparencies, contact sheets and negatives.

Payment & Terms: Pays $500-3,000/b&w photo; $500-3,000/job. Credit line given. Buys one-time and exclusive product rights. Model release required.

How to Contact: Query with samples, send unsolicited photos by mail for consideration, or submit portfolio for review. Also, "Call and set up appointment; bring 35 mm slide presentation." SASE. Reports when project is assigned.

Tips: Looks for "creative and conceptual" work in submissions.

■**LA CROSSE AREA CONVENTION & VISITOR BUREAU**, Box 1895, P.O. Box 1895, Riverside Park, La Crosse WI 54602-1895. (608)782-2366. Director Material Production: Mary Waldsmith. Estab. 1975. Provides "promotional brochures, trade show and convention planning, full service for meetings and conventions." Buys 8+ photos/year; offers "several" assignments/year through conventions. Conventions also buy photos. Photos used in brochures, newspapers, audiovisual presentations and magazines.

Subject Needs: "Scenic photos of local area; local points of interest to tourists, etc. Will be increasing slide file."

Specs: Uses 5×7 glossy b&w prints, and color slides.

Payment & Terms: Payment depends on size/scope of project. Credit line given "where possible." Buys all rights. Model release required; captions preferred.

Making Contact: Provide resume, business card, brochure, flyer or tearsheets to be kept on file for possible future assignments. Deals with local freelancers only. Solicits photos by assignment only. Does not return unsolicited material. Reports in 3 weeks.

MCGUIRE ASSOCIATES, 1234 Sherman Ave., Evanston IL 60202. (708)328-4433. FAX: (708)328-4425. Owner: James McGuire. Estab. 1982. Provides advertising and graphic design. Serves industrial, retail and service clients. Buys 2-3 freelance photos annually; gives 2-3 freelance assignments annually. Photos used for brochures, newsletters, annual reports and advertising.

Subject Needs: Buys production shots/location shots.

Specs: Uses 4×5 to 11×14 matte b&w and color prints; 35mm, 2¼×2¼, 4×5 and 8×10 transparencies; b&w contact sheets.

Payment & Terms: Pays $200/b&w photo; $300/color photo; $500-2,000/day; by the job. Credit line given depending on client usage. Buys one-time or all rights; will negotiate with photographer unwilling to sell all rights. Model release required; captions preferred.

Making Contact: Arrange a personal interview to show portfolio; query with samples; provide resume, business card, brochure, flyer or tearsheets to be kept on file for possible future assignments. Solicits photos by assignment only; interested in stock photos. Does not return unsolicited material. Reports in 2 weeks.

Tips: "Provide samples or promotional piece, or if in area call for an appointment."

■**ROB MACINTOSH COMMUNICATIONS, INC.**, 93 Massachusetts Ave., Boston MA 02115. (617)267-4912. Creative Services Director: Mr. Jamie Scott. Buys 50 photos/year; gives 24 assignments/year. Photos used in brochures, posters, audiovisual presentations, annual reports, catalogs, magazines and PR releases.

Subject Needs: People, interesting art photos.

Specs: Uses 8×10 glossy b&w prints; 35mm, 2¼×2¼, 4×5 and 8×10 transparencies; b&w contact sheet and negatives.

Payment & Terms: Pays $25-500/b&w or color photos; $600-1,800/day; per job rate varies. Use of credit line depends on job and client. Buys one-time rights or all rights. Model release required.

Making Contact: Provide resume, business card, brochure, flyer or tearsheets to be kept on file for possible future assignments. Interested in stock photos. SASE.

Tips: "There is an increasing demand on the photographer to reach beyond the expected and come up with technical solutions that challenge the viewer."

MID AMERICA DESIGNS, INC., (formerly Mid America Corvette Supplies) P.O. Box 1368, Effingham IL 62401. FAX: (217)347-2952. Operations Manager: Jeff Bloemker. Provides mail order catalog for Corvette parts & accessories. Buys 300 freelance photos annually; gives 6 freelance assignments annually.

Subject Needs: Apparel and Automotive Parts.

Specs: Uses 2¼×2¼, 4×5 and 8×10 transparencies.

Payment & Terms: Pays $65/color photo. Buys all rights. Model release required.

Making Contact: Provide resume, business card, brochure, flyer or tearsheets to be kept on file for possible future assignments. Works on assignment; interested in stock photos. Does not return unsolicited material. Reports in 2 weeks.

THE MINNESOTA OPERA, Suite 20, 400 Sibley St., St. Paul MN 55101. (612)221-0122. Public Relations: Kathy Graves. Produces five opera productions, several new works and an American musical each year. Buys 50 photos/year; gives 10 assignments/year. Photos used in brochures, posters, and PR releases/publicity.

Subject Needs: Operatic productions.

Specs: Uses 5×7 glossy b&w prints and 35mm slides.

Payment & Terms: Pays $6-12/b&w photo; $8-15/color photo; $60-85/hour. Credit line given. Model release preferred; captions required. Buys all rights; negatives/slides remain with photographer.

Making Contact: Send unsolicited photos by mail for consideration; provide resume, business card, brochure, flyer or tearsheets to be kept on file for possible future assignments. Deals with local freelancers only. Does not return unsolicited material. Reporting time depends on needs.

Tips: "We look for photography that dynamically conveys theatrical/dramatic quality of opera with clear, crisp active pictures. Photographers should have experience photographing theater and have a good sense of dramatic timing."

*MIRACLE OF ALOE, 521 Riverside Ave., Westport CT 06880. (203)454-1919. FAX: (203)226-7333. Vice President: Jess F. Clarke, Jr. Estab. 1981. Manufactures for mail order buyers of healthcare products. Works with 2 freelancers per month. Photos used in newsletters, catalogs, direct mail and consumer magazines.

Subject Needs: Uses Testimonial photos and aloe vera plants.

Specs: Uses 4×5 b&w or color prints, and 35mm transparencies.

Payment & Terms: Pays $25-35/photo. Pays on receipt of invoice. Credit line given. Buys one-time rights. Model release preferred.

Making Contact: Provide resume, business card, self-promotion piece or tearsheets to be kept on file for possible future assignments. Works with freelancers on assignment only. SASE. Reports in 1 month.

Tips: In freelancer's samples, looks for "older folks, head shots and nice white hair ladies." Also show Aloe Vera plants in fields or pots; shoot scenes of Southern Texas aloe farms."

*MISSOURI REPERTORY THEATRE, 4949 Cherry, Kansas City MO 64110. (816)276-1579. FAX: (816)276-5189. Publicity Manager: Kent Politsch. Estab. 1964. Professional theater. Photos used in newsletters, newspapers, brochures and press releases.

Markets which offer lower payment amounts, or photo credits and extra copies or tearsheets as payment are often receptive to the work of newcomers. For a list of such markets, see the First Markets Index preceding the General Index in the back of this book.

Subject Needs: Theater production photos, benefactor events (social).
Specs: Uses b&w prints 5×7 and 8×10 glossy; 35mm transparencies.
Payment & Terms: Pays $50 maximum/hour. Pays on acceptance. "We include credit lines, but they're not always used by news media." Buys all rights. Will negotiate with a photographer unwilling to sell all rights. Model release required; photo captions preferred.
Making Contact: Query with resume of credits. Work on assignment only. SASE. Reports in 3 weeks.
Tips: Freelancers should be patient. In portfolio, samples or demos, wants to see "clean, simple set up—good newspaper reproductions."

■**MSD AGVET,** Division of Merck and Co. Inc., Box 2000, Rahway NJ 07060. (201)855-3877. Manager, Marketing Communications: Gerald J. Granozio. Manufacturers agricultural and veterinary products. Buys 20-75 freelance photos/year. Photos used in brochures, posters, audiovisual presentations and advertisements.
Subject Needs: Agricultural—crops (wheat, soybean, bananas, rice, potatoes, cotton, some fruit) and livestock (cattle, horses, sheep, swine and poultry).
Specs: Uses 35mm, 2¼×2¼, 4×5 and 8×10 slides.
Making Contact & Terms: Query with samples or with a list of stock photo subjects; provide brochure and flyer to be kept on file. Interested in stock photos. SASE. Reports in 2 weeks. Pays $150-200/ b&w; $200-400/color photo. Buys one-time rights. Model release required; captions preferred.

NATIONAL ASSOCIATION OF EVANGELICALS, Box 28, Wheaton IL 60189. (708)665-0500. Editor: Don Brown. Produces a magazine centered on news events of a religious nature. Buys 15 photos/year. Photos used in brochures, posters, and magazines.
Subject Needs: Leaders in the evangelical community addressing or involved in some current issue or newsworthy event; people involved in marches, prayer vigils, and protests that have a religious/ political slant.
Specs: Uses 5×7 glossy b&w prints.
Payment & Terms: Pays $35/b&w photo. Credit line given. Buys one-time rights. Model release required; captions preferred.
Making Contact: Query with samples or list of stock photo subjects; provide resume, business card, brochure, flyer or tearsheets to be kept on file for possible future assignments; interested in stock photos. SASE. Reports in 3 weeks.
Tips: "We prefer photos that have a news or photojournalistic feel. We are looking for the *best* in b&w."

NATIONAL ASSOCIATION OF LEGAL SECRETARIES, Suite 550, 2250 E. 73rd St., Tulsa OK 74136. (918)493-3540. Director of Communications: Tammy Hailey. Publishes "an association magazine— for providing continuing legal education along with association news." Buys 12 photos/year; gives 12 assignments/year. Photos used in magazine.
Subject Needs: Needs legal, secretarial photos.
Specs: Uses b&w prints and 35mm transparencies. Uses freelance filmmakers to produce educational and promotional slideshows.
Payment & Terms: Pays $20-100/job. Credit line given. Rights purchased vary with photos.
Making Contact: Query with list of stock photo subjects. Deals with local freelancers only. Interested in stock photos. Does not return unsolicited material. Reports in 1 week.

NATIONAL BLACK CHILD DEVELOPMENT INSTITUTE, 1463 Rhode Island, Ave., NW, Washington DC 20005. (202)387-1281. Deputy Director: Vicki D. Pinkston. Photos used in brochures, newsletters, newspapers, annual reports and annual calendar.
Subject Needs: Subjects include: candid, action photos of black children and youth.
Specs: Uses 5×7 or 8×10 glossy b&w prints and b&w contact sheets.
Payment & Terms: Pays $25/cover photo and $15/inside b&w photo. Credit line given. Buys one-time rights. Model release required.
Making Contact: Query with samples; send unsolicited photos by mail for consideration. Interested in stock photos. SASE. Reports in 1 month.
Tips: "Candid, action photographs of one black child or youth or a small group of children or youths. Most photographs selected are used in annual calendar and are placed beside an appropriate poem selected by organization, therefore, photograph should communicate a message in an indirect way. Other photographs are used in quarterly newsletter and reports. Obtain sample of publications published by organization to see the type of photographs selected."

NATIONAL DUCKPIN BOWLING CONGRESS, 3703 Brownbrook Court, Randallstown, MD 21133. (301)636-BOWL. Executive Director: Manuel S. Whitman. "We are a national organization of people who enjoy the game of Duckpin bowling. We provide a wide-range of services to our members." Buys "a few photos," as needed/year; gives 2 assignments/year. Photos used in brochures, newsletters, posters, and newspapers.

Subject Needs: Pictures of people enjoying the game of Duckpin bowling.

Specs: Specifications vary from job to job.

Payment & Terms: "We pay freelance photographers on an individual job basis." Credit line given. Buys all rights. Model release and captions preferred.

Making Contact: Provide resume, business card, brochure, flyer or tearsheets to be kept on file for possible future assignments. "We don't want freelance photographers contacting us—we maintain a file and will contact them when needed." Interested in stock photos. Does not return unsolicited material. Reports in 3 weeks.

NEW EXPOSURE—A Catalog of Fine Art Photography, 4807 N. 70th St., Scottsdale AZ 85251. (602)990-2915. Executive Director: Susan Brachocki. Estab. 1987. Specializes in marketing original fine art photographic prints. Consigns approximately 80 freelance photos annually.

Subject Needs: Specializes in "a wide variety of black and white and color photographs, including landscapes, urban scenes, portraits and abstracts. We are interested in photographers who have exhibited a long-term commitment to their craft and produce *unique* images." No "commercial work, depressing or violent images."

Specs: Reviews color or b&w prints and contact sheets; also slides.

Payment & Terms: Pays 50% royalty on retail print sales. Pays on completion of sale.

Making Contact: Query with samples. SASE. Reports in 1 month. Simultaneous submissions and previously published work OK.

Tips: "We are interested in fine-art black and white and color photography. Unique perspectives, superior print quality, experience are all important. Ability to provide prints of an image on a timely basis is key as well. Prints are reproduced in a high-quality mail-order catalog; and displayed in gallery exhibitions."

PALM SPRINGS DESERT RESORT CONVENTION AND VISITORS BUREAU, Airport Park Plaza, Suite 315, 255 N. El Cielo Rd., Palm Springs CA 92262. (619)327-8411. Director of Publicity: Laurie Smith. "We are the tourism promotion entity of Palm Springs and the entire Coachella Valley." Buys 50 freelance photos/year; gives 20 assignments/year. Photos used in brochures, posters, newspapers, audiovisual presentations, magazines and PR releases.

Subject Needs: "Those of tourism interest . . . specifically in Coachella Valley."

Specs: Uses 8×10 b&w prints; 35mm slides; b&w contact sheet and negatives OK. "We buy only 35 mm transparencies."

Payment & Terms: Pays $25/b&w photo; $40-75/hour. Buys all rights—"all exposures from the job. On assignment, we provide film and processing. We own all exposures." Model release and captions required.

Making Contact: Query with resume of credits or list of stock photo subjects. Provide resume, business card, brochure, flyer, and tearsheets to be kept on file for possible future assignments. Notifies photographer if future assignments can be expected. SASE. Reports in 2 weeks.

Tips: "We will discuss only photographs of the Coachella Valley, California. No generic materials will be considered."

PGA OF AMERICA, Suite 200, 2155 Butterfield, Troy MI 48084. (313)649-1100. Contact: Heidi Russell. Services 15,500 golf club professionals and apprentices nationwide. Photos used for brochures, posters, annual reports and monthly feature magazine.

Subject Needs: Special needs include golf scenery, good color action of amateurs as well as tour stars. Buys 50 freelance photos and offers 15 freelance assignments annually.

Payment & Terms: Pays $25 minimum/b&w photo; $50-200/color photo. Credit line given. Buys one-time and all rights. Model release preferred.

Making Contact: Arrange personal interview to show portfolio and query with list of stock photo subjects. Prefers to see 35mm slides in the portfolio. Provide tearsheets to be kept on file for possible future assignments. SASE.

PHI DELTA KAPPAN, 8th & Union Sts., Box 789, Bloomington IN 47402. Design Director: Carol Bucheri. Produces Kappan magazine and supporting materials. Buys 20 photos/year; gives 3 assignments/year. Photos used in magazine, flyers, and subscription cards.

Subject Needs: Teachers, classrooms and high school students.
Specs: Uses 8×10 b&w prints, b&w contact sheets.
Payment & Terms: Pays $20-100/b&w photo; $30-400/color photo; $30-500/job. Credit line and tear-sheets given. Buys one-time rights. Model release often required.
Making Contact: Query with list of stock photo subjects; provide photocopies, brochure or flyer to be kept on file for possible future assignments. Interested in stock photos. SASE. Reports in 3 weeks.
Tips: "Don't send photos that you wouldn't want to hang in a gallery. Just because you do a photo for publications does not mean you should lower your standards. Spots should be touched up (not with a ball point pen), the print should be good and carefully done, subject matter should be in focus. Send me xeroxes of your black-and-white prints that we can look at. We don't convert slides and rarely use color."

PORTLAND-THE UNIVERSITY OF PORTLAND MAGAZINE, 5000 N. Willamette Blvd., Portland OR 97203. (503)283-7202. Editor: John A Soisson. Publishes a quarterly, 36 page magazine. Buys 20 photos/year; offers 5 assignments/year. Photos used in magazines.
Subject Needs: Subjects include people.
Specs: Uses 8×10 glossy b&w prints; b&w contact sheets; 35mm and 2¼×2¼ transparencies.
Payment & Terms: Pays $100-300/b&w photo; $100-500/color photo. Credit line given. Buys one-time rights. Model release preferred.
Making Contact: Query with resume of credits; query with list of stock photo subjects. Solicits photos by assignment only; interested in stock photos. SASE. Reports in 2 weeks.
Tips: "Our needs are fairly specific. Tell me how you can help me. We want strong, creative photos. Fewer mugs and 'grip and grins.' " In portfolio of samples wants to see "interpretive ability more so than photojournalistic work. Also show work with other magazines. Strong composition and color is important. Often buy already completed work/stock photos. University magazines are a growing market for first rate photography. Our needs are not extensive. A good promotional brochure gives me someone to contact in various areas on various subjects."

POSEY SCHOOL OF DANCE, INC., Box 254, Northport NY 11768. (516)757-2700. President: Elsa Posey. Estab. 1953. Sponsors a school of dance, and a regional dance company. Buys 10-12 photos/year; gives 4 assignments/year. Photos used in brochures and newspapers. Special subject needs include children dancing; ballet, modern dance, jazz/tap (theater dance), classes including women and men.
Subject Needs: Dancers dancing and at rest.
Specs: Uses 8×10 glossy b&w prints.
Payment & Terms: Payment negotiated individually. Pays $25-200/b&w or color photo. Credit line given if requested. Buys one-time rights. Model release required.
Making Contact: "Call us." Solicits photos by assignment only. Interested in stock photos. SASE. Reports in 1 week.
Tips: "We look for an understanding of dance (as movement), lighting for dramatic theatrical effect and sharp focus."

THE QUARASAN GROUP, INC., Suite 300, 630 Dundee Rd., Northbrook IL 60062. (708)291-0700. Contact: Randi Brill. "A complete book publishing service including design of interiors and covers to complete editorial and production stages, art and photo procurement." Buys 1,000-5,000 photos/year; offers 75-100 assignments/year. Photos used in brochures and books.
Subject Needs: "Most products we produce are educational in nature. The subject matter can vary. For textbook work, male-female/ethnic/handicapped/minorities balances must be maintained in the photos we select to ensure an accurate representation."
Specs: Prefers 8×10 b&w prints; 35mm, 2¼×2¼, 4×5, or 8×10 transparencies, or b&w contact sheets.
Payment & Terms: Fee paid is based on final use size. Pays on a per photo basis or day rate; usually buys all rights or sometimes North American rights. Credit line given, but may not always appear on page. Model release required.
Making Contact: Query with list of stock photo subjects or nonreturnable samples (photocopies OK); provide resume, business card, brochure, flyer or tearsheets to be kept on file for possible future assignments; interested in stock photos. Does not return unsolicited material. "We contact once work/project requires photos."
Tips: "Learn the industry. Analyze the books on the market to understand *why* those photos were chosen. Be organized and professional and meet the agreed upon schedules and deadlines. We are always looking for experienced photo researchers local to the Chicago area."

RSVP MARKETING, Suite 5, 450 Plain St., Marshfield MA 02050. President: Edward C. Hicks. Direct marketing consultant/agency. Buys 100-200 photos/year; gives 5-10 assignments/year. Photos used in brochures, catalogs and magazines.

Subject Needs: Industrial equipment, travel/tourism topics, and fundraising events.
Specs: Uses 2×2 and 4×6 b&w and color prints, and transparencies.
Payment & Terms: Payment per photo and per job negotiated individually. Buys all rights. Model release preferred.
Making Contact: Query with list of stock photo subjects; provide resume, business card, brochure, flyer or tearsheets to be kept on file for possible future assignments. Solicits photos by assignment only. Interested in stock photos. SASE. Reports when needs and relevant jobs dictate.
Tips: "We look for photos of industrial and office products, high-tech formats, and fashion."

RECREATION WORLD SERVICES, INC., Drawer 17148, Pensacola FL 32522. (904)477-2123. Executive Vice President: K.W. Stephens. Serves publishers and membership service organizations. Buys 5-10 photos/year; gives 2-5 assignments/year. Photos used in brochures, newsletters, newspapers, magazines and press releases.
Subject Needs: Recreation type.
Specs: Uses 3x4 prints. Buys all rights. Model release required; captions preferred.
Making Contact: Send unsolicited photos by mail for consideration; provide resume, business card, brochure, flyer or tearsheets to be kept on file for possible future assignments. SASE. Reports in 2 weeks.

RECREATIONAL EQUIPMENT, INC., Box 88126, Seattle WA 98138-2126. (306)395-5857. FAX: (206)395-5826. Contact: Christine Schmidt. Estab. 1938. Retailer of muscle-powered sporting goods. Buys varied amount of photos/year. Photos used for catalogs. Sample copy free with SASE.
Subject Needs: "We need mountain sports, scenics and outdoor activity shots for use as catalog covers." Special subject needs include action sports—outdoor activities; antique photos—participating in outdoor activities.
Specs: Uses transparencies.
Payment & Terms: Pays $50-150/b&w photo; $75-300/color photo. Buys one-time rights. Model release required.
Making Contact: Query with samples; provide resume, business card, brochure, flyer or tearsheets to be kept on file for possible future assignments. SASE. Reports in 4 weeks.
Tips: "Scenics with people doing muscle-powered sports are our main need. Use our equipment and our clothing on models in action-oriented outdoor activities; use up-to-date gear. Show people having fun in unique places, with products we sell or creating a mood where product is not identifiable."

REPERTORY DANCE THEATRE, Box 8088, Salt Lake City UT 84108. (801)581-6702. General Manager: Kathy Johnson. Uses photos of dance company for promotion. Photos used in brochures, newspapers, posters, news releases and magazines. Buys all rights. Local freelancers only. Arrange a personal interview to show portfolio. Prefers to see dance or movement photos. Queries by mail OK; SASE. Reports in 2 weeks.
Specs: Uses 8×10 b&w glossy prints; contact sheet OK. Payment negotiable.

■**RIPON COLLEGE**, Box 248, Ripon WI 54971. (414)748-8115. Contact: Director of College Relations. Photos used in brochures, newsletters, posters, newspapers, audiovisual presentations, annual reports, magazines, and PR releases. Gives 3-5 assignments/year.
Subject Needs: Formal and informal portraits of Ripon alumni, on-location shots, architecture.
Payment & Terms: Pay negotiated by job ($50-2,000). Buys all rights. Model release preferred.
Making Contact: Provide resume, business card, brochure, flyer or tearsheets to be kept on file for possible future assignments. Works on assignment only. SASE. Reports in 1 month.

C.E. RYND PHOTOGRAPHIC FINE ARTS, Box 4028, Seattle WA 98104. (206)325-3283. Director: Charles Rynd. Estab. 1985. Primarily interested in 20th century photography with an emphasis on the contemporary. Represents a wide range of styles and subject matter. Private dealer and consultant, marketing to a clientele of corporate, museum and private collectors. Also acting as exclusive national agent for a selected number of artists. Receives 50% commission. General price range: $200-2,500. Will review transparencies. Interested in unframed work and matted work only. Generally requires exclusive representation within metropolitan area. Submit slides or portfolio for review. SASE. Reports in 2 months.

SAINT VINCENT COLLEGE, Rt. 30, Latrobe PA 15650. (412)539-9761. Director of Publications: Don Orlando. Uses photos of students/faculty in campus setting. Photos used in brochures, newsletters, posters, annual reports and catalogs. Buys 50 photos/year. Credit line given. Buys all rights. Send material by mail for consideration. SASE. Reports in 1 month.

This cheerful moment for two happy college grads was captured by photographer Jim Koepnick for Ripon, Wisconsin client, Ripon College. Director of College Relations, Lorin Boone assigned Koepnick to cover the 1989 graduation, based on the photographer's "eye for the unusual" and determination "to get the right shot." This photo, originally a transparency, was used as part of a photo essay in the Summer 1989 edition of the Ripon College Magazine.

B&W: Uses 5×7 prints; contact sheet OK. Pays $10-50/photo.
Color: Uses 5×7 prints and 35mm transparencies; contact sheet OK. Pays $10 minimum/photo.
Tips: Impressed with technical excellence first, then the photographer's interpretive ability.

SAN FRANCISCO CONSERVATORY OF MUSIC, 1201 Ortega St., San Francisco CA 94122. (415)564-8086. Publications Editor: Paul Signorelli. Provides publications about the conservatory programs, concerts and musicians. Buys 25 photos/year; gives 10-15 assignments/year. Photos used in brochures, posters, newspapers, annual reports, catalogs, magazines and news releases.
Subject Needs: Musical—musicians.
Specs: Uses 5×7 b&w prints.
Payment & Terms: Payment varies by photographer; "credit line" to $25/b&w photo; $200-700/job. Credit line given "most of the time." Buys one-time rights. Deals with local freelancers only.
Tips: Prefers to see in-performance shots, and studio shots of musicians. "Contact us only if you are experienced in photographing performing musicians."

SAN FRANCISCO OPERA CENTER, War Memorial Opera House, San Francisco CA 94102. (415)861-4008. Business Manager: Russ Walton. Produces live performances of opera productions of both local San Francisco area performances and national touring companies. Estab. 1982. Buys 2-3 photos/year; gives 1 assignment/year. Photos used in brochures, newspapers, annual reports, PR releases and production file reference/singer resume photos.

Subject Needs: Production and performance shots, and artist/performer shots.
Specs: Uses 8×10 standard finish b&w prints, and b&w negatives.
Payment & Terms: Pays $8/b&w photo, $8/color photo, and $50-500/complete job. Credit line given. Buys all rights.
Making Contact: Query with resume of credits; provide resume, business card, brochure, flyer or tearsheets to be kept on file for possible future assignments. SASE. Reports in 2 weeks.
Tips: "In portfolio or samples wants to see live action shots in a wide variety of lighting—including stage and outdoor—and performance settings. We need live performance shots and action shots of individuals; scenery also. Photographers should have extensive experience in shooting live performances and be familiar with the opera product. Once good photographers are located, we contract them regularly for various production/social/public events."

SAN JOSE STATE UNIVERSITY, Athletic Department, San Jose CA 95192. (408)924-1217. Sports Information Director: Lawrence Fan. Estab. 1857. Uses sports action photos. Photos used in brochures, newspapers and posters. Buys 50 photos/year; gives 5-10 assignments/year. Credit line given. Buys all rights. Arrange a personal interview to show portfolio. SASE. Reports in 2 weeks.
Specs: Uses 8×10 b&w glossy prints; contact sheet OK. Pays $2.00/b&w photo. For color, uses 35mm transparencies. Pays $3.00/slide.
Tips: In portfolio and samples wants to see good photos, and variety. Looks for "ability to shoot indoors and outdoors, day and night."

THE SOCIETY OF AMERICAN FLORISTS, 1601 Duke St., Alexandria VA 22314. (703)836-8700. Editor: Kate Foster. National trade association representing growers, wholesalers and retailers of flowers and plants. Gives 3-5 assignments/year. Photos used in magazines and promotional materials.
Subject Needs: Needs photos of personalities, greenhouses, inside wholesalers, flower shops and conventions.
Specs: Uses b&w prints, or transparencies.
Payment & Terms: Pays $25-50/b&w photo; $50-75/color photo; $25-50/hour; $50-100/day; $125-250/job. Credit line given. Model release required; captions preferred. Buys one-time rights.
Making Contact: Query with samples; provide resume, business card, brochure, flyer or tearsheets to be kept on file for possible future assignments. Interested in stock photos. SASE. Reports in 1 week.

■**THIEL COLLEGE**, 75 College Ave., Greenville PA 16125. (412)589-2188. Director of Media Services: Ian Scott Forbes. Provides education; undergraduate and community programs. Buys 25-35 photos/year; gives 2-3 assignments/year. Photos used in brochures, newsletters, newspapers, audiovisual presentations, annual reports, catalogs, magazines and news releases.
Subject Needs: "Basically we have an occasional need for photography depending on the job we want done."
Specs: Uses 35mm transparencies.
Payment & Terms: Payment negotiated. Credit line given depending on usage. Buys all rights.
Making Contact: Query with resume of credits. Solicits photos by assignment. Reports back depending on needs.

TOPS NEWS, % TOPS Club, Inc., Box 07360, Milwaukee WI 53207. Editor: Gail Schemberger. Estab. 1948. TOPS is a nonprofit, self-help weight-control organization. Photos used in membership magazine.
Subject Needs: "Subject matter to be illustrated varies greatly."
Specs: Uses any size transparency or print.
Payment & Terms: Pays $75-125/color photo. Buys one-time rights.
Making Contact: Query with list of stock photo subjects; provide resume, business card, brochure, flyer or tearsheets to be kept on file for possible future assignments. Interested in stock photos. SASE. Reports in 1 month.
Tips: "Send a brief, well-composed letter along with a few selected samples with a SASE."

T-SHIRT GALLERY LTD., 154 E. 64, New York NY 10021. (212)838-1212. President: Finn. Estab. 1976. Manufactures clothing and printed fashions. Buys 30 photos/year; gives 20 assignments/year. Photos used in brochures, newspapers, magazines and PR releases. Retail and fashion clients; previous/current clients include *Elle*, *Seventeen* and *Vogue*.
Subject Needs: Models in T-shirts.
Specs: Uses b&w and color prints, and 8×10 transparencies.
Payment & Terms: Pays $50-200/b&w photo and $100-400/color photo. Buys exclusive product rights, all rights. Model release preferred.
Making Contact: Query with samples or send unsolicited photos by mail for consideration. SASE. Reports in 3 weeks.

Close-up

Neal Slavin
Photographer
New York City

The distinctive photographic vision of Neal Slavin, full of human vibrancy and gesture, abounds in annual reports, galleries, books, and magazines in the U.S. and throughout the world. While it might seem that such an established professional would have the luxury of choosing his markets, Slavin claims that he plays no favorites.

"I do primarily what I do," says Slavin, noting that the point of a given picture and the process are his primary motives. "I'll do anything I have to do to make that visual statement, and what I'm bounded by is not whether it's corporate, documentary or fine art but by 'What is *the* message?' Also, for me, it goes beyond the single image for a specific purpose. It's the whole series."

Typically, the kind of work which inspires Slavin involves a high degree of creative challenge. "On the commercial side, people come to me to help them solve a visual problem," he says, describing how his work is often used to illustrate a capabilities report or a magazine spread. "Basically, they say: 'Here's a subject. What can we do with it?' We then develop it along a theme, and the pictures grow out of that. On the fine arts side, there's really no difference, except there's no one on the outside telling me what to do. In this case, I pursue my own ideas."

As Slavin readily points out, no photographer involved in commercial work ever gets to do completely what he wants. But as he also stresses, photographers who strive to promote their personal vision in everything they do are more often able to do work that reflects their ideals. So *how* do you get there?

"Right from the beginning, you have to establish with the client that you work a certain way and have your own standards and ideas," Slavin advises. "You have to be honest about your work and say, 'This is what I do, and how I want to do it.' It's important that you show this in your portfolio—the type of work you firmly believe in and *want* to shoot, not just what you've shot. I do a lot of self-assignments to show people what I'm interested in shooting. If you want to get into advertising or corporate work, then obviously you have to alter and adapt. But you can't alter yourself too much. You've got to stay true to who you are. If you're not honest, it will very quickly become obvious. So the thing is to recognize your goals early on and stick it out. Eventually you will attract people who can respond to your work and offer you assignments that relate to your vision and approach."

In the end, says Slavin, love of photography is what it's all about for him—and should be for any photographer. "A photographer's job is to be an observer, to watch the way things unfold and how people relate to each other," says Slavin. "It's beyond the business; I wouldn't be in it if I didn't love the work. So, to me, first comes the work, and then the money. Since the name of the game is looking for new ways to visualize, I like to keep working with new formats and techniques. So, I'm always shooting—even when I don't have much work. At those times, my rep's out promoting my work to new clients so I *can* keep shooting."

—Sam A. Marshall

■**UNION INSTITUTE,** (formerly Union for Experimenting Colleges & Universities) 440 E. McMillan St., Cincinnati OH 45206. (513)681-6400. Contact: Don Hagerty. Provides alternative higher education, baccalaureate and doctoral programs. Photos used in brochures, newsletters, posters, newspapers, audiovisual presentations, annual reports, catalogs and news releases.
Subject Needs: Uses photos of the Union Instutute community involved in their activities. Also, photos that portray intangible themes such as peace, progress and inertia.
Specs: Uses 5×7 glossy b&w and color prints; b&w and color contact sheets; b&w and color negatives.
Payment & Terms: Payment negotiable. Credit line given. Model release required.
Making Contact: Arrange a personal interview to show portfolio. SASE. Reports in 3 weeks.
Tips: Prefers "good closeups and action shots of alums/faculty, etc. Our quarterly alumni magazine reaches an international audience concerned with major issues facing mankind. Illustrating its stories with quality photos involving our people is our constant challenge. We welcome your involvement."

U.S. SOUVENIR & NOVELTY COMPANY, 70 East Ash, Box 429, Lebanon OR 97355. (503)259-1471. President: Edward Black. Manufactures souvenirs. Buys about 100 freelance photos annually. Uses photos for souvenir photo products.
Subject Needs: Scenics, wildlife, sports and attractions.
Specs: Uses 35mm color prints, negatives or transparencies.
Payment & Terms: Pays $10-50/color photo, depending on subject and our manufacturing requirements. Buys "rights in our products only." Model releases and captions preferred.
Making Contact: Query with list of stock photo subjects. Interested in stock photos. Does not return unsolicited material. Reports in 1 month.
Tips: "Query with list of stock photo subjects first. We have strict format guidelines that must fit our products. We like to review many shots of one subject to find one or two that may be suitable for our needs since we add graphics to some products."

UNIVERSITY OF NEW HAVEN, 300 Orange Ave., West Haven CT 06516. (203)932-7243. Public Relations Director: Toni Blood. Uses University of New Haven campus photos. Photos used in brochures, newsletters, newspapers, annual reports, catalogs and news releases. Pays $2-9/b&w photo; $10-25/ color photo; $10-20/hour; $100-200 and up/day; payment negotiable on a per-photo basis. Buys one-time or all rights. Credit line often negotiable. Query with resume "and non-returnable samples for our files. We'll contact to arrange a personal interview to show portfolio." Local freelancers preferred. SASE. "Can't be responsible for lost materials." Reports in 1 week.
B&W: Uses 5×7 glossy prints; contact sheet OK.
Color: Mostly 35mm transparencies.
Tips: Looks for good people portraits, candids, interaction, news quality. Good prints b&w and color quality. Good slide color, sharp focus. Overall good versatility in mixed situations. "Call first to see if we need additional photographers. If yes, send samples and rates. Make appointment to show portfolio. Be reasonable on costs (we're a nonprofit institution). Be a resident in local area available for assignment."

UNIVERSITY OF REDLANDS, 1200 E. Colton Ave., Redlands CA 92373-0999. (714)335-4070. FAX: (714)793-2029. Director: Kip Rutty. Four-year, private, nonsectarian liberal arts university, offering a bachelor's degree in some 25 areas and limited master's programs. Buys "hundreds" photos/year; gives 50-75 assignments/year. Photos used in brochures, newsletters, posters, catalogs, magazines, press releases, ads and photo displays.
Subject Needs: On-campus scenic shots, classroom and individual student shots; "grip-and-grin" pix of donors presenting checks, receiving plaques, etc.; action shots for sports and academic events, etc. Stock photography for magazine.
Specs: Uses 5×7, 8×10 matte or glossy b&w prints; 35mm, 4×5 transparencies; b&w contact sheets; b&w and color negatives.
Payment & Terms: Pays $300-1,200/day. Credit line usually given. Buys all rights; "willing to negotiate so photographer holds copyright but we hold unlimited, lifetime access."
Making Contact: Query with samples, submit portfolio for review; provide resume, business card, brochure, flyer or tearsheets to be kept on file for possible future assignments. SASE. Reports in 1 week, usually.
Tips: "We are looking for a sensitive eye and well developed aesthetic sense. Pensive student photos are quite different from fashion photography, for example. Don't bother if you don't have the *patience* to work with college students and 'absent-minded' professors and academic administrators."

■**UNIVERSITY OF TAMPA,** 401 W. Kennedy, Tampa FL 33606. (813)253-6232. Director of Public Information: Grant Donaldson. Provides student recruitment brochures. Buys 200 photos/year; gives 30 assignments/year. Photos used for brochures, newsletters, audiovisual presentations and catalogs.

Subject Needs: Local freelancers given specific assignments.
Payment & Terms: Pays $50-150/hour. Negotiates/photos. Buys all rights.
Making Contact: Arrange a personal interview to show portfolio. Solicits photos by assignment only. SASE. Reports in 2 weeks.
Tips: "Be timely with contact sheets and prints."

■**VAC-U-MAX**, 37 Rutgers St., Belleville NJ 07109. (201)759-4600. FAX: (201)759-6449. Director of Marketing: John Andrew. Provides pneumatic conveying systems for dry powders, pellets, granules etc. in pharmaceutical, chemical, food processing, plastics plants, etc. Also, pneumatically- and electrically-operated industrial vacuum cleaners. Offers 10-12 freelance assignments/year. Photos used for brochures, audiovisual presentations, catalogs, magazines and press releases.
Subject Needs: "We will be looking for photos of installations of our products."
Audiovisual Needs: Sees possible trend toward using freelancers for video. "Most video is now done inhouse, although we are interested in video coverage of operation of equipment in the field and testimonials of users."
Specs: Uses b&w prints; 35mm, 2¼×2¼ transparencies; b&w negatives.
Payment & Terms: Payment negotiable; typically pays $50-100/b&w photo; $100-250/color photo; $50-100/hour. "We have engaged several photographers for on-site photography, and we have paid up to $1,000/day plus film, processing and travel." Buys all rights. Model release and captions preferred.
Making Contact: Query with resume of credits, send unsolicited photos by mail for consideration. SASE. Reports in 2 weeks.
Tips: "We are interested in photographer's capability in photographing industrial equipment in an operating environment. We prefer that he bring installations to our attention which he knows he will be permitted to photograph. Since our venues are strictly industrial, we look for his ability to handle adverse lighting and proper use of lenses in restricted areas."

*■**WALTER VAN ENCK DESIGN LIMITED**, 3830 N. Marshfield, Chicago IL 60613. President: Walter Van Enck. Estab. 1978. Produces corporate communications materials (primarily print). Buys 25 photos/year; gives 10 assignments/year. Photos used in brochures, newsletters, posters, audiovisual presentations, annual reports and catalogs.
Subject Needs: Corporate service related activities and product and architectural shots.
Audiovisual Needs: Uses transparencies in AV presentations.
Specs: Uses 8×10 glossy and matte b&w prints, 2¼×2¼ and 4×5 transparencies, and b&w contact sheets.
Payment & Terms: Pays $600-2,000/day. Credit line seldom given. Model release required.
Making Contact: Arrange a personal interview to show portfolio or query with samples; provide resume, business card, brochure, flyer or tearsheets to be kept on file for possible future assignments. Deals with local freelancers only. Interested in stock photos. SASE. "Queries not often reported on— only filed."
Tips: "We look for straight corporate (conservative) shots with a little twist of color or light, and ultra high quality b&w printing. Try to keep your name and personality on the tip of our minds."

■**WORCESTER POLYTECHNIC INSTITUTE**, 100 Institute Rd., Worcester MA 01609. (508)831-5000. University Editor: Michael Dorsey. Provides educators, all promotional, recruiting, fund raising printed materials. Gives "4 each" assignments/year. Photos used in brochures, newsletters, posters, audiovisual presentations, annual reports, catalogs, magazines and PR releases.
Subject Needs: On-campus, comprehensive and specific views of all elements of the WPI experience. Relations with industry, alumni.
Specs: Uses 5×7 (minimum) glossy b&w prints; 35mm, 2¼×2¼, 4×5 transparencies; b&w contact sheets.
Payment & Terms: Pays maximum $500/day. Credit line given in some publications. Buys one-time rights or all rights; negotiable. Captions preferred.
Making Contact: Arrange a personal interview to show portfolio or query with list of stock photo subjects; provide resume, business card, brochure, flyer or tearsheets to be kept on file for possible future assignments. "No phone calls." Interested in stock photos. SASE. Reports in 2 weeks.

■**WORLD WILDLIFE FUND/THE CONSERVATION FOUNDATION**, 1250 24th St. NW, Washington DC 20037. (202)293-4800. Photo Librarian: Mimi Hutchins. "WWF, a private international conservation organization, is dedicated to saving endangered wildlife and habitats around the world and to protecting the biological diversity upon which human well-being depends." Photos used in brochures, newsletters, posters, audiovisual presentations, annual reports, PR releases, and WWF Calendar. Uses photos of endangered or threatened animals, plants and habitats around the world. Write to Lindsay Lambert for calendar guidelines.

Subject Needs: Coverage of WWF projects worldwide, and endangered plants, animals, and habitat types around the world. Also, environmental problems including pollution, toxic waste, acid rain, etc.
Specs: Uses 5×7 or 8×10 glossy b&w prints and 35mm and larger format transparencies. "We are interested in photos of key WWF projects. If the location being visited is of interest or coverage of unusual species is anticipated, we would discuss paying expenses."
Payment & Terms: Pays $25-125/b&w photo; $50-350/color photo; other payment negotiable. Credit line given. Buys one-time rights. Prefers donation for on-going use in WWF publications and audiovisuals as needed. Captions required.
Making Contact: Query for list of WWF projects. Follow up with list of photo subjects and/or locations that appear to be of interest to WWF and credentials.
Tips: "We look for close-ups of wildlife and plants worldwide, candids of conservationists working in the field, and scenics worldwide. We need photographers who are already traveling to WWF project areas; we prefer experience in nature photography."

YEARBOOK ASSOCIATES, Box 91, Millers Falls MA 01349. (413)863-8093. Contact: Richard C. Baker, Jr. Provides portraits and candids for yearbooks. Gives 5,000 assignments/year. Photos used in yearbooks.
Subject Needs: Photos by assignment only.
Payment & Terms: Pays $80-160/day. Credit line sometimes given.
Making Contact: Provide resume with current address and phone number. Note: Although most of our assignments are on a national basis, we have local needs in San Francisco, Washington DC and the New England area. Does not return unsolicited material. Scheduling is set up during June, July and August. Shooting starts in September.
Tips: "In addition to portrait photographers we need people with school group and environmental portrait experience. Photographer should like to work with people and be willing to follow our directions."

Businesses and Organizations/'90-'91 changes

The following businesses and organizations appeared in the 1990 edition of *Photographer's Market* but are not in the 1991 edition. Those businesses or organizations whose presidents or communications directors did not respond to our request for an update of their listings may not have done so for a variety of reasons—they may be out of business, for example or they may be overstocked with submissions.

Air-Conditioning & Refrigeration Wholesalers (did not respond)
American Fund for Alternatives to Animal Research, The (did not respond)
Bailiwick Repertory (not reviewing work)
Civic Supply Co. (did not respond)
Club Med Sales Inc. (not reviewing work)
Dayco Corp. (did not respond)
Delta (not reviewing work)
Denmar Engineering & Control Systems (did not respond)
Design Media (moved; no forwarding address)
Four Winds Travel, Inc. (not reviewing work)
Freelance Pool (no longer in market)

Friends University (not reviewing work)
Georgia Pacific Corp. (did not respond)
Greatwest Assurance Co., The (did not respond)
Himark (did not respond)
Illinois Benedictine College, The (did not respond)
Imagination Industry, The (did not respond)
Lawrence Bender & Assoc. (did not respond)
Marycrest College (did not respond)
Menlo College (no longer in market)
National Safety Council (not reviewing work)
New Hampshire College (did not respond)
Ohio Ballet (did not respond)
Passerella, Lee (did not re-

spond)
Roller Skating Rink Operators Assoc., The (did not respond)
Salinger Academy of Fashion, Louise (did not respond)
San Diego Repertory Theatre (not reviewing work)
Schwinn Bicycle Co. (did not respond)
Sundstrand Corp. (did not respond)
Theatre IV (did not respond)
United Auto Workers, The (did not respond)
United States Tennis Assoc. (did not respond)
Unites States Yacht Racing Union (did not respond)
Wooden Canoe Heritage Assoc., Ltd. (not reviewing work)

Galleries

Photographers often think of an art or photography gallery in terms of what the gallery can do for them. For instance, will the gallery provide exposure for their work? Will the gallery buy their pictures or at least bring in collectors interested in buying them? And will the gallery give their work credibility that will open the door for other important galleries or clients to become interested in it? However, an outstanding show can do as much for the gallery as it does for the photographer. Accordingly, galleries think quite the opposite: "What can the photographer do for us?"

Quite often, because of their own motivations and concerns, galleries are looking for photographers whose work is outstanding in some important way. It may be the medium or the format or the subject matter. It may also involve such factors as the photographer's proximity to the gallery, his reputation in the region and his overall track record. On the other hand, it will often have less to do with such things and more with just the photographer's having an unusual point of view and the ability to excite viewers.

Photographic talent is assumed by most gallery directors. That is, if you approach a gallery, then the gallery expects your talent to be evident. This does not mean that you must be academically trained or solidly established in the profession before approaching a gallery with your work. However, experienced gallery directors are very tuned into established trends and techniques as well as advancing or receding trends. They look for images that express the photographer's personal point of view in a fresh, striking way. At the same time, they are disappointed in work that amateurishly echoes current visual fads or that even duplicates outright other people's work.

Interestingly, this emphasis upon creativity poses many challenges for both the aspiring and the veteran photographer who wish to work actively in the gallery market. Beginners must distinguish themselves in order to establish their credibility and attract interest from galleries. However, even seasoned photographers in the gallery market find themselves constantly in competition with other top gallery photographers — and themselves — to produce work that is compelling every time.

With the varied types of exhibit spaces listed in this section, photographers at all levels have avenues open to them in finding their niche in the gallery market. Some galleries deal only with more experienced, serious photographers, but the gallery market in general remains quite open to discovering and cultivating new talent. More than 100 galleries and museums appear in this year's edition of *Photographer's Market*. These listings include both local and regional outlets for photographic art, as well as the needs and requirements of making contact and arranging for an exhibit of your work. Additional exhibiting opportunities, though not listed, can be found in your community through art shows and in such places as libraries, restaurants, corporate lobbies and other public facilities.

Within the last couple of years, interest in film, video and other audiovisual media has been increasing among galleries and their patrons. Accordingly, we have included more information about a gallery's interest in such media in this edition. In particular, listings which are interested in seeing and exhibiting work in these various media have been marked with a special AV symbol — a solid, black square — before the listing's name for easier recognition.

Many of the issues of creativity and professionalism in the gallery market already introduced here are explored in more detail with a gallery owner in a special interview in this section. To learn more about the gallery market from a gallery director's point of view, read the Close-up interview with Herbert Ascherman, Jr., of The Ascherman Gallery, in Cleveland, on page 178.

ADAMS MEMORIAL GALLERY, (operated by *Access to the Arts Inc.*), 600 Central Ave., Dunkirk NY 14048. (716)366-7450. Director: Kay Collins. Interested in b&w and color photography of all types. All works must be insured and ready to be put on exhibit upon date of exhibit. Presents 1-2 shows/ year. Shows last 1 month. "Arrangements set up with artist." Photographer's presence at opening preferred. Receives 25% sponsor commission. General price range: $100-500. Will review transparencies. Interested in framed, mounted and matted work only. Send material by mail for consideration. SASE.

THE AFTERIMAGE PHOTOGRAPH GALLERY, The Quandrangle 250, 2800 Routh St., Dallas TX 75201. (214)871-9140. Owner: Ben Breard. Estab. 1971. Interested in any subject matter. Frequently sells landscapes.

Exhibits: Examples of recent exhibits: Ansel Adams, George Tice, and Mark Klett. Sponsor openings; "an opening usually lasts 2 hours, and we have several a year." Photographer should "have many years of experience and a history of publications and museum and gallery display; although if one's work is strong enough, these requirements may be negated." Open to exhibiting work of newer photographer; "but that work is usually difficult to sell." Prefers Cibachrome "or other fade-resistant process" for color and "archival quality" for b&w.

Terms & Making Contact: Charges 50% sales commission on most pictures handled directly (photographer sets price). Price range: $40-10,000. Query first with resume of credits and biographical data or call to arrange an appointment. SASE. Reports in 2 days-2 months. Unframed work only.

Tips: Currently landscapes sell the best. "Work enough years to build up a sufficient inventory of, say, 20-30 superb prints, and make a quality presentation. Sees trend toward more color, bigger sizes, and more hand-painted prints."

ALIAS GALLERY, #F-2, 75 Bennett St., NW, Atlanta GA 30309. (404)352-3532. Proprietor: Sarah Hatch. Estab. 1985. Interested in "extraordinary work, must go beyond—looking like a snap shot or that which looks like anyone could do it." The photographer must "pass my acceptance; shows here are booked for a fee and by prospectus and I take a minimal commission." Presents at least one show/ year; shows last 3-4 weeks." I advertise and get the information to about 10 different sources for listings." Photographer's presence at opening requested; photographer's presence during show is not necessary, but he or she must contact us by phone. Photography occasionally sold in gallery. Receives 40% commission from bins; 25% from paid shows. General price range: $100-400. "Prices are set by the artist to include gallery commission." Reviews transparencies or mounted, archival work only. Send for current prospectus. SASE.

Tips: "I will need as much information as possible about the artist; statement, resume, and photo for the newspapers. The more idealistic you are, the harder it will be to sell, but I lean toward the idealistic work. It's more creative."

a.k.a. SKYLIGHT GALLERY, 43 Charles St., Boston MA 02114. (617)720-2855. Director: John Chittick. Open to all types of photography.

Exhibits: Requirements: All images framed or matted; rent of gallery space; produce a postcard. Examples of recent exhibitions: personal photographs from The Father of American Documentary Film, Richard Leacock; large architectural Street Scenes, by Roger Baldwin; manipulated polaroids/ pinhole photography, by Fay Breed. Shows last 1 month. Sponsors openings. "Photographer pays for catering for 100-200 people—about $150 (wine, cheese, crackers, soft drinks)." Photographer's presence at opening is preferred.

Terms & Making Contact: Photography sold in gallery; photographer receives 100% commission, only pays $500 rent for space. General price range: $300-700. Will review transparencies. Interested in mounted or unmounted work. Arrange a personal interview to show portfolio. SASE. Reports in 1 month.

Tips: "If the photographer wants to receive 100% of sales and is interested in a Boston exhibit, this is a good idea." Sales prospects are rather good. "The public is looking for 'original' photos to fit in home or office."

AMERICAN SOCIETY OF ARTISTS, INC., Box 1326, Palatine IL 60078. (708)991-4748 or (312)751-2500. Membership Chairman: Helen Del Valle. "Our members range from internationally known artists to unknown artists—quality of work is the important factor. We have about 25 shows throughout the year which accept photographic art." Members and non-members may exhibit. Price range varies. Send SASE for membership information and application (state media). Reports in 2 weeks. Framed, mounted or matted work only. Accepted members may participate in lecture and demonstration service. Member publication: *ASA Artisan.*

ART CENTER OF BATTLE CREEK, 265 E. Emmett St., Battle Creek MI 49017. (616)962-9511. Director: Ann Concannon.
Exhibits: Examples of recent exhibitions: "Focus '90," statewide competition of work by Michigan photographers, March 1990. Eighty artists accepted, 132 works. All subjects, formats, and processes represented. Occasionally presents one-person exhibits and 1 competition every other year (on the even years). Shows last 1 month. Sponsors openings; press releases are mailed to area and appropriate media. Photographer's presence at opening is preferred. Receives 33.3% commission. "We also accept gifts of photography by Michigan artists into the collection." General price range: $100-500. Will review transparencies if artist wants a solo exhibit. Interested in seeing framed or unframed, mounted or unmounted, matted work only. Send material by mail for consideration. SASE. Reports after exhibits committee has met, 1-2 months.
Tips: Sees trend toward "experimentation with older formats and processes, use of hand tinting and an increase in social commentary. All photographers are invited to apply for exhibitions. The Center has a history of showing the work of emerging artists. Send examples of your best and most recent work." Classic landscapes are most popular with buying public.

ART MUSEUM OF SOUTHEAST TEXAS, Box 3703, Beaumont TX 77704. (409)832-3432. Curator of Exhibitions: Lynn Castle. Interested in 19th and 20th century American photography.
Exhibits: Requirements: Framed works only. Examples of recent exhibitions: "Uncertain to Blue," b&w prints of Texas communities, people and animals, by Keith Carter; Manipulated Poloroids by Debbie Fleming Caffery (New Orleans); $36 \times 72"$ Cibachrome prints - sets a stage and photographs by Nic Nicosia (Dallas). Presents "at least 1" exhibit/year. Shows last 6-12 weeks. Sponsors openings; includes invitations, reception with hors d'oeurves, occasional live music or performance. Photographer's presence at opening preferred.
Terms & Making Contact: "Photography can be sold in the gallery, but we do not solicit - we are nonprofit." Museum receives 20% commission on sales. Buys photography outright. General price range: $400-800. Will review transparencies. "We request that artists not schedule any other major exhibitions in the Beaumont area at least one year prior to their museum exhibition." Send slides and resumé by mail for consideration. SASE. "Sorry to say we are slow in returning material though due to volume sent." Reports in 1 month "hopefully."
Tips: "Send slides and resume, prints should be mounted on white mats-simple frames. Sometimes black mats are OK"

ARTBANQUE, 300 1st Ave. N., Minneapolis MN 55401. (612)342-9300. Director: Richard Halonen. Interested in straight, humorous, technical, abstractions, unique presentation. Examples of recent exhibitors: Horst Richelbacher and Annie Leibowitz. Photographer must have 10 years experience. Present 1 show/year. Shows last 4 weeks. Sponsors openings; split costs equally with artist for announcements, postage and entertainment costs. Photographer's presence at opening required. Photographer's presence during the show is preferred. Photography sold in gallery. Receives 50% commission. Buys photography outright. General price range: $500. Will review transparencies. Interested in framed or unframed work, mounted or unmounted work, matted or unmatted work. Requires exclusive representation within metropolitan area. Send material by mail for consideration. SASE. Reports in 1 month.
Tips: "The photography gallery market is smaller than that of painting/paints etc., but is rapidly gaining attention as a serious art medium." Somewhat receptive to the work of newer photographers: "The upcoming exhibition is by 'unknown' photographers." To have work reviewed, "submit 20 slides, resume, a bio, a price list and a SASE."

*ARTEMISIA GALLERY, 700 N. Carpenter, Chicago IL 60622. (312)226-7756. Contact: Search Committee. Estab. 1973. Interested in innovative, leading edge work and is very receptive to newer, lesser-known photographers if they demonstrate quality work and concept.
Exhibits: Requirements: send slides of work—15-20 (consistent body of work) and resume; photographer must demonstrate artistry. Examples of recent exhibitions: Sylvia Malagrino; Eleanor Antin, Biographical; and Pam Bannos, Abstract photography. Presents 6-10/year. Shows last 1 month. Sponsors openings; cash bar, we provide gallery sitters. Exhibitor provides announcements and postage, mailing service fee, ad fee and pays rental fee. Photographer's presence at opening required.
Terms & Making Contact: Occasionally sells photos in gallery. Does not charge commission. General price range: $100-500; can be more with "name" photographers. No size limits or restrictions on photography. Send 20 slides of your work, SASE and resume for jurying. Reports in 4-6 weeks.
Tips: "We are an artist's cooperative gallery; photographer installs and removes show." Opportunities for photographers in galleries are "fair to good." Sees trend toward more photo exhibitions being "treated as fine art exhibitions; also trend toward manipulated image and hand colored." The buying public is most interested in work that is "innovative, finely composed, finely crafted, or concerned

with contemporary issues. Make slides of your work and send them with a resume; we don't exhibit or sell slides, we use them for preliminary jurying."

ASCHERMAN GALLERY/CLEVELAND PHOTOGRAPHIC WORKSHOP, Suite 4, 1846 Coventry Village, Cleveland Heights OH 44118. (216)321-0054. FAX: (216)321-4372. Director: Herbert Ascherman, Jr. Estab. 1977. Sponsored by Cleveland Photographic Workshop. Subject matter: all forms of photographic art and production. "Membership is not necessary. A prospective photographer must show a portfolio of 40-60 slides or prints for consideration. We prefer to see distinctive work—a signature in the print, work that could only be done by one person, not repetitive or replicative of others." Very receptive to exhibiting work of new photographers, "they are our primary interest."
Exhibits: Presents 10 shows/year. Shows last about 5 weeks. Openings are held for some shows. Photographers are expected to contribute toward expenses of publicity. Photographer's presence at show "always good to publicize, but not necessary." Recent photography exhibits include: "Cities," work from 50 cities throughout the world, small format (35 mm), A.L. Kezys (b&w); Ohio Landscapes, b&w continuing studies of Northern Ohio, 35 mm, all seasons, Richard Wolf; New England landscapes in b&w, large format; Timothy C. Paul.
Terms & Making Contact: Receives 25-40% commission, depending on the artist. Sometimes buys photography outright. Price range: $100-1,500. "Photos in the $100-300 range sell best." Will review transparencies, matted work only for show.
Tips: Sees trend toward "traditional conservative landscapes and subject matter." "Be as professional in your presentation as possible; identify slides with name, title, etc.; matte, mount, box prints. We are a Midwest gallery and for the most part, people here respond to competent, conservative images better than experimental or trendy work, though we are always looking for innovative work that best represents the artist (all subject matter)."

THE BALTIMORE MUSEUM OF ART, Art Museum Dr., Baltimore MD 21218. (301)396-6330. Contact: Department of Prints, Drawings and Photographs. Interested in work of quality and originality; no student work. Arrange a personal interview to show portfolio or query with resume of credits. SASE. Reports in 2 weeks-1 month. Unframed and matted work only.

BC SPACE, 235 Forest Ave., Laguna Beach CA 92651. (714)497-1880. Contact: Mark Chamberlain. Interested only in contemporary photography. Presents 8 solo or group shows per year; 6 weeks normal duration. General price range: $150-3,000; gallery commission 40%. Collaborates with artists on special events, openings, etc. For initial contact submit slides and resume. Follow up by arranging personal portfolio review. SASE. Responds "as soon as possible—hopefully within a month, but show scheduling occurs several times a year. Please be patient."
Tips: "Keep in touch—show new work periodically. If we can't give a show right away, don't despair, it may fit another format later. The shows have a rhythm of their own which takes time. Salability of the work is important, but not the prime consideration. We are more interested in fresh, innovative work, and are very receptive to exhibiting the work of new photographers."

JESSE BESSER MUSEUM, 491 Johnson St., Alpena MI 49707. (517)356-2202. Chief of Resources: Robert Haltiner. Interested in a variety of photos suitable for showing in general museum. Examples of recent exhibitions: "Northern Light", black & white evening & night landscapes of the Northern Midwest by Geoffrey Peckham; "Broken Dreams", black & white images of abandoned buildings in northern Michigan by Kevin Roznowski; and "People and Places", color images of people and places around the world by Pierre Perrault, Montreal, Canada. Presents 1-2 shows/year. Shows last 6-8 weeks. Price range: $25-500. Charges 20% sales commission. "However, being a museum, emphasis is not placed on sales, per se." Submit samples to Chief of Resources, Robert Haltiner. Framed work only. Will review transparencies. SASE for return of slides. Reports in 2 weeks. "All work for exhibit must be framed and ready for hanging. Send *good* slides of work with resume and perhaps artist's statement. Trend is toward manipulative work to achieve the desired effect." Most recently, Northern Michigan scenes sell best. Very receptive to presenting newer, lesser-known photographers.

 The asterisk before a listing indicates that the market is new in this edition. New markets are often the most receptive to freelance submissions.

Close-up

Herbert Ascherman, Jr.
Gallery Owner
Ascherman Gallery
Cleveland, Ohio

"A photographer is at the same time his own worst critic and his own worst enemy," says Herbert Ascherman, Jr., owner of the Ascherman Gallery in Cleveland. "Photographers need to learn how to judge their work in comparison with what they do, what they are capable of doing and what others at the same or different levels of development have done."

Knowing the basics of photography, this gallery owner and photographer says, is essential in becoming a working photographer. However, as he also points out, learning to judge one's work and to manage the practical aspects of working in photography are also indispensable to one's success.

Developing confidence in one's own ability will help a photographer to identify the direction to take with his work, says Ascherman. He recommends taking ten favorite images and hanging them in a highly visible place, to live and become acquainted with them on a daily basis. "Every time you finish printing, walk out and look carefully at the wall and at the new work," he advises. "If what you are holding is better, take one or a few of your images down and put something else up. You will have a continuous forum for your work, be able to judge where your thinking/head/vision is, and, at the same time, watch the change in your subject, imagery and style as it evolves."

Remarking on his own entry into the field, Ascherman says that even though he was confident he had developed his artistic sensibilities at an early point in his 13-year career, he still needed to learn the business side of photography. "A young artist doesn't, can't and won't make money, let alone a legitimate living, by selling his work through a gallery," he says, explaining that galleries can be a key avenue of gaining exposure for one's work while actively pursuing clients. "A gallery introduces the public to contemporary work by up-and-coming artists on a continuous basis."

Ascherman feels a special affinity for the aspiring, talented photographer. "I would rather give an unknown artist his first show in my gallery than a master his 50th," he remarks. "I am more interested in discovering their talent. Once we have established a rapport, I help polish the photographer's image." Ascherman adds that photographers should have a vision for what they wish to accomplish, and then set out to achieve it. "He who enters my door and eventually hangs on the wall is one of any number of eclectic individuals who are aggressive enough to seek a forum for their particular vision."

Once a photographer enters Ascherman's gallery and shows him his portfolio, what the photographer says and how he says it are as important to Ascherman as the work itself. Photographers should openly discuss their pictures and reveal "what gets their juices flowing." He advises communicating "things which will not be apparent when the works hang quietly on the wall." With unsolicited submissions sent by mail, Ascherman has to read more into the work but looks for similar evidence of thought and method behind the camera lens.

Ascherman can often see when a photographer has arrived at a level of finesse in his work. As he has found in his own experience, personal confidence seems to match the quality of a photographer's work. "What I actually sell either as a photographer or as a gallery owner is an image of confidence," he says. This confidence, he explains, comes from meeting the requirements of a client or buyer while at the same time satisfying one's own creative goals. When photographers come to him for guidance, he reminds them of this and stresses that the most important opinion about the images is still the photographer's. "I always begin and end each conversation [with a photographer] with the caveat: this is one man's opinion . . . good as far as the front door."

For everyone involved in photography, learning becomes second-nature, a way of life, Ascherman observes. The Cleveland Photographic Workshop, the nonprofit, parent organization behind the gallery, is accordingly based on this philosophy. The Workshop gives as much weight to business considerations and functioning within the gallery system as to creative development. Study and training can enhance the work of already talented individuals, but the best way to learn photography, he adds, is just to live it. "I was fortunate to have had academic teachers over the years who provided me with the tools to teach myself," he says, explaining that he now learns by reading, watching and doing. His photographic library, he points out, now consists of some 1,000 books, and he reviews about 20 magazines a month for their photographic content. "Photography is a game of understanding. The more you play, the more you learn, the better you become."

— *Marcy Knopf*

This picture, titled "Ten Children" is an example of Herbert Ascherman Jr.'s own work, which has been displayed at the Ascherman Gallery. Taken by him in Paris in 1987, this image has also been reproduced in poster form and published in the book, Paris: Realist and Surrealist. As one of his colleagues in Paris had reminded him at the time, and as he also advises photographers to remember, the goal of achieving an authentic vision "is to make it better than it was."

BIRD-IN-HAND GALLERY, 323 7th St. SE, P.O. Box 15258, Washington DC 20003-0258. (202)543-0744. Owner: Christopher Ackerman. Estab. 1987. Interested in interpretive b&w, architectural, landscape and special technique; quite receptive to newer photographers..
Exhibits: Requirements: professionalism. Examples of recent exhibitions: Saguaro Cactus, Images of a Threatened Species, photographs by Madge Matteo; Cape Cod, (palladium and platinum prints) black-and-white by Slan Scherr; Photography, b&w prints by Ester Espejo; and Aerial Photography, (color and b/w prints of environmentally sensitive regions of the world and Amazonia), by Robert Perron. Presents 4-6 shows/year. Shows last 2½ weeks. Sponsors openings. Photographer's presence at opening is preferred.
Terms & Making Contact: Photography sold in gallery. Exhibitors are represented throughout the year. Receives 40% commission on works sold. General price range $75-375. Will review transparencies. Interested in framed or unframed work, matted or unmatted work. Size and quantity of photos considered on individual basis. Query with samples. SASE. Reports in 2 weeks.
Tips: "Photography is like any other business—be prepared to start at the bottom and work hard. Remain original. We have good experience with lower priced work. We receive many submissions that are obtuse and impossible to interpret without being able to read a photographer's mind. Remember form as well as content makes great art. Human subjects, landscape and special technique currently sells best at our gallery."

BOODY FINE ARTS, INC., 1425 Hanley Ind. Ct., St. Louis MO 63144. (314)961-5502. President: Steven Boody. Interested in any types, styles and subject matter.
Exhibits: Requirements: Present a proven vitae.
Terms & Making Contact: Photography sold in gallery. Receives 50% commission on works sold. General price range: $250-1,250. Will review transparencies. Interested in mounted and matted work. Requires exclusive representation in area. Minimum size accepted is 16×20. Send material by mail for consideration. SASE. Reports in 1 month.
Tips: Photographers should have 5-10 years professional experience. Landscapes and nonobjective (large format) photographic art is most popular at the present time.

*BRENT GALLERY, 908 Wood Street, Houston TX 77002. (713)236-1830. Director: Kevin Mercier. Estab. 1984. Interested in something previously not seen. Examples of recent exhibitions: Francisco Barragán, (color prints of surrealistic imagery); "Feet First," by María Inés Roqué, (b&w prints of feet in various contexts); "Contracurtis: Early American Coverups, Series #4," by Warren Neidich, (platinum prints simulations of antique photos taken from B-grade TV westerns, ala Edward S. Curtis). Presents usually one exhibit/year. Shows last 6-8 weeks. Sponsors openings; gallery pays invitations and reception. Photographer's presence at opening and during show preferred. Receives 40%. General price range: $200-950. Will review transparencies. Interested in framed or unframed, mounted or unmounted, and matted or unmatted work. Requires exclusive representation within metropolitan area. Send material by mail for consideration. SASE. Reports in 1 month.
Tips: This is a "progressive gallery looking for unique, historically important work. Landscapes/romanticized subjects seem to be leading the way for other media." The buying public is "still wrapped up in post-modernism (Sherman, et al)."

THE BROKEN DIAMOND, 19 N. Broadway, Billings MT 59101. Owner: Frederick R. Longan. Shows last 4-6 weeks. Photography sold in gallery. Receives 50% commission. Buys photography outright. General price range: $350-5,000+. Arrange a personal interview to show portfolio.

J.J. BROOKINGS GALLERY, Box 1237, San Jose CA 95108. (408)287-3311. Director: Timothy C. Duran. Interested in painterly works.
Exhibits: Requirements: professional presentation, realistic pricing, numerous quality images. Examples of recent exhibitors: Ansel Adams, James Crable, Geir Jordahl, Duane Michaels, Edward Curtis, John Wimberly and Cay Lang. Presents 3+ shows (not including group shows)/year. Sponsors openings. Photographers presence at opening preferred.
Terms & Making Contact: Photography sold in gallery. Receives 50% commission. Buys some photography outright. General price range: $300-10,000. Will review transparencies. Interested in "whatever the artist thinks will impress me the most. 'Painterly' work is best. No documentary, landscape or politically-oriented work." Send material by mail for consideration. Reports in 3 weeks, "if not acceptable reports immediately."

CALIFORNIA MUSEUM OF PHOTOGRAPHY, University of California, Riverside CA 92521. (714)787-4787. Curator: Edward Earle. The photographer must have the "highest quality work." Presents 12-18 shows/year. Shows last 6-8 weeks. Sponsors openings; inclusion in museum calendar, reception. Curatorial committee reviews transparencies and/or matted or unmatted work. Query with resume of credits. SASE. Reports in 90 days.

Tips: "This museum attempts to balance exhibitions among historical, technology, contemporary, etc." We do not sell photos but provide photographers with exposure. "The museum is always interested in newer, lesser-known photographers who are producing interesting work. We can show only a small percent of what we see in a year. The CMP will be moving to a renovated 23,000 sq. ft. building. A new series of exhibitions will begin after that."

CAMBRIDGE MULTICULTURAL ARTS CENTER GALLERY, 41 Second St., Cambridge MA 02141. (617)577-1400. Gallery Coordinator. Interested in fine arts, historical, and documentary work which examines ethnicity, nationalism, and cultural representation in the traditional and contemporary worlds. The photographer must be willing to participate in a group show, share costs of printed announcements and reception costs. Presents 4-5 shows/year. Shows last 5-6 weeks. Photographer's presence at opening preferred. "Appropriate if there is a gallery talk, does *not* have to serve as gallery attendant." Photography sold in gallery. Receives 20% commission. General price range: $175-500. Will review transparencies. Interested in slides. Arrange a personal interview to show portfolio, query with resume of credits and sample slides. SASE. Reports when jury review panel meets—4-6 months.
Tips: Work demonstrating ethnographic cultural elements will receive highest interest. Smaller works, works under $200 are being considered by new collectors, as interest and appreciation for artwork increases.

THE CAMERA OBSCURA GALLERY, 1307 Bannock St., Denver CO 80204. (303)623-4059. Director: Hal Gould. Shows last 6 weeks. Sponsors openings. Photographer's presence at opening preferred. Photography sold in gallery. Receives 40-50% commission. Buys photography outright. General price range: $200-25,000. Will review transparencies. Interested in mounted or unmounted work, matted or unmatted work. Requires exclusive representation within metropolitan area. Arrange a personal interview to show portfolio. SASE. Reports in 2 weeks.
Tips: Sees trend toward "more traditional principles of photography."

THE CANTON ART INSTITUTE, 1001 Market Ave., Canton OH 44702. (216)453-7666. Executive Director: M.J. Albacete. "We are interested in exhibiting all types of quality photography, preferably using photography as an art medium, but we will also examine portfolios of other types of photography work as well: architecture, etc.
Exhibits: The photographer must send preliminary letter of desire to exhibit; send samples of work (upon our request); have enough work to form an exhibition; complete *Artist's Form* detailing professional and academic background, and provide photographs for press usage." Presents 2-5 shows/year. Shows last 6 weeks. Sponsors openings. Major exhibits (in galleries), postcard or other type mailer, public reception.
Terms & Making Contact: Submit letters of inquiry first, with samples of photos. Photography sold in gallery. Receives 20% commission. General price range: $50-500. Interested in exhibition-ready work. No size limits. Query with samples. SASE. Reports in 2 weeks.
Tips: "We look for photo exhibitions which are unique, not necessarily by 'top' names. Anyone inquiring should have some exhibition experience, and have sufficient materials; also, price lists, insurance lists, description of work, artist's background, etc. Most photographers and artists do little to aid galleries and museums in promoting their works—no good publicity photos, confusing explanations about their work, etc. We attempt to give photographers—new and old—a good gallery exhibit when we feel their work merits such. While sales are not our main concern, the exhibition experience and the publicity can help promote new talents. If the photographer is really serious about his profession, he should design a press-kit type of package so that people like me can study his work, learn about his background, and get a pretty good concept of his work. This is generally the first knowledge we have of any particular artist, and is a bad impression is made, even for the best photographer, he gets no exhibition. How else are we to know? We have a basic form which we send to potential exhibitors requesting all the information needed for an exhibition. My article, 'Artists, Get Your Act Together If You Plan to Take it on the Road,' shows artists how to prepare self-promoting kits for potential sponsors, gallery exhibitors, etc. Copy of article and form sent for $2 and SASE."

CATSKILL CENTER FOR PHOTOGRAPHY, 59 Tinker St., Woodstock NY 12498. (914)679-9957. Exhibitions Director: Kathleen Kenyon. Interested in all creative photography. Presents 10 shows/year. Shows last 4 weeks. Sponsors openings. Receives 25% sales commission. Price range: $75-1,000. Send 20 slides plus resume by mail for consideration. SASE. Reports in 4 months.
Tips: "Visit us first—set up an appointment, or write us a brief letter, enclose resume, statement on the work, 20 slides, SASE. We are closed Wednesdays and Thursdays. We show contemporary and historical photography."

■**C.E.P.A. (CENTER FOR EXPLORATORY & PERCEPTUAL ART)**, 4th Floor, 700 Main St., Buffalo NY 14202. (716)856-2717. Executive Director: Gail Nicholson. Estab. 1974. "C.E.P.A. is a nonprofit organization whose *raison d'etre* is the advancement of photography that engages contemporary issues within the visual arts. C.E.P.A.'s varied programs explore aesthetic and intellectual issues within the camera arts of still photography, photo installation, video, film and multimedia performance. An artist must meet the aesthetic standards of the director and also must produce work that conforms to the aesthetic mission stated above. C.E.P.A. provides a venue of innovative work as well as original visions by known and unknown artists that break new ground in the photo-related arts."

Exhibits: Examples of recent exhibits: Contemporary Black British Photographers, (photography and painting, mixed subjects, group show); Carrie Mae Weems, (photographs & installations, Polaroids and silver prints); Against Interpretation (towards a Non-Representational Photography), (mixed media, group show curated by Stephen Frailey). Very receptive to the work of new, lesser-known photographers. Presents 8 major exhibitions of 1-3 artists and/or group exhibitions per show with three satellite and 12 public transit exhibits on one bus eights times a year. Shows last 4-6 weeks. Sponsors openings; provides postcard announcement and curator's statement in the C.E.P.A. Journal. Cash bar at reception. Photography sold in gallery.

Terms and Making Contact: General price range: $250-5,000. No commission charged. Requires exclusive representation in this area. Provide slide portfolio, a resume and a statement of intent or explanation of the work proposed for exhibition. Will review portfolio or slides. Considers any size, shape, form, or permutation of any camera art. Send material by mail for consideration. SASE. Prefers to keep work on file.

Tips: The trend is toward large format Polaroid, installation, Cibachrome printing, photo-collage and assemblage. "Keep updating material sent. In galleries it's not what you know, it's who you know."

CITY OF LOS ANGELES PHOTOGRAPHY CENTERS, 412 S. Parkview St., Los Angeles CA 90057. (213)383-7342. Director: Glenna Avila. Estab. 1960. Interested in all types of photography.

Exhibits: Presents 8 shows/year. Exhibits last 4-6 weeks. Examples of recent exhibits: "Contemporary African-American Photography," group exhibit 23 photographers (documentary, portrait, conceptual); "Portrait of Bodie," group exhibit 34 photographer (landscape/still-life); and "Steven Josefsberg: Gum Ammonium Diochromate Prints," (still-lifes). Offers rental darkrooms, studio space, outings, lectures, classes, bi-monthly newsletter, juried annual photography contest, a photo library and photographer's slide registry. "Send up to 20 slides with resume for us to keep on file. Send SASE if you want them returned." Reports in 1 month. Matted work only. Gallery retains 20% of sold photographs.

Tips: "We are interested in seeing professional photography which explores a multitude of techniques and styles, while expanding the notion of the art of photography. We have been extremely receptive to exhibiting the work of newer, lesser-known photographers. We are interested in seeing series of works that are unique, that hold together with a theme, that explore a particular subject matter, that have extremely high print quality and excellent presentation (mats)."

COLLECTOR'S CHOICE GALLERY, 20352 Laguna Canyon Rd., Laguna Beach CA 92651-1137. (714)494-8215. Director: Beverly Inskeep. Estab. 1968. Presents "color, b&w and mixed media photography, including Xerography in contemporary expression. Any subject matter. We do have two annual theme shows: Eroticism and Art and Technology. Interested in lesser-known photographers.

Exhibits: Examples of recent exhibits: Jennifer Griffith, Antoinette Geldun, Jim Nordstrom, Beverly Richardson and Kornelius Schorle; all exhibited in contemporary color photography exhibition of general subject matter but with a high percentage of works of metaphor. "Our annual Erotic theme show usually holds the most work of photographers compared to other exhibitions." Presents 10 shows/year. Sponsors openings. Photographer's presence is preferred at opening "if it's a one-person exhibition."

Terms & Making Contact: Rarely buys photography outright. Receives 25-40% commission. Will review transparencies. Interested in mounted, matted or unmatted work. Query with resume of credits, query with samples. SASE. Reports in 1 week.

Tips: "We're always looking for some special 'eye' or mixing of media. The public is still learning the difference between graphic commercial photography and fine art photography. We're still educating the public, but the field is getting much easier than it was two years ago. Customers are preferring large formatted sizes for drama. We're also seeing more interest in Cibachromes since they don't fade as other photos do over long periods of time."

THE CONTEMPORARY ARTS CENTER, 115 E. Fifth St., Cincinnati OH 45202. (513)721-0390. Curator: Jack Sawyer. Nonprofit arts center. Interested in avant garde, innovative photography. Photographer must be selected by the curator and approved by the board. Examples of recent exhibits: "Warhol/

■ *The solid, black square before a listing indicates that the market uses various types of audiovisual materials, such as slides, film or videotape.*

Makos," the work of New York photographer, Christopher Makos; "Images of Desire," contemporary advertising photography; "The Perfect Moment: Robert Mapplethorpe." Presents 1-3 shows/year. Exhibits last 6 weeks. Sponsors openings; provides printed invitations, music, refreshments, cash bar. Photographer's presence at opening preferred. Photography sometimes sold in gallery. Receives 10% commission. General price range: $200-500. Will review transparencies. Send query with resume and slides of work. SASE. Reports in 1 month.

CREATIVE PHOTOGRAPHY GALLERY, University of Dayton, Dayton OH 45469. (513)229-2230. Directors: Sean Wilkinson and Jack Teemer. Interested in "all areas of creative photography."
Exhibits: "Untitled", by Peter Miraglia, (b&w prints, double portraits); "Cadences", by Dan Ellsbroock, (b&w prints, various subjects); and "Gender Series", by Barbara Ellen Adelman, (color prints surrealistic and collages, mixed imagery). Very receptive to the work of newer, lesser-known photographers. Photographers with exhibition experience are preferred.
Terms & Making Contacts: Submit 20 slides of work (including dimensions) with resume of credits and SASE in February. Decision is in March, material returned by end of month. No commission.
Tips: "We are nonprofit so there are no sales. Be sure photos are well-considered, and show some maturity and development."

CATHERINE EDELMAN GALLERY, 2nd Fl., 300 W. Superior, Chicago IL 60610. (312)266-2350. Director: Catherine Edelman. "We exhibit works ranging from traditional landscapes to painted photo works done by artists who use photography as the medium through which to explore an idea."
Exhibits: Requirements: "The work must be engaging and not derivative of a well known photographer." Examples of recent exhibitions: "Silent Dramas: The Landscape," works by Carl Chiarenza, Mark Klett and Michael Kenna; "Men on Men," b&w prints, polaroid transfers, gelatin mural prints by Duane Michaels, John Reuter and Joe Ziolkowski; "Submerged Realities," by Jeff Millikan, (large Cibachromes). Presents 9-10 exhibits/year. Shows last 4 weeks. Sponsors openings; free wine and nuts. Photographer's presence at opening preferred.
Terms & Making Contact: Photography sold in gallery. Receives 50% commission. General price range: $300-5,000. Will review transparencies. Interested in matted or unmatted work. Requires exclusive representation within metropolitan area. Shows are limited to works no larger than $40 \times 60''$. Send material by mail for consideration. SASE. Reports in 2 weeks.
Tips: "Try to not be overly eager and realize that the process of arranging an exhibition takes a long time. The relationship between gallery and photographer is a partnership - there must be open lines of communication. I'm seeing more and more 'art' galleries exhibit photography. Photography is becoming more of an acceptable art form to collect, although photography collectors are still the most knowledgeable about the art form."

*PAUL EDELSTEIN GALLERY, 766 South White Station Rd., Memphis TN 38119. (901)682-7724. Director: Paul Edelstein/Lisa Dattel. Estab. 1985. Interested in modern and figurative work.
Exhibits: Examples of recent exhibits: William Eggleston, (type C prints and dye transfers); Vivus Darwin, (35mm Type C prints); and Deck Reeks, (35mm Type C prints). Presents 4 /year. Shows last 1 month.
Terms & Making Contact: Receives 50% commission. General price range: k$800; some work priced much higher, in $5,000-10,000 range. Will review transparencies. Interested in framed or unframed work, mounted or unmounted work, and matted or unmatted work. Send material by mail for consideration. Cannot return material. Reports in 1 month.
Tips: The buying public "likes big names like Eggleston, Mapplethorpe, Weston, etc."

ETHERTON/STERN GALLERY, 135 S. 6th Ave., Tucson AZ 85701. (602)624-7370. Director: Terry Etherton. Interested in contemporary photography with emphasis on artists in Western and Southwestern US. Photographer must "have a high-quality, consistent body of work—be a working artist/ photographer—no 'hobbyists' or weekend photographers." Presents 8-9 shows/year. Shows last 5 weeks. Sponsors openings; provides wine and refreshments, publicity, etc. Photographer's presence at opening and during show preferred. Receives 50% commission. Occasionally buys photography outright. General price range: $200-20,000. Will review transparencies. Interested in matted or unmatted unframed work. Arrange a personal interview to show portfolio or send material by mail for consideration. SASE. Reports in 3 weeks.
Tips: "You must be fully committed to photography as a way of life. I'm not interested in 'hobbyists' or weekend amateurs. You should be familiar with photo art world and with my gallery and the work I show. Do not show more than 20 prints for consideration—show only the best of your work—no fillers. Have work sent or delivered so that it is presentable and professional."

FOCAL POINT GALLERY, 321 City Island Ave., New York NY 10464. (212)885-1403. Photographer/Director: Ron Terner. Subject matter open. Presents 9 shows/year. Shows last 4 weeks. Photographer's presence at opening preferred. Charges 30% sales commission. Price range: $175-700. Artist should call for information about exhibition policies."

Tips: Sees trend toward more use of alternative processes. "The gallery is geared toward exposure—letting the public know what contemporary artists are doing—and is not concerned with whether it will sell. If the photographer is only interested in selling, this is not the gallery for him/her, but if the artist is concerned with people seeing the work and gaining feedback, this is the place. We are receptive to newer photographers—most of the work shown at Focal Point Gallery is of lesser-known artists. Don't be discouraged if not accepted the first time. But continue to come back with new work when ready."

FRIDHOLM FINE ARTS, Broadway Arts Bldg., 49 Broadway, Asheville NC 28801. (704)258-9206. Owners: Bonnie or David Hobbs. Estab. 1989. Interested in any types, styles and subject matter of photography.

Exhibits: Requirements: professionalism. Examples of recent exhibitors: Doug Van de Zande, Seny Norasingh, Tom Norman and Bole Cirovic. Number of photography exhibits presented each year varies. Shows last 2 months. Sponsors openings; includes invitation and opening reception. Photographer's presence at opening/during show preferred.

Terms & Making Contact: Photography sold in gallery when available. Receives 50% commission. General price range: $250-500. Will review transparencies. All work up in gallery framed, unmounted, matted or unmatted. Requires exclusive representation within metropolitan area. No size or quantity limits. Query with resume of credits, send material by mail for consideration. SASE. Reports in 3-4 weeks.

Tips: Opportunities for photographers are "poor to fair." Number of exhibitions increasing; but still difficult to sell photography in general.

THE GALLERY, (formerly The Mill Gallery), % Arts Council for Franklin County, Ballard Mill Center for the Arts, S. William St., Malone NY 12953. (518)483-0909. Interested in photojournalism, color, fine b&w images and new techniques. Presents 2 shows/year. Shows last 6 weeks. Sponsors openings. "We print invitations, mail them, send press releases, and offer opening receptions." Photographer's presence at opening preferred. Sponsor receives 15% commission. General price range: $100 (depends on matting). Will review transparencies. Interested in framed work only. Query with resume of credits or samples. SASE. Reports in 2 weeks.

Tips: "Our patrons are from the rural area around Adirondack Park, but we also have a large influx of Canadians in the summer. Realism is strong, but also some abstract work.

GALLERY EAST, THE ART INSTITUTE OF BOSTON, 700 Beacon St., Boston MA 02115. (617)262-1223. Co-Gallery Directors: Janet Cavallero Martin Mugar. All types and styles of photography considered.

Exhibits: Examples of recent exhibitions: "Hawaii: Landscape of Transformation," by David Ulrich; "Off Season," Contemporary and Historic Photographs on Baseball by well-known photographers; and "Scenes from Paris," by Lucien Aigner. Presents 2-3 shows/year. Shows last 4-6 weeks. Sponsors openings; fixed allowance for printing, refreshments and publicity. Photographer's presence at opening/during show preferred.

Terms & Making Contact: Accepts percentage donation at artist's discretion. General Price Range: $40-2,500 per print. Will review transparencies. Interested in unframed work only, mounted or unmounted and matted or unmatted work. No quantity or size limits. Arrange a personal interview to show portfolio, query with resume of credits, query with samples, send material by mail for consideration or submit portfolio for review. SASE. Reports in 1 month; sometimes longer in summer.

GALLERY OF ART, UNIVERSITY OF NORTHERN IOWA, Cedar Falls IA 50614-0362. (319)273-2077. Interested in all styles of high-quality contemporary art and photojournalistic works. "The photographer must meet a standard of artistic quality, and we do review credentials." Presents average of 4 shows/year. Shows last 4 weeks. Open to the public. Sometimes buys photography to include in gallery's photographic collection. General price range: varies $50-500. Will review transparencies. Interested in framed or unframed work, mounted or unmounted work, matted or unmatted work; for review, have *limited* framing for exhibitions. Arrange a personal interview to show portfolio, query with resume of credits, query with samples, send material by mail for consideration, submit portfolio for review. SASE. Report time varies.

Tips: Advice to interested photographers: "Patience—we schedule over long term."

GALLERY 614, 0350 County Rd. #20, Corunna IN 46730. (219)281-2752. Contact: Robert Green. Interested only in carbro and carbon prints (nonsilver processes). Examples of recent exhibitions: carbro/carbon prints by Margaret Viles; and a tri-color/carbro print by Robert Green. "The only

The Gallery, sponsored by the Arts Council for Franklin County in Malone, New York, selected this stunning piece by photographer Michael Hart for one of its regional exhibitions in 1989. Though, as the photographer points out, his only "payment" was the opportunity for exposure in the exhibit and later promotional materials published by the Council, "the exhibition initiated dialogue and resulted in subsequent sales."

limitations are the imagination." Sponsors openings. Receives 30% sales commission or buys outright. Price range: $750-3,000. Call to arrange an appointment. No unsolicited material. SASE. Mounted, matted work. Also, teaches monochrome, tri-chrome carbro/carbon printing.

Tips: Open to the work of newer, lesser-known photographers, especially in nonsilver work. Sees "a return to style—classicism and black and white." Portraits and pictorials sell most frequently.

FAY GOLD GALLERY, 247 Buckhead Ave., Atlanta GA 30305. (404)233-3843. FAX: (404)365-8633. Owner/Director: Fay Gold. Hours: Monday-Saturday 9:30 a.m. to 5:30 p.m. Interested in surreal, nudes, allegorical, landscape (20th century); strong interest in contemporary color photography. The photographer must be inventive, speak a new language, something not seen before of quality, historical importance or corporate oriented material.

Exhibits: Presents 12 shows/year. Shows last 4 weeks. Sponsors openings, provides invitation, mailing, press releases to all media, serves wine, contacts all private and corporate collectors. Photographer's presence at opening preferred. Photography sold in gallery.

Terms & Making Contact: Receives 50% commission. Buys photography outright. General price range: $350-15,000. Will review transparencies. Interested in unframed work, mounted work and matted work only. Generally requires exclusive representation within metropolitan area. Send slides and resume. SASE.

Tips: Trends are toward more surreal, figurative work for collectors; contemporary color for corporate collections.

W.A. GRAHAM GALLERY, 1431 W. Alabama, Houston TX 77006. (713)528-4957. Director: William A. Graham. Interested in contemporary innovations.
Exhibits: Examples of recent exhibitions: "Photograms" by Alain Clement; "Photographs" by Linda Connor; and "Photographs," by Sharon Stewart. Presents 2 shows/year. Shows last 4-5 weeks. Sponsors openings. Photographer's presence at opening preferred. Receives 50% commission on works sold. Seldom buys photos outright. General price ranges $100-8,000. Will review transparencies if accompanied by SASE. Interested in unframed work only. Requires exclusive representation within metropolitan area. Send material by mail for consideration. SASE. Reports in 1 month.

THE HALSTED GALLERY INC., 560 N. Woodward, Birmingham MI 48011. (313)644-8284. Contact: Melanie S. Johns or Thomas Halsted. Interested in 19th and 20th century photographs and out-of-print photography books. Sponsors openings. Presents 5 shows/year. Shows last 8 weeks. Receives 50% sales commission or buys outright. General price range: $500-25,000. Call to arrange a personal interview to show portfolio only. Prefers to see 10-15 prints overmatted. Send no slides or samples. Unframed work only.

O.K. HARRIS WORKS OF ART, 383 W. Broadway, New York NY 10012. (212)431-3600. Director: Ivan C. Karp. Estab. 1969. Interested in urban and industrial scenes and photo journalistic/documentary. Very receptive to newer photographers.
Exhibits: Examples of recent exhibitions: "Brothels of Nevada," Dye Transfer Photographs, by Timothy Hursley; "Homeless of Las Vegas," black & white and color photographs, by Andrew Garn; "Home Altars of Mexico," C-Type Ektacolor Plus Prints, by Dana Salvo. Presents 6-10 shows/year. Shows last 3 weeks. Photographer's presence at opening preferred.
Terms & Making Contact: Photography sold in gallery. Receives 40% commission on works sold. General price range $175-850. Will review transparencies. Interested in matted or unmatted work. "The gallery looks at work without portfolio for review. (Summer hours are different and the gallery closes from mid-July to early September.) SASE. Reports in 1 week.
Tips: "Be informed of the kind of photography we are interested in. Present a body of photographs that illustrate a theme or idea."

G. RAY HAWKINS GALLERY, 7224 Melrose, Los Angeles CA 90046. (213)550-1504. Interested in all types of fine art photography. Conducts 1 photo auction/year. "Primarily vintage and established artists." Wants photographers with minimum of 10 years in fine art photography and with work represented in at least 5 museum collections and shown in at least 10 major galleries or museums. Presents 4-6 shows/year. Shows last 4-7 weeks. Photographer's presence during shows preferred. Receives 40-50% sales commission or buys outright. Price range: $100-70,000. Query with non-returnable resume of credits, include statement regarding work for permanent files. Will review transparencies (dupe slides).
Tips: "Be patient. Produce innovative, fresh and new work. Understand origins of your specific media."

*HUGHES FINE ARTS CENTER, Dept. of Visual Arts, Box 8134, Grand Forks ND 58202-8134. (701)777-2257. Director: Brian Paulsen. Estab. 1979. Interested in any subjects. Newer, lesser-known photographers are welcome.
Exhibits: "Works should be framed and matted." Examples of recent exhibitions: Dana Sherman, Roger Sopher, and Harley Strauss. All three exhibited b&w 35mm and 4×5 formats. Presents 1-3/ year. Shows last 2-3 weeks. Does not charge commission; sales are between artist-buyer. Will review transparencies. Will exhibit framed work only. No size limits or restrictions. Send transparencies only. SASE. Reports in 2 weeks.
Tips: "Send slides of work . . . we will dupe originals and return ASAP and contact you later."

IMAGES, Images, Images, 328 West Fourth St., Cincinnati OH 45202. (513)241-8124. Gallery Manager: Jacqui Phlipot. Interested in fine quality photographs in all mediums. No commercial work or travel photography. Documentary photographs which speak to social issues will be considered. Must have a portfolio of work which contains a strong thematic series dealing with a subject or art concern. Presents 6 shows/year. Shows last 6 weeks. Sponsors openings, evening open hours; invitation (no food or beverage). Photographer's presence at opening is preferred. Charges 40% commission. General price range: $150-800. Rarely buys photographs. Will review transparencies. Interested in mounted and matted work only. Arrange a personal interview to show portfolio or send material for consideration. SASE. Reports in 2 months.
Tips: "We have a portion of the gallery used primarily for emerging artists and we have a members' show." Seeing trend toward "more manipulated and computer images, but fine art b&w landscapes have sold best."

INTERNATIONAL CENTER OF PHOTOGRAPHY, 1130 5th Ave., New York NY 10128. (212)860-1773. Contact: Department of Exhibitions. Estab. 1974. Portfolio reviews are held the first Monday of each month. "The norm is for more established photographers, however for our *New Directions Series*, newer work is shown. Submit portfolio to the receptionist at 9:00 a.m. and pick up in the afternoon. Call Friday prior to drop-off date to confirm. This is strictly drop-off. For a personal portfolio review, please call Ruth Lester at (212)860-1770 to schedule appointment.

JANAPA PHOTOGRAPHY GALLERY LTD., 402-A E. 12th St., New York NY 10009-4020. FAX: (800)423-8011. Director: Stanley Simon. Estab. 1980. Interested in contemporary, fine-art, avant-garde photography.
Exhibits: Examples of recent exhibitors: Diana Parrish Cull, Linda Sutton and women photographers of the 80s. Photographers must be professional. Sponsors openings; provides press and public relations, mailing list, local newspaper listings and advertising with all costs at photographer's expense. "We charge a fee of $250 for one-person show, or proportionate amount for more than one." Photographer's presence preferred at openings and during show. Photographer should be aggressive and willing to participate in own marketing.
Terms & Making Contact: Commission 25-50%, depending on artist. General price range: $150-250/ b&w; $250-500/color, (16×20), archival work, matted and normally sold in portfolio groups. "We request exclusive area representation, if possible." Interviews are arranged by appointment for portfolio reviews. Mail queries including workprints, slides, resume and credits (incl. SASE); will send reply in two weeks.
Tips: "JANAPA has changed its concept toward becoming a consulting and resource organization, in which gallery viewing is arranged by appointment (except for openings). We are also seeking staff to work in sales, administrative and managerial career positions for expansion nationally. We look for exceptional work in composition, originality and technical concepts. We lean toward innovative styles, multi-imaging, abstracts, hand coloring, infrared toning. Fine art and contemporary photos sell most frequently. Submit good quality portfolio with cohesive body of work or a theme; could be style, technique or many things but must work together as a whole."

JEB GALLERY, INC., 295 Albany St., Fall River MA 02720. (508)673-8010. Contact: Ronald Caplain or Claire Caplain. All contemporary photographers are represented. Color is accepted. Photographer receives 40% commission, with prices ranging from $300-5,000. No slides. "Portfolios of photographers are reviewed by appointment."

KENT STATE UNIVERSITY SCHOOL OF ART GALLERY, KSU, 201 Art Building, Kent OH 44242. (216)672-7853. Director: Fred T. Smith. Interested in all types, styles and subject matter of photography. Photographer must present quality work. Presents 1 show/year. Exhibits last 3 weeks. Sponsors openings; provides cheese, crackers, vegetables, dip, wine and non-alcoholic punch. Photographer's presence at opening preferred. Photography can be sold in gallery. Receives 20% commission. Buys photography outright. Will review transparencies. Send material by mail for consideration. SASE. Reports usually in 1 month, but it depends on time submitted.
Tips: Write a proposal and send with slides.

*KIRKLAND ART CENTER, Box 213, East Park Row, Clinton NY 13323. (315)853-8871. Activities Coordinator: Nancy Robinson. Estab. 1962. Interested in "all types/styles/subjects which are suitable for a community arts center."
Exhibits: Work "must be approved by the exhibition committee." Examples of recent exhibitions: Susan Landgraf, "Remembering: Women and Their Relationships"; Jenni Lukac and Katharine Kreisher, "The Painted Photograph"; and "KAC Photography Annual." Presents 2-3/year. Shows last 3½ weeks. Sponsors openings; "We send out and print black & white announcement cards, provide a wine and cheese reception, and encourage an artist's talk by the artist." Photographer's presence at opening preferred.
Terms & Making Contact: KAC takes a 25% commission on any works sold in an exhibit. No size limits or restrictions on photography. Send material by mail for consideration. SASE. Reports in 1 month, "after review by exhibition committee."
Tips: "We pay a $150 Honorarium to each exhibiting artist." The opportunities for photographers in galleries are "less than with other media such as painting/sculpture." Sees trend toward "more experimental works—combining photography with other media." Interest of public in buying photography "seems to remain stable . . . not great and yet not indifferent."

ROBERT KLEIN GALLERY, 207 South St., Boston MA 02116. (617)482-8188. Contact: Robert Klein or Michael Freed. Interested in museum quality, fine 19th and 20th century art photos. Presents 8 shows/ year. Shows last 6 weeks. Sponsors openings; provides book signing, reception, radio, TV, newspaper coverage. Photographer's presence at opening preferred. Photographer's presence during show is

preferred. Photography sold in gallery. Recieves 50% commission. Buys photography outright. General price range: $300-15,000. Will review transparencies. Interested in matted or unmatted work. Arrange a personal interview to show portfolio, submit portfolio for review. SASE. Reports in 1 week.
Tips: Be aware of what is happening in world of revolutionary-trends — be flexible, able to accept criticism. Be organized, dependable.

*KOSLOW GALLERY, 2507 W. 7th St., Los Angeles CA 90057. (213)487-7610. Contact: Owner. Estab. 1987. Interested in portraits, nudes and narratives.
Exhibits: To exhibit in gallery, "must have prior exhibitions at major galleries or museums." Examples of recent exhibitions: solo exhibtions by Regina DeLuise, Jonathan Reff, Radeka and Steven Josefsberg. Presents 6/year. Shows last 1 month. Sponsors openings. Photographer's presence at opening required; presence during show preferred.
Terms & Making Contact: Charges 50% commission. Will review transparencies. Interested in framed or unframed work, mounted or unmounted work, and matted or unmatted work. Requires exclusive representation within metropolitan area. No size limites or restrictions on photography. Send material by mail for consideration. SASE. Reports in 1 week.
Tips: "Create interest with art critics by writing about your work." Sees trend toward "fewer exhibits of 'traditional' photography, and increased interest in non-silver processes."

KRESGE ART MUSEUM, Michigan State University, East Lansing MI 48824. (517)355-7631. Estab. 1959. Curator: Phyllis Floyd. Presents 2-3 photography shows/year. Exhibits last 5-6 weeks. "Museum membership group sponsors openings for shows usually Sundays 2-4." Photographer's presence at opening and during show is preferred. Photography sold in gallery; receives 20% commission. Buys photography outright. General price range: $200-600. Reviews transparencies. Interested in matted or unmatted work. Send material by mail for consideration. SASE. Reports in 1 month.
Tips: "If the quality of the work is high we are receptive to the work of newer, lesser known photographers." Sees trend toward wide range of works "from documentary to surrealist-type" images of work. "As an art museum, we are particularly interested in innovation, historic importance and significance, and the originality of concept or technique. This does not necessarily apply to all galleries or museums."

*LAGUNA BEACH GALLERY OF PHOTOGRAPHY, Suite 103, 303 Broadway, Laguna Beach CA 92651. (714)494-4470. Owner/Director: Betsy Smith. Estab. 1990. Interested in all types, including landscapes, nudes, abstracts, documentary, experimental, vintage and hand colored.
Exhibits: Requirements: Prints must be of the highest quality, museum-calibre and archival, but "we are open to viewing and promoting the works of newer photographers if they meet these standards." Examples of recent exhibitions: Joyce Tenneson, (nudes and still life); Cole Weston, (color landscapes); and Christopher Broughton, (b&w landscapes). Presents 9-12 shows/year. Shows last approx. 4-6 weeks but "we'll continue to sell prints after close of exhibit." Sponsors openings; provides invitations, publicity, catering, champagne, musicians and promotional pieces. Photographer's presence at opening preferred.
Terms & Making Contact: Photography sold in gallery. Charges 50% commission on works sold. Sometimes buys photography outright. General price range: $500-50,000. Will review transparencies. Interested in framed or unframed work, mounted, matted or unmatted work. Requires exclusive representation within Laguna Beach. Query with samples; send material by mail for consideration; submit portfolio for review with return postage. SASE. Reports in 3 weeks, "if not sooner."
Tips: "Presentation is very important. Have a cohesive body of work and at least 20 extraordinary prints. Trend is toward tremendous variety and photography as 'collectible art.' I would say the opportunity for exposure and volume sales through our gallery is excellent. We have an aggressive sales staff and sell thousands of prints to large corporations, law firms, and decorators. We print promotional mailers and catalogs of our photographer's works. In addition to the 20-40 prints shown during the exhibition, the photographer should be able to supply us with numerous prints as they are ordered. Ideally, we prefer to have one additional portfolio of the photographer's work to be available for corporate presentations year round."

*LEDEL GALLERY, 168 Mercer St., New York NY 06840. (212)966-7659. Director: Lee Male. Estab. 1981. "We have at least 2 group shows per year — 'Stairways and Empty Chairs'; and 'New York, New York.' "
Exhibits: Examples of recent exhibitions: Jill Enfield, (hand-colored prints); Tom Baril, (black & white); and Dan Powell, (C prints with drawn-in detail). Presents 6/year. Sponsors openings; wine reception. Photographer's presence at opening required; presence at show required "off and on."
Terms & Making Contact: Charges 50% commission. Occasionally buys photography. General price range: $400-2,000. Will review transparencies. Interested in framed or unframed work, mounted or unmounted work, and matted or unmatted work. Requires exclusive representation in metropolitan

Evoking a strong "sense of presence and references to art history," this image by photographer Carolyn Demeritt caught the eye of Ken Bloom, director of The Light Factory Photographic Arts Center, in Charlotte, North Carolina . Rather than exhibiting the photograph in its space, however, the gallery purchased the image for use as a cover in a Light Factory publication. Photographer DeMerritt says that having this piece published "helped generate more interest" in all of her work and brought her "more sales and exhibition offers." Since then, the photo has been published in Charlotte Magazine and exhibited widely.

area "for one year." Shows are limited to pieces at 30×40 inches. Send material by mail for consideration. SASE. Reporting time varies.

Tips: "We mail out packets to museums, etc. including bios, press prints, and press releases." Opportunities for photographers in galleries are "improving constantly." Sees trend among the buying public toward "historical/vintage works; also increased interest in contemporary work."

*LEEDY-VOULKOS GALLERY, 1919 Wyandotte, Kansas City MO 64108. (816)474-1919. Director: Sherry Leedy. Estab. 1985. Open to all styles and subject matter.

Exhibits: Photographer must have "an established exhibition record." Examples of recent exhibitions: "Constructed Images," Peter Feldstein (cibachrome); "Current Works," group exhibit (contemporary photography); and "Group Show," (b&w). Photography "usually included in group shows." Shows last 6 weeks. Sponsors openings. Photographer's presence at opening preferred.

Terms & Making Contact: Charges 50% commission. Does not buy photography outright. Price range: $200-600. Will review transparencies. Interested in framed or unframed work. Requires exclusive representation within metropolitan area. Send slides by mail for consideration. SASE. Reports in 1 month.

Tips: "Visit the gallery to get the general 'feel' of work exhibited."

LEWIS LEHR INC., Box 1008, Gracie Station, New York NY 10028. (212)288-6765. Director: Lewis Lehr. "Private dealer." Photography sold in gallery; receives 50% commission. Buys photography outright. General price range: $500 plus. Reviews transparencies. Interested in mounted or unmounted work. Requires exclusive representation in area. Query with resume of credits. SASE. Member AIPAD.

Tips: Somewhat receptive to exhibiting work of newer, lesser-known photographers. Sees trend toward "more color and larger" print sizes. To break in, "keep trying."

JANET LEHR PHOTOGRAPHS, INC., Box 617, New York NY 10028. (212)288-1802. Contact: Janet Lehr. We offer "fine photographs both 19th and 20th century. For the contemporary photographer needing public exhibition I offer minimal resources. Work is shown by appointment only." Presents 8 shows/year. Shows last 6 weeks. Receives 50% commission or buys outright. General price range: $350-15,000. Send a letter of introduction with resume; do not arrive without an appointment. Will review transparencies, but prints preferred. SASE. Reports in 2 weeks.

■THE LIGHT FACTORY PHOTOGRAPHIC ARTS CENTER, (formerly The Light Factory), P.O. Box 32815, Charlotte NC 28232. (704)333-9755. Contact: Gallery Manager. Nonprofit. Estab. 1978. Interested in contemporary and vintage art photography, documentary photography, any subject matter. Photographer must have a professional exhibition record for main gallery. Presents 6-7 shows per year. Shows last 1-2 months. Sponsors openings; reception (3 hours) with food and beverages, artist lecture following reception; accommodations provided by The Light Factory Photographic Arts Center. Photographer's presence at opening preferred. Photography sold in the shop. Receives 33% commission. Rarely buys photography outright. General price range: $100-3,000. Will review transparencies. Interested in unframed, mounted or unmounted, matted or unmatted work. Query with resume of credits and slides. SASE. Reports in 2 months.

Tips: Among various trends such as fine art prints and documentary work, "we are seeing more mixed media using photography, painting, sculpture and videos." Currently, documentary and landscape subjects are selling best through this gallery. "I feel an artist interested in showing work should have a strong purpose and statement about the work. The photographs should also be a cohesive body of work which reflect the artist intent and purpose."

LIGHT IMPRESSIONS SPECTRUM GALLERY, 439 Monroe Ave., Rochester NY 14607. Contact: Gallery Director. "Shows 20th century silver and non-silver photography by photographers of national reputation."

Exhibits: To be considered to show work in the Light Impressions Spectrum Gallery, an artist must have a national reputation. Presents 6 shows/year. Examples of recent exhibits: "Aaron Siskind: Photogravures & Platinum Prints," (large format gravures); "Duane Michals: The Nature of Desire," (silver photographic prints); "Italy by Armchair: Stereographs and Their Antecedents," (large format etchings, albumen prints, and stereographs, by multiple artists and photographers). Exhibits last 4-6 weeks. Sponsors openings; provides invitation, press releases as well as food and beverage for the opening. Photographer's presence at opening is preferred.

Terms & Making Contacts: Photography sold in gallery; receives 40% commission. General price range: $300-3,500. Query with resumé of credits. SASE. Reports as soon as possible.

Tips: Sees continued trend toward individual expressive directions, eclecticism and a rejection of some of the ideas of the Postmodern Aesthetic. Currently selling best are traditional high-focus landscapes as well as the untraditional and emerging technology based imagery. "Photographer's presentation must be clean, well prepared, and completely professional. This presentation is your one chance to make an impression."

*MARBLE HOUSE GALLERY, 44 Exchange Place, Salt Lake City UT 84111. (801)532-7338. Owner: Dolores Kohler. Estab. 1987. Photographers must produce about 20 or more outstanding photographs a year. Examples of recent exhibitions: John Stevens, abstract landscapes; Linda Barnes, situation art; and Richard Kohler, architectural images. Presents 1 exhibit/year. Show lasts one month. Sponsors openings; provides invitation, mailings, refreshments. Also handles all promotion with newspapers, TV and radio. Photographer's presence at openings preferred. Charges 50% commission. Reviews transparencies. Interested in framed or unframed, mounted, matted or unmatted work. Requires exclusive representation. No limits on size; quality is only possible restriction. Arrange a personal interview to show a portfolio; query with resume of credits; query with samples, send material by mail for consideration, submit portfolio for review. SASE. Reports in 3 weeks.

PETER MILLER GALLERY, 150 Merchandise Mart, Chicago IL 60654. (312)951-0252, (312)951-2628. Assistant Director: Natalie R. Domchenko. "We are interested in innovative, contemporary and original photography—no blue-chip repeats. Technical facility is very important, but must be used creatively and not be the sole end. These are both requirements and style." Variable number of shows/year. Sponsors openings. Gallery space open for 3 weeks, Friday evenings. Photography sold in gallery. Receives 50% commission. Price range varies. Will review transparencies. Send material by mail for consideration. "A sheet of slides of the work is the preferred review method." Reports in 1 month. Must include SASE for return of materials.

MONTEREY PENINSULA MUSEUM OF ART, 559 Pacific St., Monterey CA 93940. (408)372-5477. Director: Jo Farb Hernandez. Estab. 1959. Interested in all subjects. Presents 2-4 shows/year. Shows last 6-12 weeks. Sponsors openings. Buys photography outright. Will review transparencies. Work must be framed to be displayed; review can be by slides, transparencies, unframed or unmatted. Send material by mail for consideration. SASE. Reports in 1 month.
Tips: "Very receptive" to working with newer, lesser-known photographers. Send 20 slides and resume at any time, attention museum director.

MUSEUM OF CONTEMPORARY PHOTOGRAPHY OF COLUMBIA COLLEGE, 600 South Michigan Ave., Chicago IL 60605-1996. (312)663-5554. FAX: (312)663-1707. Director: Denise Miller-Clark. Assistant Director: Ellen Ushioka. Estab. 1984. Interested in fine art, documentary, photojournalism, commercial, technical/scientific. "All high quality work considered." Presents 5 main exhibitions and 8-10 smaller exhibitions/year. Exhibits last 8 weeks. Sponsors openings, announcements. Photography sold in gallery. Receives 30% commission. Buys photos outright. General price range: $300-2,000. Will review transparencies. Interested in reviewing unframed work only, matted or unmatted. Submit portfolio for review. SASE. Reports in 2 weeks. No critical review offered.
Tips: "Professional standards apply; only very high quality work considered."

NEIKRUG PHOTOGRAPHICA LTD., 224 E. 68th St., New York NY 10021. (212)288-7741. Owner/Director: Marjorie Neikrug. Estab. 1970. Interested in "photography which has a unique way of showing the contemporary world. Special needs include photographic art for our annual Rated X exhibit." Sponsors openings "in cooperation with the photographer." Retrospective b&w photographs, by Paul Caponigro; Retrospective b&w, by Charles Gatewood; and Rated X group exhibit, all forms of photography, color or b&w by Louis Stettner and Eric Krull. Photographer's presence preferred. Receives 50% sales commission. Price range: $100-5,000. Call to arrange an appointment or submit portfolio in person. "We view portfolio twice a month. They should be left on Friday between 1-5 pm and picked up Saturday between 1-5 pm." SASE. Size: 11×14, 16×20 or 20×30. Requires exclusive representation in area.
Tips: "We are looking for meaningful and beautiful images—images with substance and feeling! Edit work carefully and make it easy for the viewer. Have neat presentation." Receptive to lesser-known photographers who have excellent work. Nudes and vintage currently sell best at this gallery.

NEW ENGLAND PHOTOGRAPHIC WORKSHOP PHOTO GALLERY, 30 Bridge St., New Milford CT 06776. (203)355-8578. Curator: Jo Brenzo. Interested in general fine art photography, with emphasis on contemporary fine art photography. Does not accept commercial or editorial photography. "We are interested in work by professionals or semi-professionals who have a good understanding of the photographic craft and expression. There are no size requirements, however all prints should be mounted on white rag board." Presents 8-10 shows/year. Shows last 4-6 weeks. Sponsors openings; provides a three hour wine and cheese opening, and invitation to our mail list. Photographer's presence at opening preferred. Photography sold in gallery. Receives 35% commission. Sometimes buys photos outright: it depends on the work. Will review transparencies; preferred. Interested in mounted or unmounted, matted or unmatted work. "All work must be mounted and matted on gallery white rag board. Artist is responsible for framing prints." Arrange a personal interview to show portfolio, query with resume of credits, or submit portfolio for review. SASE. Reports in 2 weeks.

Tips: "We are looking for good quality photographic images that represent craftmanship and personal expression. Arrange for personal interview or sent transparencies by mail. Include as much biographical information as possible. More than 300 visitors visit the gallery each month. "The visitors include students, art directors, educators and top professional photographers." Gallery offers unlimited exposure. We are seeing a trend back to good clean imagery, away from the gimmickry and contrived images of the last few years.

NEW ORLEANS MUSEUM OF ART, Box 19123, City Park, New Orleans LA 70179. (504)488-2631. Curator of Photography: Nancy Barrett. Interested in all types of photography. Presents shows continuously. Shows last 1-3 months. Buys photography outright. Present budget for purchasing contemporary photography is very small. Query with resume of credits only. SASE. Reports in 1-3 months.

NORTHERN ILLINOIS UNIVERSITY ART MUSEUM, (formerly Illinois University School of Art Gallery) Altgeld Hall, De Kalb IL 60115. (815)753-1936. Director: Lynda K. Martin. Accepts all types, styles and subject matter but especially fine art photographs.

Exhibits: Examples of recent exhibitions: "Color Photos of Las Vegas," by Jay Wolke; "Group Show of NE Atlantic Fishermen," Men's Lives; "Corporeal Arenas," by Lucinda Devlin. Presents 6 shows/year. Shows last 6-7 weeks. Sponsors openings; indludes invitations, food and drink. Photographer's presence at opening preferred.

Terms & Making Contact: Refers sales inquiries to artist. Buys photography outright. Will review transparencies. Interested in framed or unframed work, mounted or unmounted work and matted or unmatted work. Send material by mail for consideration. SASE. Reports in 1 month.

OPEN SPACE ARTS SOCIETY, (formerly Open Space Gallery), 510 Fort St., Victoria BC V8W 1E6 Canada. (604)383-8833. Director: Sue Donaldson. Interested in photographs as fine art in an experimental context, as well as interdisciplinary works involving the photograph. Especially open to newer, lesser-known photographers. No traditional documentary, scenics, sunsets or the like.

Exhibits: Sponsors openings. Presents 5 shows/year. Shows last 3-4 weeks. Pays the C.A.R.F.A.C. fees no commission. Price range: $100-830. Query with transparencies of work. SAE, IRCs. Reports 2 times a year.

Tips: Sees trend toward more installations, larage format and hand tinting. To be considered for the next year's schedule, send 10-12 slides and "a one-page exhibition proposal outline explaining why work would suit this 1500 sq. ft. venue (by Feb. 28 or Sept. 30). Artists in this artist-run center receive exhibition fees. It is their decision if they wish to sell work of the exhibition."

ORLANDO GALLERY, 14553 Ventura Blvd., Sherman Oaks CA 91403. (818)789-6012. Director: Philip Orlando. Interested in photography demonstrating "inventiveness" on any subject. Examples of recent exhibitions: mixed media photos by Joan Weber; Cibacrome prints by Jerry McGrath and Roger Camp. Sponsors openings. Open to work of newer photographers. Shows last 4 weeks. Receives 50% sales commission. Price range: $550-10,000. Submit portfolio. SASE. Framed work only. Requires exclusive representation in area.

THE PHOTO GALLERY AT PORTLAND SCHOOL OF ART, 619 Congress St., Portland ME 04101. (207)775-3052. Head, Photo Department: John Eide. Estab. 1972. Requires work that has been matted and ready to hang. Very receptive to newer, lesser-known photographers. Recent photography exhibits include: Boxers & Brokens, b&w photos of Boxers, stock brokers, Larry Fink; Recent Photographs, color images of street gangs, Paul D'Amato; New Landscapes, b/w large format images of western landscape, Mark Klett; Zetting, group show of young European photographers. Presents 6 shows/year. Shows last 5 weeks. Photography could be sold in gallery. General price range: $100-500. Will review transparencies. Interested in unmounted work only. Submit portfolio for review. SASE. Reporting time varies.

THE PHOTOGRAPHIC CENTER OF MONTEREY PENINSULA, Box 1100, San Carlos at 9th Ave., Carmel CA 93921. (408)625-5181. Gallery Director: Gail Pierce. Exhibition gallery interested in all types of photography. Open to "work of newer, lesser-known photographers as long as they are professional in their presentation and have something unique/exciting to show. Look at portfolios on Fridays by appointment only.

Exhibits: Examples of recent exhibitions: Polish Photographers - 10 photographers who live and work in Poland; Three Color Views - Therese Kopin, Jerri Nemiro and Dar Spain; and Abstraction Photographs, group invitational. Reviews transparencies of those photographers living outside of the area, but prefers a personal interview to show portfolios. Exhibition includes: traveling national exhibits, exhibits organized internationally, regional group (2-4) exhibits, exhibits with a theme, (abstraction) and an annual membership exhibit.

Tips: Photographers should recognize that only a few exhibitions each year are selected from unsolicited portfolios. "Photography can not be sold in the gallery, but we will give out the photographer's phone number and/or address. If any sales should occur, 25% donation is appreciated. Be professional in your presentation. Come to appointment prepared with a cohesive body of work that is finished in every detail. So often we see prints that are spotted, and not matted or printed properly. We can't guess what the finished print will look like. Bring a resume and a drop-off flyer or prints for our files. We look at a large volume of work and it is difficult to remember every photographer's prints."

■**PHOTOGRAPHIC RESOURCE CENTER,** 602 Commonwealth Ave., Boston MA 02215. (617)353-0700. Curator: Anita Douthat. Interested in contemporary and historical photography and mixed-media work incorporating photography. "The photographer must meet our high quality requirements."

Exhibits: Examples of recent exhibitions: "Marc Riboud: Lasting Moments," ICP retrospective, photojournalism, Marc Riboud; "Heaven Home & Weightless," holography installation, Doris Vila; "The Show Isn't Over," photographic installation, Louise Lawler; "Locomotion," photography, video, precinematic & cinematic devices and flipbooks, study of movement, Muybridge, Edgertoon, Morgan, Abbott, Blume, Frampton/Faller, Greenfield, Mandel and Michals. Presents 5-6 group thematic exhibitions in the David and Sandra Bakalar Gallery and 8-10 one- and two-person shows in the Natalie G. Klebenov Gallery/year. Shows last 6-8 weeks. Sponsors openings; receptions with refreshments for the Bakalar Gallery shows. Will review transparencies. Interested in matted or unmatted work. Query with samples or send material by mail for consideration. SASE. Reports in 2-3 months "depending upon frequency of programming committee meetings."

*****PHOTOGRAPHY AT OREGON GALLERY,** University of Oregon Museum of Art, Eugene OR 97403. (503)343-4415. Contact: Susie Morrill, Chairperson. "We are interested in all approaches to the photographic medium in which both technical virtuosity and serious intent on the part of the artist are displayed." Presents 5-7 shows/year. Shows last 6 weeks. "Review to be held in May for individual shows in the following year." Receives 30% sales commission. Submit portfolio for review in early May. Will review transparencies or copy slides with 1 print example. Send resume and letter of interest. No portfolios returned without prepaid postage.

Tips: "There seems to be a stylistic return to straight imagery. Our clients are interested in seeing first-rate photography of all types/styles. They rarely buy, except at our annual auction of donated photographs."

PRAKAPAS GALLERY, 19 E. 71st St., New York NY 10021. (212)737-6066. Director: Eugene J. Prakapas. "Primary interest is Modernism of the 20s and 30s. But, we are interested in any work that is not just good or accomplished but remarkable—genuinely outstanding." Examples of exhibitors: Ralph Steiner, Lazlo Moholy-Nagy and Man Ray. Presents up to 8 exhibits/year. Shows last 6 weeks. Photography sold in gallery; commission received "depends entirely upon the situation." Buys photography outright. General price range: $500-100,000. Will review transparencies, "but only if we request them — i.e., if prior arrangements are made." Requires exclusive representation in area. Query with resume of credits. "We are not interested in seeing unsolicited material."

Tips: Opportunities offered photographers by galleries in general are "excellent, better than ever before. But in exhibiting a photographer's work, a gallery makes a substantial commitment in terms of reputation and money. If a photographer hopes for/expects such commitment, he should ensure that his submission reflects at least equal commitment on his part. All too often, submissions are sloppy, haphazard, unprofessional—an immediate turnoff."

THE PRINT CLUB, 1614 Latimer St., Philadelphia PA 19103. (215)735-6090. Administrator: Richard Frey. Interested in the work of student nonprofessionals, professionals, all persons. Does some photography shows. Receives 40% sales commission. General price range: $100-1,000. Prefers unframed work. The Print Club reserves the right to photograph and reproduce any work accepted in the exhibition, in catalogues, publications and other publicity materials, as well as distribute slide sets of the show for educational purposes. Proper credit will be given. Sponsors annual competition each fall. The range of the audience of The Print Club Annual International Competition of Prints and Photographs is quite diverse: students, members, collectors, dealers, curators. Estimated number of viewers: 1,000-1,500. Send SASE for prospectus. Over $8,000 in prizes, including possible museum purchase.

Tips: "We prefer high quality experimental work. The Print Club takes advantage of the arrival of recent works from artist members to select works for other exhibitions and for consignment and travel, in addition to inviting other dealers, curators to view new work."

RANDOLPH STREET GALLERY, 756 N. Milwaukee Ave., Chicago IL 60622. (312)666-7737. Exhibition Coordinator: Mitchell Kane. "RSG's commitment is to new and innovative art regardless of medium. We would NOT exhibit *traditional* photography; any and all non-traditional forms welcomed."
Exhibits: Examples of recent exhibitions: "Out of Eastern Europe: Private Photography," group exhibit featuring 20 photographers from Eastern Europe; "In Evidence," large Cibachromes by Andres Serrano; "Metropolitan Tits," series by Diane Neumaier, as part of "Representation/Re-presentation. Exhibitions are usually mixed media, often with photographs included." Sponsors openings. Lists opening in calendar of events to 2,800 name mailing list and sends press releases to local and national press. Holds reception for artists. Also pays honoraria. Photographer's presence at opening/during show preferred.
Terms & Making Contact: Photography sold in gallery. Commission received on works sold varies with artist; average is 20%. General price range is $300-3,000. Will review transparencies. Interested in framed or unframed work, and matted or unmatted work. Write or call for prospectus. SASE. Materials reviewed quarterly. Reports in 3 months.
Tips: "We have shown an increasing amount of photography over the last two years. Unfortunately, photography doesn't seem to be as collectible as well as painting."

REAL ART WAYS, 56 Arbor St., Hartford CT 06106. (203)232-1006. Curator: Leslie Tonkonow. Interested in avant-garde/experimental, styles. Examples of recent exhibitors: Nan Goldin, Anne Turyn, Tira Burney, Joan Fitzsimmons and Mary Frey. Presents 6 shows/year. Shows last 4 weeks. Sponsors openings; provides refreshments from 6 pm to 8 pm. Will review slides. Interested in framed or unframed work, matted or unmatted work. Send material by mail for consideration, slides/resume/clippings. SASE. Reports in 2 months.
Tips: "Looks for work that is on the cutting edge of artistic experimentation. As a nonprofit arts organization we seek only to present the best work around, not what will 'sell.' For proposals send about 25 of your best slides, along with resume, and any reviews or articles which you feel represent your work."

REFLECTIONS, 199 River St., Leland MI 49654. (616)256-7120. Contact: Richard Braund. Interested in all types and subjects from nature to nude. Presents 3 shows/year. Shows last 2 months. Receives 45% sponsor commission. General price range: $5-100. Will review transparencies. Interested in framed or unframed; mounted or unmounted; matted or unmatted work. Requires exclusive area representation. No works larger than 20 × 30. Query with samples; send material by mail for consideration or submit portfolio for review. SASE. Reports in 3-4 weeks.

HOLLY ROSS ASSOC., 516 "C" St. NE, Washington DC 20002. (202)544-0400. Art Consultant: Melanie Blesse. Seeking contemporary color photos of all types. Subjects include landscape, architectural, whimsical, abstract and Deco-50s. Photographers must pass a quality review by the gallery. Sponsors openings; provides 50/50 split on invitations, advertising and refreshments. Photographer's presence at opening preferred. Photography sold in gallery. Receives 50% commission. Does not buy photography outright. General price range: $500 and up. Will review transparencies. Does not require exclusive representation. Send slides by mail for consideration. SASE. Reports in 1 month or as soon as possible.
Tips: "We are constantly reviewing new artists and would be happy to see new work. Opportunities offered by galleries are "getting much better." Trend is toward showing more moderately priced photos regularly."

SANDFORD GALLERY, Clarion University, Clarion PA 16214. (814)226-2412 or 226-2282. Director: Dr. Charles Marlin. Interested in contemporary straight and mixed media. Examples of recent exhibitors: Larry Smith, Keith A. Smith and Michael Northrup. "We require a contract covering delivery dates and documentation." Presents 2 shows/year. Shows last 4 weeks. Sponsors openings; "we print and mail the announcements and provide refreshments and hospitality." Photography sold in gallery. Buys photography outright. General price range: $200-1,500. Will review transparencies. Interested in framed or unframed work, mounted or unmounted work, matted work only. Query with resume of credits. SASE. Reports in 3 weeks.

SCHOMBURG CENTER FOR RESEARCH IN BLACK CULTURE, 515 Lenox Ave., New York NY 10037. (212)491-2247. Estab. 1978. Head of Prints and Photography: Deborah Willis. Interested in historical, documentary, contemporary, pertaining to African-American history. Every photographer's work goes before the exhibitions committee. Sponsors opening. Photographer's presence at opening preferred. Photography sometimes sold in gallery. Sometimes buys photography outright. General price range: ranges from $30/print. Reviews transparencies. Interested in seeing mounted and unmounted work. Arrange personal interview to show portfolio; or send material by mail for consideration. SASE. Reports in 1 month.

Tips: Very receptive to exhibiting work of newer, lesser-known photographers. "We are interested in contemporary African-American life in general in the U.S."

SCOTTSDALE CENTER FOR THE ARTS, 7383 Scottsdale Mall, Scottsdale AZ 85251. (602)994-2315. Assistant Director: Debra Hopkins. Interested in all fine art styles. Present 3-4 shows/year. Shows last 3-6 weeks. Sponsors openings; refreshments, no-host bar, sometimes music. If interested in exhibition send 20 non-returnable slides, résumé and proposal. Will review transparencies. Interested in framed or unframed work, mounted or unmounted work, matted or unmatted work. SASE. Reports in 1 month or depends upon review panel deadline.
Tips: Exhibits traditional artwork in all media.

SEA CLIFF PHOTOGRAPH CO., 310 Sea Cliff Ave., Sea Cliff NY 11579. (516)671-6070. Coordinators: Don Mistretta, Diann Mistretta. Estab. 1978. Interested in serious vintage and contemporary works. Quite receptive to lesser-known photographers. Are expanding to include other media. "The images must stand on their own either separately or in a cohesive grouping." Presents 10-15 show/year. Shows last 4-8 weeks. Provides press coverage; artist provides reception invitations. Photographer's presence at opening preferred. Receives 40% sales commission on photographs, 30% on other media. Occasionally buys photography outright. General price range: $100-500. Will review transparencies. Arrange a personal interview to show portfolio or query with resume of credits. Does not return unsolicited material. Reports in 2 weeks.
Tips: "Come to us with specific ideas and be willing to explore alternative avenues of thought. All forms of photographic imagery are acceptable. The buying public is looking for good contemporary and fine, vintage photography."

THE SILVER IMAGE GALLERY, 318 Occidental Ave. S., Seattle WA 98104. (206)623-8116. Director: Dan Fear. The gallery opened in 1973, primary interests include: masters, traditional landscapes, nudes and contemporary photography. General price range: $250 and up.
Tips: "The Silver Image Gallery is interested in working with photographers who are committed and have been working seriously in fine art photography for at least five years."

SIOUX CITY ART CENTER, 513 Nebraska St., Sioux City IA 51101. (712)279-6272. Contemporary expressive photography (color/b&w); altered/alternative; conceptual; generative. No student work (except advance graduate). Send slides, resume first. SASE.
Tips: "The graphics gallery contains 107 running feet of display space. Send 25-40 *good quality* slides, resume, SASE for return of materials, and letter of introduction."

SOMERSTOWN GALLERY, Box 379, Somers NY 10589. (914)277-3461. Photography Curator: Leandra Pope. Interested in straight, unmanipulated and antique processes. The photographer must be "committed to creativity." Present 8 shows/year. Shows last 4 weeks. Photographer's presence at opening preferred. Separate space in gallery for photography at all times. Buys photography outright. General price range: $75-1,000. Will review transparencies. Interested in framed or unframed work, mounted or unmounted work, matted or unmatted work. All work must be archivally processed and presented. Submit portfolio for review. SASE. Reports in 3 weeks.
Tips: "Edit. Edit. Edit. Bring works which you feel very good about."

SOUTH SHORE ART CENTER, INC., 119 Ripley Rd., Cohasset MA 02025. (617)383-9548. Executive Director: Lanci Valentine. Interested in "all types of fine arts photography." A small entry fee (usually $8) to subsidize costs of hanging and operating gallery. Presents at least 2 shows/year—all New England (juried) and at least 1 invitational. Shows last 4 weeks. Sponsors openings; cost of announcements with photo (usually 5×7) b&w. All opening costs of juried shows—artists pay part of costs of an invitational show (gallery rental). Photographer's presence at opening is preferred. Photography sold in gallery. Receives 40% commission. General price range: $100-500. Reviews transparencies. Interested in seeing framed work only. Limitations: work "must be framed in wood or metal—no bare glass edges. Send resumé and slide sheet."

SOUTHERN LIGHT, Box 447, Amarillo TX 79178. (806)371-5000. Director: Robert Hirsch. Sponsored by Amarillo College. "Very open to work of newer photographers. We don't believe that the only good artist is a dead artist." Presents 12 shows/year. Shows last 4 weeks. Receives 10% sales commission. General price range: $100 and up. Include resume, statement and postage in all cases. For still works, will review transparencies. Prefers to see portfolio of 20-40 pieces. Wants to see unmounted work for preview; matted work for shows.
Tips: "We are open to anything since we don't rely on sales to stay open. We want show work that is on the cutting edge. People photographs currently sell best at our gallery. We are presently interested in any type of computer or video generated images, nonsilver processes and time sequence work."

SUSAN SPIRITUS GALLERY, #330, 3333 Bear St., Costa Mesa CA 92626. (714)549-7550. Owner: Susan Spiritus.
Exhibits: Requirements: "All photos must be archivally printed, mounted and overmatted acid-free." Examples of recent exhibitors: George Tice, Denny Moers and Yousuf Karsh. Presents 10 shows/year. Shows last 4-6 weeks. Sponsors openings. Photographer's presence at opening preferred.
Terms & Making Contact: Photography sold in gallery. Receives 50% commission on works sold. Sometimes buys photography outright. General price range $250-10,000. Prefers not to review transparencies. Interested in unframed, mounted, or matted work only. Requires exclusive representation within metropolitan area. Photos "must be overmatted to standard frame sizes—not to exceed 40 × 50. Arrange a personal interview to show portfolio or send material by mail for consideration. SASE. Reports in 2 weeks.
Tips: Likes to see hand-colored prints and platinum/palladium photos. "We show one exhibit of hand-colored photos per year. Be unique. Buyers buy what _they_ like."

SUNPRINT CAFE & GALLERY, 638 State St., Madison WI 53703. Also at 2701 University Ave. Madison WI 53703. (608)231-1111. Directors: Rena Gelman, Linda Derrickson. Interested in all types of photography; very receptive to exhibiting the works of newer, lesser-known photographers. Examples of recent exhibitions: Photos of Bolivia by Zane Williams; Cibachrome portraits by Mary North Allen; Cibachrome scapes by Bruce Fritz. Sponsors openings. General price range: $50-400. Call for more information. Framed work only. "We need 1 month to view each portfolio and expect a follow-up phone call from us."
Tips: "On State Street we have a cafe inside the gallery which allows people to sit and view the work in a relaxed atmosphere. The University Ave. location is a full-scale restaurant. Work exhibited on all walls. Floor to ceiling windows for good light. We have 2 showrooms for the exhibits which hang approximately 6 weeks."

SUNY PLATTSBURGH ART MUSEUM, (formerly Plattsburgh State Art Galleries) SUNY College at Plattsburgh, Plattsburgh NY 12901. (518)564-2813 or 564-2178. Director: Edward Brohel. Assistant Director: Phyllis Freedman. "Professional work only." Presents "about 2 shows per year." Shows last 7 weeks. Sponsors openings. "Generally 4 gallery spaces have openings on the same day. One general reception, or tea, is held, it varies as to which gallery hosts." Photographer's presence at opening preferred. General price range: $25-200. Will review transparencies. Interested in framed work only. Requires exclusive representation to a degree within metropolitan area. Send material by mail for consideration or submit portfolio for review. Returns material "if requested—some are kept on file." Reporting time "varies with gallery pressures."

TIDEPOOL GALLERY, 22672 Pacific Coast Hwy., Malibu CA 90265. (213)456-2551. Partner: Jan Greenberg. Estab. 1969. Interested in "any photography related to the ocean—sea life, shore birds, etc." Sponsors openings; "we have 2 shows every year, with a reception for the artists. The shows last 4-6 weeks." Photographer must be present for opening. Artist receives 60% sales commission. General price range: $25-1,500. Call to arrange an appointment or submit material by mail for consideration. SASE. Dry mounted work only. "The work must be able to be hung, and protected by being framed or in acetate sleeves." Size: "nothing smaller than 1′ square or larger than 3′ long or wide." Requires exclusive representation in area "for a certain period of time when we are sponsoring the show."
Tips: "Keep the price as low as possible."

TOUCHSTONE GALLERY, 2130 P St. NW, Washington DC 20037. (202)223-6683. Director: Luba Dreyer. Interested in fine arts photography. Photographer "must be juried in and pay the membership fee. We are an artists' cooperative." Presents one feature show per Washington area artist; plus group shows each year for all member artists. Shows last 3 weeks. Photographer's presence at opening preferred. Receives 35% sponsor commission. General price range: $90-500. Submit portfolio consisting of current work plus transparencies for review at time of jurying, once a month must be picked up next day. Reports "one day after jurying."
Tips: Sees trend toward "large scale, personalized imagery." Color photos currently sell best.

UNIVERSITY OF ARIZONA, Union Gallery, Hall of Fame Gallery, Rotunda Gallery, S.U.P.O. Box 10,000, Tucson AZ 85720. (602)621-3546. Arts Coordinator: Karin Ericson. Interested in historical, traditional, contemporary and experimental. "Jury selection committee meets once a year in the spring." Presents 8-12 photography shows/year. Exhibits last 3-4 weeks. Photographer's presence at opening preferred and optional at receptions. Charges 25% commission based on exhibition price. Buys photography outright. Purchases are optional and "only if we sponsor a competition." General price range: $40-500. Reviews slides only. Prefers framed work. Unframed work is hung with glass and brackets—our stock sizes: 8 × 10, 16 × 20, 20 × 24. Send material by mail for consideration. SASE. We review once a year, send for guidelines and deadline.

Exhibits: Examples of recent exhibitions: "Beach Photographs," color photos parodies nation's idea of sun and fun by Joe Labate; "Reflections," photomontage by Carol Martin Davis; "The Group of Photographic Intentions," one photographer of group exhibit by newly assembled nonprofit group by Camille Bonzani.

Tips: "Galleries offer an opportunity for the photographers to be seen by the public. As part of the exposure that we offer, we seek and often receive press coverage. Portraits, landscapes and experimental with collage have all sold. Yet our main emphasis is not to gain a stronghold in the marketplace, we wish to give exposure to quality work. We are very receptive to newer, lesser known artists. Complete a series of 20 quality prints, have them duplicated in slides and submit to the arts coordinator for review. Formal scheduling is performed in the spring of every year." Sees trend toward "more experimentation with the technical aspects of the photographic process and more personal interest in the printed image."

UPHAM GALLERY, 348 Corey Ave., St.Petersburg Beach FL 33706. (813)360-5432. Director: Carol Ann Upham. Interested in b&w, Cibachrome, C prints and sepia prints. All subjects, "but no nudes or pornography." Receptive to newer phtographers.

Exhibits: Requirements: "Write first and we will send our policy which is self-explanatory as to our requirements. Recent exhibitions: Invitational in celebration of 150th Anniversary of Photography, featuring 60 photographers in *all* processes, 120 images. Presents 6 shows/year. "With each exhibit we also have multi-media." Shows last 6 weeks. Sponsors openings. Printing and mailing of invitation (includes gallery's and exhibitor's mailing lists), advertising and reception for opening. Photographer's presence at opening preferred. Must be working professionals doing exceptional work.

Terms & Making Contact: Receives 40% commission on works sold. General price range: $35-2,000. Will review transparencies. Interested in framed or unframed work and mounted or unmounted work. No restriction on size. Query with resume of credits. SASE. Reports in 3 weeks.

Tips: "We look for a professional resume and professionally priced works, plus the ability to be flexible in working with the Gallery Director." Presently the gallery is generating a great deal of interest. The trend is toward larger images, more experimental and Cibachromes. Beach images for tourists (hand-colored b&w) currently sells best. "Be professional. Learn how to market your art, make a good presentation, and a professional portfolio."

USL UNION ART GALLEY, Box 42611, Lafeyette LA 70504. (318)231-6939. Assistant Director, Union: Michael Flaherty. Interested in b&w and color experimental, contemporary, narrative, figurative, landscape, architectural, etc. "All works prepared to install must supply labels. Must pay all freight insurance while in transit and while installed. All submittals and requests subject to evaluation by above person. All press and advertising by the artist." Presents 1 photo show/year. Exhibits last 4-6 weeks. Sponsors opening; limited catering through contracted caterer on campus. Photographer's presence at opening is preferred. Receives 25% commission. General price range: $50-175. Reviews transparencies. Interested in framed or unframed, mounted, matted or unmatted work. 150 running linear feet of wall space, 10' ceiling, track lights. Send material by mail for consideration. SASE. Reports in 3 weeks.

Tips: "There is always a differentiation in quality aesthetic work and highly commercial 'sellable' works. The Union Gallery places higher emphasis on exhibiting than sales."

*VIRIDIAN GALLERY, 52 West 57 St., New York NY 10019. (212)245-2882. Director: Paul Cohen. Estab. 1968. Interested in eclectic. Is receptive to exhibiting work newer, photographers "if members are cooperative."

Exhibits: Requirements: Member of Cooperative Gallery. Examples of recent exhibitions: "Curtain Time & Coast to Coast," abstract & figurative images, by Robert Smith; "Re-Visioned," Computer-enhanced works, ink jet & monitor-shot work, by Glenn Rothman; "Ties that Bind, " exploration of self and mores in sequenced sets, predominantly b&w, by Yoland Skeete. Presents 3/year. Shows last 3 weeks. Photographer's presence at opening preferred.

Terms & Making Contact: Charges 20% commission. Will review transparencies only if submitted as membership application. Interested in framed or unframed work, mounted work, and matted or unmatted work. Request membership application details. SASE. Reports in 2 weeks.

Tips: "Highest degree of professionalism is expected at all times." Opportunities for photographers in galleries are "improving." Sees trend toward "a broad range of styles" being shown in galleries. "Cibachromes seem a 'given.' There are fewer hand-painted and altered types of work. More abstracts." The buying public seems open to this, too. The less 'complicated' and explicit pieces sell best. Presentation is vital! Initially, at least, offer less 'explicit' work. Be persistent!!"

This brooding shot of the Everglades, captured by Ft. Myers photographer Clyde Butcher, is an example of the kind of work the St. Petersburg-based Upham Gallery likes to spotlight. Butcher says he has exhibited numerous works through the gallery since it opened five years ago. "The gallery gives me lots of exposure," he says, explaining that he sells limited editions of his prints for about $350 while the gallery takes a 40% commission. He also notes that because of the interest he has generated in his Florida landscapes he has now published them in a book with the Everglades shot for cover art.

VISION GALLERY INC., 1155 Mission St., San Francisco CA 94103. (415)621-2107. FAS: (415)621-5074. President: Joseph G. Folberg. Interested in contemporary and vintage 19th century. Estab. 1980.
Exhibits: Presents 8 shows/year. Shows last 6 weeks. Sponsors openings. Photographer's presence at opening is preferred. Receives 50% sales commission. Buys photography outright. General price range: $200-15,000. Interested in mounted work only. Does not return unsolicited material. Arrange a personal interview to show portfolio. Reports immediately.
Tips: "Landscapes, stills and nudes sell best."

■**VISUAL STUDIES WORKSHOP GALLERY**, 31 Prince St., Rochester NY 14607. (716)442-8676. Exhibitions Coordinator: James B. Wyman. Interested in contemporary mid-career and emerging artists working in photography, video, and artists' books; new approaches to the interpretation of historical photographs.
Exhibits: No requirements except high quality. Presents 15-20 shows/year. Shows last 4-8 weeks. Sponsors openings; provides lectures, refreshments. Photographer's presence at opening preferred.
Terms & Making Contacts: Receives 40% commission. Rarely buys photography outright. General price range: $150-800. Prefers to review transparencies. Send material by mail for consideration. SASE. Submissions are reviewed twice yearly—spring and fall. "We prefer slides which we can keep and refer to as needed."
Tips: "It is important that the photographer be familiar with the overall programs of the Visual Studies Workshop. We respond to what imagemakers are producing. We represent mostly younger, emerging photographers whose work we see as being significant in our time. Therefore, I feel that most of our clients buy the work they do because they are responding to the qualities of the image itself."

*A. MONTGOMERY WARD GALLERY, 750 S. Halsted, Chicago IL 60607. (312)413-5070. Assistant Program Director: Teresa Gimpel. Estab. 1960. Interested in contemporary, political/documentary, historical, color, black & white, collaboration, photoworks and collage.
Exhibits: Examples of recent exhibitions: "The Many Faces of Hull-House," by Wallace Kirkland (silver prints from glass plate and nitrite negs); also documentary work c. 1925-35; "Work," by Michael Ensdorf (photo murals and computer generated photo images); and Sherry Antonini (large abstract b&w photos). Presents varying number of exhibits/year. Shows last 4 weeks. Sponsors openings with reception for 60, light snacks, etc. Photographer's presence at opening and during show preferred.
Terms & Making Contact: "We are a nonprofit gallery but, we will sell work and publish a price list." Charges 20% commission. Prefers to review transparencies. "Call or write and request proposal form." SASE. "Work is selected by a student committee which meets once a month during the school year. Work must meet University guidelines."
Tips: "Submit high-quality slides with a complete artist's statement or statement of intent." Sees trend toward "more murals, photoworks, appropriation of images from media, photo history, etc. We feel our gallery offers opportunities to photographers who have limited exhibition records and smaller bodies of work. Commercial galleries in this area may not be willing to offer a show to less experienced artists."

THE WITKIN GALLERY, INC., 415 W. Broadway, New York NY 10012. (212)925-5510. Director: Evelyne Z. Daitz. Interested in photography on any subject. Examples of recent exhibits: Evelyn Hofer (b&w and dye-transfer photographs); Jerry N. Uelsmann and George A. Tice."We will also be showing some work in the other media: drawing, litho, painting — while still specializing in photography." Will not accept unsolicited portfolios. Query first with resume of credits. "Portfolios are viewed only after written application *and* recommendation from a gallery, museum, or other photographer known to us." Photography sold in gallery. Receives 50% commission. Buys photography outright. Price range: $10-14,000.

WOODSTOCK GALLERY OF ART, Gallery Place, Rt. 4 East, Woodstock VT 05091. (802)457-1900. Gallery Owner: Charles Fenton. Estab. 1972. Represents professional artists of Vermont and New England. Interested in experimental and new forms. "Very receptive" to exhibiting the work of newer, lesser-known photographers. Submit portfolio and resume for consideration. All work should be archivally mounted and matted, preferably framed. Presents 2 photography-only exhibits/year. Shows last 1 month. Sponsors openings; shares expenses. Photographer's presence at opening is preferred. Charges 40% commission. Occasionally buys outright. General price range: $300-2,500. Generally requires exclusive representation in area. Unless labeled and priced accordingly, color photographs should be Cibachrome or Dye Transfer prints. Arrange a personal interview to show portfolio, query with samples, send material by mail for consideration or submit portfolio for review. Slides reviewed 4 times/year.
Tips: Sees trend toward painting with light. "Best sellers are innovative works with strong use of imagery and technique. Non-traditional work is coming on fast." Photographs carried and displayed in gallery at all times.

WORCESTER CENTER FOR CRAFTS, 25 Sagamore Rd., Worcester MA 01605. (508)753-8183. Media Communications: Ann Rogol. All types, styles and subject matter considered. Photographer must submit resume, and portfolio of work upon request.
Exhibits: The exhibitions vary in media — 6 in the Center Gallery and 6 in the Atrium Gallery. Shows last 6 weeks. Sponsors openings. Provides printed announcement for the exhibition, opening reception, and extensive news releases. Photographer's presence at opening and during show preferred.
Terms & Making Contact: Photography sold in gallery. Charges 30% commission. General price range: $60-12,000. Will review transparencies. Interested in framed or mounted work only. Main gallery size is approximately 40 × 40. Arrange a personal interview to show portfolio; query with resume of credits; send material by mail for consideration. Submit portfolio after submitting resume (upon request). Does not return unsolicited material. Reports in 1 month.
Tips: "The gallery at the Worcester Center for Crafts hosts the finest in contemporary craft exhibitions and plays a vital role in improving the cultural life in New England by providing national and international exhibitions, retrospective shows and individual artists works. The Center for Crafts has recently presented the works of Peter Faulkner, Tom Turner, Fred Fenster and John Dunnigan. In addition, the center has a two-year professional craft school.

*THE WORKING GALLERY, 2407 Pacific Ave., Virginia Beach VA 23451. (804)491-8918. Director: Rabiah Levinson. April 1989. Interested in fine art photography, urban, abstract (no industrial) and political. All work must be matted in white with silver frames; present a body of work with a theme. Examples of recent exhibitions: "Photo Expressionist Nudes," by Ron Terner, (chemical painting); "Death, Beauty and Truth," by George Elsasser, (manipulated photos); and the ATT photos of Tidewater Community College students. Presents 3 exhibits/year. Shows last 4-5 weeks. Sponsors openings; "arrangements are the artist's responsibility." Photographer's presence at opening preferred. Charges 20% commission. Does not buy photography outright. General price range: $85-950. Will review transparencies. Interested in framed work only. Requires exclusive representation. No restrictions on photography sold in gallery. Send material by mail for consideration. SASE. Reports in 2 weeks.

Tips: "Please present a theme." The opportunities for photographers by galleries are constantly improving. "Manipulated photography is becoming extremely popular and the general public seems to be leaning in that direction in their purchases."

CHARLES A. WUSTUM MUSEUM OF FINE ARTS, 2519 Northwestern Ave., Racine WI 53404. (414)636-9177. Director: Bruce W. Pepich. "Interested in all fine art photography. It's regularly displayed in our Art Sales and Rental Gallery and the Main Exhibition Galleries. Many of our exhibitors are emerging artists. We sponsor a biennial exhibit of Wisconsin Photographers."

Exhibits: The biennial show is limited to residents of Wisconsin; the sales and rental gallery is limited to residents of the Midwest. Many new and lesser-known photographers are featured. There is no limit to applicants for solo, or group exhibitions, but they must apply in November of each year. Presents an average of 3 shows/year. Shows last 4-6 weeks. Examples of recent exhibitions: Wisconsin Photography '89; Women Photographers from the Permanent Collection; William F. Lemke: Recent Portraits. Sponsors openings. "We provide refreshments and 50 copies of the reception invitation to the exhibitor." Photographer's presence at opening preferred.

Terms & Making Contact: Receives 30% commission from exhibitions, 40% from sales and rental gallery. General price range: $125-350. Will review transparencies. Interested in framed or unframed work. "Must be framed unless it's a 3-D piece. Sale prices for sales and rental gallery have a $1,000 ceiling." Query with resume of credits or send material by mail for consideration. SASE.

Tips: "Photography seems to fare very well in our area. Both the exhibitors and the buying public are trying more experimental works. The public is very interested in presentation and becoming increasingly aware of the advantage of archival mounting. They are beginning to look for this additional service. Our clients are more interested in work of newer (and more affordable) photographers. Landscapes currently sell best at our gallery. Sees trend toward increasing uses of combinations of drawing and painting media with photography. We always look for the best quality in the photographs we exhibit. The technical process involved is not as important to us as the idea or message in the work."

Galleries/'90-'91 changes

The following galleries appeared in the 1990 edition of *Photographer's Market* but are not in the 1991 edition. Those galleries whose owners or directors did not respond to our request for an update of their listings may not have done so for a variety of reasons—they may be out of business, for example, or they may be overstocked with submissions.

Akron Art Museum (did not respond)
Anderson Gallery (did not respond)
Armory Art Gallery (no longer in market)
Art Research Center (moved; no forwarding address)
Bell Gallery, Cecelia Coker (not reviewing work)
Berkshire Artisans Gallery (did not respond)
Brea Civic Cultural Center (did not respond)
Brookfield/Sono Photographic Workshop (did not respond)
Brown Contemporary Art, Robert (did not respond)
Bry Gallery, The (did not respond)
Evanston Art Center (did not respond)

Film in the Cities (did not respond)
Ft. Smith Art Center (did not respond)
Gallery at Cornerstone, The (did not respond)
Imprimatur, Ltd. (moved; no forwarding address)
International Museum of Photography at George Eastman House (did not respond)
Kirkland Fine Arts Building (did not respond)
Kondos Art Gallery, Peter J. (did not respond)
Lee Gallery (did not respond)
Midtown Y Photography Gallery (did not respond)
Minot Gallery (did not respond)
Museum of New Mexico (did not respond)

Muskegon Museum of Art (not reviewing work)
Nikon House (did not respond)
Normandale Gallery (did not respond)
Now Gallery (no longer in market)
Photographics Unlimited Gallery (not reviewing work)
Santa Barbara Museum (not reviewing work)
Schneier Fine Arts, Donna (did not respond)
Sol Del Rio (not reviewing work)
T.M. Gallery (did not respond)
Tempe Arts Center (no longer in market)
University of MA Medical Center Gallery (did not respond)
White Gallery—Portland State University (deleted)

Newspapers & Newsletters

As different as newspapers and newsletters can be in terms of subject matter, publication frequency and readership, photo editors of both types of publications readily agree that newsworthiness is the decisive factor behind every photo they choose. Accordingly, photographers who are serious about working in these markets go beyond random, speculative shooting and learn to see the news through the photo editors'—and readers'—eyes.

Initially, photographers may be drawn to a particular subject or field of business out of personal interest or access to covering it. As their knowledge of the subject and understanding of its related audience grow, so does their ability to recognize news value. They learn to make distinctions between the ordinary event and the truly newsworthy one. They also strive to stay on top of the story, to be where the news is likely to happen and to get pictures as news takes place.

Photographers can cover general news for a newspaper or shoot for a more specialized audience with most newsletters. Some photographers prefer just to shoot spot news, and so they keep alert to any situations or locations that may present photo opportunities. Such photographers take their cameras with them everywhere they go. Other photographers, especially those aiming for the special interest audiences, cultivate news leads by taking part in community activities or by keeping in touch with particular fields of interest, such as politics, business, sports or entertainment. Both types of photographers watch for scheduled events and monitor other news sources such as TV and radio for tips on upcoming meetings, performances, games and other potentially newsworthy events.

Many of the photos that appear in metropolitan dailies are shot by staff photographers, but some opportunities exist for freelancers to work on a "stringer," or as-needed, basis. Though weekly papers are generally not represented in the listings in this section, many freelancers find that working with them first is an ideal way to gain experience and news insight, to build a portfolio of clips, and to establish a pricing structure before approaching some of the regional and national markets listed in this section. Newsletters, like newspapers, provide current news for readers. However, because of a tendency among newsletters toward monthly, bimonthly and quarterly publication cycles, the news in these markets will often be less time-bound. Like weekly newspapers, newsletters can also provide beginning photographers with excellent opportunities to break in and gain experience.

If you find yourself on the scene of a breaking news event, cover it from a variety of news angles and rush it to editors of publications which may already be covering the story. Explain the story angles to each editor. If they are already planning coverage of the event which takes similar angles but do not have photos lined up, chances are that they will want to use your photos. From there, they will negotiate a price and terms for using the photos, and you will have proved both your news sense and photojournalistic skills.

Since both of these market areas are businesses, they usually pay as little as possible. Accordingly, try to retain resale rights to shots of major news events. High news value means high resale value, and strong news photos can be resold repeatedly to the right newspapers or newsletters (see Bob Sacha's comments in the close-up interview, on page 218). Another option in making up for low payment is syndicating images to newspapers around the country. However, most photographers break into syndication from fulltime newspaper work, and usually not until they have track records which show they're capable of producing newsworthy images on a consistent basis.

With newsletters in particular, payment often varies widely according to the publisher's budget. Corporations generally will have higher budgets for photos than will nonprofit organizations. Whether or not you decide to work with a particular newsletter will depend largely upon your interest in the type of business or activity the newsletter covers, your existing inventory of relevant images that might be purchased, or your potential to break in or receive steady work and income.

ALASKA FISHERMAN'S JOURNAL, 1115 NW 46th St., Seattle WA 98107. (206)789-6506. Art Director: Martha Brouwer. Monthly tabloid. Emphasizes Alaska commercial fishing for commercial fishermen. Circ. 15,000. Sample copy for $1.50 and 9×12 SAE plus $1 postage.
Photo Needs: Uses about 50 photos/issue; 10 supplied by freelancers. Special needs include commercial fishing boats in Alaska. Model release and captions preferred.
Making Contact & Terms: Call Chris Horton about specific shots needed. SASE. Reports in 1 month. Pays $50/b&w cover photo; $100/color cover photo; $15/b&w inside photo; and $50/color inside photo. Pays on publication. Credit line given. Buys one-time rights. Previously published work OK.
Tips: "Only submit slides or photos that we request."

ALLIED PUBLISHING, 430 Haywood Rd., Asheville NC 28006. (704)253-7175. Editor: Linda Hagan. Publishes *North Carolina Veterans News* and *Sagebrush Journal*. Bimonthly newspapers. Emphasizes veterans, cowboys, books and western movies. Readers are age 30-up, interested in western movies or veterans. Circ. combined: 15,000. Sample copy $2 each.
Photo Needs: Uses 30-40 photos/issue; 50% supplied by freelance photographers. Needs photos of western stars as they are today, western conventions, veterans, etc. Special needs include western conventions. Model releases and captions preferred.
Making Contact & Terms: Query with list of stock photo subjects or send any size b&w glossy print by mail for consideration. SASE. Reports in 1 month. Pay negotiated. Pays on publication. Credit line given. Buys one-time rights. Simultaneous submissions and previously published work OK.
Tips: Prefers to see "good, sharp, clear b&w photos, especially western stars as they are now, at conventions. Unable to use slides."

AMERICAN METAL MARKET, 7 E. 12th St., New York NY 10003. (212)741-4160. FAX: (212)337-3222. Fairchild Publications, A Capital Cities/ABC Inc. Co. Editor: Michael G. Botta. Daily newspaper. Emphasizes metals production and trade. Readers are top level management (CEO's, chairmen, and presidents) in metals and metals related industries. Circ. 13,500. Estab. 1882. Sample copies free with 10×13 SASE.
Photo Needs: 90% of photos supplied by freelance photographers. Needs photos of press conferences, executive interviews, industry action shots and industry receptions. Photo captions required.
Making Contact & Terms: Provide resume, business card, brochure, flyer or tearsheets to be kept on file for possible assignments. Cannot return material. Credit line given. Buys all rights; will negotiate with a photographer unwilling to sell all rights. Simultaneous submissions OK.
Tips: "We tend to avoid photographers who are unwilling to release all rights. We produce a daily newspaper and maintain a complete photo file. We cover events worldwide and often need to hire freelance photographers. Best bet is to supply business card, phone number and any samples for us to keep on file. Keep in mind action photos are difficult to come by. Much of the metals industry is automated and it has become a challenge to find good 'people' shots."

AMERICAN SPORTS NETWORK, Box 6100, Rosemead CA 91770. (818)572-4727. President: Louis Zwick. Publishes four newspapers covering "general collegiate, amateur and professional sports; i.e., football, baseball, basketball, track and field, wrestling, boxing, hockey, powerlifting and bodybuilding, etc." Circ. 50,000-755,000.
Photo Needs: Uses about 10-85 photos/issue in various publications; 90% supplied by freelancers. Needs "sport action, hard-hitting contact, emotion-filled, b&w glossy 8×10s and 4×5 transparencies. Have special bodybuilder annual calendar, collegiate and professional football pre- and post-season editions." Model release and captions preferred.
Making Contact & Terms: Send 8×10 b&w glossy prints and 4×5 transparencies by mail for consideration; provide resume, business card, brochure, flyer or tearsheets to be kept on file for possible future assignments. SASE. Reports in 1 week. Pays $1,000/color cover photo; $250/inside b&w photo; negotiates rates by the job and hour. Pays on publication. Buys first North American serial rights. Simultaneous and previously published submissions OK.

ANCHORAGE DAILY NEWS, 1001 Northway Dr., Anchorage AK 99508. (907)257-4347. Editor: Howard Weaver. Photo Editor: Richard Murphy. Daily newspaper. Emphasizes all Alaskan subjects. Readers are Alaskans. Circ. 60,000. Estab. 1946. Sample copy free with 11×14 SAE and $2 postage.

Photo Needs: Uses 10-50 photos/issue; 5% supplied by freelance photographers; most from assignment. Needs photos of all subjects, primarily Alaskan subjects. In particular, looking for freelance images for travel section; wants photos of all areas, especially Hawaii. Model release and captions required.

Making Contact & Terms: Contact photo editor with specific ideas. SASE. Reports in 1-3 weeks. Pays $25 minimum/b&w photo; $35 minimum/color photo: photo/text package negotiable. Pays on publication. Credit line given. Buys one-time rights. Simultaneous submissions OK.

Tips: "We, like most daily newspapers, are primarily interested in timely topics, but at times will use dated material." In portfolio or samples, wants to see "eye-catching images, good use of light and active photographs. More color is being used on a daily basis."

AVSC NEWS, (formerly AVSC) 122 E. 42nd St., New York NY 10168. (212)351-2500. Publications Manager: Pam Harper. Publication of the Association for Voluntary Surgical Contraception. Quarterly newsletter. Emphasizes health care, contraception. Readers are health care professionals in the US and abroad. Circ. 4,500. Estab. 1962. Sample copies for 4×9 SASE.

Photo Needs: Uses 2-3 photos/issue; 1 supplied by freelancer. Needs photos of mothers and fathers with children in US and developing worlds. Photos only; do not accept mss. Special needs include annual report 15-20 photos; brochures throughout the year. Model release required; captions preferred.

Making Contact & Terms: Query with list of stock photo subjects. Reports in 2 weeks. Pays $100-200/b&w cover photo; $50-100/b&w inside photo. Pays on publication. Buys one-time rights. Previously published work OK.

Tips: Prefers to see a "sharp, good range of tones from white through all greys to black, and appealing pictures of people."

*BAJA TIMES, Box 755, 5577 Chula Vista CA 92012. (706)612-1244. General Manager: Carlos Chabert. Editor: John W. Utley. Monthly. Circ. 60,000. Emphasizes Baja California and Mexico travel and history. Readers are travelers to Baja California, Mexico, and Baja aficionados from all over US and Canada. Free sample copy with SASE (9×12).

Photo Needs: Uses about 12 photos/issue; most supplied by freelance photographers. Needs current travel, scenic, wildlife, historic, women, children, fishing, Baja fashions and beach photos. Photos purchased with or without accompanying ms. Special needs include: History of cities in Baja California and resorts, Baja shopping, sports, and general recreation. Model release and captions preferred.

Making Contact & Terms: Send by mail for consideration b&w prints, or query with list of stock photo subjects. Now using full color photos for front cover. Avidly seeking outstanding Baja California, Mexico subjects. Will review color prints, but prefer transparencies for publication. Reports in 6 weeks. Pays $5-10/b&w photo; $45/color cover photo. Buys one-time rights.

Tips: "We need sharp photography with good definition. Photo essays are welcome but please remember the basic subject matter is Baja California and Mexico."

BANJO NEWSLETTER INC., Box 364, Greensboro MD 21639. (301)482-6278. Editor: Hub Nitchie. Monthly. Emphasizes 5-string banjo information. Readers include musicians, teachers. Circ. 8,000.

Photo Needs: Uses 3-8 photos/issue; very few supplied by freelance photographers. Needs musical instruments, cases, well known banjo players, band, PR shots; could include technical instruction. Model release preferred.

Making Contact & Terms: Query with samples; usually writers provide photos from banjo manufacturers or musicians. Reports in 1 month. Pays $40-50/b&w cover photo, $10-15/b&w inside photo. Pays on publication. Credit line given. Buys one-time rights. Simultaneous submissions and previously published work OK with permission from publisher.

BOOK AUTHOR'S NEWSLETTER, published by Writer's Digest School, 1507 Dana Ave., Cincinnati OH 45207. (513)531-2222. Editor: Kirk Polking. Semi-annual newsletter. Circ. 3,000. For students in WDS's book workshops for novel and nonfiction book writing. News items and brief articles on writing and selling novels and nonfiction books.

The asterisk before a listing indicates that the market is new in this edition. New markets are often the most receptive to freelance submissions.

Photo Needs: Uses 8×10 glossy prints for inside or cover photos. Celebrity/personality photos of well-known writers in the book field. No photos without related text of interest/help to writing students. Model release preferred; captions required.

Making Contact & Terms: Pays $15/photo. Photos purchased with accompanying mss. Buys 1-2 photos per issue. Credit line given. Pays on acceptance. Buys one-time rights. Send material by mail for consideration. SASE. Reports in 3 weeks. Simultaneous and previously published work OK.

Tips: "Material must be relevant to would-be book authors."

*CALIFORNIA SCHOOL EMPLOYEE, P.O. Box 640, San Jose CA 95106. (408)263-8000, ext. 215. Director, Member/Public Relations: Frances VanZanelt. Publication labor union, California School employees Association (CSEA). Monthly (October-July) newspaper. Circ. 100,000+. Estab. 1932. Sample copy free upon request.

Photo Needs: Needs photos of people. Special photo needs include crowds, school and college related.

Making Contact & Terms: Provide resume, business card, brochure, flyer or tearsheets to be kept on file for possible assignments. SASE. Payment varies and is negotiable. Pays on publication. Credit line given. Right purchased are negotiable. Simultaneous submissions and previously published work OK.

Tips: "Know publisher's subject matter."

THE CAPITAL, 2000 Capital Dr., Annapolis MD 21401. (301)268-5000. Graphics Editor: Brian Henley. Daily newspaper. Circ. 43,000. Estab. 1877.

Photo Needs: Uses 25 photos/issue; 1 supplied daily by freelance photographer; one monthly from freelance stock. Needs stock slides on boating, football, aging (senior citizens). Model release, photo captions preferred.

Making Contact & Terms: Query with list of stock photo subjects, send unsolicited photos by mail for consideration, submit portfolio for review. Uses b&w and color prints; 35mm transparencies. Reports in 1 week. Pays $50/color cover photo; $30/b&w cover photo; $20/color inside photo; $15/b&w inside photo. Pays on publication. Credit line given. Buys one-time rights.

Tips: "We need clarity and simplicity. We use mostly spot news from freelancers."

CAPPER'S, 616 Jefferson, Topeka KS 66607. (913)295-1108. Editor: Nancy Peavler. Estab. 1879. Bi-monthly tabloid. Emphasizes human-interest subjects. Readers are "mostly Midwesterners in small towns and on rural routes." Circ. 390,000. Sample copy 85¢.

Photo Needs: Uses about 20-25 photos/issue, "one or two" supplied by freelance photographers. "We make no photo assignments. We select freelance photos with use in specific issues in mind." Needs "35mm color slides of human-interest activities, nature (scenic), etc., in bright primary colors. We often use photos tied to the season, a holiday or an upcoming event of general interest." Captions preferred.

Making Contact & Terms: "Send for guidelines and a sample copy (SASE + 85¢). Study the types of photos in the publication, then send a sheet of 10-20 samples with caption material for our consideration. (Include postpaid return envelope.) Although we do most of our business by mail, a phone number is helpful in case we need more caption information. Phone calls to try to sell us on your photos don't really help." Reporting time varies. Pays $10-15 b/w photo; $15-25/color photo; Only cover photos receive maximum payment. Pays on publication. Credit line given. Buys one-time rights.

Tips: "Generally, we're looking for photos of everyday people doing everyday activities. If the photographer can present this in a pleasing manner, these are the photos we're most likely to use. Season shots are appropriate for Capper's, but they should be natural, no posed. We steer clear of dark, "mood" shots; they don't reproduce well on newsprint. Most of our readers are small town or rural Midwesterners, so we're looking for photos with which they can identify. Although our format is tabloid, we don't use "celebrity" shots and won't devote an area much larger than 5″ × 6″ to one photo."

CATHOLIC HEALTH WORLD, 4455 Woodson Rd., St. Louis MO 63134. (314)427-2500. Editor: Suzy Farren. Publication of Catholic Health Association. Semi-monthly newspaper emphasizing healthcare—primary subjects dealing with our member facilities. Readers are hospital and long-term care facility administrators, PR people. Circ. 7,000. Sample copy free with 9×12 SASE.

Photo Needs: Uses 4-15 photos/issue; 1-2 supplied by freelancers. Any photos that would help illustrate health concerns (i.e., pregnant teens, elderly). Model release required.

Making Contact & Terms: Send unsolicited photos by mail for consideration. Uses 5×7 or 8×10 b&w glossy prints. SASE. Reports in 2 weeks. Pays $40-60/photo. Pays on publication. Credit line given. Buys one-time rights. Simultaneous submissions OK.

CDA UPDATE, 818 K St., Sacramento CA 95814. (916)443-0505. Director of Publications: Douglas K. Curley. Publication of California Dental Association. Monthly newsletter; tabloid format. Readers are dentistry professionals. Circ. 16,000. Sample copy $4.
Photo Needs: Number of photos used each issue varies; 1-3 supplied by freelance photographers. Needs photos of concept, art and news.
Making Contact & Terms: Query with resume of credits, include list of references. SASE. Reports in 1 month. Pays $300/color cover photo. Photographers give film directly to CDA. Payment is based on time and labor rather than per shot. Pays $40-80/hour. Pays within 2 weeks of acceptance. Buys all rights, but willing to negotiate.
Tips: CDA wants to develop a list of photographers available in various regions such as Midwest, Hawaii and West Coast. The association also has affiliation with National Dentistry Association, American Dental Association, and so, participates in numerous conventions and meetings. As a result, will need photos for publication on a regular basis. "Just about anybody who's in a major convention market has a very good likelihood of producing work for us."

THE CHICAGO TRIBUNE MAGAZINE (formerly Sunday), Room 570, 532 N. Michigan Ave., Chicago IL 60611. (312)222-3535. Managing Editor: Ruby Scott. Weekly. Profiles, in-depth stories, photo essays, book excerpts. Readers are basically the Tribune's audience (general), with slightly higher demographics. Circ. 1.1 million. Sample copy free with 11 × 14 SASE.
Photo Needs: Uses 25 photos/issue; number supplied by freelancers varies. Needs photos of various kinds of stock and occasional out-of-town assignments. Also photo essays. "We need good travel stock, particularly unusual locales." Model release preferred; captions required.
Making Contact & Terms: Query with list of stock photo subjects; provide resume, business card, brochure, flyer or tearsheets to be kept on file for possible future assignments. SASE. Reports in 2 weeks. Pays $400-500/color cover photo; $100-150/b&w inside photo; $150-350/color inside photo; b&w page rate varies; $225/color page rate; by the day, $350 and expenses; photo and text package, $1,000. Pays on publication. Credit line given. Buys one-time rights, first North American serial rights or all rights for assignment photography. Will negotiate with photographer unwilling to sell all rights. Simultaneous submissions and previously published work OK.
Tips: "We're looking for photos that tell a story, not just random samples of photographers work. The Tribune has a staff of almost 50 photographers, so make sure that what you're offering is something that we can't get ourselves. Prefers regional subjects."

*CITIZEN NEWSPAPER GROUP, 412 E. 87th St., Chicago/Harvey IL 60619. (312)487-7700. Managing Editor: Brenda Garth or Hyde Park Editor: Lisa Ely. Black-owned community newspaper. Weekly tabloid. Emphasizes community. Readers are males and females, ages 17-70, home owners, business owners, primarily black audience. Circ. 112,000. Estab. 1965. Free sample copy with SASE.
Photo Needs: Uses 10+ photos/issue. 25-30% supplied by freelance photographers. Model release preferred. Photo captions required.
Making Contact & Terms: Send 35mm b&w prints; 5 × 7's preferred; by mail for consideration. Reports in 1-2 weeks. Pays up to $25/b&w cover photo. Pays on publication. Credit line given. Buys one-time rights. Simultaneous submissions OK.
Tips: "We are a small staff but largely circulated publication. We have an African American market and would appreciate many photo submissions of various topics, local and national."

COMMERCIAL PROPERTY NEWS, (formerly Real Estate Times), 1515 Broadway, New York NY 10036. (212)869-1300. Editor-in-chief: Mark A. Klionsky. Biweekly tabloid emphasizing commercial real estate. Readers are commercial real estate developers, brokers, property managers and financial institutions. Circ. 33,000. Sample copy available.
Photo Needs: Uses 60 photos/issue; 5% supplied by freelancers. Needs photos of people and buildings. Model release required; captions preferred.
Making Contact & Terms: Query with samples or list of stock photo subjects. Reports in 2 weeks. Pays $250/b&w cover; $300/color cover; $50/b&w inside photo; $125/hour; $100/job. Pays on publication. Credit line sometimes given. Simultaneous and previously published work OK.

CONSTRUCTION TODAY, 3110 Columbia Pike, Arlington VA 22204. Editor: Calvin Oren. Weekly tabloid. Emphasizes construction. Readers are construction company executives and estimators. Circ: 4,000. Sample copy free with SASE.
Photo Needs: Uses 2-10 photos/issue; 1 supplied by freelance photographer. Needs photos of construction. Model release, photo captions preferred.
Making Contact & Terms: Provide resume, business card, brochure, flyer or tearsheets to be kept on file for possible assignments. SASE. Reports in 1 month. Payment negotiable. Pays on publication. Credit line given. Buys all rights; will negotiate with a photographer unwilling to sell all rights. Simultaneous submissions and previously published work OK.

CRAIN'S CLEVELAND BUSINESS, Suite 412, 140 Public Square, Cleveland OH 44114. (216)522-1383. Assistant Managing Editor/Production: Patrick J. Hendrick. Weekly tabloid emphasizing business. Readers are Northeast Ohio business and industry. Circ. 26,000. Sample copy free for 9 × 12 SASE; photo guidelines free with SASE.
Photo Needs: Uses about 6 photos/issue; all supplied by freelancers. Needs photos of office environmentals, architecturals. Model release preferred; captions required.
Making Contact & Terms: Arrange a personal interview to show portfolio. SASE. Reports in 2 weeks. Pays the job, $50 + 20¢/mile. Pays on publication. Credit line given. Buys all rights. Previously published work OK.
Tips: Prefers to see "work that shows an ability to interact with the person being photographed in order to obtain a natural, interesting image. Work which shows a sensitivity to 'playing angles' in architectural shots. Be prompt. Be available. Follow directions. After doing the assigned shot, try to find a new, imaginative angle that might offer the editor a more creative shot."

*CRAIN'S DETROIT BUSINESS, 1400 Woodbridge, Detroit MI 48207. (313)446-6000. Graphics Editor: Nancy Kassen. Trade publication. Weekly tabloid. Emphasizes business. Estab. 1985. Sample copy for 11 × 14 SAE and 2 first-class stamps.
Photo Needs: Uses 30 photos/issue; 9-10 supplied by freelance photographers. Needs environmental portraits of business executives illustrating product and/or specialty. Model release preferred; photo captions required.
Making Contact & Terms: Arrange a personal interview to show a portfolio; submit portfolio for review; provide resume, business card, brochure, flyer or tearsheets to be kept on file for possible assignments. SASE. Reports in 2 weeks. Pays on acceptance. Credit line given. Buys one-time rights.

CYCLE NEWS, Box 498, Long Beach CA 90801. (213)427-7433. Publisher: Sharon Clayton. Editor: Jack Mangus. Weekly tabloid. Circ. 45,000. Emphasizes motorcycle news for enthusiasts and covers nationwide races.
Photo Needs: Needs photos of motorcycle racing to accompany written race reports; prefers more than one bike to appear in photo. Wants current material. Buys 1,000 photos/year. Buys all rights, but may revert to photographer after publication.
Making Contact & Terms: Send photos or contact sheet for consideration or call for appointment. "Payment on 15th of the month for issues cover-dated the previous month." Reports in 3 weeks. SASE. For b&w: send contact sheet, negatives (preferred for best reproduction) or prints (5 × 7 or 8 × 10, glossy or matte), captions required, pays $10 minimum. For color: send transparencies. captions required, pays $50 minimum. For cover shots: send contact sheet, prints or negatives for b&w; transparencies for color, captions required, payment negotiable.
Tips: Prefers sharp action photos utilizing good contrast. Study publication before submitting "to see what it's all about." Primary coverage area is nationwide.

CYCLING U.S.A., U.S. Cycling Federation, 1750 E. Boulder St., Colorado Springs CO 80909. Editor: Kyle Woodlief. Emphasizes bicycle racing for active bicycle racers. Circ. 35,000. Sample copy free with 9 × 12 SASE.
Photo Needs: Uses about 10 photos/issue; 100% supplied by freelance photographers. Needs action racing shots, profile shoots or competitors. Captions required.
Making Contact & Terms: Query with samples. Send 5 × 7 or 8 × 10 b&w prints by mail for consideration, submit photos on speculation. SASE. Reports in 3 weeks. Pays $100/color cover photo; $10 minimum/b&w inside photo, depending on size; 10¢/word. Pays on publication. Credit line given. Buys one-time rights "unless other arrangements have been made."
Tips: "Study European and American bicycle racing publications. Initially, it's a tough sport to shoot, but if a photographer gets the hang of it, he'll get his stuff published regularly."

DAILY SHIPPING NEWS, 2014 NW 24th, Portland OR 97210. (503)227-6543. Editor: Philip S. Moore. Daily newspaper. Covers maritime news (not military, fishing or recreational). Focus upon steamships, barge lines and port authorities. Readers are international trade and transportation personnel, ages 21-65. Circ. 1,000. Sample copy free with 9 × 12 SASE and 2 first-class stamps. Photo guidelines free with SASE.
Photo Needs: Uses 1 photo/issue; 100% supplied by freelance photographers. Needs more photos of merchant marine vessels, ("preferably tied to very newsworthy stories."). Photo captions required.
Making Contact & Terms: Send unsolicited photos by mail for consideration. Uses any size or finish, b&w or color prints. SASE. Reports in 1 week. Pays $10 for most photos. Pays $20-100/photo/text package. Pays on publication. Credit line given. Buys one-time rights. Simultaneous submissions OK.
Tips: "The harder the news, the more likely photos will be published. We never print 'art' photography."

*DEKALB DAILY CHRONICLE, 2815 Barber Greene Rd., DeKalb IL 60115. (815)756-4841. Head Photographer: Robb Perea. Daily newspaper. Emphasizes agriculture and features on DeKalb people. Circ. 15,000. Estab. 1869. Sample copy for 50¢.
Photo Needs: Feature pages run every week on Sunday—must pertain to DeKalb County. Photos purchased with accompanying manuscript only. Model release preferred; photo captions required.
Making Contact & Terms: Query with resume of credits; send unsolicited b&w 8×10 glossy photos by mail for consideration. Also, call to query. Cannot return material. Reports in 1 month. Pays on acceptance. Credit line given. Buys one-time rights.
Tips: "No 'set' pay scale per se; payment negotiable depending on several factors including quality of photo and need."

*EL DORADO NEWS TIMES, 111 N. Madison, Box 912, El Dorado AR 71730. (501)862-6611. Photo Editor: James Lemon. Daily newspaper. Emphasizes South Arkansas. Readers are family. Circ. 12,000. Estab. 1926. Sample copies for 25¢. Photo guidelines free with SASE.
Photo Needs: Uses 5-6 photos/issue. Needs photos of Arkansas-related news. Special photo needs unknown. Photo captions required.
Making Contact & Terms: Provide resume, business card, brochure, flyer or tearsheets to be kept on file for possible assignments. Cannot return unsolicited material. Payment variable; negotiable. Buys one-time rights.

EXCHANGE & COMMISSARY NEWS, Box 1500, Westbury NY 11590. (516)334-3030. Senior Editor: Bob Moran. Monthly tabloid. Emphasizes "military retailing: grocery and mass merchandising stores." Readers are buyers and managers.
Photo Needs: Uses about 40-50 photos/issue. Needs "store shots." Captions preferred.
Making Contact & Terms: Send b&w prints or contact sheets, also 35mm or 4×5 transparencies, b&w contact sheets by mail for consideration. SASE. Reports in 2 weeks. Payment varies. Pays on acceptance. Credit line given. Buys all rights.

EYECARE BUSINESS, 50 Washington St., Norwalk CT 06854. (203)838-9100. Art Director: Maryanne Gjersvik. Monthly tabloid emphasizing the eyecare industry—frames, contact lenses, service and fashion. Readers are opticians and optometrists. Circ. 35,000. Sample copy available.
Photo Needs: Uses 60 photos/issue; 12 supplied by freelancers. Needs photos of people in eyeglasses; eyeglasses. Model release and captions required.
Making Contact & Terms: Query with samples; provide resume, business card, brochure, flyer or tearsheets to be kept on file for possible future assignments. Does not return unsolicited material. Pays $400/color cover photo; $200/color inside photo. Pays on publication. Credit line given. Buys all rights; willing to negotiate with photographer unwilling to sell all rights.

FINANCIAL SERVICES WEEK, 7 E. 12th St., New York NY 10003. (212)741-6644. FAS: (212)337-3248. Art Director: Yvonne Picioccio. Company publication of Fairchild Publications. Estab. 1987. Biweekly newspaper. Emphasizes financial planners. Readers are certified financial planners. Circ. 70,000. Sample copy free upon request.
Photo Needs: Uses 5-10 photos/issue; 50% supplied by freelancers. Needs photos dealing with money matters, business transactions. Model release and captions required. About 50% of photos shot on assignment.
Making Contact & Terms: Send unsolicited photos by mail for consideration or submit portfolio for review. Uses any size b&w prints; b&w contact sheets and negatives. Reports in 1 month. Pays $75/hour; also pays expenses, film, mileage, overnight shipping costs. Pays on publication. Credit line given. Buys one-time rights.
Tips: Looks for "good portraits and corporate photos." Prefers to see "clear, strong darks and lights, high-contrast shots. Try to make simple head shots, more interesting, less boring. Unusual angles and different settings for personality shots."

FISHING AND HUNTING NEWS, 511 Eastlake Ave. E., Box C-19000, Seattle WA 98109. (206)624-3845. Managing Editor: Vence Malernee. Photo Editor: Scott Liles. Bi-weekly tabloid. Circ. 133,000. Buys 300 or more photos/year. Emphasizes how-to material, fishing and hunting locations and new products for hunters and fishermen.
Subject Needs: Wildlife—fish/game with successful fishermen and hunters. Captions required.
Specs: Uses 5×7 or 8×10 glossy b&w prints or negatives for inside photos. Uses color covers and some inside color photos—glossy 5×7 or 8×10 color prints, 35mm, 2¼×2¼ or 4×5 color transparencies. When submitting 8×10 color prints, negative must also be sent.
Payment & Terms: Pays $5-15 minimum/b&w print, $50-100 minimum/cover and $10-20 editorial color photos. Credit line given. Pays on acceptance. Buys all rights, but may reassign to photographer after publication. Submit model release with photo.

Making Contact: Send samples of work for consideration. SASE. Reports in 2 weeks. Free sample copy and photo guidelines.

Tips: Looking for fresh, timely approaches to fishing and hunting subjects. Query for details of special issues and topics. "We need newsy photos with a fresh approach. Looking for near-deadline photos from Oregon, California, Utah, Idaho, Wyoming, Montana, Colorado, Texas, Alaska and Washington (sportsmen with fish or game)."

FLORIDA GROWER AND RANCHER, 1331 N. Mills, Orlando FL 32803. (407)894-6522. Editor: Jim Fisher. Monthly. Emphasizes commercial agriculture in Florida. Readers are "professional farmers, growers and ranchers in the state of Florida." Sample copy and photo guidelines free with 9 × 12 SAE and $1 postage.

Photo Needs: Uses about 20-25 photos/issue; "presently few" supplied by freelance photographers. Needs photos of "Florida growers and ranchers in action in their day-to-day jobs. Prefer modern farm scenes, action, of specific farm which can be identified." Model release preferred; captions required.

Making Contact & Terms: Query with list of stock photo subjects. Provide resume, business card, brochure, flyer or tearsheets to be kept on file for possible future assignments. SASE. Reports in 3 weeks. Pays $10/b&w; $50/color cover. Pays by the line plus photo for text/photo package. Pays on publication. Credit line given if required. Buys one-time rights.

Tips: "Query first—photography usually tied in with writing assignment."

*FRANCE TODAY NEWSLETTER, 1051 Divisadero St., San Francisco CA 94115. (415)921-5100. Editor: Anne Prah-Perochon. Published 10 times/year. Emphasizes modern-day France. Readers are Americans who travel often to Europe; teachers and students of the French language. Circ. 8,000. Estab. 1984. Sample copy free with SASE.

Photo Needs: Uses 10 photos/issue. Needs photos depicting travel, food and wine, products, personalities and holiday activities. Reviews photos with or without accompanying ms. Captions preferred.

Making Contact & Terms: Query with samples; send unsolicited photos by mail for consideration. Send b&w 8 × 10 prints. SASE. Reports in 1 month. Pays $35-75/b&w inside photo; $100/b&w cover photo. Pays on publication. Credit line given. Buys one-time rights. Simultaneous submissions OK.

Tips: "We especially seek unusual visual perspectives on France: either seldom photographed locales, people and events or idiosyncratic interpretations of familiar scenes. It might be good to send us a listing of available shots, plus only a few samples, rather than sending a large random sampling. We usually solicit photos around a certain theme, depending on the content of a specific issue."

GIFT AND STATIONERY BUSINESS, 1515 Broadway, New York NY 10036. (212)869-1300. Editor: Joyce Washnik. Monthly tabloid. Emphasizes gifts and stationery retailers. Readers are gift retailers. Circ. 40,000. Sample copy free with SASE.

Photo Needs: "Cover shot and 5 inside shots by assignment only" supplied by freelance photographers. Needs environmental portraits, plus store shots or showroom shots. Special needs include 1 cover shot per month in various geographic locations.

Making Contact & Terms: Provide resume, business card, brochure, flyer or tearsheets to be kept on file for possible future assignments. Does not return unsolicited material. Reports in 1 month. Pays $350-500/job. Pays on acceptance. Credit line given on cover. Buys all rights. Will negotiate with photographer unwilling to sell all rights.

Tips: Wants "imaginative and insightful portraits of retailers and manufacturers in their work environment."

GLOBE, 5401 NW Broken Sound Blvd., Boca Raton FL 33487. (407)997-7733. Photo Editor: Ron Haines. Weekly tabloid. Circ. 2,000,000. "For everyone in the family. *Globe* readers are the same people you meet on the street, and in supermarket lines—average, hard-working Americans." Needs human interest photos, celebrity photos, humorous animal photos, anything unusual or offbeat. Buys all photos from freelancers. Pays $75/b&w photo (negotiable); $125/color photo (negotiabel); day and package rates negotiable. Buys first serial rights. Send photos for consideration. Pays on publication unless otherwise arranged. Reports in 1 week. SASE. Previously published work OK.

B&W: Send 8 × 10 glossy prints. Captions required.

Color: Transparencies or prints.

Tips: Advises beginners to look for the unusual, offbeat shots. "Do not write for photo guidelines. Study the publication instead. Tailor your submission to my market." Use of color is increasing.

GRAIN MATTERS, Box 816, 423 Main St., Winnipeg MB, R3C 2P5 Canada. (204)983-3423. Information Officer: Brian Stacey. Bimonthly newsletter. Emphasizes grain industry, transportation (rail and water). Readers are farmers (ages 18 and over). Circ. 150,000. Sample copy free with SASE.

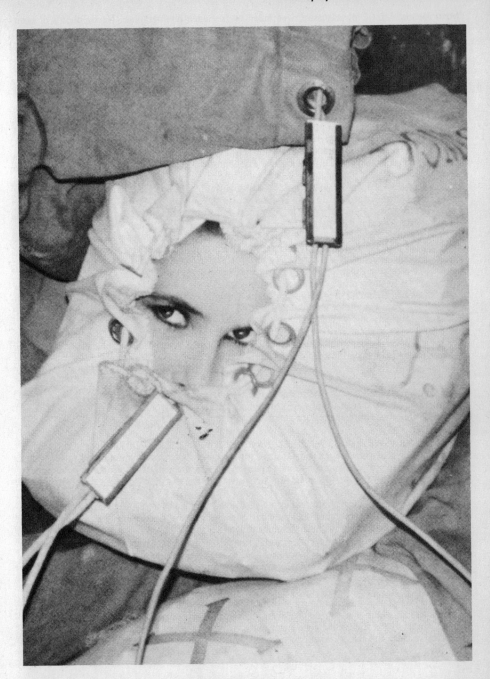

Longmont, Colorado photographer/postal service employee Ralph Williams never goes to work without his camera. On one particular day, he was especially rewarded for his readiness with this eye-opener which he calls the "Mail Order Bride." Williams explains that when he saw the magazine cover girl "peeking out from a mail sack" he grabbed his camera from his locker and got this shot under available light. Williams doubled his luck with sales of $75 to the magazine, Outdoor & Travel Photography and $150 to the weekly news tabloid, The Globe.

Photo Needs: Uses 2 photos/issue; 1 supplied by freelance photographer. Needs photos of farm scenes, grain deliveries, country elevators, terminal elevators, railcars, lake vessels and farm meetings. Photo captions required.

Making Contact & Terms: Provide resume, business card, brochure, flyer or tearsheets to be kept on file for possible assignments. Cannot return material. Pays $100 (Canadian)/inside photo. Pays on acceptance. Buys one-time rights. Previously published work OK.

GRIT, 208 W. 3rd St., Williamsport PA 17701. (717)326-1771. Contact: Assignment Editor. Weekly tabloid. Circ. 600,000. Emphasizes "people-oriented material which is helpful, inspiring and uplifting. When presenting articles about places and things, it does so through the experiences of people. Readership is small-town and rural America." Photos purchased with or without accompanying ms. Buys "hundreds" of photos/year. Buys one-time, first serial or second serial (reprint) rights. Send material by mail for consideration. SASE. Previously published work OK. Pays on acceptance. Reports in 2-3 weeks. Sample copy $1, photo guidelines free with SASE.

Subject Needs: Needs on a regular basis "photos of all subjects, provided they have up-beat themes that are so good they surprise us. Human interest, sports, animals, celebrities. Get action into shot, implied or otherwise, whenever possible. Make certain pictures are well composed, properly exposed and pin sharp. All color transparencies for the cover are square in format. We use 35mm and up." Captions required. "Single b&w photos that stand alone must be accompanied by 50-100 words of meaningful caption information." Model release preferred. "No cheesecake. No pictures that cannot be shown to any member of the family. No pictures that are out of focus or grossly over/or underexposed. No ribbon-cutting, check-passing or hand-shaking pictures."

B&W: Uses 8 × 10 glossy prints. "Because we print on newsprint, we need crisp, sharp b&w with white whites, black blacks and all the middle gray tones. Use fill-in flash where needed. We also want good composition." Pays $35/photo; $15/photo for second rights. Pays $25/photo for pix accompanying mss, $10 for reprint rights on pix accompanying mss.

Color: Uses transparencies for cover only. "Remember that *Grit* publishes on newsprint and therefore requires sharp, bright, contrasting colors for best reproduction. Avoid sending shots of people whose faces are in shadows; no soft focus." Pays $100/front cover color.

Accompanying Mss: Pays 12¢/word, first rights; 6¢/word for second or reprint rights. Free writer's guidelines for SASE.

Tips: "Good major-holiday subjects seldom come to us from freelancers. For example, Easter, 4th of July, Christmas or New Year. Using newsprint we need crisp b&w. Avoid shadows on people's faces — when photo requires action make sure action is *in* photo."

GUARDIAN NEWSWEEKLY, 33 W. 17th St., New York NY 10011. (212)691-0404. Photo Editor: Mahmood Nadia. Weekly newspaper. Emphasizes "progressive politics and national and international news; focuses on Third World and on women's movement, disarmament, labor, economy, environment, grassroots community groups." Readers are "activists, students, workers; we have subscribers around the world." Circ. 20,000. Sample copy for SASE and 90¢ postage.

Photo Needs: Uses about 25 photos/issue; "at least 50%" supplied by freelance photographers. Needs "news photos — local, international and national. Includes mugs of figures in the news, local rallies, features; most to accompany stories." Captions preferred.

Making Contact & Terms: Prefers query with 2 samples or list of stock photo subjects. Send any size b&w glossy prints by mail for consideration. SASE. Reports in 1 month "or sooner." Pays $15/b&w inside photo. Pays on publication. Credit line given. Buys one-time rights. Simultaneous and previously published submissions OK.

Tips: Prefers to see "good quality, good sense of political side of subject *and* human interest aspect" in samples. "We pay low rates, but our photos are often requested by other publications for reprinting and they will pay photographer, too. We feature photos on cover and in centerfold." In portfolio or samples, wants to see "flexibility, good news sense, full compositions which make a statement, boldness. Get up close to subjects, avoid posed shots." Needs "more coverage from geographical areas other than Northeast US."

Markets which offer lower payment amounts, or photo credits and extra copies or tearsheets as payment are often receptive to the work of newcomers. For a list of such markets, see the First Markets Index preceding the General Index in the back of this book.

GULF COAST GOLFER, Suite 212, 9182 Old Katy Rd., Houston TX 77055. (713)464-0308. Editor: Bob Gray. Monthly tabloid. Emphasizes golf in the gulf coast area of Texas. Readers are average 48.5 years, $72,406 income, upscale lifestyle and play golf 2-5 times weekly. Circ. 27,000. Sample copy free with SASE and $2.00 postage.
Photo Needs: Uses about 20 photos/issue; none supplied by freelance photographers. "Photos are bought only in conjunction with purchase of articles." Photos purchased with accompanying ms only. Model release and captions preferred.
Making Contact & Terms: "Use the telephone." SASE. Reports in 2 weeks. Pays on publication. Credit line given. Buys one-time rights or all rights, if specified.

HOUSEWARES, Harcourt Brace Jovanovich Publications, 7500 Old Oak Blvd., Cleveland OH 44130. (216)243-8100. Editor: Elliot Maras. Trade. Biweekly newspaper, tabloid size on glossy stock. Emphasizes the housewares retail business. Readers are merchandise managers of housewares and electric housewares; buyers; and chain store top management personnel who are involved in buying and selling housewares products. Circ. 13,500. Sample copy free with 11 × 17 SAE and 40¢ postage.
Photo Needs: Uses "10 photos, not counting new products"/issue; up to 2 supplied by freelance photographers. Needs retail display photos of houseware products. Model release required. "We rarely use models; prefer static display shots."
Making Contact & Terms: Provide resume, business card, brochure, flyer or tearsheets to be kept on file for possible future assignments. Does not return unsolicited material. Payment negotiable. Pays $125-250/complete package. Credit line given. Buys all rights.

INSIDE TEXAS RUNNING, 9514 Bristlebrook, Houston TX 77083. (713)498-3208. Publisher/Editor: Joanne Schmidt. Monthly tabloid. Circ. 30,000. Estab. 1977. Emphasizes running and jogging with biking insert. Readers are Texas runners and joggers of all abilities. Sample copy $2.50
Photo Needs: Uses about 20 photos/issue; 10 supplied by freelance photographers. 80 percent of freelance photography in issue comes from assignment from freelance stock. Needs photos of "races, especially outside of Houston area; scenic places to run; how-to (accompanying articles by coaches); also triathlon and bike tours and races." Special needs include "top race coverage; running camps (summer); variety of Texas running terrain." Captions preferred.
Making Contact & Terms: Send b&w or color glossy prints by mail for consideration. SASE. Reports in 1 month. Pays $10-25/b&w photo, $10-50/color photo; $25 per photo/text package. Pays on publication. Credit line given. Rights—"negotiable." Simultaneous submissions and previously published work OK.
Tips: Prefers to see "human interest, contrast and good composition" in photos. Transparencies are now used for covers. "Look for the unusual. Race photos tend to look the same." Wants "clear photos with people near front; too often photographers are too far away when they shoot and subjects are a dot on the landscape." Wants to see road races in Texas outside of Houston area.

*INTENSIVE CARING UNLIMITED, 910 Bent Lane, Philadelphia PA 19118. (215)233-4723. Editor: Lenette S. Moses. Bimonthly newsletter. Covers children with medical or developmental problems. Readers are families—all ages. Circ. 3,000. Estab. 1983. Samples copy free with 65¢ postage. Photo guidelines free with SASE.
Photo Needs: Uses 2-3 photos/year; all supplied by freelance photographers. Needs photos of parents with babies or children, parents or children alone, medical professionals with babies. Special photo needs include premature babies, high-risk pregnant mothers, grieving parents, families. Model release required; photo captions preferred.
Making Contact & Terms: Query with list of stock photo subjects; send unsolicited 2¼ × 2¼ or 4 × 5 glossy or matte b&w photos by mail for consideration. SASE. Reports 1 month. Credit line given. Buys one-time rights. Simultaneous submissions and previously published work OK.
Tips: "Ours is a nonprofit organization. We offer no pay, but photographers get nationwide exposure."

JAZZ TIMES, Suite 312, 8055 13th St., Silver Spring MD 20910. (301)588-4114. Managing Editor: David Zych. Assignment Editor: W. Royal Stokes. Monthly tabloid. Emphasizes jazz. Readers are jazz fans, record consumers, music industry. Circ. 56,000. Sample copy $3.
Photo Needs: Uses about 35 photos/issue; all supplied by freelance photographers. Needs performance shots, portrait shots of jazz musicians. Captions preferred.
Making Contact & Terms: Send 5 × 7 b&w prints by mail for consideration. SASE. "If possible, we keep photos on file till we can use them." Pays $25/b&w cover slide; $10/b&w inside photo. Pays $25/color photo. Pays on publication. Credit line given. Buys one-time or reprint rights.
Tips: "Send whatever photos you can spare. We keep them on file until we can use them. Name and address should be on back."

JEWISH EXPONENT, 226 S. 16th St., Philadelphia PA 19102. (215)893-5740. Managing Editor: Al Erlick. Weekly newspaper. Circ. 70,000. Emphasizes news of impact to the Jewish community. Buys 15 photos/issue. Photos purchased with or without accompanying mss. Pays $15-50/hour; $10-100/job; or on a per photo basis. Credit line given. Pays on publication. Buys one-time, all, first serial, first North American serial and all rights. Rights are open to agreement. Query with resume of credits or arrange a personal interview. "Telephone or mail inquiries first are essential. Do not send original material on speculation." Provide resume, business card, letter of inquiry, samples, brochure, flyer and tearsheets to be kept on file. SASE. Model release required "where the event covered is not in the public domain." Reports in 1 week. Free sample copy.
Subject Needs: On a regular basis, wants news and feature photos of a cultural, heritage, historic, news and human interest nature involving Jews and Jewish issues. Query as to photographic needs for upcoming year. No art photos. Captions are required.
B&W: Uses 8×10 glossy prints. Pays $10-35/print.
Color: Uses 35mm or 4×5 transparencies. Pays $10-75/print or transparency.
Cover: Uses b&w and color covers. Pays $10-75/photo.
Tips: "Photographers should keep in mind the special requirements of high-speed newspaper presses. High contrast photographs probably provide better reproduction under newsprint and ink conditions."

THE JOURNAL OF LIGHT CONSTRUCTION, (formerly New England Builder), Box 146, RR2, Richmond VT 05477. (802)864-5495. Art Director: Theresa Sturt. Monthly tabloid. Emphasizes light construction. Readers are architects, remodelers. Circ. 25,000. Sample copy free for 10x13 SAE with $2 postage; photo guidelines free with SASE.
Photo Needs: Uses 20 photos/issue; 5 supplied by freelancers. Needs photos of contruction work in progress. Model release preferred; captions required.
Making Contact & Terms: Query with samples; send unsolicited photos by mail for consideration; or provide resume, business card, brochure, flyer or tearsheets to be kept on file for possible future assignments. Uses 35mm, 2¼×2¼, 4×5 and 8×10 transparencies. SASE. Reports in 1 month. Pays $150/color cover photo; $20/color inside photo. Pays on acceptance. Credit line given. Buys first North American serial rights. Previously published work OK.
Tips: *New England Builder* has 12 themes for its issues. Covers reflect these themes. An editorial calendar is available by request."

*KANE COUNTY CHRONICLE, P.O. Box 190, St. Charles IL 60174. (708)584-3873. Chief Photographer: Robert Gerrard. Semi-weekly newspaper; scheduled to expand. Newspaper. General readership in Kane County, Illinois. Circ. 20,000. Estab. 1881. Sample copy 35¢.
Photo Needs: Uses 15-20 photos/issue; number of freelance photographers varies. Needs photos mostly of sports action, but also news/feature and food/fashion. "No unsolicited work is considered for publication." Photo captions required.
Making Contact & Terms: Arrange a personal interview to show portfolio. Provide resume, business card, brochure, flyer or tearsheets to be kept on file for possible assignments. Reports in 1-2 weeks. Pays $40/color cover photo; $25/b&w cover photo; $25/b&w inside photo. Pays on publication. Buys one-time rights.
Tips: In photographer's portfolio, wants to see "strictly photojournalism/newsphotography work, with an emphasis on clean, strong images, especially news and sports. No art/scenic or travel. Primary interest is b&w, but transparencies are also needed. This publication is a goldmine for a person who has the talent to make high-quality news and sports pictures in our area. Freelance and stringer work may also lead to full-time employment."

THE LIBERTY REPORT, 2020 Tate Springs Rd., Lynchburg VA 24501. (804)528-5051. Editor: Mark Smith. Monthly tabloid. Emphasizes conservative activism. Publication is geared toward the politically conservative audience. Circ. 600,000. Sample copy free, we supply envelope and postage.
Photo Needs: Uses 10-15 photos/issue; about 10% supplied by freelancers. Needs photos of newsmakers, politicians, political activists. Reviews photos with accompanying ms only. "We are always seeking photographers to attend rallies, demonstrations, litigations or public forums nationwide." Model release required; captions preferred.
Making Contact & Terms: Provide resume, business card, brochure, flyer or tearsheets to be kept on file for possible future assignments. SASE. Reports in 3 weeks. Pays $300/color cover photo; $75/b&w inside photo; $125/color inside photo. Pays on publication. Credit line given. Buys one-time rights. Previously published work OK.
Tips: Photographer should have "the willingness to get close to an event, avoiding the usual standard cover shots."

MARYLAND FARMER, VIRGINIA FARMER, GEORGIA FARMER, AND ALABAMA FARMER, Box 65120, Baltimore MD 21209. (301)377-0202. Contact: Photo Editor. Monthly tabloid. Emphasizes agriculture. Readers are agri-related. Circ. 80,000. Sample copy with 11×14 SAE and $1.50 postage.

Photo Needs: Uses about 45-60 photos/issue; 75% supplied by freelance photographers. Needs photos of agri-related subjects. "Prefer states that we publish for." Reviews photos with accompanying ms only. Model release and captions required.

Making Contact & Terms: Query with list of stock photo subjects. SASE. Reports in 1 month. Payment depends on assignment. Pays on publication. Credit line given. Buys one-time rights.

Tips: Composition, good to excellent exposures, and color and b&w film work are considered in reviewing a photographer's portfolio or samples.

MEDICAL TRIBUNE, 257 Park Ave. South, New York NY 10010. (212)674-8500. FAX: (212)982-4398. Photo Editor: John Griffin. Tri-monthly broadsheet. Emphasizes medical news. Readers are physicians. Circ. 150,000. Estab. 1960. Sample copy free with 8×11 SAE and $1 postage.

Photo Needs: Uses 20 photos/issue; 5 supplied by freelancers. Needs photos of doctors, medical devices to illustrate a specific story. Reviews photos with accompanying ms only. Model release preferred; captions required.

Making Contact & Terms: Provide resume, business card, brochure, flyer or tearsheets to be kept on file for possible future assignments. SASE. Reports in 1 week. Pays $50-100/b&w photo; $150-250/color photo; $75-100/hour; $200-350/day; $150-600/complete package. Pays on publication. Credit line given. Buys one-time rights; one-time rights include right to use in our foreign edition. Simultaneous submissions and previously published work OK.

Tips: Wants "versatility (close-up shots as well as over-all shots), good use of lighting, ability to shoot color. To contribute he/she should not be from NYC area. We do not hire photographers from here. Should be from areas in which we need photos ."

THE MERCURY, Hanover & King Sts., Pottstown PA 19464. (215)323-3000. Photo Editor: John Strickler. Daily and Sunday newspaper. Emphasizes daily news, features and sports, food and human interest. Circ. 31,000. Sample copy $1.00 (current issue) with 9×12 SAE and $1 postage.

Photo Needs: Uses about 20 photos/issue; 2 supplied by freelance photographers. Needs photos of animal or wildlife shots, how-to, travel, scenic, sports; and especially news and human interest. Captions required.

Making Contact & Terms: Submit portfolio for review; provide resume, business card, brochure, flyer or tearsheets to be kept on file for possible future assignments. SASE. Reports in 2 weeks. Pays $25-35/cover photo and $20/b&w inside photo. Pays on publication. Credit line given. Buys one-time and all rights, but will negotiate.

Tips: "Best chance for publication in our newspaper are photos from immediate circulation area (west of Philadelphia) or dramatic news photos from anywhere."

METRO, 410 S. First St., San Jose CA 95113. (408)298-8000. Managing Editor: Sharon Street. Alternative newspaper, weekly tabloid format, emphasizing news, arts and entertainment. Readers are adults ages 25-44, in Silicon Valley. Circ. 50,000. Sample copy free with SASE and 3 first-class stamps.

Photo Needs: Uses 15 photos/issue; 100% supplied by freelance photographers. Model release required for model shots; photo captions preferred.

Making Contact & Terms: Query with resume of credits, list of stock photos subjects; provide resume, business card, brochure, flyer or tearsheets to be kept on file for possible assignments. Does not return unsolicited material. Pays $75-100/color cover photo, $50-75/b&w cover photo, $25/b&w inside photo. Pays on publication. Credit line given. Buys one-time rights. Simultaneous submissions and previously published work OK "if outside of San Francisco/Bay area."

MISSISSIPPI PUBLISHERS, INC., 311 E. Pearl St., Jackson MS 39201. (601)961-7073. Photo Editors: Chris Todd and Dinah Rogers. Daily newspaper. Emphasizes photojournalism: news, sports, features, fashion, food and portraits. Readers are very broad age range of 18-70 years; male and female. Circ. 100,000. Sample copy for 11×14 SASE and 35¢.

Photo Needs: Uses 10-15 photos/issue; 1-5 supplied by freelance photographers. Needs news, sports, features, portraits, fashion and food photos. Special photo needs include food and fashion. Model release, photo captions required.

Making Contact & Terms: Provide resume, business card, brohcure, flyer or tearsheets to be kept on file for possible assignments. Uses 8×10 matte b&w and color prints; 35mm, 2¼×2¼, 4×5, 8×10 transparencies. SASE. Reports 1 week. Pays $50-100/color cover photo; $25-50/b&w cover photo; $25/b&w inside photo; $20-50/hour; $150-400/day. Pays on publication. Credit line given. Buys one-time or all rights; will negotiate with a photographer unwilling to sell all rights.

MODERN TIRE DEALER MAGAZINE, 341 White Pond Dr., Akron OH 44320. (216)867-4401. Editor: Lloyd Stoyer. Monthly tabloid, plus January, April and September special emphasis magazines. Circ. 36,000. Emphasizes the operation of retail and wholesale tire business. For independent tire dealers and tire company executives. Buys 15 photos/year. Sample copy for $2.50.

Subject Needs: Head shot, how-to, photo essay/photo feature, product shot and spot news. Captions required.

Accompanying Mss: Needs features on successful dealers and businesses with new twists in promotions. Seldom uses stories without good pictures. Pays $275-350/ms with photos. Writer's guidelines free on request. "We seldom use photographs except to illustrate our magazine articles. Exceptions would be unusual photos involving tires—such as burning scrap tires, tire feature shots, etc. In these cases we pay $50-100 per photo."

Specs: Prefers 35mm 8×10 b&w and color glossy prints and contact sheets but uses 35mm color transparencies. Uses b&w glossy contact sheet or color 35mm transparencies for cover.

Payment & Terms: Pays $5-150/job, $125-300 for text/photo package or on a per-photo basis. Pays $5-20/b&w photo. Pays $10-150/color photo. Pays $50-300/cover photo. Pays on acceptance. Buys all rights. Previously published work OK.

Making Contact: Send material by mail for consideration. SASE. Reports in 1 month.

MOM GUESS WHAT NEWSPAPER, 1725 L St., Sacramento CA 95814. (916)441-NEWS (6397). Editor: Linda Birner. Every two weeks tabloid. Gay newspaper that emphasizes political, entertainment, etc. Readers are gay and straight people. Circ. 21,000. Estab. 1978. Sample copy $1. Photo guidelines free with SASE.

Photo Needs: Uses about 8-10 photos/issue; all supplied by freelance photographers, 80% from assignment and 20% from stock. Model release and captions required.

Making Contact & Terms: Arrange a personal interview to show portfolio. Send 8×10 glossy b&w prints by mail for consideration. SASE. Pays $5-200/b&w photo; $10-15/hour; $25-50/day; $5-200 per photo/text package. Pays on publication. Credit line given. Buys one-time rights. Previously published work OK.

Tips: Prefers to see gay related stories/human rights/civil rights and some artsy stuff, photos in portfolio; *no* nudes or sexually explicit photos.

NATIONAL EXAMINER, 5401 NW Broken Sound Blvd., Boca Raton FL 33487. (407)997-7733. Editor: Lee Harrison. Photo Editor: Linda McKune. Weekly tabloid. General interest. Circ. 1,000,000.

Photo Needs: Uses 80-100 photos/issue; 90% supplied by freelancers. Needs general photos. Model release preferred; captions required.

Making Contact & Terms: Query with samples and list of stock photo subjects, send transparencies by mail for consideration. SASE. Pays $125/color and $50/b&w; payment varies according to page/hour/job. Pays on acceptance or publication. Buys one-time rights. Previously published work OK.

NATIONAL MASTERS NEWS, Box 2372, Van Nuys CA 91404. (818)785-1895. FAX: (818)989-7118. Editor: Al Sheahen. Monthly tabloid. Official world and US publication for Masters (age 35 and over) track and field, long distance running and race walking. Circ. 5,200. Estab. 1977. Sample copy free with 8×12 SAE and $1.05 postage.

Photo Needs: Uses 25 photos/issue; 20% assigned and 80% from freelance stock. Needs photographers of Masters athletes (men and women over age 35) competing in T&F events, LDR races or racewalking competitions. Captions preferred.

Making Contact & Terms: Send any size matte or glossy b&w print by mail for consideration, "may write for sample issue." SASE. Reports in 1 month. Pays $20/b&w cover photo; $7.50-10/inside b&w photo. Pays on publication. Credit line given. Buys one-time rights. Simultaneous submissions and previously published work OK.

NATIONAL NEWS BUREAU, 1318 Chancellor St., Philadelphia PA 19107. (215)546-8088. Editor: Andrea Diehl. Weekly syndication packet. Circ. 400 member publications. Emphasizes entertainment. Readers are leisure/entertainment-oriented, 17-55 years old.

Photo Needs: Uses about 20 photos/issue; 15 supplied by freelance photographers. Captions required.

Making Contact & Terms: Arrange a personal interview to show portfolio, query with sample, submit portfolio for review. Send 8×10 b&w prints, b&w contact sheet by mail for consideration. SASE. Reports in 1 week. Pays $50 minimum/job. Pays on publication. Credit line given. Buys all rights.

NEW YORK TIMES MAGAZINE, 229 W. 43 St., New York NY 10036. (212)556-7525. Photo Editor: Kathy Ryan. Weekly. Circ. 1.65 million.

Photo Needs: Uses 30 photos/issue; 28 supplied by freelance photographers (varies; some staff, some freelance). Model release and photo captions required.

Making Contact & Terms: Arrange a personal interview to show portfolio or drop off portfolio for review. SASE. Reports in 1 week. Pays $200/b&w page rate; $250/color page rate; $175/half page; $200-250/job (day rates); $550/color cover photo. Pays on acceptance. Credit line given. Buys one-time rights.

An unsolicited submission of this photo of long distance runner, Bill Rodgers, to the athletics-oriented tabloid, National Masters News, brought photographer Victor Sailer a ready sale. The publication bought one-time rights to the photo and used it as a cover shot. In particular, Sailer notes, being published in this official publication for world Masters in track sports gave him good "name exposure."

THE NEWS HERALD, Box 1940, Panama City FL 32444. (904)763-7622. Editor: Bill Salter. Chief Photographer: Vern Miller. Daily newspaper. Circ. 38,000.
Photo Needs: Uses dozens of photos/issue; uses limited number of freelance photos. Model release, photo captions preferred.
Making Contact & Terms: Send unsolicited photos by mail for consideration. Uses b&w prints or 35mm transparencies..SASE. Reports in 1 week. Pays $25/color cover photo; $10/b&w cover photo; $5/b&w inside photo. Pays on acceptance. Credit line given. Buys one-time rights.

*NEWS-GAZETTE, P.O. Drawer 2068, Kissimmee FL 32741. (407)846-7600. Photography Editor: Michael Dibari. Triweekly newspaper. Emphasizes local interests. Readers are all ages, all sexes and all occupations. Circ. 26,000. Sample copy for 25¢ with legal SASE and $2 postage.
Photo Needs: Uses 20 photos/issue; approx. one supplied by freelancer photographers. Needs photos of local interest only for Osceola County. Model release preferred. Photo captions required.
Making Contact & Terms: Send 35mm and 8×10 b&w prints by mail for consideration. Cannot return unsolicited material. Reports in 3 weeks. Pays on publication. Buys one-time rights.
Tips: "We are looking for *all* local interest for the Kissimmee/St. Cloud area."This includes Walt Disney World (EPCOT Center) and Sea World.

NORTHWEST MAGAZINE/THE OREGONIAN, 1320 SW Broadway, Portland OR 97201. (503)221-8235. Graphics Coordinator: Kevin Murphy. Sunday magazine of daily newspaper. Emphasizes stories and photo essays of Pacific Northwest interest. "Estimated readership of 1,000,000 is affluent, educated, upscale." Sample copy and photo guidelines available.
Photo Needs: Uses about 12-15 photos/issue; 4-6 supplied by freelance photographers. Needs photos "depicting issues and trends, travel, scenics, interiors and fashion. Thematic photo essays particularly encouraged." Model release and captions required.
Making Contact & Terms: Arrange a personal interview to show, or send portfolio. Returns unsolicited material on request. Reports in 2 weeks. Pays $150/page rate or $150/half day "assignment rate." Pays on acceptance. Credit line given. Buys one-time rights. All work accepted "on spec." Previously published work OK "but first-time rights in Pacific Northwest preferred."
Tips: Prefers to see "examples of color, showing range of style (portraits, editorial, landscape, interiors)."

NUMISMATIC NEWS, 700 E. State St., Iola WI 54990. (715)445-2214. Editor: Robert E. Wilhite. Weekly tabloid. Circ. 40,000. Emphasizes news and features on coin collecting. Photos purchased only on assignment. Buys 40 photos/year. Credit line given. Pays on publication. Buys all rights, but may reassign to photographer after publication. Phone or write for consideration. SASE.
Photo Needs: Spot news (must relate to coinage or paper money production or the activities of coin collectors). No photos of individual coins unless the coin is a new issue. Captions required.
Specs: Uses 5 × 7 b&w and color prints. Pays $5 minimum/b&w photo and $25 minimum/color photo. Pays $40 minimum/job or on a per-photo basis.
Accompanying Mss: Needs "documented articles relating to issues of coinage, medals, paper money, etc., or designers of same." Pays $30-100/ms.
Tips: "Devise new techniques for covering coin conventions and depicting the relationship between collectors and their coins."

OLD CARS WEEKLY, (formerly Old Cars Newspaper) 700 E. State St., Iola WI 54990. (715)445-2214. FAX: j(715)445-4087. Publisher: John Gunnell. Weekly tabloid. Circ. 85,500. Estab. 1971. *"Old Cars Weekly* is edited to give owners of collector cars information — both of a news and of a historical nature — about their cars and hobby." Photos used with or without accompanying ms, or on assignment.
Photo Needs: Uses 35 photos/issue, 20% assigned and 80% from freelance stock. Credit line given. Buys all rights, but may reassign to photographer after publication. Send material by mail for consideration. Provide business card and samples to be kept on file for future assignments. SASE. Reports in 2 weeks. Sample copy $1.50.
Subject Needs: Documentary, fine art, how-to (restore autos), human interest ("seldom — no 'I did it myself' restoration stories"); humorous, photo essay/photo feature and spot news (of occasional wrecks involving collector cars). Wants on a regular basis photos of old cars along with information. Captions preferred.
Specs: Uses 5 × 7 b&w glossy prints.
Accompanying Mss: Brief news items on car shows, especially national club meets.
Tips: Wants to see "clearness of photo and angle of photo. Subject must be cars from model year 1975 and older. Usually all photos, except good color slides/transparencies, are printed black and white. Do *not* send photos *without* a manuscript."

ON TRACK, Unit M, 17165 Newhope St., Fountain Valley CA 92708. (714)966-1131. Photo Coordinator: Pat Oxman. Bimonthly magazine. Emphasizes auto racing. Readers are auto racing enthusiasts. Estab. 1981. Sample copy $1.50. Photo guidelines free with SASE.
Photo Needs: Uses about 120 photos/issue; all supplied by freelance photographers. Needs photos of auto racing action and drivers. Special needs filled by assignment. Captions, dates, locality required.
Making Contact & Terms: Send 5 × 7 or 8 × 10 glossy b&w prints with borders; 35mm transparencies by mail for consideration. SASE. Reports in 1 month. Pays $10/b&w photo, $25-100/color photo. Pays on publication. Credit line given. Buys first North American serial rights. "Address photo submissions to the attention of Photo Coordinator."
Tips: In samples, wants to see that the photographer can "catch the news and story of a car race on film. Stay away from autofocus cameras, the cars move too fast. Our photos are moving toward action rather than static car shots. We're also seeing more creative photographs." Looks for "photos that complement our writers' styles; photos that add a human element to a mechanical subject. Get to know the subject. One needs to understand the sport in order to photograph it well. Try to shoot important events during a race — not just race cars going by. Look for relationships between drivers and cars and try to find excitement — it's harder than it seems."

PARENTS' CHOICE, A REVIEW OF CHILDREN'S MEDIA, Box 185, Newton MA 02168. (617)965-5913. Editor-in-Chief: Diana H. Green. Emphasizes children's media. Readers are parents, teachers, librarians and professionals who work. Sample copy $2.50.
Photo Needs: Uses photos occasionally. Needs "photos of parents and children; children's TV, books, movies, etc. and children participating in these media." Columns: Parents' Essay, Opinion, Profile uses photos of the author and the subject of interview. Model release not required; captions required.
Making Contact & Terms: Send sample photos. Arrange personal interview to show portfolio. Provide brochure, flyer and samples to be kept on file for future assignments. SASE. Pays on publication $30/photo. Credit line given.

THE PATRIOT LEDGER, 400 Crown Colony Dr., Quincy MA 02169. (617)786-7084. FAX: (617)786-7025. Photo Editor: Joe Lippincott. Estab. 1837. "Daily except Sunday" newspaper. General readership. Circ. 100,000. Photo guidelines free with SASE.
Photo Needs: Uses 15-25 photos/issue; most photos used come from freelance stock; some assigned.Needs general newspaper coverage photos — especially spot news and "grabbed" features from circulation area. Model release preferred; photo captions required.

Making Contact & Terms: Query with resume of credits. Cannot return material. Pays $15-75/b&w inside photo or more if material is outstanding and especially newsworthy, $10-15/hour. Pays on publication. Credit line given. Buys "negotiable" rights. Simultaneous submissions and previously published work OK "depending on time and place."

Tips: Looks for "diversity in photojournalism: use NPPA pictures of the year categories as guidelines. Dynamite grabber qualities: unique, poignant images properly and accurately identified and captioned witihich concisely tell what happened. We want images we're unable to get with staff due to immediacy of events, shot well and in our hands quickly for evaluation and possible publication. To break in to our publication call and explain what you can contribute to our newspaper that is unique. We'll take it from there, depending on the results of the initial conversation."

PC WEEK, 800 Boylston St., Boston MA 02199. (617)375-4000. Photo Editor: Ann Rahimi-Assa. Art Director: Thea Shapiro. Weekly tabloid. Emphasizes IBM PC's. Readers are IBM PC and PC compatible users. Sample copy available.

Photo Needs: Uses about 15-30 photos/issue; 25% supplied by freelance photographers. Needs photos of "business, PC's and users, and hires photographers to cover companies who are large volume users of PC's." Model release preferred.

Making Contact & Terms: Arrange a personal interview to show portfolio; provide resume, business card, brochure, flyer or tearsheets to be kept on file for possible future assignments. Does not return unsolicited material. Reports in 2 weeks. Payment varies. Pays on publication. Credit line given. Buys one-time rights.

Tips: Looks for "good candid, journalistic photography. Clear shots of computer products. Photographs should be crisp."

THE PRODUCE NEWS, 2185 Lemoine Ave., Fort Lee NJ 07024. (201)592-9100. Editor: Gordan Hochberg. Weekly tabloid. Estab. 1897. Circ. 10,000. For people involved with the fresh fruit and vegetable industry: growers, shippers, packagers, brokers, wholesalers and retailers. Needs feature photos of fresh fruit and vegetable shipping, packaging, growing, display, etc. Buys 5-10 photos annually, usually with articles only. Majority of photos submitted on assignment. Pays $8-10/b&w photo. Pays on publication. Reports in 2 weeks. SASE. Sample copy free with 10 × 13 SASE; $1.25 postage. Free photo guidelines.

B&W: Send 4 × 5 or larger glossy prints. Captions required.

Tips: "Nothing fancy—just good quality."

*QUEENS TRIBUNE, 46-25 Kissena Blvd. Flushing NY 11355. (718)7777. Executive Editor: David Oats. Weekly community newspaper. Emphasizes topics of interest to residents of Queens. Readers are females, ages 34-52, "home" audience. Circ. 92,500. Estab. 1970. Sample copy for $12/year with 9 × 12 SASE and 2 first class stamps.

Photo Needs: Uses 5 photos/issue; 35% supplied by freelance photographers. Needs photos of people and/or events. Photos purchased with accompanying ms only. Model release preferred. Photo captions required. Query with resume of credits. Provide resume, business card, brochure, flyer or tearsheets to be kept on file for possible assignments. SASE. Reports in 1-2 weeks. Pays for film and development. Pays on publication. Credit line given. Buys one-time rights.

*REGISTER CITIZEN, 190 Water St., Torrington CT 06790. (203)489-3121. Chief Photographer: John Murray. Daily newspaper. Covers all Northwestern Connecticut. Circ. 17,000.

Photo Needs: Uses 10-12 photos/issue. Less than 10% supplied by freelance photographers. Needs photos of spot news, fires, accidents and rescues. Special photo needs include spot news. Photo captions required.

Making Contact & Terms: "Call when have a 'hot' photo." Otherwise send 8 × 10 b&w prints. SASE. Reports that day. Payment varies. Pays on publication. Credit line given. Buys one-time rights.

Tips: "Be in the right place at the right time and have film in your camera."

*REVIEW PUBLICATIONS, 100 N.E. 7th St., Miami FL 33132. (305)347-6638. Chief Photographer: Andrew Itkoff. Daily newspaper. Emphasizes law, business and real estate. Readers are 25-55 yrs., average net worth of 750,000 dollars, male and female. Circ. 18,000. Estab. 1926. Sample copy for $1 with 9 × 11 SASE.

Photo Needs: Uses 8-15 photos/issue; 20-40% supplied by freelance photographers. Needs mostly portraits, however we use live news events, sports and building mugs. Photo captions "an absolute must".

Making Contact & Terms: Arrange a personal interview to show portfolio. Submit portfolio for review. Send 35mm, 8 × 10 b&w and color prints. Accepts all types of finishes. Cannot return unsolicited material. If used, reports immediately. Pays $85 for most photos; pays more if part of photo/text package. Credit line given. Buys all rights. Rights negotiable. Previously published work OK.

Close-up

Bob Sacha
News/Magazine Photographer
New York City

For freelance news/magazine photographer Bob Sacha, a good career strategy is like a three-legged table. "Technical ability, professionalism and creativity are three legs of a table: the stronger the legs, the stronger the table; and the taller the legs, the more the table is noticed," says the New York-based photographer, adding that "if one leg is weak, the table falls."

Photographers will find "fierce" competition in newspapers and magazines, says Sacha. "Anyone who owns a camera can be a photographer . . . and almost everyone owns a camera," he quips, noting that a four-legged strategy is often necessary to make it in the long run. "The fourth leg on that table would be a business sense. Everyone knows that with four legs, a table is even sturdier than with only three."

As Sacha sees it, photography and business are two different skills and one doesn't necessarily follow the other. "Most freelancers don't devote even a fraction of the time or interest to business that they do to shooting." Unlike being on staff, he explains, working as a freelancer requires a number of survival skills: marketing and self-promotion, pricing and negotiating, bookkeeping and billing, among others.

One of the more important business considerations, he points out, is protecting your copyright. "Think long and hard before selling the rights to your pictures," he says, noting that developing a sense for the future salability of your work is essential to successful freelancing. "I've resold photos for thousands of dollars. If I didn't hold the rights to those pictures, though, I would have never made a dime after the original assignment. Some publications want to own all rights. Try to find out why—then negotiate."

Similarly, says Sacha, freelance news photographers find more pressure on themselves to generate assignments than do staffers. This requires a keen sense for good photo stories and the ability to sell the ideas. "Proposing ideas is always a good way to get in the door with a newspaper, but the ideas have to be fresh and unique," he says, recommending that you always suggest subjects you know very well, from angles not already covered. "To be honest, good story ideas are rare, and especially if you're unknown, you run the risk of having a great idea but not being able to convince the publication that you can pull it off. That's where self-assigned ideas help. If you want to shoot a certain subject, then 'assign' yourself some picture stories about that subject to show you can handle the assignment. Also, stick close to home and close to what you know—it's cheaper and makes you an expert."

The 33-year-old Sacha started this way, shooting sports and local events for a small daily newspaper in upstate New York while still in high school. His first big step up came in stringing (freelancing) for United Press International through the Buffalo bureau. To this foundation he added a college degree in photojournalism and psychology, with summer intern work with the *Buffalo News* and *Newsday* in New York City. Then, until he returned to fulltime freelance work in 1982, he held staff positions with the *Philadelphia Inquirer* and ABC Broadcasting.

Being on staff certainly has its privileges, says Sacha. "It's like having a scholarship in college: you get paid to learn. There's always a paycheck at the end of the week, no matter how badly you might have screwed up that week. That is a double-edged sword, though. No matter how well you do, you usually receive the same check at the end of the week. If you're freelance and you screw up, you might not work for that client again. But if you do a great job, other people see it and call you. Take your choice: as a freelancer, the stakes are higher, but the rewards are greater too."

Whether you're on-staff or stringing, news photography presents an above average challenge. "Newspapers are mostly a young person's game," he says. "It takes tremendous stamina, physically and mentally, to work fulltime and do a good job at a newspaper. The hours are long, the equipment heavy and sometimes, the subjects don't cooperate. On the other hand, I see some very wise, older newspaper photographers who have a tremendous amount of experience and just *know* what will make a great picture. They make it look easy."

In spite of the apparent ease in news photography, Sacha observes, "there is no yellow brick road to success. An education is important, but many of the best people are self-educated and have an innate ability to see the world in a fresh way. Internships, too, can be helpful, but numerous accomplished photographers have interned in other fields that have helped them more than a photo internship."

As a case in point, Sacha recalls a key learning experience of his own. "When I applied to a college with a famous photography program, I met a cigar chomping photography teacher there who had his photographs from *National Geographic* (now one of Sacha's major clients) on his office wall. He asked me: 'Kid, do you want to be a photojournalist?' 'Yes,' I replied eagerly. 'Yes sir.' He looked at me and said, 'Well, let me tell you something: Don't go to this school. Get a liberal arts education and learn how to take pictures on the side. Taking pictures is easy. Thinking . . . that's the tough part. Work on that.'"

—Sam A. Marshall

Newspaper/magazine photographer Bob Sacha has worked both freelance and full-time with a number of newspapers since his first job as a sports/local events shooter with a small daily in upstate New York. Sacha points out that for stringers and staffers alike, "news photography presents an above average challenge." This photo, titled "Steam on Fifth Avenue," is a self-assignment shot which captures urban drama in high contrast.

Tips: In photographer's portfolio, looks for "a good grasp of lighting and composition; the ability to take an ordinary situation and make an extraordinary photograph. We work on daily deadlines so promptness is a must and extensive cutline information is needed."

ROLL CALL NEWSPAPER, Suite 107, 900 2nd St. NE, Washington DC 20002. (202)289-4900. FAX: (202)289-2205. Photo Editor: Laura Patterson. Semi-weekly newspaper. Emphasizes U.S. Congress and politics. Readers are politicians, lobbyists and congressional staff. Circ. 18,000. Estab. 1955. Sample copy free with 8½ × 11 SAE with $1 postage.
Photo Needs: Uses 20-30 photos/issue; up to 5 supplied by freelancers. Needs photos of anything involving current congressional issues, good or unusual shots of congressmen. Captions required.
Making Contact & Terms: Query with samples or list of stock photo subjects; send unsolicited photos by mail for consideration. Uses b&w 8 × 10 glossy prints; 35mm transparencies. Does not return unsolicited material. Reports in 1 month. Pays $25-50/b&w; $30-75/color (if cover); $50-75/hour or job. Pays on publication. Credit line given. Buys one-time rights. Simultaneous submissions OK.
Tips: "We're always looking for unique candids of congressmen; or political events." In reviewing photographer's samples wants to see good composition, pictures that tell a story and good use of light for newsprint. Should have knowledge of recognizing members of congress.

RUBBER AND PLASTICS NEWS, 1725 Merriman Rd., Akron OH 44313. (216)836-9180. Editor: Edward Noga. Weekly tabloid. Emphasizes rubber industry. Readers are rubber and plastic product makers. Circ. 17,000. Sample copy free.
Photo Needs: Uses 10-15 photos/issue. Needs photos of company officials, in-plant scenes, etc. to go with stories staff produces.
Making Contact & Terms: Query with samples. SASE. Reports in 2 weeks. Pays $25-200/b&w or color cover photo; $25-100/b&w or color inside photo. Pays on publication. Credit line given. Buys all rights; will negotiate with photographer unwilling to sell all rights. Simultaneous submissions OK.
Tips: Prefers to see "news photo; mood shots suitable for cover; business-related photos. Call us. We'd like to use more freelance photographers throughout the US and internationally, to produce photographs that we'd use in stories generated by our staff."

*THE SENTINEL, 1200 Gulf Breeze Pkwy., Gulf Breeze FL 32561. (904)934-1200. Publisher: Duane B. Cook. Weekly newspaper. Emphasizes local people. Readers are middle age and older, upper income. Circ. 10,000. Estab. 1960. Sample copy free with 9 × 12 SASE and 6 first class stamps.
Photo Needs: Uses 30-50 photos/issue; 50% supplied by freelance photographers. Needs photos of local people—scrapbook material.
Making Contact & Terms: Send b&w prints by mail for consideration. SASE. Reports in 1-2 weeks. Pays $5/b&w cover photo; $5/color inside photo. Pays on publication. Credit line given. Buys all rights, negotiable. Simultaneous and previously published work OK.
Tips: "Catch a local person doing something they would be proud to see in the local paper!"

SERVICE REPORTER, 651 W. Washington, Chicago IL 60606. (312)993-0929. Editorial Director: Steve Read. Monthly tabloid. Emphasizes heating, air conditioning, ventilating and refrigeration. Circ. 48,000. Sample copy $2.
Photo Needs: Uses about 12 photos/issue; no more than one supplied by freelance photographers, others manufacturer-supplied. Needs photos pertaining to the field of heating, air conditioning, ventilating and refrigeration. Special needs include cover photos of personnel installing and servicing. Model release and captions required.
Making Contact & Terms: Query with list of stock photo subjects; query on needs of publication. SASE. Reports in 2 weeks. Pays $50-100/color cover photo; $10/b&w and $25/color inside photo. Pays on publication. Credit line given. Buys one-time rights.

SINGER MEDIA CORP., INC., 3164 Tyler Ave., Anaheim CA 92801. (714)527-5650, 527-5651. FAX: (714)527-0268. Picture Editor: Donna Hollingshead. Newspaper syndicate (magazine, journal, newspaper, newsletter, tabloid). Emphasizes books and interviews. Circ. worldwide. Estab. 1940.
Photo Needs: Needs photos for book covers, celebrities, text features with transparencies (35mm, 2¼ × 2¼, 4 × 5). Reviews photos with accompanying ms only. Will use dupes only, cannot guarantee returns. No models.
Making Contact & Terms: Query with list of stock photo subjects. Reports in 3 weeks. 50:50 of all syndication sales. Pays after collection. Credit line given. Buys one-time rights. Previously published work OK.
Tips: "World wide mass market, text essential. Trend is toward international interest. Survey the market for ideas."

SKIING TRADE NEWS, 2 Park Ave. New York NY 10036. (212)779-5000. Editor: Isevlt Devlin. Tabloid published 8 times/year. Circ. 16,000. Emphasizes news, retailing and service articles for ski retailers. Photos purchased with accompanying ms or caption. Buys 2-6 photos/issue. Credit line given. Pays on publication. Buys one-time rights. Send material by mail for consideration. SASE. Reports in 1 month. Free sample copy with 12 × 24 SASE.
Subject Needs: Celebrity/personality; photo essay/photo feature ("if it has to do with ski and skiwear retailing"); spot news; and humorous. Photos must be ski related. Model release and captions preferred.
B&W: Uses 5 × 7 glossy prints. Pays $25-35/photo.
Tips: Uses 4 colors as well; prices vary.

SKYDIVING, Box 1520, DeLand FL 32721. (904)736-9779. Editor: Michael Truffer. Readers are "sport parachutists worldwide, dealers and equipment manufacturers." Monthly newspaper. Circ. 8,600. Sample copy $2; photo guidelines for SASE.
Photo Needs: Uses 12-15 photos/issue; 8-10 supplied by freelance photographers. Selects photos from wire service, photographers who are skydivers and freelancers. Interested in anything related to skydiving—news or any dramatic illustration of an aspect of parachuting.
Making Contact & Terms: Send by mail for consideration actual 5 × 7 or 8 × 10 b&w photos. SASE. Reports in 2 weeks. Pays on publication minimum $25 for b&w photo. Credit line given. Buys one-time rights. Simultaneous submissions (if so indicated) and previously published work (indicate where and when) OK.

SOCCER AMERICA, Box 23704, Oakland CA 94623. (415)528-5000. Editor-in-Chief: Lynn Berling. Managing Editor: Paul Kennedy. Weekly magazine. Circ. 25,000. Emphasizes soccer news for the knowledgeable soccer fan. "Although we're a small publication, we are growing at a very fast rate. We cover the pros, the international scene, the amateurs, the colleges, women's soccer, etc." Photos purchased with or without accompanying ms or on assignment. Buys 10 photos/issue. Credit line given. Pays on publication. Buys one-time rights. Query with samples. SASE. Previously published work OK, "but we must be informed that it has been previously published." Reports in 1 month. Sample copy and photo guidelines for $1 with 8½ × 11 SAE and 85¢ postage.
Subject Needs: Sport. "We are interested in soccer shots of all types: action, human interest, etc. Special subject needs include shots of national-level players emerging from youth ranks, shots of college action. Our only requirement is that they go with our news format." Captions required.
B&W: Uses 8 × 10 glossy prints. Pays $12 minimum/photo.
Cover: Uses b&w glossy prints. Pays $25 minimum/b&w photo, $75 minimum/color photo.
Accompanying Mss: "We are only rarely interested in how-to's. We are interested in news features that pertain to soccer, particularly anything that involves investigative reporting or in-depth (must be 'meaty') personality pieces." Pays 50¢/inch to $100/ms. Free writer's guidelines. SASE required.
Tips: "Our minimum rates are low, but if we get quality material on subjects that are useful to us we use a lot of material and we pay better rates. Our editorial format is similar to *Sporting News*, so newsworthy photos are of particular interest to us. If a soccer news event is coming up in your area, query us."

SOUTHERN MOTORACING, Box 500, Winston-Salem NC 27102. (919)723-5227. Associates: Greer Smith, Randy Pettitt. Editor/Publisher: Hank Schoolfield. Biweekly tabloid. Emphasizes autoracing. Readers are fans of auto racing. Circ. 18,000-19,000. Sample copy 75¢ postpaid.
Photo Needs: Uses about 10-15 photos/issue; some supplied by freelance photographers. Needs "news photos on the subject of Southeastern auto racing." Captions required.
Making Contact & Terms: Query with samples; send 5 × 7 or larger matte or glossy b&w prints; b&w negatives by mail for consideration. SASE. Reports in 1 month. Pays $25-50/b&w cover photo; $5-25/ b&w inside photo; $50-100/page. Pays on publication. Credit line given. Buys first North American serial rights. Simultaneous submissions OK.
Tips: "We're looking primarily for *news* pictures, and staff produces many of them—with about 25% coming from freelancers through long-standing relationships. However, we're receptive to good photos from new sources, and we do use some of those. Good quality professional pictures only, please!"

THE SPORTING NEWS, 1212 N. Lindberg Blvd., St. Louis MO 63132. (314)997-7111. Contact: Rich Pilling. Weekly tabloid. Emphasizes major league and minor league baseball, pro and college football, pro and college basketball, pro hockey and major sporting events in other sports. Readers are 18-80 years old, 75% male, sports fanatics. Circ. 700,000.
Photo Needs: Uses about 25 b&w photos/issue; 2-4 color photos for cover; all supplied by freelance photographers. Needs photos of athletes, posed or in action, involved in all sports covered by the magazine. Captions required.

Making Contact & Terms: Send 8×10 b&w glossy prints by mail for consideration. "35mm transparencies by special request." SASE. Pays $300/main color photo, $175/smaller color; $50/b&w inside photo; $350/day for assignments. Pays on publication. Credit line given for covers only. Buys one-time rights on covers; all rights on b&w photos.
Tips: "Once accepted, call for tips on upcoming needs."

SUN, 5401 NW Broken Sound Blvd., Boca Raton FL 33487. (407)997-7733, ext. 287. Photo Editor: Maureen Scozzaro. Weekly tabloid. Readers are housewives, college students, middle Americans. Sample copy free with extra large SAE and 44¢ postage.
Photo Needs: Uses about 60 photos/issue; 90% supplied by freelance photographers. Wants color spread material, varied subjects, action, car crashes, unusual pets, medical, human interest, inventions, sports action; 5 or 6 color shots for center spread for each issue; black and white human interest and offbeat pix and stories; and b&w celebrity photos. "Color, color, color. We use color of celebrity on cover each week. Also—we are always in need of interesting, offbeat color photos for the center spread." Model release and captions preferred.
Making Contact & Terms: Query with list of stock photo subjects. Send b&w 8×10 prints, 35mm transparencies, b&w contact sheet or b&w negatives by mail for consideration. "Contact by phone or send through mail at any time." SASE. Reports in 2 weeks. Pays $75/b&w cover photo; $200/color cover photo; $50/b&w inside photo; $125/color inside photo; and $50/text/photo package. Pays on publication. Buys one-time rights. Simultaneous submissions and previously published work OK.
Tips: "We are specifically looking for the unusual, offbeat, true stories and photos. We would suggest you send for a sample copy and take it from there."

SUNSHINE: THE MAGAZINE OF SOUTH FLORIDA, 101 N. New River Dr., Ft. Lauderdale FL 33301-2293. (305)761-4037. Editor: John Parkyn. Art Director: Kent H. Barton. "*Sunshine* is a Sunday newspaper magazine emphasizing articles of interest to readers in the Broward and Palm Beach Counties region of South Florida. Readers are "the 750,000 readers of the Sunday edition of the *Sun-Sentinel.*" Sample copy and photo guidelines free with SASE.
Photo Needs: Uses about 12-20 photos/issue; 30% supplied by freelance photographers. Needs "all kinds of photos relevant to the interests of a South Florida readership." Photos purchased with accompanying ms. Model release and captions preferred.
Making Contact & Terms: Query with samples; provide resume, business card, brochure, flyer or tearsheets to be kept on file for possible future assignments. SASE. Reports in 1 month. "All rates negotiable; the following are as a guide only." Pays $150-200/color cover photo; $25-75/b&w and $75-100/color inside photo; $100-150/color page; $250-1,000 for text/photo package. Pays within 1 month of acceptance. Credit line given. Buys one-time rights. Simultaneous and previously published submissions OK.
Tips: "Study the magazine and our guidelines."

TIMES JOURNAL, 6883 Commercial Dr., Springfield VA 22159. (703)750-8170. Director of Photography: Kate Patterson. Publishes weekly newspapers: *Federal Times, Defense News, Army Times, Navy Times, Air Force Times,* and *Space News.* Emphasizes military. Readers are military, federal government, defense contractors. Combined circ. 330,000.
Photo Needs: Uses approximately 40 photos/issue; 5% supplied by freelance photographers. Needs photos of military equipment, military people, military planes, ships, people for the news. Special needs include photos from worldwide relatives to military and their families. Model release and captions required.
Making Contact & Terms: Query with list of stock photo subjects. Provide resume, business card, brochure, flyer or tearsheets to be kept on file for future assignments. Does not return unsolicited material. Reports in 2 weeks. Pays $60/job. Pays on publication. Credit line given if requested. Buys one-time rights; paid extra if used at later date. Simultaneous submissions and previously published work OK.
Tips: In reviewing photos, consider quality, composition and news value. "Let us know you are out there and what you have to offer."

*THE TOWNSHIPS SUN, Box 28, Lennoxville, Quebec J1M 1Z3 Canada. Editor: Patricia Ball. Monthly magazine, tabloid format. Estab. 1972. Circ. 2,500. "Aimed at the rural, English-speaking people of Quebec. Emphasizes local history, agriculture, organic gardening, country living, ecology, wildlife and survival, both economically and politically." Buys up to 10 photos/issue.
Subject Needs: Animal, photo essay/photo feature, scenic, how-to, human interest, humorous, nature, still life and wildlife. "Quebec subjects only please. No nudes, urban scenes, or glamour or fashion shots." Captions preferred.

Specs: Uses 5×7 b&w matte prints. Uses b&w cover only; vertical format required.
Payment & Terms: Pays $35-50/text and photo package, $5-10/b&w, and $5-10/cover. Credit line given. Pays 1 month after publication. Buys one-time rights. Simultaneous submissions and previously published work OK.
Making Contact: Send material by mail for consideration. Usually works on assignment only. Uses 20% stock photos; 80% of photos assigned. Provide letter of inquiry, samples and tearsheets to be kept on file for future assignments. SAE and IRCs. Reports in 2-4 weeks. Sample copy $1.50.
Tips: "Photos must be very clear and clean. We publish on newsprint stock. We use seasonal photos on our cover or animals but very seldom people."

UNIVERCity, 1318 Chancellor St., Philadelphia PA 19107. (215)546-8088. Editor: Andy Edelman. College weekly free tabloid distributed on 33 Philadelphia area campuses. Circ. 82,000. Readers are college students. Sample copy $1.
Photo Needs: Uses about 20 photos/issue; 15 supplied by freelance photographers. Model release and captions required. "We use a lot of 'campus cheesecake' coed photos."
Making Contact & Terms: Arrange a personal interview to show portfolio, query with samples, submit portfolio for review. Send 8×10 b&w prints, b&w contact sheet by mail for consideration. SASE. Reports in 1 week. Pays $50 minimum/job. Pays on publication. Credit line given. Buys all rights. Simultaneous submissions OK.

UPSTATE MAGAZINE, Democrat and Chronicle, 55 Exchange Blvd., Rochester NY 14614. (716)232-7100. Editor: James Leunk. Photo Editor: Frank Breithaupt. Weekly Sunday (newspaper) magazine. Circ. 250,000. Estab. 1968. Emphasizes stories, photo layouts of interest to upstate New York and greater Rochester readers. Sample copy free with SASE.
Photo Needs: Uses about 10 photos/issue; very few supplied by freelance photographers. Needs specific photo story ideas; study the magazine for examples. Special needs include seasonal upstate material. Model release and captions required.
Making Contact & Terms: Send b&w prints and 35mm transparencies by mail for consideration. SASE. Reports in 1 month. Payment per cover and inside photo open. Pays $25/b&w photo or color photo. Pays on publication. Credit line given. Buys one-time rights.
Tips: "We're looking for photojournalists, people who can illustrate a story. All photos are done on assignment, and whenever possible our staff handles."

VELONEWS, Suite G, 5595 Arapahoe Ave., Boulder CO 80303. (303)440-0601. FAX: (303)444-6788. Managing Editor: Tim Johnson. Paid circ. 30,000. The journal of competitive cycling. Covers road racing and mountain bike events on a national and international basis. Photos purchased with or without accompanying ms. Credit line given, payment on publication for one-time rights. Send samples of work or tearsheets with assignment proposal. SASE. Reports in 3 weeks. Sample copy free with 9×12 SASE; $1.05 postage.
Subject Needs: Bicycle racing and nationally important races. Looking for action shots, not just finish-line photos with the winner's arms in the air. Captions and identification of subjects required. No bicycle touring.
B&W: Uses glossy prints. Pays $16.50-34.50.
Color: Transparencies only. Pays $33-69.
Cover: $50 for b&w, $100 for color.
Accompanying Mss: News, features, profiles. Query first. Pays $15-100.
Tips: We're a newspaper; photos must be timely.

*VENTURA COUNTY & COAST REPORTER, 1583 Spinnaker Dr., #213, Ventura CA 93001. (805)658-2244. Editor: Nancy S. Cloutier. Weekly tabloid newspaper. Circ. 35,000. Estab. 1977.
Photo Needs: Uses 12-14 photos/issue; 40-45% supplied by freelancer photographers. Photos purchased with accompanying ms only. Model release required.
Making Contact & Terms: Send sample b&w original photos. SASE. Reports in 1-2 weeks. Pays $10/b&w cover photo; $10/b&w inside photo. Pays on publication. Credit line given. Buys one-time rights. Simultaneous submissions OK.
Tips: "We prefer locally (Ventura County, CA) slanted photos."

*VOYAGER INTERNATIONAL, Box 2773, 7 Northgate, Westport CT 06880. (203)226-1647. Feature Editor: Lois Anderson. Consumer publication. Monthly newsletter. Emphasizes travel. Readers are middle age, upscale. Circ. 20,000. Estab. 1986. Samples copy for $4. Photo guidelines not available.

Photo Needs: Uses 10 b&w photos/issue; 20% supplied by freelancers. Needs photos of travel. Model release required; photo captions preferred.

Making Contact & Terms: Provide resume, business card, brochure, flyer or tearsheets to be kept on file for possible assignments; b&w prints. SASE. Reports in 3 weeks. Pays $25/b&w cover photo; $10/b&w inside photo. Pays on publication. Buys first N.A. serial rights. Does not consider simultaneous submissions or previously published work.

THE WASHINGTON BLADE, 8th Floor, 724 9th St. NW, Washington DC 20001. (202)347-2038. Managing Editor: Lisa M. Keen. Weekly tabloid. Estab. 1969. Circ. 27,300. For and about the gay community. Readers are gay men and lesbians; moderate to upper level income; primarily Washington, DC metropolitan area. Sample copy free with 8½ × 11 SAE plus 73¢ postage.

Photo Needs: Uses about 6-7 photos/issue; only out-of-town photos are supplied by freelance photographers. Needs "gay-related news, sports, entertainment events, profiles of gay people in news, sports, entertainment, other fields." Photos purchased with or without accompanying ms. Model release and captions preferred.

Making Contact & Terms: Query with resume of credits. SASE. Reports in 1 month. Provide resume, business card and tearsheets to be kept on file for possible future assignments. Pays $25/inside photo. Pays within 45 days of publication. Credit line given. Buys all rights when on assignment, otherwise one-time rights. Simultaneous submissions and/or previously published work OK.

Tips: "Be timely! Stay up-to-date on what we're covering in the news and call us up if you know of a story about to happen in your city that you can cover. Also, be able to provide some basic details for a caption (*Tell* us what's happening, too)." Especially important to "avoid stereotypes."

WDS FORUM, 1507 Dana Ave., Cincinnati OH 45207. (513)531-2222. Editor: Kirk Polking. Quarterly newsletter. Circ. 13,000. For students of Writer's Digest School; emphasizes writing techniques and marketing, student and faculty activities and interviews with freelance writers. Photos purchased with accompanying ms. Credit line given. Pays on acceptance. Buys one-time rights. Send material by mail for consideration. SASE. Simultaneous submissions and previously published work OK. Reports in 3 weeks. Free sample copy.

Photo Needs: Buys 1-2 photos/issue. Celebrity/personality of well-known writers. Photos purchased with accompanying ms. No photos without related text of interest/help to writing students. Model release preferred; captions required.

Making Contacts & Terms: Uses 8 × 10 glossy prints for inside or cover photos. Pays $15/photo. SASE. Reports in 3 weeks. Pays on acceptance. Credit line given. Buys one-time rights. Send material by mail for consideration. Simultaneous submissions and previously published work OK. Accompanying mss include interviews with well-known writers on how they write and market their work; technical problems they overcame; people, places and events that inspired them, etc. 500-1,000 words. Pays $10-25/ms.

Tips: "Get a sample if you are interested in working with our publication."

WESTART, Box 6868, Auburn CA 95604. (916)885-0969. Editor-in-Chief: Martha Garcia. Emphasizes art for practicing artists, artists/craftsmen, students of art and art patrons, collectors and teachers. Circ. 5,000. Free sample copy and photo guidelines.

Photo Needs: Uses 20 photos/issue, 10 supplied by freelance photographers. "We will publish photos if they are in a current exhibition, where the public may view the exhibition. The photos must be b&w. We treat them as an art medium. Therefore, we purchase freelance articles accompanied by photos." Wants mss on exhibitions and artists in the western states. Model release not required; captions required.

Making Contact & Terms: Send by mail for consideration 5 × 7 or 8 × 10 b&w prints. SASE. Reports in 2 weeks. Payment is included with total purchase price of ms. Pays $25 on publication. Buys one-time rights. Simultaneous and previously published submissions OK.

WESTERN FLYER, Box 98786, Tacoma WA 98498-0786. (206)588-1743. Editor: Dave Sclair. Biweekly tabloid. Circ. 35,000. General aviation newspaper for private pilots, homebuilders, and owner-flown business aviation. Readers are pilots, experimental aircraft builders. Sample copy $2.50; photo guidelines free with SASE (57¢ postage).

Photo Needs: Uses about 25-30 photos/issue; 40-50% supplied by freelance photographers. Needs photos of aircraft, destinations, aviation equipment. Photos purchased with accompanying ms only. Complete captions required for each photo.

Making Contact & Terms: Query with samples; "news photos may be sent unsolicited." Send b&w prints, color prints, contact sheets, negatives by mail for consideration. "Query first on slides." SASE. Reports in 2 weeks. Pays $10-25/b&w inside photo; $15-50/color photo; up to $3/column inch plus $10/ photo used for text/photo package. Credit line given. Buys one-time rights.

Tips: "Learn something about aviation subjects—we don't need or use pictures of air show teams flying maneuvers, airplanes flying overhead, people patting their airplanes affectionately, etc."

THE WESTERN PRODUCER, Box 2500, Saskatoon SK S7K 2C4 Canada. (306)665-3500. FAX: (306)653-1255. Editor: Keith Dryden. News Editor: Mike Gillgannon. Weekly newspaper. Circ. 134,000. Estab. 1923. Emphasizes agriculture and rural living in western Canada.
Photo Needs: Buys up to 10 photos/issue. Livestock, nature, human interest, scenic, rural, agriculture, day-to-day rural life and small communities. Captions required.
Making Contact & Terms: Send material by mail for consideration. SASE. Pays $15-25/photo, $35/color photo; $50-250 for text/photo package. Credit line given. Pays on acceptance. Buys one-time rights. SASE. Previously published work OK. Reports in 2 weeks. Free photo guidelines.
Tips: "Don't waste postage on abandoned, derelict farm buildings or sunset photos. We want modern scenes with life in them—people or animals, preferably both. Farm kids are always a good bet. Also seeks mss on agriculture, rural Western Canada, history, fiction and contemporary life in rural western Canada. Pays $50-200/ms."

*THE WICHITA EAGLE, 825 E. Douglas, Wichita KS 67201. (316)268-6468. Director of Photography: Joel Sartore. Daily newspaper. Emphasizes news. General readership. Circ. 190,000. Estab. 1900.
Photo Needs: Occasionally needs freelance submissions. "We have our own staff, so we don't require much freelance work. What little we do want, however, has to do with Kansas people." Model release preferred. Photo captions required.
Making Contact & Terms: Query with list of stock photo subjects. Submit portfolio for review. Provide resume, business card, brochure, flyer or tearsheets to be kept on file for possible assignments. Send 35mm b&w and color prints, or transparencies by mail for consideration. SASE. Reports in 3 weeks. Pays $50/color cover photo; $30/b&w cover photo. Pays on publication. Credit line given. Buys one-time rights. Simultaneous and previously published work OK.
Tips: In photographer's portfolio or samples, wants to see "20 or so images that show off what that shooter does best, i.e., news spots, fashion." To break in with newspapers, "work hard, shoot as much as possible, and *never* give up!"

WISCONSIN, The Milwaukee Journal Magazine, Box 661, Milwaukee WI 53201. (414)224-2341. Editor: Alan Borsuk. Weekly magazine. General-interest Sunday magazine focusing on the places and people of Wisconsin or of interest to Wisconsinites. Circ. 510,000. Free sample copy with SASE.
Photo Needs: Uses about 12 photos/issue; 1 supplied by freelance photographers. Needs "human-interest, wildlife, adventure, still life and scenic photos, etc." About 90% of photos are on assignment; very little stock. Model release and captions required.
Making Contact & Terms: Query with samples. SASE. Reports in 3 months. Pays $125/color cover photo; $25-50/b&w inside photo, $75/color inside photo. Pays on publication. Buys one-time rights, "preferably first-time rights."
Tips: "In reviewing samples, interesting people scenes, demonstrating technical proficiency and creativity, appeal to me most. We remain very Wisconsin-oriented."

YACHTSMAN, 2019 Clement Ave., Alameda CA 94501. (415)865-7500. Editor: Bill Parks. Monthly tabloid. Circ. 25,000. Emphasizes recreational boating for boat owners of northern California. Photos purchased with or without accompanying ms. Buys 5-10 photos/issue. Credit line given. Pays on publication. Buys all rights. Send material by mail for consideration. SASE. Simultaneous submissions or previously published work OK but must be exclusive in Bay Area (nonduplicated). Reports in 1 month. Sample copy $1.
Subject Needs: Sport; power and sail (boating and recreation in northern California); spot news (about boating); travel (of interest to boaters); and product shots. Model release and captions preferred.
B&W: Uses 5×7 or 8×10 glossy prints or screen directly from negatives. Pays $5 minimum/photo.
Cover: Uses color slides. Vertical (preferred) or horizontal format required. Pays $75 minimum/photo.
Accompanying Mss: Seeks mss about power boats and sailboats, boating personalities, locales, piers, harbors, and flora and fauna in northern California. Pays $1 minimum/inch. Writer's guidelines free with SASE.
Tips: Prefers to see action b&w, color slides, water scenes. "We do not use photos as stand-alones; they must illustrate a story. The exception is cover photos, which must have a Bay Area application—power, sail or combination; vertical format with uncluttered upper area especially welcome."

Newspapers and Newsletters/'90-'91 changes

The following newspapers and newsletters appeared in the 1990 edition of *Photographer's Market* but are not in the 1991 edition. Those publications firms whose editors or photo editors did not respond to our request for an update of their listings may not have done so for a variety of reasons—they may be out of business, for example, or they may be overstocked with submissions.

Boston Phoenix (did not respond)
Camera Bug/Video Bug (not reviewing work)
Connecticut Law Tribune (did not respond)
Corona-Norco Independent Daily Times (did not respond)
Daily Times (did not respond)
Feedstuffs Newspaper (did not respond)
FMI Issues Bulletin (did not respond)
Gifted Children Monthly (no longer published)
Gun Week (did not respond)
International Living (no longer in market)
Japan Economic Survey (moved; no forwarding address)
Jews for Jesus Newsletter (did not respond)
Parade (did not respond)
Personal Marketing Co. (did not respond)
Poetry Flash (did not respond)
Psychiatric News (did not respond)
Sailboat News (moved; no forwarding address)
Travel Weekly (did not respond)
Tundra Times (did not respond)
Weekly World News (did not respond)
Wesleyan Christian Advocate (not reviewing work)
Yankee Homes (did not respond)

Paper Products

While the word "publishing" immediately calls to mind images of books and magazines, photographers will find that the paper products industry expands greatly on the definition. Posters and calendars, postcards and greeting cards, framing prints and wall decor, stationery and gift materials . . . all of these products present photographers with numerous publishing opportunities.

Unlike other segments of publishing, this industry is relatively narrow in the total number of companies. Nonetheless, it is quite prosperous, with annual sales in the range of several billion dollars. Many of the larger companies have staff photographers for routine assignments, but also look to freelancers to supply images. Usually, this is in the form of stock images, and images are especially desirable if they are of unusual subject matter or remote scenic areas for which assignments—even to staff shooters—would be too costly. Freelancers are usually offered assignments once they have established a track record with a company and demonstrate a flair for certain techniques, subject matters or locations. Also, smaller companies are more receptive to working with freelancers, though they are less likely to assign work because of smaller budgets for photography.

The pay in this market can be quite lucrative if you can provide the right image at the right time for a client desperately in need of it, or if you develop a working relationship with one or a few of the better paying markets. You should be aware, though, that one reason for higher rates of payment in this market is that these companies may want to buy all rights to images. With changes in the copyright law (see Copyright and Work for Hire article, on page 26), many companies are more willing to negotiate sales which specify all rights for limited time periods or exclusive product rights rather than complete surrender of copyright.

Another key consideration is that an image with good market value can effectively be taken out of the market during the selection process. Many paper products companies work on lead times of up to two years before products are ready to market. It can be weeks, months or as much as a year before they report to photographers on their interest in using their images. In addition, some companies will pay only on publication or on a royalty basis after publication. For these reasons as well as the question of rights, you may want to reconsider selling images with high multiple resale potential in this market. Certainly, you will want to pursue selling to companies which do not present serious obstacles in these ways or which offer exceptionally good compensation when they do.

As with other markets, paper products is rapidly becoming a competitive field in which many accomplished professionals are becoming well established. Accordingly, companies expect to see work that is high quality and that meets their needs very closely. One way to study their needs is to look over various paper products in card and gift shops, bookstores and other specialty stores. Another is to read through trade publications such as *Greetings* magazine for news of creative and business trends; public libraries are a good place to find these publications.

One tendency within this market which photographers should also keep in mind is varying degrees of professionalism among the companies. For instance, some smaller companies can be a source of headaches in a number of ways, including failing to report in a timely manner on submissions, delaying return of submissions or using images without authorization. This sometimes happens with the seemingly more established companies, too, though it's less common. Typically, many smaller companies have started as one- or two-person operations, and not all have acquired adequate knowledge of industry practices which are standard among the more established firms.

Since smaller firms usually offer the freelancer more opportunity in terms of breaking in and learning the industry, it's best not to write them off entirely but study them sufficiently before doing business with them. An excellent resource for studying companies both large and small is the Greeting Card Association, which publishes an annual directory of paper products companies. Contact the Association at: Suite 615, 1350 New York Ave. NW, Washington DC 20005. Phone: (202)393-1778.

After your initial research, query to the companies you are interested in working with and send a stock photo list. Since these companies receive large volumes of submissions, they often appreciate knowing what is available rather than actually receiving it. This kind of query can lead to future sales even if your stock inventory doesn't meet their needs at the time because they know they can request a submission as their needs change. Some listings in this section advise sending quality samples along with your query while others specifically request only the list. As you plan your queries, it's important that you follow their instructions. It will help you establish a better rapport with the companies from the start.

Many aspects of the professionalism and creativity necessary for success in the paper products market are explored in more detail in a special interview in this section. To learn more about the market from a leader in the industry, read the Close-up interview with Carol Gibson of Hallmark Cards, Inc., on page 236.

A&A CREATIONS, Box 444, Westville NJ 08093. (609)853-5252. FAX: (609)853-1739. President: Bob Steen. Estab. 1980. Postcards, posters, framing prints and wall decor. Publishes and frames novelty prints. Makes 50-75 assignments/year.
Subject Needs: "We need material that appeals to teenagers and young men and women. Of particular interest are sexy girls and guys in novel and humorous settings. We also use cars, animals and humorous photos."
Specs: Uses 35mm transparencies.
Payment & Terms: Pays $100 minimum/color photo. Pays $250 for one time use. Pays for exclusive rights. Pays % of sales. Pays on acceptance or on a royalty basis. Credit line can be arranged. Buys one time rights, exclusive product rights and all rights.. Model release required; captions preferred.
Making Contact: Arrange a personal interview to show portfolio, send unsolicited photos by mail for consideration. Photo guidelines free upon request. Interested in stock photos. "We buy year round." SASE. Reports in 2 weeks. Simultaneous submissions and previously published work OK.
Tips: "We are interested in imaginative photos that are humorous or different in an offbeat way. Humor is most important."

ADVANCED GRAPHICS, 982 Howe Rd., Martinez CA 94553. (415)370-9200. FAX: (415)370-9623. Photo Editor: Steve Henderson. Estab. 1984. Provides posters, note cards, greeting cards, post cards. Buys 100-200 photos/year; gives 10-15 assignments/year. Photos used in posters.
Subject Needs: Subject matter includes wildlife and scenic, tigers, lions, dogs, cute cats, celebrities, sunsets, Indians, horses, still life, African and North American wildlife. Black and white scenics.
Specs: Uses 35mm, 2¼×2¼, 4×5, and 8×10 transparencies. "Bigger is better."
Payment & Terms: Pays $50-300/photo b&w and color. Credit line given. Buys one-time and exclusive product rights.
Making Contact: Send unsolicited photos by mail for consideration, submit portfolio for review. Interested in stock photos. SASE. Reports in 6 weeks.
Tips: Needs wildlife, white and orange tigers, foot prints on the beach with sunset, etc., still life, kids room subjects. "Submit, submit, submit. Looking for that 'something new & hot.'" Looks for "nice moods, sharp focus, popular subject, unusual shots and creative work." Needs photos of contemporary florals as well as all kinds of other contemporary photographs. To break in, "Get acquainted with what A.G. has done and what the market wants give us ideas be creative."

AFRICA CARD CO., INC., Box 91, New York NY 10108. (212)725-1199. President: Vince Jordan. Specializes in all occasion cards. Buys 25 photos annually. Call to arrange an appointment, query with resume of credits, or submit material by mail for consideration. Submit seasonal material 2 months in advance. Buys all rights. Submit model release with photo. Reports in 6-10 weeks. SASE.
Color: Send 35mm or 2¼×2¼ transparencies, or 5×7 glossy prints. Pays $15 minimum.
Tips: "Do an assortment of work and try to be as original as possible."

"When an eagle comes roaring in, you just aim your camera and try to get the best shot you can," says photographer Alan Carey. This image, which was purchased by Advanced Graphics and reproduced as a high-gloss, four-color poster, is one of several eagle shots which the Bozeman, Montana-based photographer has successfully marketed to magazines, book publishers and paper products companies. Carey explains that he was looking for a national poster distributor to help market a poster he had already produced when he discovered Advanced Graphics. "The company suggested producing the poster themselves and also ended up buying another 2 or 3 images for about $250 apiece."

*AGENT ANDY, 221 Orient Way, Lyndhurst NJ 07071. (201)933-8098. President: Andrew Abrams. Estab. 1981. Specializes in all of the following: greeting cards and calendars, post cards, posters, framing prints, stationery, gift wrap, playing cards and wall decor. Number of freelance photos bought/ assigned annually varies.

Subject Needs: Wide variety of subject matter.

Specs: Specifications for material submitted varies depending on product.

Payment & Terms: Pays in royalties on sales: 6-10%. Pays royalty advance, then paid quarterly royalties. Credit line given. Rights purchased are for term of contract.

Making Contact: Query with samples. Accepts seasonal material any time. SASE. Reports on queries or photos only if interested. Simultaneous submissions and previously published work OK. No guidelines.

Tips: In photographer's samples, "interested in conceptual work that leads to a series that can be applied to a line of products, i.e., greeting cards, calendars, etc."

ALASKA WILD IMAGES, Box 13149, Trapper Creek AK 99683. (907)733-2467. Editorial Director: Rollie Ostermick. Estab. 1976. Specializes in greeting cards, postcards and posters. Minimum of five freelance photos assigned annually.

Subject Needs: Alaskan and Canadian wildlife and wilderness. Does not want non-Alaska/Canadian material.

Specs: Uses 35mm, 2¼ × 2¼, or 4 × 5 transparencies.

Payment & Terms: Pays $75 and up/color photo. Pays on publication. Credit line given. Buys exclusive product rights. Captions preferred.

Making Contact: Interested in stock photos. Query with list of stock photo subjects. SASE. Reports in 1 month. Simultaneous submissions and previously published work OK. Photo guidelines free with SASE.

Tips: Looking for "dramatic close-ups of wildlife, wildflowers, awesome scenics especially with pleasant mood lighting. We print primarily once a year and contact photographers to request submissions and to discuss actual needs prior to this time."

AMBER LOTUS DESIGNS, 1241 21st St., Oakland CA 94607. (415)839-3931. FAX: (415)839-0954. Contact: Jerry Horovitz. Photos used for calendars, cards and book covers. Buys varying number photos annually.

Subject Needs: Innovative approaches to art, science, culture and nature.

Specs: Uses color and b&w transparencies; no special requirements.

Payment & Terms: Payment negotiated. Credit line given. Rights negotiated; no competing uses for images published. Simultaneous submissions and previously published work OK.

Making Contact: Query with samples, send unsolicited photos by mail for consideration. Occasionally interested in stock photos. SASE. Reports in 6 weeks.

Tips: In reviewing a photographer's work Horovitz looks for "unusual insight." To break in, "submit broad selection of work that shows your style. Think in terms of a theme for 12 calendar shots. Images should have enough depth to hold interest for a whole month."

*AMERICAN ARTS & GRAPHICS, INC., 10915 47th Avenue W., Everett WA 98204. (206)353-8200. Estab. 1948. Licensing Manager: Shelley Pedersen. Estab. 1948. Specializes in posters. Buys 25-30 photos/year.

Subject Needs: Humorous, cute animals, exotic sports cars, male and female models (not too risque), some scenic. Images that would be appealing to our 12-20 year-old poster market.

Specs: Uses 2¼ × 2¼, 4 × 5 transparencies.

Payment & Terms: Pays an advance of $500-1,000, with royalties on sales of 10¢ per poster. Pays on acceptance. Credit line given. Model release required.

Making Contact: Query with samples; contact by phone to request guidelines and catalog. Interested in stock photos. Submit seasonal material 5 months in advance. SASE. Reports in 2 weeks. Simultaneous submissions and previously published work OK (if not posters). Photo guidelines free with SASE.

Tips: There has been an increase in the use of black & white photography reflecting moods or emotions (sad, romantic, playful, etc.). We find that the use of a caption with a good, expressive photo image often works well to create a successful poster. Since our market is mainly in the teen age group we are looking for images that age group would put on their bedroom walls and doors."

ARPEL GRAPHICS, Box 21522, Santa Barbara CA 93121. (805)965-1551. President: Patrick O'Dowd. Estab. 1981. Specializes in note cards, calendars, postcards, posters, and books. Clients include: retail, zoos and national parks. Buys 150 freelance photos/year. Uses nature/wild animal imagery.

Subject Needs: "Product lines are developed by artist not by subject, so coverage is very broad with most all genre of photography included." Uses 35mm, 2¼ × 2¼, 4 × 5 and 8 × 10 transparencies. Royalty and other payments negotiated by artist. Credit line given. Buys one-time rights. Model release and captions required.

Making Contact: Arrange a personal interview to show portfolio; query with resume of credits; provide resume, business card, brochure, flyer or tearsheets to be kept on file for possible future assignments. "SASE required for reply." Solicits photos by assignment. Reports in 1 month. Previously published work OK.

Tips: "Photographers interested in submitting work for review by *Arpel* should study the existing line carefully. We generally look for artists who have already established themselves in their field and have solid archives of work to draw upon. In order to more fully do each artist justice, we usually work with

 The asterisk before a listing indicates that the market is new in this edition. New markets are often the most receptive to freelance submissions.

a limited number of artists in each genre of photography." Return postage and mailer must be provided with all work sent to *Arpel Graphics* for review.

*ART RESOURCE INTERNATIONAL LTD., 98 Commerce Rd., Stamford CT 06902-4506. (203)967-4545. Vice President: Robin Bonnist. Estab. 1980. Specializes in posters and fine art prints. Buys 500 photos/year.
Subject Needs: All types but does not wish to see regional.
Specs: Uses transparencies: 35mm, 4×5, 8×10.
Payments & Terms: Pays $3-250 per photo; Royalties on sales: $1-10. Pays on publication. Credit line given if required. Buys all rights; exclusive product rights. Model release required; photo captions preferred.
Making Contact: Send unsolicited photos by mail for consideration. Submit portfolio for review. Must send SASE for return. We solicit photos by assignment only. We are interested in stock photos. Accepts seasonal material anytime. SASE. Reports in 1 month. Simultaneous submissions and previously published work OK. Photo guidelines free with SASE.
Tips: Looks for "new and exciting material; subject matter with universal appeal."

CAROLYN BEAN PUBLISHING, LTD., 2230 W. Winton Ave., Hayward CA 94545. Creative Director: Andrea Axelrod. Specializes in greeting cards and stationery. Buys 50-100 photos/year for the Sierra Club Note card and Christmas card series and new line of ASPCA cards.
Subject Needs: Sierra Club—wilderness and wildlife; ASPCA—cats, dogs, puppies, kittens.
Specs: Uses 35mm, 2¼×2¼, 4×5, etc., transparencies.
Payment & Terms: $200/color photo. Credit line given. Buys exclusive product rights; anticipates marketing broader product lines for Sierra Club and may want to option other limited rights. Model release required.
Making Contact: Submit by mail. Interested in stock photos. Prefers to see dramatic wilderness and wildlife photographs "of customary Sierra Club quality." Provide business card and tearsheets to be kept on file for possible future assignments. Submit seasonal material 1 year in advance; all-year-round review. Publishes Christmas series December; everyday series January and May. SASE. Reports in 1 month. Simultaneous submissions and previously published work OK.
Tips: "Send only your best—don't use fillers."

BEAUTYWAY, Box 340, Flagstaff AZ 86002. (602)779-3651. President: Kenneth Schneider. Specializes in postcards, note cards and posters. Estab. 1979. Uses 300-400 freelance photos/year (fee pay and joint venture). Joint Venture is emphasized and is a program within Beautyway in which the photographer invests in his own images and works more closely in overall development. Through Joint Venture, photographers may initiate new lines or subjects with Beautyway which emanate from the photographer's strongest images.
Subject Needs: (1)Nationwide landscapes, emphasizes subjects of traveler interest and generic scenes of sea, lake and river. (2) Animals, birds and sealife, with particular interest in young animals, eyes and interaction. (3) Air, water and winter sports, as well as hiking, fishing and hunting. (4) The most important attractions and vistas of major cities, emphasizing sunset, storm, cloud and night settings.
Specs: All transparency formats OK. Ship in protective sleeves with photographer name and title on frame. Model releases required. Pays $30 per each 2400 units printed.
Making Contact: Query with samples, stock list and statement of interests or objectives. SASE. Previously published work OK if not potentially competitive. First report averages two weeks, others vary.
Tips: Looks for "very sharp photos with bright colors and good contrast. Subject matter should be easily identified at first glance. We seek straightforward, basic scenic or subject shots. Obvious camera manipulation such as juxtaposing shots or unnatural filter use is almost always rejected. When submitting transparencies, the person's name, address and name and location of subject should be upon each transparency sleeve. All transparencies should be in protective sleeves."

BERLIN PUBLICATIONS, INC., Box 283, Overland Park KS 66201. (913)262-6191. FAX: (913)268-5995. President: Margaret Berlin. Specializes in calendars and posters including "Flying High—Naval Aviators Calendar," "Thunderbirds—America's Team," and "Blue Angels—Heroes of the Sky," "Silent Service—Submarines of the Fleet" among others.
Subject Needs: Naval aviators, Thunderbirds, Blues Angels, military aircraft subs, ships and related material.
Payment & Terms: Pays on publication. Credit line given. Rights purchased are negotiable. Model release required; captions preferred.
Making Contact: Provide resume, business card, brochure, flyer or tearsheets to be kept on file for possible future assignments. Interested in stock photos. Does not return unsolicited material. Reports in 1 month. Simultaneous submissions and previously published work OK.

Tips: "I'm looking for good lighting skills in outdoor-on-location aircraft shots, and the ability to shoot human models attractively; knowledge of the military complex, experience with the rules and regulations on military bases."

BOKMON DONG COMMUNICATIONS, Box 75358, Seattle WA 98125. (206)364-0882. Photo Editor: Jean Haner. Specializes in greeting cards. Estab. 1981.
Subject Needs: "The subject matter is not as important as the treatment. We are looking for a strong, original image that creates a mood and evokes positive feelings. It is essential that the photograph be unusual and innovative in style. A good balance of foreground and background interest, strong color, composition, and lighting are important. Avoid cliches; no pictures of people. Special needs for 1990 include animals or flowers in uncommon situations."
Specs: Uses any size transparencies.
Payment & Terms: Payment is negotiable; depends on purchase, $150 minimum. Pays on publication. Credit line given. Buys one-time and exclusive product rights. Model release and captions required.
Making Contact: Send SASE for photographer's guidelines. For a sample card, send a 5 × 7 or larger SASE and include $1 in loose postage stamps (don't send cash or checks). Interested in stock photos. Submit seasonal material 8-12 months in advance. Reports in 2 weeks on queries; 2 months on photos. Simultaneous and previously published submissions OK "but not if submitted, published or sold to another card publisher."
Tips: "The photographer must remember the function of a greeting card—to communicate positive feelings from one person to another. The image must create a mood and have strong visual impact. The kinds of photographs we are looking for are ones that: you can recall without having to look through your files; people remember you by; are hanging on your walls." To break in, "be persistent. Study market to see what is selling. Keep submitting with our needs in mind. Avoid copying previously published material."

BRAZEN IMAGES INC., 269 Chatterton Pky., White Plains NY 10606. (914)949-2605. FAX: (914)683-7927. President/Art Director: Kurt Abraham. Estab. 1981. Specializes in greeting cards. Buys 50 photos annually.
Subject Needs: We publish adult sexually-oriented greeting cards with a humorous edge. We lampoon and parody sexual situations, psychological hang-ups and taboos.
Specs: Uses glossy b&w and color prints; 35mm, 2¼ × 2¼, 4 × 5 and 8 × 10 transparencies, and b&w and color contact sheets.
Payment & Terms: Pays $100-150/b&w and color photo. Pays on publication. Credit line given "if wanted." Buys one-time rights. Model release required.
Making Contact: Query with samples, send unsolicited photos by mail for consideration, submit portfolio for review. Interested in stock photos. Material may be submitted "anytime. We go to press once a year. We store images until that time. If you miss one printing, you'll make the next. Press time is April/June." Reports in 1 month. Simultaneous submissions and previously published work OK "as long as it is not greeting cards." Photo guidelines sheet free with SASE.
Tips: To break in, "just send the work . . . it speaks for itself. Wants to see a sense of humor in samples and *not* impatient or pushy. We are looking for sexually explicit photography with either a humorous, editorial or situational bent. Nudity is required. We also have a specific need for erotic seasonal photos, especially for Christmas. Try to understand the limitations of our business—we are not Hallmark, we are a small company with a limited market."

*BRIGHT OF AMERICA, 300 Greenbriar Rd., Summersville WV 26651. (304)872-3000. Art Directors: Penny Casto, James Pikaart and Tony Raffa. Specializes in calendars, posters and placemats. Uses freelancers once or twice a year to develop poster and calendar line.
Specs: Uses 35mm and 4 × 5 transparencies. "Four by five format is preferred, but will use 35mm if subject matter is strong enough."
Payment & Terms: "We purchase reproduction rights on a two-year, non-exclusive contract. Usual fee for poster usage would be $300-600, calendar usage, $200-400." Credit line given. Buys one-time rights and all rights (work-for-hire). Model release required.
Making Contact: Query with samples; query with list of stock photo subjects; provide resume, business card, brochure, flyer or tearsheets to be kept on file for possible future assignments. "We will solicit transparencies by category/subject matter." Solicits photos by assignment only. SASE. "Reports if interested and have immediate need right away. Otherwise we will place samples in active files."

CATCH AMERICA, INC., 32 South Lansdowne Ave., Lansdowne PA 19050. (215)626-7770. Contact: Michael Markowicz. Estab. 1988. Specializes in post cards and posters.
Subject Needs: Contemporary.
Specs: Uses 8×10 b&w prints and 35mm transparencies.
Payment & Terms: Pays quarterly or monthly on sales. Credit line given. Rights purchased vary, usually exclusive. Model release required; captions preferred.
Making Contact: Query with samples; or send unsolicited photos by mail for consideration. SASE.

CLASS PUBLICATIONS, INC., 71 Bartholomew Ave., Hartford CT 06106. (203)951-9200. Contact: Leo Smith. Specializes in posters. Buys 50 photos/year.
Subject Needs: Creative photography, especially humorous, also James Dean.
Specs: Uses b&w and color prints, contact sheets, negatives; 35mm, 2¼×2¼, 4×5 and 8×10 transparencies.
Payment & Terms: Pays per photo or royalties on sales. Pays on acceptance or publication. Credit line sometimes given. Buys one-time and exclusive poster rights. Model release and captions preferred.
Making Contact: Query with samples; submit portfolio for review. Interested in stock photos. SASE. Reports in 2 weeks. Simultaneous submissions and previously published work OK.
Tips: Looks for "creativity that would be widely recognized and easily understood."

*ELDERCARDS, INC., P.O. Box 202, Piermont NY 10968. (914)359-7137. President: Steve Epstein. Estab. 1983. Specializes in greeting cards, calendars, post cards, posters, stationery, gift wrap. Buys 20-30 photos/year.
Subject Needs: Humorous, nature, children, romantic, sexy women, sports and cars; black & white as well as color. No religious.
Specs: Uses any size glossy or matte b&w or color prints; 35mm, 2¼×2¼ and 4×5 transparencies; b&w or color contact sheets; b&w or color negatives.
Payment & Terms: Pays $50/b&w or color photo. Pays on acceptance. Credit line given. Buys exclusive product rights. Model release required.
Making Contact: Query with samples; query with list of stock photo subjects; send unsolicited photos by mail for consideration. Interested in stock photos. Submit seasonal material 3-6 months in advance. SASE. Reports in 2 weeks. Previously published work OK. Photo guidelines not available.
Tips: In photographer's samples, wantsd to see humorous treatments. Children in innocent yet loving poses; adults in less innocent, lightly risque loving poses. No 'hard core' please."

FLASHCARDS, INC., 781 W. Oakland Park Blvd., Fort Lauderdale FL 33311. (305)467-1141. Photo Researcher: Micklos Huggins. Estab. 1980. Specializes in postcards, greeting cards, notecards and posters. Buys 500 photos/year.
Subject Needs: Humorous, human interest, animals in humorous situations, nostalgic looks, Christmas material, valentines, children in interesting and humorous situations. No traditional postcard material; no florals or scenic. "If the photo needs explaining, it's probably not for us."
Specs: Uses any size color or b&w prints, transparencies and color or b&w contact sheets.
Payment & Terms: Pays $100 for exclusive product rights. Pays on publication. Credit line given. Buys exclusive product rights. Model release required.
Making Contact: Query with sample; send photos by mail for consideration; or provide resume, business card, brochure, flyer or tearsheets to be kept on file for possible future assignments. SASE. Interested in stock photos. Submit seasonal material 8 months in advance. Reports in 3 weeks. Simultaneous and previously published submissions OK. Photo guidelines free with SASE.

FREEDOM GREETINGS, 1619 Hanford St., Levittown PA 19057. (215)945-3300. FAX: (215)547-0248. Vice President: Jay Levitt. Estab. 1969. Specializes in greeting cards. Buys 200 freelance photos/year.
Subject Needs: General greeting card type photography of scenics and stills, etc., and black ethnic people.
Specs: Uses larger than 5×7 color prints; 35mm and 2¼×2¼ transparencies.
Payment & Terms: Payment negotiable, typically pays $100-225/color photos. Pays on acceptance. Model release required. "Looking for exclusive rights only."
Making Contact: Query with samples. Submit seasonal material 1½ years in advance. SASE. Reports in 1 month. Simultaneous submissions OK. Photo guidelines free on request.
Tips: "Keep pictures bright—no 'soft touch' approaches. Having difficult time finding black ethnic photos. Willing to pay premium for fine quality greeting card photos."

*FREEZEFRAME GREETING CARD CO., 36 N. Moore St., Suite 6W, New York NY 10013. (212)966-3852. Partner: Cathi Rosengren. Estab. 1989. Specializes in greeting cards, calendars and posters. Buys 25-75 photos/year.

Subject Needs: Abstract, landscape, florals, seasonal, children, humorous—any strong, visually graphic image suitable for sophisticated greeting cards. "No erotic shots."

Specs: Uses 8×10 matte or gloss (no textures) b&w/color prints; 35mm, 2¼×2¼, 4×5, 8×10 transparencies; b&w/color contact sheets.

Payment & Terms: Pay for b&w/color photo negotiable. Royalties on sales negotiable. Pays on publication. Credit line given. Buys exclusive product rights. Model release required; photo captions preferred.

Making Contact: Provide query with samples. Send unsolicited photos by mail for consideration. Submit portfolio for review. Provide resume, business card, brochure, flyer or tearsheets to be kept on file for possible future assignments. "We are interested in stock photos." Submit seasonal material 9 months in advance. SASE. Reports in 1 month. Simultaneous submissions and previously published work OK. No photo guidelines.

Tips: "We need to see a cross section of the photographer's best work: series, collections, story images and any variety of well-composed subjects in b/w or color (including hand-tinted). Please limit submissions to 25-50 at one time."

GOES LITHOGRAPHING CO., 42 W. 61st St., Chicago IL 60621. (312)684-6700. FAX: (312)684-2065. Art Buyer: W.J. Goes. Estab. 1879. Specializes in calendars.

Subject Needs: Western and Eastern seaboard harbors, such as Camden Bay; fall scenes, covered bridges, Western mountain scenes, coastal scenes, historic sights, country, Americana; forest, streams, lakes. Does not wish to see people in any scenes submitted.

Specs: Uses 2¼×2¼, 4×5 and 8×10 transparencies only; primarily 4×5's. No photographs.

Payment & Terms: Pays $50-200/transparency. Buys all rights for certain lines and usage rights. "We purchase rights to republish in future years with original purchase."

Making Contact: Send unsolicited transparencies by mail for consideration. SASE. Photo guidelines sheet available. Always enclose envelope and return postage/insurance.

Tips: "Send horizontal work. A vertical can usually be taken out of horizontal work. We hardly use any veriticals. Be sure the transparencies you send in have good lighting. This enhances all colors throughout the slide. Many submissions that we receive have colors which are washed out. If the subject is a desirable subject for our calendar line and the colors are flat and washed out, it will be rejected. Deep shadows are definitely discouraged for our use."

GRAND RAPIDS CALENDAR CO., 906 S. Division Ave., Grand Rapids MI 49507. Photo Buyer: Rob Van Sledright. Specializes in retail druggist calendars. Buys 10-12 photos/year. Pays on acceptance. Model release required. Submit material January through June. SASE. Simultaneous submissions and previously published work OK. Free photo guidelines; SASE.

Subject Needs: Used for drug store calendars. Baby shots, family health, medical/dental (doctor/patient situations), pharmacist/customer situations, vacationing shots, family holiday scenes, winter play activities, senior citizen, beauty aids and cosmetics. No brand name of any drug or product may show.

B&W: Uses 5×7 and 8×10 glossy prints. Pays $10-20/photo.

*GREETWELL, D-24, M.I.D.C., Satpur., Nasik 422 007 India. Phone: 30181. Chief Executive: Ms. V.H. Sanghavi. Estab. 1974. Specializes in greeting cards and calendars. Buys approx. 100 photos/year.

Subject Needs: Landscapes, wildlife, nudes. No graphic illustrations.

Specs: Uses any size color prints.

Payment & Terms: Pays $25/color photo. Pays on publication. Credit line given. Model release preferred.

Making Contact: Query with samples. Interested in stock photos. Submit seasonal material anytime throughout the year. SASE. Reports in 1 month. Previously published work OK. Photo guidelines not available.

Tips: In photographer's samples, "quality of photo is important; would prefer nonreturnable copies. No originals please."

HALLMARK CARDS, INC., 2501 McGee, Drop #152, Kansas City MO 64108. Photography Buyer: Carol Gibson. Assistant: Sharon Schreiber. Specializes in calendars and puzzles, greeting cards, postcards, stationery, albums and plaques.

Subject Needs: Scenics (domestic and international including recognizable cities), seasonal scenics (snow scenes, etc.), florals (dramatic set-ups, close-ups, gardens, seasonal,etc.), animals (dogs, cats, horses, pigs, cows, wildlife, African animals, etc.), tropical fish in natural environments, people—couples, singles, senior citizens in action or romantic situations; fathers with children or babies, sports (snow skiing, sailing, bicycling—must be model released), moody or romantic subject matters, inspirational skies or clouds. Black and white photography accepted (humorous animals, babies with funny expressions, humorous situations, and snow scenes).

Specs: Uses 35mm, 2¼×2¼, 4×5 and 8×10 transparencies; or black and white negatives only.
Payment & Terms: Fees negotiable. Pays on application of photo to product. Buys one-time exclusive product rights, perpetual product rights or all rights. Model release required.
Making Contact: Send letter requesting copy of guidelines. SASE. Interested in stock photos. Submissions accepted on an open basis, no set schedule. Materials returned with analysis. Reports in 2 months. Simultaneous submissions OK.
Tips: For review, prefer dupe color transparencies, but will accept originals. Negatives accepted only for black and white film. Credit lines and assignments are not given. People shots must show current fashions. Photography should be "bright, clear, colorful and unusual as in angles or subject matter which could be reproduced on social expression products. Suggest you tour a Hallmark or Ambassador card shop and see examples of photography purchased in the past. Then, write and get a copy of our guidelines."

*INTERCONTINENTAL GREETINGS, 176 Madison Ave., New York NY 10016. (212)683-5830. Estab. 1967. Specializes in greeting cards, calendars, post cards, posters, framing prints, stationery, gift wrap and playing cards. Buys 20-50 photos/year.
Subject Needs: Graphics, sports, occasions (i.e. baby, birthday, wedding), "soft-touch" romantic themes, graphic studio photography. No nature, landscape or cute children.
Specs: Uses glossy color prints; 35mm, 2¼×2¼, 4×5 and 8×10 transparencies.
Payment & Terms: 20% royalties on sales. Pays on publication. No credit line given. Buys one-time rights and exclusive product rights. Model release preferred.
Making Contact: Query with samples; send unsolicited photos by mail for consideration; submit portfolio for review; provide resume, business card, brochure, flyer or tearsheets to be kept on file for possible future assignments. Deals with local freelancers only. Accepts seasonal material any time. SASE. Reports in 3 weeks. Simultaneous submissions and previously published work OK. Photo guidelines free with SASE.
Tips: In photographer's portfolio samples, wants to see "a neat presentation, perhaps thematic in arrangement." The trend is toward "modern, graphic studio photography."

ARTHUR A. KAPLAN CO., INC., 460 West 34th St., New York NY 10001. (212)947-8989. President: Arthur Kaplan. Art Director: Kim Greenhall. Specializes in posters, wall decor, and fine prints and posters for framing. Buys the rights to 50-100 freelance photos/year.
Subject Needs: Flowers, scenes, animals, ballet, autos, still life, Oriental motif, musical instruments, abstracts, Americana, b&w, hand-colored and unique imagery.
Specs: Uses any size color prints; 35mm, 2¼×2¼, 4×5 and 8×10 transparencies.
Payment & Terms: Royalty 5-10% on sales. Pays on publication. Buys all rights, exclusive product rights. Model release required.
Making Contact: Send unsolicited photos or transparencies by mail to Kim Greenhall, for consideration. Interested in stock photos. Reports in 1-2 weeks. Simultaneous submissions OK.
Tips: "We are looking for unique, creative work. Our needs constantly change, so we need diversity of imagery. We are especially interested in images with international appeal."

KOGLE CARDS, INC., #212, 5575 S. Sycamore St., Littleton CO 80120. (303)795-3090. President: Patricia Koller. Estab. 1982. Specializes in greeting cards and post cards. Buys about 12 photos/year.
Subject Needs: Thanksgiving and Christmas holiday; also humorous.
Specs: Will work with b&w or color, all formats.
Payment & Terms: Works under royalty with no advance. "The photographer makes more that way." Monthly royalty check. Buys all rights; will negotiate with photographer unwilling to sell all rights. Model release required; captions preferred.
Making Contact: Query with samples. "Be sure and enclose SASE." Interested in stock photos. Submit seasonal material 9 months in advance. SASE. Reports in 2 weeks.

LANDMARK CALENDARS, Box 6105, Novato CA 94948-6105. Contact: Photo Department. Specializes in calendars. Buys 3,000 photos/year. Guidelines available with SASE.
Subject Needs: Scenic/nature, travel, collectibles, European, sports, animals, food, people, automobiles and miscellaneous. "Do not wish to see unfocused, grainy, dark photos or 'animal kill' photos."
Specs: Uses 35mm, 2¼×2¼, 4×5 and 8×10 color transparencies.
Payment & Terms: Pays $50-100/b&w photo; $100/color photo. Pays in April of each year. Credit line given on all except calendars printed for private label companies. Buys one-year, exclusive rights for calendar only, plus sales material and catalogs. Model release and captions required.
Making Contact: Send SASE for guidelines. Interested in stock photos. Submit seasonal material between January 15 and April 15. SASE. Reports in 2 weeks. Previously published material OK.
Tips: In portfolio of samples, wants to see "various subject themes and very bright colors, clear-focus, action in the shots, personality on the faces of animals and so on. Submit the best of your work according to our guidelines."

Close-up

Carol Gibson
Photography Buyer
Hallmark Cards, Inc.
Kansas City, Missouri

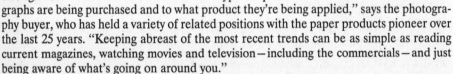

As Carol Gibson of Hallmark Cards observes, clues to up-coming visual trends in the ever-changing paper products industry can be found not only in the usual places—like card shops and drug stores—but also in the media and pop culture.

"I strongly recommend that photographers browse through their local card stores to see what types of photographs are being purchased and to what product they're being applied," says the photography buyer, who has held a variety of related positions with the paper products pioneer over the last 25 years. "Keeping abreast of the most recent trends can be as simple as reading current magazines, watching movies and television—including the commercials—and just being aware of what's going on around you."

In this highly competitive, multi-billion-dollar-a-year industry, the trends literally change almost as quickly as the stars on TV and in pop music. But as Gibson also notes, certain constants remain. Accordingly, the photographer who is not distracted by gimmicks and fads too much and keeps the basics in mind will find more success in the long run. "We tend to shy away from photos using the artificial gels and colored filters," she comments. "The consumer buying a photographic greeting card prefers to look deep within the photo to see the real, natural beauty."

Traditionally, paper products companies have built their markets around greeting cards, calendars, posters and related items. In recent years, industry leaders such as Hallmark have expanded into many other product areas such as gift items which often use photography for illustration.

"More than 50% of the freelance photographs we purchase for our products are reproduced on calendars," says Gibson, noting that the majority of these are scenics involving both nature and city settings. Additional calendar subjects include animals and birds, sports scenes, hot air balloons, and inspirational subjects such as sky, clouds and rainbows. "We also use photos on greeting cards and additional products such as puzzles, mugs, albums, stickers, stationery and note cards."

With a large internal staff of photographers, Hallmark does not give assignments to freelancers. However, with the continued expansion of product lines, says Gibson, the company has come to rely on freelance stock in meeting its growing needs. However, because of Hallmark's stature in the industry, competition among freelance photographers wanting to sell their work to the company is quite fierce. "We can afford to be extremely selective in the work we accept for review by our designers," Gibson points out. "In 1989 alone, we accepted for review only about half of close to 2,500 submissions involving some 100,000 images. Out of those submissions, we are now using about 80 photographers as sources. So, photographers should make sure their work is of the utmost quality and content before sending it off to us."

Generally, Hallmark is favorable to personal expression in the images submitted to them. "Creativity is certainly not discouraged. We look for truly exceptional photographs, not just vacation pictures or grandma's new grandchild," Gibson says, noting that she also looks for a command of color, clarity, depth and the general appeal of subject matter. "Photographers should bear in mind, though, that with greeting cards a type of story—the sentiment—has to be written to go with the photo. If the photograph is too 'far out,' the writer will find it more difficult to blend the photo and the sentiment."

With so many product lines and specialties within them, Hallmark is always looking for a variety of photographic styles, subjects and formats, says Gibson. "We have recently been using hand-tinted [black-and-white] photos as well as a modernistic approach to floral arrangements in natural settings in a variety of greeting cards," she says. "These approaches can be used for all types of occasions, such as birthdays, anniversaries, Mother's Day, Valentine's Day and so on. We are also purchasing a great many nostalgic black-and-white photographs of people and animal situations that lend themselves humorously to various greeting card lines."

Remarking on the various elements that go into an irresistible greeting card photo, Gibson reminds photographers not to forget the most important ingredient of all. "Humor is still one of life's 'cure-alls,'" she says. "Also, we all love animals. So when a photographer can put these two elements together and capture it on film and then our writers give it a good sentiment, we have a winning combination and a salable product."

—Sam A. Marshall

California-based photographer Richard Stacks submitted this humorous photo to Hallmark photo buyer Carol Gibson, and it was just what she was looking for. "Richard is an excellent animal photographer, who has been submitting to us for many, many years," she says. "He has an uncanny knack for capturing the most unusual expressions on the faces of animals. Fortunately, this enables our writers to adapt a message and create a very funny greeting card."

LIKE IT IS, Box 8125, Garden City NY 11530. (516)741-1114. President: George Christ. Specializes in greeting cards, posters and gift wrap.
Subject Needs: "We would like to see photo scenes of Harley Davidson motorcycles (only) to use in a Christmas theme. Models on bike or scenery." Important—the company's logo and the words Harley Davidson can not be used/seen in photo. Humorous settings also are all right. Does not want to see "any photos not relating to Harley Davidson motorcycles."
Specs: Uses 4×5 transparencies and color negatives. Payment negotiated, on per photo basis. Pays on acceptance. Credit lines negotiated with price. Buys all rights; will negotiate with a photographer unwilling to sell all rights. Model release required.
Making Contact: Send unsolicited photos by mail for consideration. Submit photos in March/April "for Christmas of that year." SASE. Reports in 2 weeks.
Tips: Company has fairly exclusive market. "We are the only company producing Harley Motorcycle Christmas cards/wrapping paper. We advertise in motorcycle magazines and we buy names of Harley owners through motor vehicle bureaus."

LOVE GREETING CARDS, INC., 663 N. Biscayne River Dr., Miami FL 33169. (305)685-LOVE. Vice President: Norman Drittel. Specializes in greeting cards, post cards and posters. Buys 75-100 photos/year.
Subject Needs: Nature, flowers, boy/girl (contemporary looks).
Specs: Uses 5×7 or 8×10 color prints; 35mm, 2¼×2¼ and 4×5 transparencies; color contact sheets, color negatives.
Payment & Terms: Pays $75-150/color photo. Pays on publication. Credit line given. Buys exclusive product rights. Model release preferred.
Making Contact: Query with samples or list or stock photo subjects, send unsolicited photos by mail for consideration. Provide resume, business card, brochure, flyer or tearsheets to be kept on file for possible future assignments. Interested in stock photos. Submit seasonal material 6 months in advance. SASE. Reports in 1 month. Previously published work OK.
Tips: "We are looking for outstanding photos for greeting cards and New Age posters." There is a "larger use of photos in posters for commercial sale."

MAGIC MOMENTS GREETING CARDS PUBLISHING CO., 10 Connor Ln., Deer Park NY 11729. (516)842-9292. Vice President: David Braunstein. Specializes in greeting cards. Buys 500 photos/year.
Subject Needs: All greeting card subjects, still libes—holiday themes, (Christmas, Valentines, etc.).
Specs: Uses 35mm, 2¼×2¼, 4×5 and 8×10 transparencies.
Payment & Terms: Pays $25-35/color photo. Pays on acceptance. Buys all rights, greeting cards only. Model release required.
Making Contact: Query with samples. Deals with local freelancers only. Submit seasonal material 1 year in advance. SASE. Reports in 1 month. Film submitted without return postage.

NEW HEIGHTS, a division of Museum Graphics, 703 Sandoval Way Hayward CA 94544. (415)429-1452. President: Alison Mayhew. Estab. 1988. Specializes in greeting cards, postcards and framing prints. Buys 40 photos/year.
Subject Needs: Needs humorous, seasonal, colorful, contemporary or cute photos. No scenic shots.
Specs: Uses 8×10 b&w and color prints.
Payment & Terms: Pays 10% royalties on sales. Credit line given. Buys 10-year "stationery" rights, i.e., exclusive product rights. Model release, photo captions required.
Making Contact: Send unsolicited photos by mail for consideration, submit portfolio for review; provide resume, business card, brochure, flyer or tearsheets to be kept on file for possible future assignments. Interested in stock photos. Submit seasonal material 6-8 months in advance for printing. Look at samples at any time. SASE. Reports in 1 month. Simultaneous submissions and previously published work OK. Photo guidelines free with SASE.
Tips: "New Heights is now looking for contemporary photographers to contribute to our card line. We are interested in fine art photography that is technically excellent and embodies a fresh, creative and humorous approach."

***NORMAILY MARKETING SYSTEMS,** 2467 Newport St., Burlington, ON L7M3X8 Canada. (416)332-1455. Contact: John Mignardi. Estab. 1989. Specializes in brochures, posters, magazines and other paper products. Advertisement use also.
Subject Needs: Exotic cars, jets, people, "cheesecake and beefcake," nudes, nature, travel and humorous.
Specs: Uses 4×6 glossy b&w/color prints; 35mm and 2¼×2¼ transparencies. Slides preferred.
Payment & Terms: Pays per photo; $50-200/photo; Royalties on sales. Pays on usage. Credit line given on occasion. Buys one-time rights, all rights. Will negotiate with a photographer unwilling to sell all rights. Model release and photo captions preferred. However, both are required on sale.

Making Contact: Query with samples. Provide resume, business card, brochure, flyer or tearsheets to be kept on file for possible future assignments. Deals with freelancers only. Reports in 4 weeks.

Tips: "Be original, show sense of style and develop marketable shots (i.e. for postcards, etc.). We're looking for originality. Ask yourself if this photo would be one that someone would look at for more than 5 seconds. High degree of emphasis on colors, sending a message and promoting healthy body/lifestyle."

P.S. GREETINGS, INC., D/B/A FANTUS PAPER PRODUCTS, 4345 West Division St., Chicago IL 60651. (312)384-0234. FAX: (312)384-0502. Art Director: Kevin Lahvic. Estab. 1979. Specializes in greeting cards. Buys 50-100 photos/year.

Subject Needs: Everyday—photo floral, photo pets, photo anniversary, photo scenery and photo religious. Christmas-photos: winter scenes, religious, candles, bells, ornaments, etc.

Specs: 35mm or 2¼ × 2¼ transparencies.

Payment & Terms: "Our rates are very competitive, (depending on size, subject matter, etc.)" Pays $50-150/color photo. Pays on acceptance. "Our company is willing to work with all freelance artists in a suitable arrangement for all." Buys all rights.

Making Contact: Query with resume of credits, samples and list of stock photo subjects; send unsolicited photos by mail for consideration; submit portfolio for review; provide resume, business card, brochure, flyer or tearsheets to be kept on file for possible future assignments. "We prefer seeing photo submittals before an interview is scheduled." Solicits photos by assignment; interested in stock photos. Submit Christmas and Easter material only 1 year in advance. SASE. Reports in 3-4 weeks. Buys exclusive product rights. Simultaneous submissions and previously published work OK to view style of artist. Photo guidelines free with SASE.

Tips: Prefers to see illustrations or photos suitable for greeting cards.

Photographer John von Dorn worked his way up to this photo floral concept piece for P.S. Greetings, Inc. through other assignments for the paper products company. According to Marti Ibarra in the company's art department, the idea for this card—printed in muted colors—came when P.S.'s Art Director Kevin Lahvic saw the photographer's technique of hand-painting black-and-white photos. Lahvic assigned the project, art-directed the shot and acquired all rights to the photo.

PAPER PEDDLER, INC., 1201 Pennsylvania Ave., Richmond CA 94801. (415)237-5656. FAX: (415)237-6135. President/Art Director: David McPhail. Estab. 1979. Specializes in postcards. Buys 20-25 photos/year.

Subject Needs: Humorous, nature (i.e., animals), candid shots, everyday American life teenagers, rock stars, movie stars and pictures of signs.
Specs: Uses 8×10 b&w prints.
Payment & Terms: Pays $75-125/b&w photo. Pays on publication. Advance against 5% royalties. Credit line given. Buys exclusive product rights. Model release and titles preferred.
Making Contact: Send unsolicited photos by mail for consideration. SASE. Reports in 1 month. Simultaneous submissions and previously published work OK.
Tips: Wants to see "good photo quality (in-focus, good contrast, spotted prints, etc.) pictures that tell a story. No abstract. Send b&w photos of work suitable for postcards; wants to see humor, personalities and samples that are cute."

PEMBERTON & OAKES, Department PM, 133 E. Carrillo St., Santa Barbara CA 93101. (805)963-1371. Photo Editor: Marian Groff. Specializes in limited edition lithographs and collector's porcelain plates. Buys 20-25 photos/year.
Subject Needs: "Interested only in photos of children between the ages of two and five using specific guidelines; photos capturing that moment in a million in a child's world."
Specs: Uses any size or finish color or black & white prints, and any size transparencies.
Payments & Terms: Pays $1,000 minimum/color or b&w photo. Payment on acceptance. Buys all rights. No model release necessary, photos used for artist inspiration for paintings.
Making Contact: Send for free photo guidelines.
Tips: "Submit a good selection, carefully following guidelines. Keep us in mind when shooting new material. We're always interested in new photos. Child must be actively involved in an activity, not just looking at the camera. No man-made toys. Showing interaction with pet, something from nature or one other child is best."

PHOTO/CHRONICLES, LTD., 500 West End Ave., New York NY 10024-4344. (212)595-8498. President: David W. Deitch. Estab. 1983. Specializes in postcards and posters. Buys 60-75 photos/year.
Specs: Uses b&w prints, size irrelevant. Must be excellent quality if used.
Payment & Terms: Pays flat fee based on size of press run. Pays 30 days of publication. Copyright/credit line always given. Buys exclusive only product rights. Model release and captions may be required.
Making Contact: Call to arrange a portfolio interview or send photocopies. Not interested in stock photos. SASE. Reports in 2 weeks.

PICTURE GOLD, P.O. Box 6780, Ocala FL 32678. (904)687-8307. President: Ron Gross. Estab. 1987. Specializes in post cards, posters and inspirational photo cards. Buys 10-15 photos/year.
Subject Needs: "Picture Gold is a Christian family-owned company specializing in inspirational, image-building products. We need pictures of babies, children, teens and adults showing emotions, tenderness, playing games, praying, family outings, etc. No bathing suit pictures! Only highly moral, positive life pictures."
Specs: Uses 3½×5 or 4×6 glossy b&w and color prints; 35mm transparencies.
Payment & Terms: Pays $10-100/b&w photo or $10-100/color photo; 25% royalties on sales. Also, offers joint venture program; contact for details. Pays on publication. Credit line given. Buys one-time rights. Model release required; captions preferred.
Making Contact: Send unsolicited photos by mail for consideration. Submit seasonal material as available. SASE. Reports in 2 weeks. Simultaneous submissions and previously published work OK. Photo guidelines sheet free with SASE.
Tips: Portfolios should include photos that convey "positive, inspirational feelings, moods, emotions and life situations. Also pictures we can put verses to whether they are proverbs, quotes, motivational, etc. As far as we can tell, quite possibly, our company may be one-of-a-kind! We are setting a precedent in publishing baby, children, teens, adult pictures to build positive self-images and inspire other people."

PLYMOUTH, INC., 361 Benigno Blvd., Bellmawr NJ 08031. (609)931-8700. Art Director: Alene Sirott-Cope. Specializes in back to school products. Buys 6-18 (possibly more, demand varies) photos/year.
Subject Needs: Cars, surrealistic, futuristic, outerspace.
Specs: Uses 4×5 transparencies; color negatives.
Payment & Terms: Pays $250/color photo. Pays on acceptance. Buys exclusive product rights for these particular products. Model release required.
Making Contact: Query with samples or with list of stock photo subjects. Interested in stock photos. SASE. Reports in 1 month. Simultaneous submissions and previously published work OK.
Tips: Prefers to see "graphics to catch the eye of pre-teens to teens. Graphics that appeal to grade schoolers and pre-schoolers. Only the most unique and innovative concepts will sell."

PORTAL PUBLICATIONS, Suite 400, 770 Tamalpais Dr., Corte Madera CA 94925. (415)924-5652. Specializes in greeting cards, calendars, posters, wall decor and note cards. Gives up to 100 or more assignments annually.
Subject Needs: Contemporary graphics (florals, landscapes, art deco, etc. in a variety of media and techniques), nostalgia and memorabilia, nature and wildlife, sports and travel, food and children's illustration, and youth oriented popular icons such as celebrities, movie posters and sports cars. Nothing too risque.
Specs: Uses 35mm, 2¼×2¼, 4×5 and 8×10 transparencies.
Payment & Terms: Determined by the product format. Pays on acceptance or publication. Credit line given. Buys one-time rights. Model release and captions required.
Making Contact: Query with samples; submit portfolio for review. Deals with local freelancers on assignment basis only. Interested in stock photos. SASE. Reports in 1 month (within 6-8 weeks during busy seasons). Simultaneous submissions and previously published work OK. Photo guidelines free with SASE.
Tips: "Ours is an increasingly competitive business, so we look for the highest quality and most unique imagery that will appeal to our diverse market of customers."

PRODUCT CENTRE-S.W. INC., THE TEXAS POSTCARD CO., P.O. Box 860708, Plano TX 75086. (214)423-0411. Art Director: Susan Hudson. Specializes in postcards, melamine trays and coasters. Buys approximately 100 freelance photos/year.
Subject Needs: Texas towns, Texas scenics, Oklahoma towns/scenics, regional (Southwest only) scenics, humorous, inspirational, nature (including animals), staged studio shots—model and/or products. No nudity.
Specs: Uses "C" print 8×10; 35mm, 2¼×2¼, 4×5 transparencies.
Payment & Terms: Pays up to $100/photo. Pays on publication. Buys all rights. Model release required.
Making Contact: Send insured samples with return postage/insurance. Include Social Security number and telephone number. Submit seasonal material 1 year in advance. SASE. No material returned without postage. Reports usually 3-4 months, depending on season.
Tips: "Submit slides only for viewing. Must be in plastic slide sleeves and each labeled with photographer's name and address. Include descriptive material detailing where and when photo was taken."

QUADRIGA ART, INC., 11 E. 26th St., New York NY 10010. (212)685-0751. Creative Director: Ira Kramer. Specializes in greeting cards, calendars, postcards, posters and stationery. Buys 400-500 photos/year; all supplied by freelance photographers.
Subject Needs: Religious, all-occasion, Christmas, Easter, seasonal, florals, sunsets. No buildings or sports.
Specs: Uses 4×5 or 8×10 transparencies. Transparencies only submitted in sets of 4 to 6. Will not use color photos.
Payment & Terms: Pays $50-200/color shot; payment varies. Pays on acceptance.
Making Contact: Arrange a personal interview to show portfolio; query with samples; send photos by mail for consideration, or submit portfolio for review. Interested in stock photos. Submit seasonal material 1 year in advance. SASE. Reports in 1 week. Simultaneous submissions OK.
Tips: "We prefer shots that focus on a singular subject, rather than a subject hidden in a busy backdrop."

RECYCLED PAPER PRODUCTS, INC., 3636 N. Broadway, Chicago IL 60613. (312)348-6410. Art Director: Melinda Gordon. Specializes in greeting cards and post cards. Buys 30-50 photos/year.
Subject Needs: "Primarily humorous photos for postcards and greeting cards. Photos must have wit and a definite point of view. Unlikely subjects, offbeat themes have the best chance, but will consider all types.
Specs: Uses 4×5 b&w and color prints; 4×5 transparencies; b&w or color contact sheets.
Payment & Terms: Pays $200 per b&w or color photo. Pays on acceptance. Credit line given. Buys all rights; will negotiate with photographer unwilling to sell all rights. Model release and captions required.
Making Contact: Send for artists' guidelines. SASE. Reports in 1 month. Simultaneous submissions OK.
Tips: Prefers to see "up to 10 samples of photographer's best work. Our cards are printed 5×7 vertical format. Please include messages if applicable. The key word for submissions is wit."

REEDPRODUCTIONS, Suite #650, 123 Townsend St., San Francisco CA 94107. (415)974-5767. Partner/Art Director: Susie Reed. Estab. 1978. Specializes in postcards, notebooks, key rings, address books, date books, etc. Number of freelancers assigned varies.

Subject Needs: Celebrity portraits, Hollywood images and rock n' roll photographs. Does not want to see noncelebrity or non-Hollywood images.

Specs: Uses 8 × 10 glossy b&w or color prints or contact sheets.

Payment & Terms: Pays 2% and up royalties on sales or onetime fee. For royalties pays either quarterly or annually. Credit line negotiable. Buys one-time rights. Model release preferred.

Making Contact: Query with samples or send unsolicited photos by mail for consideration. Include resume, business card, brochure, flyer or tearsheets to be kept on file for possible future assignments. SASE. Reports in 1 month. Simultaneous submissions and previously published work OK.

Tips: "We're looking for classic celebrity portraits, black and white or color, shot in clean style."

ROCKSHOTS, INC., 632 Broadway, New York NY 10012. FAX: (212)353-8756. Art Director: Bob Vesce. Estab. 1978. Specializes in greeting cards. Buys 20 photos/year.

Subject Needs: Sexy (including nudes and semi-nudes), outrageous, satirical, ironic, humorous photos. Buys all rights; may settle for greeting card and postcard rights.

Specs: Uses b&w and color prints; 35mm, 2¼ × 2¼ and 4 × 5 slides. "Do not send originals!"

Payment & Terms: Pays $75-150/b&w, $125-300/color photo; other payment negotiable. Pays on acceptance. Model release required.

Making Contact: Interested in stock photos. Provide flyer and tearsheets to be kept on file for possible future assignments. Submit seasonal material at least 6 months in advance. SASE. Reports in 8-10 weeks. Simultaneous submissions and previously published work OK.

Tips: Prefers to see "greeting card themes, especially birthday, Christmas, Valentine's Day. We like to look at life with a very zany slant, not holding back because of society's imposed standards."

THE RYTEX CO., 440 N. Capitol Ave., Indianapolis IN 46204. (317)634-5588. Vice President: Mike Herndon. Specializes in stationery and wedding invitations. Buys 80-120 photos/year.

Subject Needs: Shots of personalized stationery.

Specs: Uses 4 × 5 or 8 × 10 transparencies.

Payment & Terms: Pays $100-250/color photo, "open"/hour or job. Pays on acceptance. Buys all rights. Model release required.

Making Contact: Query with samples; provide resume, business card, brochure, flyer or tearsheets to be kept on file for possible future assignments. Deals with local freelancers only. Submit seasonal material 8 months in advance. SASE. Reports in 1 week.

SANDPIPER PUBLISHING, Box 5143, Stateline NV 89449. (916)544-3506. Publisher: Annette Schoonover. Estab. 1984. Specializes in calendars. Buys 25-50 photos/year.

Subject Needs: River rafting, canoeing, white water kayaking as well as calm water sea kayaking. Action as well as mood shots depicting river life.

Specs: Uses 35mm and 2¼ × 2¼ transparencies. "Please package slides properly."

Payment & Terms: Pays $100/color photo maximum. Pays on publication. Credit line given. Buys one-time rights. Model release and captions required.

Making Contact: Deals with freelancers only. Submit seasonal material 1 year in advance. Reports "when final shots are selected prior to calendar production." Query with SASE for free photo guidelines. No previously published work.

Tips: Please only send materials during the dates on our guidelines. Photos sent prior or past those dates will be returned without being looked at. Prefers to see "clear, crisp, well-composed shots. Try fast shutter speeds, unusual angles and subjects. Best light on the river is mornings and late afternoon. No trick shots, double exposures or other concocted surrealism. Be honest. Photos of previously unpublished rivers, especially protected scenic waterways, have the best chance of acceptance. Study '86 thru '90 calendars to know what we've used in the past."

SCAFA-TORNABENE PUBLISHING CO., 100 Snake Hill Rd., West Nyack NY 10994. (914)358-7600. Contact: Rosemary J. Mashack. Specializes in inspirationals, religious, contemporary florals, dramatic wildlife, nostalgia and children of yesteryear.

Specs: Uses camera ready prints, 35mm, 2¼ × 2¼, 4 × 5 and 8 × 10 transparencies.

Payment & Terms: Pays $150-250/b&w photo; $150-400/color photo. Also pays royalty, negotiated individually. Pays on acceptance. Credit line sometimes given. Buys all rights, depending on use. Model release required.

Making Contact: Query with samples. Deals with local freelancers only. SASE. Reports in 2-3 weeks. Simultaneous submissions and previously published work OK.

Tips: "Send a good cross section of your work. (35 mm slides, 4 × 5 transparencies). Prefer prints of hand colored work." In samples wants to see "florals, still life, animals (cats, teddybears), autos, trucks, musical instruments. Black and white, hand-colored, sepia. Dramatic unique imagery."

SIERRA CLUB BOOKS, 730 Polk St., San Francisco CA 94109-7813. Photo Editor: Geoffrey Hiller. Calendar Editor: Frances Spear. Specializes in nature calendars. Request guidelines by post card only. Buys 143 photos annually. Send for free photo guidelines (mailed in May of every year), then submit material by mail for consideration. "We accept submissions *only* March 1 to April 3 of each year for calendars covering the year after the following" (i.e., photos for the 1992 calendar will be reviewed in the summer of 1990). Buys exclusive calendar rights for the year covered by each calendar. Reports in 6-10 weeks. Simultaneous submissions OK.
Subject Needs: Needs photos of wildlife, natural history, scenery, hiking, etc. Captions required. Calendars: nature/scenic; wildlife; "Trail" (people in the outdoors); engagement (nature and wildlife). No animals in zoos; no people engaged in outdoor recreation with machines.
Color: Send transparencies. Pays $150-400.
Tips: "We're using international, as opposed to strictly North American, subjects in some of the calendars. We get lots of good scenics but not as many good wildlife shots or shots appropriate for the 'Trail' calendar (can include human subjects in activities such as climbing, canoeing, hiking, cross country skiing, etc.). *Be selective.* Don't submit more than 100 transparencies. Follow the guidelines in the spec sheet. Send only work of the highest quality/reproducibility. We're looking for strong images and seasonal appropriateness." Pays on publication.

SORMANI CALENDARS, 613 Waverly Ave., Mamaroneck NY 10543. (203)531-7400. Vice President: Donald H. Heithaus. Estab. 1954. Specializes in calendars. Buys 50 freelance photos/year. Previous campaigns included making calendars for banks and corporations.
Subject Needs: Scenics of the USA.
Specs: Uses 4×5 and 8×10 transparencies.
Payment & Terms: Pays $100 maximum/color photo. Pays on publication. Buys one-time rights. Model release preferred.
Making Contact: Query with samples or send unsolicited photos by mail for consideration. SASE. Reports in 2 weeks. Simultaneous submissions and previously published work OK.
Tips: Prefers to see "scenic pictures of the USA (chrome slides, 4×5 or larger) . . . lots of color and distance."

SOUNDYCARDS, division of Surf Sounds Inc., Box 420007, Naples FL 33939. (813)566-8343. President: William Leverick. Specializes in greeting cards. Buys 50+ photos/year.
Subject Needs: Nature photos only, featuring water (lakes, rivers, streams, waterfalls, rain, oceans, beaches etc.; winter and summer scenes OK). Animals and people OK in photos as long as they are not primary subjects. Ex: a couple in a canoe on a beautiful mountain lake with breathtaking scenery but the couple is secondary interest . . . silhouetted against sky.
Specs: Uses 8×10 color prints; 35mm, 2¼×2¼, 4×5 and 8×10 transparencies.
Payment & Terms: Pays $150/color photo. Pays on acceptance. Buys exclusive product rights. Model release preferred.
Making Contact: Send unsolicited photos by mail for consideration. Deals with local freelancers only; interested in stock photos. Submit seasonal material 6 months in advance. SASE. Reports in 2 weeks. Simultaneous submissions and previously published work OK. Photo guidelines free upon request.

SYRACUSE CULTURAL WORKERS, Box 6367, Syracuse NY 13217. (315)474-1132. Research/Development Director: Dik Cool. Posters, cards and calendars. Buys 50-75 freelance photos/year. Uses photos for posters, cards and calendars.
Subject Needs: Images of social content, reflecting a consciousness of peace/social justice.
Specs: Uses any size b&w; 35mm, 2¼×2¼, 4×5 or 8×10 color transparencies.
Payment & Terms: Pays $50-350/b&w or color photo. Credit line given. Buys one-time rights. Model release and captions preferred.
Making Contact: Send unsolicited photos by mail for consideration. SASE. Reports in 1-2 months.
Tips: "We are interested in photos that reflect a consciousness of peace and social justice, that portray the experience of people of color, disabled, elderly, gay/lesbian — must be progressive, feminist, nonsexist. Look at our catalog (available for $1) — understand our philosophy and politics. Send only what is appropriate and socially relevant. No signs/banners from demonstrations. We are looking for positive, upbeat and visionary work."

TIDE MARK PRESS, Box 280311, East Hartford CT 06128-0311. Editor: Scott Kaeser. Art Director: C. Cote. Specializes in calendars. Buys 50-100/year; few individual photos.
Subject Needs: Complete calendar concepts which are unique, but also have identifiable markets; groups of photos which could work as on entire calendar; ideas and approach must be visually appealing and innovative but also have a definable audience. No general nature or varied subjects without a single theme.

Specs: Uses 35mm, 2¼×2¼, 4×5 and 8×10 transparencies.
Payment & Terms: Pays $150-250/color photo; royalties on sales if entire calendar supplied. Pays on publication or per agreement. Credit line given. Buys one-time rights. Model release preferred; captions required.
Making Contact: "Contact us to offer specific topic suggestion which reflect specific strengths of your stock." Interested in stock photos. Submit seasonal material June-Sept. for next calendar year. SASE. Reports as soon as possible.

VAGABOND CREATIONS, INC., 2560 Lance Dr., Dayton OH 45409. (513) 298 1124. President: George F. Stanley, Jr. Specializes in greeting cards. Buys 2 photos/year.
Subject Needs: General Christmas scene . . . non-religious.
Specs: Uses 35mm transparencies.
Payment & Terms: Pays $100/color photo. Pays on acceptance. Buys all rights.
Making Contact: Query with list of stock photo subjects. Interested in stock photos. Submit seasonal material 9 months in advance. SASE. Reports in 1 week. Simultaneous submissions OK.

WARNER PRESS, INC., 1200 E. 5th St., Anderson IN 46012. (317)644-7721. Contact: John Silvey. Specializes in weekly church bulletins. Buys 100 photos/year. Submit material by mail for consideration; submit only in December. Buys all rights. Present model release on acceptance of photo. Reports when selections are finalized.
Subject Needs: Needs photos for 2 bulletin series; one is of "conventional type"; the other is "meditative, reflective, life- or people-centered. May be 'soft touch.' More 'oblique' than the conventional, lending itself to meditation or worship thoughts contributive to the Sunday church service."
Color: Uses transparencies (any size 35mm-8×10). Pays $100-150.
Tips: "Send only a few (10-20) transparencies at one time. Identify *each* transparency with a number and your name and address. Avoid sending 'trite' travel or tourist snapshots. Don't send ordinary scenes and flowers. Concentrate on *verticals*—many horizontals eliminate themselves. Do not resubmit rejections. If we couldn't use it the first time, we probably can't use it later!"

WISCONSIN TRAILS, Box 5650, Madison WI 53705. (608)231-2444. Production Manager: Nancy Mead. Estab. 1960. Bimonthly magazine. Calendar portraying seasonal scenics, some books and activities from Wisconsin.
Subject Needs: Needs photos of nature, landscapes, wildlife and Wisconsin activities. Buys 35 photos/issue.
Making Contact: Submit material by mail for consideration or submit portfolio. Makes selections in January for calendar-6 months ahead for issues; "we should have photos by December." Buys one-time rights. Reports in 4 weeks. Simultaneous submissions OK "if we are informed, and if there's not a competitive market among them." Previously published work OK.
Color: Send 35mm, 2¼×2¼ and 4×5 transparencies. Captions required. Pays $25-100/b&w photo, $50-175/color photo.
Tips: "Be sure to inform us how you want materials returned and include proper postage. Calendar scenes must be horizontal to fit 8½×11 format. See our magazine and books and be aware of our type of photography. Submit only Wisconsin scenes."

Paper Products/'90-'91 changes

The following paper products companies appeared in the 1990 edition of *Photographer's Market* but are not in the 1991 edition. Those companies whose owners or art directors did not respond to our request for an update of their listings may not have done so for a variety of reasons—they may be out of business, for example, or they may be overstocked with submissions.

Advance Cellocard Co. (did not respond)
Argonaut Press (did not respond)
Art Source (did not respond)
Bright Products, Inc. (out-of-business)
Broom Designs Inc. (did not respond)
C.R. Gibson (did not respond)
Contenova Gifts, Inc. (no longer in market)
K&L Custom Photographic (not reviewing work)
Mulligan Graphics, Robert (out of business)
Paramount Cards, Inc. (not reviewing work)
Rich Designs, Ltd., Rose (did not respond)
Scandecor International (did not respond)

Publications

With tremendously diverse subject matter and an endless need for photographic illustration, the Publications market offers photographers everywhere many creative challenges and considerable potential for income. Many of these publications are the typical monthly magazines available either over the counter or by subscription. Some are more infrequent, ranging from catalogs to academic journals. Some annuals are also included which have very specific readerships as well as particular format and subject needs.

Consumer publications, available through both newsstands and subscriptions, are by far the most varied in subject matter and readership since their readers are from a broad cross-section of the general public. Special Interest publications—a new category in this edition of *Photographer's Market* consisting of the previously separate categories, Association publications and Company publications—encompass both membership and corporate audiences. In some cases, depending upon circulation and marketing methods, these overlap with both Consumer publications and the third category in this section, Trade publications. Trade publications, of course, cover topics that are audience-specific to various professions and industries. These are usually available only through subscription on a controlled circulation basis.

Because of the widespread availability and highly visual nature of most publications, photographers often think of this as an ideal market. This remains generally true for breaking in and gaining experience, but less so for working fulltime and earning a steady income. Recent economic trends (see section introduction for Advertising, on page 33) have been forcing some publications to go out of business or to tighten their freelance budgets. As a result, many photographers who once worked exclusively or primarily in the Publications market have recently been branching into other markets, such as stock photography.

If you have little experience in marketing your photography, this market does still represent one of the better avenues for entering the field. However, it's important to realize that with the increased competition, setting your work apart from that of other photographers with quality, a creative approach to the subject and overall professionalism is more vital than ever to your success.

You can benefit a great deal from studying the markets and doing some self-assignment work before actually querying a specific publication. Aside from reading the listing carefully, request a publication's guidelines or a sample copy. With the insights you gather, you can then set up a few self-assignments. Then, when you do query or send samples, your work will be much closer to meeting the unique needs and problems of the publication. Remember: Your work must be more than just pretty pictures or technically perfect images; they must also say something to the publication's readers.

Once you have arrived at a clear understanding of the publication and its audience, your next step is actually to submit work or solicit assignments. Some publications are flexible and advise contacting them in various ways—querying, sending unsolicited materials or calling—while others are more particular and will not tolerate deviations. In any case, it's important that you follow their directions as specified to make the best first impression and promote your working relationship with them.

The standards of professional freelancing practiced in other markets are recognized too in the publications market. Such practices as providing clear, accurate captions and signed model releases are nearly universal needs. Enclosing a self-addressed, stamped envelope (SASE) facilitates a response from the publication, and is also an often-stated requirement.

Providing adequate packaging and postage is also important if you are mailing your submissions and expect to have them returned safely. In particular, when a listing indicates it cannot return material you must take this direction seriously or risk loss of your images.

One special note for photographers who are also skilled as writers is to look for publications that indicate text as well as photo needs. This is usually indicated by a "ms" or "mss"—manuscript(s)—in the listing. Some publications will purchase photos only in a photo/text package for a flat fee while others will purchase photos from existing stock, on assignment or as part of a package. Publications which purchase packages only will often recommend that photographers team up with a writer with expertise in that particular subject as a way of working for them. Generally, shooting for packages tends to pay better and can give you an advantage over other photographers.

If you are just breaking into photography or have not worked in this market previously, you may find it helpful to start with some smaller publications. Perhaps you will want to try those that feature subjects in which you have a personal interest or expertise. The smaller markets are generally less lucrative than higher-circulation national markets. However, working for them first is an excellent way to learn about the publications market, to get photos published and to build a strong portfolio. With published photos to your credit, you will then be able to build upon your success by selling to larger publications.

Another guide to help you in locating some of these smaller, lower-paying markets is a new feature in this edition, the First Markets Index. This reference, located in the back of this book, contains some 200 markets, most of which are listed within the Publications section.

Currently, more magazines are buying stock images—from both stock photo agencies and photographers' stock—because it's more economical to pay for existing photos than to assign special shoots. However, story outlines are occasionally specific enough to justify the extra expense of assigning new photos. It's much more likely that as a newcomer you will be successful in selling stock initially. As you develop a working relationship with an editor or photo editor, though, you will be offered assignments. Building a reputation as someone who understands a publication's needs and deadlines takes time and persistence, but it's worth the effort.

The combined total of publications in the three categories is more than 1,000, with nearly 175 new listings. You will see from the list, '90-'91 Changes, at the end of the Trade listings in this section that many listings from last year's edition are not currently seeking photographic submissions or have ceased publication. Also listed among the changes in the Consumer listings are a number of popular publications which photographers have frequently asked us to include in the book. These publications, in particular, either declined our invitation to be listed or simply did not respond. Such markets, generally are not currently soliciting submissions or typically do not use the work of freelancers.

Consumer

Containing more than 500 listings, the Consumer publications market is the most extensive section in *Photographer's Market*. Traditionally, this market has offered photographers the most variety in terms of subject matter, professional challenge and income. For these reasons, it remains the most popular among beginning and veteran photographers alike.

Many magazines in this category are household names, well-known regional publications and highly specialized, topic-oriented magazines. Nearly every kind of interest is represented—from nature to sports, from economics to religion, from home to health and beauty. Regardless of subject, however, these publications all have a great need in common—to communicate visually to their readers the excitement, intricacies or special values of the particular subjects.

In general, many listings in this section include substantial changes. For instance, some publications have provided new descriptions of their photo needs, or have revised their payment rates and terms concerning rights. Also, the listings reflect the usual changing of the guard on editorial and art staffs, as well as relocation of offices.

In light of the highly competitive nature of this market, you may find the two Close-up interviews with guest experts in this section to be quite insightful. The first of these is with editorial photographer D. Gorton, whose work has been published in a variety of publications, including *Esquire*, *People* and *Newsweek*. In particular, he emphasizes the importance of shooting with a multiple marketing strategy in mind. Also quite relevant to the changing market conditions now facing photographers are the comments of M.C. Marden, photo editor for *People* magazine. She points out various aspects of professionalism as well as photography trends of which editorial photographers should be aware.

ABOARD MAGAZINE, 100 Almeria Ave. Suite 220, Coral Gables, FL 33134. (305)441-9744. Editor: Georgina Fernandez. Photo Editor: Alex Sanchez. Inflight magazine for 8 separate Latin American national airlines. Bilingual; bimonthly. Emphasizes travel through Central and South America. Readers are mainly Latin American businessmen, and American tourists and businessmen. Circ. 94,000. Sample copy free with SASE. Photo guidelines free with SASE.
Photo Needs: Uses 50 photos/issue; 30 supplied by freelance photographers. Needs photos of travel, scenic, fashion, sports and art. Special needs include good quality pix of Latin American countries, particularly Chile, Guatemala, Ecuador, Bolivia, Rep. Dominicana, El Salvador, Venezuela, Honduras. Model release and captions preferred.
Making Contact & Terms: Query with samples; provide business card, brochure, flyer or tearsheets to be kept on file for possible future assignments. SASE. Reports in 1 month. Payment varies; pays $20/color photo; $150 for photo/text package. Pays on publication. Credit line given. Buys one-time rights. Previously published work OK.
Tips: If photos are accompanied by an article, chances are much better of them being accepted.

ACCENT ON LIVING, Box 700, Bloomington IL 61702. (309)378-2961. Editor: Betty Garee. Quarterly magazine. Circ. 19,500. Emphasizes successful disabled people who are getting the most out of life in every way and *how* they are accomplishing this. For physically disabled individuals of all ages and socioeconomic levels and professionals. Buys 20-50 photos annually. Buys first-time rights. Query first with ideas, get an OK, and send contact sheet for consideration. Provide letter of inquiry and samples to be kept on file for possible future assignments. Pays on publication. SASE. Reports in 2 weeks. Simultaneous submissions and previously published work OK "if we're notified and we OK it." Sample copy $2.50 with 5×7 SAE and 90¢ postage. Free photo guidelines; enclose SASE.
Photo Needs: Photos dealing with coping with the problems and situations peculiar to handicapped persons: how-to, new aids and assistive devices, news, documentary, human interest, photo essay/ photo feature, humorous and travel. "All must be tied in with physical disability. We want essentially action shots of disabled individuals doing something interesting/unique or with a new device they have developed. Not photos of disabled people shown with a good citizen 'helping' them." 90% from freelance.
B&W: Send contact sheet. Uses glossy prints. Manuscript required. Pays $5 minimum.
Cover: Cover is usually tied in with the main feature inside. Also use color photos, transparencies preferred. Pays $50-up/cover.
Tips: Needs photos for Accent on People department, "a human interest photo column on disabled individuals who are gainfully employed or doing unusual things." Also uses occasional photo features on disabled persons in specific occupations: art, health, etc. Pays $25-200 for text/photo package; and $10 min. color photo. Send for guidelines. "Concentrate on improving photographic skills. Join a local camera club, go to photo seminars, etc. We find that most articles are helped a great deal with *good* photographs—in fact, good photographs will often mean buying a story and passing up another one with very poor or no photographs at all." Looking for *good* quality photos depicting what article is about. Query first. We almost always work on speculation.

ADIRONDACK LIFE, Rt. 86, Box 97, Jay NY 12941. (518)946-2191. Art Director: Ann Eastman. Bimonthly. Circ. 50,000. Emphasizes the people and landscape of the north country of New York State. Sample copy $4 with 9×12 SAE and $1.10 postage; photo guidelines free with SASE.
Photo Needs: "We use about 40 photos/issue, most supplied by freelance photographers. All photos must be taken in the Adirondacks and all shots must be identified as to location and photographer."
Making Contact & Terms: Send one sleeve (20 slides) of samples. Send b&w prints (preferably 8×10) or 35mm color transparencies. SASE. Reports in 1 month. Pays $300/cover photo; $25-75/ b&w photo; $50-200/color photo; $75-125/day (Day- $125 plus expenses, $75 per half day). Pays on

publication. Credit line given. Buys first North American serial rights. Simultaneous submissions OK.
Tips: "Send quality work pertaining specifically to the Adirondacks. In addition to technical proficiency, we look for originality and imagination. We avoid using typical shots of sunsets, lakes, reflections, mountains, etc. We are using more pictures of people and action."

AFRICA REPORT, 833 UN Plaza, New York NY 10017. (212)949-5666. Editor: Margaret A. Novicki. Bimonthly magazine. Circ. 12,000. Emphasizes African political, and economic affairs, especially those significant for US. Readers are Americans with professional or personal interest in Africa. Photos purchased with or without accompanying ms. Buys 20 photos/issue. Provide samples and list of countries/subjects to be kept on file for future assignments. Pays on a per-photo basis. Credit line given. Pays on publication. Buys one-time rights. SASE. Simultaneous submissions and previously published work OK. Reports in 1 month. Free sample copy.
Subject Needs: Personality, documentary, photo feature, scenic, spot news, human interest, travel, socioeconomic and political. Photos must relate to African affairs. "We will not reply to 'How I Saw My First Lion' or 'Look How Quaint the Natives Are' proposals." Wants on a regular basis photos of economics, African international affairs, development, conflict and daily life. Captions required.
B&W: Uses 8 × 10 glossy prints. Pays $25-35/photo.
Cover: Uses b&w glossy prints. Vertical format preferred. Pays $25-75/photo.
Accompanying Mss: "Read the magazine, then query." Pays $150-250/ms. Free writer's guidelines.
Tips: "Read the magazine; live and travel in Africa; and make political, economic and social events humanly interesting."

*AFTER FIVE MAGAZINE, P.O. Box 492905, Redding CA 96049. (800)637-3540 only from northern California. Otherwise (916)335-4533. Publisher: Katie Harrington. Monthly tabloid. Emphasizes news, arts and entertainment. Circ. 18,043. Estab. 1986. Sample copy $1.
Photo Needs: Uses 8-12 photos/issue; 25% supplied by freelance photographers. Needs photos of animal/wildlife shots, travel and secnics. Model release and photo captions preferred.
Making Contact & Terms: Provide resume, business card, brochure, flyer or tearsheets to be kept on file for possible assignments. SASE. Reports in 1-2 weeks. Pays $50/color cover photo; $50/b&w cover photo; $20/b&w inside photo; $60/b&w page rate. Pays on publication. Credit line given. Buys one-time rights. Previously published work OK.
Tips: "Need photographs of subjects north of Sacramento to Oregon-California border, plus southern Oregon."

AIR & SPACE/SMITHSONIAN, National Air & Space Museum, 370 Lenfant Promenade SW, Washington DC 20024. (202)357-1300. Photo Editor: Lee E. Battaglia. Bimonthly magazine. Emphasizes aviation and space. Circ. 350,000.
Photo Needs: Uses 75-100 photos/issue; 80% supplied by freelancers. Model release preferred; captions required.
Making Contact & Terms: Provide resume, business card, brochure, flyer or tearsheets to be kept on file for possible future assignments. SASE. Reports in 3 weeks. Pays on publication. Credit line given. Buys one-time rights. Previously published work OK.

ALABAMA LITERARY REVIEW, 253 Smith Hall, Troy State University, Troy AL 36082. (205)566-3000, ext. 3286. Editor: Theron Montgomery. Semi-annual journal. Emphasizes short stories, poetry, essays, short drama, art and photography. Readers are anyone interested in literature and art of all ages. Circ. 600 + . Estab. 1987. Sample copy for $4/issue and 8 × 11 SASE.
Photo Needs: Uses 5-6 photos/issue; 100% supplied by freelance photographers. Will consider all kinds of photos. Special needs include anything artistic or thought-provoking. Written release required.
Making Contact & Terms: Send 8 × 10 b&w glossy prints by mail for consideration. SASE. Reports in 1-2 months. Pays in copies. Pays on publication. Credit line given. Buys one-time rights. Simultaneous submissions OK.

The asterisk before a listing indicates that the market is new in this edition. New markets are often the most receptive to freelance submissions.

For photographer Charles Orlofsky, this image symbolizes "getting one's foot in the door." And that's just what he did with this picture when he first submitted it to Alabama Literary Review. Noting that he received a modest payment and several contributor's copies of the issue in which his photo appeared, Orlofsky says the Review is an excellent first market.

Tips: "We take pride in discovering amateur photographers and presenting their work to a serious audience across the U.S. *ALR* is a good place for a new photographer to break in." Looks for "Playoff on b&w, people and forms. Also, if it 'tells' a story." The trend is towards b/w art forms. "Think of the completeness, proportion & metaphoric implications of the pictures"

ALASKA, Suite 200, 808 E St., Anchorage AK 99501. Editor: Ron Dalby. Managing Editor: Shannon Lowry. Monthly magazine. Circ. 235,000. Estab. 1963. For residents of, and people interested in Alaska. "Photos may depict any aspect of 'Life on the Last Frontier'—wildlife, scenics, people doing things they can only do in the North country." Buys 300 photos annually;25% freelance photography/issue from assignment, 50-60% from stock or from writers. Buys one-time rights. Send photos for consideration. Pays on publication. Reports in 3-4 weeks. SASE. Sample copy $2; free photo guidelines.

Making Contact & Terms: Send 8×10 b&w prints, but prefers color submissions. Pays $35-100 minimum. Send color 35mm, 2¼×2¼ or 4×5 transparencies. Pays $150/2-page spread, $100/full page or $50/half page. per color photo $35-500.Send for covers 35mm, 2¼×2¼ or 4×5 color transparencies. Pays up to $500. $250-500/day; $350-1250/photo/text package.

Tips: "Each issue of *Alaska* features a 6-10-page photo feature. We're looking for themes and photos to support those ideas." We want"clear, sharp pictures taken by someone with an eye for detail and beauty. We want to use more pictures of people. Most photographers send us pictures of things."

*ALASKA GEOGRAPHIC, P.O. Box 93370, Anchorage AK 99509. (907)258-2515. Editor: Penny Rennick. Quarterly magazine. Covers Alaska and Northwestern Canada only. Readers are professional men and women, ages 30 and up. Circ. 9,000. Estab. 1972. Guidelines free with SASE.

Photo Needs: Uses about 70 photos/issue; most supplied by freelancers. Needs photos of scenics, animals, natural history and people. Each issue covers a special theme. Especially interested in seeing pictures of Yukon River region. Model release preferred; photo captions required.

Making Contact & Terms: Query with list of stock photo subjects. SASE. Usually reports in 1 month. "We don't have time to deal with inappropriate submissions, so know the area and subjects very well to avoid wasting time." Pays $200/color cover photo; $100/inside full page color; $50/inside half page color. Pays on publication. Credit line given. Buys one-time rights. Simultaneous submissions and previously published work OK.

Tips: Do not send mss, "just photos. Our freelance writing is done by assignment only."

alive now! MAGAZINE, 1908 Grand Ave., Box 189, Nashville TN 37202. (615)340-7218. Assistant Editor: Beth A. Richardson. Bimonthly magazine published by The Upper Room. "*alive now!* uses poetry, short prose, photography and contemporary design to present material for personal devotion and reflection. It reflects on a chosen Christian concern in each issue. The readership is composed of primarily college-educated adults." Circ. 80,000. Sample copy free with 6×9 SAE and 85¢ postage; themes list free with SASE; photo guidelines available.

Photo Needs: Uses about 25-30 b&w prints/issue; 90% supplied by freelancers. Needs b&w photos of "family, friends, people in positive and negative situations; scenery; celebrations; disappointments; ethnic minority subjects in everyday situations—Native Americans, Hispanics, Asians and blacks." Model release preferred.

Making Contact & Terms: Query with samples; send 8×10 glossy b&w prints by mail for consideration; submit portfolio for review. SASE. Reports in 2 months; "longer to consider photos for more than one issue." Pays $20-30/b&w inside photo; no color photos. Pays on publication. Credit line given. Buys one-time rights. Simultaneous and previously published submissions OK.

Tips: Prefers to see "a variety of photos of people in life situations, presenting positive and negative slants, happy/sad, celebrations/disappointments, etc. Use of racially inclusive photos is preferred."

ALOHA, THE MAGAZINE OF HAWAII, Suite 309, 49 South Hotel St., Honolulu HI 96813. (808)523-9871. Editor: Cheryl Tsutsumi. Art Director: Sanford Mock. Emphasizes Hawaii. Readers are "affluent, college-educated people from all over the world who have an interest in Hawaii." Bimonthly. Circ. 65,000. Sample copy $2.95 with 9×11 SAE and $1.58 postage; photo guidelines with SASE.

Photos: Uses about 50 photos/issue; 40 of which are supplied by freelance photographers. Needs "scenics, travel, people, florals, strictly about Hawaii. We buy primarily from stock. Assignments are rarely given and when they are it is to one of our regular local contributors. Subject matter must be Hawaiian in some way. A regular feature is the photo essay, 'Beautiful Hawaii,' which is a 6-page collection of images illustrating that theme." Model release required if the shot is to be used for a cover; captions required.

Making Contact & Terms: Send by mail for consideration actual 35mm or 2¼×2¼ color transparencies; or arrange personal interview to show portfolio. SASE. Reports in 6-8 weeks. Pays $25/b&w photo; $60/color transparency; $125 for photo running across a two-page spread; $175 for cover shots. Pays on publication. Credit line given. Buys one-time rights. Previously published work OK if other publications are specified.

Markets which offer lower payment amounts, or photo credits and extra copies or tearsheets as payment are often receptive to the work of newcomers. For a list of such markets, see the First Markets Index preceding the General Index in the back of this book.

Tips: Prefers to see "a unique way of looking at things, and of course, sharp, well-composed images. Generally we are looking for outstanding photos of Hawaii scenery that are not standard sunset scenes printed in every Hawaii publication. We need to see that the photographer can use lighting techniques skillfully, and we want to see pictures that are sharp and crisp. Many photographers break in to being published by submitting transparencies for Beautiful Hawaii, a photo essay section that is run in every issue. Competition is fierce, and it helps if a photographer can bring in his portfolio to show to our art director. Then the art director can give him ideas regarding our needs."

*AM MAGAZINE, 3510 E. Ventura, Fresno CA 93702. (209)237-9661. Managing Editor: Melissa S. Haze. Consumer publication. Monthly magazine. Emphasizes Southeast Asian acculturation. Readers are Southeast Asian refugee families. Circ. 7,000. Estab. 1989. Sample copy for $1.95.
Photo Needs: Uses 25 photos/issue; 60% supplied by freelance photographers. In near future, will need "photos that include Southeast Asian individuals, travel pictures and all holiday celebrations." Model release required; photo captions preferred.
Making Contact & Terms: Send unsolicited photos by mail for consideration; submit portfolio for review. Uses 35mm, 2¼ × 2¼, 4 × 5, 8 × 10 b&w or color prints; 35mm, 2¼ × 2¼, 4 × 5, 8 × 10 transparencies. SASE. Reports in 1 month. Pays $50/color cover photo; $25/color inside photo; $25/b&w inside photo. Pays on publication. Credit line given. Buys all rights. Simultaneous submissions OK.
Tips: In freelancer's portfolio or samples, looks for "southeast Asian refugees involved in daily activities, holiday celebrations; geographical points of interest; miscellaneous. Make lots of submissions. Be a *nice* pest. Keep your name in the forefront of the publishers' mind. Remember that getting into the business means starting at the bottom and working your way up."

*AMBASSADOR (Inflight Magazine of TWA), Halsey Publishing Co., 12955 Biscayne Blvd., N. Miami FL 33181. (305)893-1520. Photo Editor: Coni Kaufman. Monthly magazine. Emphasizes general interest and travel topics. Circ. 360,000. Sample copy $3 and 9 × 12 SASE.
Photo Needs: Uses about 70 photos/issue; 35% supplied by freelance photographers. Needs photos of travel, consumer, entertainment, business, lifestyle and technology. Reviews photos with accompanying ms only. Model release and captions required.
Making Contact & Terms: Send 35mm and 2¼ × 2¼ transparencies by mail for consideration; provide resume, business card, brochure, flyer or tearsheets to be kept on file for possible future assignments. SASE. Reports in 1 month. Pays $300/color cover photo; $100/lead photo or feature story; $50/ color inside photo; $300-500/text/photo package. Pays on publication. Credit line given. Buys one-time rights. Simultaneous submissions and previously published work OK.

*AMBERGRIS, P.O. Box 29919, Cincinnati OH 45229. Editor: Mark Kissling. Consumer publication. Semi-annual journal. Emphasizes short stories and poems. Readers range of ages 16-75, educated, literary. Circ. 1,000. Estab. 1987. Sample copy for $3. Photo guidelines free with SASE.
Photo Needs: Uses 10 photos/issue; 50% supplied by freelance photographers. "We do not usually assign photos, but would consider it in future." Needs photos of "anything appropriate to a literary journal. We prefer photos that have vertical format." Special consideration to Ohio or Midwestern scenes. Model release and photo captions preferred.
Making Contact & Terms: "Send photocopies only with SASE." Uses 35mm, 2¼ × 2¼, 4 × 5 glossy or matte, b&w prints. SASE. Reports in 1 month. Pays with 2 contributor copies. Pays on publication. Credit line given. Buys first N.A. serial rights. No simultaneous submissions or previously published work.
Tips: "Photos should be appropriate to a 5½ × 8½ journal. Most emphasis on vertical format. Landscapes, cityscapes and any interesting angle. We give extra consideration to Ohio scenes. Send 5 clear photocopies of best work, brief cover letter and bio."

AMELIA MAGAZINE, 329 "E" St., Bakersfield CA 93304. (805)323-4064. Editor: Frederick A Raborg, Jr. Quarterly magazine. Emphasizes literary: fiction, non-fiction, poetry, reviews, fine illustrations and photography etc. "We span all age groups, the three genders and all occupations. We are also international in scope. Average reader has college education." Circ. 1,250. Sample copy $7.95 and SASE. Photo guidelines free with SASE.
Photo Needs: Uses up to 4 photos/issue depending on availability; 100% supplied by freelance photographers. "We look for photos in all areas and try to match them to appropriate editorial content. Sometimes use photos alone; color photos on cover. We use the best we receive; the photos usually convince us." Model release required; photo captions preferred.
Making Contact & Terms: Send unsolicited photos by mail for consideration. Send b&w or color, 5 × 7 and up, glossy or matte prints, or 35mm or 2¼ × 2¼ transparencies. SASE. Reports in 2 weeks. Pays $100/color cover photo, $50/b&w cover photo and $5-25/b&w inside photo. Pays on acceptance. Credit line given. Buys one-time rights or first N.A. serial rights. "We prefer first N.A., but one-time is fine." Simultaneous submissions OK.

Tips: In portfolio or samples, looks for "a strong cross-section. We assume that photos submitted are available at time of submission. Do your homework. Examine a copy of the magazine, certainly. Study the 'masters of contemporary' photography, i.e. Adams, Avedon etc. Experiment. Remember we are looking for photos to be married to editorial copy usually."

AMERICA WEST AIRLINES MAGAZINE, Suite 236, 7500 N. Dreamy Draw Dr., Phoenix AZ 85020. (602)997-7200. Art Director: Elizabeth Krecker. America West Airlines inflight magazine. Monthly. Emphasizes general interest—including: travel, interviews, business trends, food, etc. Readers are primarily business people and business travelers; substantial vacation travel audience. Circ. 125,000. Sample copy $2.
Photo Needs: Uses about 60-100 photos/issue; all supplied by freelance photographers. "Each issue varies immensely, we primarily look for stock photography of places, people, subjects such as animals, plants, scenics—we assign some location and portrait shots. We publish a series of photo essays with brief, but interesting accompanying text." Model release and captions required.
Making Contact & Terms: Provide resume, business card, brochure, tearsheets or color samples to be kept on file for possible future assignments. Pays $100-225/color inside photo, depends on size of photo and importance of story; $75-100/hour; $350/dayplus film and expenses. Pays on publication. Credit line given. Buys one-time rights. Previously published work OK. Will send photographers guidelines for SASE. Sample issues are $2.
Tips: "We judge portfolios on technical quality, consistency, ability to show us that you can give us what we ask for with a certain uniqueness in style or design, versatility and creativity. Photographers we work with most often are those who are both technically and creatively adept, and who can take the initiative conceptually by providing new approaches or ideas."

AMERICAN CAGE-BIRD MAGAZINE, One Glamore Court, Smithtown NY 11787. (516)979-7962. Editor: Arthur Freud. Photo Editor: Anne Frizzell. Monthly. Emphasizes care, breeding and maintenance of pet cage birds. Readers include bird fanciers scattered throughout the United States, Canada and other countries. Circ. 50,000. Estab. 1928. Sample copy $3.
Photo Needs: Uses about 15 photos/issue; 6 supplied by freelance photographers. Needs sharp, clear black & white and color photos of budgies, cockatiels, canaries, parrots, toucans and people with such birds. Clever seasonal shots also good (Xmas, etc.). "We choose photos which inform and/or entertain. Identification of the bird type or species is crucial." Special needs include Christmas theme, Fourth of July theme, etc. Model release preferred; captions required.
Making Contact & Terms: Send 5×7 glossy b&w prints, 35mm color slides or 2¼×2¼ transparencies by mail for consideration. SASE. Reports in 2 weeks. Pays $25-75 photo. "Vertical format color slides with dead space at top of slide are considered for cover with a higher payment." Pays on publication. Credit line given. Buys one-time rights. Previously published work OK.

AMERICAN DANE MAGAZINE, 3717 Harney St., Omaha NE 68131. (402)341-5049. Editor-in-Chief: Pamela K. Dorau. Monthly magazine. Circ. 11,000. Estab. 1916. For an audience of "primarily Danish origin, interested in Danish traditions, customs, etc." Wants no scenic photos "unless they are identifiably Danish in origin." Avoid general material. Buys approximately 6 photos annually. Buys all rights, but reassigns to photographer after publication. Send contact sheet or prints for consideration. Pays on publication. Reports in 1-3 weeks. SASE. Previously published work OK. Sample copy $1 with 8½×11 SAE and 75¢ postage.
Making Contact & Terms: Send b&w contact sheet or 5×7 glossy or semigloss prints. Send cover contact sheet or glossy or semigloss prints for b&w. Pays $20. Pays $10-20/color photo; $20-40/photo/text package.
Tips: "Photos must be identifiably Danish in content and have the ability to capture Danish culture." Contact by mail.

AMERICAN FILM, Suite 1514, 6671, Sunset Blvd., Hollywood CA 90028. (213)856-5350. Editor: Wolf Schneider. Art Director: Donna Agajanian. Published 12 times/year. Circ. 108,000. Emphasizes film video and television arts. Readers are "single, well educated, high income, avid movie-goers." Sample copy $2.50 with 10×12 SASE.
Photo Needs: Uses about 50 photos/issue, 5-10 supplied by freelance photographers. Needs current b&w and color portraits of film and TV personalities, on-set photos, photo essays regarding filmmaking.
Making Contact & Terms: Query with samples or with list of stock photo subjects. SASE. Reports in 3 weeks. Pays $500-1,000/color cover; $100-300/b&w or color page; $250-500/job. Pays on publication. Credit line given. Buys one-time rights. No simultaneous submissions or previously published mss; previously published photos OK.

AMERICAN HORTICULTURIST, 7931 East Boulevard Dr., Alexandria VA 22308. (703)768-5700. FAX: (703)765-6032. Editor: Kathleen Fisher. Monthly. "Alternate four-color magazine with two-color newsletter." Emphasizes horticulture. Readers are advanced amateur gardeners. Circ. 25,000. Estab. 1927. Sample copy $2.50. Photo guidelines free with SASE.
Photo Needs: Uses 20-25 (color/magazine), 5 (b&w/news edition) photos/issue; all supplied by free-lancers. "Assignments are rare. 2-3/year need portraits to accompany profiles."Needs shots of people gardening, people engaged in horticulture research public gardens, close-ups of particular plant species showing detail. "We only review photos to illustrate a particular ms which has already been accepted." Sometimes uses seasonal cover shots. Model release preferred; captions and botanical names required.
Making Contact & Terms: Query with list of stock photo subjects; provide resume, business card, brochure, flyer or tearsheets to be kept on file for possible future assignments. SASE. Reports in 3 weeks. Pays $50/color inside photo; $80/color cover photo; $25-50 for b&w photo. Pays on publication. Buys one-time rights.
Tips: Wants to see "ability to identify precise names of plants, clarity and vibrant color."

*AMERICAN SURVIVAL GUIDE, 2145 W. La Palma Ave., Anaheim CA 92801. (714)778-5773. Editor: Jim Benson. Monthly magazine. Emphasizes firearms, military gear, food storage and self defense products. Average reader is male, mid-30s, 37 years all occupations and with conservative views. Circ. 60,000. Estab. 1980. Sample copy $2.95. Photo guidelines free with SASE.
Photo Needs: Uses 125 photos/issue; 30% supplied by freelance photographers. Photos purchased with accompanying manuscript only. Model release and photo captions required.
Making Contact & Terms: Send written query detailing article and photos. Note: Will not accept text without photos or other illustrations. Reports in 1-2 weeks. Pays $70/color and b&w page rate. Pays on publication. Credit line given. Buys all rights. Rights negotiable.
Tips: Wants to see "Professional looking photographs—in focus, correct exposure, good lighting, interesting subject and people in action. Look at sample copies to get an idea of what we feature. We only accept photos with an accompanying manuscript. The better the photos, the better chance you have of being published."

AMERICANA MAGAZINE, 29 W. 38 St., New York NY 10018. (212)398-1550. Editor: Sandra Wilmot. Bimonthly magazine. Circ. 300,000. Estab. 1973. Emphasizes an interest in American history and how it relates to contemporary living. Photos purchased with or without accompanying mss. Freelancers supply 95% of the photos. Pays by assignment or on a per-photo basis. All payments negotiable. Credit line given. Pays on publication. Buys one-time rights and first North American serial rights. Model release is requested when needed. Send query with resume of credits. "Look at several issues of the magazine and then have story ideas before talking to us." SASE. "Make envelope large enough to hold material sent." Previously published work OK. Reports in 2 months. Sample copy $3 and free photo guidelines.
Subject Needs: Celebrity/personality (outstanding in the field of Americana—curator of White House, head of National Trust, famous painter, etc.); fine art; scenic (US—must relate to specific article); human interest; humorous; photo essay/photo feature (majority of stories); US travel; fashion; museum collections and old photography. Captions are required. Uses 8×10 b&w matte prints. Uses color 35mm, 2¼×2¼, 4×5 and 8×10 transparencies. Pays $25-300, depending on size. Uses color covers only with vertical format.
Accompanying Mss: "*Americana*'s stories should open the door on the past by giving the reader the opportunity to participate in the activity we are covering, be it crafts, collecting, travel or whatever. Travel, crafts, collecting, cooking and people are only a few of the subjects we cover. We often rely on contributors to point out new areas that are suitable for *Americana*. Many of the articles are very service-oriented, including practical advice and how-to information."
Tips: "We rarely accept freelance work that does not relate to a specific story we are doing."

AMÉRICAS, Organization of American States, (OAS), 19th Constitution Ave. NW, Washington DC 20006. (202)458-3000. Photo Editor: Beth Mullen. Bimonthly magazine in separate English and Spanish language editions. Circ. 75,000. For people with a special interest in contemporary Latin America and the Caribbean. Needs photos "dealing with the history, culture, arts, wildlife, tourism and development of the nations of the Americas. Prefers to see wide variety of subjects of a human interest nature taken in any country of Latin America or the Caribbean. Special need for modern, developed, urban pix." Wants no shots of "picturesque poverty" or political turmoil in Latin America. Not copyrighted "unless specifically requested." Query first with resume of credits. "Photos are not purchased without accompanying manuscript unless specifically solicited." Pays $250-300/text/photo package. Pays on acceptance. Reports in 2 months. SASE. Previously published work OK. Free sample copy and photo guidelines.

B&W: Send 8×10 matte or glossy prints. Captions required. Pays $20.

Color: Send transparencies. Captions required. Pays $25.

Cover: Send color transparencies. Captions required. Allow space in upper left hand corner for insertion of logo. Pays $75.

Tips: "First, send us a stock photo list, by subject matter, location, dates, etc. Be as specific as possible. Request a sample copy to get a feel for the types of photos we publish. Then submit proposed story ideas or photo essays in query form. Recently our approach has been a fresh new emphasis on pictures that need few captions; stylized color photos; and increasing our coverage of Latin American and Caribbean personalities and endangered wildlife indigenous to the region."

***AMIGA PLUS MAGAZINE,** 544 2nd Street, San Francisco CA 94107. (415)957-0886. Creative Service Director: Julianne Ososke. Bimonthly consumer magazine. Emphasizes Commodore computer. Readers are males, ages 25-40. Circ. 65,000. Estab. 1989. Sample copy with 9×11 SAE and $3.95; photo guidelines free.

Photo Needs: Uses 5 photos/issue; 100% supplied by freelance photographers. Needs photos of technology. Model release required.

Making Contact & Terms: Arrange a personal interview to show portfolio. Uses 35mm prints. Cannot return unsolicited material. Reports in 3 weeks. Pays $500/color cover photo; $400/b&w cover photo; $350 color inside photo; $200/b&w inside photo. Credit line given. Buys all rights; negotiable. Simultaneous submissions OK.

***AQUARIUM FISH MAGAZINE,** P.O. Box 6050, Mission Viejo CA 92690. (714)855-8822. Editor: Edward Bauman. Bimonthly magazine. Emphasizes aquarium fish. Readers are both genders, all ages. Circ. 75,000. Estab. 1988. Sample copy $3.50. Photo guidelines free with SASE.

Photo Needs: Uses 30 photos/issue; 100% supplied by freelance photographers. Needs photos of aquariums and fish, freshwater and saltwater ponds.

Making Contact & Terms: Query with list of stock photo subjects. Submit portfolio for review. Send 35mm, 2¼×2¼ transparencies by mail for consideration. SASE. Reports in 1 month. Pays $150/color cover photo; $50-75/color inside photo; $25/b&w inside photo; $75/color page rate; $25/b&w page rate. Pays on publication. Credit line given. Buys one-time rights. Previously published work OK.

ARCHITECTURAL DIGEST, 5900 Wilshire Blvd., Los Angeles CA 90036. (213)937-4740. Art Director: Thomas Sullivan. For people interested in fine interior design. "We are interested in seeing the work of photographers with background and portfolio of architecture, interiors and/or gardens. We cannot accept tearsheets or prints; only 2¼×2¼ or 4×5 transparencies. We have no staff photographers." Works with freelance photographers on assignment only basis. Provide transparencies.

Tips: Looks for "crisp and sharp lighting, knowledge of composition with interiors, capability of not losing exterior views out of windows. Keep portfolio limited to your best work. Interiors, architecture, and/or gardens."

ARIZONA BUSINESS GAZETTE, Box 1950, Phoenix AZ 85001. (602)271-7341. Editor: Bill Chronister. Weekly newspaper. Circ. 15,000.

Making Contact & Terms: Provide resume, business card, brochure, flyer or tearsheets to be kept on file for possible assignments. Cannot return unsolicited material. Reports when possible. Pays $25/color cover photo, $15/color inside photo and $10/b&w inside photo. Pays on publication. Buys one-time rights. Does not consider simultaneous submissions or previously published work.

***ATLANTA JEWISH TIMES,** Suite 470, 1575 Northside Dr., Atlanta GA 30318. (404)352-2400. Managing Editor: Fran Rothbard. Weekly tabloid. Emphasizes news of interest to Jewish community. Readers are well educated, upscale and knowledgeable. Circ. 10,000+. Estab. 1925. Sample copy free with 9×13 SAE and 4 first class stamps.

Photo Needs: Uses approximately 15 photos/issue; 15% supplied by freelance photographers. Needs photos of Jewish holidays, personalities and events of interest (like rallies against the Klan, for example). Photo captions required.

Making Contact & Terms: Provide resume, business card, brochure, flyer or tearsheets to be kept on file for possible assignments. SASE. Reports in 1 month. Pays $75/color cover photo; $50/b&w cover photo; $25/b&w inside photo. Photo/text package negotiable. Pays on publication. Credit line given. Buys with rights for use with 2 sister publications. Simultaneous and previously published work OK.

Tips: "Call us first if you have an idea so we can discuss options."

ATLANTIC CITY MAGAZINE, 1270 West Washington Ave., Cardiff NJ 08232. (609)641-8959. Editor: Tom McGrath. Monthly. Circ. 50,000. Sample copy $2 plus $1 postage.
Photo Needs: Uses 50 photos/issue; all are supplied by freelance photographers. Model release and captions required. Prefers to see b&w and color fashion, product and portraits, sports, theatrical.
Making Contact & Terms: Query with portfolio/samples. Does not return unsolicited material. Reports in 3 weeks. Provide resume and tearsheets to be kept on file for possible future assignments. Payment negotiable; usually $35-50/b&w photo; $50-100/color; $250-450/day; $175-300 for text/photo package. Pays on publication. Credit line given. Buys one-time rights.
Tips: "We promise only exposure, not great fees. We're looking for imagination, composition, sense of design, creative freedom and trust."

AUDUBON MAGAZINE, 950 3rd Ave., New York NY 10022. Picture Editor: Martha Hill. Bimonthly magazine. Circ. 475,000. Emphasizes wildlife. Photos purchased with or without accompanying mss. Freelancers supply 100% of the photos. Credit line given. Pays on publication. Buys one-time rights. No simultaneous submissions. SASE. Reports in 1 month. Sample copy $4. First-class $5.
Subject Needs: Photo essays of nature subjects, especially wildlife, showing animal behavior, unusual portraits with good lighting and artistic composition. Nature photos should be artistic and dramatic, not the calendar or post card scenic. Important: Query first before sending material; include tearsheets or list previously published credits. Portfolios should be geared to the magazine's subject matter. Must see original transparencies as samples. Also uses some journalistic and human interest photos. No trick shots or set-ups; no soft-focus, filtered or optical effects like those used in some commercial photography. Captions are required.
B&W: Uses 8 × 10 glossy prints. Pays $125-300 inside.
Color: Uses 35mm, 2¼ × 2¼ and 4 × 5 transparencies. Pays $125-300 inside; $700 cover; table-of-contents $450. Plastic sheets only. No prints. No dupes.
Cover: Uses color covers only. Horizontal wraparound format requires subject off-center. Pays $700.
Accompanying Mss: Seeks articles on environmental topics, natural areas or wildlife, predominantly North America.
Tips: "Because of an inventory backlog, *Audubon* is not encouraging photographers to send unsolicited material. If you do submit unsolicited material, it should be accompanied by return postage. We cannot assume the cost of sending back unsolicited material. All photos submitted must be accompanied by adequate captions or they will not be considered for publication."

*BABY TIMES MAGAZINE, 5005 Riviera Ct., Ft. Wayne IN 46825. (219)484-9600. National Advertising Director: A. Elaine Fortmeyer. Quarterly magazine. Emphasizes babies first 12 months of life. Readers are mostly women, ages 25-40. Circ. 250,000. Estab. 1989. Sample copy for 9 × 12 SASE with 4 first class stamps.
Photo Needs: Number of photos used/issue varies. "We only use photos of celebrities and their children at this time." Model release required.
Making Contact & Terms: Send color prints by mail for consideration. Cannot return unsolicited material. Reports in 3 weeks. Payment depends on agreement. Buys one-time rights. Simultaneous and previously published work OK.

BACK HOME IN KENTUCKY, P.O. Box 1627 Franklin TN 37064. (615)794-4338. Editor: Naci Gregg. Consumer bimonthly magazine. Emphasizes the state of Kentucky. Readers are interested in promoting the heritage and future of Kentucky. Circ. 20,000. Sample copy free with 9 × 12 SAE and $1.25 postage (first class).
Photo Needs: Uses 25 photos/issue; all supplied by freelance photographers. Needs photos of scenic, specific places, events. Reviews photos with accompanying ms only. Special needs include holidays in Kentucky; Christmas, especially in 1990; the Kentucky Derby sights and sounds. Captions required.
Making Contact & Terms: Send any size, glossy b&w and color prints, 35mm transparencies by mail for consideration. Reports in 2 weeks. Pays $15/text/photo package. Pays on publication. Credit line given. Buys one-time rights. Simultaneous submissions and previously published work OK.
Tips: "Have a great story to go with the photo—by self or another."

BALLOON LIFE, 3381 Pony Express Dr., Sacramento CA 95834. (916)922-9648. Editor: Glen Moyer. Monthly. Emphasizes sport ballooning. Readers are sport balloon enthusiasts. Circ. 3,500. Estab. 1986. Sample copy free with 9 × 12 SAE and $1.65 postage; photo guidelines free with SASE.
Photo Needs: Uses about 15-20 photos/issue; 90% supplied by freelance photographers. Needs how-to photos for technical articles, scenic for events. Model release and captions preferred.
Making Contact & Terms: Send b&w or color prints; 35mm or 2¼ × 2¼ transparencies by mail for consideration. SASE. Reports in 2 weeks. Pays $50/color cover photo; $15/b&w or color inside photo. Pays on publication. Credit line given. Buys first North American serial rights. Simultaneous submissions and previously published work OK.

Tips: "Photographs, generally, should be accompanied by a story. Cover the basics first. Good exposure, sharp focus, color saturation, etc. Then get creative with framing and content. Often we look for one single photograph that tells the reader all they need to know about a specific flight or event. We're evolving our coverage of balloon events into more than just 'pretty balloons in the sky.' I'm looking for photographers who can go the next step and capture the people, moments in time, unusual happenings, etc. that make an event unique. Query first with interest in sport, access to people and events, experience shooting balloons or other outdoor special events."

BASEBALL CARDS, 700 E. State St., Iola WI 54990. (715)445-2214. FAX: (715)445-4087. Editor: Kit Kiefer. Monthly. Emphasizes sports memorabilia collecting. Readers are 12 to 45-year-old male collectors. Circ. 310,000. Estab. 1981. Sample copy for 8½×11 SASE with $1.25 postage.
Photo Needs: Uses about 10 photos/issue; all supplied by freelance photographers. Needs photos of baseball players, portrait and action. Model release and captions preferred.
Making Contact & Terms: Send color prints and 35mm and 2¼×2¼ transparencies. SASE. Reports in 2 weeks. Pays $25-50/b&w photo, $50-100/color photo. Pays on publication. Credit line given. Buys first and one-time reprint rights. Previously published work OK.
Tips: Seeing trend toward "more use of photographs. Since introducing a line of baseball cards bound in the publication, our photo needs are now 8-10 an issue." In portfolio or samples, "I'm looking for candid-portrait and action shots of baseball players, shots that capture a player's personality." To break in, "Look at the magazine. See what we use. Then go out and shoot that sort of photo. And please don't ask us to credential you until you send us something we can use."

BASKETBALL DIGEST, 990 Grove St., Evanston IL 60201-4370. (708)491-6440. Editor-in-Chief: Michael K. Herbert. Monthly. Emphasizes pro-basketball. Circ. 85,000.
Photo Needs: Uses about 40 photos/issue; 100% supplied by freelance photographers. Needs sports action and portraits.
Making Contact & Terms: Provide resume, business card, brochure, flyer or tearsheets to be kept on file for possible future assignments. Uses 5×7 glossy b&w prints and 35mm transparencies. Pays on publication. Buys one-time rights.

BASSIN', 15115 S. 76th East Ave., Bixby OK 74008. (918)366-4441. Contact: Editor. Published 8 times/ year. Emphasizes bass fishing. Readers are predominantly male, adult; nationwide circulation with heavier concentrations in South and Midwest. Circ. 275,000 subscribers, 100,000 newsstand sales. Sample copy $2.50. Photo guidelines free.
Photo Needs: Uses about 50-75 photos/issue; "almost all of them" are supplied by freelance photographers. "We need both b&w and Kodachrome action shots of freshwater fishing; close-ups of fish with lures, tackle, etc., and scenics featuring lakes, streams and fishing activity." Captions required.
Making Contact & Terms: Query with samples. SASE. Reports in 6 weeks. Pays $250-300/color cover photo; $25/b&w inside photo; $35-150/color inside photo. Pays on publication. Credit line given. Buys first North American serial rights.
Tips: "Send lots of photos and give me a specific deadline in which to send them back. Don't send lists—I can't pick a photo from a grocery list. In the past, we used only photos sent in with stories from freelance writers. However, we would like higher quality stuff. I urge freelance photographers to participate."

BC OUTDOORS, 202-1132 Hamilton St., Vancouver, BC V6B 2S2 Canada. (604)687-1581. Editor: George Will. Emphasizes fishing, both fresh water and salt; hunting; RV camping; wildlife and management issues. Published 7 times/year (January/February, March, April, May, June/July/August, September, October/November/December). Circ. 42,000. Free sample copy with $2 postage.
Photo Needs: Uses about 30-35 photos/issue; 99% of which are supplied by freelance photographers. "Fishing (in our territory) is a big need—people in the act of catching, not standing there holding a dead fish. Hunting, canoeing and camping. Family oriented. By far most photos accompany mss. We are always on lookout for good covers—fishing, wildlife, recreational activities, people in the outdoors—horizontal and square format, primarily of B.C., and Yukon. Photos with mss must, of course, illustrate the story. There should, as far as possible, be something happening. Photos generally dominate lead spread of each story. They are used in everything from double-page bleeds to thumbnails. Column needs basically supplied inhouse." Model release preferred; captions or at least full identification required.
Making Contact & Terms: Send by mail for consideration actual 5×7 or 8×10 b&w prints; 35mm, 2¼×2¼, 4×5 or 8×10 color transparencies; color contact sheet; if color negative send jumbo prints and negatives on request; or query with list of stock photo subjects. SASE, Canadian stamps. Reports in 4-6 weeks normally. Pays $25 and up/b&w photo; $25 and up/color photo; and $150 and up/cover photo. "Payment for photos when layout finalized so we know what we're using. We try to give 'photos-only' contributors an approximate publication date at time of acceptance. We reach an

arrangement with the contributor in such cases (usually involving dupes)." Credit line given. Buys one-time rights inside; with covers "we retain the right for subsequent promotional use." Simultaneous submissions not acceptable if competitor; previously published work OK.

BC WOMAN TO WOMAN, 2nd Fl., 535 W. 10th Ave., Vancouver BC V5K 1K9 Canada. (604)874-7611. Editor: S. Massingham-Pearce. Art Director: Peter Manning. Monthly magazine. Emphasizes women's issues and mainstream, human interest. Readers are 25-65 year old BC women; 50/50 split between those who work inside and outside of the home. Circ. 48,000. Sample copy available with 9 × 12 SASE.
Photo Needs: Uses 20-40 photos/issue; 100% supplied by freelancers. Needs photos of people and human interest subjects. Model release preferred.
Making Contact & Terms: Arrange a personal interview to show portfolio; submit porfolio for review; provide resume, business card, brochure, flyer or tearsheets to be kept on file for possible assignments. Reviews b&w and color contact sheets; 35mm transparencies. SASE. Reports in 4-6 weeks. Payment by assignment. Pays 50% on acceptance, 50% on publication. Credit line given. Buys one-time rights.
Tips: "Don't use US stamps for mailing in Canada. SASE's with U.S. stamps cannot be returned." Looks for "natural, spontaneous, or action shots" in photos used. "Study your target audience/market."

BEST WISHES, EXPECTING, Suite 101, 77 Mowat St., Toronto ON M4E 3L3 Canada. (416)537-2608. Editor: Kathy Fremes. Magazine published 2 times per year. Emphasizes concerns of expectant women and new families. Readers are mothers and/or new families. Circ. 200,000.
Photo Needs: Needs photos of mothers, babies, expectant woman, young family shots. Written release preferred.
Making Contact & Terms: Send unsolicited photos by mail for consideration. SASE. Reports in 1 month. Pays $200-400/color cover photo. Pays on publication. Credit line given. Buys one-time rights (for covers); all rights (for everything else). Simultaneous submissions and previously published work OK.

BICYCLING, 33 E. Minor St., Emmaus PA 18098. (215)967-5171. Editor and Publisher: James C. McCullagh. Photo Editor: Mike Shaw. 10 monthly issues, 6 bimonthly issues. Circ. 300,000. Emphasizes touring, commuting, health, fitness and nutritional information, recreational riding and technical gearing for the beginning to advanced bicyclist. Buys 10-20 photos/issue. Photos purchased with accompanying ms. Credit line given. Pays on publication. Buys one-time rights. Send material by mail for consideration or query with resume of credits. SASE a must. Reports in 3 months. Sample copy $2; photo guidelines free with SASE.
Subject Needs: Celebrity/personality, documentary, how-to, human interest, photo essay/photo feature, product shot, scenic, special effects and experimental, sport, spot news and travel. "No cheesecakes nor beefcakes." Model release and captions required.
B&W: Uses negatives. Pays $35-75/photo.
Color: Uses 35mm, 2¼ × 2¼, 4 × 5 transparencies. Pays $75-300/photo.
Cover: Uses 35mm, 2¼ × 2¼, 4 × 5 color transparencies. Vertical format required. Pays $400/photo.
Accompanying Mss: Seeks mss on any aspects of bicycling (nonmotorized); commuting, health, fitness and nutritional information, touring or recreational riding. Pays $25-300/ms. Writer's guidelines on photo guidelines sheet.
Tips: "We prefer photos with ms. Major bicycling events (those that attract 500 or more) are good possibilities for feature coverage in the magazine. Use some racing photos. The freelance photographer should contact us and show examples of his/her work; then, talk directly to the editor for guidance on a particular shoot. For covers: Shoot vertical. The logo and blurbs run on every cover. These are constant; be aware of their location and what that means while shooting. A large single image that creates a simple cover often works best. Riding: While shooting people riding, be aware of the background. Watch out for wires, shadows, or other major distractions. Make sure people are riding in proper positions; must be wearing a helmet, dressed properly and on the correct side of the road."

BILLIARDS DIGEST, Suite 850, 101 E. Erie, Chicago IL 60611. (312)266-7179. Editor: Michael Panozzo. Bimonthly magazine. Circ. 10,000. Emphasizes billiards and pool for tournament players, room owners, tournament operators, dealers, enthusiasts and beginning players, distributors, etc. Buys 5-10 photos/issue. Pays on publication. Not copyrighted. Send material by mail for consideration. Works with freelance photographers on assignment only basis. Provide resume, tearsheet and samples (photostats of 6 are adequate) to be kept on file for possible future assignments. Credit line given. Reports in 2 weeks. SASE.
Subject Needs: "Unusual, unique photos of billiards players, particularly at major tournaments. Should also stress human emotions, their homelife and outside interests." No stock hunched-over-the-table shots. "We want photos that convey emotion, either actively or passively. Show pool people as human beings." Captions required.

B&W: Uses prints; contact sheet OK. Pays $5-50/photo.
Color: Uses transparencies. Pays $10-50/photo.
Cover: Uses transparencies. Pays $10-50/photo.

*BIOLOGY DIGEST, 143 Old Marlton Pike, Medford NJ 08055. (609)654-6500. FAX: (609)654-4309. Editor: Mary Suzanne Hogan. Photo Editor: Dorothy Whitaker. Monthly. Comprehensive abstracts journal covering all the life sciences from anatomy to zoology. Readers include high school and undergraduate college students. Circ. 1,700. Estab. 1974. Sample copy $12.
Photo Needs: Uses about 20 photos/issue. Photos purchased with descriptive captions only.
Making Contact & Terms: Send 8×10 or 5×7 b&w prints by mail for consideration. SASE. Reports in 1 month. Pays $10-15/b&w cover photo; b&w inside photo. Pays on acceptance. Credit line given. "If photographer desires one-time rights, we will honor that but prefer to have all rights (non-exclusive) so that we may use again."

BIRD TALK, Box 6050, Mission Viejo CA 92690. (714)855-8822. Editor: Karyn New. Monthly magazine. Emphasizes "better care of pet birds through informative and entertaining articles. Some birds of interest are: canaries, finches, parrots, parakeets, toucans, macaws, conures, lovebirds, cockatiels, cockatoos, mynahs." Readers are "owners of one pet bird or breeders of many." Sample copy $3.50. Photo guidelines free with SASE.
Photo Needs: Uses 50-75 photos/issue; all by freelance photographers. Needs photos of "any and all pet birds either in portraits or in action—doing anything a bird is able to do." Model release and captions preferred.
Making Contact & Terms: Send 5×7, 8×10 b&w prints; 35mm, 2¼×2¼, 4×5, 8×10 transparencies; b&w contact sheets by mail for consideration. SASE. Reports in 4 weeks. Pays $15/b&w (partial page) inside photo; $50/color (partial page) inside photo; full pages: $25/b&w, $75/color. Color prints acceptable but will often be used b&w. Pays on publication. Credit line given. Buys one-time rights.
Tips: Prefers to see "sharp feather focus. Cage bars acceptable, cages and perches must be clean. More black and white photos are used per issue than color. Send us clear shots of any pet birds with cover letter specifying *species* of bird. We also need a variety of shots of people interacting with their birds."

BIRD WATCHER'S DIGEST, Box 110, Marietta OH 45750. (614)373-5285. Associate Editor/Photography and Art: Bill Thompson III. Bimonthly. Circ. 80,000. Emphasizes birds and bird-watchers. Readers are bird watchers/birders (backyard and field, veterans and novices). Digest size. Sample copy $3.
Photo Needs: Uses 25-35 photos/issue; all supplied by freelance photographers. Needs photos of North American species. For the most part, photos are purchased with accompanying ms. Model release preferred.
Making Contact & Terms: Query with list of stock photo subjects and samples. SASE. Reports in 2 months. Pays from $25/color inside. Pays on publication. Credit line given. Buys one-time rights. Previously published work OK.

THE BLACK COLLEGIAN, 1240 S. Broad St., New Orleans LA 70125. (504)821-5694. FAX: (504)821-5713. Managing Editor: K. Kazi-Ferrouillet. Quarterly. Emphasizes career information for African-American college students. Readers are African-American college students and recent graduates. Circ. 121,000. Estab. 1970. Sample copy $2.50 with 9×12 SAE and $1.50 postage. Photo guidelines free with SASE.
Photo Needs: Uses about 70 photos/issue; 25% supplied by freelance photographers. Needs include Afro-American professionals in job situations, Afro-American students on campus and in work situations, celebrity candids. Model release preferred; captions required.
Making Contact & Terms: Query with samples. SASE. Reports in 3 months. Pays $250/color cover photo; $25-50/b&w photo; $50-200/color photo. Pays on publication. Credit line given. Buys one-time rights.

BLADE MAGAZINE, Box 22007, Chattanooga TN 37422. (615)894-0354. FAX: (615)892-7254. Managing Editor: Steve Shackleford. Bimonthly magazine. Specializes in handmade and factory knives. Readers are aged 30-70, blue collar, outdoors types, collectors. Circ. 100,000. Estab. 1973. Sample copy free with 9×11 SAE and $2 postage. Photo guidelines free with SASE.
Photo Needs: Uses 130 photos/issue; freelancer photography/issue—10% assignment and 60% freelance stock. Needs photos of how-tos on knifemaking, knife shots with artsy backgrounds, knives being used, knives on display, etc. Special needs include shots of the latest factory and handmade knives; any kind of colorful knife shot. Model release required; captions required.
Making Contact & Terms: Send unsolicited photos by mail for consideration. Uses 4×5 or 5×7 color prints or 35mm transparencies. SASE. Reports in 1 month. Pays $50+/b&w or color cover photo; $7/color or b&w inside photo. Pays on acceptance. Credit line given. Buys all rights; will negotiate

with photographers unwilling to sell all rights. Also publishes *Edges*, a pocketknife collector's tabloid. Black and white photos only used; read *Blade Magazine* listing for *Edges* information. Also publishes Blade Trade, b&w only; same rates and rules apply as for Blade magazine.

Tips: Looks for "A true appreciation for the subleties of knife design. Closeups of individual knife parts that tell more about the knife than any editorial can are also telling. Appreciation of appropriate props, ability to keep glare off blades (or to keep it on in an artistic manner). Make the shot as animate as possible, even though knives are inanimate objects. Provide a variety of shots at reasonable prices and in plent of time for each deadline."

*BLUE RIDGE COUNTRY, Box 21535, Roanoke VA 24018. (703)989-6138. Art Director: David Harris. Consumer publication. Bimonthly magazine. Emphasizes outdoor scenics of Blue Ridge Mountain Region. Readers are upscale couples, ages 30's-50's. Circ. 55,000. Estab. 1988. Sample copy for 9×12 SASE and $1.65. Photo guidelines free with SASE.

Photo Needs: Uses up to 20 photos/issue; 100% supplied by freelance photographers; 10% assignment and 90% freelance stock. Needs photos of travel, scenics and wildlife. Future photo needs include themes of the Blue Ridge region. Model release preferred; photo captions required.

Making Contact & Terms: Query with list of stock photo subjects; send unsolicited photos by mail for consideration. Uses 35mm, 2¼×2¼, 4×5 transparencies. SASE. Reports in 1 month. Pays $100/color cover photo; $25-75/b&w phot; $25-100/color photo. Pays on publication. Credit line given. Buys one-time rights.

Tips: In photographer's samples looks for "Photos of Blue Ridge Region, color saturated, focus required and photo abilities. Freelance should present him/herself neatly and organized."

THE B'NAI B'RITH INTERNATIONAL JEWISH MONTHLY, 1640 Rhode Island Ave. NW, Washington DC 20036. (202)857-6645. Editor: Jeff Rubin. Monthly magazine. Circ. 200,000. Estab. 1886. For Jewish family members. Emphasizes religious, cultural and political happenings worldwide. Buys 30 photos annually, 100% on assignment. Occasional photo essays.

Making Contact & Terms: Present samples and text (if available). Buys first serial rights. Pays on publication. Reports in 6 weeks. SASE. Pays $25-300/b&w or color photo (cover); $50-300/day; $100-500/photo/text package.

Tips: Be familiar with our format and offer suggestions or experience relevant to our needs. Looks for "Technical expertise, ability to tell a story within the frame."

BOAT JOURNAL, (formerly The Small Boat Journal), 2100 Powers Ferry Rd., Atlanta GA 30339. (404)955-5656. FAX: (404)952-0669. Editor: Richard Lebovitz. Emphasizes quality small craft for recreation, regardless of construction material. "Focus is primarily on those boats less than 30-feet long, traditional, contemporary and unusual. All types of boats are covered, including sailboats, powerboats, canoes and kayaks. Bimonthly. Circ. 65,000. Estab. 1979. Free sample copy and photo guidelines with 9×12 SAE and $2.05 postage.

Photo Needs: Buys 30-40 photos/issue; "80% assigned to freelancers who are known to us. We need good photos of small boats being built, repaired and maintained. We're also on the lookout for photos of special boat gatherings, cruises, regattas and the like. Black and white often purchased with ms, but strong photo essays with full caption information welcome. Color covers should communicate the high excitement inherent in the ownership and use of small boats. We're always looking for cover photos showing people having fun on their boats." No cute or humorous photos; no scantily clad females; no mundane points of view/framing/composition. Model release and captions required.

Specs: Black and white film and contacts with 5×7 or 8×10 unmounted glossies; 35mm or larger transparencies for interior color or cover.

Making Contact & Terms: Query with samples. Provide resume, business card, brochure and tearsheets to be kept on file for possible future assignments. Prefers to see exterior photos with natural light in a portfolio. SASE. Pays $15-75/b&w photo; $50-125/color photo; $225-350/day; $100-500/photo/text package. Pays on publication. Credit line given. Reports in 2-4 weeks.

Tips: "We are always eager to see new material. We look for sharp focus, clear, bright colors, interesting subjects and good natural light. Professionalism in marine photography. Our best photographers have ability to capture boats (and people) from a perspective that conveys useful information to our readers. We are always eager to see new material. Routine boat shots and travelogue-type photos won't work for us. We are assigning in-depth boat text/photo sessions in all parts of the country. Nautical experience a plus. We're looking for photographers with a journalistic approach. Especially need action photos of boats. Do your best work. Know how to photograph boats; know what angles to shoot from."

BOAT PENNSYLVANIA, Box 1673, Harrisburg PA 17105-1673. (717)657-4518. Editor: Art Michaels. Quarterly magazine. Emphasizes "non-angling boating in Pennsylvania: powerboating, canoeing, kayaking, sailing, personal watercraft and water skiing." Published by the Pennsylvania Fish Commission. Sample copy and guidelines free with 9×12 SASE and 85¢ postage.

Photo Needs: Uses about 30 photos/issue; 80% supplied by freelance photographers. Model release and complete identifying captions required.

Making Contact & Terms: Query with resume of credits. Send 35mm, 2¼ × 2¼ transparencies by mail for consideration. SASE. Reports in 1 week on queries; 3 months on submissions. Pays on acceptance. Credit line given. Buys variable rights, most often first rights.

Tips: "We are hungry for top-quality materials, but no matter how good a picture is, we insist on a few items. We feature subjects appropriate to Pennsylvania, so we can't use pictures with obviously non-Pennsylvania backgrounds. We prefer to show boats registered in Pennsylvania. If this is a problem, try to hide the boat registration completely. Finally, *Boat Pennsylvania* stresses safety, so pictures must show boaters accordingly. For instance, we would not publish a picture of a powerboat under way with people lying on the gunwale or leaning over the side. Submit a selection of cover possibilities. We look for verticals mostly, but we'd love to see horizontals for possible wrap-arounds. Learn how to use back-lighting effectively, and remember to shoot in early morning light or in early evening light."

BODYBOARDING MAGAZINE, Suite C, 950 Calle Amanecer, San Clemente CA 92672. (714)492-7873. Photo Editor: Peter Brouillet. Bimonthly magazine. Emphasizes hard core bodyboarding action and bodyboarding beach lifestyle photo and personalities. Readers are 15-16 years old, mostly males (96%). Circ. 40,000. Photo guidelines free with SASE.

Photo Needs: Uses roughly 70 photos/issue; 30-50% supplied by freelancers. Needs photos of hardcore bodyboarding action, surf lineups, beach scenics, lifestyles and bodyboarding personalities. Special needs include bodyboarding around the world; foreign bodyboarders in home waves, local beach scenics.

Making Contact & Terms: Send unsolicited photos by mail for consideration. Uses 35mm and 2¼ × 2¼ transparencies; b&w contact sheets & negatives. SASE. Reports in 2 weeks. Pays $500/color cover photo; $40/b&w page rate; $75/color page rate. Pays on publication. Credit line given. Buys one-time rights.

Tips: "We look for clear, sharp, high action bodyboarding photos preferably on Kodachrome 64. We like to see a balance of land and water shots. Be persistent and set high standards."

BOSTON MAGAZINE, 300 Massachusetts Ave., Boston MA 02115. (617)262-9700. Associate Art Director: Lisa Puccio. Art Asst.: Doran Putka. Monthly magazine. Emphasizes a wide variety of subjects with Boston/New England focus. Readers are primarily residents of greater Boston metro area, and most of Eastern Massachusetts, Cape Cod, Southern New England; largely college-educated professionals who regard Boston as focal point of their lives. Circ. 140,000. Sample copy free with 9 × 12 SAE and $2.40 postage.

Photo Needs: Uses about 70 photos/issue; 50 supplied by freelance photographers. Needs portraits, dramatized, journalistic or documentary, food, design, interiors, sports, fashion, travel, slice-of-life, photo-essays. All city (Boston)-oriented. Model release and captions required.

Making Contact & Terms: Query with samples; submit portfolio for review. Does not return unsolicited material. Photographers should follow up for report. Pays $600/color cover photo; $75-300/b&w inside photo; $100-400/color inside photo; $300/b&w page; $400/color page; $800-1,500/text/photo package. Pays on publication. Credit line given. Buys one-time rights.

Tips: Prefers to see "editorial work, preferably portraits in portfolio or samples. Examine the magazine carefully before the interview and edit your portfolio to suit it."

BOSTONIA MAGAZINE, 10 Lenox St., Brookline MA 02146. (617)353-3081. Editor: Keith Botsford. Art Director: Douglas Parker. Bimonthly. Circ. 150,000. Sample copy $2.50.

Photo Needs: Uses 100 photos/issue; many photos are supplied by freelance photographers. Works with freelance photographers on assignment only basis. Provide resume, brochure and samples to be kept on file for possible future assignments. Needs include documentary photos related to Boston research; celebrity/personality, sports, spot news, and travel photos related to Boston city region; photo essay/photo features and human interest related to city region; and possibly scenic photos. Also seeks feature articles on people and the New England area accompanied by photos. Model releases and captions required.

Making Contact & Terms: Send by mail for consideration actual 5 × 7 b&w glossies for inside. SASE. Reports in 2 weeks. Pays on acceptance $30-40 for b&w photos; 10¢/word or flat fee (depending on amount of preparation) for feature articles. Credit line given. Buys all rights, but may reassign to photographer after publication. No simultaneous submissions or previously published work.

BOW & ARROW, Box HH, Capistrano Beach CA 92624. (714)493-2101. Editor: Jack Lewis. Bimonthly magazine. Circ. 106,000. For archers and bowhunters. "We emphasize bowhunting—with technical pieces, how-tos, techniques, bowhunting tips, personality profiles and equipment tests." Photos purchased with accompanying ms; rarely without. "We buy approximately 4 text/photo packages per issue.

Most cover shots are freelance." Pays $50-300 for text/photo package or on a per-photo basis for photos without accompanying ms. Credit line given. Pays on acceptance. Buys first rights. Query with samples OK, but prefers to see completed material by mail on speculation. SASE. Reports in 2-3 weeks.

Subject Needs: Animal (for bowhunting stories); celebrity/personality (if the celebrity is involved in archery); head shot (occasionally used with personality profiles, but we prefer a full-length shot with the person shooting the bow, etc.); how-to (must be step-by-step); human interest; humorous; nature, travel and wildlife (related to bowhunting); photo essay/photo feature; product shot (with equipment tests); scenic (only if related to a story); sport (of tournaments); and spot news. "No snapshots (particularly color snapshots), and no photos of animals that were not hunted by the rules of fair chase. We occasionally use photos for Bow Pourri, which is a roundup of archery-related events, humor, laws and happenings." Captions required.

B&W: Uses 5×7 or 8×10 glossy prints.

Color: Uses 35mm or 2¼×2¼ transparencies.

Cover: Uses 35mm or 2¼×2¼ transparencies. Vertical format preferred.

Accompanying Mss: Technical pieces, personality profiles, humor, tournament coverage, how-to stories, bowhunting stories (with tips), equipment tests and target technique articles. Writer's guidelines included with photo guidelines.

Tips: "We rarely buy photos without an accompanying manuscript, so send us a good, clean manuscript with good-quality b&w glossies (our use of color is limited)."

BOWBENDER, Box 912, 65 McDonald Close, Carstairs AB T0M 0N0 Canada. (403)337-3023. FAX: (403)337-3460. Editor: Mrs. Kathleen Windsor. Five times/year. Emphasizes archery in Canada, especially bowhunting. Readership consists of married, professional males, 25-40 years of age with $20-40,000 annual income. Circ. 45,000. Estab. 1984. Sample copy for $2.50 and 9×12 SASE. Photo guidelines free with SASE; postage from U.S. must be sumitted thru Canadian mail order; postage from Canada, 39¢ stamp.

Photo Needs: Uses 30 photos/issue; 100% supplied by freelance photographers; 99% comes from freelance stock and rest freelance photography from assignment. Uses big game animal shots only. Written release and captions preferred.

Making Contact & Terms: Query with list of stock photos or send unsolicited photos by mail for consideration. Send color and b&w, all sizes, all formats. SASE. Reports in 3 weeks maximum. Pays $200/color cover photo; $60/color inside photo; $30/b&w inside photo;8-10¢ word/phot/text package (Canadian currency). Pays on publication. Credit line given. Buys first North American serial rights. Does not consider simultaneous submissions or previously published work.

Tips: Looking for shots of "any huntable big game for front cover: vertical shots clear, especially eyes. Close-up shots are best. Trend is mostly b/w inside shots. Submit samples first along with stock file. Label slides somehow. If photos are not catalogued by some code, at least label them. Slides especially are irreplaceable. We use as many photos as we can each issue." Look at a past issue before submitting."

BOWHUNTER, 2245 Kohn Rd., Harrisburg PA 17105. (717)657-9555. Editor/Publisher: M.R. James. Managing Editor: Dave Canfield. Published 8 times/year. Circ. 250,000. Emphasizes bow and arrow hunting. Photos purchased with or without accompanying ms. Buys 50-75 photos/year. Credit line given. Pays on acceptance. Buys one-time publication rights. Send material by mail for consideration or query with samples. SASE. Reports on queries in 1-2 weeks; on material in 4-6 weeks. Sample copy $2.

Subject Needs: Scenic (showing bowhunting) and wildlife (big and small game of North America). No cute animal shots or poses.

B&W: Uses 5×7 or 8×10 glossy prints; both vertical and horizontal format. Pays $20-75/photo.

Color: Uses 5×7 and 8×10 glossy prints or 35mm and 2¼×2¼ transparencies; vertical format. Pays $50-100/photo.

Cover: Uses 35mm and 2¼×2¼ color transparencies. Vertical format preferred. Pays $200/photo, "more if photo warrants it."

Accompanying Mss: "We want informative, entertaining bowhunting adventure, how-to and where-to-go articles." Pays $25-250/ms, occasionally more. Writer's guidelines free with SASE.

Tips: "Know bowhunting and/or wildlife and study several copies of our magazine before submitting. We're looking for better quality and we're using more color on inside pages. Get to know our magazine before submitting any material. Most purchased photos are of big game animals. Hunting scenes are second. In b&w we look for sharp, realistic light, good contrast. Color must be sharp; early, late light is best. We avoid anything that looks staged; we want natural settings, quality animals. Send only your best, and if at all possible let us hold those we indicate interest in. Very little is taken on assignment; most comes from our files or is part of the manuscript package. If your work is in our files it will probably be used."

BOWHUNTING WORLD, (formerly Archery World), Suite 101, 319 Barry Ave. South, Wayzata MN 55391. (612)476-2200. Managing Editor: Tim Dehn. Bimonthly magazine. *"Bowhunting World* is the oldest and most respected magazine in print for the hunting archer. It focuses editorially on all aspects of hunting with a bow and arrow in North America. Circ. 250,000. Estab. 1952. Readers are primarily male, college-educated, avid bowhunters who participate in their sport year-round and who make an above-average income. Free sample copy and photo guidelines.

Photo Needs: Uses 10-25 photos/issue; all from freelancer stock. "We want to see wildlife subjects commonly hunted as big game and small game species in North America." Special needs include "big game species for cover selections."

Making Contact & Terms: Send 35mm by mail for consideration. SASE. Reports in 2-4 weeks. Pays $50/color cover photo; $40/b&w inside photo; $75-125 color/inside photo; and $200-400/text/photo package. Pays on publication. Credit line given. Buys one-time rights. Simultaneous submissions and previously published work OK "but please so state in cover letter."

Tips: "We look for technically excellent phots with tropy-class animals and/or unusual and beautiful settings. We're using more color than ever before, far less freelance b&w. And our covers are no longer limited to deer—we're using elk, bear and are open to moose, caribou and antelope as well. Send small, carefully screened submissions—not more than 60 slides. 20 excellent ones will get a far better reception than 20 excellent mixed with 40 average. Be prepared for us to hold your slides on file up to a year, and if there's a limit to the number we should hold, say so."

BOWLERS JOURNAL, 101 E. Erie St., Chicago IL 60611. (312)266-7171. Editor: Mort Luby. Managing Editor: Jim Dressel. Monthly magazine. Circ. 22,000. Emphasizes bowling. For people interested in bowling: tournament players, professionals, dealers, etc. Needs "unusual, unique photos of bowlers." Buys 20-30 annually. Not copyrighted. Send contact sheet or photos for consideration. Pays on publication. Reports in 3 weeks. SASE. Simultaneous submissions OK.

B&W: Send contact sheet or 8 × 10 glossy prints. Captions required. Pays $5-50.

Color: Send transparencies. Captions required. Pays $10-75.

Cover: See requirements for color.

Tips: "Bowling is one of the most challenging areas for photography, so try it at your own risk . . . poor lighting, action, etc."

BOWLING DIGEST, 990 Grove St., Evanston IL 60201-4370. (708)491-6440. Editor-in-Chief: Michael K. Herbert. Bimonthly. Emphasizes pro and amateur bowling. Circ: 150,000.

Needs: Uses 50 photos/issue; 100% provided by freelance photographers. Needs sports action and portraits.

Making Contact & Terms: Provide resume, business card, brochure, flyer or tearsheets to be kept on file for possible future assignments. Pays on publication. Buys one-time rights.

BRIDAL FAIR MAGAZINE, 4151 Knob Dr., St. Paul MN 55122. (612)452-0571. Publisher: Russ Moore. Quarterly magazine. Circ. 175,000. Sample copy free with 9 × 11 SASE.

Photo Needs: Uses 60 photos/issue; 100% supplied by freelance photographers. Purchases photos with accompanying ms only. Written release required; captions preferred.

Making Contact & Terms: Arrange a personal interview to show portfolio or query with resume of credits and list of stock photo subjects. Also send unsolicited photos by mail for consideration or submit portfolio for review. Send color transparencies. SASE. Reports in 1 month. Pays $150/color inside photo, $100/b&w inside photo, $100/color page rate, $100/b&w page rate, $100-200/hour, $500-1,000/day or $250-500/photo/text package. Pays on publication. Credit line given. Buys one-time rights.

BRIGADE LEADER, Box 150, Wheaton IL 60189. (312)665-0630. Editor: Steven P. Neideck. Art Director: Robert Fine. Quarterly magazine. Circ. 9,000. Estab. 1959. For Christian men, age 20 and up. Seeks "to make men aware of their leadership responsibilities toward boys in their families, churches and communities." Buys 2-7 photos/issue;50% freelance photography/issue comes from assignment and 50% from freelance stock. Buys first and second serial rights. Arrange a personal interview to show portfolio or send photos for consideration. Pays on publication. Reports in 6 weeks. SASE. Simultaneous submissions and previously published work OK. Sample copy $1.50 with 9 × 12 SAE and 85¢ postage. Photo guidelines available. Include a SASE.

Subject Needs: Photos of men in varied situations (alone, with their sons, with groups of boys or with one boy, with their families or at work), head shot, photo essay/photo feature and scenic.

B&W: Send 8 × 10 glossy prints. Pays $35.

Cover: Send glossy b&w prints. Pays $75-100.

Tips: The trend seems to be "An increased emphasis on dads and their young children (ages 3-6)."

BRITISH HERITAGE, Historical Times, Inc., 2245 Kohn Rd., Box 8200, Harrisburg PA 17105. (717)657-9555. FAX: (717)657-9526. Editor: Mrs. Gail Huganir. Bimonthly magazine. Emphasizes British history, Commonwealth travel and history. Readers are professional, middle-aged. Circ. 110,000. Estab. 1974. Sample copy $4.85, author guidelines available with SASE.
Photo Needs: Uses about 50 photos/issue; 95% supplied by freelance photographers; 95% freelance stock and 5% assignment. Needs travel, scenic and historical photos. Captions required.
Making Contact & Terms: Provide resume, business card, brochure, flyer or tearsheets to be kept on file for possible future assignments. SASE. Reports in 4-6 weeks. Negotiates pay for cover photos. Pays $50-100/b&w inside photo; $75-250/color inside photo. Pays on publication. Credit line given. Buys one-time rights.
Tips: Looks for "Good focal point, bright colors and sharp image. Sees trend towards mood shot and unusual angle. Call before submitting and for photographic guidelines."

*BUZZWORM: The Environmental Journal, 1818 16th St., Boulder CO 80302. (303)442-1969. Photo Editor: Ann Carey. Bimonthly magazine. Emphasizes environmental issues and worldwide conservation. Readers are affluent, educated, active, both sexes and a median age of 38. Circ. 80,000. Estab. 1988. Sample copy $5.00. Photo guidelines free with SASE.
Photo Needs: Uses 50 photos/issue. Most are supplied by freelance photographers. Photo needs are specific to articles in issue, mostly wildlife and environment. Model release and photo captions are preferred.
Making Contact & Terms: Query with resume of credits and list of stock photo subjects. Provide resume, business card, brochure, flyer or tearsheets to be kept on file. No unsolicited calls or photos. SASE. Reports in 1 month. Pays $400/color cover photo; $200/color page rate. Pays 60-90 days after publication. Credit line given. Buys one-time rights.
Tips: Wants to see photographer's tearsheets, stock lists, resume, specialties and future travel plans. "Send information requested and update us by mail as to your most recent photography, travels, etc."

CALIFORNIA ANGLER, 1921 E. Carnegie St. N., Santa Ana CA 92705. (714)261-9779. Editor: John Skarabo. Monthly magazine. Emphasizes fresh and saltwater fishing in California and travel destinations. Readers are dedicated California sport fishermen. Circ. 30,000. Sample copy free.
Photo Needs: Uses 40-50 photos/issue; all supplied by freelance photographers. Needs shots depicting angling action rather than dead fish, and pictures illustrating angling how-to, technical skills. Special needs include underwater pictures of game fish, especially saltwater species. Model release preferred; captions required.
Making Contact & Terms: Query with samples; send 35mm or 2¼ × 2¼ transparencies by mail for consideration. SASE. Reports in 2 weeks. Pays $300/color cover photo; $25/b&w inside photo; $25-100/color inside photo; $300 for text/photo package. Pays on publication. Credit line given. Buys one-time rights or first North American serial rights. Simultaneous submissions and previously published work sometimes OK.
Tips: Looks for "someone who has good action, scenic, supplemental, and people photos of fishing. Send samples. We get so little honestly good material, we hug the good stuff."

*CALIFORNIA MAGAZINE, 11601 Wilshire Blvd., Brentwood CA 90025. (213)479-6511. Photo Editor: Hilary Johnston-Barton. Monthly magazine. Covers travel, restaurants, fashion and lifestyle subjects for young adults in their 30's. Circ, 350,000. Estab. 1965.
Photo Needs: Uses 20-30 photos/issue. Needs photos of "everything but celebrities." Model release and photo captions required.
Making Contact & Terms: Arrange a personal interview to show portfolio. Query with resume of credits. Send unsolicited b&w and color prints, 35mm and 2¼ × 2¼ by mail consideration; also transparencies, all formats. SASE. Reports in 3 months. Payment varies according to usage. Pays on publication. Credit line given. Buys one-time rights. Simultaneous submissions and previously published work OK.
Tips: Wants to see photos that are "unusual and creative with lots of energy." To break in, shoot for consistency. Also keep him "posted with what you're doing."

CAMPUS LIFE, 465 Gundersen Dr., Carol Stream IL 60188. (708)260-6200. Managing Editor: Jim Long. Art Director: Jeff Carnehl. Photo Coordinator, Assistant: Susan Mikottis. Monthly magazine except May/June and July/August. Circ. 120,000. *"Campus Life* is a magazine for high school and college-age youth. We emphasize balanced living—emotionally, spiritually, physically and mentally." Photos purchased with or without accompanying ms. Buys 20 photos/issue. Credit line given. Pays on publication. Buys one-time rights. SASE. Simultaneous submissions and previously published work OK. Reports in 4-6 weeks. Sample copy $2; photo guidelines for SASE.

Subject Needs: Head shots (of teenagers in a variety of moods); humorous, sport and candid shots of teenagers/college students in a variety of settings. "We want to see multiracial teenagers in different situations, and in every imaginable mood and expression, at work, play, home and school. No travel, how-to, still life, travel scenics, news or product shots. We stay away from anything that looks posed. Shoot for a target audience of 18-year-olds."

B&W: Uses 8×10 glossy prints. Pays $35-125/photo.

Color: Uses 35mm or larger format transparencies. Pays $60-225 minimum/photo.

Cover: Uses 35mm or larger format color transparencies. Pays $250/photo.

Accompanying Mss: Query. Pays $125 minimum/ms. Writer's guidelines for SASE.

Tips: "We try to choose photos that portray a variety of types of teenagers. Our guiding philosophy: that readers will 'see themselves' in the pages of our magazine." Looks for ability to catch teenagers in real-life situations that are well-composed but not posed. Technical quality; communication of an overall mood or emotion, or action. "Look at a few issues to get a feel for what we choose. We're not interested in posed shots. Cover shots are usually tight head shots."

*CAMPUS VOICE, 505 Market St., Knoxville TN 37902. (615)595-5000. Editor: Margo Leske. Senior Art Director: Bett McLean. Picture Researcher: Ruth Ann Reeve. Distributed nine times during the school year on college campuses. Emphasizes college life, careers, job hunting and consumer articles. Circ. 1.2 million. Sample copy and SASE (9×12 envelope).

Photo Needs: Uses about 25 color photos/issue to illustrate features in both the Youth and Adult Divisions (e.g. the college experience, the world of business, the world of travel, etc.); 10-15 supplied by freelance photographers. Wants to hear from photographers who can supply photos of students and their activities. Interested in classroom situations, fads, fashions, leisure activities and travel appropriate to college students. Model release and captions required.

Making Contact & Terms: Query with resume of photo credits and tearsheets; or samples along with SASE. Also indicate availability and location for assignments. Submit 35mm, 2¼×2¼ or 4×5 transparencies. All slides sent on speculation will be returned. Payment ASMP rates. Buys one-time North American rights.

CANADIAN BIKER MAGAZINE, P.O. Box 4122, Station A, Victoria, BC V8X 3X4 Canada. (604)384-0333. Editor: Len Creed. Monthly magazine, published 8 times a year. Emphasizes motorcycles. Readers are motorcycle enthusiasts of all ages. Circ. 15,000. Sample copy free with 8½×11 SASE. Photo guidelines free with SASE.

Photo Needs: Uses 55 photos/issue; 90% supplied by freelance photographers. Needs photos of motorcycles; people involved in related activities. Model release and photo captions required.

Making Contact & Terms: Query with list of stock photo subjects or send unsolicited photos by mail for consideration. Send b&w or color, any size, format or finish. SASE. Reports "according to situation." Pays $30-50/cover photo ($40 is standard). Pays on publication. Credit line given.

Tips: "Most photographs published in the magazine should be accompanied by articles. The most helpful contributors to the magazine are photo-journalists (with good writing ability as well)."

CANADIAN FICTION MAGAZINE, Box 946, Station F, Toronto, ON M4Y 2N9 Canada. Editor: Geoffrey Hancock. Quarterly literary magazine. Circ. 1,800. Emphasizes Canadian fiction, short stories and novel excerpts. "Each issue is an anthology devoted exclusively to the work of writers and artists resident in Canada and Canadians living abroad." Buys 8-16 photos/issue, plus cover. Buys first North American serial rights. Model release required. Submit portfolio. Credit line given. Pays on publication. Reports in 6 weeks. SAE and International Reply Coupons. Sample copy $7.50, in Canadian funds.

Cover: Uses 5×7 glossy b&w prints of "exhibition quality." Pays $50.

Tips: "Please examine back issues for the type of work required. Previous contributors include Sam Tata, Walter Curtin, Kryn Taconis, John Reeves, Kéro, Paul Orenstein, Arnaud Maggs, Peter Milroy, Helena Wilson. Especially receptive to portraits of contemporary Canadian writers, musicians, actors, playwrights and artists."

CANOE, Box 3146, Kirkland WA 98083. (206)827-6363. Editor: Barton Parrott. Bimonthly magazine. Circ. 60,000. Emphasizes a variety of paddle sports as well as how-to material and articles about equipment. For upscale canoe and kayak enthusiasts at all levels of ability. Also publishes special projects/posters. Photos only occasionally purchased without accompanying mss. Thirty photos used/issue; 90% supplied by freelancers. Pays $50-150 on a per-photo basis. Credit line given. Pays on publication. Buys one-time rights, first serial rights and exclusive rights. Model release required "when potential for litigation." Query or send material. "Let me know those areas in which you have particularly strong expertise and/or photofile material. Send best samples only and make sure they relate to the magazine's emphasis and/or focus. (If you don't know what that is, pick up a recent issue first, before sending me unusable material.) We will review dupes for consideration only. Originals required for publication. Also, if you have something in the works or extraordinary photo subject matter of interest to our audience, let me know! It would be helpful to me if those with substantial reserves would supply indexes by subject matter." SASE. Simultaneous submissions and previously published work OK, in noncompeting publications. Reports in 1 month. Free sample copy with 9 × 12 envelope and postage only.

Subject Needs: Canoeing, kayaking, ocean touring, canoe sailing, fishing when compatible to the main activity, canoe camping but not rafting. No photos showing disregard for the environment, be it river or land; no photos showing gasoline-powered, multi hp engines; no photos showing unskilled persons taking extraordinary risks to life, etc. Captions are required, unless impractical.

B&W: Uses 5 × 7 and 8 × 10 glossy prints.

Color: Uses 35mm, 2¼ × 2¼ and 4 × 5 transparencies.

Cover: Uses color transparencies; vertical format preferred. Pays $250. Pays $150/full page b&w or color photos; $100/half to full page photos; $75/quarter to half page photos; $50/quarter or less.

Accompanying Mss: "Editorial coverage strives for balanced representation of all interests in today's paddling activity. Those interests include paddling adventures, both close to home and far away; camping; fishing; flatwater; whitewater; ocean kayaking; poling; sailing; outdoor photography; how-to projects; instruction and historical perspective. Regular columns feature paddling techniques, conservation topics, safety, interviews, equipment reviews, book/movie reviews, new products and letters from readers."

Tips: "We have a highly specialized subject and readers don't want just any photo of the activity. We're particularly interested in photos showing paddlers' *faces*; the faces of people having a good time. We're after anything that highlights the paddling activity as a lifestyle and the urge to be outdoors." All photos should be "as natural as possible with authentic subjects. We receive a lot of submissions from photographers to whom canoeing and kayaking are quite novel activities. These photos are often clichéd and uninteresting. So consider the quality of your work carefully before submission if you are not familiar with the sport. We are always in search of fresh ways of looking at our sport."

CAPE COD HOME & GARDEN, 60 I Munson Meeting, Chatham MA 02633. (508)945-3542. Photo Editor: Betsy Morin. Consumer publication. Quarterly, oversized magazine format. Emphasizes regional magazine for Cape Cod and the outlying islands of Nantucket and Martha's Vineyard, Massachusetts. General readership. Circ. 20,000. Sample copy $4. Photo guidelines free with SASE.

Photo Needs: Uses 50-70 photos/issue; 100% supplied by freelance photographers. Needs home and garden photos of Cape Cod, Martha's Vineyard and Nantucket. "We periodically issue a 'stock request list' free for the asking." Written release preferred.

Making Contact & Terms: Query with resume of credits; include business card, brochure, flyer or tearsheets to be kept on file for possible assignments. Query with list of stock photo subjects, send unsolicited photos by mail for consideration or submit portfolio for review. Send b&w prints, any size and format, and 35mm, 2¼ × 2¼ or 4 × 5 transparencies. SASE. Reports in 4-8 weeks. Pays $300/color cover photo, $70/color or b&w inside photo and $90/color or b&w page rate. Pays on acceptance. Credit line given. Buys one-time rights. Simultaneous submissions and previously published work OK.

THE CAPE ROCK, Southeast Missouri State University, Cape Girardeau MO 63701. (314)651-2156. Editor-in-Chief: Harvey Hecht. Emphasizes poetry and poets for libraries and interested persons. Semiannual. Circ. 1,000. Free photo guidelines.

Photo Needs: Uses about 13 photos/issue; all supplied by freelance photographers. "We like to feature a single photographer each issue. Submit 30 thematically organized 8 × 10 glossies, or send 5 pictures with plan for complete issue. We favor most a series that conveys a sense of place. Seasons are a consideration too: we have spring and fall issues. Photos must have a sense of place: e.g., an issue featuring Chicago might show buildings or other landmarks, people of the city (no nudes), travel or scenic. No how-to or products. Sample issues and guidelines provide all information a photographer needs to decide whether to submit to us." Model release not required "but photographer is liable"; captions not required "but photographer should indicate where series was shot."

Making Contact & Terms: Send by mail for consideration actual 8 × 10 b&w photos, query with list of stock photo subjects, or submit portfolio by mail for review. SASE. Reporting time varies. Pays $100 and 10 copies on publication. Credit line given. Buys "all rights, but will release rights to photographer on request." No simultaneous submissions or previously published work.

Tips: "We don't make assignments, but we look for a unified package put together by the photographer. We may request additional or alternative photos when accepting a package."

THE CAPILANO REVIEW, 2055 Purell Way, North Vancouver, BC V7J 3H5 Canada. (604)984-1712. Editor: Pierre Coupey. Quarterly magazine. Emphasizes poetry, fiction and visual arts. Audience consists of primarily of readers of literature. Circ. 800. Estab. 1972. Sample copy $8 and 8 × 10 SASE.

Photo Needs: Needs photos of art; all freelance photography from assignment. Model release and captions required.

Making Contact & Terms: Query with resume of credits or list of stock photo subjects. SASE with Canadian postage or IRC. Reports in 3 months. Pays $15/color or b&w page rate ($120/10pages). Credit line given. Simultaneous submissions OK.

Tips: "Query one page first before sending work. Theme issues require editorial selection" in advance.

CAR COLLECTOR & CAR CLASSICS, Suite 144, 8601 Dunwoody Place, Atlanta GA 30350. (404)998-4603. Editor: Donald R. Peterson. Monthly. Emphasizes collector automobiles. Readers are 98% male, average age 41. Circ. 30,000. Estab. 1977. Sample copy $2 postpaid. Photo and writers guidelines free with SASE.

Photo Needs: Uses about 50-75 photos/issue; "nearly all" supplied by freelance photographers; 30% of photos on assignment per issue. Needs photos of "automobiles of the 1925-1965 era." Photos purchased with accompanying manuscript only. Model release required; captions required.

Making Contact & Terms: Telephone first; send b&w prints; 35mm, 2¼×2¼, 4×5 and/or 8×10 transparencies by mail for consideration. SASE. Reports ASAP, but no schedule. Pays $5/b&w inside photo; $10/color inside photo; $50-400/text/photo package. Pays on publication. Credit line always given. Buys all rights, but will negotiate with photographer.

Tips: "Do not submit photos to us without accompanying story and captions. Get connected with a writer so that a complete package can be offered. We are looking for cars shot from pleasing angles with good backgrounds." No 'fish-eye' or other 'trick lens' photos purchased."

*CAR CRAFT MAGAZINE, 8490 Sunset Blvd., Los Angeles CA 90069. (213)854-2320. Editor: Jim McGowan. Monthly magazine. Emphasizes street machines and muscle cars. Readership is mostly males ages 18-34. Circ. 500,000. Estab. 1935. Sample copy free with SASE. Model release required.

Photo Needs: Uses 100+ photos/issue. Uses freelancers occasionally. Model release required.

Making Contact & Terms: Query with resume of credits. Provide resume, business card, brochure, flyer or tearsheets to be kept on file for possible assignments. Send 35mm and 8×10 b&w prints; 35mm and 2¼×2¼ transparencies by mail for consideration. SASE. Reports in 1 month. Pays $75-150/color photo, cover or text. Payment for b&w varies according to subject ad needs. Pays on publication. Credit line given. Buys all rights.

Tips: "We use primarily black-and-white shots. When we need something special in color or see an interesting color shot, we'll pay more for that. Review a current issue for our style and taste."

CAREER WOMAN, (formerly *The Collegiate Career Woman*), Equal Opportunity Publications, Inc., 44 Broadway, Greenlawn NY 11740. (516)261-8917. FAX: (516)261-8935. Associate Editor: Eileen Nester. Published 3 times a year. Emphasizes career guidance and career opportunites for women at the college and professional level. Readers are college-age and young professional women. Circ. 10,500. Estab. 1972. Sample copy free with 9×12 SASE and 5 first-class stamps.

Photo Needs: Uses at least one photo per issue (cover); planning to use freelance work for covers and possibly editorial; many photos come from freelance writers who submit photos with their articles. Contact for needs. Model release preferred; photo captions required.

Making Contact & Terms: Query with list of stock photo subjects; send unsolicited prints or 35mm transparencies by mail for consideration. SASE. Reports in 2 weeks. Pays $15/color and b&w photo. Pays on publication. Credit line given. Buys one-time rights. Simultaneous submissions and previously published work OK, "but not in competitive career-guidance publications."

Tips: "We are looking for clear color shots of women professionals in their work environment. Photos should focus on head/shoulder shots of the women. We are looking primarily for women (ages 30-35) who represent role models for our readers. They should be attractive and professional. We've decided to use more cover photos than we have in the past. We are also open to using inside photos, but freelancers should contact us and discuss upcoming stories before sending photos. Read our magazine to get an idea of the editorial content. Cover photos do not have to tie in to anyone particular story in the magazine, but they have to be representative of the magazine's editorial content as a whole. Query with list of stock photo subjects or sent unsolicited prints or 35mm transparencies by mail for consideration."

CAREERS & THE HANDICAPPED, EQUAL OPPORTUNITY PUBLICATIONS, INC., 44 Broadway, Greenlawn NY 11740. (516)261-8917. Art Director: Andrew Elias. Magazine published two times a year. Emphasizes career guidance for people with disabilities at the college and professional levels. Readers are disabled college students and young working professionals of all occupations that require a college degree. Circ. 10,000. Sample copy free with 9×12 SASE and 6 first-class stamps.

Photo Needs: Uses at least one photo per issue (cover); planning to use freelance work for covers and possibly editorial. Contact for needs. Model release preferred; photo captions required.

Making Contact & Terms: Query with list of stock photo subjects; send unsolicited prints or 35mm transparencies by mail for consideration. SASE. Reports in 2 weeks. Pays $25/color cover photo. Pays on publication. Credit line given. Buys one-time rights. Simultaneous submissions and previously published work OK, "but not in competitive career-guidance publications."

Tips: "We are looking for clear color shots of disabled students and young professionals who are involved in activities related to their academic studies or professions. We've decided to use more cover photos than we have in the past. We are also open to using inside photos, but freelancers should contact us and discuss upcoming stories before sending photos. Read our magazine to get an idea of editorial content. Cover photos do not have to tie in with any one particular story in the issue, but they have to be representative of magazine's editorial content as a whole."

CARIBBEAN TRAVEL AND LIFE MAGAZINE, 8403 Colesville Rd., Silver Spring MD 20910. (301)588-2300. Editor: Veronica Stoddart. Published 6 times a year. Emphasizes travel, culture and recreation in islands of Caribbean, Bahamas and Bermuda. Circ. 100,000. Estab. 1985. Sample copy free with 9×12 SAE with $1.30 postage. Photo guidelines free with SASE.

Photo Needs: Uses about 57 photos/issue; 75% supplied by freelance photographers; 20% assignment and 80% freelance stock. "We combine scenics with people shots. Where applicable, we show interiors, food shots, resorts, water sports, cultural events, shopping and wildlife/underwater shots." Special needs include "cover shots—attractive people on beach; striking images of the region, etc." Captions required. "Provide throrough caption information. Don't submit stock that is mediocre."

Making Contact & Terms: Arrange a personal interview to show portfolio; query with samples; query with list of stock photo subjects. Provide stock list, business card, brochure, flyer or tearsheets to be kept on file for possible future assignments. Uses 4-color photography. SASE. Reports in 2 weeks. Pays $400/color cover photo; $150/color full page; $125/color ¾ page; $100/color ½ page and $75/color ¼ page; $75-400/color photo; $1,200-1,500 per photo/text package. Pays on publication. Buys one-time rights.

Tips: Seeing trend toward "fewer but larger photos with more impact and drama. We are looking for particularly strong images of color and style, beautiful island scenics and people shots—images that are powerful enough to make the reader want to travel to the region; photos that show people doing things in the destinations we cover; originality in approach, composition, subject matter. Good composition, lighting and creative flair. Images that are evocative of a place, creating story mood. Good use of people. Submit stock photography for specific story needs, if good enough can lead to possible assignments. Let us know exactly what coverage you have on a stock list so we can contact you when certain photo needs arise."

CAROLINA QUARTERLY, Greenlaw Hall, CB#3520, University of North Carolina, Chapel Hill NC 27599-3520. (919)962-0244. Editor: Becky Barnhouse. Circ. 800. Estab. 1948. Emphasizes "current poetry, short fiction." Readers are "literary, artistic—primarily, though not exclusively, writers and serious readers." Sample copy $5.

Photo Needs: Uses 1-8 photos/issue; all supplied by freelance photographers. "No set subject matter. Artistic outdoor as well as interior scenes. Attention to form. No photojournalism, please."

Making Contact & Terms: Send b&w prints by mail for consideration. SASE. Reports in 1-3 months, depending on deadline. Pays $25 per artist. Pays on publication. Credit line given. Buys one-time rights.

Tips: Prefers to see "high quality artistic photography. Attention to form, design. Look at a few high quality small literary magazines which use photos. Subject matter is up for grabs."

CAT FANCY, Fancy Publications, Inc., Box 6050, Mission Viejo CA 92690. (714)855-8822. Editor-in-Chief: K. E. Segnar. Readers are "men and women of all ages interested in all phases of cat ownership." Monthly. Circ. 280,000. Estab. 1965. Sample copy $3.50; photo guidelines for SASE.

Photo Needs: Uses 20-30 photos/issue; 100% freelance supplied. "For purebred photos, we prefer shots "that show the various physical and mental attributes of the breed. Include both environmental and portrait-type photographs. We also need good-quality, interesting b&w and color photos of mixed-breed cats for use with feature articles and departments." Model release required.

Making Contact & Terms: Send by mail for consideration actual 8×10 b&w photos, 35mm or 2¼×2¼ color transparencies. SASE. Reports in 6 weeks. Pays $15-25/b&w photo; $50-150/color photo; and $50-300 for text/photo package. Credit line given. Buys first North American serial rights.

Tips: "Nothing but sharp, high contrast shots, please. Send SASE for list of specific photo needs. We are using more color photos and prefer more action shots, fewer portrait shots. We look for photos of all kinds and numbers of cats doing predictable feline activities—eating, drinking, grooming, being

This amusing image is one of five from a two-page photo essay titled "Cat and Bug Encounter," which was featured in Cat Fancy magazine. Photographer Ed Swanzey submitted the black-and-white images along with some other unsolicited shots to Managing Editor Kathryn Segnar. Segnar matched the photos with a limerick and turned the essay into a very entertaining piece. Noting that he received $125 in exchange for one-time reprint rights for the five photos, Swanzey says he wanted to convey the message that "Into every life a little humor ought to fall."

groomed, playing, scratching, taking care of kittens, fighting, being judged at cat shows and accompanied by people of all ages."

CATHOLIC DIGEST, St. Paul's Square, Box 64090, St. Paul MN 55164. (612)647-5323. Editor: Henry Lexau. Photo Editor: Susan Schaefer. Monthly magazine. Emphasizes religion, family life. Readers are mostly Catholic, mature with teenagers or grown children. Circ. 620,000. Sample copy free with SASE (6½×9½ envelope, 88¢ postage).
Photo Needs: Uses 6-9 photos/issue; 1 supplied by freelance photographer. Needs photos of family life, children, teenagers, senior citizens, middle-age, young adults, religious symbols and scenes, food, health, medical. Special needs include Catholic photos of all kinds, holiday/religious feasts. Model release required; captions preferred.
Making Contact & Terms: Send b&w and color prints, contact sheets, negatives or color slides by mail for consideration. SASE. Reports in 3 weeks. Pays on publication. Credit line given. Buys one-time rights. Previously published work OK.
Tips: "More of a demand for pictures which tell the thoughts and emotions of the people in them—pictures which draw the viewer into the 'private moment' of the shot, and which tell a lot of the emotional tone or mood of the article the pictures accompany." Looks for "candid, natural expressions of people in photos—limited use of (appropriate) props—classic, simple clothing—high contrast in b&w photos; rich harmony in 4/color. Indoor photos less problematic because they work in more seasons. Seasonal photos should be received 4 to 5 months in advance of month of issue. Avoid clichés."

CATHOLIC NEAR EAST MAGAZINE, 1011 First Ave., New York NY 10022-4195. FAX: (212)838-1344. Editor: Thomas McHugh. Quarterly magazine. Circ. 170,000. Estab. 1974. Emphasizes "the living faith of native peoples in the Near East; charitable work conducted among poor and refugees in Near East; religious history and contemporary culture of Near East; Eastern Rites of the Church (both Catholic and Orthodox)." General readership, mainly Catholic; wide educational range. Buys 40 photos/year;40% supplied by freelancers. Buys first North American serial rights. Query first. Credit line given. "Credits appear on page 3 with masthead and table of contents." Pays on publication. Reports in 3 weeks; acknowledges receipt of material immediately. SASE. Simultaneous submissions and previously published work OK, "but neither one is preferred. If previously published please tell us when and where." Sample copy and photo guidelines free with 6½×9½ SASE with 60¢ postage.

Subject Needs: "Evocative photos of people, places and activity in the Middle East and India. Mainly, though, we require people pictures, especially those which show current and historical Christian influences in the Near East. We are also interested in good shots of artistic and cultural objects/painting, crafts and of the Eastern Rite Churches/priests/sacraments/etc." No posed shots, or "purely political pictures of the area." Payment varies; $50 and up, depending on size, quality, etc.
B&W: Uses 8 × 10 glossy prints. Captions required.
Color: Uses 35mm or larger transparencies. Captions required.
Cover: Send color negatives or color transparencies. "Generally, we use shots which show our readers what the people and places of the Middle East really look like. In other words, the shot should have a distinctly Eastern look." Captions required.
Tips: "We always need *people* pictures. Additionally, we use shots of the Eastern Rites of the Catholic Church. Finally, we do a 'day in the life' story on the people of different places and cultures of the Middle East and India in almost every issue. If the pictures were good enough, we would consider doing a photo story in any of the above categories." Also, "try to put the photos you send into some kind of specific context of a family, community or religious heritage. We welcome a ms accompanying photos, especially when the freelancer has a detailed knowledge about the area and its people."

THE CATHOLIC WORLD, (formerly *New Catholic World*), 997 Macarthur Blvd., Mahwah NJ 07430. (201)825-7300. Managing Editor: Laurie Felknor. Bimonthly magazine. Circ. 9,000. Estab. 1865. Buys 5-10 photos/issue. Credit line given. Pays on publication. Buys one-time rights. Send material by mail for consideration. SASE. Simultaneous submissions and previously published work OK. Reports in 1 month.
Subject Needs: Human interest, nature, fine art and still life, religious (Roman Catholic).
B&W: Uses 8 × 10 glossy prints. Pays $20-35/photo.
Tips: "Photos of people must reflect current hairstyles, clothing, etc. Each issue of *The Catholic World* is on a specific theme. Send query as to themes for the 6-issues per year."

CATS MAGAZINE, Box 290037, Port Orange FL 32029. (904)788-2770. FAX: (904)788-2710. Editor: Linda J. Walton. Monthly magazine. Circ. 150,000. For cat owners and breeders. Buys 30-50 photos/ year. Buys first serial rights. Send contact sheet or photos for consideration. Pays on publication. Reports in 8-12 weeks. SASE. Free sample copy (must include 9 × 12 SASE must include $1.25 postage) and photo guidelines. Provide tearsheets to be kept on file for possible future assignments.
Subject Needs: Felines of all types; celebrity/personality (with their cats); fine art (featuring cats); head shot (of cats); how-to (cat-oriented activities); human interest (on cats); humorous (cats); photo essay/photo feature (cats); sport (cat shows); travel (with cats); and wildlife (wild cats). No shots of clothed cats or cats doing tricks.
Making Contact & Terms: Send b&w contact sheet or 5 × 7 or 8 × 10 glossy prints. Wants no silk finish. Pays $15-50. Send 2¼ × 2¼ color transparencies for covers. Prefers "shots showing cats in interesting situations." Pays $150; $50/photo/text package.
Tips: "We are always receptive to seasonal themes." If purebred cats are used as subjects, they must be representative specimens of their breed. Should be clear, sharp photographs of cats. "Our most frequent causes for rejection: cat image too small; backgrounds cluttered; uninteresting; poor quality purebred cats; dirty pet-type cats; shot wrong shape for cover; colors untrue; exposure incorrect. Cats should be protrayed in a realistic manner—no clothed cats. Just submit your best work."

CD REVIEW, Forest Rd., Hancock NH 03449. (603)525-4201. FAX: (603)525-4423. Executive Editor: Larry Canale. Art Director: Bob Dukette. Monthly magazine. Emphasizes recorded music; hi-fi equipment. Readership is primarily men, mid to late thirties. Circ. 125,000. Estab. 1984. Sample copy free with 8 × 11 SASE.
Photo Needs: Uses 24 photos/issue; 10% supplied by freelance photographers. Needs photos of music personalities. Model release and photo captions preferred.
Making Contact & Terms: Query with list of stock photo subjects. Provide resume, business card, brochure, flyer or tearsheets to be kept on file for possible assignments. SASE. Reports in 2 weeks. Credit line given; payment varies. Rights vary; negotiable. Previously published work OK.

CHANGING MEN: Issues in Gender, Sex & Politics, 306 N. Brooks St., Madison WI 53715. Editor: Mike Biernbaum. Triannual. Emphasizes men's issues, feminist, male politics, gay and heterosexual personal and political issues. Readers are anti-sexist men, feminists, gay and political activists. Circ. 3,000. Sample copy $4.50.
Photo Needs: Uses 6-8 photos/issue; 100% supplied by freelance photographers. Needs art photography, male body shots, images of men at work, play, in social and emotional relationships, etc.; journalism on gay and male feminist gatherings. Special needs include features on men's issues, AIDS, relationships with women, men's health, gay issues, antiporn, 3rd world masculinities, etc. Model release preferred.

Making Contact & Terms: Query with list of sample relevant stock photo subjects. Send b&w prints and b&w contact sheets. SASE. Reports in 1 month. Pays $15-50/text/photo package. Pays on publication. Credit line given. Buys one-time rights.

Tips: "Display sensitivity to subject matter; provide political photos showing conscience, strong journalism on gay issues." In samples, wants to see "emotional content of image; or strong statement about a man's situation; or humor/irony in 'changing' situations." To break in, shoot "well-composed images that stand on their own, by showing emotional feeling or mood or by making a statement."

CHARISMA MAGAZINE, 600 Rinehart Rd., Lake Mary FL 32746. (407)333-0600. Art Director: Eric T. Jessen. Monthly magazine. Emphasizes Christians. General readership. Circ. 200,000. Sample copy $2.50.

Photo Needs: Uses approximatly 20 photos/issue; 100% supplied by freelance photographers. Needs editorial photos—appropriate for each article. Model release required; photo captions preferred.

Making Contact & Terms: Send unsolicited photos by mail for consideration. Provide resume, business card, brochure, flyer or tearsheets to be kept on file for possible assignments. Send color 35mm, 2¼ × 2¼, 4 × 5 or 8 × 10 transparencies. Cannot return unsolicited material. Reports ASAP. Pays $300/color cover photo, $150/b&w inside photo, $50-150/hour or $400-600/day. Pays on publication. Credit line given. Buys all rights, but willing to negotiate. Simultaneous submissions and previously published work OK.

Tips: In portfolio or samples, looking for "good color and composition with great technical ability. To break in, specialize; sell the sizzle rather than the steak!"

CHATTANOOGA LIFE & LEISURE, 1085 Bailey Ave., Chattanooga TN 37404. (615)629-5375. Managing Editor: Eileen Hoover. Editor: Mark Northern. Monthly magazine. Emphasizes articles and photos of interest to Chattanoogans. Readers are late 20s to late 40s, above average income with varied interests; from hiking to haute cuisine to local history to business. Sample copy $1.95.

Photo Needs: Uses about 4-25 photos/issue; over 50% supplied by freelance photographers. Needs photos of animal/wildlife, local travel, feature portraits, photojournalism, photo spreads on a single subject. "Everything must have a strong Chattanooga region emphasis, but, please, no postcard scenes. Assignments are given on an individual basis." Model release preferred; captions required.

Making Contact & Terms: Arrange a personal interview to show portfolio. Does not return unsolicited material. Reports in 1 month. All payments are upon agreement of editor and photographer. Pays on publication. Buys one-time rights. Simultaneous submissions and previously published work OK.

Tips: "We are very interested in good b&w photos. Portfolio should show all the photographer's abilities: portraits, nature, staged, photojournalism, etc. We are looking for photographers who capture the flavor of Chattanooga without resorting to postcard style. We find there are a lot of good outdoor photographers available. We lack photographers who can capture 'people' on film or illustrate a story without using a cliché shot."

THE CHESAPEAKE BAY MAGAZINE, 1819 Bay Ridge Ave., Annapolis MD 21403. (301)263-2662, (DC)261-1323. Art Director: Christine Gill. Monthly. Circ. 32,000. Estab. 1972. Emphasizes boating—Chesapeake Bay only. Readers are "people who use Bay for recreation." Sample copy available.

Photo Needs: Uses "approximately" 21 photos/issue;60% supplied by freelances; 20% by freelance assignment. Needs photos that are "Chesapeake Bay related (must); vertical power boat shots are badly needed (color)." Special needs include "vertical 4-color slides showing boats and people on Bay."

Making Contact & Terms: Query with samples or list of stock photo subjects; send 35mm, 2¼ × 2¼, 4 × 5 or 8 × 10 transparencies by mail for consideration. SASE. Reports in 3 weeks. Pays $200/color cover photo;$25-75/b&w photo; $25-250/color photo; $150-1,000/photo/text package. Pays on publication. Credit line given. Buys one-time rights. Simultaneous submissions OK.

Tips: "We prefer Kodachrome over Ektachrome. Vertical shots of the Chesapeake bay with *power* boats badly needed. Looking for: Boating, bay and water oriented subject matter. Qualities and abilities include: Fresh ideas, clarity, exciting angles and true color. We're using larger photos—more double page spreads. Photos should be able to hold up to that degree of enlargement. When photographing boats on the Bay—keep the 'safety' issue in mind. (People hanging off the boat, drinking, women 'perched' on the bow are no-no's!)"

CHICAGO PARENT NEWS MAGAZINE, 141 South Oak Park Ave., Oak Park IL 60302. Managing Editor: Mary Haley. News magazine published 12 times/year. Emphasizes parenting. Readers are parents. Circ. 70,000. Sample copy $1.

Photo Needs: Uses about 10 photos/issue; 2-5 supplied by freelance photographers. Needs photos of children. Model release required; photo captions preferred.

Making Contact & Terms: Query with samples; query with list of stock photo subjects; send b&w prints or contact sheets by mail for consideration. SASE. Reports in 3 weeks. Pays $25/b&w photo. Pays on publication. Credit line given. Simultaneous submissions and previously published work OK.

Tips: "Send us great photos of children. We will use them."

CHICKADEE MAGAZINE, Suite 306, 56 the Esplanade, Toronto ON M5E 1A7 Canada. (416)868-6001. FAX: (416)868-6009. Editor: Catherine Ripley. Published 10 times/year. Circ. 110,000. Estab. 1979. A natural science magazine for children 3-9 years. Sample copy for $3.50 with SAE and $1 money order to cover postage.
Photo Needs: Uses about 3-6 photos/issue; 2-4 supplied by freelance photographers. Needs "crisp, bright, close-up shots of animals in their natural habitat." Model release required.
Making Contact & Terms: Write to request a photo package. Query with list of stock photo subjects and/or photo story ideas. SAE with $1 money order to cover postage. Reports in 6-8 weeks. Pays $200 Canadian/color cover; $200 Canadian (centerfold); pays $75-300/color photo (cover); text/photo package negotiated separately. Pays on acceptance. Credit line given. Buys one-time rights, nonexclusive, to reproduce in *Owl* and *Chickadee* in Canada and affiliated children's publications in remaining world countries.

CHILD LIFE, Box 567, Indianapolis IN 46206. (317)636-8881. Editor: Steve Charles. Magazine published 8 times/year. For children ages 7-9. Photos purchased only with accompanying ms. Credit line given. Pays on publication. Buys all rights to editorial material, but usually one-time rights on photographs. Send material by mail for consideration. Query not necessary. SASE. Reports within 10 weeks. Sample copy 75¢; free writer's guidelines with SASE.
Subject Needs: Health, medical and safety articles are always needed "but we are looking for photo stories on any subject which will entertain and inform our readers." Captions and model release required.
B&W: Prefer 5×7 or 8×10 glossy to accompany mss. Pays $10/photo.
Color: Transparencies 35mm or larger. Pays $20/photo. Will consider photo accompanying photo story for cover, pay $50/cover.
Tips: "Address all packages to Editor and mark 'Photo Enclosed.' "

CHILDREN'S PLAYMATE, Box 567, Indianapolis IN 46206. (317)636-8881. Editor: Elizabeth A. Rinck. Published 8 times/year. Emphasizes better health for children. Readers are children between the ages of 6-8. Circ. 115,000. Sample copy 75¢ with 5×7 SAE. Photo guidelines free with SASE.
Photo Needs: Number of photos/issue varies; 100% supplied by freelancers. Reviews photos with accompanying ms only. Model release required; captions preferred.
Making Contact & Terms: Send unsolicited photos, accompanied by ms. Uses b&w prints and 35mm transparencies. SASE. Reports in 8-10 weeks. Pays $10/b&w inside photo; $20/color inside photo. Pays on publication. Credit line given. Buys one-time rights.

CHRISTIAN BOARD OF PUBLICATION, Box 179, St. Louis MO 63166. Director, Product Development: Guin Stemmler. Religious age-level magazines/curriculum; monthly, quarterly and annual. For various age levels (children, youth, adults) engaging in educational and recreational activities. Buys 4-6 or more photos/issue for each publication.
Subject Needs: Uses educational activities, recreation and some closeups. Does not want posed "pretty" pictures, industrial or fashion models.
Specs: Uses 5×7 and 8×10 glossy b&w. Uses b&w and some color covers; format varied.
Payment/Terms: Pays $20 minimum/b&w print. Credit line given. Pays on publication. Buys one-time rights. Simultaneous submissions and previously published work OK.
Making Contact: Send photos by mail for consideration. SASE. Reports in 4 weeks.
Tips: "Send about 25 samples with return postage; then we can comment."

THE CHRISTIAN CENTURY, 407 S. Dearborn St., Chicago IL 60605. (312)427-5380. FAX: (708)427-1302. Editor: James M. Wall. Photo Editor: Matt Giunti. Magazine published 36 times/year. Circ. 35,000. Estab. 1884. Emphasizes "concerns that arise at the juncture between church and society, or church and culture." Deals with social problems, ethical dilemmas, political issues, international affairs, the arts, and theological and ecclesiastical matters. For college-educated, ecumenically minded, progressive church clergy and laypersons. Photos purchased with or without accompanying ms. Buys 50 photos/year. Credit line given. Pays on publication. Buys one-time rights. Send material by mail for consideration. SASE. Simultaneous submissions OK. Reports in 4 weeks. Free sample copy and photo guidelines for SASE.
Subject Needs: Celebrity/personality (primarily political and religious figures in the news); documentary (conflict and controversy, also constructive projects and cooperative endeavors); scenic (occasional use of seasonal scenes and scenes from foreign countries); spot news; and human interest (children, human rights issues, people "in trouble," and people interacting). Model release and captions preferred.

B&W: Uses 5×7 or 8×10 glossy prints. Pays $20-75/photo.

Cover: Uses glossy b&w prints. Alternates among vertical, square and horizontal formats. Pays $20 minimum/photo.

Accompanying Mss: Seeks articles dealing with ecclesiastical concerns, social problems, political issues and international affairs. Pays $35-l00. Free writer's guidelines for SASE.

Tips: Needs sharp, clear photos. "We use photos sparingly. Since we use photos primarily to illustrate articles, it is difficult to determine very far in advance or with much specificity just what our needs will be. Therefore, we prefer to keep photos in our files for extended periods of time."

CHRISTIAN HERALD, 40 Overlook Dr., Chappaqua NY 10514. (914)769-9000. Art Director: Peter A. Gross. Bi-monthly magazine. "The magazine of People Making a Difference." Readers are "evangelical Christian families." Circ. 165,000. Sample copy $2 with 9×12 SAE. Photo guidelines free with SASE.

Photo Needs: Uses 8-10 photos/issue; all supplied by freelance photographers. Looking for photographers with a knack for good "people" photos. Knowledge of the evangelical Christian scene is a plus. Model release and captions preferred.

Making Contact & Terms: Send 8×10 b&w prints, 35mm, 2¼×2¼ transparencies by mail for consideration. SASE. Reports in 5-6 weeks. Pays $350/color cover photo; $75-200/b&w inside photo, $75-300/color inside photo and $200-350/text/photo package. Pays on publication. Credit line given. Buys one-time rights. Previously published work OK.

*THE CHRONICLE OF THE HORSE, P.O. Box 46, Middleburg VA 22117. (703)687-6341. Editor: John Strassburger. Weekly magazine. Emphasizes English horse sports. Readers range from young to old. "Average reader is a college educated female, middle-aged, well off financially." Circ. 23,500. Estab. 1937. Sample copy for $1.25 with 11×14 SAE and 4-5 first class stamps. Photo guidelines free with SASE.

Photo Needs: Uses 10-25 photos/issue; 90% supplied by freelance photographers. Needs photos from competitive events (horse shows, dressage, steeplechase, etc.) to go with news story or to accompany personality profile. "A few stand alone. Must be cute, beautiful or news-worthy. Reproduced in black and white." Prefer purchasing photos with accompanying ms. Special photo needs include good photos to accompany our news stories, especially horse shows. Photo caption required with every subject identified.

Making Contact & Terms: Query with what photographer has in mind. Send b&w and color prints. SASE. Reports in 3 weeks. Pays $15-30/photo/text package. Pays on publication. Credit line given. Buys one-time rights. Prefer first North American rights. Simultaneous and previously published work OK.

Tips: "We do not want to see portfolio or samples. Contact us first, preferably by letter."

THE CHURCH HERALD, 6157 28th St. SE, Grand Rapids MI 49546-6999. (616)957-1351. Editor: John Stapert. Photo Editor: Christina Van Eyl. Monthly magazine. Circ. 45,000. Emphasizes current events, family living, evangelism and spiritual growth, from a Christian viewpoint. For members and clergy of the Reformed Church in America. Needs photos of life situations—families, couples, vacations, school; religious, moral and philosophical symbolism; seasonal and holiday themes; nature scenes—all seasons. Buys 1-2 photos/issue; 50% freelance photography/issue comes from assignment and 50% from freelance stock. Buys first serial rights, second serial (reprint) rights, first North American serial rights or simultaneous rights. Send photos for consideration. Pays on acceptance. Reports in 4 weeks. SASE. Simultaneous submissions and previously published work OK. Sample copy $2 with 9×12 SAE.

B&W: Send 8×10 glossy prints. Pays $25-35. Color: pays $50/inside photo.

Cover: Color. Pays $50-100 color photo.

Tips: Looks for "good photo quality—photos that our readers will relate to in a positive way—a lot of what we get is junk photos we can't use; have an understanding of the kinds of articles we run. I want to see interesting photos of good quality which depict real-life situations. We're using more color and commissioning more. Don't send me a list of what you have unless it's accompanied by a selection of photos. I'm happy to look at someone's work, but I'm frustrated by resumes and checklists."

CIRCLE K MAGAZINE, 3636 Woodview Trace, Indianapolis IN 46268. (317)875-8755. Executive Editor: Nicholas K. Drake. Published 5 times/year. Circ. 10,000. For community service-oriented college leaders "interested in the concept of voluntary service, societal problems, leadership abilities and college life. They are politically and socially aware and have a wide range of interests." Assigns 5-10 photos/issue. Works with freelance photographers on assignment only basis. Provide calling card, letter of inquiry, resume and samples to be kept on file for possible future assignments.

Subject Needs: General interest, "though we rarely use a nonorganization shot without text. Also, the annual convention (Baltimore, Maryland, 1991) requires a large number of photos from that area." Captions required, "or include enough information for us to write a caption."

Specs: Uses 8×10 glossy b&w prints or color transparencies. Uses b&w and color covers; vertical format required for cover.
Accompanying Mss: Prefers ms with photos. Seeks general interest features aimed at the better-than-average college student. "Not specific places, people topics."
Payment/Terms: Pays up to $225-350 for text/photo package, or on a per-photo basis—$15 minimum/b&w print and $50 minimum/cover. Credit line given. Pays on acceptance. Previously published work OK if necessary to text.
Making Contact: Send query with resume of credits. SASE. Reports in 3 weeks. Free sample copy.

CIRCLE TRACK MAGAZINE, 8490 Sunset Blvd., Los Angeles CA 90069. (213)854-2350. Editor: C.J. Baker. Monthly magazine. Emphasizes American oval track racing. Readers are male, age 32, income $37,000, some college, car racing hobby. Circ. 110,000. Photo guidelines free with SASE.
Photo Needs: Uses about 70-100 photos/issue; 80% supplied by freelance photographers. Needs photos of race cars, racing personalities, parts. Special needs include continuing coverage of major events. Model release and captions required. Uses 35mm or larger color transparencies (no prints), b&w prints (5×7 or larger).
Making Contact & Terms: Query with samples. SASE. Reports in 3 weeks. Pays $150-250/color cover photo; $10-100/b&w inside photo; $10-150/color inside photo; $100/b&w page; $150/color page; $100-500/text/photo package. Pays on publication. Credit line given. Buys all rights, but will negotiate.
Tips: Prefers to see "action shots, slides, unique race car shots."

*CITY & COUNTRY CLUB LIFE MAGAZINE, 665 LaVilla Dr., Miami Springs FL 33166. (305)887-1700. Art Director: Liliana Dones-Mozer. Bi-monthly magazine/tabloid. Emphasizes society and charity events, travel, fashion, food/wine and health. Readers are over 30, upper income, socialites. Circ. 18,000. Estab. 1983. Sample copy $2.50 with 9½×12 SASE and $1.45 postage.
Photo Needs: Uses over 50 photos/issue. Features and possible cover supplied by freelancers. Needs photos of travel, scenics, personalities, still life, food and wine etc. "Most of our photos are sent in by the clubs we cover, however, we do have occasion to use cover and travel, food shots (stock)." Model release required. Photo captions preferred.
Making Contact & Terms: Query with list of stock photo subjects. Provide resume, business card, brochure, flyer or tearsheets to be kept on file for possible assignments, list of available photos (stock) (brief description). Reports in 1 month. Both color/b&w cover photo payment to be discussed with individual photographers. Pays $20/color inside photo; $10/b&w inside photo. Pays on publication. Credit line given. Rights purchased are negotiated with photographer. Simultaneous submissions OK.
Tips: "Welcome local and national photographers who have good stock photos to accompany editorials on travel, food, etc. Send us a listing of stock photos you have available—we'll keep them on file and contact you as we need them."

CLASS ACT MAGAZINE, 315 Queenstone St., Winnipeg MB R3N 0W9 Canada. (204)488-6419. Editor: Guy Rochom. Monthly journal. Emphasizes teen news. Readers are teens, 12-19; also young adults, teachers, parents. Circ. 15,000. Sample copy free with SASE.
Photo Needs: Uses 10-15 photos/issue; 80% supplied by freelance photographers; 75% assigned. Needs teens in the news, fashion, hobbies, etc. Looking especially for "broad mix of teens in action in a different parts of the country, US and Canada." Model release and photo captions required.
Making Contact & Terms: Send unsolicited photos by mail for consideration. Send b&w and color 5×7 prints. Reports in 2 weeks. Pays $50/b&w cover photo and $10/b&w inside photo. Pays on publication. Credit line given. Buys first N.A. serial rights. Simultaneous submissions and previously published work OK.
Tips: To break in, provide "good, lengthy caption with a good clear photo." In portfolio or samples, wants to see how photographer captures expressions.

COBBLESTONE: THE HISTORY MAGAZINE FOR YOUNG PEOPLE, Cobblestone Publishing, Inc., 30 Grove St., Peterborough NH 03458. (603)924-7209. Photo Editor: Sarah D. Elder. Monthly. Emphasizes American history; each issue covers a specific theme. Readers are children 8-14, parents, teachers. Circ. 45,000. Sample copy for $3.95 and 7½×9½ SAE with $1.05 postage. Photo guidelines free with SASE.
Photo Needs: Uses about 30 photos/issue; 3-5 supplied by freelance photographers. "We need photographs related to our specific themes (each issue is theme-related) and urge photographers to request our themes list." Model release required; captions preferred.
Making Contact & Terms: Query with samples or list of stock photo subjects; send 8×10 glossy b&w prints, or 35mm or 2¼×2¼ transparencies. SASE. "Photos must pertain to themes, and reporting dates depend on how far ahead of the issue the photographer submits photos; we work on issues 6 months ahead of publication. Pays $50-75/cover photo; $10-15/inside photo. Pays on publication. Credit line given. Buys one-time rights. Simultaneous submissions and previously published work OK.

Tips: "In general, we use few contemporary images; most photos are of historical subjects. However, the amount varies with each monthly theme."

COLLECTOR EDITIONS, 170 5th Ave., New York NY 10010. (212)989-8700. Editor: Joan Pursley. Bimonthly magazine. Emphasizes limited edition ceramic and glass collectibles. Circ. 75,000. Sample copy $2.
Photo Needs: Uses about 60 photos/issue; 5-10 supplied by freelance photographers. Photos purchased with accompanying ms only. Captions preferred.
Making Contact & Terms: "Ideally, suggest an article idea and send sample photos with it—transparencies (any size) and/or b&w prints, no color prints." Provide resume, business card, brochure, flyer or tearsheets to be kept on file for possible future assignments. SASE. Reports in 6 weeks. Pays $200-400/day. Pays within 30 days of acceptance. Credit line given. Buys first North American rights only.
Tips: "We don't purchase stock photos. About 25% of our photos are by assignment. The majority of our photos are product-type shots, so we're looking for someone who excels in close-up work of porcelain and glass objects, often under one foot in height. Good lighting is essential."

COLONIAL HOMES MAGAZINE, 1790 Broadway, New York NY 10019. (212)247-8720. Editor: Richard Beatty. Bimonthly. Circ. 600,000. Emphasizes traditional architecture and interior design. Sample copy available.
Photo Needs: All photos supplied by freelance photographers. Needs photos of "American architecture of 18th century or 18th century style—4-color chromes—no people in any shots; some food shots." Special needs include "American food and drink; private homes in Colonial style, historic towns in America." Captions required.
Making Contact & Terms: Submit portfolio for review. Send 4×5 or 8×10 transparencies by mail for consideration. Provide resume, business card, brochure, flyer or tearsheets to be kept on file for possible future assignments. SASE. Reports in 1 month. Pays $500/day. Pays on acceptance. Credit line given. Buys all rights. Previously published work OK.

COLUMBUS MONTHLY, 171 E. Livingston Ave., Columbus OH 43215. (614)464-4567. Editor: Lenore Brown. Assistant Editor: Laura Messerly. Art Director: Jane Fuller. Monthly magazine. Circ. 38,000. Emphasizes local and regional events, including feature articles; personality profiles; investigative reporting; calendar of events; and departments on politics, sports, education, restaurants, movies, books, media, food and drink, shelter and architecture and art. "The magazine is very visual. People read it to be informed and entertained." Photos purchased on assignment. Buys 150 photos/year. Pays $45-80/assigned photo. Covers negotiated. Credit line given. Pays on acceptance. Buys one-time rights. Arrange personal interview with art director to show portfolio or query with resume of credits. Works with freelance photographers on assignment only basis. Provide calling card, samples and tearsheet to be kept on file for possible future assignments. SASE. Previously published work OK. Sample copy $3.57.
Subject Needs: Celebrity/personality (of local or regional residents, or former residents now living elsewhere); fashion/beauty (local only); fine art (of photography, fine arts or crafts with a regional or local angle); head shot (by assignment); photo essay/photo feature on local topics only; product shot; scenic (local or regional Ohio setting usually necessary, although once or twice a year a travel story, on spots far from Ohio, is featured); and sport (should accompany an article unless it has a special angle). No special effects or "form art photography." Model release required; captions preferred.
B&W: Uses 8×10 glossy prints; contact proofsheet requested.
Color: Uses 35mm, 2¼×2¼ or 4×5 transparencies; contact proof sheet requested for negative color.
Cover: Uses 2¼×2¼ or 4×5 color transparencies. Vertical format required.
Tips: "Live in the Columbus area. Prior publication experience is not necessary. Call for an appointment."

CONNECTICUT MAGAZINE, 789 Reservoir Ave., Bridgeport CT 06606. (203)374-3388. Art Director: Joan Barrow. Monthly. Circ. 85,000. Emphasizes issues and entertainment in Connecticut. Readers are Connecticut residents, 40-50 years old, married, average income of $55,000. Sample copy $3.50; photo guidelines free with SASE.
Photo Needs: Uses about 100 photos/issue; all supplied by freelance photographers. Needs photos of Connecticut business, arts, education, interiors, people profiles, restaurants. Model release required.
Making Contact & Terms: Arrange a personal interview to show portfolio; query with samples or list of stock photo subjects; provide resume, business card, brochure, flyer or tearsheets to be kept on file for possible future assignments. SASE. Does not return unsolicited material. Reports in 3 months. Pays $400-800/color cover photo; $50-175/b&w inside photo; $100-300/color inside photo. Pays on publication. Credit line given. Buys one-time rights. Previously published work OK.

CONSERVATIONIST MAGAZINE, NYSDEC, 50 Wolf Rd., Albany NY 12233. (518)457-5547. Art Director: Wayne Trimm. Bimonthly. Emphasizes natural history and environmental interests. Readers are people interested in nature and environmental quality issues. Circ. 200,000. Sample copy $3 and 8½×11 SASE. Photo guidelines free with SASE.

Photo Needs: Uses 40 photos/issue; 80% supplied by freelance photographers. Needs wildlife shots, forest and land management, fisheries and fisheries management, environmental subjects (pollution shots, a few) effects of pollution on plants, buildings, etc. Model release and captions required.

Making Contact & Terms: Arrange personal interview to show portfolio; query with samples; send 35mm, 2¼×2¼, 4×5 or 8×10 transparencies by mail for consideration; submit portfolio for review; provide resume, business card, brochure, flyer or tearsheets to be kept on file for possible future assignments. SASE. Reports in 3 weeks. Pays $15/b&w or color inside photo. Pays on publication. Buys one-time rights. Simultaneous submissions and previously published work OK.

Tips: Looks for "artistic interpretation of nature and the environment," unusual ways of picturing environmental subjects (even pollution, oil spills, trash, air pollution, etc.); wildlife and fishing subjects from above and underwater at all seasons. Try to have the camera see the subject differently."

CONTEMPORARY CHRISTIAN MUSIC, 1913 21st Ave. S., Nashville TN 37212. (615)386-3011. Art Director: Dede Franz. Monthly. Emphasizes music profiles of well-known contemporary Christian artists, reviews and current events. Circ. 40,000. Sample copy $2.50 with 9×12 SAE and $1 postage.

Photo Needs: Uses about 25 photos/issue; 2 or 3 supplied by freelance photographers. Needs photos of Christian artists and some Christian concerts. Model release and captions preferred. "Must include date, place, photo credit and phone number on back of photo."

Making Contact & Terms: Query with resume of credits; with sample or with list of stock photo subjects; send 8×10 b&w glossy prints, 35mm transparencies, b&w or color contact sheet by mail for consideration; provide resume, business card, brochure, flyer or tearsheets to be kept on file for possible future assignments. Does not return unsolicited material. Reports "as needed." Pays $100-500/color cover photo; $10-75/b&w and $30/color inside photo; $300-500 maximum/job "or as per discussed." Pays 30 days after publication. Credit line given. Buys one-time rights. Simultaneous submissions and previously published work OK ("must be marked where published or submitted").

Tips: "We look for dynamic quality and style. Read our magazine. Get a feeling for what we want and need."

DAVID C. COOK PUBLISHING CO., 850 N. Grove, Elgin IL 60120. (708)741-2400. Director of Design Services: Randy Maid. Photo Acquisition Coordinator: Brenda Fox. Publishes books and Sunday school material for pre-school through adult readers. Photos used primarily in Sunday school material for text illustration and covers, particularly in *Sunday Digest* (for adults), *Christian Living* (for senior highs) and *Sprint* (for junior highs). Younger age groups used, but not as much. Buys 200 photos minimum/year; gives 20 assignments/year. Uses more b&w than color photos. Pays $50-250/job or on a per-photo basis. Credit line given. Usually buys one-time rights. Model release preferred.

Subject Needs: Prefers to see Sunday school, church activities, social activities, family shots, people, action, sports. SASE. Previously published work OK. Mostly photos of junior and senior high age youth of all races and ethnic backgrounds, also adults and children under junior high age, and some preschool.

B&W: Uses glossy b&w and semigloss prints. Pays $30-50/photo. 8×10 prints are copied or kept on file for ordering at a later date.

Color: Uses 35mm and larger transparencies; contact sheet OK. Pays $75-200/photo.

Jacket/Cover: Uses glossy b&w prints and 35mm and larger color transparencies. Pays $50-250/photo.

Tips: "Make sure your material is identified as yours. Send material to the attention of Brenda Fox, Photo Acquisitions Coordinator. We use black and white people shots almost daily. Submissions can be sent 1-2 times per month. We are always looking for new photos. Send only high quality shots in good condition."

COOK'S MAGAZINE, 2710 North Ave., Bridgeport CT 06604. (203)366-4155. Photo Director: Jenny Chan. Monthly magazine. Emphasizes cooking in America. Readers are sophisticated home cooks, both men and women in the upper income bracket. Circ. 200,000. Sample copy and photo guidelines free with SASE.

Photo Needs: Uses 10-15 photos/issue; 100% supplied by freelance photographers. Needs photos of food; location shots of chefs, etc.; how-to steps; products. "We are always on the lookout for new talent, especially with food of course, and people and b&w ability."

Making Contact & Terms: Submit portfolio for review. Provide resume, business card, brochure, flyer or tearsheets to be kept on file for possible assignments. Cannot return unsolicited material. Reports in 2 weeks. Pays $650/day, plus ½ day rates and $200 single shots. Pays on acceptance. Buys all rights "if printed in context that was originally intended." Simultaneous submissions and previously published work OK.

Tips: In portfolio or samples, "looking for people and food, locations and studio. We prefer editorial styles, not slick advertising looks—as natural as possible. Show range (b&w and color). Show experimental works, too." To break in, "shoot beautiful pictures with character and personality."

COPING MAGAZINE, Box 1677, Franklin TN 37065. (615)371-8474. Publisher/Editor: Betty Webb. Pulse Publications Inc. Quarterly magazine. Emphasizes oncology and news in cancer treatment and AIDS. Readers are "everyone effected by cancer." Circ. 30,000+. Photo guidelines with SASE.
Photo Needs: Uses 30 photos/issue; majority of photos supplied by freelancers. Needs photos related to the medical field showing pitfalls of research, emotional experiences, etc. Model release required; photo captions preferred.
Making Contact & Terms: Arrange a personal interview to show portfolio, query with resume of credits or list of stock photo subjects, send unsolicited photos by mail for consideration or submit portfolio for review. Provide resume, business card, brochure, flyer or tearsheets to be kept on file for possible assignments. Send b&w or color 5×7 prints and 35mm, 2¼×2¼, 4×5, or 8×10 transparencies. SASE. Reports in 3 weeks. Pays $400/color cover photo; all other rates are negotiable. Pays on publication. Credit line given. Buys all rights, but willing to negotiate. Simultaneous submissions and previously published work OK.
Tips: In portfolios, prefers any photos related to content of magazine. Some special effects OK. Include variety of 8×10 glossies, b&w or 35mm transparencies, 3×5 color prints. Promote yourself. Be consistent. Don't spread yourself thin; there is too much competition. Find a select market and create the expertise."

CORNERSTONE, 4707 N. Malden, Chicago IL 60640. (312)561-2450. Editor: Dawn Herrin. Bimonthly magazine. Emphasizes "contemporary issues in the light of evangelical Christianity." Readers are "active, dedicated Christians interested in today's issues." Circ. 90,000. Sample copy on request.
Photo Needs: Uses about 1-3 photos/issue; "usually none" supplied by freelance photographers. Subject needs "depend on what we're writing on."
Making Contact & Terms: Send prints, transparencies and b&w negatives by mail for consideration. SASE. Payment negotiable. Credit line given if requested. Buys one-time rights. Simultaneous and previously published submissions OK.

*COUNTRY JOURNAL, P.O. Box 8200, 2245 Kohn Rd., Harrisburg PA 17105. (717)657-9555. Art Editor: Sheryl O'Connell. Bi-monthly magazine. Emphasizes practical concerns and rewards of life in the country. Readers are mostly male, ages 35-55, occupations varied—most have good disposable income. Circ. 315,000. Estab. 1974. Sample copy for $3. Phogo guidelines free with SASE.
Photo Needs: Uses 40 photos/issue; 95% supplied by freelance photographers. Needs photos of animal/wildlife, country scenics, vegetable and flower gardening, home improvements, personality profiles, environmental issues and other subjects relating to rural life. Model release and photo captions required.
Making Contact & Terms: Provide resume, business card, brochure, flyer or tearsheets to be kept on file for possible assignments. Send b&w prints prints and 35mm, 2¼×2¼, 4×5 and 8×10 prints with SASE by return mail for consideration. SASE. Reports in 1 month. Pays $500/color cover photo; $500/b&w cover photo; $135/¼ page color inside photo; $135/b&w ¼ page inside photo; $235/color page rate; $235/b&w page rate; $275-325/day. Pays on publication. Credit line given. Buys one-time rights. Simultaneous submissions OK.
Tips: "Know who you are submitting to. You can waste time, money and a possible opportunity by sending inappropriate samples and queries. If you can't find samples of the publication, call or send for them."

COUNTRY MAGAZINE, Box 246, Alexandria VA 22313. (703)548-6177. Managing Editor: Tim Sayles. Monthly magazine. Emphasizes the "*Mid-Atlantic* region: travel, leisure, lifestyles, people, history, sports, nature, food, gardening, architecture, etc." Readers are 43 median age, 50-50 male/female, affluent, educated, well-read, who travel extensively. Circ. 116,000. Sample copy $3.50 plus SASE. Guidelines free with SASE.
Photo Needs: Uses about 30-35 photos/issue; all supplied by freelance photographers. Captions preferred. Looking for region-specific covers.
Making Contact & Terms: Query with resume of credits. Send 5×7 b&w glossy prints; 35mm, 2¼×2¼, 4×5 or 8×10 transparencies; b&w or color contact sheet; no negatives. Provide resume, business card, brochure, flyer or tearsheets to be kept on file for possible future assignments. SASE. Reports in 5-8 weeks. Pays up to $300/color cover photo if assigned, $150 if "found" in submitted file photos; $50/full page b&w inside photo; $50/full page color inside photo. Pays on publication. Credit line given. Buys one-time rights.

COUNTRY WOMAN, Box 643, Milwaukee WI 53201. Managing Editor: Kathy Pohl. Circ. 700,000. Emphasizes rural life and a special quality of living to which country women can relate; at work or play in sharing problems, etc. Photos purchased with or without accompanying ms. Uses 75-100 photos/ issue. Pays $100-225 for text/photo package depending on quality of photos and number used. Good quality photo/text packages featuring interesting country women are much more likely to be accepted than photos only. Pays on acceptance. Buys one-time rights. Send material by mail for consideration. Provide brochure, calling card, letter of inquiry, price list, resume and samples to be kept on file for possible future assignments. SASE. Previously published work OK. Reports in 2-3 months. Sample copy $2. Free photo guidelines with SASE.
Subject Needs: "We're always interested in seeing good shots of farm, ranch and country women (in particular) and rural families (in general) at work and at play." Uses photos of farm animals, children with farm animals, farm and country scenes (both with and without people), and nature. Want on a regular basis scenic (rural), seasonal, photos of rural women and their family. "We're always happy to consider cover idea. Covers are seasonal in nature. Additional information on cover needs available." Captions are required. Work 6 months in advance. "No poor quality color prints, posed photos, etc."
Color: Uses transparencies. Pays $35-225 (cover only), depending on size used. Many photos are used at ¼ page size or less, and payment for those is at the low end of the scale. (No b&w photos used).
Tips: Prefers to see "rural scenics, in various seasons; emphasis on farm women, ranch women, country women and their families. Slides appropriately simple for use with poems or as accents to inspirational, reflective essays, etc."

THE COVENANT COMPANION, 5101 N. Francisco Ave., Chicago IL 60625. (312)784-3000. Editor: James R. Hawkinson. Managing Editor: Jane K. Swanson-Nystrom. Art Director: David Westerfield. Monthly denominational magazine of The Evangelical Covenant Church. Circ. 24,000. Emphasizes "gathering, enlightening and stimulating the people of our church and keeping them in touch with their mission and that of the wider Christian church in the world." Credit line given. Pays within one month following publication. Buys one-time rights. Send photos. SASE. Simultaneous submissions OK. "We need to keep a rotating file of photos for consideration." Sample copy $2.00 postpaid.
Subject Needs: Mood shots of nature, commerce and industry, home life, church life, church buildings and people. Also uses fine art, scenes, city life, etc.
B&W: Uses 5×7 and 8×10 glossy prints. Pays $15.
Color: Uses prints only. Pays $15.
Cover: Uses b&w prints. Pays $25.
Tips: "Give us photos that illustrate life situations and moods. We use b&w photos which reflect a mood or an aspect of society—wealthy/poor, strong/weak, happiness/sadness, conflict/peace. These photos or illustrations can be of nature, people, buildings, designs, and so on. Give us a file from which we can draw—rotating all the time—and we will pay per use in month after publication."

CROSSCURRENTS, 2200 Glastonbury Rd., Westlake Village CA 91361. (818)991-1694. Editor-in-Chief: Linda Brown Michelson. Photo Editor: Michael Hughes. "This is a literary quarterly that uses a number of photos as accompaniment to our fiction and poetry. We are aimed at an educated audience interested in reviewing a selection of fiction, poetry and graphic arts." Circ. 3,000. Sample copy $5. Free photo guidelines with SASE.
Photo Needs: Uses about 8-11 photos/issue; half supplied by freelance photographers. Needs "work that is technically good: sharp focus, high b&w contrast. We are also eager to see arty, experimental b&w shots." Photos purchased with or without accompanying ms.
Making Contact & Terms: "Send us a sampling. Include SASE with all submissions." Reports in 1 month. Pays $15/b&w photo; $50-75/color photo. Pays on acceptance. Credit line given. Buys first one-time use.
Tips: "We are seeing higher quality submissions; therefore, the situation here has become more competitive. We want the following: b&w submissions—5×7 vertical print, publication quality, glossy, no matte; color submissions—slide plus 5×7 vertical print. Almost all work we use is purchased from stock. Study our publication. We are in greatest need of b&w material."

CRUISE TRAVEL, 990 Grove St., Evanston IL 60201. (708)491-6440. Managing Editor: Charles Doherty. Bimonthly magazine. Emphasizes cruise ships, ports, vacation destinations, travel tips, ship history. Readers are "those who have taken a cruise, plan to take a cruise, or dream of taking a cruise." Circ. 150,000. Estab. 1980. Sample copy $2.50 with 8½×11 SAE with $1.08 postage. Photo guidelines free with SASE.
Photo Needs: Uses about 50 photos/issue; 75% supplied by freelance photographers. Needs ship shots, interior/exterior; scenic shots of ports; shopping shots; native sights, etc. Photos purchased with or without accompanying ms, but manuscript strongly preferred. Model release preferred; captions required.

Reflecting the growing awareness of the drug and alcohol problem among youth, this photo by Cheryl Meyer dramatically communicates the power of peer pressure. The Minnesota-based photographer explains that the photo, which was first shot after a request from Group magazine to see material on peer pressure and then sold to the magazine, has been resold on numerous occasions to both editions of Current Health, I and II, Network and the New Jersey Educational Association. Reselling one-time reprint rights on this striking image has already brought the photographer more than $130 to date.

Making Contact & Terms: Query with samples. Uses color prints; 35mm (preferred), 2¼ × 2¼, 4 × 5, 8 × 10 transparencies. SASE. Reports in 2 weeks. Pays variable rate for color cover; $25-150/color inside photo; $200-500/text/photo package for original work. Pays on acceptance or publication; depends on package. Credit line usually given, depends on arrangement with photographer. Buys one-time rights. Simultaneous submissions and previously published work OK.
Tips: "We look for bright colorful travel slides with good captions. Nearly every purchase is a photo/manuscript package, but good photos are key. We prefer 35mm originals for publication, all color."

CRUISING WORLD MAGAZINE, 5 John Clark Rd., Newport RI 02840. (401)847-1588. Photo Editor: Kim Curran. Circ. 130,000. Emphasizes sailboat maintenance, sailing instruction and personal experience. For people interested in cruising under sail. Needs "shots of cruising sailboats and their crews anywhere in the world. Shots of ideal cruising scenes. No identifiable racing shots, please." Buys 25 year. Buys all rights, but may reassign to photographer after publication; or first North American serial rights. Credit line given. Pays on publication. Reports in 2 months. Sample copy free for 8½ × 11 SASE.
B&W: "We rarely accept miscellaneous b&w shots and would rather they not be submitted unless accompanied by a manuscript." Pays $25-100.
Color: Send 35mm transparencies. Pays $50-300.
Cover: Send 35mm Kodachrome transparencies. Photos "must be of a cruising sailboat with strong human interest, and can be located anywhere in the world." Prefers vertical format. Allow space at top of photo for insertion of logo. Pays $500. "Submit original Kodachrome slides; sharp focus works best. *No* duplicates, no Ektachrome. Most of our editorial is supplied by author. We look for good color balance, very sharp focus, the ability to capture sailing, good composition, and action. Always looking for *cover shots*."
Tips: "For 1991 calendar. Horizontal only. Leisure sailing (no racing). Any locale around the world. Sailboats of all sizes. *Boat can be under sail or at anchor*, with emphasis on the boat, not the people on it. Depiction of sailing as tranquility, serenity and beauty. Unusually sharp focus, outstanding color balance, required. Pays $200-300."

CURRENT HEALTH 1, 60 Revere Dr., Northbrook IL 60062. (312)564-4070. Photo Editor: Terry Noto. Monthly health magazine for 4th-7th grade students. List of upcoming article topics and sample copy free with 8 × 11 SASE. Simultaneous submissions and previously published work OK. Pays on publication. Credit line given. Buys one-time rights.
Subject Needs: Black and white: "Junior high aged children, geared to our health themes for inside use." Color: "35mm or larger transparencies geared to our monthly focus article for cover use."
Making Contact & Terms: Send 8 × 10 b&w prints or transparencies. Pays $25/b&w, up to $200/color cover. Pays on publication. "Include tearsheets to be kept on file for possible future assignments."

CURRENT HEALTH 2, 60 Revere Dr., Northbrook IL 60062. (312)564-4070. Photo Editor: Terry Noto. Monthly health magazine for 7th-12th grade students. List of upcoming article topics and sample copy free with 8 × 11 SASE. Simultaneous submissions and previously published work OK. Pays on publication. Credit line given. Buys one-time rights.
Subject Needs: Black and white: teens, with emphasis on health themes for inside use. Color: "35mm or larger transparencies geared to our monthly focus article for cover use." Send 8 × 10 b&w prints or transparencies. Payment negotiable. Provide tearsheets to be kept on file for possible future assignment.
Tips: "Study our publication and future article topics. We need sharp, clear photos of teens interacting with friends and family. Don't let one rejection stop you from sending in another submission."

CYCLE WORLD MAGAZINE, 853 W. 17th St., Costa Mesa CA 92627. (714)646-4455. Editorial Director: Paul Dean. Monthly magazine. Circ. 350,000. For active motorcyclists who are "young, affluent, educated and very perceptive." For motorcycle enthusiasts. Needs "outstanding" photos relating to motorcycling. Buys 10 photos/issue. Buys all rights. Send photos for consideration. Pays on publication. Reports in 6 weeks. SASE.
B&W: Send 8 × 10 glossy prints. Pays $50-100.
Cover: Uses 35mm color transparencies. "Cover shots are generally done by the staff or on assignment." Pays $150-225.
Columns: Slipstream: see instructions in a recent issue.
Tips: Prefers to buy photos with mss. "Read the magazine. Send us something good. Expect instant harsh rejection. If you don't know our magazine, don't bother us."

DAILY WORD, Unity School of Christianity, Unity Village MO 64065. (816)524-3550. Editor: Colleen Zuck. Monthly. Emphasizes daily devotional—nondenominational. General audience. Circ. 2,500,000. Free sample copy.

Photo Needs: Uses 3-4 photos/issue; all submitted by freelance photographers. Needs scenic and seasonal photos.
How to Contact: Send 35mm, 2¼ × 2¼ or 4 × 5 transparencies by mail for consideration. SASE. Reports in 1 month. Pays $175/color cover photo; $175/inside color photo. Pays on acceptance. Credit line given. Buys one-time rights. Prefers previously unpublished work.

DALLAS LIFE MAGAZINE, DALLAS MORNING NEWS, Communications Center, Dallas TX 75265. (214)977-8433. Editor: Melissa Houtte. Art Director: Lesley Becker. Weekly magazine. Emphasizes Dallas. Circ. 530,000. Sample copy free with SASE.
Photo Needs: Uses 20 photos/issue; 5% supplied by freelance photographers. Reviews photos with accompanying ms only. Captions required.
Making Contact & Terms: Query with resume of credits; provide resume, business card, brochure, flyer or tearsheets to be kept on file for possible future assignments. SASE. Reports in 1 month. Pays $50-200/color inside photo. Pays on acceptance. Credit line given. Buys one-time rights.

DANCE MAGAZINE, 33 W. 60th St., New York NY 10023. (212)245-9050. FAX: (212)956-6487. Photo Editor: Katy Matheson. Monthly magazine. Estab. 1942. Emphasizes "all facets of the dance world." Readers are 85% female, age 18-40. Circ. 50,000.
Photo Needs: Uses about 60 photos/issue; almost all supplied by freelance photographers. Needs photos of all types of dancers—from ballroom to ballet. Dance, dancer, company and date of photo must accompany all submissions.Occasionally buys stock images; 95% of photos are assigned.
Making Contact & Terms: Send 8 × 10 b&w or color prints; 35mm transparencies by mail for consideration. SASE. Reports in 1 month. Pays up to $285/color cover photo; $15-150/b&w inside photo; $40-200/color inside photo. Pays on publication. Credit line given. Buys one-time rights. Previously published work OK.
Tips: "We look for a photojournalistic approach to the medium—photos that catch the height of a particular performance or reveal the nature of a particular dancer. We occasionally will print a photo that is strikingly revealing of life backstage, or in rehearsal."

DARKROOM PHOTOGRAPHY MAGAZINE, Suite 300, 9171 Wilshire Blvd., Beverly Hills CA 90210. (213)858-7100. Editorial Director: Thom Harrop. Executive Editor: Anna Ercegovac. Monthly publication. Circ. 80,000. Emphasizes darkroom-related and general photographic subjects.
Subject Needs: Any subject if photography related. Model release preferred, captions required.
Specs: Uses 8 × 10 or 11 × 14 glossy b&w prints and 35mm, 2¼ × 2¼, 4 × 5 or 8 × 10 color transparencies or 8 × 10 glossy color prints. Uses color covers; vertical format required.
Payment/Terms: Pays $50-500/text and photo package, $30-75/b&w photo, $50 minimum/color photo and $400/cover; $500/portfolio. Credit line given. Pays on publication. Buys one-time rights.
Making Contact: Query with samples. SASE. Reports in 1 month-6 weeks. Free editorial guide.

DEER AND DEER HUNTING, Box 1117, Appleton WI 54912. (414)734-0009. Managing Editor: Al Hofacker. 8 issues a year. Distribution 200,000. Emphasizes whitetail deer and deer hunting. Readers are "a cross-section of American deer hunters—bow, gun, camera." Sample copy and photo guidelines free with 9 × 11 SASE with $2 postage.
Photo Needs: Uses about 25 photos/issue; 20 supplied by freelance photographers. Needs photos of deer in natural settings. Model release preferred.
Making Contact & Terms: Query with resume of credits and samples. "If we judge your photos as being usable, we like to hold them in our file. It is best to send us duplicates because we may hold the photo for a lengthy period." SASE. Reports in 2 weeks. Pays $500/color cover; $40/b&w inside; $125/color inside. Pays within 10 days of publication. Credit line given. Buys one-time rights. Simultaneous submissions and previously published work OK.
Tips: Prefers to see "adequate selection of b&w 8 × 10 glossy prints and 35mm color transparencies, action shots of white tail deer only as opposed to portraits. We also need photos of deer hunters in action. We are using more color photos and spreads. Submit a limited number of quality photos rather than a multitude of marginal photos. Have your name on all entries. Cover shots must have room for masthead."

THE DIVER, Box 249, Cobalt CT 06414. (203)342-4730. Publisher/Editor: Bob Taylor. 6 issues/year. Emphasizes springboard and platform diving. Readers are divers, coaches, officials and fans. Circ. 3,000. Sample copy $2 with SASE and 54¢ postage.
Photo Needs: Uses about 10 photos/issue; 30% supplied by freelance photographers. Needs action shots, portraits of divers, team shots and anything associated with the sport of diving. Special needs include photo spreads on outstanding divers and tournament coverage. Captions required.

Making Contact & Terms: Send 4×5 or 8×10 b&w glossy prints by mail for consideration; "simply query about prospective projects." SASE. Reports in 4 weeks. Pays $15-25/b&w cover photo; $5-15/b&w inside photo; $35-100 for text/photo package; $15-100/day. Pays on publication. Credit line given. Buys one-time rights. Simultaneous submissions and previously published work OK.
Tips: "Study the field, stay busy."

DIVER MAGAZINE, 295-10991 Shellbridge Way, Richmond BC V6X 3C6 Canada. (604)273-4333. Publisher: Peter Vassilopoulos. Magazine published 9 times/year. Emphasizes sport scuba diving, ocean science, technology and all activities related to the marine environment. Photos purchased with accompanying ms only. Credit line given. Pays within 4 weeks of publication. Buys first North American serial rights or second serial rights. Send material by mail for consideration. SAE and International Reply Coupons must be enclosed. Previously published work OK. Reports in 4 weeks. Guidelines available for SAE and International Reply Coupon.
Subject Needs: Photo/text packages on dive sites around the world; diving travel features; marine life—habits, habitats, etc.; personal experiences, ocean science/technology; commercial, military and scientific diving; written in laymen's terms. Model release preferred; captions required.
Tips: Prefers to see "a variety of work: close-ups, wide angle—some imagination!"

DOG FANCY, Box 6050, Mission Viejo CA 92690. (714)855-8822. Editor: Kim Thornton. Readers are "men and women of all ages interested in all phases of dog ownership." Monthly. Circ. 150,000. Sample copy $3; photo guidelines available with SASE.
Photo Needs: Uses 20-30 photos/issue, all supplied by freelance photographers. Specific breed featured in each issue. Prefers "photographs that show the various physical and mental attributes of the breed. Include both environmental and portrait-type photographs, but in both cases we would prefer that the animals be shown without leashes or collars. We also have a major need for good-quality, interesting b&w photographs of any breed dog or mutts in any and all canine situations (dogs with veterinarians; dogs eating, drinking, playing, swimming, etc.) for use with feature articles." Model release required.
Making Contact & Terms: Send by mail for consideration actual 8×10 b&w photos, 35mm or 2¼×2¼ color transparencies. Reports in 6 weeks. Pays $15-20/b&w photo; $50-150/color photo and $100-300 per text/photo package. Credit line given. Buys first North American serial rights.
Tips: "Nothing but sharp, high contrast shots. Send SASE for list of photography needs. We're looking more and more for good quality photo/text packages that present an interesting subject both editorially and visually. Bad writing can be fixed, but we can't do a thing with bad photos. Subjects should be in interesting poses or settings with good lighting, good backgrounds and foregrounds, etc. We are very concerned with sharpness and reproducibility; the best shot in the world won't work if it's fuzzy, and it's amazing how many are. Submit a variety of subjects—there's always a chance we'll find something special we like."

DOLLS—The Collector's Magazine, 170 5th Ave., New York NY 10010. (212)989-8700. Editor: Krystyna Poray Goddu. 8 times a year. Circ. 85,000. Emphasizes dolls—antique and contemporary. Readers are doll collectors nationwide. Sample copy $2.
Photo Needs: Uses about 75-80 photos/issue; 12 supplied by freelance photographers. Needs photos of dolls to illustrate articles. Photos purchased with accompanying ms only. "We're looking for writers/photographers around the country to be available for assignments and/or submit queries on doll collections, artists, etc."
Making Contact & Terms: Query with samples; provide resume, business card, brochure, flyer or tearsheets to be kept on file for possible future assignments. SASE. Reports in 6-8 weeks. Pays $100-300/job; $150-350 for text/photo package. Pays within 30 days of acceptance. Credit line given. Buys one-time or first North American serial rights ("usually"). Previously published work "sometimes" OK.
Tips: Prefers to see "relevant (i.e., dolls) color transparencies or black and white prints; clear, precise—not 'artsy'—but well-lit, show off doll."

DOWN BEAT MAGAZINE, Jazz Blues & Beyond, 180 West Park Ave., Elmhurst IL 60126. (708)941-2030. Art Director: Dan Czubak. Monthly. Emphasizes jazz musicians. Circ. 50,000. Sample copy available.
Photo Needs: Uses about 30 photos/issue; 95% supplied by freelancers. Needs photos of live music performers/posed musicians/equipment. Captions preferred.
Making Contact & Terms: Query with list of stock photo subjects; send 8×10 b&w prints; 35mm, 2¼×2¼, 4×5, 8×10 transparencies; b&w or color contact sheets by mail. Unsolicited samples for consideration will not be returned unless accompanied by SASE. Provide resume, business card, brochure, flyer or tearsheets to be kept on file for possible future assignments. Reports only when

needed. Credit line given. Buys one-time rights. Simultaneous submissions and previously published work OK.

DOWN EAST MAGAZINE, Camden ME 04843. (207)594-9544. Art Director: F. Stephen Ward. Monthly magazine. Circ. 80,000. Emphasizes Maine contemporary events, outdoor activities, vacations, travel, history and nostalgia. For residents and lovers of the Pine Tree State. Buys 25-40 photos/issue. Buys first North American serial rights. Virtually all photographs used are shot on assignment. Very few individual stock photos purchased. Query with portfolio and/or story ideas. Reports in 6 weeks SASE.
Subject Needs: Varies widely according to individual story needs, but heavy emphasis is on landscape and "photo-illustration." Photos must relate to Maine people, places and events.
B&W: Send 8×10 or larger prints; brief captions required. Pays $25 minimum.
Color: Send 35mm or larger transparencies. Brief captions required. Transparencies must be in sleeves and stamped with photographer's name. Do *not* submit color prints. Pays $25 minimum.
Tips: Prefers to see landscapes, people. In portfolios, on-location lighting. Submit seasonal material 6 months in advance.

EASYRIDERS MAGAZINE, P.O. Box 3000, Agoura Hills CA 91301. (818)889-8740. FAX: (818)889-4726. Editor: Keith R. Ball. Estab. 1971. Monthly. Emphasizes "motorcycles (Harley-Davidsons in particular), motorcycle women, bikers having fun." Readers are "adult men—men who own, or desire to own, custom motorcycles. The individualist—a rugged guy who enjoys riding a custom motorcycle and all the good times derived from it." Free sample copy. Photo guidelines free with SASE.
Photo Needs: Uses about 60 photos/issue; "the majority" supplied by freelance photographers; 70% assigned. Needs photos of "motorcycle riding (rugged chopper riders), motorcycle women, good times had by bikers, etc." Model release required. Also interested in technical articles relating to Harley-Davidson.
Making Contact & Terms: Send b&w prints, 35mm transparencies by mail for consideration. SASE. Reports in 1 month. Pays $30-100/b&w photo, $40-250/color photo and $30-2,500/complete package. Other terms for bike features with models to satisfaction of editors. For usage on cover, gatefold and feature. Pays 30 days after publication. Credit line given. Buys all rights. All material must be exclusive.
Tips: Trend is toward "more action photos, bikes being photographed by photographers on bikes to create a feeling of motion." In samples, wants photos "clear, in-focus, eye-catching and showing some emotion. Read magazine before making submissions. Be critical of your own work. Check for sharpness. Also, label photos/slides clearly with name and address."

EDUCATIONAL PROGRAMS, INC., (formerly EDN Corporation), 8003 Old York Rd., Elkins Park PA 19117-1410. (215)635-1700. Editor: Deana C. Jamroz. Quarterly magazines; *Prenatal Educator*, *Pediatrician*, "Moving" publication, "Financial" publication. Combined circ. 3,000,000. Sample copy free with 9×12 SASE.
Photo Needs: Uses about 12-20 photos/issue; all supplied by freelance photographers. Needs include pregnant women, couples with pregnant women, newlyweds, toddlers, infants, couples with children, home furnishings. Model release required.
Making Contact & Terms: If in Philadelphia area, arrange a personal interview to show portfolio; query with list of stock photo subjects. Provide resume, business card, brochure, flyer or tearsheets to be kept on file for possible future assignments. Reports in 1 month. Payment dependent on assignment. Buys all rights. Simultaneous submissions and previously published work OK.
Tips: "Keep in touch—our needs change from week to week."

ENTREPRENEUR, 2392 Morse Ave., Irvine CA 92714. (714)261-2325. Publisher: Clare Thain. Editor: Rieva Lesonsky. Design Director: Richard R. Olson. Photo Editor: Stephanie Patton. Monthly. Circ. 325,000+. Emphasizes business. Readers are existing and aspiring small business owners.
Photos Needs: Uses about 30 photos/issue; many supplied by freelance photographers. Needs "editorially specific, conceptual and how-to, and industrial" photos. Model release required.
Making Contact & Terms: Arrange a personal interview to show portfolio; query with sample or list of stock photo subjects; provide resume, business card, brochure, flyer or tearsheets to be kept on file for possible future assignment; "follow-up for response." Pays $75-200/b&w photo; $125-225/color photo; $50-75/hr.; $400-600/day. Pays on publication. Credit line given. Rights individually negotiated.

ENVIRONMENT, 4000 Albemarle St., Washington DC 20016. (202)362-6445. Editor: Barbara T. Richman. Photo Editor: Ann Rickerich. Magazine published 10 times/year. Covers science and science policy from a national, international, and global perspective. "We cover a wide range of environmental topics —acid rain, tropical deforestation, nuclear winter, hazardous waste disposal, worker safety, energy topics and environmental legislation." Readers include libraries, colleges and universities, and professionals in the field of environmental science and policy. Circ. 12,500. Sample copy $4.50.

Photo Needs: Uses 15 photos/issue; varying number supplied by freelance photographers. "Our needs vary greatly from issue to issue—but we are always looking for good photos showing human impacts on the environment worldwide—industrial sites, cities, alternative energy sources, pesticide use, disasters, third world growth, hazardous wastes, sustainable agriculture and pollution. Interesting and unusual landscapes are also needed." Model release preferred; captions required.

Making Contact & Terms: Query with list of stock photo subjects; send unsolicited photos by mail for consideration; provide business card, brochure, flyer or tearsheets to be kept on file for possible future assignments. Send any size b&w print by mail for consideration. SASE. Reports in 2 months. Pays $35-100/b&w inside photo; $50-300/color photo. Pays on publication. Credit line given. Buys one-time rights. Simultaneous submissions and previously published work OK.

Tips: "We are looking for international subject matter—especially environmental conditions in developing countries."

EQUAL OPPORTUNITY, Equal Opportunity Publications, Inc., 44 Broadway, Greenlawn NY 11740. (516)261-8917. Art Director: Andrew Elias. Magazine published 3 times a year. Emphasizes career guidance for members of minority groups at the college and professional levels. Readers are college-age women, minority, students and young working professionals of all occupations that require a college degree. Circ. 15,000. Sample copy free with 9×12 SASE and 5 first class stamps.

Photo Needs: Uses at least one photo per issue (cover); planning to use freelancers for cover and possibly editorial. Contact for needs. Model release preferred; photo captions required.

Making Contact & Terms: Query with list of stock photo subjects or send unsolicited photos by mail for consideration. Send color 35mm transparencies. SASE. Reports in 2 weeks. Pays $25/color cover photo. Pays on publication. Credit line given. Buys one-time rights. Simultaneous submissions and previously published work OK, "but not in competitive career-guidance publications."

Tips: "We are looking for clear color shots of minority students and young professionals who are involved in activities related to their academic studies or professions. We've decided to use more cover photos than we have in the past. We are also open to using inside photos, but freelancers should contact us and discuss upcoming stories before sending photos. Read our magazine to get an idea of the editorial content. Cover photos do not have to tie in to any one particular story in the issue, but they have to be representative of the magazine's editorial content as a whole."

EQUINOX MAGAZINE, 7 Queen Victoria Rd., Camden East, ON K0K 1J0 Canada. (613)378-6661. Editor: Bart Robinson. Bimonthly. Circ. 166,000. Emphasizes "Canadian subjects of a general 'geographic' and scientific nature." Sample copy $5 with 8½×14 SAE; photo guidelines free with SAE and International Reply Coupon.

Photo Needs: Uses 80-100 photos/issue; all supplied by freelance photographers. Needs "photo stories of interest to a Canadian readership as well as occasional stock photos required to supplement assignments. Story categories include wildlife, international travel and adventure, science, Canadian arts and architecture, and Canadian people and places." Captions required.

Making Contact & Terms: Query with samples; submit portfolio for review. SASE. Reports in 6 weeks. "Most stories are shot on assignment basis—average $1,500 price. We also pay expenses for people on assignment. We also buy packages at negotiable prices and stock photography at about $225 a page if only one or two shots used." Pays on publication. Credit line given. Buys first North American serial rights.

Tips: We look for "excellence and in-depth coverage of a subject, technical mastery and an ability to work intimately with people. Ninety-five percent of the photographs we use are of people, so any portfolio should emphasize people involved in some activity. Stick to Kodachrome/Ektachrome transparencies."

ERIE & CHAUTAUQUA MAGAZINE, Charles H. Strong Bldg., 1250 Tower Lane, Erie PA 16505. (814)452-6070. Editor: K.L. Kalvelage. Twice yearly magazine covering the City of Erie, Erie County, Crawford County, Warren County, Pennsylvania and Chautauqua County, New York, for upscale readers with above average education and income. Circ. 30,000. Sample copy $2.50. Photo guidelines free with SASE.

Photo Needs: Uses about 125 photos/issue; 60-70 supplied by freelance photographers. "Because so much of our content is region-oriented, most of our photography work has to be done on an assignment basis, by photographers who live in the region. May need photos for specific sports: sailing, boating, skiing, ice skating, horseback riding, golf, tennis, etc." Model release and captions required.

Making Contact & Terms: Query with samples or list of stock photo subjects; provide resume, business card, brochure, flyer or tearsheets to be kept on file for possible future assignments. "Photographers living in our coverage area are encouraged to arrange for personal interview to show portfolio." SASE. "All photographic fees are negotiated with photographer, according to type of assignment." Pays $15-25/b&w photo; $15-25 + film/color photo; "occasionally negotiates on a per-job basis. Will not consider an hourly or daily basis." Pays 30 days after publication. Credit line given. Buys all rights on assignments; "will buy one-time or first North American serial rights only on stock photos." Previously published submissions OK.

Tips: "We want to know that the photographer's work has the quality and clarity we are looking for — ours is a quality book with excellent reproduction on coated stock. Most new photographers show us b&w work that does *not* have the clarity and contrasts that will reproduce well; color shots are often fuzzy or faded. We welcome seeing portfolios of any photographers living in our coverage area. Those outside our coverage area would have their best opportunity via stock photos and should let us know what kinds of subjects they've covered."

THE EVANGELICAL BEACON, 1515 E. 66th St., Minneapolis MN 55423. (612)866-3343. Editor: George M. Keck. Circ. 37,500. Magazine of the Evangelical Free Church of America. Emphasizes Christian living, evangelism, denominational news; inspiration and information. Sample copy $1 postpaid. Uses approx. 3-4 freelance photos/issue. Photos purchased with or without accompanying mss. Credit line usually given. Pays on acceptance for photos; on publication for articles. Buys all or one-time rights. Model release preferred. Send material. SASE. Simultaneous submissions and previously published work OK. Reports in 4-8 weeks.
Subject Needs: Human interest: children and adults in various moods and activities; scenic shots: churches and city scenes. Captions not required, but helpful (especially locations of scenes). No cheesecake.
B&W: Uses 8×10 glossy prints. Pays $15 minimum.
Cover: Uses glossy color prints, transparencies or slides; vertical format required. Pays $50 minimum.
Accompanying Mss: Seeks personal testimonies, Christian living, Christian and life issues and concerns, and church outreach ideas.

EVANGELIZING TODAY'S CHILD, Child Evangelism Fellowship Inc., Warrentown MO 63383. (314)456-4321. Editor: Mrs. Elsie Lippy. Bimonthly magazine. Circ. 26,000. Written for people who work with children, ages 5-12, in Sunday schools, Bible clubs and camps. Buys 1-4 photos/issue. Pays on a per-photo basis. Credit line given. Buys one-time rights. Prefers to retain good quality photocopies of selected glossy prints and duplicate slides in files for future use. Send material by mail with SASE for consideration. Publication is under no obligation to return materials sent without SASE. Simultaneous submissions and previously published work OK. Sample copy for $1; free photo guidelines with SASE.
Subject Needs: Children, ages 5-12. Candid shots of various moods and activities. "We use quite a few shots with more than one child and some with an adult, mostly closeups. The content emphasis is upon believability and appeal. Religious themes may be especially valuable." No nudes, scenery, fashion/beauty, glamour or still lifes.
B&W: Uses 8×10 glossy prints. Pays $25/photo.
Color: Uses 35mm or larger transparencies, inside photo/$30-35; cover shots $100.

*EVENT, Douglas College, Box 2503, New Westminster, BC V3L 5B2 Canada. (604)527-5298. Editor: Dale Zieroth. Visuals Editor: Ken Hughes. Magazine published every 4 months. Circ. 1,000. Emphasizes literature and fine art graphics (essays, short stories, plays, reviews, poetry, verse, photographs and drawings). Photos purchased with or without accompanying ms. Buys 20 photos/issue. Pays $10-30/b&w photo. Credit line given. Pays on publication. Query, send material by mail for consideration or submit portfolio for review. SAE and International Reply Coupons or Canadian stamps. Simultaneous submissions OK. Reports in 2-4 weeks. Sample copy $3.50; free photo guidelines or writer's guidelines.
Subject Needs: Animal, celebrity/personality, documentary, fine art, human interest, humorous, nature, nude, photo essay/photo feature, scenic, special effects/experimental, still life, travel and wildlife. Wants any "nonapplied" photography, or photography not intended for conventional commercial purposes. Needs excellent quality. Must be a series. Model release and captions required. "No unoriginal, commonplace or hackneyed work."
B&W: Uses 8×10 prints. Any smooth finish OK.
Color: "No color work unless the photographer agrees to reproduction in b&w and unless work is of a sufficient standard when in b&w."
Cover: Uses b&w prints. Any smooth finish OK. Vertical format preferred.
Tips: "We prefer work that appears as a sequence: thematically, chronologically, stylistically. Individual items will only be selected for publication if such a sequence can be developed. Photos should preferably be composed for vertical, small format (6×9) and in b&w."

EXECUTIVE TRAVEL, 242 Vauxhall Bridge Rd., London SW1V 1AU England. (01)821-1155. Editor: Mike Toynbee. Monthly magazine. Emphasizes business travel. Readers 25-50 years old, male or female, and from all walks of life. Circ. 50,000. Sample copy free with SASE.
Photo Needs: Uses 30 photos/issue; 15 supplied by freelance photographers. Photo captions preferred.
Making Contact & Terms: Query with resume of credits or send unsolicited photos by mail for consideration. SASE. Reports in 1 month. Pays on publication. Credit line given. Buys one-time rights.

EXPECTING MAGAZINE, 685 3rd Ave., New York NY 10017. (212)878-8642. Art Director: Robin Zachary. Quarterly. Circ. 1,200,000. Emphasizes pregnancy and birth. Readers are pregnant women 18-40.

Photo Needs: Uses about 12 photos/issue. Works with freelance photographers on assignment basis only for fashion, food, nursery design and mothers with newborns; more than half the issue comes from assignment. Provide card to be kept on file for future assignments. Occasionally uses stock color transparencies of women during labor and birth, and newborn babies, hospital or doctor visits. Model release required.

Making Contact & Terms: Arrange for drop off to show portfolio. SASE. No b&w photos used. Payment varies;$150-300/color photo. Pays on publication. Credit line given. Buys one-time rights. Previously published work OK.

Tips: In photographer's portfolio looks for "nice lighting, warm, friendly people, babies, and candid lifestyle shots. Should not look too 'cataloguey'. Present a portfolio of transparancies and tear sheets of published work. I hire experienced professionals only."

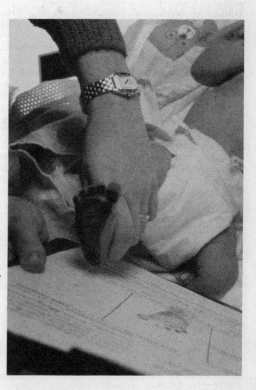

Combining somewhat unusual subject matter with an irresistibly cute model, this picture of a baby getting foot-printed was a sure thing for Robin Zachary, art director for Expecting *magazine. She explains that photographer Penny Gentieu made the first contact and pointed out her "expertise in baby photography" to the art director. Paying $750, Zachary bought one-time rights to this and two other pictures which ran with an article on tests for newborn babies. Gentieu remarks that this sale was good for her in terms of both "exposure and money."*

FACES: The Magazine About People, 30 Grove St., Peterborough NH 03458. (603)924-7209. Photo Editor: Sarah D. Elder. Monthly (except July and August) magazine. Emphasizes cultural anthropology for young people ages 8 to 14. Circ. 14,000. Sample copy $3.95 with 7½×10½ SAE and $1.05 postage.

Photo Needs: Uses about 15-20 photos/issue. "Photos (b&w) for text must relate to themes; cover photos (color) should also relate to themes. Send SASE for themes. Model release and captions preferred.

Making Contact & Terms: Query with samples. SASE. Reports in 1 month. Pays $10-15/text photos; approximately $50-75 for cover photos. Pays on publication. Credit line given.

Tips: "Most of the photographs we use are of people from other cultures; therefore, we look for an ability to capture people in action—at work or play. We primarily appreciate action shots of children from different cultures. Remember: All submissions must relate to a specific upcoming theme."

FARM & RANCH LIVING, 5400 S. 60th St., Greendale WI 53129. (414)423-0100. Editor: Bob Ottum. Bimonthly. Circ. 400,000. "Concentrates on people and places in agriculture, but not the 'how to increase yields' type. We show farming and ranching as a way of life, rather than a way to make a living." Readers are "farmers and ranchers in all states in a wide range of income." Sample copy for $2; photo guidelines free with SASE.

Photo Needs: Uses about 100-125 photos/issue; all supplied by freelance photographers. Needs "agricultural photos: farms and ranches, farmers and ranchers at work and play. Work one full season ahead—send summer photos in spring, for instance." Special needs include "good-looking seasonal photos of a rural nature."

Making Contact & Terms: Query with samples or list of stock photo subjects; send 35mm, 2¼×2¼ or 4×5 transparencies by mail for consideration. SASE. Reporting time varies; "immediately to a month." Pays $150/color cover photo; $75-150/color inside photo; $200-400 for text/photo package. Pays on acceptance. Buys one-time rights. Previously published work OK.

Tips: "Looking for brilliant colors in photos of agricultural and rural nature. Also looking for shots of photogenic farms and ranches to feature in series 'Prettiest Place in the Country.' A little imagination goes a long way with us. We like to see an unusual angle or approach now and then, but don't see nearly enough like that."

FIELD & STREAM, 2 Park Ave., New York NY 10016. (212)779-5294. Art Director: Victor Closi. This is a broad-based service magazine. The editorial content ranges from very basic "how it's done" filler stories that tell in pictures and words how an outdoor technique is accomplished or device is made, to feature articles of penetrating depth about national conservation, game management, and resource management issues; and recreational hunting, fishing, travel, nature and outdoor equipment.

Subject Needs: Photos using action and a variety of subjects and angles in both b&w and color. "We are always looking for cover photographs, in color, which may be vertical or horizontal. Remember: a cover picture must have room at the left for cover lines."

Specs: Uses 8×10 b&w photos; 35mm and 2¼×2¼ transparencies. Will also consider 4×5 or 8×10 transparencies, but "majority of color illustrations are made from 35mm or 2¼ film."

Payment & Terms: Pays $75+/per b&w photo, $450/color photo depending on size used on single page; $700/partial color spread; $900/full color spread; $1,000+/color cover. Buys First World Rights; rights returned after publication. Needs photo information regarding subjects, the area, the nature of the activity and the point the picture makes. Don't attach caption information to color photos.

Making Contact: Submit photos by registered mail. Send slides in 8½×11 plastic sheets, and pack slides and/or prints between cardboard. SASE. Reports in 60 days. Writer's/photographer's guidelines available.

FIGHTING WOMAN NEWS, P.O. Box 1459, Grand Central Station, New York NY 10163. Editor: Valerie Eads. Photo Editor: Muskat Buckby. Quarterly. Circ. 5,000. Estab. 1975. Covers women's martial arts. Readers are "adult females actively practicing the martial arts or combative sports." Sample copy $3.50 postpaid; photo guidelines free with SASE.

Photo Needs: Uses several photos/issue; most supplied by freelance photographers. Needs powerful images of female martial artists; "action photos from tournaments and classes/demonstrations; studio sequences illustrating specific techniques and artistic constructions illustrating spiritual values. Obviously, photos illustrating text have a better chance of being used. We have little space for fillers. We are always short of photos suitable to our magazine." Model release preferred; captions and identification required.

Making Contact & Terms: Query with resume of credits or with samples or send 8×10 glossy b&w prints or b&w contact sheet by mail for consideration; provide resume, business card, brochure, flyer or tearsheets to be kept on file for possible future assignments. SASE. Reports "as soon as possible." Pays $20 cover/photo; payment for text/photo package to be negotiated; "our most frequent payment is *copies*". Pays on publication. Credit line given. Buys one-time rights. Simultaneous submissions and previously published work OK; "however, we insist that we are *told* concerning these matters; we don't want to publish a photo that is in the current issue of another martial arts magazine."

Tips: Prefers to see "technically competent b&w photos of female martial artists in action; good solid images of powerful female martial artists. We don't print color. No glamour, no models; no cute little kids unless they are also skilled. Get someone knowledgeable to caption your photos or at least tell you what you have—or don't have if you are not experienced in the art you are photographing. We are a poor alternative publication chronically short of material, yet we reject 90% of what is sent because the sender obviously never saw the magazine and has no idea what it's about. Five of our last seven covers were live action photos and we are using fewer "enhancements" than previously. Best to present yourself and your work with samples and a query letter indication that you have *seen* our publication. The cost of buying sample copies is a lot less than postage these days."

*FINANCIAL INDEPENDENCE MONEY MANAGEMENT MAGAZINE, P.O. Box 1222, Ft. Washington MD 20744. (301)292-3030. Managing Editor: D. Young. Bimonthly magazine. Emphasizes money management. Readers are ages 23-50, black, 53% female, 47% male and middle incomes. Estab. 1984.

Photo Needs: Uses 10-12 photos/issue; 50% supplied by freelance photographers.Needs photos of black families—personalities—how to make money and finance related. Model release required. Photo captions preferred.
Making Contact & Terms: Provide resume, business card, brochure, flyer or tearsheets to be kept on file for possible assignments. SASE. Reports in 1 month. Pays $150/color cover photo; $15/color inside photo; $12/b&w inside photo. Pays on publication. Buys first North American serial rights. Simultaneous submissions OK.

FINE HOMEBUILDING, 63 S. Main St., Box 5506, Newtown CT 06470. (203)426-8171. Editor: Mark Feirer. Bimonthly plus 7th issue each spring. Emphasizes residential architecture and construction. Readers are architects, builders, owner/builders, contractors and craftsmen. Circ. 230,000. Sample copy for 9×12 SAE with $2.40 postage.
Photo Needs: Uses 120 photos/issue; 20 supplied by freelancers. Needs photos of unusual houses; photos of carefully crafted architectural details; wood, stained glass, wrought iron, etc. Special needs include unusual windows, doors, stairs, chimneys, fences and gates. Model release and captions required.
Making Contact & Terms: Send unsolicited photos by mail for consideration or call. Uses 35mm, 2¼×2¼, 4×5 or 8×10 transparencies. SASE. Reports in 1 month. Pays on publication. Credit line given.
Tips: Prefers to see "good, clear compositions with lots of detail, not 'art' shots."

FINESCALE MODELER, 21027 Crossroads Circle, P.O. Box 1612, Waukesha WI 53187. (414)796-8776. Editor: Bob Hayden. Photo Editor: Paul Boyer. Published 8 times per year. Circ. 82,000. Emphasizes "how-to-do-it information for hobbyists who build nonoperating scale models." Readers are "adult and juvenile hobbyists who build nonoperating model aircraft, ships, tanks and military vehicles, cars and figures." Sample copy $2.95; photo guidelines free with SASE.
Photo Needs: Uses more than 50 photos/issue; "anticipates using" 10 supplied by freelance photographers. Needs "in-progress how-to photos illustrating a specific modeling technique; photos of full-size aircraft, cars, trucks, tanks and ships." Model release and captions required.
Making Contact & Terms: Provide resume, business card, brochure, flyer or tearsheets to be kept on file for possible future assignments. "Phone calls are OK." Reports in 8 weeks. Pays $25 minimum/color cover photo; $5 minimum/b&w inside photo, $7.50 minimum/color inside photo; $30/b&w page; $45/color page; $50-500 for text/photo package. Pays for photos on publication, for text/photo package on acceptance. Credit line given. Buys one-time rights. "Will sometimes accept previously published work if copyright is clear."
Tips: Looking for "clear b&w glossy 5×7 or 8×10 prints of aircraft, ships, cars, trucks, tanks and sharp color positive transparencies of the same. In addition to photographic talent, must have comprehensive knowledge of objects photographed and provide copious caption material. Freelance photographers should provide a catalog stating subject, date, place, format, conditions of sale and desired credit line before attempting to sell us photos. We're most likely to purchase color photos of outstanding models of all types for our regular feature, FSM Showcase."

FINGER LAKES MAGAZINE, 108 S. Albany St., Ithaca NY 14850. (607)272-3470. Editor: Linda McCandless. Quarterly magazine. Emphasizes life in the Finger Lakes of New York. Circ. 20,000. Sample copy $1.95 with 9½×11 SAE and $1 postage.
Photo Needs: Uses about 20-30 photos/issue; all supplied by freelance photographers. Needs photos on Finger Lake scenics, people, animals, photo essays. Model release preferred; captions required.
Making Contact & Terms: Arrange a personal interview to show portfolio; query with samples; query with list of stock photo subjects; send 35mm transparencies and b&w contact sheets by mail for consideration. Provide resume, business card, brochure, flyer or tearsheets to be kept on file for possible future assignments. SASE. Reports in 1 month or longer. Pays $10-30/b&w inside photo; $15-25/color inside photo. Pays 1 month after publication. Buys first North American serial rights. Simultaneous submissions OK.
Tips: "Keep trying. Sell us on a story idea as well as the pictures."

FIRSTHAND MAGAZINE, GUYS, MANSCAPE, Box 1314, Teaneck NJ 07666. (201)836-9177. Executive Editor: Jerry Douglas. Monthly magazines; *Guys* 8 times a year. "*FirstHand* and *Guys* deal with all aspects of homosexuality; *Manscape* leans toward the kinky." Readers are gay men in the U.S. and Canada. Circ. 70,000. Sample copy $5.00. Photo guidelines free with SASE.
Photo Needs: All magazines use front and back color cover shots. No frontal nudity, but rear nudity okay. For *Manscape*, two b&w shots are used for the inside front and back covers, for which frontal nudity is desirable. Written model release required including two pieces of proof of age, one of which must be photographic.

Making Contact & Terms: Best bet is to mail query with samples. Send 35mm, 2¼×2¼, 4×5 transparencies, contact sheet by mail for consideration. SASE. Reports in 3 weeks. Pays $100 front cover color photo; $100 back cover color photo; $50 b&w inside photo (*Manscape*). Credit line given. Pays on publication. Buys first North American serial and all rights; will negotiate.
Tips: "Don't overload the company with your work. It's better to send 20 slides than 100."

FISHING FACTS MAGAZINE, Box 609, Menomonee Falls WI 53051. (414)255-4800. Managing Editors: Carl Malz and Spence Petros. Monthly magazine. Circ. 150,000. For people interested in freshwater fishing. "The publication is heavily how-to oriented." Needs photos dealing with freshwater fishing. "Of particular interest are scenes of freshwater fish jumping while battling anglers." Buys 20-50 annually. Buys first serial rights. Send photos for consideration. Pays on acceptance. Reports in 2 months. SASE. Sample copy $1.95 with 10×13 SASE.
B&W: Uses 8×10 glossy prints. Captions "helpful." Pays $25 minimum.
Color: Send transparencies only. Captions "helpful." Pays $50.

FISHING WORLD, 51 Atlantic Ave., Floral Park NY 11001. (516)352-9700. FAX: (516)437-6841. Editor: Keith Gardner. Bimonthly magazine. Circ. 300,000. Emphasizes techniques, locations and products of both freshwater and saltwater fishing. For men interested in sport fishing. Needs photos of "worldwide angling action." Buys 18-30/annually; all freelance photography comes from freelance stock. Buys first North American serial rights. Send photos for consideration. Photos purchased with accompanying ms; cover photos purchased separately. Pays on publication. Reports in 3 weeks. SASE. Free sample copy and photo guidelines.
Color: Send transparencies. Requires originals. Captions essential. Pays $300 for complete text/photo package.
Cover: Send color transparencies. "Drama is desired rather than tranquility. Good-looking women are a plus." Requires originals. Captions essential. Pays $300.
Tips: "First, look at the magazine. In general, queries are preferred, though we're very receptive to unsolicited submissions accompanied by smashing photography." Inside photos are color. Trend is more boats.

FLY FISHERMAN, Cowles Magazines, Inc., Editorial Offices, 2245 Kohn Rd., Box 8200, Harrisburg PA 17105. (717)657-9555. Editor and Publisher: John Randolph. Associate Editor: Philip Hanyok. Emphasizes all types of fly fishing for readers who are "99% male, 79% college educated, 79% married. Average household income is $62,590 and 55% are managers or professionals. 85% keep their copies for future reference and spend 35 days a year fishing." Bimonthly. Circ. 140,000. Sample copy $3 with 9×12 SAE and $1 postage; photo/writer guidelines for SASE.
Photo Needs: Uses about 45 photos/issue; 70% of which are supplied by freelance photographers. Needs shots of "fly fishing and all related areas—scenics, fish, insects, how-to." Column needs are: Fly Tier's Bench (fly tying sequences); Tackle Bag; and Casting About (specific streams and rivers). Captions required.
Making Contact & Terms: Send by mail for consideration 5×7 or 8×10 b&w prints or 35mm, 2¼×2¼, 4×5 or 8×10 color transparencies. SASE. Reports in 4-6 weeks. Pays on publication. Credit line given. Buys one-time rights. No simultaneous submissions; previously published work OK.

FLYING, 1633 Broadway, New York NY 10019. (212)767-6950. FAX: (212)767-5620. Art Director: Nancy Bink. Monthly magazine. Emphasizes airplanes. Readers are male pilots. Circ. 325,000. Estab. 1928.
Photo Needs: 90% of photos supplied by freelance photographers. Needs photos of airplanes and related scenes and settings.
Making Contact & Terms: Provide resume, business card, brochure, flyer or tearsheets to be kept on file for possible assignments. Reports when interested. Pays $400-500/day. Credit line given. Buys one-time rights.
Tips: Send cover letter; "be brief and straightforward."

FOOD & WINE, 1120 Avenue of the Americas, New York NY 10036. (212)382-5600. Art Director: Elizabeth Woodson. Monthly. Circ. 850,000. Estab. 1978. Emphasizes food and wine. Readers are an "upscale audience who cook, entertain, dine out and travel stylishly."
Photo Needs: Uses about 25-30 photos/issue; freelance photography on assignment basis 85%, 15% freelance stock. "We look for editorial reportage specialists who do restaurants, food on location and travel photography." Model release and captions required.
Making Contact & Terms: Drop-off portfolio by appointment. Submission of flyers, tearsheets, etc. to be kept on file for possible future assignments and stock usage. Pays $450/color page; $100-450 color photo. Pays on acceptance. Credit line given. Buys one-time world rights.

THE FORERUNNER, P.O. Box 4103, Gainesville FL 32613. Managing Editor: Jay Rogers. Monthly tabloid. Emphasizes campus evangelism, world news, political events and Christian events. Readers are ages 18-35, male and female students and Christian leaders. Circ. 20,000. Estab. 1981. Sample copy for $2 and 10×13 SASE with 85¢ postage.
Photo Needs: Uses 20-50 photos/issue; 25-50% supplied by freelance photographers. Needs photos of famous personalities, international scenes and current events photos. Model release and photo captions preferred.
Making Contact & Terms: Query with list of stock photo subjects. Send 8×10 b&w prints by mail for consideration. SASE. Reports in 1 month. Pays $10/b&w inside photo. Pays on publication. Credit line given. Simultaneous submissions and previously published work OK.
Tips: "We are a Christian newspaper distributed on college campuses. We are looking for visually stimulating photos of news events. We also will print articles that go along with photos."

FORMULA MAGAZINE, Suite 311, 5595 Côte de Liesse, St-Laurent PQ H4M 1V2 Canada. (514)744-2270. FAX: (514)744-4937. Executive Editor: Denyse Ramacieri. Consumer publication. Magazine published 10 times a year, combined issues for Jan/Feb and Mar/Apr Emphasizes motorsports and automobiles. Better than 80% male readers, 34-45 years old. Circ. 50,000. Sample copy free with 8×10 SASE.
Photo Needs: Uses 40-45 photos/issue; 90% supplied by freelance photographers. Looking for photos of motorsport events, including CART, INDY, F-1, European Rallies, Canadian Series, road tests, etc. Model release and photo captions preferred.
Making Contact & Terms: Send unsolicited photos by mail for consideration along with resume, business card, brochure, flyer or tearsheets to be kept on file for possible assignments. Send color transparencies, any format. SASE. Reports in 1 month. Pays $100/color or b&w cover photo, $40/color or b&w inside photo and $40/color or b&w page rate. Pays on publication. Credit line given. Buys one-time rights. Simultaneous submissions OK.
Tips: "Photographs have to be neat, clear, original with action, style and movement. Angles, colors are very important. A picture *is* worth a thousand words. If photographers are good, they know it and we will know it. Needs more photos of drivers, candids and portraits, for profiles of race drivers. If motor racing events are attended in order to submit material, we advise that a list of events attended be submitted in advance to our publication." If interested in observing and shooting road tests, then contact to discuss "ahead of time."

FORT LAUDERDALE MAGAZINE, 2901 Gateway Dr., Pompano Beach FL 33069. (305)979-6212. Editor: Judy Wilson. Bimonthly magazine. Emphasizes business lifestyles. Readers are men and women, ages 35-55, professionals, business owners, corporate officers, with high income. Circ. 10,000. Sample copy free with 8×10 SASE and 6 first class stamps.
Photo Needs: Uses 25-30 photos/issue; 25% supplied by local freelancers. Needs photos with Florida-oriented interest only. Special needs include South Florida lifestyle, families, residential neighborhoods, arts and culture, business, industry and building. Model release required; photo captions preferred.
Making Contact & Terms: Provide resume, business card, brochure, flyer or tearsheets to be kept on file for possible assignments. SASE. Pays $300/color cover photo, $250/color inside photo and $50-100/b&w inside photo. Pays on publication. Credit line given. Buys all rights, but willing to negotiate. Does not consider simultaneous submissions or previously published work.

FORTUNE, Time-Life Bldg., New York NY 10020. (212)522-3803. Managing Editor: Marshall Loeb. Picture Editor: Michele F. McNally. Picture Editor reviews photographers' portfolios on an overnight drop-off basis. Emphasizes analysis of news in the business world for management personnel. Photos purchased on assignment only. Day rate on assignment (against space rate): $350; page rate for space: $400; minimum for b&w or color usage: $150.

FOUR WHEELER MAGAZINE, 6728 Eton Ave., Canoga Park CA 91303. (818)992-4777. Editor: John Stewart. Monthly magazine. Emphasizes four-wheel drive vehicles and enthusiasts. Circ. 277,000. Sample copy free with SASE. Photo guidelines free with SASE.
Photo Needs: Uses 100 color/100 b&w photos/issue; 10% supplied by freelance photographers. Needs how-to, travel/scenic/action (off-road 4×4s only) photos. Reviews photos with accompanying ms only. Model release and captions required.
Making Contact & Terms: Provide resume, business card, brochure, flyer or tearsheets to be kept on file for possible future assignments. Does not return unsolicited material. Reports in 1 month. Pays $10-50/inside b&w photo; $20-100/inside color photo; $100/b&w and color page; $200-600/text/photo package. Pays on publication. Credit line given. Buys all rights.
Tips: "Be creative; accurate exposures; sharp focus; fine grain films; use a variety of focal length."

*FREEDOM MAGAZINE, 6331 Hollywood Blvd., #1200, Hollywood CA 90028. (213)960-3500. Editor: Tom Whittle. Production Manager: Geoff Brown. Bimonthly magazine. News magazine: Emphasizes investigative reporting, news and current events. Estab. 1968. Sample copy $2 with 9×12 SASE.
Photo Needs: Uses 30-40 photos/issue; 70% supplied by freelance photographers. Needs photos of current news and new journalism. Special photo needs include new current news stories—particular current issues in alignment with stories. Model release and photo captions preferred.
Making Contact & Terms: Query with list of stock photo subjects. Send unsolicited photos by mail for consideration. Provide resume, business card brochure flyer or tearsheets to be kept on file for possible assignments. No specific specifications for samples. SASE. Reports in 1 month. Payment varies depending on photo. Pays on publication. Credit line given. Buys one-time rights.

FREEWAY, Scripture Press, Box 623, Glen Ellyn IL 60138. Editor: Kyle Olund. Four-page magazine. Circ. 50,000. For older Christian teens. Photos purchased with or without accompanying ms. Freelancers supply 90% of the photos. Pays on acceptance. Buys one-time rights and simultaneous rights. "Mail portfolio with SASE; we will photocopy prints we're interested in for future ordering." Simultaneous submissions and previously published work OK. Reports in 1 month. Free sample copy and photo guidelines available on request.
Subject Needs: "Photos should include teenage subjects. We need action photos, human relationships, objects, trends and sports." Also uses some religious and mood photos. No fine art; no photos with too-young subjects or outdated styles; no overly posed or obviously gimmicky shots. No scenery.
B&W: Uses 8×10 b&w prints. Pays $20-35.
Accompanying Mss: "*Freeway* emphasizes personal experience articles which demonstrate God working in the lives of older teens and young adults. Most of our readers have an interest in Christian growth."
Tips: "We would like to use a greater percentage of photos in our layouts. Thus, we'd like to see more action photos of teenagers which we can use to illustrate stories and articles (teen personal crisis, self-help, how-to). We'd like to see some creativity and real-life situations. We're overstocked with close-up reflective shots." Looks for "teens in real-life, everyday situations; teens struggling with problems; teens helping others; relationships with friends, parents, teachers, dates" in photos.

FRIENDLY EXCHANGE MAGAZINE, Meredith Publishing, 1716 Locust St., Des Moines IA 50336. (515)284-2769. Art Director: Jann Williams. Quarterly magazine. Emphasizes family travel and leisure activities. Readers are family audience, mainly in western half of U.S. Circ. 4,500,000. Sample copy free with 5 first class stamps and 9×12 SAE. Photo guidelines free with SASE.
Photo Needs: Uses about 35-45 photos/issue; 90% supplied by freelance submissions or stock. List of special photo needs available with SASE. Model release required; captions preferred.
Making Contact & Terms: Query with list of stock photo subjects. Provide resume, business card, brochure, flyer or tearsheets to be kept on file for possible future assignments. Pays negotiable rate/color cover photo; $150/⅙ color page; $175/¼ page; $50/b&w; $200/½ color page; $250/full page color. Pays on publication. Credit line given. Buys one-time rights.
Tips: "Style, lighting, composition are considered in reviewing portfolio or photo samples."

FUN IN THE SUN, 5436 Fernwood Ave., Los Angeles CA 90027. (213)465-7121. Publisher: Ed Lange. Quarterly. Emphasizes nudism/naturism/alternative lifestyles. Circ. 10,000. Photo guidelines free with SASE.
Photo Needs: Uses about 50 photos/issue; 20 supplied by freelance photographers. Needs photos of "nudity; fun in sun (nonsexist)." Nudist, naturist, body self acceptance. Model release and captions required.
Making Contact & Terms: Query with samples. SASE. Reports in 3 weeks. Pays $50/b&w cover photo; $100/color cover photo; $25/b&w inside photo; $25/color inside photo. Pays on acceptance. Credit line given. Buys one-time or all rights. Previously published work OK.

FUN/WEST, Box 2026, North Hollywood CA 91610-0026. Editor: John D. Adlai. Managing Editor: Ms. Tracey. Quarterly magazine. Emphasizes living on the West Coast for young, single people; resorts in the US and jet set activities. Monthly features on best wines of France, Germany, Italy and California. Photo and text.
Subject Needs: Travel, fashion/beauty, glamour, ("good taste only"), product shots, wine and gourmet food. Captions preferred; model release required.
Specs: Uses 8×10 b&w and color prints. Uses b&w and color covers.
Payment/Terms: Payment negotiable. Credit line given. Pays on publication. Buys all rights. Simultaneous submissions and previously published work OK.
Making Contact: Query only with list of stock photo subjects. Unsolicited materials will be discarded. SASE. Reports in 1 month or more.
Tips: Has added a movie section dealing with Hollywood personalities, recent movies and entertainment. Articles dealing with Hollywood and stars are encouraged, especially those with photos. "Exercise good taste at all times. Concentrate on showing the same subjects under different light or style."

FUTURIFIC MAGAZINE, The Foundation for Optimism, Suite 1210, 280 Madison Ave., New York NY 10016. Editor-in-Chief: Mr. Balint Szent-Miklosy. Monthly. Circ. 10,000. Emphasizes future-related subjects. Readers range from corporate to religious leaders, government officials all the way to blue collar workers. Sample copy with $5—for postage and handling.
Photo Needs: Uses 10 photos/issue; all supplied by freelance photographers. Needs photos of subjects relating to the future. Photos purchased with or without accompanying ms. Captions preferred.
Making Contact & Terms: Send by mail for consideration b&w prints or contact sheets. Reports in 1 month. Payment negotiable. Pays on publication. Buys one-time rights. Simultaneous submissions and/or previously published work OK.
Tips: "Photographs should illustrate what directions society and the world are heading. Optimistic only."

GALLERY MAGAZINE, FOX MAGAZINE, POCKETFOX MAGAZINE, 401 Park Ave. S., New York NY 10016-8802. Photo Editor: Judy Linden. Emphasizes men's interests. Readers are male, collegiate, middle class. Estab. 1972. Free photo guidelines with SASE.
Photo Needs: Uses 80 photos/issue;10% supplied from freelancers (no assignments). Needs photos of nude women and celebrities, plus sports adventure pieces. Model release required.
Making Contact & Terms: Send by mail for consideration at least 100 35mm transparencies. SASE. Reports in 4 weeks. Girl sets: pays $800-1800; cover extra. Buys First North American serial rights plus nonexclusive international rights. Girl Next Door contest: $250 entry photo; $2500 monthly winner; $25,000 yearly winner. Photographer: entry photo/receives 1 year free subscription, monthly winner $500; yearly winner $2500. Send by mail for contest information.
Tips: In photographer's samples, wants to see "Beautiful models and good composition. Trend in our publication is outdoor settings—avoid soft focus! Send complete layout."

GAME & FISH PUBLICATIONS, Box 741, Marietta GA 30061. (404)953-9222. Photo Editor: Tom Evans. Publishes 34 monthly magazines: *Alabama Game & Fish, Arkansas Sportsman, Georgia Sportsman, Louisiana Game & Fish, Mississippi Game & Fish, Oklahoma Game & Fish, Tennessee Sportsman, Texas Sportsman, Florida Game & Fish, Missouri Game & Fish, Kentucky Game & Fish, North American White Tail, Michigan Sportsman, West Virginia Game & Fish, North Carolina Game & Fish, South Carolina Game & Fish, New England Game & Fish, New York Game & Fish, Pennsylvania Game & Fish, New Jersey Game & Fish, Maryland and Delaware Game & Fish, Nebraska Game & Fish, Kansas Game & Fish, Ohio Game & Fish, Indiana Game & Fish, Illinois Game & Fish, Iowa Game & Fish, Dakota Game & Fish, Washington-Oregon Game & Fish, Rocky Mountain Game & Fish, California Game & Fish, Minnesota Sportsman* and *Wisconsin Sportsman.* Circ. 425,000 (total). All emphasize "hunting the game species of the respective states and fishing for species native to the respective states and their contiguous waters." Readers are hunters/fishermen. Sample copy $2.50 with 10×12 SASE; photo guidelines free with SASE.
Photo Needs: 50% of photos supplied by freelance photographers; 10% assigned. Needs photos of live deer or tastefully photographed dead deer; action fishing shots. Model release preferred; captions encouraged.
Making Contact & Terms: Query with samples. Send 8×10 b&w glossy prints or 35mm transparencies (preferably Kodachrome) by mail for consideration. SASE. Reports in 1 month. Pays $250/color cover photo; $75/color inside photo; $25/b&w inside photo. Pays on acceptance. Credit line given. Buys one-time rights. Simultaneous submissions not accepted.
Tips: "Study the photos we are publishing. *Do not send dupes.* Because of our volume of photo needs we must have the photos in-house to be able to use them. Be prepared to have photos on file for 4-6 months, minimum."

GAMUT, Cleveland State University, Cleveland OH 44115. (216)687-3953. Editor: Louis T. Milic. Triannual journal. General interest. Circ. 1,500. Sample copy $2.50.
Photo Needs: Uses about 25-50 photos/issue; "several" supplied by freelance photographers. Subject needs "depend on the sort of articles we print. But we also print groups of interesting photographs (portfolios) on any subject." Model release preferred; captions required.
Making Contact & Terms: Query with b&w samples. SASE. Reports in 2 months. Pays in cash and contributor's copies. Range is $25 for a single full-page photo to $125 for a group (portfolio). Pays on publication. Credit line given. Buys first North American serial rights.

GARDEN, New York Botanical Garden, Bronx NY 10458. Photo Editor: Karen Polyak. Bimonthly magazine. Circ. 20,000. Emphasizes botany, agriculture, horticulture and the environment for members of botanical gardens and arboreta. Readers are largely college graduates and professionals, united by a common interest in plants and the environment. Provide letter of inquiry and samples with SASE, especially related to plants, gardening and the environment, "however, we are adding *very* few new photographers. We call for photos on subjects wanted." Photos purchased with or without accompanying ms. Buys 12 photos/issue. Credit line given. Pays on publication. Buys one-time rights. SASE. Reports in 1 month. Sample copy $3.50 with 9×12 SAE.

Subject Needs: Nature and wildlife (of botanical and environmental interest) and scenic (relating to plants, especially to article subjects). Captions not required, "but plants must be accurately identified."

B&W: Uses 5×7 glossy prints. Pays $35-50/photo.

Color: Uses 35mm or 4×5 transparencies. Pays $40-70/photo.

Cover: Uses 35mm or 4×5 color transparencies. Vertical format preferred. Pays $100-150/photo.

Accompanying Mss: Articles relating to emphasis of the magazine. No photo essays. Length: 1,500-2,500 words. Pays $100-300/ms. Request writer's guidelines separately.

Tips: Looks for "high quality—mastery of the basics—focus, light, composition—plus a unique or original vision. We look for photographers who have a large stock file of unusual plant subjects, well identified. Also those with many environment-related photos, and with photos of gardens all over the world. Quality is our first criterion, but your chances are better if you have many unusual plant-related subjects, not just pretty flowers."

GARDEN DESIGN, 4401 Connecticut Ave. NW, Washington DC 20008. (202)686-2752. FAX: (202)686-1001. Associate Editor: Cheryl Weber. Quarterly. Emphasizes residential landscape architecture and garden design. Readers are gardeners, home owners, architects, landscape architects, garden designers and garden connoisseurs. Estab. 1982. Sample copy $5; photo guidelines free with SASE.

Photo Needs: Uses about 80 photos/issue; nearly all supplied by freelance photographers; 80% from assignment and 20% from freelance stock. Needs photos of "public and private gardens that exemplify professional quality design." Needs to see both the design intent and how garden subspaces work together. Model release and captions required.

Making Contact & Terms: Submit proposal with resume and samples. Reports in 2 months or sooner if requested. Publishes color only, and uses original transparencies only for separation-do not send dupes. Pays $300/color cover photo; $150/inside photo over ⅓ page; $200/double page special; $75/⅓ page or smaller. Credit line given. Buys one-time first North American magazine publication rights. Previously published work may be acceptable but is not preferred.

Tips: "Show both detailed and comprehensive views that reveal the design intent and content of a garden, as well as subjective, interpretive views of the garden. A letter and resume are not enough—must see evidence of the quality of your work, in samples or tearsheets. Need excellent depth of field and superior focus throughout. Our trend is away from the large state and/or public gardens, to smaller scale, well-conceived and executed residential ones."

GARDENS WEST, 4962 Granville St., Vancouver, BC V6M 3B2 Canada. (604)266-2655. FAX: (604)266-2484. Editor: Dorothy Horton. Consumer publication. Magazine published 8 times per year. Emphasizes gardens. Readers are men and women, at least 30 years old. Circ. 40,000. Estab. 1987. Sample copy for $1.17 postage (Canadian).

Photo Needs: Uses 30 photos/issue; 100% supplied by freelance photographers; approximately 70% freelance stock and 30% assignment. Needs photos of gardens and flowers. Prefers to review photos with accompanying ms. Model release and photo captions required.

Making Contact & Terms: Query with list of stock photo subjects or send unsolicited photos by mail for consideration. Send gloss 4×6 color prints or 35mm transparencies. SASE. Reports in 1 month. Pays $125/color cover photo; inside rates vary. Pays on publication. Credit line given. Buys one-time rights. Simultaneous submissions and previously published work OK.

Tips: Looks for "Quality, printable slides or photos of named plants and/or flowers. Also looking for possible cover shots. We're not a trendy magazine. Sumbit samples of named plants/flowers to be kept on file for possible use in future editions of magazine."

GENERAL LEARNING CORP., 60 Revere Dr., Northbrook IL 60062-1563. (312)564-4070. Photo Editor: Terry Noto. 5 monthly magazines published from September to May. Emphasizes consumer and health education for interpersonal relationships for students in junior and senior high.

Photo Needs: Pays on publication. Buys one-time rights. Credit line given. Model release "preferred." Simultaneous submissions and previously published work OK. Free sample copy and subject outline with 8x11 SASE. Provide tearsheets to be kept on file for possible future assignments.

B&W: Uses 8×10. Pays $25/photo.

Color: Pays $150-200/photo.

Tips: "Research our publication; we don't use photos of cute puppies or sunsets. We *do* use contemporary photos of teens: mood shots showing a particular emotion like happiness, loneliness, etc. Be patient. Be persistent. We like to work with *new* photographers."

GENT, Suite 204, 2355 Salzedo St., Coral Gables FL 33134. (305)443-2378. Editor: Bruce Arthur. Monthly magazine. Circ. 150,000. Showcases full-figured nude models. Credit line given. Pays on publication. Buys one-time rights or second serial (reprint) rights. Send material by mail for consideration. SASE. Previously published work OK. Reports in 2 weeks. Sample copy $5 (postpaid). Photo guidelines free with SASE.

Subject Needs: "Nude models must be extremely large breasted (minimum 38" bust line). Sequence of photos should start with woman clothed, then stripped to brassiere and then on to completely nude. Bikini sequences also recommended. Cover shots must have nipples covered. Chubby models also considered if they are reasonably well attractive and measure up to our 'D-Cup' image." Model release and photocopy or photograph of picture ID required. Buys in sets, not by individual photos.

Color: Uses transparencies. Prefer Kodachrome. Pays 1st rights, $150/page; 2nd rights, $80/page.

Cover: Uses color transparencies. Vertical format required. Pays $300/photo.

Accompanying Mss: Seeks mss on travel, adventure, cars, racing, sports, gambling, grooming and fashion. Pays $200-300 for text and photo package.

GEORGIA SPORTSMAN MAGAZINE, Box 741, Marietta, GA 30061. (404)953-9222. Editor: Jimmy Jacobs. Monthly magazine. Circ. 80,000. For people interested in hunting and fishing and related outdoor recreational opportunities in Georgia. Credit line given. Pays on publication. Buys one-time rights. Query with resume of credits. SASE. Simultaneous submissions and previously published work unacceptable. Reports in 1 month. Sample copy $2.50 and free photo guidelines.

Subject Needs: Live action shots of whitetail deer, bass, small game, etc. — any huntable or fishable species in Georgia.

B&W: Uses 5×7 and 8×10 prints.

Color: Uses 35mm and 2¼×2¼ transparencies.

Cover: Uses color transparencies; vertical or horizontal format required. Pays $250 maximum.

Tips: Photos and/or illustrations complementing articles are considered extremely important. No cartoons.

GEORGIA STRAIGHT, 2nd Floor, 1235 W. Pender St., Vancouver BC V6E 2V6 Canada. (604)681-2000. FAX: (604)681-0272. Managing Editor: Charles Campbell. Weekly tabloid. Emphasizes entertainment. Readers are generally well-educated people between 20 and 45 years old. Circ. 70,000. Estab. 1967. Sample copy free with 10×12 SASE.

Photo Needs: Uses 20 photos/issue; 35% supplied by freelance photographers on assignment. Needs photos of entertainment events and personalities. In particular looking for "portraits of high-profile movie stars." Photo captions preferred.

Making Contact & Terms: Query with list of stock photo subjects. Include resume, business card, brochure, flyer or tearsheets to be kept on file for possible assignments. Reports in 1 month. Pays $100/b&w cover photo and $15-45/b&w inside photo. Pays on publication. Credit line given. Buys one-time rights. Simultaneous submissions and previously published work OK.

Tips: In portfolio or samples, wants to see "portraits and concert photos. Almost all needs are for in-Vancouver assigned photos, except for high quality portraits of film stars."

*GOLDEN YEARS, 233 E. New Haven Ave., Melbourne FL 32902-0537. (407)725-4888. Editor-in-Chief: Carol B. Hittner. Bimonthly magazine. Emphasizes interest of active people ages 50-64. Readers are male and female, but predominantly female, 50-64, some retired and some still working. Circ. 450,000. Estab. 1978. Sample copy $2. Photo guidelines free with SASE.

Photo Needs: Uses 32-50 photo/issue; 50% supplied by freelance photographers. Needs photos of mostly travel, but also celebrities, scenics, animals, people in action and still shots. Model release required. Photo captions preferred.

Making Contact & Terms: Send 35mm transparency or print by mail for consideration. Provide resume, business card, brochure, flyer or tearsheets to be kept on file for possible assignments. SASE. Reports in 2-3 months. Base rate for any unsolicited submissions professional photographs are negotiated: pays $25/color inside photo; $10/b&w inside photo. Pays on publication. Credit line given. Buys one-time rights. Simultaneous submissions OK (separate SASEs required).

Tips: Wants to see "an example of the photographer's point-of-view and composition capabilities as well as quality of product (to be examined by art director)."

GOLF DIGEST, 5520 Park Ave., Box 0395, Trumbull CT 06611. (203)373-7000. Art Director/Graphic Administrator: Nick DiDio. Monthly magazine. Circ. 1,350,000. Emphasizes golf instruction and features on golf personalities and events. Buys 10-15 photos/issue from freelance photographers. Pays $100 minimum/job and also on a per-photo or per-assignment basis. Credit line given. Pays on publication. Send material by mail for consideration. "The name and address of the photographer must appear on every slide and print submitted." SASE. Simultaneous submissions OK. Reports in 1 month. Free sample copy. Free photo guidelines with SASE.

Subject Needs: Celebrity/personality (nationally known golfers, both men and women, pros and amateurs); fashion/beauty (on assignment); head shot (golfing personalities); photo essay/photo feature (on assignment); product shot (on assignment); scenics (shots of golf resorts and interesting and/

Close-up

D. Gorton
Editorial Photographer
Jackson, Mississippi

© Linda Hanselman

"A photographer must develop a unique vision, then find where this work is desired," says D. Gorton, the Jackson, Mississippi-based freelance editorial photographer with a decidedly global view. "If you don't find that special way of seeing, you become just another commodity, the only difference between yourself and other photographers being your price. And that can ultimately mean death."

One of Gorton's first freelance projects following a lengthy stint in newspaper work taught him an important lesson: "seeing" involves recognizing both the photographic and marketing opportunities in a shoot. In 1985, he heard about the world's largest earth sculpture being created just west of Chicago, along the Illinois River. The structure was to be so large that it could be viewed from outer space, yet it failed to attract much curiosity from the news media. So being curious himself, Gorton lined up magazine assignments and drove out to cover it. And when he got there, he found a multiple marketing opportunity.

"Everything you see you can sell," says Gorton. "I took pictures of the bulldozers, the landscaping, the excelsior mats. . . ." Gorton explains he shot everything and then got on the phone with the various equipment manufacturers, the contractors and anyone else remotely connected with the project. When he reminded the companies of how they were involved in the project and told them of the photo coverage, he found they all wanted to buy photos.

The initial magazine assignments covered his expenses, including film, processing and the helicopter rental, which he used to get the needed perspective to show the sculpture in its entirety. And the assignments brought him about $7,000 in sales. But the real payoff—about $15,000 in side sales—came from all of the suppliers and contractors who wanted the photos for their company publications and advertising or public relations use.

Initially, Gorton studied to become an historian. Through his college studies as well as his experiences during the social upheaval of the late 1960s, he became increasingly fascinated in photography. "When I started, most of the photographers were World War II vets who had no interest in the Blacks, the women's movement, the gays, the migrant workers," says the one-time organizer of student protest groups in Southern California. "They didn't realize that times were changing and these were becoming the big stories. I'd go to newspapers and magazines and offer to cover the new movements. Usually, they'd let me do it because no one else was doing it."

Accordingly, Gorton began to build his list of credits which have come to include *Time*, *Newsweek* and *The New York Times*, among others. He traveled to Russia to shoot and edit for the *Day in the Life of the Soviet Union* project. Similarly, he was a photographer and editor for the *Day in the Life of America* volume. He also put in fulltime service with the *Philadelphia Inquirer*, the *Cincinnati Enquirer* and various bureaus of *The New York Times*, including the Washington DC operation where he served as a White House press photographer. Though his work had earned him several Pulitzer Prize nominations, the politics and restrictions of newspaper photography motivated him to return to freelancing.

Seeking to broaden his market, Gorton found stock photography to be a viable outlet for his body of work. His stock agency of choice was Onyx, through which he currently syndicates his stock images and acquires new assignments. Gorton also explored corporate photography as another way to develop his vision. Among several projects with the Cincinnati-based Procter & Gamble Co. was an annual report shoot which involved an around-the-world trip.

During this period, Gorton took a giant step in developing a singular style by breaking a "rule" of magazine work that color images should be shot only in transparency form. Working with high-speed (ISO 1000) color print film and darkroom manipulation, Gorton achieved a gritty, grainy photojournalistic look not possible with transparencies.

As Gorton soon found, these images were very attractive to emerging markets such as Whittle Communications Special Division. And though Whittle art directors, who liked the images, had to argue with the printers about how to reproduce them on the printed page, eventually everyone got comfortable with using prints. Suddenly finding himself with fairly large numbers of clients wanting the same "look," Gorton came to command much higher fees than his previous day rate of $350 plus expenses.

While in Japan for the Procter & Gamble annual report shoot, Gorton gained perhaps the most important perspective on the necessity of a singular vision. He readily observed that photographers in Japan and elsewhere are constantly developing new styles of "seeing" that win awards and set new standards. Because of this competitive emphasis upon innovation, Gorton warns, imitation can be deadly to one's photographic career.

"Don't be a commodity," Gorton urges once again, noting that survival in business depends upon looking beyond current trends as well as state and national boundaries. The keys, he explains, are to anticipate future changes in the social, political and economic spheres, and to strive to "see" them in your own way. "The internationalization of the marketplace means only those who are original are likely to succeed."

— Ted Schwarz

This photograph, titled "Near Wayside, Mississippi," is one example of the documentary treatment which D. Gorton often gives his work. The original — shot on ultra-high-speed color stock with darkroom manipulation — demonstrates both Gorton's gritty, photojournalistic technique and keen eye for human variety.

or unusual shots of golf courses or holes); and sport (golfing). Model release preferred; captions required. "The captions will not necessarily be used in print, but are required for identification."
B&W: Uses 8×10 glossy prints. No contact sheet. Pays $75-200/photo.
Color: Uses 35mm transparencies. No duplicates. Pays $100-600/photo.
Cover: Uses 35mm color transparencies. Vertical format required. Pays $500 minimum/photo.
Tips: "We are a very favorable market for a freelance photographer who is familiar with the subject. Most of the photos we use are done on specific assignment, but we do encourage photographers to cover golf tournaments on their own with an eye for unusual shots, and to let the magazine select shots to keep on file for future use. We are always interested in seeing good quality color and b&w work." Prefers Kodachrome-64 film; no Ektachrome.

GOLF JOURNAL, Golf House, Far Hills NJ 07931. (201)234-2300. Editor: Robert Sommers. Managing Editor: George Eberl. Art Director: Diane Chrenko-Becker. Emphasizes golf for golfers of all ages and both sexes. Readers are "literate, professional, knowledgeable on the subject of golf." Eight issues per year. Circ. 243,000. Free sample copy.
Photo Needs: Uses 20-25 photos/issue, 5-20 supplied by freelance photographers. "We use color photos extensively, but usually on an assignment basis. Our photo coverage includes amateur and professional golfers involved in national or international golf events, and shots of outstanding golf courses and picturesque golf holes. We also use some b&w, often mugshots, to accompany a specific story about an outstanding golfing individual. Much of our freelance photo use revolves around USGA events, many of which we cover. As photo needs arise, we assign photographers to supply specific photo needs. Selection of photographers is based on our experience with them, knowledge of their work and abilities, and, to an extent, their geographical location. An exceptional golf photo would be considered for use if accompanied by supportive information." Column needs are: Great Golf Holes, a regular feature of the magazine, calls for high quality color scenics of outstanding golf holes from courses around the country and abroad. Model release not required; captions required.
Making Contact & Terms: Query Managing Editor George Eberl with resume of photo credits; or call (do not call collect). Works with freelance photographers on assignment only basis. Provide calling card, resume and samples to be kept on file for possible future assignments. SASE. Reports in 2 weeks. Pays on acceptance. Negotiates payment based on quality, reputation of past work with the magazine, color or b&w and numbers of photos. Pays $25 minimum. Credit line given. Rights purchased on a work-for-hire basis. No simultaneous or previously published work.

GOLF MAGAZINE, 2 Park Ave., New York NY 10016. (212)779-5000. Editor: George Peper. Art Director: Ron Ramsey. Monthly magazine. Circ.1,000,000. Emphasizes golf. Readers are male, ages 15-80, college educated, professional. Photos purchased with accompanying ms. Pays $50 minimum/job and on a per-photo basis. Pays on acceptance. Buys first serial rights. Query with samples. SASE. Simultaneous submissions OK. Reports in 3 weeks. Free sample copy; photo guidelines free with SASE.
Subject Needs: Celebrity/personality, head shot, golf travel photos, scenic, special effects and experimental, spot news, human interest, humorous and travel. Photos must be golf-related. Model release preferred; captions required. No cartoons.
B&W: Uses 8×10 glossy prints. Pays $50 minimum/photo.
Color: Uses transparencies. Pays $50-600/photo.
Cover: Uses 2¼×2¼ transparencies. Vertical format preferred. Pays $200-350/photo.
Accompanying Mss: Golf related articles. Pays $25-750/ms. Free writer's guidelines.

GOOD HOUSEKEEPING, 959 8th Ave., New York NY 10019. (212)649-2000. Editor: John Mack Carter. Art Director: Herb Bleiweiss. Monthly magazine. Circ. 5,500,000. Emphasizes food, fashion, beauty, home decorating, current events, personal relationships and celebrities for homemakers. Photos purchased on assignment. Buys 200 photos/issue. Pays $50-400/printed page, or on a per-photo basis. Credit line given. Pays on acceptance. Buys all rights. Drop off portfolio for review or send with SASE. Reports in 2 weeks.
Subject Needs: Submit photo essay/photo feature (complete features on children, animals and subjects interesting to women that tell a story with only a short text block) to the Articles Department. All other photos done on assignment only basis. Model release required; captions preferred.
B&W: Uses 8×10 prints. Pays $50-300/photo.
Color: Uses 35mm, 2¼×2¼, 4×5 or 8×10 transparencies. Pays $150-400/photo.
Cover: Query. Vertical format required. Pays $1,200 maximum/photo.

GOSPEL HERALD, 4904 King St., Beamsville ON L0R 1B6 Canada. (416)563-7503. Editor: Roy D. Merritt or Managing Editor: Eugene Perry. Consumer publication. Monthly magazine. Emphasizes Christianity. Readers are primarily members of the Churches of Christ. Circ. 1,600. Sample copy free with SASE.

Photo Needs: Uses 2-3 photos/issue; percentage supplied by freelancers varies. Needs scenics, shots, especially those relating to readership—moral, religious and nature themes.
Making Contact & Terms: Send unsolicited photos by mail for consideration. Send b&w, any size and any format. Payment not given, but photographer receives credit line.
Tips: "We have never paid for photos. Because of the purpose of our magazine, both photos and stories are accepted on a volunteer basis."

GRAND RAPIDS MAGAZINE, 1040 Trust Bldg., 40 Pearl St., NW, Grand Rapids MI 49503. (616)459-4545. FAX: (616)459-4800. Publisher: John H. Zwarensteyn. Editor: Carole Valade Smith. Monthly magazine. Estab. 1963. Emphasizes community-related material of Western Michigan; local action and local people. Freelance photos assigned and accepted. Provide business card to be kept on file for possible future assignments; "only people on file are those we have met and personally reviewed." Buys one-time rights. Arrange a personal interview to show portfolio, query with resume of credits, send material by mail for consideration, or submit portfolio for review. SASE. Reports in 3 weeks. Model release and captions required.
Subject Needs: Animal, nature, scenic, travel, sport, fashion/beauty, photo essay/photo feature, fine art, documentary, human interest, celebrity/personality, humorous, wildlife, vibrant people shots and special effects/experimental. Wants on a regular basis western Michigan photo essays and travel-photo essays of any area in Michigan.
B&W: Uses 8×10 or 5×7 glossy prints; contact sheet OK. Pays $25-35/photo.
Color: Uses 35mm, 120mm or 4×5 transparencies or 8×10 glossy prints. Pays $35-50/photo.
Cover: Uses $2\frac{1}{4} \times 2\frac{1}{4}$ and 4×5 color transparencies. Pays $100-150/photo. Vertical format required.
Tips: "Most photography is by our local freelance photographers, so freelancers should sell us on the unique nature of what they have to offer."

GRAY'S SPORTING JOURNAL, P.O. Box 130, On the Common, Lyme NH 03768. (603)795-4757. FAX: (603)795-2238. Editor: Ed Gray. Magazine published 6 times/year. Circ. 35,000. Estab. 1975. Covers strictly hunting, fishing and conservation. For "readers who tend to be experienced outdoorsmen." Needs photos relating to hunting, fishing and wildlife. "We have 6 issues/year. We want no 'hunter or fisherman posed with an idiot grin holding his game.' No snapshots." Buys 150 photos/year. Buys first North American serial rights. Send photos for consideration. Pays on publication. Reports in 6-8 weeks. SASE. Sample copy $6.95; photo guidelines free with SASE.
Color: Send transparencies; Kodachrome 64 preferred. Pays $50 minimum.
Tips: "We like soft, moody, atmospheric shots of hunting and fishing scenes, as well as action. We like to blow our pix up *big* i.e., clarity is a must. Look at the photos we have published. They are absolutely the best guide in terms of subject matter, tone, clarity, etc."

*GREAT LAKES FISHERMAN, 1432 Parsons Ave., Columbus OH 43201. (614)445-7507. Editor: Dan Armitage. Monthly. Circ. 41,000. Estab. 1974. Emphasizes fishing for anglers in the 8 states bordering the Great Lakes. Sample copy and photo guidelines free with SASE.
Photo Needs: 12 covers/year supplied by freelance photographers; 100% from freelance stock. Needs transparencies for covers; 99% used are verticals. No full frame subjects; need free space top and left side for masthead and titles. Fish and fishermen (species common to Great Lakes Region) action preferred. Photos purchased with or without accompanying ms. "All b&w is purchased as part of ms package. Covers are not assigned but purchased as suitable material comes in." Model release required for covers; captions preferred.
Making Contact & Terms: Query with tearsheets or send unsolicited photos by mail for consideration. Prefers 35mm transparencies. SASE. Reports in 1 month. Provide tearsheets to be kept on file for possible future assignments. Pays $150/color photo; covers only. Pays on 15th of month preceding issue date. Credit line given. Buys one-time rights.
Tips: Sees trend toward: "More close-ups of *live* fish." To break in, freelancer should "look at 1990 covers" for insight.

GUIDE MAGAZINE, Box 23070, Seattle WA 98102. (206)323-7374. Editor: Jenny Peterson. Monthly. Emphasizes current events, social and political commentary, research as they relate to lives of gay men and lesbians. Readers are lesbians, gay men and those interested in issues surrounding homosexuality in the NW United States and Canada. Circ. 12,000. Sample copy with $8\frac{1}{2} \times 11$ SAE with $2 postage.
Photo Needs: Uses about 10 photos/issue; 5 supplied by freelance photographers. Needs photography to illustrate topical themes of gay men and lesbians with Northwest interests. Usually work on assignment only. Model release and captions required.
Making Contact & Terms: Query with samples. Send 4×5 or 8×10 glossy b&w prints by mail for consideration. Provide resume, business card, brochure, flyer or tearsheets to be kept on file for possible future assignments. SASE. Reports in 1 month. Pays on publication. Usually buys all rights.

GUIDEPOSTS ASSOCIATES, INC., 747 3rd Ave., New York NY 10017. (212)754-2225. FAX: (212)832-4870. Photo Editor: Courtney Reid-Eaton. Monthly magazine. Circ. 4,000,000. Estab. 1945. Emphasizes tested methods for developing courage, strength and positive attitudes through faith in God. Pays by job or on a per-photo basis; pays $125-400/color photo; $300-500/day. Credit line given. Pays on acceptance. Buys one-time rights. Send photos or arrange a personal interview. SASE. Simultaneous submissions OK. Reports in 1 month. Free sample copy and photo guidelines with 6×9 SAE and 65¢ postage.

Photo Needs: 85% assignment, 15% stock; variable. "Photos mostly used are of an editorial reportage nature or stock photos, i.e., scenic landscape, agriculture, people, animals, sports. We work four months in advance. It's helpful to send stock pertaining to upcoming seasons/holidays. No lovers, suggestive situations or violence."

Color: Uses 35mm; pays $150-400.

Cover: Uses transparencies; vertical format required. Pays $400-500. Usually shot on assignment.

Tips: "I'm looking for photographs that show people in their environment well. I like warm, saturated color for portraits and scenics. We're trying to appear more contemporary. We want to stimulate a younger audience and yet maintain a homey feel. For stock—scenics; graphic images with intense color. *Guideposts* in an 'inspirational' magazine. NO violence, nudity, sex. No more than 60 images at a time. Write first and ask for a photo guidelines/sample issue; this will give you a better idea of what we're looking for. I will review transparencies on a light box or in a carousel. I am interested in the experience as well as the photograph. I am also interested in the photographer's sensibilities—Do you love the city? Mountain climbing? Farm life?"

*GULF MARINER, P.O. Box 1220, Venice FL 34284. (813)488-9307. Editor: Thomas Kahler. Biweekly tabloid. Readers are recreational boaters, both power and sail. Circ. 15,000 +. Estab. 1984. Sample copy free with 9×12 SASE and $1 postage.

Photo Needs: Uses cover photo each issue—24 a year; 100% supplied by freelance photographers. Needs photos of boating related fishing, water skiing, racing and shows. Use of swimsuit-clad model or fisherman with boat preferred. All photos must have *vertical* orientation to match our format. Model release required. Photo captions preferred.

Making Contact & Terms: Send 35mm transparencies by mail for consideration. SASE. Reports in 1-2 weeks. Pays $25/color cover photo. Pays on acceptance. Credit lines optional. May use photo more than once for cover. Simultaneous and previously published work.

Tips: "We are willing to accept outtakes from other assignments which is why we pay only $25. We figure that is better than letting an unused shot go to waste or collect dust in the drawer."

GUN WORLD, Box HH, 34249 Camino Capistrano, Capistrano Beach CA 92624. (714)493-2101. Editor: Jack Lewis. Photo Editor: Dean Grennell. Monthly. Emphasizes firearms, all phases. Readers are middle to upper class, aged 25-60. Circ. 136,000. Sample copy $3 postpaid; photo guidelines free with SASE.

Photo Needs: Uses 70-80 photos/issue; about 50% (with mss) supplied by freelance photographers. Needs hunting and shooting scenes. Reviews photos with accompanying ms only. Model release preferred; captions required.

Making Contact & Terms: Query with samples; send unsolicited photos by mail for consideration at your own risk. Send 5×7 minimum glossy b&w prints and 35mm, 2¼×2¼ and 4×5 transparencies. SASE. Reports in 1 month. Pays $100/color cover photo; $10-100/inside b&w photo; $40/color inside photo; $100-350/text/photo package. Pays on acceptance. Credit line given if requested. Buys all rights, will release to author on request.

GUNS & AMMO MAGAZINE, 8490 Sunset Blvd., Los Angeles CA 90069. (213)854-2160. Editor: E.G. "Red" Bell, Jr. Art Director: Carol Winet. Monthly. "Technical to semi-technical firearms journal." Readers are shooters, gun collectors, do-it-yourselfers. Circ. 500,000 +. "Writer's guide with brief tips on photo packages free with SASE."

Photo Needs: Uses about 450 photos/issue. Needs photos of generally top-quality, still shots of firearms, action shots of guns being fired, sometimes wildlife shots and how-tos. Photos purchased with accompanying ms only. Model release preferred; captions required.

Making Contact & Terms: Submit photos with mss on speculation. SASE. Pays on acceptance. Credit line given. Buys one-time rights and all rights; will negotiate. Simultaneous submissions OK. Prefers to see "sharp, well-lit photos with uncluttered backgrounds. In our case, photos are most likely accepted with an article. It would be easier to 'break into' *G&A* for the writer/photographer, rather than the photographer."

HADASSAH MAGAZINE, 50 W. 58th St., New York NY 10019. (212)355-7900. FAX: (212)303-8282. Photo Editor: Adam Dickter. Magazine about Zionism and world Jewish concerns. Estab. 1914. Buys 50-75 photos/year. Photos used in magazines. Sample copy for $2.50 with 9×12 SAE and 90¢ postage.

Subject Needs: Israel and Jewish topics. "We can always uses good photos on the Jewish holidays; transparencies for our cover depicting the holiday from a unique or out-of-the-ordinary view."
Specs: Uses 5×7 glossy b&w prints, 35mm transparencies.
Payment & Terms: Pays $50/b&w photo; $75/color photo; $175/cover transparency. Credit line given. Buys one-time rights. Captions preferred.
Making Contact: Query with samples. SASE. Reports in 1 month.
Tips: Prefers to see interesting, fresh approaches to photographing Israel and Jewish life in general. "The larger the sample, the better the chances we'll like something. However, please note that we mainly deal with established freelance contacts."

HANDMADE ACCENTS: THE BUYER'S GUIDE TO AMERICAN ARTISANS, 488-A River Mtn. Rd., Lebanon VA 24266. (703)873-7402. Editor: Steve McCay. Quarterly magazine, "part catalog." Emphasizes fine art and fine crafts. Readers are arts patrons, collectors, consumers and retailers of fine arts and crafts. Circ. 45,000. Sample copy $5.
Photo Needs: "We need articles/photos from photographers who market their work as fine art." Photos purchased with accompanying ms only. "Need photos/stories of the collections or displays of fine arts/crafts of individual patrons." Photo captions required.
Making Contact & Terms: Query with samples. Send 35mm, 2¼×2¼, or 4×5 transparencies. SASE. Reports in 1 month. Pays $25-100/job or $25-100/text/photo package. Pays on publication. Credit line given. Buys one-time rights. Previously published work OK.

HARROWSMITH, 7 Queen Victoria Rd., Camden East, ON K0K 1J0 Canada. (613)378-6661. Editor-in-chief: Michael Webster. Magazine published 6 times/year. Circ. 154,000. Emphasizes alternative lifestyles, self-reliance, energy conservation, gardening, solar energy and homesteading. Photos purchased with or without accompanying ms and on assignment. Provide calling card, samples and tearsheet to be kept on file for possible future assignments. Buys 400 photos/year, 50 photos/issue; 40% assigned. Pays $50-500/job or $200-1,000 for text/photo package. Credit line given. Pays on acceptance. Buys first North American rights. Query with samples and list of subjects. SASE. Previously published work OK. Reports in 4 weeks. Sample copy $5 with 8½×14 SASE; free photo guidelines.
Subject Needs: Animal (domestic goats, sheep, horses, etc., on the farm); how-to; nature (plants, trees, mushrooms, etc.); photo essay/photo feature (rural life); horticulture and gardening; scenic (North American rural); and wildlife (Canadian, nothing exotic). "Nothing cute. We get too many unspecific, pretty sunsets, farm scenes and landscapes." Captions preferred.
B&W: Uses 8×10 glossy prints. Contact sheet and negatives OK. Pays $75-250/photo.
Color: Uses 35mm and 2¼×2¼ transparencies and 8×10 glossy prints. Pays $75-300/photo.
Accompanying Mss: Pays $125-1,000/ms. Free writer's guidelines.
Tips: Prefers to see portfolio with credits and tearsheets of published material. Samples should be "preferably subject oriented. In portfolio or samples, wants to see "clarity, ability to shoot people, nature and horticulture photo essays. Since there's a trend toward strong photo essays, success is more likely if a submission is made in a photo essay type package."

HARROWSMITH COUNTRY LIFE (formerly HARROWSMITH Magazine), Ferry Road, Charlotte VT 05445. (802)425-3961. FAX: (802)425-3307. Editorial Administrator: Regan Eberhart. Bimonthly. Emphasizes country living, environmental issues, and gardening and horticultural subjects. Readers are married couples, living in rural settings, higher than average income; college educated. Circ. 225,000. Estab. 1985. Sample copy $4. Photo guidelines free with SASE.
Photo Needs: Uses 50-60 photos/issue; 100% supplied by freelancers; assignment—30-50%; stock 50-70%. Model release and captions required.
Making Contact & Terms: Submit portfolio for review with return postage guaranteed. Provide credits and tearsheets to be kept on file for possible future assignments; "prefer to keep sheet of dupes on file." SASE. Reports in 1 month. Pays $500/color cover photo; $100-325, color page rate; by the job $200-600. Pays on acceptance. Buys first North American serial rights. Previously published work OK.
Tips: Prefers to see "technically flawless photos and fresh approaches to old subjects. Horticultural pictures must be identified; know the subject matter very well. If it's gardening, wildlife, or science—we need to know details about the photos that only a knowledgeable photographer can provide. Review many past issues. Send only top quality-best photos. We form impressions based on entire submission."

HARTFORD WOMAN, 595 Franklin Ave., Hartford CT 06114. (203)278-3800. Editor: Susan Plese. Monthly tabloid. Emhasizes women's issues. Readers are well-educated, professional women, 30 years of age and older. Circ. 40,000. Sample copy $1.85 and 10×13 SASE.

Photo Needs: Uses 8 photos/issue; 25% supplied by freelance photographers. Needs photos "usually of persons profiled." Model release and photo caption required.

Making Contact & Terms: Query with resume of credits. Provide resume, business card, brochure, flyer or tearsheets to be kept on file for possible assignments. SASE. Reports in 3 weeks. Pays $10/b&w inside photo or $7-9/hour. Pays on publication. Credit line given. Buys first N.A. serial rights. Simultaneous submissions OK.

Tips: "If the photographer is a good writer and photographer, and local, she has a good chance to get published. We're on a very tight budget, however."

HAWAII REVIEW, % University of Hawaii, 1733 Donaghho Rd., Dept. of English, Honolulu HI 96822. (808)948-8548. Editor-in-Chief: Elizabeth Lovell. Triannual journal. Literary and arts readership. Circ. 2,000. Sample copy $5 with 9 × 12 SASE and 60¢ postage.

Photo Needs: Prefers b&w experimental or "art" photos. No scenic or postcard-type shots. Special photo needs include cover photos. Model release and captions required.

Making Contact & Terms: Send unsolicited photos by mail for consideration; submit portfolio for review. Send 35mm and 8 × 10 transparencies by mail for consideration. Reports in 3 months. Payment varies. Pays on publication. Credit line given. Buys first North American rights; copyright reverts to artist upon publication. Will consider simultaneous submissions.

HAWAII-GATEWAY TO THE PACIFIC, Box 6050, Mission Viejo CA 92690. (714)855-8822. Editor: Dennis Shattuck. Bimonthly. Emphasizes the islands of Hawaii. Readers are both tourists from the mainland and residents of the state of Hawaii. Circ. 65,000. Sample copy $3.95.

Photo Needs: Uses 25-30 photos/issue; 15-20 supplied by freelancers. "We use photos for specific articles; no generalizations apply." Model release required. "Identities are necessary."

Making Contact & Terms: Query with samples. SASE. Reports in 3 weeks. Pays $250/color cover photo; $35/b&w or color inside photo. Pays on publication. Credit line given. Buys one-time rights. Previously published work OK.

HEALTH MAGAZINE, 3 Park Ave., 37th Floor, New York NY 10016. (212)779-6200. Assistant Art Director: Gordon Reynolds. Monthly magazine. Emphasizes health, sports and general well-being for women. Readers are women, median age 35, college graduates, both working and homemakers. Circ. 800,000.

Photo Needs: Uses approximately 35 photos/issue. Needs photos of "women in health situations—jogging, sports; some beauty; some generic scenes—family, office situations—all geared towards women." Model release preferred; captions required.

Making Contact & Terms: Submit portfolio for review. Provide resume, business card, brochure, flyer or tearsheets to be kept on file for possible future assignments. Rates given "upon photo submissions." Pays on publication. Credit line given. Buys one-time rights. Simultaneous submissions and previously published work OK.

Tips: In a portfolio, prefers to see "women—health, sports, some fashion, outdoors, food, beauty slots."

THE HERB QUARTERLY, Box 548, Boiling Springs PA 17007. (717)245-2764. Contact: Linda Sparrowe. Readers are "herb enthusiasts interested in herbal aspects of gardening, cooking or crafts." Quarterly. Circ. 25,000. Sample copy $6.

Photo Needs: Needs photo essays related to some aspect of herbs. Captions required.

Making Contact & Terms: Query with resume of credits. SASE. Reports in 1 month. Pays on publication $50/essay. Credit line given. Buys first North American serial rights or reprint rights.

HIDEAWAYS GUIDE, Box 1464, Littleton MA 01460. (508)486-8955. Publisher: Michael Thiel. Published 2 times/year. Circ. 12,000. Emphasizes "travel, leisure, real estate, vacation homes, yacht/house boat charters, inns, small resorts." Readers are "professional/executive, affluent." Sample copy $14.95.

Photo Needs: Uses 12-15 photos/issue; half supplied by freelance photographers. Needs "travel, scenic photos, especially horizontal format for covers." Special needs include "spectacular and quaint scenes for covers, snow on mountains, lakes and tropics, etc." Model release and captions preferred.

Making Contact & Terms: Arrange for personal interview to show portfolio; query with samples; send 8 × 10 b&w glossy prints by mail for consideration. SASE. Reports in 3 weeks. Payment is "negotiable but not more than $100." Pays on publication. Credit line given. Buys one-time rights. Simultaneous submissions and previously published work OK.

HIGH SCHOOL SPORTS, Suite 2000, 1230 Avenue of the Americas, New York NY 10020. (212)765-3300. FAX: (212)265-7278. Editor: Joe Guise. Bimonthly during school year. Emphasizes the efforts and achievements of high school athletes. Readers include teenagers who participate in high school athletics across the United States. Circ. 500,000. Estab. 1985. Sample copy $2; free photo guidelines with SASE.

Photo Needs: Uses 30-35 photos/issue; 100% supplied by freelance photographers; from assignment—85%, from stock—15%. Needs photos of boys and girls participating in high school sports. Photos that accompany feature stories will be assigned. Reviews photos with or without accompanying ms. Black/white or color transparencies of outstanding performances for 6-page news roundup. Also, humorous sports photo for full-page. Caption contest: "Photo Finish."

Making Contact & Terms: Query with samples; send unsolicited photos by mail for review; provide resume, business card, brochure, flyer or tearsheets to be kept on file for possible future assignments. Uses 35mm transparencies. SASE. Reports in 1 month. Pays $50-100/b&w photo; $50-250/color photo; $350/day. Pays on acceptance. Credit line given. Buys one-time rights. Previously published work "in some situations."

Tips: "Prefers samples of color sports action as well as set ups. When possible, we would like to see published feature assignments. We are people oriented and are not interested in still life or scenics."

ALFRED HITCHCOCK'S MYSTERY MAGAZINE, 380 Lexington Ave., New York NY 10017. (212)557-9100. Editor: Cathleen Jordan. Published every four weeks. Emphasizes short mystery fiction. Readers are mystery readers, all ages, both sexes. Circ. 225,000. Sample copy $2.75. Photo guidelines free with SASE.

Photo Needs: Uses 1 photo/issue; all supplied by freelance photographers. Needs mysterious photographs that contain a narrative element, should allow for a variety of possible interpretations. No gore; no accidents; no crime scenes. Black and white photos only. Model release required.

Making Contact & Terms: Query with samples, "nonreturnable photocopies only." Does not return unsolicited material. Reports in 2 months. Pay negotiated. Pays on acceptance. Credit line given. Buys one-time rights.

HOCKEY DIGEST, 990 Grove St., Evanston IL 60201-4370. (708)491-6440. Editor-in-Chief: Michael K. Herbert. Monthly. Emphasizes pro hockey for sports fans. Circ. 90,000.

Photo Needs: Uses about 40 photos/issue; 100% supplied by freelance photographers. Needs photos of sports action and portraits.

Making Contact & Terms: Provide resume, business card, brochure, flyer or tearsheets to be kept on file for possible future assignments. Uses 5×7 glossy b&w prints and 35mm transparencies. Pays on publication. Buys one-time rights.

HOCKEY ILLUSTRATED, 355 Lexington Ave., New York NY 10017. (212)391-1400. FAX: (212)986-5926. Editor: Stephen Ciacciarelli. Published 3 times per year, in season. Emphasizes hockey superstars. Readers are hockey fans. Circ. 50,000. Sample copy $2.25 with 9×12 SAE.

Photo Needs: Uses about 60 photos/issue; all supplied by freelance photographers. Needs color slides of top hockey players in action. Captions preferred.

Making Contact & Terms: Query with action color slides. SASE. Pays $150/color cover photo; $75/color inside photo. Pays on acceptance. Credit line given. Buys one-time rights.

HOME, 140 E. 45th St., New York NY 10017. (212)682-4040. Editor: Joseph Ruggiero. Contact: Art Department. Monthly. Circ. 925,000. Emphasizes "home remodeling, home building, home improving and interior design with special emphasis on outstanding architecture, good design and attractive decor." Readers are "home owners and others interested in home enhancement." Sample copy free with SASE.

Photo Needs: Uses 50-70 photos/issue; 100% provided by freelancers; "however, 95% are assigned rather than over the transom." Needs "four-color transparencies of residential interiors and exteriors—any subject dealing with the physical home. No lifestyle subjects covered." Model release and captions required.

Making Contact & Terms: Portfolio drop-off 5 days/week; same day pick-up; query with resume and samples; send transparencies ("2¼ and 4×5 are preferred") by mail for consideration; provide resume, business card, brochure, flyer or tearsheets to be kept on file for possible future assignments. "Material submitted on spec paid on publication. Assigned material paid on acceptance." Credit line given. Buys all rights.

Tips: Prefers to see "recent residential work showing a variety of lighting situations and detail shots as well as overall views. We accept only quality material and only use photographers who have the equipment to handle any situation with expertise."

*HOME EDUCATION MAGAZINE, Box 1083, Tonasket WA 98855. (509)486-1351. Managing Editor: Helen Hegener. Consumer publication. Bimonthly magazine. Emphasizes home schooling. Readers are parents of children, ages 2-18. Circ. 4,700. Estab. 1983. Sample copy for $4.50. Photo guidelines free with SASE.

Photo Needs: Number of photos used/issue varies based on availability; 75% supplied by freelance photographers. Needs photos of parent/child or children. Special photo needs include home school personalities and leaders. Model release and photo captions preferred.

Making Contact & Terms: Send unsolicited b&w prints by mail for consideration. SASE. Reports in 1 month. Pays $25-50/b&w cover photo; $5-20/b&w inside photo; $20/b&w page rate; $10-50/photo/text package. Pays on publication. Credit line given. Buys first N.A. serial rights. Simultaneous submissions and previously published work OK.

Tips: In photographer's samples, wants to see "sharp clear photos of children doing things alone, in groups, or with parents." Recommends that you "know your market—study the periodical."

HOME PLAN MAGAZINES, #115, 6800 France Ave. S., Minneapolis MN 55435. (612)927-6707. Editor: Roger Heegaard. Publishes three quarterly magazines, Homestyles Home Planes, Distinguished Home Plans and Designers' Collection Home Plans. Each is published quarterly, for a total of 12 issues/year. All three emphasize home designs, "for which we sell construction blueprints." Readers are people of all ages who plan to build a new home. Circ. 70,000. Sample copy free with 9 × 12 SAE with $1.75 postage.

Photo Needs: Uses about 8 photos/issue; all supplied by freelance photographers. "We use only photos of homes built from our designs. Our designs are marketed nationally, and thus homes built from those designs are scattered throughout the US. I typically need photographers in small-town and rural areas." Model release required.

Making Contact & Terms: Provide resume, business card, brochure, flyer or tearsheets to be kept on file for possible future assignments. SASE. Reports in 1 month. Pays $300-1,000/job. Pays on acceptance. Credit line given. Buys all rights; will negotiate.

HORSE & RIDER MAGAZINE, 941 Calle, Negocio CA 92672. (714)361-1955. Photo Editor: LeRoy Hinton. Monthly consumer magazine. Emphasizes training and care of horses. Circ. 100,000. Sample copy $2; free photo guidelines with SASE.

Photo Needs: Uses 45 photos/issue; 40 supplied by freelance photographers or photojournalists; 10% assigned. Needs photos of horses, prefer action, verticals, slides or 8 × 10 prints. Riders must be wearing Western hats and boots. The horse should be the emphasis of the photo; the horse's expression is also important. If horse is wearing bit, bridle, saddle, etc., all gear must be Western. Reviews photos with or without accompanying ms. Captions a must. Little use for pretty scenery or pasture shots.

Making Contact & Terms: Send 8 × 10, matte b&w or color prints; 35mm, 2¼ × 2¼ transparencies; b&w contact sheets with ms, b&w negatives with ms by mail for consideration. SASE. Reports in 1 month unless used in magazines. Pays $100/color cover photo; $5-20/inside b&w photo; $5-25/color photo; $25/page. Pays upon publication. Credit line given. "Be patient if your material is not published right away."

Tips: "We use predominantly 1 page/1 photo, however 2-4 shot series are also used. Shots being considered should be simple and get the feeling of Western training or riding across quickly. Contrast and sharpness are crucial. Good solid areas in background are preferred over busy or areas of contrasting lights and darks. *A horse photographer must know his subject.* Go vertical format as much as possible. Concentrate on the subject not the scenery. Be double sure subjects are in full Western gear. Leave room for cropping, logo, bleed, etc."

HORSE ILLUSTRATED, Box 6050, Mission Viejo CA 92690. (714)855-8822. FAX: (714)855-3045. Managing Editor: Sharon Ralls. Assistant Editor: Kathryn Shayman. Readers are "primarily adult horse-women between the ages of 18 and 40 who ride and show mostly for pleasure and who are very concerned about the well being of their horses." Circ. 120,000. Sample copy $3.50; photo guidelines free with SASE.

Photo Needs: Uses 20-30 photos/issue, all supplied by freelance photographers; 50% from assignment and 50% from freelance stock.. Specific breed featured every issue. Prefers "photos that show various physical and mental aspects of horses. Include environmental, action and portrait-type photos. Prefer people to be shown only in action shots (riding, grooming, treating, etc.). We like riders—especially those jumping—to be wearing protective headgear. We also need good-quality, interesting b&w photos of any breed for use in feature articles." Model release usually required.

The asterisk before a listing indicates that the market is new in this edition. New markets are often the most receptive to freelance submissions.

Making Contact & Terms: Send by mail for consideration actual 8×10 b&w photos or 35mm and 2¼×2¼ color transparencies. Reports in 6 weeks. Pays $15-25/b&w photo; $50-150/color photo and $100-350 per text/photo package. Credit line given. Buys one-time rights.
Tips: "Nothing but sharp, high contrast shots. Looks for clear, sharp color & b/w shots of horse care and training. Healthy horses, saferiding and care atmosphere is the current trend in our publication. Send SASE for a list of photography needs and for photoguidelines and submit work (pref. color trans.) on spec."

HORSE WORLD USA, Box 249, Huntington Station NY 11746. (516)549-3557. FAX: (516)423-0567. Editor: Diana De Rosa. 13 issues/year: 12 monthly and 1 special calendar issue. Emphasizes horses. Circ. 17,000. Estab. 1978. Sample copy $2 and 9×12" manila envelope with $1.50 postage. Photo guidelines free with SASE.
Photo Needs: Uses 25-50 photos/issue; 10 supplied by freelance photographers. Needs photos of horse shots from specific events, and horse-related photos for special features. Reviews photos with or without accompanying ms. Special needs include "photos taken at major national and international equine events. We sometimes do photo essays tied in with our editorial themes." Model release preferred; captions required; name/address/phone on back of photo, no name on front of photo.
Making Contact & Terms: Query with samples; send unsolicited photos by mail for consideration. Provide resume, business card, brochure, flyer or tearsheets to be kept on file for possible future assignments. Uses b&w prints and color. SASE. Reports in 2 months. Pays $10/inside photo; $100 for photo essays of 10-20 photos. Pays on publication. Credit line given. Buys first North American serial rights. "We keep photos published."
Tips: Looks for people "who understand horse photography. Clear, crisp, good contrast and cropped so the subject fills the photo, a knowledge of how to shoot horses. We like to work with new people who want and need the exposure and would supply us with complimentary photos in exchange for a credit line."

***HORSEPLAY MAGAZINE**, P.O. Box 130, 11 Park Ave., Gaithersburg MD 20884. (301)840-1866. Art Director: Cathy Kuehner. Monthly magazine. Emphasizes English riding (show jumping, fox hunting, dressage, eventing). Readers are ages 15-35, female, middle to upper middle class. Circ. 50,000. Estab. 1972. Sample copy $2.95. Photo guidelines free with SASE.
Photo Needs: Uses 45 photos/issue; 95% supplied by freelance photographers. Needs photos of horse shows, training photos and general horses being ridden. Special photo needs include world championship events, major grand prix, major 3-day, major dressage competitions. Photo captions required and must identify horse and rider.
Making Contact & Terms: Send b&w prints and 35mm transparencies by mail for consideration. Pays $200/color cover photo; $45/color inside photo; $22.50/b&w inside photo; $75 assignment fee. SASE. Buys first North American serial rights. Previously publised work OK.
Tips: Wants to see "good quality photo for reproduction, knowledge of subject matter with an artistic flair."

***HORSES MAGAZINE**, 21 Greenview, Carlsbad CA 92009. (619)931-9958. Managing Editor: Doug Fiske. Magazine published 8 times per year. Emphasizes show jumping and dressage. Readers are from teens to active seniors, primarily female with substantial number of males. Circ. 6,500. Estab. 1961. Sample copy $5. Call for specs (619)931-9958.
Photo Needs: Uses approximately 134 photos/issue; 35% supplied by freelance photographers. Needs photos of people, ring, jumps and performance. Special needs include "photos to accompany show reports of 'A' rated horse shows to which we do not send staff photographers."
Making Contact & Terms: Send 35mm, 2¼×2¼, 4×5, and 8×10 glossy b&w and color prints and 35mm and 2¼×2¼ transparencies by mail for consideration. SASE. Reports in 1-2 weeks. Pays $10-15/color inside photo; $10-15/b&w inside photo. Pays 30 days after publication. Credit line given. Buys first North American serial rights.
Tips: In photographer's samples "no proof sheets; 3×5, 5×7 and 8×10 b&w or color prints of action, people and 'win' photos. Know the subject, do good work and look at what kinds of photos we publish."

HOT ROD MAGAZINE, 8490 Sunset Blvd., Los Angeles CA 90069. (213)854-7155. Editor: Jeff Smith. Monthly magazine. Circ. 850,000. For enthusiasts of high performance and personalized automobiles. Typical subject areas include drag racing, street rods, customs, modified pickups, off-road racing, circle track racing. Will consider b&w and color photo features on individual vehicles; of race or event coverage with information; or b&w photos of technical or how-to subjects accompanied by text. However, best market is for "Roddin at Random" section, which uses single photo and/or short copy on any "newsy" related subject, and "Finish Line," which runs short pieces on a wide variety of vehicular racing or other competition. These sections pay $50-150 per photo or item used. Model release necessary. Buys all rights. Credit line given. Pays on acceptance. Reports in 2 weeks.

B&W: Send 8×10 glossy prints or contact sheets with negs. Pays $50-250.
Color: Send transparencies. Pays $100-500.
Tips: "Look at the magazine before submitting material. Use imagination, bracket shots, allow for cropping, keep backgrounds clean. We generally need very sharp, crisp photos with good detail and plenty of depth of field. Majority of material is staff generated; best sell is out-of-area (non-Southern California) coverage or items for news/human interest/vertical interest/curiosity columns (i.e., 'Roddin' at Random' and 'Finish Line'). Again, study the magazine to see what we want."

HUDSON VALLEY MAGAZINE, Box 429, Poughkeepsie NY 12602. (914)485-7844. FAX: (914)485-5975. Art Director: Felicia Webster. Emphasizes contemporary living in the Hudson Valley. Readers are upscale, average age 45, average combined income $81,000. Circ. 26,000. Estab. 1986. Sample copy for 9×12 SASE.
Photo Needs: Uses 30-40 photos/issue; 50% supplied by freelancers. Needs photos of scenic portraiture, architecture . . . all pertinent to the Hudson Valley. Model release and captions required.
Making Contact & Terms: Uses 8×10 glossy b&w and color prints; 35mm, 2¼×2¼, 4×5 and 8×10 transparencies. SASE. Reports in 1 month. Pays $50-250/b&w photo; $75-350/color photo; $20/hour ½ day rate; $400/day. Pays on publication. Credit line given. Previously published work OK.
Tips: Prefers to see "clear, sharp imagery capable of summing up the story at a glance; impact with subtlety and only excellence! Initial contact should be a excellent quality color or b/w promotion piece with printed example of their work on it."

*HUMM'S GUIDE TO THE FLORIDA KEYS, P.O.Box 2921, Key Largo FL 33037. (305)451-4429. Publisher: John Criswell. Quarterly consumer magazine; digest size. Emphasizes Florida Keys travel and leisure-oriented subjects. Readers are visitors and seasonal residents. Circ. 55,000. Estab. 1972. Sample copy free with 5½×8½SAE and 6 first-class stamps; photo guidelines sheet free with SASE.
Photo Needs: Uses 25-30 photos/issue; 100% supplied by freelancers. Needs photos of animal/wildlife, travel and scenics. Especially needs cover photos in vertical composition. Model release and captions preferred.
Making Contact & Terms: Query with list of stock photo subjects. Send unsolicited photos by mail for consideration; send 35mm and 2¼×2¼transparencies. SASE. Reports in 1 month. Pays $100/color cover photo; $50/color inside photo. Pays on publication. Buys one-time rights. Simultaneous submissions and previously published work OK.

IDEALS MAGAZINE, Ideals Publishing Corp., Nelson Place at Elm Hill Pike, Nashville TN 37214. Photo/Permissions Editor: Kathleen Gilbert. Magazine published 8 times/year. Emphasizes "seasonal themes—bright flowers and scenics for Thanksgiving, Christmas, Valentine, Easter and Mother's Day—all thematically related material. Other 3 issues are variable from year to year, but still overall seasonal in appearance." Readers are "mostly college-educated women who live in rural areas, aged 35-70." Sample copy $4.95 plus $1.75 postage and handling. Photo guidelines free with SASE.
Photo Needs: Uses about 21 or 22 color photos/issue. Needs photos of "bright, colorful flowers, scenics, primarily; subject-related shots depending on issue. We regularly send out a letter listing the photo needs for our upcoming issue." Model release required. No research fees.
Making Contact & Terms: Query with samples. Send 2¼×2¼, 4×5 or 8×10 transparencies by insured mail for consideration. SASE. Reports in 1 month. Payment varies. Pays on publication. Credit line given. Buys one-time rights. Simultaneous submissions OK.
Tips: "Would suggest the photographer purchase several recent issues of *Ideals* magazine and study photos for our requirements. *Ideals'* reputation is based on quality of its color reproduction of photos."

ILLINOIS MAGAZINE, P.O. Box 40, Litchfield IL 62056. (217)324-3425. Editor: Peggy Kuethe. Bimonthly. Emphasizes travel, history, current events, points of interest, people—all in Illinois. Readers are people primarily interested in Illinois history, (e.g., genealogists, teachers, students, historians), mostly rural. Circ. 12,000. Estab. 1964. Sample copy $1.50 with 9×12 SAE. Photo guidelines free with SASE.
Photo Needs: Uses about 35-40 photos/issue; 50% supplied by freelance stock. Needs "cover photos: 35mm vertical photos of Illinois scenes, natural attractions, points of interest, botanical subjects." Model release preferred; photo captions required.
Making Contact & Terms: Query with list of stock photo subjects; send 35mm transparencies by mail for consideration. SASE. Reports in 2 months. Pays $50/color cover photo; $10-100/color photo; $5-15/b&w inside photo;$50-200/photo/text package. Pays on publication. Credit line given. Buys one-time rights. Previously published work OK.
Tips: "Obtain a sample copy to see what we've published in the past—and stick to the standards *already* set—we do *not* deviate."In photographer's samples looks for "composition, clarity, subject and we're not impressed by special effects. Uses fewer wildflowers and more scenics. Look at several back issues and then talk to us."

*IN THE WIND, Box 3000, Agoura Hills CA 91301. (818)889-8740. Photo Editor: Kim Peterson. Bimonthly magazine. Emphasizes riding Harley-Davidson motorcycles and the enjoyment derived therein. Readers are 18, male/female working people. Circ. 263,529. Estab. 1979. Sample copy for $2 with 8×10 SASE. Photo guidelines free with SASE.

Photo Needs: Uses hundreds of photos/issue; 75% supplied by freelance photographers. Needs b&w or color prints and transparencies of riding and lifestyle situations. Always in need of action photos, bikes being ridden, no helmets if possible and people having fun with motorcycles worldwide. Model release required; photo captions preferred.

Making Contact & Terms: Send 35mm b&w and color glossy prints and 35mm and 2¼×2¼ transparencies by mail for consideration. Provide resume, business card, brochure, flyer or tearsheets to be kept on file for possible assignments. Reports in 3 months. Pays $200/color cover photo, $35/color inside photo; $35/b&w inside photo; and $50-250/photo/text package. Pays on publication. Buys all rights; will negotiate.

Tips: "Read the magazine, be sure to include name and address on photos in Sharpie Permanent Marker ink. Not ball-point as it shows through. Include model releases with submissions of nudity or posed photos."

*INDEPENDENT LIVING, 44 Broadway, Greenlawn NY 11740. (516)261-8899. Art Director: Andrew Elias. Consumer publication. Quarterly magazine. Emphasizes lifestyles for people with disabilities. Readers are ages 18 and up, male and female with disabilities. Circ. 25,000. Estab. 1988. Sample copy free with 9×12 SASE. Photo guidelines not available.

Photo Needs: Uses 25 photos/issue; trend is towards using more freelancers. Needs photos of lifestyle (work recreation, etc.) for people with disabilities. Model release and photo captions preferred.

Making Contact & Terms: Query with list of stock photo subjects; send unsolicited prints or transparencies by mail for consideration; provide resume, business card, brochure, flyer or tearsheets to be kept on file for possible assignments. SASE. Reports in 1-2 months. Pays $25/color cover photo; $15/color inside photo; $15/b&w inside photo. Pays on publication. Buys one-time rights. Simultaneous submissions and previously published work OK.

THE INDEPENDENT SENIOR, (formerly Seniors Advocate), 1268 W. Pender St., Vancouver BC V6E 2S8 Canada. (604)688-2271. Editor: Roderick MacDonald. Monthly tabloid. Emphasizes primarily senior activities. Other features include Canadian personalities, travel, health, finance, sports, news and veterans. Readers are male and female, working or retired. Circ. 45,000. Sample copy free with 10×12 SASE.

Photo Needs: Uses 20-30 photos/issue; 50-75% supplied by freelance photographers. Needs photos of active, interesting seniors. Photo captions required.

Making Contact & Terms: Query with list of stock photo subjects or send unsolicited photos by mail for consideration. Send b&w or color 5×7 prints. SASE. Reports in 1-4 weeks. Pays $20-50/photo depending on how used. Pays on publication. Credit line given. Buys one-time rights. Does not accept simultaneous submissions or previously published work.

Tips: "We will buy killer stand-alone photos with cutlines. We prefer graphically strong photos."

INDIANAPOLIS MONTHLY, Suite 225, 8425 Keystone Crossing, Indianapolis IN 46240. (317)259-8222. Art Director: Marie Cronin. Monthly. Emphasizes regional/Indianapolis. Readers are upscale, well-educated. Circ. 50,000. Sample copy for $3.05 and 9×12 SASE.

Photo Needs: Uses 50-60 photos/issue; 10-12 supplied by freelance photographers. Needs seasonal, human interest, humorous, regional. Model release and captions preferred.

Making Contact & Terms: Query with samples; send 5×7 or 8×10 glossy b&w prints or 35mm or 2¼×2¼ transparencies by mail for consideration. SASE. Reports in 1 month. Pays $25/b&w inside photo; $35/color inside photo. Pays on publication. Credit line given. Buys first North American serial rights. Previously published work on occasion OK, if different market.

Tips: "Read publication. Send photo similar to those you see published. If we do nothing like what you are considering, we probably don't want to."

Markets which offer lower payment amounts, or photo credits and extra copies or tearsheets as payment are often receptive to the work of newcomers. For a list of such markets, see the First Markets Index preceding the General Index in the back of this book.

INSIDE MAGAZINE, 226 S. 16th St., Philadelphia PA 19102. (215)893-5700. Editor: Jane Biberman. Quarterly magazine. Circ. 70,000. Sample copy free with SASE.
Photo Needs: 100% of photos supplied by freelance photographers. Needs photos of travel, health, auto, fashion, food, etc. Model release and photo captions preferred.
Making Contact & Terms: Arrange a personal interview to show portfolio. Provide resume, business card, brochure, flyer or tearsheets to be kept on file for possible assignments. SASE. Reports in 2 weeks. Pays $125-600, "depending on b&w or 4/c, amount, size, etc." Pays on acceptance. Credit line given. Buys one-time rights. Simultaneous submissions and previously published work OK.

INSIGHT, 3600 New York Ave. NE, Washington DC 20002. (202)636-8800. Executive Editor/Operations: Linda E. Moore. Photo Director: Brig Cabe. Photo Editor: Anne Alvarez. Weekly full-color newsmagazine. Readers are highly educated (66% are college graduates), affluent ($51,000-plus median family income), largely professional, managerial and VIP. Sample copy $3.
Photo Needs: Uses about 80 photos/issue; 5-10 supplied by freelance photographers on Insight assignments; one-third by stock photo agencies.. Needs photos of personalities and places figuring in stories. Photos reviewed with or without accompanying ms. "We don't buy freelance writing." Special needs include historic persons and events; names in the news, especially government officials, authors and thinkers around the world; some news events; many stock 'generic' images. Model release preferred; captions required.
Making Contact & Terms: Send for "Freelance Photography Terms" pamphlet, contract. Call before sending samples or portfolio; 35mm transparencies in sheets preferred. Provide resume, business card, brochure, flyer or tearsheets to be kept on file for future assignments. SASE. Reports in 2 weeks. Pays $200-400/job. Pays on publication. Credit line given. Buys all rights to a small select edit; buys first-use rights when assignment is made through a stock photography agency. Simultaneous submissions and previously published work OK.
Tips: Prefers to see a mixture of people, places, things and events. Looks for both field and studio expertise; reproducible quality; a variety of poses, backgrounds, etc.; the ability to create photographs that communicate issues and concepts, generic situations.

INTERNATIONAL GYMNAST, 225 Books, Oceanside CA 92054. (619)722-0030. Publisher: Glenn M. Sundby. Editor: Dwight Normile. Monthly magazine. Circ. 26,000. Primarily for youngsters and teens interested in gymnastics; also for coaches, teachers, athletes, international gymnasts and their associations, schools and libraries. Rights purchased vary. Needs action shots. Send photos for consideration. Credit line given. Buys 10-15 photos/issue. Pays on publication. Reports in 1 month. SASE. Previously published work OK if published outside U.S. Sample copy $3.25; editorial guidelines for SASE.
B&W: Send 5×7 or 8×10 glossy prints with "loose cropping." Captions required. Pays $5-10.
Color: Send 35mm or 2¼×2¼ transparencies. Captions required. Pays $10-40; pays up to $50 for full color spread or for photos used as posters.
Cover: Captions required. Pays $40.
Tips: "The magazine was born on, and grows on, voluntary writers and photographers. It is on limited newsstands, so has a limited readership and therefore limited payments. We do encourage writers/photographers and will pay for *quality* material if need be. Must be gymnastic-oriented and all sources identified. We are looking for good action & personality photos of top and up-and-coming gymnasts. Sharpness, peak action and a clearly recognizable face are components of a good gymnastics photo. Clean background a must, as is identification of subject."

***INTERNATIONAL PHOTOGRAPHER**, P.O. Box 18205, Washington DC 20036. (919)945-9867. Photography Editor: Vonda H. Blackburn. Quarterly magazine. Emphasizes photography. Readers are 90% male photographers. Circ. 100,000. Estab. 1986. For sample copy, send 9×12 envelope. Photo guidelines free with SASE.
Photo Needs: Uses 100 photos/issue; all supplied by freelance photographers. Model release required. Photo captions preferred.
Making Contact & Terms: Send 35mm, 2¼×2¼, 4×5, 8×10 b&w and color prints or transparencies by mail for consideration. SASE. Reports at end of the quarter. Payment negotiable. Credit line given. Buys one-time rights, per contract. Simultaneous submissions and previously published work OK.
Tips: Wants to see "consistently fine quality photographs, good captions or other associated information. Present a portfolio which is easy to evaluate—keep it simple and informative. Be aware of deadlines. Submit early to several publishers."

INTERNATIONAL WILDLIFE, 8925 Leesburg Pike, Vienna VA 22184. (703)790-4419. Senior Photo Editor: Steve Freligh. Photo Editor: John Nuhn. Bimonthly magazine. Emphasizes world's wildlife, nature, environment, conservation. Readers are people who enjoy viewing high quality wildlife and nature images, and who are interested in knowing more about the natural world and man's inter-relationship with animals and environment in all parts of the globe. Circ. 650,000. Estab. 1970. Sample copy $3 from National Wildlife Federation Membership Services (same address); do not include order with guidelines request. Photo guidelines free with SASE.

Subject Needs: Uses about 45 photos/issue; all supplied by freelance photographers. Needs photos of world's wildlife, wild plants, nature-related how-to, conservation practices, conservation minded people (tribal and individual), environmental damage, environmental research, outdoor recreation. Special needs include single photos for cover possibility (primarily wildlife but also plants, scenics, people); story ideas (with photos) from Canada, Europe, Pacific, China; black and whites accompanying unique story ideas that should not be in color. Model release preferred; captions required.

Making Contact & Terms: Send 8×10 glossy b&w prints; 35mm, 2¼×2¼, 4×5, 8×10 transparencies by mail for consideration. Query with samples, credits and stock listings. SASE. Reports in 3 weeks. Pays $750/color cover photo; $255-705 /color inside photo; $100-400/day; $750-2,500/complete package. Pays on acceptance. Credit line given. Buys one-time rights with limited magazine promotion rights. Previously published work OK.

Tips: Looking for a variety of images that show photographer's scope and specialization, organized in slide sheets, along with tearsheets of previously published work. "Study our magazine; note the type of images we use and send photos equal or better; think editorially when submitting story queries or photos; assure that package is complete—sufficient return postage (no checks), proper size return envelope, address inside, and do not submit photos in glass slides, trays or small boxes."

THE IOWAN MAGAZINE, Suite 350, 108 Third St., Des Moines IA 50309. (515)282-8220. FAX: (515)282-0125. Editor: Charles W. Roberts. Quarterly magazine. Emphasizes "Iowa—its people, places, events and history." Readers are over 30, college-educated, middle to upper income. Circ. 25,000. Estab. 1952. Sample copy $4.50 with 9×12 SAE and $2.25 postage. Photo guidelines free with SASE.

Photo Needs: Uses about 50 photos/issue; 95% by freelance photographers on assignment and 5% freelance stock. Needs "Iowa scenics—all seasons." Captions required.

Making Contact & Terms: Send b&w prints; 35mm, 2¼×2¼ or 4×5 transparencies; or b&w contact sheet by mail for consideration. SASE. Reports in 1 month. Pays $25-50/b&w photo; $50-100/color photo; $200-500/day. Pays on publication. Credit line given. Buys one-time rights.

THE ISLAND GROWER, 7007 Richview, RR4, Sooke BC V0S 1N0 Canada. (614)642-4129. Publisher: Chuck Seitz. Monthly magazine (excluding January). Emphasizes gardening. Readers are middle to senior age retired male and female professionals. Circ. 8,000. Sample copy free with 9×11 SAE and 76¢ Canadian postage.

Photo Needs: Uses 2-7 photos/issue. Needs gardening-related photos. Special needs include cover Christmas photo. Model release, photo captions required.

Making Contact & Terms: Send 5×7 or 8×10 color prints by mail for consideration. SASE. Reports "ASAP." Pays $50/color cover photo, $25/color inside photo. Pays on publication. Credit line given. Buys one-time rights.

JAZZIZ MAGAZINE, Box 8309, Gainesville FL 32605-8309. (904)375-3705. Publisher: Michael Fagien. Bimonthly magazine. Emphasizes "the spectrum of contemporary music." Circ. 65,000. Sample copy $3.50 with 8½×11 SAE and $1.15 postage. Photo guidelines free with SASE.

Photo Needs: Uses about 35 photos/issue; 20 supplied by freelance photographers. Needs photos of "jazz musicians, color and b&w, playing or posed."

Making Contact & Terms: Query with samples and list of stock photo subjects. Send color or b&w prints by mail for consideration. Submit portfolio for review. SASE. Reports in 1 month. Payment by the job negotiable by contact. Pays on publication. Credit line given. Rights purchased negotiable.

Tips: Prefers to see "high quality photos with expression—photos which give the essence of inner feeling of the person photographed. Avoid resume shots. Unusual crops, angles and lighting always welcome."

JUNIOR SCHOLASTIC, 730 Broadway, New York NY 10003. (212)505-3000. Editor: Lee Baier. Photo Researcher Editor: Deborah Thompson. Biweekly educational school magazine. Emphasizes junior high social studies (grades 6-8): world and national news, US history, geography, how people live around the world. Circ. 725,000. Sample copy $1.75 with 9×12 SASE.

Photo Needs: Uses 20 photos/issue. Needs photos of young people ages 11-14; non-travel photos of life in other countries; US news events. Reviews photos with accompanying ms only. Model release (under 18) and captions required.

Making Contact & Terms: Arrange a personal interview to show portfolio. "Please do not send samples—only stock list or photocopies of photos. Non returnable." Reports in 1 month. Pays $200/color cover photo; $75/b&w inside photo; $100/color inside photo. Pays on acceptance. Credit line given. Buys one-time rights. Simultaneous submissions OK.

Tips: Prefers to see young teenagers; in US and foreign countries. "Personal interviews with teenagers worldwide with photos."

KANSAS, 5th Floor, 400 W. 8th St., Topeka KS 66603. (913)296-3479. Editor: Andrea Glenn. Quarterly magazine. Circ. 54,000. Emphasizes Kansas scenery, arts, recreation and people. Photos are purchased with or without accompanying ms or on assignment. Buys 60-80 photos/year. Credit line given. Pays on acceptance. Not copyrighted. Send material by mail for consideration. No b&w. SASE. Previously published work OK. Reports in 1 month. Free sample copy and photo guidelines. Photos are returned after use.
Subject Needs: Animal, documentary, fine art, human interest, nature, photo essay/photo feature, scenic, sport, travel and wildlife, all from Kansas. No nudes, still life or fashion photos. Transparencies must be identified by location and photographer's name on the mount.
Color: Uses 35mm, 2¼ × 2¼ or 4 × 5 transparencies. Pays $50 minimum/photo.
Cover: Uses 35mm 2¼ or 4 × 5 color transparencies. Vertical format required. Pays $100 minimum/photo.
Accompanying Mss: Seeks mss on Kansas subjects. Pays $100 minimum/ms. Free writer's guidelines.
Tips: Kansas-oriented material only. Prefers Kansas photographers.

KARATE/KUNG FU ILLUSTRATED, Box 7728, Burbank CA 91510-7728. (818)843-4444. Executive Editor: Tim Vandehey. Bimonthly magazine. Readers are enthusiasts of martial arts and fighting styles. Circ. 85,000. Photo guidelines free with SASE.
Photo Needs: Uses 50-75 photos/issue; at least 50% supplied by freelance photographers. Needs photos on how to maintain arts; some how-to fitness and exercise shots. Model release required; captions preferred.
Making Contact & Terms: Query with samples; send 3½ × 5 or larger glossy or matte b&w and color prints; 35mm, 2¼ × 2¼ transparencies; b&w and color contact sheets; b&w negatives or color slides by mail for consideration. Phone query. SASE. Reports in 1 week. Pays $150-175/color cover photo; $10-50/b&w inside photo; $50-150/job; and $50-150 for text/photo package. Pays on publication. Credit line given. Buys all rights. Previously published work OK.
Tips: Wants crisp, clean, captivating shots. "Rarely, if ever, buys photos without accompanying manuscript."

KASHRUS MAGAZINE—The Guide for the Kosher Consumer, Box 96, Parkville Station, Brooklyn NY 11204. (718)998-3201. Editor: Rabbi Yosef Wikler. Bimonthly. Emphasizes kosher food and food technology. Readers are kosher food consumers, vegetarians, and producers. Circ. 10,000. Sample copy for 9 × 12 SAE with $1.25 postage.
Photo Needs: Uses 3-5 photos/issue; all supplied by freelance photographers. Needs photos of travel, food, food technology and seasonal nature photos. Model release and captions preferred.
Making Contact & Terms: Send unsolicited photos by mail for consideration; provide resume, business card, brochure, flyer or tearsheets to be kept on file for possible future assignments. Uses 2¼ × 2¼, 3½ × 3½ or 7½ × 7½ matte b&w prints. SASE. Reports in 1 week. Pays $50-100/b&w cover photo; $25-50/b&w inside photo; $75-200/job; $50-200/text/photo package. Pays part on acceptance; part on publication. Buys one-time rights, first N.A. serial rights, all rights. Will negotiate with photographer unwilling to sell all rights. Simultaneous submissions and previously published work OK.

KEEPIN' TRACK OF VETTES, Box 48, Spring Valley NY 10977. Editor: Shelli Finkel. Monthly magazine. Circ. 30,000. For people interested in Corvette automobiles. Buys all rights. Send contact sheet or photos for consideration. Credit line given. Photos purchased with accompanying ms. Pays on publication. Reports in 8 weeks. Free sample copy and editorial guidelines with 9 × 12 SAE and $1.20 postage.
Subject Needs: Needs interesting and different photos of Corvettes and picture essays. Human interest, documentary, celebrity/personality, product shot and humorous.
B&W: Send contact sheet or 5 × 7 or 8 × 10 glossy prints. Pays $10-150 for text/photo package.
Color: Send transparencies. Pays $50-200 for text/photo package.

KEYBOARD, 20085 Stevens Creek Blvd., Cupertino CA 95014. (408)446-1105. Editor: Dominic Milano. Photo Editor: Richard Leeds. Monthly magazine. Circ. 82,000. Emphasizes "biographies and how-to feature articles on keyboard players (pianists, organists, synthesizer players, etc.) and keyboard-related material. It is read primarily by musicians to get background information on their favorite artists, new developments in the world of keyboard instruments, etc." Photos purchased with or without accompanying ms and infrequently on assignment. Buys 10-15 photos/issue. Pays on a per-photo or per-job basis. Pays expenses on assignment only. Credit line given. Pays on publication. Buys rights to one-time use with option to reprint. Query with list of stock photo subjects. SASE. Send first class to Richard Leeds. Simultaneous submissions OK. Reports in 2-4 weeks. Free sample copy and photo guidelines.

Subject Needs: Celebrity/personality (photos of pianists, organists and other keyboard players at their instruments). No "photos showing only the face, unless specifically requested by us; no shots where either the hands on the keyboard or the face are obscured." Captions required for historical shots only.

B&W: Uses 8×10 glossy prints. Pays $35-100/photo.

Color: Uses 35mm color transparencies for cover shots. Vertical format preferred. Leave space on left-hand side of transparencies for cover shots. Pays $250/photo for cover, $50-150 for shots used inside.

Accompanying Mss: Free photographer's and writer's guidelines.

Tips: "Send along a list of artist shots on file. Photos submitted for our files would also be helpful— we'd prefer keeping them on hand, but will return prints if requested. Prefer live shots at concerts or in clubs. Keep us up to date on artists that will be photographed in the near future. Freelancers are vital to *KM*."

KITE LINES, P.O. Box 466, Randallstown MD 21133-0466. (301)922-1212. Publisher-Editor: Valerie Govig. Quarterly. Circ. 13,000. Estab. 1977. Emphasizes kites and kite flying exclusively. Readers are international adult kiters. Sample copy $3.50; photo guidelines free with SASE.

Photo Needs: Uses about 40-70 photos/issue; "50-70% are unassigned and over-the-transom—but nearly all are from *kiter*-photographers." Needs photos of "unusual kites in action (no dimestore plastic kites), preferably with people in the scene (not easy with kites). Needs to relate closely to *information* (article or long caption)." Special needs include major kite festivals; important kites and kiters. Captions required. "Identify *kites* as well as people."

Making Contact & Terms: Query with samples or send 2-3 b&w 8×10 uncropped prints or 35mm or larger transparencies by mail for consideration. Provide relevant background information, i.e., knowledge of kites or kite happenings. SASE. Reports in "2 weeks to 2 months (varies with workload, but any obviously unsuitable stuff is returned quickly—in 2 weeks." Pays $0-30 per inside photo; $0-50 for color photo; special jobs on assignment negotiable; generally on basis of expenses paid only. We provide extra copies to contributors. Our limitations arise from our small size, and we hope to do better as we grow. Meantime, *Kite Lines* is a quality showcase for good work and helps build reputations. Also we act as a referral service between paying customers and kite photographers. Pays on acceptance. Buys one-time rights. Usually buys first world serial rights. Previously published work OK.

Tips: In portfolio or samples wants to see "ability to select important, *noncommercial* kites. Just take a great kite picture, and be patient with our tiny staff. We are using more color—but we are still in need of black-and-white. Considers good selection of subject matter; good composition—angles, light, background; and sharpness. But we don't want to look at "portfolios"—just *kite* pictures, please. As we said before, just take great kite pictures—& show an interest in kites."

L.A. WEST, Suite 245, 919 Santa Monica Blvd., Santa Monica CA 90401. (213)458-3376. Editor-in-chief: Jan Loomis. Monthly magazine. *L.A. West* is the magazine for West Los Angeles. Readers are affluent, well-educated, average age 39; 50% college educated. Circ. 60,000. Sample copy available for large size envelope and 73¢ postage.

Photo Needs: Uses 15 photos/issue; all supplied by freelance photographers; 95% on assignment. Needs photos of travel, locally oriented to story. Will review photos with accompanying ms only. Model release required; captions preferred.

Making Contact & Terms: Arrange a personal interview to show portfolio. SASE with $2.40 postage. Reports in 1 month. Pays $35-75/b&w photo; $35-150/color photo. Pays on publication. Credit line given. Buys all rights.

Tips: Looks for "good composition, use of lights, style, clarity, creativity, ability to handle medium. Be organized, meet deadlines, etc. " To break in, "be consistent, have a varied portfolio and take direction well."

*LADIES HOME JOURNAL, 100 Park Ave, New York NY 10017. (212)351-3563. Contact: Photo Editor. Monthly magazine. Features women's issues. Readership consists of women with children and working women in 30's age group. Circ. 6 million.

Photo Needs: Uses 90 photos per issue; 100% supplied by freelancers. Needs photos of children, celebrities and women's lifestyles/situations. Reviews photos only without ms. Model release and captions preferred.

Making Contact & Terms: Provide resume, business card, brochure, flyer or tearsheet to be kept on file for possible assignment. Reports in 3 weeks. Pays $185/b&w inside photo; $185/color page rate. Pays on acceptance. Credit line given. Buys one-time rights.

*LAKE SUPERIOR MAGAZINE, P.O. Box 16417, Duluth MN 55816-0417. (218)722-5002. FAX: (218)722-1341. Editor: Paul L. Hayden. Consumer publication. Bimonthly magazine. "Beautiful picture magazine about Lake Superior." Readers are ages 35-55, male and female, highly educated, upper middle and upper management level through working. Circ. 20,000. Estab. 1979. Sample copy for $4.95, 8½×11 SASE and 5 first-class stamps. Photo guidelines free with SASE.

Photo Needs: Uses 30 photos/issue; 70% supplied by freelance photographers. Needs photos of scenic, travel, wildlife, personalties, underwater, all photos Lake Superior related. Photo captions preferred.

Making Contact & Terms: Send unsolicited photos by mail for consideration; provide resume, business card, brochure, flyer or tearsheets to be kept on file for possible assignments. Uses b&w prints; 35mm, 2¼×2¼, 4×5 transparencies. SASE. Reports in 3 weeks. Pays $50-75/color cover photo; $30/color inside photo; $20/b&w inside photo. Pays on publication. Credit line given. Buys first N.A. serial rights; reserves 2nd rights for future use. Simultaneous submissions OK.

Tips: "Be aware of the focus of our publication—Lake Superior. Photo features concern only that. Features with text can be related. We are known for our fine color photography. It has to be 'tops.' We try to use image large, therefore detail quality & resolution must be good. We look for unique outlook on subject, not just snapshots. Must communicate emotionally."

*LAKELAND BOATING MAGAZINE, Suite 500, 1600 Orrington Ave., Evanston IL 60201. (708)869-5400. Editor: Douglas Seibold. Monthly magazine. Emphasizes boating in the Great Lakes. Readers are affluent professionals, predominantly men over 35. Circ. 40,000. Estab. 1945. Sample copy for $5.50 with 9×12 SAE and $2.40 postage.

Photo Needs: Needs shots of particular Great Lakes ports and waterfront communities. Model release and photo captions preferred.

Making Contact & Terms: Query with list of stock photo subjects. Provide resume, business card, brochure, flyer or tearsheets to be kept on file for possible assignments. SASE. Reports back in 1 month. Will give photo credit; payment negotiable. Pays on acceptance. Credit line given. Buys one-time rights.

LEISURE WORLD (formerly LEISURE ONTARIO), 1215 Ouellette Ave., Windsor, ON N9A 6N3 Canada. (519)255-1212. Editor-in-Chief: Doug O'Neil. Bimonthly magazine. Emphasizes travel and leisure. Readers are auto club members, 50% male, 50% female, middle to upper middle class. Circ. 260,000. Estab. 1988. Sample copy $2.

Photo Needs: Uses 40-50 photos/issue; 25-30% supplied by freelance photographers. Needs photos of travel, scenics. Special needs include exotic travel locales. Model release preferred; photo captions required.

Making Contact & Terms: Send unsolicited photos by mail for consideration. Provide resume, business card, brochure, flyer or tearsheets to be kept on file for possible assignments. Send b&w or color 35mm, 2¼×2¼, 4×5, or 8×10 transparencies. SASE. Reports in 2 weeks. Pays $100/color cover photo, $80/b&w cover photo, $40/color inside photo, $25/b&w inside photo, or $100-300/photo/text package. Pays on publication. Credit line given. Buys one-time rights. Mail to Carmel Ravanello, Managing Editor.

Tips: "We expect that the technical considerations are all perfect—frames, focus, exposure, etc. Beyond that we look for a photograph that can convey a mood or tell a story by itself. We would like to see more subjective and impressionistic photographs. Don't be afraid to submit material. If your first submissions are not accepted, try again. We encourage talented and creative photographers who are trying to establish themselves."

LET'S LIVE, 444 N. Larchmont Blvd., Los Angeles CA 90004. (213)469-3901. Art Director: John DeDominic. Monthly. Circ. 125,000. Emphasizes nutrition, health and recreation. Readers are "health-oriented, typical family-type Americans seeking advice on food, nutritional supplements, dietary and exercise guidelines, preventive medicine, drugless treatment and latest research findings. Ages: 20-35 and 49-70." Sample copy $1.50; photo guidelines for SASE.

Photo Needs: Uses 9-15 photos/issue, 6 supplied by freelance photographers. Needs "candid life scenes; before-and-after of people; celebrities at work or leisure; glamour close-ups; organic uncooked foods; 'nature' views; sports; human organs (internal only); cross-sections of parts and systems (from color art or models); celebrities who are into nutrition and exercise; travel is OK if connected with food, medical research, triumph over disease, etc.; 'theme' and holiday motifs that tie in with health, health foods, clean living, preferably staged around known celebrity. Emphasis on upbeat, wholesome, healthy subject or environment with strong color values for bold full-page or double-truck layouts." Model release required; captions not required, but preferred when explanatory.

Making Contact & Terms: Send by mail for consideration 5×7 or 4×5 b&w or color prints; 35mm color transparencies; or tearsheets with publication name identified; write or call (do *not* call collect); or query with list of stock photo subjects. Provide calling card, club/association membership credits,

Photo spreads are one way to increase the monetary value of sales to a particular market. This photo, showing the Minnesota coast of Lake Superior, is one of six which Iowa-based photographer Michael Whye sold to Lake Superior Magazine out of a larger, initial submission. The magazine paid Whye $180 for the photos and a brief block of text describing the photos. According to Whye, the benefits of such a sale are three-fold. "Being paid is an obvious benefit," he says, noting the primary incentive. "Listing another credit also helps when querying to new editors. Plus, whenever a photo is used, it develops a bond between a photographer and that magazine which may result in future assignments or stock sales."

flyer, samples and tearsheets to be kept on file for possible future assignments. SASE. Reports in 3-5 weeks. Pays $17.50/b&w photo; $20/color transparency; $50-200 for text/photo package. Pays on publication. Credit line given. Buys first North American serial rights. Simultaneous submissions and previously published work OK.

LETTERS, 310 Cedar Lane, Teaneck NJ 07666. Associate Editor: Lisa Rosen. Monthly. Emphasizes "sexual relations between people, male/female; male/male; female/female." Readers are "primarily male, older; some younger women." Sample copy $3.
Photo Needs: Uses 1 photo/issue; all supplied by freelance photographers. Needs photos of scantily attired females; special emphasis on shots of semi- or completely nude buttocks. Model release required.
Making Contact & Terms: Query with samples. Send 2¼×2¼ slides by mail for consideration. Provide brochure, flyer and tearsheets to be kept on file for possible future assignments. SASE. Reports in 2-3 weeks. Pays $150/color photo. Pays on publication. Buys first North American serial rights.
Tips: Would like to see "material germane to our publication's needs. See a few issues of the publication before you send in photos. Please send slides that are numbered and keep a copy of the list, so if we do decide to purchase we can let you know by the number on the slide. All of our covers are bought from freelance photographers."

LIFE, Time-Life Bldg., Rockefeller Center, New York NY 10020. (212)522-1212. Photo Editor: Barbara Baker Burrows. Monthly magazine. Circ. 1,400,000. Emphasizes current events, cultural trends, human behavior, nature and the arts, mainly through photojournalism. Readers are of all ages, backgrounds and interests.
Photo Needs: Uses about 100 photos/issue. Prefers to see topical and unusual photos. Must be up-to-the-minute and newsworthy. Send photos that could not be duplicated by anyone or anywhere else. Especially needs humorous photos for last page article "Just One More."
Making Contact & Terms: Send material by mail for consideration. SASE. Uses 35mm, 2¼×2¼, 4×5 and 8×10 slides. Pays $500/page; $600/page in color news section; $1,000/cover. Credit line given. Buys one-time rights.
Tips: "Familiarize yourself with the topical nature and format of the magazine before submitting photos and/or proposals."

***LIFESTYLE**, 421 W MacArthur, Oakland CA 94609. (415)420-1381. Contact: Publisher. Bimonthly magazine. Covers self-improvement for singles, ages 25-60. Circ. 90,000. Estab. 1975.
Photo Needs: Uses up to 10/issue; 50% supplied by freelancers. Needs photos of personalities. Expects to be using more action photos of men and women in the coming year. Model release and photo captions preferred.
Making Contact & Terms: Send unsolicited b&w prints for consideration. SASE. Reports in 2 weeks. Pays $35/b&w photo. Pays on publication. Credit line given. Buys first North American serial rights.
Tips: "Send small sample photos."

LIGHTS AND SHADOWS, Box 27310, Market Square, Philadelphia PA 19150. (215)885-3355. Editor: H.M. Lambert. Magazine consisting entirely of freelance photography. Buys first rights. Submit material by mail with SASE only for consideration. Reports in 1 month. SASE. Previously published work OK.
B&W: Send 8×10 glossy prints, contacts or negatives.
Color: Send 35mm or up to 4 × 5 transparencies. Payments are competitive.

LIVE STEAM MAGAZINE, Box 629, Traverse City MI 49685. (616)941-7160. Editor-in-Chief: Joe D. Rice. Monthly. Circ. 13,000. Emphasizes "steam-powered models and full-size equipment (i.e., locomotives, cars, boats, stationary engines, etc.)." Readers are "hobbyists—many are building scale models." Sample copy free with 9×12 SAE and 90¢ postage; photo guidelines free with SASE.
Photo Needs: Uses about 80 photos/issue; "most are supplied by the authors of published articles." Needs "how-to-build (steam models), historical locomotives, steamboats, reportage of hobby model steam meets. Unless it's a cover shot (color), we only use photos with ms." Special needs include "strong transparencies of steam locomotives, steamboats, or stationary steam engines."
Making Contact & Terms: Query with samples. Send 3x5 b&w glossy prints by mail for consideration. SASE. Reports in 3 weeks. Pays $40/color cover photo; $8/b&w inside photo; $30/page plus $8/photo; $25 minimum for text/photo package (maximum payment "depends on article length"). Pays on publication—"we pay quarterly." Credit line given. Buys one-time rights. Simultaneous submissions OK.
Tips: "Be sure that mechanical detail can be seen clearly. Try for maximum depth of field."

THE LOOKOUT, Standard Publishing, 8121 Hamilton Ave., Cincinnati OH 45231. (513)931-4050. Contact: Photo Editor, Standard. Weekly magazine. Circ. 150,000. For adults in conservative Christian Sunday schools interested in family, church, Christian values, answers to current issues and interpersonal relationships. Buys 2-5 photos/issue. Buys first serial rights, second serial (reprint) rights or simultaneous rights. Send photos for consideration; office will circulate your work among about two dozen other editors at our company for their consideration. Credit line given. Pays on acceptance. Reports in 2-6 weeks. SASE. Simultaneous submissions and previously published work OK. Sample copy 50¢; free photo guidelines for SASE.
Subject Needs: Head shots (adults in various moods/emotions); human interest (families, scenes in church and Sunday school, groups engrossed in discussion).
B&W: Send contact sheet or 8 × 10 glossy prints. Pays $10-35.
Color: Send 35mm or 2¼ × 2¼ transparencies. Pays $25-150.
Cover: Send 35mm or 2¼ × 2¼ color transparencies. Needs photos of people. Pays $50-150. Vertical shots preferred; but "some horizontals can be cropped for our use."

LOS ANGELES MAGAZINE, 1888 Century Park E., Los Angeles CA 90067. (213)552-1021. Editor: Lew Harris. Design Director: William Delorme. Executive Art Director: James Griglak. Editorial Coordinator and Photo Editor: Nancy Clare. Monthly magazine. Circ. 170,000. Emphasizes sophisticated southern California personalities and lifestyle, particularly Los Angeles area. Most photos are purchased on assignment, occasionally with accompanying ms. Provide brochure, calling card, flyer, resume and tearsheets to be kept on file for possible future assignments. Buys 45-50 photos/issue. Pays $100 minimum/job. Credit line given. Pays on publication. Buys first serial rights. Submit portfolio for review. SASE. Simultaneous submissions and previously published work OK. Reports in 2 weeks.
Subject Needs: Celebrity/personality, fashion/beauty, human interest, head shot, photo illustration/ photo journalism, photo essay/photo feature (occasional), sport (occasional), food/restaurant and travel. Most photos are assigned.
B&W: Send contact sheet or contact sheet and negatives. Pays $100-300/photo.
Color: Uses 4 × 5, 2¼ × 2¼ or 35mm transparencies. Pays $100-500/photo.
Cover: All are assigned. Uses 2¼ × 2¼ color transparencies. Vertical format required. Pays $450/ photo.
Accompanying Mss: Pays 10¢/word minimum. Free writer's guidelines.
Tips: To break in, "bring portfolio showing type of material we assign. Leave it for review during a business day (a.m. or p.m.) to be picked up later. Photographers should mainly be active in L.A. area and be sensitive to different magazine styles and formats."

LOUISIANA LIFE MAGAZINE, Box 308, Metairie LA 70004. (504)456-2220. Editor: Maria McIntosh. Art Director: Julie Dalton Gourgues. Bimonthly magazine. Emphasizes topics of special interest to Louisianians; a people-oriented magazine. Readers are statewide; upper middle class; college educated; urban and rural. Circ. 46,000. Sample copy $4 including postage. Photo guidelines free with SASE.
Photo Needs: Uses 45 photos/issue; all supplied by freelance photographers, 80% on assignment. Photos are assigned according to stories planned for each issue. Color transparencies are used for features, b&w for columns. Special needs include people, places, events in Louisiana. Identification required.
Making Contact & Terms: Arrange a personal interview to show portfolio; query with resume of credits and with samples; provide resume, business card, brochure, flyer or tearsheets to be kept on file for possible future assignments. "Follow up on the interview. Continue to send samples. Send story queries along with slides." Send 8 × 10 glossy b&w prints; 35mm, 2¼ × 2¼, 4 × 5, 8 × 10 transparencies; b&w contact sheet by mail for consideration. SASE. Reports in 3 weeks. Pays $50-135/b&w photo; $50-225/color photo; $200/day; $300-2,000/complete package. Pays on publication. Credit line given. Buys one-time rights.
Tips: In portfolio or samples, wants to see "technical excellence. Portraits, interiors, landscapes, *industrial* shots with a creative style." Seeks quality, not quantity. Can send duplicates for review. "Study *Louisiana Life* to become familiar with our needs. We have recently been focusing on industry in the state of Louisiana. We also are more interested in b&w photography and infrared techniques."

LOUISVILLE MAGAZINE, Suite 604, One Riverfront Plaza, Louisville KY 40202. (502)566-5050. Editor: James Oppel Jr.. Managing Editor: Cammie Cox. Monthly magazine. Circ. 24,000. Emphasizes community and business developments for residents of Louisville and vicinity who are involved in community affairs. Buys 12 photos/issue. Buys all rights, but may reassign to photographer after publication. Model release required "if photo presents an apparent legal problem." Submit portfolio. Photos purchased with accompanying ms; "photos are used solely to illustrate accompanying text on stories that we have already assigned." Works with freelance photographers on assignment only basis. Provide calling card, portfolio, resume, samples and tearsheets to be kept on file for possible future assignments. Pays on publication. Reports in 1 week. SASE. Sample copy $1.

Subject Needs: Scenes of Louisville, nature in the park system, University of Louisville athletics, fashion/beauty and photo essay/photo feature on city life. Needs photos of people, places and events in and around the Louisville area.

B&W: Send 8×10 semigloss prints. Captions required. Pays $10-25.

Color: Send transparencies. Captions required. Pays $10-25.

Cover: Send color transparencies. Uses vertical format. Allow space at top and on either side of photo for insertion of logo and cover lines. Captions required. Payment negotiable.

Tips: "All ideas must focus on the Louisville market. A photographer's portfolio, of course, may be broader in scope." Wants no prints larger than 11×14 or smaller than 5×7; 8×10 preferred. Annual Kentucky Derby issue needs material dealing with all aspects of Thoroughbred racing. Deadline for submissions: January 1.

*LUTHERAN FORUM, at the Wartburg/Bradley Ave., Mt. Vernon NY 10552. (914)699-1226. Editor: Paul Hinlicky. Emphasizes "Lutheran concerns, both within the church and in relation to the wider society, for the leadership of Lutheran churches in North America." Quarterly. Circ. 4,500.

Photo Needs: Uses cover photo occasionally. "While subject matter varies, we are generally looking for photos that include people, and that have a symbolic dimension. We use *few* purely 'scenic' photos. Photos of religious activities, such as worship, are often useful, but should not be 'cliches'—types of photos that are seen again and again." Model release not required; captions not required but "may be helpful."

Making Contact & Terms: Query with list of stock photo subjects. SASE. Reports in 1-2 months. Pays on publication $15-25/b&w photo. Credit line given. Buys one-time rights. Simultaneous or previously published submissions OK.

MAC USER MAGAZINE, 950 Tower Ln., Foster City CA 94404. Art Director: Lisa Orsini. Monthly magazine. Emphasizes Macintosh computers. Readers are Macintosh Computer users and owners. Circ. 300,000.

Photo Needs: Uses 10 photos/issue; all supplied by freelance photographers. Needs photos of product and conceptual product shots. Model release required.

Making Contact & Terms: Arrange a personal interview to show portfolio; query with samples; provide resume, business card, brochure, flyer or tearsheets to be kept on file for possible future assignments. Uses 35mm, 2¼×2¼, 4×5, 8×10 transparencies. SASE. Reports in 2 weeks. Pays $2500/color cover photo; $600/color inside photo. Pays on publication. Credit line given. Buys one-time rights.

Tips: Wants "well-lighted innovative, sharp, defined style. Only put your best work in your portfolio. I would rather see 10 perfect photos than 20 almost perfect. Establish a style in lighting and composition. This makes it easier for us to assign a photographer to a job. Use past issues as a reference. Seeing trend toward special effects, dramatic lighting and primary colors."

MACLEAN'S MAGAZINE, 777 Bay St., Toronto ON M5W 1A7 Canada. (416)596-5379. Photo Editor: Peter Bregg. Weekly. Emphasizes news. Circ. 650,000.

Photo Needs: Uses 40-70 photos/issue; 20 supplied by freelance photographers. Needs photos of news, environmental portraits. Model release and captions required.

Making Contact & Terms: Provide resume, business card, brochure, flyer or tearsheets to be kept on file for possible future assignments. Pays per cover photo, per inside photo, or by the hour. Pays on acceptance. Credit line given. Buys one-time rights. Previously published work OK.

MAGICAL BLEND, Box 11303, San Francisco CA 94101. (415)673-1001. Art Director: Matthew Courtway. Consumer publication. Quarterly magazine. Emphasizes New Age consciousness, visionary painting, collage and photography. Readers include people of "all ages interested in an alternative approach to spirituality." Circ. 45,000. Sample copy $4.

Photo Needs: Uses 1-12 photos/issue; 100% supplied by freelance photographers. Looks for creative, visionary and surreal work. Model release preferred if needed. Send without captions.

Making Contact & Terms: Send unsolicited photos by mail for consideration. Send b&w color prints, 35mm, 2¼×2¼, 4×5, and 8×10 transparencies. SASE. Reports in 3 weeks. Payment not given; credit line only. Buys one-time rights.

Tips: In portfolio or samples, looking for "photos with a new age theme: images that are inspiring to look at that show people in celebration of life. Try to include positive images. The best way to see what we're interested in printing is by sending for a sample copy."

MARRIAGE PARTNERSHIP, Christianity Today, Inc. 465 Gundersen Dr., Carol Stream IL 60188. (312)260-6200. Contact: Art Director, Gary Gnidevic. Quarterly magazine. Emphasizes all issues of marriage and family life. Readers are 24-44 years old, middle to upper-middle class and are 60%

women. Circ. 80,000. Estab. 1988. Sample copy for 9×12 SASE, "to people I'm interested in after seeing their work."

Photo Needs: Uses 15 photos/issue; 100% supplied by freelance photographers. Model release required.

Making Contact & Terms: Provide resume, business card, brochure, flyer or tearsheets to be kept on file for possible assignments. SASE. Reports in 2 weeks. Pays $800/b&w and color cover photo and $400/b&w and color page rate for assigned work. Pays $400-800/day. Approximately $200-300 page rate for stock b&w or color. Simultaneous submissions and previously published work OK.

Tips: Looks for "a strong sense of individual approach. I'd rather not see a portfolio that 1,000 other photographers could have done."

MARTIAL ARTS TRAINING, (formerly *fighting Stars*), 1813 Victory Place, Box 7728, Burbank CA 91510-7728. (818)843-4444. FAX: (818)953-9244. Editor: Marian K. Castinado. Bimonthly. Emphasizes martial arts training. Readers are martial artists of all skill levels. Circ. 20,000. Sample copy $1.50. Photo guidelines free with SASE.

Photo Needs: Uses about 100 photos/issue; 50 supplied by freelance photographers. Needs "photos that pertain to story on known martial artists' training. Only stories on nationally rated fighters, forms, weapons or full-contact are needed." *Photos purchased with accompanying ms only.* "We need freelance photographers around the country who can be called upon if we have a story idea in their area." Model release and captions required.

Making Contact & Terms: Send 5×7 or 8×10 b&w prints; 35mm transparencies; b&w contact sheet or b&w negatives by mail for consideration. SASE. Reports in 1 month. Pays $50-150 for text/photo package. Pays on publication. Credit line given. Buys all rights.

Tips: Photos "must be razor-sharp, b&w. Technique shots should be against neutral background. Concentrate on training-related articles and photos."

MASTER OF LIFE, Box 38, Malibu CA 90265. (818)889-1575. Editor: Dick Sutphen. Quarterly magazine. Emphasizes metaphysical, psychic development, reincarnation, self-help with tapes. Everyone receiving the magazine has attended a Sutphen Seminar or purchased Valley of the Sun Publishing books or tapes from a line of over 300 titles: video and audio tapes, subliminal/hypnosis/meditation/ New Age music/seminars on tape, etc. Circ. 120,000. Sample copy free with 12×15 SAE and $1.27 postage.

Photo Needs: "We purchase about 50 photos per year for the magazine and also for cassette album covers. We are especially interested in surrealistic photography which would be used as covers, to illustrate stories and for New Age music cassettes. Even seminar ads often use photos which we purchase from freelancers." Model release required.

Making Contact & Terms: Send b&w and color prints; 35mm, 2¼×2¼ transparencies by mail for consideration. SASE. Reports in 2 weeks. Pays $100/color photo; b&w negotiated. Pays on publication. Credit line given if desired. Buys one-time rights. Simultaneous submissions and previously published work OK.

MENNONITE PUBLISHING HOUSE, 616 Walnut Ave., Scottdale PA 15683. (412)887-8500. Photo Secretary: Debbie Cameron. Publishes Story Friends (ages 4-9), On The Line (ages 10-14), Christian Living, Gospel Herald, Purpose (adults).

Photo Needs: Buys 10-20 photos/year. Needs photos of children engaged in all kinds of legitimate childhood activities (at school, at play, with parents, in church and Sunday School, at work, with hobbies, relating to peers and significant elders, interacting with the world); photos of youth in all aspects of their lives (school, work, recreation, sports, family, dating, peers); adults in a variety of settings (family life, church, work, and recreation); abstract and scenic photos. Model release preferred.

Making Contact & Terms: Send 8½×11 b&w photos by mail for consideration; provide resume, business card, brochure, flyer or tearsheets to be kept on file for possible future assignments. SASE. Reports in 1 month. Pays $20-50/b&w photo. Credit line given. Buys one-time rights. Simultaneous submissions and previously published work OK.

MEN'S HEALTH, 33 East Minor, Emmaus PA 18098. (215)967-5171. Photo Editor: Margaret Skrovanek. Bimonthly magazine. Emphasizes active men, sports, travel. Circ. 250,000. Sample copy $3.50 and 8½×11 SASE.

Photo Needs: Uses 70 photos/issue; 50% supplied by freelance photographers. Needs men playing sports and in travel and business settings. Model release required.

Making Contact & Terms: Query with resume of credits or list of stock photo subjects. Does not return unsolicited material. Reports in 1 week. Pays ASMP rates. Credit line given. Buys first N.A. serial rights.

Tips: "In samples wants to see interesting light and upbeat compositions. Send samples of men in various situations."

METAL EDGE, 355 Lexington Ave., New York NY 10017. (212)949-6850. FAX: (212)986-5926. Editor: Gerri Miller. Monthly magazine. Emphasizes heavy metal music. Readers are young fans. Circ. 250,000. Estab. 1985. Sample copy free with large manila SASE.
Photo Needs: Uses 125 photos/issue; 100 supplied by freelance photographers. Needs studio b&w and color, concert shots, and behind-the-scenes (b&w) photos of heavy metal artists.
Making Contact & Terms: Arrange a personal interview to show portfolio, query with samples, and list of stock photo subjects. Reports ASAP. Pays $25-35/b&w inside photo; $75+/color; job. Pays on publication. Buys one-time rights for individual shots. Buys all rights for assigned sessions or coverage. Previously published work OK.
Tips: Prefers to see very clear, exciting concert photos; studio color with vibrancy and life, that capture subject's personality.

MICHIGAN NATURAL RESOURCES MAGAZINE, P.O. Box 30034, Lansing MI 48909. (517)373-9267. Editor: Norris McDowell. Photo Editor: Gijsbert van Frankenhuyzen. Bimonthly. Circ. 120,000. Estab. 1931. Emphasizes natural resources in the Great Lakes region. Readers are "appreciators of the out-of-doors; 15% readership is out of state." Sample copy $3; photo guidelines free with SASE.
Photo Needs: Uses about 40 photos/issue; freelance photography in given issue—50% from assignment and 50% from freelance stock. Needs photos of Michigan wildlife, Michigan flora, how-to, travel in Michigan, energy usage (including wind, water, sun, wood). Also, photos of people, especially minorities and handicapped, enjoying outdoor pursuits. Captions preferred. Query with samples or list of stock photo subjects; send 35mm color transparencies by mail for consideration. SASE. Reports in 1 month. Pays $75-250/color page; $500/job; $800 maximum for text/photo package. Pays on acceptance. Credit line given. Buys one-time rights.
Tips: Prefers "Kodachrome 64 or 25 or Fuji 50 or 100, 35mm, *razor sharp in focus!* Send about 20 slides with a list of stock photo topics. Be sure slides are sharp, labeled clearly with subject and photographer's name and address. Send them in plastic slide filing sheets. Looks for unusual outdoor photos. Flora, fauna of Michigan and Great Lakes region. We also need good photos of minoirities involved in outdoor pursuits. Provides some indication that he has read our magazine and is familiar with its approach."

MICHIGAN OUT-OF-DOORS, Box 30235, Lansing MI 48909. (517)371-1041. FAX: (517)371-1505. Editor: Kenneth S. Lowe. Monthly magazine. Circ. 130,000. Estab. 1947. For people interested in "outdoor recreation, especially hunting and fishing; conservation; environmental affairs." Buys first North American serial rights. Credit line given. Send photos for consideration. Reports in 1 month. SASE. Previously published work OK "if so indicated." Sample copy $2; free editorial guidelines.
Photo Needs: Animal; nature; scenic; sport (hunting, fishing and other forms of noncompetitive recreation); and wildlife. Materials must have a Michigan slant. Use 1-6 from freelance stock/issue.
B&W: Send any size glossy prints. Pays $15 minimum.
Cover: Send 35mm transparencies or 2¼×2¼. Pays $75 for cover photos, $25 for inside color photos.
Tips: Submit seasonal material 6 months in advance. Wants to see "new approaches to subject matter."

MICHIGAN SPORTSMAN, Box 741, Marietta GA 30061. (404)953-9222. Editor: Jim Schlender. Emphasizes fishing, hunting and related outdoor activities in the state of Michigan. Sample copy $1.95 with a SASE; photo guidelines free with SASE.
Photo Needs: Uses 15-20 photos/issue; mostly supplied by freelance photographers. Reviews photos with or without accompanying ms. Captions preferred.
Making Contact & Terms: Query with list of stock photo subjects; send 5×7 or larger color or b&w glossy prints, 35mm and 2¼×2¼ transparencies by mail for consideration; submit portfolio for review. SASE. Reports in 3-5 weeks. Pays $250/color cover photo; $25 b&w inside photo; $75/color inside photo. Pays 2½ months prior to publication. Credit line given. Buys one-time rights. No simultaneous submissions. Previously published work OK.
Tips: "We're looking for hunting/fishing actions scenes in a wide variety of settings, as well as outstanding photos of game animals and birds in natural situations. We need excellent sharpness, simple and 'non-busy' backgrounds and a sense of movement or animation whenever possible. We also prefer a good mix of horizontal and vertical treatments. Study our publication(s) to see what types of photos we use and duplicate that approach. Send sleeved slides with caption info that identifies species or activities shown in the photos. About half of our photos are purchased either as part of text/photo packages or from freelance files that we maintain in the office."

MID-ATLANTIC COUNTRY, 300 N. Washington St., Suite 305, Alexandria VA 22314. (703)548-6177. Art Director: Randy Clark. Monthly magazine. Emphasizes travel. Readers are middle-aged professional men and women. Circ. 115,000. Sample copy $2, 9×12 SASE and $1.65 postage. Photo guidelines free with SASE.
Photo Needs: Uses 30-35 photos/issue; 100% supplied by freelance photographers, 85% assigned. Needs travel and scenics from New Jersey, Pennsylvania, Delaware, Washington DC, Virginia, West Virginia, North Carolina and Maryland. Model release and photo captions required.
Making Contact & Terms: Arrange a personal interview to show portfolio, query with resume of credits along with business card, brochure, flyer or tearsheets to be kept on file for possible assignments, send unsolicited photos by mail for consideration or submit portfolio for review. Send b&w prints, any size, any finish and 35mm or 2¼×2¼ transparencies. SASE. Reports in 1 month. Pays $300/color cover photo, $100/color inside photo, $50/b&w inside photo, $200-500/day. Pays on publication. Credit line given. Buys one-time rights.
Tips: In portfolios, prefers to see "color transparencies (35mm and 2¼×2¼) of artful/unusual travel photography of Mid-Atlantic region." Also looks for "Interesting use of light and lenses. Shoot early morning and late afternoon." To break in with the magazine, "show me the kind of photos (and quality) that I'm already using in the magazine."

MIDDLER TEACHER, 6401 The Paseo, Kansas City MO 64131. (816)333-7000. Editor: Molly Mitchell. Quarterly Sunday school publication. Circ. 7,500. Emphasizes Christian principles for children 8-9. Freelancers supply 95% of the photos. Pays on acceptance. Model release required. Send photos. SASE. Simultaneous submissions and previously published work OK. Reports in 2-3 weeks. Free photo guidelines. SASE.
Subject Needs: Sunday school settings, action pictures showing children in different Sunday school situations and activities, families in different activities and situations. No fashion, sport or celebrity photos.
Cover: Color slides or photos only.
Making Contact & Terms: Pays $30-40/b&w photo; $75/color photo.
Tips: "Subjects must be suitable for a conservative Christian denomination and geared toward 8-9 year olds. Children prefer pictures with which they can identify. For children, realistic, uncluttered photos have been the standard for many years and will continue to be so. Photographing children in their natural environment will yield photos that we will buy. Send all photos to Editorial Librarian at address above."

MILITARY COLLECTORS NEWS, Box 702073, Tulsa OK 74170. (918)743-6048. Editor: Jack Britton. Magazine. Circ. 18,000. For collectors of military medals, badges, and insignia. Photos purchased with or without accompanying ms. Buys 72 photos/year. Pays $5-25 for text/photo package or on a per-photo basis. Credit line given. Pays on publication. Buys all rights. Send material by mail for consideration. SASE. Simultaneous submissions and previously published work OK. Reports in 1 month. Sample copy $1.
Photo Needs: Only photos of military items used or worn on uniforms (preferably foreign or old US) or men in uniform. Model release and captions preferred.
B&W: Uses 8×10 or smaller prints. Pays 50¢-$2/photo.
Color: Uses 8×10 or smaller prints. Pays 50¢-$3/photo.
Cover: Uses b&w or color prints. Vertical format preferred.
Accompanying Mss: Needs mss on military collecting. Pays $3-25/ms.

MINNESOTA SPORTSMAN, Box 741, Marietta GA 30067. Editorial Director: Jim Schlender. Emphasizes fishing, hunting and related outdoor activities in Minnesota. Sample copy $1.95 with a SASE; photo guidelines free with SASE.
Photo Needs: Uses 15-20 photos/issue; about half supplied by freelance photographers. Reviews photos with or without accompanying ms. Captions preferred.
Making Contact & Terms: Send slide sleeves and/or 5×7 or larger glossy prints by mail for consideration. SASE. Reports in 3-5 weeks. Pays $250/cover photo, $75/inside color and $25/b&w photo. Pays 2½ months prior to publication. Credit line given. Buys one-time rights. Previously published work OK.

MINORITY ENGINEER, Equal Opportunity Publications, Inc., 44 Broadway, Greenlawn NY 11740. (516)261-8917. Art Director: Andrew Elias. Quarterly. Emphasizes career guidance for minority engineers at the college and professional levels. Readers are college-age minority engineering students and young working minority engineers. Circ. 16,000. Sample copy free with 9×12 SASE and 6 first class stamps.

Photo Needs: Uses at least one photo per issue (cover); planning to use freelance work for covers and possibly editorial. Contact for needs. Model release preferred; photo captions required.
Making Contact & Terms: Query with list of stock photo subjecis; send unsolicited prints or 35mm transparencies. SASE. Reports in 2 weeks. Pays $25/color cover photo. Pays on publication; provide résumé, business card, brochure flyer or tearsheets to be kept on file for possible assigments. Credit line given. Buys one-time rights. Simultaneous submissions and previously published work OK, "but not in competitive career-guidance publications."
Tips: "We are looking for clear color shots of minority students and young professionals who are involved in activities related to their academic studies or professions. Most of the photography we use is submitted by the freelance writer with his or her manuscript. Also looking for more stock photos. We've decided to use more cover photos than we have in the past. We are also open to using inside photos, but freelancers should contact us and discuss upcoming stories before sending photos. Read our magazine to get an idea of the editorial content. Cover photos do not have to tie in to any one particular story in the magazine, but they have to be representative of the magazine's editorial content as a whole."

MODERN DRUMMER MAGAZINE, 870 Pompton Ave., Cedar Grove NJ 07009. (201)239-4140. FAX: (201)239-7139. Editor: Ron Spagnardi. Photo Editor: Scott Bienstock. Magazine published 12 times/year. Circ. 85,000. Buys 200-300 photos annually. For drummers at all levels of ability: students, semiprofessionals and professionals. Sample copy with 8½×11 SAE and $1.50 postage.
Subject Needs: Celebrity/personality, product shots, action photos of professional drummers and photos dealing with "all aspects of the art and the instrument."
Specs: Uses b&w contact sheet, b&w negatives, or 5×7 or 8×10 glossy b&w prints; 35mm, 2¼×2¼, 8×10 color transparencies. Uses color covers.
Payment/Terms: Pays $150/cover, $50-100/color, $25-50/b&w photos. Credit line given. Pays on publication. Buys one-time international usage rights per country. Previously published work OK.
Making Contact: Send photos for consideration. SASE. Sample copy $2.95.
Tips: Submit freelance photos with letter. Looking for "clean photos with good composition and imagination."

MODERN LITURGY, 160 E. Virginia St., Box 290, San Jose CA 95112. Editor: John Gallen, Sr. Magazine published 10 times annually. Circ. 15,000. For "religious artists, musicians, pastors, educators and planners of religious celebrations," who are interested in "aspects of producing successful worship services." Buys one-time rights. Present model release on acceptance of photo. Query first with resume of credits "or send representative photos that you think are appropriate." Pays on publication. Reports in 6 weeks. SASE. Sample copy $4.
B&W: Uses 8×10 glossy prints. Pays $5-25.
Color: Note: color photos will be reproduced in b&w. Uses 35mm transparencies. Pays $5-25.
Cover: Send 8×10 glossy b&w prints. Pays $5-25.
Tips: "Not currently buying many freelance submissions, but will talk to anyone with a keen interest in shooting liturgical space or ceremonies."

MOMENT, Suite 300, 3000 Connecticut Ave. NW, Washington DC 20008. (202)387-8888. FAX: (202)483-3423. Managing Editor: Charlotte Anker. Bimonthly magazine. Emphasizes Jewish issues—social, political, religious, historical, cultural, literary and artistic. Readers are English-speaking Jews in U.S. and elsewhere. Circ. 30,000. Sample copy free with 8½×11 SASE.
Photo Needs: Uses 10-20 photos/issue; 80% supplied by freelance photographers. Needs photos of people events, scenic and art.
Making Contact & Terms: Query with resume of credits, query with samples or list of stock photo subjects. Provide resume, business card, brochure, flyer or tearsheets to be kept on file for possible future assignments. Reports in 1 month. Pays $100-150/b&w cover photo; $50/¼ b&w or color page; $75/½ b&w or $100/¾ b&w or color page. Pays on publication. Credit line given. Buys first N.A. serial rights. Previously published work.

MONEY MAKER MAGAZINE, 5705 N. Lincoln Ave., Chicago IL 60659. (312)275-3590. Editor: Dennis Fertig. Art Director: Debora Clark. Bimonthly magazine. Emphasizes personal finance and investments. Readers are upper income, 30-65 age, college educated, home owners. Circ. 130,000. Sample copy free with 9×12 SASE; 2nd 54¢ postage.
Photo Needs: Uses 10 photos/illustrations/issue; all supplied by freelance photographers and illustrators. Needs photos prepared per assignment. Special needs are determined according to articles. Model release required.
Making Contact & Terms: Arrange a personal interview to show portfolio; query with resume of credits, list of stock photo subjects; provide resume, business card, flyer or tearsheets to be kept on file for possible future assignments. SASE. Reports in 1 month. Pays up to $2,000/color cover photo;

$450/b&w page; $900/color page. Pays on acceptance. Credit line given. Previously published work OK.

Tips: "Contact Art Director to show or send samples, tailor material to subject matter—in this case, investment materials—and to illustrative skills, i.e., creativity, sources, facilities."

MONITORING TIMES, Box 98, Brasstown NC 28902. (704)837-9200. Editor: Larry Miller. Monthly. Emphasizes radio communications, scanners and shortwave. Circ. 20,000. Sample copy for $2.50 (postpaid) and 8½×11 envelope; photo guidelines for SASE.
Photo Needs: Uses about 40 photos/issue; 20 supplied by freelance photographers. Needs photos of radio equipment, action scenes involving communications, individuals connected with storyline. Special needs include b&w and color (cover) concerning radio, antennas, equipment, boats, planes, military exercises, anything dealing in radio communications. Model release and captions preferred.
Making Contact & Terms: Query with samples or list of stock photo subjects. SASE. Reports in 2 weeks. Pays $25-50/color cover photo; $10-50/b&w inside photo; $50-100/text/photo package. Pays on acceptance. Credit line given if requested. Buys one-time rights. Simultaneous submissions and previously published work OK.
Tips: "First, acquaint yourself with the publication and anticipate its reader profile; second write to the publisher or editor and describe your services. Product shots must be contrasty and sharp, suitable for camera-ready application. Action shots must revolve around story lines dealing with radio broadcasting (international), news events, scanner excitement: air shows, emergencies."

MONTANA MAGAZINE, Box 5630, Helena MT 59604. (406)443-2842. Publisher: Rick Graetz. Editor: Carolyn Cunningham. Bimonthly magazine. Circ. 72,000. Emphasizes history, recreation, towns and events of Montana. Buys 10-15 photos/issue. Credit line given. Pays $25/b&w photo and $35-75/color photo. Pays on publication. Buys one-time rights. Send material by mail for consideration. SASE. Simultaneous submissions and previously published work OK. Reports in 4-6 weeks. Sample copy $2; photo guidelines free with SASE.
Subject Needs: Animal, nature (generally not showing development, roads, etc.), scenic, travel (to accompany specific travel articles) and wildlife; "photos showing lesser known places in Montana as well as the national parks." Captions required.
Color: Uses transparencies. Pays $35-50/inside photo.
Cover: Uses 35mm, 2¼×2¼ or 4×5 color transparencies. Pays $75 minimum/photo.
Tips: Wants to see "heavily saturated colors, more bright and snappy than subtle or misty; more scenic panoramas than close-ups. We're overloaded on Glacier Park and Yellowstone Park, but short on central and eastern Montana. We are using fewer articles so that we now have more room for photos."

MOTHER EARTH NEWS, 80 Fifth Ave., New York NY 10011. (212)242-2460. Photo Editor: Linda Eger. Bimonthly. Emphasizes country skills and living. Readers are young, sophisticated, ex-urban. Circ. 800,000.
Photo Needs: Uses about 65 photos/issue; 35 supplied by freelance photographers. Needs photos of garden and yard, food, country skills, back country, home, animals and wild animals. Model release and captions required for cover.
Making Contact & Terms: Query with list of stock photo subjects; query by phone about dropping off portfolio. Does not return unsolicited material. Pays on publication. Credit line given. Buy one-time rights. Previously published work OK.

MOTHERING MAGAZINE, Box 1690, Santa Fe NM 87504. (505)984-8116. Associate Editor: Susanne Miller. Quarterly magazine. Emphasizes parenting. Readers are progressive parents, primarily aged 25-40, with children of all ages, racially mixed. Estab. 1976. Free sample copy, photo guidelines and current photo needs..
Photo Needs: Uses about 40-50 photos/issue; nearly all supplied by freelance photographers. Needs photos of children of all ages, mothers, fathers, breastfeeding, birthing, education. Model release required.
Making Contact & Terms: Send 5×7 or 8×10 (preferred) b&w or color prints or slides by mail for consideration. SASE. Reports in 3 months. Pays $200/color cover photo; $25/b&w inside photo; $50/color inside photo. Pays on acceptance or publication. Credit line given. Buys one-time rights.
Tips: "For cover: we want technically superior, sharply focused image evoking a strong feeling or mood, spontaneous and unposed; unique and compelling; eye contact with subject will often draw in viewer; color slide or print. For inside: b&w or color (slide only), sharply focused, action or unposed shots; 'doing' pictures—family, breastfeeding, fathering, midwifery, birth, reading, drawing, crawling, climbing, etc. No disposable diapers, no bottles, no pacifiers."

MOTOR BOATING & SAILING MAGAZINE, 224 W. 57th St., New York NY 10019. (212)649-2000. Editor: Peter A. Janssen. Art Director: Erin Kenney. Emphasizes powerboats and large sailboats for those who own boats and participate in boating activities. Monthly magazine. Circ. 145,000. Information on and enjoyment of boating. Photos are purchased on assignment. Buys 30-50 photos/issue. Pay negotiated. Credit line given. Pays on acceptance. Buys one-time rights. Send material by registered mail for consideration. SASE. Reports in 1-3 months. Provide flyer and tearsheets to be kept on file for possible future assignments.

Subject Needs: Power boats; scenic (with power and sail, high performance, recreational boats of all kinds and boat cruising). "Sharp photos a must!" Model release and captions required.

Color: Kodachrome 25 preferred; Kodachrome 64 OK; Ektachrome and Fuji Film OK.

Cover: Uses 35mm color transparencies. Vertical format preferred.

MOTORHOME, 29901 Agoura Rd., Agoura CA 91301. (818)991-4980. Editor: Bob Livingston. Managing Editor: Gail Harrington. Monthly. Circ. 150,000. Emphasizes motorhomes and travel. Readers are "motorhome owners with above-average incomes and a strong desire for adventurous travel." Sample copy free; photo guidelines for SASE.

Photo Needs: Uses 25 photos/issue; at least 12 from freelancers. Needs "travel-related stories pertaining to motorhome owners with accompanying photos and how-to articles with descriptive photos. We usually buy a strong set of motorhome-related photos with a story. Also we are in the market for cover photos. Scenes should have maximum visual impact, with a motorhome included but not necessarily a dominant element. Following a freelancer's query and subsequent first submission, the quality of his work is then evaluated by our editorial board. If it is accepted and the freelancer indicates a willingness to accept future assignments, we generally contact him/her when the need arises." Captions required.

Making Contact & Terms: Send by mail for consideration 8×10 (5×7 OK) b&w prints or 35mm or 2¼×2¼ (4×5 or 8×10 OK) slides. Also send standard query letter. SASE. Reports as soon as possible, "but that sometimes means up to one month." Pays on acceptance $300-500 for text/photo package; up to $600 for cover photos. Credit line given. Buys first rights. No simultaneous submissions or previously published work.

*MULTINATIONAL MONITOR, P.O. Box 19405, Washington DC 20036. (202)387-8030. Associate Editor: Amy Allina. "We are a political-economic magazine covering operations of multinational corporations." Monthly magazine. Emphasizes multinational corporate activity. Readers are in business, academia and many are activists. Circ. 3,500. Estab. 1978. Sample copy free with 8½×11 SAE.

Photo Needs: Uses 12 photos/issue. Number of photos supplied by freelancers varies. "We need photos of industry, people, cities, technology, agriculture and many other business related subjects."

Making Contact & Terms: Query with list of stock photo subjects. SASE. Reports in 3 weeks. Will give photo credit, will pay in copies and in special circumstances will negotiate pay. Pays on publication. Buys one-time rights.

MUSCLE/MAG INTERNATIONAL, Unit 7, 2 Melanie Dr., Brampton ON L6T 4K8 Canada. (416)457-3030. FAX: (416)796-3563. Editor: Robert Kennedy. Monthly magazine. Circ. 130,000. Estab. 1974. Emphasizes male and female physical development and fitness. Photos purchased with accompanying ms. Buys 1000 photos/year; 50% assigned; 50% stock. Credit line given. Pays $85-100/hour and $1,000-3,000 per complete package. Pays on acceptance. Buys all rights. Send material by mail for consideration; send $3 for return postage. Reports in 2-4 weeks. Sample copy $3.

Subject Needs: Celebrity/personality, fashion/beauty, glamour, how-to, human interest, humorous, special effects/experimental and spot news. "We require action exercise photos of bodybuilders and fitness enthusiasts training with sweat and strain." Wants on a regular basis "different" pics of top names, bodybuilders or film stars famous for their physique (i.e., Schwarzenegger, The Hulk, etc.). No photos of mediocre bodybuilders. "They have to be among the top 20 in the world or top film stars exercising." Captions preferred.

B&W: Uses 8×10 glossy prints. Query with contact sheet. Pays $15-35/photo.

Color: Uses 35mm, 2¼×2¼ or 4×5 transparencies. Pays $25-500/photo.

Cover: Uses color 35mm, 2¼×2¼ or 4×5 transparencies. Vertical format preferred. Pays $100-500/photo.

Accompanying Mss: Pays $85-300/ms. Writer's guidelines $3.

Tips: Hulk image. "We would like to see photographers take up the challenge of making exercise photos look like exercise motion." In samples wants to see "sharp, color balanced, attractive subjects, no grain, artistic eye. Someone who can glamorize bodybuilding on film." To break in, "get serious: read, ask questions, learn, experiment and try, try again. Keep trying for improvement – don't kid yourself that you are a good photographer when you don't even understand half the attachments on your camera. Immerse yourself in photography."

NATIONAL PARKS MAGAZINE, 1015 31st St. NW, Washington DC 20007. (202)944-8530. Editor: Michele Strutin. Bimonthly magazine. Circ. 90,000. Emphasizes the preservation of national parks and wildlife. Pays on publication. Buys one-time rights. SASE. Reports in 1 month. Sample copy $3; free photo guidelines with SASE.

Subject Needs: Photos of wildlife and people in national parks, scenics, national monuments, national recreation areas, national seashores, threats to park resources and wildlife.
B&W: Uses 8×10 glossy prints. Pays $25-70/photo.
Cover: Pays $150 full-bleed color covers. Pays $50-125/4×5 or 35mm color transparencies.
Accompanying Mss: Seeks mss on national parks, wildlife with accompanying photos.
Tips: "Send stock list with example of work if possible. Photographers should be more specific about areas they have covered. We are a specialized publication and are not interested in extensive lists on topics we do not cover. Trends include 'more dramatic pictures.'"

NATIONAL RACQUETBALL, Suite B, 400 Douglas Ave., Dunedin FL 34698. (813)736-5616. Editor: Judi Schmidt. Published 10 times/year. Circ. 51,000. Emphasizes racquetball. Readers are "racquetball players and court club owners; median age 18-35; college educated and professionals; health-conscious and sports minded." Sample copy free with SASE.
Photo Needs: Uses 30-40 photos/issue; 10 supplied by freelance photographers. Looking for "action shots of racquetball players, head and informal shots of personalities in the racquetball world and shots illustrating principles." Model release required.
Making Contact & Terms: Query with samples; send 3×5 and up b&w glossy or matte prints, 35mm transparencies by mail for consideration; provide resume, business card, brochure, flyer or tearsheets to be kept on file for possible future assignments. SASE. Reports in 3 weeks. Pays $50/color cover photo; $5/b&w inside photo, $10/color inside photo; negotiates payment per job; $50-150 for text/photo package. Pays on publication. Credit line given. Buys all rights. Previously published work OK.
Tips: "Make sure you know what you are doing. Racquetball is very difficult to photograph."

NATIONAL WILDLIFE, 8925 Leesburg Pike, Vienna VA 22184. (703)790-4419. Photo Editor: John Nuhn. Senior Photo Editor: Steve Freligh. Bimonthly magazine. Estab. 1962. Emphasizes wildlife, nature, environment and conservation. Readers are people who enjoy viewing high quality wildlife and nature images, and who are interested in knowing more about the natural world and man's interrelationship with animals and environment. Circ. 975,000. Sample copy $3; send to National Wildlife Federation Membership Services (same address). Photo guidelines free with SASE. Please keep sample copy and guidelines requests separate.
Photo Needs: Uses 45 photos/issue; all supplied by freelance photographers; 80% stock vs. 20% assigned. Needs photos of wildlife, wild plants, nature-related how-to, conservation practices, environmental damage, environmental research, outdoor recreation. Subject needs include single photos for cover possibility (primarily wildlife but also plants, scenics, people); black and whites accompanying unique story ideas that should not be in color. Model release preferred; captions required.
Making Contact & Terms: Send 8×10 glossy b&w prints; 35mm, 2¼×2¼, 4×5, 8×10 transparencies (magazine is 95% color) by mail for consideration. Query with samples, credits and stock listings. SASE. Reports in 3 weeks. Pays $255-705/b&w inside photo; $750/color cover photo; $255-705/color inside photo; text/photo negotiable. Pays on acceptance. Credit line given. Buys one-time rights with limited magazine promotion rights. Previously published work OK.
Tips: Interested in a variety of images that show photographer's scope and specialization, organized in slide sheets, along with tearsheets of previously published work. "Study our magazine; note the types of images we use and send photos equal or better. We look for imagination (common subjects done creatively, different views of animals and plants); technical expertise (proper exposure, focusing, lighting); and the ability to go that one step further and make the shot unique. Think editorially when submitting story, queries or photos; assure that package is complete—sufficient return postage (no checks), proper size return envelope, address inside, and do not submit photos in glass slides, trays or small boxes."

NATURAL HISTORY MAGAZINE, Central Park W. at 79th St., New York NY 10024. (212)769-5500. Editor: Alan Ternes. Picture Editor: Kay Zakariasen. Monthly magazine. Circ. 520,000. Buys 400-450 annually. For primarily well-educated people with interests in the sciences.
Subject Needs: Animal behavior, photo essay, documentary, plant and landscape. Photos used must relate to the social or natural sciences with an ecological framework. Accurate, detailed captions required.
Specs: Uses 8×10 glossy, matte and semigloss b&w prints; and 35mm, 2¼×2¼, 4×5, 6×7 and 8×10 color transparencies. Covers are always related to an article in the issue.
Payment/Terms: Pays $75-250/b&w print, $75-400/color transparency and $500 minimum/cover. Credit line given. Pays on publication. Buys one-time rights. Previously published work OK but must be indicated on delivery memo.
Making Contact: Query with resume of credits. SASE. Reports in 2 weeks. Free photo guidelines.
Tips: "Study the magazine—we are more interested in ideas than individual photos. We do not have the time to review portfolios without a specific theme in the social or natural sciences."

NATURAL LIFE MAGAZINE, 4728 Byrne Rd., Burnaby BC V5H 3X7 Canada. (604)438-1919. Photo Editor: Siegfried Gursche. Consumer publication. Bimonthly magazine. Readers are health and nutrition, lifestyle and fitness-oriented. Circ. 110,000. Sample copy $2.50 (Canadian) and 9½×11 SASE. Photo guidelines free with SASE.

Photo Needs: Uses 12 photos/issue; 50% supplied by freelance photographers. Looking for photos of healthy people doing healthy things. Subjects include environment, ecology, organic farming and gardening, herbal therapies, vitamins, mineral supplements and good vegetarian food, all with a family orientation. Model release required; photo captions preferred.

Making Contact & Terms: Send unsolicited photos by mail for consideration with resume, business card, brochure, flyer or tearsheets to be kept on file for possible assignments. Send color 4×5 prints and 35mm, 2¼×2¼, or 4×5 transparencies. SASE. Reports in 2 weeks. Pays $125/color cover phot, $60/color inside photo. Pays on publication. Credit line given. Buys all rights; will negotiate. Simultaneous submissions and previously published work OK.

Tips: "Get in touch with the 'Natural Foods' and 'Alternative Therapies' scene. Observe and shoot healthy people doing healthy things."

NEVADA MAGAZINE, Capitol Complex, Carson City NV 89710. (702)687-5416. Art Director: Brian Buckley. Bimonthly. Circ. 80,000. State tourism magazine devoted to promoting tourism in Nevada, particularly for people interested in travel, people, history, events and recreation; age 30-70. Buys 40-50 photos/issue; 30-35 supplied by freelance photographers. Credit line given. Buys first North American serial rights. Pays on publication. Reports in 2 months. Send samples of *Nevada* photos. SASE. Sample copy $1.

Subject Needs: Towns and cities, scenics, outdoor recreation with people, people, events, state parks, tourist attractions, travel, wildlife, ranching, mining, and general Nevada life. Must be Nevada subjects. Special photo needs include futuristic cities, rural towns, ghost towns, Tahoe skiing, camping.

B&W: Send 8×10 glossy prints. Must be labeled with name, address, and captions on back of each. Pays $15-75.

Color: Send 35mm, 2¼×2¼, 4×5, 8×10 transparencies. Must be labeled with name, address, and captions on each. Pays $15-75.

Cover: Send color transparencies. Prefers vertical format. Captions required. Pays $100.

Tips: "Send variety of good-quality Nevada photos, well-labeled and self-edited. Label each slide or print properly with name, address, and caption on each, not on a separate sheet. Send 35mm slides in 8×10 see-through slide sleeves."

NEW AGE JOURNAL, 342 Western Ave., Brighton MA 02135. (617)787-2005. Editor: Dr. Phillip M. Whitten. Art Director: Dan Mishkind. Bimonthly. Emphasizes alternative thinking, human potential. Readers are people interested in non-traditional lifestyle and thinking. Circ. 180,000. Sample copy $5.

Photo Needs: Uses 12-15 photos/issue; all supplied by freelance photographers. Model release required; captions preferred.

Making Contact & Terms: Query with samples and list of stock photo subjects; send unsolicited photos by mail for consideration; provide business card, brochure, flyer or tearsheets to be kept on file for possible future assignments. Uses color prints and transparencies. SASE. Reports in 1 month. Pays page rate, $175/b&w and $325/color. Pays 30 days from publication. Credit line given. Buys one-time rights. Simultaneous submissions and previously published word OK.

Tips: "Be flexible and be willing to accept low editorial rates to get work printed."

NEW CLEVELAND WOMAN JOURNAL, 104 E. Bridge St., Berea OH 44107. (216)243-3740. Editorial Director: June Vereeke-Hutt. Monthly magazine. Emphasizes "news and features pertaining to working women in the Cleveland/Akron area." Readers are working women, 50% married, average age 35. Circ. 34,000.

Photo Needs: Uses about 6 photos/issue; half supplied by freelance photographers. Needs "photo illustrations of subject-careers, travel, finance, etc." Model release and captions required.

Making Contact & Terms: Query with samples. Provide business card and brochure to be kept on file for possible future assignments. SASE. Reports in 1 month. Pays $25/b&w inside photo. Pays on publication. Credit line given. Buys first North American serial rights. Simultaneous submissions OK.

*NEW DOMINION MAGAZINE, Suite 730, 2000 N. 14th St., Arlington VA 22201. (703)527-1199. Monthly magazine. Emphasizes business and lifestyle for northern Virginia. Readers are 65% male, 35% female, affluent, median age early 40's. Circ. 50,000. Estab. 1987. Sample copy for $2.95 with 9×12 SASE.

Photo Needs: Uses 40 photos/issue; 60% supplied by freelance photographers. Needs photos of stock landscape, tourism, architecture; assignment people, studio (still lifes, concept shots). *No* newspaper photo journalism, no fashion. Model release and photo captions preferred.

Making Contact & Terms: Provide resume, business card, brochure, flyer or tearsheets to be kept on file for possible assignments. SASE. Reports in 1 month. Pays $250/day; $125/half day plus expenses. Buys one-time rights. Previously published work OK.

Tips: Wants to see "a brief selection of the photographer's work that demonstrates his/her style and capabilities. For samples, we prefer tearsheets, printed samples, or even xeroxes."

*NEW ENGLAND BRIDE, 215 Newbury St., Peabody MA 01960. (508)535-4186. Art Director: Ron Brown. Monthly magazine. Emphasizes weddings. Readers are ages 18-40. Circ. 20,000. Estab. 1982.

Photo Needs: Uses 20 photos/issue; 25% supplied by freelance photographers. Needs photos of travel and people.

Making Contact & Terms: Provide resume, business card, brochure, flyer or tearsheets to be kept on file for possible assignments. Cannot return unsolicited material. Pays $150/color cover photo; $50/b&w cover photo. Pays on publication. Credit line given. Buys one-time rights. Rights negotiable. Simultaneous submissions and previously published work OK.

Tips: In photographer's samples looks for photos "well exposed, well thought out. And keep trying."

NEW ENGLAND MONTHLY, P.O. Box 446, 132 Main St., Haydenville MA 01039. (413)268-7262. Art Director: Tim Gabor. Monthly. Emphasizes regional matters, interests. Readers are concerned, interested New Englanders. Circ. 100,000. Estab. 1984. Sample copy and photo guidelines free with SASE.

Photo Needs: Model release and captions preferred. 50% freelance photography in a given issue comes from assignment and 50% from freelance stock.

Making Contact & Terms: Query with samples and list of stock photo subjects; send unsolicited photos by mail for consideration; or submit portfolio for review. Uses b&w and color transparencies. SASE. Pays $700/color cover photo; $300/b&w inside photo; $450/color inside photo. Pays on acceptance or publication. Credit line given. Buys one-time rights.

Tips: "Please *send in* your samples/portfolio. Due to the small staff size, we rarely can grant in-person interviews."

NEW HAMPSHIRE PROFILES, P.O. Box 370, Stratham NH 03885. (603)772-5252. Editor: Suki Casanave. Bimonthly. Circ. 25,000. Editorial content, both written and photographic; addresses the social, historical and cultural climate of New Hampshire, exploring what is unique and exciting in the state, especially profiles of people. Bimonthly special sections on homes, getaways, boating, recreation, dining and fashion. Photos purchased with or without accompanying ms and on assignment. Buys 10-20 photos/issue (b&w or color). Credit line given. Pay recieved 30 days after publication. Buys first North American serial rights. Write for editorial and photography guidelines, then submit query with story idea or list of stock photo subjects. Samples are returned. SASE. Reports in 2 months. Sample copy $2.50 plus 9 × 12 SASE. Photo guidelines free with SASE.

Subject Needs: "We will publish photos of a subject idea captured by several different photographers as well as a series by one photographer. We accept freelance submissions and make specific photo assignments."

B&W: Uses 5 × 7 and 8 × 10 glossy prints.

Color: Uses 2¼ × 2¼ or 4 × 5 transparencies, and 35mm slides. Vertical and horizontal.

Cover: Same requirements as for color photos, generally related to feature in magazine. Also uses artist's drawings and graphics.

Tips: "We are seeking photographers who are excited by what we are trying to do at *Profiles* and show an eagerness to submit photo essay ideas. We want clear, concise non-cluttered photos stating/showing one specific subject matter. Rates vary accordingly."

NEW HOME, Box 2008, Laconia NH 03246. (603)528-4285. Managing Editor: Steven Maviglio. Art Director: Kevin Wells. Consumer publication. Bimonthly magazine. Emphasizes interiors and exteriors of houses and home-related products. Readers are new homeowners. Circ. 300,000. Sample copy $5.

Photo Needs: Uses 50 photos/issue; 80% supplied by freelance photographers. Needs photos of homes (interiors and exteriors) and home-related topics and products. Model release required; photo captions preferred.

Making Contact & Terms: Send unsolicited photos by mail for consideration. Provide resume, business card, brochure, flyer or tearsheets to be kept on file for possible assignments. Send 4 × 5 color transparencies, any format. SASE. Reports in 3 weeks. Pays $300/color cover photo, pays $100-250 per page for inside color, depending on size. Pays on acceptance. Credit line given. Buys one-time rights. Simultaneous submissions and previously published work OK.

Tips: In portfolios, prefers to see photos of "topics covered in New Home. Please get your hands on an issue first to see our sense of style and use."

NEW MEXICO MAGAZINE, Joseph Montoya State Building, 1100 St. Francis Dr., Santa Fe NM 87503. Editor: Emily Drabanski. Monthly magazine. Circ. 100,000. For people interested in the Southwest or who have lived in or visited New Mexico.

Photo Needs: Needs New Mexico photos only—landscapes, people, events, architecture, etc. "Most work is done on assignment in relation to a story, but we welcome photo essay suggestions from photographers." Buys 40 photos/issue; 50% on assignment, 50% on stock. Buys one-time rights.

Making Contact & Terms: Submit portfolio to Mary Sweitzer. Credit line given. Pays on publication. SASE. Sample copy $2.25 with 8½×11 SAE and 75¢ postage; free photo guidelines with SASE.

Color: Send transparencies. Captions required. Pays $50-100.

Cover: Cover photos usually relate to the main feature in the magazine. Pays $100.

Tips: Prefers transparencies submitted in plastic pocketed sheets. Interested in different viewpoints, styles not necessarily obligated to straight scenic. "All material must be taken in New Mexico. Representative work suggested. If photographers have a preference about what they want to do or where they're going, we would like to see that in their work. Transparencies or dupes are best for review and handling purposes."

*NEW MEXICO PHOTOGRAPHER, Box 2582—ENMU, Portales NM 88130. (505)562-2253. Publisher: Wendel Sloan. Biennial magazine. Emphasizes high-quality b&w photography taken anywhere in the world. Readers are photographers and patrons of high-quality photography. Circ. 2,000. Estab. 1989. Sample copy for $5. Photo guidelines free with SASE.

Photo Needs: Uses 50 photos/issue; 100% supplied by freelancers. "We are devoted to all subject matters from black-and-white photographers everywhere." Likes to see seasonal photos for summer and winter issues; deadlines—April 15, October 15. Model release and photo captions preferred.

Making Contact & Terms: Send unsolicited b&w prints by mail for consideration. SASE. Reports after selections made, prior to publication. Photos selected on basis of semi-annual contest; photos are published and cash prizes also offered. Credit line given. Buys one-time rights. Simultaneous submissions and previously published work OK.

Tips: "Since we run very little advertising, we sponsor a contest for each issue to help pay for publication of the magazine." A $5 entry is charged for each entry. "We look for high-quality b&w photos with a new way of looking at old subjects—something visually exciting or emotional."

NEW REALITIES, 4000 Albemarle St., N.W., Washington DC 20016. (202)362-6445. FAX: (202)537-0287. Editor: Neal Vahle. Bimonthly. Emphasizes new age: holistic health; consciousness, parapsychology. Circ. 18,000. Estab. 1977.Sample copy for 8½×11 with $1.88 postage.

Photo Needs: Uses 13-15 photos/issue; 4 supplied by freelance photographers. Needs specific topic shots for subject articles; abstract shots/art photos of more issue- or idea-related articles. Model release required; captions preferred.

Making Contact & Terms: Provide resume, business card, brochure or tearsheets to be kept on file for possible future assignments. SASE. Reports in 1 month. Pays up to $300/cover photo; $50/b&w inside photos; $150/color inside photo (full page). Pays on publication. Credit line given. Simultaneous submissions and previously published work OK.

Tips: Prefers to see "creative photos that could enhance articles on growth, human potential, etc. whether people-oriented or nature-oriented shots. Please send us clips, photocopies, color photocopies and/or extra slides for our file."

*NEW WOMAN, 215 Lexington Ave., New York NY 10016. (212)685-4790. Picture Editor: C. Howard. Monthly magazine. Covers all subjects related to women for women, ages 20-40. Circ. 1.5 million. Estab. 1970. Sample copy with 11×14 SAE and $1.25 postage.

Photo Needs: Uses 50 photos/issue; 25% supplied by freelancers. Needs wide range of subjects, including beauty & fashion, travel, scenics, personalities and animals. Model release required.

Making Contact & Terms: Submit portfolio for review. Reports in 2 weeks. Pays $1500/color cover photo; $350 day rate. Pays on publication. Credit line given. Buys all rights; negotiable.

NEW YORK ALIVE, 152 Washington Ave., Albany NY 12210. (518)465-7511. Editor/Photo Editor: Mary Grates Stoll. Bimonthly. Emphasizes the people, places and events of New York State. Readers include young adults to senior citizens, well-educated, fairly affluent, who enjoy reading about life (past and present) in New York State. Circ. 35,000. Sample copy $2.50; photo guidelines free with SASE.

Photo Needs: Uses 40-50 photos/issue; 75% supplied by freelance photographers. Needs scenic (appropriate to season of cover date) and illustrations for specific features. Reviews photos with or without accompanying ms. Model release preferred.

Making Contact & Terms: Query with samples. SASE. Pays $250/color cover photo; $15-30/b&w inside photo; $30-125/color inside photo; $100/halfday; $250/fullday; and $500 maximum/text/photo package. Pays on publication. Credit line given. Buys one-time rights. Previously published work OK.

N.Y. HABITAT, 928 Broadway, New York NY 10010. (212)505-2030. Managing Editor: Lloyd Chrein. Magazine published 8 times/year. Emphasizes real estate, co-op/condo management. Readers are board members and owners at co-ops, condos and are all ages, occupations (mid- upper-middle class). Circ. 10,000. Estab. 1982. Sample copy $5. Photo guidelines free with SASE.
Photo Needs: Uses 11 photos/issue. Half freelance photography in a given issue comes from assignment and half from freelance stock. Needs photos of people, candid, action—photojournalism.
Making Contact & Terms: Provide resume, business card, brochure, flyer or tearsheets to be kept on file for possible assignments. Reports in 1 month. Pays $50/b&w inside photo. Pays on publication. Credit line given. Buys one-time rights. Previously published work OK.
Tips: Looks for "Photojournalism with depth, action, and expression." The trend is "People, show me people in situations. Give me black & white photos with depth and contrast."

NEW YORK MAGAZINE, 755 Second Ave., New York NY 10017. (212)880-0829. Editor: Edward Kosner. Photography Director: Jordan Schaps. Picture Editor: Susan Vermazen. Weekly magazine. Full service city magazine: national and local news, fashion, food, entertaining, lifestyle, design, profiles, etc. Readers are 35-55 years average with $90,000+ average family income. Professional people, family people, concerned with quality of life and social issues affecting them, their families and the community. Circ. 450,000. Estab. 1968. Sample copy free with SASE.
Photo Needs: Uses about 50 photos/issue; 85% assigned; 15% stock. Needs full range: photojournalism, fashion, food, product still lifes, conceptual, and stock (occasionally). Always need great product still life, and studio work. "Model release and captions preferred for professional models; require model release for 'real' people."
Making Contact & Terms: Arrange a personal interview to show portfolio, submit portfolio for review, "as this is a FAST paced weekly, phone appointments are ESSENTIAL, time permitting." Drop offs, every Thursday. *Does not return unsolicited material.* Reports as soon as possible. Pays $1,000/color cover photo; $300/page of color; $125-150/photo spot; $150-300/b&w and color photo; $300/day. Pays on publication and receipt of original invoices. Credit line given. Buys one-time rights, possible minimum to-the-trade in-house advertising.
Tips: "We're looking for strong, high quality work that works with the text but tells its own story as well. We look for the kind of photographer who can deliver those kinds of images whether it be on his own in photo-journalism or being spiritedly art directed. We prefer a traditional approach (strong, accessible images, well lit, in focus) but we must evince an awareness of the current stylish trends and directions in which photography is moving. You need to really get to know the magazine and its various departments ("Intelligencer", "Fast Track", "Hot Line", "Best Bets", etc.) as well as the way we do fashion, entertaining, life-style, etc. *New York* is a great showcase for the talented new-comer looking for prestige editorial exposure, the solid working photojournalist, and the well established advertising specialist looking for the creative freedom to do our kind of editorial work. We lean towards traditional high-quality photographic solutions to our visual needs, but are ever mindful of and sensitive to the trends and directions in which photography is moving." Freelancer interested in working with us should: "1. Make an appointment. 2. Be on time. 3. Have materials geared to what we need and what you'd like to do for us. 4. Leave a photo image with phone #. 5. Don't call frequently asking for work. 6. Remember that this is a fast paced weekly magazine. We're courteous but on constant deadlines."

NORTH SHORE MAGAZINE, 874 Green Bay Rd., Winnetka IL 60093. (708)441-7892. Publisher/Editor: Asher Birnbaum. Monthly magazine. City/regional magazine for upscale, well educated, politically/socially oriented readers. Circ. 45,000. Sample copy free with SASE and $1 postage.
Photo Needs: Uses about 50-75 photos/issue; all supplied by freelance photographers. Needs portraits and photos of fashion, food, Chicagoland scenics, society events and humorous local shots for picture-of-the-month use. Written release and captions required.
Making Contact & Terms: Query with resume of credits. SASE. Reports in 2 weeks. Pays on acceptance or publication. Buys one-time rights.

*NORTHERN OHIO LIVE, 11320 Juniper Rd., Cleveland OH 44106. (216)721-1800. Art Director: Laura Goldfarb. Monthly magazine. Emphasizes arts, entertainment, lifestyle and fashion. Readers are upper income, ages 25-60, professionals. Circ. 38,000. Estab. 1980. Sample copy for $2 with 9×12 SAE.
Photo Needs: Uses 30 photos/issue; 20-100% supplied by freelance photographers. Needs photos of people in different locations, fashion and local. Model release preferred. Photo captions preferred (names only is usually OK).
Making Contact & Terms: Arrange a personal interview to show portfolio. Send 35mm, 2¼×2¼, b&w and color prints by mail for consideration. Provide resume, business card, brochure, flyer or tearsheet to be kept on file for possible assignments. Follow up phone call OK. SASE. Reports in 3 weeks. Pays $250/color cover photo; $250/b&w cover photo; $100/color inside photo; $50/b&w inside

photo; $30-50/hour; $250-500/day. Pays on publication. Credit line given. Buys one-time rights. Previously published work OK.

Tips: In photographer's portfolio wants to see "good portraits, people on location, photo journalism strengths, quick turn-around and willingness to work on *low* budget. Mail sample of work, follow up with phone call. Portfolio review should be short—only *best quality* work!"

NORTHWEST LIVING, 130 Second Ave. S., Edmonds WA 98020. (206)774-4111. FAX: (206)672-2824. Editor: Terry W. Sheely. Bimonthly magazine. Emphasizes natural resources, people, places, the northwest. Circ. 28,000. Estab. 1983. Sample copy free with 10×13 SASE. Photo guidelines free with SASE.
Photo Needs: Uses 50 photos/issue; 95% supplied by freelance photographers. Model release preferred; captions required.
Making Contact & Terms: Query with samples; send b&w prints; 35mm, 2¼×2¼ transparencies by mail for consideration. SASE. Reports in 3 weeks. Pays $50-175/b&w/color photos. Pays on publication. Credit line given. Buys one-time rights. Simultaneous submissions and previously published work OK.
Tips: "Study our editorial content; query first and often. Submit what we need, not what you want to sell."

NUGGET, Suite 204, 2355 Salzedo St., Coral Gables FL 33134. (305)443-2378. Editor: Jerome Slaughter. Bimonthly magazine. Circ. 100,000. Emphasizes sex and fetishism for men and women of all ages. Uses 100 photos/issue. Credit line given. Pays on publication. Buys one-time rights or second serial (reprint) rights. Submit material (in sets only) for consideration. SASE. Previously published work OK. Reports in 2 weeks. Sample copy $5 postpaid; photo guidelines free with SASE.
Subject Needs: Interested only in nude sets; single woman, female/female or male/female. All photo sequences should have a fetish theme (sadomasochism, leather, bondage, transvestism, transsexuals, lingerie, infantilism, wrestling—female/female or male/female—women fighting women or women fighting men, amputee models, etc.). Model release required. Buys in sets, not by individual photos. No Polaroids or amateur photography.
B&W: Uses 8×10 glossy prints; contact sheet OK. Pays $200 minimum/set.
Color: Uses transparencies. Prefers Kodachrome. Pays $200-300/set.
Cover: Uses color transparencies. Vertical format required. Pays $150/photo.
Accompanying Mss: Seeks mss on sex, fetishism and sex-oriented products. Pays $200/ms.

***OCEAN NAVIGATOR**, 18 Danforth St., Portland ME 04101. (207)772-2466. Art Director: Denny Ryus. Magazine publishing 8 issues annually. Emphasizes marine navigation and ocean voyaging. Readers are primarily male, 40 and up, inboard auxiliary sailboat owners. Circ. 35,000. Estab. 1985. Sample copy $3.50.
Photo Needs: Uses 20 photos/issue; 100% supplied by freelance photographers. Needs photos of boats and related machinery, marine hardware, marine situations, marine technology and events—commercial and recreational. Model release and photo captions required.
Making Contact & Terms: Send 35mm, 2¼×2¼, 4×5 b&w and color prints; 35mm, 2¼×2¼, 4×5 transparencies by mail for consideration. SASE. Reports in 1 month. Pays $400/color cover photo; $50/color inside photo. Pays on publication. Credit line given. Buys one-time rights. Simultaneous and previously published work OK.
Tips: Looks for "almost anything that has to do with marine navigation or ocean voyaging. Get a copy of the magazine to get a feel for what we write about."

OFFSHORE, The Boating Magazine of New England, New York and New Jersey, Box 817, Needham MA 02194. (617)449-6204. Executive Editor: Martha Lostrom. Monthly. Emphasizes boating in New England, New York and New Jersey for boat owners. Circ. 35,000.
Photo Needs: Uses about 24 photos/issue; 12 supplied by freelance photographers. Needs photos of "boats, harbors and waterfronts." Captions preferred.
Making Contact & Terms: Query with samples—contact sheets are sufficient. SASE. Reports in 1 week. Pays $150/color cover; $150 plus $15/photo for photo essays which include extensive captions. Pays on acceptance. Credit line given. Buys one-time rights "plus the right to use in promotional materials."
Tips: "We prefer interesting rather than pretty subjects. We look for unique photos, readily printable on uncoated paper."

OHIO MAGAZINE, 40 S. 3rd St., Columbus OH 43215. (614)461-5083. Contact: Brooke Wenstrup. Monthly magazine. Emphasizes features throughout Ohio for an educated, urban and urbane readership. Sample copy $3 postpaid. Pays $150/day plus color film expenses for photojournalism or on a per-photo basis. Credit line given. Pays within 90 days after acceptance. Buys first world rights and permission to reprint in later issues or promotions. Send material by mail for consideration; query with samples; or arrange a personal interview to show portfolio. SASE. Reports in 1 month.

Subject Needs: Travel, photo essay/photo feature, black & white scenics, personality, sports and spot news. Photojournalism and concept-oriented studio photography.

B&W: Uses 8×10 glossy prints; contact sheet requested. Pays $25-75/in-stock shot.

Color: Pays $50-100/35mm, 2¼×2¼ or 4×5 transparencies.

Cover: Uses 35mm, 2¼×2¼ or 4×5 transparencies. Vertical square format preferred. Pays $350 maximum/photo.

Tips: "Send sheets of slides and/or prints with return postage and they will be reviewed. Dupes for our files are always appreciated—and reviewed on a regular basis. We are leaning more towards well-done documentary photography and less toward studio photography. Trends in our use of editorial photography include scenics, single photos that can support an essay, photo essays on cities/towns, more use of 180° shots. In reviewing a photographer's portfolio or samples we look for humor, insight, multi-level photos, quirkiness, thoughtfulness; ability to work with subjects (i.e., an obvious indication that the photographer was able to make subject relax and forget the camera—even difficult subjects); ability to work with givens, bad natural light, etc.; creativity on the spot—as we can't always tell what a situation will be on location."

OLD WEST, Box 2107, Stillwater OK 74076. Editor: John Joerschke. Quarterly. Circ. 30,000. Estab. 1963. Emphasizes history of the Old West (1830 to 1910). Readers are people who like to read the history of the West. Sample copy free with 8½×11 SAE and $2 postage.

Photo Needs: Uses 100 or more photos/issue; "almost all" supplied by freelance photographers. Needs "mostly Old West historical subjects, some travel, some scenic (ghost towns, old mining camps, historical sites). Prefers to have accompanying ms. Special needs include western wear, cowboys, rodeos, western events.

Making Contact & Terms: Query with samples, b&w only for inside, color covers. SASE. Reports in 1 month. Pays $75-150/color cover photos; $10/b&w inside photos. Payment on publication. Credit line given. Buys one-time rights.

Tips: "Looking for transparencies of existing artwork as well as scenics for covers, pictures that tell stories associated with Old West for the inside. Most of our photos are used to illustrate stories and come with manuscripts; however, we will consider other work (scenics, historical sites, old houses)."

ON THE LINE, 616 Walnut Ave., Scottdale PA 15683. (412)887-8500. Contact: Editor. Weekly magazine. Circ. 10,000. Estab. 1875. For children, ages 10-14. Needs photos of children, age 10-14. Buys one-time rights. Send photos for consideration. Pays on acceptance. Reports in 1 month. SASE. Simultaneous submissions and previously published work OK. Free sample copy and editorial guidelines.

B&W: Send 8×10 prints. Very little photography from assignment and 95%+ from freelance stock. Pays $20-50/b&w (cover).

Tips: "We need quality black & white photos only. Prefers vertical shots, use some horizontal. We need photos of children, age 10-14 representing a balance of male/female, white/minority/international, urban/country. Clothing and hair styles must be contemporary, but not faddish. Wants to see children interacting with each other, with adults and with animals. Some nature scenes as well (especially with kids)."

1001 HOME IDEAS, 3 Park Ave., New York NY 10016. (212)779-6200. Art Director: Robert Thornton. Monthly magazine. Emphasizes interiors, some food. Sample free with SASE.

Photo Needs: Uses about 30-40 photos/issue; all supplied by freelance photographers. Needs photos of interiors. "We welcome scouting photos of photography possibilities."

Making Contact & Terms: Arrange a personal interview to show portfolio. Send 2¼×2¼, 4×5 or 8×10 transparencies by mail for consideration. Reports in 3 weeks. Payment varies. Pays on publication. Credit line given. Buys all rights.

Tips: Trends in editorial photography include details, close-ups. In reviewing a portfolio or samples looks for "inventiveness."

OPEN WHEEL MAGAZINE, Box 715, 27 S. Main St., Ipswich MA 01938. (508)356-7030. FAX: (508)356-2492. Editor: Dick Berggren. Monthly. Circ. 50,000-100,000. Estab. 1981. Emphasizes sprint car, supermodified and midget racing with some Indy coverage. Readers are fans, owners and drivers of race cars and those with business in racing. Photo guidelines free for SASE.

Photo Needs: Uses 100-125 photos/issue supplied by freelance photographers; almost all comes from freelance stock. Needs documentary, portraits, dramatic racing pictures, product photography, special effects, crash. Photos purchased with or without accompanying ms. Model release required for photos not shot in pit, garage or on track; captions required.

Making Contact & Terms: Send by mail for consideration 8×10 b&w or color glossy prints and any size slides. Kodachrome 64 preferred. SASE. Reports in 1 week. Pays $20-25/b&w inside; $35-250/color inside. Pays on publication. Buys all rights.

Tips: "Send the photos. We get dozens of inquiries but not enough pictures. We file everything that comes in and pull 80% of the pictures used each issue from those files. If it's on file, the photographer has a good shot."

OPERA NEWS, 1865 Broadway, New York NY 10023. (212)582-3285. Senior Editor: Jane L. Poole. Published by the Metropolitan Opera Guild. Biweekly (December-April) and monthly (May-November) magazine. Emphasizes opera performances and personalities for operagoers, members of opera and music professionals. Circ. 120,000. Sample copy $2.50.

Photo Needs: Uses about 45 photos/issue; 15 supplied by freelance photographers. Needs photos of "opera performances, both historical and current; opera singers, conductors and stage directors." Captions preferred.

Making Contact & Terms: Query with samples; provide resume, business card, brochure, flyer or tearsheets to be kept on file for possible future assignments. SASE. Reporting time varies. Payment negotiated. Pays on publication. Credit line given. Buys one-time rights. Simultaneous submissions OK.

ORANGE COAST MAGAZINE, 245 D Fischer Ave., Suite D, Costa Mesa CA 92626. (714)545-1900. Editor: Palmer Jones. Photo Editor: Sarah McNeill. Monthly. Circ. 40,000. Emphasizes general interest—all subjects. Sample copy $3.

Photo Needs: Uses 35 photos/issue; all supplied by freelance photographers. Needs graphic studio shots, travel shots, food shots; mostly 4×5 format. Special needs include travel shots of the world. Model release preferred; captions required.

Making Contact & Terms: Query with samples. SASE. Reports in 1 month. Credit line given. Buys one-time rights. Simultaneous submissions and previously published work OK.

Tips: "Studio and location work, graphic still life and travel shots."

OREGON COAST MAGAZINE, Box 18000, Florence OR 97439. (503)997-8401. Managing Editor: Lynne LaReau Owens. Bimonthly. Emphasizes Oregon coast life. Readers are middle class, middle age. Circ. 56,000+. Sample copy $2.50 with 9×12 SASE and $1.85 postage; photo guidelines available for SASE with 45¢.

Photo Needs: Uses 15-20 photos/issue; 100% supplied by freelance photographers. Needs photos of animals, wildlife, travel, scenic. Model release and captions required.

Making Contact & Terms: Send 35mm, 2¼×2¼, 4×5 transparencies by mail for consideration. SASE with sufficient postage.. Reports in 6 weeks. Pays $150/color cover photo; $50/color inside photo. Pays on publication. Credit line given. Buys one-time rights.

Tips: Wants "mostly coastal scenics. Artistry is less important than spectacle and fully saturated natural color."

ORGANIC GARDENING, 33 E. Minor St., Emmaus PA 18098. (215)967-5171. Photo Editor: Rob Cardillo. 10 issues/year, magazine. Circ. 1,000,000. Emphasizes the entire range of gardening topics: annual/perennial flowers, vegetables, herbs, shrubs, trees/vines. Free photo guidelines/want lists with SASE.

Photo Needs: Uses 80-100 photos/issue; 50% supplied by freelance photographers. Needs "photographs of the entire life-cycle of garden plants, overall organic gardens in all four seasons and geographic settings, photo essays of interesting organic gardeners and their creative solutions to local conditions, close-up photographs of companion plantings, unique flower combinations, garden wildlife. Also uses shots of attractive people of all ages working in the garden—planting, pruning, harvesting, etc." Photo captions (as to species and variety) required.

Making Contact & Terms: "Submissions should be sent in clear plastic slide pages with each item identified as to subject and photographer." Uses 35mm and larger transparencies (prefer Kodachrome or Fujichrome). Pays $75/¼ page; $125/½ page; $200/page; $300/double page; $400-600/cover shot. Pays on publication. Credit line given. Buys one-time rights.

Tips: "Shoot using the entire range of lighting (especially early morning and late afternoon), under all weather conditions (after a frost or late spring snow, during a summer shower or early morning mist). Vary camera angles and focal lengths." To break in, "know the subject throughly. Know how to shoot people as well as plants. Caption with specific varietal names as often as possible. Don't shoot at high noon!"

THE ORIGINAL NEW ENGLAND GUIDE, 177 E. Industrial Dr., Manchester NH 03103-1899. (603)668-7330. Editor: Catherine H. Smith. Annual magazine. Circ. 160,000, nationwide and international. For vacationers and visitors to New England. Forty-two percent are New Englanders. Buys 60-75 photos/issue. Sample copy $5; free photo guidelines.

Photo Needs: "All photos must be contemporary shots of the six New England states. We use scenics taken in the spring or summer; photos of landmarks and attractions; pictures of individuals or small groups biking, hiking, boating and camping; and events such as crafts, fairs and festivals."

Making Contact & Terms: Uses 35mm and larger transparencies. "ID subjects in photos including the town and state where shot was taken." Buys one-time rights. Credit line given. Pays on publication (early spring). Reports in 3 weeks. SASE. Previously published work OK.

THE OTHER SIDE, 300 W. Apsley St., Philadelphia PA 19144. (215)849-2178. Art Director: Cathleen Boint. Bimonthly magazine. Circ. 12,000. Estab. 1965. Emphasizes social justice issues from a Christian perspective. Buys 6 photos/issue; 95-100% from stock, 0-5% on assignment. Credit line given. Buys one-time rights. Send samples or summary of photo stock on file. SASE. Simultaneous submissions and previously published work OK. Sample copy $1.

Subject Needs: Documentary, human interest and photo essay/photo feature. "We're interested in photos that relate to current social, economic or political issues, both here and in the Third World."

B&W: Uses 8×10 glossy prints. Pays $15-30/photo.

Cover: Uses color transparencies. Vertical format required. Pays $100-150/photo.

Tips: Send samples of work to be photocopied for our files and/or photos; a list of subjects is difficult to judge quality of work by. Materials will be returned on request. In reviewing photographs/samples looks for "sensitivity to subject, good quality darkroom work and good contrast."

*OUR ANIMALS, 2500 16th St., San Francisco CA 94103. (415)554-3000. Editor: Paul Glassner. Quarterly magazine. Emphasizes pets. Readers are animal lovers of all ages. Circ. 40,000. Estab. 1906. Sample copy free with SASE.

Photo Needs: Uses 25 photos/issue; 25% supplied by freelance photographers. Needs photos of pets (especially cats and dogs of mixed breed backgrounds) and especially in interactions with humans. Model release preferred.

Making Contact & Terms: Send b&w prints by mail for consideration. SASE. Reports in 3 weeks. Pays $100/b&w cover photo; $40/b&w inside photo. Pays on acceptance. Buys one-time rights. Simultaneous and previously published work OK.

Tips: "We also hire local photographers for assignments."

OUR FAMILY, P.O. Box 249, Battleford SK S0M 0E0 Canada. FAX: (306)937-7644. Editor: Nestor Gregoire. Monthly magazine. Circ. 14,265. Estab. 1949. Emphasizes Christian faith as a part of daily living for Roman Catholic families. Photos are purchased with or without accompanying ms. Buys 5 photos/issue; cover by assignment, contents all freelance. Credit line given. Pays on acceptance. Buys one-time rights and simultaneous rights. Send material by mail for consideration or query with samples after consulting photo spec sheet. Provide letter of inquiry, samples and tearsheets to be kept on file for possible future assignments. SAE and International Reply Coupons. (Personal check or money order OK instead of International Reply Coupon.) Simultaneous submissions or previously published work OK. Reports in 4 weeks. Sample copy $2.50 with 9×12 SAE and 99¢ Canadian postage. Free photo guidelines with SAE and 45¢ postage.

Subject Needs: Head shot (to convey mood); human interest ("people engaged in the various experiences of living"); humorous ("anything that strikes a responsive chord in the viewer"); photo essay/photo feature (human/religious themes); and special effects/experimental (dramatic—to help convey a specific mood). "We are always in need of the following: family (aspects of family life); couples (husband and wife interacting and interrelating or involved in various activities); teenagers (in all aspects of their lives and especially in a school situation); babies and children; any age person involved in service to others; individuals in various moods (depicting the whole gamut of human emotions); religious symbolism; and humor. We especially want people photos, but we do not want the posed photos that make people appear 'plastic', snobbish or elite. In all photos, the simple, common touch is preferred. We are especially in search of humorous photos (human and animal subjects). Stick to the naturally comic, whether it's subtle or obvious." Model release required if editorial topic might embarrass subject; captions required when photos accompany ms.

B&W: Uses 8×10 glossy prints. Pays $35/photo.

Color: Transparencies or 8×10 glossy prints are used on inside pages, but are converted to b&w. Pays $75-100/photo.

Accompanying Mss: Pays 7-10¢/word for original mss; 4-6¢/word for nonoriginal mss. Free writer's guidelines with SAE and 45¢ postage.

Tips: "Send us a sample (20-50 photos) of your work after reviewing our Photo Spec Sheet. Looks for "photos that center around family life—but in the broad sense — i.e., our elderly parents, teenagers, young adults, family activities. Our covers (full color) are a specific assignment. We do not use freelance submissions for our cover."

OUTDOOR CANADA, Suite 301, 801 York Mills Rd., Don Mills, ON M3B 1X7 Canada. (416)429-5550. Editor: Teddi Brown. Magazine published 9 times annually. Circ. 141,000. Needs Canadian photos of people fishing, hunting, hiking, wildlife, cross-country skiing. Action shots. Buys 70-80 annually. Buys first serial rights. Send photos for consideration. Pays on publication. Reports in 3 weeks; "acknowledgement of receipt is sent the same day material is received." SAE and International Reply Coupons for American contributors; SASE for Canadians *must* be sent for return of materials. Free writers' and photographers' guidelines "with SASE or SAE and International Reply Coupons only." No phone calls, please.
B&W: Send 8×10 glossy prints. Pays $25-75.
Color: Send transparencies. Pays $30-225 depending on size used; $500/complete package.
Cover: Send color transparencies. Allow undetailed space along left side of photo for cover lines. Pays $400 maximum.
Tips: "Study the magazine and see the type of articles we use and the types of illustration used" and send a number of pictures to facilitate selection. "We are using more photos. We are looking for pictures that tell a story. We also need photos of people in the outdoors. A photo that captures the outdoor experience and shows the human delight in it. Take more fishing photos. It's the fastest-growing outdoor pastime in North America."

OUTDOOR LIFE MAGAZINE, 2 Park Ave., New York NY 10016. (212)779-5000. Art Director: Jim Eckes. Monthly. Circ. 1,500,000. Emphasizes hunting, fishing, shooting, camping and boating. Readers are "outdoorsmen of all ages." Sample copy "not for individual requests." Photo guidelines free with SASE.
Photo Needs: Uses about 50-60 photos/issue; 75% supplied by freelance photographers. Needs photos of "all species of wildlife and fish, especially in action and in natural habitat; how-to and where-to. No color prints—preferably Kodachrome 35mm slides." Captions preferred. No duplicates.
Making Contact & Terms: Send 5×7 or 8×10 b&w glossy prints; 35mm or 2¼×2¼ transparencies; b&w contact sheet by mail for consideration. Pays $35-275/b&w photo, $50-700/color photo depending on size of photos; $800-1,000/cover photo. SASE. Reports in 1 month. Rates are negotiable. Pays on publication. Credit line given. Buys one-time rights. "Multi subjects encouraged."
Tips: "Have name and address clearly printed on each photo to insure return, send in 8×10 plastic sleeves."

OUTDOOR PHOTOGRAPHER, 16000 Ventura Blvd., Encino CA 91436. (818)986-8400. Art Director: Ruth McKinney. Published 10 times per year magazine. Emphasizes professional and semi-professional scenic, travel, wildlife and sports photography. Readers are photographers of all ages and interests. Circ. 100,000+. Photo guidelines free with SASE.
Photo Needs: Uses about 50-60 photos/issue; 90% supplied by freelance photographers. Model release and captions preferred.
Making Contact & Terms: Query with samples; send b&w prints or color transparencies by mail for consideration. SASE. Reports in 60 days. Payment for cover photos, inside photos and text/photo package to be arranged. Pays on publication. Credit line given. Buys one-time rights but will negotiate. Previously published work OK.

OVERSEAS!, Kolpingstr. 1, 6906 Leimen, West Germany (06 224) 7060. Editorial Director: Charles L. Kaufman. Managing Editor: Greg Ballinger. Monthly magazine. Circ. 83,000. Emphasizes entertainment and European travel information of interest to military personnel and their families in Europe. Read by American and Canadian military personnel stationed in Europe, mostly males ages 20-35. Sample copy free with 9×12 SAE and 4 IRC. Photo guidelines available.
Photo Needs: Needs cover photos of unusual or dramatic travel scenes in Europe. Don't want the standard "Leaning Tower of Pisa" or "Eifel Toer" photo, but something with a little more energy and excitement.
Making Contact & Terms: Query with samples; send b&w or color prints; 35mm, 2¼×2¼ transparencies; color contact sheets by mail for consideration. SASE. Reports in 3 weeks. Pays $250-400. Pays on publication. Credit line given. Buys first European serial rights. Previously published work OK.
Tips: Send 15-50 slides. "The more color and action in the photo the better chance of being selected."

PAINT HORSE JOURNAL, Box 18519, Fort Worth TX 76118. (817)439-3412. Editor: Bill Shepard. Emphasizes horse subjects—horse owners, trainers and show people. Readers are "people who own, show or simply enjoy knowing about registered Paint horses." Monthly. Circ. 12,500. Sample copy $1 postpaid; photo guidelines for SASE.
Photo Needs: Uses about 50 photos/issue; 3 of which are supplied by freelance photographers. "Most photos will show Paint (spotted) horses. Other photos used include prominent Paint horse showmen, owners and breeders; notable Paint horse shows or other events; overall views of well-known Paint

horse farms. Most freelance photos used are submitted with freelance articles to illustrate a particular subject. The magazine occasionally buys a cover photo, although most covers are paintings. Freelance photographers would probably need to query before sending photos, because we rarely use photos just for their artistic appeal—they must relate to some article or news item." Wants on a regular basis Paint horses as related to news events, shows and persons. No "posed, handshake and award-winner photos." Model release and captions required.

Making Contact & Terms: Query with resume of photo credits or state specific idea for using photos. Provide resume, business card, brochure, flyer and tearsheets to be kept on file for possible future assignments. SASE. Reports in 3-6 weeks. Pays on acceptance $7.50 minimum/b&w photo; $10 minimum/color transparency; $50 minimum/color cover photo; $50-200 for text/photo package. Credit line given. Buys first North American serial rights or per individual negotiation.

Tips: "Send us a variety of Paint horse photos. We buy action, unusual situations, humor, but rarely buy halter shots."

PALM BEACH LIFE, 265 Royal Poinciana Way, Palm Beach FL 33480. (407)837-4762. Design Director: Anne Wholf. Monthly magazine. Circ. 32,000. Emphasizes entertainment, gourmet cooking, affluent lifestyle, travel, personalities, decorating and the arts. For regional and general audiences. Freelance photographers supply 20% of the photos. Pays $300-700/job, or on a per-photo basis. Credit line given. Pays on acceptance. Query or make appointment. SASE. Simultaneous submissions OK. "*Palm Beach Life* cannot be responsible for unsolicited material." Reports in 4-6 weeks. Sample copy $4.18.

Subject Needs: Fine art, scenic, human interest and nature. Captions are required.

B&W: Uses any size glossy prints. Pays $25-50.

Color: Uses 35mm, 2¼ × 2¼ and 4 × 5 transparencies. Pays $50-75.

Cover: Uses color transparencies; vertical or square format. Payment negotiable.

Tips: "Don't send slides—make an appointment to show work. We have staff photographers, are really only interested in something really exceptional or material from a location that we would find difficult to cover."

PALM SPRINGS LIFE MAGAZINE, 303 N. Indian Ave., Palm Springs CA 92262. (619)325-2333. FAX: (619)325-7008. Editor: Jamie Pricer. Monthly. Emphasizes Palm Springs/California desert area. Readers are extremely affluent, 45+ years old. Primarily for our readers, Palm Springs is their second/vacation home. Circ. 80,000. Estab. 1957. Sample copy $3.95. Photo guidelines free with SASE.

Photo Needs: Uses 50+ photos/issue; 50% supplied by freelance photographers; 80% from assignment. Needs desert photos, scenic wildlife, gardening, fashion, beauty, travel and people. Special needs include photo essays, art photography. Model release required; captions preferred.

Making Contact & Terms: Arrange a personal interview to show portfolio; query with list of stock photo subjects; or send unsolicited photos by mail for consideration. Uses 35mm, 2¼ × 2¼, 4 × 5 or 8 × 10 transparencies. SASE. Reports in 1 week. Pays $250/color cover photo; $50-100/color inside photo; $100/color page; $25-100/b&w photo; $50-250/color photo. Pays on publication. Credit line given. Buys all rights. Will negotiate with photographer unwilling to sell all rights. Simultaneous submissions and previously published work OK.

Tips: In photographer's portfolio looks for "published photographs, the 'unusual' bend to the 'usual' subject. We will try anything new photographically as long asd it's gorgeous! Must present professional-looking portfolio."

PARENTS & TEENAGERS MAGAZINE, (formerly Parents & Teenagers Newsletter) 2890 N. Monroe Ave., Box 481, Loveland CO 80539. (303)669-3836. Published by Group Publishing. Editorial Director: Joani Schultz. Art Director: Jean Bruns. Bimonthly. Circ. 25,000. Estab. 1988. For Christian parents of teenagers. Emphasizes ideas and support for raising healthy, mature teenagers. Photos purchased with or without accompanying ms. Buys up to 10 freelance photos/issue. Credit line given. Pays on publication. Buys one-time rights. Send material by mail for consideration with SASE. Simultaneous submissions and previously published work OK. Reports in 4 weeks. Sample copy with 9 × 12 SAE with $1 first-class postage. Photo guidelines free with SASE.

Photo Needs: Uses mostly people photos—parents (of teenagers), individuals, couples or groups; individual or groups of teenagers, parents interacting with their teenagers. All kinds of settings and activities common to families—at home, work, play, church, etc.—and depiction of a range of emotions are desired. Emphasis on ethnic and cultural diversity. Almost exclusively uses freelance stock. Model release preferred and sometimes required, depending on subject matter.

B&W: Uses 8 × 10 b&w prints. Pays $25-50/photo, one-time inside editorial use. (Will also convert color transparencies to b&w with photographer's permission—all interior photography is b&w.).

Accompanying Mss: Seeks articles to help parents understand, discipline and communicate with their teenagers, as well as family involvement activities and family success stories. Pays $25-100/ms. Writer's guidelines free with SASE.

Close-up

M.C. Marden
Photo Editor, People
New York City

© Harry Benson

"When you leaf through the pages of *People*," says M.C. Marden, photo editor for the popular weekly magazine, "it looks like a 'piece of cake' to get those pictures." But, she adds quickly, "it is anything *but* easy."

Marden, a member of the magazine's photo staff since 1978, has learned the territory—photography—and the subject matter—people—very, very well in her tenure. She has seen the magazine, its audience *and* its competition evolve dramatically over the last dozen or so years. So, as she observes, keeping the visual element "surprising, lively and different" in light of these factors plus a relentless weekly deadline has become more—not less—challenging.

"Basically, the photographer is told to get something incredible, something that shows the reader a real side to the person we're presenting in the article," she explains. "If we show a person in a playroom playing with their dog and children, it's going to be *their* playroom, not a studio. That's getting harder and harder to do because other publications are willing to not push hard to get that personal side of the story, and just settle for getting the person, particularly celebrities. We do a lot of negotiating to get the story, before we even get the photographer involved. Then, the photographer walks in with his or her cameras and persuades the people to do something interesting. That's a *lot* harder. We often use many of the same [photographers] we have worked with before because they know how to do it. They also have a great allegiance to the magazine and will push really hard to get the pictures we need."

Since the photographer represents the magazine just as much as the reporter does, interpersonal skills are essential, says Marden. "It's really important to me that they're professional and honest. I don't hire photographers to be intrusive or harass people. I believe a photographer should be able to get on well with the subject, and be pleasing and personable."

Sometimes, as she elaborates, this translates into no less than grace under pressure. "There are times when a photographer will go in with a subject and all he gets is 10 minutes. Covers sometimes even have to be shot in five minutes. You really have to know what you're doing and be the utmost professional to deal with the obstacles that come up. It's really the top-notch photographer who can deal with the problems of time."

While Marden is always looking for good, new photographers to bring on board, she doesn't discover new talent quite as frequently as she would like. "It's so exciting to get new, fresh 'blood' shooting for the magazine. But each year, I see only one or two portfolios—ones that are well-presented, with really exciting photos,—where I say 'That person could really do a piece for *People*' or that I'll just want to kiss their feet. Sometimes it's hard to give people a try because we know all the obstacles, and we just want to be sure of getting the shots." For that reason, she explains, "We will give a photographer a first try on a one-page story."

In particular, freelancers should be aware of trends in the magazine market but avoid trendiness, Marden advises. "A lot of the trendy, popular shots today are portraits," she says, remarking on the over-exposure of that style. "I worry sometimes because there's such a sameness . . . so many people are shooting the *same* [kind of] picture. That type of photography will wane, I think, and we'll see it go back more to reportage. Of course, I say that because that's what I love. So I suggest that a photographer strive to be versatile. Know the trade and how to shoot a lot of different things. And then, present a portfolio to places needing that kind of variety. It really is magic when you see that kind of determination in a portfolio."

Interestingly enough, Marden sees story opportunities in the major markets heading for a burnout, but fresh, fertile territory waiting to be found in outlying regions. "I'm always telling people to move to Wyoming and North Dakota," she remarks. "There's a whole part of the world that I don't see stuff from, and I'm sure there are really good stories, just some incredible *people* out there. Coverage doesn't even have to be a news event, like the Yellowstone fires. Just folks." Not only is this desirable, but in fact the magazine has already been working in that direction, she adds. "We have two people working for us regularly out of Kansas City, where we have a lot of work, so they're pretty busy. Also, they're located in such a way that we often get them to fly up to North Dakota, or wherever. We got two strong people in Florida, and a couple in Seattle. But it's the middle part of the country I'd like to develop. I think a photographer who went there rather than fight the mobs in New York and L.A. — I might be totally wrong — would find a lot more stories to cover."

All in all, Marden observes that breaking in with *People* is possible by following her suggestions: work hard, be personable and professional, know your craft and market, oh, and one more . . . travel light. "A lot of photographers today have become encumbered with equipment, I think, so I try to get them to lighten up on gear," she says, once again noting her preference for reportage over portraiture. "Photographer's have this 'love affair' with the 2¼ and the Hasselblad. They've been living with the tripod. It has diminished their ability to do really candid pictures, to get that 'moment.' My idea of THE *People* picture is having the family romping in the back yard instead of a staid picture of them sitting on the back steps. So that's sort of my crusade . . . long live the 35mm without strobes and everything else."

— Sam A. Marshall

"Strive to be versatile," People's *picture editor, M.C. Marden recommends to aspiring editorial photographers. "Know the trade and how to shoot a lot of different things. And then, present a portfolio to places needing that kind of variety. It really is magic when you see that kind of determination in a portfolio."*

Tips: "Dated, obviously posed, and poorly focused or exposed photos are typically rejected. We look for good technical ability (lighting, printing, etc.); ability to capture emotion, expressions; good compositional ability; ability to edit out poorer quality work and present only the best work; ability to bring out the subject from the background, and to have a strong center of interest in each photo. We're also attracted to shots with an unusual perspective on a situation. A current, contemporary look (in fashions, styles) is essential; a real-life, "natural setting" highly desirable, while not looking snapshot-y. Experience working with religious publicaltions can be helpful. Don't send too much work at once — it can be overwhelming and is often more unhelpful than helpful. Focus on fewer subjects and only the best of each in each of your submissions."

PENNSYLVANIA, Box 576, Camp Hill PA 17011. (717)761-6620. Editor: Albert E. Holliday. Bimonthly. Emphasizes history, travel and contemporary issues and topics. Readers are 40-60 years old professional and retired; average income is $46,000. Circ. 40,000. Sample copy $2.95; photo guidelines free with SASE.
Photo Needs: Uses about 40 photos/issue; most supplied by freelance photographers. Needs include travel and scenic. Reviews photos with or without accompanying ms. Captions required.
Making Contact & Terms: Query with samples and list of stock photo subjects; send 5×7 and up b&w prints and 35mm and 2¼×2¼ transparencies (duplicates preferred) by mail for consideration. SASE. Reports in 2 weeks. Pays $100-150/color cover photo, $15-25/inside photo, $50-400/text/photo package. Credit line given. Buys one-time rights. Simultaneous submissions and previously published work OK.

PENNSYLVANIA GAME NEWS, 2001 Elmerton Ave., Harrisburg PA 17110-9797. (717)787-3745. Editor: Bob Bell. Monthly magazine. Circ. 150,000. Published by the Pennsylvania Game Commission. For people interested in hunting, wildlife management and conservation in Pennsylvania. Buys all rights, but may reassign after publication. Photos purchased with accompanying ms. Pays on acceptance. Reports in 2 months. SASE. Free sample copy with 8½×11 SASE; free editorial guidelines.
Subject Needs: Considers photos of "any outdoor subject (Pennsylvania locale), except fishing and boating."
B&W: Send 8×10 glossy prints. Pays $5-20.
Tips: Buys photos without accompanying ms "rarely." Submit seasonal material 6 months in advance.

*PENNSYLVANIA SPORTSMAN, P.O. Box 90, Lemayne PA 17043. (717)761-1400. Managing Editor: Sherry Ritchey. Regional magazine, published 8 times/year. Features nonfiction, how-to's, where-to's, various game and wildlife in Pennsylvania. Readers are men and women of all ages and occupations.Circ. 62,000. Estab. 1971. Sample copy for $2. Photo guidelines free with SASE.
Photo Needs: Uses 40 photos/issue; 5 supplied by freelancers. Primarily needs animal/wildlife shots. Especially interested in shots of deer, bear, turkeys and game fish such as trout and bass. Photo captions preferred.
Making Contact & Terms: Query with list of stock photo subjects. SASE. Reports in 1 month. Payment negotiable. Pays on acceptance. Credit line given. Buys one-time rights. Simultaneous submissions OK.
Tips: "Read the magazine to determine needs."

PEOPLE MAGAZINE, Time & Life Bldg., Rockefeller Center, New York NY 10024. (212)522-2606. Photo Editor: M.C. Marden. Weekly. "We are concerned with people, from the celebrity to the person next door. We have a dual audience, men and women, primarily under 40. Circ. 1.5 million subscribers; 1.7 newsstand buyers.Estab. 1974.
Photo Needs: Uses approximately 100 photos/issue. "We have no staff photographers therefore all work in PEOPLE is done by freelancers. About 75% is from assignments, the rest of the material is from photo agencies and pickups from freelancers, movie companies, and n networks, record companies and publishers." . We are always looking for recent lively photojournalistic photos. We are less interested in studio portraits than in photo reportage. Our needs are specific people rather than generic people." Model release and captions required.
Making Contact & Terms: "PEOPLE has a portfolio drop-off system. This enables them to let PEOPLE see their work. They should call and make a drop-off apointment. Pays $1,250/b&w or color cover photo; "space rates: minimum $125 to $350 for full page." Pays $350/day. Pays on publication. Credit line given. Buys one-time rights.
Tips: "Our photographs must tell a story. I have to see reportage, not portraits. I am looking for pictures with impact, pictures that move one, make one laugh. It is valuable to include contact sheets to show how the photographer really works a story. It is also important to have a portfolio that relates to the appropriate market, i.e. advertising for advertising, editorial for editorial. Submit lively, interesting, newsworthy recent photos. It really should be timely and exclusive."

PERSONAL INVESTOR, Suite 280, 18818 Teller Ave., Irvine CA 92715. (714)851-2220. Art Director: Bob Tambo. Bimonthly. Emphasizes financial investing. Readers are affluent working professionals with financial interests. Circ. 90,000. Sample copy $2.50.
Photo Needs: Uses about 8 photos/issue; 5 supplied by freelance photographers. Needs environmental portraits of investment personalities, and conceptual shots of financial ideas, all by assignment only. Model release and captions preferred.
Making Contact & Terms: Arrange a personal interview to show a portfolio; query with samples and list of stock photo subjects; provide resume, business card, brochure, flyer or tearsheets to be kept on file for possible future assignments. Does not return unsolicited material. Pays $300-900/b&w or color cover photo; $150-300/b&w or color inside photo. Pays 30 days after publication. Buys one-time rights. Simultaneous submissions and previously published work OK.

PETERSEN'S HUNTING MAGAZINE, Petersen Publishing Co., 8490 Sunset Blvd., Los Angeles CA 90069. (213)854-2222. Editor: Craig Boddington. Monthly magazine. Circ. 300,000. For sport hunters who "hunt everything from big game to birds to varmints." Buys 4-8 color and 10-30 b&w photos/issue. Buys one-time rights. Present model release on acceptance of photo. Send photos for consideration. Identify subject of each photo. Pays on publication. Reports in 3-4 weeks. SASE. Free photo guidelines.
Subject Needs: "Good sharp wildlife shots and hunting scenes. No scenic views or unhuntable species."
B&W: Send 8×10 glossy prints. Pays $25.
Color: Send transparencies. Pays $75-250.
Cover: Send color transparencies. Pays $500.
Tips: Prefers to see "photos that demonstrate a knowledge of the outdoors, heavy emphasis on game animal shots, hunters and action. Try to strive for realistic photos that reflect nature, the sportsman and the flavor of the hunting environment. Not just simply 'hero' shots where the hunter is perched over the game. Action—such as running animals, flying birds, also unusual, dramatic photos of same animals in natural setting. Submit a small selection of varied subjects for review—20-40 slides. Majority of photographs used are author-supplied; approx. 20% from outside photographers."

PETERSEN'S PHOTOGRAPHIC MAGAZINE, 8490 Sunset Blvd., Los Angeles CA 90069. (213)854-2200. FAX: (213)854-6823. Editor: Bill Hurter. Monthly magazine. For the beginner and professional advanced amateur in all phases of still photography. Circ. 275,000. Estab. 1972. Sample copy $3. Photo guidelines free with SASE.
Photo Needs: Uses about 100 photos/issue; 50 supplied by freelance photographers. Needs imaginative photos on all subjects. Model release and captions required.
Making Contact & Terms: Query with samples. Uses 8×10 b&w and color glossy or matte prints or transparencies. Send article outline with sample photos. SASE. Reports back approximately 1 month. Pays $35/b&w or color inside photo; $60/b&w or color page. Pays on publication. Credit line given. Buys one-time rights or all rights, but will negotiate.
Tips: Prints should have wide margins; "the margin is used to mark instructions to the printer." Photos accompanying how-to articles should demonstrate every step, including a shot of materials required and at least one shot of the completed product. "We can edit our pictures if we don't have the space to accommodate them. However, we cannot add pictures if we don't have them on hand. Hit as many markets as frequently as possible. Seek feedback."We look for the ability to apply photographic techniques to successfully solve creative and practical challenges. The work should be exemplary of the technique(s) employed, and be appealing viually as well. We do not look for specific trends, per se, but rather photographic techniques that will be of interest to our readers. A freelancer should have a good working knowledge of photographic techniques, and be able to discuss and communicate them clearly, both in his/her imagery as well as editorially. Even if not a writer, the freelancer should be able to supply some form of an outline to accompany his/her work, whether this be verbal or written. We welcome submissions from freelancers."

PETS MAGAZINE, Moorshead Publications, 1300 Don Mills Rd., Toronto ON M3B 3M8 Canada. (416)445-5600, FAX: (416)445-8149. Editor: Marie Hubbs. Bimonthly magazine. Emphasizes pets (mainly cats and dogs). Readers are about 85% female, 30 yrs.+, middle income and better. Circ. 67,000. Sample copy for 8½×11 SASE. "Please use internat'l reply coupon 95¢ or *Canadian* stamps."
Photo Needs: Uses 10-15 photos/issue; 3-5 supplied by freelance photographers. Needs animal shots. Model release and photo captions preferred.
Making Contact & Terms: Provide resume, business card, brochure, flyer or tearsheets to be kept on file for possible assignments. SASE. Reports in 1-5 weeks (or more). Pays $25/color cover photo or b&w inside photo. Pays on publication. Credit line given. Buys all rights; will negotiate. Previously published work OK.

Tips: "To be frank, we rarely buy just photos—our writers (all freelance) send any photos needed for specific articles, or we use "generic" photos from our (large) collection of photos (gathered through four photo contests)."

PHOENIX MAGAZINE, 4707 N. 12th St., Phoenix AZ 85014. (602)248-8900. Executive Editor: Dick Vonier. Monthly magazine. Circ. 50,000. Emphasizes "subjects that are unique to Phoenix: its culture, urban and social achievements and problems, its people and the Arizona way of life. We reach a professional and general audience of well-educated, affluent visitors and long-term residents." Buys 10-35 photos/issue.
Subject Needs: Wide range, all dealing with life in metro Phoenix. Generally related to editorial subject matter. Wants on a regular basis photos to illustrate features, as well as for regular columns on arts. No "random shots of Arizona scenery, etc. that can't be linked to specific stories in the magazine." Special issues: *Restaurant Guide*, *Valley "Superguide"* (January); *Desert Gardening Guide*. Photos purchased with or without an accompanying ms.
Payment & Terms: B&w: $25-75; color: $50-200; cover: $400-1,000. Pays within two weeks of publication. Payment for manuscripts includes photos in most cases. Payment negotiable for covers and other photos purchased separately.
Making Contact: Query. Works with freelance photographers on assignment only basis. Provide resume, samples, business card, brochure, flyer and tearsheets to be kept on file for possible future assignments. SASE. Reports in 3-4 weeks.
Tips: "Study the magazine, then show us an impressive portfolio."

PHOTO LIFE, 130 Spy Court, Markham, ON L3R 5H6 Canada. (416)475-8440. Editor: Jane Griffen. Consumer publication. Magazine published eleven times a year. Readers are advanced amateur photographers. Circ. 65,000. Sample copy or photo guidelines free with SASE.
Photo Needs: Uses 50 photos/issue; 80% supplied by freelance photographers. Needs animal/wildlife shots, travel, scenics, and so on. Usually only by Canadian photographers, though. Model release and photo captions required.
Making Contact & Terms: Query with resume of credits. SASE. Reports in 1 month. Pays $200-500/photo/text package. Pays on publication. Buys first N.A. serial rights.

PHOTOGRAPHER'S MARKET, 1507 Dana Ave., Cincinnati OH 45207. (513)531-2222. Editor: Sam Marshall. Annual hardbound directory for freelance photographers. Credit line given. Pays on publication. Buys one-time and promotional rights. Send material by mail for consideration. SASE. Simultaneous submissions and previously published work OK.
Subject Needs: "We look for all subjects. The photos must be of work you have sold (but still own the rights to) to buyers listed in *Photographer's Market*. Photos are used to illustrate to readers of the book the types of images being sold. Captions should explain how the photo was used by the buyer, how you got the assignment or sold the photo, what was paid for the photo, your own self-marketing advice, etc. We hold all potential photos and make our choice in mid-April. We report after April deadline. We recommend submitting photos in fall and winter to ensure sufficient time to review them; the selection deadline does fluctuate from year to year. For the best indication of the types of photos used, look at the photos in the book." Buys 20-50 photos/year.
Specs: Uses 5×7 or 8×10 b&w glossy prints; also 35mm transparencies; sometimes use tearsheets. Pays $25 plus complimentary copy of book for photos previously sold to listings in *Photographer's Market*.
Tips: "We prefer original prints or transparencies instead of tearsheets when possible. Usually, we will use tearsheets if photos are used in an interesting collage or striking cover layout."

PLANE & PILOT, 16000 Ventura Blvd., Encino CA 91436. (818)986-8400. Art Director: Steve Curtis. Monthly magazine. Emphasizes personal, business and home-built aircraft. Readers are private, business and hobbyist pilots. Circ. 70,000-100,000.
Photo Needs: Uses about 50 photos/issue; 90% supplied by freelance photographers. Needs photos of "production aircraft and homebuilt experimentals." Special needs include "air-to-air, technical, general aviation and special interest" photos. Written release and captions preferred.
Making Contact & Terms: Query with samples. Send 5×7 or 8×10 b&w glossy prints; 35mm transparencies; b&w contact sheets. SASE. Reports in 1 month. Pays $150-200 color cover photo; $25-50/inside photo; $100-150/color inside photo; $500/job; $250-500/text/photo package. Pays on acceptance. Credit line given. Buys one-time rights. Simultaneous submissions and previously published work OK.
Tips: Prefers to see "a variety of well-shot and composed color transparencies and b&w prints dealing with mechanical subjects (aircraft, auto, etc.)" in samples. "Use good technique, a variety of subjects and learn to write well."

*PLAYBOY MAGAZINE, 680 North Lake Shore Dr., Chicago IL 60611. (312)751-8000. Associate Photography Editor: James Larson. Monthly magazine. Emphasizes men's entertainment. Circ. 3.4 million copies per month—over 12 million readers. Wide range from college kids to CEOs. Estab. 1953. Photo guidelines free with SASE.
Photo Needs: Uses 100-150 photos/issue; 40% supplied by freelance photographers. Needs photos for glamour nudes, personalities, fashion and sill life. Model release required.
Making Contact & Terms: Send unsolicited photos by mail for consideration. Submit portfolio for review. SASE. Reports in 3 weeks. Pays 1,500/color cover photo; $1,000/color page. Credit line given. Buys all rights; negotiable.

PLEASURE BOATING, 1995 NE 150th St., North Miami FL 33181. (305)945-7403. FAX: (305)947-6410. Managing Editor: Connie Frocchi. Monthly. Circ. 30,000. Estab. 1971. Emphasizes recreational fishing and boating in Florida and the Caribbean. Readers are "recreational boaters interested in this area, regardless of where they live." Sample copy $2.
Photo Needs: Uses about 35-40 photos/issue; most freelance photography comes from assignment. Needs photos of "people in, on, around boats and water." Model release and captions preferred.
Making Contact & Terms: Query with samples. Provide brochure to be kept on file for possible future assignments. SASE. Reports in 4 weeks. Pays $15-75/b&w photo; $25-200/color photo; $100-300/color photo/feature illustrations; $250-375/day and per photo/text package. Pays month of publication. Credit line given. Buys one-time rights and full rights. Simultaneous submissions OK.
Tips: Prefers 35mm slides, good quality. Prefers verticals, strong colors; people involved in water and/or boating activity. Interested in boating related and watersports related that have composition originality, etc. "Contact editorial department on telephone regarding photos available. Submit in envelope with stiffener for protection. Most freelance photography comes from assignment. Include SASE."

PODIATRY MANAGEMENT, Suite 210, 7000 Terminal Square, Upper Darby PA 19082. (215)925-9744. Editor: Dr. Barry Block, DPM. Photo Editor: M.L. Goldberg. Published 9 times/year. Emphasizes podiatry. Readers include podiatrists. Circ. 12,500. Free sample copy with 9 × 12 SASE.
Photo Needs: Uses 4 photos/issue; 3 supplied by freelance photographers. Needs cover—office or surgical shots. Reviews photos with accompanying ms only. Model release and captions required.
Making Contact & Terms: Query with resume of credits. SASE. Payment individually negotiated; $100-250. Pays on publication. Buys all rights.
Tips: "Also looking for photos of Hi Tech items podiatrists use in their practice."

POLO MAGAZINE, 656 Quince Orchard Rd., Gaithersburg MD 20878. (301)977-3900. Managing Editor: Martha LeGrand or Art Director: Florence Jones Hobbs. Publishes monthly magazine 10 times/year with combined issues for January/February and June/July. Emphasizes the sport of polo and its lifestyle. Readers are primarily male; average age is 40. Some 90% of readers are professional/managerial levels, including CEO's and presidents. All are affluent. Circ. 6,000. Sample copy free with 10 × 13 SASE. Photo guidelines free with SASE.
Photo Needs: Uses 50 photos/issue; 70% supplied by freelance photographers; 20% of this by assignment. Needs photos of polo action, portraits, travel, party/social and scenics. Most polo action is assigned, but freelance needs range from dynamic action photos to spectator fashion to social events. Photographers may write and obtain an editorial calendar for the year, listing planned features/photo needs. Model release and photo captions preferred, where necessary.
Making Contact & Terms: Query with list of stock photo subjects. Provide resume, business card, brochure, flyer or tearsheets to be kept on file for possible assignments. SASE. Reports in 2 weeks. Pays $25-150/b&w photo, $30-300/color photo, $150/½ day, $300/full day, $200-500/complete package. Pays on publication. Credit line given. Buys one-time or all rights; will negotiate. Simultaneous submissions and previously published work OK "in some instances."
Tips: "In assigning action photography, we look for close-ups that show the dramatic interaction of two or more players rather than a single player. On the sidelines, we encourage photographers to capture emotions of game, pony picket lines, etc."

POOL & SPA MAGAZINE, 46 Crockford Blvd., Scarborough ON M1R 3C3 Canada. (416)752-2500. Editor: David Barnsley. Consumer publication. Quarterly. Emphasizes swimming pools, spas, hot tubs, outdoor entertaining, landscaping (patios, decks, gardens, lawns, fencing). Readers are homeowners and professionals 30-55 years old. Equally read by men and women. Circ. 40,000.
Photo Needs: Uses 20-30 photos/issue; 30% supplied by freelance photographers. Looking for shots of models dressed in bathing suits, people swimming in pools/spas, patios. Plans annual bathing suit issue late in year. Model release required.

Making Contact & Terms: Send unsolicited photos by mail for consideration. Send color, glossy, 35mm or 8×10 prints. SASE. Reports in 2 weeks. Will negotiate payment. Pays on publication. Credit line given. Buys all rights; will negotiate. Simultaneous submissions and previously published work OK.

Tips: Looking for "photos of families relaxing outdoors around a pool, spa or patio. We are always in need of visual material, so send in whatever you feel is appropriate for the magazine. Photos will be returned."

POPULAR ELECTRONICS, (formerly Hands-On Electronics), 500-B Bi-County Blvd., Farmingdale NY 11735. (516)293-3000. Managing Editor: Carl Laron. Monthly magazine. Emphasizes hobby electronics. Readers are hobbyists in electronics, amateur radio, CB, audio, TV, etc. "Mostly male, ages 13-59." Circ. 100,000. Sample copy free with 9×12 SAE and 90¢ postage.

Photo Needs: Uses about 20 photos/issue; 20% supplied by freelance photographers. Photos purchased with accompanying ms only. Special needs include regional photo stories on electronics. Model release and captions preferred.

Making Contact & Terms: Arrange a personal interview to show portfolio; query with samples. SASE. Reports in 2 weeks. Pays $250-400/color cover photo; $200-350 for text/photo package. Pays on acceptance. Credit line given. Buys all rights but will negotiate. Simultaneous submissions and previously published work OK.

Tips: "Read the magazine before you write to the editor."

POPULAR PHOTOGRAPHY, 1515 Broadway, New York NY 10036. Editorial Director: Jason Schneider. Picture Editor: Jeanne Stallman. Monthly magazine. Circ. 725,000. Emphasizes good photography, photographic instructions and product reports for advanced amateur and professional photographers. Buys 15+ photos/issue. "We look for photographs in color and b&w showing highly creative, interesting use of photography. Also, authoritative, well-written and well-illustrated how-to articles on all aspects of amateur photography." Buys first serial rights and promotion rights for the issue in which the photo appears; or all rights if the photos are done on assignment, but may reassign to photographer after publication. Present model release on acceptance of photo. Submit portfolio or arrange a personal interview to show portfolio. Pays on publication. Reports in 4 weeks. SASE. Previously published work generally OK "if it has not appeared in another photo magazine or annual." Free photo guidelines.

B&W: Send 8×10 semigloss prints. Captions are appreciated: where and when taken, title and photographer's name; technical data sheets describing the photo must be filled out if the photo is accepted for publication. Pays $250/printed page; but "prices for pictures will vary according to our use of them."

Color: Send 8×10 prints or any size duplicate transparencies. Captions required; technical data sheets describing the photo must be filled out. Pays $250/printed page; but "prices for pictures will vary according to our use of them."

Cover: Send color prints or duplicate color transparencies. Caption required; technical data sheets describing the photo must be filled out. Pays $500.

Tips: "We see hundreds of thousands of photographs every year; we are interested only in the highest quality work by professionals or amateurs." No trite, cornball or imitative photos. Submissions should be insured.

POPULAR SCIENCE, 2 Park Ave., New York NY 10016. (212)779-5000. Art Director: W. David Houser. Monthly magazine. Circ. 1,850,000. Emphasizes new developments in science, technology, automotive and consumer products. Freelancers provide 25% of photos. Works on an assignment basis. Credit line given. Pays on acceptance. Buys one-time rights and first North American serial rights. Model release required. Send photos by mail for consideration or arrange a personal interview. SASE. Reports in 1 month.

Subject Needs: Documentary photos related to science, technology and new inventions; automotive technology product photography. Captions required.

Color: Uses transparencies. Pay variable.

Cover: Uses color covers; vertical format required.

Tips: "Our major need is for first-class photos of new products and examples of unusual new technologies. A secondary need is for photographers who understand how to take pictures to illustrate an article." Prefers innovative photography.

POWDER MAGAZINE, Box 1028, Dana Point CA 92629. (714)496-5922. Editor/Photo Editor: Steve Casimaro. Published September through March. Circ. over 100,000. Emphasizes skiing. Sample copy $1; photo guidelines free with SASE.

Photo Needs: Uses 70-80 photos/issue; 90% supplied by freelance photographers. Needs "ski action, ski action, ski action! Also. scenics, personalities and humorous ski photos. Always needs photos from the East—Vermont, New Hampshire, Maine, New York." Model release preferred.

Making Contact & Terms: Query with samples or call to discuss requirements, deadlines, etc. SASE. Reports in 2 weeks. Pays $500/color cover photo; $200/color page, $50/color minimum. Pays on publication. Credit line given. Buys first North American serial rights. Simultaneous submissions OK.

Tips: "Our readers are advanced and expert skiers. Your submissions should reflect that. Be bold and exciting—lots of action. Avoid static, staged photos. Be creative (and weird). We *are* a market for experimental photos as well as 'traditional' action shots. We look for photographers who break the standards of ski photography."

PRAYING, P.O. Box 419335, Kansas City MO 64141. (800)821-7926. Editor: Art Winter. Photo Editor: Rich Heffern. Bimonthly. Emphasizes spirituality for everyday living. Readers include mostly Catholic laypeople. Circ. 20,000. Estab. 1986. Sample copy and photo guidelines free with SASE.

Photo Needs: Uses 3 photos/issue; 100% supplied by freelance photographers. Needs quality photographs which stand on their own as celebrations of people, relationships, ordinary events, work, nature, etc. Reviews photos with or without accompanying ms.

Making Contact & Terms: Query with samples; send 8×10 b&w prints by mail for consideration. SASE. Reports in 2 weeks. Pays $50/b&w cover, $25/b&w inside photo. Pays on publication. Credit line given. Buys one-time rights. Simultaneous submissions and previously published work OK.

Tips: Looking for "good *printing*, composition. We get a lot of really *poor* stuff! Know how to take and print a quality photograph. Don't try to add holy element or reflective moment. Natural, to us, is holy. We have one rule: never to run a picture of someone praying."

PREVENTION MAGAZINE, 33 E. Minor St., Emmaus PA 18098. (215)967-5171, ext. 1601. Executive Art Director: Wendy Ronga. Monthly magazine. Emphasizes health. Readers are mostly female, 35-50, upscale. Circ. 2,500,000.

Photo Needs: Uses 12-15 photos/issue; 60% on assignment, 40% from stock, but seeing trend toward "more assignment work than usual." Photo needs very specific to editorial, health, beauty, food. Model release and captions required.

Making Contact & Terms: Provide resume, business card, brochure, flyer or tearsheets to be kept on file for possible future assignments; tearsheets and/or dupes very important. Does not return unsolicited material. Reports in 2 weeks. Pays $100-300/b&w photo; $150-600/color photo; and $250-1,000/day. Pays on publication. Credit line given. Buys one-time rights.

Tips: Prefers to see ability to do one thing very well. "Good lighting technique is a must." Wants to see "something different, taking a different twist to an ordinary subject."

PROBLEMS OF COMMUNISM, U.S. Information Agency, Room 402, 301 4th St. SW, Washington DC 20547. (202)485-2230. FAX: (202)485-2173. Editor: Wayne Hall. Bimonthly magazine. Circ. 32,500. Estab. 1952. Emphasizes scholarly, documented articles on the politics, economics and sociology of Communist states and related movements. For all scholars, government officials, journalists, business people, opinion-makers—with higher education. Needs current photography of Communist societies, leaders and economic activities and of related leftist movements and leaders. Not interested in nature shots or travelogues, but in good incisive photos capturing economic and social life and political events. Although the magazine is not copyrighted, it does bear the following statement on the index page: "Graphics and pictures which carry a credit line are not necessarily owned by *Problems of Communism*, and users bear responsibility for obtaining appropriate permissions." Query first with resume of credits, summary of areas visited, dates and types of pix taken. Pays on acceptance. Reports in 1 month. SASE. Simultaneous submissions and previously published work OK. Free sample copy and photo guidelines.

B&W: Uses 8×10 glossy prints. "Captions with accurate information are essential." Pays $50-100.

Cover: Uses 8×10 glossy b&w prints. Also uses 35mm color transparencies, but will be converted to b&w. "The stress is on sharp recent personalities in Communist leaderships, although historical and mood shots are occasionally used." Pays $100-250.

Tips: "Photos are used basically to illustrate scholarly articles on current Communist affairs. Hence, the best way to sell is to let us know what Communist countries you have visited and what Communist or leftist movements or events you have covered." In samples, wants to see "clear, factural documentation with good contrast."

THE PROGRESSIVE, 409 E. Main St., Madison WI 53703. Art Director: Patrick JB Flynn. Monthly. Circ. 40,000. Estab. 1909. Emphasizes "political and social affairs—international and domestic." Free sample copy and photo guidelines upon request.

Photo Needs: Uses 5 or more b&w photos/issue; all supplied by freelance photographers and photo agencies. Looking for images documenting the human condition and the social/political structures of contemporary society. (Central America, Middle East, Africa, etc.). Special photo needs include "Third World societies, labor activities, environmental issues and war resistance." Captions and credit information required.
Making Contact & Terms: Query with photocopies to be kept on file for possible future assignments. SASE. Reports in 1 month. Pays $200/b&w cover photo; $30-150/b&w inside photo; $150/b&w full-page. Pays on publication. Credit line given. Buys one-time rights. Simultaneous submissions and previously published work fine.
Tips: "Interested in photo essays, and in images that make a visual statement."

The point of this picture, explains photographer Jim West, was "to illustrate the labor organizing that's sweeping South Korea." Noting that he queried to The Progressive on the story idea first, West said he knew it "would be of interest" to the magazine because of its coverage of similar themes. When West contacted the magazine, he also mentioned that he had photos to go with the story, and so the magazine asked him to supply both the text and illustration. He received $75 for the text and $25 for the photo. Another magazine, Union, also paid him $300 for a color version and a similar story.

THE QUARTER HORSE JOURNAL, Box 32470, Amarillo TX 79120. (806)376-4811. Executive Editor: Audie Rackley. Monthly magazine. Circ. 70,000. Emphasizes breeding and training of quarter horses. Buys first North American serial rights and occasionally buys all rights. Photos purchased with accompanying ms only. Pays on acceptance. Reports in 2-3 weeks. SASE. Free sample copy and editorial guidelines.
B&W: Uses 5×7 or 8×10 glossy prints. Captions required. Pays $50-250 for text/photo package.
Color: Uses 2¼×2¼, 35mm or 4×5 transparencies and 8×10 glossy prints; "we don't accept color prints on matte paper." Captions required. Pays $50-250 for text/photo package.
Cover: Pays $150 for first publication rights.
Tips: "Materials should be current and appeal or be helpful to both children and adults." No photos of other breeds. "The only freelance photos we use are for our covers. Write for particulars."

QUILT WORLD, QUICK & EASY QUILTING, STITCH 'N SEW QUILTS, 306 E. Parr Rd., Berne IN 46711. (219)589-8741. Editor: Sandra L. Hatch. Bimonthly. Quarterly (*Quilting Omnibook*). Emphasizes quilts. Readers are quilters, traditionally oriented, not contemporary. Circ. 120-140,000. Sample copy $2.50.
Photo Needs: Uses 30-50 photos/issue 75% supplied by freelancers. Needs photos of quilts—close-ups and set-ups with 1 over-all photo of quilt. Special needs include coverage of shows all over country and the world. Model release preferred; captions required.
Making Contact & Terms: Send unsolicited photos by mail for consideration; provide resume, business card, brochure, flyer or tearsheets to be kept on file for possible future assignments. Uses 35mm and 2¼ × 2¼ transparencies. SASE. Reports in 4 weeks. Pays $50/color cover photo; $15/b&w inside photo; $15/color inside photo. Pays on publication usually. Credit line given. Buys all rights. Will negotiate with photographer unwilling to sell all rights. Previously published work OK.
Tips: "Quilts are difficult to photograph, especially at shows, You should know something about the patterns. We have printed most common ones. I prefer the convenience of having photographers in many locations."

*RADIANCE, The Magazine for Large Women, Box 31703, Oakland CA 94604. (415)482-0680. Publisher/Editor: Alice Ansfield. Consumer publication. Quarterly magazine. "We're a positive/self-esteem magazine for large women. We have diverse readership, 90% women, ages 25-70 from all ethnic groups, lifestyles and interests." Circ. 25,000. Estab. 1984. Sample copy for $2.50, 8½ × 11 SASE and 1 first-class stamp. Photo guidelines not available.
Photo Needs: Uses 15+ photos/issue; 100% supplied by freelance photographer. Needs portraits, cover shots, fashion photos. Our photo needs are "more of what we're already doing." Model release and photo captions preferred.
Making Contact & Terms: Arrange a personal interview to show portfolio; send unsolicited photos by mail for consideration; provide resume, business card, brochure, flyer or tearsheets to be kept on file for possible assignments. SASE. Reports in 1-2 months. Pays $1-200/color cover photo; $15-25/ b&w inside photo; $2,200/color page rate; $975/b&w page rate; $8-12/hour; $400/day. Pays on acceptance and publication. Credit line given. Buys one-time rights. Simultaneous submissions OK.
Tips: In photographer's porfolio or samples wants to see "clear, crisp photos, creativity, setting, etc." Recommends freelancers "get to know the magazine they're talking with a little bit. Work with the publisher (or photo editor) and get to know " his requirements. "Try to help the magazine with its goals."

RAILROAD MODEL CRAFTSMAN, Box 700, Newton NJ 07860. (201)383-3355. Editor: W. Schaumburg. Monthly. Emphasizes scale model railroading. Readers are adults interested in the hobby of model railroading. Circ. 75,000. Sample copy $2.50. Photo guidelines free with SASE.
Photo Needs: Uses 100+ photos/issue; 95% supplied by freelance photographers. Needs photos of creative and good railroad modeling, as well as photos accompanying "how-to" articles. Reviews photos with accompanying ms only. Model release preferred; captions required.
Making Contact & Terms: SASE. Reports in 1 month. Pays $125/color cover photo. Pays on publication. Credit line given. Buys all rights. Will negotiate with a photographer unwilling to sell all rights.

RANCH & COAST MAGAZINE, Suite 204, 462 Stevens Ave., Solana Beach CA 92075-2065. (619)481-7659. Editor: Kit Ladwig. Monthly magazine. Circ. 50,000. Sample copy $2.50.
Photo Needs: Uses 30 photos/issue; 100% supplied by freelance photographers. Needs animal/wildlife, travel, scenics, how-to, and any other shots that convey Southern California living. Foresees some "on assignment" work in next year. Model release and photo captions required.
Making Contact & Terms: Arrange a personal interview to show portfolio; query with resume of credits and list of stock photo subjects; provide business card, brochure, flyer or tearsheets to be kept on file for possible assignments. Cannot return unsolicited material. Pays $500/day. Pays on acceptance. Credit line given. Buys one-time rights.

RAND MCNALLY ROAD ATLAS, 8255 N. Central Park, Skokie IL 60076. (708)673-9100. Retail Marketing Manager: Anne Adams. Annually. Emphasizes domestic auto travel. Readers are adults 25-65. Sample copy for 12 × 16 SASE. Photo guidelines free with SASE.
Photo Needs: Uses 1 (cover) photo/issue. Needs photos of vacation-oriented summer scenery with paved road with later model auto(s) on it. No RVs, trucks; no heavy traffic shots. Other needs include several dozen line extensions of this product which require similar annual cover photo updates. Model release and captions required; location clearly identified.
Making Contact & Terms: Query with samples. Reports in 1 month. Pays up to $500/color cover photo. Pays on acceptance. Credit line given. Buys one-time rights. Simultaneous submissions and previously published work OK.

Tips: "Current shots are a must. For our travel guides and cover, we need clean, colorful 4×5 photos appropriate for destinations. For covers, we need plenty of blue sky above the subject."

RANGER RICK, 8925 Leesburg Pike, Vienna VA 22184-0001. Photo Editor: Robert L. Dunne. Monthly magazine. Circ. 850,000. Estab. 1967. For children interested in the natural world, wildlife, conservation and ecology; age 6-12. Buys 400 photos annually; 90% from freelancers. Credit line given. Buys first serial rights and right to reuse for promotional purposes at half the original price. Submit portfolio of 20-40 photos and a list of available material. Photos purchased with or without accompanying ms, but query first on articles. Pays 3 months before publication. Reports in 2 weeks. SASE. Previously published work OK. Sample copy $2; free photo guidelines.

Subject Needs: Wild animals (birds, mammals, insects, reptiles, etc.), humorous (wild animals), pet animals children would keep (no wild creatures), nature (involving children), wildlife (US and foreign), photo essay/photo feature (with captions), celebrity/personality (involved with wildlife—adult or child) and children (age 6-12, especially girls or racial minorities) doing things involving wild animals, outdoor activities (caving, snowshoeing, backpacking), crafts, recycling and helping the environment. No plants, weather or scenics. No soft focus, grainy, or weak color shots.

Color: Uses original transparencies. Pays $180 (half page or less); $480 (2-page spread).

Cover: Uses original color transparencies. Uses vertical format. Allow space in upper left corner or across top for insertion of masthead. Prefers "rich, bright color." Pays $300.

Tips: "Come in close on subjects." Wants no "obvious flash." Mail transparencies inside 20-pocket plastic viewing sheets, backed by cardboard, in a manila envelope. "Don't waste time and postage on fuzzy, poor color shots. Do your own editing (we don't want to see 20 shots of almost the same pose). We pay by reproduction size. Check *printed* issues to see our standards of quality which are high. Looking for fresh, colorful, clean images. New approaches to traditional subject matter welcome. If you have a choice, work with girls or minority children and you'll increase your sales chances."

RELAX, 2333 Waukegan Rd., Bannockburn IL 60015. (708)940-8333. Editor-in-Chief: Mary Kaye Stray. Monthly. Emphasizes global travel. Readers are practicing physicians in the specialties of cardiology, family practice, internal medicine, osteopathy and psychiatry. Circ. 120,000. Sample copy free with SASE with $2.40 postage. Photo guidelines free with SASE.

Photo Needs: Buys about 50 color/issue; 45 supplied by freelance photographers. Needs photos of destinations—scenes, people, and activities that help define the character of the place. Transparencies captions required.

Making Contact & Terms: Query with list of stock photo subjects. SASE. Reports in 1 month. Pays $450/color cover photo; inside photo "depends on size"; $250-750/text/photo package. Pays on publication. Credit line given. Buys one-time rights for photos. Previously published work OK; "not exact photos; not similar market."

Tips: "Photos should make an impact, create interest, and make a lasting impression. Pictures and text should support each other. Send a variety of original color slides: overview, close-up, verticals, horizontals, scenes, people, actions."

*RELIX MAGAZINE, Box 94, Brooklyn NY 11229. (212)645-0818. Editor: Toni A. Brown. Bimonthly. Circ. 30,000. Estab. 1974. Emphasizes rock and roll music. Readers are music fans, ages 13-40. Sample copy $3.

Photo Needs: Uses about 50 photos/issue; "about 30%" supplied by freelance photographers; assignment—20%; stock—80%. Needs photos of "music artists—in concert and candid, backstage, etc." Special needs: "Photos of rock groups, especially the Grateful Dead, San Francisco-oriented groups and sixties related bands."

Making Contact & Terms: Send 5×7 or larger b&w and color prints by mail for consideration. SASE. Reports in 1 month. "We try to report immediately; occasionally we cannot be sure of use." Pays $100-150/b&w or color cover; $10-50/b&w inside full page; $40-150/color photo. Pays on publication. Credit line given. Buys all rights. Simultaneous submissions and previously published material OK.

Tips: "B&w photos should be printed on grade 4 or higher for best contrast."

*REPTILE & AMPHIBIAN MAGAZINE, RD3, Box 3709, Pottsville PA 17901. (717)622-1098. Editor: Dr. Norman Frank. Bimonthly magazine. Emphasizes reptiles and amphibians. Readers are college-educated, interested in nature and animals, familiar with basics of herpetology, many are breeders and conservation oriented. Circ. 5,000. Estab. 1989. Sample copy $4. Photo guidelines with SASE.

Photo Needs: Uses 20-30 photo/issue; 80% supplied by freelance photographers. Needs photos of related subjects. Model release and captions preferred; clearly identify animals. Photos purchased with or without ms.

Making Contact & Terms: Query with list of stock photo subjects. Send unsolicited photos by mail for consideration. Provide resume, business card, brochure, flyer or tearsheets to kept on file for possible assignments. Send b&w and glossy prints; 35mm transparencies. SASE. Reports in 2 weeks. Pays $25-50/color cover photo; $25/color inside photo; and $10/b&w inside photo. Pays on acceptance. Credit line given. Buys one-time and first North American serial rights. Considers previously published work.
Tips: In photographer's samples, looks for quality—eyes in-focus. "Avoid field-guide type photos— try to get shots with action and/or which have 'personality.' "

RESTAURANT ROW MAGAZINE, Suite P-10, 100 Ocean Gate, Long Beach CA 90802. (213)437-6565. Editor: Ron Hodges. Monthly. Emphasizes restaurants, resorts, food, wine, spirits, celebrities in these contexts. An affluent readership through home delivery, through restaurants and hotels. Circ. 50,000 mostly free targeted distribution. Sample copy free with 9×12 SAE with $1 postage.
Photo Needs: Uses about 25 photos/issue; 2 supplied by freelance photographers. Needs photos almost always related to specific subjects in articles, however, striking photos, illusionary photos or trick photos will be considered. Special needs include culinary olympics in Frankfort, Germany. Model release and captions preferred.
Making Contact & Terms: Query with samples and list of stock photo subjects. Send b&w or color prints; 35mm, $2\frac{1}{4} \times 2\frac{1}{4}$, 4×5 or 8×10 transparencies by mail for consideration. Submit portfolio for review. SASE. Reports in 2 weeks. Pays $100-200/color cover photo; $10-50/b&w inside photo; $15-100/color inside photo; $25-300/text/photo package. Pays on publication. Credit line given if requested. Buys one-time rights. Simultaneous and previously published submissions OK.
Tips: "Because food and beverage is usually static, the use of special effects, chefs or celebrities add the needed interest. How-to photos can be of interest to demonstrate a recipe or technique."

RICHMOND SURROUNDINGS MAGAZINE, Ste. 110, 7814 Carousel Ln., Richmond VA 23294. (804)346-4130. Managing Editor: Frances Helm. Bimonthly magazine; "includes special newcomer annual edition." Emphasizes lifestyle, including business, health, education, leisure. Readers are upper income, college-educated, 30 and up. Circ. 20,000. Estab. 1979. Sample copy free with $8\frac{1}{2} \times 11$ SASE and $1.50 postage.
Photo Needs: Special photo needs, creative cover, editorial humor, advertising. 90% freelance photography in given issue from assignment and 10% from freelance stock. Model release and photo captions required.
Making Contact & Terms: Query with samples, send unsolicited photos by mail for consideration. Provide resume, business card, brochure, flyer or tearsheets to be kept on file for possible future assignments. Send 5×7 glossy transparencies, b&w contact sheet, color negatives. SASE. Reports in 4-6 weeks. Pays $150/b&w cover photo and $30-400/color cover photo, $25-150/b&w photo; $25-100/color photo; $10-100/hour; $100-500/day. Pays on publication. Credit line given. Buys all rights; willing to negotiate.
Tips: Looks for "creativity, photographs conveying emotion, as well as good technical quality. Be flexible. Be willling to accept lower fees for exposure and portfolio. Show versatility."

RIDER, 29901 Agoura Rd., Agoura CA 91301. (818)991-4980. Editor: Mark Tuttle. Monthly magazine. Circ. 160,000. For dedicated motorcyclists with emphasis on long-distance touring, with coverage also of general street riding, commuting and sport riding. Needs human interest, novelty and technical photos; color photos to accompany feature stories about motorcycle tours. Buys first-time rights. Query first. Photos rarely purchased without accompanying ms. Pays on publication. Reports in 4 weeks. SASE. Sample copy $2 with $8\frac{1}{2} \times 11$ SAE. Free guidelines.
B&W: Send 8×10 glossy or matte prints. Captions required. Pay is included in total purchase price with ms.
Color: Send 35mm transparencies. Captions required. Pay is included in total purchase price with ms.
Tips: "We emphasize quality graphics and color photos with good visual impact. Photos should be in character with accompanying ms and should include motorcyclists engaged in natural activities. Read our magazine before contacting us."

RIVER RUNNER MAGAZINE, Box 697, Fallbrook CA 92028. (619)723-8155. Editor: Rand Green. Published 7 times/year. Emphasizes whitewater river running. Readers are predominately male, college grads, aged 18-40. Circ. 18,000. Sample copy $2.50; photo guidelines free with SASE.
Photo Needs: Uses 30 + photos/issue; all supplied by freelance photographers. Needs shots of canoeing, kayaking, rafting or anything that might be of interest to whitewater enthusiasts. Reviews transparencies with or without accompanying ms.
Making Contact & Terms: Query with samples, list of stock photo subjects; send b&w prints, 35mm transparencies by mail for consideration. SASE. Reports in 1 month. Pays $125/color cover, $15-65/ inside b&w, $20-175/inside color photo. Pays on publication. Credit line given. Buys first North Ameri-

can serial rights. Simultaneous submissions in nonrelated publications OK.

Tips: "We like to see a mix of tight, action shots, with more expansive views showing the river environment. Study us. Don't submit flower and birds and such unless they directly relate to a river feature. Shoot more verticals; magazine pages are vertical."

ROAD KING MAGAZINE, 23060 S. Cicero, Richton Park IL 60471. (708)481-9240. Editor: William A. Coop. Photo Editor: Rich Vurva. Bimonthly magazine. Emphasizes trucks, truckers and trucking. Readers are over-the-road, long-haul truckers. Circ. 224,000. Sample copy free with 6×9 SAE and 85¢ postage.

Photo Needs: Uses 20-25 photos/issue; 10-15 supplied by freelance photographers. Needs photos of trucks, truckstops and facilities, truckers. "We will need and use freelancers to accompany our reporters gathering stories. Our reporters also take back-up pictures simultaneously." Model release required.

Making Contact & Terms: "Let us know who you are, where you are, if you are available for story assignments and your day rate." SASE. Pays $150-250/text/photo package. Buys all rights.

THE ROANOKER, Box 12567, Roanoke VA 24026. (703)989-6138. Editor: Kurt Rheinheimer. Monthly. Circ. 14,000. Emphasizes Roanoke and western Virginia. Readers are upper income, educated people interested in their community. Sample copy $2.

Photo Needs: Uses about 60 photos/issue; most are supplied on assignment by freelance photographers. Need "travel and scenic photos in western Virginia; color photo essays on life in western Virginia." Model release preferred; captions required.

Making Contact & Terms: Send any size b&w or color glossy prints and transparencies by mail for consideration. SASE. Reports in 1 month. Pays $15-25/b&w photo; $20-35/color photo; $100/day. Payment negotiable. Pays on publication. Credit line given. Rights purchased vary. Simultaneous submissions and previously published work OK.

THE ROBB REPORT—The Magazine for Connoisseurs, One Acton Place, Acton MA 01720. (508)263-7749. Art Director: Russ Rocknak. Monthly. Emphasizes "the good life, e.g., yachting, exotic autos, investments, art, travel, lifestyle and collectibles." The magazine is aimed at the connoisseur who can afford an affluent lifestyle. Circ. 50,000.

Subject Needs: Uses 30-50 photos/issue. Generally uses existing photography; freelance work is assigned once story manuscripts have been reviewed for design treatment.

Specs: Uses 35mm (Kodachrome preferred), 2¼×2¼, 4×5 or 8×10 color transparencies.

Payment & Terms: Pay is individually negotiated prior to assignment. Rates vary depending on whether photography purchased is stock or assigned. Pays on publication. Prefers to buy all rights, but will negotiate. Credit lines given. Captions preferred.

Making Contact: Arrange a personal interview to show portfolio or send promotional mailers to be kept on file for possible future assignments. Photo guidelines are free with a SASE. Reports within 1 month.

ROCK & ICE, P.O. Box 3595, Boulder CO 80307. (303)499-8410. Managing Editor: Sally Moser. Bimonthly magazine. Emphasizes rock and ice climbing and mountaineering. Readers are predominantly professional males, ages 20-40. Circ. 16,500. Estab. 1982. Sample copy for $4. Photo guidelines free with SASE.

Photo Needs: Uses 40 photos/issue; 100% supplied by freelance photographers. Needs photos of climbing action shots, personalities and scenics. Buys photos with or without ms. Model release preferred; photo captions required.

Making Contact & Terms: Query with list of stock photo subjects. Send unsolicited photos by mail for consideration. Send b&w prints; 35mm, 2¼×2¼ and 4×5 transparencies. SASE. Pays $250/color cover photo; $100/color page rate; $100/b&w page rate. Pays on publication. Credit line given. Buys one-time rights and first North American serial rights. Previously published work OK.

ROLLING STONE, 745 5th Ave., New York NY 10151. (212)758-3800. Photo Editor: Laurie Kratochvil. Associate Photo Editor: Jodi Peckman. Emphasizes all forms of entertainment (music, movies, politics, news events).

Photo Needs: "All our photographers are freelance." Provide brochure, calling card, flyer, samples and tearsheet to be kept on file for future assignments. Needs famous personalities and rock groups in b&w and color. No editorial repertoire. SASE. Reports immediately. Pays $150-350/day.

Tips: "Drop off portfolio at front desk any Wednesday between 10 am and noon. Pickup same day between 4 pm and 6 pm or next day. Leave a card with sample of work to keep on file so we'll have it to remember."

RUNNER'S WORLD, 135 N. 6th St., Emmaus PA 18049. (215)967-5171. FAX: (215)965-5670. Executive Editor: Amby Burfoot. Photo Editor: M. T. B. Bois-Byrne. Monthly magazine. Emphasizes running. Readers are median aged: 32, 65% male; median income $37,000, college-ed. Circ. 435,000. Photo guidelines free with SASE.

Photo Needs: Uses 100 photos/issue; 55 supplied by freelance photographers; features are generally assigned; columns and departments often come from stock. Needs photos of action, features, photojournalism. Model release and captions preferred.

Making Contact & Terms: Query with samples; send b&w and color prints, and 35mm transparencies by mail for consideration; submit portfolio for review; provide resume, business card, brochure, flyer or tearsheets to be kept on file for possible future assignments. SASE. Pays as follows: color—$200/ full page, $125/half page, $75/quarter page, $300/spread; b&w—$100/full page, $60/half page, $35/ quarter page, $150/spread. Cover shot negotiable. Pays on publication. Credit line given. Photographic rights vary with assignment. Simultaneous submissions and previously published work OK.

Tips: "Become familiar with the publication and send photos in on spec. Also send samples that can be kept in our source file. Show full range of expertise; lighting abilities—quality of light—whether strobe sensitivity for people—portraits, sports, etc.. Both action and studio work if applicable, should be shown." Current trend is non-traditional treatment of sports coverage and portraits. Call prior to submitting work. Be familiar with running as well as the magazine.

RURAL HERITAGE, Box 516, Albia IA 52531. (515)932-5084. Publisher: D.H. Holle. Quarterly. Emphasizes "the draft horse, rural nostalgia, country antiques, country crafts." Published primarily for individuals interested in nostalgia, back-to-basics, ecology and rural life." Circ. 5,000. Estab. 1975. Sample copy for $4.50; photo guidelines for SASE.

Photo Needs: Uses about 60 photos/issue; 25 supplied by freelance photographers usually with accompanying mss. "Draft horse, mule and oxen photos showing beauty and power of these animals are most welcome. Also want human interest shots with owner, driver or farmer working with the animal. Capture the animal and people in creative and engaging angles." Special needs include draft horses captured in action in an attractive, attention-getting manner. Model release and captions preferred.

Making Contact & Terms: Send 5 × 7 b&w prints (limit: 10 prints/submission) by mail for consideration. SASE. Reports in 3 months. Payment varies. Pays $10-25/b&w photo; $10-25/color photo; pays more if mss included. Pays on acceptance. Credit line given. "Prefer to buy first rights."

Tips: "Peruse our magazine before sending any materials. Know magazine audience well and submit only photos that apply to the specific market. Clear photos that print well and exemplify the topics Rural Heritage covers.

SACRAMENTO MAGAZINE, 1021 Second St., Sacramento CA 95814. (916)446-7548. Managing Editor: Ann McCully. Design Director: Chuck Donald. Assistant Design Director: Derek Davalos. Emphasizes business, government, culture, food, outdoor recreation, and personalities for middle- to upper middle class, urban-oriented Sacramento residents. Monthly magazine. Circ. 27,000. Free photo guidelines.

Photo Needs: Uses about 40-50 photos/issue; mostly supplied by freelance photographers. "Photographers are selected on the basis of experience and portfolio strength. No work assigned on speculation or before a portfolio showing. Photographers are used on an assignment only basis. Stock photos used only occasionally. Most assignments are to area photographers and handled by phone. Photographers with studios, mobile lighting and other equipment have an advantage in gaining assignments. Darkroom equipment desirable but not necessary." Needs news photos, essay, avant-garde, still life, landscape, architecture, human interest and sports. All photography must pertain to Sacramento and environs. Captions required.

Making Contact & Terms: Send slides, contact sheets (no negatives) by mail or arrange a personal interview to show portfolio. Also query with resume of photo credits or mail portfolio. SASE. Reports up to 4 weeks. Pays $5-45/hour; pays on acceptance. Average payment is $15-20/hour; all assignments are negotiated to fall within that range. Credit line given on publication. Buys rights on a work-for-hire basis. Will consider simultaneous submissions and previously published work, providing they are not in the Northern California area.

SADDLE & BRIDLE MAGAZINE, 375 N. Jackson Ave., St. Louis MO 63130. (314)725-9115. Editor: Jeffrey A. Thompson. Monthly magazine. Emphasizes show horses and the people involved with them. Readers are from ages 13-80; average age 35. Circ. 7,000. Sample copy $4 with 11 × 14 SAE and $1.50 postage.

Photo Needs: Uses about 350 photos/issue; 150 supplied by freelance photographers. (Customers pay for most of the photography.) Needs photos of animal shots of horses in action or natural. Also people shots. Photos purchased with accompanying ms only. Special subjects include photo essays on specific subjects involving the show horses (preparations, cooling down, the life of a groom, etc.). Model release and captions required.

Making Contact & Terms: Query with samples; query with list of stock photo subjects. SASE. Reports in 2 weeks. Payment for b&w inside photo negotiable. Pays on publication. Credit line given. Buys first North American serial rights. Simultaneous submissions and previously published work OK.
Tips: "It is important that the photographer be familiar with the show circuit and know how to best photograph the show animal."

SAILING, 125 E. Main St., Box 248, Port Washington WI 53074. (414)284-3494. Editor: Micca L. Hutchins. Monthly magazine. Circ. 40,000. Emphasizes sailing. Our theme is "the beauty of sail." Readers are sailors with great sailing experience – racing and cruising. Sample copy free with 11 × 15 SAE and $2.40 postage. Photo guidelines free with SASE.
Photo Needs: "We are a photo journal-type publication so about 50% of issue is photos. "Needs photos of exciting sailing action, onboard deck shots; sailor-type boat portraits seldom used. Special needs include largely b&w, some inside color – mainly good *sailing* (not simply sailboats) shots. "We must have area sailed, etc. identification."
Making Contact & Terms: Query with samples; send 8 × 10 glossy b&w prints, 35mm transparencies by mail for consideration. "Request guidelines first – a big help." SASE. Reports in 1 month. Pays $100/color cover photo; $15-50/b&w inside photo; $50-100/color inside photo (depends on size used); text/photo package by arrangement. Pays 30 days after publication. Credit line given. Buys one-time rights. Simultaneous submissions and previously published work OK "if not with other sailing publications who compete with us."
Tips: "We are looking for good, clean, sharp photos of sailing action – exciting shots are for us. No 'fly-spec' sails against the horizon – we use close work from a sailor's perspective. Please request a sample copy to become familiar with format. Knowledge of the sport of sailing a requisite for good photos for us."

SAILING WORLD, 5 John Clarke Rd., Newport RI 02840. (401)847-1588. FAX: (401)848-5048. Editor: John Burnham. Art Director: Rachel Cocroft. Magazine published monthly. Circ. 62,000. Estab. 1961. Emphasizes sailboat racing and performance cruising for sailors, upper income, age group 30s-40s. Credit line given. Pays on publication. Buys first North American serial rights. Reports in 1 month. Sample coy $2.50 with 10 × 12 SAE and $1.50 postage; free photo guidelines with SASE.
Subject Needs: "We will send an updated photo letter listing our needs on request. Freelance photography in a given issue: 20% assignment and 80% freelance stock. "We are using more 4/c photos and need high quality work." Covers most sailing races.
Cover: Uses 35mm and 2¼ × 2¼ color transparencies. Vertical and square (slightly horizontal) formats. Pays $500 for cover shot; regular color $50-150 (varies with use).
Tips: We look for photos that are unusual in composition, lighting, and/or color that feature performance sailing at its most exciting. We would like to emphasize speed, skill, fun and action. Photos must be of high quality. We prefer kodachrome 64 film. We have a format that allows us to feature work of exceptional quality. A knowledge of sailing and experience with on-the-water photography is really a requirement." Please call with specific questions or interests.

ST. LOUIS MAGAZINE, 612 N. 2nd, Box 88908, St. Louis MO 63188. (314)231-7200. Art Director: Christine Kiester. Jon Davis. Paid circ. 38,330. Emphasizes life in St. Louis for "those interested in the St. Louis area, recreation issues, lifestyles, etc."
Subject Needs: Celebrity/personality, documentary, fine art, scenic, local color, sport, human interest, travel, fashion/beauty and political. Photos purchased with or without accompanying mss. Freelancers supply 90% of the photos. Pays by assignment or on a per-photo basis.
Making Contact & Terms: Provide calling card, resume and samples to be kept on file for possible future assignments. Credit line given. Pays on publication. Arrange a personal interview or submit portfolio for review. SASE. Reports in 1 month. Sample copy $1.95 and free photo guidelines.
B&W: Uses 8 × 10 glossy prints. Pays $50-250/photo.
Color: Uses 35mm, 2¼ × 2¼ and 4 × 5 transparencies. Pays $100-300/photo.
Cover: Uses color covers only. Vertical format required. Pays $200-350/photo.
Tips: Prefers to see "b&w prints, color photos or transparencies of St. Louis people, events and places, fashion and history. Any printed samples, especially from magazines. Don't be a jack-of-all-trades. Any photographer who has an 'I can do it all' portfolio is not as likely to get a general assignment as a specialty photographer."

SALT WATER SPORTSMAN, 280 Summer St., Boston MA 02111. (617)439-9977. FAX: (617)439-9357. Editor: Barry Gibson. Monthly magazine. Circ. 135,000. Estab. 1939. Emphasizes all phases of salt water sport fishing for the avid beginner-to-professional salt water angler. "Only strictly marine sport fishing magazine in the world." Buys 1-3 photos/issue (including covers) without ms; 20-30 photos/issue with ms. Pays up to $750/text/photo package. Accepting slides and holding them for 1 year and will pay as used. Pays on acceptance. Buys one-time rights. Send material by mail for consideration or query with samples. SASE. Provide resume and tearsheets to be kept on file for possible future assignments. Reports in 1 month. Sample copy free with 9×11 SAE and $2 postage. Free photo guidelines.

Subject Needs: Salt water fishing photos. "Think scenery with human interest, mood, fishing action, storytelling close-ups of anglers in action. Make it come alive – and don't bother us with the obviously posed 'dead fish and stupid fisherman' back at the dock. Wants, on a regular basis, cover shots, vertical Kodachrome (or equivalent) original slides depicting salt water fishing action or 'mood.' "

B&W: Uses 8×10 glossy prints. Pay included in total purchase price with ms, or pays $20-200/photo.

Color: Uses 8×10 glossy prints and 35mm or 2¼×2¼ transparencies. Pay included in total purchase price with ms, or pays $50-400/photo.

Cover: Uses 35mm and 2¼×2¼ transparencies. Vertical format required. Pays $600 minimum/photo.

Accompanying Mss: Fact/feature articles dealing with marine sportfishing in the U.S., Canada, Caribbean, Central and South America. Emphasis on how-to. Free writer's guidelines.

Tips: "Prefers to see a selection of fishing action or mood – no scenics, lighthouses, birds, etc. – must be sport fishing oriented. Be familiar with the magazine and send us the type of things we're looking for. Example: no horizontal cover slides with suggestions it can be cropped etc. Don't send Ektachrome. We're using more 'outside' photography – that is, photos not submitted with ms package. Take lots of verticals and experiment with lighting. Most shots we get are too dark."

SANTA BARBARA MAGAZINE, 216 East Victoria St., Santa Barbara CA 93101. (805)965-5999. FAX: (805)965-7627. Editor: Janet Nancarrow. Photo Editor: Kimberly Kavish. Bimonthly magazine. Emphasizes Santa Barbara community and culture. Circ. 11,000. Estab. 1975. Sample copy $2.95 with 9×12 SASE.

Photo Needs: Uses 50-60 photos/issue; 40% supplied by freelance photographers. Needs portrait, environmental, architectural, travel, celebrity, et al. Reviews photos with accompanying ms only. Model release required; captions preferred.

Making Contact & Terms: Provide resume, business card, brochure, flyer or tearsheets to be kept on file for possible future assignments; "portfolio drop off Thursdays, pick up Fridays." Does not return unsolicited material. Reports in 4-6 weeks. Pays $75-250/b&w or color photo. Pays on acceptance. Credit line given. Buys first N.A. serial rights."

Tips: Prefers to see strong personal style and excellent technical ability. "Work needs to be oriented to our market. Know our magazine and its orientation before contacting me."

THE SATURDAY EVENING POST SOCIETY, Benjamin Franklin Literary & Medical Society, 1100 Waterway Blvd., Indianapolis IN 46202. (317)634-1100. Editor: Cory SerVaas, M.D. Photo Editor: Patrick Perry. Magazine published 9 times annually. Circ. 600,000. For family readers interested in travel, food, fiction, personalities, human interest and medical topics – emphasis on health topics. Prefers the photo essay over single submission. Prefers all rights. Model release required. Send photos for consideration. Provide business card to be kept on file for possible future assignments. Pays on publication. Reports in 1 month. SASE. Simultaneous submissions and previously published work OK. Sample copy $4; free photo guidelines with SASE.

B&W: Send 8×10 glossy prints. Pays $50 minimum/photo or by the hour; pays $150 minimum for text/photo package.

Color: Send 35mm or larger transparencies. Pays $75 minimum; $300/cover photo.

SCIENCE OF MIND MAGAZINE, 3251 West Sixth St., Los Angeles CA 90020. (213)388-2181. Editor: Kathy Juline. Photo Coordinator: Sheri Cady. Monthly. Emphasizes Science of Mind philosophy. Readers include positive thinkers, holistic healing, psychological thinkers. Circ. 100,000. Sample copy and photo guidelines free with 6×9 SASE.

Photo Needs: Uses 7-10 photos/issue; 4-8 supplied by freelance photographers. Needs scenic nature, sensitive (e.g., baby, baby animals, people situations). Reviews with or without accompanying ms.

Making Contact & Terms: Send 5×7, 8×10 b&w prints, high quality duplicate 35mm transparencies by mail for consideration. Include 6×9 SASE. Reports in 4 weeks. Pays $100/color cover photo, $25/inside b&w photo, $50/inside color photo. Pays 30 days after masthead date. Credit line given. Buys one-time rights unless otherwise specified. Simultaneous submissions and previously published work OK.

Tips: "First contact do not send more than 24 slides. Send duplicates only."

SCORE, Canada's Golf Magazine, 287 MacPherson Ave., Toronto, ON M4V 1A4 Canada. (416)928-2909. FAX: (416)928-1357. Managing Editor: John Gordon. Magazine published 7 times/year. Emphasizes golf. "The foundation of the magazine is Canadian golf and golfers." Readers are affluent, well-educated, 80% male, 20% female. Circ. over 125,000. Estab. 1980. Sample copy $2 (Canadian). Photo guidelines free with SAE with IRC.

Photo Needs: Uses between 15 and 20 photos/issue; approximately 95% supplied by freelance photographers. Needs "professional-quality, golf-oriented color and b&w material on prominent Canadian male and female pro golfers on the US PGA and LPGA tours, as well as the European and other international circuits, scenics, travel, closeups and full-figure." Model releases (if necessary) and captions required.

Making Contact & Terms: Query with samples and with list of stock photo subjects. Send 8 × 10 or 5 × 7 glossy b&w prints and 35mm or 2¼ × 2¼ transparencies by mail for consideration. Provide resume, business card, brochure, flyer or tearsheets to be kept on file for possible future assignments. SASE with IRC. Reports in 3 weeks. Pays $75-100/color cover photo, $30/b&w inside photo, $50/color inside photo, $40-65/hour, $320-520/day, and $80-2,000/job. Pays on acceptance. Credit line given. Buys all rights. Simultaneous submissions OK.

Tips: "When approaching *Score* with visual material, it is best to illustrate photographic versatility with a variety of lenses, exposures, subjects and light conditions. Golf is not a high-speed sport, but invariably presents a spectrum of location puzzles: rapidly changing light conditions, weather, positioning, etc. Capabilities should be demonstrated in query photos. Scenic material follows the same rule. Specific golf hole shots are certainly encouraged for travel features, but wide-angle shots are just as important, to 'place' the golf hole or course, especially if it is located close to notable landmarks or particularly stunning scenery. Approaching *Score* is best done with a clear, concise presentation. A picture is absolutely worth a thousand words, and knowing your market and your particular strengths will prevent a mutual waste of time and effort. Sample copies of the magazine are available and any photographer seeking to work with *Score* is encouraged to investigate it prior to querying."

SCUBA TIMES MAGAZINE, Ste. 16, 14110 Perdido Key Dr., Pensacola FL 32507. (904)492-7805. Art Director: Blair Fischrupp. Bimonthly magazine. Emphasizes scuba diving. Circ. 30,000. Sample copy $3. Photo guidelines free with SASE.

Photo Needs: Uses 50-60 photos/issue; 100% supplied by freelance photographers. Needs animal/wildlife shots, travel, scenics, how-to, all with an underwater focus. Provides an editorial schedule with SASE. Model release and photo captions preferred.

Making Contact & Terms: Send unsolicited photos (dupes only) by mail for consideration. Send 35mm transparencies. SASE. Reports in 1 to 2 months. Pays $75-100/color cover photo, $75/color page rate and $75/b&w page rate. Pays 30 days after publication. Credit line given. Buys one-time rights. Previously published work OK "under certain circumstances."

Tips: In portfolio or samples, likes to see "broad range of samples, majority underwater."

SEA, The Magazine of Western Boating, Suite C-2, 1760 Monrovia, Costa Mesa CA 92627. Mailing Address: Box 1579, Newport Beach CA 92663. (714)646-0173. FAX: (714)642-8980. Executive Editor: Linda Yuskaitis. Art Director: Jeffrey Fleming. Monthly magazine. Circ. 60,000. Emphasizes "recreational boating in 13 western states (including some coverage of Mexico and British Columbia) for owners of recreational power boats." Sample copy and photo guidelines free with 9½ × 13 SASE.

Photo Needs: Uses about 50-75 photos/issue; most supplied by freelance photographers; 30% assignment—"but this is growing"; 70% requested from freelancers existing photo files or submitted unsolicited. Needs people enjoying boating activity and scenics shots; shots which include parts or all of a boat are preferred." Special needs include "square or vertical-format shots involving power boats for cover consideration." Photos should have West Coast angle. Model release required; captions preferred.

Making Contact & Terms: Query with samples. SASE. Reports in 1 month. Pays $250/color cover photo; inside photo rate vary according to size published. Range is from $25 for b&w and $50-150 for color. Pays on publication. Credit line given. Buys one-time North American rights.

Tips: "We are looking for sharp color transparencies with good composition showing pleasureboats in action, and people having fun aboard boats in a West Coast location. We also use studio shots of marine products and do personality profiles. Black and white also accepted, for a limited number of stories. Color preferred. Send samples or work with a query letter and a resume or clips of previously published photos."

SEACOAST LIFE MAGAZINE, Box 594, North Hampton NH 03862. (603)964-9898. Art Director: Heidi Illingworth. Bimonthly. Emphasizes lifestyle and general interest to New England Seacoast area: Newburyport, Massachusetts to Kennebunk, Maine. Readers are urban upwardly mobile, rural upwardly mobile, professional, nature-oriented. Circ. 20,000. Sample copy $2.50 with 9 × 12 SAE and $1.85 postage. Photo guidelines free with SASE.

Photo Needs: Uses about 30 photos/issue; 15 supplied by freelance photographers. "We are open to any photos (color) that reflect our circulation area—wildlife, nature, seasons, outdoor sports, beaches, boats, etc." Special needs include seasonal themes, Christmas holidays, Americana, nautical, home & gardens etc. Model release and captions required.

Making Contact & Terms: Query with samples. Send 35mm, 2¼×2¼ or 4×5 transparencies by mail for consideration. SASE. Reports in 6 weeks or less. Pays $150/color cover photo; $40-65/color page, depending on location. Pays 30 days after publication. Credit line given. Simultaneous submissions and previously published work (published outside circulation area only) OK.

Tips: "Samples should directly relate to our market and should be available for immediate publication. We need only highest quality transparencies, displayed in sleeves. Identify each side with photographer's name and subject matter; shoot location preferable. We do not require previous publishing credentials, just great shots. Specify whether submissions may be retained on file longer than 6 weeks. Know the magazine, know the terrain. Surprise us."

SELF, 350 Madison Ave., New York NY 10017. (212)880-8834. Editor-in-Chief: Alexandra Penney. Emphasizes self-improvement and physical and mental well being for women of all ages. Monthly magazine. Circ. 1,091,000.

Photo Needs: Uses up to 200 photos/issue; all supplied by freelancers. Works with photographers on assignment basis only. Provide tearsheets to be kept on file for possible future assignments. Pays $200 day rate. Needs photos emphasizing health, beauty, medicine, relationships and psychology relating to women.

*SENIOR MAGAZINE, 3565 Sough Higuera, San Luis Obispo CA 93401. (805)544-8711. Pubisher: Gary Suggs. Monthly magazine, tabloid. Emphasizes "the wonderful life over 50. Readers are m/f, ages 50 and older. Circ. 500,000. Estab. 1981. Sample copies for 9×12 SAE and $1.25 postage.

Photo Needs: Uses 5-15 photos/issue; most supplied by freelance photographers. Needs mainly personality shots. Special photo needs include WWII photos—people, planes and famous wartime people. Buys photos with or without ms. Model release required.

Making Contact & Terms: Query with list of stock photo subjects. SASE. Reports in 1-2 weeks. Pays $100/b&w cover photo; $50-75/b&w inside photo. Pays on acceptance. Credit lines given. Buys one-time rights, also second reprint rights. Previously published work OK if not from competitive 'senior' publications.

Tips: "We really need photos of the famous; photos of unknowns and people over 50 with ms, only."

*SHAPE, 21100 Erwin St., Woodland Hills CA 91367. Art Director: Charles Hess. Monthly magazine. Emphasizes women's health and fitness: exercise, psychology, portraits, fashion and beauty. Readers are women ages 18-35. Circ. 800,000.

Photo Needs: Uses 40-80 photos/issue; 100% supplied by freelance photographers. Needs photos of exercise, psychology, portrait, lifestyle, fashion, beauty and travel. Model release and photo captions required.

Making Contact & Terms: Provide resume, business card, brochure, flyer or tearsheets to be kept on file for possible assignments. Pays on publication. Credit line given. Buys all rights. Rights negotiable. Simultaneous submissions and previously published work OK.

*SILVER CIRCLE, 4900 Rivergrade Rd., Irwindale CA 91706. Editor: Jay Binkly. Quarterly magazine. Readers are ages 50 and older, middle-upper income men and women. Circ. 600,000. Estab. 1973. Sample copy $1.50 with SAE.

Photo Needs: Uses 15-20 photos/issue; 100% supplied by freelance photographers. Needs photos of scenics, how-to, active couples, personal finance, consumer interests and travel. Buys photos with or without manuscript. Uses 35mm transparencies. Model release and photo captions required.

Making Contact & Terms: Provide resume, business card, brochure, flyer or tearsheets to be kept on file for possible assignments. SASE. Reports in 3 weeks. Pays $500/color cover photo; $25/color inside photo; $200/color page rate. Pays on acceptance. Credit line given. Buys one-time rights.

SINGLELIFE MILWAUKEE, 606 W. Wisconsin Ave., Milwaukee WI 53203. (414)271-9700. Art Director: Paul Rosanski. Bimonthly. Emphasizes recreation and special interests for single adults. Readers are 18- to 70-year-old single adults. Circ. 24,000. Sample copy $2.50.

Photo Needs: Uses about 20 photos/issue; all supplied by freelance photographers. Need photos of skiing, biking, dining, dancing, picnics, sailing—single people, couples or groups of people in recreational settings. Model release and captions required.

Making Contact & Terms: Send b&w or color glossy prints, 2¼×2¼ transparencies, b&w contact sheet by mail for consideration. SASE. Pays $30-100/b&w photo; $40-300/color photo; $50-300/job. Pays on publication. Credit line given. Buys all rights. Previously published work OK.

Tips: "We look for recreational scenes (active and passive) of couples or individuals in a portfolio. We also are getting very active in fashion photography."

SKATE MAGAZINE, Box 81846, Lincoln NE 68501. (402)489-8811. Art Director: Janet Denison. A recreational and competitive roller skating magazine for readers ages 6-16; brochures and other promotional pieces also published. Buys 20 photos/year; gives 4 assignments/year. Photos used in brochures, newsletters, and magazines. Sample copy free with 9×12 SAE and $1.24 postage.

Subject Needs: Athletes in regional and national roller skating competitions, and all aspects of roller skating. "We also have a section called 'Gears' for new products coming on the market."

Specs: "No set specs—negotiated per assignment."

Payment & Terms: Pay negotiated. Credit line given. Rights negotiated per photo or project. Model release required; captions preferred.

Making Contact: Provide resume, business card, brochure, flyer or tearsheets to be kept on file for possible future assignments. Solicits photos by assignment only. SASE. Reports in 1 month.

*SKI, 2 Park Ave, New York NY 10016. (212)779-5000. FAX: (212)779-5469. Editor: Dick Needham. Art Director: Steve Wierzbicki. Monthly. Circ. 440,000. Estab. 1936. Emphasizes skiing for skiers.

Photo Needs: All photos supplied by freelance photographers, 20% assigned; 80% freelance stock. Model release and captions required.

Making Contact & Terms: Send 35mm, 2¼×2¼ or 4×5 transparencies by mail (dupes OK) for consideration. SASE. Reports in 1 week. Pays $750 color cover photo; $50-250/b&w inside photo, $50-350/color inside photo; $75-100/b&w half page; $150 b&w page, $250/color page; $200-600/job; $75-750/b&w or color photo; by the day, $350; $500-850 for text/photo package. Pays on acceptance. Credit line given. Buys one-time rights.

Tips: "I look for a particular style or point of view that the photographer may have. We are getting more involved with the 'ski-lifestyle' in an effort to show our readers what the *total* ski experience will be like—food, lodging, local color."

SKI CANADA, 227 Front St. E, Toronto, ON M5A 1E8 Canada. (416)368-0185. FAX: (416)941-9113. Editor: Cathy Carl. Monthly magazine published six times a year, fall and winter only. Readership is 75% male, ages 19-40, with high income. Circ. 60,000. Sample copy free with SASE.

Photo Needs: Uses 80 photos/issue; 100% supplied by freelance photographers. Needs photos of skiing—competition, equipment, travel (within Canada and abroad), instruction, news and trends. Model release required; photo captions preferred.

Making Contact & Terms: Send unsolicited photos by mail for consideration. Provide resume, business card, brochure, flyer or tearsheets to be kept on file for possible assignments. Send color and 35mm transparencies. SASE. Reports in 1 month. Pays $100/photo/page or smaller; $200/ photo larger than 1 page; cover $400; rates are for (b&w or color). Pays on publication. Credit line given. Buys first N.A. serial rights. Simultaneous submissions OK.

Tips: In samples, wants to see "sharp, good action shots. Also, shots that depict ski areas accurately, in good variety." And "be a skier. In addition to payment receives 1 issue of our summer magazine SunSports—on newsstands 1st week of May each year—all summer sports: tennis, golf, windsurfing, waterskiing, cycling, footwear, fashion, beach activities, triathlon, etc."

SKI RACING MAGAZINE, Box 1125, Waitsfield VT 05673-1125. (802)496-7700. Editor: Andrew Bigfard. Published 20 times/year by Ski Racing International. First issue each season in September is a glossy magazine; 19 issues published between October and May are tabloid newpapers. Circ. 40,000. Covers ski competition, alpine, nordic and freestyle, from junior to World Cup levels. Our readers are serious skiers—racers, coaches and those involved in the ski industry. Sample copy and photo guidelines with SASE.

Photo Needs: Use about 25 photos per issue, most supplied by photographers working with Sports File, Ski Racing International's photo agency. Occasionally purchases photos from unaffiliated freelancers.

Making Contact & Terms: All photos are taken on assignment. "In most cases, we negotiate a flat fee for a photo shoot and supply photographers with film. The photos taken belong to Ski Racing and Sports File, and the photographer receives a percentage of any revenue generated by sale of the photos to Ski Racing advertisers or Sports File clients." Credit line given.

Tips: "We shoot only color slides, usually Fuji 100. For us, the perfect photographer is someone who can provide sharp photos of World Cup downhillers traveling at 80 mph and then head for the bottom of the course to get colorful personality shots in the finish area. Send a resume and samples during the summer if you're interested in working the following winter."

SKIING MAGAZINE, 40 E. 33 St., New York NY 10016. (212)779-5000. FAX: (212)779-5465. Art Director: Jeffrey Tennyson. Published monthly (September through March). Circ. 454,266. Emphasizes skiing for Alpine skiers. Photo guidelines free with SASE.

Photo Needs: Uses 75-120 photos/issue; 75% supplied by freelance photographers; 70% from assignment and 10% freelance stock.. Needs photos of ski action, people, resorts and competitions. Name on slides and captions required.

Making Contact & Terms: Query with dupes, not original samples or with list of stock photo subjects; send 8×10 b&w prints, 35mm transparencies or b&w contact sheet by mail for consideration; submit portfolio for review; or provide resume, business card, brochure, flyer or tearsheets to be kept on file for possible future assignments. SASE. Reports in 1 month. Pays $750/color cover photo; $350/color full page photo; $100 minimum color inside photo; $250/b&w full page photo; $75 minimum/b&w inside photo. Pays on acceptance. Buys one-time rights.

Tips: "Show work *specifically* suited to *Skiing*—and be familiar with the magazine before submitting We look for skiing experience—ski action, ski people and ski resorts. High quality a must, unique lighting and a sense of drama. Trend is fashionable clothing, bright colors and people skiing not as much jumping photos. Study the publication, variety is always good. (action, people, scenics)."

SKIN DIVER, Suite 503, 8490 Sunset Blvd., Los Angeles CA 90069. (213)854-2222. Editor/Publisher: Bill Gleason. Executive Editor: Bonnie J. Cardone. Monthly magazine. Circ. 219,035. Emphasizes scuba diving in general, dive travel and equipment. "The majority of our contributors are divers-turned-writers." Photos purchased with accompanying ms only; "particularly interested in adventure stories." Buys 60 photos/year; 85% supplied by freelance photographers. Pays $50/published page. Credit line given. Pays on publication. Buys one-time rights. Send material by mail for consideration. SASE. Free photo guidelines.

Subject Needs: Adventure; how-to; human interest; humorous (cartoons); wreck diving, game diving, local diving. All photos must be related to underwater subjects. Model release required; captions preferred.

B&W: Uses 5×7 and 8×10 glossy prints.

Color: Uses 35mm and 2¼×2¼ transparencies.

Cover: Uses 35mm color transparencies. Vertical format preferred.

Accompanying Mss: Free writer's guidelines.

Tips: "Read the magazine; submit only those photos that compare in quality to the ones you see in *Skin Diver.*"

SKY (Inflight Magazine of Delta Air Lines), Halsey Publishing Co., 12955 Biscayne Blvd., N. Miami FL 33181. (305)893-1520. Photo Editor: Coni Kaufman. Monthly magazine. Emphasizes general interest and business/finance topics. Circ. 410,000 (print run). Sample copy $3 and 9×12 SASE.

Photo Needs: Uses about 70 photos/issue; 35% supplied by freelance photographers. Needs photos of travel, consumer, entertainment, business, lifestyle, sports, technology, collectibles. Reviews photos with accompanying ms only unless submitting for "Cityscapes" department. "We are actively seeking materials for 'Cityscapes' department, our photo end page that features interesting perspectives on Delta destination cities (vertical format only)." Model release and captions required.

Making Contact & Terms: Send 35mm and 2¼×2¼ transparencies by mail for consideration; provide resume, buisness card, brochure, flyer or tearsheets to be kept on file for possible future assignments. SASE. Reports in 1 month. Pays $300/color cover photo; $50/color inside photo; $300-500/text/photo package. Pays on publication. Credit line given. Buys one-time rights. Simultaneous submissions and previously published work OK.

SNOW WEEK, Ste. 101, 319 Barry Ave., Wayzata MN 55391. (612)476-2200. Editor: Dick Hendricks. Tabloid published 16 times from July through March. Emphasizes snowmobile racing. Circ. 30,000. Photo guidelines free with SASE.

Photo Needs: Uses 30-40 photos/issue; 30% supplied by freelance photographers. Needs race photos. Purchases photos with accompanying ms only. Model release preferred; photo captions required.

Making Contact & Terms: Query with resume of credits. SASE. Reports in 3 weeks. Pays $75/b&w cover photo, $25/b&w inside photo and $50-250/photo/text package. Pays on publication. Credit line given. Buys first N.A. serial rights.

SNOWMOBILE MAGAZINE, Suite 101, 319 Barry Ave., Wayzata MN 55391. (612)476-2200. Editor/Associate Publisher: Dick Hendricks. Published 3 times/year. Emphasizes "snowmobiles and snowmobiling, people, industry, places." Readers are 500,000 owners of two or more registered snowmobiles. Sample copy $2. Photo guidelines free with SASE.

Photo Needs: Uses about 70 photos/issue; 5 or more supplied by freelance photograhers. Needs "scenic photography of winter, primarily with snowmobiles as primary subject interest—travel slant is needed—people." Special needs include "scenics, great snowmobiling tour places, snowmobiling families and family activities, snowmobiles together with other winter activities." Written release preferred.

Making Contact & Terms: Query with samples. SASE. Reports in 1 month. Pays $25 and up/b&w inside photo; $40 and up/color inside photo. Pays on publication. Credit line negotiable. Buys one-time rights. Simultaneous submissions and previously published work OK.

Tips: "Snowmobiling is a beautiful and scenic sport that most often happens in places and under conditions that make good pictures difficult; capture one of these rare moments for us and we'll buy."

SNOWMOBILE WEST, 520 Park Ave., Idaho Falls ID 83402. (208)524-7000. Editor: Steve Janes. Magazine published 4 times/year. Circ. 135,000. Emphasizes where to go snowmobiling, new machine previews and tips on modifying. Buys 6-8 photos/issue. Credit line given. Pays on publication. Buys one-time rights. Send material by mail for consideration or phone. SASE. Reports in 1 month. Sample copy $1; free photo guidelines. Provide business card and tearsheets to be kept on file for possible future assignments.

Subject Needs: Celebrity/personality, photo essay/photo feature, special effects/experimental, sport, how-to, human interest, nature and travel. Captions preferred.

B&W: Uses 8×10 glossy prints. Pays $5-15/photo.

Color: Uses 35mm transparencies. Pays $10-35/photo.

Cover: Uses 35mm color transparencies. Square format preferred. Pays $25-50/photo.

Accompanying Mss: Seeks features on snowmobiling. Free writer's guidelines.

Tips: "We want photos that focus on people having fun, not so much on speed of machines. The photos of people should be with helmets off. We want family-oriented, fun-oriented pix. Send query. Let us know who you are. Then send a follow-up letter to remind us every now and then. Once we use a photographer, we tend to go back to him time and time again."

SOAP OPERA DIGEST, 45 W 25th St., New York NY 10010. (212)645-2100. Executive Editor: Meredith Berlin. Art Director: Catherine Connors. Biweekly. Circ. 1 million. Emphasizes daytime and nighttime TV serial drama. Readers are mostly women, all ages. Sample copy free with 5×7 SAE and 73¢ postage.

Photo Needs: Needs photos of people who appear on daytime and nighttime TV soap operas; special events in which they appear. Uses mostly color and some b&w photos.

Making Contact & Terms: Query with resume of credits to the art director. Send unsolicited material to Lynn Davey with SASE. Reports in 1 week. Provide business card and promotional material to be kept on file for possible future assignments. Pays $60-75/b&w photo; $100/color photo. Pays $200-750/complete package. Pays on publication. Credit line given. Buys dual rights.

Tips: "Have photos of the most popular stars and of good quality." Sharp color quality is a must. "I look for something that's unusual in a picture, like a different pose instead of head shots. We are not interested in people who happened to take photos of someone they met. Show variety of lighting techniques and creativity in your portfolio."

SOCIETY, Rutgers University, New Brunswick NJ 08903. (201)932-2280. FAX: (201)932-3138. Editor: Irving Louis Horowitz. Bimonthly magazine. Circ. 31,000. Estab. 1962. For those interested in the understanding and use of the social sciences and new ideas and research findings from sociology, psychology, political science, anthropology and economics. Needs photo essays—"no random photo submissions." Essays (brief) should stress human interaction; photos should be of people interacting (not a single person) or of natural surroundings. Include an accompanying explanation of photographer's "aesthetic vision." Buys 75-100 photos/annually. Buys all rights to one time usage. Send photos for consideration to Rebecca L. Woolston. Pays $250/photo-essay. Pays on publication. Reports in 3 months. SASE. Free sample copy and photo guidelines.

Photo Needs: Human interest, photo essay and documentary.

B&W: Send 8×10 glossy prints.

SOLDIER OF FORTUNE MAGAZINE, Box 693, Boulder CO 80306. (303)449-3750. Editor: John Coleman. Monthly magazine. Emphasizes adventure, combat, military units and events. Readers are mostly male—interested in adventure and military related subjects. Circ. 175,000. Sample copy $5.

Photo Needs: Uses about 60 photos/issue. Needs photos of combat—under fire, or military units, military—war related. "We always need front-line combat photography." Model release and captions preferred.

Making Contact & Terms: Query first; send 8×10 glossy b&w, color prints, 35mm transparencies, b&w contact sheets by mail for consideration. SASE. Reports in 3 weeks. Pays $300-1,200 (occasionally higher)/text/photo package; will negotiate a space-rate payment schedule for photos alone. Pays on acceptance. Credit line given. Buys all rights, but will negotiate.

Tips: "Combat action photography gets first consideration for full-page and cover layouts. Photo spreads on military units from around the world also get a serious look, but stay away from 'man with gun' shots. *Give us horizontals and verticals!* The horizontal-shot syndrome handcuffs our art director. *Get close!* Otherwise, use telephoto. Too many photographers send us long distance shots that just don't work for our audience. *Give us action!* People sitting, or staring into the lens, mean nothing. *Consider using b&w* along with color. It gives us options in regard to layout; often, b&w better expresses the combat/military dynamic."

SOUNDINGS, 35 Pratt St., Essex CT 06441. (203)767-3200. Graphics Editor: Milton Moore. Monthly tabloid. Emphasizes recreational boating. Readers are men, ages 40-60, with approximately $70,000 annual income. Circ. 105,000. Sample copy free with 12 × 18 SASE and $2.50 postage. Photo guidelines free with SASE.

Photo Needs: Uses 50 photos/issue; 40% supplied by freelance photographers. Needs photos for story illustrations, plus a few pictures of boating enterprises. Editorial calendar available. Model release preferred; photo captions required.

Making Contact & Terms: Send unsolicited photos by mail for consideration. Provide resume, business card, brochure, flyer or tearsheets to be kept on file for possible assignments. Send b&w prints, any size and format, or 35mm transparencies. SASE. Reports in 1 month. Pays $200-400/color cover photo, $35 and up/b&w inside photo and $400/day. Pays on publication. Credit line given. Buys one-time rights. Previously published work OK.

Tips: In portfolios, looking for a range of skills: action, fill flash, portrait, etc."

SOUTHERN ACCENTS, 2100 Lakeshore Dr., Birmingham AL 35209. (205)877-6000. Art Director: Lane Gregory. 10 issues. Emphasizes interiors, gardens. Readers are "upper class." Circ. 500,000. Sample copy available for 8½ × 11 SAE and 50¢ postage.

Photo Needs: Uses 200 photos/issue, 75% supplied by freelancers. Needs interior photos exclusively; our choice of locations. Model release required.

Making Contact & Terms: Provide resume, business card, brochure, flyer or tearsheets to be kept on file for possible future assignments. SASE. Reports in 1 month. Pays $500-1,000/job (day rate). Pays on publication. Credit line given. Buys all rights; will negotiate with photographer unwilling to sell all rights.

Tips: "Send only samples of interiors, table scapes and gardens—no food or fashion."

SOUTHERN EXPOSURE, Box 531, Durham NC 27702. (919)688-8167. Managing Editor: Eric Bates. Quarterly. Emphasizes the politics and culture of the South, with special interest in women's issues, black affairs and labor. Estab. 1972. Photo guidelines free with SASE. Sample copy $4 with 8½ × 11 SASE.

Photo Needs: Uses 30 photos/issue; most supplied by freelance photographers. Needs news and historical photos; photo essays. Model release and captions preferred.

Making Contact & Terms: Query with samples; send b&w glossy prints by mail for consideration. SASE. Reports in 3-6 weeks. Pays $50/b&w cover photo; $75/color cover photo; $15-30/b&w inside photo. Credit line given. Buys all rights "unless the photographer requests otherwise." Simultaneous submissions and previously published work OK.

SPORT FISHING, Box 2456, Winter Park FL 32790. (407)628-4802. Photo Editor: Doug DuKane. Monthly magazine. Emphasizes off-shore fishing. Readers are upscale boat owners and off-shore fishermen. Circ. 70,000. Sample copy $2.50 with 9 × 12 SAE and $1.58 postage. Photo guidelines free with SASE.

Photo Needs: Uses 50 photos/issue; 75% supplied by freelance photographers. Needs photos of off-shore fishing—big boats/big fish, travel destinations. "We are working more from stock—good opportunities for extra sales on any given assignment." Model release and captions preferred.

Making Contact & Terms: Query with samples; send unsolicited photos by mail for consideration; provide resume, business card, brochure, flyer or tearsheets to be kept on file for possible future assignments. Send 35mm, 2¼ × 2¼ and 4 × 5 transparencies by mail for consideration. "Kodachrome and slow Fuji are preferred." Reports in 3 weeks. Pays $20-100/b&w page; $30-300/color page. Buys one-time rights unless otherwise agreed upon. Simultaneous submissions OK.

Tips: "We need razor sharp images. The best guideline is the magazine itself. Get used to shooting on, in or under water. Most of our needs are found there."

SPORT MAGAZINE, 8490 Sunset Blvd., Los Angeles CA 90069. (213)854-2268. Picture Editor: Ira Gabriel. Monthly magazine. Emphasizes sports, both professional and collegiate. Readers are ages "9-99, male and female." Circ. 1 million. Photo guidelines free with SASE.

Photo Needs: Uses 80+ photos/issue; 20% supplied by freelance photographers. Needs photos of sports action, strobed basketball, hockey, football, baseball.

Making Contact & Terms: Query with resume of credits or stock photo subjects. "No unsolicited work accepted." Reports in 1 month. Pays $600/color cover photo or $350/day. Pays on publication. Credit line given. Buys one-time rights.

Tips: In portfolio or samples looking for "tight, sharp, action—hockey and basketball must be strobed, color transparencies preferred, well-lighted portraits of athletes. No prints. Shoot as much as you can on your own. Continue to call upon publications. Don't get let down; be patient. Freelance photographers have a good opportunity to do a lot of work for our magazine on an assignment basis. More assignments are being given to those who continue to excellence and are creative."

SPORTS AFIELD, 250 W. 55th St., New York NY 10019. (212)649-4015. Art Director: Gary Gretter. For persons of all ages interested in the out-of-doors (hunting and fishing) and related subjects. Write by registered mail. Credit line given.

Subject Needs: Animal, nature, scenic, travel, sports, photo essay/photo feature, documentary, still life and wildlife. "We are only viewing duplicate transparencies."

Tips: "We are looking for photographers who can portray the beauty and wonder of the outdoor experience." Don't send originals, only duplicate slides.

SPORTS ILLUSTRATED, Time-Life Bldg., Rockfeller Center, New York NY 10020. (212)522-1212. Photo Editor: Karen Mullarky. A newsweekly of sports; emphasizes sports and recreation through news, analysis and profiles for participants and spectators. Circ. 2,250,000. Almost *everything* is done on assignment; has photographers on staff and on contract. Freelancers may submit portfolio by appointment in person if in the area or by mail; also looking for feature ideas by mail. Reports on portfolios in 2 weeks. SASE. Pays a day rate of $350 against $500/page, $1,000/cover.

Tips: "On first contact with the photographer, we want to see a portfolio only. Portfolios may be varied, not necessarily just sport shots. We like to meet with photographers after the portfolio has been reviewed."

SPUR, 13 W. Federal, Box 85, Middleburg VA 22117. (703)687-6314. Editor: Cathy Laws. Bimonthly magazine. Emphasizes Thoroughbred horses. Readers are "owners, breeders, trainers and enthusiasts in the sports of racing, steeplechasing, polo, fox hunting, horse showing and three-day eventing." Circ. 10,000+. Sample copy $4. Photo guidelines free with SASE.

Photo Needs: Uses about 45-55 photos/issue; all supplied by freelance photographers. Needs photos of "horses—Thoroughbreds only—and action (racing, steeplechasing, polo), scenic shots." Special needs include "covers—colorful, original approaches." All photos must be identified.

Making Contact & Terms: Query with samples. Send transparencies, slides or prints by mail for consideration. Provide resume, business card, brochure, flyer or tearsheets to be kept on file for possible future assignments. SASE. Reports in 3 weeks. Pays $75 and up/color cover photo, $20-100/ b&w inside photo, and $40-150/color inside photo. Pays on publication. Credit line given.

THE STATE: Down Home in North Carolina, 128 S. Tryon St. Suite 2200, Charlotte NC 28202. (704)375-7404. Editor: Jim Duff. Monthly magazine. Circ. 21,000. Estab. 1933. Regional publication, privately owned, emphasizing travel, history, nostalgia, folklore, humor, all subjects regional to North Carolina for residents of, and others interested in, North Carolina.

Subject Needs: Photos on travel, history and human interest in North Carolina. Freelance photography used; 5% assignment and 5% stock. Captions required.

Specs: Uses 5×7 and 8×10 glossy b&w prints; also glossy color prints and slides. Uses b&w and color cover photos, vertical preferred.

Making Contact & Terms: Send material by mail for consideration. SASE. Reporting time depends on "involvement with other projects at time received." Pays $15-25/b&w photo; $15-25/color photo; $50-125/photo/text package. Sample copy $3. Credit line given. Pays on acceptance.

Tips: Looks for "North Carolina material; solid cutline information." Send samples of work with return postage."

STOCK CAR RACING MAGAZINE, 27 S. Main St., Box 715, Ipswich MA 01938. (508)356-7030. FAX: (508)356-2492. Editor: Dick Berggren. Monthly magazine. Circ. 105,000. Estab. 1966. Emphasizes all forms of stock car competition. Read by fans, owners and drivers of race cars and those with racing businesses. Photos purchased with or without accompanying ms and on assignment. Buys 50-70 photos/ issue. Credit line given. Pays on publication. Buys one-time rights. Send material by mail for consideration. Free photo guidelines for SASE.

Subject Needs: Documentary, head shot, photo essay/photo feature, product shot, personality, crash pictures, special effects/experimental, technical and sport. No photos unrelated to stock car racing. Model release required unless subject is a racer who has signed a release at the track; captions required.

B&W: Uses 8×10 glossy prints. Pays $20/photo.

Color: Uses 35mm or 2¼×2¼ transparencies. Pays $35-250/photo. Kodachrome 64 or Fuji 100 preferred.

Cover: Pays $35-250/photo.

Tips: "Send the pictures. We will buy anything that relates to racing if it's interesting, if we have the first shot at it, and it's well printed and exposed. Eighty percent of our rejections are for technical reasons—poorly focused, badly printed, too much dust, picture cracked, etc. We get far fewer cover submissions than we would like. We look for full bleed cover verticals where we can drop type into the picture and fit our logo too."

STRAIGHT, 8121 Hamilton Ave., Cincinnati OH 45231. (513)931-4050. FAX: (513)931-0904. Editor: Carla J. Crane. Readers are ages 13 through 19, mostly Christian; a conservative audience. Weekly. Circ. 65,000.

Photo Needs: Uses about 4 photos/issue; all supplied by freelance photographers. Needs color and black and white photos of teenagers involved in various activities such as sports, study, church, part-time jobs, school activities, classroom situations. Outside nature shots, groups of teens having good times together are also needed. "Try to avoid the sullen, apathetic look—vital, fresh, thoughtful, outgoing teens are what we need. Any photographer who submits a set of quality b&w glossies or color transparencies for our consideration, whose subjects are teens in various activities and poses, has a good chance of selling to us. This is a difficult age group to photograph without looking stilted or unnatural. We want to purport a clean, healthy, happy look. No smoking, drinking or immodest clothing. We especially need masculine-looking guys, and minority subjects. Submit photos coinciding with the seasons (i.e., winter scenes in December through February, spring scenes in March through May, etc.) Model release and captions not required, but noting the age of the model is often helpful.

Making Contact & Terms: Send 5×7 or 8×10 b&w photos and color transparencies by mail for consideration. Enclose sufficient packing and postage for return of photos. Reports in 4-6 weeks. Pays on acceptance. Pays $20-45/b&w photo, $75-125/color photo. Credit line given. Buys one-time rights. Simultaneous submissions and previously published work OK. Sample copy free with SASE and 39¢ postage. Photo guidelines for SASE.

Tips: "Our publication is almost square in shape. Therefore, 5×7 or 8×10 prints that are cropped closely will not fit our proportions. Any photo should have enough 'margin' around the subject that it may be cropped square. This is a simple point, but absolutely necessary. Look for active, contemporary teenagers. For our publication, keep up with what teens are interested in."

*THE STRAIN, Box 330507, Houston TX 77233-0507. (713)733-6042. For articles contact: Alicia Adler; for columns, Charlie Mainze. Monthly magazine. Emphasizes interactive arts and 'The Arts'. Readers are mostly artists and performers. Circ. 1,000. Estab. 1987. Sample copy $5 with 9×12 SASE and 7 first class stamps. Photo guidelines free with SASE.

Photo Needs: Uses 5-100 photos/issue; 95% supplied by freelance photographers. Needs photos of scenics, personalities, portraits, but the main emphasis for the upcoming year are "enigmas" and distortions. Model release required. Photo captions preferred.

Making Contact & Terms: Send any format b&w and color prints or transparencies by mail for consideration. SASE. The longer it is held, the more likely it will be published. Reports in 1 year, however. Pays $50/color cover photo; $100/b&w cover photo; $5 minimum/color inside photo; $5 minimum/b&w inside photo; $5/b&w page rate; $50-500/photo/text package. Pays on publication. Credit line given. Buys one-time rights or first North American serial rights. Simultaneous submissions and previously published work OK.

Tips: "We have categories for almost any photographic images that aspire to the notion that photography can be 'high art'. Our advice to the freelancer trying to break in is to study the great art works of the past."

STREET & SMITH'S COLLEGE PREP BASKETBALL, 304 E. 45th St., New York NY 10017. (412)221-3580. Editor: Jim O'Brien. Send submissions to: 1603 Terphin Dr., Pittsburgh PA 15241. Consumer publication. Annual magazine. Emphasizes all aspects of college/prep basketball. Readers are "red hot basketball fans." Circ. 275,000. Sample copy and photo guidelines free with SASE.

Photo Needs: Uses 300 photos/issue; 100% supplied by contributors. Needs "game action photos of returning college prep players. Always looking for shots of top prep and All-America caliber players, as well as cheerleaders, dancing girls, fans, etc." Model release preferred; photo captions required ("must identify players; that's sufficient").

Making Contact & Terms: Send unsolicited photos by mail for consideration. Provide resume, business card, brochure, flyer or tearsheets to be kept on file for possible assignments. Send b&w prints or 35mm, 4×5 or 8×10 transparencies. Returns unsolicited material, but SASE "not necessary." Reports in 2 weeks. Pays $250/color cover photo, $100/color inside photo and $30/b&w inside photo. Pays on publication. Credit line given. Buys one-time rights. Simultaneous submissions OK.

Tips: To break in, "Try me—that's how I've gotten most of my regular photographers."

 The asterisk before a listing indicates that the market is new in this edition. New markets are often the most receptive to freelance submissions.

STREET & SMITH'S PRO BASKETBALL, 304 E. 45th St., New York NY 10017. (412)221-3580. Editor: Jim O'Brien. Send submissions to: 1603 Terphin Dr., Pittsburgh PA 15241. Consumer publication. Annual magazine. Emphasizes all aspects of pro basketball. Readers are "red hot basketball fans." Circ. 275,000. Sample copy and photo guidelines free with SASE.
Photo Needs: Uses 300 photos/issue; 50% supplied by freelance photographers. Needs "game action photos of pro players. Always looking for shots of top pro players." Model release preferred; photo captions required ("must identify players; that's sufficient").
Making Contact & Terms: Send unsolicited photos by mail for consideration. Provide resume, business card, brochure, flyer or tearsheets to be kept on file for possible assignments. Send b&w prints or 35mm, 4×5 or 8×10 transparencies. Returns unsolicited material, but SASE "not necessary." Reports in 2 weeks. Pays $250/color cover photo, $100/color inside photo and $30/b&w inside photo. Pays on publication. Credit line given. Buys one-time rights. Simultaneous submissions OK.
Tips: To break in, "try me—that's how I've gotten most of my regular photographers."

SUCCESS MAGAZINE, 342 Madison Ave., New York NY 10173. (212)503-0700. Art Director: David Bayer. Picture Editor: Gail Toivanen. Monthly magazine. Circ. 450,000. Emphasizes business and entrepreneurs, self-improvement and goal-attainment for men and women. Buys 30 photos/an issue. Credit line given. Buys one-time rights or all rights. Query with samples which may be kept on file for future reference for assignments and stock list.
Subject Needs: Business, human interest, and still life. Model release preferred; captions required.
B&W: Uses 8×10 prints.
Color: Uses transparencies.
Cover: Uses transparencies.
Tips: "We are always looking for new photographers, especially those who are located in places other than the major metropolitan areas, the midwest, south and southwest."

*SUMMIT, The Mountain Journal, 111 Schweitz Rd., Fleetwood PA 19522. (215)682-1701. Art Director: Adele Hammond. Quarterly magazine. Features news related to the world of mountains. Readers are mostly male professionals, ages 35-45. Circ. 20,000. Estab. 1990. Sample copy for $3.00 with 10×13 SAE and $2.40 postage.
Photo Needs: Uses up to 40 photos/issue; 100% supplied by freelancers. Needs "landscape shots of mountains, flowers, mountain people, animals and mountain environments from all over the world." Photos must be high quality b&w or color only. Model release preferred (when applicable); photo captions required.
Making Contact & Terms: Query with list of stock photo subjects. Provide resume, business card, brochure, flyer or tearsheets to be kept on file for possible assignment. Reports in 3 weeks. Pays $200-250/color cover photo; $50-170/various page rates. Pays on publication. Credit line given. Buys one-time rights.

THE SUN, 107 North Roberson, Chapel Hill NC 27516. (919)942-5282. Editor: Sy Safransky. Monthly magazine. Circ. 12,000. Sample copy $3 and 9×12 SAE with $1 postage. Photo guidelines free with SASE.
Photo Needs: Uses about 3 photos/issue; all supplied by freelance photographers. Model release preferred.
Making Contact & Terms: Send b&w prints by mail for consideration. SASE. Reports in 1 month. Pays $25/b&w cover and inside photo. Pays on publication. Credit line given. Buys one-time rights. Previously published work OK.
Tips: Looks for "artful and sensitive photographs that are not overly sentimental. We use many photos of people. All the photographs we publish come to us as unsolicited submissions."

SURFING MAGAZINE/BODYBOARDING MAGAZINE, Box 3010, San Clemente CA 92672. Editor: David Gilovich. Photo Editor: Larry Moore. Monthly. Circ. 120,000. Emphasizes "surfing and bodyboarding action and related aspects of beach lifestyle. Travel to new surfing areas covered as well. Average age of readers is 18 with 92% being male. Nearly all drawn to publication due to high quality, action packed photographs." Free photo guidelines with SASE. Sample copy free with legal size SAE and $2.25 postage.
Photo Needs: Uses about 80 photos/issue; 35%+ supplied by freelance photographers. Needs "in-tight front-lit surfing and bodyboarding action photos as well as travel-related scenics. Beach lifestyle photos always in demand."
Making Contact & Terms: Send by mail for consideration 35mm or 2¼×2¼ transparencies; b&w contact sheet and negatives. SASE. Reports in 2-4 weeks. Pays $500/color cover photo; $30-125/color inside photo; $20-70/b&w inside photo; $500/color poster photo. Pays on publication. Credit line given. Buys one-time rights.

Tips: Prefers to see "well-exposed, sharp images showing both the ability to capture peak action as well as beach scenes depicting the surfing and bodyboarding lifestyle. Color, lighting composition and proper film usage are important. Ask for our photo guidelines prior to making any film/camera/lens choices."

TAMPA BAY MAGAZINE, Suite 101, 2531 Landmark Dr., Clearwater FL 34621. (813)791-4800. Editor: Aaron Fodiman. Bimonthly magazine. Emphasizes Tampa Bay and surrounding area. Readers are upwardly mobile. Circ. 20,000.
Photo Needs: Uses 100 photos/issue; 100% supplied by freelance photographers. Model release and photo captions required.
Making Contact & Terms: Send unsolicited photos by mail for consideration. SASE. Reports in 1 weeks. Pays $100/color cover photo, $40/color or b&w inside photo. Pays on publication. Credit line given. Buys one-time rights.

*TATTOO ADVOCATE JOURNAL, P.O. Box 8390, 380 Belmont Avenue, Haledon NJ 07580. (201)790-0429. Publisher: Shotsie Gorman. Consumer publication. Semi-annual magazine. Emphasizes tattoo art. Readership crosses all boundaries. Circ. 5,000. Estab. 1988. Sample copy for $5. Photo guidelines not available.
Photo Needs: Uses 200 photos/issue; 60% supplied by freelance photographers; 80% assignment; 20% freelance stock. Needs quality artistic documentation of tattoo art, editorial black & whites. Usually purchases photos with accompanying ms.; in addition purchases separate photos. Special photo needs include rock & roll and pop stars with tattoos. Model release and photo captions required.
Making Contact & Terms: Arrange a personal interview to show portfolio; query with resume of credits. Reports in 1 month. Pays $25-250/b&w (cover); $40-300/color photo; $50-150; and $100-500/photo/text package. Pays on acceptance. Credit line given. Buys first N.A. serial rights, all rights; will negotiate with photographer unwilling to sell all rights. Simultaneous submissions and previously published work OK.
Tips: In portfolio, looks for "creative dramatic, personal point of view; I need tasteful lyrical photos of tattooed people. High quality color work or strong journalistic content. Query letter and samples of published work or work that fits our editorial needs."

*TAVERN SPORTS INTERNATIONAL, 101 E. Erie, Suite 850, Chicago IL 60611. (312)266-9499. Managing Editor: Jocelyn Hathaway. Consumer publication. Bimonthly magazine. Emphasizes the coin-operated game industry and action/players within organized tavern-based sports. Readers are ages 21-45; male and female; vendor/operators, manufacturers, location owners and players. Circ. 25,000. Estab. 1988. Sample copy free with 9 × 12 SASE and $1.25 postage. Photo guidelines not available.
Photo Needs: Uses 20 photos/issue; 25% supplied by freelance photographers. Needs photos of personalties and sports action. Photo captions required.
Making Contact & Terms: Provide resume, business card, brochure, flyer or tearsheets to be kept on file for possible assignments. Reports in 1 month. Pays $150/color cover photo; $50/color inside photo; $125-175/photo/text package. Credit line given. Buys all rights. Simultaneous submissions OK.
Tips: Keep in mind this publication "is on a tight budget; therefore, the more reasonable photographers can work for, the more assignments Tavern Sports International can offer to freelancers." Also, there is a growing demand and expectation of participatory entertainment.

TEENS TODAY, 6401 The Paseo, Kansas City MO 64131. (816)333-7000, ext. 214. Editorial Accountant: Rosemary Postel. Editor: Karen DeSollar. Weekly magazine. Circ. 60,000. Read by junior- and senior-high-school/age persons. Buys 100 photos/year; 2 photos/issue. Credit line given. Pays on acceptance. Buys one-time rights. Simultaneous submissions and previously published work OK.
Subject Needs: Needs shots of high-school age young people. Junior and senior highs (grades 7-12) must be the subjects. Shots of driving, talking, eating, walking, sports, singles, couples, groups, etc.
B&W: Uses 8 × 10 glossy prints. Pays $15-25/photo.
Accompanying Mss: Pays 3½¢ minimum/word first rights, 3¢/word for second rights. Free writer's guidelines with SASE.
Making Contact: Send material by mail for consideration. "Send photo submissions to our central distribution center to Rosemary Postel and they will be circulated through other editorial offices." SASE. Reports in 6-8 weeks. Free sample copy with 9 × 12 SAE and 54¢ postage; photo guidelines free only with SASE.
Tips: "Make sure your work has good contrast and is dealing with the teen-age group."

TENNIS MAGAZINE, 5520 Park Ave., Trumbull CT 06611. (203)373-7000. Art Director: Kathleen Burke. Monthly magazine. Circ. 500,000. Emphasizes instructional articles and features on tennis for young, affluent tennis players. Freelancers supply 60% of photos. Payment depends on space usage. Credit line given. Pays on acceptance. Buys first North American and overseas affiliates rights or on

agreement with publisher. Send material by mail for consideration. SASE. Reports in 2 weeks.
Subject Needs: "We'll look at all photos submitted relating to the game of tennis. We use color action shots of the top athletes in tennis. Also uses studio setups and instructional photography, but rarely freelance.
B&W: Uses 5×7 glossy prints.
Color: Uses 35mm transparencies Kodachrome 64 ASA preferred.

TENNIS WEEK, 124 East 40th St., New York NY 10016. (212)808-4750. Publisher: Eugene L. Scott. Editor: Reneé L. Dussault. Readers are "tennis fanatics." Biweekly. Circ. 62,000. Sample copy $2.
Photo Needs: Uses about 16 photos/issue. Needs photos of "off-court color, beach scenes with pros, social scenes with players, etc." Emphasizes originality. No captions required; subject identification required.
Making Contact & Terms: Send by mail for consideration actual 8×10 or 5×7 b&w photos. SASE. Reports in 2 weeks. Pays on publication, $15/b&w photo; $50/cover; $100/color cover. Credit line given. Rights purchased on a work-for-hire basis.

TEXAS FISH & GAME, Box 1000, 903 Third St., Marble Falls TX 78654. (512)693-5725. Editor: Marvin Spivey. Magazine published monthly, 10 times per year. Features all types of hunting and fishing. Must be Texas only. Circ. 70,000. Sample copy $1.95 and 9×12 SASE. Photo guidelines free with SASE.
Photo Needs: Uses 20-30 photos/issue; 95% supplied by freelance photographers. Needs photos of fish: action, close up of fish found in Texas; hunting: Texas hunting and game of Texas. Model release preferred; photo captions required.
Making Contact & Terms: Query with list of stock photo subjects. SASE. Reports in 1 month. Pays $150/color cover photo and $50/color inside photo. Pays on publication. Credit line given. Buys one-time rights.
Tips: "Query first. Ask for guidelines. No b&w used. For that 'great' shot, prices will go up. Send best shots and only of subjects the publication you're trying to sell to uses."

TEXAS FISHERMAN MAGAZINE, Suite 150, 4550 Post Oak Place Dr., Houston TX 77027. (713)626-3474. Contact: Mike Haines. Publishes 9/year. Circ. 75,237. Emphasizes all aspects of fresh and saltwater fishing in Texas, plus hunting, boating and camping when timely. Readers: 90% are married, with 47.4% earning over $35,000 yearly. Sample copy free with SASE.
Photo Needs: Use 25 photos/issue; 75% supplied by freelance photographers. Needs "action photos of fishermen catching fish, close-ups of fish with lures, 'how-to' rigging illustrations, some wildlife." Especially needs photos of Texas coastal fishing (saltwater). Captions required.
Making Contact & Terms: Query with samples; if submitting ms, include contact sheets. "Mug shots with ms." SASE. Reports in 6 weeks. Pays $200-400/color cover photo; $25-75/b&w inside photo. Extensive use of 4-color inside. Pays $35-125, based on column-size use. Pays on acceptance. Credit line given. Buys one-time rights.
Tips: Prefers to see "*action* shots—no photos of fishermen holding up fish, but tasteful stringer shots OK. Concentrate on taking photos that tell something, such as how-to." Knowledge of fishing, presentation of fishing material from unusual perspectives, and technical expertise in color selection are qualities looked for in photo samples submitted.

TEXAS GARDENER, Box 9005, Waco TX 76714. (817)772-1270. Editor/Publisher: Chris S. Corby. Bimonthly. Circ. 37,000. Emphasizes gardening. Readers are "65% male, home gardeners, 98% Texas residents." Sample copy $1.
Photo Needs: Uses 20-30 photos/issue; 90% supplied by freelance photographers. Needs "color photos of gardening activities in Texas." Special needs include "photo essays on specific gardening topics such as 'Weeds in the Garden.' Must be taken in Texas." Model release and captions required.
Making Contact & Terms: Query with samples. SASE. Reports in 3 weeks. Pays $100-200/color cover photo; $5-15/b&w inside photo, $10-200/color inside photo. Pays on acceptance. Credit line given. Buys all rights.

Markets which offer lower payment amounts, or photo credits and extra copies or tearsheets as payment are often receptive to the work of newcomers. For a list of such markets, see the First Markets Index preceding the General Index in the back of this book.

Tips: "Provide complete information on photos. For example, if you submit a photo of watermelons growing in a garden, we need to know what variety they are and when and where the picture was taken."

TEXAS HIGHWAYS, P.O. Box 141009, Austin TX 78714. (512)483-3675. Editor-in-Chief: Frank Lively. Photo Editor: Bill Reaves. Monthly. Circ. 430,000. *"Texas Highways* interprets scenic, recreational, historical, cultural and ethnic treasures of the state and preserves the best of Texas heritage. Its purpose is to educate and entertain, to encourage recreational travel to and within the state, and to tell the Texas story to readers around the world." Readers are "45 and over (majority); $24,000 to $60,000 per year salary bracket with a college education." Sample copy and photo guidelines free.
Photo Needs: Uses about 50 photos/issue; 50% supplied by freelance photographers. Needs "travel and scenic photos in Texas only." Special needs include "fall, winter, spring, and summer scenic shots and wildflower shots (Texas only)." Captions required.
Making Contact & Terms: Query with samples. Provide business card and tearsheets to be kept on file for possible future assignments. SASE. Reports in 1 month. Pays $120 for ½ page color inside photo and $170/full-page color photo, $400 for front cover photo. Pays on acceptance. Credit line given. Buys one-time rights. Simultaneous submissions OK.
Tips: "Know our magazine and format. We take only color originals, 35mm Kodachrome or Fujichrome 2¼ × 2¼ or 4 × 5 transparencies. No negatives. Don't forget to caption and name names. We publish only photographs of Texas. We accept only high-quality, professional level work—no snapshots."

*THANATOS, P.O. Box 6009, Tallahassee FL 32314. (904)224-1969. Associate Editor: Alana Schwermer. Quarterly magazine. Covers death, dying and bereavement. Readers include healthcare professionals, thanatologists, clergy, funeral directors, counselors, support groups, volunteers, bereaved family members, students, et al. Circ. 6,000. Estab. 1975. Sample copy free upon request. Photo guidelines free with SASE.
Photo Needs: Uses 8 photos/issue; 100% supplied by freelancers. Needs many scenic and people shots to accompany articles. Especially looking for pictures of people of different ethnic groups. Also, full-color scenics to illustrate seasons for each quarterly edition. Model release required; photo captions preferred.
Making Contact & Terms: Query with list of stock photo subjects. Provide resume, business card, brochure, flyer or tearsheets to be kept on file for possible assignment. Cannot return unsolicited material. Reports in 2 weeks. Pays $50/color cover photo; $25/b&w inside photo. Pays on acceptance. Buys all rights; negotiable. Simultaneous submissions OK.

THINKING FAMILIES MAGAZINE, 605 Worcester Rd., Towson MD 21204. (301)321-0121. Bimonthly. "We are a magazine for families with children in elementary school. Our two main areas of coverage are 1.) Developmental issues relating to children ages 6-12 and 2.) education issues relating to this age group." Readers are parents with kids in elementary school. Concentrated in the age group of 35-42; extremely well educated—70% hold more than one college degree. Circ. 50,000. Estab. 1988. Sample copy for 9 × 12 SASE with $1.05 postage.
Photo Needs: Uses about 12 photos/issue; all supplied by freelance photographers; nearly all from assignment. Need various shots of school kids; possibility of needing shots of parents, too. Special needs include good shots of kids who look as if they are going to school and liking it. Model release and captions required.
Making Contact & Terms: Query with samples; send unsolicited photos by mail for consideration; provide resume, business card, brochure, flyer or tearsheets to be kept on file for possible future assignments. SASE. Reports back "as subject is needed." Pays $350/color cover photo; $25-150/b&w inside photo; $50-350/color photo; $500 maximum/job; $35/hour. Pays on publication. Credit line given. Buys one-time rights. Simultaneous submissions and previously published work OK.
Tips: Looks for "photographers who are experienced with photography of school children—in all situations. Also, good, clean shots with tight composition and xeroxes of prints."

*THIRD WORLD, Rua da Glória, 122-Sala 105, Rio de Janeiro RJ 20241 Brazil. (5521)222-1370/242-1957. Editor: Bill Hinchberger. News and current affairs magazine. Bimonthly magazine. Emphasizes The Third World (Asia, Africa, Latin America, The Caribbean and the Middle East). Readers are adults, male and female, professionals, university professors, development activists, etc. Circ. 5,000. Estab. 1986. Sample copy free with SASE. "No guidelines, but we are willing to answer any questions that potential contributors have."
Photo Needs: Uses 100 photos/issue; up to 50% supplied by freelance photographers. Needs photos of Third World leaders, popular movements, environment, industry, agriculture, population, cultural events and groups. "Our needs are fairly constant. We need photos of current events in the Third World and of conditions in various countries." Model release and photo captions preferred.

Making Contact & Terms: Query with resume of credits and send copies to be kept on file for future reference if needed; provide resume, business card, brochure, flyer or tearsheets to be kept on file for possible assignments. Uses 4×5 or 8×10 b&w prints. Cannot return material. Reports in 1-2 weeks allow extra time for international mail. Pays $10/color cover photo; $10/b&w cover photo; $5/b&w inside. "We pay Brazilian union scale. The exact amount depends on the exchange rate." Pays on publication. Credit line given in the staff box. Buys one-time rights. Simultaneous submissions and previously published work OK.

Tips: "Our publication is a good starting point for aspiring photojournalists. We encourage young photographers to contact us."

THUNDER BAY MAGAZINE, 1184 Roland St., Thunder Bay, ON P7B 5M4 Canada. (807)623-8545. FAX: (807)623-7110. Art Director: Jack Hudolin. Editorial Coordinator: Jean Pendziwol. Bimonthly magazine. Emphasizes city lifestyle. "Our audience is primarily between the ages of 30 and 50 with an average household income of over $40,000. Occupation is generally professional/business." Circ. 32,000. Estab. 1983. Sample copy free with 9×12 SAE and 76¢ postage.

Photo Needs: Uses 7-15 photos/issue; 1-2 supplied by freelance photographers. "Usually look for good quality cover shots along theme of magazine." Model release preferred; photo captions required.

Making Contact & Themes: Query with list of stock photo subjects, send 35mm, $2\frac{1}{4} \times 2\frac{1}{4}$, 4×5, 8×10 transparencies by mail for consideration. SASE. Reports in 2 weeks. Pay rates negotiable. Pays on publication. Buys one-time rights. Simultaneous submissions and previously published work OK.

Tips: Wants to see "Sites around Thunder Bay, food, fashion and travel. Regional and local interest photos are the trend."Gear photos submitted to the publication to the themes of that particular issue. Keep in mind the 5-6 month lead time necessary when choosing cover photos. Submit list of photos available."

TQ, Box 82808, Lincoln NE 68501. (402)474-4567. Managing Editor: Karen Christianson. Monthly magazine. Circ. 70,000. Emphasizes Christian living for Christian young people, ages 13-17. Buys 5-10 photos/issue. Buys one-time-use rights. Send photos for consideration, or send contact sheet. Address to Photo Coordinator. Pays on acceptance. Reports in 2-4 weeks. SASE. Simultaneous submissions and previously published work OK. Free sample copy (with 9×12 SAE) and photographer's guidelines.

Subject Needs: Photos of young people 13-16 years old in unposed, everyday activities. Scenic, sport, photo essay/photo feature, human interest, head shot, still life, humorous and special effects/experimental. Especially interested in photos of minorities. Current fashion.

B&W: Send contact sheet or 8×10 glossy prints. Pays $35 for most.

Color: Send color transparencies. Pays $60 for most.

Tips: "Close-up shots featuring moody, excited or unusual expressions needed. Would like to see more shots featuring unusual and striking camera and darkroom techniques. Looks for "wholesome youth 13-17 in fun situations, school, family: good quality technically and creative work. We have a limited budget but high standards. Take care in printing your black and white photos. Also review your work and send only those pictures that have a shot at being printed. Limit your submissions."

TRACK AND FIELD NEWS, Suite 606, 2570 El Camino Real., Mountain View CA 94040. (415)948-8417. Feature/Photo Editor: Jon Hendershott. Monthly magazine. Circ. 35,000. Emphasizes national and world-class track and field competition and participants at those levels for athletes, coaches, administrators and fans. Buys 10-15 photos/issue. Credit line given. Captions required. Payment is made bimonthly. Query with samples or send material by mail for consideration. SASE. Reports in 1 week. Sample copy free with $8\frac{1}{2} \times 11$ SASE. Free photo guidelines.

Subject Needs: Wants on a regular basis photos of national-class athletes, men and women, preferably in action. "We are always looking for quality pictures of track and field action as well as offbeat and different feature photos. We always prefer to hear from a photographer before he/she covers a specific meet. We also welcome shots from road and cross-country races for both men and women. Any photos may eventually be used to illustrate news stories in *T&FN*, feature stories in *T&FN* or may be used in our other publications (books, technical journals, etc.). Any such editorial use will be paid for, regardless of whether or not material is used directly in *T&FN*. About all we don't want to see are pictures taken with someone's Instamatic or Polaroid. No shots of someone's child or grandparent running. Professional work only."

B&W: Uses 8×10 glossy prints; contact sheet preferred. Pays $20/photo, inside.

Color: Pays $50/photo.

Cover: Uses 35mm color transparencies. Pays $150/photo, color.

Tips: "No photographer is going to get rich via *T&FN*. We can offer a credit line, nominal payment and, in some cases, credentials to major track and field meets to enable on-the-field shooting. But we can offer the chance for competent photographers to shoot major competitions and competitors up close as well as the most highly regarded publication in the track world as a forum to display a photographer's talents."

TRAILER BOATS MAGAZINE, Poole Publications Inc., 20700 Belshaw Ave., Carson CA 90746. (213)537-6322. FAX: (213)537-8735. Editor: Chuck Coyne. Monthly magazine. Circ. 85,000. Estab. 1971. "Only magazine devoted exclusively to legally trailerable boats and related activities" for owners and prospective owners. Photos purchased with or without accompanying ms. Uses 15 photos/issue with ms. Pays per text/photo package or on a per-photo basis. Credit line given. Pays on publication. Buys all rights. Query or send photos or contact sheet by mail for consideration. SASE. Reports in 1 month. Sample copy $1.25.
Subject Needs: Celebrity/personality, documentary, photo essay/photo feature on legally trailerable boats or related activities (i.e., skiing, fishing, cruising, etc.), scenic (with ms), sport, spot news, how-to, human interest, humorous (monthly "Over-the-Transom" funny or weird shots in the boating world), travel (with ms) and wildlife. Photos must relate to trailer boat activities. Captions required. Needs funny photos for Over the Transom column. No long list of stock photos or subject matter not related to editorial content.
B&W: Uses 5×7 glossy prints. Pays $7.50-50/photo.
Color: Uses transparencies. Pays $15-100/photo.
Cover: Uses transparencies. Vertical format required. Pays $150-300/photo.
Accompanying Mss: Articles related to trailer boat activities. Pays 7-10¢/word and $7.50-50/photo. Free writer's guidelines.
Tips: "Shoot with imagination and a variety of angles. Don't be afraid to 'set-up' a photo that looks natural. Think in terms of complete feature stories; photos and manuscripts. It is rare any more that we publish freelance photos only, without accompanying manuscript; with one exception, 'Over the Transom'—a comical, weird or unusual boating shot."

TRAILER LIFE, 29901 Agoura Rd., Agoura CA 91301. (818)991-4980. Editor: Bill Estes. Monthly magazine. Circ. 315,000. Emphasizes the why, how and how-to of owning, using and maintaining a recreational vehicle for personal vacation or full-time travel. The editors are particularly interested in photos for the cover; an RV must be included. Pays $50-150/b&w photo, $75-300+/color photo. Credit line given. Pays on acceptance. Buys first North American rights. Send material by mail for consideration or query with samples. SASE. Reports in 3 weeks. Send for editorial guidelines.
Subject Needs: Human interest, how-to, travel and personal experience.
B&W: Uses 8×10 glossy prints.
Color: Uses 35mm and 2¼×2¼ transparencies.
Accompanying Mss: Related to recreational vehicles and ancillary activities.

TRAILS-A-WAY, 9425 S. Greenville Rd., Greenville MI 48838. (800)334-6808. Publisher: Jerry Zeilhofer. Monthly tabloid. Emphasizes camping and recreational vehicle travel. Readers are "middle-aged, mid- to upper-income with RVs and a strong desire to travel." Circ. 57,000.
Photo Needs: Uses about 12-15 photos/issue; "maybe half" supplied by freelance photographers. Needs photos of "travel, camping, RVs, etc." Captions required.
Making Contact & Terms: Query with samples. Send 5×7, 8×10 glossy prints or 35mm, 2¼×2¼ transparencies by mail for consideration. SASE. Reports in 1 month. Pays $25-35/color cover photo and $10/b&w inside photo. Pays on publication. Credit line given if requested. Buys one-time rights. Simultaneous submissions and previously published work OK.

TRAINS MAGAZINE, P.O. Box 1612, 21027 Crossroads Circle, Milwaukee WI 53187. (414)796-8776. Art Director: George Gloff. Monthly magazine. Emphasizes railroads. Readers are railroad enthusiasts and hobbyists. Most readers are males of all ages. Circ. 200,000. Sample copy $2.75, 9×12 SASE and 2 first-class stamps. Photo guidelines free with SASE.
Photo Needs: Uses 70 photos/issue; 90% supplied by freelance photographers. Needs photos of trains, and railroad scenes including equipment and people. Model release preferred; photo captions required.
Making Contact & Terms: Send unsolicited photos by mail for consideration. Uses 8×10 b&w prints, any finish, or 35mm transparencies. SASE. Reports in 1 month; acknowledges receipt at once, though. Pays $100/color cover photo, $30-100/color inside photo and $10-50/b&w inside photo. Pays on publication. Credit line given. Buys one-time rights.
Tips: To break in, "keep submissions small in volume—a sheet of 35mm slides, or a dozen b&w prints; they'll get reviewed more quickly. We also have a new quarterly publication, *Trains Illustrated*." Contact for further information.

Santa Barbara photographer Terence A. Miller found a unique photo opportunity when he came upon this custom-built motorhome. Miller got the shot, wrote a short feature and submitted them on speculation to Trailer Life. The magazine, with a readership of 315,000, liked the results and paid him $50 for the article and one-time rights for the photo. According to him, the sale has continued to have positive effects, including "exposure, feedback from such a large readership and the incentive to continue pursuing [his] ultimate love—photography."

*TRANSITIONS ABROAD, 18 Hulst Road, Box 344, Amherst MA 01004. (413)256-0373. Assistant Publisher: Lisa Aciukewicz. Consumer publication. Bimonthly magazine. Emphasizes travel. Readers are people interested in traveling, learning, living, or working abroad, all ages, both sexes. Circ. 10,000. Estab. 1978. Sample copy for $3.50. Photo guidelines free with SASE.

Photo Needs: Uses 15 photos/issue; all photographers are freelancers. Needs photos of travelers in international settings or the people of other countries. Each issue has an area focus: Jan/Feb.—Asia and the Pacific Rim; Mar./Apr.—Europe and the Soviet Union; May/June—The Mediterranean Basin and the Near East; Nov./Dec.—The Americas and Africa (South of the Sahara).

Making Contact & Terms: Query with list of stock photo subjects; send unsolicited 8×10 b&w prints by mail for consideration. SASE. Reports in 1 month. Pays $10-125/b&w cover photo. Pays on publication. Credit line given. Buys one-time rights. Simultaneous submissions and previously published work OK.

Tips: In freelance photographer's samples, wants to see "mostly people shots—travelers and people of other countries. We use very few landscapes or abstract shots and use only vertical shots on cover."

TRAVEL & LEISURE, 1120 Avenue of the Americas, New York NY 10036. (212)382-5600. Editor: Ila Stanger. Art Director: Bob Ciano. Picture Editor: Hazel Hammond. Monthly magazine. Circ. 1,200,000. Emphasizes travel destinations, resorts, dining and entertainment. Credit line given. Pays on publication. Buys first World serial rights, plus promotional use. Sometimes pays $450-1,200/day; $1,200 minimum/complete package. Previously published work OK. Free photo guidelines. SASE.

Subject Needs: Nature, still life, scenic, sport and travel. Model release and captions required.
B&W: Uses 8 × 10 semigloss prints. Pays $200-500.
Color: Uses transparencies. Pays $200-500.
Cover: Uses 35mm, 2¼ × 2¼, 4 × 5 and 8 × 10 transparencies. Vertical format required. Pays $1,000/ photo or payment negotiated.
Tips: Seeing trend toward "more editorial/journalistic images, more use of b&w with color, use of photographers in proximity to destination, larger formats and 35mm." Demonstrate prior experience or show published travel-oriented work. Have a sense of "place" in travel photos. "Allow me to become familiar with your work, perhaps with stock requests, and then grow from there with smaller stories leading up to more comprehensive stories. We are proximity oriented when we can and are not likely to fly people great distances at great expense."

TRAVEL/HOLIDAY, 28 W. 23rd St., New York NY 10010. (212)633-4633. Editor: Margaret Simmons. Art Director: Windy Palitz. Monthly magazine. Circ. 816,000. Emphasizes quality photography on travel destinations, both widely known and obscure. For people "with the time and money to actively travel. We want to see travel pieces, mostly destination-oriented." Wants no "posed shots or snapshots." Readers are experienced travelers who want to be shown the unusual parts of the world. Credit line given. Buys 30 photos/issue. Buys first North American serial rights. Do not send samples for consideration. Pays on acceptance. Reports in 6 weeks. SASE. Write for free photo guidelines. Send printed stock list.
Subject Needs: Quality photography of all areas of world—scenics, people, customs, arts, amusements, etc. "We prefer shots which have people in them whenever possible."
B&W: Send 8 × 10 glossy or semigloss prints. Captions required. Pays $25.
Color: Send transparencies 35mm and larger. Captions required. Pays $75/¼ page, $100/½ page, $125/ ¾ page, $150/full page, $200/2-page spread.
Cover: Send color transparencies. Captions required. Pays $400. No research or holding fees paid.
Tips: "Send us a list that catalogues by geographic area the transparencies that you have on stock. Include, if applicable, a listing of recent publications in which your work has appeared. When we are seeking photography on a specific subject entered on your stock list, we will contact you at that time. We will be reviewing our payment schedule sometime in coming year."

TREASURE, 6278 Adobe Rd., 29 Palms CA 92277. (619)367-3531. FAX: (619)367-0039. Editor: Jim Williams. Photo Editor: Lee Chandler. Monthly magazine. "We cover all aspects of treasure hunting— including prospecting, archaeological digs, relic hunting, all applications of metal detectors, beach combing and so forth." Readers are searchers, taking as much delight in hunting as in finding their particular kind of "treasure." Circ. 40,000. Estab. 1970. Sample copy free with SASE. Photo guidelines free with SASE.
Photo Needs: Uses 35 photos/issue; 30 supplied by freelance photographers. "We need photos for how-to articles, of treasures that have actually been found, and of people involved in a search. What we would most like to see are photos of valuables that have actually been found and photos for how-to projects that would help readers." Model release preferred.
Making Contact & Terms: Send 35mm transparencies and b&w contact sheets by mail for consideration. SASE. Reports in 1 week. Pays $75/color cover photo; $3/b&w inside photo; $30/page; $30-50/text/photo package (page). Pays on publication. Credit line given. Buys all rights. Simultaneous submissions and previously published work OK.
Tips: "Photographers should study a copy of the magazine to understand the breadth of the subject matter and our needs. Since we report only what has actually been found or done, we avoid fabricated stories and photos, except for cover shots. We hope to improve the quality of our photos, which are often of a snapshot variety. If the freelance photographer can supply a manuscript of interest to our readers as well as photos, there is a good chance he or she will be published."

TREASURE SEARCH/FOUND, (formerly Treasure Search), 6278 Adobe Rd., Twenty-Nine Palms CA 92277. (619)367-3531. FAX: (619)367-0039. Executive Editor: Jim Williams. Editor: Lee Chandler. Monthly magazine. Emphasizes metal detecting, prospecting and underwater salvage. Readers are 35-65 years old, male, all occupations. Circ. 40,000. Estab. 1973. Sample copy free with 8½ × 11 SAE and $1.05 postage. Photo guidelines free with SASE.
Photo Needs: Uses 50 photos/issue; 40 supplied by freelance photographers. Needs photos of products, treasures found, subjects pertinent to stories about lost treasures. Reviews photos with accompanying manuscript only. Special photo needs include mainly cover photos, unless the photographer can supply an article with photo submissions. Model release, photo captions preferred.
Making Contact & Terms: Provide resume, business card, brochure, flyer or tearsheets to be kept on file for possible assignments. SASE. Reports in 2 weeks. Pays $75/color cover photo; $30/photo/ text package per magazine page. Pays on publication. Credit line given. Buys all rights; will negotiate with a photographer unwilling to sell all rights. Previously published work OK.

Tips: "Photographers should be able to supply manuscripts with their photos or willing to work with us in developing leads to stories."

*TRIATHLETE MAGAZINE, #303, 1415 Third St., Santa Monica CA 90401. (213)394-1321. Contact: Richard Graham. Monthly magazine. Covers multi-sport events: biathlon, triathlon, etc. Circ. 60,000. Sample copy free upon request.
Photo Needs: Uses 50-80 photos/issue; 30% supplied by freelances. Needs action photos of athletes. "Photos should be dramatic, exciting coverage of events." Model release and photo captions preferred.
Making Contact & Terms: Query with resume of credits. Send unsolicited 35mm transparencies by mail for consideration. SASE. Reports in 1 month. Pays $300/color cover photo. Pays on publication. Credit line given. Buys one-time rights.
Tips: "Know triathlon; know the stars."

TROPICAL FISH HOBBYIST MAGAZINE, One T.F.H. Plaza, Neptune NJ 07753. (201)933-8400. Contact: Editor. Monthly magazine. Emphasizes tropical and marine fishes. General readership. Circ. 60,000. Sample copy $3, 9×12 SASE and 4 first-class stamps.
Photo Needs: Needs photos of fresh and saltwater fishes, garden ponds and other marine hobby related photos. Uses approx. 100 photos/issue; 100% supplied by freelance photographers. Model release and photo captions preferred.
Making Contact & Terms: Send unsolicited photos by mail for consideration. Send color 35mm transparencies. SASE. Reports in 1 month. Pays $10/color inside photo. Pays on acceptance. Credit line given. Buys all rights, but "photographer may sell elsewhere after TFH publication." Previously published work OK.
Tips: In porfolio or samples, looking especially for shots of endangered and rare species.

TRUE WEST, Box 2107, Stillwater OK 74076. (405)743-3370. Editor: John Joerschke. Monthly. Circ. 30,000. Emphasizes "history of the Old West (1830 to about 1910)." Readers are "people who like to read the history of the West." Estab. 1953. Sample copy $1 with 8½×11 SASE.
Photo Needs: Uses about 100 or more photos/issue; almost all are supplied by freelance photographers. Needs "mostly Old West historical subjects, some travel, some scenic, (ghost towns, old mining camps, historical sites). We prefer photos with manuscript." Special needs include western wear; cowboys, rodeos, western events.
Making Contact & Terms: Query with samples—b&w only for inside; color for covers. SASE. Reports in 1 month. Pays $75-150/color cover photo; $10/b&w inside photo; "minimum of 3¢/word for copy." Pays on acceptance. Credit line given. Buys one-time rights.
Tips: Prefers to see "transparencies of existing artwork as well as scenics for cover photos. Inside photos need to tell story associated with the Old West. Most of our photos are used to illustrate stories and come with manuscripts; however, we will consider other work, scenics, historical sites, old houses. Even though we are Old West history, we do need current photos, both inside and for covers—so don't hesitate to contact us."

TURN-ONS, TURN-ON LETTERS, UNCENSORED LETTERS, OPTIONS, BEAU, Box 470, Port Chester NY 10573. Photo Editor: Wayne Shuster. Periodical magazines. Emphasizes "sexually oriented situations. We emphasize good, clean sexual fun among liberal-minded adults." Readers are mostly male; age range 18-65. Circ. 75,000. Sample copy $2.95 with 6×9 SAE and 85¢ postage (*Uncensored Letters* $3.50 with 9×12 SASE and $1.05 postage).
Photo Needs: Uses approximately 20-30 b&w photos/issue, all stock. Needs a "variety of b&w photos depicting sexual situations of boy-girl, girl-girl, boy-boy, girl-boy-girl scenes. Also need color transparencies of single girls, girl-girl, and single boys for cover; present in a way suitable for newsstand display." Model release and picture ID's required.
Making Contact & Terms: Query with samples. Send 8×10 glossy b&w prints or 35mm, 2¼×2¼, 4×5 transparencies by mail for consideration. SASE. Reports in 2 weeks. Pays $250/color cover photo and $20/b&w inside photo. Pays on publication. Buys one-time rights on covers, second rights OK for b&ws.
Tips: "Please examine copies of our publications before submitting work. In reviewing samples we consider composition of color photos for newsstand display and look for recently photographed b&w's for inside."

TV GUIDE, Radnor PA 19088. (215)293-8500. Editor, National Section: David Sendler. Art Director: Jerry Alten. Picture Editors: Maureen Griffin (Los Angeles), Ileane Rudolph (New York). Emphasizes news, personalities and programs of TV for a general audience. Weekly. Circ. 16,300,000.
Photo Needs: Uses 20-25 photos/issue; many supplied by freelance photographers. Selection "through photo editors in our New York and Los Angeles bureaus. Most work on assignment. Interested in hearing from more photographers."

Making Contact & Terms: Call or write photo editors to arrange personal interview to show portfolio. Buys one-time rights. Credit line given. No simultaneous submissions or previously published work.

TWINS MAGAZINE, Box 12045, Overland Park KS 66212. (913)722-1090. Editor: Barbara Unell. Bimonthly. Emphasizes parenting twins, triplets, quadruplets, or more and being a twin, triplet, quadruplet or more. Readers include the parents of multiples. Circ. 40,000. Sample copy free with SASE. Free photo guidelines with SASE.
Photo Needs: Uses about 10 photos/issue; all supplied by freelance photographers. Needs family related — children, adults, family life. Usually needs to have twins, triplets or more included as well. Reviews photos with or without accompanying ms. Model release and captions required.
Making Contact & Terms: Query with resume of credits and samples; provide resume, business card, brochure, flyer or tearsheets to be kept on file for possible future assignments. SASE. Reports in 4-6 weeks. Pays $100 minimum/job. Pays on publication. Credit line given. Buys all rights. Simultaneous submissions OK.

ULTRA MAGAZINE, Suite 350, 1400 Post Oak Blvd., Houston TX 77056. (713)622-1967. Asst. Art Director: Connie Willhite. Monthly magazine. Emphasizes upscale lifestyles. Readers are women (70%) in top management, average age of 48. Circ. 100,000. Sample copy $3.95 and 11×14 SASE.
Photo Needs: Uses 40-50 photos/issue; 100% supplied by freelance photographers. Needs people profile photos, fashion, architecture, travel, products and food. Model release and photo captions preferred.
Making Contact & Terms: Query with resume of credits with business card, brochure, flyer or tearsheets to be kept on file for possible assignments. Query with list of stock photo subjects. "Query first, then we'll request portfolio." Reports in 1 month. Pays on publication. Credit line given. Buys one-time rights. Previously published work OK.
Tips: In porfolio or samples, looking for "originality in treatment of difficult subjects; also technical perfection." To break in, "be persistent, provide excellent references and spell the art director's name correctly."

UNITY, Unity Village MO 64065. Editor: Philip White. Associate Editor: Janet McNamara. Monthly magazine. Circ. 430,000. Emphasizes spiritual, self-help, poetry and inspirational articles. Photos purchased with or without accompanying ms or on assignment. Uses 20-25 photos/issue. Buys 280 photos/year, 90% from freelancers. Credit line given. Pays on acceptance. Buys first North American serial rights. Send insured material by mail for consideration; no calls in person or by phone. SASE. Reports in 4-8 weeks. Free sample copy and photo guidelines.
Subject Needs: Wants on a regular basis people and nature scenics for covers and 10-20 b&w scenics. Also human interest, nature, still life and wildlife. Animal photos used sparingly. Model release required; captions preferred.
B&W: Uses 5×7 or 8×10 semigloss prints. Pays $35/photo.
Cover: Uses 4×5 color transparencies. Vertical format required, occasional horizontal wraparound used. Pays $200/cover, $65-125 inside color photo.
Accompanying Mss: Pays $25-200/ms. Rarely buys mss with photos. Free writer's guidelines.
Tips: "Don't overwhelm us with hundreds of submissions at a time. We look for nature scenics, human interest, some still life and wildlife, photos of active people (although the primary interest of the photo is not on the person or persons). We are looking for photos with a lot of color and contrast."

UP HERE, Box 1350, Yellowknife NT X1A 2N9 Canada. (403)920-4652. FAX: (403)873-2844. Editor: R. Allerston. Bimonthly magazine. Estab. 1980. Emphasizes Canada's north. Readers are white collar men and women ages 30 to 60. Circ. 25,000. Sample copy $3 and 9×12 SASE. Photo guidelines free with SASE.
Photo Needs: Uses 20-30 photos/issue; 90% supplied by freelance photographers. Purchases photos with accompanying ms only. Photo captions required.
Making Contact & Terms: Provide resume, business card, brochure, flyer or tearsheets to be kept on file for possible assignments. SASE. Reports in 1-2 months. Pays $35-100/b&w photo; $35-500/color photo; $150-500/cover. Pays on publication. Credit line given. Buys one-time rights.
Tips: "We are a PEOPLE magazine. We're moving more into "outdoor adventure" — soft type, as they say in the industry — and wildlife. Few scenics as such. We approach local freelancers for given subjects, but are building a library. We can't always make use of photos alone, but a photographer could profit by sending sheets of dupes for our stock files." Wants to see "Sharp, clear photos, good color & composition — We always need verticals to consider for the cover, but they usually tie in with an article inside."

UTAH HOLIDAY MAGAZINE, Suite 200, 8th Floor, 807 E. Southtemple, Salt Lake City UT 84102. (801)532-3737. Art Director: Jeff Ray. Monthly magazine. Emphasizes Salt Lake City and Utah in general. Readers are professional, business or self-employed people, 30-49 years of age. Circ. 18,000. Sample copy free with 9×12 SASE and 5 first class stamps.
Photo Needs: Uses 30-40 photos/issue; 100% supplied by freelance photographers. Needs photos of travel, scenics, people. Purchases photos with accompanying ms only. Model release and photo captions required.
Making Contact & Terms: Query with resume of credits and list of stock photo subjects. SASE. Reports in 1 month. Pays $300/color cover photo, $200/color inside photo and $100-150/b&w inside photo. Pays on publication. Credit line given. Buys one-time rights. Simultaneous submissions and previously published work OK.

UTNE READER, 1624 Harmon Pl., Minneapolis MN 55403. (612)338-5040. Managing Editor: Lynette Lamb or Art Director: Consumer publication. Bimonthly magazine. Readers are half and half men and women, very well educated, professional/managerial, ages 25-45. Circ. 200,000. Estab. 1984. Sample copy $4.
Photo Needs: Uses 40-50 photos/issue; 100% supplied by freelance photographers; 95% freelance and stock; 5% assigned. "We do a lot on urban issues, the environment, social issues, international politics and domestic politics." Reviews photos only; "no manuscripts please." Model release and photo captions preferred.
Making Contact & Terms: Query with list of stock photo subjects; "do not send photos—we want stocklists only." Does not return unsolicited material. Pays $75-150/color inside photo, $50-125/b&w inside photo. Pays on publication. Credit line given. Buys one-time rights. Simultaneous submissions and previously published work OK.
Tips: Plan on "More color in the next year. Send stock list, don't expect to hear back unless we have a specific photo request."

***VAIL MAGAZINE**, 2077 N. Frontage Rd. West, Vail CO 81657. (303)476-6600. Editor: Charles McNamara. Managing Editor: Mary Morgan Parker. Consumer magazine, published 3 times/year. Emphasizes Vail and the surroundings. Circ. 20,000. Estab. 1976. Sample copy free with SASE.
Photo Needs: Uses 40 photos/issue; 85% supplied by freelance photographers. Needs wide range of subject matter. Model release and photo captions preferred.
Making Contact & Terms: Query with list of stock photo subjects. SASE. Reports in 1-2 weeks. Pays $300/color cover photo. $200-250/color inside photo; $250/day. Pays on acceptance. Credit line given. Buys one-time rights. Previously published work OK.

VEGETARIAN TIMES, Box 570, Oak Park IL 60303. (708)848-8100. Art Director: Gregory Chambers. Published 12 times annually. Circ. 100,000. Buys 80 photos/year; 90% specific, 10% stock. Credit line given. Pays 30 days after acceptance. Rights vary. Send material by mail for consideration. SASE. Simultaneous submissions OK. Reports in 6 weeks. Sample copy $2.
Subject Needs: Primary: food (with styling) to accompany articles. Celebrity/personality (if vegetarians), sport, spot news, how-to (cooking and building), humorous. Model release and captions preferred.
B&W: Uses 8×10 glossy prints. Pays $40 minimum/photo.
Cover: Pays $300 and up (color slide).
Tips: "We consider composition, color usage, flair with food when reviewing photographer's samples."

VENTURE, Box 150, Wheaton IL 60189. (312)665-0630. Editor: Steven P. Neideck. Art Director: Robert Fine. Magazine published 6 times annually. Circ. 23,000. Estab. 1959. Sample copy $1.50 with 9×12 SAE and 85¢ postage. "We seek to provide entertaining, challenging, Christian reading for boys 10-15." Needs photos of boys in various situations: alone; with other boys; with their families; in school; with animals; involved in sports, hobbies or camping, etc. Buys 1-2 photos/issue; freelance photography/issue-75% assignment; 25% stock. Buys first serial rights. Arrange a personal interview to show portfolio or send photos for consideration. Pays on publication. Reports in 6 weeks. SASE. Simultaneous submissions and previously published work OK. Photo guidelines available (SASE).
B&W: Send 8×10 glossy prints. Pays $35.
Cover: Send glossy b&w prints. Pays $75-100.

VERMONT LIFE, 61 Elm St., Montpelier VT 05602. (802)828-3241. Editor: Tom Slayton. Quarterly magazine. Circ. 130,000. Emphasizes life in Vermont: its people, traditions, way of life, farming, industry, and the physical beauty of the landscape for "Vermonters, ex-Vermonters and would-be Vermonters." Buys 30 photos/issue; 75% original, 25% stock/regular "scenic" submissions. Buys first serial rights. Query first. Credit line given. Pays day rate of $200. Pays on publication. Reports in 3 weeks. SASE. Simultaneous submissions OK. Sample copy $4 with 8½×11 SAE; free photo guidelines.

Subject Needs: Wants on a regular basis scenic views of Vermont, seasonal (winter, spring, summer, autumn), submitted 6 months prior to the actual season; animal; documentary; human interest; humorous; nature; photo essay/photo feature; still life; travel and wildlife. "We are using fewer, larger photos and are especially interested in good shots of wildlife, birds." No photos in poor taste, nature close-ups, cliches or photos of places other than Vermont.

Color: Send 35mm or 2¼ × 2¼ transparencies. Captions required. Pays $75.

Cover: Send 35mm or 2¼ × 2¼ color transparencies. Captions required. Pays $200.

Tips: "We look for clarity of focus; use of low-grain, true film (Kodachrome is best); unusual composition or subject."

VERMONT MAGAZINE, Box 288, 14 School St., Bristol VT 05443. (802)453-3200. Picture Editor: Lisa Furgatch. Bimonthly magazine. Emphasizes all facets of Vermont and nature, politics, business, sports, restaurants, real estate, people, crafts, art, architecture, etc. Readers are all people interested in state of Vermont, including residents, tourists and summer home owners. Circ. 50,000. Estab. 1989. Sample copy for $3, 9 × 12 SASE and 5 first class stamps. Photo guidelines free with SASE.

Photo Needs: Uses 50 photos/issue; 75% supplied by freelance photographers. Needs animal/wildlife shots, travel, scenics, how-to, portraits, products and architecture. Special photo needs include Vermont scenics and Vermont activities such as skiing, ice skating, swimming, biking, hiking, etc. Model release preferred; photo captions required.

Making Contact & Terms: Arrange a personal interview to show portfolio; query with resume of credits and samples of work. Send 8 × 10 b&w prints or 35mm or larger transparencies by mail for consideration; submit portfolio for review; provide tearsheets to be kept on file for possible assignments. SASE. Reports in 1 month. Pays $450/color cover photo, $200/color page rate. Pays on publication. Credit line given. Buys one-time rights and first N.A. serial rights. Previously published work OK, depending on "how it was previously published."

Tips: In portfolio or samples, wants to see "tearsheets of published work, and at least 40 35mm or transparencies. Get some copies of the magazine, see if your skill and style will fit, send in portfolio with query."

VICTIMOLOGY: AN INTERNATIONAL JOURNAL, 2333 N. Vernon St., Arlington VA 22207. (703)536-1750. Editor: Emilio C. Viano. Quarterly journal. Circ. 2,500. "We are the only magazine specifically focusing on the victim, on the dynamics of victimization." For social scientists; criminologists; criminal justice professionals and practitioners; social workers; volunteer and professional groups engaged in crime prevention and in offering assistance to victims of rape, spouse abuse, child abuse, etc.; victims of accidents, neglect, natural disasters, and occupational and environmental hazards. Needs photos related to those themes. Buys 20-30 photos/annually. Buys all rights, but may reassign to photographer after publication. Submit model release with photo. Query with resume of credits or submit material by mail for consideration. Pays on publication. Reports in 6 weeks. SASE. Simultaneous submissions and previously published work OK. Sample copy $5; free editorial guidelines.

B&W: Send contact sheet or 8 × 10 glossy prints. Captions required. Pays $25-50 depending on subject matter.

Color: Send 35mm transparencies, contact sheet, or 5 × 7 or 8 × 10 glossy prints. "We will look at color photos only if part of an essay with text." Captions required. Pays $30 minimum. "Collages OK."

Cover: Send contact sheet or glossy prints for b&w; contact sheet, glossy prints, or 35mm transparencies for color. Captions required. Pays $200 minimum.

Tips: "Contact us so that we can tell what themes we are going to be covering. Send us pictures around a theme, with captions and, if possible, a commentary—some text, even if not extensive. We will look at any pictures that we might use to break the monotony of straight text, but we would prefer essays with some text. A very good idea would be for a photographer to look for a writer and to send in pictures accompanying text as a package. For instance, an interview with the staff of a Rape Crisis Center or Abused Spouses Center or Crisis Intervention Hotline or victims of a natural or industrial disaster accompanied by photos would be very well received. Other topics: accident prevention, earthquake monitoring, emergency room services, forensic pathologists, etc. A good example of what we are looking for is the work of the Smiths on the victims of mercury poisoning in Japan. We will pay well for good photo essays."

THE VIRGINIAN MAGAZINE, P.O. Box 7480, Atlantic Station, VA Beach VA 23458. (804)422-5577. Editor: Jeffrey Wexler. Art Director: Ron Wright. Bimonthly magazine. Emphasizes the state of VA (leisure, travel, history, food, people, etc.). Readers are upscale, college-educated. Circ. 25,000. Sample copy $4. Photo guidelines free with SASE.

Photo Needs: Uses 100 photos/issue; 25% supplied by freelance photographers. Needs photos of scenics, wildlife, seasonal activities.

Making Contact & Terms: Send transparencies (35mm preferred) by mail for consideration; provide resume, business card, brochure, flyer or tearsheets to be kept on file for possible future assignments; or drop off and pick up policy. "We are not liable for loss or damage of material." SASE. Reports in 1 month. Payment negotiated. Pays 30 days after publication. Credit line given. Buys one-time rights. Simultaneous submissions OK.

Tips: "Past issues will give photographers a clearer idea of what we need. The magazine aspires to quality of *National Geographic* photos and leans toward photos which stand by themselves or Norman Rockwell-type story pictures."

VIRTUE MAGAZINE, 548 Sisters Parkway, Box 850, Sisters OR 97759. (503)549-8261. Art Director: Geoff Sprague. Magazine published 6 times/year. Emphasizes Christian growth, marriage, family, food and fashion. Readers are women—mostly married, ages 25-45, Christian, family-oriented. Circ. 230,000. Sample copy $30.

Photo Needs: Uses about 25-30 photos/issue; all supplied by freelance photographers. "Most freelance photos are assigned." Needs photos of "people relating to each other and to their environment, scenics, wildlife, travel; mood shots which would be difficult for us to set up." Model release required.

Making Contact: Query with samples or "send Xerox prints or printed copies to be kept on file. Besides submitting examples of current work, please submit tear sheets from previous assignments with other publications. Also please submit stock lists and any information on particular specialties and interests." Reports in 2 months. Pays $40-150/b&w inside photo, and $75-250/color inside photo. Transparencies only for color photos. Pays on publication. Credit line given. Buys one-time rights. Simultaneous submissions OK.

Tips: "Black and white must be very well printed—very smooth, little grain. They shouldn't be too contrasting, plenty of grays, good range white to black. Color transparencies should have rich color; they should be crisp. Send b&w prints on spec.—10-15 to be held for 2 months. Family oriented but also scenics. Transparencies OK too, but printed samples/promos, etc., are preferred. Freelance work we use is specifically assigned to fit an article's subject matter."

VISION MAGAZINE, Box 7259, Grand Rapids MI 49510. (616)241-5616. FAX: (616)241-5558. Editor: Dale Dieleman. A general interest magazine for young adults 18 to 30. Buys 40 photos annually; 90% freelance from stock. Sample copy free with 9×12 SAE and 3 first class stamps.

Subject Needs: Subjects include young adults in the work-a-day world, recreational settings, individual and group shots; multi-racial.

Specs: Uses 8×10 glossy b&w prints.

Payment & Terms: Pays $20-50/photo. Credit line given. Buys one-time rights. Model release required.

Making Contact: Send samples. Interested in stock photos. SASE. Reports in 1 month.

Tips: In samples wants to see "More than faces, we look for activity, unusual situations or settings, and symbolism. Good contrast in b&w and no out-of-date fashion or hair. We are trying to tie photos in with story content, using more symbolic or abstract photography. We've used photo's of pigs, sun beams from behind a cloud, a booted foot about to step on a coiled snake. For people shots we need a multi-ethnic variety. Send a packet of photos. We will photocopy and return photos, requesting those we wish to use when we are ready to publish."

*VOICE OF SOUTH MARION, P.O. Box 700, Belleview FL 32620. (904)245-3161. Editor: Jim Waldron. Weekly tabloid. Readers are male and female, ages 12-65, working in agriculture and various small town jobs. Circ. 1,700. Estab. 1969. Sample copy $1.

Photo Needs: Uses 5-10 photos/issue; 2 supplied by freelance photographers. Feature pictures that can stand alone with a cutline. "Must have a cutline." Photo captions required.

Making Contact & Terms: Send 35mm and 2¼×2¼ b&w prints by mail for consideration. SASE. Reports in 1-2 weeks. Pays $10/b&w cover photo; $5/b&w inside photo. Pays on publication. Buys one-time rights. Credit line given.

VOLLEYBALL MONTHLY, Box 3137, San Luis Obispo CA 93401. (805)541-2294. FAX: (805)541-2438. Co-Publishers/Editors: Jon Hastings, Dennis Steers. Monthly. Emphasizes volleyball. Readers are volleyball enthusiasts. Circ. 60,000. Estab. 1982. Sample copy free with 9×12 SASE and $2 postage.

Photo Needs: Model release preferred; captions required.

Making Contact & Terms: Query with samples. Send b&w prints or transparencies by mail for consideration. SASE. Reports in 2 weeks. Pays $150/color cover photo; $25-50/b&w photo; $50-150/color photo; $150-300/day. Pays on publication. Credit line given. Buys one-time rights.

WASHINGTON, The Evergreen State Magazine, 200 W. Thomas, Seattle WA 98119. (206)285-9009. Photo Editor: Karen Gutowsky. Bimonthly magazine. "We're a regional publication covering the entire state of Washington." Readers are "anybody and everybody living in the state, who wants to live in the state, or who is going to visit the state." Circ. 70,000. Sample copy $3.10; photo guidelines for SASE.

Photo Needs: Uses approximately 50 photos/issue; 35 supplied by freelance photographers. Needs "any and all subjects, provided all subjects are in Washington state. No ringers, please." Model release and captions required. "Captions need not be elaborate; they must, however, identify the subject matter and provide names of persons."

Making Contact & Terms: Submit portfolio for review; provide resume, business card, brochure, flyer or tearsheets to be kept on file for possible future assignments. "Preference is to set up an appointment and come in." SASE. Reports in 2 months. Pays $325/color cover photo, $250/b&w cover photo; $125-275/color inside photo, $50-200/b&w inside photo; $200/color page, $125/b&w page. Pays on publication. Credit line given "either individually for single shots or by-lined for multiple." Buys one-time rights or inclusive of use for magazine promotion. Simultaneous and previously published submissions OK, "depending on the subject and where published."

WASHINGTON POST MAGAZINE, 1150 15th St., NW, Washington DC 20071. (202)334-7585. Art Director: Mark Danzig. Photo Editor: Molly Roberts. Weekly. Circ. 1,200,000. Emphasizes current events, prominent persons, cultural trends and the arts. Readers are all ages and all interests.

Photo Needs: Uses 30 photos/issue; all are supplied by freelance photographers. Needs photos to accompany articles of regional and national interest on anything from politics to outdoors. Photo essays of controversial and regional interest. Model release required.

Making Contact & Terms: Call for appointment. Uses 8×10 or larger b&w prints; 35mm, 2¼×2¼, 4×5 or 8×10 slides. Color preferred. Reports in 2 weeks. Credit line given. Payment on publication. "Call first; just don't send samples."

WASHINGTONIAN, Ste. 200, 1828 L St. NW, Washington DC 20036. (202)296-3600. Photo Editor: Kathleen Hennessy. Monthly city/regional magazine emphasizing Washington metro area. Readers are in their 30s and 40s; 54% female-46% male and middle to upper-middle professionals. Circ. 160,000.

Photo Needs: Uses 75-150 photos/issue; 50% supplied by freelance photographers. Needs photos of people for illustration, portraits, reportage; table-top for illustration, products, food; restaurants; nightlife; house and garden; fashion; and local and regional travel. Model release preferred; photo captions required.

Making Contact & Terms: Submit portfolio for review; provide resume, business card, brochure, flyer or tearsheets to be kept on file for possible assignments. Cannot return material. Reports in 1 month. Pays $175/half day-$350/day. Credit line given. Buys one-time rights.

Tips: "Read the magazine you want to work for. Show work that relates to their needs. Offer photo-story ideas. Send samples occasionally of good new work."

*WATER SCOOTER, Suite 101, 319 Barry Ave. S., Wayzata MN 55391. (612)476-2200. Editor: Michael Dapper. Bimonthly magazine. Emphasizes personal watercraft. Readers are mostly male, ages 16-40 (concentrated in 19-25), all occupations. Circ. 100,000. Estab. 1987. Sample copy for $3.50.

Photo Needs: Uses 40+ photos/issue; 10% supplied by freelance photographers. Needs photos of personal watercraft action; water-oriented vacation site coverage. Model release and captions preferred.

Making Contact & Terms: Query with resume of credits. SASE. Reports in 1 month. Pays $200/color cover photo; $40/color inside photo; $20/b&w inside photo. Pays on publication. Credit line given. Buys first North American serial rights.

Tips: "Color and action are the keys to our photography."

WATERWAY GUIDE, 6255 Barfield Rd., Atlanta GA 30328. FAX: (404)256-3116. Editor: Judith Powers. Quarterly cruising guide. Emphasizes recreational boating. Readers are men and women ages 25-65, management or professional, with average income $95,000 a year. Circ. 70,000. Estab. 1947. Sample copy $25.95 and $3 shipping. Photo guidelines free with SASE.

Photo Needs: Uses 25-50 photos/issue; 100% supplied by freelance photographers. Needs photos of boats, intercoastal waterway, bridges, landmarks, famous sights and scenic waterfronts. Expects to use more coastal shots from Maine to the Bahamas; also, more Great Lakes and Gulf of Mexico. Model release and photo captions required.

Making Contact & Terms: Send unsolicited photos by mail for consideration. Send b&w and color prints or 35mm transparencies. SASE. Reports in 1 month. Pays $500/color cover photo or $25/b&w inside photo;$50-500/color photo. Pays on publication. Credit line given. Buys first N.A. serial rights.

WEIGHT WATCHERS, 360 Lexington Ave., New York NY 10017. (212)370-0644. Editor: Lee Haiken. Art Director: Lisa Moore. Monthly magazine. Circ. 1,000,000. For those interested in weight control, fitness, nutrition, inspiration and self-improvement. Photos purchased on assignment only. Buys approximately 12 photos/issue. Pays $300/single page; $500/spread; and $700/cover. Credit line given. Pays on acceptance. Buys first rights. Portfolio—drop-off policy only.

Subject Needs: All on assignment: food and tabletop still life, beauty, health and fitness subjects, fashion, personality portraiture. All photos contingent upon editorial needs.

WESTERN HORSEMAN, 3850 N. Nevada Ave., Box 7980, Colorado Springs CO 80933. (719)633-5524. Editor: Pat Close. Monthly magazine. Circ. 180,598. For active participants in horse activities, including pleasure riders, ranchers, breeders and riding club members. Buys first rights. Submit material by mail for consideration. "We buy mss and photos as a package. Payment for 1,500 words with b&w photos ranges from $100-225. Articles and photos must have a strong horse angle, slanted towards the western rider—rodeos, shows, ranching, stable plans, training."

WESTERN OUTDOORS, 3197-E Airport Loop, Costa Mesa CA 92626. Editor-in-Chief: Burt Twilegar. Monthly magazine. Circ. 151,001. Estab. 1961. Emphasizes hunting, fishing for 11 western states, Alaska, Western Mexico and Canada. Needs cover photos of hunting and fishing in the Western states. "We are moving toward 100% four-color books, meaning we will be buying only color photography in the near future. A special subject need will be photos of boat-related fishing, particularly small and trailerable boats." Buys one-time rights "but will negotiate." Query or send photos for consideration. Most photos purchased with accompanying ms. Pays on acceptance for covers. Reports in 4 weeks. SASE. Sample copy $1.50 with SASE. Free editorial guidelines; with SASE.

B&W: Pays $25-100/b&w photo.

Color: Send 35mm Kodachrome II transparencies. Captions required. Pays $25-100/color photo; $200-250/cover photo; $300-500 for text/photo package.

Tips: "Submissions should be of interest to western fishermen or hunters, and should include a 1,120-1,500 word ms; a Trip Facts Box (where to stay, costs, special information); photos; captions; and a map of the area. Emphasis is on fishing and hunting how-to, some where-to-go. Submit seasonal material 6 months in advance. Make your photos tell the story and don't depend on captions to explain what is pictured. Avoid 'photographic cliches' such as 'dead fish with man,' dead pheasants draped over a shotgun, etc. Get action shots, live fish and game. We avoid the 'tame' animals of Yellowstone and other national parks. In fishing, we seek individual action or underwater shots. For cover photos, use vertical format composed with action entering picture from right; leave enough left-hand margin for cover blurbs, space at top of frame for magazine logo. Add human element to scenics to lend scale. Get to know the magazine and its editors. Ask for the year's editorial schedule (available through advertising department) and offer cover photos to match the theme of an issue. In samples, looks for color consistency, naturalness of the scene, amount of action, alertness and pose of wildlife and composition. Send duplicated transparencies as samples, but be prepared to provide originals."

WESTERN SPORTSMAN, Box 737, Regina, Saskatchewan S4P 3A8 Canada. (306)352-8384. FAX: (306)565-2440. Editor: Roger Francis. Bimonthly magazine. Audited Circ. 30,000. Estab. 1967. Emphasizes fishing, hunting and outdoors activities in Alberta and Saskatchewan. Photos purchased with or without accompanying ms. Buys 100 freelance photos/year; 90% freelancers "who send stuff on a whim" and 10% stock.. Pays on acceptance. Send material by mail for consideration or query with a list of stock photo subjects. SASE. Reports in 3 weeks. Sample copy $4; free photo guidelines with SASE.

Subject Needs: Sport (fishing, hunting, camping); nature; travel; and wildlife. Captions required.

B&W: Uses 8×10 glossy prints. Pays $35-50/photo.

Color: Uses 35mm and 2¼×2¼ transparencies. Pays $75-150/photo for inside pages.

Cover: Uses 35mm and 2¼×2¼ transparencies. Vertical format preferred. Pays $250-350/photo.

Accompanying Mss: Fishing, hunting and camping. Pays $75-325/ms. Free writer's guidelines with SASE.; $350/photo/text package.

Tips: Looks for "Covers—strong vertical components that work well within our established masthead layout; Interiors—crisp, clear definition of main figure. Animal *action* rather than animal portraiture. Close up shots or still shots of animals and fish often look posed. Reality comes through with movement and dimension. Don't let the main subject look like a stuffed museum piece! Send a small selection for the photo editor to review. We keep notes on many photographers, their strengths and weaknesses—and often call back for specfic items."

WESTWAYS, Box 2890, Los Angeles CA 90051. (213)741-4760. Art Director: Paul Miyamoto. Emphasizes Western US and world travel, leisure time activities, people, history, culture and western events.
Making Contact & Terms: Query first with sample of photography enclosed. Pays $25/b&w photo; $50/color transparency; $300-350 plus $50 per photo published for text/photo package.
Tips: "We like to get photos with every submitted manuscript. We take some photo essays (with brief text), but they must be unusual and of interest to our readers. All photos should be tack sharp originals for final reproduction and well captioned. Trends in our use of editorial photography include high drama and high photographic art."

WHEELINGS, Box 389, Franklin MA 02038. (508)528-6211. Editor: J.A. Kruza. Published 6 times/year, tabloid-size magazine. Emphasizes auto body shops, auto paint shops, auto dealers, auto paint manufacturers. Readers are auto industries with 8 or more employees. Circ. 14,000. Photo guidelines free.
Photo Needs: Uses 25 photos/issue; usually 10-15 supplied by freelance photographers. "We need news-type photos relating to the industry." Captions required.
Making Contact & Terms: Query with samples. SASE. Reports in 2 weeks. Pays $25 first photo, $10 for each additional photo; buys 3-5 photos in a series. Pays on acceptance. Credit line given. Prefers all rights; reassigns to photographer after use. Simultaneous submissions and previously published work OK.
Tips: "Do some work and get in touch with us."

WHERE MAGAZINE, 15th Fl., 600 Third Ave., New York NY 10016. (212)687-4646. Editor-in-Chief: Michael Kelly Tucker. Monthly. Emphasizes points of interest, shopping, restaurants, theater, museums, etc., in New York City (specifically Manhattan). Readers are visitors to New York staying in the city's leading hotels. Circ. 125,000/month. Sample copy available in hotels.
Photo Needs: Covers showing New York scenes. No manuscripts. Model release and captions preferred.
Making Contact & Terms: Arrange a personal interview to show portfolio. Does not return unsolicited material. Payment varies. Pays on publication. Credit line given. Rights purchased vary. Simultaneous submissions and previously published work OK.

WILDLIFE CONSERVATION MAGAZINE, (formerly Animal Kingdom), New York Zoological Park, Bronx NY 10460. (212)220-5121. FAX: (212)584-2625. Editor: Eugene J. Walter, Jr. Photo researcher: Miriam Helbok. Bimonthly. Emphasizes wildlife conservation and natural history, especially of endangered species. Readers include mature people (over 12), interested in wildlife and nature. Circ. 125,000. Sample copy available for $2.95; photo guidelines free with SASE.
Photo Needs: Uses 25 photos/issue; supplied by freelance photographers and researchers. Needs wildlife photos. Captions required.
Making Contact & Terms: Query with list of stock photo subjects. Send ideas for photo-essays but do not send unsolicited photos. Reports in 1 month. Pays $50-200/b&w photo; $75-300/color photo. Other page sizes and approximate rates available; request rate sheet. Pays on publication. Credit line given. Buys one-time rights. Simultaneous submissions OK.
Tips: "We're looking for very striking images that can be blown up large and still be very clear." In portfolio or samples, wants to see "brilliant color, unusual views and wildlife in action." To break in, "compile a fairly specific list of species and geographic areas; concentrate on specific species; get series of behavioral shots."

WINDSOR THIS MONTH, Box 1029, Station "A", Windsor, ON N9A 6P4 Canada. (519)977-0007. Monthly. Circ. 25,000. "*Windsor This Month* is mailed out in a system of controlled distribution to 25,000 households in the area. The average reader is a university graduate, middle income and active in leisure area." Sample copy free with 8½ × 11 SAE and 50¢ Canadian postage (IRC).
Photo Needs: Uses 12 photos/issue; all are supplied by freelance photographers. Selects photographers by personal appointment with portfolio. Uses photos to specifically suit editorial content; specific seasonal material such as skiing and other lifestyle subjects. Provide resume and business card to be kept on file for possible future assignments. Model release and captions required.
Making Contact & Terms: Send material by mail for consideration and arrange personal interview to show portfolio. Uses 8 × 10 prints and 35mm or larger format transparencies. SASE. Reports in 2 weeks. Pays $100-300/photo/text package; $50/color cover; $25/b&w inside; $35/color inside. Credit line given. Payment on publication. Simultaneous and previously published work OK provided work hasn't appeared in general area.
Tips: "*WTM* is a city lifestyle magazine; therefore most photos used pertain to the city and subjects about life in Windsor."

WINE TIDINGS, 5165 Sherbrooke St. W., #414 Montreal, PQ H4A 1T6 Canada. (514)481-5892. Editor: Barbara Leslie. Published 8 times/year. Circ. 27,000. Estab. 1973. Emphasizes "wine for Canadian wine lovers, 85% male, ages 25 to 65, high education and income levels." Sample copy free with 9 × 12 SAE and International Reply Coupons.

Photo Needs: Uses about 15-20 photos/issue; most supplied by freelance photographers. Needs "wine scenes, grapes, vintners, pickers, vineyards, bottles, decanters, wine and food; from all wine producing countries of the world. Many fillers also required." Photos usually purchased with accompanying ms. Captions preferred.

Making Contact & Terms: Send any size b&w and color prints; 35mm or 2¼ × 2¼ transparencies by mail for consideration. SAE and International Reply Coupons. Reports in 5-6 weeks. Pays $150/color cover photo; $10-25/b&w inside photo; $25-100/color used inside. Pays on publication. Credit line given. Buys "all rights for one year from date of publication." Previously published work accepted occasionally.

Tips: "Send sample b&w prints with interesting, informed captions."

WINNING!, 15115 S. 76th E. Ave., Bixby OK 74008. (918)366-4441. FAX: (918)366-6250. Editor: Simon P. McCaffery. Monthly magazine. Emphasizes winning at casinos, state lotteries and creative contests. Readers are men and women ages 21-65. Circ. 175,000. Estab. 1976. Sample copy free with 8½ × 11 SASE and 2 first class stamps.

Photo Needs: Uses 15-20 photos/issue; 40% supplied by freelance photographers. Needs photos of exotic travel, casinos and gaming (lottery, bingo, etc.). Plans to use more "exotic" photos of resorts and casinos in U.S. and abroad. Model release and photo captions required.

Making Contact & Terms: Query with list of stock photo subjects, send unsolicited photos by mail for consideration. Provide resume, business card, brochure, flyer or tearsheets to be kept on file for possible assignments. Send b&w or color 3½ × 5 and larger gloss prints or 35mm transparencies. SASE. Reports in 2 weeks. Pays $250/color cover photo; $75-100/b&w cover photo; $50-150/color inside photo; or $50/b&w inside photo. Pays on acceptance. Credit line given. Buys one-time rights and first N.A. serial rights. Does consider previously published work.

Tips: In portfolio or samples, looking for "splashy, vividly colorful shots of people at casinos, resorts, cruise ships, race tracks, etc. Shots must show action and excitement. *Winning!* needs high-quality photos (of the aforementioned) that convey action, excitement and romance—not boring, static shots of buildings or objects."

WISCONSIN SPORTSMAN, Box 741, Marietta GA 30061. Editor: Jim Schlender. Monthly magazine. Emphasizes fishing, hunting, humor, nostalgia and the outdoors of Wisconsin. Sample copy $1.95. Photos purchased with or without accompanying ms. Buys 100 photos/year; 50% on assignment, 50% stock. Pays $175-350 for text/photo package, and on a per-photo basis; $250 for cover, $75 for inside color and $25 for black and white. Credit line given. Pays 2½ months prior to publication. Send material by mail for consideration or query with list of stock photo subjects. SASE. Previously published work OK.

Subject Needs: Animal (upper Midwest wildlife); sport (fishing, hunting); still life (hunting/fishing oriented). "Good fishing/hunting action scenes." Captions preferred.

B&W: Uses 8 × 10 glossy prints. Pays $25.

Color: Uses transparencies. Pays $75/inside photo.

Cover: Uses color transparencies. Vertical format preferred. Pays $250.

Accompanying Mss: How-to oriented toward fishing, hunting and outdoor activities in the upper Midwest; where/to for these activities in Wisconsin. *Wisconsin Sportsman* frequently buys in combination with sister publications in Minnesota, Michigan and other states.

Tips: "We look for dramatic, well-exposed photos of game fish, game animals or game birds, preferably alive and in a natural-looking environment."

WISCONSIN TRAILS, Box 5650, Madison WI 53705. (608)231-2444. Photo Editor: Nancy Mead. Bimonthly magazine. Circ. 30,000. For people interested in history, travel, recreation, personalities, the arts, nature and Wisconsin in general. Needs seasonal scenics and photos relating to Wisconsin. Annual Calendar: uses horizontal format; scenic photographs. Pays $175. Wants no color or b&w snapshots, color negatives, cheesecake, shots of posed people, b&w negatives ("proofs or prints, please") or "photos of things clearly not found in Wisconsin." Buys 200 photos annually. Buys first serial rights or second serial (reprint) rights. Query with resume of credits, arrange a personal interview to show portfolio, submit portfolio or submit contact sheet or photos for consideration. Provide calling card and flyer to be kept on file for possible future assignments. Pays on publication. Reports in 3 weeks. SASE. Simultaneous submissions OK "only if we are informed in advance." Previously published work OK. Photo guidelines with SASE; sample copy $3.

B&W: Send contact sheet or 5×7 or 8×10 glossy prints. "We greatly appreciate caption info." Pays $50. Most done on assignment.

Color: Send transparencies; "we use all sizes." Locations needed. Pays $50-150.

Cover: Send 35mm, 2¼×2¼ or 4×5 color transparencies. Photos "should be strong seasonal scenics or people in action." Uses vertical format; top of photo should lend itself to insertion of logo; or a square to be boxed. Locations preferred. Pays $150.

Tips: "Because we cover only Wisconsin and because most b&w photos illustrate articles (and are done by freelancers on assignment), it's difficult to break into *Wisconsin Trails* unless you live or travel in Wisconsin." Also, "be sure you specify how you want materials returned. Include postage for any special handling (insurance, certified, registered, etc.) you request."

WITH, Box 347, Newton KS 67114. (316)283-5100. Editor: Susan E. Janzen. Monthly magazine. Circ. 6,500. Estab. 1968. Emphasizes "Christian values in lifestyle, vocational decision making, conflict resolution for US and Canadian high school students." Photos purchased with or without accompanying ms and on assignment. Buys 120 photos/year; 10 photos/issue. Pays $20-35/b&w photo, 4¢/word for text/photo packages, or on a per-photo basis. Credit line given. Pays on acceptance. Buys one-time rights. Send material by mail for consideration or submit portfolio and resume for review. SASE. Simultaneous submissions and previously published work OK. Reports in 6 weeks. Sample copy $1.25 with 9×12 SAE and 85¢ postage; photo guidelines free with SASE.

Subject Needs: Documentary (related to concerns of high school youth "interacting with each other, with family and in school environment"); fine art; head shot; photo essay/photo feature; scenic; special effects & experimental; how-to; human interest; humorous; still life; and travel. Particularly interested in mood/candid shots of youths. Prefers candids over posed model photos. Less literal photos, more symbolism. Few religious shots, e.g., crosses, Bibles, steeples, etc.

B&W: Uses 8×10 glossy prints. Pays $25-35/photo.

Cover: Uses b&w glossy prints. Pays $30-50/photo.

Accompanying Mss: Issues involving youth—school, peers, family, hobbies, sports, community involvement, sex, dating, drugs, self-identity, values, religion, etc. Pays 4¢/printed word. Writer's guidelines free with SASE.

Tips: "Freelancers are our lifeblood. We're interested in photo essays, but good ones are scarce. Candid shots of youth doing ordinary daily activities and mood shots are what we generally use. Photos dealing with social problems are also often needed. We rely greatly on freelancers, so we're interested in seeing work from a number of photographers. *With* is one of several periodicals published at this office, and we also publish Sunday school curriculum for all ages here, so there are many opportunities for photographers. Needs to relate to teenagers—either include them in photos or subjects they relate to; using a lot of 'nontraditional' roles, also more ethnic and cultural diversity, more emphasis on current global events. Use models who are average-looking, not obvious model-types. Teenagers have enough self esteem problems without seeing 'perfect' teens in photos."

WOMAN ENGINEER, Equal Opportunity Publications, Inc., 44 Broadway, Greenlawn NY 11740. (516)261-8917. FAX: (516)261-8935. Associate Editor: Eileen Nester. Quarterly magazine. Emphasizes career guidance for women engineers, at the college and professional levels. Readers are college-age and young professional women in engineering. Circ. 16,000. Estab. 1979. Sample copy free with 9×12 SASE and 6 first class stamps.

Photo Needs: Uses at least one photo per issue (cover); planning to use freelance work for covers and possibly editorial; most of the photos are submitted by freelance writers with their articles. Contact for needs. Model release preferred; photo captions required.

Making Contact & Terms: Query with list of stock photo subjects. Send unsolicited photos by mail for consideration. Send color and 35mm transparencies. SASE. Reports in 2 weeks. Pays $25/color cover photo; $15/b&w photo; $15/color photo. Pays on publication. Credit line given. Buys one-time rights. Simultaneous submissions and previously published work OK, "but not in competitive career-guidance publications."

Tips: "'We are looking for strong, sharply focused photos or slides of women engineers. The photo should show a woman engineer at work, but the background should be uncluttered. The photo subject should be dressed and groomed in a professional manner. Most important—the photo should be in focus! Cover photo should represent a professional woman engineer at work, convey a positive and professional image. Read our magazine, and find actual women engineers to photograph. We are not against using cover models, but we prefer the cover subjects to be women engineers working in the field."

WOMAN'S WORLD, 270 Sylvan Ave., Englewood Cliffs NJ 07632. (201)569-0006 Ext. 400. Editor-in-Chief: Dena Vane. Photo Editor: Melinda Patelli. Weekly. Circ. 1,200,000. Emphasizes women's issues. Readers are women 25-60 nationwide of low to middle income. Sample copies available.

In a composition which balances between photojournalism and fine art, this photo of homeless people on a park bench was used to bring to life a poem about human suffering in With *magazine. The magazine, which emphasizes Christian values to its high school readers, selected the striking image by photographer Jeffrey High "because of its crispness and poignancy." In addition to being paid for one-time rights, High notes that he was especially pleased with the page layout. "The way the photo was used made for good reprints for promo purposes," he points out.*

Photo Needs: Uses up to 100 photos/issue; all supplied by freelancers and stock houses. Needs travel, fashion, crafts and celebrity shots. "For editorial pages we look for informative straightforward photos of women's careers, travel, people in everyday personal situations and medicine. Photographers should be sympathetic to the subject, and our straightforward approach to it." Photos purchased with or without accompanying ms. Model release and captions required. "Not responsible for any materials sent on spec. Please talk with someone at the magazine before sending anything."
Making Contact & Terms: Query with 8×10 b&w glossy prints or 35mm transparencies or provide basic background and how to contact. Prefers to see tearsheets of published work, or prints or slides of unpublished work, as samples. SASE. Reports in 1 month. Provide resume and tearsheets to be kept on file for possible future assignments. Pays $250/day plus expenses; $300/page for color and fashion; $150-200/day for b&w. Pays on acceptance. Credit line given. Buys one-time rights.

WOMEN'S SPORTS AND FITNESS MAGAZINE, Suite 421, 1919 14th St., Boulder CO 80302. (303)440-5111. Photo Editor/Art Director: Ian Paton. Monthly. Circ. 300,000. Readers are active women who are vitally interested in health and fitness. Recreational interests include participation in two or more sports, particularly cycling, running and swimming. Sample copy and photo guidelines free with SASE.
Photo Needs: 80% of photos supplied by freelance photographers. "Photo needs mailed out for each issue." Model release and captions preferred.
Making Contact & Terms: Send 35mm, 2¼×2¼ or 4×5 transparencies by mail for consideration. Provide resume, business card, brochure, flyer or tearsheets to be kept on file for possible future assignments. SASE. Reports in 1 month. Pays $400/color cover; $50-300/color inside; $200/color page. Pays on publication. Credit line given. Buys one-time rights.
Tips: Looks for "razor sharp images and nice light. Check magazine before submitting query."

WOODENBOAT MAGAZINE, Naskeag Rd., Box 78, Brooklin ME 04616. (207)359-4651. Art Director: Lindy Gifford. Bimonthly magazine. Emphasizes wooden boats. Readers are builders, designers, owners, and lovers of wooden boats. Circ. 120,000. Sample copy $3.50 with 8½ × 11 SAE and $1.50 postage. Photo guidelines free with SASE.

Photo Needs: Uses 100-150 photos/issue; 50% supplied by freelance photographers. Needs photos relating to articles. "Much better chance of purchase with ms." Model release required only for advertising purposes; captions preferred.

Making Contact & Terms: Query with samples. SASE. Reports in 3 weeks. Pays $350/color cover photo (according to size used). Pays on publication. Credit line given. Buys first North American serial rights. Simultaneous submissions and previously published work OK with notification.

Tips: "Please become familiar with our publication before contacting us."

WORKBENCH MAGAZINE, 4251 Pennsylvania Ave., Kansas City MO 64111. Editor: Robert N. Hoffman. Managing Editor: A. Robert Gould. Bimonthly magazine. Circ. 850,000. Emphasizes do-it-yourself projects for the woodworker and home maintenance craftsman. Photos are purchased with accompanying ms. "We also purchase photos to illustrate articles, including 'beauty' lead photographs." Photographs of tools, home interiors and exteriors, furniture, wood crafts and home accessories. Pays $150-300/published page. Credit line given with ms. Pays on acceptance. Buys all rights, but may reassign to photographer after publication. Ask for writer's guidelines, then send material by mail for consideration. SASE. Reports in 4 weeks. Free sample copy and photo guidelines.

Subject Needs: How-to; needs step-by-step shots. Model release required; captions preferred.

B&W: Uses 5 × 7 or 8 × 10 glossy prints. Pay is included in purchase price with ms.

Color: Uses 2¼ × 2¼ or 4 × 5 transparencies and 8 × 10 glossy prints. Pays $125 minimum/photo.

Cover: Uses 4 × 5 color transparencies. Vertical format required. Pays $450 minimum/photo.

Accompanying Mss: Seeks how-to mss. Pays $150-300/published page. Free writer's guidelines.

Tips: Prefers to see "sharp, clear photos; they must be accompanied by story with necessary working drawings. See copy of the magazine. We are happy to work with photographers in developing story ideas."

WORLD OF WHEELS MAGAZINE, 2061 McCowan Rd., #207, Scarborough ON M1S 3Y6 Canada. (416)297-9277. Editor: Joe Duarte. Magazine published 5 times yearly, (Feb., Apr., June, Oct., Dec.). Emphasizes automotive. Readers are mostly male, average age of 37, average household income of $50,000. Circ. 140,000. Sample copy free with 8½ × 11 SASE.

Photo Needs: Uses approximately 50 photos/issue. Automobile related spy photos preferred. Model release and photo captions required.

Making Contact & Terms: Send unsolicited photos by mail for consideration. Send b&w and color prints, 35mm, 2¼ × 2¼, 4 × 5 and 8 × 10 transparencies. Does not return photos if used. Reports in 1 week. Pays $100/color cover photo, $50/color or b&w inside photo. Pays on publication. Credit line given. Buys all rights. "Photo becomes our property." Simultaneous submissions and previously published work OK.

Tips: "Look for original angles."

WRESTLING WORLD, Lexington Library, Inc., 355 Lexington Ave., New York NY 10017. FAX: (212)986-5926. Editor: Stephen Ciacciarelli. Magazine published bimonthly. Emphasizes professional wrestling superstars. Readers are wrestling fans. Circ. 50,000. Sample copy $2.25 with 9 × 12 SAE and 75¢ postage.

Photo Needs: Uses about 60 photos/issue; all supplied by freelance photographers. Needs photos of wrestling superstars, action and posed, color slides and b&w prints.

Making Contact & Terms: Query with representative samples, preferably action. SASE. Reports ASAP. Pays $150/color cover photo; $75/color inside photo; $50-125/text/photo package. Pays on acceptance. Credit line given on color photos. Buys one-time rights.

YANKEE PUBLISHING, INC., Dublin NH 03444. (603)563-8111. Managing Editor: Tim Clark. Editor: Judson D. Hale. Editorial Director: John Pierce. Photography Editor: Stephen O. Muskie. Monthly magazine. Circ. 1,000,000. Emphasizes the New England lifestyle of residents of the 6-state region for a national audience. Buys 50-70 photos/issue. Credit line given. Buys one-time rights. Query only. Provide calling card, samples and tearsheets to be kept on file for possible future assignments. SASE. Previously published work OK. Reports in 4-6 weeks. Free photo guidelines.

Subject Needs: "Outstanding photos are occasionally used as centerspreads; they should relate to surrounding subject matter in the magazine. Photo essays ('This New England') must have strong and specific New England theme, i.e., town/region, activity or vocation associated with the region, etc. All *Yankee* photography is done on assignment." No individual abstracts. Captions required.

B&W: Uses 8×10 glossy prints; contact sheet OK.
Color: Uses 35mm, 2¼×2¼ and 4×5 transparencies. Pays $150/printed page; $50-300/b&w and color photo; $150-300/day; $1,500/maximum package.
Tips: "Send in story ideas after studying *Yankee* closely. We look for pro-level quality. Shouldn't have to make excuses or apologies for *anything* in a portfolio. Be persistent. Study the magazine."

*YELLOW JERSEY PUBLICATIONS: TEXAS BICYCLIST, FLORIDA BICYCLIST AND CALIFORNIA BICYCLIST, 490 Second St., #304, San Francisco CA 94107. (415)546-7291. Managing Editor: Ms. Shawn McAndrew. Monthly tabloid. Emphasizes bicycling. Readers are 80% male-20% female professionals, ages 18 and older. Circ. 300,000. Estab. 1983. Sample copy for 10×14 SAE with $1 postage.
Photo Needs: Uses 15-20 photos/issue; most supplied by freelance photographers. Needs photos of bicycling—all aspects. Model release preferred.
Making Contact & Terms: Query with list of stock photo subjects. SASE. Reports "when we can get to it." Pays $300/color cover photo; $50/color inside photo; $50/b&w inside photo. Pays on publication. Credit line given.

YELLOW SILK: Journal of Erotic Arts, Box 6374, Albany CA 94706. (415)644-4188. Editor: Lily Pond. Quarterly magazine. Circ. 15,000. Emphasizes literature, arts and erotica. Readers are well educated, creative, liberal. Sample copy $6.
Photo Needs: Uses about 15-20 photos "by one artist" per issue. Have published the work of Judy Dater, Tee Corinne, Sandra Russell Clark and Stephen John Phillips. "All photos are erotic; none are cheesecake or sexist. No porn. We define 'erotic' in its widest sense; trees and flowers can be as erotic as humans making love. They are fine arts." Model release required.
Making Contact & Terms: Query with samples; submit prints, transparencies, contact sheets or photocopies by mail for consideration; submit portfolio for review. SASE. Reports in 3 months. Payment to be arranged." Pays on publication. Credit line given. Buys one-time rights; "use for promotional and/or other rights arranged."
Tips: "Get to know the publication you are submitting work to and enclose SASE in all correspondence. Interested in color work at this time."

YM, 685 Third Ave., New York NY 10017. (212)878-8602. Photo Editor: Martha Maristany. Monthly magazine. Readers are girls from ages 17-21. Magazine emphasizes fashion/beauty. Circ. 1 million and growing. Sample copy free upon request. Photo guidelines available.
Photo Needs: Needs "street photos of fashion, fashion, beauty and celebrities. Model release and photo captions preferred; "depending on subject."
Making Contact & Terms: Submit portfolio for review. Reports in 2 weeks, sometimes longer. Pays $300/color page rate or $200-250/b&w page rate. Buys all rights; non-negotiable. Simultaneous submissions and previously published work OK.
Tips: In portfolio or samples, looking for "good sense of color, light and composition." Also, photos that are "natural, fun, hip, well-styled and fairly unique." To break in, "send only your best and favorite work. Look at our magazine before contacting us."

YOUR HEALTH, 5401 NW Broken Sound Blvd., Boca Raton FL 33487. (800)233-7733, (407)997-7733. Editor: Susan Gregg. Photo Editor: Judy Browne. Biweekly tabloid. Emphasizes healthy lifestyles: aerobics, sports, eating, celebrity fitness plans, plus medical advances and the latest technology. Readers are consumer audience; males and females from early 20's through 70's. Circ. 40,000. Estab. 1963. Sample copy free wtih 9×11 SASE. Call for photo guidelines.
Photo Needs: Uses 40-45 photos/issue; all supplied by freelance photographers. Needs photos depicting nutrition and diet, sports (runners, tennis, hiking, swimming, etc.), food, celebrity workout, pain and suffering, arthritis and bone disease, skin care and problems. Also any photos illustrating exciting technological or scientific breakthroughs. Model release required.
Making Contact & Terms: Provide resume, business card, brochure, flyer or tearsheets to be kept on file for possible future assignments, and call to query interest on a specific subject. SASE. Reports in 2 weeks. Pay depends on photo size and color. Pays on publication. Pays $25-75/b&w photo; $75-200/color photo; $75-150/photo/text package. Buys one-time rights. Simultaneous submissions and previously published work OK.
Tips: "Pictures and subjects should be interesting; bright and consumer-health oriented. We are using both magazine-type mood photos, and hard medical pix. We are looking for different, interesting, unusual ways of illustrating the typical fitness, health nutrition story; e.g. an interesting concept for fatigue, insomnia, vitamins. Send prints or dupes to keep on file. Our first inclination is to use what's on hand."

YOUR HOME, Meridian Publishing, Box 10010, Ogden UT 84409. Editor/Publisher: Caroll Shreeve. Distributed to businesses to be used, with their inserts, as their house magazine. "A monthly pictorial magazine with emphasis on home decor, buying, home construction, financing, landscaping and working with realtors. We prefer manuscripts (800 to 1,200 words) with color transparencies." No do-it-yourself pieces, emphasize using professionals.

Payment & Terms: 15¢/word; $35 for color transparencies. Also needed are vertical transparencies for covers. $50/cover. "These should have dramatic composition with sharp, contrasting colors." Six-month lead time. Buys first North American rights. Credit line given. Payment on acceptance. Send SASE for guidelines. Sample copy $1 plus 9 × 12 envelope.

Tips: Prefers to see "interior and exterior views of homes; good interior decor ideas; packages (photos with text) on home, garden, decorating and improvement ideas." Photos and text are commonly purchased as a package. About 95% of work is assigned. Send clear sharp pictures with contrasting colors for our review. The photo department is very strict about the quality of pictures chosen for the articles. Send queries to the attention of the editor."

Special Interest

Many corporations and nonprofit organizations use publications to communicate to their primary audiences as well as to interested secondary audiences in the general public. Typically, the primary audience consists of association members, professional staff and personnel, investors or business affiliates in allied industries. Generally, these special interest publications are available either by subscription or on controlled-circulation basis only. However, when the publications cover highly specialized topics that also have some popular or wider industry appeal, there is some overlap in audiences and the publications are sometimes also made available to those readers.

In this edition of *Photographer's Market*, two previously separate categories of publications—Association and Company Publications—have been combined to form this one new category, Special Interest Publications. Most of these publications are for clearly defined readerships, which are indicated in the beginning of the listing. For instance, association publications will generally be described with the phrase, "Publication of The (Name) Association." For company publications, the identifying phrase is, "Company publication for the (Name) Co. or Corp." Some publications which are published by associations or companies but are generally intended for consumer or trade audiences may be found in one of those other market sections.

Though the subject matter, readerships and circulation sizes of these publications vary, their photo editors do share a need for top-notch photos. Also, an ability to write can often make your work more desirable to photo editors with publications that look primarily for photo/text packages. These publications include a description of their subject and manuscript needs in the listing. When you query such a publication, be sure to point out your knowledge or expertise with their particular subject, activities or business.

As with most publications, breaking in will probably happen in stages. You may be assigned smaller projects at first, but once you supply quality material—on time and within budget—you may quickly find yourself a regular contributor to the publication. In addition to shooting editorial work, you may also be offered additional noneditorial opportunities as you become known within the parent company or organization. Among these would be shooting publicity materials, executive portraits, product advertising and documentation of company or organization events.

There are more than 200 listings in this newly combined section, including 50 new listings. Also, there are a number of listings returning to the book after being inactive over the last couple of editions. Like other categories of publications, this category includes many listings with substantial changes. All of these changes—in contact people, addresses, photo needs and payment rates—are updated in this year's *Photographer's Market*.

If you are looking to break into publication work through listings in this section, you may want to check the First Markets Index in the back of this book for any Special Interest titles. Generally, markets such as these, which offer lower payment or photo credits and contributor's copies in place of payment, are the most receptive to working with photographers who are new to the market.

For both the beginner and the established photographer, the Close-up interview in this section will offer numerous insights about shooting for association publications. The interview, which appears early in the section, features Doug Damerst, editor and publisher for *AAA World*, magazine of the American Automobile Association.

AAA MICHIGAN LIVING, 17000 Executive Plaza Dr., Dearborn MI 48126. (313)336-1211. FAX (313)336-1897. Editor: Len Barnes. Managing Editor: Jo-Anne Harman. Monthly magazine. Estab. 1918. Circ. 1,023,000. Emphasizes auto use, as well as travel in Michigan, US and Canada.
Photo Needs: Scenic and travel. Captions required. "We rarely buy photos without accompanying ms. We maintain a file on stock photos and subjects photographers have available." Buys 100-200 photos/year. For b&w, uses 8×10 glossy prints. Pays $25-35/b&w. For color, uses 35mm, 2¼×2¼ or 4×5 transparencies. Pays $16-125/depending on quality and size. For covers in particular, uses 35mm, 4×5 or 8×10 color transparencies. Vertical format preferred. Pays up to $350.
Making Contact & Terms: Query with list of stock photo subjects. SASE. Simultaneous submissions and previously published work OK. Reports in 6 weeks. Free sample copy and photo guidelines. Credit line given. Pays on publication for photos, on acceptance for mss. Buys one-time rights.
Tips: Seeks mss about travel in Michigan, US and Canada. Pays $150-300/ms.

AAA WORLD, 1000 AAA Drive, Heathrow, FL 32746-5063. (703)222-6386. Editor/Associate Publisher: Doug Damerst. Association publication of AAA. Bimonthly magazine emphasizing how to drive, car care, how to travel and travel destinations. Readers are above average income and age. Circ. 2,180,000. Sample copy free.
Photo Needs: Uses 60 photos/issue; 20 supplied by freelancers. Needs photos of people enjoying domestic and international vacation settings. Model release required; captions preferred. Provide resume, business card, brochure, flyer or tearsheets to be kept on file for possible future assignments. Does not return unsolicited material. Reports in 3 weeks. Pays $75/color inside photo. Pays on acceptance. Credit line given. Buys one-time rights. Simultaneous and previously published submissions OK.
Tips: "Our need is for travel photos, but not of places as much as of people enjoying travel."

ACADEME: BULLETIN OF THE AAUP, Suite 500, 1012 14th St. NW, Washington DC 20005. (202)737-5900. Managing Editor: Kathryn Evans. Publication of the American Association of University Professors. Bimonthly. Emphasizes higher education. Readers are college and university professors, all disciplines. Circ. 43,000.
Photo Needs: Uses about 4 photos/issue. Needs photos of classroom shots, campus scenes, general faculty photos. Model release preferred.
Making Contact & Terms: Query with samples; query with list of stock photo subjects; send 8×10 glossy b&w prints or b&w contact sheets by mail for consideration; or submit portfolio for review. Provide resume, business card, brochure, flyer or tearsheets to be kept on file for possible future assignments. SASE. Reports in 2 weeks. Pays approximately $250/b&w cover; $400/color cover; $50-100/b&w inside photo. Pays on publication. Credit line given. Buys one-time rights. Simultaneous submissions and previously published work OK.
Tips: "In reviewing a photographer's portfolio or samples, we look for ability to capture environment of college/university campus and the people who inhabit that environment."

*****ADVENTURE ROAD,** 200 E. Randolph Dr., Chicago IL 60601. (312)856-2583. Editor: Marilyn Holstein. Publication of Amaco Motor Club. Bimonthly magazine. Emphasizes vacation travel. Readers are 60% male and 40% female, typically ages 48 and up. Circ. 1,500,000. Estab. 1965. Sample copy free for SASE.
Photo Needs: Uses 30-50 photos/issue; 100% supplied by freelance photographers. Model release and photo captions required.
Making Contact & Terms: Query with resume of credits. Pays $1,000/color cover photo; $200/color inside photo. Pays on publication. Credit line given. Buys one-time rights.

*****AG ALERT,** 1601 Exposition Blvd., Sacramento CA 95815. (916)924-4140. Editor: Steve Adler. Publication of the California Farm Bureau. Weekly tabloid. Covers agriculture for farmers of all ages. Circ. 50,000. Estab. 1978. Sample copy free with SASE.
Photo Needs: Uses approx. 5 photos/issue; occasionally uses freelancers. Needs photos that cover agriculture in California. Especially wants to see transparencies of cotton production in California. Model release preferred; photo captions required.
Making Contact & Terms: Query with suggestions of photo possibilities. If sending samples, include SASE. Reports in 3 weeks. Pays $50-150/color cover photo; $50-100/b&w inside photo. Pays on acceptance. Credit line given. Buys first North American serial rights. Does not accept simultaneous submissions and previously published work.

Tips: Call editor and discuss publication's needs personally.

AI MAGAZINE, 445 Burgess Dr., Menlo Park CA 94025. (415)328-3123. FAX: (415)321-4457. Publishing Consultant: David Hamilton. Publication of American Association of Artificial Intelligence (AAAI). Quarterly. Estab. 1980. Emphasizes artificial intelligence. Readers are research scientists, engineers, high-technology managers, professors of computer science. Circ. 13,000. Sample copy $4 with 9 × 12 SAE and $2.40 postage.
Photo Needs: Uses about 3-5 photos/issue; all supplied by freelance photographers. Needs photo of specialized computer applications. Model release and captions required.
Making Contact & Terms: Arrange a personal interview to show portfolio; query with list of stock photo subjects; provide resume, business card, brochure, flyer or tearsheets to be kept on file for possible future assignments. SASE. Reports in 3 weeks. Pays $100-1,000/color cover photo; $25-250/color inside photo. Pays on publication. Credit line given. Buys one-time and first North American serial rights. Simultaneous submissions and previously published work OK.
Tips: Looks for "editorial content of photos, not artistic merit."

AIR LINE PILOT, 535 Herndon Parkway, Box 1169, Herndon VA 22070. (703)689-4172. Photography Editor: Bob Moeser. Association publication of Air Line Pilots Association. Monthly. Emphasizes news and feature stories for commercial airline pilots. Circ. 40,000. Estab. 1933. Photo guidelines for SASE.
Photo Needs: Uses 12-15 photos/issue; 25% comes from by freelance stock. Needs dramatic 35mm Kodachrome transparencies of commercial aircraft, pilots and co-pilots performing work-related activities in or near their aircraft. Special needs include dramatic 35mm Kodachromes technically and aesthetically suitable for full-page magazine covers. Especially needs vertical composition scenes. Model release and captions required.
Making Contact & Terms: Query with samples; send unsolicited photos by mail for consideration. Uses 35mm transparencies. SASE. Pays $35/b&w photo; $35-250/color photo. Pays on acceptance. Buys one-time rights or all rights; willing to negotiate with photographer unwilling to sell all rights. Simultaneous submissions and previously published work OK.
Tips: In photographer's samples, wants to see "strong composition, poster-like quality and high technical quality. Photos compete with text for space so they need to be very interesting to be published. Be sure to provide brief but accurate caption information and send in only top, professional quality work. For our publication, cover shots do not need to tie in with current articles. This means that the greatest opportunity for publication exists on our cover."

ALABAMA MUNICIPAL JOURNAL, 535 Adams Ave., P.O. Box 1270, Montgomery AL 36102. (205)262-2566. Publications Manager: Anne Roquemore. Association publication of Alabama League of Municipalities. Monthly magazine. Emphasizes municipal government and its responsibilities. Readers are municipal officials—mayors, councilmembers, judges, clerks, attorneys, male and female; ages 20-80; black and white, varied occupations besides municipal offices. Circ. 4,200. Estab. 1945. Sample copy and guidelines free with 8½ × 11 SAE.
Photo Needs: Uses 2-3 photos/issue (more depending on availability and appropriateness of subjects). Needs photos of daily operations of municipal government—police, fire, courts, sanitation, etc. Model release required; photo captions preferred.
Making Contact & Terms: Query with resume of credits and list of stock photo subjects. Provide resume, business card, brochure, flyer or tearsheets to be kept on file for possible assignments. Returns unsolicited material if SASE is enclosed. Reports in 1 month. Does offer photo credit and pays in copies (usually 3). Credit line given. Previously published work OK.
Tips: "Photos which grab the reader's attention and contribute to the story we are telling are most welcome. Don't strive for fanciness yet maintain some artistry in the photos."

*THE ALABAMIAN, Drawer Q University of Montevallo, Montevallo AL 35115. (205)665-6336/665-8615. Photo Editor/Editor-in-Chief: James Olliff/D.L. Richardson. Publication of University of Montevallo. Biweekly newspaper. Emphasizes news pertinent to college students. Readers are male and female students ages 17-23.. Circ. 2,500. Estab. 1922. Sample copy free with SASE.

The asterisk before a listing indicates that the market is new in this edition. New markets are often the most receptive to freelance submissions.

Close-up

Doug Damerst
Editor and Associate Publisher
AAA World
Heathrow, Florida

Are you an assignment or stock photographer trying to get freelance work with a magazine? The best tack, suggests Doug Damerst of the Florida-based association publication *AAA World*, is to review sample copies of a prospective magazine before randomly submitting photos. If you study the publication's use of photos, this editor says, you will have a clear idea of its needs and can avoid the pitfalls of submitting subjects just recently covered. Lack of such awareness, he warns, will most often lead to automatic rejection of your work.

About 25 percent of the photos used in *AAA World*, the publication of the American Automobile Association with a monthly readership of 2.3 million, comes from stock images supplied by freelancers. The shots are exclusively travel-oriented, specifically of people visiting various destinations and enjoying all types of travel experiences. "It seems a never ending complaint from travel editors; we can't find travel stock that includes [people] in the scene," Damerst remarks. As travel magazines increase in number in the 1990s, Damerst says he expects this to be an even greater problem. The stock photographer must "offer interesting perspective and make vicarious travel possible for the magazine's readers," he advises. "A great travel photo should include strong foreground interest full of textures or action."

Photographers who have various categories of stock images available should always include a list of subjects on file, says Damerst. This list (and subsequent updates) is used for researching future images that a magazine may need, and without the list, photographers will rarely attract any attention. Model releases are frequently required and should be included, too. A further necessity is a price quote. Damerst points out that he looks for lower rates [from freelancers] than those currently being charged by stock photo agencies.

As Damerst also notes, many more of the photos used in *AAA World*—about three-fourths—are assigned rather than bought from freelance stock. A high level of skill and expertise is necessary for these, says Damerst, since assigned photos involve setups used to illustrate editorials. These often take the form of large productions requiring scene-building and the directing of a cast of actors or models, he explains. The photographer, who is always accompanied on a shoot by an editor to insure that the photo accurately illustrates the text, is given license to work out imaginative perspectives and compositions, and to summon believable, natural action from the actors.

There is a great need for tight control of a situation while shooting assignment photos, Damerst stresses. Rather than traveling to the more remote setting that may be dictated by a magazine article, he often prefers to enhance a nearby location. With one project, he notes, he "needed photos for an article about driving in Europe. While it was within our means to go to Europe for the shoot, we chose to set up a French street in Georgetown. Unless the budget is unlimited, you can simply lose too much control going overseas to shoot."

Damerst prefers to assign work to photographers based in Washington DC or Orlando, Florida. After contacting *AAA World* about its needs, a photographer who seems interesting to the magazine will be invited for a portfolio review with the magazine's art director. Assignments are offered to those freelancers skilled and experienced in the type of people-oriented production shot that meets the magazine's visual style. Then, after a couple of assignments, the photographer is reevaluated before being given more work.

Although *AAA World* is open to photo/text packages by photographer/writer teams, rarely have any such duos contacted the magazine, says Damerst. He also notes that he has never found a person strong in both areas, and accordingly, he refuses to compromise quality in either copy or photos.

According to Damerst, one of the most memorable shoots he has assigned since he came to *AAA World* three and a half years ago was of a completely setup freeway scene. "We needed to photograph the interaction between drivers when they change lanes at highway speeds," he explains. "Utilizing an unfinished highway—yes, we had to put stripes on the road!—cars and trucks were placed at appropriate intervals. While the finished photo looked like simple stop-action with the camera looking rearward from a moving vehicle, the fact that the scene was shot standing still avoided a certainly dangerous and possibly uncontrollable photo session. Sometimes a photographer's best creative and re-sourceful work goes on well off-camera."

— Connie Springer

Photographer Barry M. Winiker says this photo, which he took while on a Caribbean cruise, "conveys the vitality of the cruise experience." AAA World apparently agreed and paid the New York City-based freelancer $150 to use the photo in illustrating a cruise-related article for its readers. Winiker points out that he made his first contact with the magazine by sending a stock list to the editor, and she called him not long after that to discuss her photo needs.

Photo Needs: Uses 7-10 photos/issue. Needs photos of anything of interest to college students in SE area. Special photo needs include advertising. Model release preferred; photo captions required.
Making Contact & Terms: Query with list of stock photo subjects. Send unsolicited 5×7 or 8×10 b&w glossy prints, 35mm or 2¼×2¼ color prints by mail for consideration. No resume but flyers, brochures, etc. accepted. Will return unsolicited material if a SASE is enclosed. Reports in 1-2 weeks. Pays $5/b&w cover photo; $5/b&w inside photo. Pays on publication. Credit line given. Buys one-time rights. Silumtaneous submissions and previously published work OK if credit is given to original publication.
Tips: Looks for "anything the photographer feels would be of interest for a college newspaper. Local."

ALCALDE MAGAZINE, Box 7278, Austin TX 78713. (512)471-3799. FAX: (512)471-8832. Editor: Ernestine Wheelock. Publication of the University of Texas Ex-Students' Association. Bimonthly magazine. Emphasizes University alumni. Readers are graduates, former students and friends who pay dues in the Association. Circ. 48,000. Estab. 1913. Sample copy free with 8½×11 SAE and $1.10 postage.
Photo Needs: Uses 65 photos/issue; 2-3 supplied by freelance photographers. Needs UT campus shots, professors, students, buildings, city of Austin, UT sports. Will review photos with accompanying ms only. Model release preferred; captions required.
Making Contact: Query with list of stock photo subjects; send 5×7 or 8×10 glossy b&w and color prints; 35mm, 2¼×2¼ or 4×5 transparencies by mail for consideration. SASE. Reports in 1 month. Fee negotiable. Pays $100/color cover photo; $25/b&w and color inside photo. Pays on publication. Credit line given. Buys one-time rights. Simultaneous submissions and previously published work OK if details of use are supplied.

ALFA OWNER, 1385 E. Warner Ave., Suite C, Tustin CA 92680. (714)259-8240. Editor: Julie Nichols. Publication of the Alfa Romeo Owners Club association. Monthly magazine. Emphasizes Alfa Romeo automobiles. Audience is upscale with median household income of $70,180. Majority hold executive, technical or professional positions. Average age is 35, with three quarters male readership. Circ. 5,500. Sample copy free with 9×12 SASE and 4 firstclass stamps.
Photo Needs: Uses 12 photos/issue; 50% supplied by freelance photographers. Needs shots of Alfa Romeos on the road, under-the-hood tech shots, photos of historical figures related to Alfa and "glamour" shots of Alfas. Written release and captions preferred.
Making Contact & Terms: Submit portfolio for review. SASE. Reports in 2 weeks. Pays $75-100/ color cover photo and $10/b&w inside photo. Negotiates hour and day rate. Pays on publication. Credit line given. Simultaneous submissions and previously published work OK.
Tips: "We would like to see the photographer's background in automotive photography. Experience in automotive photography is preferable, though such a background isn't crucial if the person's work is good enough. Photographers should send a combination of color slides and/or 5×7 prints (if possible), plus some b&w prints. For *Alfa Owner*, knowledge of the tech aspects of automobiles is very valuable, as we need technical shots almost as much as we need glamour and "on-the-road" photos. Focus and, for the cover, a vertical format are crucial."

*AMERICAN BAR ASSOCIATION JOURNAL, 750 N. Lake Shore Drive, Chicago IL 60611. (312)988-6002. Photo Editor: Beverly Lane. Publication of the American Bar Association. Monthly magazine. Emphasizes law and the legal profession. Readers are lawyers of all ages. Circ. 400,000. Estab. 1915. Photo guidelines available.
Photo Needs: Uses 50-100 photos per month; 80% supplied by freelance photographers. Needs vary; mainly shots of lawyers and clients.
Making Contact & Terms: Send non-returnable printed samples with resume and two business cards with rates written on back. "If samples are good, portfolio will be requested. ABA Journal keeps film. However, if another publication requests photos, we will release and send the photos. Then, that publication pays the photographer." Cannot return unsolicited material. Credit line given.
Tips: "NO PHONE CALLS. The ABA does not hire beginners."

AMERICAN BIRDS, 950 3rd Ave., New York NY 10022. (212)546-9193. Editor: Susan Roney Drennan. Managing Editor: Victoria Leidner. Publication of National Audubon Society. Published 5 times/year. Circ. 12,000. "Our major areas of interest are the changing distribution, population, migration and rare occurrence of the avifauna of North and South America, including Middle America and the West Indies. Readers are 'bird people only.' Of our 29,000 readers, 11% are professional ornithologists or zoologists, 79% serious amateurs, the rest novices." Sample copy $5; photo guidelines free with SASE.
Photo Needs: Uses one cover-quality shot, vertical format, color/issue. This most often supplied by freelance photographer. Also very interested in excellent b&w photos for inside use. Birds can be flying or perched, singly or in flocks, in any wild American habitat; picture essays on bird behavior.

Avoid zoo or back-yard shots. "Since we never know our needs too far in advance, best to send representative sampling."

Making Contact & Terms: Query with samples; send transparencies by mail for consideration; provide resume, business card, brochure, flyer or tearsheets to be kept on file for possible future assignments. SASE. Reports in 4 months. Pays up to $100/color cover photo. Pays on publication. Credit line given.

Tips: "We will probably be able to publish more photos this year than we have in the past. With rare exceptions, we look for very clear, easily identifiable birds. Diagnostic marks should be clearly visible, eyes open."

AMERICAN CRAFT, 45 W. 45th St., New York NY 10036. (212)869-9422. Editor: Lois Moran. Senior Editor: Pat Dandignac. Bimonthly magazine of the American Craft Council. Circ. 45,000. Estab. 1941. Emphasizes contemporary creative work in clay, fiber, metal, glass, wood, etc. and discusses the technology, materials and ideas of the artists who do the work. Pays on publication. Buys one-time rights. Arrange a personal interview to show portfolio. SASE. Previously published work OK. Reports in 1 month. Free sample copy with 9 × 12 SAE and 64¢ postage.

Photo Needs: Visual art. Shots of crafts: clay, metal, fiber, etc. Captions required.

B&W: Uses 8 × 10 glossy prints. Pays according to size of reproduction; $40 minimum.

Color: Uses 4 × 5 transparencies and 35mm film. Pays according to size of reproduction; $40 minimum.

Cover: Uses 4 × 5 color transparencies. Vertical format preferred. Pays $175-350.

*AMERICAN FITNESS, The Magazine of the Aerobics and Fitness Association of America, Suite 310, 15250 Ventura Blvd., Sherman Oaks CA 91403. (818)905-0040. Editor: Peg Jordan. 6 issues/year. Estab. 1983. Emphasizes exercise, fitness, health, sports nutrition, aerobic sports. Readers are fitness enthusiasts and professionals, 75% college educated, 66% female, majority between 20-45. Circ. 30,000. Sample copy $2.50.

Photo Needs: Uses about 20-40 photos/issue; most supplied by freelance photographers. Assigns 90% of work. Needs action photography of runners, aerobic classes, especially high drama for cover: swimmers, bicyclists, aerobic dancers, runners, etc. Special needs include food choices, male and female exercises, people enjoying recreation, dos and don'ts. Model release required.

Making Contact & Terms: Query with samples or with list of stock photo subjects; send b&w prints, 35mm, 2¼ × 2¼ transparencies, b&w contact sheets by mail for consideration. SASE. Reports in 2 weeks. Pays $20-35/b&w or color photo; $50-100 for text/photo package. Pays on publication. Credit line given. Buys first North American serial rights. Simultaneous submissions and previously published work OK.

Tips: Wants work that is "sharp, well-lighted, with good action."

AMERICAN FORESTS MAGAZINE, 1516 P St. NW, Washington DC 20005. Editor: Bill Rooney. Publication for the American Forestry Association. Emphasizes use, enjoyment and management of forests and other natural resources. Readers are "people from all walks of life, from rural to urban settings, whose main common denominator is an abiding love for trees, forests, or forestry." Monthly. Circ. 30,000. Sample copy and free photo guidelines with magazine-size envelope and $1.25 postage.

Photo Needs: Uses about 40 photos/issue, 35 of which are supplied by freelance photographers (most supplied by article authors). Needs woods scenics, wildlife, woods use/management and forestry shots. Model release and captions preferred.

Making Contact & Terms: Query with resume of credits. SASE. Reports in 6-8 weeks. Pays on acceptance $250/color cover photo; $25-40/b&w inside; $50-100/color inside; $350-800 for text/photo package. Credit line given. Buys one-time rights.

Tips: Seeing trend away from "static woods scenics, toward more people and action shots." In samples wants to see "overall sharpness, unusual conformation, shots that accurately portray the highlights and 'outsideness' of outdoor scenes."

AMERICAN HUNTER, Suite 1000, 470 Spring Park Place, Herndon VA 22070. (703)481-3360. Editor: Tom Fulgham. Monthly magazine. Circ. 1,400,000. Sample copy free with 9 × 12 SASE.

Photo Needs: Uses wildlife shots and hunting action scenes. Captions preferred.

Specs: Uses 8 × 10 glossy b&w prints and 35mm color transparencies. (Uses 35mm color transparencies for cover.) Vertical format required for cover.

Accompanying Mss: Photos purchased with or without accompanying mss. Seeks general hunting stories on North American game. Free writer's guidelines with SASE.

Payment & Terms: Pays $25-75/b&w print; $40-275/color transparency; $300/color cover photo; $200-450 for text/photo package. Credit line given. Pays on publication for photos. Buys one-time rights.

Making Contact: Send material by mail for consideration. SASE. Reports in 1 month. Free sample copy and photo guidelines with SASE.

AMERICAN LIBRARIES, 50 E. Huron St., Chicago IL 60611. (312)944-6780. Senior Production Editor: Edith McCormick. Publication of the American Library Association. Magazine published 11 times/year. Emphasizes libraries and librarians. Readers are "chiefly the members of the American Library Association but also subscribing institutions who are not members." Circ. 50,000. Sample copy free with SASE. General guidelines free with SASE.

Photo Needs: Uses about 5-20 photos/issue; 1-3 supplied by freelance photographers. "Prefer vertical shots. Need sparkling, well-lit color prints or transparencies of beautiful library exteriors. Dramatic views; can be charming old-fashioned structure with character and grace or striking modern building. Library should be *inviting*. Added color enrichment helpful: colorful foliage, flowers, people engaged in some activity natural to the photo are examples." Special needs include "*color* photos of upbeat library happenings and events—must be unusual or of interest to sophisticated group of librarian-readers. Special need for school and academic library shots." All inside shots must be in color.

Making Contact & Terms: "Supply possible cover photos of library exterior—as many views as possible of same subject." Send transparencies or contact sheet by mail for consideration. SASE. Reports in 2-8 weeks. Pays $200-400/color cover photo; $75-150/color inside photo; and $100-450/text/photo package. Credit line always given. Buys first North American serial rights.

Tips: "Read or scan at least two issues thoroughly. We look for excellent, focused, well-lit shots, especially in color, of interesting events strongly related to library context—off-beat and upbeat occurrences in libraries of interest to sophisticated librarian audience. Also looking for rich color photos of beautiful library exteriors, both old-fashioned and charming and modern structures . . . people should be included in photos (e.g., one or two entering library building)."

AMERICAN MOTORCYCLIST, Box 6114, Westerville OH 43081-6114. (614)891-2425. Executive Editor: Greg Harrison. Managing Editor: Bill Wood. Monthly magazine. Circ. 150,000. For "enthusiastic motorcyclists, investing considerable time in road riding or competition sides of the sport." Publication of the American Motorcyclist Association. "We are interested in people involved in, and events dealing with, all aspects of motorcycling."

Photo Needs: Buys 10-20 photos/issue. Subjects include: travel, technical, sports, humorous, photo essay/feature, and celebrity/personality.

Making Contact & Terms: Query with samples to be kept on file for possible future assignments. Sample copy and photo guidelines available for $1.50. Reports in 3 weeks. SASE. Send 5×7 or 8×10 semigloss prints; pays $20-50/photo. Also uses transparencies; pays $30-100/slide. Also buys photos in photo/text packages according to same rate; pays $4/column inch minimum for story. Captions preferred for all photos. Buys all rights. Pays on publication.

Tips: Uses transparencies for covers. "The cover shot is tied in with the main story or theme of that issue and generally needs to be with accompanying ms." Pays minimum $100/cover photo. "Work to be returned *must* include SASE. Show us experience in motorcycling photography and suggest your ability to meet our editorial needs and complement our philosophy."

ANCHOR NEWS, 75 Maritime Dr., Manitowoc WI 54220. (414)684-0218. Editor: Joan Kloster. Publication of the Manitowoc Maritime Museum. Bimonthly magazine. Emphasizes Great Lakes maritime history. Readers include learned and lay readers interested in Great Lakes history. Circ. 1,900. Sample copy free with 9×12 SAE and $1 postage. Guidelines free with SASE.

Photo Needs: Uses 8-10 photos/issue; infrequently supplied by freelance photographers. Needs historic/nostalgic, personal experience, and general interest articles on Great Lakes maritime topics. How-to and technical pieces and model ships and shipbuilding are OK. Special needs include historic photography or photos that show current historic trends of the Great Lakes. Photos of waterfront development, bulk carriers, sailors, recreational boating, etc. Model release and captions required.

Making Contact & Terms: Query with samples, send 4×5 or 8×10 glossy b&w prints by mail for consideration. SASE. Reports in 1 month. Pays in copies only on publication. Credit line given. Buys first North American serial rights. Simultaneous submissions and previously published work OK.

Tips: "Besides historic photographs I see a growing interest in underwater archaeology, especially on the Great Lakes, and underwater exploration—also on the Great Lakes. Sharp, clear photographs are a must. Our publication deals with a wide variety of subjects; however, we take a historical slant with our publication. Therefore photos should be related to a historical topic in some respect. Also current trends in Great Lakes shipping. A query is most helpful. This will let the photographer know exactly what we are looking for and will help save a lot of time and wasted effort."

ANGUS JOURNAL, 3201 Frederick Blvd., St. Joseph MO 64506. (816)233-0508. FAX: (816)233-0563. Editor: Jerilyn Johnson. Publication of the American Angus Association. Monthly. Circ. 17,000. Estab. 1979. Emphasizes purebred Angus cattle. Readers are Angus cattle breeders. Sample copy and photo guidelines free with 10×14 SAE and $2 postage.

Photo Needs: "Cover shots only" are supplied by freelancers; 10% assigned and 10% from freelance stock. Needs scenic color shots of Angus cattle. Special needs include "cover shots, especially those depicting the four seasons. Winter scenes especially needed—vertical shots only." Identify as to farm's location.

Making Contact & Terms: Send slides and 8×10 color prints; 35mm, color contact sheet; and color negatives (all vertical shots). Provide resume, business card, brochure, flyer or tearsheets to be kept on file for possible future assignments. SASE. Pays $25-50/b&w photo; $150-225 color photo (cover); $150-200 photo/text package (Photo story). Pays on acceptance. Credit line given. Buys all rights; rights purchased are negotiable.

Tips: "For covers: looks for creativity, pleasing-to-the eye scenery and compositions. Professional work *only*; perfect lighting, sharpness and composition. Would like to see more people (Angus farmers—kids, grandpa or grandma shots). Angus cattle shots should be purebred animals (black only) and quality animals preferred. Send us letter, sample of work and photo would like to submit. Follow-up with a phone call or letter. We are often busy and may put letter aside. Be patient—allow us at least 2 month to reply."

ANIMALS, 350 S. Huntington Ave., Boston MA 02130. (617)522-7400. FAX: (617)522-4885. Photo Researcher: Laurie Ten Eyck. Publication of the Massachusetts Society for the Prevention of Cruelty to Animals. Bimonthly. Emphasizes animals, both wild and domestic. Readers are people interested in animals, conservation, animal welfare issues, pet care and wildlife. Circ. 75,000. Estab. 1868. Sample copy $2.50 with 9×12 SASE. Photo guidelines free with SASE.

Photo Needs: Uses about 45 photos/issue; approx. 95% supplied by freelance photographers. "All of our pictures portray animals, usually in their natural settings, however some in specific situations such as pets being treated by veterinarians, or captive breeding programs." Special needs include clear, crisp shots of animals, wild and domestic, both close-up and distance shots with spectacular backgrounds, or in the case of domestic animals, a comfortable home or backyard. Model release and captions required.

Making Contact & Terms: Query with resume of credits; query with list of stock photo subjects. Provide resume, business card, brochure, flyer or tearsheets to be kept on file for possible future assignments. SASE. Reports in 1 month. Fees are usually negotiable; pays $50-150/b&w photo; $75-300/color photo. Pays on publication. Credit line given. Buys one-time rights.

Tips: "Offer original ideas combined with extremely high-quality technical ability. Suggest article ideas to accompany your photos, but only propose yourself as author if you are qualified. We have a never-ending need for sharp, high-quality portraits of mixed-breed dogs and cats for both inside and cover use. Keep in mind we seldom use domestic cats outdoors; we often need indoor cat shots."

APA MONITOR, American Psychological Association, 1200 17th St. NW, Washington DC 20036. (202)955-7690. Editor: Laurie Denton. Managing Editor: John Bales. Monthly newspaper. Circ. 80,000. Emphasizes "news and features of interest to psychologists and other behavioral scientists and professionals, including legislation and agency action affecting science and health, and major issues facing psychology both as a science and a mental health profession." Photos purchased on assignment. Buys 60-90 photos/year. Pays by the job; $50/hour; or $25-50/b&w photo; or $300-400/day. Credit line given. Pays on receipt. Buys first serial rights. Arrange a personal interview to show portfolio or query with samples. SASE. Sample copy with $3 and 9×12 envelope.

Photo Needs: Portraits; feature illustrations; and spot news.

B&W: Uses 5×7 and 8×10 glossy prints; contact sheet OK.

Tips: "Become good at developing ideas for illustrating abstract concepts and innovative approaches to cliches like meetings and speeches. We look for quality in technical reproduction and innovative approaches to subjects."

APERTURE, 20 E. 23rd St., New York NY 10010. (212)505-5555. Editor: Charles Hagen. Publication of Aperture. Quarterly. Emphasizes fine art and contemporary photography. Readers include photographers, artists, collectors. Circ. 16,000.

Photo Needs: Uses about 60 photos/issue; all supplied by freelance photographers. Model release and captions required.

Making Contact & Terms: Submit portfolio for review. SASE. Reports in one month. Pay varies. Pays on publication. Credit line given.

Tips: "We are a nonprofit foundation and do not pay for photos." Also does not assign work.

APPALACHIA, Appalachian Mountain Club, 5 Joy St., Boston MA 02108. (617)523-0636. Editor: Catherine Buni. Monthly. Circ. 37,500. Emphasizes "outdoor activities, conservation, environment, especially in the Northeastern USA. We run extensive listings of club outings, workshops, etc." Readers are "interested in outdoor activities and conservation." Sample copy available for $2.50, including postage and handling. Photo guidelines free with SASE.

Photo Needs: Uses about 10 photos/issue; all supplied by freelance photographers. Needs "hiking, skiing, canoeing, kayaking, scenics, wildlife; color slides for covers (prefer vertical); b&w for inside." Model release preferred for inside photos; required for cover photos. Subject description required.
Making Contact & Terms: Arrange a personal interview to show portfolio; query with samples and stock list or send unsolicited photos by mail for consideration. Send 8 × 10 b&w glossy prints, 35mm transparencies by mail for consideration. SASE. Reports in 1 month. No payment. Credit line given. Simultaneous submissions and previously published work (with permission) OK.
Tips: "Capture people enjoying the outdoors. Photos have a greater chance of selection for the cover if they relate to editorial material. Call or query for relevant material."

APPALACHIAN TRAILWAY NEWS, Box 807, Harpers Ferry WV 25425. (304)535-6331. Editor: Judith Jenner. Publication of the Appalachian Trail Conference. Bimonthly. Circ. 24,500. Emphasizes the Appalachian Trail. Readers are conservationists, hikers. Guidelines free with SASE; sample copy $3 (includes postage and guidelines).
Photo Needs: Uses about 20-30 b&w photos/issue; 4-5 supplied by freelance photographers (plus 13 color slides each year for calendar). Needs scenes from/on the Appalachian Trail; specifically of people using or maintaining the trail. Special needs include candids—people/wildlife/trail scenes. Photo information required.
Making Contact & Terms: Query samples. Send glossy 5 × 7 or larger b&w prints; b&w contact sheet; or 35mm transparencies by mail for consideration. SASE. Reports in 3 weeks. Pays on acceptance. Pays $100/b&w cover photo; $200 minimum/color slide calendar photo; $10-50/b&w inside photo. Credit line given. Rights negotiable. Simultaneous submissions and previously published work OK.

*APPALOOSA JOURNAL, P.O. Box 8403, Moscow ID 83843. (208)882-5578. Editor: Chris Olney. Association publication of Appaloosa Horse Club, Inc. Monthly magazine. Emphasizes Appaloosa horses. Readers are Appaloosa owners, breeders and trainers, child through adult. Circ. 17,000. Estab. 1946. Sample copy for $3. Photo guidelines sheet free with SASE.
Photo Needs: Uses 30 photos/issue; 20% supplied by freelance photographers. Needs photos (color and b&w) to accompany features and articles. Special photo needs include photographs of Appaloosas (high quality horses) in winter scenes. Model release and photo captions required.
Making Contact & Terms: Send unsolicited 8 × 10 b&w and color prints or 35mm and 2¼ × 2¼ transparencies by mail for consideration. Reports in 3 weeks. Pays $100-300/color cover photo; $50-100/color inside photo; $25-50/b&w inside photo. Pays on acceptance. Credit line given. Buys first N.A. serial rights. Will consider previously published work.
Tips: In photographer's samples, wants to see "high quality color photos of high quality Appaloosa horses with people in outdoor environment. We often need a freelancer to illustrate a manuscript we have purchased. We need specific photos and usually very quickly."

ARCHAEOLOGY MAGAZINE, 15 Park Row, New York NY 10038. (212)732-5154. Art Director: Alex Isley. Publication of the Archaeological Institute of America. Bimonthly. Emphasizes popular accounts of archaeological work, worldwide. Readers are upscale, highly educated, with avocational interest in archaeology. Circ. 100,000. Sample copy free with SASE.
Photo Needs: Uses about 40 photos/issue; 5 supplied by freelance photographers. Needs photos of archaeological sites that are the subject of editorial features. Special needs include archaeological sites. Captions required.
Making Contact & Terms: Query with list of stock photo subjects. Uses 35mm transparencies. SASE. Reports in 3 weeks. Pays $500/color cover photo. Pays on publication. Buys one-time rights. Simultaneous submissions OK.
Tips: "Read the magazine carefully."

ARCHITECTURE CALIFORNIA, 1303 J St., #200, Sacramento CA 95814. (916)448-9082. Editor: Julie Knisely. Publication of the California Council of the America Institute of Architects Association. Semi-annual magazine. Emphasizes architecture. Readers are architects. Circ. 11,000. Sample copy $5.
Photo Needs: Uses 20 photos/issue. Needs photos of buildings. Model release preferred; captions required.
Making Contact & Terms: Query with resume of credits. Does not return unsolicited material. Reports in 2 months. Payment negotiated. Pays on publication. Credit line given. Rights negotiated. Simultaneous submissions and previously published work OK.

*ARKANSAS FARM & COUNTRY, 912 South Grand, Stuttgart AR 72160. (501)673-3276/673-6283. Editor: Jeffrey E. Tennant. Publication of AgCom Inc. Monthly tabloid. Emphasizes agricultural/farming. Readers are male farmers, ages 20-70. Circ. 11,700. Estab. 1986. Sample copy free with 9 × 12 SAE and 3 first class stamps. No photo guidelines available.

Photo Needs: Uses 10-15 photos/issue; 50% supplied by freelance photographers. Needs photos of farmers with families or at work and agricultural scenes and farming conferences. Model release and photo captions preferred.

Making Contact & Terms: Query with list of stock photo subjects; send unsolicited b&w photos by mail for consideration; provide resume, business card, brochure, flyer or tearsheets to be kept on file for possible assignments. SASE. Reports in 3 weeks. Pays $20/cover photo, $5/b&w cover photo. Credit line given. Buys one-time rights. Simultaneous submissions and previously published work OK.

Tips: "This is a specialized market which requires specialized photography. Arkansas farmers or agricultural scenes are most needed."

*ARMY RESERVE MAGAZINE, 1815 N. Fort Myer Dr., Room 501, Arlington VA 22209-1805. (202)696-3962. Editor: Lt. Col. B.R. Devlin. Publication for U.S. Army Reserve. Quarterly magazine. Emphasizes training and employment of Army Reservists. Readers are ages 17-60, 60% male, 40% female, all occupations. No particular focus on civilian employment. Circ. 575,000. Estab. 1955. Sample copy free with 8½ × 11 SAE and 2 first-class stamps. No photo guidelines.

Photo Needs: Uses 35-45 photos/issue; 85% supplied by freelance photographers. Needs photos related to the mission or function of the U.S. Army Reserve. Uses 5 × 7 b&w prints, also 35mm or 2¼ × 2¼ transparencies. Model release is preferred (if of a civilian or non-affiliated person); photo captions required.

Making Contact & Terms: "Contact editor to discuss potential job before execution." SASE. Reports in 1 month. "No pay for material; credit only since we are a nonprofit operation." Unable to purchase rights, but consider as "one-time usage." Simultaneous and previously published work OK.

Tips: "Make contact with the Public Affairs Officer of a local Army Reserve unit, preferably a major unit, to determine if you can photograph unit events or training which may be usable."

*ATLANTA CHAMBER OF COMMERCE, 235 International Blvd. NW, Atlanta GA 30303. (404)586-8493. Production Manager: Stephanie Saxon. Publication of Atlanta Chamber of Commerce. Annual magazine; includes International Directory. Readers are business community needing information on foreign businesses and opportunities in the Atlanta Metro area. Circ. 15,000. Estab. 1990. No sample copy or guidelines available.

Photo Needs: Uses 20-40 photos/issue; 100% supplied by freelance photographers. Needs photos of architectural, technology, foreigners at work, etc. Special photo needs include something that illustrates "our" presence in Japan (example: a Delta airline jet in Toyko) or the USSR (example: Coca Cola in Moscow). Model release and photo captions are preferred.

Making Contact & Terms: Query with list of stock photo subjects; send unsolicited photos by mail for consideration; provide resume, business card, brochure, flyer or tearsheets to be kept on file for possible assignments. Phone first. Accepts all formats. Reports in 1 month. Pays $250/color cover photo; $250/b&w cover photo; $50/color inside photo; $50/b&w inside photo. Pays on acceptance. Credit line given. Buys all rights. Negotiates with a photographer unwilling to sell all rights. Simultaneous submissions and previously published work OK.

Tips: "Bear in mind that these are not vacation photos! A picture may be worth a thousand words, but we need photos that make one, clear point."

AUTO TRIM NEWS, 9255 Lazy Ln., Tampa FL 33614. (813)935-0952. Editor: Nat Danas. Publication of National Association of Auto Trim Shops. Monthly. Circ. 8,000. Emphasizes automobile restoration and restyling. Readers are upholsterers for auto/marine trim shops; body shops handling cosmetic soft goods for vehicles. Sample copy $2.40 with SASE; photo guidelines free with SASE.

Photo Needs: Uses about 15 photos/issue; 6-10 supplied by freelance photographers. Needs "how-to photos; photos of new store openings; restyling showcase photos of unusual completed work." Special needs include "restyling ideas for new cars in the after market area; soft goods and chrome add-ons to update Detroit." Captions preferred.

Making Contact & Terms: Provide resume, business card, brochure, flyer or tearsheets to be kept on file for possible future assignments; submit ideas for photo assignments in local area. Photographer should be in touch with a cooperative shop locally. SASE. Reports in 1 week. Pays $35/b&w cover photo; $75-95/job. Pays on acceptance. Credit line given if desired. Buys all rights. Simultaneous submissions and previously published work OK.

Tips: "First learn the needs of a market or segment of an industry. Then translate it into photographic action so that readers can improve their business."

THE B.C. PROFESSIONAL ENGINEER, 2210 W. 12th Ave., Vancouver BC V6K 2N6 Canada. (604)736-9808. FAX: (604)736-2984. Editor: Mike Painter. Publication of the Professional Engineers Association. Monthly magazine. Emphasizes engineering. Readers are professional engineers of all ages. Circ. 12,000. Estab. 1950. Sample copy and photo guidelines free with 9 × 12 SASE.

Photo Needs: Uses approximately 6 photos/issue; 50% supplied by freelance photographers. Needs photos including anything relating to any one of the many engineering disciplines: biomedical, chemical, mining, forestry, civil and so on. Each year, needs a scenic winter photo for December issue. Model release preferred. Captions required.

Making Contact & Terms: Send unsolicited photos by mail for consideration; b&w 5 × 7 glossy prints. SASE. Reports in 1 week. Unable to offer payment, but gives full credit. Simultaneous submissions and previously published work OK.

Tips: In portfolio or samples, wants to see "unique perspectives, sharp images, good print contrast, suitability. Prefers photos taken in B.C."

BICYCLE USA, Suite 209, 6707 Whitestone Rd., Baltimore MD 21207. (301)944-3399. Editor: Arlene Plevin. Publications of the League of American Wheelmen Association. Magazine published 8 times a year. Emphasizes bicycling. Audience consists of avid, well-educated bicyclists of all ages, occupations and sexes. Circ. 19,000. Photo guidelines free with SASE.

Photo Needs: Uses 15-20 photos/issue; 100% supplied by freelance photographers. Needs photos of travel, scenics and how-to. Cyclists must be shown with helmets. Prefers photos with accompanying manuscript but will also consider without. Model release preferred; captions required.

Making Contact & Terms: Send unsolicited photos by mail for consideration; b&w prints and 35mm transparencies. SASE. Reports in 1 month. Offers membership in the organization as payment. Credit line given. Buys one-time rights. Previously published work OK.

BIKE REPORT, Box 8303, Missoula MT 59801. (406)721-1776. Editor: Dan D'Ambrosio. Publication of Bikecentennial Association. Magazine published 9 times a year. Emphasizes bicycle touring. Readers are mid-30s, mostly male, professionals $30,000+ income. Circ. 18,000. Estab. 1974. Samples copy free with 9 × 12 SAE and 65¢ postage. No photo guidelines available.

Photo Needs: Uses 12 photos/issue; 50% supplied by freelancers. Needs scenics with bicycles. Photos purchased with accompanying ms only. Model release preferred; photo captions required.

Making Contact & Terms: Submit portfolio for review. SASE. Reports in 3 weeks. Pays $100/color cover photo; $50/color page rate; $35/b&w page rate. Pays on publication. Credit line given. Buys one-time rights. Simultaneous submissions and previously published work OK.

BILANS, 7th Fl., 680 Sherbrooke, Montreal, PQ H3A 2S3 Canada. (514)288-3256. Contact: Odile Civitello. Bimonthly magazine. Emphasizes accounting, economy, finance and taxation. Readers are chartered accountants in the province of Quebec; 15% women, 85% men, ages 20-65. Circ. 16,000.

Photo Needs: Uses 20 photos/issue; 50% supplied by freelancers. Photo captions preferred.

Making Contact & Terms: Arrange a personal interview to show portfolio. Cannot return unsolicited material. Reports in 3 weeks. Pays $500/color cover photo. Pays on publication. Credit line given for covers only. Buys all rights. Simultaneous submissions OK.

*BIONICS, P.O. Box 1553, Owosso MI 48867. Publisher: Ben Campbell. Quarterly publication of Bionics Industry Association. Emphasizes bionics, bio-sensors, bio-medical and cybernetics. Readers are corporate executives, bionic scientists, inventors and investors. Circ. 3,000. Estab. 1988. Samples copies for $10. Photo guidelines available.

Photo Needs: Uses 3-5 photos/issue; most supplied by freelancers. Special needs include photos of renowned bionic inventors, and bionic industry leaders. Model release and photo captions preferred.

Making Contact & Terms: Query with resume of credits; query with list of stock photo subjects; send unsolicited 2¼ × 2¼, 4 × 5, or 8 × 10 b&w or color photos by mail for consideration; provide resume, business card, brochure, flyer or tearsheets to be kept on file for possible assignments. SASE. Reports in 3 weeks. Pays $25/color cover photo; $20/b&w cover photo; $15/color inside photo; $10/b&w inside photo; $20/color page rate; $15/b&w page rate; $10-300/photo/text package. Pays on publication. Credit line given. Buys all rights; negotiable. Previously published work OK.

Tips: "Because of the difficulty in acquiring photographs of bionic products, and bionic research & development facilities we do not require the photographer(s) to submit portfolios. Be extra sensitive while on an assignment, because, you are dealing with a very top-secret and valuable industry. It's best if you work with a writer."

Markets which offer lower payment amounts, or photo credits and extra copies or tearsheets as payment are often receptive to the work of newcomers. For a list of such markets, see the First Markets Index preceding the General Index in the back of this book.

*THE BLACK WRITER, P.O. Box 1030, Chicago IL 60690. (312)995-5195. Editor: Mable Terrell. Publication of International Black Writers Association. Quarterly magazine. Emphasizes current African-American writers. Readers are ages 15-75 and of various occupations. Circ. 500. Estab. 1970. Sample copy free for 9½×12 SAE and 90¢ postage.
Photo Needs: Uses 20 photos/issue; 100% supplied by freelance photographers. Needs photos of travel and personalities. Model release preferred; photo captions required.
Making Contact & Terms: Provide resume, business card, brochure, flyer or tearsheets to be kept on file for possible assignments. SASE. Reports in 1 month. Pays $25/b&w cover photo; $20/b&w inside photo. Pays on acceptance. Credit line given. Buys one-time rights. Previously published work OK.
Tips: Looking for "quality of the photography."

*BOAT/U.S. REPORTS, 880 S. Pickett Street, Alexandria VA 22304. (703)832-9550. FAX: (703)461-2847. Managing Editor: Elaine Dickinson. Publication of the Boat Owners Association of the United States. Bimonthly tabloid. Emphasizes recreational boating. Readers are middle income adults who are boat owners and outdoor-oriented. Circ. 340,000. Estab. 1966. Sample copy free with 8½×11 SAE and 4 first-class stamps. Photo guidelines not available.
Photo Needs: Uses approximately 20 photos/issue. Needs photos of boating scenes, sail and power, people at play, working on boats, marine weather, harbors and marinas, law enforcement, Coast Guard, marine police, some travel. No sunsets! Model release and photo captions preferred.
Making Contact & Terms: Query with resume of credits; query with list of stock photo subjects; provide resume, business card, brochure, flyer or tearsheets to be kept on file for possible assignments. Uses color prints or 35mm transparencies. SASE. Reports in 3-4 weeks. Pays up to $250 and up/color cover photo; $50/color inside photo. Rates negotiable depending upon usage. One time or unlimited use; Pays on acceptance. Credit line given. Buys one-time rights. Simultaneous submissions previously published work.
Tips: "We buy or borrow photos on a case-by-case basis. Must be flexible; know boats and boating."

BOWLING MAGAZINE, 5301 S. 76th St., Greendale WI 53129. (414)421-6400. Editor: Dan Matel. Published by the American Bowling Congress. Emphasizes bowling for readers who are bowlers, bowling fans or media. Published 11 times annually. Circ. 140,000. Free sample copy; photo guidelines for SASE.
Photo Needs: Uses about 20 photos/issue, 1 of which, on the average, is supplied by a freelance photographer. Provide calling card and letter of inquiry to be kept on file for possible future assignments. "In some cases we like to keep photos. Our staff takes almost all photos as they deal mainly with editorial copy published. Rarely do we have a photo page or need freelance photos. No posed action." Model release and captions required.
Making Contact & Terms: Send by mail for consideration actual 5×7 or 8×10 b&w or color photos. SASE. Reports in 2 weeks. Pays on publication $10-15/b&w photo; $15-20/color photo. Credit line given. Buys one-time rights but photos are kept on file after use. No simultaneous submissions or previously published work.

*CALIFORNIA LABOR FEDERATION, 417 Montgomery St., Suite 300, San Francisco CA 94104. (415)986-3585. Editor: Floyd Tucker. Association publication of California Labor Federation, AFL-CIO. Weekly tabloid. Readers are officers of unions affiliated with the AFL-CIO in California; legislators and members of Congress; employer groups; law firms; some union rank and file. Circ. 6,000. Estab. 1958. Sample copy free with SASE.
Photo Needs: Uses 2-10 photos/issue; Number of freelance photographers varies. Needs photos of labor-related news. Photo captions are required.
Making Contact & Terms: "Call when you have something." Send any size or finish b&w prints. Will return unsolicited material with SASE. Reports in 1-2 weeks. Pays $25/b&w cover photo. Pays on acceptance. Credit line given. Buys one-time rights. Simultaneous submissions and previously published work OK.

CALIFORNIA LAWYER, 1016 Fox Plaza, 1390 Market St., San Francisco CA 94102. (415)558-9888. Editor and Publisher: Ray Reynolds. Art Director: Gordon Smith. Director of Photography: Max Ramirez. Monthly. Emphasizes law/lawyers. Readers are lawyers and judges; some other subscribers. Circ. 115,000.
Photo Needs: Innovative photos to illustrate stories on topical legal issues. Uses 12-18 photos/issue. Needs artistic interpretations of lawyers/courts/related issues. Model release required; captions preferred.
Making Contact & Terms: Query with samples; send 8×10 glossy b&w prints or 35mm and 2¼×2¼ transparencies by mail for consideration. SASE. Reports in 2 weeks. Pays $650/color cover photo; $100-350 color inside; $75/b&w inside photo. Pays on acceptance. Credit line given. Buys one-time rights. Simultaneous submissions OK.

Tips: "We look for an artistic eye; dramatic lighting. Offer new and innovative ways to illustrate legal stories, not simply variations on the scales of justice."

*CALIFORNIA MONTHLY, Alumni House, Berkeley CA 94720. (415)642-0760. Managing Editor: William Rodarmor. Publication of UC-Berkeley Alumni. Six times/year magazine. Readers are University of California, Berkeley graduates. Circ. 90,000. Estab. 1870. Sample copy available for 11 × 14 SAE.
Photo Needs: Uses 25-30 photos/issue; 90% supplied by freelance photographers. "Photos must relate to Berkeley grads or campus." Model release preferred; photo captions required.
Making Contact & Terms: Query with resume of credits. Provide resume, business card, brochure, flyer or tearsheets to be kept on file for possible assignments. Material is not returned. Reports in 3 weeks. Pays $200-400/color cover photo; $100/b&w inside photo; $75/color page rate. Pays on publication. Credit line given. Buys one-time rights. Simultaneous submissions and previously published work OK.
Tips: "Photo tie-in with the Berkeley campus is a must."

*CALIFORNIA NURSE, Suite 670, 1855 Folsom St., San Francisco CA 94103. Managing Editor: Catherine Direen. Association publication of California Nurses Association. Monthly tabloid. Emphasizes nursing. Readers are adults, mixed male and female nurses. Circ. 25,000. Estab. 1904. Sample copy free with SAE.
Photo Needs: Uses 15-20 photos/issue; 10% supplied by freelance photographers. Needs photos of nurses, medical technology and populations served by health professionals, (e.g. elderly, infants, uninsured). Model release and photo captions required.
Making Contact & Terms: Send unsolicited 4 × 5 or 5 × 7 glossy b&w prints by mail for consideration. Provide resume, business card, brochure, flyer or tearsheets to be kept on file for possible assignments. Phone calls accaptable. SASE. Reports in 3 weeks. Pays $20/b&w cover photo; $20/b&w inside photo. Pays on publication. Buys one-time rights. Simultaneous submissions OK.
Tips: "Mostly we use photos only of CNA members. Best choice besides that are sensitive shots of people needing or receiving health care. Send sample photos, well-tailored to individual publications and follow-up."

CALYPSO LOG, 8440 Santa Monica Blvd., Los Angeles CA 90069. (213)656-4422. FAX: (213)656-4891. Editor: Mary Batten. Publication of The Cousteau Society. Bimonthly. Emphasizes expedition activities of The Cousteau Society; educational/science articles; environmental activities. Readers are members of The Cousteau Society. Circ. 50,000. Sample copy $2 with 9 × 12 SAE and 65¢ postage. Photo guidelines with SASE.
Photo Needs: Uses 10-14 photos/issue; 1-2 supplied by freelancers; 2-3 photos per issue come from freelance stock. Preference for underwater creature shots in natural habitats. We review duplicates only. Captions preferred.
Making Contact & Terms: Query with samples; query with list of stock photo subjects; send unsolicited photos (duplicates) by mail for consideration. Uses color prints; 35mm and 2¼ × 2¼ transparencies (duplicates only). SASE. Reports in 5 weeks. Pays $25-100/color photo. Pays on publication. Buys one-time rights and translation rights for our French publication. Previously published work OK.
Tips: Send "sharp, clear images of underwater life/creatures in duplicate form only." In samples, wants to see "photos that tell a story of animals interacting with each other and/or the environment. "Also sharp, clear, good composition and color; unusual animals or views of environmental features. Prefers transparencies over prints. "We look for ecological stories, food chain, prey-predator interaction, and impact of people on environment. Please request a copy of our publication to familiarize yourself with our style, content and tone and then send samples that best represent underwater and environmental photography."

CANADA LUTHERAN, 1512 St., James St., Winnipeg MB R3H 0L2 Canada. (204)786-6707. FAX: (204)783-7548. Art Director: Darrell Dyck. Editor: Ferdy Baglo. Publication of Evangelical Lutheran Church in Canada. Monthly. Emphasizes faith/religious content; Lutheran denomination. Readers are members of the Evangelical Lutheran Church in Canada. Circ. 32,000. Sample copy for $1.50/copy, 8½ × 11 SASE and 76¢ (Canadian).
Photo Needs: Uses 4-10 photos/issue; most supplied though article contributors; 1 or 2 supplied by freelance photographers. Needs photos of people (in worship/work/play etc.); scenics. Model release and captions preferred.
Making Contact & Terms: Send 5 × 7 glossy prints or 35mm transparencies by mail for consideration. SASE. Pays $25-50/b&w photo; $50-150/color photo. Pays on publication. Credit line given. Buys one-time rights.
Tips: "Trend toward more men and women in non-stereotypical roles. Do not restrict photo submissions to just the categories you believe the client needs. Keep the submissions coming regularly—you never know when a client's need will match your submission. Give us a pile of shots that show your

range. Let us keep them on file—then we will turn to that file each month when we need to illustrate something on short notice."

CDA JOURNAL, 818 K St., Sacramento CA 95814. (916)443-0505. Director of Publications: Douglas K. Curley. Publication of California Dental Association. Monthly magazine. Readers are dentistry professionals. Circ. 18,000. Sample copy $6.
Photo Needs: Number of photos used each issue varies, supplied by 1-3 freelancers. Needs concept, art and news photos. Reviews photos with or without manuscript.
Making Contact & Terms: Query with resume of credits include list of references. SASE. Reports in 1 month. Pays within 2 weeks of acceptance. Credit line given. Buys all rights, but willing to negotiate.
Tips: CDA wants to develop a list of photographers available in various regions such as Midwest, Hawaii and West Coast. The association also has affiliation with national dentistry association, American Dental Association, and so participates in numerous conventions and meetings. As a result, will need photos for publication on a regular basis. "Just about anybody who's in a major convention market has a very good likelihood of producing work for us."

CHESS LIFE, 186 Route 9W, New Windsor NY 12550. (914)562-8350. FAX: (914)561-CHES. Editor-in-Chief: Julie Anne Desch. Art Director: Jami Anson. Publication of the U.S. Chess Federation. Monthly. Circ. 60,000. *Chess Life* covers news of all major national and international tournaments; historical articles, personality profiles, columns of instruction, occasional fiction, humor . . . for the devoted fan of chess. Sample copy and photo guidelines free with SAE and 75¢ postage.
Photo Needs: Uses about 10 photos/issue; 7-8 supplied by freelance photographers. Needs "news photos from events around the country; shots for personality profiles." Special needs include "Chess Review" section. Model release and captions preferred.
Making Contact & Terms: Query with samples. Provide business card and tearsheets to be kept on file for possible future assignments. SASE. Reports in "2-4 weeks, depending on when the deadline crunch occurs." Pays $100-150/b&w or color cover photo; $10-25/b&w inside photo; $15-30/hour; $150-250/day. Pays on publication. Credit line given. Buys one-time rights; "we occasionally purchase all rights for stock mug shots." Simultaneous submissions and previously published work OK.
Tips: Using "more color, and more illustrative photography. The photographer's name and date should appear on the back of all photos. 35mm color transparencies are preferred for cover shots. Looks for 'clear images, good composition and contrast—with a fresh approach to interest the viewer. Increasing emphasis on strong portraits of chess personalities, especially Americans. Tournament photographs of winning players and key games are in high demand."

CHEVY OUTDOORS, 30400 Van Dyke Ave., Warren MI 48093. (313)574-9100. Art Director: Steve Szablewski. Publication of the Chevrolet company. Quarterly magazine. Emphasizes outdoor life and travel, recreational vehicles, and fishing. Readership consists of men and women of all occupations, ages 20 to 70. Circ. 1,080,000. Sample copy free with 9 × 12 SASE and $1.50 postage. Photo guidelines free with SASE.
Photo Needs: Uses 80 photos/issue; 70% supplied by freelance photographers. Needs photos of animal/wildlife shots, travel, scenics. Model release and photo captions required.
Making Contact & Terms: Query with list of stock photo subjects. SASE. Reports in 2-6 weeks. Pays $350-600/b&w page. Pays on acceptance. Credit line given. Buys one-time rights. Simultaneous submissions and previously published work OK.
Tips: "Looking for intelligent, well-exposed and insightful outdoor photography. Photographers should have a genuine interest in subject."

CHILDHOOD EDUCATION, Suite 200, 11141 Georgia Ave., Wheaton MD 20902. (301)942-2443. Director of Publications/Editor: Lucy Prete Martin. Assistant Editor: Joan Saidel. Publication for the Association for Childhood Education International. Bimonthly journal. Circ. 15,000. Emphasizes the education of children from infancy through early adolescence. Readers include teachers, administrators, day care workers, parents, psychologists, student teachers, etc. Sample copy free with 8½ × 11 SASE and $1 postage; photo guidelines free with SASE.
Photo Needs: Uses 5-10 photos/issue; 2-3 supplied by freelance photographers. Subject matter includes children ages 1-14 years in groups or alone, in or out of the classroom, at play, in study groups; boys and girls of all races, and in all cities and countries. Reviews photos with or without accompanying ms. Special needs include photos of minority children; photos of children from different ethnic groups together in one shot; boys and girls together. Model release required.
Making Contact & Terms: Send unsolicited photos by mail for consideration. Uses 8 × 10 glossy b&w prints and colored transparencies and prints. SASE. Reports in 1 month. Pays $50-75/b&w cover photo; $25-50/b&w inside photo. Pays on publication. Credit line given. Buys one-time rights. No simultaneous submissions or previously published work.
Tips: "Send pictures of unposed children, please."

"I've sold over 10 images to this market, so I had an idea of what would best meet their needs," photographer John J. Morgan, Jr. says of the association publication, Christian Home & School. This humorous image, which Morgan submitted unsolicited and was used for text illustration, earned him $30. Morgan advises targeting your mailing list to publishers who use your type of images. "Each time I sell an image," he says, "I'm encouraged to get busy and produce more images for possible publication."

CHRISTIAN HOME & SCHOOL, 3350 E. Paris Ave. SE, Grand Rapids MI 49512. (616)957-1070. Associate Editor: Judy Zylstra. Publication of Christian Schools International. Published 8 times a year. Estab. 1922. Emphasizes Christian family issues. Readers are parents who support Christian education. Circ. 10,000. Sample copy free with 9 × 12 SAE with $1 postage; photo guidelines free with SASE.

Photos Needs: Uses 10-15 photos/issue; 7-10 supplied by freelance photographers. Needs photos of children, family activities, school scenes. Model release preferred.

Making Contact & Terms: Query with samples; query with list of stock photo subjects; send b&w prints or contact sheets by mail for consideration. SASE. Reports in 3 weeks. Pays $100/color cover photo; $30/b&w inside photo. Pays on publication. Credit line given. Buys one-time rights. Simultaneous submissions and previously published work OK.

Tips: Assignment work is becoming rare. Freelance stock most often used. "Photographers who allow us to hold duplicate photos for an extended period of time stand more chance of having their photos selected for publication than those who require speedy return of submitted photos."

*CITROËN CAR CLUB NEWS, 350 Hulbe Dr., Boise ID 83705. (208)323-1000. Editor: Karl A. Petersen. Publication of the Citroën Car Club Association. Monthly magazine. Emphasizes Citroen and Panhand cars. Readers are individualists ages 18-70. Circ. 1,100. Estab. 1964. Sample copy free with 9 × 12 SAE and 3 first class stamps.

Photo Needs: Uses 15 photos/issue; 30% supplied by freelancer photographers. Needs Citroen topics. Model release preferred; photo captions required.

Making Contact & Terms: Send unsolicited b&w or color prints any size or finish by mail for consideration. SASE. Reports in 2 weeks. Pays $20/b&w cover photo; $10/b&w inside photo; $10-20/photo/ text package. Pays on publication. Credit line given. Buys one-time rights. Previously published work OK.

Tips: In freelancer's samples, wants to see "square cover format showing car or detail in good composition." Be aware that "our publication is a NASA and Old Cars winner and is seen by major automotive journalists (and editors) as personal reading material and in competition."

*CIVITAN MAGAZINE, P. O. Box 130744, Birmingham AL 35213-0744. (205)591-8910. Editor: Dorothy Wellborn. Association publication of Civitan International. Bimonthly magazine. Emphasizes work with mental retardation/developmental disabilities. Readers are men and women, college age to retirement and usually managers or owners of businesses. Circ. 36,000. Estab. 1920. Sample copy free with 8½×11 SAE and 2 first class stamps. No photo guidelines.

Photo Needs: Uses 8-10 photos/issue; 50% supplied by freelance photographers. Always looking for good cover shots (travel, scenic and how-to's). Model release and photo captions preferred.

Making Contact & Terms: Send unsolicited 2¼×2¼ or 4×5 transparencies or b&w prints by mail for consideration. Provide resume, business card, brochure, flyer or tearsheets to be kept on file for possible assignments. Reports in 1 month. Pays $50/color cover photo; $10 b&w inside photo. Pays on acceptance. Buys one-time rights. Simultaneous submissions and previously published work OK.

CLEARWATERS, New York Water Pollution Control Assoc. Inc., Suite 122, 90 Presidential Plaza, Syracuse NY 13202. (315)422-7811. Editor: Laurie Harrington. Quarterly magazine. Circ. 3,500. Publication of the New York Water Pollution Control Association, Inc. *Clearwaters* publishes articles aimed at identifying problems and finding solutions to a broad range of environmental issues, particularly those relating to all aspects of water pollution and those affecting New York State. Each issue of the magazine focuses on a specific topic—past topics have included hazardous waste recycling, groundwater contamination, state fisheries industry, and the environmental impact of agricultural practices.

Photo Needs: Freelance photographers are occasionally needed to illustrate hard-to-illustrate articles. Uses 5×7 or 8×10 b&w glossy prints; color slides (preferred) or 8×10 prints. Color photos (verticle format preferred) for cover, b&w only on inside.

Making Contact & Terms: Photographers (preferably those in or near New York State) should send a preliminary list of the kinds of photographs they have taken concerning environmental issues. We look for the ability to take an interesting photo of a sometimes "dry" subject. Credit line given. "We will pay incidentals, mileage, phone, etc." Pays on acceptance. Buys all rights, but may reassign to photographer after publication.

*COAL VOICE, % National Coal Association, 1130 17th St. NW, Washington DC 20036. (202)463-2640. Editor: Aundrea Cika. Publication of the National Coal Association. Bimonthly magazine. Covers coal and energy issues. Readers are coal producers, major coal consumers, industry representatives and allies, and state and local regulatory/legislature members. Circ. 13,000. Estab. 1978. Sample copies free upon request.

Photo Needs: Uses 15 photos/issue; 25% supplied by freelancers. Needs photos of technology, people and scenics.

Making Contact & Terms: Arrange personal interview to show portfolio. Query with list of stock photo subjects. Provide resume, business card, brochure, flyer or tearsheets to be kept on file for possible future assignment. Reports in 2 weeks. Payment varies according to use. Pays on publication. Credit line given. Rights purchased vary. Simultaneous submissions and previously published work OK.

Tips: "Looking for someone who can break through stereotypes and help enhance a misunderstood industry."

*COMMERCIAL INVESTMENT REAL ESTATE JOURNAL, Suite 500, 430 N. Michigan Ave., Chicago IL 60611. (312)321-4464. Editor: Kerry J. Otto. Publication of Commercial-Investment Real Estate Council. Quarterly journal. Emphasizes commercial real estate brokerage and consulting. Readers are commercial real estate brokers, consultants, developers, mortgage bankers, attorneys. Circ. 12,000. Estab. 1983. Sample copy free with 9×12 SAE and $1.45 postage.

Photo Needs: Uses 3-6 photos/issue; 100% supplied by freelance photographers. Photo needs vary; may be office scenes, buildings, high-resolution close-ups for special effects, etc.

Making Contact & Terms: Provide resume, business card, brochure, flyer or tearsheets to be kept on file for possible assignments. Pays $800-900/b&w cover photo; $250/b&w inside photo. Pays on acceptance. Credit line given. Buys first North American serial rights. Will consider previously published work.

*COMMUNICATION WORLD, Suite 600, One Hallidie Plaza, San Francisco CA 94102. (415)433-3400. Editor: Gloria Gordon. Publication of International Association of Business Communicators. Monthly magazine. Emphasizes public relations, business and organizational communications. Readers are members in corporate communication, consultants, ages 30+. Circ. 15,000. Estab. 1969.

Photo Needs: Uses 2-3 photos/issue; all supplied by freelance photographers. Needs photos that reflect communication in corporate atmosphere. Model release preferred; photo captions required.

Making Contact & Terms: Arrange a personal interview to show portfolio. Query with resume of credits. Submit portfolio for review. Provide resume, business card, brochure, flyer or tearsheets to be kept on file for possible assignments. SASE. Pays $350/color cover photo; $250/b&w cover photo; $275+/color inside photo; $100/b&w inside photo; $250/color page rate. Pays on publication. Credit line given. Buys one-time rights. Simultaneous submissions and previously published work OK.

COMPANY: A MAGAZINE OF THE AMERICAN JESUITS, 3441 N. Ashland Ave., Chicago IL 60657. (312)281-1534. FAX: (312)281-0555. Editor: E.J. Mattimoe. Published by the Jesuits (Society of Jesus). Quarterly magazine. Emphasizes people; "a human interest magazine about people helping people." Circ. 153,000. Estab. 1983. Sample copy free with 9×12 SAE with 73¢ postage. Photo guidelines free with SASE.

Photo Needs: All photos supplied by freelancers. Needs photo-stories of Jesuit and allied ministries and projects, only photos related to Jesuit works. Photos purchased with or without accompanying ms. Model release and captions required.

Making Contact & Terms: Query with samples. Provide resume, business card, brochure, flyer or tearsheets to be kept on file for possible future assignments. SASE. Reports in 1 month. Pays $300/color cover photo; $100-400/job. Pays on publication. Credit line given. Buys one-time rights.

Tips: "Avoid large-group 'smile at camera' photos. We are interested in people photographs that tell a story in a sensitive way—the eye-catching look that something is happening."

COMPUTER MAGAZINE, 10662 Los Vaqueros Circle, P.O. Box 3014, Los Alamitos CA 90720-1264. (714)821-8380. Editor: Marilyn Potes. Association publication of IEEE Computer Society. Monthly magazine. Emphasizes computer industry and research. Readers are electrical engineers, technical managers, computer designers, value-added resellers and system integrators. Circ. 90,000. Sample copy free with 8½×11 SAE and $2 postage.

Photo Needs: Uses 1 cover photo/issue; usually supplied by freelance photographers or stock photo house. Needs high-technology-oriented images or analogous images from other fields or nature.

Making Contact & Terms: Query with samples, query with list of stock photo subjects. Send 8×10½ color prints, 35mm transparencies by mail for consideration. SASE. Reports in 1-4 weeks. Pays $300/color cover photo. Pays on publication. Credit line given. Buys one-time rights. Previously published work OK "depends on where published."

*****CONFIDENT LIVING**, Box 82808, Lincoln NE 68501. (402)474-4567. Managing Editor: Jan Reeser. Publication of Back to the Bible. Monthly (July-Aug. combined) magazine. Emphasizes religious subjects (Protestant, conservative). Readers are adults, primarily ages 50 and up, conservative, middle class. Circ. 85,000. Estab. 1944. Sample copy for $1.75. Photo guidelines free with SAE.

Photo Needs: Uses 25 photos/issue; 70% supplied by freelance photographers. Most photos are used to illustrate specific article topics, but interested in seeing seniors of all ages in numerous activities. Model release preferred.

Making Contact & Terms: Send unsolicited photos by mail for consideration. Uses 8×10 glossy b&w prints; 35mm, 2¼×2¼ transparencies; duplicates preferred. SASE. Reports in 1 month. Pays up to $85/color cover photo; up to $25/b&w inside photo. Pays on acceptance or publication (if accompanying article ms). Credit line given. Buys one-time rights. Simultaneous submissions and previously published work OK.

Tips: "Be familiar with the magazines you want to sell to."

*****THE CONSTRUCTION SPECIFIER**, 601 Madison St., Alexandria VA 22314. (703)684-0300. FAX: (703)684-0465. Editor: Kimberly Young. Publication of the Construction Specifications Institute. Monthly magazine. Emphasizes construction. Readers are architects and engineers in commercial construction. Circ. 20,000. Estab. 1949. Sample copy free with 8½×11 SAE and 1 first-class stamp. Photo guidelines not available.

Photo Needs: Uses 40 photos/issue; 15% supplied by freelance photographers; 85% from freelance stock. Needs architectural and construction shots. Model release and photo captions required.

Making Contact & Terms: Provide resume, business card, brochure, flyer or tearsheets to be kept on file for possible assignments. SASE. Pays $25-200/b&w photo; $50-400/color photo. Pays on publication. Credit line given. Buys one-time rights. Simultaneous submissions OK if in unrelated field. Previously published work OK.

Tips: Wants to see "photos depicting commercial construction: jobsite shots."

CONTACT MAGAZINE, IDS Financial Services, IDS Tower 10, T21/745, Minneapolis MN 55440. (612)372-8513. Editor: Ron Lee. Publication of IDS Financial Services, Inc. Bi-monthly. Circ. 10,000. Emphasizes financial services. Readers are home office employees, registered representatives throughout the country, retirees and others. Sample copy free.

Photo Needs: Uses about 25 photos/issue; some are supplied by freelance photographers. Needs "photojournalistic coverage of IDS people at work."

Making Contact & Terms: Query with samples. SASE. Reports in 1 month. Pays $40-50/hour. Pays on acceptance. Credit line given. Buys all rights.

Tips: Prefers to see "b&w photojournalism" in samples, "bringing the human element into any type of story, use of natural light." Offers good work and pleasant client/photographer working arrangements. Editor is involved in the whole project, from concept through completion.

CURRENTS, Voice of the National Organization for River Sports, Suite 200, 314 N. 20th St., Colorado Springs CO 80904. (719)473-2466. Editor: Eric Leaper. Quarterly magazine. Circ. 10,000. Estab. 1979. Membership publication of National Organization for River Sports, for canoeists, kayakers and rafters. Emphasizes river conservation and river access, also techniques of river running. Provide tearsheets or photocopies of work to be kept on file for possible future assignments.

Subject Needs: Photo essay/photo feature (on rivers of interest to river runners). Need features on rivers that are in the news because of public works projects, use regulations, Wild and Scenic consideration or access prohibitions. Sport newsphotos of canoeing, kayaking, rafting and other forms of river paddling, especially photos of national canoe and kayak races; nature/river subjects, conservation-oriented; travel (river runs of interest to a nationwide membership). Wants on a regular basis close-up action shots of river running and shots of dams in progress, signs prohibiting access. Especially needs for next year shots of rivers that are threatened by dams showing specific stretch to be flooded and dam-builders at work. No "panoramas of river runners taken from up on the bank or the edge of a highway. We must be able to see their faces, front-on shots. We always need photos of the twenty (most) popular whitewater river runs around the U.S." Buys 10 photos/issue; 25% assigned and 75% unsolicited. Captions required.

Specs: Uses 5×7 and 8×10 glossy b&w prints. Occasional color prints. Query before submitting color transparencies.

Accompanying Mss: Photos purchased with or without accompanying ms. "We are looking for articles on rivers that are in the news regionally and nationally—for example, rivers endangered by damming; rivers whose access is limited by government decree; rivers being considered for Wild and Scenic status; rivers hosting canoe, kayak or raft races; rivers offering a setting for unusual expeditions and runs; and rivers having an interest beyond the mere fact that they can be paddled. Also articles interviewing experts in the field about river techniques, equipment, and history." Pays $25 minimum. Free writer's and photographer's guidelines with SASE.

Payment & Terms: Pays $20-60/b&w print or color prints or transparencies; $35-150 for text/photo package. Credit line given. Buys one-time rights. Simultaneous submissions and previously published work OK if labeled clearly as such.

Making Contact: Send material or photocopies of work by mail for consideration. "We need to know of photographers in various parts of the country." SASE. Reports "up to" 3 months. Sample copy $1; free photo guidelines with #10 SASE.

Tips: Looks for close-up action shots of whitewater river runners in kayaks, rafts, canoes or dories. Little or no red. Show faces of paddlers. Photos must be clear and sharp. Tell us where the photo was taken—name of river, state, and name of rapid, if possible."

CYCLING: BC, 332-1367 W. Broadway, Vancouver, BC V6H 4A9 Canada. (604)737-3034. Editor: Allen McIntyre. Monthly newsletter. Publication of Bicycling Association of British Columbia. Emphasizes bicycling. Readers are ages 14-75, male and female. Circ. 2,600. Sample copy with #10 SASE.

Photo Needs: Uses 1 photo/issue, supplied by 1 freelance photographer. Needs action photos of bicycling. Special photo needs include all photos for newsletters, promo materials.

Making Contact & Terms: Send b&w and color prints by mail for consideration. SASE. Reports in 2 weeks. Credit line given. Previously published work OK.

Tips: Bicycling Association of British Columbia asks for donations of photos. Will give photographer credit and send sample copy of publication.

DEALER PROGRESS MAGAZINE, (formerly Progress Magazine), 314 At the Barn, 15444 Clayton Rd., Baldwin MO 63011. (314)527-4001. Editor: K. Elliott Nowels. Publication of The Fertilizer Institute. Bimonthly. "We focus on managers of retail fertilizer and agricultural chemical dealerships. Our aim is to be the business magazine for agribusiness managers." Readers are retail business people dealing directly with farmers. Most readers are in small, rural communities and many are in the Midwest. Circ. 22,000. Sample copy free with 9×12 SASE. Photo guidelines free with SAE.

Photo Needs: Uses 3-4 photos/issue; all covers are assigned and 1-2 editorial photos are bought each year. Cover: studio shot based on *Dealer Progress* concept. Editorial photos should be illustrative of the topic. Scenes of actual retail facilities and activities are sought. No brand/chain affiliations visible if possible. Special needs include artistic photos suitable to accompany broad discussions of industry trends. Model release required; captions preferred.

Making Contact & Terms: Arrange a personal interview to show portfolio; provide resume, business card, brochure, flyer, or tearsheets to be kept on file for possible future assignments. Uses 8×10 glossy b&w prints; 35mm transparencies. SASE. Pay varies by the job. Pays on publication. Credit line given. Buys one-time rights. Simultaneous submissions OK.

Tips: Prefers to see "familiarity with our industry; variety of subjects and techniques; originality of approach; quality workmanship. Capitalize on your strengths. Be ambitious and persistent. Create opportunities."

DEFENDERS, 1244 19th St. NW, Washington DC 20036. (202)659-9510. FAX: (202)833-3349. Editor: James G. Deane. Membership publication of Defenders of Wildlife. Bimonthly. Circ. 73,000. Emphasizes wildlife and wildlife habitat. Sample copy free with 9×12½ SAE and $1.25 postage; photo guidelines free with SASE.

Photo Needs: Uses 35 or more photos/issue; "almost all" from freelance photographers. Caption information required.

Making Contact & Terms: Query with list of stock photo subjects. SASE. Reports ASAP. In portfolio or samples, wants to see "wildlife group action and behaviorial shots in preference to static portraits. High technical quality." Pays $50-100/b&w photo; $75-450/color photo. Pays on publication. Credit line given. Buys one-time rights.

Tips: "*Defenders* focuses heavily on endangered species and destruction of their habitats, wildlife refuges and wildlife management issues, primarily North American, but also some foreign. Images must be sharp. Cover images usually must be vertical, able to take the logo up top, and be arresting and *simple*. Think twice before submitting anything but low speed (preferably Kodachrome) transparencies."

DIMENSIONS IN HEALTH SERVICE, Suite 100, 17 York St., Ottawa, ON K1N 9J6 Canada. (613)238-8005. Editor, Journals: Jackie Barlow. Publication of Canadian Hospital Association. Magazine published eight times a year. Emphasizes health care management issues. Readers are professional health care managers and chief executive officers, ages 25-65. Circ. 12,500. Sample copy $5.25 Canadian with 9×12 SAE.

Photo Needs: Uses 1 photo/issue; supplied by freelance photographer. Model release required; captions preferred.

Making Contact & Terms: Query with list of stock photo subjects. SASE. Reports in 2 weeks. Pays $335 Canadian/color cover photo and $335 Canadian/b&w cover photo. Pays on publication. Credit line given. Buys one-time rights. Simultaneous submissions and previously published work OK.

DISCOVERY MAGAZINE, Suite 1700, One Illinois Center, 111 E. Wacker Dr. Chicago IL 60601. (312)565-1200. Art Director: Tim Prendergast. Publication of Allstate Motor Club. Quarterly. Emphasizes U.S. travel, especially by car and destinations—particular places or regions. Readers are middle-aged, average income, who like to travel by car. Circ. 1.6 million. Sample copy for 9×12 SASE and $1 postage. Photo guidelines free with SASE.

Photo Needs: Uses 35 photos/issue; all supplied by freelance photographers. Needs photos of U.S. travel destinations—both urban and rural scenes, with people. Model release preferred; captions required.

Making Contact & Terms: Query with list of stock photo subjects. Provide resume, business card, brochure, flyer or tearsheets to be kept on file for possible future assignments. Reports in 1 month. Pays $450 maximum/day. Pays on acceptance. Credit line given. Buys first North American serial rights. Simultaneous submissions and previously published work OK.

Tips: "Write for photo guidelines and a sample issue, sending us a SASE. Don't call or send unsolicited photos."

THE DOLPHIN LOG, 8440 Santa Monica Blvd., Los Angeles CA 90069. (213)656-4422. Editor: Pamela Stacey. Publication of The Cousteau Society, Inc., a nonprofit organization. Bimonthly magazine. Emphasizes "ocean and water-related subject matter for children ages 7 to 15." Circ. 96,000. Estab. 1981. Sample copy $2 with 9×12 SAE and 65¢ postage. Photo guidelines free with SASE.

Photo Needs: Uses about 15 photos/issue; 8 supplied by freelance photographers; 60% stock. Needs "selections of images of individual creatures or subjects, such as architects and builders of the sea, how sea animals eat, the smallest and largest things in the sea, the different forms of tails in sea animals, resemblances of sea creatures to other things. Also excellent potential cover shots or images which elicit curiosity, humor or interest." Please request photographer's guidelines. Model release required; captions preferred.

Making Contact & Terms: Query with samples, list of stock photos or send duplicate 35mm transparencies or b&w contact sheets by mail for consideration. Send duplicates only. SASE. Reports in 1 month. Pays $25/b&w photo; $25-100/color photo. Pays on publication. Credit line given. Buys one-time rights and worldwide translation rights. Simultaneous and previously published submissions OK.

Tips: Prefers to see "rich color, sharp focus and interesting action of water-related subjects" in samples. "No assignments are made. A large amount is staff-shot. However, we use a fair amount of freelance photography, usually pulled from our files, approx. 45-50%. Stock photos purchased only when an author's sources are insufficient or we have need for a shot not in file. These are most often hard-to-find creatures of the sea." To break in, "send a good submission of dupes which are in keeping with our magazine's tone/content; be flexible in allowing us to hold slides for consideration."

*DUCKS UNLIMITED, One Waterfowl Way, Long Grove IL 60047, (708)438-4300. Senior Editor: Niki Barrie. Association publication of Ducks Unlimited. Bimonthly magazine. Emphasizes waterfowl conservation. Readers are professional males, ages 40-50. Circ. 550,000. Estab. 1937. Sample copy $2.50. Guidelines free with SASE.
Photo Needs: Uses 20-30 photos/issue; 70% supplied by freelance photographers. Needs wildlife shots (waterfowl/waterfowling), scenics and personalities. Special photo needs: "I like to see photos with ideas on how to use them in photo stories."
Making Contact & Terms: To contact: Sample 20 to 40 or so 35mm or larger transparencies with ideas. SASE. Reports in 1 month. Pays $250/color cover photo; $50-150/color inside photo; $150-300/day plus expenses for assignemnts; $500/photoessay. Pays on acceptance. Credit line given. Buys one-time rights plus permission to reprint in our Mexican and Canadian publications. Previously published work OK.

EDUCATIONAL THEATRE ASSOCIATION, (formerly Dramatics), 3368 Central Pkwy., Cincinnati OH 45225. (513)559-1996. Editor: Don Corathers. Publication of the International Thespian Society. Monthly (except June, July, August). Emphasizes performing arts, especially, but not limited to, educational theatre. Readers are high school and college theatre students and teachers. Circ. 34,000. Sample copy free with 9 × 12 SAE and $1.05 postage.
Photo Needs: Uses about 12-20 photos/issue; about 25% supplied by freelance photographers. Needs photos of theatre performances; candids of theatre personalities. Most photos are purchased with ms. Model release preferred (unless permission is implicit, as is the case with most photos of public figures); captions required.
Making Contact & Terms: Send photos with ms for consideration: 8 × 10 glossy or pearl b&w prints; 35mm, 2¼ × 2¼, 4 × 5, 8 × 10 transparencies; b&w contact sheet or negatives. Provide resume, business card, brochure, flyer or tearsheets to be kept on file for possible future assignments. SASE. Reports in 1 month. Pays $200/color cover photo; $35/b&w inside photo; $50/color inside photo; $100-300/job; $25-300/text-photo package. Pays on acceptance. Credit line given. Buys first North American serial rights. Simultaneous submissions and previously published work OK.
Tips: "Hook up with a good freelance writer and submit photo-illustrations with his/her manuscript."

ELCIC SUNDAY BULLETINS, 1512 St. James St., Winnipeg MB R3H 0L2 Canada. (204)786-6707. Art Director: Darrell Dyck. Publication of the Division for Parish Life, Evangelical Lutheran Church in Canada. "Weekly bulletins printed semi-annually; 8½ × 11 bi/tri fold bulletin. Emphasizes faith/religious content; worship; seasons of the liturgical church year. Readers are members of the Evanglical Lutheran Church in Canada. Circ. 40,000.
Photo Needs: Uses 1 photo/issue; supplied by freelance photographer. Uses 100% from stock. Model release is preferred.
Making Contact & Terms: Send b&w or color 5 × 7 gloss prints or 35mm transparencies by mail for consideration. SASE. Reports in 1 month. Pays $50/color or b&w cover photo. Pays on publication. Credit line given. Buys one-time rights.
Tips: In portfolio or samples, wants to see "photos of people that tell a story, illustrate a situation or a mood. Good lighting and natural posing are important. Send a lot. Let us keep it for review. This publication is an ongoing project and many of the topics we illustrate happen over and over, so we might need a similar but different shot in future issues. We try to balance between our changing Canadian mosaic and tradition. Modern Canadian life reflects changing roles for men & women and a changing ethnic pattern. We try to illustrate this as well as tell the story."

ELECTRICAL CONTRACTOR, Suite 1300 West, 7315 Wisconsin Ave., Bethesda MD 20814. Managing Editor: Walt Albro. Publication of National Electrical Contractors Association. Monthly magazine. Emphasizes management of electrical contracting companies. Readers are the owners and key personnel of electrical construction businesses. Circ. 66,000. Sample copy free with SASE.
Photo Needs: Uses 1-8 photos/issue; 1-3 supplied by freelancers. "Usually illustrations for feature articles on specific electrical construction companies."
Making Contact & Terms: Provide resume, business card, brochure, flyer or tearsheets to be kept on file for possible future assignments. SASE. Reports in 1 month. Pays $100-400/job. Pays on acceptance or on publication. Credit line given if requested. Buys all rights or "negotiable" rights.
Tips: "Give evidence that you have done previous magazine work. Make known your area of geographic availability. When we have an assignment in your area, we will contact you."

THE ELKS MAGAZINE, 425 W. Diversey, Chicago IL 60614. (312)528-4500. Editor: Fred D. Oakes. Publication of the B.P.O. Elks of the U.S. Monthly magazine. Emphasizes general interest including travel, history, nostalgia, sports, business and self-improvement. Readers are 50+, 54% male, 46% female, broad occupational spectrum. Circ. 1.5 million. Estab. 1922. Sample copy for 9 × 12 SAE and 85¢ postage.

Photo Needs: "We frequently use scenics for cover." Model release and photo captions preferred.
Making Contact & Terms: SASE. Reports in 3 weeks. Pays $450/color cover photo. Pays on acceptance. Credit line given. Buys first North American serial rights. Will consider simultaneous submissions.

EXECUTIVE FEMALE, 127 W 24th St., New York NY 10011. (212)371-0470. Editor: Ingrid Eisenstadter. Art Director: Helen Serfling. Association publication of National Association for Female Executives. Bimonthly. Emphasizes career advancement, problems/solutions in work place. Readers are "middle to upper level managers looking to move up in career. Also entrepreneurs and women starting or expanding small businesses." Circ. 200,000. Sample copy free with 10×13 SAE and $1.07 postage.
Photo Needs: Uses about 20 photos/issue; 5 supplied by freelancers. Needs portraits of professional women, informal and formal. Model release required; captions and storyline preferred.
Making Contact & Terms: Query with resume of credits; provide resume, business card, brochure, flyer or tearsheets to be kept on file for possible future assignments. SASE. Reports in 4-6 weeks. Pays $600/color cover photo; $100/quarter page; $200/half page. Pays on publication. Credit line given. Buys one-time and all rights. Simultaneous submissions and previously published work OK.
Tips: Looks for "interesting portraits of women; professional but not boring business photos." Send transparencies only for best color.

FAMILY MOTOR COACHING, 8291 Clough Pike, Cincinnati OH 45244. (513)474-3622. Editor: Pamela Wisby Kay. Publication of Family Motor Coach Association. Monthly. Emphasizes motor homes. Readers are members of national association of motor home owners. Circ. 75,000. Sample copy $2.50. Photo guidelines free with SASE.
Photo Needs: Uses about 45-50 photos/issue; 40-45 supplied by freelance photographers. Each issue includes varied subject matter—primarily needs travel and scenic shots and how-to material. Photos purchased with accompanying ms only. Model release preferred; captions required.
Making Contact & Terms: Query with resume of credits. SASE. Reports in 1 month. Pays $100-500/ text/photo package. Pays on acceptance. Credit line given if requested. Prefers first North American rights, but will consider one-time rights on photos *only*.

FELLOWSHIP, Box 271, Nyack NY 10960. (914)358-4601. FAX: (914)358-4924. Editor: Virginia Baron. Publication of the Fellowship of Reconciliation. Estab. 1935. Publishes 32-page b&w magazine 8 times/ year. Emphasizes peace-making/social justice/nonviolent social change. Readers are religious peace fellowships—interfaith pacifists. Circ. 8,500. Sample copy free with SASE on request.
Photo Needs: Uses 8-10 photos/issue; 90% supplied by freelance photographers. Needs stock photos of monuments/civil disobedience/demonstrations—Middle East; South Africa; prisons; anti-nuclear; children; farm crisis; USSR. Captions required. Also natural beauty and scenic; b&w only.
Making Contact & Terms: Provide resume, business card, brochure, flyer or tearsheets to be kept on file for possible future assignments. "Call on specs." SASE. Reports in 3 weeks. Pays $25/b&w cover photo; $13.50/b&w inside photo. Pays on publication. Credit line given. Buys one-time rights. Simultaneous submissions and previously published work OK.
Tips: "You must want to make a contribution to peace movements. Money is simply token; (our authors contribute without tokens)."

FIRE JOURNAL/FIRE COMMAND, 1 Batterymarch Park, Quincy MA 02269. (617)770-3000. ext. 566. Art Director: Jane Reed. Publication of National Fire Protection Association. Bimonthly magazine. Emphasizes fire professionals. Readers are predominately male fire professionals, ages 20-65. Circ. 45,000. Sample copy for 9×12 SASE.
Photo Needs: Uses 25-30 photos/issue; 50% supplied by freelance photographers. Needs photos of fires and fire related incidents. Especially wants to use more photos for Fire Fighter Injury Report and Fire Fighter Fatality Report. Model release and photo captions preferred.
Making Contact & Terms: Query with list of stock photo subjects, send unsolicited photos by mail for consideration or provide resume, business card, brochure, flyer or tearsheets to be kept on file for possible assignments. Send color prints and 35mm transparencies. SASE. Reports in 3 weeks or "as soon as I can." Payment negotiated. Pays on publication. Credit line given. Buys rights depending "on article and sensitivity of subject."
Tips: "Send cover letter, 35mm color slides preferably with manuscripts and photo captions."

*FLORIDA FOLIAGE MAGAZINE, P.O. Box 2507, Apopke FL 32703. (407)886-1036. Contact: Editor. Publication of Florida Foliage Association. Monthly magazine. Emphasizes foliage. Readers are growers, nurserymen, retail outlets and grocery stores. Circ. 3,000. Estab. 1977. Sample copy free with SASE.

Photo Needs: Usage of photos/issue varies. Needs cover photos of plants, nurseries and people. Needs monthly cover photos. Model release required; photo captions preferred.

Making Contact & Terms: Provide resume, business card, brochure, flyer or tearsheets to be kept on file for possible assignments. Report time varies depending on deadlines. Payment varies. Pays within 10 days of acceptance. Buys "mainly the right to keep photo at our convenience." Simultaneous submissions and previously published work OK.

FLORIDA WILDLIFE, 620 S. Meridian St., Tallahassee FL 32399-1600. (904)488-5563. FAX: (904)488-6988. Editor: Andrea Blount. Estab. 1947. Publication of the Florida Game & Fresh Water Fish Commission. Bimonthly magazine. Emphasizes wildlife, hunting, fishing, conservation. Readers are wildlife lovers, hunters, and fishermen. Circ. 29,000. Sample copy $1.25. Photo guidelines free with SASE.

Photo Needs: Uses about 20-40 photos/issue; 75% supplied by freelance photojournalists. Needs 35mm color transparencies and b&w glossies of southern fishing and hunting, all wildlife (flora and fauna) of southeastern USA; how-to; covers and inside illustration. Do not feature products in photographs, where they can be subdued. No alcohol or tobacco. Special needs include hunting and fishing activities in southern scenes; showing ethical and enjoyable use of outdoor resources. Model release preferred.

Making Contact & Terms: Query with samples, or send "mostly 35mm transparencies, but we use some b&w enlarged prints" by mail for consideration. "Do not send negatives." SASE. Reports in 1 month or longer. Pays $50/back color cover; $100/front color cover; $20-50/b&w or color inside photo. Pays on publication. Credit line given. Buys one-time rights; "other rights are sometimes negotiated." Simultaneous submissions OK "but we prefer originals over duplicates." Previously published work OK but must be mentioned when submitted.

Tips: "Use flat slide mounting pages or individual sleeves. Show us your best."

FLYFISHER, 1387 Cambridge Dr., Idaho Falls ID 83401. (208)523-7300. Editor: Dennis G. Bitton. Quarterly magazine. Circ. 11,000. Emphasizes fly fishing for members of the Federation of Fly Fishers. Uses 100 photos/year, most bought with ms. Pays $25-200 for text/photo package, or on a per-photo basis. Credit line given. Pays after publication. Buys first North American serial rights. Query with resume of credits or samples. "Send us 20-40 slides on spec with due date for returning." SASE. Reports in 1 month. Sample copy $3, available from Federation of Fly Fishers, Box 1088, West Yellowstone MT 59758. Photo guidelines free with SASE.

Photo Needs: How-to (on tying flies, fishing techniques, etc.); photo essay/photo feature; and scenic. No photos of angling unrelated to fly fishing. Captions required.

B&W: Uses 8 × 10 glossy prints. Pays $15-50/photo.

Color: Uses 35mm, 2¼ × 2¼ or 4 × 5 transparencies. Pays $25-100.

Cover: Uses 35mm, 2¼ × 2¼ or 4 × 5 color transparencies. Needs scenics. Vertical or square formats required. Pays $100-150.

Accompanying Mss: "Any mss related to fly fishing, its lore and history, fishing techniques, conservation, personalities, fly tying, equipment, etc." Writer's guidelines free with SASE.

FOCUS, Owens-Corning Fiberglas, Toledo OH 43659. (419)248-8000. FAX: (419)241-5210. Editor: Bill Hamilton. Monthly tabloid. Circ. 23,000. For employees of Owens-Corning Fiberglas. "We assign photo jobs based on our needs. We do not use unsolicited material. We use photojournalism; photography that tells a story. We do not use contrived, posed shots." Hires at least 12 photographers annually. Query first with resume of credits. "Send photocopies of shots you think show your talent as a visual communicator." Free sample copy.

B&W: Uses 8 × 10 glossy prints; must send negatives. Captions required.

Cover: See requirements for b&w.

Tips: Employee communications are coordinated by outside agency. Contact: Kristin Paquette, %Funk Luetke, Inc. 405 Madison Ave., 12th Floor, Toledo OH 43604. "We have a need for freelancers in all parts of the country for special assignments determined by story content."

FORD TIMES, Suite 1700, One Illinois Center, 111 E. Wacker Dr., Chicago IL 60601. Art Director: James Prendergast. Monthly. Circ. 1,200,000. General interest; current upbeat lifestyle subjects with a magazine featuring slant. Free sample copy and photo guidelines with 9 × 12 SAE and 56¢ postage.

Photo Needs: Photos purchased with accompanying ms or by assignment. Model release and caption information required.

Making Contact & Terms: Query with samples. Prefers to see published works in a printed form and original photography as samples. SASE. Reports in 1 month. Pays $350-500/b&w or color inside photo, full page or more; $150/b&w or color inside photo, less than page size; $500/cover photo; payment on complete package negotiable. Pays on publication. Credit line given. Buys (first time when applicable) one-time rights.

Tips: In portfolio or samples, wants to see "ability to take the mundane and creatively produce a variety of interesting images." To break in, "continually mail in printed samples which parallel type used in our magazines—general interest and travel." Go beyond the obvious requirements of an assignment, and come up with the unexpected." Sees trend toward more use of people shots.

THE FUTURIST, 4916 St. Elmo Ave., Bethesda MD 20814. (301)656-8274. Managing Editor: Timothy Willard. Publication of the World Future Society, general readership. Bimonthly magazine. Emphasizes the future. Circ. 32,000.
Photo Needs: Uses variable number of photos/issue. Model release required; captions preferred.
Making Contact & Terms: Query with stock photo list. SASE. Reports within 6 weeks. Pays $25-100/b&w photo; $25-250/color photo. Pays on acceptance. Credit line given. Buys one-time rights.

GOLF COURSE MANAGEMENT, 1617 St. Andrews Dr., Lawrence KS 66047. (913)841-2240. FAX: (913)841-2407. Editor: Clay Lloyd. Estab. 1926. Publication of the Golf Course Superintendents Association of America. Monthly. Circ. 22,000. Emphasizes "golf course maintenance/management." Readers are "golf course superintendents and managers." Sample copy free with 9 × 12 SAE plus $1 postage; photo guidelines free with SASE.
Photo Needs: Uses about 25 photos/issue; 1-5 supplied by freelance photographers. Needs "scenic shots of famous golf courses, good composition, unusual holes dramatically portrayed." Also, golf course construction, maintenance, and renovation photos. Model release required; captions preferred.
Making Contact & Terms: Query with samples. Provide business card, brochure, flyer or tearsheets to be kept on file for possible future assignments. SASE. Reports in 3 weeks. Pays $125-250/color cover photo. Pays on acceptance. Credit line given. Buys one-time rights.
Tips: Prefers to see "good color, unusual angles/composition for vertical format cover."

THE GREYHOUND REVIEW, Box 543, Abilene KS 67410. (913)263-4660. Contact: Gary Guccione or Tim Horan. Publication of the National Greyhound Association. Monthly. Circ. 7,000. Emphasizes greyhound racing and breeding. Readers are greyhound owners and breeders. Sample copy with SASE and $2.50 postage.
Photo Needs: Uses about 10 photos/issue; 2 supplied by freelance photographers. Needs "anything pertinent to the greyhound that would be of interest to greyhound owners." Captions required.
Making Contact & Terms: Query with samples; send b&w or color prints and contact sheets by mail for consideration; submit portfolio for review; provide resume, business card, brochure, flyer or tearsheets to be kept on file for possible future assignments. Can return unsolicited material if requested. Reports within 1 month. Pays $75/color cover photo; $10-50/b&w; and $25-100/color inside photo. Pays on acceptance. Credit line given. Buys one-time North American rights. Simultaneous and previously published submissions OK.
Tips: "We look for human-interest or action photos involving greyhounds. No muzzles, please, unless the greyhound is actually racing. When submitting photos for our cover, make sure there's plenty of cropping space on all margins around your photo's subject; full bleeds on our cover are preferred."

GROWTH MAGAZINE, Georgia-Pacific Corp., 133 Peachtree St. NE, Atlanta GA 30303. Editor: Carole Siracusa. Publication of Georgia-Pacific Corp. Monthly. Circ. 44,000. Emphasizes items of interest to Georgia-Pacific employees worldwide. Readers are 44,000 Georgia-Pacific employees, plus stockholders, retirees and friends of the company. Sample copy free.
Photo Needs: Uses about 10 photos/issue; 10% supplied by freelance photographers. Wants color shots for duotone cover reproduction. Needs "product shots; on-site plant photography; good candid people shots; occasional 'how-to' (standard industrial photojournalism)." Model release and caption required.
Making Contact & Terms: Query with samples. Provide resume, business card, brochure, flyer or tearsheets to be kept on file for possible future assignments. Reports in 3 weeks. Rates vary; ranges around $500/color cover; $150/b&w inside; $300/color inside; $20-50/by the hour. Pays on acceptance. Credit line given. Buys all rights. Terms include purchase of negative.
Tips: Prefers to see "industrial photography showing creative approach to plant, people and operations."

GUERNSEY BREEDERS' JOURNAL, Box 666, Reynoldsburg OH 43068-0666. (614)864-2409. Co-editors: Cheri Schroer and Lisa Knapps. Publication of American Guernsey Association. Magazine published 10 times a year. Emphasizes Guernsey dairy cattle, dairy cattle management. Readership consists of male and female dairymen, 20-70 years of age. Circ. 2,800. Sample copy free with 8½ × 11 SASE.

Photo Needs: Uses 40-100 photos/issue; uses less than 5% of freelance photos. Needs scenic photos featuring Guernsey cattle. Model release and captions preferred.

Making Contact & Terms: Query with resume of credits business card, brochure, flyer or tearsheets to be kept on file for possible assignments. SASE. Reports in 1 month. Pays $100/color cover photo and $50/b&w cover photo. Pays on publication. Credit line given. Buys all rights; will negotiate. Simultaneous submissions and previously published work OK.

HARVARD MAGAZINE, 7 Ware St., Cambridge MA 02138. (617)495-5746. FAX: (617)495-0324. Managing Editor: Christopher Reed. Photo Editor: Jean Martin. Bimonthly magazine. Emphasizes Harvard University, Radcliffe College and alumni/alumnae of those schools. Readers are primarily alumni/alumnae of Harvard University and Radcliffe College. Circ. 150,000. Estab. 1898.

Photo Needs: Uses 60+ photos/issue; 30-50% supplied by freelance photographers. Needs photos of the Cambridge area, university area. Local photographers preferred. Captions preferred.

Making Contact & Terms: Provide resume, business card, brochure, flyer or tearsheets to be kept on file for possible future assignments. SASE. Reports in 1 month or longer. Pays $300/b&w cover photo; $300 and expenses/color cover photo; $50 minimum/inside b&w or color photo shot on assignment; $35/b&w or color stock photo. Pays on publication. Credit line given. Buys one-time rights. Simultaneous submissions and previously published work OK.

Tips: "We need a fairly limited range of photos, but are happy to pay for variety within that range."

*HEADWATERS, Friends of the River, Ft. Mason Ctr., Bldg C, San Francisco CA 94123. (415)771-0400. Director: Ted Cuzzillo. Publication of Friends of the River. Bimonthly tabloid. Emphasizes river recreation and conservation. Readers are all ages and genders, mostly professional occupations and education above average. Circ. 20,000. Estab. 1976. Sample copy for $1 or 9×12 SAE and 2 first-class stamps. Guidelines free with SASE.

Photo Needs: Uses 5 photos/issue; up to 100% supplied by freelance photographers. Needs photos of river recreation, (i.e. rafting, kayaking, camping and activities incidental to this with clear reference to boating). Model release preferred; photo captions required.

Making Contact & Terms: Send unsolicited b&w glossy prints and 35mm, 2¼×2¼, 4×5 transparencies by mail for consideration. SASE. Reports in 1 month. Credit line given. Buys one-time rights. Simultaneous submissions and previously published work OK.

HEALTHCARE EXECUTIVE, 840 N. Lakeshore, Chicago IL 60611. (312)943-0544. Art Director: Kirk Horlbeck. American College of Healthcare Executives. Bimonthly. Emphasizes healthcare management. Circ. 24,000. Sample copy free with 8½×11 SAE.

Photo Needs: Uses 6-12 photos/issue; 50% supplied by freelancers Model release required; captions preferred.

Making Contact & Terms: Query with samples or list of stock photo subjects; send unsolicited photos by mail for consideration; provide resume, business card, brochure, flyer or tearsheets to be kept on file for possible future assignments. SASE. Reports in 2 weeks. Pays on publication. Credit line given. Buys one-time rights.

HICALL, Church School Literature Department, 1445 Boonville Ave., Springfield MO 65802. (417)862-2781. Editor: Deanna S. Harris. Publication of The General Council of the Assemblies of God. Thirteen weekly, 8-page issues published quarterly. Readers are primarily high school students (but also junior high). Circ. 85,000. Sample copy free for 6×9 SAE and 50¢ postage; photo guidelines free with SASE.

Photo Needs: Uses 2-3 photos/issue; 75% supplied by freelance photographers. Uses 5% assigned; 95% from stock.Needs photos of teens in various moods (joy, loneliness, prayer, surprise). Some scenics used, also nature close-ups; high school settings and activities. Reviews photos with or without accompanying ms.

Making Contact & Terms: Query with list of stock photo subjects, send 8×10 glossy b&w prints, 35mm, 2¼×2¼, and 4×5 transparencies by mail for consideration. SASE. Pays $25-30/b&w photo; $30-40/color photo. Pays on acceptance. Credit line given. Buys one-time rights. Simultaneous submissions and previously published work OK.

Tips: Wants to see "sharp, clear, usually close-ups of teens involved in various activities and with other people." For submission, wants good "composition and contrast of teens working, playing eating, partying, relaxing, at school, home, church, etc. Also, mood shots, closeups."

HISTORIC PRESERVATION, 1785 Massachusetts Ave., NW, Washington DC 20036. (202)673-4084. Art Director: Jeff Roth. Publication of National Trust for Historic Preservation. Bimonthly. Emphasizes people involved in historic homes, towns, neighborhoods, restoration. Readers are upper income. Average age fifties. Also restoration professionals, architects, etc. Circ. 224,000. Sample copy $2.50 and 8½×11 SAE. Photo guidelines with SASE.

Photo Needs: Uses about 45 photos/issue; almost all supplied by freelance photographers. Needs photos of historic homes, restoration in progress, craftspeople, exteriors and interiors. Needs strong photo portfolio ideas, black & white or color, relating to the preservation of buildings, craftspeople, interiors, furniture, etc. Model release, captions required.

Making Contact & Terms: Arrange a personal interview to show portfolio; query with samples. SASE. Reports in 1 month. Pays $25-100/b&w photo; $50-200/color photo; $200-400/day. Other terms negotiable. Pays on acceptance. Credit line given. Buys first North American serial rights.

Tips: Prefers to see "interestingly or naturally lit architectural interiors and exteriors. Environmental portraits, artfully done. Become familiar with our magazine. Suggest suitable story ideas. Will use stock when applicable."

HOBIE HOTLINE, Box 1008, Oceanside CA 92054. (619)758-9100. Publisher: Bonnie Hepburn. Publication of the World Hobie Class Association. Bimonthly. Circ. 48,000. Emphasizes "Hobie Cat sailing in the US and foreign countries." Readers are "young adults and sailing families, average age 28 to 38. Enthusiastic active group of people who love sailing." Sample magazine $1 with 9 × 12 SAE and $1.50 postage; photo guidelines free with SASE.

Photo Needs: Uses about 30-35 photos/issue; 90% supplied by freelance photographers. Needs "action photos of Hobie Cats; scenics that correspond to location of shoot." Special needs include "mid-America photo essays; lake sailing on a Hobie Cat; wave surfing on a Hobie Cat."

Making Contact & Terms: Send 8 × 10 b&w glossy prints; 35mm or 2¼ × 2¼ transparencies or b&w contact sheet by mail for consideration. Prefers Kodachrome. SASE. Reports in 1 month. Pays $200/color cover photo; $10-60/b&w and $25-100/color inside photo; $35/b&w and $65/color page; and $150-300 for text/photo package. Pays on publication. Credit line given. Buys one-time rights. Simultaneous submissions and previously published work OK.

Tips: "We are looking for sharp, clear, exciting Hobie Cat action shots as well as mood shots."

HOME & AWAY MAGAZINE, Box 3535, Omaha NE 68103. (402)390-1000. Photo Editor: Jill Carstens-Faust. Bimonthly. Circ. 1,750,000. Emphasizes travel (foreign and domestic), automotive, auto safety, consumerism from the viewpoint of auto ownership. Readers are between 45-50 years of age, above average income, broadly traveled and very interested in outdoor recreation and sports. Free sample copy with 8½ × 11 SAE and $1.50 postage.

Photo Needs: Uses 20-30 photos/issue; 75% supplied by freelance photographers/travel writers. Needs photos on travel subjects. "Interested in scenics alone; but prefer people in the photos — not posed, but active." Photos should reinterpret a sense of place. Captions required.

Making Contact & Terms: Query with list of stock photo subjects. SASE. Reports in 2 weeks. Provide resume, brochure, flyer and tearsheets to be kept on file for possible future assignments. Pays an average of $400/color photo (cover); $50-150/color photo (inside); $300-1,000 for text/photo package. Pays on acceptance. Credit line given. Buys one-time rights. Simultaneous submissions and/or previously published work OK, as long as not in territory of magazine circulation.

Tips: Seeing trend toward "use of larger photos and more people-oriented images." In portfolio or samples, wants to see "a unique style. The ability to interpret a sense of place or a person in a single shot. Review the publication and send me images that are interesting to you and that grab your attention. SASE is a must."

HOOF BEATS, 750 Michigan Ave., Columbus OH 43215. (614)224-2291. FAX: (614)228-1385. Executive Editor: Dean Hoffman. Design/Production Manager: Jenny Gilbert. Publication of the US Trotting Association. Monthly. Circ. 24,000. Estab. 1933. Emphasizes harness racing. Readers are participants in the sport of harness racing. Sample copy free.

Photo Needs: Uses about 30 photos/issue; about 20% supplied by freelance photographers. Needs "artistic or striking photos that feature harness horses for covers; other photos on specific horses and drivers by assignment only."

Making Contact & Terms: Query with samples. SASE. Reports in 3 weeks. Pays $25-150/b&w photo; $50-200/color photo; $150+/color cover photo; freelance assignments negotiable. Pays on publication. Credit line given if requested. Buys one-time rights. Simultaneous submissions OK.

Tips: "We look for photos with unique perspective and that display unusual techniques or use of light. Send query letter first. Know the publication and its needs before submitting blindly. Be sure to shoot pictures of harness horses only, not Thoroughbred or riding horses." There is "more artistic use of b&w photography instead of color. More use of fill-flash in personality photos. We always need good night racing action or creative photography."

HOSPITAL PHYSICIAN (& PHYSICIAN ASSISTANT), PW Communications — 400 Plaza Dr., Secaucus NJ 07094. (201)865-7500. Art Director: Sharyl Sand Carow. Publication of Association for Hospital Medical Education. Monthly. Emphasizes health care, medical technology, medicine, science. Readers are doctors, residents, medical students, physician assistants. Circ. 178,000. Sample copy free with 9x11 SASE.

Photo Needs: Uses 5-10 photos/issue. Needs medical photos; health care, hospital, technology, medicine, etc. Reviews photos with accompanying ms only. Special photo needs include healthcare; nurses, doctors, surgery, patients, elderly, etc.; medical technology—procedures. Model release and captions required.

Making Contact & Terms: Query with list of stock photo subjects; send unsolicited b&w and color prints, 35mm transparencies, b&w and color contact sheets and negatives by mail for consideration; provide resume, business card, brochure, flyer or tearsheets to be kept on file for possible future assignments. Does not return unsolicited material. Reports back only if material is considered. Pays $100/b&w cover or inside photo; $200/color cover or inside photo. Pays on publication. Credit line given. Buys all rights; will negotiate with photographer unwilling to sell all rights. Simultaneous submissions and previously published work OK.

Tips: "Please don't call—our need for photographers is limited to medical."

HOSPITAL TRUSTEE, Suite 100, 17 York St., Ottawa, ON K1N 9J6 Canada. Editor, Journals: Jackie Barlow. Publication of Canadian Hospital Association. Bimonthly magazine. Emphasizes hospital trusteeship. Readers are hospital trustees, ages 40-70, upper income bracket. Circ. 5,600. Sample copy $4.50 Canadian with 9 × 12 SAE.

Photo Needs: Uses 1 photo/issue; 100% supplied by freelancers. Needs photos of "business: decision-making, meetings, etc." Model release required; photo captions preferred.

Making Contact & Terms: Query with list of stock photo subjects. SASE. Reports in 2 weeks. Pays $335 Canadian/color and b&w cover photo. Pays on publication. Credit line given. Buys one-time rights. Simultaneous submissions and previously published work OK.

HOUSTON MAGAZINE, Suite 400, 2323 S. Voss, Houston TX 77057. (713)784-0555. Editor: D. Ann Shiffler. Publication of the Houston Chamber of Commerce. Monthly magazine. Emphasizes Houston businesses and business executives. Readers are Chamber of Commerce members. Circ. 25,000. Sample copy for $2.50, 8½ × 10½ SASE and 2-3 first class stamps.

Photo Needs: Uses 10 photos/issue; 100% supplied by freelance photographers. Needs photos of people, offices, business activities and how-to. Model release and captions required.

Making Contact & Terms: Query with resume of credits, business card, brochure, flyer or tearsheets to be kept on file for possible assignments; query with list of stock photo subjects, or send any size glossy b&w or color print by mail for consideration. SASE. Reports in 1 month. Contact for revised payment rates. Buys all rights; will negotiate. Does not consider simultaneous submissions or previously published work.

Tips: "Being in Houston is essential. Contact editor for information."

HR MAGAZINE (formerly Personnel Administrator), 606 N. Washington St., Alexandria VA 22314. (703)548-3440. Publisher/Editor: John T. Adams III. Art Director: Caroline Foster. Association publication of SHRM. Monthly magazine. Estab. 1956. Emphasizes human resource management. Readers are human resource professionals. Circ. 42,000. Sample copy $7.50.

Photo Needs: Uses 10-25 photos/issue; 90% supplied by freelance photographers on assignment. Needs photos of worklife situations—software use, technology, work environments, human resource or personal situations/issues. Model release and captions preferred.

Making Contact & Terms: Query with samples and list of stock photo subjects; provide resume, business card, brochure, flyer or tearsheets to be kept on file for possible future assignments. Does not return unsolicited material. Reports in 2 weeks. Pays $600/color cover photo. Also pays $300-800/day. Pays on acceptance. Credit line given. Buys one-time reproduction world rights. Previously published work OK.

Tips: SHRM also publishes a monthly newspaper uses b&w photos, HRNews. Editor: Ceel Pasternak. Art Director: Caroline Foster. In samples, looks for corporate portraits on location.

***■THE ICF BUGLE**, E-11376 Shady Lane Rd., Baraboo WI 53913. (608)356-9462. Education Director: David Thompson. Publication of International Crane Foundation (nonprofit organization). Quarterly newsletter. Emphasizes worldwide conservation of cranes and wetlands. Readers are conservationists and scientists interested in conservation and cranes. Circ. 5,000. Estab. 1975. Sample copy for $1 and 9 × 12 SAE.

Photo Needs: Uses 9 photos/issue; 45% supplied by freelance photographers. Needs striking, beautiful color slides of cranes in a magnificdent natural setting; crane behavior and biology; and people involved with cranes (i.e. crane counting) Needs photos for the newsletter, slide shows, brochures, and miscellaneous publications. Special photo needs include photos of people in The Annual Wisconsin Sandhill Crane Count, in mid April. Model release preferred. Photo captions required.

Making Contact & Terms: "Query with details about specific crane or wetlands subjects you have photos of." SASE. Reports in 1 month. Pays $25/color inside photo; $15/b&w inside photo. Pays on publication. Buys one-time rights. Simultaneous submissions and previously published work OK.

Tips: "Do not send photos taken in zoos unless they are truly exceptional or extremely funny. The photos you submit should be really exceptional. We have scientists who are good photographers making submissions, so yours have to be better. If there is a research or conservation project in your area involving cranes or wetlands, attach yourself to it and provide striking photos that document its progress."

"IN THE FAST LANE", ICC National Headquarters, 2001 Pittston Ave., Scranton PA 18505. (717)347-5839. Editor: D.M. Crispino. Publication of the International Camaro Club. Bimonthly. 20-page newsletter. Emphasizes camaro car shows, events, cars, stories, etc. Readers are auto enthusiasts/Camaro exclusively. Circ. 2,000+. Sample copy $1.

Photo Needs: Uses 20-24 photos/issue; 90% assigned. Needs Camaro-oriented photos only. Reviews photos with accompanying ms only. Model release and captions required.

Making Contact & Terms: Send 3½×5 and larger b&w or color prints by mail for consideration. SASE. Reports in 2 weeks. Pays $5-20 for text/photo package. Pays on publication. Credit line given. Buys one-time rights. Previously published work OK.

Tips: "We need quality photos that put you at the track, in the race or in the midst of the show. Magazine is bi-monthly; timeliness even more important than with monthly."

JAYCEES MAGAZINE, Box 7, Tulsa OK 74121-0007. (918)584-2481. Editor: Bob Hardy. Publication of the Jaycees. Bimonthly magazine. Emphasizes volunteerism. Readers are men and women 21 to 39. Circ. 234,000. Sample copy $2.

Photo Needs: Uses 6-10 photos/issue; 1 supplied by freelance photographers. Needs of photos varies, primarily people, also meetings. Model release required; captions preferred.

Making Contact & Terms: Query with list of stock photo subjects. SASE. Reports in 3 weeks. Pay varies by assignment. Pays on acceptance. Credit line given. Buys one-time rights. Previously published work OK.

JOURNAL OF PHYSICAL EDUCATION, RECREATION & DANCE, American Alliance for Health, Physical Education, Recreation & Dance, Reston VA 22091. (703)476-3400. Managing Editor: Frances Rowan. Monthly magazine. Emphasizes "teaching and learning in public school physical education, youth sports, youth fitness, dance on elementary, secondary or college levels (not performances; classes only), recreation for youth, children, families, girls and women's athletics and *physical* education and fitness." Circ. 35,000. Estab. 1896. Sample copy free with 9×12 SAE and $1.80 postage. Photo guidelines free with SASE.

Photo Needs: Freelancers supply cover photos only; 80% from assignment. Written release and captions preferred. Buys b&w by contract.

Making Contact & Terms: Query with list of stock photo subjects. Buys 5×7 or 8×10 color prints, and 35mm transparencies. Pays $30/b&w photo; $250/color photo. Returns unsolicited photos with SASE. Reports in 2 weeks. Credit line given. Buys one-time rights. Previously published work OK.

Tips: "Innovative transparencies relating to physical education, recreation and sport are considered for publication on the cover—vertical format." Looks for "action shots, cooperative games, no competitive sports and classroom scenes. Send samples of *relevant* photos."

JOURNAL OF SOIL AND WATER CONSERVATION, 7515 NE Ankeny Rd., Ankeny IA 50021. (515)289-2331. FAX: (515)289-1227. Editor: Max Schnepf. Association publication for the Soil and Water Conservation Society. Bimonthly journal. Estab. 1946. Emphasizes land and water conservation. Readers include a multidisciplinary group of professionals and laymen interested in the wise use of land and water resources. Circ. 13,500. Free sample copy with 9×12 SAE and $1 postage.

Photo Needs: Uses 25-40 photos/issue; 0-2 supplied by freelance photographers. Needs photos illustrating land and water conservation problems and practices used to solve those problems; including items related to agriculture, wildlife, recreation, reclamation, and scenic views. Reviews photos with or without accompanying ms. Model release and captions preferred.

Making Contact & Terms: Send unsolicited photos by mail for consideration. Uses 5×7, 8×10 b&w prints, and 35mm, 2¼×2¼, 4×5 and 8×10 color transparencies; b&w contact sheet. SASE. Reports in 2 weeks. Pays $50-100/color cover; $10 up/inside b&w. Pays on acceptance. Credit line given. Buys one-time rights.

Tips: In samples wants to see "good quality photos of people involved in conservation-related activities."

JOURNAL OF THE NATIONAL MEDICAL ASSOCIATION, Slack Incorporated, 6900 Grove Rd., Thorofare NJ 08086. (800)257-8290. Managing Editor: Sandra Patterson. Publication of National Medical Association. Monthly journal. Emphasizes clinical research that is related to the health problems of the urban patient. Readers are inner-city minority physicians. Circ. 29,000. Sample copy $7. Free photo guidelines.

Photo Needs: Needs "photos depicting black physicians in medical settings, and photos that illustrate black history in general and black medical history specifically."

Making Contact & Terms: Send 35mm, 2¼ × 2¼ transparencies by mail for consideration. SASE. Reports in 1 month. Pays $350/color cover photo. Pays on publication. Credit line given. Buys one-time rights.

JOURNAL OF THE NATIONAL TECHNICAL ASSOCIATION, 1240 S. Broad St., New Orleans LA 70125. (504)821-5694. FAX: (504)821-5713. Production Manager: K. Kazi Ferrouillet. Publication of National Technical Association. Quarterly journal. Emphasizes engineering/science. Readers are experienced African-American technical professionals. Circ. 10,000. Estab. 1970. Sample copy for $5 and $1.50 postage.

Photo Needs: Uses 12 photos/issue; 4 supplied by local freelance photographers; assigns—10-15%, buys 85% stock. Needs photos of engineering, science and computers. Model release and captions preferred.

Making Contact & Terms: Arrange a personal interview to show a portfolio; query with resume or credits, samples or list of stock photo subjects. Reports in 1 month. Pays $25-50/b&w photo; $50-200/color photo. Pays on publication. Credit line given. Buys one-time rights.

Tips: Wants to see "African-American college students and young professionals in campus/work settings. Show sensitivity to the African-American experience. The trend is towards more action and more social/political activism. Examine our publication thoroughly before making proposal."

JUDICATURE, Suite 1600, 25 E. Washington, Chicago IL 60602. (312)558-6900. Editor: David Richert. Publication of the American Judicature Society. Bimonthly. Emphasizes courts, administration of justice. Readers are judges, lawyers, professors, citizens interested in improving the administration of justice. Circ. 21,000. Sample copy free with 9 × 12 SAE with $1.45 postage.

Photo Needs: Uses 2-3 photos/issue; 1-2 supplied by freelance photographers. Needs photos relating to courts, the law. "Actual or posed courtroom shots are always needed." Model release and captions preferred.

Making Contact & Terms: Send 5 × 7 glossy b&w prints by mail for consideration. Provide resume, business card, brochure, flyer or tearsheets to be kept on file for possible future assignments. SASE. Reports in 2 weeks. Pays $200/b&w cover photo; $125/b&w inside photo. Pays on publication. Credit line given. Buys one-time rights. Simultaneous submissions and previously published work OK.

Tips: "We only want to see photos relevant to our interests."

KIWANIS MAGAZINE, 3636 Woodview Trace, Indianapolis IN 46268. (317)875-8755. FAX: (317)879-0204. Executive Editor: Chuck Jonak. Art Director: Jim Patterson. Published 10 times/year. Circ. 300,000. Estab. 1915. Emphasizes organizational news, plus major features of interest to business and professional men and women involved in community service. Send resume of stock photos. Provide brochure, calling card and flyer to be kept on file for future assignments. Assigns 95% of work. "We work regularly with local freelancers who make an appointment with the art director or production manager to show portfolio." Buys one-time rights.

B&W: Uses 5 × 7 or 8 × 10 glossy prints. Pays $50-700/b&w photo.

Color: Uses 35mm but would rather use 2¼ × 2¼ and 4 × 5 transparencies. Pays $75-1,000/color photo.

Accompanying Mss: Pays $400-1,000/ms with photos. Free sample copy and writer's guidelines with SASE.

Tips: "We are a nonprofit organization and subsequently do not have a large budget. But we can offer the photographer a lot of freedom to work *and* worldwide exposure. And perhaps an award or two if the work is good. We are now using more conceptual photos. We also use studio set-up shots. When we assign work, we want to know if a photographer can follow a concept into finished photo without on-site direction." In portfolio or samples, wants to see "studio work with flash and natural light."

LACMA PHYSICIAN, P.O. Box 3465, Los Angeles CA 90051-1465. (213)483-1581. Managing Editor: Michael Villaire. Published 20 times/year—twice a month except January, July, August and December. Circ. 11,000. Estab. 1875. Emphasizes Los Angeles County Medical Association news and medical issues. Readers are physicians and members of LACMA.

Photo Needs: Uses about 1-20 photos/issue; from both assignment and freelance stock. Needs photos of meetings of the association, physician members, association events—mostly internal coverage. Photos purchased with or without accompanying ms. Model release required.

Making Contact & Terms: Arrange a personal interview to show portfolio. Does not return unsolicited material. Pays by hour, day or half day; negotiable. General range is $5-8/b&w photo; $50-75/hour. Pays on publication with submission of invoice. Credit line given. Buys one-time rights or first North American serial rights "depending on what is agreed upon."

Tips: "We want photographers who blend in well, and can get an extraordinary photo from what may be an ordinary situation. We need to see work that demonstrates an ability to get it right the first time. without a lot of set-up on most shoots."

LANDSCAPE ARCHITECTURE, Fifth Fl., 4401 Conn. Ave. NW, Washington DC 20008. (202)686-2752. Managing Editor: Susan Waterman. Publication of the American Society of Landscape Architects. Monthly magazine. Emphasizes "landscape architecture, urban design, parks and recreation, architecture, sculpture" for professional planners and designers. Circ. 18,000. Sample copy $4; photo guidelines free with SASE.

Photo Needs: Uses about 50-75 photos/issue; 50% supplied by freelance photographers. Needs photos of landscape- and architecture-related subjects as described above. Special needs include aerial photography. Model release required, captions preferred. "We also need American and international landscape photographs for our international sections of the magazine."

Making Contact & Terms: Query with samples or list of stock photo subjects; provide resume, business card, brochure, flyer or tearsheets to be kept on file for possible future assignments. SASE. Reporting time varies. Pays $250/color cover photo; $100/b&w inside; $100/color inside ($50/quarter page). Pays on publication. Credit line given. Buys two-time rights. Previously published work OK.

LAW PRACTICE MANAGEMENT, (formerly Legal Economics), Box 11418, Columbia SC 29211. (803)754-3563. Editor/Art Director: Delmar L. Roberts. Published 8 times/year. Circ. 23,000. Publication of the Section of Law Practice Management, American Bar Association. For practicing attorneys and law students. Sample copy $7 (make check payable to American Bar Association).

Photo Needs: Uses 4-5 photos/issue; all supplied by freelance photographers. Needs photos of some stock subjects such as group at a conference table; someone being interviewed; scenes showing staffed office-reception areas; *imaginative* photos illustrating such topics as time management, employee relations, automatic typewriters, computers and word processing equipment, computer graphics of interest, record keeping, filing, malpractice insurance protection, abstract shots or special effects illustrating almost anything concerning management of a law practice. "We'll exceed our usual rates for exceptional photos of this latter type." No snapshots or Polaroid photos.

Making Contact & Terms: Uses 5×7 glossy b&w prints; 35mm, 2¼×2¼, 4×5 transparencies. Reports in 1-3 months. Pays $150-175/color cover photo (vertical format); $50-60/b&w inside photo; $100-200/job. Pays on publication. Credit line given. Usually buys all rights, and rarely reassigns to photographer after publication. Model releases and captions required. Send unsolicited photos by mail for consideration. They are accompanied by an article pertaining to the lapida "if requested." SASE. Simultaneous submissions OK.

LEADERSHIP, 465 Gundersen Dr., Carol Stream IL 60188. (312)260-6200. FAX: (708)260-0114. Editor: Marshall Shelley. Company publication for Christianity Today, Inc. Quarterly. Emphasizes the clergy. Circ. 90,000. Estab. 1980. Sample copy $6.

Photo Needs: Uses about 12 photos/issue; 100% supplied by freelance photographers, most assigned. Reviews photos with accompanying ms only.

Making Contact & Terms: Reviews photos only with ms. Send b&w contact sheet. SASE. Reports in 2 weeks. Payment individually negotiated; $250/half day, plus expenses and prints. Pays on acceptance. Credit line given. Buys first North American serial rights. Simultaneous submissions and previously published work OK; depends on material.

THE LION, 300 22nd St., Oak Brook IL 60521-8842. (708)571-5466. Editor: Robert Kleinfelder. Monthly magazine. Estab. 1918. Circ. 650,000. For members of the Lions Club and their families. Emphasizes Lions Club service projects. Works with freelance photographers on assignment only basis. Provide resume to be kept on file for possible future assignments. Buys 10 photos/issue. Buys all rights. Submit model release with photo. Query first with resume of credits or story idea. "Generally photos are purchased with ms (300-1,500 words) and used as a photo story. We seldom purchase photos separately." Pays $50-500/page; $50-400/text/photo package. Pays on acceptance. Reports in 2 weeks. SASE. Free sample copy and photo guidelines.

Photo Needs: Photos of Lions Club service or fundraising projects. "All photos must be as candid as possible, showing an activity in progress. Please, no award presentations, meetings, speeches, etc." For b&w, uses 5×7 or 8×10 glossy prints. Also accepts color prints and 35mm transparencies. Captions required. Pays $10-25.

*THE LOOKOUT, 50 Broadway, New York NY 10004. (212)269-2710. Editor: Carlyle Windley. Publication of Seamen's Church Institute of New York/New Jersey. Triannually. Circ. 6,000. Emphasizes the maritime/shipping industry. Sample copy available.

Photo Needs: Uses about 14-20 photos/issue; 2-3 supplied by freelance photographers. Needs "ocean shots; aboard ships at sea—seafarers at work." Captions required.
Making Contact & Terms: Query with resume of credits or with list of stock photo subjects. Reports in 2 weeks. Pays $50-100/color 35mm slide for cover; will return slide; $50-150 for text/photo package. Pays on publication. Credit line given. Buys one-time rights unless on assignment, then all rights plus negatives. Previously published work OK.

*LOYOLA MAGAZINE, 820 N. Michigan, Chicago IL 60611. (312)915-6157. Editor: William S. Bike. Loyola University Alumni Publication. Magazine published 3 times/year. Emphasizes issues related to Loyola University of Chicago. Readers are Loyola University of Chicago alumni—professionals, ages 22 and up. Circ. 90,000. Estab. 1971. Sample copy free with 9×12 SAE and 3 first-class stamps.
Photo Needs: Uses 50 photos/issue; 40% supplied by freelancers. Needs Loyola-related or Loyola alumni-related photos only. Model release and photo captions preferred.
Making Contact & Terms: Send unsolicited photos by mail for consideration. Provide resume, business card, brochure, flyer or tearsheets to be kept on file for possible assignments. Send 8×10 b&w/color prints; 35mm and 2¼×2¼ transparencies. SASE. Reports within 3 months. Pays $300/b&w and color cover photo; $85/b&w and color inside photo; $50-150/hour; and $400-1200/day. Pays on acceptance. Credit line given. Buys one-time rights. Simultaneous submissions and previously published work OK.
Tips: "Send us information, but don't call."

THE LUTHERAN, 8765 West Higgins Rd., Chicago IL 60631. (312)380-2546. Art Director: Jack Lund. Publication of Evangelical Lutheran Church in America. Triweekly magazine. Circ. 1,000,000+. Estab. 1988. Sample copy 75¢ and 9×12 SAE.
Photo Needs: Assigns 35-40 photos/issue; 4-5 supplied by freelancers. Needs current news, family, mood shots. Model release and captions preferred.
Making Contact & Terms: Query with list of stock photo subjects; provide resume, business card, brochure, flyer or tearsheets to be kept on file for possible future assignments. SASE. Reports in 3 weeks. Pays $35-100/b&w photo; $50-175/color photo; and $175-300/day. Pays on publication. Credit line given. Buys one-time rights.
Tips: Trend toward "more dramatic lighting. Careful composition." In portfolio or samples, wants to see "candid shots of people active in church life, preferably Lutheran. Just churches or landscapes have little chance of publication. Submit sharp well-composed photos with borders for cropping."

MAINSHEET, 208 Glenwood St., Mobile AL 36606. (205)476-5952. Editor: David Johnson. Publication of Rhodes 19 Class Association. Quarterly newsletter. Emphasizes all aspects of sailing, racing and maintaining The Rhodes 19 (a one design sailboat). Readers are present and prospective owners of the boat. Circ. 150-200. Sample copy free with SASE.
Photo Needs: Uses 3-6 photos/issue; none supplied by freelance writers so far. Needs on or off water photos of R-19 or closely related subjects.
Making Contact & Terms: Send any size glossy b&w prints by mail for consideration. Provide resume, business card, brochure, flyer or tearsheets to be kept on file for possible future assignments. SASE. Reports in 2 weeks. Pays $50-100/b&w cover and inside photo. Pays on acceptance. Credit line possible. Buys all rights, but will negotiate. Simultaneous submissions and previously published work OK.
Tips: "Send action photos of boats/sailors."

MAINSTREAM—ANIMAL PROTECTION INSTITUTE OF AMERICA, Box 22505, Sacramento CA 95822, or 2831 Fruitridge Rd., Sacramento CA 95820. (916)731-5521. Contact: Art Assistant. Official Publication of the Animal Protection Institute of America. Quarterly. Circ. 90,000. Emphasizes "humane education toward and about animal issues and events concerning animal welfare." Readers are "all ages; people most concerned with animals." Sample copy and photo guidelines available with 9×12 SASE ($1.25 first class mail).
Photo Needs: Uses approximately 30 photos/issue; 15 supplied by freelance photographers. Needs images of animals in natural habitats. All species, wild and domestic: marine mammals, wild horses, primates, companion animals (pets), farm animals, wildlife from all parts of the world and endangered species. Animals in specific situations: factory farming, product testing, animal experimentation, and their alternatives; people and animals working together; trapping and fur ranching; animal rescue and rehabilitation; entertainment (rodeos, circuses, amusement parks, zoos); etc. *API* also uses high quality images of animals in various publications besides its magazine. Submissions should be excellent quality—sharp with effective lighting. Prefer tight to medium shots with good eye contact. Vertical format required for Mainstream covers. Model release and captions required.
Specs: Black and white rarely used. However, will accept b&w images of outstanding quality or hard-to-get issue-oriented situations such as experimentation, product testing, factory farming etc. For color, original transparencies only; 35mm Kodachrome 64 preferred; larger formats accepted.

Making Contact & Terms: Query with resume, credits, stock list, and samples submission of no more than 20 of best slides. Provide business card, brochure, flyer, or tearsheets for *API* files for future reference. We welcome all "excellent quality" contacts with SASE. Reports in 2-4 weeks. Pays $150-200/color cover, $35/b&w (from slide) inside, and $50-150/color inside. Pays on publication. Credit line given; please specify. Buys one-time rights. Simultaneous submissions and previously published work OK.

Tips: "The images used in Mainstream touch the heart."

Mainstream, the magazine of the Animal Protection Institute of America, requested this frequently purchased image after photographer Jeff Myers sent the magazine his stock photo list. The magazine paid him $150 for one-time rights and featured the color photo as a cover. Myers, who sells a great deal of stock, notes that over the last eight years this image has been bought for use in numerous magazines, textbooks and filmstrips.

MANAGEMENT ACCOUNTING, 10 Paragon Dr., Montvale NJ 07645. (201)573-9000. FAX: (201)573-8185). Editor: Robert Randall. Association publication of National Association of Accountants. Estab. 1919. Monthly. Emphasizes management accounting. Readers are financial executives. Circ. 87,000.
Photo Needs: Uses about 25 photos/issue; 99% from freelance stock. Needs stock photos of business, high-tech, production and factory. Model release and captions preferred.
Making Contact & Terms: Query with samples; provide resume, business card, brochure, flyer or tearsheets to be kept on file for possible future assignments. Uses prints and transparencies. SASE. Reports in 2 weeks. Pays $125/b&w photo; 150/color photo. Pays on acceptance. Credit line given. Buys one-time rights. Simultaneous and previously published submissions OK.
Tips: Prefers to see "ingenuity, creativity, dramatics (business photos are often dry), clarity, close-ups, simple but striking. Aim for a different slant."

THE MANITOBA TEACHER, 191 Harcourt St., Winnipeg, MB R3J 3H2 Canada. (204)888-7961. Editor: Mrs. Miep van Raalte. Publication of The Manitoba Teachers' Society. Quarterly magazine. Emphasizes education in Manitoba—emphasis on teachers' interest. Readers are teachers and others in education. Circ. 16,900. Sample copy free with 10 × 14 SASE and Canadian stamps.
Photo Needs: 80% of photos supplied by freelancers; approx. 4 photos per issue. Needs action shots of students and teachers in education-related settings. "Good cover shots always needed." Model release and captions required. Send 8 × 10 glossy b&w prints by mail for consideration. Submit portfolio for review. Provide resume, business card, brochure, flyer or tearsheets to be kept on file for possible assignments. SASE. Reports in 1 month. Does not pay; only gives credit line.
Tips: "Always submit action shots directly related to major subject matter of publication and interests of readership of that publication."

MAP INTERNATIONAL, Box 50, Brunswick GA 31520. (912)265-6010 or (800)-225-8550 (interstate toll free). Publication of MAP International. Bimonthly. Reports on the organization's annual distribution of $35 million in donated medicines and supplies to relief agencies in 75 countries in the developing world, as well as work in community health development projects. Sample copy and photo guidelines free with SASE.
Photo Needs: "Specifically, we need photos depicting the health needs of people in the developing countries of Africa, Asia and Latin America, and the work being done to meet those needs. Also use photos of disaster situations like the El Salvador earthquake of '86, *while situation is current*." Captions required.
Making Contact & Terms: Query with resume of credits; query with samples; query with list of stock photo subjects. Uses b&w 5×7 glossy prints; 35mm transparencies. SASE. Reports in 1 month. Pays $75/b&w cover photo; $25+/b&w inside photo; payment for color photos individually negotiated. Pays on acceptance. Credit line given. Buys one-time rights. Simultaneous submissions and previously published work OK, "depending on where else they had been submitted or used."
Tips: "Photos should center on people: children, patients receiving medical treatment, doctors, community health workers with the people they are helping, hospitals, health development projects and informal health education settings. Our interest is much broader than crisis situations and emergency aid alone, and we try to show the hopeful side of what is being done. Care about people. We are a people-developing agency and if a photographer cares about the problems of people in developing nations it will come through in the work."

MATURE YEARS, 201 Eighth Ave. S., Nashville TN 37203. (615)749-6438. Editor: Donn Downall. Publication of the United Methodist Church. Quarterly magazine. "*Mature Years* is a leisure-time resource for older adults in The United Methodist Church. It contains fiction, articles dealing with health, faith and fun matters related to aging, poetry and lesson material." Readers are "adults over fifty-five. The magazine may be used in Sunday school class, at home, or in nursing and retirement homes." Circ. 100,000. Sample copy available for $2.00 and 9×12 SAE.
Photo Needs: Uses about 15 photos/issue; many supplied by freelance photographers. Needs "mainly photos showing older adults in various forms of activities. We have problems finding older adults pictured as healthy and happy. We *desperately* need pictures of older adults who represent ethnic minorities."
Making Contact & Terms: Query with list of stock photo subjects. Send 8×10 b&w glossy prints and any transparencies by mail for consideration. SASE. Reports in 3-6 weeks. Pays $65-175/cover photo; $10-45/inside photo. Pays on acceptance. Credit line given on copyright page. Buys one-time rights. Simultaneous submissions and previously published work OK. Include social security number with submissions.
Tips: Prefers to see "ethnic minority older adults, older adults who are healthy and happy—pictures portraying the beauty and wonder of God's creation. Remember that all older adults are not sick, destitute or senile."

*MDA NEWSMAGAZINE, Muscular Dystrophy Assn., 810 7th Avenue, New York NY 10019. (212)586-0808. Editor: Cathy Carlson. Publication of Muscular Dystrophy Association. Quarterly magazine. Emphasizes research into neuromuscular diseases and helpful features for persons with disabilities. Readers are all ages, patients and their families, volunteers and others; both sexes, with cross-section of occupations. Circ. 96,000. Estab. 1950. Sample copy free with 9×12 SASE and 4 first-class stamps.
Photo Needs: Uses 45 photos/issue; 15-30% supplied by freelance photographers. Needs photos specific to feature articles. Photos purchased with accompanying ms only. Model release and photo captions required.
Making Contact & Terms: Provide resume, business card, brochure, flyer or tearsheets to be kept on file for possible assignments. Will return unsolicited material if a SASE is enclosed. Reports in 1 month. Payment varies. Pays on acceptance. Credit line given. Buys all rights. Will negotiate with a photographer unwilling to sell all rights.
Tips: "I keep file of photographers around the country in case I need someone for a specific assignment."

*THE MEETING MANAGER, Infomart, 1950 Stemmons Freeway, Dallas TX 75207. (214)746-5262. Art Director: Robin Gailey. Publication of Meeting Planners International. Monthly magazine. Emphasizes planning meetings. Readers are ages 30-60, male and female, meeting planners. Circ. 10,000. Estab. 1972. Sample copy available.
Photo Needs: Uses 10-20 photos/issue; 100% supplied by freelance photographers. Needs: cover shots vary, other photos are specific events, some promotional material requiring photography. Special photo needs include cover photos and feature photos, some stock. Model release required; photo captions preferred.

Making Contact & Terms: Provide resume, business card, brochure, flyer or tearsheets to be kept on file for possible assignments. Reports as needed. Pays on publication. Credit line given. Buys all rights. Will negotiate with a photographer unwilling to sell all rights. Will consider previously published work.

Tips: Wants to see photographers "slicks or printed samples. Send samples of photography to be kept on file until matched with a specific job."

MENNONITE BRETHREN HERALD, 3-169 Riverton Ave., Winnipeg MB R2L 2E5 Canada. (204)669-6575. FAX: (204)667-0680.Art Director: Fred Koop. Publication of the Mennonite Brethren Church. Biweekly magazine. Publication emphasizes "anything related to the church, which touches on all of life." Readers are adult church members. Circ. 13,000. Sample copy free with SASE. (Canadian).
Photo Needs: Uses 10-15 photos/issue; most are supplied by freelancers. Approximately 75% purchased from stock; 25% on assignment. Looking for people-oriented shots. Some religious, some scenics, some symbolic, but mostly people of all ages in activity of all sorts. "We simply need to update our present photo file with current subject matter, etc." Model release required; captions preferred. Send glossy or matte finish 8 × 10 b&w prints by mail for consideration. SASE. Reports in 3 months. Pays $25/b&w cover and $15-20/b&w inside photo. Pays on publication. Credit line given. Buys one-time rights and first N.A. serial rights. Simultaneous submissions and previously published work OK.

THE MIDWEST MOTORIST, Auto Club of Missouri, 12901 N. Forty Dr., St. Louis MO 63141. (314)576-7350. Editor: Michael Right. Emphasizes travel and driving safety. Readers are "members of the Auto Club of Missouri, ranging in age from 25-65 and older." Bimonthly. Circ. 385,000. Free sample copy and photo guidelines when request is accompanied by SASE; use large manilla envelope.
Photo Needs: Uses 8-10 photos/issue, most supplied by freelancers. "We use four-color photos inside to accompany specific articles. Our magazine covers topics of general interest, historical (of Midwest regional interest), humor (motoring slant), interview, profile, travel, car care and driving tips. Our covers are full color photos mainly corresponding to an article inside. Except for cover shots, we use freelance photos only to accompany specific articles. Model release not required; captions required.
Making Contact & Terms: Send by mail for consideration 5 × 7 or 8 × 10 b&w photos; 35mm, 2¼ × 2¼ or 4 × 5 color transparencies; query with resume of credits or query with list of stock photo subjects. SASE. Reports in 3-6 weeks. Pays $100-250/cover; $10-25/photo with accompanying ms; $10-50/b&w photo; $50-200/color photo; $75-200 for text/photo package. Pays on publication. Credit line given. Rights negotiable. Simultaneous or previously published submissions OK.
Tips: "Send an 8½ × 11 SASE for sample copies and study the type of covers and inside work we use."

MODERN MATURITY, 3200 E. Carson St., Lakewood CA 90712. (213)496-2277. Photo Editor: M.J. Wadolny. Bimonthly. Readers are 50 years old and over. Circ. 17 million. Sample copy free with 9 × 12 SASE; guidelines sheet free with SASE.
Photo Needs: Uses about 50 photos/issue; 5 supplied by freelancers; 75% from assignment and 25% from stock. Needs nature, scenic, personality and travel photos. Model release and captions preferred.
Making Contact & Terms: Arrange a personal interview to show portfolio. SASE. Pays $50-200/b&w photo; $150-1,000/color photo; $350/day. Pays on acceptance. Credit line given. Buys one-time and first North American serial rights.
Tips: Prefers to see clean, crisp images on a variety of subjects of interest to people 50 or over. "Present yourself and your work in a professional manner.Be familiar with Modern Maturity. Wants to see creativity, ingenuity and perserverance."

*MODERN STEEL CONSTRUCTION, Suite 3100, One East Wacker Dr., Chicago IL 60601-2001. (312)670-5407. Editor: Scott Melnick. Publication of the American Institute of Steel Construction. Bimonthly magazine. Covers steel construction for structural engineers, architects, building owners, fabricators, creators and detailers. Circ. 35,000. Estab. 1960. Sample copy free with 10 × 13 SAE.
Photo Needs: Uses 35 photos/issue; 10% supplied by freelancers. Needs shots of buildings and bridges, both completed and under construction. Photo captions preferred.
Making Contact & Terms: Query with list of stock photo subjects. Send unsolicited color prints by mail for consideration. SASE. Reports in 1 month. Payment negotiable; typically tries to arrange payment through architects being featured in articles. Credit line given. Buys one-time rights. Simultaneous submissions and previously published work OK.
Tips: Include architect's name when sending in sample photos.

*THE MORGAN HORSE, P.O. Box 960, Shelburne VT 05482. (802)985-4944. Editor: Suzy Lucine. Publication of official breed journal of The American Morgan Horse Association Inc. Monthly magazine. Emphasizes Morgan horses. Readers are all ages. Circ. 10,000. Estab. 1941. Sample copy for $4.

Photo Needs: Uses 25 photos/issue; 50% supplied by freelance photographers. Needs photos of Morgan horses—farm scenes, "showing," trail riding, how-to and photos with owners. Special photo needs include covers and calendars. Model release and photo captions preferred.
Making Contact & Terms: Send unsolicited 35mm, 2¼×2¼, 4×5, 8×10 glossy b&w/color prints by mail for consideration. Will return unsolicited material if a SASE is enclosed. Reports in 3 weeks. Pays $150/color cover photo; $25/color inside photo; $5/b&w inside photo. Pays on publication. Credit line given. Buys either one-time or all rights. Will negotiate with a photographer unwilling to sell all rights.
Tips: "Artistic color photographs of Morgan horses in natural settings, with owners, etc., are needed for calendars and covers."

MOTORLAND MAGAZINE, 150 Van Ness Ave., San Francisco CA 94102. (415)565-2464. Editor: John Holmgren. Photo Editor: Al Davidson. Company publication for the California State Auto Association. Bimonthly. Emphasizes travel. Readers include RVH travelers 40-45 median age. Circ. 1,900,000. Free sample copy and photo guidelines with SASE.
Photo Needs: Uses 35 photos/issue; 30 supplied by freelance photographers. Needs include travel, scenic. Reviews photos with or without accompanying ms. Model release and captions required.
Making Contact & Terms: Arrange a personal interview to show portfolio. SASE. Reports in 3 weeks. Pays $450/color cover photo, $175/inside color photo, $400-600/text/photo package. Pays on acceptance. Credit line given. Buys one-time rights. Previously published work OK.

MUZZLE BLASTS, Box 67, Friendship IN 47021. (812)667-5131. Editor: Sharon Cunningham. Publication of The National Muzzle Loading Rifle Association. Monthly. "Our publication relates to the muzzle-loading firearms (rifles, pistol, shotguns), primitive aspects of these firearms and to our heritage as signified within early Americana history." Readers are "a membership audience of shooters of muzzle-loading firearms, hunters, and historians desiring general information of the muzzle-loading era." Circ. 29,000+. Sample copy free. Photo guidelines free upon request. Uses color only.
Photo Needs: Most photos are purchased from writers as part of text/photo packages, but "we will have a need for cover photos depicting the muzzle-loading era. We also use photos of paintings or will be glad to accept cover work in order to promote cover work of photographer. This only upon review of the material presented." Model release preferred; captions required.
Making Contact & Terms: Call to discuss needs. Reports in 2 weeks. "No rate schedule set up at present." Credit line given. Previously published work OK.
Tips: "Past experience in rejecting photos has been due to poor lighting on subject matter. To bring out the richness of wood, embellished with silver inlay work, a photographer's knowledge of highlighting comes into play. When photographing a group of people, do not pose to face camera other than if it is only suitable with photo captions to identify those in the picture."

NACLA REPORT ON THE AMERICAS, 475 Riverside Dr., Rm 454, New York NY 10015. (212)870-3146. Photo Editor: Mark Fried. Association publication of North American Congress on Latin America. Bimonthly journal. Emphasizes Latin American political economy, US foreign policy toward Latin America and the Caribbean and domestic development in the region. Readers are academic, church, human rights, political activists, the foreign policy interested. Circ. 11,500. Sample copy for $4.40 (includes postage).
Photo Needs: Uses about 25 photos/issue; all supplied by freelancers. Model release and captions preferred.
Making Contact & Terms: Arrange a personal interview to show portfolio; query with samples; or send b&w prints or contact sheets by mail for consideration. SASE. Reports in 2 weeks. Pays $25/b&w photo. Pays on publication. Credit line given. Buys one-time rights. Simultaneous and previously published work OK.

NATIONAL CATTLEMEN, Box 3469, Englewood CO 80155. (303)694-0305. FAX: (303)694-0305. Editor: Scott Cooper. Publication of the National Cattlemen's Association. Monthly tabloid. Emphasizes all aspects of beef production. Readers are cattle ranchers and feedlot operators; most are male, median age 57. Circ. 41,000. Estab. 1985. Sample copy free with 11×17 SASE.
Photo Needs: Buys photos "as needed." Beef cattle shots, ranch shots, beef industry photography. Written release required, captions preferred.
Making Contact & Terms: Arrange a personal interview to show portfolio, query with list of stock photo subjects or send 8×10 glossy color prints by mail for consideration. SASE. All rates negotiated; pricing structure in progress. Pays on publication. Credit line given. Buys one-time rights. Simultaneous submissions and previously published work OK.

*NATIONAL ENGINEER, 2350 E. Devon Avenue, Suite 115, Des Plaines IL 60018. (708)298-0600. Association publication of National Association of Power Engineers. Monthly magazine. Emphasizes energy production, plant operation and maintenance and new technology. Readers are predominantly male stationary and chief engineers, working and retired. Circ. 5,000. Estab. 1897. Sample copy free for 8½×11 SASE and 5 first-class stamps.

Photo Needs: Uses 15 photos/issue; a few are supplied by freelance photographers. Needs photos of Power Plants, Cooling Towers, Stationary Engineers, Chief Engineers, etc. at work; Classes in Session; and new technology. Can almost always use photos in the coming year. Model release preferred. Photo captions required.

Making Contact & Terms: Query with list of stock photo subjects. Send 4×5, 8×10 b&w prints by mail for consideration. Will return unsolicited material if a SASE is enclosed. Reports ASAP. Payment in copies. Credit line given. Simultaneous submissions and previously published work OK.

Tips: "Budget does not allow for payment, but this is a great way for beginning photographers to begin a published portfolio! If you can provide a quick turn around, call to discuss photos needed for magazine in production."

NATIONAL GARDENING, 180 Flynn Ave., Burlington VT 05401. (802)863-1308. Editor: Warren Schultz. Publication of the National Gardening Association. Monthly. Circ. 200,000. Covers fruits, vegetables and ornamentals. Readers are home and community gardeners. Sample copy free with 9×12 SAE and $1 postage. Photo guidelines free with SASE.

Photo Needs: Uses about 50 photos/issue; 90% supplied by freelance photographers. "Most of our photographers are also gardeners or have an avid interest in gardening or gardening research." Needs photos of "people gardening; special techniques; how to; specific varieties (please label); unusual gardens and food gardens in different parts of the country. We often need someone to photograph a garden or gardener in various parts of the country for a specific story." Model release required; captions preferred.

Making Contact & Terms: Query with samples or list of stock photo subjects. SASE. Reports in 3 weeks. Pays $350/color cover photo; $30/b&w and $50/color inside photo. Also negotiates day rate against number of photos used. Pays on acceptance. Credit line given. Buys one-time rights.

Tips: "We're becoming more selective all the time, need top quality work. Most photos used are color. We look for general qualities like clarity, good color balance, good sense of lighting and composition. Also interesting viewpoint, one that makes the photos more than just a record (getting down to ground level in the garden, for instance, instead of shooting everything from a standing position). Look at the magazine carefully and at the photos used. We work at making the stories friendly, casual and personal. When we write a story on growing broccoli, we love to have photos of people planting, harvesting or eating broccoli, not a formal shot of broccoli on a black background. We like to show process, step-by-step."

THE NATIONAL RURAL LETTER CARRIER, 1448 Duke St., Alexandria VA 22314. Managing Editor: RuthAnn Saenger. Weekly magazine. Circ. 70,000. Emphasizes Federal legislation and issues affecting rural letter carriers and the activities of the membership for rural carriers and their spouses and postal management. Photos purchased with accompanying ms. Buys 52 photos/year. Credit line given. Pays on publication. Buys first serial rights. Send material by mail for consideration or query with list of stock photo subjects. SASE. Previously published work OK. Reports in 4 weeks. Sample copy 34¢; photo guidelines free with SASE.

Photo Needs: Animal; wildlife; sport; celebrity/personality; documentary; fine art; human interest; humorous; nature; scenics; photo essay/photo feature; special effects and experimental; still life; spot news; and travel. Needs scenes that combine subjects of the Postal Service and rural America; "submit photos of rural carriers on the route." Especially needs for next year features of the state of Iowa, particularly the city of Des Moines. Model release and captions required.

B&W: Uses 8×10 glossy prints. Pays $60/photo.

Color: Uses 8×10 glossy prints. Pays $60/photo.

Cover: Uses b&w or color glossy prints. Vertical format preferred. Pays $50/photo.

Tips: "Please submit sharp and clear photos with interesting and pertinent subject matter. Study the publication to get a feel for the types of rural and postal subject matter that would be of interest to the membership. We receive more photos than we can publish, but we accept beginners' work if it is good."

THE NATURE CONSERVANCY MAGAZINE, (formerly The Nature Conservancy News), 1815 N. Lynn St., Arlington VA 22209. (703)841-8742. Photo Editor: Susan Bournique. Publication of The Nature Conservancy. Bimonthly. Emphasizes "nature, rare and endangered flora and fauna, ecosystems in North and South America." Readers are the membership of The Nature Conservancy. Circ. 533,000+. Estab. 1950. Sample copy for 7½×10½ SAE and $1.05 postage.

Special Needs: The Nature Conservancy welcomes permission to make duplicates of slides submitted to the *Magazine* for use in slide shows only.
Photo Needs: Uses about 20-25 photos/issue; 99% comes from freelance stock. Captions preferred (location and names of flora and fauna).
Making Contact & Terms: Write for guidelines. Many photographers contribute the use of their slides. Uses color transparencies. Pays $150/color cover photo; $50-100/color inside photo. Pays on publication. Credit line given. Buys one-time rights.
Tips: "Membership in the Nature Conservancy is only $15/year and the *Magazine* will keep photographers up to date on what the Conservancy is doing in your state. Many of the preserves are open to the public. Occasionally submit updated stock photo lists as to where and what (species) you have added to your collection. We look for rare and endangered species, wetlands and flyways, including Latin America and Canada."

NETWORK, for Public Schools, Suite 301, 10840 Little Patuxent Pkwy., Columbia MD 21044. (301)997-9300. Editor: Chrissie Bamber. Publication of the National Committee for Citizens in Education. flexi published 6 times/year. Circ. 8,000. Estab. 1975. Emphasizes "parent/citizen participation in public school." Readers are "parents, citizens, educators." Sample copy available.
Photo Needs: Uses various number photos/issue; 90% freelance photography/issue from freelance stock and 10% from assignment. Needs photos of "children (elementary and high school) in school settings or with adults (parents, teachers) shown in helping role; meetings of small groups of adults." Model release required; captions preferred.
Making Contact & Terms: Query with samples. Send glossy prints, contact sheets or good quality duplicator facsimiles by mail for consideration. SASE. Reports in 2 weeks. Pays $35/b&w cover photo; $25-35/b&w inside photo. Pays on acceptance. Credit line given. Negotiates rights purchased. Simultaneous submissions and previously published work OK.
Tips: "Photos of school buildings and equipment are more appealing when they include children. In reviewing samples we look for appropriate subject matter—school age children, often with helping adults (parents or teachers); good resolution, sharp focus of print; a picture conveying a mood and capturing expressions, telling a story with a message; picture must have focal point, good composition. Need to represent ethnic diversity among teachers and school children. Send b&w prints, not contacts. Include full name, address and phone number on back of every print. Enclose return postage."

NEVADA FARM BUREAU AGRICULTURE AND LIVESTOCK JOURNAL, 1300 Marietta Way, Sparks NV 89431. (702)358-7737. Contact: Norman Cardoza. Monthly tabloid. Emphasizes Nevada agriculture. Readers are primarily Nevada Farm Bureau members and their families. Members are farmers and ranchers. Readers are men, women and youth of various ages. Circ. 2,800. Sample copy free with 10×13 SASE with 3 first-class stamps.
Photo Needs: Uses 5 photos/issue; 30% occasionally supplied by freelancers. Needs photos of Nevada agriculture people, scenes and events. Model release preferred; captions required.
Making Contact & Terms: Send b&w 3×5 and larger prints, any format and finish by mail for consideration. SASE. Reports in 1 week. Pays $10/b&w cover photo and $5/b&w inside photo. Pays on acceptance. Credit line given. Buys one-time rights. Does not consider simultaneous submissions or previously published work.
Tips: "In portfolio or samples, wants to see "newsworthiness, 50%; good composition, 20%; interesting action, 20%; photo contrast, resolution, 10%. Try for new angles on stock shots: awards, speakers, etc., We like 'Great Basin' agricultural scenery such as cows on the rangelands and high desert cropping. We pay little, but we offer credits for your resume."

NEW WORLD OUTLOOK, Rm. 1351, 475 Riverside Dr., New York NY 10115. (212)870-3758/3765. Executive Editor: Susan Keirs N. Kester. Magazine published 6 times/year. Circ. 38,000. Features Christian mission and involvement in evangelism, social concerns and problems around the world. Primarily for United Methodist lay persons, but clergy are encouraged to subscribe. Credit line given. Pays on publication. Buys one-time rights. Send material by mail for consideration; submit portfolio for review or query with samples. SASE. Previously published work OK. Reports in 3 weeks. Sample copy and photo guidelines available for $2 with 9×12 SAE.
Photo Needs: Query for needs. Captions preferred.
B&W: Uses 8×10 glossy prints. Pays $15-35 minimum/photo.
Color: Uses 35mm or larger transparencies. Pays $50-100/photo.
Cover: Uses color transparencies. Vertical format required. Pays $150-250/photo.

*NEWS PHOTOGRAPHER, 1446 Conneaut Avenue, Bowling Green OH 43402. (419)352-8175. FAX: (419)354-5435. Editor: James R. Gordon. Publication of National Press Photographers Association, Inc. Monthly magazine. Emphasizes photojournalism and news photography. Readers are newspaper, magazine, television freelancers and photojournalists. Circ. 11,000, Estab. 1946. Sample copy free with 9×12 SASE and 9 first-class stamps.

Photo Needs: Uses 50 photos/issue. Needs photos of photojournalists at work; photos which illustrate problems of photojournalists. Special photo needs include photojournalists at work, assaulted, arrested; groups of news photographers at work, problema and accomplishments of news photographers. Photo captions required.

Making Contact & Terms: Send glossy b&w/color prints, 35mm, 2¼×2¼ transparencies by mail for consideration. Provide resume, business card, brochure, flyer or tearsheets to be kept on file for possible assignments; make contact by telephone. Reports in 3 weeks. Pays $75/color page rate; $50/b&w page rate; $50-150/photo/text package. Pays on acceptance. Credit line given. Buys one-time rights. Simultaneous submissions and previously published work OK.

*NORTH AMERICAN WHITETAIL MAGAZINE, P.O. Box 741, Marietta GA 30067. (404)953-9222. Photo Editor: Tom Evans. Company publication of Game and Fish Publications. June-January magazine. Emphasizes trophy whitetail deer hunting. Circ. 150,000. Estab. 1982. Sample copy for $3. Photo guidelines free with SASE.

Photo Needs: Uses 20 photos/issue; 40% supplied by freelance photographers. Needs photos of large live whitetail deer, clean kill shots with man holding trophy. Habitat, record book material, photo of mounted head from past. Special photo needs include trophy whitetails live or dead—clean kill shots. Photo captions preferred.

Making Contact & Terms: Query with resume of credits. Query with list of stock photo subjects. Send unsolicited 8×10 b&w prints, 35mm, 2¼×2¼ transparencies by mail for consideration. Will return unsolicited material if a SASE is enclosed. Reports in 1-2 weeks. Pays $250/color cover photo; $75/color inside photo; $25/b&w inside photo. Pays 30 days before publication. Buys one-time rights. No simultaneous submissions and no previously published work.

Tips: "Use a lupe at least 8×10, be professional in quality and presentation, name on all slides and prints, with identifying number. If not sharp, don't send it. We are always looking for good, sharpe, new material!"

N.S. CONSERVATION, Box 68, Truro NS B2N 5B8 Canada. (902)893-5660. FAX: (902)895-9616. Editor: Bob Bancroft. Publication of Nova Scotia Dept. of Lands & Forests. Quarterly magazine. Emphasizes wildlife conservation and ecology specific to Nova Scotia and Maritime Provinces. Readers include school age to elderly. Circ. 20,000. Estab. 1977. Sample copy free with 9×12 SASE.

Photo Needs: Uses 4-6 photos/issue; 50% supplied by freelance photographers. Needs photos of animals, scenery—topic dependent.

Making Contact & Terms: Query with list of stock photo subjects. Send 35mm transparencies by mail for consideration. SASE. Reports in 1-2 weeks. "We do not pay for photos." Credit line given. Previously published work OK.

Tips: Looks for photos of "wildlife, conservation, ecological sites and wildflowers found in Nova Scotia. Keep photo subjects, clear and to the point. Most photogenic shots are designed."

OAK RIDGE BOYS "TOUR BOOK" AND FAN CLUB NEWSLETTER, 329 Rockland Rd., Hendersonville TN 37075. (615)824-4924. Art Director: Kathy Harris. Publication of The Oak Ridge Boys, Inc. Annual tour book and quarterly newsletter. Tour book: 24 pages, full color. Emphasizes The Oak Ridge Boys (music group) exclusively. Readers are fans of Oak Ridge Boys and country music. Circ. newsletter: 15,000; tour book: 50,000. Free sample copies available of newsletter; tourbook for $10.

Photo Needs: Uses 2-4 photos/issue of newsletter, 2 supplied by freelance photographers; 20-150/tour book, 1-50 supplied by freelance photographers. Needs photos of Oak Ridge Boys. Will review photos with or without accompanying ms; subject to change without notice. "We need *good* live shots or candid shots—won't accept just average shots." Model release required; captions preferred.

Making Contact & Terms: Arrange a personal interview to show portfolio, query with samples. SASE. Reports vary, 1-6 weeks. Pays $250/pg b&w inside; $500/pg color inside; $500/pg b&w or color cover; $50/b&w or color cover photo, $35/color inside photo for newsletter; rates can vary and subject to change without notice. Pays on publication. Credit line usually given. Buys one-time rights. Simultaneous submissions and previously published work OK.

Tips: "We are interested in Oak Ridge Boys photos only!!! Send only a few, good shots at one time—send prints only. No original slides or negatives please."

OKLAHOMA TODAY, Box 53384, Oklahoma City OK 73152. (405)521-2496. Managing Editor: Jeanne M. Devlin. Bimonthly magazine. "We are the official publication of the state of Oklahoma, published by the Department of Tourism and Recreation. We cover all aspects of Oklahoma, from history to people profiles, but we emphasize travel and tourism." Readers are "Oklahomans, whether they live in state or are exiles; studies show them to be above average in education and income." Circ. 38,000. Estab. 1950. Sample copy $2.50; photo guidelines free with SASE.

Photo Needs: Uses about 50 photos/issue; 90-95% supplied by freelance photographers. Needs photos of "Oklahoma subjects only; the greatest number are used to illustrate a specific story on a person, place or thing in the state. We are also interested in stock scenics of the state." Model release preferred; captions required. No color prints.

Making Contact & Terms: Query with samples or send 8 × 10 b&w glossy prints, 35mm, 2¼ × 2¼, 4 × 5, 8 × 10 transparencies or b&w contact sheets by mail for consideration. SASE. Reports in 4-6 weeks. Pays $50-100/b&w photo, $50-200/color photo and $50-800/complete package. Payment for text material on acceptance; payment for photos as soon as layout is final and rate can be figured. Buys one-time rights, plus right to reproduce photo in promotions for magazine, without additional payment with credit line. Simultaneous and previously published submissions OK (on occasion). To break in, "read the magazine. Look at the magazine every issue. Then go out and find the most original, striking shots of Oklahoma, Oklahoma landmarks, Oklahoma people and Oklahoma places. We work a year in advance so when a season's over, send stuff."

Tips: In samples, wants to see "a look that evokes a sense of person or place." Trend is toward "more for scenics or recreational activities against a scenic backdrop. We're moving away from wildlife, but have greater interest in photo essays, be they b&w or color. We love to see large-format color transparencies of people and places in Oklahoma; also high quality b&w prints and original approaches. We purchase little from stock, because we want the freshness of photography shot with the story we're doing in mind. It's not enough for us to get close with a photograph; we want it to be such a perfect fit that it actually makes the story stronger than it would be alone. We're small — try us!"

THE ONTARIO TECHNOLOGIST, Suite 404, 10 Four Seasons Place, Islington, ON M9B 6H7 Canada. (416)621-9621. FAX: (416)621-8694. Editor-in-Chief: Ruth M. Klein. Publication of the Ontario Association of Certified Engineering Technicians and Technologists. Bimonthly. Circ. 18,000. Emphasizes engineering technology. Sample copy free with SASE.

Photo Needs: Uses 10-12 photos/issue. Needs how-to photos — "building and installation of equipment; similar technical subjects." Prefers business card and brochure for files. Model release and captions preferred.

Making Contact & Terms: Send 5 × 7 b&w or color glossy prints for consideration. SASE. Reports in 1 month. Pays $25/b&w photo; $50/color photo. Pays on publication. Credit line given. Buys one-time rights. Previously published work OK.

OUTDOOR AMERICA, 1401 Wilson Blvd., Level B, Arlington VA 22209. (703)528-1818. FAX: (703)528-1836. Editor: Kristin Merriman. Estab. 1922. Published quarterly. Circ. 50,000. Emphasizes natural resource conservation and activities for outdoor enthusiasts, including hunters, anglers, hikers and campers. Readers are members of the Izaak Walton League of America and all members of Congress. Sample copy $1.50 with 9 × 12 envelope; free photo guidelines with SASE.

Photo Needs: Needs outdoor scenics, wildlife or shots of anglers or hunters for cover; buys pictures to accompany articles on conservation and outdoor recreation for inside. Captions (identification) required.

Making Contact & Terms: Query with resume of photo credits. Tearsheets and non-returnable samples only. Not responsible for return of unsolicited material. Uses 35mm and 2¼ × 2¼ slides. SASE. Pays $200-250/color cover; $35-75/inside photo. Credit line given. Pays on publication. Buys one-time rights. Simultaneous and previously published work OK.

Tips: "*Outdoor America* seeks photos of wild life (particular game species); outdoor recreation subjects (fishing, hunting, camping or boating) and scenics (especially of the Chesapeake Bay and Upper Mississippi river). We also like the unusual shot — new perspectives on familiar objects or subjects — for use on inside covers." "Color work should be 35 mm or 2¼ × 2¼, (cover shots must be cropped square). Send tearsheets or non-returnable samples only and/or stocklist. We do not assign work. Approximately one half of the magazine's photos are from freelance sources."

*PACIFIC DISCOVERY, California Academy of Sciences, Golden Gate Park, San Francisco CA 94118. (415)750-7116. Art Director: Susan Schneider. Publication of California Academy of Sciences. Quarterly magazine. Emphasizes natural history and culture of California, the western U.S., the Pacific, and Pacific Rim countries. Circ. 26,000. Estab. 1948. Sample copy for $1.25, 9 × 12 SASE and postage. Photo guidelines free with SASE.

Photo Needs: Uses 60 photos/issue; most supplied by freelance photographers. Scenics of habitat as well as detailed photos of individual species that convey biological information. "Scientific accuracy in identifying species is essential." "We do extensive photo searches for every story." Current needs listed in Guilfoyle Reports, natural history photographers' newsletter published by AG Editions. "Photo captions preferred, but captions are generally staff written."

Making Contact & Terms: Query with list of stock photo subjects; file stock lists, but recommend consulting Guilfoyle Report and calling first. Uses color prints, 35mm, 2¼ × 2¼, or 4 × 5 transparencies. SASE. Reports in 1 month. Pays $200/color cover photo; $75-90/color inside photo; $100/color page rate; $125 color 1 ⅓ pages. Also buys phot/text packages, but payment varies according to length of text and number of photos.Pays on publication. Credit line given. Buys one-time rights and first N.A. serial rights. Previously published work (for individual images) OK.

Tips: *"Pacific Discovery* has a reputation for high-quality photo reproduction and favorable layouts, but photographers must be meticulous about identifying what they shoot."

*PACIFIC UNION RECORDER, Box 5005, Westlake Village CA 91359. (805)497-9457. Editor: C. Elwyn Platner. Company publication of Pacific Union Conference at Seventh-day Adventist. Biweekly magazine. Emphasizes religion. Readers are primarily 18-90 church members. Circ. 60,000. Estab. 1901. Sample copy free with 8½ × 11 SASE and 3 first-class stamps. Photo guidelines sheet free with SASE.

Photo Needs: Uses photos for cover only; 80% supplied by freelance photographers. Needs photos of animal/wildlife shots, travel, scenics, limited to subjects within Nevada, Utah, Arizona, California and Hawaii. Special photo needs include annual contest held Nov. 1 each year; submit entries in October only. Model release and photo captions required.

Making Contact & Terms: Send unsolicited 35mm, 2¼ × 2¼, 4 × 5, 8 × 10 transparencies by mail for consideration. Limit of 10 transparencies or less/year per photographer. Will return unsolicited material if a SASE is enclosed. Reports in 1-2 months after contest. Pays $50/color cover photo. Pays on publication. Credit line given. Buys first one-time rights. No simultaneous submissions or previously published work.

Tips: "Avoid the trite e.g. Yosemite Falls, Half Dome, etc."

PENNSYLVANIA ANGLER, Box 1673, Harrisburg PA 17105-1673. (717)657-4518. Editor: Art Michaels. Monthly. Circ. 53,000. *"Pennsylvania Angler* is the Keystone State's official fishing magazine, published by the Pennsylvania Fish Commission." Readers are "anglers who fish in Pennsylvania." Sample copy and photo guidelines free with 9 × 12 SASE and 85¢ postage.

Photo Needs: Uses about 25 photos/issue; 80% supplied by freelance photographers. Needs "action fishing and boating shots." Model release preferred; captions required.

Making Contact & Terms: Query with resume of credits. Send 8 × 10 glossy b&w prints; 35mm or larger transparencies by mail for consideration. SASE. Reports in 2 weeks. Pays up to $200/color cover photo; $25-100/b&w inside photo; $25 and up/color inside photo; $50-250 for text/photo package. Pays on acceptance. Credit line given. Buys variable rights.

Tips: "Crisp, well-focused action shots get prompt attention. Study the magazine before submitting material."

PENNSYLVANIA HERITAGE, Box 1026, Harrisburg PA 17108-1026. (717)787-7522. FAX: (717)783-1073. Editor: Michael J. O'Malley, III. Published by the Pennsylvania Historical & Museum Commission. Quarterly magazine. Estab. 1974. Emphasizes Pennsylvania history, culture and art. Readers are "varied—generally well-educated with an interest in history, museums, travel, etc." Circ. 10,000. Sample copy free with SASE and 65¢ postage. Photo guidelines free with SASE.

Photo Needs: Uses approximately 75 photos/issue; supplied by freelance photographers. Uses about "60% on specific assignment; 40% from stock." Needs photos of "historic sites, artifacts, travel, scenic views, objects of material culture, etc." Photos purchased with accompanying ms only. "We are generally seeking illustrations for specific manuscripts." Captions required.

Making Contact & Terms: Query with samples and list of stock photo subjects. Provide resume, business card, brochure, flyer or tearsheets to be kept on file for possible future assignments. SASE. Reports in 1 month. Pays $5-50/b&w photo and $25-100/color photo. Pays on acceptance. Credit line given. Simultaneous submissions OK.

Tips: "Send query *first* with sample and ideally, a list of Pennsylvania subjects that are available. Quality is everything. Don't bombard an editor or photo buyer with everything—be selective."

THE PENTECOSTAL MESSENGER, Box 850, Joplin MO 64802. (417)624-7050. FAX: (417)624-7102. Editor: Don Allen. Monthly magazine. Circ. 10,000. Estab. 1919. Official publication of the Pentecostal Church of God. Buys 20-30 photos/year; all supplied from freelance stock. Credit line given. Pays on publication. Buys second serial rights. Send samples of work for consideration. SASE. Simultaneous submissions and previously published work OK. Reports in 4 weeks. Free sample copy with 9 × 12 SASE; free photo guidelines with SASE.

Photo Needs: Scenic; nature; still life; human interest; Christmas; Thanksgiving; Bible and other religious groupings (Protestant). No photos of women or girls in shorts, pantsuits or sleeveless dresses. No men with cigarettes, liquor or shorts.

Cover: Uses 3½ × 5 and 8 × 10 color prints and 2¼" transparencies. Pays $2-5/inside; $10-25/outside cover (front). Vertical format required.

Tips: "We must see the actual print or slides (120 or larger). Do not write on back of picture; tape on name and address. Enclose proper size envelope and adequate postage. We need open or solid space at top of photo for name of magazine. We also print in the foreground often. Several seasonal photos are purchased each year. In selecting photos, we look for good composition, good color, sharp focus, interesting subject and detail. We anticipate the use of *more* photography (and less art) on covers. Most of our cover material comes from stock material purchased from freelance photographers. We are needing more photos of people related to issues of our day, e.g. abortion, AIDS, suicide, etc. Keep in mind our holiness requirements and look for subjects that would lend themselves to proclaiming the gospel and speaking out on the issues by which we are confronted in today's world."

PHI DELTA KAPPAN, Box 789, Bloomington IN 47402. (812)339-1156. Editor-in-Chief: Pauline Gough. Design Director: Carol Bucheri. Publication of Phi Delta Kappa, Inc. Monthly (September-June). Circ. 150,000. Education magazine. Readers are "higher education administrators, K-12 teachers and administrators, curriculum and counseling specialists, teacher educators, professional staffs, consultants, and state and federal education specialists." Sample copy free with 8½×11 SASE.
Photo Needs: Uses 1-2 b&w photos/issue; "very few supplied by freelancer—we would use more if appropriate photos were submitted." Needs: 1) news photos of education and related events; 2) thematic shots that symbolically portray current issues: i.e., desegregation, computer learning; 3) teacher/child interaction, classroom scenes." Model release required.
Making Contact & Terms: Query with samples or with list of stock photo subjects. Send 5×7 or 8×10 b&w prints or photo copies by mail for consideration. "We do not use color photos." Provide business card to be kept on file for possible future assignments. SASE. Reports in 3 weeks. Pays $35-100/b&w inside photo. Pays on acceptance. Credit line given. Buys one-time rights. Simultaneous submissions and previously published work OK. Not responsible for unsolicited materials.
Tips: Prefers to see "good technical quality, good composition; content related to our editorial subject matter and style. *Read* the publication before submitting—most libraries have copies. Send a list of stock photos and one or two pieces that I can keep on file."

THE PILOT'S LOG, 501 Boylston St., Boston MA 02117. (617)578-3668. Editor: Earl Marchand. Quarterly. Circ. 5,000. Publication of New England Mutual Life Insurance Co. Emphasizes selling insurance and related products and services. "*The Pilot's Log* is New England Life's feature magazine for its national sales force of 5,000." Free sample copy with SASE.
Photo Needs: Uses about 6-10 photos/issue; 2-3 are supplied by freelance photographers. Needs photos of "mostly New England Life agents in business settings. Occasionally, we assign a photographer to take photos for illustrative purposes." Photos purchased with or without accompanying ms. Model release required.
Making Contact & Terms: Arrange a personal interview; query with samples or submit portfolio for review. "Absolutely no unsolicited photos." Does not return unsolicited material. Reports in 1 month. Provide brochure, flyer, tearsheets and samples to be kept on file for possible future assignments. Pays $50-100/b&w photo, $150-250 cover/color photo; $100-200 for text/photo package. Pays on acceptance. Buys all rights.
Tips: "We need quality freelancers in almost every major metropolitan area in the country for sporadic photo assignments." Prefers to see b&w candid shots and cover shots for business periodicals.

PLANNING, American Planning Association, 1313 E. 60th St., Chicago IL 60637. (312)955-9100. Monthly magazine. Circ. 25,000. Estab. 1972. Editor: Sylvia Lewis. Photo Editor: Richard Sessions. "We focus on urban and regional planning, reaching most of the nation's professional planners and others interested in the topic." Photos purchased with accompanying ms and on assignment. Buys 50 photos/year, 95% from stock. Credit line given. Pays on publication. Buys all rights. Query with samples. SASE. Previously published work OK. Reports in 1 month. Free sample copy with 9½×12½ SAE ($1.10 first class, 70¢ 4th class) and photo guidelines.
Subject Needs: Photo essay/photo feature (architecture, neighborhoods, historic preservation, agriculture); scenic (mountains, wilderness, rivers, oceans, lakes); housing; and transportation (cars, railroads, trolleys, highways). "No cheesecake; no sentimental shots of dogs, children, etc.; no trick shots with special filters or lenses. High artistic quality is very important." Captions required.
B&W: Uses 8×10 glossy and semigloss prints; contact sheet OK. Pays $25-100/photo.
Cover: Uses 4-color; 35mm or 4×5 transparencies. Pays up to $250/photo (cover only);$25-200/color photo.
Accompanying Mss: "We publish high-quality nonfiction stories on city planning and land use. Ours is an association magazine but not a house organ, and we use the standard journalistic techniques: interviews, anecdotes, quotes. Topics include energy, the environment, housing, transportation, land use, agriculture, neighborhoods and urban affairs." Pays $200-600/ms. Writer's guidelines included on photo guidelines sheet.
Tips: "Just let us know you exist. Eventually, we may be able to use your services. Send tearsheets or photocopies of your work, or a little self-promo piece. Subject lists are only minimally useful. How the work looks is of paramount importance."

PNEUMATIC PACKAGING, 65 Newport Ave., Quincy MA 02171. (617)328-6100. FAX (617)770-3845. Editor: Arbey Feigenson. Issued periodically. Circ. 12,000. Estab. 1934. Features histories of customer companies that package food, cosmetics, chemicals, drugs and beverages. For customers, prospects and stockholders of Pneumatic Scale Corporation. Provide flyer to be kept on file for possible future assignments. Uses 15-25 photos/issue; all freelance photography in a given issue comes from frelance stock. Pays on acceptance. Buys one-time rights. SASE. Previously published work OK. Reports in 3 weeks. Pays $100-200/b&w; $150-300/color. Free sample copy with 8½ × 11 SAE and 50¢ postage.
Photo Needs: Scenic, sport (action), human interest and nature. Interested in "any eye-catching, unusual photo." Model release and captions required.
Cover: Uses color glossy prints and 35mm or larger transparencies. Vertical format preferred. Pays $75-250/color cover photo. Looks for cover photos that are "unusual or eye-catching."
Tips: "Don't send individual flower, insect and snow track views. Use imagination, creativity and common sense."

*POPULATION BULLETIN, 777 14th St., NW Suite 800, Washington D.C. 20005. (202)639-8040. Production Assistant: Martha Herr. Publication of the Population Reference Bureau. Quarterly journal. Emphasizes demography. Readers are educators (both high school and college) of sociology, demography and public policy. Circ. 15,000. Estab. 1929.
Photo Needs: Uses 8-10 photos/issue; 70% supplied by freelance photographers. Needs vary widely with topic of each edition – primarily people, families, mothers and children. Special photo needs include world labor force, people working and all countries. Model release preferred.
Making Contact & Terms: Query with list of stock photo subjects. Send unsolicited photos by mail for consideration. Send b&w prints. SASE. Reports in 1-2 weeks. Pays $15/b&w page rate. Pays on acceptance. Buys one-time rights. Simultaneous submissions and previously published work OK.
Tips: Publishes other population-related publications, including a monthly newsletter.

PRESERVATION NEWS, 1785 Massachusetts Ave. NW, Washington DC 20036. (202)673-4075. Editor: Arnold Berke. Publication of the National Trust for Historic Preservation. Monthly tabloid. Emphasizes historic preservation and building restoration. Readers are professional men and women, 20 years of age and older. Circ. 210,000. Estab. 1969. Sample copy free with 8½ × 11 SASE.
Photo Needs: Uses 20 photos/issue; 15% supplied by freelance photographers. Needs photos of buildings, people with buildings, "event" shots (ceremonies, parties, openings, etc.) and scenics. Model release and captions preferred.
Making Contact & Terms: Query with list of stock photo. Provide resume, business card, brochure, flyer or tearsheets to be kept on file for possible assignments. SASE. Reports in 3 weeks. Pays $25-100/b&w cover or inside photo and $300-400/day. Pays on publication. Credit line given. Buys one-time rights. Previously published work OK.

PRINCETON ALUMNI WEEKLY, 41 William St., Princeton NJ 08540. (609)258-4885. Editor-in-Chief: J.I. Merritt. Photo Editor: Stacey Wszola. Biweekly. Circ. 52,000. Emphasizes Princeton University and higher education. Readers are alumni, faculty, students, staff and friends of Princeton University. Sample copy $1.50 with 8½ × 11 SAE and 37¢ postage.
Photo Needs: Uses about 15 photos/issue; 10 supplied by freelance photographers. Needs b&w photos of "people, campus scenes; subjects vary greatly with content of each issue. Show us photos of Princeton." Captions required.
Making Contact & Terms: Arrange a personal interview to show portfolio. Provide brochure to be kept on file for possible future assignments. SASE. Reports in 1 month. Pays $100/b&w and $200/color cover photos; $25/b&w inside photo; $50/color inside photo; $45/hour. Pays on publication. Buys one-time rights. Simultaneous submissions and previously published work OK.

PRINCIPAL MAGAZINE, 1615 Duke St., Alexandria VA 22314-3406. (703)684-3345. Editor: Lee Greene. Publication of the National Association of Elementary School Principals. Bimonthly. Emphasizes public education – Kindergarten to 8th grade. Readers are mostly principals of elementary and middle schools. Circ. 25,000. Sample copy free with SASE.
Photo Needs: Uses 5-10 b&w photos/issue; all supplied by freelance photographers. Needs photos of school scenes (classrooms, playgrounds, etc.); teaching situations; school principals at work; computer use and technology and science activities. The magazine sometime has theme issues, such as back to school, technology and early childhood education. *No posed groups*. Close-ups preferred. Reviews photos with or without accompanying ms. Model release preferred; captions required.
Making Contact & Terms: Query with samples and list of stock photo subjects; send b&w prints, b&w contact sheet by mail for consideration. SASE. Reports in 1 month. Pays $50/b&w photo. Pays on publication. Credit line given. Buys one-time rights. Simultaneous submissions and previously published work OK.

*PROCEEDINGS/NAVAL HISTORY, U.S. Naval Institute, Annapolis MD 21402. (301)268-6110. Photo Editor: Linda Cullen. Association publication. *Proceedings* is a monthly magazine and *Naval History* is a quarterly publication. Emphasizes Navy, Marine Corps, Coast Guard. Readers are age 18+, male and female, naval officers, enlisted, retirees, civilians. Circ. 110,000. Estab. 1873. Sample copy free with 9×12 SASE and 1 first-class stamp. Photo guidelines free with SASE.
Photo Needs: Uses 25 photos/issue; 40% supplied by freelance photographers. Needs photos of foreign and US Naval, Coast Guard and Marine Corps vessels, personnel, and aircraft. Photo captions required.
Making Contact & Terms: Send unsolicited photos by mail for consideration: 35mm or 8×10, glossy or matte, b&w or color prints; 35mm transparencies. SASE. Reports in 1 month. Pays $200/color cover photo; $200/b&w cover photo; $25/color inside photo; $25/b&w page rate; $250-500/photo/ text package; pays $50 opener/inside. Pays on publication. Credit line given. Buys one-time rights. Simultaneous submissions and previously published work OK.

PTA TODAY, 700 N. Rush St., Chicago IL 60611-2571. (312)787-0977. Photo Editor: Moosi Raza Rizvi. Published 7 times/year. Circ. 40,000. Emphasizes parent education. Readers are parents living in the US—rural, urban, suburban and exurban. Sample copy $2.50 with 9×12 SAE.
Photo Needs: Uses about 20-25 photos/issue; all are supplied by freelance photographers; uses 100% stock. Needs "candid, not cutesy, shots of kids of all ages who live in the 1990s—their parents and teachers; anything to do with infancy through adolescence." Model release required "allowing photo to be used at the editor's discretion in *PTA Today* and other PTA publications."
Making Contact & Terms: Send b&w prints only (any size) by mail for consideration. SASE. Reports within 2 weeks. Pays $35/b&w inside and $75/b&w cover each time used. Pays on publication. Credit line given on contents page. Simultaneous submissions and previously published work OK. Every photo should have the name and address of photographer.
Tips: "Our preference is for the dramatic, uncluttered, strong contrast, crisp and clean photo. Desperately need minority children and/with parents, talking, discussing—all ages. Should be recent shots. Send SASE for schedule of topics to be covered in upcoming issues."

PUBLIC CITIZEN, 2000 P St. NW, Washington DC 20036. (202)293-9142. Editor: Anna Rodelot. Bimonthly. "*Public Citizen* is the magazine of the membership organization of the same name, founded by Ralph Nader in 1971. The magazine addresses topics of concern to today's socially aware and politically active consumers on issues in consumer rights, safe products and workplaces, a clean environment, safe and efficient energy, and corporate and government accountability." Circ. 45,000. Sample copy free with 9×12 SAE and 2 first class stamps.
Photo Needs: Uses 5 photos/issue; 2 supplied by freelancers. Needs photos to go along with articles on various consumer issues—assigns for press conference coverage or portrait shot of interview; buys stock for other purposes.
Making Contact & Terms: Provide resume, business card, brochure, flyer or tearsheets to be kept on file for possible future assignments. Does not return unsolicited material. Pays $50-75/b&w inside photo. Pays on publication. Credit line given. Buys first North American serial rights. Simultaneous and previously published work OK.
Tips: Prefers to see "good photo copies of photos and list of stock to keep on file. Common subjects: nuclear power, Bush administration, health and safety issues, citizen empowerment, union democracy, etc."

*THE PUBLIC EMPLOYEE MAGAZINE, AFSCME, 1625 L St. NW, Washington DC 20036. (202)429-1150. Production Supervisor: Judy Sugar. Association Union publication of American Federation of AFL-CIO. State, County and Municipal Employees, 8 times/year color magazine. Emphasizes public employees—our members. Readers are "our members." Circ. 1.2 million.
Photo Needs: Uses 35 photos/issue; majority supplied by freelance photographers. Assignment only.
Making Contact & Terms: Provide resume, business card, brochure, flyer or tearsheets to be kept on file for possible assignments. Will try to return unsolicited material if a SASE is enclosed, but no guarantee. Reports back as needed. Depends on assignment, usually negotiate price. Pays on acceptance. Credit line given. Buys all rights. Will negotiate with a photographer unwilling to sell all rights in particular situations.
Tips: "Color transparencies, no fast film. Well lighted; use flash when needed. Show strong photojournalism skills and be skilled in use of flash."

PURE—BRED DOGS/AMERICAN KENNEL GAZETTE, 51 Madison Ave., New York NY 10010. (212)696-8332. Photo Editor: Jeff Dorl. Publication of the American Kennel Club. Monthly. Emphasizes AKC pure-bred dogs. Readers are pure-bred dog fanciers and owners. Circ. 58,000. Estab. 1889. Photo guidelines free with SASE.

Photo Needs: Uses about 50 photos/issue; 50% supplied by freelance photographers. Needs photos of AKC pure-bred dogs. Model release and captions preferred. About "50% of covers are on assignment; most other work is submitted by professional and freelance 'dog' photographers."

Making Contact & Terms: Query with samples; send 5×7 b&w and color prints; 35mm, 2¼×2¼ transparencies by mail for consideration. SASE. Reports in 3 weeks. Pays $250/color cover photo; $25-100/color or b&w inside photo. Pays on publication. Buys first North American serial rights.

Tips: Prefers to see candids with attractive backgrounds. No show poses. Excellent show-quality representatives of AKC breeds, naturally posed or in action "extremely sharp, with good contrast and lots of detail." Prefers transparencies. "Read the magazine and attend dog shows where quality dogs can be found as subjects." Trend is "more elegant rather than cute. No props or costumes. Simple backgrounds. Dog should be primary focus. Casual, not overly posed."

REAL ESTATE FINANCE TODAY, 1125 15th St. NW 3rd Fl., Washington DC 20005. (202)861-1927. FAX: (202)861-0736. Production Editor: Patricia Curran. Publication of the Mortgage Bankers Association. Weekly tabloid. Emphasizes housing, commercial buildings, banking, finance. Readership consists of predominantly male mortgage banking professionals, 30-65 years of age. Circ. 11,000. Estab. 1983. Sample copy free with 9×12 SASE and 2 first-class stamps.

Photo Needs: Uses 1-2 photos/issue; 50% supplied by freelance photographers. Needs photos of some legislative work. Also, scenes of cities in which conferences are held. "We often use photos of housing or housing construction as backgrounds for graphs." Model release and captions preferred.

Making Contact & Terms: Query with list of stock photo subjects. Send b&w prints (any size of format) by mail for consideration. Provide resume, business card, brochure, flyer or tearsheets to be kept on file for possible assignments. SASE. Reports in 2 weeks. Pays $100/color cover photo, $75/b&w cover photo, $50/color or b&w inside photo. Pays on publication. Credit line given. Buys one-time rights. Simultaneous submissions and previously published work OK.

REGARDS, La Revue de l'assurance, 300 rue Léo-Pariseau, Bureau 801, Succ. Place du Parc C.P. 985, Montréal PQ H2W 2N1 Canada. (514)842-2591. Publication of the Professional Body of the Insurance Brokers Association of the Province of Quebec. Bimonthly magazine. Emphasizes insurance industry, financial institution. Readers are 25 and over, average early 40s–30% women, 70% men, Insurance industry—lawyers, notary, doctors, bankers, financial institutions. Circ. 6,100. Sample copy free with SASE.

Photo Needs: Uses about 10 photos/issue; 80% supplied by freelance photographers. Photos purchased with accompanying ms only. Special needs include aviation (crash) and political risks. Model release and captions required.

Making Contact & Terms: Arrange a personal interview to show portfolio. SASE. Will negotiate payment. Pays on publication. Credit line given. Buys all rights; will negotiate. Previously published work OK.

Tips: Looking for "variety, complexity of the picture, imagination. Recommends punctuality, professionalism, imagination and open mind."

THE RETIRED OFFICER MAGAZINE, 201 N. Washington St., Alexandria VA 22314. (800)245-8762. FAX: (703)838-8173. Contact: Associate Editor. Monthly. Circ. 365,000. Publication represents the interests of retired military officers from the seven uniformed services: recent military history (particularly Vietnam and Korea), travel, health, hobbies, humor, second-career job opportunities, military family lifestyle and current military/political affairs. Readers are officers or warrant officers from the Army, Navy, Air Force, Marine Corps, Coast Guard, Public Health Service and NOAA. Free sample copy and photo guidelines with 9×12 SAE and $1.25 postage.

Photo Needs: Uses about 24 photos/issue; 8 (the cover and some inside shots) usually supplied by freelance photographers. "We're always looking for good color slides of active duty military people and healthy, active mature adults with a young 50s look—our readers are 55-65."

Making Contact & Terms: Query with list of stock photo subjects. Provide resume, brochure, flyer to be kept on file. Do not send original photos unless requested to do so. Uses original 35mm, 2¼×2¼ or 4×5 transparencies. Pays $250/color cover photo; $25/b&w inside photo; $75-175 transparencies for inside use (in color). Other payment negotiable. Pays on acceptance. Credit line and complimentary copies given. Buys one-time rights.

Tips: "A photographer who can also write and submit a complete package of story and photos is valuable to us. Much of our photography is supplied by our authors as part of their manuscript package. We periodically select a cover photo from these submissions—our covers relate to a particular feature in each issue." In samples, wants to see "good color saturation, well-focused, excellent composition."

RETIREMENT LIFESTYLES, 104, 1260 Hornby St., Vancouver BC U62 1W2 Canada. (403)295-0567. Editor: David Todd. Publication of Club 55. Magazine published 10 times/year; Jan./Feb. and July/Aug. issues combined. Emphasizes retirement topics. Readers are age 49 plus, male and female and are retired or planning a retirement. Circ. 50,000. Photo guidelines sheet free with SASE.

Photo Needs: Uses 10 photos/issue. Needs photos of people ages 45-55; prefers action pictures such as hiking, skiing, boating or at travel sites. Model release and photo captions preferred.

Making Contact & Terms: Send color prints by mail for consideration. SASE. Reports in 1 month. Pays $150/color cover photo, $25/color inside photo and $10/b&w inside photo. Pays on publication. Credit line given. Buys one-time rights. Simultaneous submissions and previously published work OK.

Tips: "We admire the cover pictures on *New Choices* magazine (formerly *50 PLUS*) and would suggest review of past issues as samples."

THE ROTARIAN, 1560 Sherman Ave., Evanston IL 60201. (312)866-3000. FAX: (312)328-8554. Editor: Willmon L. White. Photo Editor: Judy Lee. Monthly magazine. Estab. 1911. Circ. 538,000. For Rotarian business and professional men and women and their families in 167 countries and geographical regions. "Our greatest need is for the identifying face or landscape, one that says unmistakably, 'This is Japan, or Minnesota, or Brazil, or France or Sierra Leone,' or any of the other countries and geographical regions this magazine reaches." Buys 10 photos/issue. Buys first-time international rights. Query with resume of credits or send photos for consideration. Pays on acceptance. Payment varies. Reports in 1-2 weeks. SASE. Free sample copy and photo guidelines.

B&W: Uses 8×10 glossy prints; contact sheet OK.

Color: Uses 8×10 glossy prints or transparencies.

Cover: Uses color transparencies. Photos are "generally related to the contents of that month's issue."

Tips: "We prefer vertical shots in most cases. The key words for the freelance photographer to keep in mind are *internationality* and *variety*. Study the magazine. Read the kinds of articles we publish. Think how your photographs could illustrate such articles in a dramatic, story-telling way. Key submissions to general interest, art-of-living material." Plans special pre-convention promotion coverage of 1991 Rotary International convention in Mexico City, Mexico.

SAFARI MAGAZINE, 4800 W. Gates Pass Rd., Tucson AZ 85745. (602)620-1220. Editor: W.R. Quimby. Publication of Safari Club International. Bimonthly magazine. Emphasizes big game hunting. Readers are international big game hunters. Circ. 18,000. Sample copy $3.50 with 8×10 SASE. Photo guidelines free with SASE.

Photo Needs: Uses 50 photos/issue; all supplied by freelance photographers. Needs photos of live, trophy-size, big game animals, especially Asian.

Making Contact & Terms: Query with samples. Send b&w prints and 35mm transparencies by mail for consideration. SASE. Reports in 1 month. Pays $150/color cover photo; $35/b&w inside photo; $50-100/color inside photo. Pays on publication. Credit line given. Buys one-time rights.

Tips: Prefers to see live big game animals in natural settings, not zoo shots—must be trophy size.

THE SCIENCE TEACHER, NSTA, 1742 Connecticut Ave. NW, Washington DC 20009. (202)328-5800. Managing Editor: Shelly Carey. Publication of the National Science Teachers Association. Publishes 9 monthly issues per year. Emphasizes high school science education. Readers are adult science teachers. Circ. 29,000. Sample copy and photo guidelines free upon request.

Photo Needs: Uses 5-10 photos/issue; 50% supplied by freelance photographers. Needs color and b&w shots of high school students and teachers; no nature/scenics needed. Model release "required only if run with article on special education."

Making Contact & Terms: Arrange personal interview to show portfolio, query with stock photo list, or send 8×10 glossy b&w prints or 8×10 transparencies by mail for consideration. Provide resume, business card, brochure, flyer or tearsheets to be kept on file for possible assignments. SASE. "Often reports in 6 months for prints; sooner for queries." Pays $150/color cover; $50/b&w or color full page; or $35/b&w smaller page rate. Pays on publication. Credit line given. Buys one-time rights. Simultaneous submissions and previously published work OK.

Tips: Looks for samples that show "high-school-age students in the science classroom and science teachers."

***SCRAP PROCESSING**, Suite 700, 1627 K St. NW, Washington DC 20006. (202)466-4050. Editor: Elise Browne. Publication of the Institute of Scrap Recycling Industries. Bimonthly magazine. Covers scrap recycling for owners and managers of private recycling operations worldwide. Circ. 5,800. Estab. 1988. Sample copy for $5.00.

Photo Needs: Uses approx. 100 photos/issue; 15% supplied by freelancers. Needs studio concept shots and company operation shots of companies being profiled. Model release and photo captions required.

Making Contact & Terms: Arrange personal interview to show portfolio. Query with list of stock photo subjects. Provide resume, business card, brochure, flyer or tearsheets to be kept on file for possible assignment. SASE. Reports in 1 month. Payment negotiable. Pays on publication. Credit line given. Rights negotiable. Previously published work OK.

Tips: "We are always looking for good color photographers to accompany our staff writers on visits to companies being profiled. Other photography is usually assigned through freelance art director."

SEA FRONTIERS, 4600 Rickenbacker Causeway, P.O. Box 499900, Miami FL 33149-9900. (305)361-4888. Executive Editor: Jean Bradfisch. Editor: Bonnie Bilyeu Gordon. Bimonthly magazine. Circ. 55,000. For anyone with an interest in any aspect of the sea, the life it contains and its conservation. Buys 80 photos annually. Buys one-time rights. Send photos for consideration. Credit line given. Pays on publication. Reports in 10 weeks. SASE. Sample copy $3 postpaid; photo guidelines.
Photo Needs: Animal, nature, photo feature, scenic, wildlife, industry vessels structures and geological features. Ocean-related subjects only.
B&W: Send 8×10 glossy prints. Captions required. Pays $20 minimum.
Color: Send 35mm or 2¼×2¼ transparencies. Captions required. Pays $30 minimum.
Cover: Send 35mm or 2¼×2¼ color transparencies. Captions required. Uses vertical format. Allow space for insertion of logo. Pays $125 for front cover and $75 for back cover.

THE SENTINEL, Industrial Risk Insurers, 85 Woodland St., Hartford CT 06102. (203)520-7300. Editor: Anson Smith. Quarterly magazine. Circ. 54,000. Emphasizes industrial loss prevention for "insureds and all individuals interested in fire protection." Pays on acceptance. Send material by mail for consideration. Previously published work OK. Reports in 2 weeks. Free sample copy and photo guidelines.
Photo Needs: Uses 4-8 photos/issue; 2-3 supplied by freelance photographers. Needs photos of fires, explosions, windstorm damage and other losses at industrial plants. Prefers to see good industrial fires and industrial process shots, industrial and commercial fire protection equipment. No photos that do not pertain to industrial loss prevention (no house fires). Model release preferred. Credit line given. Buys one-time rights.
B&W: Uses glossy prints. Pays $35/photo.
Color: Uses glossy prints. Pays $100/photo.
Cover: Uses b&w or color glossy prints. Vertical format required. Pays $100/photo.

SERVICES, Suite 225, 10201 Lee Highway, Fairfax VA 22030. (703)359-7090. or (800)368-3414. Editor: Robert E. Simanski. Publication of the Building Service Contractors Association International. Monthly. Emphasizes building service contracting (janitorial mostly). Readers largely consist of building service contractors, manufacturers and distributors of sanitary supplies, building owners and managers, and hospitals. Circ. 12,300. Sample copy free with 9×12 SAE and $1.50 postage.
Photo Needs: Needs photos of building maintenance services performed by outside contractors—office cleaning, floor and carpet care, window washing, lighting maintenance, exterior maintenance. Always need good material on janitorial cleaning, floor and carpet care, upholstery and drapery care, water and fire damage restoration, window washing. Also need photos for managerial articles—financial management, staff training, etc. Model release and captions required.
Making Contact & Terms: Arrange a personal interview to show portfolio. Send 8×10 matte b&w prints; 35mm transparencies; b&w contact shets by mail for consideration. SASE. Reports in 1 week. Pays $350/color cover photo; $400-600/day. Pays on acceptance. Credit line given. Buys one-time rights. Simultaneous submissions and previously published work OK.
Tips: Prefers to see "strong communication values—photos that *tell me* something about the subject. Don't want something that looks like a set-up stock photo."

SHOOTING SPORTS USA, 1600 Rhode Island Ave. NW, Washington DC 20036. (202)828-6000. Editor: Glynda Lyon. Publication of the National Rifle Association of America. Monthly. Emphasizes competitive shooting sports (rifle, pistol and shotgun). Readers are mostly NRA-classified competitive shooters including Olympic-level shooters. Circ. 125,000. Sample copy free with 9×12 SAE with $1 postage. Editorial guidelines for SASE.
Photo Needs: Uses 1-10 photos/issue; about half or less supplied by freelance photographers. Needs photos of how-to, shooting positions, specific shooters. Model release required; captions preferred. Photos preferred with ms, but will accept quality photos for covers.
Making Contact & Terms: Query with photo and editorial ideas by mail. Uses 8×10 glossy b&w prints. SASE. Reports in 2 weeks. Pays $150-250 for photo/text package; amount varies for photos alone. Pays on publication. Credit line given. Buys first North American serial rights. Previously published work OK when cleared with editor.
Tips: Looks for "generic photos of shooters shooting—obeying all safety rules—proper eye protection and hearing protection. If text concerns certain how-to advice, photos are needed to illuminate this. Always query first. We are in search of quality photos to interest both beginning and experienced shooters."

SIERRA, 730 Polk St., San Francisco CA 94109. Art & Production Manager: Silvano Nova. Magazine published 6 times annually. Circ. 450,000. For members of the Sierra Club, an environmental organization as well as small newsstand circulation. Emphasizes outdoor activities, enjoyment of the land and the problems of preserving the environment. Pays $500-1,800 for text/photo package. Credit line given. Buys one-time rights. Contact Art and Production Manager, Silvano Nova, by mail (send SASE) for editorial and/or photography guidelines before sending photos. Sample copy available for $3.00 (includes postage and handling.)

Photo Needs: Animal (wildlife, endangered species, general—no pet shots); nature/scenic (general scenics of wide variety of places, foreign and domestic, wilderness areas, National Parks, forests, monuments, etc., BLM or Forest Service lands, out-of-the-way places; seasonal shots); outdoor recreation (camping, rafting, skiing, climbing, backpacking); documentary (areas of environmental crises, pollution/industrial damage etc.). "No dupes, superimposed photos, urban/commercial style photos, zoos or nightlife. No submissions *strictly* of butterflies, flowers, etc."

B&W: Captions required. Pays $100-250. Black and white submissions not encouraged.

Color: Captions required. Pays $125 minimum; $175/half page, $200/full page, $250/spread.

Cover: Verticals. Captions required. Pays $350.

Tips: "Keep submissions concise and only send best and most representative work. Stock list a necessity. Follow guidelines. Almost all work is stock. Assignments are *rarely* offered. We keep a list of photographers who have sent us samples of their work and contact them when we require subjects they have on hand. Assignments are rarely offered. Looking for high quality, good color, sharp focus, interesting composition. Also, the unusual hard-to-find or out-of-the-way on stock list. We have increasing coverage of hot spots environmentally related problems around the world and in obscure (or oft-ignored) areas of North America. Show good range of stock available."

SIGNPOST MAGAZINE, #518, 1305 Fourth Ave., Seattle WA 98101. (206)625-1367. Editor: Ann Marshall. Publication of the Washington Trails Association. Monthly. Emphasizes "backpacking, hiking, cross-country skiing, all nonmotorized trail use, outdoor equipment, and minimum-impact camping techniques." Readers are "people active in outdoor activities, primarily backpacking; residents of the Pacific Northwest, mostly Washington. Age group: 9-90, family-oriented, interested in wilderness preservation, trail maintenance." Circ. 3,800. Estab. 1966. Free sample copy with 10 × 12 SASE. Photo guidelines free with SASE.

Photo Needs: Uses about 10-15 photos/issue; 30% supplied by freelance photographers. Needs "wilderness/scenic; people involved in hiking, backpacking, canoeing, skiing; wildlife; outdoor equipment photos, all with Pacific Northwest emphasis." Captions required.

Making Contact & Terms: Send 5 × 7 or 8 × 10 glossy b&w prints by mail for consideration. SASE. Reports in 1 month. No payment for inside photos. Pays $25/b&w cover photo. Pays on publication. Credit line given. Buys one-time rights. Simultaneous submissions and previously published work OK.

Tips: "We are a b&w publication and prefer using b&w originals for the best reproduction. Photos must have a Pacific Northwest slant. Photos that meet our cover specifications are always of interest to us. Familiarity with our magazine would greatly aid the photographer in submitting material to us; a sample copy is free. Contributing to *Signpost* won't help pay your bills, but sharing your photos with other backpackers and skiers has its own rewards."

THE SINGLE PARENT, 8807 Colesville Rd., Silver Spring MD 20910. (301)588-9354. FAX: (301)588-9216. Contact: Editor. Publication of Parents Without Partners, Inc. Published 6 times/year. Circ. 120,000. Estab. 1957. Emphasizes "issues of concern to single parents, whether widowed, divorced, separated or never-married, and their children, from legal, financial, emotional, how-to, legislative or first-person experience." Readers are "parents mainly between 30-55, US and Canada." Sample copy free with SAE plus postage at 3 oz. rate.

Photo Needs: Uses 8-10 photos/issue; all supplied by freelance photographers; 5-10% from assignment and 90-95% from stock. "We usually make assignments for a particular story. All photos relate to and illustrate articles in the magazine." Model release and captions required.

Making Contact & Terms: Query with samples. Send 8 × 10 b&w prints, b&w contact sheets and color slides/photos by mail for consideration. Provide resume, business card, brochure, flyer or tearsheets to be kept on file for possible future assignments. SASE. Reports in 2 months. Pays $75-150/color cover photo; $35-50/b&w inside photo. Pays on publication. Credit line given. Negotiates rights purchased. Simultaneous submissions OK.

Tips: "We have received photo selections on long-term hold from several freelancers. Our first search for each issue is within these selections, and up to 6 photos in each issue are from these selections. We also have contact sheets and tear sheets from freelancers we query periodically for specific subjects and situations. I am hoping to increase the use of inside color phots during the forthcoming year. We occasionally need, and never find, children who are not on their best behavior. I am usually looking for a photo that easily relates to some aspect of the article I want to illustrate. Often, this will establish a mood; sometimes it is symbolic of the theme of the article. Once in a great while, one will exactly match some situation portrayed in the article."

SNACK WORLD, 1711 King St., Alexandria VA 22314. (703)836-4500. Editor: Al Rickard. Publication of the Snack Food Association. Monthly. Emphasizes snacks (salted only—potato chips, pretzels, corn chips, popcorn, etc.). Readers are snack manufacturers and suppliers to the snack industry. Circ. 5,500. Sample copy free with 9×12 SASE.

Photo Needs: Uses about 30 photos/issue; 1-2 supplied by freelance photographers. Needs photos of snacks in unique settings, ingredients and machinery used to make snacks. Model release and captions required.

Making Contact & Terms: Query with samples and list of stock photo subjects; provide resume, business card, brochure, flyer or tearsheets to be kept on file for possible future assignments. Will return unsolicited material with SASE. Reports in 1 month. Pays $500/color cover photo; $100/b&w inside photo; $100/color inside photo. Pays on acceptance. Credit line given. Buys all rights. Will negotiate with a photographer unwilling to sell all rights. Simultaneous submissions and previously published work OK.

Tips: Prefers to see "good quality color photos showing snacks in generic settings. Send samples and identify specialties."

SOARING, Box E, Hobbs NM 88241. (505)392-1177. FAX: (505)392-8154. Art Director: Steve Hines. Association publication. Monthly magazine. Emphasizes the sport of soaring in sailplanes and motor-gliders. Readership consists of white collar and professional males and females, ages 14 and up. Circ. 15,600. Estab. 1937. Sample copy and photo guidelines free with SASE.

Photo Needs: Uses 25+ photos/issue; 95% supplied by freelance photographers. "We hold freelance work for a period of usually 6 months, then it is returned. If we have to keep work longer, we notify the photographer. The photographer is always updated on the status of his or her material." Needs sharply focused transparencies, any format. Especially needs aerial photography. "We need a good supply of sailplane transparencies for our yearly calendar." Model release preferred; captions required.

Making Contact & Terms: Send unsolicited photos by mail for consideration. Uses b&w prints, any size and format. Also color transparencies, any format. SASE. Reports in 2 weeks. Pays $50/color cover photo. Pays $100 for calendar photos. Pays on publication. Credit line given. Buys one-time rights. Simultaneous submissions OK.

Tips: "Exciting air-to-air photos, creative angles and techniques are encouraged. We pay only for the front cover of our magazine and photos used in our calendars. We are a perfect market for photographers that have sailplane photos of excellent quality. Send work dealing with sailplanes only and label all material."

SOUND BUSINESS, (formerly Seattle Business), Suite 200, 3000 Northup Way, Bellevue WA 98004. Editor: Michele A. Dill. Monthly magazine. Emphasizes business-related news, analysis, tips, columns. Readers are business executives in the greater Seattle area. Circ. 13,000. Sample copy $4 with 9×12 SAE and 85¢ postage.

Photo Needs: Uses 4-7 photos/issue; 0-1 supplied by freelance photographers. Needs photos of business, business people—"most of our stories are directly related to business in Seattle." Model release preferred; captions required.

Making Contact & Terms: Arrange a personal interview to show portfolio; query with resume of credits and list of stock photo subjects. Does not return unsolicited material. Reports in 3 months. Payment negotiable for color cover photo; $15-100/b&w and color inside photo. Pays on publication. Credit line given. Buys one-time rights or more. Simultaneous submissions and previously published work OK.

Tips: "Business stories can be dry. I look for the ability to illustrate a story in an interesting, unique way. We don't want to run mug shots only."

*SOURCES—THE JOURNAL OF UNDERWATER EDUCATION, P.O. Box 14650, Montclair CA 91763-1150. (714)621-5801. Production Manager: Lisa Ambrose. Editor: Mike Williams. Association publication of National Association of Underwater Instructors. Bimonthly journal. Emphasizes scuba diving-safety. Readers are male and female, ages 12+. "Since diving is an expensive hobby, our audience tends to be more elite." Circ. 10,000. Estab. 1962. Sample copy with 9×12 SASE.

Photo Needs: Uses 50-70 photos/issue; up to 50% supplied by freelance photographers. Needs photos of scuba diving, pretty beaches and underwater shots. Model release and photo captions preferred.

Making Contact & Terms: No set procedure for making contact, photographer can choose preference. Will return unsolicited material if a SASE is enclosed. Pays $1 per column inch. Pays on acceptance. Credit line given. Will negotiate rights. Simultaneous submissions and previously published work OK.

Tips: "National Association of Underwater Instructors (NAUI) is a nonprofit organization. I prefer b/w negs/or quality b/w prints, but I can use color slides."

*SOUTH AMERICAN EXPLORER, P.O. Box 18327, Denver CO 80218. (303)320-0388. Contact: Linda Rojas. Association publication. Quarterly magazine. Emphasizes Latin America: adventure, travel and field science. Circ. 5,500. Estab. 1977. Sample copy for $3.

Photo Needs: Uses 30 photos/issue; 100% supplied by freelance photographers. Needs historical photos. Photos purchased with accompanying ms only. Photo captions required.

Making Contact & Terms: Send manuscript and photos. Send 35mm, 4×5, 8×10 b&w/color prints, 35mm, 2¼×2¼, 4×5, 8×10 transparencies. Will return unsolicited material if a SASE is enclosed. Reports in 2-3 months. Pays $50/color cover photo; $50/b&w cover photo; $50/photo/text package. Pays on publication. Credit line given. Buys one-time rights. Simultaneous submissions and previously published work OK.

*SOUTHERN CALIFORNIA BUSINESS, 404 S. Bixel, Los Angeles CA 90017. (213)629-0671. Editor: Christopher Volker. Association publication of L.A. Chamber of Commerce. Monthly newspaper. Emphasizes business. Readers are mostly business owners, M/F, ages 21-65. Circ. 12,000. Estab. 1901. Sample copy for $2. No photo guidelines.

Photo Needs: Uses 10-20 photos/issue; 25% supplied by freelance photographers and public relations agencies. Needs photos of technology, business people and new products. Special photo needs include specialty shots on various subjects (mainly business-oriented).

Making Contact & Terms: Query with list of stock photo subjects. Send b&w prints by mail for consideration. Provide resume, business card, brochure, flyer or tearsheets to be kept on file for possible assignments. Will return unsolicited material if a SASE is enclosed. Reports in 3 weeks. Pays $100/b&w cover photo; $25-50/hour; $100-150/day; $100-250/photo/text package. Pays on publication. Credit line given. Buys first N.A. serial rights. Will negotiate with a photographer unwilling to sell all rights. Will consider simultaneous submissions.

Tips: In photographer's samples, wants to see "work that shows photographer's ability to capture subjects in the best possible way. Send in detailed letter and description of work."

SPECTRUM, The Horace Mann Companies, One Horace Mann Plaza, Springfield IL 62715. Manager, Photographic Services: Dave Waugh. Mail number L102. Monthly publication for employees. Includes articles on company programs, monthly employee honors, and human interest features on employees and their families.

Photo Needs: Uses about 35 photos/issue; 3-4 supplied by freelancers. "We need photos of our agents at work and with their families." Captions (at least names) preferred.

Making Contact & Terms: Provide resume, business card, brochure, flyer or tearsheets to be kept on file for possible future assignments. SASE. Reports "as soon as we would need a photographer from his/her area of the country." Pays $25-30/hour; $125 maximum/job. Pays on acceptance. Credit line given. Buys all rights. Simultaneous submissions and previously published work OK.

*SPIRITUAL LIFE, 2131 Lincoln Road NE, Washington D.C. 20002. (202)832-6622. Editor: Steven Payne, O.C.D. Publication of the Discalced Carmelites. Quarterly journal. Emphasizes contemporary spirituality. Readers are adult, college-educated, male/female and largely Roman Catholic. Circ. 13,000. Estab. 1955. Sample copy free with 6×9 SAE and 4 first-class stamps.

Photo Needs: Uses 1-4 photos/issue; all supplied by freelance photographers. Needs photos of landscapes, portraits, candids and such that are appropriate to religious or spiritual themes (understood broadly). Special photo needs include spirituality in USA and John of the Cross. Model release preferred.

Making Contact & Terms: Send small selection of b&w glossy prints by mail for consideration. SASE. Reports in 1 month. Pays $50-100/b&w cover photo and $25-75/b&w inside photo. Pays on acceptance. Credit line given. Buys one-time rights. Simultaneous submissions and previously published work OK.

Tips: Submissions "should be appropriate to spirituality journal, though they need not be explicitly religious activities (symbols, etc. OK)."

SPORT SCENE: FOCUS ON YOUTH PROGRAMS, 4985 Oak Garden Dr., Kernersville NC 27284. (919)784-4926. Editor: Jack Hutslar, Ph.D. Publication of North American Youth Sport Institute. Quarterly. Also publishes newletters and skill manuals. Emphasizes children in sport and recreation, ages 12-13 and younger mainly. Readers are parents, youth and school coaches, teachers, program directors. Sample copy free with SASE.

Tips: "Do not send samples. Provide resume, business card, etc. Can sell photos through *Sport Scene*."

SPORTS CAR, 1385 E. Warner, Suite C, Tustin CA 92680. (714)259-8240. Editor: John Zimmermann. Publication of the Sports Car Club of America. Monthly magazine. Emphasizes sports car racing and competition activities. Circ. 50,000. Estab. 1944. Sample copy for $2.95.

Photo Needs: Uses 75-100 photos/issue;75% freelance photography issue come from assignment and 25% from freelance stock. Needs action photos from competitive events, personality portraits and technical photos.

Making Contact & Terms: Query with resume of credits or send 5×7 color or b&w glossy/borders prints or 35mm or 2¼×2¼ transparencies by mail for consideration. Provide resume, business card, brochure, flyer or tearsheets to be kept on file for possible assignments. SASE. Reports in 1 month. Pays $25/color inside photo or $10/b&w inside photo;$25-250/color photo (covers only at this rate). Negotiates all other rates. Pays on publication. Credit line given. Buys first N.A. serial rights. Simultaneous submissions OK.

Tips: To break in with this or any magazine, "always send only the absolute best work; try to accommodate the specific needs of your clients. Have a relevant subject, strong action, crystal sharp focus, proper contrast and exposure. We seem to need good candid personality photos of key competitors and officials."

STATE GOVERNMENT NEWS, Iron Works Pike, Box 11910, Lexington KY 40578. (606)252-2291. Publications Manager: Doug Dill. Publication of The Council of State Governments. Monthly. Emphasizes state government issues. Readers are state legislators and officals. Circ. 18,000. Sample copy free for 9×12 SAE and $1 postage.

Photo Needs: Uses about 12 photos/issue, for covers only. Contact publications manager for needs. Model release and captions required.

Making Contact & Terms: Query with list of stock photo subjects. Provide resume, business card, brochure, flyer or tearsheets to be kept on file for possible future assignments. SASE. Reports in 2 weeks. Pays $150/color cover photo; $25/b&w inside photo. Pays on publication. Credit line not given. Buys one-time rights. Simultaneous submissions OK.

Tips: "Check with us for our current needs. Photograph people that are active and expressive. We may begin using more color."

STUDENT LAWYER, 750 N. Lake Shore Dr., Chicago IL 60611. Editor: Sarah Hoban. Managing Editor: Miriam R. Krasno. Publication of the American Bar Association. Magazine published 9 times/school year. Emphasizes social and legal issues for law students. Circ. 35,000. Sample copy $3.

Photo Needs: Uses about 3-5 photos/issue; all supplied by freelance photographers. "All photos are assigned, determined by story's subject matter." Model release and captions required.

Making Contact & Terms: Arrange a personal interview to show portfolio or send samples. SASE. Reports in 3 weeks. Pays $300/color cover photo; $75-200/b&w; $100-250/color inside photo. Pays on acceptance. Credit line given. Buys one-time rights. Previously published work OK.

THE SUNFLOWER, 4023 State, Bismarck ND 58501. (701)224-3019. FAX: (701)224-2798. Contact: Larry Kleingartner. Publication of National. Sunflower Association. Magazine published 5 times/year. Emphasizes sunflower production and other industry news such as research and product utilization. Readers are sunflower producers, male, ages 18 and older. Circ. 20,000. One sample copy free with SASE; additional copies $2.

Photo Needs: Uses 3-5 photos/issue; 30% by freelancers; freelance stock—80%; from assignment—20%. Uses cover shots featuring aspects of sunflower. For text, all sunflower-related photos needed. Also, some machinery shots. Photo captions required.

Making Contact & Terms: Query with list of stock photo subjects, provide resume, business card, brochure, flyer or tearsheets to kept on file for possible assignments. Send 35mm transparencies and slides by mail for consideration. SASE. Reports in 1 month. Pays $25-50/b&w or color photo. Credit line given. Buys one-time and other rights; negotiable. Simultaneous submissions and previously published work OK.

Tips: Wants to see "All sorts of sunflower shots—should be ag related. For instance, a sunflower field rather than a flower bed. Samples are good; will return them. May want to write for a sample issue so they understand the magazine."

THE SURGICAL TECHNOLOGIST, 8307 Shaffer Parkway, Littleton CO 80127. (303)978-9010. Editor: Michelle Armstrong. Publication of the Association of Surgical Technologists. Bimonthly. Circ. 11,000. Emphasizes surgery. Readers are "20-60 years old, operating room professionals, well educated in surgical procedures." Sample copy free with 9×12 SAE and $1.25 postage. Photo guidelines free with SASE.

Photo Needs: Uses 1 photo/issue. Needs "surgical, operating room photos that show members of the surgical team in action." Model release required.

Making Contact & Terms: Query with samples; submit portfolio for review. Send 5×7 or 8½×11 glossy or matte prints; 35mm, 2¼×2¼ or 4×5 transparencies; b&w or color contact sheets; b&w or color negatives by mail for consideration. Provide resume, business card, brochure, flyer or tearsheets to be kept on file for possible future assignments. SASE. Reports in 4 weeks after review by Editorial

Board. Pays $75/b&w cover photo, $150/color cover photo; $25/b&w inside photo, $50/color inside photo. Pays on acceptance. Credit line given. Buys one-time rights. Simultaneous submissions and previously published work OK.

*SYMPHONY, 777 14th St., NW, Suite 500, Washington DC 20005. (202)628-0099. Editor: Matthew Sigman. Association publication of American Symphony Orchestra League. Bimonthly magazine. Emphasizes symphony orchestras. Readers are trustees, orchestra managers, volunteers and staff. Circ. 17,000. Sample copy for $6.
Photo Needs: Uses 15-20 photos/issue; occasionally uses freelancers. Needs photos of orchestras and personalities. Model release is required; photo captions preferred.
Making Contact & Terms: No specific submission guidelines, can contact in various methods but "our needs are limited." Will return unsolicited material if a SASE is enclosed. Reporting time varies depending on needs. Credit line given. Buys first N.A. serial rights.

TANK TALK, 728 Anthony Trail, Northbrook IL 60062. (708)498-1980. FAX: (708)498-3173. Contact: Jim Wisuri. Publication of Steel Tank Institute. Monthly. Emphasizes matters pertaining to the underground storage tank industry. Readers are tank owners, installers, government officials, regulators, manufacturers. Circ. 11,500. Free sample copy with 9×12 SAE and 39¢ postage.
Photo Needs: Uses about 4-6 photos/issue; 50-75% supplied by freelance photographers. Needs photos of installations, current developments in the industry, i.e., new equipment and features for tanks, author photos, fiberglass tank leaks. Photos purchased with accompanying ms only.
First Contact & Terms: "Call if you have photos of interest to the tank industry." Uses at least 5×7 glossy b&w prints. SASE. Reports in 2 weeks. Pays on publication. Buys all rights; will negotiate with photographer unwilling to sell all rights. Simultaneous submissions and previously published work OK.

TEAM MAGAZINE, publication of the Young Calvinist Federation, P.O. Box 7259, Grand Rapids MI 49510. (616)241-5616. FAX: (616)241-5558. Editor: Dale Dieleman. *Team* magazine is a quarterly digest for volunteer church youth leaders. It promotes shared leadership for holistic ministry with high school young people. Buys 25-30 photos/year. Photos used in magazines and books—"we produce 1-2 books annually for youth leaders, an additional 5-25 pix."
Subject Needs: High school young people in groups and as individuals in informal settings—on the street, in the country, at retreats, at school, having fun; racial variety; discussing in two's, three's, small groups; studying the Bible, praying, dating, doing service projects, interacting with children, adults, the elderly.
Specs: Uses 5×7 or 8×10 b&w glossy prints. Also uses color for cover.
Payment & Terms: Pays $20-50/b&w photo; $50-150/color photo. Credit line given. Buys one-time rights.
Making Contact: Query with samples, query with list of stock photo subjects, send unsolicited photos by mail for consideration. SASE. "We like to keep those packages that have potential on file for 2 months. Others (with no potential) returned immediately."
Tips: "Ask us for our Contributor's Guidelines and a sample issue of the magazine, *Team*. We appreciate a SASE for return." In samples, looks for "more than just faces. We look for activity, unusual situations or settings, symbolic work. No out-of-date fashion or hair." To break in "Send us a selection of photos. We will photocopy and request as needed. We expect good contrast in black and white."

TEXTILE RENTAL MAGAZINE, Box 1283, Hallandale FL 33009. (305)457-7555. Managing Editor: Nancy Ashmore. Publication of the Textile Rental Services Association of America. Monthly magazine. Emphasizes the "linen supply, industrial and commercial laundering industry." Readers are "heads of companies, general managers of facilities, predominantly male audience; national and international readers." Circ. 6,000.

The asterisk before a listing indicates that the market is new in this edition. New markets are often the most receptive to freelance submissions.

Photo Needs: Photos "needed on assignment basis only." Model release preferred; captions preferred or required "depending on subject."

Making Contact & Terms: "We contact photographers on an as-needed basis selected from a directory of photographers." Does not return unsolicited material. Pays $350/color cover plus processing; "depends on the job." Pays on acceptance. Credit line given if requested. Buys all rights. Previously published work OK.

Tips: "Meet deadlines; don't charge more than $100-500 for a series of b&w photos that take less than half a day to shoot."

TRAILBLAZER MAGAZINE, 1000 124th Ave NE, Bellevue WA 98005. (206)455-8585. Editor: Gregg Olsen. Thousand Trails, Inc. Monthly magazine. Emphasizes the outdoors, destinations, RV travel, leisure time, hobbies and self-improvement. Readers are 55+, $30,000 a year, who enjoy traveling and camping; active, fairly well educated. Circ. 180,000. Sample copy $2 with SASE. "Please send appropriate sized envelope for sample copy." Photo guidelines free with SASE.

Photo Needs: Uses 25-30 photos/issue; 5 supplied by freelance photographers. Needs "photos to accompany articles, photographers who work with writers." Photos purchased with accompanying ms. Model release preferred; captions required.

Making Contact & Terms: Provide resume, business card, brochure, flyer or tearsheets to be kept on file for possible future assignments. SASE. Reports in 1 month. Pays $500/color cover photo; $50-200/color inside photo. Pays on publication. Credit line given. Buys first North American serial rights.

Tips: Looks for *"sharpness* of image, quality of light, camera cropping, professional presentation— good b&w prints would be a pleasant surprise! Hook up with a writer—complete, high-quality packages are *very* attractive."

TROT, 233 Evans Ave., Toronto, ON M8Z 1J6 Canada. (416)252-3565. Editor: Harold Howe. Monthly magazine. Emphasizes harness racing. Readers are a cross section of all Canadians. Circ. 21,500. Sample copy available.

Photo Needs: Uses 3-5 photos/issue; 100% supplied by freelance photographers. Uses horse photos from various angles and moods. Photos purchased with accompanying ms only. Looking for Christmas and fall mood shots in particular. Model release preferred; captions required.

Making Contact & Terms: Submit portfolio for review. Uses 8 × 10 glossy color prints. SASE. Reports in 2 weeks. Pays $100/color cover photo, $50/color inside photo and $25/b&w inside photo. Pays on publication. Credit line given. Buys one-time rights. Simultaneous submissions and previously published work OK.

TROUT, Box 6225, Bend OR 97708. (503)382-2327. FAX: (503)382-5421. Associate Editor: James A. Yuskavitch. Publication of Trout Unlimited. Quarterly magazine. "Trout is published for the members and supporters of Trout Unlimited. Editorial focus is on trout, salmon and steelhead fishing and conservation in waters throughout North America. Each issue features well illustrated articles on fishing techniques, famous streams, salmonid species and current coldwater conservation issues. The average readers is male, 40s, and avid trout and salmon fisherman. He has a bachelor's degree and works as a white collar professional." Circ. 65,000. Estab. 1959. Sample copy for $4. Photo guidelines free with SASE.

Photo Needs: Uses 15-40 mostly color shots/issue. Nearly all supplied by freelancers; "Occasional assignments, usually only when photographer has a good story idea and we know his or her work." Needs "Scenics of trout and salmon rivers and streams, anglers fishing in beautiful surroundings, close-ups of trout and salmon, including underwater photography, close-ups of flies, lures and fishing equipment, abstract art and nature photographs related to trout and salmon angling." "We feature a 1⅓ page photograph on the table of contents and ad index pages of each issue. The subject matter is open, from realistic to abstract. The only criteria are that it be stunning and relate to trout and salmon. "We're especially interested in seeing large format transparencies for these pages." Model release and captions preferred; "be brief—just the who, what, when, where and why."

Making Contact & Terms: Query with list of stock photo subjects, send b&w prints or 35mm, 2¼ × 2¼, 4 × 5 or 8 × 10 transparencies by mail for consideration or submit portfolio for review. Provide resume, business card, brochure, flyer or tearsheets to be kept on file for possible assignments. SASE. Reports in 1-3 months. Pays $300/color cover photo, $50-200/color or b&w inside photo and $100-650/ photo text package. Negotiates hour and day rate. Pays on publication. Credit line given. Buys one-time and first N.A. serial rights. Previously published work OK.

Tips: In portfolio of samples, "emphasize what you're good at." Trend is more medium and large format use. "We're also beginning to branch out into the posters and calendars which should eventually open additional opportunities to photographers, besides magazine pages. We like to see photographers work. Although most of our photography is assigned or solicited from a small group of photographers, it's a club you can join if you do good work. Send us some of your work and prepare to be rejected. But how else will we know who you are and what kind of photography you do? If we like you, you'll hear from us. And it isn't rare for us to find a use for an unsolicited photograph that we like."

TURKEY CALL, P.O. Box 530, Edgefield SC 29824. (803)637-3106. Publisher: National Wild Turkey Federation, Inc. (nonprofit). Editor: Gene Smith. Bimonthly magazine. Circ. 53,000. Estab. 1973. For members of the National Wild Turkey Federation—people interested in conserving the American wild turkey. Needs photos of "wild turkeys, wild turkey hunting, wild turkey management techniques (planting food, trapping for relocation), wild turkey habitat." Buys 40-50 photos/annually. Copyrighted. Send photos to editor for consideration. Credit line given. Pays on acceptance. Reports in 4 weeks. SASE. Sample copy $3 with 9 × 12 SAE. Free contributor guidelines for SASE.
B&W: Send 8 × 10 glossy prints. Captions required. Pays $20.
Color: Send color transparencies. Uses any format. For covers, requires space for insertion of logo. Pays $50-75/inside photo; cover negotiated.
Tips: Wants no "poorly posed or restaged shots, mounted turkeys representing live birds, domestic turkeys representing wild birds, or typical hunter-with-dead-bird shots."

UNITED EVANGELICAL ACTION, 450 Gundersen, Carol Stream IL 60188. (708)665-0500. Editor: Don Brown. Bimonthly. Circ. 11,000. Emphasizes religious concerns as those concerns relate to current news events. Readers are evangelicals concerned about putting their faith into practice. Free sample copy for 9 × 12 SAE and 65¢ postage; photo guidelines with SASE.
Photo Needs: Uses about 15 photos/year; all are supplied by freelance photographers. No travel or scenic photos. "Think 'news.' On the lookout for photos depicting current news events that involve or are of concern to evangelicals. Interested in photos demonstrating current moral/social problems or needs; Christians reaching out to alleviate human suffering; Christians involved in political rallies, marches or prayer vigils; and leading evangelicals addressing current moral/social issues." Photos purchased with or without accompanying ms. Model release required.
Making Contact & Terms: Query with samples; list of stock photo subjects and send by mail 8 × 10 b&w glossy prints for consideration. Provide brochure, flyer and periodic mailings of shots available to be kept on file for possible future assignments. SASE. Reports in 1 month. Pays $35-100/b&w photo. Pays on publication. Credit line given. Buys one-time rights.
Tips: "Would like to see 'people' shots with a strong news or current events, or religious orientation. Please no family or children shots. Send a wide variety of samples. This will allow us to see if your work fits our editorial needs."

V.F.W. MAGAZINE, Broadway at 34th St., Kansas City MO 64111. (816)756-3390. Editor: Richard Kolb. Monthly magazine. Circ. 2,000,000. For members of the Veterans of Foreign Wars (V.F.W.)—men who served overseas—and their families. Needs photos illustrating accompanying mss on personalities, accounts of "military actions of consequence," combat stories and humor. Buys all rights. Present model release on acceptance of photo. Do not submit poetry. Send photos for consideration. Photos purchased with accompanying mss. Pays on acceptance. Reports in 4 weeks. SASE. Sample copy free with SASE and 50¢ postage.
B&W: Send 8 × 10 glossy prints. Captions required.
Cover: Send glossy b&w prints or color transparencies. "Cover shots must be submitted with a ms. Price for cover shot will be included in payment of manuscript." Captions required. Pays $250 minimum.
Tips: "Go through an issue or two at the local library (if not a member) to get the flavor of the magazine."

VIRGINIA WILDLIFE, 4010 W. Broad St., Box 11104, Richmond VA 23230. (804)367-1000. Art Director: Emily Pels. Monthly magazine. Circ. 55,000. Emphasizes Virginia wildlife, as well as outdoor features in general, fishing, hunting and conservation for sportsmen and conservationists. Photos purchased with accompanying ms. Buys 350 photos/year; about 95% purchased from freelancers. Credit line given. Pays on acceptance. Buys one-time rights. Send material by mail for consideration. SASE. Reports (letter of acknowledgement) within 30 days; acceptance or rejection within 45 days of acknowledgement. Free sample copy and photo guidelines.
Photo Needs: Good action shots relating to animals (wildlife indigenous to Virginia); action hunting and fishing shots; photo essay/photo feature; scenic; human interest outdoors; nature; outdoor recreation (especially boating); and wildlife. Photos must relate to Virginia.
Color: Uses 35mm and 2¼ × 2¼ transparencies. Pays $30-50/photo.
Cover: Uses 35mm and 2¼ × 2¼ transparencies. Vertical format required. Pays $125/photo.
Accompanying Mss: Features on wildlife; Virginia travel; first-person outdoors stories. Pays 10¢/printed word. Free writer's guidelines included on photo guidelines sheet.
Tips: "We don't have time to talk with every photographer who submits work to us. We discourage phone calls and visits to our office, since we do have a system for processing submissions by mail. Our art director will not see anyone without an appointment. In portfolio or samples, wants to see a good

eye for color and composition and both vertical and horizontal formats. We are seeing higher quality photography from many of our photographers. It is a very competitive field. Show only your best work. Name and address must be on each slide. Plant and wildlife species should also be identified on slide mount. We look for outdoor shots (must relate to Virginia); close-ups of wildlife."

VOLKSWAGEN'S WORLD, Volkswagen of America, 888 W. Big Beaver Rd., Box 3951, Troy MI 48007-3951. (313)362-6770. Editor: Marlene Goldsmith. Quarterly magazine. Circ. 300,000. For owners of Volkswagen (VW) automobiles. Buys 25 photos annually. Buys first North American rights. Submit model release with photo or present model release on acceptance of photo. Query first with story and/ or photo essay idea. Photos purchased with accompanying ms; "features are usually purchased on a combination words-and-pictures basis." Credit line given. Pays on acceptance. Pays $150/printed page; $300/2-page spread. Reports in 6 weeks. 8×10 SASE. Previously published work OK. Free sample copy and contributor's guidelines.
Photo Needs: Travel (US, Europe, Brazil), how-to, human interest, humorous, photo essay/photo feature, sport, German high-tech products (how they're made), and celebrity/personality.
Color: Send transparencies; prefers 35mm but accepts any size. Captions required. Pay is included in total purchase price with ms.
Cover: Submit 35mm slides or color transparencies. Uses vertical format. Captions required. Pays $350.

THE WAR CRY, The Salvation Army, 799 Bloomfield Ave., Verona NJ 07044. (201)239-0606. Editor-in-Chief: Lt. Colonel Henry Gariepy. Publication of The Salvation Army. Biweekly. Circ. 300,000. Emphasizes the inspirational. Readers are general public and membership. Sample copy free with SASE.
Photo Needs: Uses about 6 photos/issue. Needs "inspirational, scenic, general photos."
Making Contact & Terms: Send color or b&w glossy prints or color slides by mail for consideration. SASE. Reports in 2 weeks. Pays $35/b&w photo; up to $150/color photo; payment varies for text/photo package. Pays on acceptance. Credit line given "if requested." Buys one-time rights. Simultaneous submissions and previously published work OK.

WASTE AGE MAGAZINE, 10th Floor, 1730 Rhode Island Ave. NW, Washington DC 20036. (202)659-4613. Editor: Tom Naber. Publication of the National Solid Wastes Management Association. Monthly magazine. Emphasizes management of solid wastes. Readers are sanitation departments, refuse haulers, etc. Circ. 30,000.
Photo Needs: Uses about 12-20 photos/issue; 3-5 supplied by freelance photographers. Needs "cover shots in color illustrating main story in magazine; inside shots to go with that story. We need names of artists who can take cover photos of quality in various areas of the country."
Making Contact & Terms: Provide resume, business card, brochure, flyer or tearsheets to be kept on file for possible future assignments. SASE. Reports in 3 weeks. Pays $200/color cover. Pays on acceptance. "Sometimes" gives credit line. Buys all rights.
Tips: "Print up a cheap brochure, resume or similar item describing experience, covers taken, etc., (maybe include a photocopy, offering sample on request) and price range."

THE WATER SKIER, 799 Overlook Dr., Winter Haven FL 33884. (813)324-4341. Editor: John Baker. Publication of the American Water Ski Association. Bi-monthly magazine. Emphasizes water skiing. Readers are members of American Water Ski Association, active, competitive and recreational water skiers. Circ. 25,000. Sample copy for $1 and 9×12 SAE; photo guidelines free with SASE.
Photo Needs: Uses 40-50 photos/issue; "few" supplied by freelance photographers. Photos purchased with accompanying manuscript only except for color used on the cover. Model release and captions required.
Making Contact & Terms: Query with photo story ideas. SASE. Reports in 3 weeks. Pays lump sum for text/photo package. Pays on acceptance. Credit line given. Buys one-time rights.
Tips: "Prefers to see a knowledge of water skiing techniques. We are a very specialized market. Query first."

WFCD COMMUNICATOR, Box 1301, Brandon, MB R7A 6N2 Canada. (204)725-4236. Editor: Rosalie I. Tennison. Publication of the Western Fertilizer and Chemical Dealers Association. Quarterly magazine. Emphasizes fertilizer and chemical, related equipment and products. Audience consists of independent fertilizer and chemical dealers who are primarily male (although this changing), of various ages. Circ. 2,700. Estab. 1980.
Photo Needs: Uses approximately 10 photos/issue; 20% supplied by freelance photographers. Looking for agricultural shots related to fertilizer and chemical industry, e.g., application equipment and field work in progress. Written release and captions preferred.

Making Contact & Terms: Provide resume, business card, brochure, flyer or tearsheets to be kept on file for possible assignments. SASE. Reports in 1 month. Pays $25/b&w inside photo. Pays on publication. Credit line given. Buys one-time rights.
Tips: "Be very specific in the shots you take; match them exactly to the requirements of the publication. For example, a picture of a tractor and hay baler is useless to a publication that focuses on chemical application."

WILDLIFE PHOTOGRAPHY, P.O. Box 224, Greenville PA 16125. (814)371-6818. Editor: Rich Faler. Quarterly. Emphasizes pursuit and capture of wildlife on film. Circ. 3,000. Sample copy $2; writer's guidelines free with SASE.
Photo Needs: Uses about 20 photos/issue; 18 supplied by freelance photographers. Needs photos of wildlife, how-to. Photos purchased with accompanying ms only. Special needs include photographers in action under field conditions. Model release preferred; captions required.
Making Contact & Terms: Preferably submit queried manuscript with photos. SASE. Reports in 6 weeks. Pays $20-75 for text/photo package. "But articles with more thought put into them, better writing, photos shot with us in mind, and sidebars and sketches will have a payment ceiling at more than double the previous rate." Pays on publication. Credit line given. Buys one-time rights. Simultaneous submissions and previously published work OK.
Tips: "Select one photo challenge or species of wildlife and give us a ms/photo package which describes the photo target, the challenge and the methods used."

*WOMAN BOWLER, 5301 S. 76th St., Greendale WI 53129. (414)421-9000. FAX: (414)421-4420. Editor: Karen Sytsma. Publication of Women's International Bowling Congress. Magazine published 8 times/year. *Woman Bowler* emphasizes women's bowling. Circ. 140,000. Estab. 1936. Sample copy for 10×13 SASE and $2.50 postage. Photo guidelines free with SASE.
Photo Needs: Uses 75 photos/issue; up to 70% supplied by freelance photographers; 30-50% freelance/issue from assignment. Needs photos of sports action shots, portraits in sports settings, competition and bowling interest shots. Use freelancers nationwide to help fill voids when staff members cannot travel." In near future, needs "available photographers nation wide for assignments in various areas." Model release and photo captions preferred.
Making Contact & Terms: Provide resume, business card, brochure, flyer or tearsheets to be kept on file for possible assignments. Reports in 1-2 weeks. Pays $200/color cover photo; $100/b&w cover photo; $25/color inside photo; $10/b&w inside photo; $75/color page rate; $50/b&w page rate; $75-200/photo/text package. Pays on acceptance. Credit line given (if requested). Buys all rights. Simultaneous submissions and previously published work OK.
Tips: "Looking for skilled photographers with "strong portrait and action abilities. Quality lighting abilities important as well." *Woman Bowler* is an excellent opportunity for photographers looking for additional portfolio clips. Use 85-100% color photographs—very limited use of b&w. However, creative use of b&w welcomed. Prefer photographs that make lighting look natural, center lighting poses many problems. Send letter of interest and samples of published work, tearsheets."

*WOMENWISE, CFHC, 38 S. Main St., Concord NH 03104. (603)225-2739. Contact: Editorial Team. Publication of the New Hampshire Federation of Feminist Health Centers. Quarterly tabloid. Emphasizes women's health from a feminist perspective. Readers are women, all ages and occupations. Circ. 3,000+. Estab. 1978. Sample copy for $2.
Photo Needs: Varies; 100% supplied by freelance photographers. Needs photos of primarily women, women's events and demonstrations, etc. Model release required; photo captions preferred.
Making Contact & Terms: Arrange a personal interview to show portfolio. Send b&w prints. Pays $15/b&w cover photo; sub per b&w inside photo. Pays on publication. Credit line given. Buys first N.A. serial rights. Simultaneous submissions and previously published work OK.
Tips: "We don't publish a lot of 'fine-arts' photography now. We want photos which reflect our commitment to empowerment of all women. We work as a collective; our process can often be lengthy. We prefer work by women."

WOODMEN OF THE WORLD, 1700 Farnam St., Omaha NE 68102. (402)342-1890, ext. 302. Editor: Leland A. Larson. Monthly magazine. Circ. 470,000. Estab. 1890. Official publication for Woodmen of the World Life Insurance Society. Emphasizes American family life. Photos purchased with or without accompanying ms. Buys 25-30 photos/year. Credit line given on request. Pays on acceptance. Buys one-time rights. Send material by mail for consideration. SASE. Previously published work OK. Reports in 1 month. Free sample copy and photo guidelines.
Photo Needs: Historic; animal; celebrity/personality; fine art; photo essay/photo feature; scenic; special effects and experimental; how-to; human interest; humorous; nature; still life; travel; and wildlife. Model release required; captions preferred.

According to Karen Sytsma, editor of Woman Bowler *magazine, she assigned this portrait of award-winning bowler Jane Amlinger to photographer Rob Skeoch on the basis of his previous photos of the Canadian female Bowler of the Year. "We have found newspaper photographers like Rob to be excellent in producing high-quality freelance photos," says Sytsma, noting that she tracked him from his photo credit in the press clipping. "This is a perfect example of the type of photos we seek—portraits in a sports setting with natural lighting." Sytsma used the photo for full-page illustration with text and paid the photographer $90 for all rights to the photo.*

B&W: Uses 8×10 glossy prints. Pays $25/photo.
Color: Uses 35mm, 2¼×2¼ and 4×5 transparencies. Pays $50 minimum/photo; $150/cover use.
Cover: Uses b&w glossy prints and 4×5 transparencies. Vertical format preferred. Pays $25-150/photo.
Accompanying Mss: "Material of interest to the average American family." Pays 10¢/printed word. Free writer's guidelines.
Tips: "Submit good, sharp pictures that will reproduce well. Our organization has local lodges throughout America. If members of our lodges are in photos, we'll give them more consideration."

*WORLD ENCOUNTER, % ELCA-DGM, 8765 W. Higgins, Chicago IL 60631. (312)380-2642. Art Director: Kathryn Hillert. Publication of the Lutheran Church. Quarterly magazine. Emphasizes global mission. Readers are members of the Lutheran Church, men and women of all ages. Circ. 10,000. Estab. 1970. Sample copy $1.00 with 10×13 SAE.
Photo Needs: Uses 10-15 photos/issue; 50-75% supplied by freelancers. Needs photos with a global view of people, places and work of the Church. Reviews photos with or without ms, but does not accept unsolicited mss. Foresees special needs of photos of Asia, Latin America and Middle East in next year. Model release and captions preferred.
Making Contact & Terms: Query with list of stock photo subjects. Provide resume, business card, brochure, flyer or tearsheets to be kept on file for possible assignments. SASE. Reports in 1 month. Pays $100/color cover photo; $50/color inside photo. Pays on publication. Credit line given. Buys one-time rights. Simultaneous submissions and previously published work OK.
Tips: "Be neat and punctual. Professionalism pays."

WYOMING RURAL ELECTRIC NEWS, P.O. Box 380, 340 W. B St., Casper WY 82602. (307)234-6152. Contact: Editor. Publication of Rural Electric. Estab. 1950. Monthly. Circ. 30,000. "Electricity is the primary topic. We have a broad audience whose only common bond is an electrical line furnished by their rural electric system. Most are rural, some are ranch." Sample copy free with SASE and 54¢ postage.
Photo Needs: Uses about 4 photos/issue; 1 supplied by freelance photographers. Needs "generally scenic or rural photos—wildlife is good, something to do with electricity—ranch and farm life." Model release and captions preferred.
Making Contact & Terms: Query with samples or list of stock photo subjects; 100% of freelance photos bought from stock. SASE. Reports in 1 month. Pays up to $50/color cover photo; $10-15/b&w inside photo. Pays on publication. Credit line given. Buys one-time rights. Simultaneous submissions and previously published work OK.
Tips: In samples, wants to see "sharp, clear photo with documentary, human interest or rural orientation. Keep in mind that we have a basically rural audience with a broad variety of interests."

YOUNG CHILDREN, 1834 Connecticut Ave., NW, Washington DC 20009-5786. (202)232-8777. Photo Editor: Ellyn Kestnbaum. Bimonthly journal. Circ. 32,000. Emphasizes education, care and development of young children and promotes education of those who work with children. Read by teachers, administrators, social workers, physicians, college students, professors and parents. Photos purchased with or without accompanying ms. Buys 20-30 photos/issue. Credit line given. Pays on publication. Also publishes 8 books/year with photos. Query with samples. Simultaneous submissions and previously published work OK. SASE. Reports in 2 weeks. Free sample copy and photo guidelines.
Photo Needs: Children (from birth to age 8) unposed, with/without adults. Wants on a regular basis "children engaged in educational activities: dramatic play, scribbling/writing, playing with blocks— typical nursery school activities. Especially needs photos of minority children and children with disabilities." No posed, "cute" or stereotyped photos; no "adult interference, sexism, unhealthy food, unsafe situations, old photos, children with workbooks, depressing photos, parties, religious observances." Model release required.
B&W: Uses glossy prints. Pays $25/inside photo; $75/posters and covers.
Color: Uses color transparencies. Pays $25/inside photo; $75/posters and covers.
Accompanying Mss: Professional discussion of early childhood education and child development topics. No pay. Free writer's guidelines.
Tips: "Write for our guidelines and sample issue. We are using more photos per issue and using them in more creative ways, such as collages and inside color." Looks for "photos that depict children actively learning through interactions with the world around them; sensitivity to how children grow, learn and feel."

Trade

Traditionally, publications in the "trade" category have been oriented specifically toward the business community. Sometimes, these have been geared to as broad an audience as the finance industry, while in other cases, they have been intended for highly specialized professions, such as microsurgery. Interestingly, the trade market has opened itself somewhat to include areas of seemingly general interest, such as fitness, musical education and performing arts. Even with these allowances, the overall emphasis with these newer publications remains upon more indepth coverage for a more sophisticated readership.

For photographers interested in shooting for trade publications, this emphasis offers an important clue to crafting images for this market. Primarily, photos in trade publications, as in other publication markets, serve to attract the reader to the articles and illustrate the text in an informative way. Trade publication readers are usually well-educated and very knowledgeable about their businesses or professions. The editors and photo editors, too, are often experts in their particular fields. So, with both the readers and the publications staffs, you are dealing with a much more discriminating audience. To be taken seriously, your photos must not be merely technically good pictures but also communicate a solid understanding of the subject and reveal greater insights.

In particular, photographers who can communicate their knowledge in both verbal and visual form will often find their work more in demand. If you have such expertise, you may wish to query about submitting a photo/text package that highlights a unique aspect of working in that particular profession or that deals with a current issue of interest to that specific trade or profession.

Many of the photos purchased by these publications come from stock—both that of freelance inventories and of stock photo agencies. Generally, these publications are more conservative with their freelance budgets and use stock as an economical alternative. For this reason, listings in this section will often advise sending a stock list as an initial method of contact. Some of the more established publications with larger circulations and advertising bases will sometimes offer assignments as they become familiar with a particular photographer's work. For the most part, though, stock remains the primary means of breaking in and doing business with this market.

Overall, this is a very active market, as reflected in the gain in listings in this edition of *Photographer's Market*. The section now lists nearly 300 trade publications, including 40 to 50 new listings. Also, as in other publications markets, there is a great deal of change in locations and primary staff people as well as photo needs. You will also want to pay close attention to changes in rates of payment.

Offering a look at the highly specialized nature of the trade publications market, the Close-up interview in this section features observations from Mike Delia, art director for *Firehouse* magazine. In the interview, Delia discusses his work with the magazine and what he likes to see from photographers.

ABA BANKING JOURNAL, 345 Hudson St., New York NY 10014. (212)620-7256. Art Director: Robert Supina. Monthly magazine. Circ. 38,000. Estab. 1909. Emphasizes "how to manage a bank better. Bankers read it to find out how to keep up with changes in regulations, lending practices, investments, technology, marketing and what other bankers are doing to increase community standing." Photos purchased with accompanying ms or on assignment. Buys 12 photos/year; freelance photography is 50% assigned; 50% from stock. Pays $100 minimum/job, or $200/printed page for text/photo package. Credit line given if requested. Pays on acceptance. Buys one-time rights. Query with samples. SASE. Reports in 1 month.
Photo Needs: Personality ("We need candid photos of various bankers who are subjects of articles"), and occasionally photos of unusual bank displays. Also, photos of small-town bank buildings including their surroundings. Captions required.
Making Contact & Terms: For b&w contact sheet preferred, uses 8×10 glossy prints "if prints are ordered." For color: Uses 35mm transparencies and 2¼×2¼ transparencies. For cover: Uses color transparencies, square format required. Pays $100-500/photo.
Tips: "I look for the ability to take a portrait shot in a different and exciting way, not just 'look at the camera and smile.'"

ACCESS CONTROL, 6255 Barfield Rd., Atlanta GA 30328. (404)256-9800. Editor: Steven Lasky. Monthly tabloid. Emphasizes electronic security for corporate, governmental and energy facilities. Readers are fortune 1000 corporate executives; also, military and government officials. Circ. 31,000. Sample copy free with SASE.
Photo Needs: Uses 30 photos/issue; 30% supplied by freelance photographers. Needs photos of how-to, products, facility installations. Model release required; photo captions preferred.
Making Contact & Terms: Provide resume, business card, brochure, flyer or tearsheets to be kept on file for possible assignments. Uses b&w and color 4×5 matte prints. SASE. Reports in 2 weeks. Contact for rates of payment. Pays on publication. Does not give credit line. Buys one-time rights. Previously published work OK.

ACROSS THE BOARD MAGAZINE, published by the Conference Board, 845 Third Ave., New York NY 10022. (212)759-0900. Picture Editor: Bill Schiffmiller. Trade magazine with 10 monthly issues (January/February and July/August are double issues). Readers are upper-level managers in large corporations. "Mission is to keep these guys well rounded." Recent articles have covered foreign ownership in the U.S., corporate teamwork and computer security.
Photo Needs: Use 20 to 30 photos/issue for both cover and text, including a number of photos supplied by freelancers. Visuals vary from month to month—need photos of all corporate conditions from A to Z. Model release and photo captions preferred.
Making Contact and Terms: Query with resume of credits or list of stock photo subjects (include business card, brochure or tearsheets to be kept on file for possible assignments), or arrange a personal interview to show portfolio. We buy one-time rights, or six-month exclusive rights "if we assign the project." We pay $150-500/color cover; $100-200/b&w cover photo; or $350 per day, plus expenses.
Tips: "We are looking for plenty of b&w. Photos should be in a corporate setting with both white- and blue-collar workers."

AGRI FINANCE MAGAZINE, 6201 Howard St., Niles IL 60648. (312)647-1200. Editor: David Pelzer. Photo Editor: Judy Henderson. Monthly (September through April, plus July issue). Emphasizes agricultural finance, banking, state-of-the art production practices, commodity marketing. Readers are farm managers, bankers, crop consultants and large-scale farmers. Circ. 21,000. Sample copy $5.
Photo Needs: Uses 10-15 photos/issue; 2-3 supplied by freelance photographers. Needs portrait shots of farmers, crop consultants, bankers or farm managers, production shots of agricultural practices. Model release required.
Making Contact & Terms: Query with samples and list of stock photo subjects; provide resume, business card, brochure, flyer or tearsheets to be kept on file for possible future assignments. SASE. Reports in 1 month. Pays $350-500/color cover photo, $25-50/hour. Pays on acceptance. Credit line given. Buys one-time rights. Simultaneous submissions and previously published work OK.
Tips: Prefers to see specific shots that focus directly on subject. Shots that will blow up well if needed. Shots that have good contrast, especially b&w. "Query us to let us know you're there. Provide examples of your style and subject range. Past experience with agricultural subjects is a plus. Once given an assignment, be prompt on turnaround time."

AGRICHEMICAL AGE, 731 Market St., San Francisco CA 94103-2011. (415)495-3340. Managing Editor: Sam Wilson. Art Director: Larry Bruderer. Monthly magazine. Emphasizes agricultural chemicals, including fertilizer, insecticides and herbicides; application, business management, crops, diseases and insects. Readers are national dealers, applicators of agrichemicals and crop consultants. Circ. 46,000. Sample copy and photo guidelines free with SASE.
Photo Needs: All features use photos; half supplied by freelance photographers. Wants vertical format for covers. Subjects include weeds, insects, major crops, diseased crops, agricultural chemical application, equipment, tillage and machinery. Model release required, photo captions preferred.
Making Contact & Terms: Send 35mm transparencies by mail for consideration; query with samples. SASE. Reports in 1 month. Pays $300/color cover photo; $50-125/color photo depending on use. Pays on publication. Credit line given. Buys first N.A. serial rights.
Tips: "I like to see people shots, scenic, specific crop and/or application, but all pertaining to agriculture and ag chemicals. Please, no out-of-focus, poorly-lit shots. Get a copy of magazine before sending slides. We use photography on all aspects of pest control in agriculture, particularly photos which feature people and new technologies."

AGRI-TIMES NORTHWEST, 206 SE Court, Box 189, Pendleton OR 97801. (503)276-7845. Editor: Virgil Rupp. Weekly newspaper. Emphasizes agriculture of Eastern Oregon, eastern Washington and Northern Idaho. Readers are agribusiness people and farmers, both men and women, of all ages. Circ. 5,500. Sample copy free with 9×12 SASE and 4 first class stamps. Photo guidelines free with SASE.

Photo Needs: Uses 15-20 photos/issue; 70% supplied by freelance photographers. Uses all agriculturally related photos including crop production and animals such as cattle, hogs, horses and sheep. Request editorial calendar for special subject needs. Model release preferred; photo captions required.

Making Contact & Terms: Query with list of stock photo subjects or send unsolicited photos by mail for consideration. Send b&w 5×7 or 8×10 glossy prints. SASE. Reports in 1 month. "All b&w $10 per photo except 1 column photo, which is $5. Pays on publication. Credit line given. Buys one-time rights. Simultaneous submissions OK.

Tips: Especially looking for "photos of farmers and farming in our circulation area."

*AIPE FACILITIES MANAGEMENT OPERATIONS AND ENGINEERING, 3975 Erie Ave., Cincinnati OH 45208. (513)561-6000. FAX: (513)527-5914. Contact: Editor. Bimonthly. Circ. 10,000. Emphasizes technical and problem solving information related to facilities management. Readers are plant and facilities engineers (members in U.S., international and Canada), many of whom are in charge of commercial building and industrial plant operations or related services. Sample copy and photo guidelines for 9×12 SASE.

Photo Needs: Uses 10 photos/issue; 50% assignment and 50% stock. "Subjects must be of interest to our audience; i.e., plant engineers who look to the journal for technical information and data." Captions required. Also needs photos for special publications and promotional materials.

Making Contact & Terms: Query with resume of photo credits. SASE. Reports in 2 weeks. Pays $10-50 b&w photo; $50-400/color photo; $250-1,000/day; pay is negotiable. Credit line given. Pays on publication. Buys one-time rights.

Tips: "The biggest need is for 4-color photos illustrating the central topic for that issue. Square finish shots are preferred. Stylized, clean, professionally-done photos of industrial operations, machinery, commercial office building and hospital engineering focus. Trend toward the human element in facilities management, operations and engineering and away from simply a high-tech, mechanized look. Understand our audience and editorial focus throroughy first."

AIR CONDITIONING, HEATING & REFRIGERATION NEWS, Box 2600, Troy MI 48007. (313)362-3700. Editor: Thomas A. Mahoney. Weekly newspaper. Emphasizes heating, air conditioning and refrigeration service, manufacturing, etc. Readers are industry servicemen, manufacturers, contractors, wholesalers. Sample copy free with SASE.

Photo Needs: Uses 40 photos/issue; 2-15 supplied by freelance photographers. Needs photos of action service and installation shots, some product shots.

Making Contact & Terms: Send b&w prints and b&w contact sheets by mail for consideration. SASE. Reports in 3 months. Payment negotiable. Pays on acceptance. Credit line given. Buys one-time rights. Simultaneous submissions OK if exclusive to trade.

AIRPORT SERVICES MAGAZINE, 50 S. 9th St., Minneapolis MN 55402. (612)333-0471. Managing Editor: Karl Bremer. Monthly magazine. Emphasizes management of airports and airport-based businesses. Readers are managers of airports and airport-based businesses. Circ. 21,000. Sample copy free with 9×12 SASE.

Photo Needs: Only buys cover photo; color transparencies preferred. Needs photos of scenes depicting articles relating to above subject. Special subject needs include airport hangar planning, airport pavement maintenance, terminal maintenance, airport passenger handling, flight training. Model release preferred; captions required.

Making Contact & Terms: Arrange a personal interview to show portfolio; query with samples; query with list of stock photo subjects. Does not return unsolicited material. Reports in 3 weeks. Pays $150-300/color cover photo. Pays on acceptance. Credit line given. Buys first North American serial rights, exclusive within our industry.

Tips: "Learn the magazine, slant, topics and audience."

ALTERNATIVE ENERGY RETAILER, Box 2180, Waterbury CT 06722-2180. (203)755-0158. FAX: (512)693-4327. Editor: Ed Easley. Monthly magazine. Emphasizes solid fuel industry. Readers are retailers of wood stoves, coal stoves, fireplace inserts, factory-built fireplaces, central heaters and

The asterisk before a listing indicates that the market is new in this edition. New markets are often the most receptive to freelance submissions.

accessories for the same. Circ. 15,000. Estab. 1980. Sample copy free with #10 SAE and $1 postage. Photo guidelines free with SASE.

Photo Needs: Uses about 30-40 photos/issue; up to 10% supplied by freelance photographers. Needs photos of retailers in their environment, at a task, concept color work at the direction of the art director, how-to and generic environment showroom shots. Editorial guidelines free with SASE. Model release and captions required.

Making Contact & Terms: Submit idea query; send 5×7 glossy b&w prints; transparencies; b&w or color contact sheets by mail for consideration. SASE. Reports in 3 weeks. Pays $125/color cover photo; $25/b&w inside photo; $100-350/text/photo package. Pays on publication. Credit line given. Rights negotiable. Simultaneous submissions and previously published work OK "if we know who the other principals are."

Tips: "We look for a dynamic, interesting angle, good use of lines of force, detail, without harsh lighting; good use of color; quality printing, good middle tones and color that jumps off a page. Unfortunately we're doing less photojournalism. Seems like everything is done with lights and tripods." In photographer's samples, looks for "clarity and communication value. Query first. Have a solid idea in mind."

ALUMI-NEWS, Box 400, Victoria Station, Westmount, PQ H3Z 2V8 Canada. (514)489-4941. Editor: Nachmi Artzy. Bimonthly magazine. Emphasizes renovation, construction. Readers are constructors/renovators. Circ. 18,000. Sample copy free with SASE.

Photo Needs: Uses 20 photos/issue; 25-50% supplied by freelance photographers. Needs photos of construction and renovations. Model release and photo captions preferred.

Making Contact & Terms: Query with list of stock photo subjects. SASE. Reports in 2 weeks. Pays $300/color cover photo, $100-200/color inside photo and $300-500/day. Pays in 30 days. Credit line given. Buys one-time rights; will negotiate. Simultaneous submissions and previously published work OK.

Tips: "We prefer 'people on the job' photos as opposed to products/buildings."

AMERICAN AGRICULTURIST, Box 370, Ithaca NY 14851. (607)273-3507. Editor: Gordon Conklin. Art Director: Elise Gold. Monthly. Emphasizes agriculture in the Northeast—specifically New York, New Jersey, Pennsylvania and New England. Circ. 75,000. Free photo guidelines with SASE.

Photo Needs: Uses 1-2 photos/issue supplied by freelance photographers. Needs photos of farm equipment, general farm scenes, animals. Geographic location: only New York, New Jersey, Pennsylvania and New England. Reviews photos with or without accompanying ms. Model release required.

Making Contact & Terms: Query with samples and list of stock photo subjects; send 8×10 vertical, glossy color prints, and 35mm transparencies by mail for consideration. SASE. Reports in 3 months. Pays $100/color cover photo and $75/inside color photo. Pays on acceptance. Credit line given. Buys one-time rights.

Tips: "We need shots with modern farm equipment with the newer safety features. Also looking for shots of women actively involved in farming. Most of our photos are purchased from stock. We send out our editorial calendar with our photo needs yearly."

AMERICAN BEE JOURNAL, 51 S. 2nd St., Hamilton IL 62341. (217)847-3324. Editor: Joe M. Graham. Monthly trade magazine. Emphasizes beekeeping for hobby and professional beekeepers. Circ. 16,000. Sample copy free with SASE.

Photo Needs: Uses about 100 photos/issue; 1-2 supplied by freelance photographers. Needs photos of beekeeping and related topics, beehive products, honey and cooking with honey. Special needs include color photos of seasonal beekeeping scenes. Model release and captions preferred.

Making Contact & Terms: Query with samples; send 5×7 or 8½×11 b&w and color prints by mail for consideration. SASE. Reports in 2 weeks. Pays $25/b&w or color cover photo; $5/b&w or color inside photo. Pays on publication. Credit line given. Buys all rights.

AMERICAN BOOKSELLER, Production Dept., 137 W. 25th St., New York NY 10001. (212)463-8450. Editor: Dan Cullen. Art Director: Joan Adelson. Monthly magazine. Circ. 8,700. "*American Bookseller* is a journal for and about booksellers. People who own or manage bookstores read the magazine to learn trends in book selling, how to merchandise books, recommendations on stock, and laws affecting booksellers." Photos purchased with or without accompanying ms. Works with freelance photographers on assignment only. Pays $25 minimum/job, $70 minimum for text/photo package, or on a per-photo basis. Credit line given. Pays on acceptance. Buys one-time rights, but may negotiate for further use. Provide resume, business card, tearsheets and samples to be kept on file for possible future assignments. Arrange personal interview to show portfolio; submit portfolio for review; query with list of stock photo subjects and samples. SASE. Previously published work OK. Reports in 5 weeks. Sample copy $3.

B&W: Uses 5 × 7 prints. Pays $25 minimum/inside photo.
Color: No color used inside.
Cover: Uses 35mm color transparencies. Vertical format preferred. Pays $600/photo.
Accompanying Mss: On assignment only. Payment negotiable. Pays $40-80 for text/photo package. Model release preferred; captions required.

AMERICAN CITY & COUNTY MAGAZINE, 6255 Barfield Rd., Atlanta GA 30328. (404)256-9800. Editor: Janet Ward. Monthly magazine. Emphasizes "activities/projects of local governments." Readers are city and county government officials and department heads; engineers. Circ. 67,000.
Photo Needs: Uses 4-6 photos/issue; all supplied by freelance photographers. Needs "pictures of city and county projects, activities—prefer depictive, artsy photos rather than equipment and facility shots." Special needs include "cover photos to illustrate major themes, (editorial calendar with themes listed is available)."
Making Contact & Terms: Query with samples. Send 5 × 7 or 8 × 10 glossy b&w prints; 35mm, 2¼ × 2¼, 4 × 5 transparencies for consideration. SASE. Reports in 2 weeks. Pays $500/cover photo; $25/b&w inside photo; $200/color inside photo. Paste-up. Credit line given. Buys all rights.

AMERICAN DEMOGRAPHICS, Box 68, Ithaca NY 14851. (607)273-6343. Editor: Cheryl Russell. Art Director: Michael Rider. Monthly. Circ. 35,000. Emphasizes "demographics—population trends." Readers are "business decision makers, advertising agencies, market researchers, newspapers, banks, professional demographers and business analysts." Sample copy $5.
Photo Needs: Uses 10-12 photos/issue, all supplied by freelance photographers. Needs b&w photos of "people (crowds, individuals), ethnic groups, neighborhoods; people working, playing, and moving to new locations; regional pictures, cities, single parent families, aging America, baby boom and travel trends. Photographers submit prints or photocopies that they feel fit the style and tone of *American Demographics*. We may buy the prints outright or may keep a file of photocopies for future use and order a print when the photo is needed. No animals, girlie photos, politicians kissing babies, posed cornball business shots or people sitting at a computer keyboard." Model release required.
Making Contact & Terms: Send by mail for consideration actual 8 × 10 b&w or photocopies; submit portfolio by mail for review. SASE. Pays on publication $35-100/b&w photo. Credit line given on "Table of Contents" page. Buys one-time rights. Simultaneous and previously published submissions OK.

AMERICAN FARRIERS JOURNAL, 63 Great Rd., Maynard MA 01754. FAX: (508)897-6824. Editor: Susan Philbrick. 7/year magazine. Circ. 7,000 paid. Estab. 1974. Emphasizes horseshoeing and horse health for professional horseshoers. Sample copy free with SASE. Photos purchased with or without accompanying ms. Credit line given. Pays on publication. Buys all rights, but may reassign to photographer after publication.
Photo Needs: Documentary, how-to (of new procedures in shoeing), photo essay/photo feature, product shot and spot news. Captions required.
Making Contact & Terms: Query with printed samples. SASE. Uses 5 × 7 or 8 × 10 semigloss b&w prints for covers; Uses 4-color transparencies for covers. Vertical format. Artistic shots.
Accompanying Mss: Useful information for horseshoers.

AMERICAN FIRE JOURNAL, Suite 7, 9072 E. Artesia Blvd., Bellflower CA 90706. (213)866-1664. FAX: (213)867-6434. Editor: Carol Carlsen Brooks. Monthly magazine. Circ. 6,000. Estab. 1952. Emphasizes fire protection and prevention. Buys 5 or more photos/issue; 90% supplied by freelancers. Credit line given. Pays on publication. Buys one-time rights.
Photo Needs: Documentary (emergency incidents, showing fire personnel at work); how-to (new techniques for fire service); and spot news (fire personnel at work). Captions required.
Making Contact & Terms: Query with samples to Lauree Godwin, art director. Provide resume, business card or letter of inquiry. SASE. Reports in 1 month. Sample copy $2 with 10 × 12 SAE and $1.49 postage. Free photo guidelines. Uses b&w semigloss prints. Pays $4-15/photo, negotiable. For color: pays $10-30/photo. For cover: Uses 35mm color transparencies; pays $30/photo. Covers must be verticals.
Accompanying Mss: Seeks short description of emergency incident and how it was handled by the agencies involved. Pays $1.50-2/inch. Free writer's guidelines.
Tips: "Don't be shy! Submit your work. I'm always looking for contributing photographers (especially if they are from outside the L.A. area). I'm looking for good shots of fire scene activity with captions. The action should have a clean composition with little smoke and prominent fire and show good firefighting techniques, i.e., firefighters in full turnouts, etc. It helps if photographers know something about firefighting so as to capture important aspects of fire scene. We like photos that illustrate the drama of firefighting—large flames, equipment and apparatus, fellow firefighters, people in motion."

Write suggested captions. Give us as many shots as possible to choose from." Most of our photographers are firefighters or 'fire buffs.'

*AMERICAN FITNESS MAGAZINE, 15250 Ventura Blvd., Suite 310, Sherman Oaks CA 91403. (818)905-0040. FAX: (818)990-5468 Managing Editor: Rhonda J. Wilson. Trade publication. Bimonthly magazine. Emphasizes fitness and health awareness. Readers are women, ages 30-40, who are highly involved in exercise. Circ. 25,100. Estab. 1982. Sample copy for $2.50 and 8×10 SASE. Photo guidelines not available.
Photo Needs: Uses 35 photos/issue; most supplied by freelance photographers. Needs photos of anything sports or fitness related. Special photo needs include water sports, running, youth and fitness, winter sports, fit trip locations and generic shots of people exercising. Model release and photo captions preferred.
Making Contact & Terms: Query with list of stock photo subjects; provide resume, business card, brochure, flyer or tearsheets to be kept on file for possible assignments. Reports in 6 weeks. Pays $35/ color inside photo; $10/b&w inside photo. Pays 30 days after publication. Credit line given. Buys one-time rights. Simultaneous submissions and previously published work OK.
Tips: Editor is looking for "first-hand fitness experiences—we frequently publish personal photo essays." Fitness-oriented outdoor sports are the current trend (i.e. mountain bicycling, hiking, rock climbing). Over 40 sports leagues and senior fitness are also hot trends. We look for high-quality, professional photos of people participating in high-energy activities—anything that conveys the essence of a fabulous fitness lifestyle. Since we don't have a big art budget, freelancers usually submit piggyback pictures from their larger assignments.

AMERICAN OIL & GAS REPORTER, Box 343, Derby KS 67037. (316)681-3560. Editor: Bill Campbell. "A monthly business publication serving the domestic exploration, drilling and production markets within the oil/gas industry. The editorial pages are designed to concentrate on the domestic independent oilman. Readers are owners, presidents and other executives." Circ. 12,000. Estab. 1957. Sample copy free with SASE.
Photo Needs: Uses 1 color photo for cover/issue; others are welcome; virtually all from stock. Needs "any photo dealing with the oil & gas industry. We prefer to use only independent oil and gas photos; we discourage anything that would have to do with a major oil company, i.e., Standard, Exxon, Shell, etc." Written release and captions required.
Making Contact & Terms: Send 35mm transparencies and unsolicited photos by mail for consideration. Returns unsolicited material with SASE. Pays $50-100/color cover photo; $10-15/b&w inside photo. Pays on publication. Credit line given. Buys one-time rights. Simultaneous submissions OK.
Tips: Prefers to see "any picture which depicts a typical or picturesque view of the domestic oil and gas industry." Prefers shots depicting "drilling rigs at work and working well sites, not abandoned well sites or equipment 'grave yards'. Wants to show active industry, people in the shots. Do not have special assignments. Need stock photos that match editorial material in issue."

AMERICAN SQUAREDANCE, Box 488, Huron OH 44839. (419)433-2188. Editor: Stan & Cathie Burdick. Monthly magazine. Emphasizes square dancing (also clogging, round dancing, folk dancing). Readers are callers, cuers, leaders, dancers, cloggers. Circ. 24,000. Sample copy for 6½×9½ SAE with 90¢ postage. Photo guidelines free with SASE.
Photo Needs: Uses about 30-40 photos/issue; 2-3 supplied by freelance photographers. Needs photos of dance subjects (above); club activities; festival shots, people. Model release and captions preferred.
Making Contact & Terms: Query with samples; query with list of stock photo subjects; submit portfolio for review; send any size b&w, color prints; 35mm, 2¼×2¼ transparencies; b&w, color contact sheets by mail for consideration. SASE. Reports in 2 weeks. Pays $50-75/b&w cover photo; $75-100/ color cover photo; $5-10/b&w inside photo. Lump sum for text/photo package and other arrangements. Pays on publication. Credit line given. Buys all rights, but will negotiate.
Tips: "It takes many shots of dance action to produce good ones with no blur and with dancers in appealing form—a challenge!"

APPAREL INDUSTRY MAGAZINE, Suite 300 N, 180 Allen Rd., Atlanta GA 30328. (404)252-8831. Editor: Karen Schaffner. Art Director: Linda Wilson. Monthly magazine. Circ. 18,600. Emphasizes management and production techniques for apparel manufacturing executives; coverage includes new equipment, government news, finance, marketing, management and training in the apparel industry. Sample copy $3. Works with freelance photographers on assignment only. Provide resume, brochure and business card to be kept on file for possible future assignments. Buys 3 photos/issue. Pays $50/ b&w photo; $200/color photo; and $400/complete package. Pays on publication. SASE. Reports on queries in 4-6 weeks.
Subject Needs: Cover photos depicting themes in magazines; feature photos to illustrate articles.

ARCHITECTURAL & ENGINEERING SYSTEMS MAGAZINE, Suite 100, Bldg A., 760 Whalers Way, Ft. Collins CO 80525. (303)229-0029. Editor: Mary Benke. Monthly. Emphasizes CAD and automation in the AEC industry (architectural, engineering, construction). Readers are architects, engineers, contractors, facility managers. Circ. 40,000. Sample copy free with SASE.

Photo Needs: Needs photos of computer graphics related to AEC industry; people working on computers, buildings of design interest. Special needs include custom-generated computer renderings of architectural models. Model release preferred; captions required.

Making Contact & Terms: Query with sample or list of stock photo subjects; send 35mm, 2¼ × 2¼, 4 × 5 or 8 × 10 transparencies by mail for consideration; submit portfolio for review; provide resume, business card, brochure, flyer or tearsheets to be kept on file for possible future assignments. SASE. Pays $150/color cover photo; $100-500/text/photo package. Pays on publication. Simultaneous submissions and previously published work OK.

Tips: "Learn to take pictures of computer screens. Actual computer hardcopy is difficult to publish."

ART DIRECTION, 6th Floor, 10 E. 39th St., New York NY 10016. (212)889-6500. Monthly magazine. Circ. 12,000. Emphasis is on advertising design for art directors of ad agencies. Buys 5 photos/issue. Sample copy for $3 and $1 postage.

Accompanying Mss: Photos purchased with an accompanying mss only.

Payment/Terms: Pays $50/b&w photo. Pays on publication. Credit line given. Buys one-time rights.

Making Contact: Works with freelance photographers on assignment only basis. Send query to Soshanna Sommer. Provide tearsheets to be kept on file for possible future assignments. SASE. Reports in 2 weeks.

ASBESTOS ISSUES 91, Suite 100, 760 Whalers Way, Ft. Collins CO 80525. (303)229-0029. Art Director: Craig VanWechel. Monthly magazine. Emphasizes asbestos. Circ. 30,000. Sample copy $5 and 11 × 14 SASE.

Photo Needs: Uses 4-10 photos/issue; 50% supplied by freelance photographers. Model release required.

Making Contact & Terms: Send unsolicited photos by mail for consideration or submit portfolio for review. Provide resume, business card, brochure, flyer or tearsheets to be kept on file for possible assignments. Send color 4 × 5 transparencies. SASE. Reports in 1 month. Pays $100-300/color cover photo and $100-200/b&w inside photo. Pays in 30 days. Credit line given. Buys one-time rights. Simultaneous submissions and previously published work OK.

ASSEMBLY ENGINEERING, 191 S. Gary Ave., Carol Stream IL 60188. (708)462-2215. Publisher: Donald E. Hegland. Editor: John Coleman. Art Director: Sarah Ann Cummings. Monthly. Emphasizes design and manufacturing technology where individual parts become useful products (the processes and equipment needed to assemble a finished product). Readers include corporate executives, managers, design engineers, manufacturing engineers, professionals. Circ. 79,000. Sample copy free with SASE.

Photo Needs: Uses about 30-40 photos/issue; few (so far) are supplied by freelance photographers. Needs high-tech photos of assembly systems, robots, conveyors, lasers, machine vision equipment, electronics, printed circuit boards, computers, software, fasteners, welders, etc. Special needs include any general shot where parts (components) become a whole (product) — conceptual in nature. Vertical format could be a series of shots. Model release required; captions preferred.

Making Contact & Terms: Query with samples or with list of stock photo subjects; send any size b&w or color print, transparencies, color contact sheet or b&w negatives by mail for consideration; submit portfolio for review; provide resume, business card, brochure, flyer or tearsheets to be kept on file for possible future assignments. SASE. Reports in 2 weeks. Pays $100-500 for text/photo package. Credit line given "only if requested." Buys all rights. Simultaneous submissions and previously published work OK.

ATLANTIC SALMON JOURNAL, Suite 1030, 1435 Saint-Alexandre Montreal PQ H3A 2G4 Canada. (514)842-8059. FAX: (514)842-3147. Editor: Terry Davis, Atlantic Salmon Federation. Quarterly magazine. Readers are avid salmon anglers and conservationists interested in fishing techniques, art and literature, management of the species, scientific discoveries and research and new places to fish. Circ. 20,000. Sample copy and photo guidelines free with SASE.

Photo Needs: Uses 20-25 photo/issue; majority provided with accompanying article. Needs action shots of Atlantic salmon fishing rivers; management techniques; salmon fishing trips to North American or European rivers; Atlantic salmon management, conservation and biology, river restoration and science; Atlantic salmon literature, art, history and politics. Model release and captions required.

Making Contact & Terms: Query with story idea, outline and clips; indicate availability of photos. Will also consider completed mss; send dupes with unsolicited mss. Prefers 8 × 10 b&w, 2¼ × 2¼ color transparencies or 35mm slides. Reports in 4-6 weeks. Pays $300/color cover photo, $50-100/color inside photo, $30/b&w photo. Pays on publication. Credit line given. Buys one-time rights.

AUTOMATED BUILDER, Box 120, Carpinteria CA 93013. (805)684-7659. Editor and Publisher: Don Carlson. Monthly. Circ. 26,000. Emphasizes home and apartment construction. Readers are "factory and site builders and dealers of all types of homes, apartments and commercial buildings." Sample copy free with SASE.
Photo Needs: Uses about 40 photos/issue; 10-20% supplied by freelance photographers. Needs in-plant and job site construction photos and photos of completed homes and apartments. Photos purchased with accompanying ms only. Captions required. Will consider dramatic, preferably vertical cover photos. Send color proof or slide.
Making Contact & Terms: "Call to discuss story and photo ideas." Send 35mm or 2¼ × 2¼ transparencies by mail for consideration. SASE. Reports in 2 weeks. Pays $300/text/photo package. Pays $150 for cover photos. Credit line given "if desired." Buys first time reproduction rights.

AVC, (formerly Technical Photography; incorporating Functional Photography), 210 Crossways Park Dr., Woodbury NY 11797. (516)496-8000. Editor-in-Chief: Bill Lewis. Monthly magazine. Emphasizes in-plant industrial, scientific, medical, educational, military and government image-production. Readers include individuals producing images — AV, video, motion picture, print — for use by non-photographic companies such as Ford, Kraft, Grumman, hospitals, educational institutions, etc. Circ. 60,000. Sample copy $2 with 8½ × 11 SAE. Photo and ms guidelines free with SASE.
Photo Needs: Uses 15 photos/issue, all supplied by freelance photographers. "Covers and inside articles produced by readers. Needs shots produced to fulfill a company need; to help our readers learn their craft." Model release and captions required.
Making Contact & Terms: Query with samples, send 4 × 5 or larger glossy b&w and color prints; 35mm, 2¼ × 2¼, 4 × 5, 8 × 10 transparencies by mail for consideration. SASE. Reports in 4-6 weeks. Pays $150/color cover photo; $75-250/text/photo package. Pays on publication. Credit line given. Buys one-time rights.
Tips: Prefers to see "materials related to our readership — industrial."

BEEF, 3rd Floor, 7900 International Dr., Maples MN 55425. (612)851-9329. Editor: Paul D. Andre. Monthly magazine. Emphasizes beef cattle production and feeding. Readers are feeders, ranchers and stocker operators. Circ. 120,000. Sample copy free with SASE. Photo guidelines free with SASE.
Photo Needs: Uses 35-40 photos/issue; "less than 1%" supplied by freelance photographers. Needs variety of cow-calf and feedlot scenes. Model release and captions required.
Making Contact & Terms: Send 8 × 10 glossy b&w prints and 35mm transparencies by mail for consideration. SASE. Reports in 1 month. Pays $25/b&w inside photo; $50/color inside photo. Pays on acceptance. Buys one-time rights.
Tips: "We buy few photos, since our staff provides most of those needed."

BEEF TODAY, Farm Journal Publishing, Inc., 6205 Earle Brown Dr. Ste. 100, Brooklyn Center MN 55430. (612)561-0300. Photo Editor: Greg Lamp. Monthly magazine. Emphasizes American agriculture. Readers are active farmers, ranchers or agribusiness people. Circ. 220,000. Sample copy and photo guidelines free with SASE.
Photo Needs: Uses 20-30 photos/issue; 75% supplied by freelance photographers. We use studio-type portraiture (environmental portraits), technical, details, scenics. Model release preferred; photo captions required.
Making Contact & Terms: Arrange a personal interview to show portfolio or query with resume of credits along with business card, brochure, flyer or tearsheets to be kept on file for possible assignments. SASE. Reports in 2 weeks. "We pay a cover bonus." Pays on acceptance. Credit line given. Buys one-time rights. Simultaneous submissions OK.
Tips: In portfolio or samples, likes to "see about 20 slides showing photographer's use of lighting and photographer's ability to work with people. Know your intended market. Familiarize yourself with the magazine and keep abreast of how photos are used in the general magazine field."

BEVERAGE DYNAMICS, (formerly Liquor Store Magazine), 352 Park Ave. S., New York NY 10010. (212)685-4848. Editor: Bob Keane. Nine times/year magazine. Emphasizes distilled spirits, wine and beer. Readers are national — retailers (liquor stores, supermarkets, etc.), wholesalers, distillers, vintners, brewers, ad agencies and media. Circ. 50,000. Sample copy free with 8½ × 11 SAE and 37¢ postage.
Photo Needs: Uses 20 photos/issue; 5 supplied by freelance photographers and photo house (stock). Needs photos of retailers, product shots, concept shots and profiles. Special needs include good retail environments; interesting store settings; special effect wine and beer photos. Model release and captions required.

Making Contact & Terms: Query with samples and list of stock photo subjects. SASE. Reports in 2 weeks. Pays $400/color cover photo; $300/job. Pays on publication. Credit line given. Buys one-time rights or all rights on commissioned photos. Simultaneous submissions OK.

BEVERAGE WORLD, 150 Great Neck Rd., Great Neck NY 11021. (516)829-9210. FAX: (516)829-5414. Editor: Alan Wolf. Monthly. Circ. 32,000. Estab. 1881. Emphasizes the beverage industry. Readers are "bottlers, wholesalers, distributors of beer, soft drinks, wine and spirits." Sample copy $3.50.
Photo Needs: Uses 25-50 photos/issue; many supplied by freelance photographers. Needs "freelancers in specific regions of the U.S. for occasional assignments."
Making Contact & Terms: Query with samples. Provide resume, business card, brochure, flyer or tearsheets to be kept on file for possible future assignments. Pays $100/day; fees paid per assignment; payment range varies according to nature of assignment. Pays on publication or per assignment contract. Rights purchased varies.
Tips: Prefers to see "interesting angles on people, products. Provide affordable quality."

BIOPHARM MANUFACTURING, 859 Willamette St., Eugene OR 97440. (503)343-1200. Art Director: Barbara A. Mickelson. Monthly. Emphasizes science. Readers are scientists and manufacturers of scientific products/equipment. Circ. 30,000. Sample copy free with 8½×11 SAE. Photo guidelines free with SASE.
Photo Needs: Uses 6-10 photos/issue; one, 4/c, supplied by freelance photographers. Needs photos of scientific topics. Photo captions preferred.
Making Contact & Terms: Query with list of stock photo subjects; provide resume, business card, brochure, flyer or tearsheets to be kept on file for possible future assignments. Does not return unsolicited material. Reports in 1 month. Pays $300/color cover photo; $100/b&w inside photo. Pays on publication. Credit line given on table of contents page or with photo. Buys one-time rights. Simultaneous submissions OK.
Tips: Looks for "an artistic look at technical scientific products/equipment. Colorful and dramatic. We seldom use people shots."

BRAKE & FRONT END, 11 S. Forge St., Akron OH 44304. (216)535-6117. FAX: (216)535-0874. Editor: Mary DellaValle. Monthly magazine. Circ. 30,000. Estab. 1931. Emphasizes automotives maintenance and repair. For automobile mechanics and repair shop owners. Needs "color photos for use on covers. Subjects vary with editorial theme, but basically they deal with automotive or truck parts and service." Wants no "overly commercial photos which emphasize brand names" and no mug shots of prominent people. May buy up to 6 covers annually. Credit line given. Buys first North American serial rights. Submit model release with photos.
Making Contact & Terms: Send contact sheet for consideration. Reports immediately. Pays on publiclation. SASE. Simultaneous submissions OK. Sample copy $1. Uses 5×7 b&w glossy prints; send contact sheet. Captions required. Pays $8.50 minimum. For cover: Send contact sheet or transparencies. Study magazine, then query. Lead time for cover photos is 2 months before publication date. Pays $150 minimum.
Tips: Send for editorial schedules; enclose SASE. Looks for "New, fresh ideas for technical automotive subjects."

BUILDER/DEALER MAGAZINE, 16 First Ave., Corry PA 16407-1894. (814)664-8624. FAX: (814)664-8506. Production Manager: Timothy S. Lee. Art Director: William E. Stright. Monthly. Circ. 28,000. Estab. 1980. Emphasizes "log, dome, modular, timber post and beam frame component, precut, and panelized housing." Readers are builders, dealers, manufacturers, product suppliers and potential builders and dealers for this industry. Free sample copy.
Photo Needs: Uses many photos/issue; many supplied by freelance photographers. Needs interiors and exteriors of manufactured structures. Also, vertical shots for possible covers. Model release and captions required.
Making Contact & Terms: Query with samples and list of stock photo subjects. Provide resume, business card, brochure, flyer or tearsheets to be kept on file for possible future assignments. Reports in 1 month. Rates established on individual basis and is negotiable. Pays on publication. Credit given. Buys all rights.
Tips: In samples looks for "upper end, vertical shots, clean and open to accept a variety of colors for blurbs & etc." Trend is "upper end and modular. Show good quality and a professional attitude with respectable competitive prices."

BUILDING SUPPLY HOME CENTERS, 1350 E. Touhy, Box 5080, Des Plaines IL 60017. FAX: (708)635-9950. Editor: Craig Shutt. Trade publication. Monthly magazine. Emphasizes lumberyards, home center retailing, residential construction. Readers are owners and managers of lumberyards and home centers. Circ. 47,000. Estab. 1917. Sample copy $10.

Photo Needs: Uses 100+ photos/issue; freelance usage varies widely; most is stock, couple issues per year are all assignment. Needs photos of retail and construction. Model release and photo captions preferred.

Making Contact & Terms: Query with list of stock photo subjects. SASE. Report time varies. Pays $100-300/color cover photo, $50-150/color inside photo or $300-600/day. Pays on publication. Credit line given. Buys one-time rights. Simultaneous submissions and previously published work OK.

Tips: Wants to see "Application to our industry, uniqueness and clean, sharp look. We're using more symbolic work for covers and lead feature. Make it applicable to market."

BUSINESS ATLANTA, 6255 Barfield Rd., Atlanta GA 30328. (404)256-9800. Editor: Ken Anderberg. Managing Editor: John Sequerth. Monthly. Emphasizes "general magazine-style coverage of business and business-related issues in the metro Atlanta area." Readers are "everybody in Atlanta who can buy a house or office building or Rolls Royce." Circ. 36,000. Sample copy $2.95

Photo Needs: Uses about 40 photos/issue; 35-40 supplied by freelance photographers. Needs "good photos mostly of business-related subjects if keyed to local industry." Model release and captions required.

Making Contact & Terms: Arrange a personal interview to show portfolio. SASE. Reports in 1 month. Pays $50/b&w photo; $350-450/color cover photo; $50-200/color inside photo; $200 minimum/job; $50-500/package. Pays on publication. Credit line given. Buys one-time rights and reprint rights.

Tips: "Study the publication for the feel we strive for and don't bring us something either totally off the wall or, at the other extreme, assume that business means boring and bring us something duller than ditchwater. People in the business community are becoming more willing to do unusual things for a photo. We need the ability to work on location with subjects who have little time to spend with a photographer. Anybody can shoot a perfume bottle in a studio. Study *Business Atlanta* to see the types of work we use. Then show me something better."

BUSINESS FACILITIES, Box 2060, Red Bank NJ 07701. (201)842-7433. Editor: Eric Peterson. Monthly magazine. Emphasizes economic development, commercial and industrial real estate. Readers are top corporate executives, public and private development organizations. Circ. 35,000. Free sample copy.

Photo Needs: Uses about 20-30 photos/issue; 2-3 supplied by freelance photographers. Needs "news-oriented shots; current events; generally illustrative of real estate development. We always need photos of nationally known political or business leaders." Captions required.

Making Contact & Terms: Query with list of stock photo subjects. SASE. Reports in 2 weeks. All rates negotiable. Pays on publication. Credit line given sometimes; all times for cover shots. Rights negotiable. Simultaneous submissions and previously published work OK.

Tips: "No telephone queries, please! Put it in writing."

BUSINESS VIEW, Box 9859, Naples FL 33941. (813)263-7525. Publisher: Eleanor Sommer. Editor: Ken Gooderham. Monthly magazine. Emphasizes business for professional and business readers. Sample copy $2.

Photo Needs: Uses about 5 photos/issue; 25% supplied by freelance photographers. "Usually needs head shots for profiles, press releases, etc. Almost all would be of local/regional interest (southwest Florida)." Captions required.

Making Contact & Terms: Query with samples. SASE. Reports in 6 weeks. Payment negotiable depending on the assignment; pays $15-50/b&w photo; $100-250/color photo. Pays on publication. Credit line given in masthead. Simultaneous submissions OK.

Tips: Prefers to see "sharp, clear b&w portraits" in samples. "Be local and available."

BUTTER FAT MAGAZINE, Box 9100, Vancouver, BC V6B 4G4 Canada. (604)420-6611. Managing Editor: C. A. Paulson. Editor: G. Hahn. Published 6 times per year. Circ. 3,500. Emphasizes dairy farming and marketing for dairy farmers in British Columbia; also emphasizes dairy consumers in British Columbia. Free sample copy.

Photo Needs: Uses 40 photos/issue; 2 are supplied by freelance photographers. Especially needs freelancers throughout the province to work on assignment only basis. Needs photos on personalities, locations and events. Special subject needs include abstracted photos related to regulation, government standards, and trade economics in the dairy industry. Captions required.

Making Contact & Terms: Arrange personal interview with managing editor to show portfolio. Provide tearsheets to be kept on file for possible future assignments. Pays $10/photo; $50-500 for text/photo package. Pay on color photos and job is negotiable. Credit line given. Payment on acceptance. Simultaneous submissions OK.

CABLE PUBLISHING GROUP, (formerly CED Magazine), Capital Cities ABC, Suite 400, 600 South Cherry St., Denver CO 80222. (303)393-7449. Art Director: Don Ruth. Monthly magazine. Emphasizes cable TV engineering. Readers are mostly male CEOs and head engineers of various ages in the cable television industry. Sample copy $2.50.

Photo Needs: Uses 3 photos/issue; uses only a few freelance photos over a year. Themes and technical shots specific to the industry. "Subject needs will vary according to editorial focus." Model release required; photo captions preferred.

Making Contact & Terms: Arrange a personal interview to show portfolio, query with resume of credits along with resume, business card, brochure, flyer or tearsheets to be kept on file for possible assignments; query with list of stock photo subjects, send unsolicited photos by mail for consideration or submit portfolio for review. Send b&w or color prints or 35mm or 2¼×2¼ transparencies. SASE. Call for report after sending. Pays $300-500/color cover photo, $100-300/color inside photo or $50-200/b&w inside photo. Pays on publication. Credit line not given. Buys all rights; willing to negotiate. Simultaneous submissions and previously published work OK.

Tips: In porfolio or samples, looks especially for "quality, the type of individual they are, how they present themselves and their work, the style of work, the quantity and type of experience as seen in their work and its volume. Don't contact us just once; be persistent. Be flexible on what to do and what to change."

CALIFORNIA BUILDER & ENGINEER, Box 10070, Palo Alto CA 94303. (415)494-8822. Publisher: David W. Woods. Bimonthly magazine. Circ. 12,500. Emphasizes the heavy construction industry. For public works officials and contractors in California, Hawaii, western Nevada and western Arizona. Send photos for consideration. Pays on publication. Reports in 2 weeks. SASE. Sample copy available.

Subject Needs: Head shot (personnel changes), photo essay/photo feature and product shot (construction equipment on the job).

B&W: Send 4×5 glossy prints. Captions required. Pays $10-15.

Cover: Cover shots should have an accompanying ms. Transparencies only. Purchase covers rarely, but will consider. Pays $15-25/4×5 color photo.

Tips: Camera on the Job column uses single photos with detailed captions. Photographers "should be familiar with their subject—for example, knowing the difference between a track dozer and a wheel loader, types and model number of equipment, construction techniques, identity of contractor, etc. We are using very little freelance material."

CALIFORNIA FARMER, 731 Market St., San Francisco CA 94103-2011. (415)495-3340. Editor: Len Richardson. Managing Editor: Ann Senuta. Photo Editor/Art Director: Larry Bruderẽr. Semimonthly magazine. Emphasizes agriculture. Readers are farmers and statewide agricultural professionals. Circ. 63,000. Sample copy $1.50.

Photo Needs: Uses 10 photos/issue; 1-2 supplied by freelance photographers.

Making Contact & Terms: Send 35mm transparencies by mail for consideration; provide resume, business card, brochure, flyer or tearsheets to be kept on file for possible future assignments. SASE. Reports in 4 weeks. Pays $300/color cover photo; $50-125/color photo page. Pays on receipt of invoice. Credit line given. Simultaneous submissions OK.

CANADIAN BUILDING OWNER AND PROPERTY MANAGER, P.O. Box 82230, North Burnaby, BC V5C 6E7 Canada. (604)433-8164. FAX: (604)433-9549. Editor: Brian Martin. Quarterly magazine. Emphasizes property management. Readers are primarily property managers, building owners who are 35 years old and older. Circ. 30,000. Sample copy available.

Photo Needs: Uses 15 photos/issue; 100% supplied by freelance photographers. Needs outstanding photos of high-rise buildings and other shots pertaining to articles.

Making Contact & Terms: Send unsolicited photos by mail for consideration. Also submit portfolio for review. Send color prints; contact for size and format. Does not return unsolicited material. Reports in 1 month. Pays on publication. Credit line given. Buys all rights; willing to negotiate. Previously published work OK.

CATECHIST, 2451 E. River Rd., Dayton OH 45439. (513)294-5785. Editor: Patricia Fischer. Monthly magazine published from July/August through April. Circ. 45,000. Emphasizes religious education for professional and volunteer religious education teachers working in Catholic schools. Buys 4-5 photos/issue. Not copyrighted. Send photos or contact sheet for consideration. Pays on publication. Reports in 2-3 months. SASE. Simultaneous submissions OK. Sample copy $2.

Subject Needs: Fine art, human interest (all generations and races), nature, scenic, still life and seasonal material (Christmas, Advent, Lent, Easter). Wants on a regular basis family photos (all economic classes and races).

B&W: Send contact sheet or 8×10 glossy, matte, semigloss or silk prints. Pays $25-35.

Cover: Send b&w glossy, matte, semigloss or silk prints. Using 4-color art on covers now.

CERAMICS MONTHLY, Box 12448, Columbus OH 43212. (614)488-8236. Contact: Editorial Department. 10 issues/year, Sept.-June. Emphasizes "handmade pottery/ceramic art—particularly contemporary American, but also international and historic." Readers are "potters, ceramic artists, teachers, professors of art, collectors of ceramics, craft institutions and libraries." Circ. 36,000. Sample copy $4. Photo guidelines free with SASE.

Photo Needs: Uses about 100 photos/issue. Needs "museum-quality shots of ceramics (pottery, sculpture, porcelain, stoneware, individual objects) shot on plain backgrounds; shots of potters in their studios; photos of ceramic processes." Photos purchased with accompanying ms only "except cover photos which *sometimes* do not have a text." Captions required.

Making Contact & Terms: Send 8×10 glossy b&w prints; 35mm (Kodachrome 25 only), 2¼×2¼, 4×5 or 8×10 transparencies by mail for consideration. SASE. Reports "as time permits." Pays $60/color cover photo; $15/b&w or $25/color inside photo. "News and exhibition coverage excluded from payment." Pays on publication. Buys magazine rights.

Tips: "Team up with a good potter to help with ceramic aesthetic decisions."

CFO MAGAZINE, 253 Summer St., Boston MA 02210. Art Director: Barbara Deem Anderson. Monthly. Emphasizes business. Readers are chief financial officers; accountants. Circ. 200,000. Sample copy for 9×12 SASE.

Photo Needs: Uses 5-10 photos/issue; 75% supplied by freelance photographers. Needs photos of interesting people, pictures of businessmen, factories, products. Special needs: occasionally need short-notice shots done on assignment in smaller cities and towns. Model release and captions preferred.

Making Contact & Terms: Arrange a personal interview to show portfolio; query with sample or list of stock photo subjects. Send "published clips only; non returnable." Reports only when photographer makes follow-up phone call." Pays $900 maximum (plus expenses)/color cover photo; $200-800/color inside photo, depending on size; $800 maximum including expenses/inside full-page opener, "but we rarely have full-page openers"; $200+ expenses/job. Pays on acceptance. Credit line given. Buys one-time rights plus reprint rights. Previously published work OK.

Tips: Prefers to see "color samples, preferably tears from other business magazines."

THE CHRISTIAN MINISTRY, 407 S. Dearborn St., Chicago IL 60605-1111. (312)427-5380. Managing Editor: Mark Halton. Bimonthly magazine. Emphasizes religion—parish clergy. Readers are 30-65 years old; 80% male, 20% female; parish clergy and well-educated. Circ. 12,000. Estab. 1969. Sample copy free for 9×12 SASE and $.65 postage. Photo guidelines free with SASE.

Photo Needs: Uses 6 photos/issue; all supplied by freelance photographers. Needs photos of clergy (especially women clergy), church gatherings, school classrooms and church symbols. Future photo needs include social gatherings and leaders working with groups. Model release and photo captions preferred.

Making Contact & Terms: Send 8×10 b&w prints by mail for consideration. SASE. Reports in 3 weeks. Pays $50/b&w cover photo; $20/b&w inside photo. Pays on publication. Credit line given. Buys one-time rights. Will consider simultaneous submissions.

Tips: "We're looking for up-to-date photos of clergy, engaged in preaching, teaching, meeting with congregants, working in social activities. We need photos of women, black and Hispanic clergy."

*THE CHRONICLE OF PHILANTHROPY, 1255 23rd Street, NW, Suite 775, Washington DC 20037. (202)466-1205. Art Director: Jojo Gragasin, Jr.. Biweekly tabloid. Readers are all aspects of the nonprofit world such as charities (large or small grant maker/giving, foundations, and relief agencies (e.g. Red Cross). Circ. 20,000. Estab. 1988. Sample copy free. No guidelines.

Photo Needs: Uses 20 photos/issue; 50-75% supplied by freelance photographers. Needs photos of people (profiles) making the news in philanthropy and environmental shots related to person(s) organization. Most shots arranged with freelancers are specific. Model release and photo captions required.

Making Contact & Terms: Arrange a personal interview to show portfolio. Send unsolicited photos by mail for consideration. Send 35mm, 2¼×2¼ b&w prints by mail for consideration. Provide resume, business card, brochure, flyer or tearsheets to be kept on file for possible assignments. Will send negatives back via certified mail. Reports in 1-2 days. Pays (all b&w) ½ day: $225+ expense; full day: $350+ expenses; reprints: $75. Pays on publication. Buys one-time rights. Will consider previously published work.

CLASSROOM COMPUTER LEARNING, Suite A4, 2169 E. Francisco Blvd, San Rafael CA 94901. (415)457-4333. Editor: Holly Brady. Art Director: Ellen Wright, c/o 2451 E. River Rd., Dayton OH 45439. Monthly. Emphasizes computer in education. Readers are teachers and administrators, grades K-12. Circ. 82,000. Sample copy $3.

Photo Needs: Uses about 7-10 photos/issue; 2 or more supplied by freelance photographers. Photo needs "depend on articles concerned. No general categories. Usually photos used to accompany articles in a conceptual manner, computer screen shots needed often." Model release required.

Making Contact & Terms: Contact Ellen Wright to arrange a personal interview to show portfolio; query with nonreturnable samples; provide resume, business card, brochure, flyer or tearsheets to be kept on file for possible future assignments. SASE. Reports in 3 weeks. Pays $300-700/color cover photo; $50-100/b&w inside photo; $100-300/color inside photo. Pays on acceptance. Credit line given. Buys one-time rights. Previously published work OK.

CLAVIER, 200 Northfield Rd., Northfield IL 60093. (708)446-5000. Editor: Kingsley Day. Magazine published 10 times/year. Circ. 20,000. Estab. 1962. For piano and organ teachers. Credit line given. Pays on publication. Buys all rights.
Photo Needs: Human interest photos of keyboard instrument students and teachers. Special needs include synthesizer photos, senior citizens performing and children performing.
Making Contact & Terms: Send material by mail for consideration. SASE. Reports in 1 month. Sample copy $2.Uses b&w glossy prints. Pays $10-25.For cover: Kodachrome, color glossy prints or 35mm transparencies. Vertical format preferred. Pays $25-75/photo.
Tips: "We look for sharply focused photographs that show action and for clear color that is bright and true. We need photographs of children and teachers involved in learning music at the piano. We prefer shots that show them deeply involved in their work rather than posed shots. Very little is taken on specific assignment except for the cover. Authors usually include article photographs with their manuscripts. We purchase only one or two items from stock each year."

COLLISION, Box M, Franklin MA 02038. Editor: Jay Kruza. Magazine published every 5 weeks. Circ. 20,000. Emphasizes "technical tips and management guidelines" for auto body repairmen and dealership managers in eastern US. Needs photos of technical repair procedures, association meetings, etc. A regular column called 'Stars and Cars' features a national personality with his/her car. Prefer 3+ b&w photos with captions as to why person likes this vehicle. If person has worked on it or customized it, photo is worth more. Buys 100 photos/year; 12/issue. Buys all rights, but may reassign to photographer after publication. In created or set-up photos, which are not direct news, requires photocopy of model release with address and phone number of models for verification. Query with resume of credits and representational samples (not necessarily on subject) or send contact sheet for consideration. Pays on acceptance. Reports in 3 weeks. SASE. Simultaneous submissions OK. Sample copy $3; free photo guidelines.
B&W: Send glossy or matte contact sheet or 5×7 prints. Captions required. Pays $25 for first photo; $10 for each additional photo in the series; pays $25-50/photo for "Stars and Cars" column depending on content. Extra pay for accompanying mss.
Tips: "Don't shoot one or two frames; do a sequence or series. It gives us choice, and we'll buy more photos. Often we reject single photo submissions. Capture how the work is done to solve the problem."

COMMERCIAL CARRIER JOURNAL, Chilton Way, Radnor PA 19089. (215)964-4513. Editor-In-Chief: Gerald F. Standley. Executive Editor: Parry Desmond. Monthly magazine. Circ. 79,000. Emphasizes truck and bus fleet maintenance operations and management. Photos purchased with or without accompanying ms, or on assignment. Pays on a per-job or per-photo basis. Credit line given. Pays on acceptance. Buys all rights. Send material by mail for consideration. SASE. Reports in 3 weeks.
Subject Needs: Spot news (of truck accidents, Teamster activities, and highway scenes involving trucks). Model release and *detailed* captions required.
Color: Uses prints and 35mm transparencies.
Cover: Uses color transparencies. Uses vertical cover only. Pays $100/photo.
Accompanying Mss: Features on truck fleets and news features involving trucking companies.

COMMUNICATIONS, Suite 350, 6300 S. Syracuse Way, Englewood CO 80111. (303)220-0600. Editorial Director: Bob Chapin. Monthly. Emphasizes mobile communications industry, e.g., cellular phones, paging, two-way radios—and matters relating to their use. Readers are dealers, manufacturers, users. Circ. 20,000. Sample copy free with SASE. Focus calendar available.
Photo Needs: Uses 15-20 photos/issue; 1-5 supplied by freelance photographers.
Making Contact & Terms: Query with list of stock photo subjects; provide resume, business card, brochure, flyer or tearsheets to be kept on file for possible future assignments. Does not return unsolicited material. Reports in 3 weeks. Pays $300/color cover photo. Pays on publication. Credit line given. Buys one-time rights. Previously published work OK.
Tips: Looks for "shots that convey any concept relating to our industry, from technical to managerial. Shots should force reader to stop and look at them."

COMMUNICATIONS WEEK, 600 Community Dr., Manhasset NY 11030. (516)365-4600. Editor: Laurel Nelson. Weekly newspaper with magazine supplement. Emphasizes communications (telecom, datacom). Readers are users and vendors of communications equipment and services. Circ. 96,000. Sample copy free with SASE.

Subject Needs: Uses 15 photos/issue; 50% supplied by freelancers. Needs photos mostly of people in the industry. Will review photos only on assignment. Photo captions required.
Making Contact & Terms: Query with samples. Does not return unsolicited material. Reports back as photographers needed. Pay negotiable. Pays on publication. Credit line given. Buys all rights.

COMPRESSED AIR MAGAZINE, 253 E. Washington Ave., Washington NJ 07882-2495. (201)850-7818. Editor: S.M. Parkhill. Monthly. Circ. 149,000. Emphasizes "industrial subjects, technology, energy." Readers hold middle to upper management positions in Graad SIC range. Sample copy free.
Photo Needs: Uses about 20 photos/issue; "very few" supplied by freelance photographers. Model release and captions preferred.
Making Contact & Terms: Provide resume, business card, brochure, flyer or tearsheets to be kept on file for possible future assignments. Does not return unsolicited material. Previously published work OK.
Tips: "We look for high quality color shots, and have increased use of 'symbolic' photos to supplement industrial shots."

*COMPUTERS IN HEALTHCARE MAGAZINE, 6300 So. Syracuse Way #650, Englewood CO 80111. (303)220-0600. FAX: (303)773-9716. Editor: Carolyn Dunbar. Monthly magazine. Emphasizes healthcare computing—management focus. Readers are hospital CEO, CFO, MIS directors, physicians, nurses, marketing managers in healthcare, HMD directors and healthcare decision makers. Circ. 17,000. Estab. 1980. Sample copy free for large manila SASE and $2.50 postage. No photo guidelines.
Photo Needs: Uses 5-10 photos/issue; 10% supplied by freelance photographers. Needs photos of very techy—abstract—covers similar to Omni, computer tech focus. "We need to build a stable of highly skilled, competent, reasonably priced freelancers. We will welcome portfolios." Model release and photo captions preferred.
Making Contact & Terms: Query with list of stock photo subjects. Send b&w/color prints by mail for consideration. Submit portfolio for review. Provide resume, business card, brochure, flyer or tearsheets to be kept on file for possible assignments. SASE. Reports in 1-2 weeks. Pays $250/color cover photo. Pays on publication. Credit line given. Buys one-time rights. Simultaneous submissions and previously published work OK.
Tips: "Mostly we are looking for 'hot' cover art. This is a good time for photographers to contact us, because we are planning for next two years. Covers are highly colorful, glitzy, high-end looking with healthcare and computer technology as a theme—but we consider abstract 'futuristic' images. Fit with our style, show an excellent portfolio, and make things easy on our end—provide full, speedy service."

*CONNSTRUCTION MAGAZINE, P.O. Box 9768, Wethersfield CT 06109. (203)774-6093. Managing Editor: Victor Bonini. 7× yearly magazine. Emphasizes horizontal construction. Readers are 21-60, M/F, Construction Co. owners and managers. Circ. 5,500. Estab. 1962. Sample copy for 9×12 SASE and 5 first-class stamps. No photo guidelines.
Photo Needs: Uses 80 photos/issue; 10% supplied by freelance photographers. Photo types include trade, on-site and personalities. Model release and photo captions required.
Making Contact & Terms: Query with resume of credits. Provide resume, business card, brochure, flyer or tearsheets to be kept on file for possible assignments. SASE. Reports in 1-2 weeks. Most rates negotiable. Pays $200-400 color cover photo. Pays on publication. Credit line given. Buys first N.A. serial rights.
Tips: "We generally use everything from event coverage to detailed, cover studio shots. But everything is issue specific. Always best to contact us to discuss a shot first."

CONSTRUCTION NEWS, Box 2421, Little Rock AR 72203. (501)376-1931. Editor: Robert J. Alvey. Weekly magazine. Emphasizes construction. Readers are contractors, architects and engineers. Circ. 8,500. Sample copy $2 and 8½×11 SASE.
Photo Needs: Uses 3-10 photos/issue; number supplied by freelancers "varies as needed." Needs photos of construction industry-related people, equipment, job sites. "We are always seeking highest quality color transparencies for covers. We average 13 full-color covers annually." Model release and photo captions required.
Making Contact & Terms: Provide resume, business card, brochure, flyer or tearsheets to be kept on file for possible assignments. SASE. Reports in 1-3 months. Color cover rate negotiable; pays $25 b&w cover. B&w inside rate negotiable. Pays on publication. Credit line given. Buys one-time rights. Previously published work OK.
Tips: "All photos must be within magazine's circulation area (Arkansas, West Tennessee, Louisiana, Mississippi, Oklahoma). Photos for cover should, in most cases, display name of equipment manufacturer and cannot show workers *not* in compliance with OSHA standards."

CONTRACTORS GUIDE, 6201 Howard St., Niles IL 60648. (708)647-1200. Editor: Russ Gager. Monthly magazine. Emphasizes "roofing, siding, insulation, solar construction business, both manufacturing and contracting." Circ. 33,000. Sample copy free with SASE.
Photo Needs: Uses about 10 photos/issue; 0-1 supplied by freelance photographers. Needs "head shots, group photos, product shots and on-site construction shots." Reviews photos with accompanying ms only. Model release and captions preferred.
Making Contact & Terms: Provide resume, business card, brochure, flyer or tearsheets to be kept on file for possible future assignment. SASE. Reports in 1 week. Pays negotiable rate for color cover photo; $25/b&w inside photo, $30/color inside photo. Pays on publication. Credit line given. Buys all rights.
Tips: Wants to see "Good location work, format larger than 35mm."

COPE MAGAZINE, P.O. Box 1700, 444 Hospital Dr., Franklin TN 37065. . (615)371-8474. Publisher/Editor: Betty Webb. Pulse Publications, Inc., publication. Magazine published monthly, 10 times a year. Emphasizes oncology and news in cancer treatment and AIDS. Readers are doctors—oncologists and hemotologists, etc. Circ. 30,000+. Sample copy and photo guidelines free with SASE.
Photo Needs: Uses 30 photos/issue; 100% supplied by freelance photographers. Photos should be medically related. Focus on details of research facilities etc. Model release required; photo captions preferred.
Making Contact & Terms: Arrange a personal interview to show portfolio, query with resume of credits or list of stock photo subjects, send unsolicited photos by mail for consideration or submit portfolio for review. Provide resume, business card, brochure, flyer or tearsheets to be kept on file for possible assignments. Send b&w and color 5×7 prints or 35mm, 2¼×2¼, 4×5 or 8×10 transparencies. SASE. Reports in 3 weeks. Pays $400/color cover photo; all other rates are negotiable. Pays on publication. Credit line given. Buys all rights, but will negotiate. Simultaneous submissions or previously published work OK.
Tips: In portfolio or samples, looking for variety of "subject-related samples for our field. Some special effects. Promote yourself—be consistent, don't spread yourself thin. There's too much competition. Find a select market and create the expertise."

*CORPORATE CASHFLOW, 6255 Barfield Road, Atlanta GA 30328. (404)256-9800. Managing Editor: Jill Lambert. Monthly magazine. Emphasizes corporate treasury management. Readers are senior financial officers of large and middle-sized U.S. corporations. Circ. 30,000. Estab. 1980. Sample copy available. No photo guidelines.
Photo Needs: Uses 1 or 2 photos/issue; all supplied by freelance photographers.
Making Contact & Terms: Provide resume, business card, brochure, flyer or tearsheets to be kept on file for possible assignments. "Atlanta photographers only." Pays $400/color cover photo. Pays on acceptance. Credit line given. Buys one-time rights.

CRANBERRIES, Box 249, Cobalt CT 06414. (203)342-4730. Publisher/Editor: Bob Taylor. Monthly. Emphasizes cranberry growing, processing, marketing and research. Readers are "primarily cranberry growers but includes anybody associated with the field." Circ. 650. Sample copy free with SASE.
Photo Needs: Uses about 10 photos/issue; half supplied by freelance photographers. Needs "portraits of growers, harvesting, manufacturing—anything associated with cranberries." Captions required.
Making Contact & Terms: Send 4×5 or 8×10 b&w glossy prints by mail for consideration; "simply query about prospective jobs." SASE. Pays $15-25/b&w cover photo; $5-15/b&w inside photo; $35-100 for text/photo package. Pays on publication. Credit line given. Buys one-time rights. Simultaneous and previously published submissions OK.
Tips: "Learn about the field."

Markets which offer lower payment amounts, or photo credits and extra copies or tearsheets as payment are often receptive to the work of newcomers. For a list of such markets, see the First Markets Index preceding the General Index in the back of this book.

DAIRY GOAT JOURNAL, 821 Ridge Rd., Telford PA 18969. (215)234-0732. Photo Editor: Ann Miller. Monthly magazine. Circ. 10,000. Estab. 1916. For breeders and raisers of dairy goats.
Photo Needs: Relate in some manner to dairy goats, dairy goat dairies, shows, sales products and life of people who raise dairy goats.
Making Contact & Terms: Send 4×5 glossy b&w prints and manuscript by mail for consideration. SASE. Reports in 1 month. Pays $5-15/b&w or color print. Pays on publication. Credit line given. Buys first N.A. serial rights.
Tips: Make sure "photo is appropriate with manuscript. Have a detailed know of dairy goat industry."

DAIRY HERD MANAGEMENT, Box 2400, Minnetoka MN 55343. (612)931-0211. Editor: Ed Clark. Monthly magazine. Circ. 105,000. Emphasizes dairy management innovations, techniques and practices for dairy producers. Photos purchased with accompanying ms, or on assignment. Pays $100-250 for text/photo package, or on a per-photo basis. Pays on acceptance. Buys one-time rights. Query with list of stock photo subjects. SASE. Reports in 2 weeks.
Subject Needs: Animal (natural photos of cows in specific dairy settings), how-to and photo essay/photo feature. Wants on a regular basis photos showing new dairy management techniques. No scenics or dead colors. Model release and captions preferred.
B&W: Uses 5×7 glossy prints. Pays $5-25/photo.
Color: Uses 35mm or 2¼×2¼ transparencies. Pays $25-100/photo.
Cover: Uses 35mm or 2¼×2¼ transparencies. Vertical format required. Pays $50-150/photo.
Accompanying Mss: Interesting and practical articles on dairy management innovations, techniques and practices. Pays $100-150/ms.

DAIRY TODAY, Farm Journal Publishing, Inc., 6205 Earle Brown Dr., Ste. 100, Brooklyn Center MN 55430. (612)561-0300. Photo Editor: Greg Lamp. Monthly magazine. Emphasizes American agriculture. Readers are active farmers, ranchers or agribusiness people. Circ. 111,000. Sample copy and photo guidelines free with SASE.
Photo Needs: Uses 20-30 photos/issue; 75% supplied by freelance photographers. We use studio-type portraiture (environmental portraits), technical, details, scenics. Model release preferred; photo captions required.
Making Contact & Terms: Arrange a personal interview to show portfolio or query with resume of credits along with business card, brochure, flyer or tearsheets to be kept on file for possible assignments. SASE. Reports in 2 weeks. "We pay a cover bonus." Pays on acceptance. Credit line given. Buys one-time rights. Simultaneous submissions OK.
Tips: In portfolio or samples, likes to "see about 20 slides showing photographer's use of lighting, and photographer's ability to work with people. Know your inteneded market. Familiarize yourself with the magazine and keep abreast of how photos are used in the general magazine field."

DARKROOM & CREATIVE CAMERA TECHNIQUES, Preston Publications, 7800 Merrimac Ave., P.O. Box 48312, Niles IL 60648. (708)965-0566. FAX: (708)965-7639. Publisher: Seaton T. Preston. Editor: David Alan Jay. Bimonthly magazine. Covers darkroom techniques, creative camera use, photochemistry and photographic experimentation/innovation—particularly in photographic processing, printing and reproduction—plus general user-oriented photography articles aimed at advanced amateurs and professionals. Lighting and optics are also very important. Circ. 44,000. Estab. 1979. SASE for free photography and writer's guidelines. Sample copy $4.50.
Photo Needs: "The best way to publish photographs in *Darkroom Techniques* is to write an article on photo or darkroom techniques and illustrate the article. Except for article-related pictures, we publish few single photographs. The two exceptions are: cover photographs—we are looking for strong poster-like images that will make good newsstand covers; and Professional Portfolio—exceptional, professional photographs of an artistic or human nature; most of freelance photography comes from what is currently in a photographer's stock. Model releases are required where appropriate."
Making Contact & Terms: "To submit for cover or Professional Portfolio, please send a selected number of superior photographs of any subject; however, we do not want to receive more than ten or twenty in any one submission. We ask for submissions on speculative basis only. Except for portfolios, we publish few single photos that are not accompanied by some type of text. "Prefer color transparencies over color prints. B&w submissions should be 8×10. For cover submissions, 4 × 5 transparencies are preferable. Payment up to $300 for covers. Articles pay up to $100/page for text/photo package, will negotiate. Pays on publication only. Credit line given. Buys one-time rights.
Tips: "We are looking for exceptional photographs with strong, graphically startling images. We look for colorful graphic images with room at top and on one side for covers; technically accurate, crisp, clear images for portfolios. No run-of-the-mill postcard shots please. We are the most technical general-interest photographic publication on the market today. Authors are encouraged to substantiate their conclusions with experimental data. Submit samples, article ideas, etc. It's easier to get photos published with an article."

DATA COMMUNICATIONS MAGAZINE, 41st Fl., 1221 Ave. of the Americas, New York NY 10020. (212)512-2639. Art Director: Ken Surabian. Monthly magazine. Emphasizes data communications. Readers are men in middle management positions. Circ. 70,000.

Photo Needs: Uses 8 photos/issue; 40-50% supplied by freelance photographers. Needs photos of people, still life, industry-related equipment or processes. Model release and photo captions required.

Making Contact & Terms: Provide resume, business card, brochure, flyer or tearsheets to be kept on file for possible assignments. Cannot return material. Reports in 2 weeks. Pays $1,000/color cover photo, $650/color inside photo, $650/color page rate, $250-350/day. Pays on acceptance. Credit line given. Buys one-time and international one-time rights.

DATAMATION MAGAZINE, 275 Washington St., Newton MA 02158-1630. (617)558-4682. Art Director: Christopher Lewis. Biweekly magazine. Emphasizes data processing for professionals—computers. Readers are the professionals in data processing. Circ. 165,000. Sample copy $3.

Photo Needs: Uses 5 photos/issue; all supplied by freelance photographers. Special needs include special effects. Model release required. Also hires photojournalists to take pictures of people in the business. Pays ½ day rates of $200, day rates of $350.

Making Contact & Terms: Arrange a personal interview to show portfolio; query with samples; submit portfolio for review; provide resume, business card, brochure, flyer or tearsheets to be kept on file for possible future assignments. Pays $1,000/b&w and color cover photo; $500/b&w and color page. Pays on acceptance. Credit line given. Buys one-time rights and international rights. Simultaneous submissions OK.

Tips: Prefers to see special effects and still life.

*DEFENSE SCIENCE MAGAZINE, 300 Orchard City Dr. Suite 124, Campbell CA 95008. (408)370-3509. Assistant Managing Editor: Laura M. Lukas. Monthly magazine. Emphasizes aerospace and defense industry. Readers are mostly male, middle-aged, top-level decision makers in the defense industry—Congress, White House, military commanders and defense company CEOs. Circ. 60,000. Estab. 1982. Sample copy for $1. No photo guidelines.

Photo Needs: Uses 8-10 photos/issue; 10-15% supplied by freelancers. Needs photos of high-tech, computer generated, simulation, aerospace-related—planes and space. Model release preferred; photo captions required.

Making Contact & Terms: Send 8×10 color prints, 35mm, 4×5 transparencies by mail for consideration. Provide resume, business card, brochure, flyer or tearsheets to be kept on file for possible assignments. SASE. Reports in 1-2 weeks. Payment varies. Pays on publication. Credit line given. Buys one-time rights. Will consider previously published work.

DENTAL ECONOMICS, Box 3408, Tulsa OK 74101. (918)835-3161. Editor: Dick Hale. Monthly magazine. Circ. 100,000. Emphasizes dental practice administration—how to handle staff, patients and bookkeeping and how to handle personal finances for dentists. Photos purchased with or without accompanying ms, or on assignment. Buys 20 photos/year. Pays $50-150/job, $75-400 for text/photo package, or on a per-photo basis. Credit line given. Pays in 30 days. Buys all rights, but may reassign to photographer after publication. Send material by mail for consideration. SASE. Reports in 2-4 weeks. Free sample copy; photo guidelines for SASE.

Subject Needs: Celebrity/personality, head shot, how-to, photo essay/photo feature, special effects/experimental and travel. No consumer-oriented material.

B&W: Uses 8×10 glossy prints. Pays $5-15/photo.

Color: Uses 35mm or 2¼×2¼ transparencies. Pays $35-50/photo.

Cover: "No outsiders here. Art/painting."

Accompanying Mss: "We use an occasional 'lifestyle' article, and the rest of the mss relate to the business side of a practice: scheduling, collections, consultation, malpractice, peer review, closed panels, capitation, associates, group practice, office design, etc." Also uses profiles of dentists. Writer's guidelines for SASE.

Tips: "Write and think from the viewpoint of the dentist—not as a consumer or patient. If you know of a dentist with an unusual or very visual hobby, tell us about it. We'll help you write the article to accompany your photos. Query please."

DENTIST, Box 7573, Waco TX 76714. (817)776-9000. FAX: (817)776-9018. Editor: Mark Hartley. Published 9 times/year. Emphasizes dentistry. Readers are dental professionals. Circ. 140,000. Estab. 1985. Sample copy free with 11½×15 SASE.

Photo Needs: Uses 20 photos/issue; 10 supplied by freelance photographers. "Usually we require photos of dentists in a specific setting, avoiding, at all costs, simple shots of dentist treating patients in chair." Almost any photo that uniquely reflects dentistry is salable. Captions preferred.

Making Contact & Terms: Send unsolicited photos by mail for consideration; provide resume, brochure, flyer or tearsheets to be kept on file for possible future assignments. Send 35mm color slides by mail for consideration. SASE. Reports in 3 weeks. Pays $100-150/color cover photo; $50-100/b&w inside photo; $150-250/color inside photo; $200-300/photo text package. Pays on acceptance. Credit line given.

Tips: "We are relying more on photographers who work on assignment. Send a business card and cover letter, so we can call if there's an assignment in your area. Otherwise, submit unusual portrayals of dentistry for our consideration. Most photos we publish are environmental portraits of dentists quoted in related articles. When reviewing samples, we look at the 'people' in photos to see if photographers work well with their subjects. We're leaning toward 'feature, human interest' shots, rather than posing a dentist in his operatory. Send a letter with address and phone number. If there's an assignment in the area, we'll call."

*DESIGN & COST DATA, 8602 N. 40th St., Tampa FL 33604. (813)989-9300. Managing Editor: Melissa Wells. Bimonthly trade magazine. Covers architecture and architectural design. Readers are architects, specifiers, designers, builders; both male and female, students and professionals. Circ. 15,000. Estab. 1958. Sample copy free with 11 × 14 SAE with $2.00 postage.

Photo Needs: Uses 15-20 photos/issue; 30% supplied by freelancers. Needs architectural photos, including newly completed buildings and newly renovated structures. Permissions and names of architect and building owner required. Also, photo captions required.

Making Contact & Terms: Send unsolicited b&w or color prints, glossy, any format; also send any format transparencies. SASE. Reports in 1 month. Pays $100/color cover photo; $75/color inside photo; $35/b&w inside photo. Pays on publication. Credit line given. Buys one-time rights. Simultaneous submissions and previously published work OK.

DESIGN FOR PEOPLE, 4129 42nd East Ave., Tulsa OK 74145. (918)622-3730. Managing Editor: Leslie Fala. Published 6 times each year. Circ. 15,000. Emphasizes floral design. Readers are "florist shop owners, managers, designers, floral service advertisers, (refrigeration, gift accessories)." Sample copy $7.

Photo Needs: Uses about 35-40 photos/issue; 2 supplied by freelance photographers. Needs photos of "events significant to floral industry (designs for prominent weddings), and how-to (series of shots describing innovative designs." Model release preferred; captions required.

Making Contact & Terms: Send color prints, 2¼ × 2¼ transparencies or color negatives by mail for consideration. SASE. Reports in 1 month. Pay "negotiable." Pays on acceptance. Credit line given. Buys all rights. Simultaneous submissions and previously published work OK.

Tips: "Be innovative, suggest new angles for articles that accompany photos, mss are not necessary— just the idea. Use photos involving Florafax members."

DIRECT MARKETING MAGAZINE, 224 Seventh St., Garden City NY 11530. (516)746-6700. Editor: Elaine Santoro. Monthly. Emphasizes direct mail, catalogs, telemarketing, building databases of customers and prospects for all kinds of businesses. Reader are marketers of all kinds—creative (copywriters, designers) and statisticians. Circ. 20,000. Sample copy free with 9 × 12 SASE.

Photo Needs: Uses about 20-40 photos/issue; 1-5 supplied by freelance photographers. Needs portraits for cover stories. Model release required; captions preferred.

Making Contact & Terms: Arrange a personal interview to show portfolio; query with resume of credits; provide resume, business card, brochure, brochure, flyer or tearsheets to be kept on file for possible future assignments. SASE. Reports in 2 weeks. Pays $200-300/color cover photo. Pays on publication. Credit line given. Buys one-time rights.

Tips: Prefers to see "ability to capture a subject's personality; getting drama into photos; making otherwise dull corporate subjects vital and engaging."

DISTRIBUTOR, Suite 300, 651 W. Washington, Chicago IL 60606. (312)993-0929. Editorial Director: Steve Read. Published 12 times/year. Circ. 14,000. Emphasizes heating, air conditioning, ventilating and refrigeration. Readers are wholesalers. Sample copy $4.

Photo Needs: Uses about 12 photos/issue; 1-2 supplied by freelance photographers. Needs photos pertaining to the wholesaling of heating, air conditioning, ventilating and refrigeration. Special needs include cover photos of interior and exteriors of wholesaling businesses. Model release and captions required.

Making Contact & Terms: Query with list of stock photo subjects; "query on needs of publications." SASE. Reports in 2 weeks. Pays $100-250/color cover photo; $10/b&w and $25/color inside photo. Pays on publication. Credit line given. Buys one-time rights. Simultaneous and previously published submissions OK "if not within industry."

DIXIE CONTRACTOR, Box 280, Decatur GA 30031. (404)377-2683. Editor: Steve Hudson. Biweekly magazine. Circ. 10,000. Emphasizes news of the heavy construction field in Alabama, Florida, Georgia, South Carolina and eastern Tennessee. Our magazine is read by heavy construction contractors, public officials, architects, engineers, construction equipment manufacturers and dealers. We buy first North American serial rights. Pays on publication. Reports in 2 weeks. Free sample copy and guidelines for 9×12 SAE and 8 first class stamps.
Subject Needs: "Currently, our greatest photo needs are for shots of construction jobs in progress. Strong preference is given to photo/manuscript packages."
B&W: Uses 5×7 or 8×10 glossy prints with ample margins.
Color: Editorial color is used on front cover only. We prefer 35mm or larger format transparencies. Pays $50 up for cover use.
Tips: "Our readers are interested in the overall job, in the machinery being used to complete it, and in innovative techniques that may be employed. If you can show that in a clear and visually interesting way, you'll catch our eye. When shooting photos for *Dixie Contractor*, remember to record details of what you're shooting—name of contractor and location of job, type and manufacturer of machine, etc. Given the choice, we prefer to see a manuscript/photo package. Write or call us with ideas. We're glad to discuss them with you."

DOMESTIC ENGINEERING MAGAZINE, 400 N. Michigan Ave., Chicago IL 60611. (312)222-2000. Editor: Stephen J. Shafer. Monthly magazine. Circ. 40,000. Emphasizes plumbing, heating, air conditioning and piping; also gives information on management marketing and merchandising. For contractors, executives and entrepreneurs. "For photos without stories, we could use a few very good shots of mechanical construction—piping, industrial air conditioning, etc.," but most photos purchased are with stories. Buys 5 photos/issue. Rights purchased are negotiable. Submit model release with photo. Send contact sheet for consideration. Pays on acceptance. Reports in 2 weeks. SASE. Simultaneous submissions and previously published work OK.
B&W: Uses 5×7 glossy prints; send contact sheet. Captions required. Pays $10-100.
Color: Uses 8×10 glossy prints or transparencies; send contact sheet. Captions required. Pays $10-100.
Cover: Uses glossy b&w prints, glossy color prints or color transparencies; send contact sheet. Captions required. Pays $50-125.

***DRYCLEANERS NEWS**, 70 Edwin Ave., Waterbury CT 06722. (203)755-0158. Editor: Ed Easley. Monthly tabloid. Emphasizes drycleaning. Readers are owners of drycleaning plants. Circ. 10,000. Estab. 1950. Sample copy free for 11×14 SAE and 8 first-class stamps.
Photo Needs: Uses 30 photos/issue. Needs photos of how-to and profiles. Model release preferred. Photo captions required.
Making Contact & Terms: Query with list of stock photo subjects. SASE. Reports in 3 weeks. Pays $50/color inside photo; $25/color page rate. Pays on publication. Credit line given. Buys one-time rights. Simultaneous submissions and previously published work OK "so long as we know where it's going and where it's been."
Tips: "Make your submission clear. Too many hit the trash because we don't get a query or SASE."

EARNSHAW'S REVIEW, Room 1212, 225 W. 34th St., New York NY 10001. (212)563-2742. Art Director: Michaele Staikas. Monthly. Emphasizes children's wear. Readers are buyers of children's apparel for specialty and department stores. Circ. 10,000.
Photo Needs: Uses about 30 photos/issue; all supplied by freelance photographers. Needs photos of "children in various settings (holiday, swimming, springtime, active, back-to-school, birthday parties, etc.)." Model release required.
Making Contact & Terms: Arrange a personal interview to show portfolio. Pays $250/color cover photo; $1,800-2,000/day. Pays on publication. Credit line given. Buys one-time rights. Simultaneous and previously published submissions OK.
Tips: "Do not mail any original work unless specifically requested. We hire only after portfolio review and a personal interview."

EDUCATION WEEK, Suite 250, 4301 Connecticut Ave. N.W., Washington DC 20008. (202)364-4114. Editor-in-Chief: Ronald A. Wolk. Photo Editor: Lisa Jennings. Weekly. Circ. 55,000. Emphasizes elementary and secondary education.
Photo Needs: Uses about 8 photos/issue; all supplied by freelance photographers. Model release preferred; captions required.
Making Contact & Terms: Query with samples. Provide resume and tearsheets to be kept on file for possible future assignments. Does not return unsolicited material. Reports in 2 weeks. Pays $50-250/ job; $50-300 for text/photo package. Pays on acceptance. Credit line given. Buys all rights. Simultaneous submissions and previously published work OK.

*ELECTRICAL APPARATUS, Barks Publications, Inc., 400 N. Michigan Ave., Chicago IL 60611-4198. (312)321-9440. Associate Publisher: Elsie Dickson. Monthly magazine. Circ. 16,000. Emphasizes industrial electrical machinery maintenance and repair for the electrical aftermarket. Readers are "persons engaged in the application, maintenance and servicing of industrial and commercial electrical and electronic equipment." Photos purchased with accompanying ms or on assignment. Credit line given. Pays on publication. Buys all rights, but "exceptions to this are occasionally made." Query with resume of credits. SASE. Reports in 3 weeks. Sample copy $4.
Subject Needs: "Assigned materials only. We welcome innovative industrial photography, but most of our material is staff-prepared." Model release required when requested; captions preferred.
Specs: Contact sheet or contact sheet and negatives OK. Pays $25-100/b&w or color photo.

ELECTRONIC BUSINESS, 275 Washington St., Newton MA 02158. (617)964-3030. FAX: (617)964-7136. Art Director: Michael Roach. Assistant Art Director: Carla Leeder. Biweekly. Emphasizes the electronic industry. Readers are CEO's, managers and top executives. Circ. 70,000.Estab. 1974.
Photo Needs: Uses 25-30 photos/issue; all supplied by freelancers; assignment-98%, stock-2%. Needs photos of corporate—people shots. Captions required.
Making Contact & Terms: Arrange a personal interview to show portfolio; provide resume, business card, brochure, flyer or tearsheets to be kept on file for possible future assignments. Does not return unsolicited material. Pays $50-250/b&w photo; $200-500/color photo; $50-100/hour; $500-800/day; $200-500/photo/text package. Pays on acceptance. Credit line given. Buys one-time rights. Simultaneous submissions and previously published work OK.
Tips: In photographer's portfolio looks for corporate location portraits.

EMERGENCY, The Journal of Emergency Services, 6300 Yarrow Dr., Carlsbad CA 92009. (619)438-2511. FAX: (619)931-5809. Editor: Tara Regan. Monthly magazine. Circ. 30,000. Emphasizes pre-hospital emergency medical and rescue services for paramedics, EMTs, firefighters, to keep them informed of latest developments in the emergency medical services field. Photos purchased with or without accompanying ms. Buys 50-75 photos/year; 5 photos/issue. Pays for mss/photo package, or on a per-photo basis. Credit line given. Pays on acceptance. Buys all rights, "nonexclusive." Sample copy $5.00.
Photo Needs: Documentary, photo essay/photo feature and spot news dealing with pre-hospital emergency (EMS) medicine. Needs shots to accompany unillustrated articles submitted and cover photos; year's calendar of themes forwarded on request with #10 SASE. Try to get close to the action; both patient and emergency personnel should be visible. Captions required and should include the name, city and state of the emergency rescue team and medical treatment being rendered in photo. Also needs color transparencies for "Action," a photo department dealing with emergency personnel in action.
Making Contact & Terms: Uses 5×7 or 8×10 glossy prints. Pays $30/photo. For color: Uses 35mm or larger transparencies. Pays $30/photo.For cover: Prefers 35mm; 2¼×2¼ transparencies OK. Vertical format preferred. Pays $100/photo. Send material by mail for consideration, especially action shots of EMTs/paramedics in action. SASE
Accompanying Mss: Instructional, descriptive or feature articles dealing with emergency medical services. Pays $100-300/ms.
Tips: Wants well-composed photos with good overall scenes and clarity that say more than "an accident happened here." "We're going toward single-focus uncluttered photos," Looking for more color photos for articles. "Good closeups of actual treatment. Also, sensitive illustrations of the people in EMS—stress, interacting with family/pediatrics etc. We're interested in rescuers, and our readers like to see their peers in action, demonstrating their skills. Mfake sure photo is presented with treatment rendered and people involved. Prefer model release if possible."

EMPLOYEE ASSISTANCE, 225 N. New Rd., Waco TX 76710. (817)776-9000. FAX: (817)776-9018. Editor: Paul Walker. Monthly magazine. Emphasizes problems in the workplace (substance abuse, stress, health issues, AIDS, drug testing). Readers are personnel directors and employee assistance consultants, both men and women, 30-60 years of age. Circ. 21,000. Estab. 1988. Sample copy free upon request.
Photo Needs: Uses approximately 6 photos/issue; 50-75% of all art is freelance. Needs "concept" shots relating to subjects featured, corporate image photos, plus portrait-style photos for featured individuals. Model release required; photo captions preferred.
Making Contact & Terms: Query with list of stock photo subjects or send unsolicited photos by mail for consideration. Provide resume, business card, brochure, flyer or tearsheets to be kept on file for possible assignments. Uses 35mm or 2¼×2¼ transparencies. SASE. Reports in 2 weeks. Pays $50-200/b&w photo; $75-200/color photo; $15-50/hour; $250/photo/text package; $400/cover art/photos. Pays on publication. Credit line given. Buys first N.A. serial rights. Does not consider simultaneous submissions or previously published work.

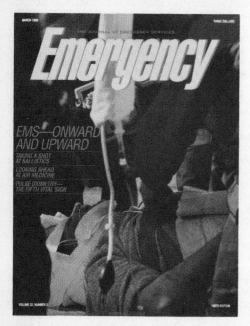

"I often send unsolicited chromes of firefighters and Emergency Service personnel to Emergency magazine," says photographer Robert DeMartin. When DeMartin first sent this color photo to photo editor Rhonda Foster, she purchased it from him as stock, for $30. Then, she decided it would make a high-impact cover and paid the photographer another $70 for one-time use. The appeal of the image, says DeMartin, is in the "action, drama and illustration of patient care by EMS personnel."

Tips: Looks for "Health, nursing, counseling, human resources and wellness programs that are people oriented. Health and wellness promotion is a hot item in our magazine, we look for art to portray this; photographs of people or of concepts.

*ENGINEERED SYSTEMS, 7314 Hart St., Mentor OH 44060. (216)255-6264. Editor: Robert L. Schwed. Bimonthly magazine. Emphasizes heating, air conditioning and refrigeration design, installation, operation. Readers are industry, engineers, contracters, building owners and operators. Sample copy $5.
Photo Needs: Uses 20 photos/issue; some occasionally supplied by freelance photographers. Needs photos of action and installation shots, people, some product shots.
Making Contact & Terms: Send inquiry by mail for consideration. SASE. Pay negotiated. Pays on publication. Credit line given. Buys one-time rights. Simultaneous submissions OK if exclusive to trade.

EUROPE MAGAZINE, Suite 707, 2100 M St. NW, Washington DC 20037. (202)862-9500. Managing Editor: Anke Middelmann. Magazine published 10 times/year. Circ. 25,000. Covers the European Common Market with "in-depth news articles on topics such as economics, trade, US-EC relations, industry, development and East-West relations." Readers are "businessmen, professionals, academic, government officials." Free sample copy.
Photo Needs: Uses about 20-30 photos/issue, most of which are supplied by stock houses and freelance photographers. Needs photos of "current news coverage and sectors, such as economics, trade, small business, people, transport, politics, industry, agriculture, fishing, some culture, some travel. Each issue we have an overview article on one of the 12 countries in the Common Market. For this we need a broad spectrum of photos, particularly color, in all sectors. If a photographer queries and lets us know what he has on hand, we might ask him to submit a selection for a particular story. For example, if he has slides or b&w's on a certain European country, if we run a story on that country, we might ask him to submit slides on particular topics, such as industry, transport or small business." Model release and captions not required; identification necessary.
Making Contact & Terms: Send query with list of stock photo subjects. Initially, a list of countries/topics covered will be sufficient. SASE. Reports in 3-4 weeks. Pays on publication $75-150/b&w photo; $100 minimum/color transparency for inside, $400 for front cover; per job negotiable. Credit line given. Buys one-time rights. Simultaneous and previously published submissions OK.

Tips: "For certain articles, especially the Member State Reports, we are now using more freelance material than previously. Good photo and color quality, not too touristic a shot, agriculture or industry if possible."

EXCAVATING CONTRACTOR, Suite 204, 26011 Evergreen Rd., Southfield MI 48076. (313)358-4900. Editor/Publisher: Andrew J. Cummins. Monthly. Circ. 26,000. Emphasizes earthmoving/small business management. Readers are owner/operator excavating contractors. Will send sample copy and photo guidelines.
Photo Needs: Uses 20 photos/issue; 2-3 are supplied by freelance photographers. "We'll use a freelance photographer, especially for covers, if it is better than we can obtain elsewhere. Usually receive photos from equipment manufacturers and their hired guns of a very high quality, but if a freelancer submits a quality photo, one that not only features an easily identifiable machine hard at work, but also some nice mountains or water in the background, it will be considered at the discretion of the publisher. Prominent credit line given. Vertical shots are a must." Photos must be of small work sites since readers are small contracting businesses. Captions preferred.
Making Contacts & Terms: Send material by mail for consideration. Uses 5×7 and 8×10 b&w and color prints, 2¼×2¼ slides and contact sheets. SASE. Reports in 2 weeks. Pays $75/color cover; $25/ color inside; $25-100 for text/photo package. Credit line given. Payment on publication. Buys all rights. Simultaneous and previously published work OK, but "please tell when and where work was published."
Tips: "We are using photography more than ever."

*EXPORT TODAY MAGAZINE, 733 15th St. NW Suite 1100, Washington DC 20005. (202)737-1060. FAX: (202)783-5966. Photo Editor: Julianne LeMense. 9 issues per year. Emphasizes exporting and international finance. Readers are upper management and CEO's of small to mid-size exporting firms. Circ. 23,000. Estab. 1985. Sample copy for $5 and #12 SASE.
Photo Needs: Uses 8-10 photos/issue. Needs photos of industry, infrastructure and technology. Special photo needs include European and Eastern European photos. Model release and photo captions preferred.
Making Contact & Terms: Query with list of stock photo subjects. Provide resume, business card, brochure, flyer or tearsheets to be kept on file for possible assignments. Reports in 3 weeks. Price negotiated per item. Pays on publication. Credit line given. Buys one-time rights. Will consider simultaneous submissions.
Tips: "We look for a very specific type of photo—business related and 'non-touristy'. Photo submissions, if appropriate, have an excellent chance of being published."

FARM CHEMICALS, 37841 Euclid Ave., Willoughby OH 44094. (216)942-2000. Editorial Director: Charlotte Sine. Editor: Parry Klassen. Emphasizes application and marketing of fertilizers and protective chemicals for crops for those in the farm chemical industry. Monthly magazine. Circ. 32,000. Needs agricultural scenes. Buys 6-7 photos/year. Not copyrighted. Query first with resume of credits. Pays on acceptance. Reports in 3 weeks. SASE. Simultaneous submissions and previously published work OK. Free sample copy and photo guidelines with 8½×11 SAE.
B&W: Uses 8×10 glossy prints. Captions required.
Color: Uses 8×10 glossy prints or transparencies.

FARM INDUSTRY NEWS, Webb Division Intertec Publishing, 1999 Shepard Rd., St. Paul MN 55116. (612)690-7292. Editor: Joseph Degnan. Graphics Editor: Lynn Varpness. Published 11 times/year. Circ. 270,000. Emphasizes "agriculture product news; making farmers better buyers." Readers are "high-volume farm operators." Sample copy free with SASE.
Photo Needs: Freelancers supply "very few photos, usually cover shots." Needs photos of "large acreage midwestern farms, up-to-date farm equipment, livestock, crops, farmshows, farm electronics, haying and chemical application." Model release required; captions preferred.
Making Contact & Terms: Query with samples or with list of stock photo subjects; send 35mm, 2¼×2¼, 4×5 or 8×10 transparencies by mail for consideration. SASE. Reports in 1 month. Payment per color cover photo negotiable. Pays on publication. Buys first publication rights.
Tips: Prefers "2¼×2¼ or larger format cover and feature material transparencies of *up-to-date* large farm operations, crops, scenics and action photos of newer farm equipment in the field."

FARM JOURNAL, INC., 230 W Washington Square, Philadelphia PA 19105. (215)829-4865. Editor: Earl Ainsworth. Photo Editor: Tom Dodge. Monthly magazine. Circ. 800,000. Emphasizes the business of agriculture: "Good farmers want to know what their peers are doing and how to make money marketing their products." Photos purchased with or without accompanying ms. Freelancers supply 60% of the photos. Pays by assignment or $125-350 for photos; more for covers. Credit line given. Pays on acceptance. Buys one-time rights,"but this is negotiable." Model release required. Arrange a personal interview or send photos by mail. Provide calling card and samples to be kept on file for possible future assignments. SASE. Simultaneous submissions OK. Reports in 1 week/1 month. Free sample copy upon request.

Subject Needs: Photos having to do with the basics of raising, harvesting and marketing of all the farm commodities. People-oriented shots are encouraged. Also uses human interest and interview photos. All photos must relate to agriculture. Captions are required.

B&W: Uses 8×10 or 11×14 glossy or semigloss prints. Pays $25-100 depending on size used.

Color: Uses 35mm or $2\frac{1}{4} \times 2\frac{1}{4}$ transparencies or prints. Pays $100-200 depending on size used.

Cover: Uses color transparencies, all sizes.

Tips: "Be original, take time to see with the camera. Be more selective, take more shots to submit. Take as many different angles of subject as possible. Use fill where needed. We also publish five titles—*Farm Journal*, *Top Producer* (photo editor is Tom Dodge), *Hogs Today*, *Beef Today*, *Dairy Today* (photo editor is Greg Lamp—(612)631-3151)."

FARM STORE MERCHANDISING, Suite 160, 12400 Whitwater Dr., Minnetonka MN 55343. (612)931-0211. Editor: Jan Johnson. Monthly magazine. Emphasizes retailing in agribusiness. Readers are feed, grain, animal health, fertilizer and chemical dealers. Circ. 35,000. Sample copy free with SASE.

Photo Needs: Uses 20 photos/issue; 2 supplied by freelance photographers. Needs photos of marketing, merchandising applications and agribusiness sales shots. Model release preferred; captions required.

Making Contact & Terms: Query with list of stock photo subjects. SASE. Reports in 1 month. Pays $25/b&w inside photo; $50/inside color photo; $25-200/job; $100-300/text/photo package. Pays on publication. Credit line given. Buys one-time rights.

THE FARMER/THE DAKOTA FARMER, 7900 International Drive, Suite 300, Minneapolis MN 55425. (612)851-4650. Editor: Tom Doughty. Published 19 times/year. Emphasizes agriculture in Minnesota, Dakotas. Readers are farmers. Circ. 120,000. Estab. 1882. Sample copy free with 11x13 SASE.

Photo Needs: Needs cover photos of farm scenes, preferably set in Upper Midwest. Model release preferred; captions required.

Making Contact & Terms: Query with samples and list of stock photo subjects. Uses 35mm transparencies. SASE. Reports in 2 weeks. Pays $200/color cover photo. Pays on acceptance. Credit line given. Buys one-time rights. Simultaneous submissions OK.

Tips: Looks for cover photos.

FIRE CHIEF MAGAZINE, 307 N. Michigan Ave., Chicago IL 60601. (312)726-7277. Editor: William Randleman. Monthly magazine. Circ. 42,000. Emphasizes administrative problem solving for management in the fire protection field. For municipal, district and county fire chiefs. Needs cover photos of "big fires with fire departments in action and fire chiefs or other officers in action at a fire. Also, photos in connection with feature articles." Buys 12 photos/year. Credit line given. Buys all rights, but may reassign to photographer after publication. Send photos for consideration. Photos purchased with accompanying ms; cover photos purchased separately. Pays 2 weeks after publication. Reports in 1 month. SASE. Free sample copy and photo guidelines.

Making Contact & Terms: Send 5×7 or 8×10 glossy b&w or color prints; 35mm color transparencies. Captions required. Pays $10 maximum/inside photo. Pays $50 minimum/cover.

FIREHOUSE MAGAZINE, 210 Crossways Park Drive, Woodbury NY 11797. (516)496-8000. FAX: (516)496-8013. Executive Editor: Thomas Rahilly. Art Director: Michael Delia. Monthly. Circ. 110,000. Estab. 1973. Emphasizes "firefighting—notable fires, techniques, dramatic fires and rescues, etc." Readers are "paid and volunteer firefighters, EMT's." Sample copy $3 with $8\frac{1}{2} \times 11$ SAE and approximately $1.65 postage; photo guidelines free with SASE.

Photo Needs: Uses about 30 photos/issue; 20 supplied by freelance photographers. Needs photos in the above subject areas. Model release preferred.

Making Contact & Terms: Send 8×10 matte or glossy b&w or color prints; 35mm, $2\frac{1}{4} \times 2\frac{1}{4}$, 4×5, 8×10 transparencies or b&w or color negatives with contact sheet by mail for consideration. "Photos must not be more than 30 days old." SASE. Reports ASAP. Pays $200/color cover photo; $15-250/b&w photo; $15-250/color photo. Pays on publication. Credit line given. Buys one-time rights.

Tips: "Mostly we are looking for action-packed photos—The more fire, the better the shot. Show firefighters in full gear, do not show spectators. Fire safety is a big concern." Much of our photo work is freelance. "Try to be in the right place at the right time as the fire occurs."

FLOORING, 7500 Old Oak Blvd., Cleveland OH 44130. (216)243-8100. FAX: (216)826-2832. Editor: Mark S. Kuhar. Monthly magazine. Emphasizes floor covering and other interior surfacing for floor covering retailers, contractors and distributors. Circ. 25,000. Estab. 1931.

Close-up

Mike Delia
Art Director
Firehouse Magazine
New York City

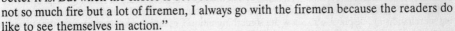

As art director for *Firehouse*, the East Coast-based magazine of firefighting, Mike Delia helps to bring the world of
fire to life for its readers every month.

"We're looking for *lots* of fire," says Delia, noting that
most of the readers are volunteer firemen and fire buffs.
"The bigger the fire, the more firemen in the picture, the
better it is. But when the choice is between a lot of fire and
not so much fire but a lot of firemen, I always go with the firemen because the readers do
like to see themselves in action."

Since some 90 percent of the readers are male, Delia accordingly gears his design and
photo picks to men. "In reality," he says, "fire is a horrible subject, but there's a certain
sensational appeal with it. So, if it's a fire shot, it's got to be dramatic."

Fire photography is intensely fascinating to those who pursue it, says Delia. "Since we
don't have the staff to do these shots, we depend a lot on unsolicited photos," he says,
noting that writers often supply their own photos. Payment, he adds, is still separate, and
based on size and placement. "Luckily, the people who send us stuff are really dedicated
to the field and publication. It's like a big fraternity."

Though this doesn't exclude other photographers from working with *Firehouse*, Delia
explains, the best images often come from being inside, where the action is. "A lot of
volunteer firemen carry cameras around with them and they get 'right in there' while a
fire's in progress," he says, pointing out that certification is necessary for shooting behind
the scenes. Anyone can apply to their local police and fire departments for the special
press card. But as he adds, even firemen find "it's very, very hard to get."

Notably, Delia says, *Firehouse* holds the top subscription rates and readership out of
several fire publications. Because of this enviable position, he explains, the magazine strives
to be first with its stories and photos. When submitting photos to *Firehouse*, always keep
newsworthiness and exclusivity in mind, Delia advises. "If the photo's been published
elsewhere, we won't do it."

Prior to coming to *Firehouse* in mid-1986, Delia was more accustomed to studio setups
and styling in his previous work as art director and food photographer for *Restaurant
Business*. Now, he never shoots his subject, and rarely, because of the magazine's journalistic treatment of fire-related events, does he ever run "set-up" shots of fires.

Occasionally, personality pieces and special theme issues, such as those dealing with
rescue and emergency medical technicians (EMT's), provide some opportunities for portraiture and lighted-interior shots. "Once in a while, we use studio-type shots," he says.
"In fact, one of my favorite projects which we assigned to a freelancer was a portrait of a
new fire chief. It was a black-and-white shot, very dramatic with harsh lighting. It definitely
captured his personality."

Photographers especially interested in portraiture of fire professionals should take note
of a recently-introduced trade journal, *Chief Fire Executive*. Since PTN Publications, the

parent company of *Firehouse*, is also behind this new title, Delia also handles its art direction.

As Delia has indicated, content and newsworthiness are always important, but striking composition is especially critical for pictures to make it into print. "I'm always looking for shots that have impact—a dramatic angle, interesting light and shadow, something going on in them," he says. He has recently been tending toward more "bleed" shots, which generally are vertical. But, vertical or horizontal, the photos that otherwise meet *Firehouse*'s visual needs will be right at home. "If I like a shot," he says confidently, "I'll make it work."

—Sam A. Marshall

Photo Needs: Uses about 25-30 photos/issue; "a few" supplied by freelance photographers. Stock photos are rarely purchased. Needs photos "to illustrate various articles—mostly showroom shots." Model release and captions preferred.
Making Contact & Terms: Prefers query with samples. Provide resume, business card, brochure, flyer or tearsheets to be kept on file for possible future assignments. SASE. Pay varies; $5/b&w photo; $5-50/color photo; $5-$50/photo/text. Pays on acceptance. Buys all rights.
Tips: "We are finding a great need to expand our contacts among photographers across the country, especially those available for simple, local assignments (general assignments). Looking for people with demonstrated abilities with 35mm cameras; prefer photojournalists. Wants showroom shots emphasizing merchandising, displays, etc. Show me something unique, creative product shots in settings (nothing that looks like *Home & Garden* magazine). Get on file. We may need someone in your area soon. Can you do the impossible in record time?"

*THE FLORIDA SPECIFIER, 385 W. Fairbanks Ave. Suite 300, Winter Park FL 32789. (407)740-7950. Publisher/President: Duane Williams. Monthly tabloid. Emphasizes engineering, construction, environmental, wastewater and design-architectural. Readers are ages 40-50's, males, (manager, design-specification). Circ. 38,000. Estab. 1979. Sample copy free for SASE. No photo guidelines.
Photo Needs: Uses 15-25 photos/issue; approximately 20-25% supplied by freelance photographers. Needs photos of technology, construction, (highway, building) environmental, water and wastewater. Special photo needs include roofing, pipes and tanks, geosynthetics, asbestos, abatement and stormwater control. Model release and photo captions preferred.
Making Contact & Terms: Query with list of stock photo subjects. SASE. Reports in 1 month. Payment negotiable. Pays on publication. Credit line given. Simultaneous submissions and previously published work OK.
Tips: "Become familiar with publications format and get a feel for the types of photos they look for and an understanding of subject matter."

FLORIDA UNDERWRITER, Suite 115, 1345 S. Missouri Ave., Clearwater FL 34616. (813)442-9189. Editor: James E. Seymour. Monthly magazine. Emphasizes insurance. Readers are insurance professionals in Florida. Circ. 10,000. Estab. 1984. Sample copy free with 8½×11½ SASE.
Photo Needs: Uses 10-12 photos/issue; 1-2 supplied by freelance photographers;80% assignment and 20% freelance stock. Needs photos of insurance people, subjects, meetings and legislators. Photo captions preferred.
Making Contact & Terms: Query first with list of stock photo subjects, send b&w prints, 35mm, 2¼×2¼, 4×5, 8×10 transparencies by mail for consideration; provide resume, business card, brochure, flyer or tearsheets to be kept on file for possible assignments. SASE. Reports in 3 weeks. Pays $50-150/b&w cover photo; $15-35/b&w inside photo; $5-20/color page rate. Pays on publication. Credit line given. Buys all rights; will negotiate with a photographer unwilling to sell all rights. Simultaneous submissions and previously published work OK (admission of same required).

FORD NEW HOLLAND NEWS, P.O. Box 1895, New Holland PA 17557. (717)355-1276. Editor: Gary Martin. Published 8 times/year. Circ. 400,000. Estab. 1960. Emphasizes agriculture. Readers are farm families. Sample copy and photo guidelines free with 8½×11 SASE.
Photo Needs: Buys 30 photos/year of scenic agriculture relating to the seasons, harvesting, farm animals, farm management and farm people; 50% freelance photography/issue from assignment and 50% freelance stock. Need photo/article combination. Model release and captions required. "Collections viewed and returned quickly."

Making Contact & Terms: "Show us your work." SASE. Reports in 2 weeks. Pays $50-500/color photo, depends on use and quality of photo; $800-$1,500/photo/text package; $500/cover. Payment negotiable. Pays on acceptance. Buys first North American serial rights. Previously published work OK.

Tips: Photographers "must see beauty in agriculture and provide meaningful photojournalistic caption material to be successful here. It also helps to team up with a good agricultural writer and query us on a photojournalistic idea."

FUTURES MAGAZINE, Suite 1150, 250 S. Wacker Dr., Chicago IL 60606. (312)977-0999. Editor-in-chief: Darrell Jobman. International Editor: Ginger Szala. Monthly magazine. Emphasizes futures and options trading. Readers are individual traders, institutional traders, brokerage firms, exchanges. Circ. 70,000. Sample copy $4.50.

Photo Needs: Uses 12-15 photos/issue; 80% supplied by freelance photographers. Needs mostly personality portraits of story sources, some mug shots, trading floor environment. Model release required; captions preferred.

Making Contact & Terms: Arrange a personal interview to show portfolio; query with list of stock photo subjects; provide resume, business card, brochure, flyer or tearsheets to be kept on file for possible future assignments. SASE. Reports in 2 weeks. Pays $150/½ day minimum. Pays on publication. Buys all rights.

Tips: All work is on an assignment basis. Be competitive on price, shoot good work without excessive film use.

GARDEN SUPPLY RETAILER, 1 Chilton Way, Radnor PA 19089. (215)964-4000. Editor: Jan Brenny. Monthly. Emphasizes "all aspects of retail garden centers—products, displays, customers, employees, power equipment, green goods, holiday goods, service and repair of lawn equipment." Readers are retailers and dealers of garden and lawn supplies. Circ. 40,190. Sample copy free with SASE and 75¢ postage.

Photo Needs: Uses about 10-20 photos/issue; "very few if any" supplied by freelance photographers. Needs "photos depicting business at a retail garden center. Prefer people with products rather than products alone." Special needs include "photographing plants in garden centers located in various areas of the country (especially outside the upper Midwest)."

Making Contact & Terms: Query with samples; list of stock photo subjects; send 35mm transparencies, b&w contact sheets by mail for consideration; provide resume, business card, brochure, flyer or tearsheets to be kept on file for possible future assignments. SASE. Tries to report in 3 weeks. Pays $25/b&w photo; $50/color photo; $100/cover photo. Pays on publication. Credit line given only "in certain cases." Buys all rights.

Tips: Prefers to see "photos illustrating retailing in a garden center, or of interest to the magazine's audience. Know the audience of the magazine and photograph what would be of interest to them. Strive for simplicity in form, using natural, spontaneous shots, people going about daily business."

*GOLF INDUSTRY, 1450 NE 123 St., Miami FL 33161. (305)893-8771. FAX: (305)893-8793. Vice President Manufacturing/Editorial: James Kukar. Bimonthly. Emphasizes golf trade. Circ. 21,000. Estab. 1970. Sample copy for $2 and 9×12 SAE with 80¢ postage.

Photo Needs: Uses 20-30 photos/issue; all supplied by freelance photographers. Model release preferred; photo captions required. 75% from assignment; 25% from stock.

Making Contact & Terms: Query with list of stock photo subjects; submit portfolio for review. SASE. Reports in 1 month. Pays $25-150/b&w; $25-500/color; $25-100/hour; $250/1,250/day; and $100-1,500/photo/text package. Buys one-time rights; all rights. Will negotiate with photographer unwilling to sell all rights. Simultaneous submissions and previously published work OK.

GOLF SHOP OPERATIONS, Box 395, 5520 Park Ave., Trumbull CT 06611. (203)373-7235. Managing Editor: Chris Davidson. Magazine published 8 times a year. Circ. 14,000. Emphasizes "methods that would allow the golf professional to be a better businessman." For golf professionals and golf retailers employed at country clubs, public and municipal golf courses, golf specialty outlets. Most work done on assignment. Special needs: human interest shots, unusual golf shops or displays. Buys 15-20 shots/year. Buys one-time reproduction rights. Provide business card, flyer and tearsheets to be kept on file for possible future assignments. Send contact sheet for consideration. Reports in one month. Free sample copy and photo guidelines. Pays on acceptance.

B&W: Send contact sheet. Captions required. Pays $25-150 per shot.

Color: Send slides or color transparencies. Captions required. Pays $100-250 per shot.

GRAIN JOURNAL, 2490 N. Water Str., Decatur IL 62526. (217)877-9660. Editor: Mark Avery. Bimonthly. Also produces monthly newsletter. Emphasizes grain industry. Readers are "elevator managers primarily as well as suppliers and others in the industry." Circ. 11,822. Sample copy free with 10×12 SAE with 85¢ postage.

Photo Needs: Uses about 6 photos (but we want more)/issue. We need photos concerning industry practices and activities. Captions preferred.
Making Contact & Terms: Query with samples and list of stock photo subjects. SASE. Reports in 1 week. Pays $100/color cover photo; $30/b&w inside photo. Pays on publication. Credit line given. Buys all rights. Will negotiate with a photographer unwilling to sell all rights.

GROCERY DISTRIBUTION, 455 S. Frontage Rd. #116, Meadowbrook Court, Burr Ridge IL 60521. (708)986-8767. Editor/Publisher: Richard W. Mulville. Bimonthly. Emphasizes the warehousing and transportation function in the food industry. Readers are specifiers, purchasers and operators of industrial equipment and services for the food industry's warehousing/transportation function. Circ. 16,000. Free sample copy with 9×12 SAE with $1.25 postage. Free photo guidelines.
Photo Needs: Uses about 40 photos/issue; uses an estimate of 4-6 freelance photographers. Needs photos of equipment and facilities relating to food warehouses, delivery trucks, etc. "We suggest that freelancers contact us by letter or phone before going to the expense of sending unsolicited photos." Model release preferred; captions required.
Making Contact & Terms: Provide resume, business card, brochure, flyer or tearsheets to be kept on file for possible future assignments. SASE. Reports in 2 weeks. Pays lump sum for text/photo package (depends on assignment). Pays on assignment. Simultaneous submissions OK.

GROUND WATER AGE, 13 Century Hill Dr., Latham NY 12110. (518)783-1281. Editor: Tom Williams. Monthly magazine. Circ. 20,000. Estab. 1966. Emphasizes management, marketing and technical information. For water well drilling contractors, water pump specialists and monitoring well contractors. Buys all rights, but may reassign to photographer after publication. Send photos for consideration. Pays on acceptance. Reports in 3 weeks. SASE. Simultaneous submissions and previously published work OK. Free sample copy and photo guidelines.
Photo Needs: Needs picture stories and photos of water well drilling activity and pump installation. Buys 10-20 annually. Send 5×7 b&w matte prints. Color: send negatives, 8×10 matte prints or transparencies. Uses vertical format for covers. Payment negotiable.
Tips: "The market is wide open. There is a great need for quality photos of on-site, job-related activity in our industry. Many photo sites are in outdoor locations. Some familiarity with the industry would be helpful, of course." In photographer's samples, wants to see "an ability to capture interesting 'action' of a water well contractor, pump installer, or monitoring well contractor actually doing his/her job in the field." We have been actively improving the quality of our color cover shots. We'd appreciate more contributions from freelancers."

GROUP MAGAZINE, 2890 N. Monroe Ave., Box 481, Loveland CO 80539. (303)669-3836. FAX: (303)669-3269. Editorial Director: Joani Schultz. Art Director: Jan Aufdemberge. Eight issues/year. Circ. 57,000. Estab. 1974. For adult leaders of senior high and junior high church youth groups. Emphasizes Christian youth ministry activities, concerns and problems. Buys up to 10 freelance photos/issue. Credit line given. Pays on publication. Buys one-time and occasionally additional rights. Send material by mail for consideration with SASE. Simultaneous submissions and previously published work OK. Reports in 4 weeks. Sample copy with 9×12 SAE with $1 first class postage. Photo guidelines free with SASE.
Subject Needs: Uses mostly people photos—individual or small groups of adults, adults with teenagers, individual or groups of teenagers, youth group activities, families with teenagers in all kinds of settings and activities. Emphasis on ethnic and cultural diversity and a male/female balance. Model release is always preferred and sometimes required, depending on subject matter.
B&W: Uses 8×10 prints. Pays $25-50/photo, one-time inside editorial use.
Color: Uses 35mm or 2¼×2¼ color transparencies. Pays $50-150/photo, one-time inside editorial use. (Sometimes converts color to b&w, with photographer's permission.)
Cover: Uses 35mm or 2¼×2¼ color transparencies. Vertical format required. Pays $200 minimum/color photo.
Accompanying Mss: Seeks how-to feature articles on activities or projects involving high school students or Christian youth groups. Pays $100 minimum/ms. Writer's guidelines free with SASE.
Tips: "Photos must look contemporary and relate to, or be appropriate for, Christian teenagers and adults. Dated, obviously posed and poorly focused or exposed shots are typically rejected. We prefer candid, natural shots, if well-composed and sharp. We're also attracted to shots with an unusual perspective on a situation."

THE GROWING EDGE, 215 SW 2nd St., Box 2046, Corvallis OR 97333. (503)757-2511. FAX: (503)757-0028. Editor: Don Parker. Quarterly. Circ. 15,000. Estab. 1989. Emphasizes "high tech indoor and outdoor cultivation of flowers, herbs, vegetables using such techniques as hydroponics, halide lighting, carbon dioxide generators. Sample copy $6.50

Photo Needs: Uses about 10-15 photos per issue; most supplied with articles by freelance photographers. Needs "how-to, use of high tech aids in cultivation of legitimate crops." Model release required.
Making Contact & Terms: Query with samples. Send b&w or color prints; 4×5 transparencies, b&w color contact sheets or color negatives. SASE. Reports in 4-6 weeks or will notify and keep material on file for future use. Pays $50/color cover photo; $10-20/b&w inside photo; $25-30/color inside photo; $50-300/text/photo package. Pays on publication. Credit line given. Buys first and reprint rights. Simultaneous submissions and previously published work OK.
Tips: "Most photos are used to illustrate processes and equipment used in high-tech gardening." "Many of our photographers are of indoor plants under artificial lighting. The ability to deal with tricky lighting situations is important."

HEARTH & HOME, Box 2008, Village West, Laconia NH 03247. (603)528-4285. Editor: Ken Daggett. Monthly magazine. Emphasizes "wood heat and energy topics in general for manufacturers, retailers and distributors of wood stoves, fireplaces and other energy centers." Circ. 32,000. Sample copy $3.
Photo Needs: Uses about 30 photos/issue; 60% supplied by freelance photographers. Needs "shots of energy stores, retail displays, wood heat installations. Assignments available for interviews, conferences and out-of-state stories." Model release required; captions preferred.
Making Contact & Terms: Query with samples or list of stock photo subjects; send b&w or color glossy prints, transparencies, b&w contact sheets by mail for consideration. SASE. Reports in 2 weeks. Pays $50-100/b&w photo; $75-150/color photo. Pays on acceptance. Credit line given. Buys various rights. Simultaneous and photocopied submissions OK.
Tips: "Call and ask what we need. We're *always* on the lookout for material."

HEAVY DUTY TRUCKING, 1800 E. Deere Ave., Santa Ana CA 92705. (714)261-1636. Editor: Deborah Whistler. Trade publication. Monthly magazine. Emphasizes trucking. Readers are mostly male — corporate executives, fleet management, supervisors, salesmen and drivers — ages 30-65. Circ. 96,000. Photo guidelines free with SASE.
Photo Needs: Uses 30 photos/issue; 30-100% supplied by freelance photographers. Needs photos of scenics (trucks on highways) how-to (maintenance snap shots). Model release is "photographers responsibility." Photo captions preferred.
Making Contact & Terms: Query with resume of credits or send unsolicited photos by mail for consideration. Send 35mm transparencies. SASE. Sends check when material is used. Pays $150/color cover photo or $75/color or b&w inside photo. Pays on publication. Buys one-time rights. Does not consider simultaneous submissions or previously published work OK.

HEAVY TRUCK SALESMAN, 1800 E. Deere Ave., Santa Ana CA 92705. (714)261-1636. Managing Editor: Deborah Whistler. Trade publication. Bimonthly magazine. Emphasizes trucking. Readers are mostly male truck dealers and salesmen, ages 30-65. Circ. 15,000. Photo guidelines free with SASE.
Photo Needs: Uses 30 photos/issue; 30-100% supplied by freelance photographers. Needs photos of truck dealerships, truck salesmen with customers, scenics (trucks on highways) how-to (maintenance snapshots). Model release is "photographer's responsibility." Photo captions preferred.
Making Contact & Terms: Query with resume of credits or send unsolicited photos by mail for consideration. Send 35mm transparencies. SASE. Sends check when material is used. Pays $150/color cover photo or $75/color or b&w inside photo. Pays on publication. Buys one-time rights. Does not consider simultaneous submissions or previously published work.

HELICOPTER INTERNATIONAL, 75 Elm Tree Rd., Locking, Weston-S-Mare, Avon BS248EL England. (934)822524. Editor: E. apRees. Bimonthly magazine. Emphasizes helicopters and autogyros. Readers are helicopter professionals. Circ. 22,000. Sample copy £1.50 and A4 SASE.
Photo Needs: Uses 25-35 photos/issue; 50% supplied by freelance photographers. Needs photos of helicopters, especially newsworthy subjects. Model release preferred; photo captions required.
Making Contact & Terms: Send unsolicited photos by mail for consideration. Send b&w or color 8×10 or 4×5 gloss prints. Cannot return unsolicited material. Reports in 1 month. Pays $20/color cover photo or $5/b&w inside photo. Pays on publication. Credit line given. Buys one-time rights. Simultaneous submissions or previously published work OK.
Tips: Magazine is growing. To break in, submit "newsworthy pictures. No arty-crafty pix; good clear shots of helicopters backed by newsworthy captions, e.g., a new sale/new type/new color scheme/accident, etc."

*HIGH VOLUME PRINTING, Box 368, Northbrook IL 60065. (312)564-5940. FAX: (708)564-8361. Editor: Catherine M. Stanulis. Bimonthly. Circ. 30,000. Emphasizes equipment, systems and supplies; large commercial printers: magazine and book printers. Readers are management and production personnel of high-volume printers and producers of books, magazines and periodicals. Sample copy $5 plus $1.41 postage; free photo guidelines with SASE.

Photo Needs: Uses about 30-35 photos/issue. Model release required; captions preferred.
Making Contact & Terms: Query with samples or with list of stock photo subjects; send b&w and color prints (any size or finish); 35mm, 2¼×2¼, 4×5 or 8×10 transparencies; b&w or color contact sheet or negatives by mail for consideration. SASE. Reports in 1 month. Pays $200 maximum/color cover photo; $50 maximum/b&w or color inside photo and $200 maximum for text/photo package. Pays on publication. Credit line given. Buys one-time rights with option for future use. Previously published work OK "if previous publication is indicated."

HOG FARM MANAGEMENT, Suite 160, 12400 Whitewater Dr., Minnetonka MN 55343. (612)931-0211. Editor: Steve Marbery. Monthly magazine. Emphasizes all phases of hog production. Circ. 45,000. Sample copy with 9×12 SAE and 69¢ postage.
Photo Needs: Some b&w are used on the inside of magazine; color slides, 35mm and larger for covers and some inside. "We are interested in photojournalism rather than basic commercial photography depicting hog scenes. They should show a modern hog scene; various management activities to run a hog farm." Model release and captions preferred.
Making Contact & Terms: Query with resume of credits; and/or with samples. Send 5×7 matte finish b&w or color prints; 35mm or 120 transparencies; b&w contact sheets and b&w negatives. SASE. Reports in 2 weeks. Prefers to work on assignment basis. Payment negotiable. Pays on publication. Buys one-time rights. Previously published work is satisfactory.
Tips: "Don't send something without understanding that we pay upon publication, no kill fee. No cute pics of pigs in hats, please."

HOGS TODAY, Farm Journal Publishing, Inc., 6205 Earle Brown Dr., Suite 100, Brooklyn Center MN 55430. (612)561-0300. Photo Editor: Greg Lamp. Monthly magazine. Circ. 125,000. Sample copy and photo guidelines free with SASE.
Photo Needs: Uses 20-30 photos/issue; 75% supplied by freelance photographers. We use studio-type portraiture (environmental portraits), technical, details, scenics. Model release preferred; photo captions required.
Making Contact & Terms: Arrange a personal interview to show portfolio or query with resume of credits along with business card, brochure, flyer or tearsheets to be kept on file for possible assignments. SASE. Reports in 2 weeks. "We pay a cover bonus." Pays on acceptance. Credit line given. Buys one-time rights. Simultaneous submissions OK.
Tips: In portfolio or samples, likes to "see about 20 slides showing photographer's use of lighting, and photographer's ability to work with people. Know your intended market. Familiarize yourself with the magazine and keep abreast of how photos are used in the general magazine field."

HOME HEALTHCARE NURSE, Appleton & Lange, Inc., Box 5630, 25 Van Zant St., E. Norwalk CT 06856. (203)838-4400. Photo Editor: Karen Genetski. Journal. Emphasizes home health care. Readers are nurses. Circ. 11,000. Sample copy $5. Photo guidelines free with SASE.
Photo Needs: Uses 1 photo/issue; all supplied by freelance photographers. "For *HHCN*, use practicing professional nurses working in home health, community health and public health areas (all noninstitutional settings). We accept photos with people in them for this publication, but the photographer must be able to obtain a signed release form from the subject(s) before publication. A release form will be forwarded to you upon acceptance of photo." Special photo needs include six covers photos. Model release required, photo captions preferred.
Making Contact & Terms: Send unsolicited 35mm transparencies by mail for consideration. Reports in 4-6 weeks. Pays $350/color cover photo. Pays on publication. Credit line given. Buys one-time rights.
Tips: "We are looking for visual impact: imaginative, vivid photographs, unique in subject or treatment, that will appeal to our discerning readership."

HOME IMPROVEMENT CENTER (formerly HOME CENTER MAGAZINE), Box 1400, Lincolnshire IL 60069. (312)634-2600. FAX: (708)634-4379. Editor: Cori Dunn. Monthly. Emphasizes retail home improvement stores/do-it-yourself home improvement products. Readers are owners and managers of retail home improvement stores. Circ. 73,500. Estab. 1911. Sample copy free.
Photo Needs: Uses 50+ photos/issue; 50% supplied by freelancers (by assignment only). Uses in-store shots and product shots. Model release required.
Making Contact & Terms: Query with samples and list of stock photo subjects; provide resume, business card, brochure, flyer or tearsheets to be kept on file for possible future assignments. SASE. Pays $50-150/b&w photo; $50-200/color photo; $400-800/day or $200-400/half-day rate plus expenses. Pays on publication. Credit line given. Buys all rights. "We keep all pictures for our files." Previously published work OK.
Tips: Looks for fast, good color, experience shooting retail, homecenters & hardware stores. We need rights to all pictures—for our files. Sees trend toward "more in-store color photography and product shots." Accordingly, prefers to see "proof of his/her ability to shoot store interiors under poor light conditions, good tabletop product shots quickly and in good color."

HOSPITAL PRACTICE, 10 Astor Place, New York NY 10003. (212)477-2727. Editorial Director: David W. Fisher. Design Director: Robert S. Herald. Publishes 18 issues/year. Circ. 190,000. *"Hospital Practice* is directed to a national audience of physicians and surgeons. Major review articles provide comprehensive information on new developments and problem areas in medicine and clinical research. Authors are nationally recognized experts in their fields." Photos purchased on assignment, "vary occasionally, as needed." Credit lines grouped in space available. Occasionally requires second serial (reprint rights). Submit portfolio for review to Design Director, or query with samples. SASE. Reports in 2 weeks. Photo guidelines provided on assignment.

Subject Needs: Documentary (narrow field); and photo essay/photo feature (assignments are made based on ms needs). "Documentary photographers must have experience with medical and/or surgical photography for editorial (not advertising) purposes. May have to travel to location on short notice with appropriate equipment." Model release and captions required if requested. No studio photos, animals, landscapes, portraits, moods.

B&W: Contact sheet and negatives OK.

Color: Prefers 2¼×2¼ Ektachrome transparencies.

*IEEE SOFTWARE, 10662 Los Vaqueros Circle, Los Alamitos CA 90720. (714)821-8380. Managing Editor: Angela Burgess. Bimonthly magazine. "We cover software engineering, but we use photos on any subject to illustrate concepts." Readers are professional software engineers. Circ. 25,000. Estab. 1984. Sample copy free with SASE. No photo guidelines.

Photo Needs: Uses 3 photos/issue; all supplied by freelance photographers. Photo needs vary from issue to issue. Model release required, although prefers not to use models.

Making Contact & Terms: Provide resume, business card, brochure, flyer or tearsheets to be kept on file for possible assignments. Reports in 3 weeks. Pays $400-500/color cover photo; $100-300/color inside photo; $75/b&w inside photo. Pays on acceptance Credit line given. North American serial rights. Simultaneous submissions and previously published work OK.

Tips: "Call for sample issue."

*ILLINOIS LEGAL TIMES, 420 W. Grand Ave., Chicago IL 60610. (312)644-4378. Managing Editor: Mara Tapp. Monthly trade publication, tabloid format. Covers law. Readers are Illinois-based lawyers, of various ages and backgrounds. Circ. 13,000. Estab. 1987. Sample copy free with 10×13 SAE.

Photo Needs: Uses 30-35 photos/issue; most supplied by freelancers. Needs photos of personalities in the profession.

Making Contact & Terms: Query with resume of credits. Provide resume business card, brochure, flyer or tearsheets to be kept on file for possible assignment. SASE. Reports in 3 weeks. Pays $100/color or b&w cover photo; $35/b&w or color inside photo. Pays on 15th of month of cover date in which photos appear. Credit line given. Buys all rights; negotiable. Will not consider simultaneous submissions or previously published work.

INDUSTRIAL PHOTOGRAPHY, PTN Publications, 210 Crossways Park Dr., Woodbury NY 11797. (516)496-8000. Editorial Director: George Schaub. Managing Editor: Steve Shaw. Monthly magazine. Circ. 46,000. "Our emphasis is on the industrial photographer who produces images (still, cine, video) for a company or organization (including industry, military, government, medical, scientific, educational, institutions, R&D facilities, etc.)." Free sample copy and writer's/photo guidelines.

Subject Needs: All mss and photos must relate to the needs of industrial photographers. Captions and releases required.

Specs: Uses 4×5, 5×7 or 8×10 glossy b&w and color prints or 35mm color transparencies; allows other kinds of photos. Photos purchased with accompanying ms. Seeks mss that offer technical or general information of value to industrial photographers, including applications, techniques, case histories of in-plant departments, etc.

Payment & Terms: Pays $150 minimum/ms, including all photos and other illustrations. Credit line given. Pays on publication. Buys first North American serial rights except photo with text.

Making Contact: Query with story/photo suggestion. Provide letter of inquiry and samples to be kept on file for possible future assignments. SASE. Reports in 1 month.

Tips: Trend toward "photo-text packages only." In samples wants to see "technical ability, graphic depiction of subject matter and unique application of technique." To break in, "link up with a writer" if not already a writer as well as photographer.

INDUSTRIAL SAFETY AND HYGIENE NEWS, 201 King of Prussia Rd., Radnor PA 19089. (215)964-4057. Editor: Dave Johnson. Monthly magazine. Circ. 60,000. Emphasizes industrial safety and health for safety and health management personnel in over 36,000 large industrial plants (primarily manufacturing). Free sample copy.

Photo Needs: Front covers, occasionally use freelance photography. Magazine is tabloid size, thus front cover photos must be powerful, graphic, with the dramatic impact of a poster.
Making Contact & Terms: Send material by mail for consideration. Uses color, 35mm and 2¼×2¼ transparencies. Photographer should request editorial schedule and sample of publication. SASE. Reports in 2 weeks. Pays $300-400/color photo; pays/job. Credit line given. Payment on publication. Buys all rights on a work-for-hire basis. Previously published work OK.

INFORMATION WEEK, 600 Community Dr., Manhasset NY 11030. (516)365-4600. Art Director: Hector W. Marrero. Weekly. Emphasizes computers, mainframes and MIS management. Readers are the nation's 100 largest MIS installations. Circ. 150,000. Sample copy for $3 and 8½×11 SASE. Photo guidelines free with SASE.
Photo Needs: Uses 20 photos/issue; 10 supplied by freelance photographers. Needs photos of corporate, communications, government and banking end/user computing. Model release preferred; captions required.
Making Contact & Terms: Send color prints, 35mm or 2¼×2¼ transparencies by mail for consideration; provide resume, business card, brochure, flyer or tearsheets to be kept on file for possible future assignments. Does not return unsolicited material. Reports next day. Payment negotiable. Pays on acceptance. Credit line given. Buys all rights. Simultaneous submissions and previously published work OK.
Tips: Prefers to see "good concepts and design."

IN-PLANT PRINTER AND ELECTRONIC PUBLISHER, P.O. Box 1387, Northbrook IL 60065. (708)564-5940. Editor: Virgil Busto. Bimonthly. Circ. 40,000. Emphasizes "in-plant printing; print and graphic shops housed, supported, and serving larger companies and organizations and electronic publishing applications in those locations." Readers are management and production personnel of such shops. Sample copy $5; free photo guidelines with SASE.
Photo Needs: Uses about 30-35 photos/issue. Needs "working/shop photos, atmosphere, interesting equipment shots, how-to." Model release required; captions preferred.
Making Contact & Terms: Query with samples or with list of stock photo subjects; send b&w and color (any size or finish) prints; 35mm, 2¼×2¼, 4×5, 8×10 slides, b&w and color contact sheet or b&w and color negatives by mail for consideration. SASE. Reports in 1 month. Pays $200 maximum/ b&w or color cover photo; $25 maximum/b&w or color inside photo; and $200 maximum for text/ photo package. Pays on publication. Credit line given. Buys one-time rights with option for future use. Previously published work OK "if previous publication is indicated."
Tips: "Good photos of a case study—such as a printshop, in our case—can lead us to doing a follow-up story by phone and paying more for photos. Photographer should be able to bring out the hidden or overlooked design elements in graphic arts equipment." Trends include artistic representation of common objects found in-plant—equipment, keyboard, etc.

INSTANT AND SMALL COMMERCIAL PRINTER, P.O. Box 1387, Northbrook IL 60065. (708)564-5940. Editor-in-Chief: Virgil Busto. Bimonthly. Circ. 40,000. Emphasizes the "instant and retail printing industry." Readers are owners, operators, managers of instant and smaller commercial (less than 20 employees) print shops. Sample copy $3; photo guidelines free with SASE.
Photo Needs: Uses about 15-20 photos/issue. Needs "working/shop photos, atmosphere, interesting equipment shots, some how-to." Model release required; captions preferred.
Making Contact & Terms: Query with samples or with list of stock photo subjects or send b&w and color (any size or finish) prints; 35mm, 2¼×2¼, 4×5 or 8×10 slides; b&w and color contact sheet or b&w and color negatives by mail for consideration. SASE. Reports in 1 month. Pays $300 maximum/ b&w and color cover photo; $50 maximum/b&w and color inside photo and $200 maximum for text/ photo package. Pays on publication. Credit line given. Buys one-time rights with option for future use. Previously published work OK "if previous publication is indicated."

THE INSTRUMENTALIST, 200 Northfield Rd., Northfield IL 60093. (708)446-5000. FAX: (708)446-6263. Managing Editor: Judy Nelson. Monthly magazine. Circ. 22,500. Estab. 1946. Emphasizes instrumental music education. Readers are school band and orchestra directors and performers. Buys 1-5 photos/issue, mostly color. Credit line given. Pays on publication. Buys all rights. Send material by mail for consideration. SASE. Reports in 2-4 weeks. Sample copy $2.50.
Subject Needs: Head shots and human interest. "All photos should deal with instrumental music in some way." Especially needs photos for Photo Essay section. Uses 5×7 or 8×10 b&w glossy prints. Pays $15-25/photo.For cover: Uses 35mm and 2¼×2¼ transparencies and glossy color prints. Vertical format preferred. Pays $100 minimum/photo.
Tips: Request sample copy to review. "We look for shots that capture a natural expression of a player or that zoom in on an instrument to show it in a new perspective. We receive more marching band shots than we can use. We are always looking for closeups of people or classical instruments (no rock

or folk instruments). Kodachrome 64 ASA works well because it can withstand enlargement. Be sure to take into account logo placement, vertical format, and room for cropping. The cover and an occasional inside shot come from assignments. Many covers are provided by freelancers introducing themselves to us for the first time."

INSURANCE WEEK, Suite 3029, 1001 Fourth Ave. Plaza, Seattle WA 98154. (206)624-6965. Editor: Richard Rambeck. Weekly magazine. Emphasizes timely news for property/casualty insurance industry. Readers are "typically white, middle-aged male, insurance agents or executives." Circ. 6,200. Sample copy free with 9×12 SASE and 3 first class stamps.
Photo Needs: Uses 1-2 photos/issue; number supplied by freelance photographers varies. Needs "shots of newsmakers, legislators, important meetings, etc. Example: President Bush addressing national insurance convention." Purchases photos with accompanying ms only. Especially needs more photos of West Coast conventions and legislative hearings. Photo captions required.
Making Contact & Terms: Provide resume and business card. Unsolicited material not returned. Reports in 2 weeks. Pays $25/b&w cover photo or $50-200/photo/text package. Pays on acceptance. Credit line given. Buys one-time rights. Simultaneous submissions OK.
Tips: "Our needs are almost always hard-news related. Good quality b&w. Send letter first—if interested, I'll answer."

*INTERLIT, 850 N. Grove, Elgin IL 60120. (708)741-2400. Editor: Tim Bascom. Quarterly journal. Emphasizes writing, editing and publishing in the third world. Readers are writers, editors, publishers and designers in third world. Circ. 6,000. Estab. 1964. Sample copy for 9×12 SASE and 45¢ postage. No photo guidelines.
Photo Needs: Uses between 5 and 7 photos/issue; approximately 40-45% supplied by freelance photographers. Needs photos of every aspect of publishing overseas; sometimes photos of other cultures. Model release and photo captions preferred.
Making Contact & Terms: Query with list of stock photo subjects. Reports in 1 month. Pays $50/b&w cover photo; $30/b&w inside photo. Buys one-time rights. Will consider simultaneous submissions.

INTERNATIONAL FAMILY PLANNING PERSPECTIVES, 111 Fifth Ave., New York NY 10003. (212)254-5656. Editor: Olivia Nordberg. Quarterly. Circ. 30,000. Emphasizes family planning (population). Readers are family planning professionals, clinicians, demographers and sociologists. Free sample copy with SASE.
Photo Needs: Uses 0-3 photos/year. 1 is supplied by freelance photographers. Needs photos of Third World women and children of all ages; large and small families; women receiving services in family planning and abortion clinics; certain medical procedures—sterilizations, abortions, Pap smears, blood pressure tests, breast exams—in clinics and hospitals; teenagers (pregnant and nonpregnant); sex education classes; women receiving services from family planning workers in developing countries; family planning and abortion counseling in hospitals and clinics; hospital nurseries, infant intensive-care units; childbirth and pregnant women. Photos purchased without accompanying ms only. Model release and captions preferred. "We write captions used in magazine, but prefer to have identifying information with photo."
Making Contact & Terms: Arrange a personal interview to show portfolio. SASE. Reports in 2 weeks. Provide resume and brochure to be kept on file for possible future assignments. Pay negotiable. Pays on publication. Credit line given. Buys one-time rights. Previously published work OK.

JEMS, the Journal of Emergency Medical Services, Box 1026, Solana Beach CA 92075. (619)481-1128. Art Director: Bob Schmitt. Monthly journal. Emphasizes emergency medical services. Readers are paramedics, emergency physicians, flight nurses, administrators. Circ. 30,000. Estab. 1980. Publication for Ashbeams, NFNA, NFPA. Sample copy free with 10×12 SAE and $2.00 postage.
Photo Needs: Uses about 6-10 photos/issue; 5-8 supplied by freelance photographers. Needs photos of paramedics in action. Special needs include comunications/extrications, water injuries, hazardous material responses. Model release and captions required.
Making Contact & Terms: Query with samples; query with list of stock photo subjects. SASE. Reports in 1 month. Pays $50-75/b&w cover photo; $150/color cover photo; $25-35/b&w inside photo; and $50-75/color inside photo. Pays on publication. Credit line given. Buys one-time rights or first North American serial rights.
Tips: "Photos most often published show pre-hospital workers involved in some form of *patient care* (We do *not* need pictures of smashed cars). "Send dupes or originals for our stock files. Photos are selected on quality of image and subject matter needs of each issue." Also publishes *Rescue* magazine(see index)—bimonthly; Circ. 20,000.

JOBBER RETAILER MAGAZINE, 341 White Pond Dr., Akron OH 44320. (216)867-4401. Editor: Mike Mavrigian. Monthly. Circ. 36,000. Emphasizes "automotive aftermarket." Readers are "wholesalers, manufacturers, retail distributors of replacement parts." Sample copy free with 11 × 14 SAE and 69¢ postage.
Photo Needs: Uses about 3-20 photos/issue; often needs freelance photographers. Needs automotive feature shots; exterior and interior of auto parts stores. Model release and captions preferred.
Making Contact & Terms: Provide resume, business card, brochure, flyer or tearsheets to be kept on file for possible future assignments. Does not return unsolicited material. Reporting time varies. Pays $50-150/b&w photo; $75-200/color photo. Pays on publication. Credit line given. Buys various rights—"generally all rights." Simultaneous submissions and previously published work OK.
Tips: "Let us know *who* and *where* you are."

*JOURNAL OF EXTENSION, 436 Lowell Hall, 610 Langdon St., Madison WI 53703. (608)262-1974. Editor: Colleen L. Schuh. Quarterly journal. A professional journal for adult educators. Readers are adult educators, extension personnel. Circ. 10,000. Estab. 1963.
Photo Needs: Uses 1 cover photo/issue; supplied by freelancers. "Each issue we try to highlight the lead article, so the subject matter varies each time." Model release required.
Making Contact & Terms: Send 4 × 6 or 5 × 7 b&w prints by mail for consideration. Call to check on current needs. SASE. Reports in 1 month. Pays $75-100/b&w cover photo. Pays on acceptance. Credit line given. Buys one-time rights.

THE JOURNAL OF FAMILY PRACTICE, 25 Van Zant St., E. Norwalk CT 06855. (203)838-4400. Photo Editor: Karen Genetski. Monthly. Circ. approx. 80,000. Emphasizes clinical application in family practice. Readers are family practitioners. Sample copy and photo guidelines free.
Photo Needs: Rural scenes (indoor and outdoor), unusual botanicals, abstracts.
Making Contact & Terms: Send 35mm or 2¼ × 2¼ transparencies by mail for consideration. SASE. Reports in 1 month. Pays $350/color cover. Pays on publication. Credit line given. Buys one-time rights.

JOURNAL OF OPHTHALMIC NURSING & TECHNOLOGY, 6900 Grove Rd., Thorofare NJ 08086. FAX: (609)853-5991. Managing Editor: John Bond. Editor: Heather Boyd-Monk. Bimonthly journal. Emphasizes ophthalmic nursing. Readers are ophthalmic nurses and technicians. Circ 4,000. Estab. 1981. Sample copy for $8 and SASE.
Photo Needs: Uses 10-15 photos/issue; cover photos—only 1 or 2 issues/year supplied by freelance photographers. Needs clinical photos of eyes or nurses and technicians in action. Model release and captions required.
Making Contact & Terms: Query with samples. SASE. Reports in 3 weeks. Pays $50/b&w cover photo; $150/color cover photo. Pays on acceptance. Credit line given. Buys all rights. Will negotiate with photographer unwilling to sell all rights.
Tips: "Must be familiar with the publication." In samples, wants to see "accuracy and interaction between nurse and patient." The best way to break in is "to know ophthalmic nursing."

JOURNAL OF PSYCHOACTIVE DRUGS, 409 Clayton St., San Francisco CA 94117. (415)626-2810. Editors: E. Leif Zerkin and Jeffrey H. Novey. Quarterly. Circ. 1,200. Estab. 1967. Emphasizes "psychoactive substances (both legal and illegal)." Readers are "professionals (primarily health) in the drug abuse treatment field."
Photo Needs: Uses 1 photo/issue; supplied by freelance photographers. Needs "full-color abstract, surreal, avant-garde or computer graphics."
Making Contact & Terms: Query with samples. Send 4 × 6 color prints or 35mm slides by mail for consideration. SASE. Reports in 2 weeks. Pays $55-100/color cover photo. Pays on publication. Credit line given. Buys one-time rights. Simultaneous submissions and previously published work OK.

JOURNAL OF PSYCHOSOCIAL NURSING, 6900 Grove Rd., Thorofare NJ 08086. (609)848-1000. FAX: (609)853-5491. Editor: Dr. Shirley Smoyak. Photo Editor: John Bond. Monthly magazine. Covers psychosocial nursing (psychiatric/mental health). Circ. 15,000. Estab. 1962.
Photo Needs: Uses 1 photo/issue; all supplied by freelance photographers. Needs photos of people, abstract concepts. Model release required.
Making Contact & Terms: Query with samples; query with list of stock photo subjects; provide resume, business card, brochure, flyer or tearsheets to be kept on file for possible future assignments. SASE. Reports in 1 month. Pay varies. Pays on publication. Credit line given. Buys one-time rights. Previously published work OK.
Tips: In samples, wants to see "imagination, unique perspective and knowledge of mental illness." Sees trend toward showing "patient *usually* in sympathetic light." Accordingly, "Use a unique perspective, not a trite picture of patients in a mental hospital."

LIQUID AND GAS CHROMATOGRAPHY, 859 Willamette St., Eugene OR 97440. (503)343-1200. Art Director: Barbara A. Mickelson. Monthly. Emphasizes science. Readers are scientists and manufacturers of scientific products/equipment. Circ. 30,000. Sample copy free with 8½×11 SASE. Photo guidelines free with SASE.
Photo Needs: Uses 6-10 photos/issue; usually one supplied by freelancer. Needs photos relating to chromatography. Photo captions preferred.
Making Contact & Terms: Query with list of stock photo subjects; provide resume, business card, brochure, flyer or tearsheets to be kept on file for possible future assignments. Does not return unsolicited material. Reports in 1 month. Pays $300/color cover photo; $100/b&w inside photo. Pays on publication. Credit line given on table of contents page or with photo. Buys one-time rights. Simultaneous submissions OK.
Tips: Looks for "an artistic look at technical scientific products and equipment. Colorful and dramatic. We seldom use people shots."

MANUFACTURING ENGINEERING, One SME Dr., Dearborn MI 48121. (313)271-1500. Editor-in-Chief: John Coleman. Monthly magazine. Emphasizes traditional and high-technology manufacturing. Readers are "members of the Society of Manufacturing Engineers and paid subscribers. Circ. 145,000. Sample copy free with $2 postage.
Photo Needs: Uses 60-75 photos/issue: 1% supplied by freelance photographers. Needs photos of "manufacturing equipment, tool show shots, high technology, people in businesses, tooling shots." Special needs include "specific cover shots, working on ideas with editor and art director." Send 5×7 b&w or color prints; or 4×5 transparencies by mail for consideration. Provide resume, business card, brochure, flyer or tearsheets to be kept on file for possible future assignments. SASE. Reports in 1 week. Pays $175-300/color cover photo; $25/b&w inside photo; $50/color inside photo. Pays $200/day maximum. Payment is made monthly. Buys one-time or all rights. Simultaneous and previously published work OK.

MD MAGAZINE, 3 E. 54th St., New York NY 10022. (212)355-5432. Picture Editor: Richard Litell. Monthly magazine. Circ. 160,000. Emphasizes the arts, science, medicine, history and travel; written with the readership (physicians) in mind. For medical doctors. Needs a wide variety of photos dealing with history, art, literature, medical history, pharmacology, activities of doctors and sports. Also interested in photo essays. Buys first serial rights. Arrange a personal interview to show portfolio. Single pictures require only captions. Picture stories require explanatory text, but not finished ms. Pays $75-100/¼ page of b&w photos; $150-180/¼ page of color photos; $1,000-1,500/photo-text package. Pays on publication. Reports ASAP. SASE. Simultaneous submissions and previously published work OK.
B&W: Send 8×10 glossy prints. Captions required.
Color: Send transparencies. Captions required.
Tips: "Do not send unsolicited material. Call or write to arrange portfolio interview. 80-100 tightly edited slides in sheets or 20-25 prints."

MEDICAL ECONOMICS MAGAZINE, 680 Kinderkamack Rd., Oradell NJ 07649. (201)262-3030. Editor: Don L. Berg. Photo Editor: (Ms.) Donna DeAngelis. Biweekly magazine. Emphasizes financial aspects of running a medical practice. Readers are physicians and financial specialists. Circ. 182,000. Sample copy free with SASE.
Photo Needs: Uses 5 photos/issue; 1-5 supplied by freelance photographers. Needs head and shoulders shots. Day-in-the-life-of shots, indoor and outdoor. Special needs include photos of doctors and their families, homes, and hobbies. Doctors interacting with/examining patients. Model release and captions required.
Making Contact & Terms: Provide resume, business card, flyer or tearsheets to be kept on file for possible future assignments, "send to Donna DeAngelis, Art Administrator." SASE. Reports in 2 weeks. Payment negotiable. Pays on acceptance. Credit line given on contents page. Buys one-time rights. Previously published work OK.
Tips: Prefers to see medical and editorial photography, location shots, photomicrography, computer-generated images. "Don't be too pushy. Don't overprice yourself. A good photographer makes a good living."

MEDICAL WORLD NEWS, 500 Howard St., San Francisco CA 94105. (415)397-1881. Editor: Don Gibbons. Photo Editors: Melanie McMullen, Andrea Wheeler, Becky Freed. Bimonthly magazine. Emphasizes medicine. Readers are family practitioners, G.P.'s, internists, D.O.'s, cardiologists and gastro-enterologists. Circ. 150,000. Estab. 1960. Sample copy free with SASE.
Photo Needs: Uses 30 photos/issue; 10 supplied by freelance photographers. Needs photos of medical people, news items. Reviews photos with accompanying ms only. Model release and captions required.
Making Contact & Terms: Provide resume, business card, brochure, flyer or tearsheets to be kept on file for possible future assignments. SASE. Reports in 2 weeks. Pays $50-$150/b&w photo; $75-600/color photo; $100/hour. Pays on publication. Credit line given. Buys one-time rights.

MICHIGAN BUSINESS MAGAZINE, Suite 303, 26111 Evergreen, Southfield MI 48076. (313)357-8300. Editor: Ron Garbinski. Monthly independent circulated to senior executives. Emphasizes Michigan business. Readers include top-level executives. Circ. 36,000. Free sample copy with 9 × 12 SASE; call editor for photo guidelines.
Photo Needs: Uses variable number of photographs; most supplied by freelance photographers. Needs photos of business people, environmental, feature story presentation, mug shots, etc. Reviews photos with accompanying ms only. Special needs include photographers based around Michigan for freelance work on job basis. Model release preferred; captions required.
Making Contact & Terms: Arrange a personal interview to show portfolio, query with resume of credits and samples. SASE. Reports in 2 weeks. Pay individually negotiated. Pays on publication. Credit line given. Buys all rights.

MISSOURI RURALIST, 2401 A Vandiver Dr., Columbia MO 65202. (314)474-9557. Editor-in-Chief: Larry S. Harper. Bimonthly. Circ. 68,000. Emphasizes agriculture. Readers are rural Missourians. Sample copy $2.
Photo Needs: Uses about 25 photos/issue; primarily color slides. "Few" are supplied by freelancers. "Photos must be from rural Missouri." Photos purchased with accompanying ms only. Pays $60/photo and page. Captions required.

MODERN BAKING, Suite 306, 2700 River Rd., Des Plaines IL 60018. (312)299-4430. Editor: Ed Lee. Monthly. Emphasizes on-premise baking, in supermarkets, foodservice establishments and retail bakeries. Readers are owners, managers and operators. Circ. 27,000. Sample copy for 9 × 12 SAE with $2.40 postage.
Photo Needs: Uses 30 photos/issue; 1-2 supplied by freelancers. Needs photos of on-location photography in above-described facilities. Model release and captions preferred.
Making Contact & Terms: Provide resume, business card, brochure, flyer or tearsheets to be kept on file for possible future assignments. SASE. Reports in 2 weeks. Payment negotiable. Pays on acceptance. Credit line given. Buys all rights; willing to negotiable with photographer unwilling to sell all rights.
Tips: Prefers to see "photos that would indicate person's ability to handle on-location, industrial photography."

MODERN OFFICE TECHNOLOGY, 1100 Superior Ave., Cleveland OH 44114. (216)696-7000. FAX: (216)696-7932. Editor: Lura K. Romei. Monthly magazine. Emphasizes office automation, data processing. Readers are middle and upper management and higher in companies of 100 or more employees. Circ. 160,000. Sample copy free with 11 × 14 SAE and 44¢ postage.
Photo Needs: Uses 15 photos/issue; 5 supplied by freelance photographers. Needs office shots, office interiors, computers, concept shots of office automation and networking. Special photo needs: "any and all office shots are welcome." Captions required.
Making Contact & Terms: Provide resume, business card, brochure, flyer or tearsheets to be kept on file for possible future assignments. Reports in 3 weeks. Pays $500/color cover photo; $50-100/b&w and color inside photo. Pays on publication. Credit line given. Buys one-time rights.
Tips: "Good conceptual (not vendor-specific) material about the office and office supplies is hard to find. Crack that and you're in business." In reviewing a photographer's samples, looks for "imagination and humor."

MODERN PLASTICS, 1221 6th Ave., New York NY 10020. (212)512-3491. Art Director: Bob Barravecchia. Monthly magazine. Readers are male buyers in the plastics trade. Circ. 65,000.
Photo Needs: Needs photos of how-to, etc. Purchases photos with accompanying ms only. Model release and photo captions required.
Making Contact & Terms: Arrange a personal interview to show portfolio. Cannot return unsolicited material. Reports in 1 week. Pays $1000/color cover photo and $75/color inside photo. Pays on acceptance. Credit line given. Buys first N.A. serial rights.
Tips: In portfolio or samples looking for concept covers.

MUSIC EDUCATORS JOURNAL, 1902 Association Dr., Reston VA 22091. (703)860-4000. Art Director: Karen Fields. Monthly magazine. Emphasizes music. Readers are music teachers. Circ. 55,000. Sample copy free with 9 × 12 SASE.
Photo Needs: Uses about 35 photos/issue; 10 supplied by freelancers. Needs photos of music students, K-12 and college, and music teachers. Model release preferred.
Making Contact & Terms: Send 5 × 7 or 8 × 10 glossy b&w prints; 35mm, 2¼ × 2¼ transparencies by mail for consideration; provide resume, business card, brochure, flyer or tearsheets to be kept on file for possible future assignments. SASE. Reports in 1 month. Payment negotiable/b&w; $15-20/b&w

inside photo. Pays on acceptance. Credit line given. Buys one-time rights. Simultaneous submissions and previously published work OK.

NATIONAL BUS TRADER, 9698 W. Judson Rd., Polo IL 61064-9049. (815)946-2341. FAX: (815)946-2347. Editor: Larry Plachno. Monthly. Circ. 5,000. Estab. 1977. "The Magazine of Bus Equipment for the United States and Canada—covers mainly integral design buses in the United States and Canada." Readers are bus owners, commercial bus operators, bus manufacturers, bus designers. Sample copy free, (no charge—just write or call).
Photo Needs: Uses about 30 photos/issue; 22 supplied by freelance photographers. Needs photos of "buses; interior, exterior, under construction, in service." Special needs include "photos for future feature articles and conventions our own staff does not attend."
Making Contact & Terms: "Query with specific lists of subject matter that can be provided and mention whether accompanying mss are available." SASE. Reports in 1 week. Pays $3-5/b&w photo; $100-3,000/photo/text package. Pays on acceptance. Credit line given. Buys rights "depending on our need and photographer." Simultaneous submissions and previously published work OK.
Tips: "We don't need samples, merely a list of what freelancers can provide in the way of photos or ms. Write and let us know what you can offer and do. We often use freelance work. We also publish *Bus Tours Magazine*—a bimonthly which uses many photos but not many from freelancers; *The Bus Equipment Guide*—infrequent, which uses many photos; and *The Official Bus Industry Calendar*—annual full-color calendar of bus photos. We also publish historical railroad books and are looking for historical photos on midwest interurban lines and railroads. Due to publication of historical railroad books, we are purchasing many historical photos. In photos looks for subject matter appropriate to current or pending article or book. Send a list of what is available with specific photos, locations, bus/interurban company and fleet number."

NATIONAL FISHERMAN, 120 Tillson Ave., Rockland ME 04841. (207)594-6222. FAX: (207)594-8978. Art Director: Marydale Abernathy. Monthly magazine. Circ. 55,000. Estab. 1960. Emphasizes commercial fishing, boat building, marketing of fish, fishing techniques and fishing equipment. For amateur and professional boatbuilders, commercial fishermen, armchair sailors, bureaucrats and politicians. Buys 5-8 photo stories monthly; buys 4-color action cover photo monthly. Free sample copy with 11x15 SAE and $2 postage.
Subject Needs: Action shots of commercial fishing, work boats, traditional sailing fishboats. No recreational, caught-a-trout photos.
Payment & Terms: Pays $10-25/inside b&w print and $250/color cover transparency. Pays on publication.
Making Contact: Query. Reports in 6 weeks.
Tips: "We seldom use photos unless accompanied by feature stories or short articles—i.e., we don't run a picture for its own sake. Even those accepted for use in photo essays must tell a story—both in themselves and through accompanying cutline information. However, we do use single, stand-alone photos for cover shots. We need sharp black and white glossy photos—5×7s are fine. For cover, please send 35mm transparencies; dupes are acceptable. We want high quality b&w images for inside that will hold detail on newsprint. Send slide samples."

NATIONAL GUARD, 1 Massachusetts Ave. NW, Washington DC 20001. (202)789-0031. Editor-in-Chief: Lt. Col. Reid K. Beveridge. Monthly. Circ. 69,000. Emphasizes news, policies, association activities and feature stories for officers of the Army and Air National Guard. Readers are National Guard officers. Free sample copy and photo guidelines with SASE.
Photo Needs: "Pictures in military situations which show ability to shoot good quality, dramatic action pictures as this is the type of photography we are most interested in." Uses 40 photos/issue; 6 are supplied by freelancers. "Normally, photography accompanies the freelance articles we purchase. Freelance photographers should query first and their photography should be of subjects not available through normal public affairs channels. We are most interested in hiring freelance work in the Midwest, South and West. We never use freelance work in the Washington area because members of our staff take those pictures. Subject matter should be relevant to information of the National Guard officer. Please submit SASE with all material."

NATIONAL LAW JOURNAL, Suite 900, 111 8th Ave., New York NY 10011. (212)741-8300. Art Director: Douglas Hunt. Photo Editor: Dave Hornor. Weekly tabloid. Emphasizes legal stories and law-related topics. Readers are lawyers, law librarians, judges and professors. Circ. 50,000. Sample copy on request.
Photo Needs: Mostly news topics and portrait photography. Captions required.
Making Contact & Terms: Arrange a personal interview to show portfolio; provide resume, business card, brochure, flyer or tearsheets to be kept on file for possible future assignments. SASE. Reports in 2 weeks. Pays on publication. Credit line given. Buys one-time rights. Simultaneous submissions and previously published work OK.

NATION'S BUSINESS, U.S. Chamber of Commerce, 1615 H St. NW, Washington DC 20062. (202)463-5447. Photo Editor: Laurence L. Levin. Assistant Photo Editor: Frances Borchardt. Monthly. Emphasizes business, especially small business. Readers are managers, upper management and business owners. Circ. 850,000. Sample copy free with 9 × 12 SASE.
Photo Needs: Uses about 30-40 photos/issue; 65% supplied by freelance photographers. Needs portrait-personality photos, business related-oriented-theme pictures relating to the story. Foreign scenics. Model release preferred; captions required.
Making Contact & Terms: Arrange a personal interview to show portfolio; submit portfolio for review. SASE. Reports in 3 weeks. Pays $200/b&w or color inside photo; $175-300/day. Pays on publication. Credit line given. Buys one-time rights.
Tips: In reviewing a portfolio, we look for the photographer's "ability to light, taking a static situation and turning it into a spontaneous, eye-catching and informative picture."

NETWORK, Suite 200, 807 Manning Rd. N.E., Calgary AB T2E 7M8 Canada. (403)569-9520. Editor: Randi Berting. Bimonthly. Emphasizes cemetery, memorialization, monument sculptors. Readers are cemeterians, cremationists and service and supply companies. Circ. 8,000. Sample copy free with 8½ × 11 SASE. Photo guidelines free with SASE.
Photo Needs: Uses 20 photos/issue; 15% supplied by freelance photographers. Needs full color shots of beautiful cemeteries, especially Canadian cemeteries. Purchases photos with accompanying ms only. Model release and photo captions required.
Making Contact & Terms: Send unsolicited photos by mail for consideration. Send color prints, any size or format. SASE. Reports as soon as possible. Will negotiate payment upon photo submission. Pays on publication. Credit line not given. Buys one-time rights. Simultaneous submissions and previously published work OK unless "published in other cemetery/funeral trade magazines."

NEW BIOTECH, Box 7131, Station J, Ottawa, ON K2A 4C5 Canada. (613)567-1417. Editor: Peter Winter. Trade publication. Monthly magazine. Emphasizes biotechnology. Readers are research professionals. Circ. 6,000. Sample copy free with 9 × 12 SASE. Photo guidelines free with SASE.
Photo Needs: Uses 8 photos/issue; 20% supplied by freelance photographers. Needs photos of scientific achievements, company developments. Purchases photos with accompanying ms only. "We have several special supplements during 1989." Contact to discuss specific needs. Model release and photo captions preferred.
Making Contact & Terms: Query with list of stock photo subjects. SASE. Reports in 2 weeks. Pays $250/color cover photo, $250/b&w cover photo, $300/color inside photo, $250/b&w inside photo, $500/color page rate, $400/b&w page rate, $12.50-15/hour, $300-400/day or $900-1,200/photo/text package. Pays on publication. Credit line given. Buys first N.A. serial rights. Simultaneous submissions and previously published work OK.
Tips: "We look for material which will "grab" our audience. New angles and themes will have the best chance of success." Magazine is looking for "illustrated material which captures mood of biotechnology research and industry. Dramatic shots are required; does not want to see "the researcher at the lab bench."

NEW METHODS, Box 22605, San Francisco CA 94122-0605. (415)664-3469. Art Director: Larry Rosenberg. Monthly. Circ. 5,600. Estab. 1976. Emphasizes veterinary personnel, animals. Readers are veterinary professionals and interested consumers. Sample copy $3.60; photo guidelines free with SASE.
Photo Needs: Uses 12 photos/issue; 2 supplied by freelance photographers. Assigns 95% of photos. Needs animal, wildlife and technical photos. Most work is b&w. Model release and captions required.
Making Contact & Terms: Arrange a personal interview to show portfolio; query with resume of credits, samples or list of stock photo subjects; provide resume, business card, brochure, flyer or tearsheets to be kept on file for possible future assignments. SASE. Reports in 2 months. Payment is rare, negotiable; will barter. Pays on publication. Credit line given. Buys one-time rights. Simultaneous submissions and previously published work OK.
Tips: Prefers to see "technical photos (human working with animal(s) or animal photos (*not cute*)" in a portfolio or samples. On occasion, needs phtographer for shooting new products and local area conventions.

NEWSPAPERS & TECHNOLOGY, Suite 700, 50 S. Steele St., Denver CO 80209. (303)355-2101. Editor: Tom Rees. Monthly tabloid. Emphasizes technology in the newspaper field. Readers are male and female newspaper department managers, ages 25-55. Circ. 25,000. Estab. 1988. Sample copy free upon request.

Photo Needs: Uses approximately 7 photos/issue; 2 supplied by freelance photographers. Needs location shots in newspaper offices and plants. Model release preferred; photo captions required.
Making Contact & Terms: Provide resume, business card, brochure, flyer or tearsheets to be kept on file for possible assignments. SASE. Reports in 3 weeks. Payment negotiated on a bid basis. Pays on acceptance. Credit line given. Buys one-time rights. Simultaneous submissions OK.

*911 MAGAZINE, Box 11788, Santa Ana CA 92711. (714)544-7776. Editor: Joe Bergman. Trade publication. Monthly magazine. Emphasizes emergency response—i.e.: police, fire, paramedic, dispatch, utilities, etc. Readers are ages 20-65 mostly male. Circ. 20,000. Estab. 1988. Sample copy free with 9×12 SASE 7 first-class stamps. Photo guidelines free with SASE.
Photo Needs: Uses up to 25 photos/issue; 75% supplied by freelance photographers. "From the Field" department photos are needed of incidents involving two or more emergency agencies in action from Law Enforcement, Fire Suppression, Paramedics, dispatch, etc., showing proper techniques and attire. Accompany with captions describing incident location by city and state, agencies involved, duration, dollar cost, fatalities and injuries." Model release and photo captions preferred.
Making Contact & Terms: Query with list of stock photo subjects; send unsolicited photos by mail for consideration; provide resume, business card, brochure, flyer or tearsheets to be kept on file for possible assignments. Uses 35mm, $2\frac{1}{4} \times 2\frac{1}{4}$, 4×5, 8×10 gloss contacts, b&w or color prints; 35mm, $2\frac{1}{4} \times 2\frac{1}{4}$, 4×5, 8×10 transparencies. SASE. Reports in 3 weeks. Pays $100-200/color cover photo; $50-150/b&w cover photo; $25-75/color inside photo; $20-50/b&w inside photo. Pays on publication. Credit line given. Rights are negotiable. Simultaneous submissions and previously published work OK.
Tips: "We need photos for unillustrated cover stories and features appearing in each issue. Topics include rescue, traffic, communications (dispatch), training, stress, media relations, crime prevention, etc. Calendar available. Assignments possible."

THE NORTHERN LOGGER & TIMBER PROCESSOR, Box 69, Old Forge NY 13420. Editor: Eric A. Johnson. Managing Editor: George F. Mitchell. Monthly magazine. Circ. 14,000. Emphasizes methods, machinery and manufacturing as related to forestry. For loggers, timberland managers and processors of primary forest products in the territory from Maine to Minnesota and from Missouri to West Virginia. Photos purchased with accompanying ms. Buys 3-4 photos/issue. Credit line given. Pays on publication. Copyrighted. Query with resume of credits. SASE. Previously published work OK. Reports in 2 weeks. Free sample copy.
Subject Needs: Head shot, how-to, nature, photo essay/photo feature, product shot; mostly b&w. Captions required. "The magazine carries illustrated stories on new methods and machinery for forest management, logging, timber processing, sawmilling and manufacture of other products of northern forests."
B&W: Uses 5×7 or 8×10 glossy prints. Pays $15-20/photo.
Color: Uses 35mm transparencies. Pays $35-40/photo.
Cover: Uses b&w glossy prints or 35mm color transparencies. Vertical format preferred. Pays $35-40/photo.
Accompanying Mss: Pays $100-250 for text/photo package.
Tips: "Send for a copy of our magazine and look it over before sending in photographs. We're open to new ideas, but naturally are most likely to buy the types of photos that we normally run. An interesting caption can mean as much as a good picture. Often it's an interdependent relationship."

NURSING MANAGEMENT, 103 N. 2nd St., W. Dundee IL 60118. (708)426-6100. Production Manager: Andrew Miller. Monthly. Circ. 125,000+. Emphasizes information on and techniques for nurse management. Readers are managerial level professional nurses.
Photo Needs: Uses 5 photos/issue; all are usually supplied by freelancers. Needs hospital-oriented photos. Model release required.
Making Contact and Terms: Query with list of stock photo subjects. SASE. Reports in 1 month. Credit line given. Pays on publication.

OCCUPATIONAL HAZARDS, 1100 Superior Ave., Cleveland OH 44114. FAX: (216)696-7932. Editor: Stephen Minter. Monthly magazine. Emphasizes occupational safety and health. Readers are professionals in the occupational safety and health field. Circ. 60,000. Estab. 1938.
Photo Needs: Uses 10-20 photos/issue; 20% supplied by freelance photographers. Uses photos of industry, safety/health duties and medical settings. Model release and photo captions preferred.
Making Contact & Terms: Provide resume, business card, brochure, flyer or tearsheets to be kept on file for possible assignments. Pays $150/b&w photo; $500/color photo. Pays on acceptance. Credit line given. Buys one-time rights. Simultaneous submissions and previously published work OK.

OCEANUS, Woods Hole Oceanographic Institution, Woods Hole MA 02543. (508)548-1400. Editor: Paul R. Ryan. Quarterly. Circ. 15,000. Estab. 1952. Emphasizes "marine science and policy." Readers are "seriously interested in the sea. Nearly half our subscribers are in the education field." Sample copy free with SASE.
Photo Needs: Uses about 60 photos/issue; 25% supplied by freelance photographers. "All four issues per year are thematic, covering marine subjects." Captions required.
Making Contact & Terms: Query with resume of credits or with list of stock photo subjects; provide resume, business card, brochure, flyer or tearsheets to be kept on file for possible future assignments. Does not return unsolicited material. Reports in 1 month. Pays $60-300/b&w photo; $80-400/color photo; $150-300/photo/text package. Payments "to be negotiated based on size of photo used in magazine." Pays on publication. Credit line given. Buys one-time rights.
Tips: "The magazine uses mainly b&w but some color photos. Color slides can be converted. Send us high contrast b&w or color photographs with strong narrative element (scientists at work, visible topographic, atmospheric alterations or events)."

OCULAR SURGERY NEWS, 6900 Grove Rd., Thorofare NJ 08086. (609)848-1000. Editor: Keith Croes. Biweekly newspaper. Emphasizes ophthalmology, medical and eye care. Readers are ophthalmologists in the U.S. Circ. 18,000. Sample copy free with 9×12 SASE and 10 first class stamps.
Photo Needs: Uses 30 photos/issue; less than 10% supplied by freelancers. Needs photos of medical subjects—tie in with special issues. Plans 6 special issues each year; contact for needs. Model release and photo captions preferred.
Making Contact & Terms: Query with list of stock photo subjects. Provide resume, business card, brochure, flyer or tearsheets to be kept on file for possible assignments. SASE. Reports in 2 weeks. Pays $300/color cover photo, $150/color inside photo and $150-250/day. Pays on publication. Credit line given. Buys one-time rights.

OH&S CANADA, 1450 Don Mills Rd., Don Mills, ON M3B 2X7 Canada. (416)445-6641. Art Director: Lynne Stevenson. Bimonthly magazine. Emphasizes occupational health and safety. Readers are health and safety professionals, mostly male, median age of 40. Circ. 6,000.
Photo Needs: Uses 3 photos/issue; 70% supplied by freelance photographers. Primarily uses photos of business, industry on-site, etc. Model release and photo captions preferred.
Making Contact & Terms: Provide resume, business card, brochure, flyer or tearsheets to be kept on file for possible assignments. Pays $600/color cover photo or $400/color inside photo. "Rates of payment vary quite substantially according to photographer experience." Pays on acceptance. Credit line given. Buys one-time rights.
Tips: In portfolio or samples, looking for "industry shots."

OHIO BUSINESS, 1720 Euclid Ave., Cleveland OH 44115. (216)621-1644. FAX: (216)621-5918. Managing Editor: Michael Moore. Monthly magazine. Emphasizes "all types of business within Ohio." Readers are executives and business owners. Circ. 50,000. Estab. 1977. Sample copy $2.
Photo Needs: Uses 20-25 photos/issue; 1-5 supplied by freelance photographers. Needs photos of "people and industrial processes within articles." Captions preferred.
Making Contact & Terms: Provide resume, business card, brochure, flyer or tearsheets to be kept on file for possible future assignments. SASE. Reports in 2 weeks. Pays $200 + /color cover photo, $25 + /b&w inside photo and $50 + /color inside photo. Pays on acceptance. Credit line given. Buys one-time rights. Simultaneous submissions and previously published work OK.
Tips: "Read the publication."

ONTARIO MOTORCOACH REVIEW, 6th Fl., 920 Yonge, Toronto, ON M4W 3C7 Canada. (416)961-1028. Executive Editor: John Howarth. Publication of the Ontario Motorcoach Association. Annual magazine. Readers are owners and motorcoach operators, tour operators, hotel and restaurant owners. Circ. 5,000. Sample copy and photo guidelines free with SASE.
Photo Needs: Uses 50 photos/issue; 50% supplied by freelance photographers. Needs travel photos. Photo captions required.
Making Contact & Terms: Provide resume to be kept on file for possible assignments. Uses b&w prints; 35mm, $2\frac{1}{4} \times 2\frac{1}{4}$, 4×5 transparencies. SASE. Reports in 2 weeks. Pays $200/color cover photo, $25/b&w and color inside photo. Pays 30 days after publication. Credit line given. Buys all rights.
Tips: Looks for "quality in composition and use of light."

OPHTHALMOLOGY MANAGEMENT, OPTOMETRIC MANAGEMENT, CONTACT LENS FORUM, Gralla Publications, 1515 Broadway, New York NY 10036. (212)869-1300. Art Director: Mark Tuchman. Monthly magazines. Circ. 13,000-14,000 each. Emphasizes eye care. Readers are optometrists and ophthalmologists.

Photo Needs: Uses 2 photos/issue; 50% supplied by freelance photographers. Needs photos of scenes of doctor's offices, eye doctors, occasional graphic look, e.g., in issue concerning optometry in the year 2000, photographer used futuristic space scene. "Our needs vary from project to project. We want photographers who can turn around quality work fast and who are resourceful in getting what is needed to do a shot." Model release and captions preferred.

Making Contact & Terms: Provide resume, business card, brochure, flyer or tearsheets to be kept on file for possible future assignments. Reports depending on need. Pays $95-230/b&w photo; $500 maximum/color cover photo. Pays on acceptance. Credit line given. Previously published work OK.

Tips: "We are trying to use photojournalistic shots more often. We're interested in expanding our file of photographers in major cities around the country for specific assignments. Also for special effects photography, I'm looking for people who can be creative without being campy. I'm most interested in photographs that have personality, not a 'stock photo' look. Aesthetic but with some grit. Don't send work 'on spec' that you need returned. We're too busy for that. Make a presentation that shows a singular style. We use stock photos for convenience but prefer assignment. In a typical issue we may use three photos including the cover, and the breakdown will be mixed as to what is assignment and what is stock."

OREGON BUSINESS MAGAZINE, Suite 407, 921 S.W. Marrisch, Portland OR 97205. (503)223-0304. Production Manager: Ervin Miller. Monthly. Circ. 20,000. Emphasizes business features. Readers are business executives. Sample copy free with SASE and 90¢ postage.

Photo Needs: Uses about 15 photos/issue; 5 supplied by freelancers. "Usually photos must tie to a story. Query any ideas." Model release and captions required.

Making Contact & Terms: Query first with idea. Reports in 1 week. Pays $20/b&w inside photo; $25/ color inside photo with stories; $25 minumum/job. Pays on publication. Credit line given. Buys one-time rights. Simultaneous submissions and previously published work OK.

Tips: "Query first, also get hooked up with an Oregon writer. Must tie photos to an Oregon business story."

OUTLOOK, Suite 222, 99 Canal Center Plaza, Alexandria VA 22314. (703)683-6422. Editor: Judith Zwolak. Monthly. Circ. 8,000. Emphasizes general business and commercial and industrial asbestos abatement insulation for personnel in the commercial and industrial insulation industries. Sample copy $2.

Photo Needs: Uses photos of industrial and commercial construction projects across the USA. Uses photographers for everything from head shots to covers. Publication features 4-color process on feature material and cover. Especially needs photos on commercial/industrial insulation projects asbestos abatement.

Making Contact & Terms: Query with resume. SASE. Reports in 1 week. Negotiates payment. Credit line given. Simultaneous and previously published work OK.

PAPER SALES, 1 E. 1st St., Duluth MN 55802. (218)723-9225. Editor: Jane Seybolt. Monthly. Emphasizes paper and allied products including plastic (disposable foodservice items), and packaging and sanitary maintenance products (cleaners, mops/brooms, soaps). Readers are the paper distributors and their sales reps. Circ. 13,000. Photo guidelines sheet available.

Photo Needs: Uses about 10 photos/issue. Needs end-user shots of products, e.g., groundwood papers, restaurant disposables, soaps, text & cover papers, floor care systems, labels, computer software, envelopes, bags and sacks, non-impact papers, plastic films, computer paper, business forms and cups (disposable). Model release preferred; captions required.

Making Contact & Terms: Query with samples; send b&w or color contact sheets by mail for consideration; or provide resume, business card, brochure, flyer or tearsheets to be kept on file for possible future assignments. SASE. Pays $200/color cover photo; $25/b&w inside photo; $50-100/color inside photo. Pays on publication. Credit line given. Buys one-time rights; usually "one-time"; "if we want to use it again, may ask for 'all'; however, prefer to be first to use photo."

Tips: "Photos need to show products being used with no brand name visible, if possible. Read trade journals; study our magazine."

PEDIATRIC ANNALS, 6900 Grove Rd., Thorofare NJ 08086. (609)848-1000. Editor: Sandra Patterson. Monthly journal. Emphasizes "the pediatrics profession." Readers are practicing pediatricians. Circ. 36,000. Sample copy free with SASE.

Photo Needs: Uses 1-4 photos/issue; all supplied by freelance photographers. Needs photos of "children in medical settings, some with adults." Written release required; captions preferred. Query with samples; provide resume, business card, brochure, flyer or tearsheets to be kept on file for possible future assignments. Reports in 6 weeks. Pays $350/color cover photo; $25/inside photo; $50/color inside photo. Pays on publication. Credit line given. Buys all rights. Simultaneous and previously published work OK.

PET BUSINESS, P.O. Box 2300, Miami FL 33243. Editor: Karen Payne. Monthly news magazine for pet industry professionals. Circ. 17,000. Sample copy $3. Guidelines free with SASE.
Photo Needs: Photos of well-groomed pet animals (preferably purebred) of any age in a variety of situations. Identify subjects. Also, news/action shots related to the pet trade.
Terms: Buys all rights. Payment upon publication; $10 for b&w glossy, $20 for color print or transparency. Credit line given. Submit photos for consideration. Reports within 1 month with SASE.
Tips: Uncluttered background. Portrait-style always welcome. Close-ups best. No humans in photo! News/action shots if timely.

PETROLEUM INDEPENDENT, 1101 16th St. NW, Washington DC 20036. (202)857-4775. Editor: Bruce Wells. Monthly magazine. Circ. 14,000. Emphasizes independent petroleum industry. "Don't confuse us with the major oil companies, pipelines, refineries, gas stations. Our readers explore for and produce crude oil and natural gas in the lower 48 states. Our magazine covers energy politics, regulatory problems, the national outlook for independent producers."
Subject Needs: Photo essay/photo feature; scenic; and special effects/experimental, all of oil field subjects. Please send your best work.
Color: Uses 35mm or larger transparencies. Pays $35-100/photo.
Cover: Uses 35mm or larger transparencies. Payment negotiable.
Tips: "We want to see creative use of camera—scenic, colorful or high contrast-studio shots. Creative photography to illustrate particular editorial subjects (natural gas decontrol, the oil glut, etc.) is always wanted. We've already got plenty of rig shots—we want carefully set-up shots to bring some art to the oil field."

PGA MAGAZINE, Suite 430, 2701 Troy Center Dr., Troy MI 48084. (313)362-0044. Art Director: Sandra Langan. Monthly. Circ. 50,000. Emphasizes golf for 15,500 club professionals and apprentices nationwide plus 13,000 amateur golfers.
Photo Needs: Uses 20 photos/issue; 5 are supplied by freelance photographers. Interested in photos of world's greatest golf courses, major tournament action, golf course scenic and junior golfers. Model release and captions required.
Making Contact & Terms: Send material by mail to keep on file, arrange personal interview to show portfolio and submit portfolio for review. Uses mostly color slides, very few color prints. SASE. Pays $50-200/color photo inside. Credit line given. Pays on publication. Buys first time rights. Previously published work OK.
Tips: "Know golf and golf course architecture."

PHARMACEUTICAL TECHNOLOGY, 859 Willamette St., Eugene OR 97440. (503)343-1200. Art Director: Barbara A. Mickelson. Monthly. Emphasizes pharmaceuticals. Readers are scientists and manufacturers of pharmaceutical products/equipment. Circ. 30,000. Sample copy free with 8½×11 SASE. Photo guidelines free with SASE.
Photo Needs: Uses 6-10 photos/issue; 1, 4/c, supplied by freelancer. Needs photos of pharmaceutical topics. Photo captions preferred.
Making Contact & Terms: Query with list of stock photo subjects; provide resume, business card, brochure, flyer or tearsheets to be kept on file for possible future assignments. Does not return unsolicited material. Reports in 1 month. Pays $300/color cover photo; $100/b&w inside photo. Pays on publication. Credit line given on table of contents page or with photo. Buys one-time rights. Simultaneous submissions OK.
Tips: Looks for "an artistic look at pharmaceutical products/equipment. Colorful and dramatic. We seldom use people shots."

PHOTOMETHODS, CS9043, Hicksville NY 11802-9043. (516)942-0190, FAX: (516)942-0230. Editor-in-Chief: David A. Silverman. Associate Editor: Mike Ballai. Art Director: Debbie Todd. Monthly magazine. Circ. 55,000. Estab. 1957. Emphasizes industrial imagemaking by the in-house (captive) visual communicator and corporate/commercial photographer. Covers all media of visual communications including traditional silver-halide still and motion pictures, still and motion video, audiovisuals, computergraphics, etc. Readers work in industry, military, government, medicine, scientific research, evidence, police departments. Buys one-time rights for cvers.
Making Contact & Terms: Query with resume of credits, samples or dupe photos for consideration. Original photos or slides sent at contributor's risk. Credit line given. Pays on publication. Reports in 5 weeks. SASE. Uses glossy, unmounted b&w prints. Captions required. Also uses color prints or any size transparencies. Captions required. Free sample copy. Photo guidelines with SASE.
Tips: Images must relate to some aspect of "industrial" imaging.

THE PHYSICIAN AND SPORTSMEDICINE, 4530 W. 77th St., Minneapolis MN 55435. (612)835-3222. Photo Editor: Ann Harste. Monthly journal. Emphasizes sports medicine. Readers are 85% physicians; 15% athletic trainers, coaches, athletes and general public. Circ. 120,000. Photo guidelines available.

Photo Needs: Uses about 25 photos/issue; 20 supplied by freelance photographers. Needs "primarily generic sports shots—color slides preferred." Model release preferred.

Making Contact & Terms: Query with list of stock photo subjects; provide resume, business card, brochure, flyer or tearsheets to be kept on file for possible future assignments. Does not return unsolicited material. Reports in 1 month. Pays $250/color cover; $75/b&w half page, $100/color half page; $100/b&w page, $150/color page. Also pays $50/hour; $250/half day; or $450/full day. Pays on publication. Credit line given. Buys one-time rights unless otherwise specified. Simultaneous and previously published submissions OK.

Tips: "Be patient, submit shots that are specific to the subject defined, and submit technically sound (clear, sharp) photos."

*PIPELINE AND UTILITIES CONSTRUCTION, Box 22267, Houston TX 77227. (713)662-0676. FAX: (713)722-0676. Editor: Chris Horner. Monthly. Emphasizes construction of oil and gas, water and sewer underground pipelines and cable. Readers are contractor key personnel and company construction managers. Circ. 18,000. Estab. 1945. Sample copy $2.

Photo Needs: "Uses photos of pipeline construction but must have editorial material on project with the photos." Will review photos with accompanying ms only.

Making Contact & Terms: Send unsolicited photos by mail for consideration. Uses 4×5 or 8×10 color or b&w prints. SASE. Reports in 1 month. Pays $100-300 for text/photo package. Buys one-time rights. Simultaneous submissions OK.

Tips: "We rarely use freelance photography. Freelancers are competing with staff as well as complimentary photos supplied by equipment manufacturers. Subject matter must be unique, striking, and 'off the beaten track' (i.e., somewhere we wouldn't travel ourselves to get photos)."

PIZZA TODAY, Box 114, Santa Claus IN 47579. (812)937-4464. Editor: Paula Werne. Monthly. Emphasizes pizza trade. Readers are pizza shop owner/operators. Circ. 41,000. Estab. 1983. Sample copy for $9\frac{1}{2} \times 12\frac{1}{2}$ SAE with $1.41 postage.

Photo Needs: Uses 80 photos/issue; 20 supplied by freelancers;100% from assignment. Needs how-tos of pizza making, product shots, profile shots. Special needs include celebrities eating pizza, politicians eating pizza. Model release and captions required.

Making Contact & Terms: Provide resume, business card, brochure, flyer or tearsheets to be kept on file for possible future assignments. SASE. Reports in 1 month. Pays $5-15/b&w photo; $20-30/color photo (prefer 35mm slides); all fees are negotiated in advance. Pays on publication. Credit line given. Buys all rights. Will negotiate with photographer unwilling to sell all rights. Previously published work OK.

Tips: Accept samples by mail only. "Team up with writer/contributor and supply photos to accompany article. We are not looking for specific food shots—looking for freelancers who can go to pizza shops and take photos which capture the atmosphere, the warmth and humor; 'The human touch.' "

PLANT, Sentry Communications, Suite 500, 245 Fairview Mall Dr., Willowdale, ON M2J 4T1 Canada. (416)490-0220. FAX: (416)490-0119. Editor: Ron Richardson. Published 20 times/year. Emphasizes manufacturing. Readers are plant managers and engineers. Circ. 52,000. Sample copy free with SASE and 67¢ Canadian postage.

Photo Needs: Uses about 6-8 photos/issue; 1-2 supplied by freelance photographers. Needs photos "to illustrate technical subjects featured in a particular issue—many 'concept' or 'theme' shots used on covers." Model release preferred; captions required.

Making Contact & Terms: Query with samples; provide resume, business card, brochure, flyer or tearsheets to be kept on file for possible future assignments. SASE. Reports in 1 month. Pays $150-300/color cover photo; $35-50/b&w and $50-200/color inside photo; $100-300/job; $120-600 for text/photo package. Pays on acceptance. Credit line given. Buys first North American serial rights.

Tips: Prefers to see "industrial experience, variety (i.e., photos in plants) in samples. Read the magazine. Remember we're Canadian."

PLASTICS TECHNOLOGY, 633 Third Ave., New York NY 10017. (212)986-4800. Editor: Matthew Naitove. Art Director: Anita Tai. Monthly magazine. Emphasizes plastics product manufacturing. Readers are engineers and managers in manufacturing plants using plastics. Circ. 41,000.

Photo Needs: Uses about 30-35 photos/issue; 1 supplied by freelance photographer. Needs manufacturing plant shots (mostly interiors) and machine close-ups, product still-lifes. Model release required; captions preferred.

Making Contact & Terms: Arrange a personal interview to show portfolio. SASE. Reports in 1 week. Pays $150-300/b&w photo, $250-400/color photo, $700/day, $350/½ day. Pays on publication. Credit line given "mainly on covers." Buys one-time rights. Simultaneous and previously published work "if in non-competition medium" OK.

Tips: In portfolio or samples, wants to see "industrial and scientific subjects. Also, creativity and consistent quality with good lighting—especially still life close-ups.

POLICE MAGAZINE, 6300 Yarrow Dr., Carlsbad CA 92009. (619)438-2511. Editor: Sean T. Hilferty. Monthly. Emphasizes law enforcement. Readers are various members of the law enforcement community: especially police officers. Sample copy $2 with 9×12 SAE and $1.50 postage. Photo guidelines free with SASE.
Photo Needs: Uses about 15 photos/issue; 99% supplied by freelance photographers. Needs law-enforcement related photos. Special needs include photos relating to daily police work, crime prevention, international law enforcement, police technology and humor. Model release required; captions preferred.
Making Contact & Terms: Arrange a personal interview to show portfolio; send b&w prints, 35mm transparencies, b&w contact sheet or color negatives by mail for consideration. SASE. Pays $100/color cover photo; $20/b&w photo; $30/color inside photo; $150-300/job; $150-300/text/photo package. Pays on acceptance. Buys all rights; rights returned to photographer 45 days after publication. Simultaneous submissions OK.
Tips: "Send for our editorial calendar and submit photos based on our projected needs. If we like your work, we'll consider you for future assignments."

POLICE TIMES/CHIEF OF POLICE, 1100 NE 125th St., North Miami FL 33161. (305)891-1700. Editor-in-Chief: Jim Gordon. Bimonthly magazines. Circ. 50,000+. For law enforcement officers at all levels. Needs photos of police officers in action, CB volunteers working with the police and group shots of police department personnel. Wants no photos that promote products or other associations. Buys 30-60 photos/year. Police oriented cartoons also accepted on spec. Buys all rights, but may reassign to photographer after publication. Send photos for consideration. Pays on acceptance. Reports in 3 weeks. SASE. Simultaneous submissions and previously published work OK. Sample copy $2.50; free photo guidelines. Model release and captions preferred. Credit line given if requested; editor's option.
B&W: Send 8×10 glossy prints. Pays $5-10 upwards.
Cover: Send 8×10 glossy color prints. Pays $25-50 upwards.
Tips: "We are open to new and unknowns in small communities where police are not given publicity."

POLLED HEREFORD WORLD, 4700 E. 63rd St., Kansas City MO 64130. (816)333-7731. Editor: Ed Bible. Monthly magazine. Circ. 11,500. Estab. 1947. Emphasizes Polled Hereford cattle for registered breeders, commercial cattle breeders and agribusinessmen in related fields.
Specs: Uses b&w prints and color transparencies and prints.
Payment & Terms: Pays $5/b&w print, $100/color transparency or print. Pays on publication.
Making Contact: Query. Reports in 2 weeks.
Tips: Wants to see "Polled hereford cattle in quantities, in seasonal &/or scenic settings."

*THE PREACHER'S MAGAZINE, E. 10814 Broadway, Spokane WA 99206. (509)926-1545. Editor: Randal E. Denny. Quarterly professional journal for ministers. Emphasizes the pastoral ministry. Readers are pastors of large to small churches in 5 denominations; most pastors are male. Circ. 18,000. Estab. 1925. No sample copy available. No photo guidelines.
Photo Needs: Uses 1 photo/issue; 100% supplied by freelance photographers. Large variety needed for cover, depends on theme of issue. Model release and photo captions preferred.
Making Contact & Terms: Send 35mm b&w/color prints by mail for consideration. Reports ASAP. Pays $60/color cover photo. Pays on acceptance. Credit line given. Buys one-time rights. Simultaneous submissions and previously published work OK.
Tips: In photographer's samples wants to see "a variety of subjects for the front cover of our magazine. We rarely use photos within the magazine itself."

PRO SOUND NEWS, 2 Park Ave., New York NY 10016. (212)213-3444. Editor: Debra Pagan. Managing Editor: Chris Kimble. Monthly tabloid. Emphasizes professional recording, and sound and production industries. Readers are recording engineers, studio owners and equipment manufacturers worldwide. Circ. 17,500. Sample copy free with SASE.
Photo Needs: Uses about 12 photos/issue; all supplied by freelance photographers. Needs photos of recording sessions, sound reinforcement for concert tours, permanent installations. Model release and captions required.
Making Contact & Terms: Query with samples; send 8×10 color glossy prints by mail for consideration. SASE. Reports in 2 weeks. Pays by the job or for text/photo package. Pays on publication. Credit line given. Buys one-time rights. Simultaneous and previously published submissions OK.

PROFESSIONAL AGENT, 400 N. Washington St., Alexandria VA 22314. (703)836-9340. Editor: John S. DeMott. Monthly. Circ. 30,000. Emphasizes property/casualty insurance. Readers are independent insurance agents. Sample copy free with SASE.
Photo Needs: Uses about 20 photos/issue; 5 supplied by freelancers. Model release and captions required.
Making Contact & Terms: Arrange a personal interview to show portfolio; query with list of stock photo subjects; provide resume, business card, brochure, flyer or tearsheets to be kept on file for possible future assignments. Uses minimum 5×7 glossy color and b&w prints, 35mm and 2¼×2¼ transparencies. SASE. Reporting time varies. Pays $500-700/color cover photo. Pays on publication. Credit line given. Buys one-time rights or first North American serial rights, exclusive in the insurance industry.

PROFESSIONAL BUILDER, 1350 E. Touhy Ave., Des Plaines IL 60018. (708)635-8800. Editor: Roy Diez. Art Director: William Patton. Monthly magazine. Emphasizes housing and light construction; also remodeling. Readers are builders of housing and light construction. Circ. 140,000.
Photo Needs: Uses 100 photos/issue; 10% supplied by freelancers. Needs photos of architectural interiors and exteriors of current, innovative projects throughout USA; 4×5 format preferred. "We make assignments based on specific editorial needs only. We do not accept unsolicited photography! We are always looking for good photographers throughout the USA." Model release required.
Making Contact & Terms: Provide resume, business card, brochure, flyer or tearsheets to be kept on file for possible future assignments. Does not return unsolicited material. Reports in 1 month. Pays on publication. Credit line given. Buys all rights.

PROFESSIONAL PHOTOGRAPHER, 1090 Executive Way, Des Plaines IL 60018. (708)299-8161. FAX: (708)299-2685. Editor: Alfred DeBat. Senior Editor: Carol Howe. Art Director: Debbie Todd. Monthly. Emphasizes professional photography in the fields of portrait, wedding, commercial/advertising, corporate and industrial. Readers include professional photographers and photographic services and educators. Approximately half the circulation is Professional Photographers of America members. Circ. 32,000+. Estab. 1907. Sample copy $3.25 postpaid; photo guidelines with SASE.
Photo Needs: Uses 25-30 photos/issue; all supplied by freelance photographers. "We only accept material as illustration that relates directly to photographic articles showing professional studio, location, commercial and portrait techniques. A majority are supplied by Professional Photographers of America members." Reviews photos with accompanying ms only. "We always need commercial/advertising and industrial success stories. How to sell your photography to major accounts, unusual professional photo assignments." Model release preferred; captions required.
Making Contact & Terms: Query with resume of credits. "We want a story query, or complete ms if writer feels subject fits our magazine. Photos will be part of ms package." Uses 8×10 glossy unmounted b&w or color prints; 35mm, 2¼×2¼, 4×5 and 8×10 transparencies. SASE. Reports in 8 weeks. PPA members submit material unpaid to promote their photo businesses and obtain recognition. Credit line given. Previously published work OK.

PROGRESSIVE ARCHITECTURE, 600 Summer St., Box 1361, Stamford CT 06904. (203)348-7531. Editor: John Morris Dixon. Monthly magazine. Circ. 75,000. Emphasizes current information on building design and technology for professional architects. Photos purchased with or without accompanying ms and on assignment; 90% assigned. Pays $500/1-day assignment, $1,000/2-day assignment; $250/half-day assignment or on a per-photo basis. Credit line given. Pays on publication. Buys one-time rights. Send material by mail for consideration. SASE. Reports in 1 month.
Subject Needs: Architectural and interior design. Captions preferred.
B&W: Uses 8×10 glossy prints. Pays $25 minimum/photo.
Color: Uses 4×5 transparencies. Pays $50/photo.
Cover: Uses 4×5 transparencies. Vertical format preferred. Pays $50/photo.
Accompanying Mss: Interesting architectural or engineering developments/projects. Payment varies.
Tips: In samples, wants to see "straightforward architectural presentation."

PSYCHIATRIC ANNALS, 6900 Grove Rd., Thorofare NJ 08086. (609)848-1000. FAX: (609)853-5991. Executive Editor: Mary Lou Jerrell. Monthly journal. Emphasizes psychiatry. Readers are practicing psychiatrists. Circ. 30,000. Estab. 1971. Sample copy free with SASE.
Photo Needs: Uses cover illustration only; supplied by freelance illustrators or photographers. Needs photos of people—abstract.
Making Contact—Terms: Query with samples; provide resume, business card, brochure, flyer or tearsheets to be kept on file for possible future assignments. SASE. Reports in 3 weeks. Pays maximum of $250/color cover photo; $150-250/color photo. Pays on publication. Credit line given. Buys one time publication rights. Simultaneous submissions and previously published work OK.

Tips: "We are a single-topic issue publication, and the illustrator receives copies of the manuscript. When looking at portfolios, we look for unusual approaches. We use illustrations, but are not averse to photographs if they illustrate our topic. Don't call several times a day."

PUBLIC WORKS MAGAZINE, 200 South Broad St., Ridgewood NJ 07451. (201)445-5800. Contact: Edward B. Rodie. Monthly magazine. Emphasizes the planning, design, construction, inspection, operation and maintenance of public works facilities. Ex: bridges, roads, water systems, landfills, etc. Readers are predominately male civil engineers, ages 20 and up. Some overlap with other planners, including consultants, department heads, etc. Circ. 52,000+. Sample copy free upon request. Photo guidelines available, but for cover only.
Photo Needs: Uses dozens of photos/issue. "Most photos are supplied by authors or with company press releases." Purchases photos with accompanying ms only. Photo captions required.
Making Contact & Terms: Provide resume, business card, brochure, flyer or tearsheets to be kept on file for possible assignments. SASE. Reports in 2 weeks. Payment negotiated with editor. Credit line given "if requested." Buys one-time rights.
Tips: "Nearly all of the photos used are submitted by the authors of articles (who are generally very knowledgeable in their field). They may occasionally use freelancers. Cover personality photos are done by staff and freelance photographers." To break in, "learn how to take good clear photos of public works projects that show good detail without clutter. Prepare a brochure and pass around to small and mid-size cities, towns and civil type consulting firms; larger (organizations) will probably have a staff photographers."

*QUALITY DIGEST, P.O. Box 1503, Red Bluff CA 96080. (916)527-6970. Editor: Scott M. Paton. Monthly digest. Emphasizes quality improvement. Readers are mainly mid-level and senior-level managers in large corporations. Circ. 4,000. Estab. 1981. Sample copy for $6.25. No photo guidelines.
Photo Needs: Uses 10-12 photos/issue; 50% supplied by freelance photographers. Needs photos of training sessions, meetings in progress, office situations and factory scenes. Special photo needs include Europe 1992 and service quality. Model release required; photo captions preferred.
Making Contact & Terms: Send b&w prints by mail for consideration. Reports in 1 month. Pays $100/b&w cover photo; $50/b&w inside photo. Pays on acceptance Credit line given. Buys all rights. Will negotiate with a photographer unwilling to sell all rights. Will consider simultaneous submissions. No perviously published work.

QUICK FROZEN FOODS INTERNATIONAL, 80 8th. Ave., New York NY 10012. Editor: John M. Saulnier. Quarterly magazine. Circ. 15,000. Emphasizes retailing, marketing, processing, packaging and distribution of frozen foods around the world. For international executives involved in the frozen food industry: manufacturers, distributors, retailers, brokers, importers/exporters, warehousemen, etc. Needs plant exterior shots, step-by-step in-plant processing shots, photos of retail store frozen food cases, head shots of industry executives, product shots, etc. Buys 20-30 photos annually. Buys all rights, but may reassign to photographer after publication. Query first with resume of credits. Pays on acceptance. Reports in 1 month. SASE. Sample copy free for 10×13 SAE and $2.40 postage.
B&W: Uses 5×7 glossy prints. Captions required. Pays $10 minimum.
Tips: A file of photographers' names is maintained; if an assignment comes up in an area close to a particular photographer, he may be contacted. "When submitting names, inform us if you are capable of writing a story, if needed."

RADIO-ELECTRONICS MAGAZINE, 500 B Bi-Country Blvd., Farmingdale NY 11735. (516)293-3000. Editor: Brian C. Fenton. Monthly magazine. Emphasizes electronics. Readers are electrical engineers and technicians, both male and female, ages 25-60. Circ. 250,000. Sample copy free with 8½×11 SASE.
Photo Needs: Uses 25-50 photos/issue; 2-3 supplied by freelance photographers. Needs photos of how-to, computer screens, test equipment and digital displays. Purchases photos with accompanying ms only. Model relesase required; photo captions preferred.
Making Contact & Terms: Submit portfolio for review. Provide resume, business card, brochure, flyer or tearsheets to be kept on file for possible assignments. SASE. Reports in 2 weeks. Pays $400/ color cover photo. Pays on acceptance. Credit line given. Buys all rights, but willing to negotiate. Simultaneous submissions OK.

RDH, The National Magazine for Dental Hygiene Professionals, 225 N. New Rd., Waco TX 76714. (817)776-9000. Editor: Laura Albrecht. Monthly magazine. Emphasizes dentistry and dental hygienists. Readers are female dental hygienists, ages 22-35. Circ. 55,000. Sample copy free upon request.

Photo Needs: Uses 12 photos/issue; 50% supplied by freelance photographers. Uses cover shots which relate to cover story. Purchases photos with accompanying ms only. Plans to use more location shots across U.S. Also, some studio and outside work. Model release and photo captions required.
Making Contact & Terms: Query with resume of credits along with business card, brochure, flyer or tearsheets to be kept on file for possible assignments. Query with list of stock photos subjects. Cannot return unsolicited material. Reports in 1 month. Pays on publication. Credit line given. Buys first N.A. serial rights.
Tips: "Since we buy so few photos for the magazine, each assignment is based on individual considerations: expenses, pay rate, processing." To break in, "read and review the publication. Write for a sample copy. Know your audience. This will save you time and money when submitting work."

RECOMMEND WORLDWIDE, Suite 120, 50979 N.W. 151st St., Miami Lake FL 33014. (305)828-0123. Art Director: Linda Ferguson. Managing Editor: Carl Von Wodtke. Monthly. Emphasizes travel. Readers are travel agents, meeting planners, hoteliers, ad agencies. Sample copy for 8½×11 SAE with $2.50 postage.
Photo Needs: Uses about 40 photos/issue; 70% supplied by freelance photographers. "Our publication divides the world up into 7 regions. Every month we use destination oriented photos of animals, cities, resorts, cruise lines, all types of travel photography from all over the world." Model release and captions preferred; identification required.
Making Contact & Terms: "We prefer a resume, stock list and sample card or tearsheets with photo review later." SASE. Pays $150/color cover photo; $10/b&w inside photo; $25/color inside photo; $50/ color page. Pays 30 days upon publication. Credit line given. Buys one-time rights. Simultaneous submissions and previously published work OK.
Tips: Prefers to see "transparencies—either 2¼ or 35mm first quality originals, travel oriented."

RECYCLING TODAY, 4012 Bridge Ave., Cleveland OH 44113. (216)961-4130, (800)456-0707. FAX: (216)961-0364. Editor: Arnie Rosenberg. Monthly magazine. Emphasizes recycling, solid-waste management and scrap metals. Readers are dealers, processors and brokers. Circ. 21,000. Estab. 1963. Sample copy available.
Photo Needs: Needs industry-related photos, not set up; should contain people. Photo captions required.
Making Contact & Terms: Payment varies. SASE. Pays on publication. Credit line given. Buys all rights; will negotiate with a photographer unwilling to sell all rights.
Tips: Looks for "ability to capture action. No tendency for set-up shots."

*REFEREE, Box 161, Franksville WI 53126. (414)632-8855. Editor: Tom Hammill. Trade publication. Monthly magazine. Readers are mostly male, ages 30-50. Circ. 35,000. Estab. 1976. Sample copy free with 9×12 SASE and 5 first-class stamps. Photo guidelines free with SASE and 25¢.
Photo Needs: Uses up to 50 photos/issue; 75% supplied by freelance photographers. Needs action officiating shots—all sports. Photo needs are ongoing. Model release and photo captions preferred.
Making Contact & Terms: Send unsolicited photos by mail for consideration. Any format is accepted. Reports in 1-2 weeks. Pays $100/color cover photo; $75/b&w cover photo; $25/color inside photo; $15/ b&w inside photo. Pays on publication. Credit line given. Rights purchased varies; will negotiate with photographer not willing to sell all rights. Simultaneous submissions and previously published work OK.
Tips: Prefers photos which bring out the uniqueness of being a sports official. Need photos primarily of officials at high school level in baseball, football, basketball, soccer, and softball in action. Other sports acceptable, but used less frequently. "When at sporting events, take a few shots with the officials in mind, even though you may be on assignment for another reason." Address all queries to Tom Hammill, editor. "Don't be afraid to give it a try. We're receptive, always looking for new freelance conributors. We are constantly looking for offbeat pix of officials/umpires. Our needs in this area have increased."

REGISTERED REPRESENTATIVE, Suite 280, 18818 Teller Ave., Irvine CA 92715. (714)851-2220. Art Director: Chuck LaBresh. Monthly magazine. Emphasizes stock brokerage industry. Magazine is "requested and read by 90% of the nation's stock brokers." Circ. 80,000. Sample copy for $2.50.
Photo Needs: Uses about 8 photos/issue; 5 supplied by freelance photographers. Needs environmental portraits of financial and brokerage personalities, and conceptual shots of financial ideas, all by assignment only. Model release and captions preferred.
Making Contact & Terms: Arrange a personal interview to show portfolio; query with sample or list of stock photo subjects; provide resume, business card, brochure, flyer or tearsheets to be kept on file for possible future assignments. Does not return unsolicited material. Pays $300-900/b&w or color cover photo; $150-300/b&w or color inside photo. Pays 30 days after publication. Credit line given. Buys one-time rights. Simultaneous submissions or previously published work OK.

REMODELING, 655 15th St. NW, Washington DC 20005. (202)737-0717. Managing Editor: Leslie Ensor. Published 11 times/year. "Business magazine for remodeling contractors." Readers are "small contractors involved in residental and commercial remodeling." Circ. 85,000. Sample copy free with 8x11 SASE.
Photo Needs: Uses 10-15 photos/issue; number supplied by freelancers varies. Needs photos of remodeled residences, both before and after. Reviews photos with "short description of project, including architect's or contractor's name and phone number." "We have three regular photo features: *Double Take* is photo caption piece about an architectural photo that fools the eye. *Close Up* is a photo caption showing architectural details."
Making Contact & Terms: Provide resume, business card, brochure, flyer or tearsheets to be kept on file for possible future assignments. Reports in 1 month. Pays $100/color cover photo; $25/b&w inside photo; $50/color inside photo; $300 maximum/job. Pays on acceptance. Credit line given. Buys one-time rights.
Tips: Wants "interior and exterior photos of residences that emphasize the architecture over the furnishings."

RESCUE MAGAZINE, Jems Publishing Co., Suite 201, 674 Via De La Valle, Box 1026, Solana Beach CA 92075. (619)481-1128. Art Director: Robert Schmitt. Bimonthly. Emphasizes techniques, equipment, action stories with unique rescues; paramedics, EMTs, rescue divers, fire fighters, etc. Rescue personnel are most of our readers. Circ. 25,000. Sample copy free with 9x11 SAE and $1.58 postage. Photo guidelines free with SASE.
Photo Needs: Uses 20-25 photos/issue; 5-10 supplied by freelance photographers. Needs rescue scenes, transport, injured victims, equipment and personnel, training. Special photo needs include strong color shots showing newsworthy rescue operations, including a unique or difficult rescue/extrication, treatment, transport, personnel, etc. Black-and-whites showing same. Model release preferred; captions required.
Making Contact & Terms: Query with samples; or send 5×7 or larger glossy b&w or color prints, 35mm or 2¼×2¼ transparencies or b&w or color contacts sheets by mail for consideration. SASE. Reports in 3 weeks. Pays $150-200/color cover photo; $25-35/b&w inside photo; $50-75/color inside photo. Pays on publication. Credit line given. Buys one-time rights. Previously published work OK (must be labeled as such).
Tips: "Ride along with a rescue crew or team. This can be firefighters, paramedics, mountain rescue teams, dive rescue teams, and so on. Get in close." Looks for "photographs that show rescuers in action, using proper techniques and wearing the proper equipment. Submit timely photographs that show the technical aspects of rescue."

RESOURCE RECYCLING, Box 10540, Portland OR 97210. (503)227-1319. Editor: Jerry Powell. Monthly. Estab. 1982. Emphasizes "the recycling of waste materials (paper, metals, glass, etc.)" Readers are "recycling company managers, local government officials, waste haulers and environmental group executives." Circ. 10,000. Sample copy free with $2 postage plus 9×12 SASE.
Photo Needs: Uses about 5-15 photos/issue; 1-5 supplied by freelancers. Needs "photos of recycling facilities, curbside recycling collections, secondary materials (bundles of newspapers, soft drink containers), etc." Model release and captions preferred.
Making Contact & Terms: Send glossy b&w prints and b&w contact sheet. SASE. Reports in 1 month. Payment "varies by experience and photo quality." Pays on publication. Credit line given. Buys first North American serial rights. Simultaneous submissions OK.
Tips: "Because *Resource Recycling* is a trade journal for the recycling industry, we are looking only for photos that relate to recycling issues."

RESTAURANT HOSPITALITY, 1100 Superior Ave., Cleveland OH 44114. (216)696-7000. Executive Editor: Michael DeLuca. Monthly. Circ. 121,000. Emphasizes "restaurant management, hotel foodservice, cooking, interior design." Readers are "restaurant owners, chefs, foodservice chain executives." Sample copy free with 8×10 SAE and $1 postage.
Photo Needs: Uses about 30 photos/issue; half supplied by freelance photographers. Needs "people with food, restaurant and foodservice interiors and occasional food photos." Special needs include "spectacular food and/or beverage shots; query first." Model release and captions preferred.
Making Contact & Terms: Query with resume of credits or samples, or list of stock photo subjects; provide resume, business card, brochure, flyer or tearsheets to be kept on file for possible future assignments. SASE. Reports in 2 weeks. Pays $150-450/job plus normal expenses. Pays on acceptance. Credit line given. Buys exclusive rights. Previously published work OK "if exclusive to foodservice press."
Tips: "Let us know you exist; we can't assign a story if we don't know you. Send resume, business card, samples, etc. along with query or introductory letter."

RESTAURANT/HOTEL DESIGN INTERNATIONAL, 633 3rd Ave., New York NY 10017. (212)984-2440. Editor-in-Chief: Mary Jean Madigan. Monthly. Circ. 40,000. Readers are architects, designers, restaurant and hotel executives.
Photo Needs: "We need high quality previously unpublished architectural photographs of restaurant/hotel/lounge/disco/senior living facilities interiors and exteriors. No people, no food set-ups, please."
Making Contact & Terms: Send material by mail for consideration. Prefers to see a variety of interior and exterior shots (location work preferred over studio shots) in a portfolio. Uses 8 × 10 b&w prints and 4 × 5 color slides. SASE. Reports in 1 month. Pays per photo. Credit line given. Buys one-time rights.
Tips: "Virtually all our photographs are supplied by design firms, architects, or photographers on spec. We make very, very few assignments."

RN MAGAZINE, 680 Kinderkamack Rd., Oradell NJ 07649. (201)262-3030. Editor-in-Chief: Richard Service. Art Director: Andrea di Benedetto. Monthly. Circ. 275,000. Readers are registered nurses. Sample copy $3.
Photo Needs: Uses approximately 2-3 photos/issue. Photographers are used on assignment basis. "We select the photographers by previous work." Needs photos on clinical how-to and some symbolic theme photos. Model release and captions required.
Making Contact & Terms: Query with resume of photo credits and submit portfolio by mail for review. SASE. Reports in 2 weeks. Payment negotiable. Credit line given. Pays on acceptance. Buys one-time reproduction rights; additional rights are renegotiated. Previously published work OK with qualifications.

ROOFER MAGAZINE, 10990 Metro Pkwy., Ft. Myers FL 33912. (813)275-7663. Editor: Ms. Kaerrie A. Simons. Art Director: Angelo Cane. Monthly. Estab. 1981. Circ. 16,000. Emphasizes the roofing industry and all facets of the roofing business. Readers are roofing contractors, manufacturers, architects, specifiers, consultants and distributors. Sample copy free with 9 × 12 SAE and $1.75 postage.
Photo Needs: Uses about 25 photos/issue; few are supplied by freelancers. Needs photos of unusual roofs or those with a humorous slant (once published a photo with a cow stranded on a roof during a flood). Needs several photos of a particular city or country to use in photo essay section. Model release required; captions preferred.
Making Contact & Terms: Query with samples. Provide resume, brochure and tearsheets to be kept on file for possible future assignments. Does not return unsolicited material. Reports in 1 month. Pays $25 maximum/b&w photo; $50 maximum/color photo. Pays maximum $125 per page for photo essays. Pays on publication. Buys all rights.
Tips: "Good lighting is a must. Clear skies, beautiful landscaping around the home or building featured add to the picture. Looking for anything unique, in either the angle of the shot or the type of roof it is. Humorous photos are given special consideration. No photos of reroofing jobs on your home will be accepted. Most of the photos we publish in each issue are contributed by our authors. Freelance photographers should submit material that would be useful for our photographic essays, depicting particular cities or countries. We've given assignments to freelance photographers before, but most submissions are the ideas of the freelancer."

SALOME: A JOURNAL FOR THE PERFORMING ARTS, 5548 N. Sawyer, Chicago IL 60625. (312)539-5745. Editor: Effie Mihopoulos. Quarterly. Emphasizes performing arts. Estab. 1975. Sample copy $4. Photo guidelines free with SASE.
Photo Needs: Uses approx. 500 photos/issue; 50% supplied by freelance photographers; 10% freelance assignment; 5-25% stock. Needs photos of performing arts subjects. Model release and photo captions preferred; identification of subject (if person) necessary.
Making Contact & Terms: Send b&w prints by mail for consideration. SASE. Reports in 2 weeks. Pays in copy of magazine. Pays on publication. Credit line given. Buys one-time rights. Simultaneous submissions and previously published work OK (must state with submission).
Tips: Looks for "good composition and a striking image that immediately grabs your attention." There is a trend of "more good photographers creating fiercer competition. Send an overview of photos - examine previous issue of magazine to prepare a sample portfolio."

SCHOOL SHOP, Box 8623, Ann Arbor MI 48107. (313)769-1211. Art Director: Sharon K. Miller. Monthly except June and July. *School Shop* is a journal for industrial arts/technology education, and trade and industrial education teachers and administrators. Circ. 47,000. Sample copy free with 9 × 12 SAE with $1 postage.
Photo Needs: Uses 10-15 photos/issue. We use only photographs depicting activities and projects in industrial/technology and trade and industrial education. Special needs include photos that show new developments in the industrial/technology education field. Captions required.

Making Contact & Terms: Send b&w or color prints by mail for consideration; provide brochure, flyer or tearsheets to be kept on file for possible future assignments. SASE. Reports in 1 month. Payment depends on usage. Pays on publication. Credit line given. Buys all rights. Will negotiate with photographer unwilling to sell all rights.

THE SCIENTIST, 3501 Market St., Philadelphia PA 19104. (215)386-0100, ext. 1553. Art Director: Amy Decker Henry. Biweekly tabloid. Emphasizes science. Readers are mostly male scientists or science administrators. Circ. 30,000.
Photo Needs: Uses 30-40 photos/issue; 30-50% supplied by freelance photographers. Uses photos of "mostly people in labs or with work." Model release and photo captions preferred.
Making Contact & Terms: Provide resume, business card, brochure, flyer or tearsheets to be kept on file for possible assignments. SASE. Reports in 1 month. Pays $125/b&w cover or inside photo. Pays on publication. Credit line given. Buys one-time rights. Previously published work OK.
Tips: "We only use black & white photographs. Since most of our stuff is people oriented, I'm looking for unusual portraits."

SEAFOOD LEADER, 1115 NW 46th St., Seattle WA 98107. (206)789-6506. Managing Editor: Wayne Lee. Published quarterly. Emphasizes seafood. Readers are buyers and brokers of seafood. Circ. 15,000. Sample copy $5 with 9 × 12 SASE.
Photo Needs: Uses about 40 photos/issue; half supplied by freelance photographers. Needs photos of international seafood harvesting and farming, supermarkets, restaurants, shrimp, many more. Model release preferred.
Making Contact & Terms: Query with list of stock photo subjects. Send photos on subjects we request. SASE. "We only want it on our topics." Reports in 1 month. Pays $100/color cover photo; $50/color inside photo. Pays on publication. Credit line given. Buys one-time rights. Previously published work OK.
Tips: "Call and ask what topics we need photos on for the next issue." Looks for "aesthetic shots of seafood, shots of people interacting with seafood in which expressions are captured (i.e. not posed shots); artistic shots of seafood emphasizing color and shape."

SECOND IMPRESSIONS, Box 930, Ganges, BC V0S 1E0 Canada. (604)537-9933. Editor: Al McGee. Bimonthly magazine. Emphasizes printing, graphic arts industry. Readers are 18 years old and up, male and female, and are in printing trade. Circ. 6,131. Sample copy available.
Photo Needs: Uses 6 photos/issue; 4 supplied by freelance photographers. Photo captions required.
Making Contact & Terms: Provide resume, business card, brochure, flyer or tearsheets to be kept on file for possible assignments. Pays $100/color cover photo, $75/b&w cover photo, $50/color inside photo, $30/b&w inside photo. Pays on acceptance. Credit line given. Buys first N.A. serial rights.

SECURITY DEALER, 210 Crossways Park Dr., Woodbury NY 11797. (516)496-8000. FAX: (516)496-8013. Editor: Susan Brady. Monthly magazines. Emphasizes security subjects. Readers are blue collar businessmen installing alarm systems. Circ. 22,000. Sample copy free with SASE.
Photo Needs: Uses 2-5 photos/issue; none at present supplied by freelance photographers. Needs photos of security-application-equipment. Model release preferred.
Making Contact & Terms: Send b&w and color prints by mail for consideration. SASE. Reports "immediately." Pays $200/color cover photo; $100/inside color photos. Pays 2 weeks after publication. Credit line given. Buys one-time rights in trade industry. Simultaneous submissions and previously published work OK.

*SERVICE STATION MANAGEMENT, 950 Lee St., Des Plaines IL 60016. (708)296-0770. Contact: Editor. Monthly magazine. Emphasizes automotive technical and service stations, past and present. Readers are men ages 20-60, service station dealers and mechanics. Circ. 90,000. Estab. 1956. No sample copies available. No photo guidelines.
Photo Needs: Uses 10-20 photos/issue; 1-2 supplied by freelance photographers. Needs photos of automotive technology. Model release required; photo captions preferred.
Making Contact & Terms: Query with list of stock photo subjects. Reports in 1 month. Pays $3-500/color cover photo; $50-100/b&w cover photo; $1-300/color inside photo; $50-100/b&w inside photo. Pays on publication. Credit line given. Buys all rights. Will negotiate with a photographer unwilling to sell all rights. Will consider simultaneous submissions.

*SHEEP! MAGAZINE, W. 2997 Market Rd., Helenville WI 53137. (414)593-8385. FAX (414)593-8384. Editor: Dave Thompson. Trade publication. Monthly tabloid. Emphasizes sheep and wool. Readers are sheep and wool producers across the US and Canada. Circ. 13,000. Estab. 1982. Sample copy for $1. Photo guidelines available.

Photo Needs: Uses 30 photos/issue; 50% supplied by freelance photographers. Needs photos of sheep, lambs, sheep producers, wool, etc. Model release and photo captions preferred.
Making Contact & Terms: Send unsolicited photos by mail for consideration; provide resume, business card, brochure, flyer or tearsheets to be kept on file for possible assignments. Uses b&w and color prints; 35mm transparencies. SASE. Reports in 3 weeks. Pays $200/color cover photo; $150/b&w cover photo; $100/color inside photo; $50/b&w inside photo. Credit line given. Buys one-time rights and all rights; will negotiate with photographer not willing to sell all rights. Previously published work OK.
Tips: To break into the market freelancer must "do quality work."

*SHELTER SENSE, 5430 Grosvenor Lane, Suite 100, Bethesda MD 20814. (301)571-8984. Editor: Rhonda Lucas Donald. Monthly newsletter. Emphasizes animal protection. Readers are animal control and shelter workers, men and women, all ages. Circ. 3,000. Estab. 1978. Sample copy for $1 with 9 × 12 SASE and 2 first-class stamps. Photo guidelines not available.
Photo Needs: Uses 15 photos/issue; 35% supplied by freelance photographers. Needs photos of domestic animals interacting with people/humane workers; animals during the seasons; animal care, obedience; humane society work and functions, other companion animal shots. "We do not pay for manuscripts." Model release required; photo captions preferred.
Making Contact & Terms: Provide resume, business card, brochure, flyer or tearsheets to be kept on file for possible assignments. SASE. Reports in 3 weeks. Pays $35/b&w cover photo; $25/b&w inside photo. Pays on acceptance. Credit line given. Buys one-time rights.
Tips: Keep in mind "much of the material and photos used in *Shelter Sense* is donated by humane society workers/volunteers. However, we will pay for good b&w photos that we think we will be able to use."

SIGNCRAFT MAGAZINE, Box 06031, Fort Myers FL 33906. (813)939-4644. Editor: Tom McIltrot. Bimonthly magazine. Estab. 1980. Readers are sign artists and sign shop personnel. Circ. 21,000. Sample copy $3. Photo guidelines free with SASE.
Photo Needs: Uses over 100 photos/issue; few at present supplied by freelance photographers. Needs photos of well-designed, effective signs. Model release and captions preferred.
Making Contact & Terms: Query with samples; send b&w, color prints; 35mm, 2¼ × 2¼ transparencies; b&w, color contact sheet by mail for consideration. SASE. Reports in 1 month. Pays on publication. Credit line given. Buys first North American serial rights. Previously published work possibly OK.
Tips: "If you have some background or past experience with sign making, you may be able to provide photos for us."

SKIES AMERICA, 7730 S.W. Mohawk St., Tualatrin OR 97069. (503)691-1955. Editor: Terri J. Wallo. Photo Editor: James Rullo. Monthly magazine. "We publish 5 inflight magazines for regional airlines on topics ranging from business to leisure and travel." Readers are affluent; frequent fliers; business owners/executives. Circ. 132,000. Sample copy $3.
Photo Needs: Uses 20 photos/issue; 5 supplied by freelance photographers. Needs photos of cityscapes, travel. Captions preferred.
Making Contact & Terms: Query with resume of credits and list of stock photo subjects. SASE. Reports in 1 month. Pays $300/text/photo package; separate photo payments negotiable. Pays on publication. Credit line given. Buys one-time rights. Simultaneous submissions and previously published work OK.

SMALL WORLD, #1212, 225 W. 34th St., New York NY 10001. (212)563-2742. Art Director: Dana Dolan. Monthly magazine. Emphasizes children's products and furniture for retailers and manufactuers. Circ. 8,000. Sample copy free with 10 × 14 SAE and $1 postage.
Photo Needs: Uses about 10 photos/issue; 2-3 supplied by freelance photographers on assignment basis. Needs photos of business people and their stores, children's fashion, still-life. Model release required.

 The asterisk before a listing indicates that the market is new in this edition. New markets are often the most receptive to freelance submissions.

Making Contact & Terms: Arrange a personal interview to show portfolio; submit portfolio for review. Provide resume, business card, brochure, flyer or tearshheets to be kept on file for possible future assignments. SASE. Pays $200/color cover photo; $125-200/color inside photo. Usually given as one assignment. Pays on publication. Credit line given. Buys all rights, but will negotiate.
Tips: Prefers to see photos of business people in portfolio. Looks for "energy, versatility, ability to deal with changes on the spot. Do not mail any original work unless specifically requested."

SOCIAL POLICY, 25 W. 43rd St., New York NY 10036. (212)642-2929. Managing Editor: Audrey Gartner. Quarterly. Emphasizes "social policy issues—how government and societal actions affect people's lives." Readers are academics, policymakers, lay readers. Circ. 3,500. Estab. 1970. Sample copy $2.50.
Photo Needs: Uses about 6 photos/issue; all supplied by freelance photographers. Needs photos of social consciousness and sensitivity. Model release preferred.
Making Contact & Terms: Arrange a personal interview to show portfolio; query with samples; provide resume, business card, brochure, flyer or tearsheets to be kept on file for possible future assignments. Send 8×10 b&w glossy prints; b&w contact sheets by mail for consideration. SASE. Reports in 2 weeks. Pays $75/b&w cover photo; $25/b&w inside photo. Pays on publication. Credit line given. Buys one-time rights. Simultaneous and previously published submissions OK.
Tips: Prefers to see "editorial content, clarity, sensitivity. Be familiar with social issues. We're always looking for relevant photos. Contact us."

*SOUND CHOICE, P.O. Box 1251, Ojai CA 93024. (805)646-6814. Office Manager: Venus Louviere. Quarterly magazine. Emphasizes music. Circ. 7,000. Estab. 1985. Sample copy $3.00.
Photo Needs: Uses 10-15 photos/issue; anywhere from 50-100% supplied by freelance photographers. Needs photos of technology, personalities and how-to.
Making Contact & Terms: Query with resume of credits. Query with list of stock subjects. Send b&w/color prints by mail for consideration; send query and unsolicited photos. Cannot return unsolicited material. Reports in 1-2 weeks. Payment rates to be arranged. Pays on publication. Rights purchased to be arranged on a per basis. Will negotiate with a photographer unwilling to sell all rights. Simultaneous submissions and previously published work OK.
Tips: In photographer's samples looks for "music related/live action photo's."

SOUNDINGS TRADE ONLY, 35 Pratt St., Essex CT 06426. (203)767-3200. Managing Editor: Milton Moore. Tabloid. Emphasizes recreational boating industry. Readers are boating industry executives. Circ. 28,000. Sample copy free with 12×18 SASE and $2 postage.
Photo Needs: Uses approx. 15 photos/issue; 30% supplied by freelance photographers. Assigns story illustrations; contact for editorial calendar. Model release preferred; photo captions required.
Making Contact & Terms: Send unsolicited photos by mail for consideration. Provide resume, business card, brochure, flyer or tearsheets to be kept on file for possible assignments. Send b&w prints and transparencies. SASE. Reports in 1 month. Pays $200-400/color cover photo, $35 and up/b&w cover photo and $400/day. Pays on publication. Credit line given. Buys one-time rights.
Tips: In portfolio or samples, looking for "a range of shooting skills. Call me."

SOUTHERN BEVERAGE JOURNAL, Box 561107, Miami FL 33256-1107. (305)233-7230. Editor: Jacqueline N. Preston. Monthly. Circ. 30,000. Emphasizes beverage alcohol products. Readers are licenses, wholesalers and executives in the alcohol beverage industry. Free sample copy for 9×12 SAE and $1.50 postage.
Photo Needs: Uses about 20 photos/issue. Needs photos of "local licensees (usually with a promotion of some kind)." Captions required. Send b&w and color prints and any size transparency by mail for consideration. SASE. Reports in 1 week. Pays $20/b&w inside photo. Pays on acceptance. Credit line given "if they ask for it." Buys all rights. Simultaneous submissions and previously published work OK.
Tips: Need product photos for cover. Price negotiable.

SOUTHERN LUMBERMAN, Suite 116, 128 Holiday Ct., Box 1627, Franklin TN 37064. (615)791-1961. FAX: (615)790-6188. Managing Editor: Nanci Gregg. Monthly. Emphasizes forest products industry-sawmills, pallet operations, logging trades. Readers are predominantly owners/operators of mid-sized sawmill operations nationwide. Estab. 1881. Circ. 12,000. Sample copy $1 with 9×12 SAE and $1.25 postage. Photo guidelines free with SASE.
Photo Needs: Uses about 4-5 photos/issue; 50% supplied by freelance photographers. "We need four-color work for our covers—forest scenes, logging operations, sawmill scenes, etc. We are looking for an attractive, creative approach. Also need black and whites of 'general interest' in the lumber industry. We need photographers from across the country to do an inexpensive black & white shoot in conjunction with a phone interview; we need 'human interest' shots from a sawmill scene—just

basic 'folks' shots—a worker sharing lunch with the company dog, sawdust flying as a new piece of equipment is started; face masks as a mill tries to meet OSHA standards, etc." Looking for photo/text packages. Model release and captions required.

Making Contact & Terms: Query with samples. Send 5×7 or 8×10 glossy b&w prints; 35mm, 4×5 transparencies, b&w contact sheets, b&w negatives by mail for consideration. SASE. Reports in 4-6 weeks. Pays a minimum of $10/b&w photos; $25-50/color photo; $125-175/photo/text package. Pays on publication. Credit line given. Buys first N.A. serial rights. No simultaneous or previously published submissions.

Tips: Prefers b&w capture of close-ups in sawmill, pallet, logging scenes. "Every year we seek a December color cover that blends a winter scene/Christmas feeling with the woods—a country church, lighted cabin, etc., complete with snow—perhaps a sleigh ride, etc. Try to provide what the editor wants—call and make sure you know what that is, if you're not sure. Don't send things that the editor hasn't asked for. We're all looking for someone who has the imagination/creativity to provide what we need. I'm not interested in 'works of art'—I want and need b&w feature photos capturing essence of employees working at sawmills nationwide. I've never had someone submit anything close to what I state we need—try that. *Read* the description, shoot the pix, send a contact sheet or a couple 5×7's."

Natural disasters always seem to provide good raw material for photographers. When Hurricane Hugo swept through South Carolina, photographer Thomas L. McLaughlin was on the scene and took this shot of severe tree damage. More important, he followed up right away with a query to Southern Lumberman. According to Managing Editor Nanci Gregg, "it was the only query" she had received from anyone on the subject. Noting that she bought one-time rights for the photo, Gregg adds: "He was timely, provided quality material and quoted a reasonable fee."

SOUVENIRS & NOVELTIES MAGAZINE, Suite 210, 7000 Terminal Square, Upper Darby PA 19082. (215)734-2420. President: Scott C. Borowsky. Magazine, published 7 times annually. Circ. 20,000. Emphasizes new products, buying and selling, and other news of the industry. For managers and owners of resort and amusement park souvenir shops; museum and zoo souvenir shops and hotel gift shops. Buys 10-15 text/photo packages/year. Buys first serial rights or first North American serial rights. Photos purchased with accompanying ms; "the photos should illustrate an important point in

the article or give an indication of how the shop looks." Credit line given. Pays on publication. Reports in 2 weeks. SASE. Simultaneous submissions and previously published work OK. Free sample copy.
Specs: Uses 8×10 glossy prints. Pays $20-40/photo.
Cover: See requirements for b&w. Captions preferred. Pays $10.
Tips: Especially interested in articles which describe how a specific manager sells souvenirs to tourists.

SOYBEAN DIGEST, 540 Maryville Centre Dr., St. Louis MO 63141-1309. (314)576-2788. FAX: (314)576-2786. Editor: Gregg Hillyer. Monthly. Circ. 205,000. Estab. 1940. Emphasizes production and marketing of soybeans for high-acreage soybean growers. Photos purchased with or without accompanying ms and on assignment. Buys 75 photos/year. Pays $200-400 for text/photo package or on a per-photo basis. Credit line given. Pays on acceptance. Buys all rights, but may reassign after publication. Send material by mail for consideration; query with list of stock photo subjects, resume, card, brochure and samples. SASE. Reports in 3 weeks. Previously published work possibly OK. Sample copy $3.
Subject Needs: Soybean production and marketing photos of modified equipment. Captions preferred. No static, posed or outdated material.
B&W: Uses 5×7 or 8×10 prints. Pays $50-200/photo.
Color: Uses 35mm or 2¼×2¼ transparencies. Pays $50-200/photo.
Cover: Uses 35mm, 2¼×2¼, 4×5 and 8×10 transparencies. Vertical format preferred. Pays $600/photo.
Accompanying Mss: Grower techniques for soybean production and marketing. Pays $100-550/ms. Prefers photos with ms.

SPECTROSCOPY, 859 Willamette St., Eugene OR 97440. (503)343-1200. Art Director: Barbara A. Mickelson. Monthly. Emphasizes science. Readers are scientists and manufacturers of scientific products/equipment. Circ. 30,000. Sample copy free with 8½×11 SASE. Photo guidelines free with SASE.
Photo Needs: Uses 6-10 photos per issue; 1 supplied by a freelancer. Needs photos of laser shots and spectroscopy. Photo captions preferred.
Making Contact & Terms: Query with list of stock photo subjects; provide resume, business card, brochure, flyer or tearsheets to be kept on file for possible future assignments. Does not return unsolicited material. Reports in 1 month. Pays $300/color cover photo; $100/b&w inside photo. Pays on publication. Credit line given on table of contents page or with photo. Buys one-time rights. Simultaneous submissions OK.
Tips: Looks for "an artistic look at technical scientific products and equipment. Colorful and dramatic. We seldom use people shots."

THE SPORTING GOODS DEALER, 1212 N. Lindbergh Blvd., St. Louis MO 63132. (314)997-7111. Editor: Steve Fechter. Monthly magazine. Circ. 27,600. Emphasizes news and merchandising ideas for sporting goods dealers. Photos purchased with or without accompanying ms or on assignment. Pays on publication. Buys all rights. Send material by mail for consideration. Simultaneous submissions and previously published work OK if not published in a sporting goods publication. Sample copy $2 with 8½×11 SAE and 50¢ postage (refunded with first accepted photo).
Subject Needs: Spot news relating to the merchandising of sporting goods. Outdoor (fishing, hunting, camping, water sports)-related photos (color preferred). Captions required.
B&W: Uses 5×7 glossy prints. Pays $3-6/photo.
Color: Uses transparencies, standard sizes. Pays $200-300 for full-page use.
Accompanying Mss: Seeks mss on the merchandising of sporting goods through trade channels. Pays 2¢/word. Free writer's guidelines.

SPORTS CAR INTERNATIONAL, #120, 3901 Westerly Pl., Newport Beach CA 92660. (714)851-3044. Art Director: Keith May. Monthly magazine. Emphasizes sports cars. Readers are male, with high income, ages 18-65. Circ. 75,000. Sample copy $8.50.
Photo Needs: Uses 90 photos/issue; 100% supplied by freelance photographers. Needs automotive shots, also people shots for profiles. Especially needs more large formal transparencies. Model release required.
Making Contact & Terms: Provide resume, business card, brochure, flyer or tearsheets to be kept on file for possible assignments. SASE. Reports in 2 weeks. Pays $600/color cover photo, $50/color inside photo, $25/b&w inside photo, $200/color page rate, $600/day or $850/photo/text package. Pays on publication. Credit line given. Buys all rights, but willing to negotiate. Simultaneous submissions OK.

*STEP-BY-STEP GRAPHICS, 6000 N. Forest Park Dr., Peoria IL 61614-3592. (309)688-2300. Managing Editor: Catharine Fishel. Bimonthly. Emphasizes the graphic communications field. Readers are graphic designers, illustrators, art directors, studio owners, photographers. Circ. 45,000. Estab. 1988. Sample copy for $7.50.

Photo Needs: Uses 130 photos/issue; all supplied by freelance photographers. Needs how-to shots taken in artists' workplaces. Model release and captions required; assignment only.
Making Contact & Terms: Query with samples; provide resume, business card, brochure, flyer or tearsheets to be kept on file for possible future assignments. SASE. Reports in 1 month. Pays by the job on a case-by-case basis. Pays on acceptance. Credit line given. Buys one-time rights or first North American serial rights.
Tips: In photographer's samples looking for "color and lighting accuracy." Recommends letter of inquiry plus samples.

SUCCESSFUL FARMING, 1716 Locust St., Des Moines IA 50336. (515)284-2579. Art Director: Jim Galbraith. 14 issues/year. Emphasizes farming production, business, family living and outdoor recreation. Circ. 575,000. Sample copy free with 9×12 SAE and $2.24 postage; photo guidelines free with SASE.
Photo Needs: Uses about 64 photos/issue; 55 supplied by freelance photographers: 95% on specific assignments; 5% from stock. Needs photos of farm livestock, farm machinery, buildings, crops (corn, soybeans, wheat, cotton mostly), farming activity, interesting farm people. "We are always looking for good cover shots with unique situations-composition-lighting, etc., farm management and people oriented." Model release required.
Making Contact & Terms: Arrange a personal interview to show portfolio; query with samples and list of stock photo subjects; provide resume, business card, brochure, flyer or tearsheets to be kept on file for possible future assignments. Reports in 2 weeks. Pays $450-600/color covers (one-time use); $100-250/color inside photo (one-time use); your daily rate, negotiable plus mileage. Pays on acceptance. Credit line given. Buys all rights on per-day assignments, one-time use on stock photos. No simultaneous submissions or previously published work.
Tips: "We need technically good (lighting, focus, composition) photos. Photographer must remember that his/her pictures must be reproducible by color separation and printing process. More and more of our needs are specific subjects. In other words, more of our photos are taken on assignment. Our needs are fewer in the areas of stock photos and photos taken on speculation. In reviewing a photographer's portfolio or samples, looks for technical excellence plus composition; must have modern agriculture practices."

SUCCESSFUL MEETINGS, 633 Third Ave., New York NY 10017. (212)986-4800. FAX: (212)983-6930. Art Director: Don Salkaln. Monthly. Circ. 77,000. Estab. 1955. Emphasizes business group travel for all sorts of meetings. Readers are business and association executives who plan meetings, exhibits, conventions and incentive travel. Sample copy $10.
Photo Needs: Uses 25 photos/issue. Needs photos of a few general travel—scenic and urban meeting groups, trade shows, conventions; mainly travel shots and corporate portraits. Special needs include *good*, high-quality meeting—group shots. Model release preferred.
Making Contact & Terms: Arrange a personal interview to show portfolio; query with resume of credits and list of stock photo subjects. SASE. Reports in 2 weeks. Pays $500-750/color cover photo; $50-150/inside b&w photo; $75-200/inside color photo; $150-250/b&w page; $200-300/color page; $200-600/text/photo package; $50-100/hour; $175-350/½ day. Pays on acceptance. Credit line given. Buys one-time rights. Simultaneous submissions and previously published work OK "only if you let us know."
Tips: "Be fair, be professional and persistent."

*SUNSHINE ARTISTS USA, 1700 Sunset Dr., Longwood FL 32750-9697. (407)323-5927. Editor: J. Wahl. Monthly. Emphasizes arts and crafts in malls and outdoors. Readers are mainly professional artists and craftsmen making a living at mall and outdoor shows. Circ. 50,000. Sample copy $2.50.
Photo Needs: Uses 25-30 photos/year; mainly submitted by readers. Also 3-4 (35mm slides) of artist's work on cover each month. Needs 5×7 b&w photos of artist's work with article. Photos purchased with accompanying ms only. Special needs include unusual artwork or craft from successful artisans on the show circuit. Model release required; captions preferred.
Making Contact & Terms: Query with resume of credits. Does not return unsolicited material. Reports in 2 weeks. Pays $10/b&w inside photo; $15-35/text/photo package. Pays on publication. Credit line given. Buys first North American serial rights.

Markets which offer lower payment amounts, or photo credits and extra copies or tearsheets as payment are often receptive to the work of newcomers. For a list of such markets, see the First Markets Index preceding the General Index in the back of this book.

SUPERMARKET NEWS, 7 East 12th St., New York NY 10003. (212)741-5471. Art Director: Peter Kelley. Weekly tabloid. Emphasizes supermarket retailing. Readers are supermarket company executives, store managers and wholesalers. Circ. 60,000.
Photo Needs: Uses 30 photos/issue; 75% supplied by freelance photographers. Needs "journalistic photos of stores, conventions and seminars, primarily b&w. Story requirements demand assignments nationwide." Photo captions required.
Making Contact & Terms: Provide resume, business card, brochure, flyer or tearsheets to be kept on file for possible assignments. Reports as needed. Pays $50-100/hour, $300-500/day. Pays on acceptance. Credit line given. Buys all rights, but willing to negotiate. Previously published work OK.
Tips: In porfolio or samples, looking for "ability to shoot on location in difficult lighting situations."

TEACHING TODAY, 6112-102 Ave., Edmonton, AB T6A 0N4 Canada. (403)465-2990. Editor: Max Coderre. Magazine published 5 times/year. Emphasizes professional development of teachers. Readers are primarily educators, from preschool through university level. Circ. 17,000. Estab. 1983. Sample copy free with 9×12 SASE and $1.17 Canadian postage.
Photo Needs: Uses 3-5 photos/issue; 100% supplied by freelance photographers; 1% freelance assignment; 99% freelance stock. Needs photos of teachers and/or students in kindergarten to university level to enhance articles. Model release required.
Making Contact & Terms: Send unsolicited photos by mail for consideration. Send b&w or color prints, any size or format. SASE. Reports in 1 month. Pays $25/b&w photo; $25-100/color photo. Pays on publication. Credit line given. Simultaneous submissions OK.
Tips: "For color photos for front cover—simple, uncluttered, vivid colors—most photos used are of 1 or 2 people, usually something that we could use pertaining to educational field. B&w or small photographs also used for inside purposes (e.g.to enhance articles). Must be sharp, clear photos. When sending work, give suggestion, reason of where, how, why his/her photos could be (should be) used in educational publication."

TELECOMMUNICATIONS, 685 Canton St., Norwood MA 02062. (617)769-9750. Senior Editor: Tom Valovic. Monthly. Emphasizes "state-of-the-art voice and data communications equipment and services." Readers are "persons involved in communications management/engineering." Circ. 85,000. Sample copy with SASE and 40¢ postage. Runs international also, in Europe.
Photo Needs: Uses about 6 photos/issue; varying number supplied by freelance photographers. Needs "applications-oriented photos of communications systems/equipment." Model release and captions required.
Making Contact & Terms: Query with list of stock photo subjects; send b&w and color prints; 35mm transparencies by mail for consideration; provide resume, business card, brochure, flyer or tearsheets to be kept on file for possible future assignments. SASE. Reports in 1 week. Pays $250/color cover photo; $25/b&w and $50/color inside photo. Pays on publication. Credit line given. Buys all rights.

*TENNIS INDUSTRY, 1450 NE 123 St., Miami FL 33161. (305)893-8771. Vice President Manufacturing: James Kukar. Magazine published 11 times/year. Emphasizes tennis trade. Circ. 30,000. Sample copy for $1 and 9×12 SAE with 80¢ postage.
Photo Needs: Uses 10-30 photos/issue all supplied by freelance photographers. Model release preferred; captions required.
Making Contact & Terms: Query with list of stock photo subjects; submit portfolio for review. SASE. Reports in 1 month. Pays $350/color cover photo; $150/color inside photos. Buys one-time rights, all rights. Will negotiate with photographer unwilling to sell all rights. Simultaneous submissions and previously published work OK.

*TEST & MEASUREMENT WORLD, 275 Washington St., Newton MA 02158. (617)964-3030. Editor: Charles Masi. Monthly magazine. Emphasizes testing of electronic and electro-optic devices, components and systems. Readers are engineers involved in testing electronic and electro-optic devices, components and systems. Circ. 65,505. Sample copy free with SASE.
Photo Needs: Uses approx. 12 photos/issue. Number supplied by freelancers varies; most come from press relations offices in our industry. Needs "close-ups or situation shots of electronics being tested, i.e. the test set-up, or the working test head." Model release and photo captions preferred.
Making Contact & Terms: Provide resume, business card, brochure, flyer or tearsheets to be kept on file for possible assignments. "However, assignments are rare." Send b&w or color 35mm glossy prints. Does not return unsolicited material. Reports when possible. "We rarely pay for our photography, as most of it is supplied by companies in our industry." Credit line given. Claims all rights, but willing to negotiate. Previously published work OK.

THOROUGHBRED RECORD, P.O. Box 8237, Lexington KY 40533. (606)223-9800. Editor: Don Clippinger. Monthly. Circ. 17,000. Emphasizes Thoroughbred racing. Readers are Thoroughbred owners and breeders. Sample copy $2.50.

Photo Needs: Uses about 50 photos/issue; 66% supplied by freelance photographers on an assignment basis, balance from files or stock. Uses a very few "spec" photos of major Thoroughbred races each year.

Making Contact & Terms: Exclusively uses established photographers in the Thoroughbred industry. No submissions prior to written query. Pays $25-75/b&w photo; $30-100/color photo; $150-300 by the day. Credit line given. Buys one-time rights.

Tips: Uses racing photographs that capture the excitement of the sport and the power of the Thoroughbred. Looks for technical quality, sharpness and exposure and composition.

Photo editor for the Thoroughbred Record, Don Clippinger, remarks that "the attractiveness of this picture speaks for itself." Noting that photographer Philippe Roca captured both the beauty of the farm and the grazing thoroughbred, Clippinger adds that the image was "not luck but the result of a great deal of hard work." Roca was paid for first rights to this and four other images assigned to create illustration for an article on a major racing trainer.

*THOROUGHBRED TIMES, 801 Corporate Dr., Suite 101, Lexington KY 40503. (606)223-9800. Managing Editor: Ray Paulick. Weekly newspaper. Emphasizes thoroughbred breeding and racing. Readers are wide demographic range of industry professionals. Circ. 24,000. Estab. 1985. No photo guidelines.

Photo Needs: Uses 18-20 photos/issue; 40-60% supplied by freelance photographers. Needs photos of specific subject features (personality, farm, or business). Model release and photo captions preferred.

Making Contact & Terms: Provide resume, business card, brochure, flyer or tearsheets to be kept on file for possible assignments. SASE. Reports in 1 month. Pays $25/b&w cover photo; $25/b&w inside photo; $25/b&w page rate; $150/day. Pays on publication. Credit line given. Buys one-time rights. No simultaneous submissions. Will consider previously published work.

Tips: "Looks for photos only from desired trade (thoroughbred breeding and racing)."

*TODAY'S TRUCKING, Suite 211, 10 Shorncliffe Rd., Toronto, ON M9B 3S3 Canada. (416)233-1243. FAX (416)237-0634. Editor: Rolf Lockwood. Trade publication. Magazine published 10 times/year. Emphasizes heavy trucking. Circ. 30,000. Estab. 1987. Sample copy free with SASE. Photo guidelines not available.

Photo Needs: Uses 35 photos/issue; 15-20% supplied by freelance photographers. Needs photos of trucks, highways, truck drivers, mechanics, etc. Model release preferred; photo captions required.

Making Contact & Terms: Arrange a personal interview to show portfolio. Send unsolicited transparencies by mail for consideration. SASE. Reports in 2 weeks. Pays $350/color cover photo; $50+/color inside photo; $35+/b&w inside photo. Pays on acceptance. Credit line not given. Buys one-time rights. Previously published work OK.

Tips: In freelancer's portfolio wants to see "trucks in action, trucking situations, trucks in seasonal situations, dramatic highways, etc." Also looks for "striking color. Prefer extreme lenses—wide, long telephoto."

TOP PRODUCER, Farm Journal Publishing, Inc., 230 W. Washington Square, Philadelphia PA 19105. (215)829-4865. Photo Editor: Tom Dodge. Monthly. Emphasizes American agriculture. Readers are active farmers, ranchers or agribusiness people. Circ. 800,000. Sample copy and photo guidelines free with SASE.
Photo Needs: Uses 20-30 photos/issue; 75% supplied by freelance photographers. "We use studio-type portraiture (environmental portraits), technical, details and scenics." Model release preferred; photo captions required.
Making Contact & Terms: Arrange a personal interview to show portfolio or query with resume of credits along with business card, brochure, flyer or tearsheets to be kept on file for possible assignments. SASE. Reports in 2 weeks. "We pay a cover bonus." Pays on acceptance. Credit line given. Buys one-time rights. Simultaneous submissions and previously published work OK.
Tips: In portfolio or samples, likes to "see about 20 slides showing photographer's use of lighting and photographer's ability to work with people. Know your intended market. Familiarize yourself with the magazine and keep abreast of how photos are used in the general magazine field."

TOURIST ATTRACTIONS AND PARKS, Suite 210, 7000 Terminal Square, Upper Darby PA 19082. (215)734-2420. President: Scott C. Borowsky. Bimonthly. Circ. 22,000. Emphasizes theme parks, carnivals, concert arenas, amusement parks, zoos and tourist attractions for managers and owners. Needs photos of new developments in amusement parks, such as new systems of promotion, handling crowds or drawing visitors. Buys 5-10 photos/year. Buys first North American serial rights. Send photos for consideration. Credit line given. Pays on publication. Reports in 2 weeks. SASE. Simultaneous submissions and previously published work OK. Free sample copy.
B&W: Send 8×10 glossy prints. Captions required. Pays $10-15.
Color: Send transparencies. Captions required. Pays $50.
Cover: See requirements for b&w and color. Pays $20-40.
Tips: Wants no nature shots; only professional quality photos of theme parks, attractions or amusement parks. "Photos can also be of food concessions, merchandise stores or arcades at leisure facilities."

TOW-AGE, Box M, Franklin MA 02038. Contact: J. Kruza. Magazine published every 6 weeks. Circ. l0,000. For owner/operators of towing service businesses.
Subject Needs: Recovery of trucks, trains, boats, etc. Prefers "how-to" approach in a series of photos. Technical articles on custom-built tow trucks and rigs are more desired and receive better payment.
Specs: Uses b&w prints and occasionally color prints.
Accompanying Mss: Photos purchased with or without accompanying ms.
Payment & Terms: Pays $25/first b&w print, $15 each additional. Pays on acceptance.
Making Contact: Query or send material. SASE. Reports in 3 weeks to 1 month.
Tips: "Befriend a towing company that has a contract with police to clear major Interstate roadways in accidents. Personality profiles and news shots are by assignment. But accident and recovery sequences are by luck." Also see *Towing and Recovery Trade News*, this section.

TOWING & RECOVERY TRADE NEWS, Box M, Franklin MA 02038. Editor: Jay Kruza. Bimonthly magazine. Circ. 15,000 tow truck operators. Needs photos of unusual accidents with tow trucks retrieving and recovering sequences for cars and trucks. Avoid gory or gruesome shots depicting burned bodies, numerous casualties, etc. Buys 50 photos/year, 8/issue showing how-to procedure. Buys all or reprint rights. Send photos for consideration. Pays on acceptance. Reports in 5 weeks. SASE. Simultaneous submissions OK. Sample copy $3; free photo/writer guidelines.
B&W: Send glossy or matte contact sheet or 5×7 prints. Captions required. Pays $25 for first photo, $15 for each additional photo in the series.
Tips: "Most shots are 'grab' shots—a truck hanging off a bridge, recovery of a ferryboat in water, but the photographer should get sequence of recovery photos. Some interviews of owners of a fleet of tow trucks are sought as well as the 'celebrity' whose car became disabled." Also see *Tow-Age*, this section.

TRADESWOMAN MAGAZINE, Box 40664, San Francisco CA 94140. (415)821-7334. Editors: Molly Martin and Helen Vozenilek. Quarterly. Emphasizes women in nontraditional blue collar trades work (carpenters, electricians, etc.). Readers are highly skilled specialized women in crafts jobs with trade unions, and self-employed women such as contractors. Women doing work which is currently considered nontraditional. Circ. 1,500. Estab. 1981. Sample copy $3.

Photo Needs: Uses about 10-15 photos/issue; one-third supplied by freelance photographers. Needs "photos of women doing nontraditional work—either job site photos or inshop photos. Occasionally we just use photos of tools." Special needs include cover quality photos—black and white only.
Making Contact & Terms: Send unsolicited photos by mail for consideration. Send high contrast b&w prints; b&w contact sheet. SASE. Reports in 1 month. Pays $25/b&w photo; payment is negotiable. Pays on acceptance. Credit line given. Rights negotiable. Simultaneous submissions and previously published work OK.
Tips: "We are looking for pictures of strong women whom we consider pioneers in their fields. Since we are nonprofit and do not have a lot of money, we often offer write-ups about authors and photographers in addition to small payments."

TRAINING: THE MAGAZINE OF HUMAN RESOURCES DEVELOPMENT, Lakewood Building, 50 S. 9th St., Minneapolis MN 55402. (612)333-0471. Editor: Jack Gordon. Art Director: Jodi Scharff. Monthly. Circ. 51,000. Covers "job-related training and education in business and industry, both theory and practice." Audience: "training directors, personnel managers, sales and data processing managers, general managers, etc." Sample copy free plus 9×12 SASE ($1.20 postage attached-no checks).
Photo Needs: Uses about 5-10 photos/issue. "We accept very few freelance submissions. Most work on assignment only. We do keep a contact file for future reference. We use b&w photos or transparencies only."
Making Contact & Terms: Query with samples or with list of stock photo subjects. Call or write art director for appointment to show portfolio. Provide business card, brochure and flyer to be kept on file for possible future assignments. Samples returned only if requested and only by SASE. Payment negotiable. Pays on acceptance. Credit line given. Buys all rights. Previously published work OK.

TREASURE CHEST, #211A, 253 W. 72 St., New York NY 10023. (212)496-2234. Editor: Howard Fischer. Monthly newspaper. Emphasizes antiques and collectibles. Circ. 50,000. Estab. 1988. Sample copy free with 9×12 SASE and 3 first class stamps. Photo guidelines free with SASE.
Photo Needs: Uses 4-6 photos/issue; 75% supplied by freelance photographers. Needs "positive depictions of antique shows, shops, auctions. Also collectors with collections, humorous happenings, unusual items, displays, people, etc." Model release preferred; photo captions required.
Making Contact & Terms: Query with list of stock photo subjects or send unsolicited photos by mail for consideration. Black and white 4×5 prints preferred. SASE. Reports in 3 weeks. Pays $30/b&w cover photo and $20/b&w inside photo. Credit line given. Buys one-time rights. Previously published work OK.
Tips: To break in, "learn about our publication and specific needs."

TRUCKERS NEWS, 1800 E. Deere Ave., Santa Ana CA 92705. (714)261-1636. Managing Editor: Deborah Whistler. Monthly magazine. Emphasizes trucking. Readers are over-the-road truck drivers. Most male, ages 30-65. Circ. 200,000. Photo guidelines free with SASE.
Photo Needs: Uses 20 photos/issue; 50% supplied by freelance photographers. Needs photos of scenics (trucks on highways), drivers at work. Model release is "photographer's responsibility." Photo captions preferred.
Making Contact & Terms: Query with resume of credits or send unsolicited photos by mail for consideration. Send 35mm transparencies. SASE. Sends check when material is used. Pays $150/color cover photo or $75/color or b&w inside photo. Pays on publication. Buys one-time rights. Does not consider simultaneous submissions or previously published work.

TRUCKSTOP WORLD, 1800 E. Deere Ave., Santa Ana CA 92705. (714)261-1636. Managing Editor: Deborah Whistler. Bimonthly magazine. Emphasizes trucking. Readers are truckstop managers. Most male, ages 30-65. Circ. 12,000. Photo guidelines free with SASE.
Photo Needs: Uses 10 photos/issue; 30-100% supplied by freelance photographers. Needs photos of truckstops. Model release is "photographer's responsibility." Photo captions preferred.
Making Contact & Terms: Query with resume of credits or send unsolicited photos by mail for consideration. Send 35mm transparencies. SASE. Sends check when material is used. Pays $150/color cover photo or $75/color or b&w inside photo. Pays on publication. Buys one-time rights. Does not consider simultaneous submissions or previously published work.

U.S. NAVAL INSTITUTE PROCEEDINGS, U.S. Naval Institute, Annapolis MD 21402. (301)268-6110. Photo Editor: Linda Cullen. Monthly magazine. Circ. 119,790. Emphasizes matters of current interest in naval, maritime and military affairs—including strategy, tactics, personnel, shipbuilding and equipment. For officers in the Navy, Marine Corps and Coast Guard; also for enlisted personnel of the sea services, members of other military services in this country and abroad, and civilians with an interest in naval and maritime affairs. Buys 15 photos/issue. Needs photos of Navy, Coast Guard and merchant ships of all nations; military aircraft; personnel of the Navy, Marine Corps and Coast Guard; and maritime environment and situations. No poor quality photos. Buys one-time rights. Query first with resume of credits. Pays $200/color cover photo; $50 for article openers; $25/inside editorial. Pays on publication. Reports in 2 weeks on pictorial feature queries; 6-8 weeks on other materials. SASE. Free sample copy. Color and b&w: Uses 8×10 glossy prints or slides. Captions required. Pays $10 for official military photos submitted with articles. Pays $250-500 for naval/maritime pictorial features. "These features consist of copy, photos and photo captions. The package should be complete, and there should be a query first. In the case of the $25 shots, we like to maintain files on hand so they can be used with articles as the occasion requires. Annual photo contest—write for details."

UNITED ARTS, Suite 6D, 141 Wooster, New York NY 10012. (212)473-6695. Publisher: Larry Qualls. Quarterly journal. Emphasizes theatre, dance and art. Readers are in the university community. Circ. 3,000. Estab. 1988. Sample copy available.
Photo Needs: Needs photos of dance, theatre and art. Special photo needs include art photos of sculpture and theatre production shots. Model release, photo captions required.
Making Contact & Terms: Query with resume of credits. Reports in 3 weeks. Credit line given. Simultaneous submissions and previously published work OK.

*UTILITY AND TELEPHONE FLEETS, P.O. Box 183, Cary IL 60013. (708)639-2200. Editor: Alan Richter. Bimonthly magazine. Emphasizes equipment and vehicle management and maintenance. Readers are fleet managers, maintenance supervisors, generally 35+ in age and primarily male. Circ. 18,000. Estab. 1987. Sample copy free with SASE. No photo guidelines.
Photo Needs: Uses 80 photos/issue; 1-2% usually supplied by a freelance writer with an article. Needs photos of vehicle and construction equipment orientated. Special photo needs include photos relating to alternate fuel vehicles and eye grabbing colorful shots of utility vehicles in action as well as utility construction equipment. Model release preferred; photo captions required.
Making Contact & Terms: Provide resume, business card, brochure, flyer or tearsheets to be kept on file for possible assignments. SASE. Reports in 1-2 weeks. Pays $50/color cover photo; $10/b&w inside photo; $50-200/photo/text package ($50/published page). Pays on publication. Credit line given. Buys one-time rights.
Tips: "Be willing to work cheap and be able to write as the only photos we have paid for so far were part of an article/photo package."

*UTILITY CONSTRUCTION AND MAINTENANCE, P.O. Box 183, Cary IL 60013. (708)639-2200. Editor: Alan Richter. Quarterly magazine. Emphasizes equipment and vehicle management and maintenance. Readers are fleet managers, maintenance supervisors, generally 35+ in age and primarily male. Circ. 25,000. Estab. 1990. Sample copy free with SASE. No photo guidelines.
Photo Needs: Uses 80 photos/issue; 1-2% usually supplied by a freelance writer with an article. Needs photos of vehicle and construction equipment oriented. Special photo needs include photos relating to eye grabbing colorful shots of utility construction equipment. Model release preferred; photo captions required.
Making Contact & Terms: Provide resume, business card, brochure, flyer or tearsheets to be kept on file for possible assignments. SASE. Reports in 1-2 weeks. Pays $50/color cover photo; $10/b&w inside photo; $50-200/photo/text package ($50/published page). Pays on publication. Credit line given. Buys one-time rights.
Tips: "Be willing to work cheap and be able to write as the only photos we have paid for so far were part of an article/photo package."

*VERMONT BUSINESS MAGAZINE, Box 6120, Brattleboro VT 05302. (802)257-4100. Editor: B.J. Lawson. Trade publication. Monthly tabloid. Emphasizes business news. Readers are business owners and managers. Circ. 15,000. Estab. 1972. No sample copies or photo guidelines available.
Photo Needs: Uses 25 photos/issue; 45% supplied by freelance photographers. Needs photos of business topics. Photos purchased with accompanying ms only. Model release and photo captions preferred.
Making Contact & Terms: Arrange a personal interview to show portfolio. SASE. Reports in 1-2 weeks. Pays $100/color cover photo; $50/b&w cover photo. Pays on publication. Credit line given. Buys one-time rights. Previously published work OK.
Tips: Editor "only needs Vermont—specific photos." Recommends freelancer "call and we'll assign out the photos."

VETERINARY LEARNING SYSTEMS, Compendium, Veterinary Technician, Equine Veterinary Journal, 425 Phyllips #100, Trenton NJ 08618. (609)882-5600. Editor: Phyllis Harris. Art Director: Vanessa Schaefer. Monthly journal. Emphasizes veterinary. Readers are veterinarians, veterinary technicians. Circ. 30,000. Sample copy available for 9×12 SAE.

Photo Needs: Uses about 40 photos/issue; only cover usually supplied by freelance photographers. Needs photos of animals-sometimes clinical. Model release and captions preferred.

Making Contact & Terms: Query with list of stock photo subjects. Does not return unsolicited material. Pays $100-200/b&w cover photo; $300-600/color cover photo. Pays on acceptance. Credit line given "in some cases." Buys one-time rights.

Tips: "Looking for stock photography of animals-*dogs*, *cats*, *cows*, *pigs*, *horses* only. Also need animals being treated by veterinarians and veterinary technicians. Sometimes need photos for 'special projects' other than our journals. These photos can be less clinical. More artistic. But *never cute*."

VIDEO SOFTWARE, (formerly Video Software Dealer), 6750 Centinela Ave., Suite 300, Los Angeles CA 90230. (213)306-2907. Editor: Jack Schember. Monthly. Emphasizes home video industry. Readers are video retailers. Circ. 38,000. Sample copy free with 9 × 12 SAE and $2 postage.

Photo Needs: Uses about 50 photos/issue; 10 supplied by freelance photographers. Needs photos of video stores, movies, celebrities. Model release preferred; captions required.

Making Contact & Terms: Provide resume, business card, brochure, flyer or tearsheets to be kept on file for possible future assignments. SASE. Reports in 2 weeks. Pay negotiable. Pays on acceptance. Credit line given. Buys all rights. Will negotiate with a photographer unwilling to sell all rights.

Tips: Prefers to see "familiarity with the home video industry. Query the editor. I'm looking for a good presentation."

B&W: Uses 8 × 10 glossy prints. Captions required. Pays $10-25.

Color: Uses 35mm, 2½x2½ or 8 × 10 transparencies. Captions required. Pays $25-50.

Cover: Uses 35mm, 2½x2½ or 8 × 10 color transparencies. Vertical format. Allow space at top of photo for insertion of logo. Captions required. Pays $100.

VM & SD (VISUAL MERCHANDISING AND STORE DESIGN), 407 Gilbert Ave., Cincinnati OH 45202. Editor: P. K. Anderson. Monthly magazine. Emphasizes store design and store display (all types of stores). Readers are visual merchandisers and store designers, store owners, presidents and chief executive officers. Circ. 18,000. Sample copy free.

Photo Needs: Number of freelance photos used varies considerably. About 20% assigned. Needs architectural shots of stores and photos of displays. Photo captions preferred.

Making Contact & Terms: Query with resume of credits; provide business card, brochure, flyer or tearsheets to be kept on file for possible assignments; or send unsolicited photos by mail for consideration. Send color 35mm, 2¼ × 2¼, or 4 × 5 photos. SASE. Reports in 3 weeks. Pays $150/color cover photo, $50/color inside photo or $20/b&w inside photo. Pays on publication. Credit line given. Buys one-time rights. Simultaneous submissions and previously published work OK.

Tips: Trend in publication toward "excellent facade shots of stores and more shots concentrating on architectural detail." In samples, wants to see "an excellent sense of composition in interior photographs depicting not only the design of the space, but also the integration of merchandise presentation." To break in, "submit 4 × 5 or 2¼ transparencies showing imaginative window displays as well as unusual store interiors. With interiors, try to convey the store from several vantage points."

WALLCOVERINGS MAGAZINE, Suite 101, 15 Bank St., Stamford CT 06901. (203)357-0028. Editor/Publisher: Martin A. Johnson. Managing Editor: James Sullivan. Monthly trade journal of the flexible wallcoverings and window treatment industries. Circ. 18,000. For manufacturers, wholesalers and retailers in the wallcovering, wallpaper and window treatment trade, and interior decorating business. Buys all rights. Submit model release with photo. Send contact sheet or photos for consideration. Pays on publication. SASE. Sample copy $2.

B&W: Send contact sheet, negatives, or 5 × 7 or 8 × 10 glossy prints. Captions required. Payment negotiated on individual basis.

WALLS & CEILINGS MAGAZINE, 8602 N. 40th St., Tampa FL 33604. (813)989-9300. Editor: Lee Reclay. Monthly magazine. Emphasizes wall and ceiling construction, drywall, lath, plaster, stucco and exterior specialty finishes. Readership consists of 98% male, wall and ceiling contractors. Circ. 17,000. Sample copy $4.

Photo Needs: Uses 15-20 photos/issue. Uses 30% freelance work. Needs photos of interior/exterior architectural shots, contractors and workers on job (installing drywall and stucco). Model release required.

Making Contact & Terms: Query with resume of credits or send unsolicited photos by mail for consideration. Send b&w or color glossy prints, any size, or 35mm, 2¼ × 2¼ or 4 × 5 transparencies. SASE. Reports in 1 month. Pays $150/color cover photo, $50/color inside photo, $25/b&w inside photo or $50-150/photo-text package. Pays on publication. Credit line given. Buys exclusive, one-time and "our industry" rights. Simultaneous submissions and previously published work OK, provided not submitted to or published by competitors.

WANG IN THE NEWS, 251 Live Oak, Marlin TX 76661. (817)883-2533. Editor: Larry Storer. Monthly tabloid. Emphasizes computers and related products—specifically Wang and Wang-compatible. Readership is 25-55, 50/50 male/female in occupations ranging from secretaries to lawyers. Basically anyone who uses Wang computers. Circ. 25,000. Sample copy free with 8½×11 SASE and 2 first class stamps.
Photo Needs: Uses about 5 photos/issue; 20-30% supplied by freelance photographers. Usually needs product-oriented shots. Model release and photo captions required.
Making Contact & Terms: Query with resume of credits, business card, brochure, flyer or tearsheets to be kept on file for possible assignments, query with list of stock photo subjects; or send unsolicited photos by mail for consideration. Send b&w glossy prints, all sizes. SASE. Reports in 2 weeks. Pays $25/b&w inside photo and $100-150/photo-text package. Pays on publication. Credit line given. Buys all rights; rights negotiable. Does not consider simultaneous submissions or previously published work.
Tips: "Doesn't hurt to try and understand content. Locate Wang installations in area, visit, visualize photo possibilities. Needs photographers in New York area and Boston area from time to time."

WARD'S AUTO WORLD, 28 W. Adams St., Detroit MI 48226. (313)962-4433. FAX: (313)962-4456. Editor: Edward K. Miller. Monthly. Circ. 92,000. Estab. 1965. Emphasizes the automotive industry. Sample copy free with 9×12 SAE and $2 postage.
Photo Needs: Uses about 40 photos/issue, mainly color transparencies; 10-30% supplied by freelance photographers; 100% assignment. Subject needs vary. "Most photos are assigned. We are a news magazine—the news dictates what we need." Model release preferred; captions required.
Making Contact & Terms: Arrange a personal interview to show portfolio or query with samples; provide resume, business card, brochure, flyer or tearsheets to be kept on file for possible future assignments. SASE. Reports in 2 weeks. Pays $50-100/b&w photo; $60-125/color photo; $10-20/hour; $350-500/day. Pays on publication. Credit line given. Buys all rights.
Tips: In reviewing a photographer's portfolio or samples, looks for "creativity, originality, and quality." Also looks for "ability to capture news subjects in good candid poses. We need photographers to accompany reporters on interviews, plant tours, etc. More photos are being printed on people; less on cars themselves. *DO NOT* send us photos of cars. We have all we need. We want freelancers with proven work abilities (who can accompany a reporter on assignment)."

WATER WELL JOURNAL, 6375 Riverside Dr., Dublin OH 43017. (614)761-3222. FAX: (614)761-3446. Associate Editor: Gloria Swanson. Monthly. Circ. 39,008. Estab. 1946. Deals with construction of water wells and development of ground water resources. Readers are water well drilling contractors, managers, suppliers and ground water scientists. Sample copy $1.50.
Photo Needs: Uses 1-3 freelance photos/issue plus cover photos. Needs photos of installations and how-to illustrations. Model release preferred; captions required.
Making Contact & Terms: Contact with resume of credits; inquire about rates. "We'll contact." Pays $10-50/hour; $200/color cover photo; $50/b&w inside photo; "flat rate for assignment." Pays on publication. Credit line given "if requested." Buys all rights.

WESTERN AND ENGLISH FASHIONS, 2403 Champa St., Denver CO 80205. (303)296-1600. Publisher/ Ad. Director: Bob Harper. Editor: Lawrence Bell. Monthly. Circ. 14,000. A trade magazine serving the needs of today's sophisticated retailers of Western and English riding apparel, accessories and square dance fashion. Features editorials, business columns and display advertisements designed to keep retailers abreast of the latest in business and fashion developments. Free sample copy and photo guidelines.
Photo Needs: Uses 30 photos/issue; 5-10 are supplied by freelance photographers. "Most of our photos accompany mss; we do use photo essays about once every 2-3 months. Photographers should query with idea. Photo essays should show Western products or events (rodeo etc.)." Model release preferred; captions required.
Making Contact & Terms: Query with photo essay idea. "We will respond quickly; if interested we will ask to see sample of photographer's work." SASE. Reports in 2 weeks. Pays $10-25/inside b&w photo; $25-50/color cover; $150 maximum for text/photo package. Pays on publication. Credit line given. Buys one-time rights. Simultaneous and previously published work OK if they were not published by a competitive magazine.

WILSON LIBRARY BULLETIN, 950 University Ave., Bronx NY 10452. (212)588-8400. FAX (212)538-2716. Editor: Mary Jo Godwin. Monthly magazine. Circ. 14,000. Emphasizes the issues and the practice of librarianship. For librarians and information professionals. Needs photos of library interiors, people reading in all kinds of libraries—school, public, university, community college, etc. No posed shots, dull scenics or dated work. Buys 10-15 photos/year; 2-5 photos assigned. Buys first serial rights.
Making Contact & Terms: Send photos for consideration. Provide business card and brochure to be kept on file for possible future assignments. For b&w: send 5×7 or 8×10 glossy prints. Pays $25/ inside photo. For cover: pays $300/color cover. Pays $300 for text/photo package. For color photos:

send color slide or transparency; pays $25-50. Credit line given. Pays on publication. Reports in 4-6 weeks.

Tips: Looks for "interesting subjects portrayed creatively and high quality. Send a brochure or business card with samples to be kept on file."

WINES & VINES, 1800 Lincoln Ave., San Rafael CA 94901. Contact: Philip E. Hiaring. Monthly magazine. Circ. 5,000. Emphasizes winemaking in the US for everyone concerned with the wine industry, including winemakers, wine merchants, suppliers, consumers, etc. Wants color cover subjects on a regular basis.

Payment & Terms: Pays $10/b&w print; $50-100/color cover photo. Pays on publication. Credit line given. Buys one-time rights.

Making Contact: Query or send material by mail for consideration. SASE. Reports in 5 weeks to 3 months. Provide business card to be kept on file for possible future assignments. Previously published work OK.

*WINGS WEST, 89 Sherman St., Denver CO 80203. (303)778-7145. FAX (303)460-8106. Editor: Babette André. Trade publication. Bimontly magazine. Emphasizes aviation, travel. Readers are midlife male, affluent, mobile. Circ. 20K. Estab. 1985. Sample copy free with SASE. Photo guidelines not available.

Photo Needs: Uses 12 photos/issue; 25% supplied by freelance photographers; both assignment and stock. Model release and photo captions required.

Making Contact & Terms: Provide resume, business card, brochure, flyer or tearsheets to be kept on file for possible assignments: contact by phone. SASE. Reports in 1 month. Pays $10-35/b&w; $35-75/color; $25-100/photo/text package. Pays on publication. Credit line given. Buys all rights; will negotiate with photographer not willing to sell all rights. Simultaneous submissions and previously published work OK.

Tips: Looks for "unusual destination pix, general aviation oriented." Trend is "imaginative." Make shot pertinent to an active pilot readership. Query first. Don't send originals—color copies acceptable. Copy machine reprints OK for evaluation.

WIRE TECHNOLOGY INTERNATIONAL, (formerly Initial Publications), Suite 101, 3869 Darrow Rd., Stow OH 44224. (216)686-9544. Editor: Thomas Dreher. Bimonthly magazine. Emphasizes technology in the manufacture and use of bare and insulated wire, and cable and optical fiber cable. Readers are management, engineering management, production management. Circ. 12,000.

Photo Needs: Uses 20-30 photos/issue; presently none supplied by freelance photographers. Needs photos used to illustrate a particular article or editorial subject. Model release required; captions preferred.

Making Contact & Terms: Provide resume, business card, brochure, flyer or tearsheets to be kept on file for possible future assignments. Does not return unsolicited material. Reports in 2 weeks. Pays on acceptance. Rights purchased varies with use.

THE WISCONSIN RESTAURATEUR, 125 W. Doty St., Madison WI 53703. Editor: Jan LaRue. Monthly magazine, except combined issue in November and December. Circ. 4,000. Trade magazine for the Wisconsin Restaurant Association. Emphasizes the restaurant industry. Readers are "restaurateurs, hospitals, schools, institutions, cafeterias, food service students, chefs, etc." Photos purchased with or without accompanying ms. Buys 12 photos/year. Pays $15-50 for text/photo package, or on a per-photo basis. Credit line given. Pays on acceptance. Buys one-time rights. Send material by mail for consideration. SASE. Simultaneous submissions and previously published work OK. Reports in 1 month. Free sample copy and photo guidelines with 8½×11 SAE and $1.85 postage. Provide photocopies of previously submitted work.

Subject Needs: Animal; celebrity/personality; photo essay/photo feature; product shot; scenic; special effects/experimental; how-to; human interest; humorous; nature; still life; and wildlife. Wants on a regular basis unusual shots of normal restaurant activities or unusual themes. Photos should relate directly to food service industry or be conceived as potential cover shots. No restaurants outside Wisconsin; national trends OK. No nonmember material except the very unusual. Ask for membership list for specific restaurants. Model release required; captions preferred.

B&W: Uses 5×7 glossy prints. Pays $7.50-15/photo.

Cover: Uses b&w glossy prints. Vertical format required. Pays $10-25/photo.

Accompanying Mss: As related to the food service industry—how-to, unusual concepts, humorous and "a better way." No cynical or off-color material. Pays $15-50 for text/photo package. Writer's guidelines free with SASE.

*WOODSHOP NEWS, 35 Pratt St., Essex CT 06426. (203)767-8227. Associate Editor: Lewis Lorini. Monthly tabloid. Emphasizes woodworking. Readers are male, 20's-60's, furniture makers, cabinet-makers, millworkers and hobbyist woodworkers. Circ. 100,000. Estab. 1986. Sample copy free with 11 × 13 SASE. No photo guidelines.
Photo Needs: Uses 40 photos/issue; up to 10% supplied by freelance photographers. Needs photos of people working with wood. Model release and photo captions required.
Making Contact & Terms: Provide resume, business card, brochure, flyer or tearsheets to be kept on file for possible assignments. SASE. Reports in 1 month. Pays $200/color cover photo; $25/b&w inside photo. Pays on publication. Credit line given. Buys one-time rights.

THE WORK BOAT, Box 1348, Mandeville LA 70470. (504)626-0298. Associate Editor: Marilyn Barrett. Bimonthly. Circ. 13,600. Emphasizes news of the work boat industry; all commercial vessels working inland and coastal waters. Readers are executives of towboat, offshore supply, crew boat, dredging and passenger vessel firms, naval architects, leasing companies, equipment companies and shipyards, captains, mates and crews. "Technically minded balance-sheet conscious." Sample copy $3 with 8½ × 11; photo and writer's guidelines for SASE.
Photo Needs: Uses 10-20 photos/issue; most supplied by freelancers. Strictly cover, vertical, of work boats in action, including people. No pleasure boats. Photos should crop 8 × 11 for full-page bleed. Reviews photos with or without manuscript. "Cover photo corresponds to calendar theme (inside). Submit work 3 months prior to issue at least." Model release preferred; captions required.
Making Contact & Terms: Query with resume of credits and list of stock subjects; provide resume, business card, brochure, flyer or tearsheets to be kept on file for possible assignments. SASE. Reports and returns slides within 4-6 weeks; cover submissions take 2 months. For cover: Pays on acceptance $250. Payment varies for color inside photo. Credit line given. Buys one-time rights and first N.A. serial rights. No simultaneous or previously published submissions.
Tips: "We solicit cover submissions—try to secure others from writers. Study the magazine—talk to people in the industry first."

WRITER'S DIGEST/WRITER'S YEARBOOK, 1507 Dana Ave., Cincinnati OH 45207. (513)531-2222. FAX: (513)531-4744. Managing Editor: Tom Clark. Monthly magazine. Circ. 250,000. Estab. 1921. Emphasizes writing and publishing. For "writers and photojournalists of all description: professionals, beginners, students, moonlighters, bestselling authors, editors, etc." Buys 15 photos/year. Buys first North American serial rights, one-time use only. Submit model release with photo. Query with résumé of credits, list of photographed writers, or send contact sheet for consideration. Uses about 10% freelance material each issue. Purchases about 5% of photos from stock or on assignment; 95% of those with accompanying ms. Provide brochure and samples (print samples, not glossy photos) to be kept on file for possible future assignments. "We never run photos without text." Credit line given. Pays on acceptance. Reports in 4 weeks. SASE. Simultaneous submissions OK if editors are advised. Previously published work OK. Sample copy $2; guidelines free with SASE.
Subject Needs: Primarily celebrity/personality ("to accompany profiles"); some how-to, human interest and product shots. All must be writer-related. "We most often use photos with profiles of writers; in fact, we won't buy the profile unless we can get usable photos. The story, however, is always our primary consideration, and we won't buy the pictures unless they can be specifically related to an article we have in the works. We sometimes use humorous shots in our Writing Life column."
B&W: Uses 8 × 10 glossy prints; send contact sheet. "Do *not* send negatives." Captions required. Pays $50-75.
Cover: "Freelance work is rarely used on the cover."
Tips: "Shots should not *look* posed, even though they may be. Photos with a sense of place, as well as persona, preferred—with a mixture of tight and middle-distance shots of the subject. Study a few back issues. Avoid the stereotyped writer-at-typewriter shots; go for an array of settings. Move the subject around, and give us a choice. We're also interested in articles on how a writer earned extra money with photos, or how a photographer works with writers on projects, etc."

YOUNG FASHIONS MAGAZINE, 8th Fl., 119 5th Ave., New York NY 10003. (212)677-7040. Editor: Kathy McFarland. Monthly magazine. Emphasizes children's fashions. Readers are retail store buyers for children's wear. Circ. 25,000+.
Subject Needs: Uses 60 photos/issue; 30 supplied by freelance photographers. Needs photos of four-color fashion shots with child models, photos of retail stores and personality profiles on manufacturing designers and retailers. Model release required.
Making Contact & Terms: Arrange a personal interview to show portfolio, submit portfolio for review. Does not return unsolicited material. Reports in 1 week. Pays $200-500/job. Pays on publication. Credit line given.
Tips: Must have experience in handling children. "No non-professionals or assistants, please."

YOUR HEALTH & FITNESS, 60 Revere Dr., Northbrook IL 60062-1563. (312)564-4070. Picture Editor: Terry Noto. Published bimonthly. Health magazine. Sample copy free with 8×11 SASE.
Photo Needs: Uses vertical 35mm or larger color transparencies of family involved in indoor/outdoor activities (no portraits); photos of adults, primarily health, fitness, safety or nutrition themes.
Making Contact & Terms: Send prints or transparencies by mail for consideration. SASE. Buys one-time rights only. Pays $500+/color cover photo; $250-600/color inside photo. Pays on publication. Credit line given. Simultaneous and previously published submissions OK. "Please include copies for our files."

Consumer Publications/'90-'91 changes

The following publications do not appear in the 1991 edition of *Photographer's Market* for a number of reasons. Primarily, they may be listings which appeared in the 1990 edition but did not respond to our request for an update of their information, have gone out of business or are overstocked with submissions. Also listed here are a number of publications which photographers have frequently asked us to have in the book but which did not return information to us.

Accent (moved; no forwarding address)
Acclaim (did not respond)
Amateur Radio (did not respond)
American Baby (did not respond)
American Heritage (did not respond)
American Legion (did not respond)
American Way (did not respond)
American West (not reviewing work)
Arizona Highways (did not respond)
Auto Magazine (did not respond)
Auto-X (did not respond)
Backpacker (not reviewing work)
Better Nutrition (did not respond)
Bicycling (did not respond)
Black Beat (did not respond)
Bloomsbury Review, The (did not respond)
Blue Grass Unlimited (did not respond)
Body, Mind & Spirit (did not respond)
Boston Globe Magazine (did not respond)
Boy's Life (did not respond)
Braniff Magazine (no longer published)
Bread (did not respond)
Bride's (did not respond)
Careers Magazine (did not respond)
Cavalier (did not respond)
Celebrity Plus Magazine (did not respond)
Cheri Magazine (did not respond)
Chic Magazine (did not respond)
Chicago (not reviewing work)

Columbia Magazine (did not respond)
Conservative Digest (did not respond)
Coral Springs Monthly (not reviewing work)
Cosmopolitan (not reviewing work)
Cross Country Skier (not reviewing work)
Daytime TV Magazine (did not respond)
Delaware Today (not reviewing work)
Disc Sports Magazine (moved; no forwarding address)
Disciple, The (did not respond)
Earthwise Review (did not respond)
Endless Vacation (not reviewing work)
Esquire (did not respond)
Family Circle (did not respond)
Final Frontier (did not respond)
Flower & Garden Magazine (did not respond)
Football Digest (did not respond)
Frets Magazine (no longer published)
Front Page Detective (did not respond)
Gambling Times (did not respond)
Genesis (did not respond)
Glamour (did not resopnd)
Gold Illustrated (did not respond)
Gulf Shore Life (did not respond)
Highlights for Children (did not respond)
Home Mechanix (did not respond)
Home Office Computing (did not respond)
Home Shop Machinist (did not respond)
HomeOwner (did not respond)

Horticulture Magazine (did not respond)
Hot Boat (did not respond)
House of White Birches (did not respond)
In Business (not reviewing work)
In Health (did not respond)
In Touch (did not respond)
Infoworld Magazine (did not respond)
Inside Detective (did not respond)
Inside Sports (did not respond)
International Bicycle Classic Official Magazine (did not respond)
Itinerary Magazine (did not respond)
Lad (did not respond)
Light and Life (did not respond)
Lilith (did not respond)
Long Island Monthly (did not respond)
Longevity (did not respond)
Los Angeles Times Magazine (did not respond)
Lottery (no longer in market)
Mademoiselle (not reviewing work)
McCall's (did not respond)
Michigan (no longer published)
Miniature Collector (did not respond)
Modern Bride (did not respond)
Mother Jones (not reviewing work)
National Geographic (not reviewing work)
National Geographic Traveler (not reviewing work)
National Geographic World (not reviewing)
New Breed (moved; no forwarding address)
New Homeowner (did not respond)
New Jersey Monthly (did not respond)

New York (did not respond)
Oceans (did not respond)
Oklahoma Home & Lifestyle (did not respond)
Outside (did not respond)
Ovation (moved; no forwarding address)
Parents Magazine (did not respond)
PC/Computing (did not respond)
Penthouse (did not respond)
Personal Computing (did not respond)
Popular Lures (no longer published)
Practical Homeowner (did not respond)
Premiere (did not respond)
Present Tense (no longer in market)
Prime Time Sports & Fitness (did not respond)
Pro (did not respond)
Psychology Today (did not respond)
Que Pasa Magazine (did not respond)
R & R Entertainment Digest, The

(did not respond)
Radio-Electronics (did not respond)
Reader's Digest (did not respond)
Redbook (did not respond)
Reform Judaism (did not respond)
Regardie's (did not respond)
Right On (did not respond)
Rock Magazine (no longer published)
Rocky Mountain Visitor (no longer published)
RV Times (no longer published)
Sail (did not respond)
Seventeen (did not respond)
Ski Guide (no longer published)
Smithsonian (not reviewing work)
Snow Country (did not respond)
South Florida (did not respond)
Southeastern Log, The (no longer in market)
Sports Parade (moved; no forwarding address)
St. Louis Weekly (no longer published)
Star (did not respond)

Sunday School Counselor (did not respond)
Surfer Magazine (not reviewing work)
Taxi (did not respond)
Texas Hi-Tech Review (no longer published)
3 & 4 Wheel Action (did not respond)
Tigerbeat (did not respond)
Today's Living (no longer published)
Toronto Life Magazine (did not respond)
Torso (moved; no forwarding address)
Turf & Sport Digest (no longer published)
Video Review Magazine (did not respond)
Vista (did not resond)
Western Flyer (did not respond)
Woman's Day (did not respond)
Woodall's (not reviewing work)
World Tennis (not reviewing work)
Wrestling Eye Magazine (did not respond)

Other Publications/'90-'91 changes

The following publications appeared in the 1990 edition of *Photographer's Market* but are not in the 1991 edition. Those publications whose editors or photo editors did not respond to our request for an update of their listings may not have done so for a variety of reasons—they may be out of business, for example, or they may be overstocked with submissions.

Special Interest

American Music Teacher (not reviewing work)
Arthritis Today (did not respond)
ATA Magazine (did not respond)
Back to Godhead (moved; no forwarding address)
Bulletin of the Atomic Scientist (did not respond)
Cattlemen, The (not reviewing work)
CEA Advisor (did not respond)
Chatter (did not respond)
China Painter (did not respond)
Chosen People, The (did not respond)
Cincinnati Bar Association Report (did not respond)
Communications (did not respond)
Diabetes Forecast (did not respond)
Explorer (not reviewing work)
Explorer, The (did not respond)
Foreign Service Journal (did not respond)
Foundation News (did not respond)
Gold Prospector Magazine (did not respond)

Green Bay Packer Yearbook (did not respond)
International Show Stopper (did not respond)
Journal of Freshwater (did not respond)
Journal of the Senses (did not respond)
Magazine for Christian Youth (did not respond)
Mayo Alumnists (did not respond)
National Future Farming (did not respond)
National Notary (did not respond)
New Physician (did not respond)
North American Hunter (did not respond)
OCAW Reporter (did not respond)
Ontario Snowmobile Magazine (moved; no forwarding address)
Pentecostal Evangel (did not respond)
Pentecostal Testimony (did not respond)
Presbyterian Record (did not respond)
Presbyterian Survey (did not re-

spond)
Professional Sanitation Management (did not respond)
Prorodeo Sports News (did not respond)
Public Power (did not respond)
Reading Teacher, The (not reviewing work)
Real Estate Today (did not respond)
SAM Advanced Management Journal, The (did not respond)
Savings Institutions (did not respond)
Scouting Magazine (did not respond)
Secretary, The (did not respond)
Survival Internationl News, Notes from SIUSA (did not respond)
Tennis USA (not reviewing work)
Today's Insurance Woman (did not respond)
Touch (did not respond)
Traffic Safety (did not respond)
Urban Land (not reviewing work)
Zymurgy (no longer in market)

Trade

Action Sports Retailer (not reviewing work)

American Trucker Magazine (moved; no forwarding address)

Architectural Lighting (no longer published)

Automatic Merchandiser (did not respond)

Business of Fur, The (did not respond)

Circuit Rider (did not respond)

City News Service (moved; no forwarding address)

Construction Comment (didnot respond)

Contemporary Radiology (moved; no forwarding address)

Contractor Magazine (not reviewing work)

Diagnostics & Clinical Testing (did not respond)

Dr. Dobbs Journal (did not respond)

Drug Topics (did not respond)

Equinews (did not respond)

Foodservice Equipment & Supplies Specialist (did not respond)

Home Builder Magazine (moved; no forwarding address)

Journal, The (moved; no forwarding address)

MSM Magazine (did not respond)

National Coin-Operated Reporter (did not respond)

Occupational Health & Safety (did not resopnd)

P.O.B. (Point of Beginning) (did not respond)

Pacific Banker (no longer published)

Portefeuille D'Assurances (did not respond)

Rural Heritage (not reviewing work)

Studio Photography (did not respond)

Study in the USA (not reviewing work)

Systems/3X World (did not respond)

Teaching & Computers Scholastic (no longer published)

Technical Analysis of Stocks & Commodities (did not respond)

TI Computing News (no longer in market)

Veterinary Economics (did not respond)

Record Companies

Photographers who like the freedom to express themselves creatively while still solving a client's creative problems can find ample opportunity in the record company market. As in other competitive markets today, however, this opportunity is not automatically open to all photographers but is a result of originality, persistence and professionalism.

Many photographers who think of working with record companies dream of shooting record cover and publicity photos for major music stars. But in reality, photographers who go on to long-term, high-profile success often start out working with the smaller, independent music companies, or "indies." Larger companies typically rely on stables of photographers who are either on staff or who work through art studios that deal with music companies. Because of this tendency, it can be quite difficult for a newcomer to break in when these companies already have their pick of talented, reliable photographers.

Currently, about six major companies take in better than 90 percent of all sales in the music industry. The balance is shared among independent companies, some of which are subsidiaries of the larger corporations. However, even within this relatively minor segment of the market, there are hundreds of companies competing for very specific music audiences, with many newer labels being born every year.

In light of this prolific growth in the independent market, freelance photographers have reason for optimism. However, for the same reason, freelancers should be alert when dealing with such companies. In most cases, it takes time for recently established companies to learn the various aspects of professionalism and ethics in doing business. In a few cases, companies can be deliberately deceptive and abusive in terms of payment and copyright. Either way, it's best to study a company well before selling stock images to them or working for them on assignment.

It's a good idea to query to prospective companies and request copies of their various forms and contracts for photographers; seeing the content and company's image in such materials can tell you a great deal about how organized and professional a company is. In addition, talk to other photographers or network within the music industry to learn more about a prospective company, even if it's listed in this section.

Shooting for the record company market draws upon various skills. There is a need for photographers who can capture good action shots under the adverse, rapidly changing lighting conditions of live performance. Also, there is a tremendous need for photographers with studio-photography skills to coordinate and shoot concept and group shots for cover art as well as promotional photos. A good portfolio for record company prospects shows off the photographer's range of skills or concentration in an imaginative way, but especially illustrates his ability to solve the creative problems facing record company art directors. Such problems may be as "simple" as coming up with a fresh concept for record art, working within the relatively limited visual format of the 5-inch compact disc liner sheet, or assembling a complex finished shot on a limited budget. Even if a photographer has not worked for a record company client previously, he can study the needs of various companies in this section and shoot a series of self-assignments which clearly show his problem-solving abilities.

The record company listings in this year's *Photographer's Market* feature many independent labels, including some that are especially well known. In the Close-up interview on page 510 in this section, Dave Bett, art director for Relativity Records, explains what independent labels expect from freelance photographers and how freelancers can get started in the industry.

ALPHABEAT, Box 12 01, D-6980 Wertheim/Main, West Germany. Phone: 9342-841 55. Managing Director: Stephan Dehn. Handles disco, dance, pop, soft ballads, wave, synth-pop, electro-disco and funk. Photographers used for portraits, studio shots and special effects for album covers, publicity, brochures, posters and product advertising. Works with freelance photographers on assignment only.
Specs: Uses color prints.
Making Contact: Send unsolicited photos by mail for consideration or submit portfolio for review; provide resume, business card, brochure, flyer or tearsheets to be kept on file for possible future assignments. SASE. Reports in 2 weeks.
Payment & Terms: Pays according to type of order. Credit line given. Buys all rights; will negotiate with a photographer unwilling to sell all rights.

AMERICAN MUSIC CO. and CUCA RECORD & CASSETTE MANUFACTURING CO., Box 8604, Madison WI 53708. Vice President/Marketing: Daniel W. Miller. Handles mostly ethnic and old-time (polka, waltz, etc.). Photographers used for portraits, in-concert shots, studio shots and special effects for album covers.
Specs: Uses 8×10 or 5×7 b&w and color prints.
Making Contact: Send photos "that may be useful on album cover or back, especially as it may relate to ethnic and old-time music albums." Provide resume, business card, brochure, flyer, tearsheets and samples to be kept on file for possible future assignments. SASE. Reports within 6 months.
Payment & Terms: Pays $1-50/b&w photo and $2-50/color photo. Credit line given. Buys all rights.
Tips: "We suggest any interested photographers review their portfolios for pictures that they feel may interest us. Since we are a modest-sized record company, our need for pictures is infrequent, but we'd like to be aware of interested photographers."

ANTONE'S RECORDS, 2928 Guadalupe St., Austin TX 78705. (512)322-0617. General Manager: Susan Piver. Handles R&B and blues. Photographers used for portraits, in-concert shots and studio shots, album covers, publicity and posters. Works with freelance photographers on assignment only; offers 5-10 assignments/year.
Specs: Uses 8×10 glossy b&w and color prints.
Making Contact: Provide resume, business card, brochure, flyer or tearsheets to be kept on file for possible future assignments. Cannot return material. Reports in 3 weeks.
Payment & Terms: Rate of payment varies. Credit line given. Buys all rights, but willing to negotiate.
Tips: To break in, "please submit photographs." There are "good chances" with record companies. More need for "retro lighting, b&w covers."

APON RECORD COMPANY, INC., Steinway Station, Box 3082, Long Island NY 11103. (212)721-5599. President: Andre M. Poncic. Handles classical, folklore and international. Photographers used for portraits and studio shots for album covers and posters. Buys 50+ assignments/year. Provide brochure and samples to be kept on file for possible future assignments.
Specs: Uses b&w prints and 4×5 transparencies.
Making Contact: Send photos by mail for consideration. Cannot return material. Reports in 3 months.
Payment & Terms: Payment negotiable. Credit line given. Buys all rights.

*BARNETT PRODUCTIONS INC., 2305 Dickey Avenue, Chicago IL 60064. (708)689-2726. Vice President: Walter T. Barnett. Estab. 1980. Handles r&b, rap, rock and ballads. Photographers used for portraits, studio shots, and special effects for album covers, publicity and product advertising. Buys unlimited number of photos/year.
Specs: Uses 10×12 and 5×6 b&w or color prints.
Making Contact: Query with resume of credits; submit portfolio for review. SASE. Reports in 1 month.
Payment & Terms: Pays $150-500/job. Credit line given on occasion. Buys all rights; will negotiate with a photographer unwilling to sell all rights.
Tips: In photographer's portfolio, looks for "creativity. Small record companies are always looking for professionals to work with."

The asterisk before a listing indicates that the market is new in this edition. New markets are often the most receptive to freelance submissions.

BOUQUET-ORCHID ENTERPRISES, Box 11686, Atlanta GA 30355-1686. (404)355-7635. President: Bill Bohannon. Photographers used for live action and studio shots for publicity flyers and brochures. Works with freelance photographers on assignment only.
Making Contact: Provide brochure and resume to be kept on file for possible future assignments. SASE. Reports in 1 month.
Tips: "We are just beginning to use freelance photography in our organization. We are looking for material for future reference and future needs."

*BRENTWOOD MUSIC, INC., 316 Southgate Ct., Brentwood TN 37027. (615)373-3950. FAX: (615)373-0386. President: Jim Van Hook. Marketing Director: Dill Beaty. Estab. 1980. Handles gospel. Photographers used for studio shots and special effects for cassette covers, publicity, brochures, posters and product advertising. Works with freelance photographers on assignment basis only. Uses some stock photographs of scenics and people.
Specs: Uses color prints or transparencies.
Making Contact: Provide resume, business card, brochure, flyer or tearsheets to be kept on file for possible future assignments. SASE. Reports in 1 month.
Payment & Terms: Pays $25-75/b&w photo; $30-80/hour; $400-1,000/day. Credit line given "most of the time." Buys all rights and one-time rights, depending on needs.
Tips: Prefers to see "warmth, inspiration, character; kids and seasonal shots (Christmas esp.)." To break in "submit printed samples. Don't send unsolicited photos."

CAMEX INC., 535 5th Ave., New York NY 10017. (212)682-8400. President: Victor Benedetto. Handles rock, classical, country, etc. Photographers used for portraits, in-concert shots, studio shots, special effects, album covers, inside album shots, publicity, brochures, posters, event/convention coverage, product advertising. Works with freelance photographers on assignment only; offers "various" assignments/year.
Specs: Uses b&w and color prints (all sizes); 35mm, 2¼ × 2¼ transparencies.
Making Contact: Send unsolicited photos by mail for consideration, submit portfolio for review. Does not return unsolicited material. Reports in 1 month.
Payment & Terms: Pay negotiated. Buys one-time rights or all rights.

*CAROLINE RECORDS INC., 114 W. 26th Street, 11th Floor, New York City NY 10001. (212)989-2929. Director of Creative Operations: Yvonne Garrett. Estab. 1985. Handles alternative rock, heavy metal. Photographers used for in-concert shots, studio shots for album covers, inside album shots, publicity. Works with freelance photographers on assignment basis only; number of assignments varies; number of photos bought varies.
Specs: Uses 8 × 10, glossy photos; also 35mm transparencies.
Making Contact: Provide resume, business card, brochure, flyer or tearsheets to be kept on file for possible future assignments. Cannot return material. Reports in 1 month.
Payment & Terms: Payment varies per photographer and job. Credit line given. Buys all rights. Will not negotiate with a photographer unwilling to sell all rights.
Tips: Wants to see "b&w promo shots and live color slides, preferably artwork akin to the type we generally use (i.e. *know the label's roster!*) Be very familiar with our roster and be aware that we are interested in quality, live/studio shots at competitive prices. We tend to hire photographers only if we've worked with them before or if our artists recommend them." The trend "depends on the indie (independent record company). We tend to use young photographers as they're more familiar with the music, more creative and less expensive."

*CHARTA RECORDS/DELUX RECORDS, 44 Music Square East, Nashville TN 37203. (615)255-2175/2176. V. President: Bernice Fields. Estab. 1977. Handles country. Photographers used for portraits and studio shots for album covers, publicity and posters. Works with freelance photographers on assignment basis only; offers 4-5 assignments/year.
Specs: Uses 8 × 10 b&w and color prints.
Making Contact: Submit portfolio for review; provide resume, business card, brochure, flyer or tearsheets to be kept on file for possible future assignments. SASE. Reports in 3 weeks.
Payment & Terms: Pays $250-400/job. "Dependent on the layout and what we need at the time." Buys one-time rights.
Tips: "What we're looking for usually depends on the artist and what kind of PR work we are doing at the time." The freelance photographer should "be on time and not waste our time and his by not knowing what to do and how to do it (posing etc., make-up etc.)."

COSMOTONE RECORDS, Box 71988, Los Angeles CA 90071-0988. Record Producer: Rafael Brom. Handles all types of records. Photographers used for portraits, studio shots and special effects for album covers, inside album shots, brochures, posters and product advertising. Works on assignment only; offers 1-3 assignments/year.

Specs: Uses all sizes, all finish b&w and color photos.
Making Contact: Cannot return material. Will contact only if interested.
Payment & Terms: Pays $30-200/b&w photo; $50-350/color photo; $30-1,000/job. Credit line given. Buys one-time rights and all rights, but will negotiate.

EARWIG MUSIC COMPANY, INC., 1818 W. Pratt Blvd., Chicago IL 60626. (312)262-0278. President: Michael Frank. Handles blues, jazz, gospel and storytelling. Photographers used for portraits, in-concert shots and studio shots for album covers, publicity, brochures and advertising. Works on assignment only; offers 4-6 assignments/year.
Specs: Uses b&w or color prints.
Making Contact: Photographers in northern Mississippi, St. Louis, Chicago, who can do location shooting. Provide resume, business card, brochure, flyer or tearsheets to be kept on file for possible future assignments. Reports in 1 month.
Payment & Terms: Pays $5-50/b&w or color photo or $25-200/job. Credit line given. Buys all rights; "my preference." Will negotiate with a photographer unwilling to sell all rights.
Tips: "I only use photographers in geographic areas where my artists are performing or where they live. I have one full time nationally touring act, and three regional ones, living in St. Louis, near Baltimore, and in Clarksdale, Mississippi. Most independent labels use freelance photographers most of the time. The photographer needs to be aware of the whole album design process, and be able to get the shot that the producer and musicians want, rather than to get the shot that he as photographer assumes would look good on the cover. The image a photographer sees may not convey the intangibles that the producer or musicians want. I function as label owner and artist manager, and I do not like the ongoing exploitative use of photos by the photographer that the label or artist paid for, or my paying for lots of rolls of film to get only a few prints. Learn how an album cover and compact disc cover are designed so that you can shoot photos easily applicable to those specifications."

*ENIGMA ENTERTAINMENT, 11264 Plaza Ct., Culver City CA 90231. (213)390-9969. Art Director: Pat Dillon. Estab. 1982. Handles rock, classical and all types except country thus far. Photographers used for portraits, in-concert shots, studio shots and special effects—"the more innovative the better"—for album covers, inside album shots, publicity, brochures, posters, event/convention coverage and product advertising. Works with freelance photographers on assignment basis only; buys 20-40 freelance photos/year.
Making Contact: Arrange a personal interview to show portfolio; provide resume, business card, brochure, flyer or tearsheets to be kept on file for possible future assignments. Cannot return unsolicited material. Reports in 3 weeks.
Payment & Terms: Pays $50-3,000/job. Credit line given. Buys one-time rights, but have varied.
Tips: Wants "creative input from the photographer, something unique—not treated as just an assignment but as an avenue for self-expression." Interested in freelance photographer who is "creative, bizarre and experimental."

FOUR WINDS RECORD PRODUCTIONS INC., 217 Highway 51-S, Box 98, Madison MS 39110. (601)856-7468. A&R: Style Wooten. Handles bluegrass, black gospel, southern gospel and country. Photographers used for portraits, in-concert shots, studio shots and publicity for album covers, inside album covers, publicity, brochures and posters.
Specs: Uses 8×10 color and b&w glossy prints.
Making Contact: Send unsolicited photos by mail for consideration. Looks for "8×10 b&w and color prints of artists they have done." SASE. Reports in 2 weeks.
Payment & Terms: Negotiates payment. Buys one-time rights.

*FOX FARM RECORDING, 2731 Saundersville Ferry Road, Mt. Juliet TN 37122. (615)754-2444. Owner: Kent Fox. Estab. 1970. Handles bluegrass and gospel. Photographers used for portraits, studio shots, special effects for album covers, inside album shots and publicity. Works with freelance photographers on an assignment basis only.
Specs: Uses b&w/color.
Making Contact: Send unsolicited photos by mail for consideration. SASE. Reports in 1 month.
Payment & Terms: Pays by the job: $100-2,000. Credit line sometimes given. Buys all rights.
Tips: Looking for album covers. Keep in mind, freelancers must "have a good attitude." Future prospects for freelancers look good.

GLOBAL PACIFIC RECORDS, 180 E. Napa St., Sonoma CA 95476. (707)996-2748. FAX: (707)996-2658. Senior Vice President: Howard L. Morris. Handles jazz, New Age, pop, classical and rock. Photographers used for portraits, in-concert shots, studio shots and special effects for album covers, inside album shots, publicity, brochures, posters and product advertising. Buys 12-18 photos/year.

Specs: Uses 8×10 glossy b&w and color prints or transparencies.

Making Contact: Submit portfolio for review; provide resume, business card, brochure, flyer or tearsheets to be kept on file for possible future assignments. SASE. Reports in 2 weeks.

Payment & Terms: Buys all rights; will negotiate with photographer unwilling to sell all rights.

Tips: Prefers "technically excellent (can be blown up, etc.), excellent compositions, emotional photographs. Be familiar with what we have done in the past. Study our music, album packages, etc., and present material that is appropriate."

*GO-RECORDS, 3345 Hollins Ferry Rd., Baltimore MD 21227. (301)247-7446. General Manager: Ernest W. Cash. Estab. 1987. Handles country, gospel and rock. Photographers used for in-concert shots, studio shots and special effects for album covers, publicity, brochures, posters, event/convention and product advertising. Works with freelance photographers on assignment basis only.

Specs: Uses 8×10 b&w and color prints.

Making Contact: Provide resume, business card, brochure, flyer or tearsheets to be kept on file for possible future assignments. Cannot return material. Reports in 2 weeks.

Payment & Terms: Pays $100-300/job. Credit line sometimes given. Buys all rights.

Tips: Consider photographer's "quality of work, years of experience in field, time demands and contracts on products. Above all, be honest with us and we will treat you the same. The opportunities are endless."

GRAMAVISION RECORDS, 260 W. Broadway, New York NY 10013. (212)226-7057. General Manager: Al Pryor. Handles jazz, New Age, contemporary. Photographers used for portraits, in-concert shots and special effects for album covers, inside album shots, publicity, posters, and event/convention coverage. Works with freelance photographers on assignment basis only; "gives 10 assignments/year."

Making Contact: Arrange a personal interview to show portfolio. Query with resume of credits. Provide resume, business card, brochure, flyer or tearsheets to be kept on file for possible future assignments. Reports in 6 weeks.

Payment & Terms: Payment negotiable.

HARD HAT RECORDS & CASSETTES, 519 N. Halifax Ave., Daytona Beach FL 32118. (904)252-0381. President: Bobby Lee Cude. Handles country, pop, disco, gospel, MOR. Photographers used for portraits, in-concert shots, studio shots, special effects for album covers, publicity and posters. Works on assignment only; offers varied number of assignments/year.

Specs: Uses 8×10 b&w glossy prints.

Making Contact: Provide resume, business card, brochure, flyer or tearsheets to be kept on file for possible future assignments. SASE. Does not return unsolicited material. Reports in 1 month.

Payment & Terms: Pays on a contract basis. Credit line sometimes given. Buys all rights.

Tips: "Submit credentials as well as work done for other record companies as a sample; also price, terms. Read *MIX/MUSICIAN* magazines."

HIGHER OCTAVE MUSIC, Suite 41, 8033 Sunset Blvd., Los Angeles CA 90046. (213)856-0039. Vice President, Creative Services: Dee Westlund. Handles New Age. Photographers used for studio shots and special effects for album covers, inside album shots, publicity and brochures.

Specs: Uses b&w and color prints.

Making Contact: Arrange a personal interview to show portfolio or submit portfolio for review; provide resume, business card, brochure, flyer or tearsheets to be kept on file for possible future assignments. SASE. Reports in 3-4 weeks.

Payment & Terms: Credit line given. Buys all rights; will negotiate with photographer unwilling to sell all rights.

Tips: "New Age album covers are finally getting away from lonely landscapes and into a more progressive look—I look for clean elegance for our covers. Freelancers are in demand with small independent record companies that don't have lots of money to spend, but have the time to work with the photographer—for the right shot at the right price."

HUSH PRODUCTIONS, 231 W. 58th St., New York NY 10019. (212)582-1095. Artist Development Director: Lynda Simmons. Handles R&B, jazz, pop. Uses photographers for portraits, studio shots, special effects for album covers, inside album shots, publicity, brochures, posters, event/convention coverage. Works with freelancers on assignment only; offers a minimum of 2 assignments/year to freelancers.

Specs: Uses primarily 8×10 flat finish b&w and color prints.

Making Contact: Submit portfolio for review; provide resume, business card, brochure, flyer or tearsheet to be kept on file for possible future assignment. Drop off portfolios on Thursdays only. Does not return unsolicited material. Reports in 2 weeks.

Payment & Terms: Pays $500-2,500/job; rates are determined per session basis—LP photo shoot, publicity photo shoot, etc. Credit line given. Buys all rights.
Tips: Prefers to see creative/styling of the subject. "Present a portfolio which shows the personal direction and attitudes of the photographer. Freelancers are the life blood of record company art departments. Few (if any) are permanent staff members. Specializing is the dominant trend, i.e., use of computer imaging, beauty, surreal still life, action/movement shots, hand-painted photos, intimate portraits."

HYBRID RECORDS, Box 333, Evanston IL 60204. (312)328-0400. Art Director: Mike Rodgers. Handles all types of records. Photographers used for portraits, in-concert shots, studio shots and special effects for album covers, inside album shots, publicity, brochures, posters, event/convention coverage, product advertising and "other forms of creative merchandising." Number of photos bought/year varies.
Specs: Uses 8 × 10 matte or glossy color prints or 35mm transparencies.
Making Contact: Send "something that shows your best work, by mail for consideration—anything with women, i.e., flashy disco covers are nice," or submit portfolio for review. SASE. Reports ASAP.
Payment & Terms: Payment negotiable. Credit line given. Negotiates rights purchased.
Tips: Prefers to see "energy, flash and uniqueness" in photographer's portfolio. "Give us your best shot or don't bother."

INVASION RECORDS, 114 Lexington Ave., New York NY 10016. (212)532-1414. A&R Director: Bill Horwedel. Photographers used for portraits, in-concert shots and studio shots for album covers, inside album shots, publicity head shots and posters.
Specs: Uses b&w and color prints.
Making Contact: Provide resume, business card, brochure, flyer or tearsheets to be kept on file for possible future assignments. SASE. Reports in 3 weeks.
Payment & Terms: Pays $100-2,500/b&w photo; $100-2,500/color photo; $100-2,500/job. Credit line given.
Tips: "Be open minded, on time, professional, to make it as easy as possible to work with. Always looking for new 'kid on the block', creative photography, innovative."

JLI RECORDS, P.O. Box 74-R, Romeoville IL 60441-0974. (815)886-3929. President: Julian Leal. Estab. 1985. Handles rock and pop-rock. Photographers used for portraits, in-concert shots, studio shots and special effects for album covers, inside album shots, publicity, brochures, posters, event/convention coverage and product advertising. Works on assignment only; offers 12 assignments/year.
Specs: Uses 8 × 10 glossy b&w prints and color.
Making Contact: Provide resume, business card, brochure, flyer or tearsheets to be kept on file for possible future assignments. SASE. Reports in 1 month.
Payment & Terms: Pays variable rate per quality. Credit line given. Buys all rights, but will negotiate.
Tips: Looks for "live shots, special effects and an original style. Take time to get acquainted with the artist's music and incorporate the style and individuality into the photo project. Emphasize the characteristics that make your work different from anyone else's. Freelance photographers have a better chance of working with major record labels by establishing their art and talent on small record labels and unknown artists. To break in with this label, simply submit with SASE and be patient."

JODY RECORD INC., 2557 E. 1st St., Brooklyn NY 11223. (718)339-8047. VP-Sales: Tom Bosco. A&R Director: Vince Vallis. Handles rock, jazz, country, pop. Photographers used for portraits, in-concert shots, studio shots and special effects for album covers, publicity, brochures and posters. Works on assignment only.
Specs: Uses b&w prints.
Making Contact: Send unsolicited photos by mail for consideration. Reports in 2 weeks. Buys all rights but will negotiate with photographer.
Payment & Terms: Credit line given.
Tips: Looks for something unusual in photos.

KIMBO EDUCATIONAL, 10 N. Third Ave., Long Branch NJ 07740. (201)229-4949. Production Coordinator: Amy Laufer. Handles educational—early childhood movement oriented records and tapes. General entertainment songs for young children. Physical fitness programs for all ages. Photographers work used for album covers, brochures and product advertising. Offers 5 assignments/year.
Specs: Uses b&w and color prints.
Making Contact: Provide resume, business card, brochure, flyer or tearsheets to be kept on file for possible future assignments. Cannot return material. "We keep samples on file and contact photographer if in need of their services."

Payment & Terms: "Each job is different. Small advertising job—$50 minimum. Album covers—$100 minimum. $300-400 maximum." Buys all rights; will negotiate with photographer unwilling to sell all rights.

Tips: "We are looking for top quality work but our budgets do not allow us to pay New York City prices (need reasonable quotes). Prefer local photographers—communication easier. We are leaning a little more towards photography especially in our catalog. In the educational marketplace, it's becoming more prevalent to actually show our products being used by children."

K-LARRCO SATELLITE RADIO & T.V., Division Larrco Industries of TX, Inc., Box 3842, Houston TX 77253. President: Dr. Lawrence Herbst. Handles all types of records and publishes magazine. Photographers used for portraits, in-concert shots, studio shots, special effects for album covers, inside album shots, publicity, brochures, posters, event/convention coverage, product advertising and special jobs. Works on assignment only.
Specs: Uses 8×10 b&w or color glossy prints.
Making Contact: Provide resume, business card, brochure, flyer or tearsheets to be kept on file for possible future assignments. SASE. Reports in 1 month.
Payment & Terms: Pays $15-10,000/job. Buys all rights, but will negotiate.

SID KLEINER ENTERPRISES, 10188 Winter View Dr., Naples FL 33942. Director: Sid Kleiner. Freelance photographers supply 20% of photos. Uses subject matter relating to health, food, mental health, music, sex, human body, etc. Query with resume of credits or send samples. SASE. Pays $25 minimum/photo. Rights negotiable.
Tips: "Show us examples of your best work. We keep a file of prospective freelancers which we examine as needs arise. Subscribe to the trade journals where inside information is offered. Form a liason with the leading personal managers and bookers. Get to know the head honchos at all leading concert halls and arenas in the area."

L.R.J. RECORDS, 1700 Plunkett Ct., Box 3, Belen NM 87002. (505)864-7441. FAX: (505)864-7441. President: Little Richie Johnson. Handles country and bilingual records. Estab. 1959. Photographers used for record album photos. Credit line given. Send material by mail for consideration. Payment negotiable; pays on receipt of completed job. Buys all rights, but may reassign to photographer.

LANDMARK COMMUNICATIONS GROUP, Box 148296, Nashville TN 37214. President: Bill Anderson, Jr. Handles country/gospel. Photographers used for in-concert shots, studio shots and special effects for album covers and product advertising. Works with freelance photographers on assignment only; offers 2-3 assignments/year. Buys 2 photos/year.
Specs: Uses color and b&w prints.
Making Contact: Provide resume, business card, brochure, flyer or tearsheets to be kept on file for possible future assignments. SASE. Reports in 1 month.
Payment & Terms: Payment depends on project. Credit line given. Buys one-time rights.

LEMON SQUARE PRODUCTIONS, Box 671008, Dallas TX 75367-8008. (214)750-0720. Owner: Bart Barton. A&R Director: Mike Anthony. Handles country and gospel. Photographers used for portraits, live action shots and special effects for album covers, publicity flyers and posters. Works with freelance photographers on assignment only. Provide resume and samples to be kept on file for possible future assignments.
Specs: Uses 8×10 color prints.
Making Contact: Send material by mail for consideration or submit portfolio for review. Prefers to see creativity, abilities and thought in a portfolio. SASE. Reports ASAP.
Payment & Terms: Negotiates payment per job. Credit line given. Buys all rights.

LIN'S LINES, Suite 1103, 150 Fifth Ave., New York NY 10011. (212)691-5630. FAX: (212)645-5038. President: Linda K. Jacobson. Estab. 1983. Handles all types of records. Uses photographers for portraits, in-concert shots, studio shots for album covers, inside album shots, publicity, brochures, posters and product advertising. Works on an assignment only; gives 6 assignments/year.
Specs: Uses 8×10 prints; 35mm transparencies.
Making Contact: Query with resume of credits; provide resume, business card, brochure, flyer or tearsheets to be kept on file for possible future assignments. "Do not send unsolicited photos." SASE. Reports in 1 month.
Payment & Terms: Pays $50-500/b&w photo; $75-750/color photo; $10-50/hour; $100-1,500/day; $75-3,000/job. Credit line given. Buys one-time rights; all rights, but may reassign to photographer.
Tips: Prefers unusual and exciting photographs such as holograms and 3-D images. "Send *interesting* material, initially in post card form."

LUCIFER RECORDS, INC., Box 263, Brigantine NJ 08203. (609)266-2623. President: Ron Luciano. Photographers used for portraits, live action shots and studio shots for album covers, publicity flyers, brochures and posters. Freelancers supply 50% of photos.
Making Contact: Provide brochure, calling card, flyer, resume and samples. Purchases photos for album covers and record sleeves. Submit portfolio for review. SASE. Reports in 2-6 weeks.
Payment & Terms: Payment negotiable. Buys all rights.

JACK LYNCH ENTERPRISES, (Nashville Country Productions/Nashville Bluegrass/Jalyn & Nashville Country Recording Companies), 351 Millwood Dr., Nashville TN 37217. (615)366-9999. President: Col. Jack Lynch. Estab. 1963. Handles country, bluegrass and gospel. Uses photographers for portraits, in-concert shots and studio shots for album covers. Works with freelance photographers on assignment only; offers 1-10 assignments/year.
Specs: Uses various size b&w and color prints/transparencies.
Making Contact: Provide resume, business card, brochure, flyer or tearsheets to be kept on file for possible future assignments. SASE. Reports in 1 month.
Payment & Terms: Pays variable rates; $50-100/b&w photo; $100-200/color photo; $50-100/hour; $500-1,000/day; and $500-1,000/job.. Credit line usually given. Buys exclusive product rights.
Tips: "Call or write for information. Looks for good service, quality work and reasonable fees."

LEE MAGID, Box 532, Malibu CA 90265. (213)463-5998. President: Lee Magid. Operates under Grass Roots Records label. Handles R&B, jazz, C&W, gospel, rock, blues, pop. Photographers used for portraits, in-concert shots, studio shots, and candid photos for album covers, publicity, brochures, posters and event/convention coverage. Works with freelance photographers on assignment only; offers about 10 assignments/year.
Specs: Uses 8×10 b&w or color buff or glossy prints and $2\frac{1}{4} \times 2\frac{1}{4}$ transparencies.
Making Contact: Send print copies by mail for consideration. SASE. Reports in 2 weeks.
Payment & Terms: Credit line given. Buys all rights.

MARICAO RECORDS/HARD HAT RECORDS, 519 N. Halifax Ave., Daytona Beach FL 32118. (904)252-0381. President: Bobby Lee Cude. Handles country, MOR, pop, disco and gospel. Photographers used for portraits, in-concert shots, studio shots and special effects for album covers, inside album shots, publicity, brochures, posters, event/convention coverage and product advertising. Works with freelance photographers on assignment only; offers 12 assignments/year.
Specs: Uses b&w and color photos.
Making Contact: Submit portfolio for review; provide resume, business card, brochure, flyer, tearsheets or samples to be kept on file for possible future assignments. SASE. Reports in 2 weeks.
Payment & Terms: Pays "standard fees." Credit line sometimes given. Rights negotiable.
Tips: "Submit sample photo with SASE along with introductory letter stating fees, etc. Read *Mix Music* magazine."

NARADA PRODUCTIONS, 1845 N. Farwell Ave., Milwaukee WI 53202. (414)272-6700. Image Researcher: Kathy Hanus. Handles contemporary instrumentals and New Age music. Estab. 1980. Photographers used for publicity portraits for album covers. Buys up to 30+ freelance photos/year.
Specs: Uses 35mm and 5×7 transparencies.
Making Contact: Send unsolicited photos by mail for consideration; submit portfolio for review; provide resume, business card, brochure, flyer or tearsheets to be kept on file for possible future assignments. "Two of our specialty labels use nature scenics — no manmade objects or animals. For the *Narada Lotus* label, images should be simple, graphic, powerful, dynamic and colorful. Will even consider abstract nature scenics. The other label, *Narada Equinox*, requires two images. Background image is soft and textural with an inset image which should have a strong focal point." SASE. Reports in 1 month.
Payment & Terms: Payment "varies depending on usage." Credit line given. Buys one-time rights.
Tips: In samples, wants to see "vibrant and simple nature scenics. Strong focal point, not a lot of detail. Generally, work should be evocative of places and experiences and be something we've never seen before."

NIGHTHAWK RECORDS, Box 15856, St. Louis MO 63114. (314)576-1569. Director: Robert Schoenfeld. Handles blues and reggae. Photographers used for portraits, in-concert shots and studio shots for album cover and publicity. Works with freelance photographers on assignment basis only.
Specs: Uses color prints.
Making Contact: Send unsolicited photos by mail for consideration. Provide resume, business card, brochure, flyer or tearsheets to be kept on file for possible future assignments. SASE. Reports in 2 weeks.
Payment & Terms: Credit line given. Buys all rights, but willing to negotiate.

*NORTHWEST INTERNATIONAL ENTERTAINMENT, 5503 Roosevelt Way N.E., Seattle WA 98105. (206)524-1020. Vice President/Marketing: David Sterling. Estab. 1986. Handles all genres. Photographers used for in-concert shots, studio shots and special effects for album covers, inside album shots, publicity, brochures, posters, event/convention coverage and product advertising. Number of photos bought varies according to number of projects.

Specs: Uses 8×10, matte/gloss b&w and color prints.

Making Contact: Arrange a personal interview to show portfolio; send unsolicited photos of special effects and music-oriented shots by mail for consideration; provide resume, business card, brochure, flyer or tearsheets to be kept on file for possible future assignments. "Looking especially for special effects and music-oriented shots." SASE. Reports in 3 weeks.

Payment & Terms: Pays $75-125/hour. Credit line given. Buys one-time rights and all rights; will negotiate with photographer unwilling to sell all rights.

Tips: Considers photographer's "variety of samples and poses. Photo work is incorporated into promo pieces. Just keep sending information." The chances of working with record companies are "excellent. Music is sold by photography. It must portray the image and style of the music."

NUCLEUS RECORDS, Box 111, Sea Bright NJ 07760. President: Robert Bowden. Estab. 1979. Handles rock, country. Photographers used for portraits, studio shots for publicity, posters and product advertising. Works with freelance photographers on assignment basis only.

Making Contact: Send still photos of people by mail for consideration. SASE. Reports in 3 weeks.

Payment & Terms: Pays $50-100/b&w photo; $100-200/color photo; $50-75/hour; $100-200/day; $500-1,000/job. Credit line given. Buys one-time rights.

ORINDA RECORDS, 111 Deerwood Place, San Ramon CA 94583. (415)831-4890. President: C.J. Black. Handles rock, classical, pop, jazz. Photographers used for portraits, studio shots and special effects for album covers and posters.

Specs: Uses 8×10 color prints and 35mm transparencies.

Making Contact: Submit portfolio for review; provide resume, business card, brochure, flyer or tearsheets to be kept on file for possible future assignments. Cannot return material. Reports in 6 weeks.

Payment & Terms: Credit line given. Buys all rights.

Tips: A cover must sell the product inside.

PARC RECORDS, INC., 2nd Fl., 3016 Dade Ave., Orlando FL 32804. (407)894-0021. Administrative Assistant: Gayle Boulware. Handles rock, dance and southern rock. Photographers used for in-concert shots and studio shots for album covers, inside album shot, publicity and posters. Works with freelance photographers on assignment only; offers 4-6 assignments/year.

Specs: Uses 8×10 glossy b&w or color prints.

Making Contact: Send unsolicited photos by mail for consideration. Provide resume, business card, brochure, flyer or tearsheets to be kept on file for possible future assignments. Looking especially for "any band/concert shots, the strange and unusual." SASE. Reports in 1 month.

Payment & Terms: Credit line given. Buys all rights, but willing to negotiate.

PLAYBACK RECORDS/GALLERY II RECORDS, INC., Box 630755, Miami FL 33163. (305)935-4880. FAX: (305)933-4007. President: Jack Gale. Estab. 1983. Handles country. Uses portraits and in-concert shots for album covers, inside album shots, publicity and posters.

Specs: Uses b&w and color prints.

Making Contact: Send unsolicited photos by mail for consideration; provide resume, business card, brochure, flyer or tearsheets to be kept on file for possible future assignments. Send 8×10 glossy, 8×10 color and poster album cover images. Cannot return material. Reports whenever need arises.

Payment & Terms: Pays per b&w or color photo or by the job. Credit line given. Buys one-time rights or all rights; will negotiate with photographer unwilling to sell all rights.

THE PRESCRIPTION CO., 70 Murray Ave., Port Washington NY 11050. (516)767-1929. President: David F. Gasman. VP (A&R): Kirk Nordstrom. Tour Coordinator: Bill Fearn. Secretary: Debbie Fearn. Handles rock, soul and country & western. Photographers used for portraits, in-concert/studio shots and special effects for album covers, inside album shots, publicity flyers, brochures, posters, event/convention coverage and product advertising. Works on assignment only.

Specs: Uses b&w/color prints.
Making Contact: To arrange interview to show portfolio, "send us a flyer or tearsheets for our files." Cannot return material. "We want no original photos submitted."
Payment & Terms: Payment negotiable. Rights purchased negotiable.
Tips: "Send us a flyer or some photos for our files. We're only a small company with sporadic needs. If interested we will set up an in-person meeting. There is always need for good photography in our business, but like most fields today, competition is growing stiffer. Art and technique are important, of course, but so is a professional demeanor when doing business."

PRO/CREATIVES, 25 W. Burda Pl., Spring Valley NY 10977. President: David Rapp. Handles pop and classical. Photographers used for record album photos, men's magazines, sports, advertising illustrations, posters and brochures. Buys all rights. Query with examples, resume of credits and business card. Reports in 1 month. SASE.

PUBLIC I PUBLICITY SERVICES, Suite 1102, 928 Broadway, New York NY 10010. (212)505-8778. FAX: (212)979-2768. President: Ida S. Langsam. Manager: Susan Burke. Estab. 1982. Handles mostly rock and roll, some pop, a lot of heavy metal artists. Uses photographers for in-concert shots, studio shots for publicity. Number of photos bought from freelancers/year varies, depending on the account and budget.
Specs: Uses 8×10 b&w prints.
Making Contact: Arrange a personal interview to show portfolio; query with resume of credits; or provide resume, business card, brochure, flyer or tearsheets to be kept on file for possible future assignments. SASE. Reports in 1 week.
Payment & Terms: Payment "depends entirely on the photographer's fees and the intended use of the photo—one time magazine feature illustration, publicity shot, etc." Credit line given when requested. Rights purchased vary depending on photographer's requests and the situation.
Tips: "Looking for photographer who is able to bring his/her creativity to making an artist/band look good in the same old cliche of a press photo—good lighting, color contrasts and excitement, poses, background, concept and image, styling and costuming—for in-studio and set-ups and for in-concert shots. Looking for clarity of subject, visual excitement and the feel of the event itself. Know the music area and when coming to an appointment, have your portfolio organized. Make sure the samples are good examples of creative work done, prints are standard sizes, slides are mounted and that the photos speak for themselves. One way to break in is to get experience through magazines. In particular, work for local market via newspapers, magazines, with coverage of local artists."

*RANDALL PRODUCTIONS, 5129 S. Harper - #405, Chicago IL 60615-4143. (708)450-8283. President: Frank Leonard. Handles all types except classical music. Photographers used for in-concert shots, postcards, magazines, photo layouts, studio shots, and video for album covers, brochures, posters, and concert promotion/artist promotion. Works with freelance photographers on assignment basis only; gives 20 assignments/year.
Specs: Uses all sizes of b&w or color glossy prints: 35mm, 2¼×2¾ and transparencies.
Making Contact: Send surrealism, new concept, idealistic, or abstract material by mail for consideration; provide resume, brochure, flyer or tearsheets to be kept on file for possible future assignments. SASE if you wish to have material returned. Reports "when needs arise."
Payment & Terms: Pays $15-25/b&w photo; $25/color photo; $15-25/hour; $50-150/day; $50-150/job. Buys all ownership rights outright. Acts as broker to major magazines.
Tips: "Freelancers have just as much to contribute as any photographer, if not more. Because of the nature of the business, record companies tend to lean towards seeking unknowns, because their styles are usually, in our opinion, more unique."

*RANDOM RECORDS/RANDOM IMAGE MUSIC, 209 Madison Ave., Toronto, ON M5R 3S7 Canada. (416)929-2349. President: Peter Randall. Estab. 1986. Handles rock, pop and country. Photographers used for studio shots and special effects for album covers, inside album shots, publicity and posters. Works with freelance photographers on assignment basis only; offers 2-3 assignments/year.
Specs: Uses b&w and color prints, various sizes.
Making Contact: Send unsolicited photos by mail for consideration; provide resume, business card, brochure, flyer or tearsheets to be kept on file for possible future assignments. SASE. Reports in 1 month.
Payment & Terms: Pays $100-1,000/b&w photo; $100-1,500/color photo; $100-200/hour; $100-2,500/job. Credit line given. Buys all rights; wil negotiate with photographer unwilling to sell all rights.

*RAPP PRODUCTIONS, including RR & R Records, Rapp Records, Rapture and Ready Records, Rt. 16 Box 560 Cain Circle, Gainesville GA 30506. (404)889-8624. Publicity Co-Ordinator: Marci Wheeler. Estab. 1966. Handles Rapp Records, commercial all types; RR & R, all categories; Rapture

Close-up

Dave Bett
Art Director
Relativity Records
Hollis, New York

© Randy Masser

"It happens most of the time that photographers help us to solve our creative problems," says Dave Bett, art director for Relativity Records. "And that's the kind of person we need, someone who can take responsibility for making things happen."

In talking about his experience with the four-year-old independent record company, Bett recalls an instance where the photographer really 'delivered the goods.' "We were having a hard time coming up with a concept for an album called *Stormy Weather* by the group Thelonius Monster," he says. "The photographer, Ed Colver, wanted to show the band 'raining down.' So, he got these five guys—who are very hard to get to sit still for more than 10 minutes—to lie down on 'no seam' and take these crazy positions, as if they were falling. He also threw in stuff he had around his studio—a dud bomb, a pitchfork, his cat and dog—and added all these assorted objects falling from the sky. And because the day of the shoot was a rainy day in Los Angeles—of all places—Ed also threw in a shot of L.A. in the rain as a backdrop."

From there, Bett continues, it all sort of 'fell' together. "It seemed like Ed sent us a ton of stuff, and we 'stripped' the different photos together so it looked as if all this was falling from the clouds," he says admiringly of Colver's final results. "It was all done, too, without me on the scene. I stayed here and Ed went out to California and took it all on himself. He impressed the hell out of me, and he did it all on an average budget."

Because independent labels typically don't have very large budgets for artwork, some photographers may be seduced by the thought of working for a major record label instead. However, as Bett points out, what independent record companies such as Relativity don't offer in terms of money-making opportunities they usually make up for with just this kind of creative freedom. "One nice thing about working with musicians," he adds, "is that they're creative to begin with and pretty interesting people. So, photographers tend to do a lot more for them than they might with corporate clients."

According to Bett, who handles art direction for Relativity and its two subsidiary labels, In-Effect and Combat, an average budget per project is in the $1,000 to $1,500 range . . . with some exceptions. "If we're expecting big sales on a record, such as with Joe Satriani, the fee can go as high as $3,000 to $5,000, but we only have two or three acts like him that would justify paying that much," says Bett, noting that guitarist Satriani was the label's first major selling artist and now has two gold records to his credit. "Because of him, we've tripled in size and we're attracting more commercial acts to the label—people we couldn't even have conceived of four years ago. But the budget's still pretty standard."

For the standard price, Bett likes to get a package of images that will be good for the entire life of the album. "We try to do it all at once . . . get all the photography done in one or two sessions right at the start of the album project," says Bett, noting that album art and publicity stills usually come from the same shoot, even if different formats are required.

"I have the photographer shoot 2¼ for covers, and 35mm color or b&w for publicity," Bett continues. He explains that because the artwork for album covers usually ends up being used in posters, the 2¼ x 2¼ format will hold greater detail when the image is blown up to poster size, 2×3 or 3×4 feet usually.

Most of Relativity's needs are very specific and vary according to the act, so Bett rarely buys stock images from freelancers. "It's really rare when you see a stock photo that is exactly what you want," he says, noting that he strives to illustrate the concept or theme of an album as precisely as possible. "When you become dependent on stock images, it's like being dictated to by the photograph. I really like to start with the idea and get that across in the photograph."

Even though Bett prefers to assign photos to have them tailored exactly to the group's image and the album's concept, he does not buy all rights or hire photographers on a 'work for hire' basis. "We buy rights for specific use, and spell this out on the contract," he says. "If we decide to buy additional rights, we renegotiate—but that's rare. The payment period is usually within 30-60 days, which is pretty typical for a record company."

Bett says that as the company grows so do his needs, and so he is always keeping an eye for new people to bring on board. "I will see anyone who's willing to make the trip to Queens to show me their portfolio," he says. "I've had photographers just walk in and I've given them work right on the spot. It doesn't happen every time, but it does happen. If they send me a portfolio, I'll look it over and return it right away. I may call if they include their card and something comes up around that time, while they're still in mind. But it really pays for them to follow up."

Finally, Bett reminds photographers that 'indies' like Relativity are a good training ground for those who aspire to someday work with major labels. "Typically, the goal for photographers is to work with the majors because that's where the money is," says Bett. "If you really sell the right company on your work and you land them, you're set. But it's hard to approach a major label and get work because you're competing with those labels' established rosters. It can be tough if you're relying on one or two independent labels for making a living, but I think there are enough opportunities in the business if you get out there and hustle. The place to start, though, is with the independent labels."

—*Sam A. Marshall*

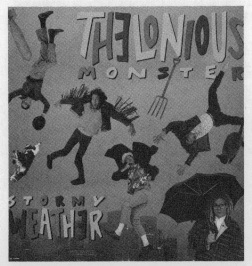

As Relativity Art Director Dave Bett points out, photographers who are successful in shooting for record companies are often those who help solve creative problems. One such problem solver was Los Angeles-based photographer Ed Colver, who produced this image for an album cover by the group, Thelonious Monster. Not only did Colver create and execute the concept mostly by himself, says Bett, but also, "he did it all on an average budget."

Records, Christian music, all categories and Ready Records, promotional. Photographers used for portraits, in-concert shots, studio shots, special effects for album covers, publicity, brochures, posters, event/convention, product advertising. Number of photos bought from freelancers per year varies.
Specs: Uses all formats and sizes.
Making Contact: Send unsolicited photos by mail for consideration. Submit portfolio for review. Cannot return material. Reports in 1 month.
Payment & Terms: Payment varies according to usage; negotiable. Credit line given. Buys all rights. Will negotiate with a photographer unwilling to sell all rights.
Tips: In photographer's portfolio or samples wants to see "originality, feeling and remembrance." Sees trend toward "less sex, violence, culture shock, more publicity or promotional shots and advertisements."

*RELATIVITY RECORDS, INC., 187-07 Henderson Ave., Hollis NY 11423. (718)740-5700. Art Director: David Bett. Estab. 1979. Handles rock, heavy metal, hardcore, pop and jazz. Photographers used for portraits, in-concert shots, studio shots and special effects for album covers, inside album shots, publicity, posters and event/convention. Works on assignment only; offers approx. 20-25 assignments/year. Examples of recent uses: "Flying in a Blue Dream," by Joe Satriani; "Passion and Warfare," by Steve Vai; "Shotgun Messiah," by Shotgun Messiah. In all three cases, photos used for album covers, posters, ads and print publicity.
Specs: Uses 35mm or 2¼×2¼ color transparencies; 8×10 b&w prints.
Making Contact: Submit portfolio for review, provide resume, business card, brochure, flyer or tearsheets to be kept on file for possible future assignments. Contact by phone to arrange submission of portfolio or send card to be kept on file. SASE. Reports when we want to hire photographer.
Payment & Terms: Uses $50-1,500/b&w photo; $50-1,500/color photo; publicity photos $50-150 per shot; album cover photo $500-1,500; back cover $150-500. Credit line given. Buys one-time rights.
Tips: In photographer's portfolio wants to see "music-oriented photos: portraits of musicians; photos used on albums, posters, or for publicity or photos that could work as album covers. We have bands all over the U.S., though mainly in NY & LA areas. Always looking for photographers with imagination and good rapport with musicians. We use freelancers exclusively, a core group of about 10-12, but willing to add good photographers to our roster. We probably use photography on about 60% of our covers, and somewhere on all our albums. Photo must have good concept or look to be on cover."

*RIPSAW RECORD CO., #805, 4545 Connecticut Ave. NW, Washington DC 20008. (202)362-2286. President: Jonathan Strong. Handles roots rock and rockabilly. Photographers used for in-concert shots and studio shots for album covers, publicity, brochures and posters. Buys up to 10 photos/year.
Specs: "Depends on need."
Making Contact: Send "material we might use" by mail for consideration. SASE. Reporting time "depends on free time; we try to be considerate and return as promptly as possible."
Payment & Terms: Pays by the job. Credit line given. Buys all rights.

*ROADRUNNER RECORDS, 225 Lafayette Street, New York NY 10012. (212)219-0077. Director of Publicity: Larry Getlen. Estab. 1986. Handles heavy metal, hard rock, alternative. Photographers used for portraits, in-concert shots, studio shots and special effects for album covers, inside album shots and publicity. Buys 20-30 photos/year.
Specs: Varies.
Making Contact: Provide resume, business card, brochure, flyer or tearsheets to be kept on file for possible future assignments. Does not return material. Reports in 3 weeks.
Payment & Terms: Pays $200-1,000/job. Credit line given. Buys all rights, but may reassign to photographer.
Tips: Editor is looking for "variety, good composition and unique shots. Pay attention to both photo quality and creativity."

ROBBINS RECORDS, INC., HC80, Box 5B, Leesville LA 71446. National Representative: Sherree Angel. Estab. 1972. Handles religious, gospel and country. Photographers used for studio shots and special effects for album covers and publicity. Works on assignment only; offers variable assignments/year.
Specs: Uses various size b&w or color prints.
Making Contact: Send religious or gospel album cover material by mail for consideration; provide resume, business card, brochure, flyer or tearsheets to be kept on file for possible future assignments. Cannot return material. Report time varies.
Payment & Terms: Pays agreed amount/job. Buys all rights, but will negotiate.
Tips: "Freelancers have a fair chance of working with record companies. Some special effects photography is being used."

*ROCK CITY RECORDS, Box 6553, Malibu CA 90264. (818)506-3789. President: Mike Danna. Estab. 1984. Handles rock. Photographers used for portraits, in-concert shots and studio shots for album covers and publicity. Works with freelance photographers on assignment basis only; offers 1-3 assignments/year.
Specs: Uses 5×7 and 8×10 glossy b&w or color prints.
Making Contact: Provide resume, business card, brochure, flyer or tearsheets to be kept on file for possible future assignments. SASE. Reports in 1 month.
Payment & Terms: Pays $25-100/b&w photo; $30-125/color photo; $100-300/job. Credit line given. Buys all rights. Will negotiate with a photographer unwilling to sell all rights 'if he does pictures on a spec basis only."
Tips: "Show us your abilities and work with us so that when we grow, you'll grow. It's a very competitive market—hold on till you get established and if you're good, you'll be rewarded down the road."

ROCKWELL RECORDS, Box 1600, Haverhill MA 01831. (617)373-6011. President: Bill Macek. Produces top 40 and rock and roll records. Photographers used for live action shots, studio shots and special effects for album covers, inside album shots, publicity, brochures and posters. Photos used for jacket design and artist shots. Buys 8-12 photos and offers 8-12 assignments/year. Freelancers supply 100% of photos.
Making Contact: Interested in seeing all types of photos. "No restrictions. I may see something in a portfolio I really like and hadn't thought about using." Arrange a personal interview; submit b&w and color sample photos by mail for consideration; or submit portfolio for review. Provide brochure, calling card, flyer or resume to be kept on file for possible future assignments. SASE. Local photographers preferred, but will review work of photographers from anywhere.
Payment & Terms: Payment varies.

*ROLL ON RECORDS®, 112 Widmar Pl., Clayton CA 94517. (415)672-8201. Owner: Edgar J. Brincat. Estab. 1986. Handles country, rock, r&b, pop/soul, gospel, middle of the road, easy listening. Photographers used for portraits, in-concert shots, studio shots and special effects for album covers, inside album shots and publicity. Works with freelance photographers on assignment basis only; offers 2-4 assignments/year.
Specs: Uses various sizes, glossy b&w or color prints.
Making Contact: Query with resume of credits; provide resume, business card, brochure, flyer or tearsheets to be kept on file for possible future assignments. SASE. Reports in 2 weeks.
Payment & Terms: Pays $300-1,500/b&w photo; $400-2,000/color photo; negotiable. Credit line given. Buys all rights.
Tips: "We expect an itemized contract and a price that does not change" when working with freelancers. The future outlook is "very good" for freelancers.

This photo, by photographer Pat Johnson, was the final choice from some 100 pictures shot while developing the art for the sleeve of this recent record by country music artist, Steve Jordan. Roll On Records owner Edgar Brincat notes that the photo was used not only for the 45 rpm single but also the cassette tape and CD liner sleeve. As in this case, where the company paid the photographer $550 for the shoot, the record company acquired all rights to all the images for the flat fee.

RUSHWIN PRODUCTIONS, Box 1150, Buna TX 77612. (409)423-2521. Manager: James Gibson. Handles Christian; all styles. Photographers used for portraits, in-concert shots, studio shots, special effects for album covers, publicity, brochures, posters. Works with freelance photographers on assignment only; offers "various" assignments/year.

Specs: Uses 4×5 transparencies.

Making Contact: Send color print, matte finish photos by mail for consideration; provide resume, business card, brochure, flyer or tearsheets to be kept on file for possible future assignments. SASE. Reports ASAP.

Payment & Terms: Payment varies/job. Credit line given. Buys all rights.

*SILKINI RECORDS, 9135 Manzanar Avenue, Downey CA 90240. (213)862-1825. Public Relations: William Delis. Handles rock, classical and country. Photographers used for portraits, in-concert shots, studio shots and special effects for album covers, inside album shots, publicity, posters and product advertising. Works with freelance photographers on assignment basis only; offers over 20 assignments/year.

Specs: Uses 8×10, glossy, b&w/color prints.

Making Contact: Arrange a personal interview to show portfolio; send unsolicited photos by mail for consideration; provide resume, business card, brochure, flyer or tearsheets to be kept on file for possible future assignments. Cannot return material. Reporting time varies.

Payment & Terms: Payment negotiable. Credit line sometimes given. Rights purchased varies. Will negotiate with a photographer unwilling to sell all rights.

Tips: "Call us—have good ideas and the ability to put them to work. Quality is important."

SIRR RODD RECORD & PUBLISHING CO., Box 58116, Philadelphia PA 19102-8116. President/A&R: Rodney Jerome Keitt. Handles R&B, jazz, top 40, rap, pop, gospel and soul. Uses photographers for portraits, in-concert shots, studio shots and special effects for album covers, inside album shots, publicity, posters, event/convention and product advertising. Buys 10 (minimum) photos/year.

Specs: Uses 8×10 glossy b&w or color prints.

Making Contact: Submit portfolio for review; provide resume, business card, brochure, flyer or tearsheets to be kept on file for possible future assignments. SASE. Reports in 1 month.

Payment & Terms: Pays $40-200/b&w photo; $60-250/color photo; $75-450/job. Credit line given. Buys all rights, but will negotiate.

Tips: "We look for the total versatility of the photographer. Of course, you can show us the more common group photos, but we like to see new concepts in group photography. Remember that you are freelancing. You do not have the name, studio, or reputation of 'Big Time' photographers, so we both are working for the same thing—exposure! If your pieces are good and the quality is equally good, your chances of working with record companies are excellent. Show your originality, ability to present the unusual, and what 'effects' you have to offer."

SOLAR RECORDS, 1635 N. Cahuenga Blvd., Hollywood CA 90028. (213)461-0390. Production Coordinator: Brenda Patrick. Handles R&B. Uses portraits, in-concert shots, studio shots for album covers, inside album shots, publicity and posters. Works on assignment only; uses 10-12 freelance photographers/year.

Specs: Uses b&w and color prints.

Making Contact: Arrange a personal interview to show portfolio; submit portfolio for review; provide resume, business card, brochure, flyer or tearsheets to be kept on file for possible future assignments. SASE. Reports in 2 weeks.

Payment & Terms: Pays $1,000-4,000/assignment. Buys all rights.

SONIC WAVE RECORDS, Box 256577, Chicago IL 60625. (312)631-8782. President: Tom Petreli. Handles new wave/punk, classical, rock, New Age and country. Photographers used for in-concert shots, studio shots and special effects for album covers, inside album shots, publicity, brochures and posters. Works on assignment only; offers 25-50 assignments/year.

Specs: Uses b&w and color prints, and 35mm and 8×10 transparencies.

Making Contact: Provide resume, business card, brochure, flyer or tearsheets to be kept on file for possible future assignments. SASE. Reports in 1 month.

Payment & Terms: Pays $50-100/b&w photo; $100-200/color photo; $25-50/hour; $125-300/job. Credit line given. Buys all rights.

*THE SOUND ACHIEVEMENT GROUP, Box 24625, Nashville TN 37202. (615)883-2600. President: Royce Gray. Estab. 1984. Handles all forms of gospel. Photographers used for in-concert shots, studio shots and location shots for album covers, publicity, brochures, posters, event/convention and product advertising. Works on assignment only; offers 10-15 assignments/year.

Specs: Uses 2¼×2¼ color transparencies, b&w prints.

Making Contact: Arrange a personal interview to show portfolio; provide resume, business card, brochure, flyer or tearsheets to be kept on file for possible future assignments. SASE. Reports in 1 month.

Payment & Terms: Pays $15-35/hour; $75-300/job. Credit line given. Buys all rights. Will negotiate with a photographer unwilling to sell all rights.

Tips: In photographer's portfolio, wants to see "album and promo shots of artists. We're a custom company, our budgets vary from job to job. Your chances are good providing you're flexible with your budget."

*SOUNDS OF WINCHESTER, Rt. 2, Box 116 H, Berkeley Springs WV 25411. Contact: Jim McCoy. Handles rock, gospel and country. Photographers used for portraits and studio shots for album covers, publicity flyers and brochures. Provide brochure to be kept on file for possible future assignments.

THE SPARROW CORPORATION, 9255 Deering Ave., Chatsworth CA 91311. (818)709-6900. Director of Creative Services: Barbara Hearn. Handles rock, classical, worship, and children's albums. Uses photographers for portraits, studio shots for album covers, inside album shots, publicity, brochures, posters, event/convention coverage, product advertising, cassette inserts and mobiles. Works with freelance photographers on an assignment basis only; gives 10 assignments/year.

Specs: Uses 8×10 color prints; 2¼×2¼ transparencies.

Making Contact: Provide resume, business card, brochure, flyer or tearsheets to be kept on file for possible future assignments. SASE. Reports "if artist calls for feedback or when we decide to use the photos."

Payment & Terms: Pays $300-1,000/job. Credit line given. Buys all rights.

Tips: "Prefer to see people shots, close-up faces, nice graphic design and elements included. Send clean-cut samples with wholesome images. No nude models, etc. Be friendly, but not pushy or over-bearing. Freelancers have very good chances. We are moving toward more detailed photo sets and designs that can carry a theme and using elements which can be used separately or together according to need. We have incorporated a new instrumental series and are always looking for mood shots."

SPHEMUSATIONS, 12 Northfield Rd., One house, Stomarket Suffolk 1P14 3HF England. 0449-613388. General Manager: James Butt. Handles classical, country and western. Uses photographers for portraits, in-concert shots, studio shots, special effects and ensemble portraits for album covers, inside album shots, publicity, brochures, posters, event/convention coverage and product advertising. Works with freelance photographers on assignment basis only; gives 2-6 assignments/year.

Specs: Uses glossy b&w or color prints.

Making Contact: Send unsolicited photos by mail for consideration; submit portfolio for review. Provide resume, business card, brochure, flyer or tearsheets to be kept on file for possible future assignments. SASE. Reports in 1 month.

Payment & Terms: Pays $10-1,000/b&w photo; $50-2,000/color photo; $5-25/hour; $30-175/day; $25-2,500/job. Credit line given. Buys all rights but may reassign rights; negotiable.

Tips: "Prefers to see good portraits of artists, and album cover to which the photographer has contributed work. Especially wants to see pictures which show a sense of character and culture. Chances of working with record companies are many, varied, and excellent. There is a trend toward visually sensitive, perceptive photography, which reveals something more than simple surface—values."

STORYVILLE RECORDS AB, Dortheavej 39, Copenhagen NV DK 2400 Denmark. (01)260757. President/Owner: Karl Emil Knudsen. Handles jazz and blues. Uses portraits, in-concert shots, studio shots, special effects for album covers, inside album shots, publicity; "We also publish books and are working on a series of picture books on jazz."

Specs: Uses b&w and color transparencies.

Making Contact: Send unsolicited photos by mail for consideration; provide resume, business card, brochure, flyer or tearsheets to be kept on file for possible future assignments. Wants to see portraits or in-concert/live shots for books only. SASE. Reports in 1 month.

Payment & Terms: Pays $40-100/b&w photo; $75-200/color photo; $2-300/assignment. Credit line given. Buys all rights; will negotiate with photographer unwilling to sell all rights.

Tips: "99% of all covers show/use photos. We issue 25-40 LP/CDs per year. Since most artists perform in New York, Los Angeles/San Francisco he should be from/live in that/those area/s. Someone who has done this work for 20-30 years with a backlog of material has a good chance for our forthcoming books."

*TEMPE RECORDS, Box 256577, Chicago IL 60625. (312)631-8782. President: Tom Petreli. Estab. 1985. Handles New Age, jazz, American Indian, opera, heavy metal, rap and spoken word. Photographers used for portraits, in-concert shots, studio shots, special effects and limited edition for album covers, inside album shots, publicity, brochures, posters, event/convention and adv. video covers.

Specs: Uses all sizes, various finishes, b&w/color prints.

Making Contact: Send unsolicited photos by mail for consideration. SASE. Reports in 1 month.

Payment & Terms: Pays $100-300/b&w photo; $250-600/color photo; $100-600/hour; $200-800/job. Credit line given. Buys one-time rights. Will negotiate with a photographer unwilling to sell all rights.

Tips: Editor wants to see all different types in samples sent. The trend is towards "different covers."

TIMELESS RECORDS, P.O. Box 201, Wageningon Holland 6700 AE. (8370)13440. FAX: (8370)21540. Administrative Director: M. Wigt. Estab. 1975. Handles jazz, traditional jazz, blues and salsa. Photographers used for portraits, in-concert shots, studio shots and special effects for album covers and publicity. Works on assignment only.

Specs: Uses b&w and color prints.

Making Contact: Arrange a personal interview to show portfolio or send unsolicited photos by mail for consideration. Cannot return material. Reports in 1 month.

Payment & Terms: Pays $100 minimum/b&w or color photo. Credit line given. Buys all rights.

Tips: Looks for "photos of musicians; good, clear, striking photos of situations/scenes."

RIK TINORY PRODUCTIONS, Box 311, Cohasset MA 02025. (617)383-9494. Art Director: Claire Babcock. Handles rock, classical, country. Photographers used for portraits, in-concert shots, studio shots, and special effects for album covers, inside album shots, publicity, brochures, posters and event/convention coverage.

Specs: Uses 8×10 b&w prints and 2¼×2¼ transparencies.

Making Contact: Query first. Does not return unsolicited material.

Payment & Terms: Pays "flat fee—we must own negatives." Credit line given. Buys all rights plus negatives.

Tips: "Be good, fast and dependable."

*T-JAYE RECORD CO., 923 Main St., Box 60412, Nashville TN 37206. (615)226-1004. President: Ted Jarrett. Estab. 1980. Handles r&b and gospel. Photographers used for portraits, in-concert shots and studio shots for album covers, publicity, posters and product advertising. Works with freelance photographers on assignment basis only; offers 3-4 assignments/year.

Specs: Uses 8×10 color prints.

Making Contact: Provide resume, business card, brochure, flyer or tearsheets to be kept on file for possible future assignments. Needs "new ideas." Cannot return material. Reports in 2 weeks.

Payment & Terms: "We pay whatever the charges are, if we want the photo." Credit line given. Buys all rights.

Tips: "We look for unique ideas. We are a small company and we use what we can afford."

*TRIPLE X MANAGEMENT., Box 1010, Hollywood CA 90078. (213)871-0605. President: Charley Brown. Estab. 1985. Handles rock and alternative. Photographers used for in-concert shots, studio shots and special effects for album covers, inside album shots, publicity and posters. Especially wants to see bizarre images. Works with freelance photographers on assignment basis only; offers 6-10 assignments/year.

Spec: Uses 8×10, matte b&w/color prints.

Making Contact: Arrange a personal interview to show portfolio; send unsolicited album cover, live performance and press shots by mail for consideration; submit portfolio for review. SASE. Reports in 1 month.

Payment & Terms: Pays $100-500/b&w photo. Credit line given. Buys all rights; not negotiable.

Tips: "Be original and cost effective."

MIKE VACCARO PRODUCTIONS INC., (formerly Mike Vaccaro Music Services and Productions) Box 7991, Long Beach CA 90807. (213)424-4958 Contact: Mike Vaccaro. Handles classical. Photographers used for portraits, in-concert shots, studio shots, special effects for album covers, publicity, brochures, event/convention coverage and product advertising. Works on assignment only; gives 2-3 assignments/year.

Making Contact: Arrange a personal interview to show portfolio; query with resume of credits; send unsolicited photos by mail for consideration or submit portfolio for review; provide resume, business card, brochure, flyer or tearsheets to be kept on file for possible future assignments. Does not return unsolicited material. Reports as needed.

Payment & Terms: Payment, credit line and rights purchased are negotiated.

Tips: "Flexibility in many styles and special effects" is advisable.

ALIX B. WILLIAMSON, 55 Central Park West, New York NY 10023. (212)769-4433. Owner: Alix B. Williamson. Estab. 1938. Publicity office handling classical music. Uses photographers for portraits, in-concert shots, studio shots and on-location candids for publicity, brochures, posters. Works on assignment only; offers 20+ freelance assignments/year.

Specs: Uses 8×10 glossy b&w and color prints and color slides.
Making Contact: Arrange a personal interview to show portfolio. Does not return unsolicited material.
Payment & Terms: Pays by the job: varies according to photographer, kind of photo, subject matter and speed of service. Credit line given. Buys all rights.
Tips: To break in with this company, "send samples and rates or call for appointment."

WINDHAM HILL PRODUCTIONS, INC., 831 High St., Palo Alto CA 94301. (415)329-0647. Art Director: Anne Robinson. Handles mostly jazz-oriented, acoustic and electronic music. Uses freelance photographers for portraits, art shots for covers, inside album shots, posters. Buys 20-30 freelance photos/year.
Specs: Uses 35mm, 2¼×2¼, 4×5 and 8×10 transparencies. "Please send dupes, if we want more accurate version we will ask for original." Submit portfolio for review. SASE. Reports in 1 month.
Payment & Terms: Payment varies. Credit line given. Buys one-time rights or all rights, "depends on the nature of the product."
Tips: "I am not looking for variations of shots we have already used. I am looking for unusual points of view, generally of natural subjects, without people or animals. Become acquainted with our covers before submitting materials. Send materials that have personal significance. I am not merely looking for technically excellent work. I want work with heart."

Record Companies/'90-'91 changes

The following record companies appeared in the 1990 edition of *Photographer's Market* but are not in the 1991 edition. Those companies whose presidents or art directors did not respond to our request for an update of their listings may not have done so for a variety of reasons—they may be out of business, for example, or they may be overstocked with submissions.

American Music Network (deleted)
Anamaze Records (deleted)
Azra Records (deleted)
Bator & Assoc., Robert (did not respond)
Byron Productions, Bill (did not respond)
Dawn Productions (deleted)
EFA-Medien-GMBH (did not respond)
Epoch Universal Publications (did not respond)

GCS Records (did not respond)
J & J Musical Enterprises (did not respond)
(KAM) Executive Record (did not respond)
Kiderian Record Products (deleted)
KLW International Inc. (did not respond)
Mirror Records, Kack Klick Inc. (did not respond)
Next Plateau Records (did not respond)

Plankton Records (not reviewing work)
Redbud Records (did not respond)
Revonah Records (did not respond)
Sauna-Music Co. (did not respond)
Sound RX (did not respond)
Terock Records (did not respond)

Stock Photo Agencies

Among the many types of markets open to photographers looking to sell their images, stock photography is one of the most exciting. The relatively recent growth in numbers and sizes of stock photo agencies—many call it a boom—is a direct reflection of the increased demand from all types of photo buyers, including ad agencies, publishers, audiovisual firms, TV stations, nonprofit organizations and a wide range of corporations.

Stock agencies will often specialize in certain subject matters—for instance, sports, fashion or science—or deal with particular types of clients, such as advertising, editorial or corporate. In particular, there has been a visible increase in the number of agencies marketing audiovisual materials.

Some agencies which are developing their AV market are primarily looking for stock transparencies to be used in audiovisual productions, while others are seeking stock film or videotape footage of a range of subjects. In this edition of *Photographer's Market*, stock photo agencies with these kinds of audiovisual needs have been marked with a special AV symbol—a solid, black square—before the listing's name for easier recognition.

In light of the escalating competition among photographers in other market areas such as advertising and editorial, some photographers are choosing stock photography as a primary, fulltime pursuit. These photographers usually sign exclusive contracts with a single agency or will contract with a small number of agencies with noncompeting inventories. This allows the photographer to spend as much time shooting as possible while one or more of the agencies market his work.

While some agencies will buy single photos or small inventories of needed subject matter, many will work only with photographers who can initially deliver a large quantity of photos—200, 500 or 1,000 images—and who will continue to submit large quantities on a regular basis. So you must be very attentive to which agencies welcome the casual submission and which ones expect a major commitment for new work.

The standards of most stock agencies are quickly being upgraded since they seek to do business with top clients and expect high multiple resales of a given image. There is little or no room for amateurish work, leftover shots or images that otherwise lack a strong ability to communicate visually. Every photo that a stock agency markets must be of the utmost quality—at least comparable to the calibre of work which they are already presenting. Accordingly, every image a photographer submits must also be top-notch. Among the best ways to learn what goes into highly marketable stock images are to study agency catalogs and stock industry references such as the *Stock Workbook*, as well as the listings in this section.

Besides shooting high-quality images, photographers must strive for professionalism in all aspects of their business. As Richard Steedman, president of the Stock Market, Inc. has noted, (see interview on page 561), "Stock photography is not a specialty—it's a legitimate business." So to work successfully in the stock field, you must know how stock agencies do business, how to do business with agencies, how to gear your images for them and their clients, and how to make the most of the marketing opportunities stock agencies provide. The "Tips" paragraphs in many of the listings in this section offer insight into the industry's practices and requirements. However, you can gain a more complete understanding of the business by reading the Stock Photography Spotlight on page 5 in this edition of *Photographer's Market*.

All in all, because of several key market factors, the stock photography industry is currently at a highwater mark. You'll find that this year's Stock Photo Agencies section reflects this "flood" with more than 175 stock agency listings, including 60 markets appearing in the section for the first time. With a high rate of return listings from last year's edition plus these new listings, the section certainly demonstrates the abundant opportunities for photographers in this market.

■ACE PHOTO AGENCY, 22, Maddox St., Mayfair, London WIR 9PG United Kingdom. (01)629-0303. FAX: (01)495-6100. Chief Editor: John Panton. Stock photo agency. Has approximately 200,000 photos. Deals with ad agencies, audiovisual firms, businesses, book/encyclopedia publishers, magazine publishers, postcard companies, calendar companies, greeting card companies, design companies and direct mail companies.
Subject Needs: People, sport, corporate, industrial, travel (world), seas and skies, still life and humor.
Specs: Uses 35mm, 2¼ × 2¼, 4 × 5 and 8 × 10 transparencies.
Payment & Terms: Pays 50% commission on color photos. General price range: $135-1,800. Offers one-time rights, first rights or mostly non-exclusive rights. Model release and captions required.
Making Contact: Arrange a personal interview to show portfolio; query with samples. SASE. Reports in 2 weeks. Photo guidelines free with SASE. Distributes tips sheet twice yearly to "ace photographers under contract."
Tips: Prefers to see "total range of subjects in collection. Must be commercial work, not personal favorites. Must show command of color, composition and general rules of stock photography. All people must be mid-Atlantic to sell in U.K. Must be sharp and also original. No dupes. Be professional and patient."

■ADAMS PICTURE LIBRARY, 156 New Cavendish St., London W1 England. Phone: 01-636-1468, FAX: 01-436-7131. Director: Ms. Carol White. Has 400,000 color transparencies. Clients include ad agencies, public relations firms, audiovisual firms, businesses, book/encyclopedia publishers, magazine publishers, newspapers, postcard companies, calendar companies, greeting card companies, poster companies, TV companies, and government offices, both in UK and overseas.
Specs: Uses all formats.
Payment & Terms: Pays 50% commission on transparencies only. General price range: 50-1,000 pounds (English currency). "The photographer signs a contract with us stating he has model release where applicable."
Making Contact: Arrange a personal interview to show portfolio, or send selection of transparencies by recorded delivery; query with samples, query with list of stock photo subjects. SASE. Reports in 1 month. Tips sheet distributed to all photographers intermittently.
Tips: "Only top-quality transparencies are accepted. Needs families, groups, pretty girls, capital cities and towns in USA, American cars, beach shots, couple shots, babies, animals — domestic and wild — and humorous pix."

*ADVENTURE PHOTO, Suite 202, 56 E. Main St., Ventura CA 93001. (805)643-7751. FAX: (805)643-4423. Owner: Rick Ridgeway. Estab. 1987. Stock agency. Has 25,000 photos. Clients include advertising agencies, public relations firms, businesses, magazine publishers and greeting card companies.
Subject Needs: Adventure Photo offers it's clients 4 principle types of images: Adventure Sports (sailing, windsurfing, rock climbing, skiing, mountaineering, mountain biking, etc.), Adventure Travel (All fifty states as well as third world and exotic locations.), Landscape, Environment and Pollution.
Specs: Uses 35mm, 2¼ × 2¼ and 4 × 5 transparencies.
Payment & Terms: Pays 50% commission on color photos. Offers one-time rights; Occasionally negotiates exclusive and unlimited use rights. Model release preferred, photo captions required.
Making Contact: Call for copy of submission guidelines. SASE. Reports in 1 month. Photo guidelines free with SASE.
Tips: In freelancer's portfolio or samples, wants to see "well-exposed, well-lighted transparencies (reproduction quality)." Unique outdoor sports, travel and wilderness images. "We love to see shots of this subject matter that portray metaphors commonly used in ad business ("risk taking," "teamwork," etc.)." To break in, "we request new photographers send us 2 to 4 20-image sheets they feel are representative of their work. Then when we sign a photographer, we pass ideas to them regularly

The asterisk before a listing indicates that the market is new in this edition. New markets are often the most receptive to freelance submissions.

about the kinds of shots our clients are requesting, and we pass them any ideas we get too. Then we council our photographers to always look at magazines and advertisements to stay current on the kinds of images art directors and agencies are using."

***■ALLSPORT PHOTOGRAPHY USA, INC.**, Suite 200, 320 Wilshire Blvd., Santa Monica CA 90401. (213)395-2955. Contact: Mike Powell. Estab. 1969 (London); 1985 (USA). Stock photo agency. Has 1 million photos. Clients include advertising agencies, public relations firms, audiovisual firms, businesses, book/encyclopedia publishers, magazine publishers, newspapers and calendar companies.
Subject Needs: "Up to date sports news as well as historical sporting events, personalities and venues."
Specs: Uses 8×10 b&w prints; 35mm transparencies.
Payment & Terms: Pays 50% commission on b&w or color photos. Offers all rights; alternatives negotiable. Model release preferred; photo captions required.
Making Contact: Submit portfolio for review. SASE. Reports in 1 week.
Tips: In portfolio, wants to see "the ability to shoot strong action as well as the feature and mood type photos. Duplicate slides OK." For breaking in, learn about lighting. "Editorially the pictures most published tend to be isolated, long lens shots in good lighting conditions. Ninety percent of indoor sporting events are shot on stadium strobes."

***■AMERICAN STOCK PHOTOGRAPHY**, 6640 Sunset Blvd. #100, Hollywood CA 90028. (213)469-3900. President: Christopher C. Johnson. Stock photo agency. Has 2 million photos. Clients include advertising agencies, public relations firms, audiovisual firms, businesses, book/encyclopedia publishers, magazine publishers, newspapers, postcard companies; calendar companies, greeting card companies and TV and movie production companies.
Subject Needs: General stock, all categories except fashion. Special emphasis upon California scenics and lifestyles.
Specs: Uses 35mm, 2¼×2¼, 4×5 transparencies; b&w contact sheets; b&w negatives.
Payment & Terms: Buys photos outright; pays $5-20. Pays 35-50% commission on b&w photos; 50% commission on color photos. General price range: $100-750. Offers one-time rights. Model release and photo captions required.
Making Contact: Contact Camerique Inc., 1701 Skyspack Rd., Box 175. Blue Bell PA 19422. (215)272-4000. SASE. Reports in 1 week. Photo guidelines free with SASE. Tips sheet distributed quarterly to all active photographers with agency; free with SASE.

AMWEST PICTURE AGENCY, 1083 Atlas Peak Rd., Napa CA 94558. (707)257-8155. Owner: Marla A. Murphy. Clients include: ad agencies, brochures, textbooks, magazines and calendar companies. Offers one-time rights; other sales negotiable.
Subject Needs: Couples and singles in everyday activity, leisure and working. Teens and active seniors in positive situations, again, sports or upbeat, happy settings. Some need for "problem" shots but people interacting is paramount. Handicapped people coping and learning. All kinds of sports, business and high-tech office settings—all the preceding in b&w and color. Needs more coverage of the western U.S./recreation areas, people enjoying the western life.
Specs: Uses 35mm, 2¼×2¼ and 4×5 transparencies; 8×10 b&w prints.
Payment & Terms: Pays 50% commission. Model released photography should be marked "MR." A four-year contract must be signed.
Making Contact: "A SASE must be enclosed with your letter of inquiry and submissions, or we cannot return our packet of information to you."
Tips: Edit down tightly. Well shot, completely focused, and perfect exposure get the most attention and sell best. We are looking for more photographers in Idaho, Montana, Wyoming, Washington and Central states. Be very specific in captioning your work.

■THE ANCIENT ART & ARCHITECTURE COLLECTION, 6, Kenton Rd., Harrow-on-the-Hill, Middlesex HA1 2BL London, England. (81)422-1214. Contact: The Librarian. Picture library. Has 200,000 photos. Clients include public relations firms, audiovisual firms, book/encyclopedia publishers, magazine publishers and newspapers.
Specs: Uses 35mm, 2¼×2¼, 4×5 or 8×10 transparencies.
Payment & Terms: Pays 50% commission. Sells one-time rights. Fully detailed captions required.
Making Contact: Query with samples and list of stock photo subjects. SASE. Reports in 2 weeks. Tips sheets for accredited photographers distributed on request; free with SASE. Photo guidelines free to accredited photographers with SASE.
Tips: "Material must be suitable for our specialist requirements. We cover historical and archeological periods from 25,000 BC to the 19th century AD, worldwide. All civilizations, cultures, religions, objects and artifacts as well as art are includable. Pictures with tourists, cars, TV aerials, and other modern intrusions not accepted."

■**ANDES PRESS AGENCY**, 26 Padbury Ct., London E2 England. (01)739-3159. Director: Carlos Reyes. Picture library and news/feature syndicate. Has 500,000 photos. Deals with audiovisual firms, book/encyclopedia publishers, magazine publishers and newspapers.
Subject Needs: "We have a large collection of photographs on social, political and economic aspects of Latin America, Africa, Asia, Europe and Britain, specializing in contemporary world religions."
Specs: Uses 8×10 glossy b&w prints, 35mm and 2¼×2¼ transparencies, b&w contact sheets and negatives.
Payment & Terms: Pays 50% commission for b&w photos. General price range: £50-200/b&w photo; £50-300/color photo; (British currency). Offers one-time rights. Captions required.
Making Contact: Query with samples; query with list of stock photo subjects. SASE. Reports in 1 week. Photo guidelines free with SASE.
Tips: "We want to see that the photographer has mastered one subject in depth."

■**ANIMALS ANIMALS/EARTH SCENES**, 17 Railroad Ave., Chatham NY 12037. (518)392-5500. Branch office: 9th Floor, 65 Bleecker St., New York NY 10012. (212)982-4442. President: Nancy Henderson. Has 850,000 photos. Clients include ad agencies, public relations firms, businesses, audiovisual firms, book publishers, magazine publishers, encyclopedia publishers, newspapers, postcard companies, calendar companies and greeting card companies.
Subject Needs: "We specialize in nature photography with an emphasis on all animal life."
Specs: Uses 8×10 glossy or matte b&w prints; 35mm and some larger format color transparencies.
Payment & Terms: Does not buy outright; pays 50% commission. Offers one-time rights; other uses negotiable. Model release required if used for advertising; captions required.
Making Contact: Send material by mail for consideration. SASE. Reports in 1-2 months. Free photo guidelines with SASE. Tips sheet distributed regularly to established contributors.
Tips: "First, preedit your material. Second, know your subject. We need captions, including Latin names, and they must be correct!"

ANTHRO—PHOTO FILE, 33 Hurlbut St., Cambridge MA 02138. (617)868-4784, 497-7227. President/Owner: Nancy S. Devore. Stock photo agency. Has approximately 10,000 color photos, 2,000 b&w photos. Clients include textbook/encyclopedia publishers, magazine publishers and newspapers. Clients include: *Primate Societies* by Smuto, U.Chicago Press, many photos of monkeys and apes; *Discover* magazine, article on chimpanzees; and *Cultural Anthropology* by Haviland, Hold, Rinehart, Winston, photos of various peoples.
Subject Needs: Anthropology and biology.
Specs: Uses 8×10 glossy b&w prints; 35mm and 2¼×2¼ transparencies.
Payment & Terms: Pays 60% commission on photos. Pays $125-600/b&w photo; $160-800/color photo. Commission 60% to photographers, 40% to agent. One year exclusive. No model release if documentary; captions required.
Making Contact: Query with samples. SASE.
Tips: Prefers to see behavioral/anthropological emphases. Send duplicates or prints labeled and captioned with emphasis on the important topics for anthrotexts and biology texts; sociology texts; geography and social studies texts. *Look at* the current best selling texts.

*****APPALIGHT**, P.O. Box 508, Spencer WV 25276. (304)927-4898. Partner(s): Chuck Conner or Chuck Wyrostok. Estab. 1988. Stock photo agency. Has 7,000 slides/10,000 b&w prints; no films. Clients include advertising agencies, public relations firms, book/encyclopedia publishers, magazine publishers, postcard companies, calendar companies and greeting card companies.
Subject Needs: General subject matter with emphasis on children, inspirational, city scapes, animals, human interest, country and urban scenes, social issues and travel.
Specs: Uses 8×10, glossy b&w prints; 35mm transparencies; b&w contact sheets; b&w negatives.
Payment & Terms: Pays 50% commission on b&w and color photos. Usual fee is $135 and up for black and white or color. Model release preferred, photo captions required.
Making Contact: Query with samples. Query with list of stock photo subjects; Call for information before submitting. SASE. Reports in 1 month. No photo guidelines.
Tips: In photographer's samples, wants to see "technical proficiency, eye for composition, creativity and high impact imagery (high success rates require an eye for images most in demand as well as an understanding of the stock business). We are getting more requests for abstract, graphics, computer

■ *The solid, black square before a listing indicates that the market uses various types of audiovisual materials, such as slides, film or videotape.*

generated and composites (fantasy landscapes) but the market for general subject matter, human activities, children, animals, etc. is still strong."

■**ASSOCIATED PICTURE SERVICE**, 394 Nash Circle, Mableton GA 30059. Has 25,000 photos. Clients include advertising agencies, AV firms, book publishers, magazine publishers, encyclopedia publishers and calendar companies.
Subject Needs: Nature, historical points, city/suburbs, scenics.
Specs: Uses 35mm transparencies only.
Payment & Terms: Does not buy outright; pays 50% commission. General price range: $500. Offers one-time rights. Model release required.
Making Contact: Query with SASE. Reports in 2 weeks.

■**A-STOCK PHOTO FINDER (ASPF)**, Suite 1100, 230 N. Michigan Ave., Chicago IL 60601. (312)645-0611. General Manager: Joanne Filippi. Has access to 1 million photos. Clients include primarily ad agencies, but also public relations firms, businesses, AV firms, book publishers, magazine publishers, encyclopedia publishers, newspapers, postcard companies, calendar companies, greeting card companies, poster companies and others.
Specs: Uses 35mm, 2¼×2¼, 4×5, 8×10 and 11×14 etc., color transparencies and color contact sheets.
Payment & Terms: Pays 50% commission on leases. Commission payments made upon collection from clients. General price range: $75-2,000. Offers one-time or first rights. Copies of model releases required *at time of* submission; releasability status indicated on each transparency in *red* ink (R; NR). Cover letter with submission list and short, to-the-point captions required at time of submission.
Making Contact: Send samples and list of stock photo subjects. SASE. Complete kits with submission guidelines supplied on request. Tips sheets distributed regularly; also bimonthly newsletter.
Tips: "ASPF is known as 'Chicago's Image Marketplace—where the advertising professional calls for stock photographic art.' ASPF's standards are very high; the company is in pursuit of excellence. Please approach us only if you know you are excellent! This company's management is very strong, marketing-oriented, and aggressive in the marketplace."

*****ATLANTA STOCK ASSOCIATES**, P.O. Box 723093, Atlanta GA 30339. (404)434-8363. President: Betsy Harbison. Photo Editor: Bob Ginn. Estab. 1987. Stock photo agency. Has more than 60,000 photos. Deals with ad agencies, public relations firms, audiovisual firms, businesses, book/encyclopedia publishers, magazine publishers, newspapers, postcard companies, calendar companies, greeting card companies. Photo guidelines free with SASE. Tips sheet available quarterly to contracted photographers.
Subject Needs: Scenics (terrain and seasonal); people and lifestyles: Occupations; industry; transportation; corporate; nature (plants and animals); travel; abstracts and still life: travel, domestic and foreign. ASA is a generalized agency. Wants to see a photographer's viewpoint of the world around him, expressed in the above categories. A key question when looking at an image is what is the concept or what does the image say? The first critical technical quality is sharpness, then proper exposure and composition.
Specs: Quality images of all subjects with emphasis on Model/Property Released Images. Uses 8×10 full frame b&w glossy prints with ½" borders and 35mm , 2¼×2¼, 4×5, 5×7 and 8×10 transparencies.
Payment & Terms: Pays 50% commission on b&w and color photos; 50% commission on films; 55% commission on released images. Pays quarterly. General price range $150 up. Larger fees are determined by use pressruns, distribution average is $300-700. Buys one-time rights; also exclusive rights with photographer's written permission. Model release and captions required.
Making Contact: Arrange a personal interview to show portfolio. Send 100 slides in slide pages. Must have return postage. "We will deal with any photographer who meets our criteria." SASE. Reports in 1 month.
Tips: In portfolio or samples, wants to see "sharp, properly exposed subject matter with good composition." Also, ability to document subject material close-up, full horizontal and vertical. If image naturally horizontal, force vertical and vice versa. Sees trend toward lots of model-released people, in all areas—workplace, lifestyles, families. People need to be somewhat attractive, happy with pleasant looks. Encourages use of families, friends and associates. Many stock shots are now being set up by photographers; trends in the environment, ecology, pollution, tourist attractions in photographer's area. Also, heavy corporate, healthy people, seasonal and holiday materials in stills, scenics, table-top and lifestyles.

■**BARNABY'S PICTURE LIBRARY**, Barnaby House, 14, Rathbone St., London WIP 1AF England. 01-636-6128. FAX: 01-637-4317. Contact: Mrs. Ruth Turner. Stock photo agency and picture library. Has 4,000,000 photos. Deals with ad agencies, public relations firms, audiovisual firms, businesses, book/

encyclopedia publishers, magazine publishers, newspapers, film production companies, BBC, all TV companies, record companies, etc.

Specs: Uses 8×10 b&w prints, 35mm, 2¼×2¼, 4×5 and 8×10 transparencies.

Payment & Terms: Pays 50% commission on b&w and color photos. Model release and captions required.

Making Contact & Terms: Arrange a personal interview to show portfolio; send unsolicited photos by mail for consideration; submit portfolio for review. SASE. Reports in 3 weeks. Photo guidelines free with SASE. Tips sheet distributed yearly to anyone for SASE.

■**BERG & ASSOCIATES**, Suite 707, 6065 Mission Gorge Rd., San Diego CA 92120. (619)284-8456. Contact: Margaret C. Berg. Has 100,000 photos. Clients include ad agencies, public relations and AV firms, businesses, textbook/encyclopedia and magazine publishers, newpapers, postcard, calendar and greeting card companies.

Subject Needs: Children, including ethnic and handicapped groups—all ages (playing, at school, sports, interacting); careers, business, industry; medical; sports and recreation; underwater; tourism; agriculture; families doing things together.

Specs: Uses transparencies only; 35mm.

Payment & Terms: Pays 50% commission. Sells one-time rights, first rights or "special rights for specific time period." Model release and captions preferred.

Making Contact: Photo guidelines free with SASE. Query with list of stock photo subjects; and list geographical areas covered. Send photos by mail for consideration. SASE. Reports in 6 weeks. Tips sheet distributed periodically only "to those with photos in stock. *Don't* send photos before studying guidelines."

Tips: "For 35mm color, send 100 maximum. Kodachrome only. Package carefully. If you want photos returned by insured mail, include insurance cost. Remember most printed pages are vertical. We need photographers from other parts of the country. Especially looking for tourism, hi-tech, science, wildlife, city skylines, business, industry, manufacturing and service industries. Families, school scenes, sports and recreation always in high demand. There is a new emphasis on health, fitness and nutrition, in advertising, calendars, magazines and textbooks. Model releases are needed. Location shots of cities and towns, landmarks, lifestyle, new city skylines, with and without people are needed. We need foreign as well as eastern, mid-west and southern United States."

BERNSEN'S INTERNATIONAL PRESS SERVICE LTD. (BIPS), 9 Paradise Close, Eastbourne, E. Sussex BN20 8BT England. Phone: (0323) 28760. Editor: E.L. Habets. International feature and stock picture agency with branch offices in USA, Germany, Italy, Holland, Belgium and Sweden. Clients include newspapers and magazines throughout the world. Stock library of more than 2,000,000 b&w and more than 600,000 color images.

Subject Needs: All general interest photo features suitable for sale on an international basis.

Specs: Uses b&w prints; 35mm transparencies.

Payment & Terms: Varies according to subject. General price range: $75/photo. Will also handle material on commission and handle second rights.

Making Contact: Query by letter in first instance, including contacts and/or cuttings. Reports within 30 days. Our leaflet "Guidelines for Photojournalists" free with two International Reply Coupons.

Tips: "Would like to see more amusing animal pictures, be it as singles with a humorous caption or as a lengthier story. We're also very interested in anything which is "the biggest, the oddest, the most expensive" . . . of well, almost anything. Look for the unusual: the oddities, the record breakers, the ones-of-a-kind. Picture content matters more that sheer photographic skill or quality. And, don't give up too easily!"

*****BILDAGENTUR MAURITIUS GMBH**, Postfach 2 09, 8102 Mittenwald Germany. Phone: 08823/5074. FAX: 08823/8881 President: Hans-Jorg Zwez. Stock photo agency. Has 1.2 million photos. Deals with advertising agencies, businesses, book/encyclopedia publishers, magazine publishers, postcard companies, calendar companies and greeting-card companies.

Subject Needs: All kinds of contemporary themes: geography, people, animals, plants, science, economy.

Specs: Uses 2¼×2¼, 4×5 and 8×10 transparencies.

Payment & Terms: Pays 50% commission for color photos. Offers one-time rights. Model release and captions preferred.

Making Contact: Query with samples; submit portfolio for review. SASE. Reports in 2 weeks. Tips sheet distributed once a year.

Tips: Prefers to see "people in all situations, from baby to grandparents, new technologies, transportation."

BIOLOGICAL PHOTO SERVICE, P.O. Box 490, Moss Beach CA 94038. (415)726-6244. Photo Agent: Carl W. May. Stock photo agency. Has 80,000 photos. Clients include ad agencies, businesses, book/encyclopedia publishers and magazine publishers. Previous clients include: Jordan and Yama Advertising, SEM of fly head, magazine ad for computer (scanner) upgrade unit; Saunders College Publishing, dozens of photos from micrographs to aerials, college general biology textbooks; and Seymour Simon, photos of volcanoes and glaciers, children's books on science.
Subject Needs: All subjects in the life sciences, including agriculture, natural history and medicine. "Stock photographers must be scientists." Subject needs include: "color enhanced scanning electron micrographs; photographic coverage of contemporary medical problems, from the biological basis of the disease to treatment; minor phyla of invertebrates; and photomicrographs of diverse bacteria and protists. All aspects of general and pathogenic microbiology. All aspects of normal human biology and the basic medical sciences, including anatomy, histology, human embryology, and human genetics.
Specs: Uses $4 \times 5 - 11 \times 14$, glossy, high-contrast b&w prints; 35mm, $2\frac{1}{4} \times 2\frac{1}{4}$, 4×5, 8×10 transparencies. "Dupes acceptable but photographer should understand some clients will not consider them."
Payment & Terms: Pays 50% commission on b&w and color photos. General price range: $70-350, sometimes higher for advertising uses. Offers one-time rights; other rights are negotiable. "Photographer is consulted during negotiations for buyouts, etc." Model release required for non-educational use; captions required.
Making Contact: Query with list of stock subjects and resume of scientific and photographic background. SASE. Reports in 2 weeks. Photo guidelines free with query and SASE. Tips sheet distributed intermittently to stock photographers only.
Tips: "When samples are requested, we look for proper exposure, maximum depth of field, adequate visual information and composition, and adequate technical and general information in captions. Requests fresh light and electron micrographs of traditional textbook subjects; applied biology such as bioengineering, agriculture, industrial microbiology, and medical research; biological careers. We avoid excessive overlap among our photographer/scientists. We are experiencing an ever-growing demand for photos covering environmental problems of all sorts—local to global, domestic and foreign. Forests are hot (and not just those on fire). Our three greatest problems with potential photographers are: 1) Inadequate captions. 2) Inadequate quantites of *good* and *diverse* photos. 3) Poor sharpness/depth of field/grain/composition in photos."

BLACK STAR PUBLISHING CO., INC., 116 E. 27th St., New York NY 10016. (212)679-3288. President: Howard Chapnick. Has 4 million b&w and color photos of all subjects. Clients include magazines, ad agencies, book publishers, encyclopedia publishers, corporations and poster companies.
Specs: Send 8×10 semigloss b&w prints. Interested in all subjects. "Our tastes and needs are eclectic. We do not know from day to day what our clients will request. Submissions should be made on a trial and error basis. Our only demand is top quality." Send 35mm color transparencies.
Payment & Terms: Does not buy outright; pays 50% commission. Offers first North American serial rights; "other rights can be procured on negotiated fees." Model release, if available, should be submitted with photos.
Making Contact: Call to arrange an appointment, submit portfolio, or mail material for consideration. Reports in 2-3 weeks. SASE. Free photo guidelines.
Tips: "We are interested in quality and content, not quantity. Comprehensive story material welcomed."

JOHN BLAKE PICTURE LIBRARY, 7 High Street, Thornbury, Bristol, Avon BS12 2AE United Kingdom. (0454)418321/413240. FAX: (0454)416636. Proprietor: John Blake. Picture library. Has 50,000 photos. Deals with ad agencies, businesses, book/encyclopedia publishers, magazine publishers, postcard companies and calendar companies.
Subject Needs: "General topographical library covering towns, villages, landscapes of Britain, Europe, USA, Mid and Far-East. People at work and at play. Horse trials, eventing and racing covered. Comprehensive section on mountains and mountaineering in Himalayas, European Alps and Antartica.
Specs: Uses 6x8 glossy b&w prints; $2\frac{1}{4} \times 2\frac{1}{4}$ and 4×5 transparencies.
Payment & Terms: Pays 50% commission for b&w and color photos. General price range: $50-250. Model release preferred; captions required.
Making Contact: Query with list of stock photo subjects. Solicits photos by assignment only. SASE. Reports in 1 month. Photo guidelines free for SASE.
Tips: Prefers to see "sharp and accurate focusing, good composition, good color saturation; ability to take less then obvious view of a commonly-seen tourist attraction. We require color shots of businesses, office situations, where VDTs, keyboards, faxes etc. are in use. Business people meeting, ancillary services such as secretarial needs are always in demand. We are always on the lookout for topical features on the USA (crime, environmental issues, etc.) which we would also need copy for. Good composition is becoming less important as ad agencies and publishers seek to achieve eye-catching

effects with logos and graphics in pictures. We often need to find images with blank areas to one side to get this effect for clients."

■**D. DONNE BRYANT STOCK PHOTOGRAPHY**, Box 80155, Baton Rouge LA 70898. (504)387-1620. President: Douglas D. Bryant. Stock photo agency. Has 250,000 photos. Clients include ad agencies, audiovisual firms, book/encyclopedia publishers and magazine publishers. Currently represents 35 professional photographs.
Subjects: Specializes in picture coverage of Latin America with emphasis on Mexico, Central America, South America, the Caribbean Basin and the Southern USA. Eighty percent of picture rentals are for editorial usage. Important subjects include agriculture, anthropology/archeology, art, commerce and industry, crafts, education, festivals and ritual, geography, history, indigenous people and culture, museums, parks, religion, scenics, sports and recreation, subsistence, tourism, transportation, travel and urban centers.
Specs: Uses 8×10 glossy b&w and 35mm, 2¼×2¼ and 4×5 color transparencies.
Payment & Terms: Pays 50% commission on b&w and color photos. General price range: $85-1,600. Offers one-time rights. Model release preferred; captions required.
Making Contact: Query with resume of credits and list of stock photo subjects. SASE. Reports in 1 month. Photo guidelines free with SASE. Tips sheet distributed every 3 months to agency photographers.
Tips: Prefers to see "developed picture stories related to one of the subject interests listed above. Would like to see more coverage of commerce and industry, as well as better coverage of the modern urban environment in Latin American countries. There is a decreasing interest in Latin American Indians and ruins and an increasing interest in the modern and dynamic urban Latin culture. A photographer interested in shooting Latin scenics will make sales through the DDB Stock Agency, but a photographer who is willing to photograph inside modern schools, factories, and hospitals will make far more. We would like to improve our coverage of Puerto Rico, especially Old San Juan. We also want to increase coverage of Cuba, the Dominican Republic, Lima, Buenos Aire, tropical rainforest destruction/colonization and illegal aliens/INS activity along the US/Mexico border. All these areas are receiving increasing interest and our files are weak in these subject areas. Freelancers interested in working successfully with DDB Stock should visit Latin America two or more times a year to shoot stock pictures. These self assignments should be co-ordinated with the agency to assure saleable subjects. Successful agency photographers submit 500-1,000 new images each year. Most successful agency photographers speak Spanish and understand Latin culture. The photographers who earn the most money at DDB Stock are those who would rather tour a Mexican steel mill or hospital than relax on the beach at Cancun. Our ideal photographer is a cultural geographer with an artist's eye and world class photography talent. We have several of these individuals and value them highly."

■**CALIFORNIA VIEWS/Pat Hathaway Collection**, 763 Lighthouse Ave., New Monterey CA 93940. (408)373-3811. Photo Archivist: Mr. Pat Hathaway. Picture library; historical collection. Has 60,000 b&w images, 2,000 35mm color. Deals with ad agencies, public relations firms, audiovisual firms, businesses, book/encyclopedia publishers, magazine publishers, newspapers, postcard companies, calendar companies, greeting card companies, television and video and historical exhibition.
Subject Needs: Historical photos of California from 1860-1990s.
Specs: Uses 8×10 b&w prints.
Payment & Terms: Buys photos outright; pays $10-100 per b&w photo. General price range: $100-150, $175-200. Offers one-time rights.
Making Contact: Deals with local freelancers only. Does not return unsolicited material. Reports in 1 month.

■**CAMERA PRESS LTD.**, Russell Court, Coram Street, London WCIH 0NB England. (01)837-4488. FAX: (01)278-5126. Telex 21654. Operations Director: Roger Eldridge. Picture library, news/feature syndicate. Deals with ad agencies, public relations firms, audiovisual firms, book/encyclopedia publishers, magazine publishers, newspapers, postcard companies, calendar companies, greeting card companies and TV stations. Clients principally press, but also advertising, publishers, etc. Previous/current clients include People magazine, Princess Diana and children. Offers one-time rights.
Subject Needs: Documentary, features, world personalities, i.e. politicians, athletes, statesmen, artists.
Specs: Uses prints; 35mm, 2¼×2¼ and 4×5 transparencies; b&w contact sheets and negatives.
Payment & Terms: Pays 50% commission for color or b&w photos. "Top rates in every country." Offers one-time rights. Model release and captions required.
Making Contact: SASE. Reports in 1 month.
Tips: Prefers to see "lively, colorful (features) series which tell a story and individual portraits of up-and-coming world personalities. Exhibit photographic excellence and originality in every field. We specialize in worldwide syndication of news stories, human interest features, show business personali-

ties 'at home' and general portraits of celebrities. Good accompanying text and/or interviews are an advantage. Remember that subjects which seem old-hat and clichéd in America may have considerable appeal overseas. Try to look at the U.S.with an outsider's eye."

■**CAMERIQUE STOCK PHOTOGRAPHY,** Main office: 1701 Skippack Pike, Box 175, Blue Bell PA 19422. (215)272-4000. Fax (215)272-7651. Representatives in Boston, Los Angeles, Chicago, New York City, Toronto, Tampa and Tokyo. Photo Director: Christopher C. Johnson. Estab. 1973. Has 300,000 photos. Types of clients: advertising agencies, public-relations firms, audiovisual firms, businesses, book/encyclopedia publishers, magazine publishers, newspapers, post-card companies, calendar companies, greeting-card companies.
Subject Needs: General stock photos, all categories. Emphasizes people activities all seasons. Always need large format color scenics from all over the world. No fashion shots; all people shots, including celebrities must have releases.
Specs: Uses 35mm, 2¼, 4×5 transparencies; b&w contact sheets; b&w negatives; "35mm accepted if of unusual interest or outstanding quality."
Payment & Terms: Sometimes buys photos outright; pays $10-25/photo. Also pays 50% commission/ b&w; 50% commission/color. General price range: $150-500. Offers one-time rights. Captions required.
Making Contact: Query with list of stock photo subjects; send unsolicited photos by mail for consideration; "send letter 1st we'll send our questionaire and spec sheet." SASE. Reports in 2 weeks. Will return material with SASE. Tips sheet distributed periodically to established contributors.
Tips: Prefers to see "well-selected, edited color on a variety of subjects. Well-composed, well-lighted shots, featuring contemporary styles and clothes. Be creative, selective, professional and loyal. Communicate openly and often."

CATHOLIC NEWS SERVICE, 3211 Fourth St., NE, Washington DC 20017-1100. (202)541-3264. Photos/ Graphics Manager: Barbara Stephenson. Photos/Graphics Researcher: Patrice Souders. Wire Service transmitting news, features and photos to Catholic newspapers. Pays $25/ photo; $75-200/job; $75-300/ text-photo package. Offers one-time rights. Captions required. Send material by mail for consideration. SASE. Photo guidelines free with SASE.
Subject Needs: News or feature material related to the Catholic Church or Catholics; head shots of Catholic newsmakers; close-up shots of news events, religious activities. Especially interested in photos aimed toward a general family audience and photos depicting modern lifestyles, e.g., family life, human interest, teens, poverty, active senior citizens, families in conflict, unusual ministries, seasonal and humor.
B&W: Uses 8×10 glossy prints.
Tips: Submit 10-20 good quality prints covering a variety of subjects. Some prints should have relevance to a religious audience. Knowledge of Catholic religion and issues are helpful; read a diocesan newspaper for ideas of the kind of photos used. Caption information should accompany photos. Photos should be up-to-date and appeal to a general family audience. No flowers, no scenics, no animals. As we use more than 1,000 photos a year, chances for frequent sales are good. Send only your best photos.

■**BRUCE COLEMAN, INC.,** 381 5th Ave., New York NY 10016. (212)683-5227. Telex: 429 093. FAX: (212)689-6140. Contact: Norman Owen Tomalin and Tina White. File consists of over 800,000 original transparencies on all subjects including natural history, sports, people, travel, industrial, medical and scientific. Clients include major ad agencies, public relations firms, corporations, magazine and book publishers, calendar companies, greeting card companies, AV firms, and jigsaw puzzle publishers. 350 photographers.
Subject Needs: "Every conceivable subject."
Specs: Uses original transparencies. "If sending 35mm, send only Kodachrome or Fujichrome professional transparencies."
Payment & Terms: Does not buy outright; pays 50% commission. Offers one-time rights. Model release preferred; captions required.
Making Contact: Write for details first. Large SASE. Reports in 4-6 weeks. Periodic "want list" distributed to contributing photographers.
Tips: "Edit your work very carefully. Include return postage with submission if you wish material returned. Photograph subject matter which interests you and do it better than anyone else. Don't try to copy other photographers because they're probably doing the work better! We need top quality original work. As the field becomes more competitive, there is more concentration on subject matter. Most photographers possess adequate technical skills, but a lack of imagination. Foreign markets provide an additional source for sales for our photographers."

EDUARDO COMESANA-AGENCIA DE PRENSA, Casilla de Correo 178 (Suc.26), Buenos Aires 1426 Argentina. (541)771-9418. FAX: (541)313-7267. Director: Eduardo Comesana. Stock photo agency, picture library and news/feature syndicate. Has 100,000 photos. Deals with ad agencies, book/encyclopedia publishers, magazine publishers and newspapers. Clients include: *Conocer* magazine: "Israel's Bionic man," cover story; *Editorial América*: "Michael Jackson's home"; and *Gente* magazine: "Wall Street," double spread.

Subject Needs: Personalities, entertainment, politics, science and technology, expeditions, archeology, travel, industry, nature, human interest, education, medicine, foreign countries, agriculture, space, ecology, leisure and recreation, couples, families and landscapes.

Specs: Uses 8×10 glossy b&w prints; 35mm, 2¼×2¼ and 4×5 transparencies.

Payment & Terms: Pays $30-60/b&w photo; $60-300/color photo; 40% commission. Offers one-time rights and one-year exclusive rights. Model release preferred; captions required.

Making Contact: Query with samples. SASE. Reports in 1 month.

Tips: Represents Black Star in South America; Woodfin Camp & Associates, Outline Press Syndicate from New York City; and Shooting Star from Los Angeles. "We would like to review magazine-oriented stories with a well-written text and clear captions. In case of hot-news material, please fax or phone before sending anything. Freelancers should send us an introductory letter staing the type of photography he intends to sell thru us. In our reply we will request him to send at least five stories of 10 to 20 colors each, for review. We would like to have some clippings of his photography."

■**COMSTOCK, INC.**, 30 Irving Place, New York NY 10003. (212)353-8600. President: Henry Scanlon. Has 1,750,000 photos. Clients include ad agencies, public relations and audiovisual firms, businesses, book/encyclopedia and magazine publishers, newspapers, and postcard, calendar and greeting card companies.

Subject Needs: Write for subject guidelines.

Specs: Uses 35mm (preferred), 2¼×2¼, 4×5 or 8×10 transparencies; 8×10 b&w double-weight fiber-based prints.

Payment & Terms: Pays 50% of stock sale, 25% to agency on assignments.. General price range: $150-20,000. Model release and captions required. Offers one-time rights or as asked for and fee reflects.

Making Contact: Jane Kinne, editorial director. Query with resume of credits or list of stock photo subjects. SASE. Reports in 3 weeks.

Tips: "We represent very few photographers all of whom are extremely productive, most of whom make their living from stock photography. We could use more coverage in the science and hi-tech areas and in child-development from birth to full adulthood. We look for creativity, originality, a recognizeable point of view, consistent technical excellence. Have an area of specialty and expertise. Present a scrupulously *edited* portfolio."

■**CUSTOM MEDICAL STOCK PHOTO**, 3819 N. Southport Ave., Chicago IL 60613. (312)248-3200. FAX: (312)248-7427. Computer access: (312)248-PICS. Image Consultant: Mike Fisher. Clients include ad agencies, magazines, textbook publishers, design firms, audiovisual firms and hospitals. All commercial and editorial markets that express interest in medical and scientific subject area. Clients include: Scott, Foresman & Co., editorial, drug abuse, psychological testing, pathology; Foote, Cone, Belding, commerical; Silhouette of Nurse and Child in Wheelchair; and Du Pont, Inc., commercial, electron microscopy, hand colored.

Subject Needs: Biomedical, scientific, healthcare environmentals and general biology for advertising illustrations, textbook and journal articles, annual reports, editorial use and patient education.

Specs: Uses 35mm, 2¼×2¼ and 4×5 transparencies. Negatives for electron microscopy. 4×5 copy transparencies of medical illustrations.

Payment & Terms: Pays per shot, rate depends on usage. Pays commission: 50% - domestic leases; 30-40% - foreign leases. Contract. Credit line given if applicable, client discretion. Offers one-time rights. Offers one-time rights; other rights can be arranged.

Making Contact: Query with list of stock photo subjects and request current Want List and submission packet. "PC captioning disk available for database inclusion, please request. Do not send uncaptioned unsolicited photos by mail. SASE. Reports in average 4 weeks. Monthly Want List available by U.S. Mail, and by FAX. Model and property release copies required.

Tips: "Our past Want Lists are a valuable guide to the types of images requested by our clients. Past Want Lists are available. Environmentals of researchers hi-tech biomedicine, physicians, nurses and patients of all ages in situations from neonatal care to mature adults are requested frequently. Almost any image can qualify to be medical if it touches an area of life: breakfast, sports, etc. Trends also follow newsworthy events found on newswires. Photos should be good clean images that portray a single idea whether it is biological, medical or scientific; the ability to recognize the newsworthiness of subjects. Put together a minimum of 100 images for submission. Call before shipping to receive computer disk and caption information and return information. Contributing to our agency can be very profitable if a solid commitment can exist."

■**CYR COLOR PHOTO AGENCY**, Box 2148, Norwalk CT 06852. (203)838-8230. Contact: Judith A. Cyr. Has 125,000 transparencies. Clients include ad agencies, businesses, book publishers, magazine publishers, encyclopedia publishers, calendar companies, greeting card companies, poster companies and record companies. Does not buy outright; pays 50% commission. Offers one-time rights, all rights, first rights or outright purchase; price depending upon rights and usage. Model release and captions preferred. Send material by mail for consideration. SASE. "Include postage for manner of return desired." Reports in 3 weeks. Distributes tips sheet periodically to active contributors; "usually when returning rejects."

Subject Needs: "As a stock agency, we are looking for all types. There has been a recent interest in family shots (with parents and children) and people in day-to-day activities. Also office-of-the-future with high tech equipment and general business/professional settings. Mood shots, unusual activities, etc. are always popular—anything not completely 'standard' and basic and common. Photos must be well exposed and sharp, unless mood shots."

Color: Uses 35mm to 8×10 transparencies.

Tips: Each submission should be accompanied by an identification sheet listing subject matter, location, etc. for each photo included in the submission. All photos should be properly numbered, with photographer's initials; also using vinyl sheets is a great time-saver in reviewing photos. "We have received more requests from clients to use 35mm in a slide presentation only (i.e. one time) and/or in a video presentation. Thus, there are more uses of a photo with limited copyright agreements."

■**DAS PHOTO**, Domaine de Bellevue, 181, Septon 5482 Belgium. (086)32 24 25. Director: David Simson. Stock photo agency. Has 50,000 photos. Clients include: advertising agencies, public relations firms, audiovisual firms, book/encyclopedia publishers, magazine publishers, calendar companies and greeting card companies. Previous/current clients include: Stern and Oggi, both features and Oxford University Press, book commission.

Subject Needs: Handles "mainly reportage—suitable for publishers and magazines although we do deal with most subjects. We are specialists in selling photo material in all European countries."

Specs: Uses 8×10 glossy b&w prints; 35mm, 2¼×2¼, 4×5 and 8×10 transparencies.

Payment & Terms: Pays 50% commission on b&w and color photos. Pays $40-500/b&w photo; $60-1000/color photo; $350/day plus expenses. Offers one-time rights; (sometimes) territory rights. Model release preferred; captions required.

Making Contact: Query with samples, send unsolicited photos by mail for consideration. SASE. Reports in 1 week. Photo guideline sheet and tips sheet free with SASE.

Tips: In photographer's samples, wants to see "high technical, quality—then unusual interesting pictures."

■**JAMES DAVIS TRAVEL PHOTOGRAPHY**, 30 Hengistbury Rd., New Milton, Hampshire BH25 7LU England. 0425-610328. FAX: 0425-638402. Library Manager: Tricia Silcox. Stock photo agency, picture library (specialist in travel photography). Has approximately 60,000 transparencies. Deals with advertising agencies, public relations firms, audiovisual firms, businesses, book/encyclopedia publishers, magazine publishers, newspapers, postcard companies, calendar companies, greeting card companies and tour and travel operators are major clients.

Subject Needs: Landscapes, seascapes, skyscapes, city view, tourist locations, people—families, couples, tourists. "Mainly high quality travel photography from all over the world."

Specs: Uses 2¼×2¼, 4×5 and 8×10 transparencies.

Payment & Terms: Pays 50% commission for color photos. General price range: from a minimum of $100 to $2,000. Offers one-time rights, first rights, and all rights. Model release preferred; captions required.

Making Contact: Arrange a personal interview; query with resume of credits, samples and list of stock photo subjects. SASE. Reports in 1 week. Photo guidelines free with SASE.

Tips: "We now require a minimum photo submission of 300 transparencies." Photos must have "good quality with good picture content." To break in, "study good quality travel publications. Photos with people at leisure, shopping, traveling, etc., are always needed, but we are also in constant need of all sorts of photographs of *the USA*, as described in Subject Needs above."

■**LEO DE WYS INC.**, 1170 Broadway, New York NY 10001. (212)689-5580. FAX: (212)545-1185. President: Leo De Wys. Office Manager: Deborah Billings. Has 350,000 photos. Clients include ad agencies, public relations and AV firms, business, book, magazine and encyclopedia publishers, newspapers, calendar and greeting card companies, textile firms, travel agencies and poster companies.

Subject Needs: Sports (368 categories); recreation (222 categories); travel and destination (1,450 categories); and released people pictures in foreign countries (i.e., Japanese business-people, German stockbrokers, English nurses, etc.).

Specs: Uses 35mm, medium format, color transparencies.

Payment & Terms: Price depends on quality and quantity. Usually pays 50% commission. General price range: $75-6,000. Offers to clients "any rights they want to have; pay is accordingly." Model release required; "depends on subject matter," captions preferred.

Making Contact: Query with samples "(about 20 pix) is the best way"; query with list of stock photo subjects or submit portfolio for review. SASE. Reporting time depends; often the same day. Photo guidelines free with SASE.

Tips: "Photos should show what the photographer is all about. They should show his technical competence—photos that are sharp, well composed, have impact, if color they should show color. Competition is terrific and only those photographers who take their work seriously survive in the top markets. Company now uses bar coded computerized filing system." Seeing trend toward more use of food shots tied in with travel such as "key lime pie for Key West and Bavarian beer for Germany. Also more shots of people—photo-released and in local costumes."

DESIGN PHOTOGRAPHERS INTERNATIONAL, INC., (DPI), Suite 901, 19 W. 21st St., New York NY 10010. (212)627-4060. FAX: (212)645-9619. President: Alfred W. Forsyth. Has approximately 300,000 photos. Clients include ad agencies, corporations, book publishers, magazine publishers, encyclopedia publishers, poster companies, postcard companies, calendar companies, greeting card companies, designers and printers. May buy photos outright; pays 50% commission on sale of existing stock shots. General price range for color: $175-10,000. Offers one-time rights; limited exclusivity when necessary. Model release and captions are required on most subjects. "Accurate caption information is absolutely necessary. We suggest photographers first request information, which explains how we work with photographers, then call for appointment for portfolio review. SASE; "state amount and type of insurance needed." Reports in 2 weeks-1 month. Free photo guidelines and monthly tips sheet distributed only to photographers under contract with DPI.

Subject Needs: Human interest, natural history, industry, people in industry, education, medicine, foreign lands, sports, agriculture, space, science, technology, people in offices, energy related, leisure and recreation, transportation, US cities, towns and villages, teenage activities, couples, families and landscapes. "In short, we're interested in everything." Especially needs photos of the Pacific Area and Caribbean Islands. Avoid brand name products or extreme styles of clothing, etc., that would date photos. Ongoing need for pictures of family group activities and teenage activities; attractive, all-American type family with boy and girl ages 6-12 years. Also family with teenage kids. Model releases are needed.

Color: Accepts original transparencies only; uses 35mm or larger; "no dupes."

Tips: "Master the fundamentals of exposure, composition and have a very strong graphic orientation. Study the work of top-notch successful photographers like Pete Turner or Jay Maisel." In portfolio, we prefer to see "100-200 top quality cross-section of photographer's best work, on 20-slide sheet clear plastic 35mm slide holders. Do not send loose slides or yellow boxes. Remember to include instructions for return, insurance needed and return postage to cover insurance and shipping. Our picture editors edit very tightly. We're looking for top-quality. Be selective."

DEVANEY STOCK PHOTOS, Suite 306, 755 New York Ave., Huntington NY 11743. (516)673-4477. FAX: (516)673-4440. President: William Hagerty. Photo Editor: Ruth Fahlbusch. Has over 1 million photos on file. Clients include: ad agencies, book publishers, magazines, corporations and newspapers. Previous/current clients: Mobil Oil Company, an eye, poster usage; MacMillan Publishing, various, books; Newsday, QEII, aft deck, editorial travel section.

Subject Needs: High technology; computers; computer chips; video games; modern offices; business meetings; breaking a tape (winning); tiger-sitting down; close-up of eagle swooping; people; nursing homes; hospital scenes and action; modern tractor trailer shots (dramatic); robot shots; automated production line; set-ups for holidays; exchange of money; teller-lobby shots; women doing housework; stress situations; modern supermarkets, drug, department and sports stores (can be empty); children at Christmas; large meetings (small, too); executives; hard hats; excited crowds; prizefighter on ropes; skylines; street scenes; major landmarks; weather; fires; fireworks; etc.—virtually all subjects. "Releases from individuals and homeowners are most always required if photos are used in advertisements."

Specs: Uses 8×10 glossy b&w prints; uses all sizes of color transparencies.

Payment & Terms: Does not buy outright. Pays 50% commission on color and 30% on b&w. Offers one-time rights. Model release preferred. Captions required.

Making Contact: Query with list of stock photo subjects or send material by mail for consideration. SASE. Reports in 1 month. Free photo guidelines with SASE. Distributes monthly tips sheet free to any photographer.

Tips: "It is most important for a photographer to open a file of at least 1,000 color and b&w of a variety of subjects. We will coach."

*■DMI PHOTO AGENCY, RR 1, Box 162, Morris NY 13808. (607)263-2090. Vice-President: Ann Clifford. Estab. 1980. Stock photo agency. Has 400,000 photos. Clients include public relations firms, book/encyclopedia publishers, magazine publishers, newspapers and postcard companies.
Subject Needs: Celebrities (film TV and stage), politics, sports, music and social.
Specs: Uses b&w prints; 35mm transparencies.
Payment & Terms: Buys photos/film outright. General price range: from $75 up. Offers one-time rights. Photo captions required.
Making Contact: Query with resume of credits. Deals with local freelancers only. Cannot return material.

■FRANK DRIGGS COLLECTION, 1235 E. 40 St., Brooklyn NY 11210. (718)338-2245. Owner: Frank Driggs. Stock photo agency. Has 100,000 photos. Clients include ad agencies, public relations firms, audiovisual firms, businesses, book/encyclopedia publishers, magazine publishers, newspapers, motion pictures.
Subject Needs: All aspects of music.
Payment & Terms: Buys and leases photos. Pays 50% commission on b&w and color photos; 50% commission on film. General price range: $75-100/photo. Rights negotiated.
Making Contact: Query with samples and list of stock photo subjects. Solicits photos by assignment only. SASE. Reports in 1 month.

■DRK PHOTO, 265 Verde Valley School Rd., Sedona AZ 86336. (602)284-9808. FAX: (602)284-9096. President: Daniel R. Krasemann. "We handle only the personal best of a select few photographers—not hundreds. This allows us to do a better job aggressively marketing the work of these photographers." Clients include ad agencies; PR and AV firms; businesses; book, magazine, textbook and encyclopedia publishers; newspapers; postcard, calendar and greeting card companies; branches of the government; and nearly every facet of the publishing industry, both domestic and foreign.
Subject Needs: "Especially needs marine and underwater coverage. Also interested in S.E.M.'s, African, European and Far East wildlife; and good rainforest coverage.
Specs: Uses 35mm, 2¼ × 2¼ and 4 × 5 transparencies.
Payment & Terms: Pays 50% commission on color photos. General price range: $75-"many thousand." Offers one-time rights; "other rights negotiable between agency/photographer and client." Model release preferred; captions required.
Making Contact: "With the exception of established professional photographers shooting enough volume to support an agency relationship we are not soliciting open submissions at this time. Those professionals wishing to contact us in regards to representation should query with a brief letter of introduction and tearsheets."

DYNAMIC GRAPHICS INC., CLIPPER & PRINT MEDIA SERVICE, 6000 N. Forrest Park Dr., Peoria IL 61614. (309)688-8800. Photo Editor: Rosemarie McShane Gardner. Clients include ad agencies, printers, newspapers, companies, publishers, visual aid departments, TV stations, etc.
Subject Needs: Generic stock photos (all kinds). "Our needs are somewhat ambiguous and require that a large number of photos be submitted for consideration. We will send a 'photo needs list' and additional information if requested."
Specs: Majority of purchases are b&w. Send 8x10's, contact sheets and high contrast conversions. Minimal use of 35mm and 4 × 5 transparencies.
Payment and Terms: Pays $50 and up/b&w photo; $100 and up/color photo. Pays on acceptance. Rights are specified in contract. Model release required.
Making Contact: Send tearsheets or folio of 8 × 10 b&w photos by mail for consideration; supply phone number where photographer may be reached during working hours. Reports in 6-8 weeks.

■EARTH IMAGES, Box 10352, Bainbridge Island WA 98110. (206)842-7793. Director: Terry Domico. Has 100,000 photos. Clients include ad agencies, filmmakers, book publishers, businesses, magazine publishers, design firms, encyclopedia publishers and calendar companies.
Subject Needs: "We specialize in color photography which depicts life on planet Earth. We are looking for natural history and documentary photography. Animals, insects, birds, fish, reptiles, science, ecology, scenics, landscapes, underwater, endangered species and action recreation—worldwide." Established professionals only.
Specs: Uses 35mm slides.
Payment & Terms: Pays 50% commission on photos. Usual price range: $100-650. Offers one-time rights. Captions required on slides.
Making Contact: Query with list of credits and introductory letter. Photo submission guidelines free with SASE. Reports in 4-6 weeks.
Tips: "We are seeking photographers who have particular talent and interests. We need to see at least 100 best images. We are looking for photographic excellence as this is a very competitive field. We are also interested in well done picture stories. Pictures of flowers, tiny ducks centered in the middle

of the frame, 'miniature' moose, and fuzzy shots taken at the zoo just don't make it. Our focus is on quality, not quantity. We only want to see top professional quality work." We're "looking for 'life history' portfolio depicting one species of animal (moose, wolf, [no bears, please], lion, tiger and gorilla)."

■EKM-NEPENTHE, Box 217, El Rito NM 87530. (505)984-9719. Cable: Ekphot. Additional Address: 7874 Tanglerod Ln. La Mesa CA 92041. Director: Robert V. Eckert. Has 100,000 photos. Clients include ad agencies, public relations firms, businesses, audiovisual firms, book publishers, magazine publishers, encyclopedia publishers and newspapers.
Subject Needs: Subjects include folk art (Americana); architecture; animals; beaches; business; cities; country; demonstrations and celebrations; ecology; education; emotions; agriculture; manufacturing; food, health, medicine and science research; law enforcement; leisure; occupations; business related (meetings, executives, minorities and women); technology/energy; non-traditional roles (working mothers-house fathers, etc.); nature; art; travel; people "our biggest category"; performers; political; prisons; religion; signs; sports and recreation; transportation; weather; historical subjects for newly formed historical section; also earth sciences, biology, geology for newly developed area, etc. "We prefer b&w and color photos of prisons, education, people, technology, radio telescopes, foreign, national parks, energy, robotics, housing, groups, medicine, science-research, interaction, races (ethnic groups), people all ages and occupations (especially nontraditional ones, both male and female). Do not want to see sticky sweet pictures."
Specs: Uses 8×10 glossy, matte and semigloss b&w contact sheets and prints; uses any size color transparency.
Payment & Terms: Rarely buys photos outright. Pays 50% commission on photos. General price range: $75-2,500. Offers one-time rights. Captions preferred.
Making Contact: Query with list of stock photo subjects. SASE. Reports in 1 month. Photo guidelines free on request.
Tips: "Realizing that stock is a slow business, photographers should have a long-term perspective toward it. It can be very rewarding if you work hard at it, but it isn't for the person who wants to place his 100 best shots and wait for money to start rolling in. Try to provide unique, technically sound photos. Be objective about your work. Study the markets and current trends. Also work on projects that you feel strongly about, even if there is no apparent need (as to make strong images). Photograph a lot, you improve with practice. We are actively seeking new photographers. Edit carefully. We see too much technically and aesthetically bad work. We are not looking to have the most photographers in the world of photo agencies but we would not mind having the best. We try to work closely with our photographers, make them more than just a number with us. There seem to be just too many photographers around who are unable to determine if a transparency is sharp or a black & white print is actually printed well. Technique is very important. Study exhibits to see what well printed work looks like; seek, and listen to criticism and comments from more advanced/professional photographers. Just shooting a good subject is not enough, you must shoot it well and then carry through with your technique. A good magnifier is imperative in determining if a slide is sharp. You cannot determine if it is sharp just by holding it up and looking at it or projecting it through a slide projector. (In fact, you want to avoid projecting originals as much as possible, the heat can damage the slide). It is always a pleasure to receive a submission from someone who obviously knows how to print his/her black & white and knows how to determine if a slide is sharp or well exposed, etc."

■ELITE PHOTOGRAPHY, INC., Box 2789, Toledo OH 43606. Director: David Thompson. Clients include advertising agencies, public relations firms, audiovisual firms, businesses, magazine publishers, postcard companies, calendar and greeting card companies, book/encyclopedia publishers, video distributors.
Subject Needs: "We are a stock agency that is specializing in photography of women, be it pretty pictures, cheesecake, nude, exotic, or erotic. Although we are strict on such rules as focusing and exposures, our needs are as varied as the marketplace—if it is salable, we will sell it. We enjoy working with new photographers."
Specs: Uses 35mm and $2\frac{1}{4} \times 2\frac{1}{4}$ transparencies. "Don't send larger transparencies or b&w unless she is a special subject."
Payment & Terms: Rarely buys photos/film outright. Pays 50% commission on b&w and color photos. General price range: $150-1,500, complete sets higher. Offers one-time and first rights. Model release required; captions preferred.
Making Contact & Terms: Query with samples; send unsolicited photos by mail for consideration. SASE. Reports in 2 weeks. Photo guidelines, tip sheet free with SASE *and* samples. (No phone calls please.)
Tips: "Be able to compose, focus and expose a photograph properly. Remember that we specialize in photographs of women, with cheesecake and nude/erotic the biggest and fastest sales. Show us you can produce marketable images, and we'll do the rest. Almost all of our magazine buyers are screaming

for cover shots—shoot them! In addition, we also direct market sets overseas to publishers. This creates a very lucrative market for those with sets that have already sold in the US. We can still market them to the rest of the world. For those with such talent, Elite now deals in video and is interested in seeing sample VHS tapes that fall within our subject guidelines. We are very interested in seeing much more photography involving women working in all career fields and in various forms of play such as sports and other leisure activities. We also want more mother and child photography."

*■ELLIS WILDLIFE COLLECTION, 69 Cranberry St., Brooklyn NY 11201. (718)935-9600. Director: Sharon Cohen. Estab. 1986. Stock photo agency. Has 100,000 photos. Clients include advertising agencies, public relations firms, audiovisual firms, businesses, book/encyclopedia publishers, magazine publishers, newspapers, postcard companies, calendar companies, greeting card companies, design firms, zoos and aquariums.
Subject Needs: "Anything to do with the natural world, including scenics, vegetation, underwater, and wildlife from around the world."
Specs: Uses color prints; 35mm transparencies.
Payment & Terms: Pays 50% commission on color photos. General price range: $100-6,000. Offers one-time rights.
Making Contact: Query with samples. SASE. Reports in 2 weeks. Photo guidelines free with SASE.
Tips: In freelancer's samples, wants to see "variety of lighting and subject matter, accurate captioning, and quality of photography: composition and focus." Sees trend toward "more requests of endangered species as well as such environments as rainforests and deserts."

■GREG EVANS PHOTO LIBRARY, 91, Charlotte St., London W1P ILB England. (071)636-8238. FAX: (071)436-2318. Manager: Greg Evans. Picture library. Has 250,000 photos. Clients include: ad agencies, public relations firms, audiovisual firms, businesses, book/encyclopedia publishers, magazine publishers, newspapers, postcard companies, calendar companies and greeting card companies and travel companies.
Specs: Uses 35mm, 2¼×2¼, 4×5 and 8×10 transparencies and 2¼×2¾.
Payment & Terms: Pays 50% commission on color photos. Offers one-time rights and also buys outright. Model release required.
Making Contact: Arrange a personal interview to show portfolio, send unsolicited photos by mail for consideration. SASE. Reports in 1 week. Quarterly tips sheet free with SASE.
Tips: Wants "creativity, sharpness, clarity, perfect exposure, precise captions" in work submitted.

*■FASHIONS IN STOCK, 21-45 78th St., East Elmhurst NY 11370. (718)721-1373. President: Nicasio Sanchez. Estab. 1987. Stock photo agency. Has 60,000 photos. Clients include advertising agencies, public relations firms, businesses, magazine publishers and calendar companies.
Subject Needs: "We specialize in stock photos that tell a story, illustrate a scenario, be it in the area of business, leisure, family, friendships, etc. Many of our stock photos are fashion-oriented. Our photos also deal with current controversial issues. The photos all include people against a backdrop of unique regional interest or interesting architecture, exotic locales. People also shown participating in sports of all kinds, in business settings, at family holidays, shopping, and in academic environments."
Specs: Uses 8×10 fiber base, b&w prints; 35mm, 2¼×2¼, 4×5 transparencies; b&w contact sheets; b&w negatives; 16mm film; VHS videotape.
Payment & Terms: Pays 50% commission on b&w/color photos. Offes one-time rights; other rights negotiable. Model release required; photo captions preferred.
Making Contact: Arrange a personal interview to show portfolio; submit portfolio for review; arrange personal interview if photographer's location is permanent. SASE. Reports in 1 week. Tips sheet distributed to photographers with fashions in stock.
Tips: "We are looking for current, fashionable stock photography that can convey an idea or sell a product or service. The photos must have flexibility, universality, a keen insight into people's feelings. We also look for unique locations in different areas of the United States as a background. Our focus is mostly on commercial print advertising." Stock is being used instead of assignment work by many advertising agencies. "They are looking for casual, upscale typesof people of all ages. I notice a large request for young women (20s to early 30s) in professional scenarios, different ethnic groups (Asian, Black, Hispanic) working and playing together, and elderly people involved in work or exercise. The photographer working with Fashions In Stock would grow rapidly and would save considerable processing and model expenses. We also push for assignment work for our photographers. We are currently establishing an office in Manhattan."

■FINE PRESS SYNDICATE, Box 112940, Miami FL 33111. Vice President: R. Allen. Has 49,000 photos and 100+ films. Clients include ad agencies, public relations firms, businesses, audiovisual firms, book publishers, magazine publishers, postcard companies and calendar companies worldwide.

Subject Needs: Nudes; figure work, seminudes and erotic subjects.

Specs: Uses color glossy prints; 35mm, 2¼ × 2¼ transparencies; 16mm film; videocasettes: VHS and Beta.

Payment & Terms: Pays 50% commission on color photos and film. Price range "varies according to use and quality." Offers one-time rights.

Making Contact: Send unsolicited material by mail for consideration or submit portfolio for review. SASE. Reports in 2 weeks.

Tips: Prefers to see a "good selection of explicit work. Currently have European and Japanese magazine publishers paying high prices for very explicit nudes and 'X-rated' materials. Clients prefer 'American-looking' female subjects. Send as many samples as possible. Foreign magazine publishers are buying more American work as the value of the dollar makes American photography a bargain."

*■FIRST LIGHT ASSOCIATED PHOTOGRAPHERS, 1 Atlantic Ave., Suite 204, Toronto ON M6K 3E7 Canada. (416)532-6108. President: Pierre Guevremont. Estab. 1984. Stock and assignment agency. Has 250,000 photos. Clients include advertising agencies, public-relations firms, audiovisual firms, businesses, book/encyclopedia publishers, magazine publishers, newspapers, post-card companies, calendar companies and greeting-card companies.

Subject Needs: Natural history, international travel, commercial imagery in all categories. Special emphasis upon model-released people, high tech, industry, and business.

Specs: Uses 35mm, 2¼ × 2¼ and 4 × 5 transparencies.

Payment & Terms: Pays 50% commmission. General price range: $5-5,000. Offers one-time rights. Model release preferred; photo captions required.

Making Contact: Query with samples; query with list of stock photo subjects. SASE. Reports in 2 weeks. Photo guidelines free with SASE. Tips sheet distributed every 6 weeks.

Tips: "Vacations and leisure are bywords to Florida developers and promoters. The key to Florida and the Caribbean is sunshine and smiling faces. People shooting for us should see the beauty around them as though it was their first time. It often is for many seeing their published work. Keep cars, telephone poles and lines out of frame. Go for happy action, sports, intimate beach shots and wildlife-nature."

*■FOCUS STOCK PHOTO, 409-950 Yonge St., Toronto, ON M4W 2J4 Canada. (416)968-6619. FAX: (416)968-7582. Estab. 1985. Stock photo agency. Has 100,000+ photos. Clients include advertising agencies, public relations firms, book/encyclopedia/magazine publishers, calendar companies.

Specs: Uses 35mm, 2¼ × 2¼, 4 × 5, 8 × 10 transparencies.

Payment & Terms: Pays 40-50% commission on color photos. General price range: $350-4,000. Offers one-time rights. Model release and photo captions required.

Making Contact: Submit portfolio for review. SASE. Reports in 2 weeks. Photo guidelines free with SASE. Tips sheet distributed quarterly to contract photographers.

Tips: "We are a general stock agency that caters primarily to the advertising and design agencies and therefore requries very clean and graphic photos that clearly represent a message, feeling or concept. We are looking for photographers who have done some homework regarding how to shoot for stock. We prefer photographes who will spend the time to obtain "The Great Shot" rather than large quantities of "average" shots."

■FOCUS—STOCK FOTOGRAFICO, Santa Fe 3192, #5 "A", Buenos Aires 1425 Argentina. (1)83-3905. Deputy Director: Carlos Goldin. Has 150,000 photos. Clients: advertising agencies, audiovisual firms, businesses, book/encyclopedia and magazine publishers, calendar companies.

Subject Needs: People in general for advertising—at work, jogging, mature couples, in the office, in meetings, beside the corporate jet, at ease during relaxing hours, in the restaurants and bars, having a drink, with children. Families in general, in all situarions. Everyday scenes and specially produced stock shots.

Specs: Uses 35m, 2¼ × 2¼, and 4 × 5 transparencies; prefers Kodachrome, but will accept other good quality slides. Works only with originals.

Payment & Terms: Somtimes buys photos/film outright. Pays $50-1,000 US/photo; pays 50% commission/color. General price range $50-300. Offers one-time rights or all rights. Model release preferred. Captions required.

Making Contact: Query with samples; send unsolicited photos by mail for consideration. SAE, IRCs. Reports in 1 month. Photo guidelines free with SAE, IRCs. Distributes tip sheet every six months "to our photographers"; free with SAE, IRCs.

Tips: "We are interested in opening our stock agency for a few good North American photographers who wish to open up their markets."

■**FOTO EXPRESSION INTERNATIONAL (Toronto),** Box 1268, Station "Q" Toronto, ON M4T 2P4 Canada. (416)841-9788. FAX: (416)841-5593. Photo Editor: Mrs. Veronika Kubik. Selective archive of photo, film and audiovisual materials. Clients include ad agencies, public relations and audiovisual firms, TV stations, networks, film distributors, businesses, book, encyclopedia and trade magazine publishers, newspapers and news magazines. Also, postcard, calendar and greeting card companies.
Subject Needs: City views, aerial, travel, wildlife, nature-natural phenomena and disasters, underwater, aerospace, weapons, warfare, industry, research, computers, educational, religions, art, antique, abstract, models, sports. Worldwide news and features, personalities and celebrities.
Specs: Uses 8×10 b&w; 35mm and larger transparencies; 16mm, 35mm film; VHS, Beta and commercial videotapes (AV). Motion Picture, news film, film strip and homemade video.
Payment & Terms: Sometimes buys transparencies outright. 40% for b&w; 50% for color and 16mm, 35mm films and AV. (If not otherwise negotiatied.) Offers one-time rights. Model release and captions required for photos.
Making Contact: Submit portfolio for review. The ideal portfolio for 8×10 b&w prints includes 10 prints; for transparencies include 60 selections in plastic slide pages. With portfolio you must send SAE with return postage (out of Canada—either money-order or International Postal Coupon). Photo guidelines free with SAE and postage. Reports in 3 weeks. Tips sheet distributed twice a year only "on approved portfolio."
Tips: "We require photos, slides, motion picture films, news film, homemade video and AV that can fulfill the demand of our clientele." Quality and content therefore is essential. Photographers, cameramen, reporters, writers, correspondents and representatives are required world wide by FOTO-PRESS, Independent News Service International, (416-841-4486/FAX: 416-841-5593), a division of the FOTO ex-PRESS-ion in Toronto. Contact Mr. Milan J. Kubik, Director, International section.

*****FOTOCONCEPT INC.,** P.O. Box 350335, Ft. Lauderdale FL 33335. (305)463-1912. FAX: (350)463-8864. Vice President: Aida Bertsch. Estab. 1985. Stock photo agency. Has 100,000 photos. Clients include magazines, advertising agencies, newspapers and publishers.
Subject Needs: General worldwide travel, medical and industrial.
Specs: Uses 35mm, 2¼×2¼, 4×5 transparencies.
Payment & Terms: Pays 50-55% commission for color photos. pays $50/b&w photo; $100/color photo. Offers one-time rights; one-year exclusive. Model release and photo captions required.
Making Contact: Query with samples; query with list of stock photo subjects. SASE. Reports in 1 month. Photo guidelines free with SASE. Tips sheet distributed annually to all photographers.
Tips: "We are looking for photographs with people of all ages with good composition, lighting and color in any material for stock use. Send 200 transparencies which best represents their work with a SASE, for consideration."

■**FOTO-PRESS TIMMERMANN,** Speckweg 34A, D-8521 Moehrendorf, West Germany. 9131/42801. FAX 9131/450528. Contact: Wolfgang Timmermann. Stock photo agency. Has 100,000 slides. Clients include ad agencies, audiovisual firms, businesses, book/encyclopedia publishers, magazine publishers, newspapers and calendar companies.
Subject Needs: All themes: landscapes, countries, towns, people, animals, nature.
Specs: Uses 35mm, 2¼×2¼, 4×5 and 8×10 transparencies.
Payment & Terms: Pays 60% commission on color prints. Buys one-time rights. Model release preferred, captions required.
Making Contact: Query with list of stock photo subjects, send unsolicited photos by mail for consideration. SASE. Reports in 2 weeks.

■**FOTOS INTERNATIONAL,** 4230 Ben Ave., Studio City CA 91604. (818)508-6400. FAX: (818)762-2181. Manager: Max B. Miller. Has 4 million photos. Clients include ad agencies, public relations firms, businesses, book publishers, magazine publishers, encyclopedia publishers, newspapers, calendar companies, TV and posters.
Subject Needs: "We are the World's Largest Entertainment Photo Agency. We specialize exclusively in motion picture, TV and popular music subjects. We want color only! The subjects can include scenes from productions, candid photos, rock, popular or classical, concerts, etc., and must be accompanied by full caption information."
Specs: Uses 35mm color transparencies only.
Payment & Terms: Pays $5-25/photo. No pay on a commission basis. Offers one-time rights and first rights. Model release optional; captions required.
Making Contact: Query with list of stock photo subjects. SASE. Reports in 1 month.

FPG INTERNATIONAL CORP., 251 Park Ave. S., New York NY 10010. (212)777-4210. Director of Photography: Rebecca Taylor. A full service agency with emphasis on images for the advertising, corporate, design and travel markets.

Minimum submission requirement per year—500 original color transparencies, exceptions for large format, 100 b&w full-frame 8 × 10 glossy prints.

Subject Needs: High-tech industry, model released human interest, foreign and domestic scenics in large formats, still life, animals, recreational sports, architectural interiors/exteriors with property releases.

Payment & Terms: Pays 50% commission. "We sell various rights as required by the client."

Making Contact: "Initial approach should be by mail telling us what kind of material you have." Photo guidelines and tip sheets provided for affiliated photographers. Model and property releases required and must be indicated on photograph; photo captions required.

Tips: "Submit regularly; we're interested in committed, high-caliber photographers only. Be selective and send only first-rate work. Our files are highly competitive."

FRANKLIN PHOTO AGENCY, 85 James Otis Ave., Centerville MA 02632. (508)428-4378. President: Nelson Groffman. Has 35,000 transparencies of scenics, animals, horticultural subjects, dogs, cats, fish, horses, antique and classic cars, and insects. Clients include: publishers, advertising and industrial.

Specs: Uses 35mm, 2¼ × 2¼ and 4 × 5 color transparencies. "More interest now in medium size format—2¼ × 2¼.

Payment & Terms: Does not buy outright; pays 50% commission. General price range: $100-300; $60/b&w photo; $100/color photo. Offers one-time rights; one-year exclusive. Present model release on acceptance of photo.

Making Contact: Query first with resume of credits. Reports in 1 month. SASE.

■FROZEN IMAGES, INC., Suite 512, 400 First Ave. N., Minneapolis MN 55401. (612)339-3191. Director: Lonnie Schroeder. Stock photo agency. Has approximately 130,000 photos. Clients include ad agencies, public relations firms, audiovisual firms, graphic designers, businesses, book/encyclopedia publishers, magazine publishers, newspapers and calendar companies.

Subject Needs: All subjects including abstracts, scenics, industry, agriculture, US and foreign cities, high tech, businesses, sports, people and families.

Specs: Uses transparencies.

Payment & Terms: Pays 50% commission on color photos. Usually offers one-time rights. Model release and captions required.

Making Contact: Query with resume of credits; query with list of stock photo subjects; call for procedures info. SASE. Reports in 1 month or ASAP (sometimes 6 weeks). Photo guidelines free with SASE. Tip sheet distributed quarterly to photographers in the collection.

Tips: Prefers to see strengths and scope of the photographer's work and technical perfection.

FUNDAMENTAL PHOTOGRAPHS, 210 Forsyth St., New York NY 10002. (212)473-5770. Partners: Kip Peticolas and Richard Megna. Stock photo agency. Clients include book/encyclopedia publishers.

Subject Needs: Science illustration—from rainbows to nuclear reactors; scientific/technical (physics, chemistry, photomicrographs and industrial illustrations). . .basic science to high technology.

Specs: Uses color: 35mm, 2¼ × 2¼, 4 × 5 and 8 × 10 transparencies; b&w: 8 × 10 prints.

Payment & Terms: Pays on commission basis; b&w 40%, color 50%. General price range $150-2,000. Offers one-time rights. Model release and captions required.

Making Contact: Arrange a personal interview to show portfolio; query with resume of credits, samples or list of stock photo subjects. SASE. Reports in 1 month. Photo guidelines free with SASE. "Tips sheet distributed to photographers we use."

Tips: "We look for excellent technical quality, an imaginative and knowledgeable approach to science illustration and good clean graphic imagery. Overall, there is a demand for high quality in images and a need for ways to communicate and illustrate the concepts of a high-tech society. The photographer is affected by seeing daily life with attention to how and why things work—whether it's rainbows, sailboats or computers."

■GAMMA/LIAISON, 11 E. 26th St., New York NY 10010. (212)447-2512. Exec. V.P./Director: Jennifer Coley. Has 5 million plus photographs. Extensive stock files include hard news (reportage), human interest stories, movie stills, personalities/celebrities, corporate portraits, industrial images. Clients include newspapers and magazines, book publishers, audiovisual producers, encyclopedia publishers and corporation/graphic designers.

Specs: Uses 35mm or 2¼ × 2¼ transparencies.

Payment & Terms: Photographer and agency split revenues 50/50.

Making Contact: Submit portfolio with description of past experience and publication credits.

Tips: Involves a "rigorous trial period for first 6 months of association with photographer." Prefers previous involvement in publishing industry.

■**MARILYN GARTMAN AGENCY, INC.**, 510 N. Dearborn, Chicago IL 60611. (312)661-1656. FAX: (312)661-0785. Vice President/Manager: John Ford. Stock photo agency. Has 500,000 photos. Deals with ad agencies, public relations firms, audiovisual firms, businesses, book/encyclopedia publishers, magazine publishers and calendar companies.

Subject Needs: Geographic (world wide) general categories going from subjects like abstracts to zoos.

Specs: Uses b&w prints, 35mm, 2¼ × 2¼ and 4 × 5 and 8 × 10 transparencies.

Payment & Terms: Pays 50% commission for b&w and color photos. Offers one-time rights. Model release and captions required.

Making Contact: Query with resume of credits, samples and list of stock photo subjects; do not send unsolicited material. Distributes tips sheet every few months to contracted photographers.

Tips: "We will speak to the individual photographer and request portfolio or samples—at that time we will tell the photographer what we desire to see."

■**GEOSCIENCE FEATURES PICTURE LIBRARY**, 6 Orchard Dr., WYE, Nr. Ashford, Kent TN25 5AU United Kingdom. 0233-812707 (UK). FAX: (0233)812707. Contact: Dr. Basil Booth. Stock photo agency, picture library, earth sciences and natural history picture library. Has 100,000+ photos; approximately 10,000 feet 16mm film, mainly volcanic eruptions. Deals with ad agencies, public relations firms, audiovisual firms, businesses, book/encyclopedia publishers, magazine publishers, newspapers, calendar companies and television companies.

Subject Needs: Zoology (all aspects, particularly animal behavior, portrait shots of mammals, birds, reptiles, etc. are required but action pictures are being requested more these days; no zoo shots). Botany (all aspects, plants, for example, should include flower close-up, entire flower head and entire plant, plant adaptations, trees, etc.). Microbiology. Earth sciences, particularly violent weather (tornados), volcanic eruptions and northern lights. General subjects.

Specs: Uses 8 × 10 glossy b&w prints; 35mm, 2¼ × 2¼, 6 × 7cm, 4 × 5 and 8 × 10 transparencies; b&w and color contact sheets, 16mm film, and VHS videotape. "No filtration material; we will add at duping stage."

Payment & Terms: Pays 55% commission for b&w photos; 60% commission for color photos; 50% for film. General price range: £20-50/b&w photo; £30-500/color photo. Offers one-year exclusive and occasionally 3 year exclusive; mostly non-exclusive, one time only, one edition and territory. Model release preferred; captions required (brief).

Making Contact: Arrange a personal interview to show portfolio; query with resume of credits, samples and list of stock photo subjects. SASE. Reports in 2 weeks to 1 month, depending on work load. Photo guidelines free with SASE. Distributes tips sheet twice a year to all our photographers. "Concentrate in fields most familiar to you—i.e., bird photographers should specialize in birds, and so on, and improve technique, especially with difficult subjects."

Tips: Prefers to see "images that are razor sharp. Full color saturation. No filter gimmicks. Good composition (artistic where relevant). Where possible each picture should tell a story (except landscape, etc). Action shots. High speed flash. No posed wild animals. No domestic animals. Several themes to show photographer's versatility. Subjects required include moods, skys, volcanic eruptions, weather, earthquakes, natural history, geology, geography, peoples, communications, sports, (no glamour). Images should be factual and well-composed, but not arty."

■**GEOSLIDES (Photography)**, 4 Christian Fields, London SW16 3JZ England. (081) 764-6292. Library Director: John Douglas. Picture library. Has approximately 100,000 photos. Deals with ad agencies, public relations firms, audiovisual firms, businesses, book/encyclopedia publishers, magazine publishers, newspapers, calendar companies and television.

Subject Needs: Only from: Central Africa (South of Sahara); Asia; Arctic and Sub-Arctic; Antarctic. Anything to illustrate these areas. Especially Nigeria and Alaska. Accent on travel/geography.

Specs: Uses 8 × 10 glossy b&w prints; 35mm and 2¼ × 2¼ transparencies.

Payment & Terms: Pays 50% commission for b&w and color photos. General price range $50-800. Offers one-time rights and first rights. Model release and captions required.

Making Contact: Query with resume of credits and list of stock photo subjects. SASE. Reports in 1 month. Photo guidelines for SASE (International Reply Coupon). No samples until called for.

Tips: Looks for "technical perfection, detailed captions, must suit lists (especially in areas). Increasingly competitive on an international scale. Quality often more important than level of reproduction fees charged. Need for very large stocks with frequent renewals." To break in, "build up a comprehensive (i.e. in subject or geographical area) collection of photographs which are well documented."

■**GLOBE PHOTOS, INC.**, 275 7th Ave., New York NY 10001. (212)689-1340. FAX: (212)627-8932. General Manager: Ray Whelan. Has 10 million photos. Clients include advertising agencies, public relations firms, businesses, AV firms, book publishers, magazine publishers, encyclopedia publishers, newspapers, postcard companies, calendar companies and greeting card companies. Does not buy outright; pays 50% commission. Offers one-time rights. Model release preferred; captions required. Arrange a personal interview to show portfolio; query with samples; send material by mail for consideration; or submit portfolio for review. Prefers to see a representative cross-section of the photographer's work. SASE. Reports in 4 weeks. Photo guidelines free with SASE; tips sheet distributed at irregular intervals to established contributors.

Subject Needs: "Picture stories in color and/or b&w with short captions and text. Single shots or layouts on celebrities. Stock photos on any definable subject."

B&W: Uses 8×10 glossy prints; contact sheet OK.

Color: Uses 35mm, 2¼×2¼, 4×5 and 8×10 transparencies.

Tips: "Find out what the markets need and produce as much as possible — regularly; but keep in mind quality is more important than quantity. It is important for the photographer to have good, technical skills as well as an imagination to shoot highly competitive stock photographs. There is a general increase in need of stock pictures, particularly photos of people doing things, but these must be released."

JOEL GORDON PHOTOGRAPHY, 112 4th Ave., New York NY 10003. (212)254-1688. Picture Agent: Elaine Abrams. Stock photo agency. Clients include ad agencies and book/encyclopedia publishers.

Specs: Uses 8×10 b&w prints, 35mm transparencies, b&w contact sheets and b&w negatives.

Payment & Terms: "Usually" pays 50% commission on b&w and color photos. Model release, photo captions preferred.

*WALLY HAMPTON PHOTOGRAPHY, INC./TRAVEL STOCK, 4190 Rockaway Beach, Bainbridge Island WA 98110. (206)842-9900. FAX: (206)842-0900. Vice President: Wendy Hampton. Estab. 1984. Commercial photography/stock agency. Has 50,000 photos. Clients include advertising agencies, public relations firms, businesses, book/encyclopedia publishers, magazine publishers and graphic artists.

Subject Needs: Needs "worldwide travel destination which show geographical areas with natives and/or tourists enjoying themselves."

Specs: Uses 35mm, 2¼×2¼, 4×5 transparencies.

Payment & Terms: Pays 50% commission on color photos. General price range: $50-300. Offers one-time rights and first rights. Model release preferred; photo captions required.

Making Contact: Query with samples. SASE. Reports in 2 weeks. Tips sheet distributed semimonthly to photographers represented by Hampton only.

Tips: "We look for colorful, sharp images of worldwide destinations that include people or are of people in costume. Show your best work professionally."

■HILLSTROM STOCK PHOTO, INC., 5483 N. Northwest Hwy., (Box 31100), Chicago IL 60630 (60631 for Box No.). (312)775-4090, 775-3557. FAX: (312)774-2929. President: Ray F. Hillstrom, Jr. Stock photo agency. Has 1 million color transparencies; 50,000 b&w prints. Clients include ad agencies, public relations firms, audiovisual firms, businesses, book/encyclopedia publishers, magazine publishers, newspapers, calendar companies, greeting card companies and sales promotion agencies.

Subject Needs: "Model released: heavy industry, medical, high-tech industry, computer-related subjects, family-oriented subjects, foreign travel, adventure sports and high-risk recreation, Midwest festivals (country fairs, parades, etc.), the Midwest. We need more color model released family, occupation, sport, student, senior citizen, high tech and on-the-job shots."

Specs: Uses 35mm, 2¼×2¼ and 4×5 transparencies; 8×10 b&w prints.

Payment & Terms: Pays $50-5,000/b&w and color photo; pays 50% commission on b&w and color photos. "We have a 22 other stock agency network." Offers one-time rights. Model release preferred; captions required; property releases.

Making Contact: Send unsolicited photos by mail for consideration. SAE and check for postage for return of submitted material; make check to pay Hillstrom Stock Photo. Reports in 3 weeks. Photo guidelines free with SASE.

Tips: Prefers to see good professional images, proper exposure, mounted, and name IDs on mount. In photographer's samples, looks for "large format, model and property release, high tech, people on the job, worldwide travel and environment. Show us at least 200 different images with 200 different subjects."

*■HISTORICAL PICTURES SERVICE, INC., Room 201, 921 West Van Buren, Chicago IL 60607. (312)346-0599. FAX: (312)733-2844. Archivist: Jeane Williams. Picture library. Has 3 million photos. Deals with ad agencies, audiovisual firms, businesses, book/encyclopedia publishers and magazine publishers.

Subject Needs: Topics from pre-history through the mid-1950s, worldwide.

Specs: Uses any size, any finish b&w and color prints; 35mm transparencies; b&w negatives.

Payment & Terms: Buys photos outright; "altogether negotiable." Offers one-time rights. Model release preferred; captions required.

Making Contact: Query with list of stock photo subjects. Will return material submitted for review. Reports in 1 week.

Tips: Looks for "antique images" in portfolio or samples. Even today the 1960s are regarded as "vintage"! "Color is almost a requisite in some media; hence we have taken to hand coloring—even photographs that could never have originally been anything but black-and-white."

■**HOLT STUDIOS LTD.**, The Courtyard, 24 High St., Hungerford, Berkshire, RG17 0NF United Kingdom. 0488-683523. Director: Nigel D. Cattlin. Picture library. Has 40,000 photos. Deals with ad agencies, public relations firms, audiovisual firms, businesses, book/encyclopedia publishers, magazine publishers and newspapers.

Subject Needs: Photographs of world agriculture associated with crop production and crop protection including healthy crops and relevant weeds, pests, diseases and deficiencies. Farming, people and machines throughout the year including good landscapes. Livestock and livestock management. Worldwide assignments undertaken.

Specs: Uses 35mm, 2¼×2¼ and 4×5 transparencies.

Payment & Terms: Occasionally buys photos outright. Pays 50% commission for color photos. General price range: $100-1,500. Offers one-time rights. Captions required.

Making Contact: Send unsolicited photos by mail for consideration. SASE. Reports in 1 week. Photo guidelines for SASE. Distributes tips sheets every 3 months to all associates.

Tips: "Holt Studios looks for high quality technically well-informed and fully labeled color transparencies of subjects of agricultural interest." Currently sees "expanding interest particularly conservation and the environment."

■**HOT SHOTS STOCK SHOTS, INC.**, 309 Lesmill Rd., Toronto, ON M3B 2V1 Canada. (416)441-3281. FAX: (416)441-1468. Attention: Editor. Clientele includes advertising and design agencies, publishers, major printing houses and product manufacturers. Previous/current clients include: McLaren : Lintas, child skating, television ad; Reidmore Books, industrial, education, historical, textbook; and Postcard Factory, Atlantic scenics, postcards, keychains and placemats.

Subject Needs: People and human interest/lifestyles, commerce and industry, wildlife, historic and symbolic Canadiana..

Specs: Color transparency material any size, b&w contacts only.

Payment & Terms: Pays 50% commission, quarterly upon collection. Price ranges: $200-2,000. Offers one-time, non-exclusive rights. Pays $100-500/b&w photo; $100-3,000/color photo. Also offers one-time rights; one-year exclusive; industry exclusive one-year..

Making Contact: Photo guidelines free with business SASE, reply in 1 week. Must send a minimum of 300 images. Unsolicited submissions must have return postage.

Tips: "Submit colorful, creative, current, technically strong images with negative space in composition." Looks for people, lifestyles, variety, bold composition, style, flexibility and productivity. "People should be model released for top sales." Prefer Kodachrome and medium format. Photographers should "shoot for business not for artistic gratification; tightly edited, good technical points (exposure, sharpness etc.) professionally mounted, captioned/labeled and good detail."

THE IMAGE BANK, 111 5th Ave., New York NY 10003. (212)529-6700. President: Stanley Kanney. Has over 50 full service library locations. Clients include ad agencies, public relations firms, corporations, book publishers, magazine, newspaper, calendar and greeting card companies, and government agencies.

Subject Needs: "With more than 4,000 subject categories including travel, scenics, sports, people, industry, occupations, animals, architecture and abstracts, we market images in virtually every subject area. We especially need leisure-time photos and upscale images of people. The people can be of any age group and any nationality, but must be attractive. Model releases are necessary. European and Asian commerce and industry are desired, as well as wildlife and released home and office interiors." Accepts only color transparencies.

Payment & Terms: Does not buy outright; pays 50% commission. Fees for sales are negotiated on the basis of usage, print run, territory, insertions and distribution. Also handles assignments for photographers under contract.

Making Contact: Send material by mail for consideration, or submit portfolio for review.

Tips: Put together about 500 representative color transparencies and submit to Lauren Wendle, Director of Photography at the New York office. Put all transparencies in clear vinyl pages. "Freelance photographers interested in working with *The Image Bank* should have a large file of technically superb color transparencies that are highly applicable to advertising sales. There is an emphasis on released people of all nationalities and ages, involved in all types of activities: work, school, play, travel etc. Computer graphics, industrial photography, commercial and financial subjects are also in demand. Although we specialize in advertising sales, we have a large and superb editorial library. Very lucrative stock sales are being made by *The Image Bank* throughout the world in areas where formerly only original assignments were considered."

■**THE IMAGE BANK/WEST**, 4526 Wilshire Blvd., Los Angeles CA 90010. (213)930-0797. General Manager: Lilly Filipow. Maintains 1,000,000 photos in Los Angeles and 3,000,000 in New York. Serves ad agencies, public relations firms, businesses, audiovisual firms, book, magazine and encyclopedia publishers, newspapers and film/TV. Also, postcard, calendar and greeting card companies.
Specs: Uses 35mm color transparencies; "some larger formats."
Payment & Terms: Pays 50% commission for photos. Model release and captions required.

IMAGE BROKER, Box 1996, Columbus OH 43216. (614)421-1919. Contact: Dave Pyles, Director. Has 40,000 images. Clients include ad agencies, public relations firms, businesses, book/encyclopedia publishers and magazine publishers.
Subject Needs: People in everyday situations, especially women, ethnics, elderly, children, occupations, office scenes, computers in use . . . Also travel images from anywhere in the world.
Specs: Uses 35mm, 2¼ × 2¼ and 4 × 5 "color" added transparencies.
Payment & Terms: Pays 50% commission on b&w and color photo required. Model release and captions required. "We do not buy images outright." Rights offered are whatever is needed.
Making Contact: Query with resume of credits, and list of stock image subjects. Professional queries with SASE, categories of work, number of images available. Do not send photos or slides on initial query. Reports in 2 weeks. Image guidelines free with SASE. "Tips sheet distributed monthly to our photographers."
Tips: Prefers to see strong coverage of one or more areas the photographer specializes in. Photographer's work should be "clean, sharp, Kodachrome and the entire image must lend (or focus) itself on the main subject matter. We need more than nature photographers, we need shooters who can interact with and photograph people in all situations. We are looking for photojournalistic images of real people in real life situations. All ages. Older, 60's, people physically active in their world. Find the largest bookstore with magazines and look at what is being used. If you think you can do better, then go for it. Become visually literate. Learn to look and see."

■**IMAGE FINDERS PHOTO AGENCY, INC.**, Suite 501, 134 Abbott St., Vancouver, BC V6B 2K4 Canada. (604)688-9818. Contact: Julia Day. Has 300,000 photos of all subjects. Clients include ad agencies, public relations firms, businesses, audiovisual firms, book publishers, magazine publishers, encyclopedia publishers, newspapers, postcard companies, calendar companies and greeting card companies. "Majority of sales are from model-released lifestyles shots. Ninety percent of our usage fees go toward advertising. Editorial material not required."
Subject Needs: All subjects that can be used for promotional, advertising, public relations, editorial or decorative items. Needs lifestyles shots of people — people of all ages engaged in all kinds of activities, especially leisure and recreational type activities, (USA and foreign — must be generic; and high-tech concept photography.) "We advise photographers to check technical quality with a loop before sending. We especially need photos on Canada, sports and recreation, couples in tropical beach settings, events, families, children and teenagers."
Specs: Uses transparencies only.
Payment & Terms: Does not buy outright; pays 50% commission. General price range: $50-500, more for large ad campaigns. Offers one-time rights, all rights or first rights. For acceptance, model release and captions must be provided.
Making Contact: Send material by registered mail for consideration (do not send in glass mounts); U.S. or other out-of-Canada photographers should contact first before mailing. Reports on queries in 2 weeks; submissions, 2-4 weeks. Photo guidelines free with SAE and International Reply Coupons. "(*Please no* US stamps—*stamps must be Canadian*)." Distributes semiannual tips sheet to established contributors.
Tips: Wants model-released people and activities suitable for sales to airlines and travel industry. People must have a clean look and wear contemporary clothing. Props must be high-quality, no $2 racquets used in tennis shots. Joggers (a salable topic) must be in fashionable jogging clothing. Food props must not contain any brand names or logos. Also, avoid shots with eaten food in them. Peoples' expressions, should be pleasant and happy."

IMAGE QUEST INC., #205, 12995 S. Cleveland Ave., Ft. Myers FL 33907. (813)278-0202. Stock Operations Director: Ed Jerrett. Stock photo agency. Clients include ad agencies, magazines, public relations firms. "Our clients are not limited to the Florida area."

Subject Needs: Human interest (people enjoying life), resort life, tropical areas, occupations, scenic, wildlife.

Specs: Uses 35mm, 2¼ × 2¼ transparencies.

Payment & Terms: Pays 50% commission on photos. Average price range: $150. Model releases required; photo captions preferred.

Making Contact: Write for information/submission guidelines. Reports in 2 weeks.

Tips: "We're looking for clean, sharp images. No snapshot type please. We have more requests than images."

■**THE IMAGE WORKS**, P.O. Box 443, Woodstock NY 12498. (914)246-8800. Directors: Mark Antman and Alan Carey. Stock photo agency. Has 250,000 photos. Clients include audiovisual firms, book/ encyclopedia publishers, magazine publishers and newspapers.

Subject Needs: "We specialize in documentary style photography of worldwide subject matter. People in real life situations that reflect their social, economic, political, leisure time and cultural lives." Topic areas include health care, education, business, family life and travel locations.

Specs: Uses 8 × 10 glossy/semi-glossy, b&w prints; 35mm and 2¼ × 2¼ transparencies.

Payment & Terms: Pays 50% commission on b&w and color photos. General price range: $100-800. Offers one-time rights. Model release preferred; captions required.

Making Contact: Query with list of stock photo subjects or samples. SASE. Reports in 1 month. Photo guidelines free with SASE. "Tips" sheet distributed monthly to contributing photographers.

Tips: "We want to see photographs that have been carefully edited, that show technical control and a good understanding of the subject matter. All photos should be thoroughly captioned and indicate if they are model released. More and more there is a need for photos shot specifically for stock. These pictures illustrate real-life situations but are more controlled than newspaper-style shooting. Still they must not look contrived. They must have strong graphic impact and can be used both editorially and for commercial markets. Stock photographers must be aware of the need to meet deadlines and they should shoot their subjects to fit various layout shapes. Quite often layouts are pre-determined and editors/art directors are looking for the right pictures to fill a space. The use of stock photography increases every year. The markets are world-wide. Once New York City was the only place you could sell photos. With overnight delivery services, publishers and photo agencies can be anywhere. Freelancers who work with us must be hard workers. They have to want to make money at their photography and do it fulltime. Freelancers have to have a high degree of self-motivation to succeed."

*■**IMAGERY UNLIMITED**, Box 2878, Alameda CA 94501. (415)769-9766. President: Jordan Coonrad. Estab. 1981. Stock photo agency. Has 50,000+ photos. Clients include advertising agencies, public-relations firms, audiovisual firms, businesses, book/encyclopedia publishers, magazine publishers, newspapers, postcard companies, calendar companies and greeting card companies.

Subject Needs: Needs photos of "military, aviation, computers, business situations, travel and high-tech industry."

Specs: Uses 35mm, 2¼ × 2¼, 4 × 5, 8 × 10 transparencies.

Payment & Terms: Sometimes buys photos outright. Pays 50% commission on b&w/color photos. General price range: $200-5,000. Buys one-time rights, first rights, all rights (work-for-hire); terms vary "by project." Model release preferred; required in some cases. Photo captions required.

Making Contact: Query with resume of credits; query with samples; query with list of stock photo subjects. Also "send photos when requested after initial contact." SASE. Reports in 1 month. Photo guidelines not available. Tips sheet not distributed at present.

Tips: In freelancer's samples, wants to see high quality, sharp, graphic images. "Prefer Kocachrome. Other film OK in 2¼ and larger formats. Submit 100-200 well-edited images in pages. *No yellow boxes.*" Confirms trend toward "increased use of stock photos."

IMAGES PRESS SERVICE CORP., 22 E. 17th St., New York NY 10003. (212)675-3707. FAX: (212)243-2308. Managers: Peter Gould and Barbara Rosen. Has 100,000+ photos. Clients include public relations firms, book publishers, magazine publishers and newspapers.

Subject Needs: Current events, celebrities, feature stories, pop music, pin-ups and travel.

Specs: Uses b&w prints, 35mm transparencies, b&w contact sheets and b&w negatives.

Payment & Terms: Pays 50% commission on b&w and color photos. General price range: $50-1,000. Offers one-time rights or first rights. Captions required.

Making Contact: Query with resume of credits or with list of stock photo subjects. Also send tearsheets or photocopies of "already published material, original story ideas, gallery shows, etc." SASE. Reports in 2 weeks.

Tips: Prefers to see "material of wide appeal with commercial value to publication market; original material similar to what is being published by magazines sold on newsstands. We are interested in ideas from freelancers that can be marketed and assignments arranged with our clients and subagents." Wants to see "features that might be of interest to the European or Japanese press, and that have already been published in local media. Send copy of publication and advise rights available." To break in, be persistent and offer fresh perspective.

*IMAGES UNLIMITED, 23 Bristol Road, Clinton NY 13323. (315)853-6342. Executive Director: Sharon Olmstead. Newly established. Stock photo agency. Clients include book/encyclopedia publishers, magazine publishers, calendar companies, greeting card companies, art publishers and galleries.
Subject Needs: We are a general interest agency at this time, with a variety of potential clients and subject matter. Of particular interest are the areas of people—especially women, ethnic, elderly, children—at work and play, childbirth, family life, education, health care, business, sports, environment, innovative scenics and nature shots, the arts, architecture, crafts, and food.
Specs: Uses 8×10, glossy b&w prints; 35mm transparencies.
Payment & Terms: Pays 50% commission on b&w and color photos. Buys one-time rights. Model release and photo captions required.
Making Contact: Arrange a personal interview to show portfolio, Query with sample. Query with list of stock photo subjects. SASE. Reports in 1 month.
Tips: "We are a small, new agency looking for part-time photographers whose work is professional in quality—clear, crisp and original—and whose supply of stock images is dependable, prolific and ongoing. Particularly receptive right now to women wishing to enter the field; committment lies in representing each one of our photographers in marketplace."

■IMPACT VISUALS PHOTO & GRAPHIC, INC., 503 Broadway, Room 512, New York NY 10012. (212)966-9619. Co-Editor: Michael Kaufman and Donna Binder. News/feature syndicate. Has 50,000 photos. Clients include public relations firms, audiovisual firms, businesses, book/encyclopedia publishers, magazine publishers, newspapers, progressive organizations, churches, unions and nonprofit organizations.
Subject Needs: Needs "b&w and color transparency work . . . news and documentary photos on issues of social concern: esp. poverty, workers, environment, racism, gay/lesbian, anti-intervention, government, Latin America, Africa, Asia; also economics, education, health, etc.
Specs: Uses 8×10 glossy or matte b&w prints; 35mm transparencies.
Payment & Terms: Does not buy outright. Pays 60% commission on b&w and color photos to members, 50% to contributors. Pays $25-2,500; most in $75-225 range. Buys one-time rights. Buys other rights by arrangement with photographer. Model release preferred, photo captions required.
Making Contact: Submit portfolio for review or write for intro brochure for "new members." SASE. Reports in 3 weeks. Photo guidelines free with SASE. Tip sheet distributed monthly to members only.
Tips: In portfolio or samples, especially looks for "20-30 b&w prints, captioned, and/or 40-60 color slides, captioned. Should show news or documentary from a progressive perspective, with strong composition and excellent technique on "issues of social concern." Also include resume or note on interests and political perspectives broadly speaking."

■INDEX STOCK INTERNATIONAL INC., 126 Fifth Ave., New York NY 10011. (212)929-4644. FAX: (212)633-1914. Manager: Chris Ferrone. Has 500,000 tightly edited photos. Clients include ad agencies, corporate design firms, graphic design agencies, in-house agencies, direct mail production houses, magazine publishers, audiovisual firms, calendar, postcard and greeting card companies.
Subject Needs: Up-to-date model-released people photos, business executives and activities in general, industry, technology (science & research) and computers, people, family, mature adults, sports, US and general scenics, major cities and local color, foreign/travel, and animals.
Specs: 35mm, 2¼×2¼, 4×5 and 8×10 transparencies. "All 35mm must be Kodachrome."
Payment & Terms: Pays 50% commission on back-up material; 25% on catalog shots. General price range: $125-5,000. Sells one-time rights plus some limited buy-outs and exclusives. Model/property releases and captions required.
Making Contact: Query with list of stock photo subjects. Responds in 2 weeks with submission guidelines and general information.
Tips: "We have expanded our foreign representation to include Korea, Australia, Hong Kong and Italy. Educate yourself to the demands and realities of the stock photography marketplace, find out where your own particular style and expertise fit in, and edit unmercifully. The demands for new images increase daily as more ad people become comfortable using stock images that rival assignment work." Looks for "technically perfect samples of that photographer's personal expertise; different examples/compositions of the same subject. Submit 200-500 originals (in person or by mail) that are representative of your work. We have opened a branch office at 6500 Wilshire Blvd., Suite 500, Los Angeles, CA (213)658-7707. FAX: (213)651-4975. Manager: Steve Tseckares."

*■INSTOCK PICTURE AGENCY, 516 NE 13 St., Ft. Lauderdale FL 33304. (305)527-4111. General Manager: Victoria Ross. Estab. 1987. Stock photo agency. Has 100,000 photos. Clients include advertising agencies, public relations firms, audiovisual firms, businesses, book/encylcopedia publishers,

magazine publishers, newspapers, postcard companies, calendar and greeting card companies.
Subject Needs: Uses 35mm, 2¼×2¼, 4×5, 8×10 transparencies.
Payment & Terms: Pays 50% commission on color photos. General price range: $350-3,500. Offers all rights, with photographers permission. Model release required; photo captions preferred.
Making Contact: Query with samples. SASE. Reports in 3 weeks. Photo guidelines free with SASE. Tips sheet distributed monthly, free with SASE.
Tips: "Send only high quality work and be committed to shoot and submit regularly." Sees trend toward more images of "active seniors and lifestyle with an ethnic mix."

*INTERNATIONAL COLOR STOCK, INC., Suite 701, 555 NE 34th St., Miami FL 33137. (305)573-5200. Contact: Dagman Fabricius or Randy Taylor. Estab. 1989. Stock photo agency and news/feature syndicate. Clients include foreign agencies distributing to all markets.
Subject Needs: "We serve as a conduit, passing top-grade photo-reportage and model-released production stock to foreign agencies. We have no US sales and no US archives."
Specs: Uses 35mm transparencies.
Payment & Terms: Offers one-time rights and first rights. Model release required for stock, but not for editorial. Photo captions required.
Making Contact: Query with resume of credits. Reports "only when photographer is of interest" to them. Photo guidelines sheet not available. Tips sheet not distributed.
Tips: "Our percentages are extremely low. Because of this, we deal only with top shooters seeking long-term success. If you are not published 20 times a month or have not worked on contract for three or more photo agencies or have less than 15 years experience, please do not call us."

INTERNATIONAL PHOTO NEWS, Box 2405, West Palm Beach FL 33402. (305)793-3424. Photo Editor: Jay Kravetz. News/feature syndicate. Has 50,000 photos. Clients include newspapers, magazines and book publishers. Previous/current clients include: Lake Worth Herald, S. Fla. Entertainment Guide and Prime-Time; all three celebrity photos with story.
Subject Needs: Celebrities of politics, movies, music and television at work or play.
Specs: Uses 5×7, 8×10 glossy b&w prints.
Payment & Terms: General price range: $5; pays $5/b&w photo; $10/color photo; 25% commission. Offers one-time rights. Captions required.
Making Contact: Query with resume of credits. Solicits photos by assignment only. SASE. Reports in 1 week.
Tips: "We use celebrity photographs to coincide with our syndicated columns. Must be approved by the celebrity."

INTERPRESS OF LONDON AND NEW YORK, 400 Madison Ave., New York NY 10017. Editor: Jeffrey Blyth. Has 5,000 photos. Clients include magazine publishers and newspapers.
Subject Needs: Offbeat news and feature stories of interest to European editors. Captions required.
Specs: Uses 8×10 b&w prints and 35mm color transparencies.
Payment & Terms: Does not buy outright. Offers one-time rights.
Making Contact: Send material by mail for consideration. SASE. Reports in 1 week.

JEROBOAM, INC., 120-D 27th St., San Francisco CA 94110. (415)824-8085. Contact: Ellen Bunning. Has 150,000 b&w photos, 100,000 color slides. Clients include text and trade books, magazine and encyclopedia publishers and editorial. Previous/current clients include: textbook publishers of Marriage and Family, Psychology and Spanish; Harper & Row, John Wiley and Harcourt, Brace.
Subject Needs: "We want people interacting, relating photos, artistic/documentary/photojournalistic images, especially minorities and handicapped. Images must have excellent print quality—contextually interesting and exciting, and artistically stimulating." Need shots of school, family, career and other living situations. Child development, growth and therapy, medical situations. No nature or studio shots.
Specs: Uses 8×10 double weight glossy b&w prints with a ¾" border. Also uses 35mm transparencies.
Payment & Terms: Consignment only; does not buy outright; pays 50% commission; pays $125/b&w photo; $160/color photo. Offers one-time rights. Model release and captions required where appropriate.
Making Contact: Call if in the Bay area; if not, query with samples, query with list of stock photo subjects, send material by mail for consideration or submit portfolio for review. "We look at portfolios the first Wednesday of every month." SASE. Reports in 2 weeks.
Tips: "The Jeroboam photographers have shot professionally a minimum of 5 years, have experienced some success in marketing their talent and care about their craft excellence and their own creative vision. Jeroboam images are clear statements of single moments with graphic or emotional tension. We look for people interacting, well exposed and printed with a moment of interaction. New trends

are toward more intimate, action shots. Be honest in regards to subject matter (what he/she *likes* to shoot)."

JOURNALISM SERVICES, 118 E. Second St., Lockport IL 60441. (312)951-0269. President: John Patsch. Stock photo agency. Has 200,000 photos. Clients include ad agencies, public relations firms, businesses, book/encyclopedia publishers, magazine publishers, newspapers, postcard companies, calendar companies and greeting card companies.
Subject Needs: Model released people, high tech, travel, medical, factory, assembly lines, transportation, families, corporate. General coverage, released pictures for advertising, industry, corporate world travel, animals, scientific/technical, family life, agricultural, sports and medical.
Specs: Uses medium and large format transparencies.
Payment & Terms: Pays 50% commission on color photos. General price range: $135-650. "ASMP rates are charged on all sales." Offers one-time rights. Model release and captions required.
Making Contact: Query with list of stock photo subjects. SASE. Reports in 3 weeks. Tips sheet distributed quarterly to photographers on file.
Tips: Prefers to see high quality color. "We look at the photographer's use of light and color as well as subject matter. Due to changes in the tax laws, stock will have an edge over pictures shot on assignment. The market in stock is beginning to go away from 35mm format and to 2¼ since the introduction of Kodachrome in this format. Our company is looking for photographers shooting medium and large format, skylines, people, scenics. We are only accepting medium and large format photographs for file at this time. We will still accept 35mm for action and sports images. Please make sure your images are captioned with detailed descriptions as to what the image is and where it was taken. The trend this year seems to be toward model-released people and life styles."

■**KIDSSTOCK AMERICA**, 139 Windfall Rd., Utica NY 13502. (315)797-9194. Photo Editor: Marie Douglas. Clients include ad agencies, audiovisual firms, book publishers, magazine publishers and calendar companies.
Subject Needs: Children from birth to early teens and families. Colorful, high quality, model-released images only. Submit releases with photos.
Specs: Uses 35mm, mounted 2¼ × 2¼ slides.
Payment & Terms: Pays 50% commission on color photos. Three-year contract. Offers one-time rights in most cases. Prices depend upon use and vary widely. Model release required; captions preferred.
Making Contact: Query with 100-200 samples. SASE. Reports in 2-6 weeks. "We prefer to deal with professionals or photographers who know better than to expect miracles in a crowded, fiercely competitive field."
Tips: "Looks for quality and freshness. Submit regularly and consistently. Be serious and realistic. Know the stock photography business and how it operates. Patience, perseverance, and steady, high-quality submissions are requirements."

■**JOAN KRAMER AND ASSOCIATES, INC.**, 5 N. Clover Dr., Great Neck NY 11021. (212)567-5545. President: Joan Kramer. Has 1 million b&w and color photos dealing with travel, cities, personalities, animals, flowers, scenics, sports and couples. Clients include ad agencies, magazines, recording companies, photo researchers, book publishers, greeting card companies, promotional companies and AV producers.
Subject Needs: "We use any and all subjects! Stock slides must be of professional quality."
Specs: Uses 8 × 10 glossy b&w prints; any size transparencies.
Payment & Terms: Does not buy outright; pays 50% commission. Offers all rights. Model release required.
Making Contact: Query or call to arrange an appointment. SASE. Do not send photos before calling.

■**LA COLOTHEQUE S.P.R.L.**, Aveune Paul Hymans, 103 (bte 23), 1200 Brussels Belgium. (02)762-48-07. FAX: (02)770-39-67. Manager: René J. Mertens von der Becke. Stock photo agency and picture library. Has 100,000 photos. Clients include advertising agencies, public-relations firms, audiovisual firms, businesses, book/encyclopedia publishers, magazine publishers, postcard companies, calendar companies, greeting card companies and tour operators.
Specs: Uses 35mm, 2¼ × 2¼ and 4 × 5 transparencies.
Payment & Terms: Pays 60% commission on color photos. General price range: 3,000-60,000 (Belgian currency). Model release preferred; captions required.
Making Contact: Arrange a personal interview to show a portfolio; send unsolicited photos by mail for consideration. SASE.
Tips: Stock photography business is "growing in quality and quantity." To break in, "furnish excellent material."

HAROLD M. LAMBERT STUDIOS, INC., Box 27310, Philadelphia PA 19150. (215)224-1400, 885-3355. Vice President: Raymond W. Lambert. Has 1.5 million b&w photos and 400,000 transparencies of all subjects. Clients include ad agencies, publishers and religious organizations. Buys photos outright— "rates depend on subject matter, picture quality and film size"; or pays 50% commission on color. Offers one-time rights. Present model release on acceptance of photo. Submit material by mail for consideration. Reports in 2 weeks. SASE. Free photo guidelines.
Subject Needs: Farm, family, industry, sports, robotics in industry, scenics, travel and people activities. No flowers, zoo shots or nudes.
B&W: Send negatives or contact sheet. Photos should be submitted in blocks of 100.
Color: Send 35mm, 2¼×2¼ or 4×5 transparencies.
Tips: "We return unaccepted material, advise of material held for our file, and supply our photo number." Also, "we have 7 selling offices throughout the US and Canada."

*∎**LGI PHOTO AGENCY,** 241 West 36th St., New York NY 10018. (212)736-4602. Vice President: Laura Giammarco. Estab. 1978. Stock photo agency and news/feature syndicate. Has 1 million photos. Clients include advertising agencies, public-relations firms, audiovisual virms, book/encyclopedia publishers, magazine publishers, newspapers and calendar companies.
Subject Needs: "We handle news events which relate to personalities in TV, music, film, sports, politics etc. We also represent special studio and at-home sessions with these people."
Specs: Uses mostly photos, some film.
Payment & Terms: Pays 50% commission on b&w/color photos; percentage on film varies. General price range: minimum $125/b&w, $175/color. Offers one-time rights.
Making Contact: Arrange a personal interview to show portfolio. Deals with local freelancers only. Solicits photos by assignment only. Cannot return material. Reports in 2 weeks.

*__**LIGHT IMAGES, INC.,** 207 Miller Ave., Mill Valley CA 94941. (415)381-5485. Senior Editor: Rob Northern. Estab. 1983. Stock photo agency. Has 300,000 photos. Clients include advertising agencies, book/encyclopedia publishers, magazine publishers, postcard companies, calendar companies and greeting card companies.
Subject Needs: "We do not specialize. However, the vast majority of requests we receive are . . . people-related . . . work, leisure, etc. Must be released. Second major category is travel, both scenics and people-related."
Specs: Uses 8×10 glossy b&w prints; 35mm, 2¼×2¼, 4×5, 8×10 transparencies.
Payment & Terms: Pays 50% commission on b&w and color photos. General price range: from $150-5,000. Average is about $300. Mostly offers one-time rights; other rights negotiable. Model release and photo captions required.
Making Contact: Query with list of stock photo subjects. SASE. Reports in 1 month. Photo guidelines free with SASE. Tips sheet distributed approximately 2 times per month to all photographers; free with SASE.
Tips: Sees an ever increasing demand for top-notch work. Wants to see "only extraordinary quality, both technically and compositionally. We cannot submit 'average' work to our clients."

LIGHTWAVE, Suite 306-114, 1430 Massachusetts Ave., Cambridge MA 02138. (617)628-1052. Contact: Paul Light. Has 200,000 photos. Clients include: ad agencies and textbook publishers. Previous/current clients include: Harcourt Brace Jovanovich, Holt Rinehart & Winston, and Houghton Mifflin; people in everyday activities.
Subject Needs: Candid photos of people in everyday activities in the U.S., France, Japan and Spain.
Specs: Uses Kodachrome and Fujichrome transparencies.
Payment & Terms: Pays $85/b&w photo; $125/color photo; commission 50/50. Offers one-time rights; mail 200 slides.
Making Contact: Mail 200 Kodachromes or Fujichromes in slide sheets for consideration. SASE.
Tips: "Photographers should enjoy photographing people in everyday activities. Work should be carefully edited before submission. Shoot constantly and watch what is being published. We are looking for photographers who can photograph daily life with compassion and originality."

*__**MAGNUM PHOTOS,** 72 Spring St., New York NY 10012. (212)966-9200. Contact: Editorial Director. Estab. 1947. Photographers cooperative. Has over 1 million photos. Clients include advertising agencies, public-relations firms, book/encyclopedia publishers, magazine publishers, newspapers, postcard companies, calendar companies and greeting card companies.
Specs: Uses 8×10 b&w prints; 35mm transparencies; b&w contact sheets and negatives.
Payment & Terms: General price range: $125 and up. Offers one-time rights and North American or world rights. Model release and photo captions preferred.
Making Contact: Arrange a personal interview to show portfolio; submit portfolio for review once a year; May 15 deadline. SASE. Reports in 3 weeks; only seen once a year. Photo guidelines free with SASE.

Tips: "We look for a personal vision, developed style and passion for whatever subject the photographer has chosen."

*■MEGA PRODUCTIONS, INC., 1714 N. Wilton Pl., Los Angeles CA 90028. (213)462-6342. FAX: (213)462-7572. Photo researcher: Kim Edwards. Estab. 1974. Stock photo agency and news/feature syndicate. Has "several million" photos. Clients include book/encyclopedia publishers, magazine publishers, television, film and newspapers.
Subject Needs: Needs "television, film, studio, celebrity, paparazzi, feature stories (sports, national and international interest events, current news stories. Written information to accompany stories appreciated. We do not wish to see fashion and greeting card-type scenics."
Specs: Uses 35mm, 2¼ × 2¼ transparencies.
Payment & Terms: Pays 50% commission on color photos. General price range: $100-20,000; 50% commission of sale. Offers one-time rights. Model release preferred; photo captions required.
Making Contact: Query with resume of credits; query with samples; query with list of stock photo subjects. Deals with local freelancers only. Occasionally assigns work. Reports in 1 week.
Tips: "Studio shots of celebrities, and home/family stories are frequently requested." In samples, looking for "marketability, high quality, recognizable personalities and current newsmaking material. Also, looks for paparazzi celebrity at local and national events. We deal mostly in Hollywood entertainment stories. We are interested mostly in celebrity photography and current events. Written material on personality or event helps us to distribute material faster and more efficiently."

■MILLER COMSTOCK INC., Suite 1102, 180 Bloor St. W., Toronto, ON M5S 2V6 Canada. (416)925-4323. FAX: (416)964-8507. Photo Editor: Carlos Maningas. More than 1 million color transparencies. Clients include ad agencies, corporations, public relations and audiovisual firms, book and magazine publishers, calendar and greeting card companies, printers and packagers.
Subject Needs: Lifestyle model released people, high-tech industrial, science and medicine.
Specs: Accepts 35mm Kodachrome, Fujichrome, 6 × 7 and larger, 8 × 10 b&w glossy prints, and b&w contact sheets.
Payment & Terms: General price range: $100-10,000. Offers one-time rights. Model release and captions required.
Making Contact: Query with resume and promotional samples.

■MONITOR SYNDICATION, 17 Old Street, London EC1V 9HL England. 01-253 7071. General Manager: David Willis. Stock photo agency and picture library. Clients include advertising agencies, public relations firms, audiovisual firms, businesses, book/encyclopedia publishers, magazine publishers, newspapers, postcard companies, calendar companies, greeting card companies and television.
Subject Needs: Handles portrait-type photographs of famous or important personalities from politics, music, sports, acting, etc.
Specs: Uses 35mm or 2¼ × 2¼ transparencies; 35mm negatives.
Payment & Terms: Buys photos outright or pays 50% commission on b&w and color photos. General price range is "too varied to list." Offers one-time rights.
Making Contact: Query with list of stock photo subjects. Does not return unsolicited material. Reports in 2 weeks. Guidelines free with SASE.
Tips: Wants "personalities looking at camera. Taken close up. Both landscape and upright color transparencies." Also, "good composition and properly exposed images."

■N.E.B. STOCK PHOTO AGENCY, Suite 112, 805 E St., San Rafael CA 94901. (415)883-0305. Owner: Norman Buller. Estab. 1988. Stock photo agency. Has 4,000 photos. Clients include advertising agencies, businesses, book/encyclopedia publishers, magazine publishers, postcard companies, calendar companies, greeting card companies and men's magazines, foreign and domestic. Previous/current clients include: Playboy, unpublished nudes of Marilyn Monroe; Baseball Cards magazine, 1958 original Dodgers team, 2¼ × 2¼ transparencies; Augsberg Fortress, Tree's in Mist.
Subject Needs: Nudes, animals, flowers, people, x-rated material of all subject matter and celebrity nudes. B&w and transparencies only.
Specs: Uses any size b&w/prints; 35mm, 2¼ × 2¼, 4 × 5 transparencies; VHS videotape.
Payment & Terms: Pays 50% commission on all sales. Offers one-time or first rights and all rights. Model release and photo captions required. Outright purchase.
Making Contact: Query with samples and list of stock photo subjects. Send unsolicited photos by mail for consideration. Reports 2 weeks.
Tips: "Work must be good. Buyers are incredibly picky! Getting harder to please everyday. We have worldwide clientele, don't edit too tightly, let me see 90% of your material on hand and critique it from there!"

■**NATIONAL BASEBALL LIBRARY**, Box 590, Cooperstown NY 13326. (607)547-9988. Photo Collection Manager: Patricia Kelly. Picture library. Has 175,000 photos. Clients include ad agencies, public relations and audiovisual firms, businesses, book/encyclopedia publishers, magazine publishers, newspapers, postcard companies, calendar companies, ball clubs, baseball fans and educational/college/high school.
Subject Needs: Uses "baseball related photos from the late 1800's to present day. Includes photos of all Hall of Famers, players not in the Hall of Fame, teams, stadiums, world series and many more, action, portraits and group photos.
Payment & Terms: "We accept donations only. We will honor copyright ownership. We refer client to photographer for permission to use and to negotiate a price for use. General price range: $20-50. Offers one-time rights.
Making Contact: Query with samples, send unsolicited photos by mail for consideration. SASE. Reports in 2 weeks.
Tips: "Our clients want good action photos of players whether modern day or turn-of-the century players in uniform."

NATIONAL NEWS BUREAU, 1318 Chancellor St., Philadelphia PA 19107. (215)546-8088. Photo Editor: Andy Edelman. Clients include book and magazine publishers, and newspapers. Distribute/syndicate to 1,100 publications.
Subject Needs: "All feature materials; fashion; celebrity."
Specs: Uses 8×10 b&w and color prints, and b&w and color contact sheets.
Payment & Terms: Buys photos outright; pays $15-500. Offers all rights. Model release and captions required.
Making Contact: Query with samples; send photos by mail for consideration; submit portfolio for review. SASE. Reports in 2 weeks.
Tips: Needs photos of "new talent—particularly undiscovered female models."

■**NATURAL HISTORY PHOTOGRAPHIC AGENCY (NHPA)**, Little Tye, 57 High St., Ardingly, Sussex, RH17 6TB England. 444-892514. FAX: 444-892168. Library Manager: Tim Harris. Stock photo agency and picture library. Has approximately 100,000 photos. Clients include ad agencies, audiovisual firms, book/encyclopedia publishers, magazine publishers, calendar companies and greeting card companies. Previous/current clients include: Reader's Digest magazine, illustrations for magazine article (turtles); Broadbent Advertising, 48 sheet poster for supermarket chain (barn owl); and Marshall Editions, wraparound cover for "The Atlas of the Living World" (antelope running).
Subject Needs: Every aspect of natural history, worldwide. This includes wild and domesticated animals, plants, marine life, landscapes, environmental and agricultural subjects, pollution, habitat destruction, hunting and fishing; Arctic wildlife, redwood trees, skunks, California condors, all aspects of rainforest wildlife and rainforest destruction, especially in Brazil.
Specs: Uses b&w prints and 35mm and medium/large format original transparencies. Also good quality large format dupes.
Payment & Terms: Pays 60% commission on b&w and color photos. Normal price range 40-300 pounds (English currency) editorial, 100-2000 pounds advertising. Offers one-time rights. Captions are required.
Making Contact: Query with list of stock photo subjects. Before sending photos, must be accompanied by funds to cover return postage. Reports in 2 months. Guidelines free with SASE. Distributes tip sheet every 6 months to all NHPA photographers.
Tips: Prefers pictures with flow and impact—behavioral interest, immediate appeal and good editorial content. Animal pictures must be dramatic, interesting and well composed. Stock photos of natural history show constant changes of subject and emphasis. Pictures showing man's impact on wildlife and the environment, pictures with cute appeal and several selling angles are most pressing needs. Send a tightly-edited selection of pictures. Concentrate on technical quality, have strong behavioral content and demonstrate as wide a range of subject matter as possible."

NATURAL SCIENCE PHOTOS, 33 Woodland Dr., Watford, Hertfordshire WD1 3BY England. 0923-245265. FAX: 0923-246067. Principals: Peter and Sondra Ward. Stock photo agency and picture library. Members of British Association of Picture Libraries and Agencies. Has 100,000 photos. Clients include ad agencies, public relations firms, audiovisual firms, businesses, book/encyclopedia publishers, magazine publishers, newspapers, postcard companies, calendar companies, greeting card companies and television. Current clients: TIB Publishers (for Image Bank), 43 Wildlife pictures in *Africa the Mighty Continent*; Ginn & Co. Science Level 5, 60 natural history pictures; International Masters Publishing, Wildlife fact file, 41 pictures first 14 packs.
Subject Needs: Natural science of all types, including wildlife (terrestrial and aquatic), habitats (including destruction and reclamation), botany (including horticulture, agriculture, pests, diseases, treatments and effects), ecology, pollution, geology, primitive peoples, astronomy, scenics (mostly

without artifacts), climate and effects, e.g. hurricane damage and etc., creatures of economic importance, e.g. disease carriers and domestic animals and fowl. "We need to expand our holdings of Antarctic subjects, both faunistic and scenic. South America and India are poorly represented in our files and we would be pleased to review material on all natural science subjects from these regions."
Specs: Uses 35mm, 2¼ × 2¼ original color transparencies.
Payment & Terms: Pays 66% commission for color photos. General price range: $55-1,400. Offers one-time rights, exclusive on calendars. Copyright not sold without written permission. Model release preferred; captions required.
Making Contact: Arrange a personal interview to show a portfolio; query with list of stock photo subjects; send unsolicited photos by mail for consideration. SASE. Reports in 1-4 weeks, according to pressure on time.
Tips: "We normally ask for 20-25 transparencies that give a good idea of both scope and quality available. These should preferably be card-mounted and must be clearly captioned with English and scientific name (where applicable), locality and photographer's name. No glass mounts will be accepted. All submissions should be registered and be accompanied by return postage. No external insurance value should be declared. Wildlife photographs in particular need to contain some action, fighting, feeding, courting, etc., or depict a form of behavior. Series shots of growth in plants or metamorphosis are always useful, also flight pictures in both birds and insects. Transparencies must generally be very sharp and there is an emphasis on accurate identification. Popular themes are destruction of environment (reclamation of same), exploitation of wildlife, preservation of same, and poaching of all kinds. Material on all cetaceans (whales and dolphins, etc.) is in short supply. We especially need high-class transparencies on geology and palaeontology, with pictures of actual fossils and reconstructions of prehistoric animals: dinosaurs, pteranodon, archaeopteryx, mammals, etc. These must be scientifically accurate and shot with realistic backgrounds. There is a consistent and expanding market."

NAWROCKI STOCK PHOTO, Suite 1630, 332 S. Michigan Ave., Chicago IL 60604. (312)427-8625. FAX: (312)427-0178. Director: William S. Nawrocki. Stock photo agency, picture library. Has over 300,000 photos and 500,000 historical photos. Clients include ad agencies, public relations firms, editorial, businesses, book/encyclopedia publishers, magazine publishers, newspapers, postcard companies, calendar companies and greeting card companies. Previous/current clients: Woman's World, Model Releases Images, magazine; Certified Tours, Travel Images, borchure; and Leu Buanett, Cityscape/Farm Images, AD.
Subject Needs: Model-released people, all age groups, all types of activities, families, couples, relationships, up-dated travel, domestic and international, food.
Specs: Uses 8 × 10 matte or glossy b&w and color prints; 35mm, 2¼, 2¼ × 2¾, 4 × 5, 8 × 10 transparencies. "We look for good composition, exposure and subject matter; good color." Also, finds large format work "in great demand."
Payment & Terms: Buys only historical photos outright. Pays $100/b&w and color photo; varies with/ use/press run. Commission depends on agent-foreign or domestic 50%/40%/35%. Offers one-time, first, exclusive and all rights. Model release and captions required.
Making Contact: Arrange a personal interview to show portfolio; query with resume of credits, samples and list of stock photo subjects; submit portfolio for review. SASE. Reports ASAP. Photo guidelines free with SASE. Tips sheet distributed "very often to our photographers. Suggest that you call first—discuss your photography with the agency, your goals, etc. NSP prefers to help photographers develop their skills. We tend to give direction and offer advice to our photographers. We don't take photographers on just for their images. NSP prefers to treat photographers as individuals and likes to work with them, whether seasoned pro or an amateur." Provide return postage. Allow 2 weeks for review. Label and caption images. Has network with domestic and international agencies.
Tips: "A stock agency uses just about everything. We are using more people images, all types—family, couples, relationships, leisure, the over 40's and 50's group. Looking for large format—variety and quality. More images are being custom shot for stock with model releases. Model releases are very, very important—a key to a photographer's success and income. Model releases are the most requested for ads/brochures."

NEW ENGLAND STOCK PHOTO, Box 815, Old Saybrook CT 06475. (203)388-1741. President: Betty Rogers Johansen. Stock photo agency. Has 50,000 photos in files. Clients include ad agencies, public relations firms, businesses, book/encyclopedia publishers, magazine publishers, postcard, calendar and greeting card companies. Previous/current clients: DC Heath, textbook cover, Sailing at Sunset; Trendsetters Advertising, tour brochures/magazines, travel; and Compton's Encyclopedia, various subjects, printed and computer versions.
Subject Needs: "We are a general interest agency with a wide variety of clients and subject matter. Always looking for good people shots—workplace, school, families, couples, children, senior citizens— engaged in everyday life situations, including recreational sports, home life, vacation and outdoor

This photo, originally in color, brings the Far East to life in the minds of viewers, says William Nawrocki of Nawrocki Stock Photo. The image, Nawrocki notes, has so far brought in "hundreds of dollars" in sales. Usages have included billboard advertising for a photographic service, illustration in a travel brochure and most recently as a cover for a Nawrocki stock catalog. Nawrocki first learned of the photographer, Steve Vidler, when he made contact with the agency. Vidler is a 20-year veteran travel photographer who has worked extensively in stock.

activities. We also get many requests for animal shots — horses, dogs, cats and wildlife (natural habitat). Special emphasis on New England — specific places, lifestyle and scenics, but have growing need for other US and international subject matter. Also use setup shots of flowers, food, nostalgia." Uses 8×10 b&w glossy prints; 35mm, 2¼×2¼, 4×5 transparencies. "We are especially interested in more commercial/studio photography, such as food and interiors, which can be used for stock purposes. Also, we get many requests for particular historical sites, annual events, and need more coverage of towns/cities, main streets and museums."

Payment & Terms: Pays 50% commission for b&w and color photos; $100-1,000/b&w photo; $100/color photo (no maximum); 50% commission/50%. Offers one-time rights; postcard and calendar rights are limited. Model release preferred; captions required.

Making Contact: Query with list of stock photo subjects or send unsolicited photos by mail for consideration. SASE. Reports in 3 weeks. Guidelines free with SASE. Distributes monthly tip sheet to contributing photographers.

Tips: "Quality, not quantity, is the key. We look for images with a clear message or mood, good depth of field, and dramatic scenics with good captions. We look for technically excellent images with good captions — who, what, where. We are not interested in bodies of work concentrated on generic scenics and nature. The need is for people involved in daily life, environmental and social issues, travel, education, specific locations, etc. People and animal shots should usually be closeup, active and vital images. We do get assignment requests for photographers, so it is helpful to get a good sense of a photographer's special skills and interests. Our clients expect us to have just about any subject — from angry bears to a man having a haircut or a retired couple playing golf. We are getting more requests for specific locations so we advise our photographers to carry a notebook or cassette recorder to gather information while shooting. There are fewer calls for so-called 'generic' scenics, so we are rejecting a lot of good images for lack of geographic location. Also see more of a trend for model-released images in editorial and textbook usage — so get that release! Also become aware of issues of today; concerns about our environment, aging, health & fitness, education & drugs are subjects we are hearing more & more about. So there are constant demands for images depicting them. We are not just looking for pretty pictures but those showing our relationship with each other and our world."

■**THE NEW IMAGE STOCK PHOTO AGENCY INC.**, Suite 200, 38 Quail Ct., Walnut Creek CA 94596. (415)934-2405. President: Tracey Prever. Estab. 1986. Stock photo agency. Has 50,000 photos. Clients include advertising agencies, public relations firms, audiovisual firms, businesses, book/encyclopedia

publishers, magazine publishers, newspapers, calendar companies and greeting card companies.
Subject Needs: "We mainly deal with commercial clients in advertising. We look for model-released people images in all different situations, . . . lifestyles, corporate, people working, etc. Also, industry, travel, technology and medical."
Payment & Terms: Pays 50% commission on color photos. General price range: $200-1,000. Offers one-time rights. Model release and photo captions required.
Making Contact: Arrange a personal interview to show portfolio. SASE. Reports in 1 month. Photo guidelines free with SASE. Tips sheet distributed quarterly to contracted photogs.
Tips: Wants to see "technical quality as well as salable subject matter, variety, model-released people images." Individual style is especially desired.

■**NEWS FLASH INTERNATIONAL, INC.**, Division of Observer Newspapers, 2262 Centre Ave., Bellmore NY 11710. (516)679-9888. Editor: Jackson B. Pokress. Has 25,000 photos. Clients include ad agencies, public relations firms, businesses and newspapers.
Subject Needs: "We handle news photos of all major league sports: football, baseball, basketball, boxing, wrestling, hockey. We are now handling women's sports in all phases including women in boxing, basketball, softball, etc." Some college and junior college sports. Wants emphasis on individual players with dramatic impact. "We are now covering the Washington DC scene. There is now an interest in political news photos."
Specs: Super 8 and 16mm documentary and educational film on sports, business and news; 8 × 10 glossy b&w prints or contact sheet; transparencies.
Payment & Terms: Pays $5 minimum/photo; also pays 40% commission/photos and films. Offers one-time rights or first rights. Model release and captions required.
Making Contact: Query with samples, send material by mail for consideration or make a personal visit if in the area. SASE. Reports in 1 month. Free photo guidelines and tip sheet on request.
Tips: "Exert constant efforts to make good photos—that newspapers call grabbers, make them different than other photos, look for new ideas. There is more use of color and large format chromes." Special emphasis on major league sports. "We cover Mets, Yankees, Jets, Giants, Islanders on daily basis. Rangers & Knicks on weekly basis. We handle bios and profiles on athletes in all sports. There is an interest in women athletes in all sports."

OKAPIA K.G., Michael Grzimek & Co., 6 Frankfurt/Main, Roderbergweg 168 Germany. President: Grzimek. Stock photo agency and picture library. Has 350,000 photos. Clients include ad agencies, book/encyclopedia publishers, magazine publishers, newspapers, postcard companies, calendar companies, greeting card companies and school book publishers.
Subject Needs: Natural history, science and technology, and general interest.
Specs: Uses 13x18cm minimum b&w prints; 35mm, 2¼ × 2¼, 4 × 5 and 8 × 10 transparencies.
Payment & Terms: Buys photos outright $40. Pays 50% commission on b&w and color photos. Offers one-time rights. Model release and captions required.
Making Contact: Send unsolicited material by mail for consideration. SASE. Distributes "tips" sheets on request.
Tips: "We need every theme which can be photographed." Looks for minimum of 200 slides in submission. For best results, "send pictures continuously." Work must be of "high standard quality."

OMEGA NEWS GROUP/USA, 1200 Walnut St., Philadelphia PA 19107-5449. (215)985-9200. FAX: (215)985-0690. Managing Editor: A.S. Rubel. Stock photo and press agency. Clients include: ad agencies, public relations firms, businesses, book publishers, magazine publishers, encyclopedia publishers, newspapers, calendar and poster companies.
Subject Needs: "All major news, sports, features, society shots, shots of film sets, national and international personalities and celebrities in the news as well as international conflicts and wars."
Specs: Uses 35mm, 2¼ × 2¼ or 4 × 5 transparencies; 8 × 10 b&w glossy prints. Photos must be stamped with name only on mounts and back of prints; prints may be on single or double weight but unmounted.
Payment & Terms: Pays 50% commission. Price depends upon usage (cover, inside photo, etc.). Offers first North American serial rights; other rights can be procured on negotiated fees. Releases required on most subjects; captions a must.
Making Contact: Submit material by mail for consideration. SASE. Send resume, including experience, present activities and interests, and range of equipment. Supply phone number where photographer may be reached during working hours.
Tips: Should have experience in news and/or commercial work on location. "We always welcome the opportunity to see new work. We are interested in quality and content, not quantity. Comprehensive story material welcomed."

■OUTLINE PRESS SYNDICATE INC., 11th Fl., 596 Broadway, New York NY 10012. (212)226-8790. President: Jim Roehrig. Personality/Portrait. Has 250,000 photos. Clients include advertising agencies, public relations firms, magazine publishers, newspapers and production/film co.

Subject Needs: Heavy emphasis on personalities, film, TV, political feature stories.

Payment & Terms: General price range: negotiable. Rights negotiable. Model release preferred; captions required.

Making Contact: Query with resume of credits. Deals with local freelancers by assignment only. Does not return unsolicited material. Reports in 3 weeks.

Tips: Prefers a photographer that can create situations out of nothing. "The market seems to have a non-ending need for celebrities and the highest quality material will always be in demand."

■OXFORD SCIENTIFIC FILMS, Lower Road, Long Hanborough, Oxford, Oxfordshire OX7 2LD England. (0993)881881. Photo Library Manager: Sandra Berry. Film Library: Jane Mulleneux. Film unit and stills and film libraries. Has 250,000 photos; 700,000 feet stock footage on 16mm, and 40,000 feet on 35mm. Clients include ad agencies, design companies, audiovisual firms, book/encyclopedia publishers, magazine and newspaper publishers, calendar, postcard and greeting card companies.

Subject Needs: Natural history: animals, plants, behavior, close-ups, life-histories, histology, embryology, electron microscopy. Scenics, geology, weather, conservation, country practices, ecological techniques, pollution, special-effects, high speed, time-lapse.

Specs: Uses 35mm, and larger transparencies; 16 and 35mm film and VHS videotapes.

Payment & Terms: Pays 50% commission on b&w and color photos. Model release preferred; captions required.

Making Contact: Query with list of stock photo subjects. SASE. Reports in 1 month. Distributes wants list quarterly to all photographers.

Tips: Prefers to see "good focus, composition, exposure. Rare or unusual natural history subjects."

*■PACIFIC STOCK, P.O. Box 90517, Honolulu HI 96835. (808)922-0975. FAX: (808)922-7881. Owner/President: Barbara Brundage. Estab. 1987. Stock photo agency. Has 50,000+ photos; 100+ films. Clients include advertising agencies, public relations firms, audiovisual firms, businesses, book/encyclopedia publishers, magazine publishers, postcard companies, calendar companies and greeting card companies. Previous/current clients: Ogilvy & Mather, Hawaiian food shot for Hawaiian airlines menu; Atlantis Submarines, 7 fish shots for ad; and Reed Kaina Schaller: couple on beach, for real estate brochure.

Subject Needs: "Pacific Stock is the *only* stock photo agency worldwide specializing in Pacific-related photography (both still and motion picture). Locations include North American west coast, Hawaii, Pacific Islands, Australia, New Zealand, Far East, etc. Subjects include: people, travel, science, sports, marine science and industrial."

Specs: Uses 35mm, 2¼×2¼, 4×5 and 8×10 (all formats) transparencies; Super 8, 16mm and 35mm film; Betacam, 1″, D2 original format videotape.

Payment & Terms: Pays 50% commission on b&w and color photos; 50% commission on films. Offers one-time or first rights and extended rights over specified time period; additional rights with photographer's permission. Model release and captions required.

Making Contact: Query with resume of credits and list of stock photo subjects. SASE. Reports in 2 weeks. Photo guidelines free with SASE. Tips sheet distributed quarterly to interested photographers; free with SASE.

Tips: Looks for "Highly edited shots preferrably captioned in archival slide pages. Photographer must be able to supply minimum of 1,000 slides (must be model released) for initial entry and must make quarterly submissions of fresh material from Pacific area destinations from areas outside Hawaii." Major trends to be aware of include: "Increased requests for 'assignment style' photography so it will be resellable as stock. The two general areas (subject) requested are: Tourism usage and economic development. Looks for focus, composition and color. As the Pacific region expands, more people are choosing to travel to various pacific destinations, while greater development occurs, i.e. construction, banking, trade, etc. Increased requests for film, particularly 35mm format of Pacific region—particularly scenery, aerials and ocean. "Be interested in working with our agency to supply what is on our want lists."

■PANORAMIC STOCK IMAGES, 230 N. Michigan Ave., #3700, Chicago IL 60601. (312)236-8545. Photo Editors: Dan Martin/Doug Segal. Estab. 1986. Stock photo agency. Has 50,000 photos. Clients include advertising agencies, audiovisual firms, businesses, magazine publishers, newspapers, postcard companies, calendar companies, corporate design firms, graphic designers and corporate art consultants.

Subject Needs: Works only with *panoramic formats* (2:1 aspect ratio or greater). Subject include: cityscapes/skylines, landscape/scenics, travel, conceptual and backgrounds (puffy clouds, sunrises/sunsets, water, trees, etc.)

Specs: Uses 35mm, 2¼×5, 2¼×7 and 2¼×10 (6×12cm, 6×17cm and 6×24cm). "2¼ formats (chromes only) preferred; will accept 35mm pans, horizontals and verticals."
Payment & Terms: Pays 50% commission on color photos. Average price: $700. Offers one-time rights and limited exclusive usage. Model release preferred "and/or property release, if necessary." Photo captions required.
Making Contact: Arrange a personal interview to show portfolio; query with samples; query with list of stock photo subjects. SASE. Reports in 1 month; also sends "response postcard immediately to all photo submissions." Photo guidelines free with SASE. Tips sheet distributed 3-4 times yarly to agencies and prospective photographers, free with SASE.
Tips: Wants to see "well-exposed chromes. Panoramic portraiture of well-known locations nation-wide and world wide. Also, generic beauty panoramics. Use of panoramic point of view is exponentially increasing in lucrative advertising and corporate design areas. PSI has doubled in gross sales, staff and number of contributing photographers over the past months and we expect strong growth to continue. We are the only stock agency dedicated to panoramic photography."

*DOUGLAS PEEBLES PHOTOGRAPHY, 445 Iliwahi Loop, Kailua, Oahu HI 96734. (808)254-1082. FAX: (808)254-1267. Owner: Douglas Peebles. Estab. 1975. Stock photo agency. Has 50,000 photos. Clients include advertising agencies, public relations firms, businesses, magazine publishers, newspapers, postcard companies and calendar companies. Previous/current clients: Travel Holiday, magazine; GTE, book; and Hill & Knowton, brochure–all scenics of Hawaii.
Subject Needs: South Pacific and Hawaii.
Specs: Uses 35mm, 2¼×2¼, 4×5 color transparencies.
Payment & Terms: Pays 50% commission on color photos. General price range: $100-5,000; $100-5,000/color photo; Commission: 50. Offers one-time rights. Model release required; photo captions preferred.
Making Contact: Contact by telephone. SASE. Reports in 1 month. Photo guideline sheet not available.
Tips: Looks for "strong color, people in activities and model released. Call first."

*PHOTO GEMS, P.O. Box 307, Newport NY 13416. (315)797-9194. Contact: Photo Editor. Estab. 1989. Stock photo agency. Has 5,000 photos. Clients include advertising agencies, public relations firms, businesses, book publishers and magazine publishers.
Subject Need: People of all ages; commercial images rather than editorial; must be model released. Hi-tech images; graphic symbolism. Scenics/sunsets; spectacular and generic; no national parks or identifiable locations. Think mood and commercial/use.
Specs: Uses 35mm, 2¼×2¼, 4×5, color transparencies; 35mm must be Kodachrome. No dupes.
Payment & Terms: Buys photos. Pays $10-100/photo+ royalties. No commission. Buys all rights; royalties in most cases. Model release required.
Making Contact: Send $1 (stamps) and #10 SASE for information packet. SASE for return of materials. Reports in 1 month. Tips sheet distributed occasionally to contributing photographers on mailing list.

■PHOTO LIBRARY INTERNATIONAL, Box 75, Leeds LS7 3NZ U.K. 0532-623005. Managing Director: Kevin Horgan. Picture library. Clients include ad agencies, public relations firms, audiovisual firms, businesses, book/encyclopedia publishers, magazine publishers, newspapers, postcard companies, calendar companies and greeting card companies.
Subject Needs: Most contemporary subjects, excluding personalities or special news events, i.e. industry, sport, travel, transport, scenics, animals, commerce, agriculture, people, etc.
Specs: Uses 35mm, 2¼×2¼ and 4×5 transparencies.
Payment & Terms: 50% commission.

■PHOTO NETWORK, 1541J Parkway Loop, Tustin CA 92680. (714)259-1244. Owners: Mrs. Cathy Aron and Ms. Gerry McDonald. Stock photo agency. Pays 50% commission. Has 300,000 photos. Works with ad agencies, AV producers, textbook companies, graphic artists, public relations firms, newspapers, corporations, calendar companies and greeting card companies. Model release required and captions preferred. Query with list of stock photo subjects and credits. SASE. Reports in 3 weeks.
Subject Needs: Needs shots of personal sports and recreation, industrial/commercial, high-tech, families, couples (all ages), animals, travel and lifestyles. Special subject needs include computer technology; people over 55 enjoying life.
Color: Uses 35mm, 2¼×2¼, 4×5 and 8×10 transparencies.
Tips: "We look for clear, sharp focus, strong colors and good composition. We'd rather have many very good photos rather than one great piece of art. Would like to see photographers with a specialty or specialties and have it covered thoroughly. You need to supply new photos on a regular basis and

be responsive to current trends in photo needs. Photographers are supplied with quarterly 'want' lists and information about current trends."

PHOTO RESEARCHERS, INC., 60 E. 56th St., New York NY 10022. (212)758-3420. FAX: (212)355-0731. President: Robert Zentmaier. Stock agency representing hundreds of photographers. Includes the National Audubon Society and Science Source Collection. Clients include ad agencies and publishers of textbooks, encyclopedias, filmstrips, trade books, magazines, newspapers, calendars, greeting cards, posters, and annual reports in US and foreign markets.
Subject Needs: All aspects of natural history and science; human nature (especially children and young adults 6-18 engaged in everyday activity); industry; "people doing what they do"; and pretty scenics to informational photos, particularly needs model released people photos and property photos such as houses, cars and boats.
Specs: Uses 8 × 10 matte doubleweight b&w prints and any size transparencies.
Payment & Terms: Rarely buys outright; works on 50% stock sales and 30% assignments. General price range: $150-7,500. Indicate model release on photo. Offers one-time and one-year exclusive rights.
Making Contact: Query with description of work, type of equipment used and subject matter available; send to Bug Sutton, Creative Director. Follow up to arrange a personal interview to show portfolio; or submit portfolio for review. Reports in 1 month maximum. SASE.
Tips: "When a photographer is accepted, we analyze his portfolio and have consultations to give the photographer direction and leads for making sales of reproduction rights. We seek the photographer who is highly imaginative, or into a specialty, enthusiastic and dedicated to technical accuracy. We are taking very few photographers—unlike the old days. We are looking for serious photographers who have many hundreds of photographs to offer for a first submission and who are able to contribute often. More advertisers are using stock. Many editorial textbook publishers are turning to color only. Electronic imaging systems for showing and selling stock will be in place before we know it."

■**PHOTOBANK,** Suite B, 17952 Skypark Circle, Irvine CA 92714. (714)250-4480. FAX: (714)752-5495. Photo Editor: Kristi Bressert. Stock photo agency. Has 1 million transparencies. Clients include ad agencies, public relations firms, audiovisual firms, businesses, book/encyclopedia publishers, magazine publishers, newspapers, postcard companies, calendar companies, greeting card companies and wall decor companies.
Subject Needs: Emphasis on active couples (age 40-60 in high demand), lifestyle, medical, family and business. High tech shots are always needed. These subjects are highly marketable, but model releases are a must.
Specs: Uses all formats: 35mm, 2¼ × 2¼, 4 × 5, 6 × 7 and 8 × 10; color only.
Payment & Terms: Pays 50% commission. Model release and captions required.
Making Contact: Arrange a personal interview to show portfolio, or query with samples and list of stock photos. SASE. Reports in 2 weeks. Photo guidelines free with SASE.
Tips: Prefers to see "The 3 'C's: clarity, color, composition. Clients are looking for assignment quality and are very discerning with their selections. Only your best should be considered for submission. Please tightly edit your work before submitting. Model released people shots in lifestyle situations (picnic, golf, tennis, etc.) sell."

*****PHOTOEDIT,** 6056 Corbin Ave., Tarzana CA 91356. (818)342-2811. Estab. 1987. Stock photo agency. Has 120,000+ photos. Clients include book/encyclopedia publishers, magazine publishers, newspapers, postcard companies and calendar companies.
Subject Needs: Needs photos of "people—families, children, ethnics. Also social issues—AIDS, poverty, homeless, aging, healthcare and sports."
Specs: Uses 8 × 10 b&w prints; 35mm, 2¼ × 2¼, 4 × 5 transparencies.
Payment & Terms: Pays 50% commission on b&w and color photos. General price range: $100-600. Offers one-time rights. Model release and photo captions preferred.
Making Contact: Contact by phone. SASE. Reports in 1 week. Tips sheet distributed to photographers in the agency.

■**THE PHOTOGRAPHIC GAME,** Box 233, Forestville, Sydney NSW 2087, Australia. (2)451-2739. Contact: Malcolm Thomas. Keeps 200,000 photos on file. Specializes in the Australian and Japanese markets. Clients include magazine, book publishers, audiovisual and record companies, public relations firms, calendars, corporate clients and ad agencies.

Subject Needs: Human interest, business-oriented shots, sport, glamour, humor and portraits. Submissions accepted from anywhere in the world.
Specs: Uses 35mm and larger format transparencies, "unless b&w is outstanding."
Payment & Terms: Pays 50% commission.
Making Contact: "Send us a few samples (10-100) so we can judge quality and a list of what you have available. Very prompt replies."
Tips: "Sharpness, color, action and impact are what sell photos. Your shots should have 1, 2, 3 or all of these in them."

■**PHOTOPHILE,** 2311 Kettner Blvd., San Diego CA 92101. (619)234-4431. Director: Laurie Walton. Clients include publishers (trade, text, reference, periodical, etc.), advertisers, broadcasters, etc. Negotiates rights for use; usually offers one-time rights. Does not buy outright; pays 50% commission. Write with SASE for photographer's information. "Professionals only, please."
Subject Needs: Lifestyle, vocations, sports, industry, travel, business and computer graphics.
Color: 35mm, 2¼ × 2¼, 4 × 5 original transparencies.
Tips: In samples, wants to see: model-released people in various activities. "Specialize, and shoot for the broadest possible sales potential. Get releases!"

*****PHOTOREPORTERS, INC.,** 875 6 Ave., New York NY 10001. General Manager: Roberta Boehm. Estab. 1958. Stock photo agency, news/feature syndicate. Has many, many, many photos. Clients include public relations firms, book/encyclopedia publishers, magazine publishers and newspapers.
Subject Needs: Celebrities, politics and photo stories such as human interest.
Specs: Uses 35mm transparencies.
Payment & Terms: Pays 50% commission on b&w and color photos. General price range: $175/ ½ page color; $125/¼ page b&w. Offers one-time rights. Model release preferred; photo captions required.
Making Contact: Contact by telephone. SASE. Reports in 3 weeks.

■**PHOTOTAKE,** 4523 Broadway, New York NY 10040. (212)942-8185. FAX: (212)942-8186. Director: Leila Levy. Stock photo agency; "also 'new wave' photo agency specializing in science and technology in stock and on assignment." Has 200,000 photos. Clients include: ad agencies, businesses, newspapers, public relations and AV firms, book/encyclopedia and magazine publishers, and postcard, calendar and greeting card companies.
Subject Needs: General science and technology photographs, medical, high-tech, computer graphics, special effects for general purposes, health-oriented photographs, natural history, people and careers.
Specs: Uses 8 × 10 prints; 35mm, 2¼ × 2¼, 4 × 5 or 8 × 10 transparencies; contact sheets or negatives.
Payment & Terms: Pays 50% commission on b&w and color photos. Offers one-time or first rights (world rights in English language, etc.). Model release and captions required.
Making Contact: Arrange a personal interview to show portfolio; query with samples or with list of stock photo subjects; or submit portfolio for review. *SASE.* Reports in 1 month. Photo guidelines "given on the phone only." Tips sheet distributed monthly to "photographers that have contracted with us at least for a minimum of 500 photos."
Tips: Prefers to see "at least 100 color photos on general photojournalism or studio photography and at least 5 tearsheets – this, to evaluate photographer for assignment. If photographer has enough in medical, science, general technology photos, send these also for stock consideration." Using more "illustration type of photography. Topics we currently see as hot are: general health, computers, news on science. Photographers should always look for new ways to illustrate concepts generally."

■**PHOTRI INC.,** 3701 South George Maxon Drive, Suite C2 North, Falls Chruch VA 22041. (703)836-4439. President: Jack Novak. Has 400,000 b&w photos and color transparencies of all subjects. Examples of recent clients: Harcourt Brace Johanovich and Rand McNally book and encyclopedia publishers, ad agencies, record companies, calendar companies, and "various media for AV presentations."
Subject Needs: Military, space, science, technology, romantic couples, people doing things, humor, picture stories. Special needs include calendar and poster subjects. Has subagents in 10 foreign countries interested in photos of USA in general.
Specs: Uses 8 × 10 glossy b&w prints; 35mm and larger transparencies.
Payment & Terms: Seldom buys outright; pays 50% commission. Pays: $50-150/b&w photo; $75-300/ color photo. Offers all rights and occasionally total "buyout." Model release required if available and if photo is to be used for advertising purposes.
Making Contact: Call to arrange an appointment or query with resume of credits. Reports in 2-4 weeks. SASE.
Tips: "Respond to current needs with good quality photos. Take other than sciences, i.e., people and situations useful to illustrate processes and professions. Send photos on energy and environmental subjects. Also need any good creative 'computer graphics.' Subject needs include major sports events."

*∎PICTOR INTERNATIONAL, LTD., Twyman House, 31-39 Camden Rd., London NW1 9LR England. (01)482 0478. Managing Director: Alberto Sciama. Stock photo agency and picture library with branch offices in Paris, Munich and Milan. Has 500,000 photos. Clients include advertising agencies, public relations firms, audiovisual firms, businesses, book/encyclopedia publishers, magazine publishers, postcard companies, calendar companies, greeting card companies and travel plus decorative posters; jigsaw companies.
Subject Needs: "Pictor is a general stock agency. We accept *all* subjects. Needs primarily people shots (released): business, families, couples, children, etc. Criteria for acceptance: photos which are technically and aesthetically excellent."
Specs: Uses 35mm, 2¼×2¼, 4×5 and 8×10 transparencies.
Payment & Terms: Buys photos outright "whenever possible, depending on subject." Pays 50% commission for color photos. General price range: $100 to $15,000. Offers one-time rights, first rights and all rights. Requires model release and photo captions.
Making Contact: Arrange a personal interview to show portfolio or query with list of stock photo subjects. Send unsolicited photos by mail for consideration. Photo guidelines sheet available for SASE. Tips sheet for "photographers we represent only."
Tips: Looks for "photographs covering all subjects. Criteria: technically and aesthetically excellent. Clients are getting more demanding and expect to receive only excellent material. Through our marketing techniques and PR, we advertise widely the economic advantages of using more stock photos. Through this technique we're attracting 'new' clients who require a whole different set of subjects."

∎PICTORIAL PARADE, INC., 130 W. 42nd St., New York NY 10036. (212)840-2026. President: Baer M. Frimer. Has 2-3 million photos. Clients include: ad agencies, audiovisual firms, public relations firms, businesses, book publishers, magazine and encyclopedia publishers, newspapers, postcard, calendar and greeting card companies—"just about anyone who can use a photograph." Does not buy outright; pays 50% commission. Offers one-time rights. Model release and captions required. Arrange a personal interview to show portfolio; query with samples; send material by mail for consideration. SASE. Reports "as rapidly as possible, depending upon the amount of material to be reviewed."
Subject Needs: News events all over the world, famous personalities and celebrities, authors, scientific discoveries, stoppers and photo features. "We cover Hollywood celebrities, Washington DC; White House, Government hearings; feature sets; oddities."
B&W: Uses 8×10 glossy prints; contact sheet and negatives OK.
Color: Uses 35mm transparencies.

∎THE PICTURE CUBE INC., Suite 1131, 89 Broad St., Boston MA 02110. (617)367-1532. FAX: (617)482-9266. President: Sheri Blaney. Has 300,000 photos. Clients include ad agencies, public relations firms, businesses, audiovisual firms, book publishers, magazine publishers, encyclopedia publishers, newspapers, postcard companies, calendar companies, greeting card companies and TV. Guidelines available upon request.
Subject Needs: US and foreign coverage, contemporary images, agriculture, industry, energy, high technology, religion, family life, multicultural, animals, transportation, work, leisure, travel, ethnicity, communications, people of all ages, psychology and sociology subjects. "We need more lifestyle, model released images of families, couples, and work situations. Also, technology. We emphasize New England/Boston scenics for our ad/design clients."
Specs: Uses 8×10 prints and 35mm, 2¼×2¼, 4×5 and larger slides.
Payment & Terms: Pays 50% commission. General price range: $120 minimum/b&w; $150 minimum/color photo. Offers one-time rights. Model release preferred; captions required.
Making Contact: Request guidelines before sending any materials. Arrange a personal interview to show portfolio. SASE. Reports in 1 month.
Tips: Serious freelance photographers "must supply a good amount (at least a thousand images per year, sales-oriented subject matter) of material, in order to produce steady sales. All photography submitted must be high quality, with needle-sharp focus, strong composition. More of our clients are using color; all of our advertising clients require model releases on all photos of people."

*PICTURE GROUP, INC., 830 Eddy St., Providence RI 02905. (401)461-9333. Managing Editor: Philip Hawthorne. Estab. 1979. Stock photo agency, news/feature syndicate. Has 500,000+ photos. Clients include book/encyclopedia publishers and magazine publishers.
Subject Needs: Needs photos of "topical, contemporary issues and news, including industry, science, health, environment, politics lifestyles and people in the news."
Specs: Uses b&w prints; 35mm and 2¼×2¼ transparencies.
Payment & Terms: Commission is negotiable. Offers one-time rights. Model release preferred; photo captions required.
Making Contact: Contact by phone before sending work. SASE. Reports ASAP. Photo guidelines available to contract photographers. Tips distributed occasionally to contract photographers.

Tips: In freelancer's samples, wants to see professionalism, originality, intelligence, relevance, integrity and hard work. "The demand for released material is growing, also for most up-to-date, distinctive, well-informed material with complete captions."

*PICTURE THAT, INC., 880 Briarwood Rd., Newtown Square PA 19073. (215)353-8833. Stock Librarian: Gail Vickrey. Estab. 1978. Stock photo agency. Has 20,000-30,000 photos. Clients include advertising agencies, public relations firms, businesses, book/encyclopedia publishers, magazine publishers, postcard companies, calendar companies and greeting card companies.
Subject Needs: Handles all subjects: nature, scenics, sports, people of all types and activities, animals, some abstracts and art, and travel (especially East Coast and Pennsylvania).
Specs: Uses 35mm and 2¼ × 2¼ transparencies.
Payment & Terms: Pays 50% commission on photos. General price range: varies with usage and circulation. Offers one-time rights. Model release and photo captions preferred.
Making Contact: Query with list of stock photo subjects; call for info.
Tips: Likes to "see good color and good exposure. Send images in plastic sheets with captions and photographer's name on slides. We are receiving more and more requests for lifestyle photos, people in all situations, especially active and sports shots; also senior citizens. They must be model-released."

*■PICTURESQUE STOCK PHOTOS, 1520 Brookside Drive #3, Raleigh NC 27604. (919)828-0023. Manager: Audra Fowler. Estab. 1987. Stock photo agency. Has 100,000 photos. Clients include: advertising agencies, public relations firms, audiovisual firms, businesses, book/encyclopedia publishers, magazine publishers, newspapers, post card companies, calendar companies and greeting card companies.
Subject Needs: Southeastern US, model released people, travel, lifestyle, agriculture, industry, and general topics.
Specs: 35mm, 2¼ × 2¼, 4 × 5 and 8 × 10 transparencies.
Payment & Terms: 50% commission on color photos. Offers various rights depending on client needs. Model releases and photo captions required.
Making Contact: For consideration send unsolicited photos by mail; contact by telephone for submissions guidelines. SASE. Reports in 1 month. Photo guidelines available. Tips sheet distributed quarterly to member photographers.
Tips: Submission requirements include 200-300 original transparencies.

■PLANET EARTH PICTURES/SEAPHOT LTD, 4 Harcourt St., London W1H IDS England. 01-262-4427. FAX: 01-706-4042. Managing Director: Gillian Lythgoe. Has 80,000 photos. Clients include ad agencies, public relations and audiovisual firms, businesses, book/encyclopedia and magazine publishers, and postcard and calendar companies.
Subject Needs: "Marine—surface and underwater photos covering all marine subjects, including water sports, marine natural history, seascapes, ships; natural history. All animals and plants: interrelationships and behavior; landscapes, natural environments, the people and the animals and plants." Special subject needs: natural history of the US including American wildlife and wilderness.
Specs: Uses any size transparencies.
Payment & Terms: Pays 50% commission on color photos. General price range: £30 (1 picture/1 AV showing), to over £1,000 for advertising use. Prices negotiable according to use. Offers one-time rights. Model release preferred; captions required.
Making Contact: Arrange a personal interview to show portfolio; send photos by mail for consideration. SAE, IRCs. Reports ASAP. Distributes tips sheet every 6 months to photographers.
Tips: "We like photographers to have received our photographer's booklet that gives details about photos and captions. In reviewing a portfolio, we look for a range of photographs on any subject—important for the magazine market—the quality. Trends change rapidly. There is a strong emphasis that photos taken in the wild are preferable to studio pictures. Advertising clients still like larger format photographs. Exciting and artistic photographs used even for wildlife photography, protection of environment."

*PLESSNER INTERNATIONAL, 121 West 27th St., Suite 502, New York NY 10001. (212)645-2121. President: Walter W. Plessner. Stock photo agency. Clients include advertising agencies, magazine publishers and calendar companies.
Payment & Terms: Pays 50% commission on photos. Offers one-time rights. Model release preferred.
Making Contact: Arrange a personal interview to show portfolio.

*■PRO FILES WEST, P.O. Box 1199, Buena Vista CO 81211. (719)395-8671. FAX: (719)395-8840. President, Photographer Representative: Allen Russell. Estab. 1988. Stock photo agency. Has 150,000 photos. Clients include advertising agencies, public relations firms, audiovisual firms, businesses, book/

encyclopedia publishers, magazine publishers, postcard companies, calendar companies, greeting card companies.

Subject Needs: "Our specialty is the American West and its people at work and play. We also have extensive files on foreign locations and people. We are very strong in leisure sports and lifestyles, people at work and Western scenes."

Specs: Uses 35mm, medium and large format transparencies.

Payment & Terms: Pays 50% commission on color photos. General price range: $100+. Offers one-time or first rights. "A wide range is offered but one-time dominates. All rights are sold only with photographers approval and is usually discouraged."

Making Contact: Query with list of stock photo subjects. Submit portfolio for review. SASE. Reports in 1 week. Photo guidelines free with SASE. Tips sheet distributed to contract photographers.

Tips: In photographer's portfolio, wants to see "an organized style which shows people and their environment in a manner which looks unposed, even when it often is. A commitment to developing a series of subjects rather than only random shots." The trend is towards "a desire for images which go beyond the limits of what has come to be expected from stock, more emotion, realism, etc. There is a tremendous need for stock photographers to accept that they are small business people and act accordingly. Most need to tighten their scope of subject and find where they can best compete."

R.D.R. PRODUCTIONS, INC., 351 W. 54th St., New York NY 10019. (212)586-4432. President: Al Weiss. Photo Editors: Joe Griffith and David Shapiro. Has 700,000 photos. Clients include ad agencies, public relations firms, book publishers, magazine publishers, newspapers and calendar companies.

Subject Needs: Uses editorial material: human interest, personalities, glamour and current news features.

Specs: Uses b&w and color glossy prints; 35mm and 2¼ × 2¼ transparencies; b&w negatives.

Payment & Terms: "Occasionally" buys photos outright; price open. Pays 60% commission for photos. General price range varies from $35/b&w to $1,500 for color series. Average for b&w $75; average for single color $150. Offers one-time rights. Model release and captions required.

Making Contact: Query with samples or with list of stock photo subjects or send unsolicited material by mail for consideration. SASE. Reports in 3 weeks. Tips sheet distributed "approximately quarterly to photographers we represent."

■**RAINBOW,** P.O. Box 573, Housatonic MA 01236. (413)274-6211. FAX: (413)274-6689. Director: Coco McCoy. Stock photo agency. Estab. 1976. Has 80,000 photos. Clients include: public relations firms, design agencies, audiovisual firms, book/encyclopedia publishers, magazine publishers and calendar companies. 20% of sales come from overseas.

Subject Needs: Although Rainbow is a general coverage agency, it specializes in high technology images and is continually looking for talented coverage in fields such as computer graphics, robotics, subatomic research, medicine, DNA, communications, lasers and space. We are also looking for graphically strong and colorful images in such areas as macro and microphotography, illustrations of physics, biology and earth science concepts; also active teenagers and elderly people."

Specs: Uses 35mm and larger transparences.

Payment & Terms: Pays 50% commission. General price range: $165-$1000. Offers one-time rights. Model release is required for advertising, book covers or calendar sales. Photo captions required for scientific photos or geographic locations, etc. Payments made quarterly.

Making Contact: Photographers may write or call us for more information. We may ask for an initial submissions of 150-300 chromes. Arrange a personal interview to show portfolio or query with samples. SASE. Published professionals only. Reports in 2 weeks. Guidelines sheet for SASE. Distributes a tips sheets twice a year.

Tips: Looks for well-composed, well-lit, sharp focused images with either a concept well illustrated or a mood conveyed by beauty or light. "Clear captions help our researchers choose wisely and ultimately improve sales. As far as trends in subject matter goes, strong, simple images conveying the American Spirit. . .families together, farming, scientific research, winning marathons, hikers reaching the top, are the winners. And include females doing 'male' jobs, black scientists, Hispanic professionals, Oriental children with a blend of others at play, etc. The importance of model releases for editorial covers, selected magazine usage and always for advertising/corporate clients cannot be stressed enough!"

CHRIS ROBERTS REPRESENTS, Box 7218, Missoula MT 59807. (406)728-2180. Owner/Art Director: Chris Roberts. Photographer's representative company, stock photo agency. Has 3,000 photos.

Subject Needs: "We are building a specialty in images from the Western and Southwestern U.S. People, animals, nature, scenics, architecture, industry and livelihoods (cowboys, Indians, loggers, fishermen).

Specs: Uses 35mm and 4×5 transparencies.

Payment & Terms: Pays 50% on color photos. General price range: $45 minimum. Offers one-time rights, limited rights. Model releases (for recognizable faces) and photo captions preferred.

Making Contact: Query with SASE, arrange a personal interview to show portfolio; send unsolicited photos by mail for consideration; submit portfolio for review; provide resume, business card, brochure, flyer or tearsheets to be kept on file for possible future assignments. SASE. Reports in 3 weeks. Submission guidelines available.

Tips: "If you've got a scenic or good location spot, put people doing something in it. Stock images 'want' people."

*■SCENIC PHOTO IMAGERY, 9208 32nd Ave. N., Mpls MN 55427. (612)542-8740. Manager: Conrad Bloomquist. Estab. 1985. Stock photo agency. Has 100,000 transparencies. Clients include advertising agencies, public relations firms, audiovisual firms, businesses, book/encyclopedia publishers, magazine publishers, postcard companies, calendar companies and greeting card companies.

Subject Needs: Needs photos of scenic landscapes, cityscapes, nature—both flora & fauna, people relating to nature, and travel subjects.

Specs: Uses 35mm, 2¼×2¼, 4×5, 8×10 transparencies.

Payment & Terms: Pays 55% commission on transparencies. General price range: $75-1,000. Offers one-time rights, first rights, or all rights (with written approval of photographer only). Model release required when applicable; photo captions required.

Making Contact: Query first with list of stock photo subjects; submit originals for review after first query. SASE. Reports ASAP, generally less than 1 month. Photo guidelines free with SASE. Tips sheet distributed yearly to accepted photographers in S.P.I agency.

Tips: "Greater competition in the marketplace means that there is little room for the "good" image in a submission. Eye-catching, great images make the vast majority of sales, and lead buyers to call again in the future." Wants to see, "quality lighting, composition, and color. Photographers with the ability to produce the best traditional views of a subject, or a great new angle on the subject will have the most success in the marketplace. Images that make visual statements beyond just being "pretty" will produce more sales. Photographers that specialize in certain subject matter and refine their abilities, while being cognizant of the latest trends in photographic style will produce the best stock photos."

■SCIENCE STOCK AMERICA, 139 Windfall Rd., Utica NY 13502. (315)797-9194. Photo Editor: Marie Douglas. Clients include: ad agencies, audiovisual firms, book publishers and magazine publishers.

Subject Needs: Science and technology, basic to advanced. Photomicrographs, SEM's, TEM's. "Astronomy to Zoology." Also special effects.

Specs: Uses 35mm, mounted 2¼×2¼ slides; 8×10 b&w prints and contact sheets.

Payment & Terms: Pays 50% commission on b&w and color photos. Three-year contract. Offers one-time rights in most cases. Prices depend upon use and vary widely. Model release preferred; captions required.

Making Contact: Query with 100-200 samples. SASE. Reports in 2-6 weeks. "We prefer to deal with professional scientists and photographers." Distributes tips and needs sheet to actively and regularly contributing photographers and contacts on immediate needs by phone.

Tips: "Looks for quality and freshness. Submit regularly and consistently. Be serious and realistic. Photographers need not be professional scientists, but should have a basic understanding of and respect for what they are photographing."

■SCOOPIX PHOTO LIBRARY, 154 Greville St., Prahran, Melbourn Victoria 3181 Australia. (03)521-2233. FAX: (03)521-2379. Managing Directors: Rennie Ellis, Dallas & John Heaton. Stock photo agency and picture library. Has over 300 transparencies on file. Clients: advertising agencies, businesses, book publishers, magazine publishers, travel industry, calendar companies, greeting card companies, art studios and printers. Clients: National Geographic, Australiana shots for *Surprising Lands Downunder*; Valentine Sands Claendars, shots for claendars and greeting cards; and Australian Airlines, beach shot for use in magazine ad.

Subject Needs: Tourist destination subjects in U.S.A., Europe, Asia, Pacific, Canada, etc. Landmarks, key tourist attractions, both natural and man made, with involvement of people. Sports action; couples—young, middle aged, retirement age in varying situations; families; modern technology/computers, etc. Wildlife, Model released shots of attractive people. Demand for photos of couples of all ages involved in, activities appropriate to their age group.

Specs: Uses 35mm, 2¼×2¼ and 4×5 transparencies.
Payment & Terms: Pays 50% commision on all sales. General price range: $150-1,500. Model release and captions required.
Making Contact: Query with resume of credits and list of stock photo subjects. Submissions must be of at least 250 shots, captioned and presented in plastic viewing files. Only interested in transparencies, all size formats from 35mm to 6×7. Offers one time rights; usually 12-mth exclusive right to transparency. SASE. Reports in 3 months. Photo guidelines free with SASE.

SHOOTING STAR INTERNATIONAL PHOTO AGENCY, Box 93368, Hollywood CA 90093. (213)876-2000 or 876-9000. FAX: (213)874-7366. President: Yoram Kahana. Clients include newspapers, magazines, magazines, book/encyclopedia publishers, ad agencies, and anyone using celebrity and human interest photos in the USA and 30 foreign countries.
Subject Needs: "We specialize in celebrity photos and photostories, with emphasis on at-home photosessions, in-studio portraits and beauty shoots, special events and location filming. No run of the mill grab shots, paparazi, parties, etc. In order of importance and salability: television, movies, music, arts and politics, etc. Human interest photos should be complete stories, timeless unusual sports, upbeat medical, animal interest, curiosities, stunts and so on."
Specs: Color transparencies only (35mm E-6 preferred).
Payment: "We pay 60% bimonthly. Fees range from a few dollars per color in some third world countries to thousands of dollars for some covers in the USA and abroad." Must have captions, ID's and brief text.
Making Contact: Query with list of subjects, photocopies of tearsheets. "We look for animation in the subjects, comprehensive coverage (not just one great shot) and, of course, good color, composition, sharpness." SASE. Replies ASAP. Will send some additional info with SASE.
Tips: "We can resell your celebrity photos if you are a pro working with celebrities, e.g., a photographer working with a fitness magazine who shoots celebrities exercising, a fashion photographer who works with celebrity models, or does celebrity homes for an interior design magazine etc.; also if you shoot celebrities outside of Hollywood: a star's winter home in Tahoe, a star living in Arizona, etc. Shooting Star distributes directly and through sub agents to more than 30 countries: American TV is seen everywhere. We have more thorough coverage of TV actors than any other agency—we have done photosessions with more than 50 actors on *Dallas*, whole casts of other popular (and obscure) series. TV names outsell other celebrities 10 to 1, but we do cover all areas, especially if they have international appeal, e.g., golf, tennis, wrestling, but not baseball or horseracing. Human interest stories are about 10% of our volume, but the good ones sell and resell; heartwarming, smile inducing, positive stories; animal trainers, medical miracles, heroic people and deeds—a one-armed surgeon, a water tower turned into a home, custom dog houses, skiing on snow shovels, etc. The kind of photostories you see in *People*, the *Star*, *Life*—they have universal appeal."

*SILVER IMAGE PHOTO AGENCY, INC., 5128 NW 58th Court, Gainesville FL 32606. (904)373-5771. President/Owner: Carla Hotvedt. Estab. 1988. Stock photo agency. Assignments in Florida/S. Georgia/Caribbean. Has 20,000 color/b&w photos. Clients include public relations firms, book/encyclopedia publishers, magazine publishers and newspapers.
Subject Needs: Florida-based travel/tourism, Florida cityscapes and people, nationally oriented topics such as drugs, environment, recycling, pollution, etc. Humorous people and animal posters.
Specs: Uses 8×10 glossy b&w prints; 35mm transparencies.
Payment & Terms: Pays 50% commission on b&w/color photos. General price range: $25-600. Offers one-time rights. Model release preferred. Non-exclusive contract required.
Making Contact: Query with list of stock photo subjects. SASE; will return if query first. Reports on queries in 2 weeks; material—up to 2 months. Photo guidelines free with SASE. Tips sheets distributed as needed. SASE. Do not submit material unless requested first.
Tips: "I will look at photographer's work if they seem to have images outlined on my stock needs list which I will send out after receiving a query letter with SASE. Because of my photojournalistic approach my clients want to see people-oriented photos, not just pretty scenics. I also get many calls for drug-related photos and unique shots from Florida."

THE SLIDE FILE, 79 Merrion Square, Dublin 2 Ireland. (0001)686086. FAX: (0001)608332. Director/Photographer: George Munday. Stock photo agency and picture library. Has 20,000 photos. Clients include ad agencies, public relations firms, businesses, book/encyclopedia publishers, magazine publishers, newspapers and designers.
Subject Needs: Overriding consideration is given to Irish or Irish-connected subjects. Has limited need for overseas locations, but is happy to accept material depicting other subjects, particularly people.

Specs: Uses 35mm, 2¼×2¼ and 4×5 transparencies.
Payment & Terms: Pays 50% commission on color photos. General price range: £60-1,000 English currency ($75-900). Offers one-time rights. Model release preferred; captions required.
Making Contact: Query with list of stock photo subjects. Deals with local freelancers only. Does not return unsolicited material. Reports in 1 month.
Tips: "Apart from growing sales of Irish-oriented material, the trend seems to indicate increasing use of people shots—executives, families, couples, etc. particularly on medium format."

*■SOUTHERN STOCK PHOTOS, Suite 33, 3601 W. Commercial Blvd., Ft. Lauderdale FL 33309. (305)486-7117. FAX: (305)485-5257. Office Manager: Catherine Sadler. Estab. 1976. Stock photo agency. Has 750,000 photos. Clients include advertising agencies, audiovisual firms, businesses, book/ encylcopedia publishers, magazine publishers, newspapers, calendar companies and greeting card companies.
Subject Needs: Needs photos of "southern U.S. cities, Bahamas, Caribbean, S. America, and model-released lifestyle photos with young families and retired people."
Specs: Uses color, 35mm, 2¼×2¼, 4×5 transparencies.
Payment & Terms: Pays 50% commission on color photos. General price range: $225-5,000. Offers one-time rights, first time rights and all rights. Model release required; photo captions preferred.
Making Contact: Query with samples. SASE. Reports in 1 month. Photo guidelines free with SASE. Tips sheet distributed every 6 months to members only.
Tips: In freelancer's portfolio or samples, wants to see approximately 200 transparencies of a cross section of their work. Photographers "must be willing to submit regular new work. Want photographers who will shoot stock for stock sale not just send us rejects of jobs they shoot."

*■SPORTING PICTURES (UK), LTD., 7A, Lambs Conduit Passage, Holborn, London, England. 071-405 4500. FAX: (071)831-7991. Picture Editor: Steve Brown. Sports picture library. Has approximately 3 million photos. Clients include advertising agencies, public relations firms, audiovisual firms, businesses, book/encyclopedia publishers, magazine publishers, newspapers, postcard companies, calendar companies and greeting card companies.
Subject Needs: All types of sport and leisure.
Specs: Uses 35mm transparencies.
Payment & Terms: Pays 50% commission for photos. Captions preferred.
Making Contact: Send unsolicited photos by mail for consideration. SASE. Reports in 1 month. Distributes a tip sheet monthly to all contracted freelancers. Free for SASE.

SPORTSLIGHT PHOTO, Suite 205, 1202 Lexington Ave., New York NY 10028. (212)996-8926. Director: Roderick Beebe. Stock photo agency. Has 25,000 photos, 5 films. Clients include: ad agencies, public relations firms, businesses, book/encyclopedia publishers, magazine publishers, newspapers, postcard companies, calendar companies, greeting card companies, design firms and sports marketing/ promotion agencies.
Subject Needs: We specialize in every sport in the world. We deal primarily in the recreational sports such as skiing, golf, tennis, running, canoeing, etc., but are expanding into pro sports, and have needs for all pro sports, action and candid close-ups of top athletes. We also handle adventure-travel photos, e.g., rafting in Chile, trekking in Nepal, dogsledding in the Arctic, etc.
Specs: Uses 35mm and 2¼ × 2¼ transparencies.
Payment & Terms: Pays 50% commission on color photos. General price range: $70-3,000. Offers one-time rights, rights depend on client, sometimes exclusive rights for a period of time. Model release required for corporate and advertising usage, captions required. (Obtain releases whenever possible).
Making Contact: Query with list of stock photo subjects, "send samples after our response." SASE must be included. Reports in 2-4 weeks. Photo guideline sheet free with SASE.
Tips: "Well edited, perfect exposure and sharpness, good composition and lighting in all photos. Seeking photographers with strong interests in particular sports. Shoot variety of action, singles and groups, youths, male/female—all combinations. Plus leisure, relaxing after tennis, lunch on the ski slope, golf's 19th hole, etc. Clients are looking for all sports these days. All ages, also. Sports fashions change rapidly, so that is a factor. Art direction of photo shoots is important. Avoid brand names and minor flaws in the look of clothing. Attention to detail is very important. Shoot with concepts/ideas such as teamwork, determination, success, lifestyle, leisure, cooperation and more in mind. Clients not only look for individual sports, but for photos to illustrate a mood or idea."

■TOM STACK & ASSOCIATES, Suite 212, 3645 Jeannine Dr., Colorado Springs CO 80917. (719)570-1000. Contact: Jamie Stack. Has 900,000 photos. Member: Picture Agency Council of America. Clients include ad agencies, public relations firms, businesses, audiovisual firms, book publishers, magazine publishers, encyclopedia publishers, postcard companies, calendar companies and greeting card companies. Does not buy outright; pays 60% commission. General price range: $150-200/color; as high as

$7,000. Offers one-time rights, all rights or first rights. Model release and captions preferred. Query with list of stock photo subjects or send at least 800 transparencies for consideration. SASE or mailer for photos. Reports in 2 weeks. Photo guidelines with SASE.

Subject Needs: Wildlife, endangered species, marine-life, landscapes, foreign geography, people and customs, children, sports, abstract, arty and moody shots, plants and flowers, photomicrography, scientific research, current events and political figures, Indians, etc. Especially needs women in "men's" occupations; whales; solar heating; up-to-date transparencies of foreign countries and people; smaller mammals such as weasels, moles, shrews, fisher, marten, etc.; extremely rare endangered wildlife; wildlife behavior photos; current sports; lightning and tornadoes; hurricane damage. Sharp images, dramatic and unusual angles and approach to composition, creative and original photography with impact. Especially needs photos on life science flora and fauna and photomicrography. No run-of-the-mill travel or vacation shots. Special needs include photos of energy-related topics—solar and wind generators, recycling, nuclear power and coal burning plants, waste disposal and landfills, oil and gas drilling, supertankers, electric cars, geo-thermal energy.

Color: Uses 35mm transparencies.

Tips: "Strive to be original, creative and take an unusual approach to the commonplace; do it in a different and fresh way." Have need for "more action and behavioral requests for wildlife. We are large enough to market worldwide and yet small enough to be personable. Don't get lost in the 'New York' crunch—try us. Use Kodachromes and Kodak processing. Competition is too fierce to go with anything less. Shoot quantity. We try harder to keep our photographers happy. We attempt to turn new submissions around within 2 weeks. We take on only the best, and so that we can continue to give more effective service, we have doubled our office space and hired new personnel to keep our efficiency."

*■STILLS, 3288 Marjan Drive, Atlanta GA 30340. (404)451-6749. FAX: (404)451-7957. Managing Editor: Tom Quinn. Estab. 1980. Stock photo agency. Clients include advertising agencies, public relations firms, audiovisual firms, businesses, book/encyclopedia publishers, magazine publishers newspapers, postcard companies, calendar companies, greeting card companies and graphic design firms.

Subject Needs: Needs photos of agriculture, animals, architecture, arts & crafts, celebrations and events, disasters, entertainment, flora, food, history, holidays, industry, medical/scientific, occupations, people (lifestyles), recreation, scenics, signs, skyscapes, special effects, sports, still life, textures, transportation, weapons, U.S., Atlanta and international countries. ("Would like to see southern styles, different points-of-view, and strong 90's conceptual images.")

Specs: Uses 35mm, 2¼×2¼, 4×5, 8×10 + 70mm +120 format transparencies.

Payment & Terms: Pays 50% commission on photos. Offers one-time rights. General price range: $150-3,000, "based on subject matter & specific usage." Model releases and photo captions required.

Making Contact: Arrange a personal interview to show portfolio; submit portfolio for review. SASE. Reports in 1 month. Photo guidelines free with SASE. Tips sheet distributed bimonthly to professional photographers.

Tips: In freelancer's portfolio, wants to see "minimum of 250 images (accepting a broad range of subjects). Looking for unique people and corporate photos. Looking for images with a new, unique point-of-view. Less emphasis on scenics, unless spectacular." Trends in stock include increased demand for "family-oriented images, environmental concerns and high-tech looks in computers and science (ie. superconductivity)."

*■STOCK BOSTON INC., 36 Gloucester St., Boston MA 02115. (617)266-2300. Manager of Editing: Jean Howard. Estab. 1970. Stock photo agency. Clients include advertising agencies, public relations firms, audiovisual firms, businesses, book/encyclopedia publishers, magazine publishers, newspapers, postcard companies, calendar companies and greeting card companies.

Subject Needs: "We seek pictures of real people in their everyday lives. Technical quality must be excellent, model releases are preferred."

Specs: Uses 8×10 b&w prints; 35mm, 2¼×2¼, 4×5, 8×10 transparencies.

Payment & Terms: Pays 50% on b&w and color photos. General price range: $175-up. Offers one-time rights. Model release and photo captions preferred.

Making Contact: Send SASE for information. SASE. Reports in 1 week. Photo guidelines available on acceptance. Tips sheet distributed quarterly to contributors.

Tips: In freelancers' portfolio or samples, wants to see "a representative sample of the type of work they typically shoot: 50-100 b&w prints, 100-200 transparencies. Please request more information." Trends in stock include "a swing away from the bland, over-lit studio set-up and move towards a realistic approach. B&w still does quite well at Stock Boston, particularly in the editorial market."

Close-up

Richard Steedman
President
The Stock Market, Inc.
New York City

According to stock agency owner Richard Steedman, success in the always competitive stock photography business can be found by reading the "signs of the times." And, as the president of The Stock Market points out, there's no better place for photographers to find them than in "the mirror of American advertising."

The signs Steedman refers to are the symbols of society's collective values which are all around us but often taken for granted and not verbalized. As he notes, symbols are especially powerful motivators exactly because they are nonverbal and influence people at the unconscious, emotional level. Naturally, he adds, advertising thrives on this kind of motivation, and that's where you'll always find symbolism being used.

"Check out the evening news on TV, newspapers and magazines," says Steedman, noting that many of his agency's clients are among these primary markets. "When you study all the ads of business, you'll notice that they are loaded with symbolic value. Most products need something to help them sell because they are not unique in themselves. Advertising tries to find an appeal, and this is why most products are sold on an emotional basis. The smart photographer is aware of this and tries to work symbolic content into his images."

Anything—a color, an object, a person—can be a symbol. However, as Steedman explains, symbols never have meaning in themselves but acquire their value through social consensus or agreement. Christmas trees, piggy banks, and teddy bears, for instance, all have obvious cultural meanings. A sandy beach, a popping bottle of champagne and a dark blue, pinstripe suit are images which conjure specific meanings yet are open to personal interpretation. On the other hand, symbols such as a national flag are deeply rooted in society's values and convey a much more profound, universal meaning. "George Bush understood the power of symbolism," Steedman observes, noting the influence of symbols upon our national identity. "He got himself elected president by wrapping himself in the American Flag."

Certainly, nostalgia and Americana, have widespread appeal among clients of stock photo agencies, says Steedman. For instance, he notes that sports are very much a part of the national mentality in the U.S., and so this often spills over into other areas. As he explains, images of sports—and the underlying themes of competition and teamplaying—are frequently used as metaphors for success.

Objects, locations and situations all have meanings in and of themselves, says Steedman. A hot dog calls to mind the national pastime, and a back porch or a country kitchen suggests a simpler time. But new meanings can also be created by using simple images and adding a twist. "You can take an ordinary object and put it into a different context to change meaning," he remarks. Pointing out an example from an actual print ad, he explains how a hammer by itself suggests 'work.' Then, he describes how the ad showed the hammer with a screw, remarking that it doesn't quite seem to fit, till you add a slogan . . . "The wrong tool for the job." Then, he explains, the symbols are modified for a particular client's needs.

While photographers can manipulate symbols for a specific client in this way, the real potential for them in stock sales is in creating symbols and themes which have high resale value, says Steedman. Accordingly, photographers should pay close attention to both established symbols and new meanings emerging from the numerous cultural trends of the next decade. Among these trends, he notes, are the aging of the Baby Boom generation; the expanding role of women in the workplace; the impact of international affairs upon national pride and identity; the widespread use of technology in the workplace; the growing emphasis upon family and interpersonal bonding; and a shift to basic values. Many products and services will be targeted to specific segments of the population on the basis of these trends, says Steedman, and so the alert stock photographer should be gearing his images for such uses.

Learning the language of symbols—for the photographer and the social scientist alike—is not a random process but a deliberate study of cultural values, social trends and human behavior, says Steedman. This study even has a formal, academic name: semiotics. Though he admits such a study is "a vast, complex, lifetime pursuit," he points out that even a casual familiarity with semiotics provides photographers with insight into crafting profitable images. "A photographer cannot work in a vacuum," Steedman advises. "He must create images that speak to people's values. If a photographer is unaware of symbolic communication or chooses to ignore its potential, it will limit his success."

—Sam A. Marshall

---

*■THE STOCK MARKET, 1181 Broadway, New York NY 10001. (212)684-7878. Contact: Sally Lloyd/ Kelly Foster. Estab. 1981. Stock photo agency. Has 1,600,000. Clients include advertising agencies, public relations firms, audiovisual firms, businesses, book/encyclopedia publishers, magazine publishers, newspapers, postcard companies, calendar companies and greeting card companies.
Specs: Uses color, any format; 35mm transparencies.
Payment & Terms: Pays 50% gross sale on color photos. General price range: $20,000-250,000. Offers one-time rights and first rights. Model release and photo captions required.
Making Contact: Arrange a personal interview to show portfolio; query with samples; submit portfolio for review. SASE. Reports in 2-3 weeks. Tips sheet distributed as needed to contract photographers only.

*■STOCK OPTIONS, 4602 East Side Ave., Dallas TX 75226. (214)826-6262. Owner: Karen Hughes. Estab. 1985. Stock photo agency. Has 25,000 photos. Clients include advertising agencies, public relations firms, audiovisual firms, businesses, book/encyclopedia, magazine publishers, newspapers, post card companies, calendar companies and greeting card companies.
Subject Needs: Emphasizes the southern US. Files include Gulf Coast scenics, wildlife, fishing, festivals, food, industry, business, people, etc. Also western folklore.
Specs: Uses 35mm, 2¼ × 2¼ and 4 × 5transparencies.
Payment & Terms: Pays 50% commission on b&w or color photos. General price range: $300-1,500. Offers one-time rights. Model release and photo captions preferred.
Making Contact: Arrange a personal interview to show portfolio; query with list of stock photo subjects. Deals with local freelancers only. SASE. Reports in 1 month. Tips sheet distributed annually to all photographers.
Tips: Wants to see "clean, in focus, relevant and current materials." Current stock requests include: elderly, environmental subjects, people in up-beat situations and food.

*■STOCK PHOTOS, Castello 124 2° "C", Madrid Spain 28006. (1)564-4095. FAX: (1)564-4353. Director: Marcelo Brodsky. Estab. 1988. Stock photo agency and news/feature syndicate. Has 100,000 photos. Clients include advertising agencies, audiovisual firms, businesses, book/encyclopedia publishers, magazine publishers and newspapers.

Subject Needs: Stock photography for advertising with model released people, top quality magazine stories with short text and people.

Specs: "We specialize in advertising in our ad section and we also handle magazine photography in our editorial section." Uses 35mm, b&w prints; 35mm, 2¼ × 2¼, 4 × 5, 8 × 10 transparencies.

Payment & Terms: Pays 50% commission on color photos. General price range: Minimum $90-1,500. Offers one-time rights. Model release required for advertising materials.

Making Contact: Query with samples. Reports in 3 weeks. Tips sheet distributed once a year to working photographers; free with SASE.

Tips: Looks for "transparencies of technical excellence, professionalism in producing stock and knowledge of the needs of this market, whether editorial or advertising. We need high tech imagery, high tech stories/reportage for mags, pictures with models, teenagers, people consuming, people doing their professions, medicine, etc. Portraits of celebrities have another area of the market and we also sell them very well in Spain."

■**STOCK PILE, INC.**, Main office: 2404 N. Charles St., Baltimore MD 21218. (301)889-4243. Branch: Box 15384, Rio Rancho NM 87174. (505)892-7288. Vice President: D.B. Cooper. 28,000 library. Clients include ad agencies, art studios, slide show producers, etc.

Subject Needs: General agency looking for well-lit, properly composed images that will attract attention. Also, people, places and things that lend themselves to an advertising-oriented marketplace.

Specs: Transparencies, all formats. Some black and white, 8 × 10 glossies.

Payment & Terms: Pays 50% commison on b&w and color photos. Offers one-time rights. Model release preferred; captions required.

Making Contact: Inquire for guidelines, submit directly (minimum 100), or call for personal interview. All inquiries and submissions must be accompanied by SASE. *Send all submissions to New Mexico address.*

Tips: Periodic newsletter sent to all regular contributing photographers.

***THE STOCK SHOP**, 232 Madison Ave., New York NY 10016. (212)679-8480. FAX: (212)532-1934. President: Barbara Gottlieb. Estab. 1975. Has 2,000,000 photos. Clients include advertising agencies, public relations firms; businesses, book/encyclopedia publishers, magazine publishers, postcard companies, calendar companies and greeting card companies.

Subject Needs: Needs photos of travel, industry and medicine. Also model released life-style including old age, couples, babies, men, women, families.

Specs: Uses 35mm, 2¼ × 2¼, 4 × 5 and 8 × 10 transparencies.

Payment & Terms: Pays 50% commission on color photos. General price range: $150 and up. Model release preferred; photo captions required.

Making Contact: Arrange a personal interview to show portfolio; submit portfolio for review. SASE. Tips sheet distributed as needed to contract photographers only.

Tips: Wants to see "a cross section of the style and subjects the photographer has in his library. 200-300 samples should tell the story. Photographers should have at least 1,000 in his library. Photographers should not photograph people *before* getting a model release. The day of the 'grab shot' is over."

THE STOCK SOLUTION, 307 W. 200 South, #3004, Salt Lake City UT 84101. (801)363-9700. FAX: (801)363-9707. President: Royce Bair. Stock photo agency. Has 100,000 photos. Clients include ad agencies, businesses, book/encyclopedia and magazine publishers, calendar companies and design studios.

Subject Needs: Leisure, outdoor recreation, business, finance, industry, health/medical, education, family/children, national parks, major cities, commerce, transportation. Nature and scenics only on a limited basis.

Specs: Uses 35mm, 2¼ × 2¼, 4 × 5 and 8 × 10 transparencies; also 8 × 10 b&w prints.

Payment & Terms: Pays 50% commission on color photos. General price range: $250-500; "minimum usually $150, maximum is unlimited." Offers one-time rights; occasionally, one-year exclusives for advertising or calendar. Model release preferred; captions required after selecting photos.

Making Contact: Query with resume of credits, samples, list of stock photo subjects; submit portfolio for review. SASE. Reports in 2 weeks. Photo guidelines free with SASE. Tips sheet sent quarterly free to contract photographers; $3 for inquiring, non-contract photographers.

Tips: "We can usually determine with a portfolio of only 100 slides if we want to represent a photographer. We actively seek photographers who photograph people in real-life situations of home, family and work, but who are willing to take the extra effort necessary to prop and light the scene in order to make it more salable to today's demanding clients in advertising and publishing. Does not require exclusive contract, but offers worldwide representation if requested. Offers photo foxing system for greater distribution of b&w photos (in half tone form)."

*■THE STOCKHOUSE, INC., Box 741008, Houston TX 77274. (713)796-8400. FAX: (713)796-8047. Sales and Marketing Director: Celia Jumonville. Stock photo agency. Has 500,000 photos. Clients include advertising agencies, public relations firms, audiovisual firms, businesses, book/encyclopedia publishers, magazine publishers, newspapers, postcard companies, calendar companies and greeting card companies.

Subject Needs: Needs photos of general topics from travel to industry, lifestyles, nature, US and foreign countries. Especially interested in Texas and petroleum and medical.

Specs: Uses 35mm, 2¼×2¼, 4×5, 8×10 transparencies; "originals only."

Payment & Terms: Pays 50% commission on color photos. General price range: $150-1,000. Offers one-time rights; other rights negotiable. Model release preferred; photographer retains written release. Photo captions required.

Making Contact: Query with samples; request guidlines and tipsheet. SASE. Photo guidelines free with SASE. Tips sheet distributed quarterly to contract photographers.

Tips: In freelancers' samples, wants to see "quality of photos-color saturation, focus and composition. Also variety of subjects and 200-300 transparencies on the first submission. Trends in stock vary depending on the economy and who is needing photos. Quality is the first consideration and subject second. We do not limit the subjects submitted since we never know what will be requested next. Industry and lifestyles and current skylines are always good choices." (Submissions send to 9261 Kirby Dr. Houston TX 77054.)

■STOCKPHOTOS INC., 373 Park Avenue South, New York NY 10016. (212)686-1196. General Manager: Ken Eichler. Has 1,000,000 transparencies. Clients include ad agencies, corporate publishing, public relations firms, audiovisual companies, book publishers, magazine and newspaper publishers, encyclopedia and textbook publishers, poster and greeting card companies, record cover and television companies, and private businesses. Exclusively marketed by the Image Bank through over 50 offices worldwide.

Subject Needs: "We have no limitation on subject matter. Practically every possible picture subject is covered: people, glamour, nudes, industry and science, travel, scenics, sports and nature. Our most popular subjects are people (at work, at play, children, teenagers, women, men, couples, families, and the elderly), and industry (high-tech, computers, office scenes, communications, oil, steel, manufacturing, and transport). We are looking for creative photographers with innovative, dynamic styles and a willingness to take direction. Needs professional and amateur sports; international and world scenics."

Specs: Accepts original transparencies, all formats.

Payment & Terms: Does not buy outright; pays 50% commission. Fees for sales are negotiated on the basis of usage, print run, territory, insertions and distribution. Also handles assignments for photographers under contract.

Making Contact: Send material by mail for consideration or submit portfolio for review. Portfolio should be sent to the ATTN of Lauren Wendley, Director of Photography, %The Image Bank, 1115th Ave., New York NY 10003.

Tips: "Portfolios should contain between 150 and 300 original transparencies that are representative of your photographic interests and that are appropriate to our markets. Portfolios will be promptly returned with an appraisal of your photographs and their marketability. We are always interested in working with energetic and creative photographers."

SUMMIT PHOTOFILE, 2037 Rhine Court, Kissimmee FL 34741-3435. FAX: (407)933-1292. Manager: Jay Jacobson. Stock photo agency. Clients include ad agencies, book/encyclopedia publishers, magazine publishers, newspapers, calendar companies, government agencies and paper products producers. Previous/current clients include: Appleton & Lange, magazine covers, people, abstracts, scenics; Hallmark Cards, scenics, greeting cards; and Reader Digest Books, editorial, travel destinations.

Subject Needs: Travel destinations, industrial, sports and activities, occupational, scenic, abstract and lifestyle. "We have a continuing need for photos of everyday activities involving minority children and families."

Specs: Color transparencies, from 35mm to 4×5 ("Larger sizes no longer seem to have an advantage—35mm has become the standard for most markets"). Sometimes uses color negatives ("We make slides from negatives, then return negs to photographer").

Payment & Terms: Pays 50% commission on all sales (gross receipts). General price range: $50-2,000. Offers one-time rights for most uses ("Sales for magazine covers, greeting cards, and calendars usually specify a one-year exclusive for the particular use"). Usually one-time nonexclusive; negotiated individually. Model release required "for all recognizable individuals." Captions required.

Making Contact: Query with SASE for free guidelines.

Tips: "Before shooting any subject, consider the potential markets. Desert scenes, however remarkable they might look, rarely sell. Flowers, blue skies, smiling faces—subjects that evoke a positive mood—appeal to many (and more lucrative) markets. One theme that always sells well is 'mood/inspirational': sunbeams, rainbows, children with puppies, improbably fabulous sunsets. Maintain the highest standards—our clients insist on technical excellence, and captions must be accurate and complete. We are very interested in working with new talent."

*SUOMEN KUVAPALVELU OY, 00241, Helsinki, Finland. 15661. Managing Director: Jolyon Tigerstedt. Stock photo agency, picture library and news/feature syndicate. Has about 5,000,000 photos. Clients include advertising agencies, book/encyclopedia publishers, and magazine publishers.
Payment & Terms: Pays 30-70% commission for b&w and color photos. General price range: $80-1,000. Offers one-time or first rights. Model release and captions preferred.
Making Contact: Query with samples. Send unsolicited photos by mail for consideration. SASE. Reports in 2 weeks.

■SUPERSTOCK INC./SUPERSTOCK CATALOG, (formerly Superstock International/Superstock Catalog), 11 W. 19th St., New York NY 10011. (212)633-0708. Director of Photographer Relations: Jane Stoffo. Stock photo agency. Has more than 300,000 photos in file. Clients include ad agencies, public relations firms, audiovisual firms, businesses, book/encyclopedia publishers, magazine publishers, newspapers, postcard companies, calendar companies, greeting card companies and major corporations.
Subject Needs: "We are a general stock agency involved in all markets, our files are comprised of all subject matter."
Specs: Uses 35mm, 2¼ × 2¼, 4 × 5 and 8 × 10 transparencies.
Payment & Terms: "We work on a contract basis." Checks and statements sent monthly. Statement reflects previous months sales. Rights offered "varies, depending on client's request." Model release and photo captions required. Query with resume of credits; query with tearsheets only; query with list of stock photo subjects; submit portfolio for review "when requested." SASE. Reports in 3 weeks. Photo guidelines sheet free with SASE or sent if requested via phone. Newsletter distributed monthly to contracted photographers.
Tips: Photographers can participate in Superstock Catalog to promote their work. "The use of catalogs as a buying source is a very effective means of promoting photographs, and a continuing trend in the industry is the importance of bigger, comprehensive catalogs. We distribute the SuperStock Photo Catalog in the US. Space is available to professional photographers regardless of any of their other photographic affiliations. Participation in this catalog provides an excellent opportunity for photographers to take advantage of the growing international market for stock, and receive the highest royalty percentage for internationally distributed photographs."

*■TAKE STOCK INC., 705, 603 7th Avenue SW, Calgary, AB T2P 2T5 Canada. (403)233-7487. FAX: (403)265-4061. Vice President: Helen Grenon. Estab. 1987. Stock photo agency. Clients include advertising agencies, public relations firms, audiovisual firms, business, book/encyclopedia publishers, magazine publishers, newpapers, postcard companies, calendar companies and greeting card companies.
Subject Needs: Model released people (all ages), Canadian images, arts/recreation, industry/occupation, business, hi-tech.
Specs: Uses 35mm, 2¼ × 2¼, 4 × 5, 8 × 10 transparencies. Prefer medium to large format.
Payment & Terms: Pays 50% commission on color transparencies. General price range: $75-600. Offers one-time rights, exclusive rights. Model release and photo caption required.
Making Contact: Query with list of stock photo subjects. SASE. Reports in 3 weeks. Photo guidelines free with SASE. Tips sheet distributed monthly to photographers on file.

TANK INCORPORATED, Box 212, Shinjuku, Tokyo 160-91, Japan. (03)239-1431. Telex: 26347 PHT-PRESS. FAX: 03230-3668.President: Masayoshi Seki. Has 500,000 slides. Clients include advertising agencies, book publishers, magazine publishers, encyclopedia publishers and newspapers.
Subject Needs: "Women in various situations, families, special effect and abstract, nudes, scenic, sports, animal, celebrities, flowers, picture stories with texts, humorous photos, etc."
Specs: Uses 8 × 10 b&w prints; 35mm, 2¼ × 2¼ and 4 × 5 slides; b&w contact sheets.
Payment & Terms: Pays 60% commission on b&w and color photos. General price range: $70-1,000. Offers one-time rights. Captions required.
Making Contact: Query with samples; with list of stock photo subjects or send unsolicited material by mail for consideration. SAE, IRCs. Reports in 1 month. Photo guidelines free with International Reply Coupons.
Tips: "We need some pictures or subjects which strike viewers. Pop or rock musicians are very much in demand. If you want to make quick sales, give us some story ideas with sample pictures which show quality, and we will respond to you very quickly. Also, give us brief bio. Color transparencies with sample stories to accompany. No color print at all. Stock photography business requires patience. Try to find some other subjects than your competitors. Keep a fresh mind to see salable subjects."

■TAURUS PHOTOS INC., 118 E. 28th St., New York NY 10016. (212)683-4025. Photo Editor: Jim Pearson. Has 500,000 photos. Clients include ad agencies, public relations firms, businesses, audiovisual firms, book publishers, magazine publishers, encyclopedia publishers and newspapers.
Specs: Uses 8 × 10 b&w prints and transparencies.
Tips: "Looking for top-notch photographers. Photographers interested in being represented by Taurus should submit a portfolio of 100 transparencies and b&w prints for evaluation along with information about the type of material which they are able to shoot. An evaluation will be returned to you. A self-addressed stamped return envelope is necessary for this step. Beautiful photos of American life, e.g., family, industry, business are particularly welcome."

*■TELEGRAPH COLOUR LIBRARY, Unit C1, Enterprise Business Estate, Mastmaker Rd., London E14 9TE England. 01-987-0121. Director of Photography: Tim Lund. Stock photo agency. Has 100,000 photos. Clients include ad agencies, public relations firms, audiovisual firms, businesses, book/encyclopedia publishers, magazine publishers, postcard companies, calendar companies and greeting card companies.
Subject Needs: Handles people (business and leisure), industry, technology, transport, travel, scenics, animals and sport.
Specs: Uses 35mm, 2¼ × 2¼ or 4 × 5 transparencies.
Payment & Terms: Pays 50/40% commission. General price range: £80-2,000. Buys one-time rights. Model release and photo captions required.
Making Contact: Query with list of stock photo subjects. SASE. Reports in 2 weeks. Photo guidelines sheet free with SASE. Tips sheet distributed quarterly to agency photographers.
Tips: Looks for "clean, colorful, bright commercial images. Clients are becoming more demanding. Successful images are usually those taken specifically for stock."

■TELEPHOTO, 8 Thomas St., New York NY 10007. (212)406-2440. FAX: 964-8027. Contact: Martin Rubenstein. Stock photo agency. Has 300,000 photos. Clients include advertising agencies, public relations firms, audiovisual firms, businesses, book/encyclopedia and magazine publishers, newspapers, postcard, calendar and greeting card companies, and design firms.
Subject Needs: Telephoto is a general interest stock photo agency seeking top-quality photographs from talented individuals worldwide, whether professional or amateur. We are currently seeking model-released lifestyle photography of children, families, romantic couples from teenage to old age, pretty girls, handsome men, grandparents; in all combinations, at work, doing sports and hobbies, and pursuing leisure-time activities. Also, model-released corporate, industrial, and computer graphics images. We are constantly seeking exceptional nature/scenic/travel/lifestyle images. Also, animals, both domestic and wild.
Specs: Uses 35mm, 2¼ × 2¼, 4 × 5, 6 × 7 and 8 × 10 transparencies. "We do not accept b&w."
Payment & Terms: Has not bought photos outright, but would consider. Pays 50% commission. General price range $100-5,000. Negotiates rights depending on needs of client and wishes of photographer. "There has been an increasing trend toward buy-outs in the advertising field. Telephoto respects the photographer's wishes in this area." Model release preferred; captions required.
Making Contact: Arrange a personal interview to show portfolio; query with resume of credits and list of stock photo subjects; submit portfolio for review. SASE. Reports in 1 month. Tips sheet sent to contract photographers.
Tips: "We constantly seek new material in all areas from talented photographers regardless of professional experience. Photographers should not hesitate to call to discuss their work with us. Sending unsolicited photos by mail is not advised. Please call or write for submission guidelines."

TERRAPHOTOGRAPHICS/BPS, Box 490, Moss Beach CA 94038. (415)726-6244. Photo Agent: Carl May. Stock photo agency. Has 25,000 photos on hand; 70,000 on short notice. Clients include ad agencies, businesses, book/encyclopedia publishers and magazine publishers. Previous/current clients: Silver Burdett & Ginn, various geological subjects, school science series; Wagner & Teldon, scenics of Midwest and Middle Atlantic states, calendars; and National Geographic Special Projects, Hawaiian volcano, pelicans, Devil's Tower, trade book on national parks.
Subject Needs: All subjects in the Earth sciences: paleontology, volcanology, seismology, petrology, oceanography, climatology, mining, petroleum industry, civil engineering, meteorology, astronomy. Stock photographers must be scientists. Currently, we need more on the processing of various ores, both natural and cut gems, economic minerals, and good photos of microbial processes (such as leach

■ *The solid, black square before a listing indicates that the market uses various types of audiovisual materials, such as slides, film or videotape.*

piles) in mining. Environmental problems associated with industry are hot topics. Much more needed from the Third World, USSR, and formerly Communist coutries.

Specs: Uses 8×10 glossy b&w prints; 35mm, $2\frac{1}{4} \times 2\frac{1}{4}$, 4×5 and 8×10 transparencies.

Payment & Terms: Pays 50% commission on color photos. General price range: $70-350. Offers one-time rights; other rights negotiable. Model release and captions required for non-educational uses.

Making Contact: Query with list, and resume of scientific and photographic background. SASE. Reports in 2 weeks. Photo guidelines free with query and SASE. Tips sheet distributed intermittently only to stock photographers.

Tips: Prefers to see proper exposure, maximum depth of field, interesting composition, good technical and general information in caption. Natural disasters of all sorts, especially volcanic eruptions, storms and earthquakes; scientists at work using modern equipment. "We are a suitable agency only for those with both photographic skills and sufficient technical expertise to identify subject matter. Captions must be neat and contain precise information on geographical locations. Don't waste your time submitting images on grainy film. Photos should be of professional photographic quality but of subjects only an Earth scientist would know enough to shoot. Our photographers should be able to distinguish between dramatic, compelling examples of phenomena and run-of-the-mill images. We need more on all sorts of weather phenomena; the petroleum and mining industries from exploration through refinement; problems and management of toxic wastes; environmental problems associated with resource development; natural areas threatened by development; and oceanography."

■**THIRD COAST STOCK SOURCE**, Box 92397, Milwaukee WI 53202. (414)765-9442. Director: Paul Henning. Managing Editor: Mary Ann Platts. Research Manager: Paul Butterbrodt. Has over 100,000 photos. Clients include: ad agencies, public relations firms, audiovisual firms, corporations, book/encyclopedia publishers, magazine publishers, newspapers, calendar companies and greeting card companies.

Subject Needs: Needs images specifically relating to the Third Coast region (Ohio, Minnesota, Wisconsin, Illinois, Iowa, Michigan, Indiana) lifestyles, business, industry, points of interest. Also needs photos of other regions of the country and overseas.

Specs: Uses 35mm, $2\frac{1}{4} \times 2\frac{1}{4}$, 4×5 and 8×10 transparencies (Kodachrome or Fujichrome 50 preferred).

Payment & Terms: Pays 50% commission. General price range: $200 and up. Offers one-time rights. Model release preferred; captions required.

Making Contact: Submit 200-300 images for review. SASE. Reports in 1 month. Photo guidelines free with SASE. Tips sheet distributed 4 times/year to "photographers currently working with us."

Tips: "We are looking for technical expertise; outstanding, dramatic and emotional appeal; photos representative of life in this region. We are extremely anxious to look at new work. Do your homework. Learn what stock photography is all about. Educate yourself before submitting work and then submit only that which is saleable, stock photography. Our biggest need is for photos of model released people; couples, seniors, business situations, recreational situations, etc. Also, we find it very difficult to get great winter activity scenes (again, with people) and photos which illustrate holidays: Christmas, Thanksgiving, Easter, etc."

■**THE TRAVEL IMAGE**, Box 9550, Marina Del Rey CA 90295. (213)823-3439. President: Greg Wenger. Has 300,000 photos and growing. Clients include ad agencies, editorial, public relations and audiovisual firms, businesses, book/encyclopedia and magazine publishers, newspapers and wholesale tour operators. Previous/current clients: SFA Adv. Conn., travel photos, Europe, UK, travel books; Halsey Publications, inflight magazines, travel articles; and Zaner, Bloser Publishers, text books, China Mongolia, Silk Route.

Subject Needs: "Travel photos—popular tourist destinations, leisure activities."

Specs: Original color; 35mm, $2\frac{1}{4} \times 2\frac{1}{4}$ and 4×5 transparencies.

Payment & Terms: Pays 50% commission on sale. Model release, captions and subject ID required. Offers one time rights.

Making Contact: By mail, request "guidelines" must include SASE.

Tips: "Best-sellers are strong in color and composition. Looks for quality images in volume of popular destinations worldwide on an ongoing basis. People-oriented subjects, scenics and activities. The US has become a travel destination for more countries. Good photos of U.S. vacation spots are in demand, as well as the Orient, Southeast Asia, Oceana, South America, Europe, Eastern Europe, Russia and Caribbean. Be prepared to commit to a great deal of time, energy creativity—and film. Submit samples by mail after requestion our guidelines."

*****TRAVEL PHOTO INTERNATIONAL**, 8 Delph Common Rd., Aughton NR Ormskirk, Lancashire L39 5DW United Kingdom 0695 423720. Director: Mrs. V. Crimes. Picture library. Has 200,000 photos. Clients include advertising agencies, tour operators, book/encyclopedia publishers, magazine publishers and calendar companies.

Subject Needs: Travel photos covering worldwide locations.

Specs: Uses 35mm, 2¼ × 2¼, and 4 × 5 transparencies.

Payment & Terms: Pays 50% commission on color photos. General price range: £20-£1,000. Offers one-time rights. Model release preferred; captions required.

Making Contact: Submit portfolio for review: must include return postage and packing. SASE. Reports in 1 week. Distributes tip sheet once a year to contributors free with SASE.

Tips: Prefers "critical sharpness, clear sunlight, salable subjects, good composition, good color saturation and *perfect* exposure. Standards have risen sharply and our reputation relies on our very high standards. Only shots taken on crystal clear sunny days have any real hope of sales today."

TSW/AFTERIMAGE, INC., (formerly Afterimage, Inc.), Suite 240, 6100 Wilshire Blvd., Los Angeles CA 90048. (213)938-1700. FAX: (213)938-0731. Interested in all subjects, particularly color photos of model released contemporary people. Sells to advertising and editorial clients. Pays 50% commission. Photographers must have a review. Send SASE for submission guidelines.

Tips: Needs "dynamic action shots of wild animals, especially mammals."

UNICORN STOCK PHOTO LIBRARY, 5400 NW 86th Terrace, Kansas City MO 64154. (816)587-4131. President/Owner: Betts Anderson. Has 80,000 color slides. Clients include ad agencies, corporate accounts, magazines, textbooks, calendars and religious publishers.

Subject Needs: Ordinary people of all ages and races doing everyday things: at home, school, work and play; current skylines of all major cities; tourist attractions, historical; wildlife; seasonal and holidays and religious subjects. Particularly need shots showing 2 or more races represented in one photo and family scenes with both parents. There is a critical need for more minority shots.

Specs: Uses 35mm color slides.

Payment & Terms: Pays 50% commission. General price range: $50-400. Offers one-time rights. Model releases are preferred and increase opportunities for sales and fro higher fees. Captions are an absolute necessity.

Making Contact & Terms: "We are looking for professionals who understand this business and will provide a steady supply of top-quality images. At least 300 images are required to open a file. Information package available for $10.00."

Tips: "We keep in close, personal contact with all our photographers. Our monthly newsletter is a very popular medium for keeping in touch. Our biggest need is for minorities and interracial shots. Because UNICORN is in the Midwest, we have many requests for framing/gardening/agriculture/winter and general scenics of the Midwest.

■**VISIONS PHOTO, INC.**, 220 W. 19th St., New York NY 10011. (212)255-4047. FAX: (212)206-0238. Editorial Director: Julie Ades. Stock photo agency and news/feature syndicate. Has 300,000 photos. Clients include public relations firms, audiovisual firms, designers, book/encyclopedia publishers, magazine publishers, newspapers and advertising agencies.

Subject Needs: "VISIONS is a news and feature photographic agency distributing material internationally. The majority of material is feature-oriented as opposed to 'hard' news or stock photography. Subject matter deals with lifestyle, social and political concerns, science, business and industry around the world. Emphasis is placed on thorough, photojournalistic coverage of a region or issue."

Specs: Uses 8 × 10 b&w prints 35mm; 2¼ × 2¼ transparencies; b&w contact sheets and negatives.

Payment & Terms: General price range: "Reproduction rights begin at $175/quarter page publication." Offers one-time, first and other rights when appropriate. Model release preferred; photo captions required.

Making Contact: Arrange a personal interview to show portfolio or query with resume of credits. Submit portfolio for review by appointment only. SASE. Reports monthly. Generally portfolio reviews are conducted in person.

Tips: Looks for "strong emphasis on reportage in black/white and color, and a completed photo essay. Photo requests reflect recent political and economic trends—photos of consumer life world-wide, industrial and economic conditions internationally."

*****VISUAL IMAGES WEST, INC.**, 600 East Baseline B6, Tempe AZ 85283. (602)820-5403. Photo Director: Jude Westake. Estab. 1985. Stock photo agency. Clients include advertising agencies, public-relations firms, businesses, book/encyclopedia publishers, magazine publishers, and newspapers. Previous/current clients: Richard Alan Medical, MI, cowboy shot used on corporation invitation; Best-western, AZ, S.F. Bay Bridge & Still Life of Poker Chips, Trade mag.; and U.S. Sprint, KS, Desert sunset (4 × 5) Corp, international poster.

Subject Needs: Needs photos of southwestern lifestyles and scenics. Also general travel and model-released lifestyles.
Specs: Uses 2¼ up to 4×5 transparencies; "scenics in large format only."
Payment & Terms: Pays 50% commission on domestic photos. General price range: editorial, $150 and up; advertising, $200 base rate. Offers one-time rights and specific print and/or time usages. Model release and photo captions required.
Making Contact: Contact by telephone for photographer's package. SASE. Reports in 1 month. Photo guidelines free with SASE. Tips sheet distributed quarterly to contract photographers.
Tips: Trend among clients is "toward medium and large format. Looks for "professional quality, sharp focus; proper exposure, simple design and a direct message. When sending work to review make sure the submission is tightly edited. Do not send soft, improperly exposed chromes. Include subject list of what work is available."

■**VISUALS**, Box 381848, Miami FL 33138. (305)681-5379. Researcher: Lou Wald. Stock photo agency and picture library. Has 2 million photos. Clients include ad agencies, public relations firms, audiovisual firms, book/encyclopedia publishers, magazine publishers, calendar companies and government. Previous/current clients: Sea Frontier, color sunset, Rio harbor; Underwater USA, ship building, in Miami; and Cosmo Magazine, art subject.
Subject Needs: Travel subjects, from Central America, South America, Caribbean, Europe, Atlantic, Middle East, Africa, Asia-Far East and Pacific.
Specs: Uses 35mm color slides; 35mm transparencies.
Payment & Terms: Pays 50% commission on color slides. General price range: $100-800. Buys one-time, first, world or all rights. Model release and key sheet required.
Making Contact & Terms: Photo guidelines free with SASE. Tip sheet free with SASE.
Tips: Wants to see well exposed, sharp, interesting, well composed shots, 2×2 or 2¼×2¼ color transparencies only—no prints. "Many of our buyers want pictures depicting the positive in travel and editorial views. Send photo and include phone number areas covered."

■**VISUALS UNLIMITED**, P.O. Box 146, Hale Hill Rd., East Swanzey NH 03446-0146. (603)352-6436. President: Dr. John D. Cunningham. Stock photo agency and photo research and developmental editing service. Has over 1,000,000 photos. Clients include ad agencies, public relations firms, audiovisual firms, businesses, book/encyclopedia publishers, magazine publishers, postcard companies, calendar companies and greeting card companies.
Subject Needs: All fields (biology, environmental, medical, natural history, geography, history, scenics, chemistry, geology, physics, industrial, astronomy and "general.").
Specs: Uses 5×7 or larger b&w prints; 35mm, 2¼×2¼, 4×5 and 8×10 transparencies; b&w contact sheets; and b&w negatives.
Payment & Terms: Pays 50% commission for b&w and color photos. General price range: flexible rates based upon publication, size of use, etc. Model release and captions preferred.
Making Contact: Query with samples or send unsolicited photos by mail for consideration. Submit portfolio for review. SASE. Reports in 1 week. Photo guidelines sheet is free with SASE. Distributes a tip sheet several times/year as deadlines allow, to all people with files.
Tips: Looks for "focus, composition, and contrast, of course. Instructional potential (e.g., behavior, anatomical detail, habitat, example of problem, living conditions, human interest). Increasing need for exact identification, behavior, and methodology in scientific photos; some return to b&w as color costs rise. Edit carefully for focus and distracting details; submit anything and everything from everywhere that is geographical, biological, geological, environmental, and people oriented."

*■**WEATHERSTOCK**, Box 44124, Tucson AZ 85733. (602)325-4207. Director/Photographer: Warren Faidley. Estab. 1987. Stock photo agency. Has basic inventory of 8,000 images with an additional collection of 10,000 images representing the work of 20 photographers. Clients include advertising agencies, public relations firms, audiovisual firms, businesses, book/encyclopedia publishers, magazine publishers, postcard companies, calendar companies, greeting card companies and scientific.

The asterisk before a listing indicates that the market is new in this edition. New markets are often the most receptive to freelance submissions.

Subject Needs: "Our greatest needs are high quality original images of all types of weather and related interests, including volcanoes, earthquakes. Our most requested photographs are those of tornadoes, hurricanes, and other similar, severe weather. Also scenics and environmental issues such as pollution, and toxic waste."

Specs: Uses 5×7, 8×10 b&w/color prints; 35mm, 2¼×2¼, 4×5, 8×10 transparencies; b&w/color negatives, with proofs only. We prefer transparencies, for most subjects, but will consider prints of dramatic weather shots.

Payment & Terms: Pays 50% commission on b&w/color photos. General price range: $200-500 average, some sales are much higher. Offers one-time rights, first rights and all rights. Any exclusive uages "are approved by represented photographers." Model release and photo captions required.

Making Contact: "*Do not send* photos with first contact." SASE. Reports in 1 week. Photo guidelines free with SASE. Tips sheet distributed quarterly to contract photographers.

Tips: "Since we are the world's first and only stock agency which specializes in weather and related images, we can offer clients a more detailed and quality selection than the general interest agencies, including even the biggest ones. We are able to fill everything from greeting card scenics for the client that demands super scenic quality to the advertiser or scientific client who has a very specific request. If we don't have the image, we can almost always locate it through our vast collection of weather references. If a photographer is interested in being represented by Weatherstock, the transparencies must be of very high quality. Dupes are welcome, as we are completely non-exclusive in our representation. Many photographers that we represent have similar images that they sell on their own or photos that they file with other agencies."

WEST STOCK, INC., Suite 520, 83 S. King St., Seattle WA 98104. (206)621-1611. FAX: (206)223-1545. Chairman: Mark Karras. President: Rick Groman. Project Director: Stephanie Webb. Files contain over 500,000 transparencies. Clients include ad agencies, design firms, major corporations, magazines, book publishers, calendar and greeting card companies.

Subject Needs: "Our files are targeted to meet the needs of advertising, corporate communications and publishing. We need strong imagery of virtually all subjects, especially people involved in business, leisure activities, sports and recreation. Model released people and property make your images far more salable."

Specs: Only original transparencies accepted, 35mm and larger.

Payment & Terms: Pays 50% commission. General price range: $200-15,000. Sells one-time rights. Model releases, property releases and captions required.

Making Contact: Send letter outlining qualifications along with tearsheets to receive guidelines. "Please, no telephone calls or portfolios sent without our request."

Tips: "We expect photographers to have a thorough understanding of stock photography prior to contacting us. We do not represent amateur photographers. The stock photography market is becoming more competitive and sophisticated. In order to stay ahead of the crowd we demand nothing but the finest in professional photography."

*■WESTLIGHT, 2223 S. Carmelina Ave., Los Angeles CA 90064. (213)820-7077. Owner: Craig Aurness. Estab. 1978. Stock photo agency. Has 1,000,000+ photos. Clients include advertising agencies, public relations firms, audiovidual firms, businesses, book/encyclopedia publishers, magazine publishers, newspapers, postcard companies, calendar companies and greeting card companies and TV.

Subject Needs: Needs photos of all subjects.

Specs: Uses 35mm, 2¼×2¼, 4×5 transparencies.

Payment & Terms: Pays 50% commission on color photos. General price range: $450+. Offers one-time rights (no exclusive) and first rights. Model release and photo captions required.

Making Contact: Query with resume of credits; query with tearsheet samples; query with list of stock photo subjects. Cannot return material. Reports in 1 month. Photo guidelines free with SASE. Tips sheet distributed monthly to contract photographers. Send tearsheets only, no unsolicited photos.

Tips: In freelancer's samples, wants to see "top professional work with a specialty."

■DEREK G. WIDDICOMBE, Worldwide Photographic Library, "Oldfield", High Street, Clayton West, Huddersfield Great Britain HD8 9NS. (011)44 484 862638. Proprietor: Derek G. Widdicombe. Picture library. Has over 100,000 photos. Clients include: ad agencies, public relations firms, audiovisual firms, businesses, book/encyclopedia publishers, magazine publishers, newspapers, postcard companies, calendar companies, greeting card companies, television, packaging, exhibition and display material, posters, etc.

Subject Needs: "The library covers many thousands of different subjects from landscape, architecture, social situations, industrial, people, moods and seasons, religious services, animals, natural history, travel subjects and many others. We have some archival material. These subjects are from worldwide sources."

WOULD YOU USE THE SAME CALENDAR YEAR AFTER YEAR?

f course not! If you scheduled your appointments
sing last year's calendar, you'd risk missing
nportant meetings and deadlines, so you keep
p-to-date with a new calendar each year. Just like
ur calendar, *Photographer's Market*® changes every
ar, too. Many of the buyers move or get promoted,
tes of pay increase, and even photo buyers' needs
ange from the previous year. You can't afford to use
n out-of-date book to plan your marketing efforts!

So save yourself the frustration of getting photos
turned in the mail, stamped MOVED: ADDRESS UNKNOWN.
d of NOT submitting your work to new listings because
u don't know they exist. **Make sure you have the most
urrent marketing information by ordering** *1992
hotographer's Market* **today.** All you have to do is
mplete the attached post card and return it with your
ayment or charge card information. Order now, and there's
e thing that won't change from your *1991 Photographer's
arket* — the price! That's right, we'll send you the 1992
lition for just $21.95. *1992 Photographer's Market* will be
blished and ready for shipment in September 1991.

Let an old acquaintance be forgot, and toast the new edition
Photographer's Market. Order today!

See other side for more books on how to sell your photos)

---

o order, drop this postpaid card in the mail.

] YES! I want the most current edition of *Photographer's Market.*® Please send me the 1992 edition
the 1991 price — $21.95.* (NOTE: *1992 Photographer's Market* will be ready for shipment in
ptember 1991.) #10207
so send me:

___(10193) Lighting Secrets For The Professional Photographer, $22.95,* (available NOW)
___(10020) Sell & Re-Sell Your Photos, $16.95,* (available NOW)
___(10175) How To Shoot Stock Photos That Sell, $16.95,* paperback, (available NOW)
lus postage & handling: $3.00 for one book, $1.00 for each additional book. Ohio residents add 5½% sales tax.
Payment enclosed (Slip this card and your payment into an envelope)
Please charge my: ☐ Visa   ☐ MasterCard

Account # _____ Exp. Date _____

Signature _____

me _____

dress _____

y _____ State _____ Zip _____

his offer expires August 1, 1992.)

1507 Dana Avenue
Cincinnati, OH 45207

5777

MORE BOOKS TO HELP YOU SELL YOUR PHOTOS!

Lighting Secrets for the Professional Photographer
by Alan Brown, Tim Grondin, & Joe Braun
As a photographer, you're always on the lookout for new ways of shooting common subjects—and new tricks to make shooting difficult subjects easier. This book is loaded with step-by-step answers to your questions, in addition to detailed exploration of highlights, shadows, highlights combined with shadows, and lighting for effect.
144 pages/300 color illus./$22.95

Sell & Re-Sell Your Photos
by Rohn Engh
This book shows you how to launch or strengthen your own photo sales business—how to sell by mail and phone to a full range of the nation's markets. You'll also find information on pricing, copyrights, taxes, recordkeeping, and much more.
336 pages/40 b&w photos/$16.95

How To Shoot Stock Photos That Sell
by Michal Heron
Don't let the lucrative market of stock photography pass you by! This book features 25 step-by-step assignments to help photographers shoot what the market needs most.
160 pages/30 b&w illus./$16.95, paperback

Use coupon on other side to order today!

Specs: Uses 20.3 × 24.4 cm. glossy b&w prints; 35mm, 2¼ × 2¼, 4 × 5, and 8 × 10 transparencies.

Payment & Terms: Pays 50% commission for b&w and color photos. General price range: reproduction fees in the range of £25-200 (English currency); pays $52-333 or higher/b&w photo; $73-500 or higher/color photo. Offers one-time rights usually but all rights are by agreement before publication. Model release and captions required.

Making Contact: Query with samples. Send small selection at own risk with return postage/packing. SASE.

Tips: Looks for "technical suitability (correct exposure, sharpness, good tonal range, freedom from defects, color rendering [saturation] etc.). Subject matter well portrayed without any superfluous objects in picture. Commercial suitability (people in pictures in suitable dress, up-to-date cars — or none, clear-top portions for magazine/book cover titles). Our subject range is so wide that we are offering the whole spectrum from very traditional (almost archival) pictures to abstract, moody, out-of-focus shots. Send material in small batches — normally a hundred images at a time, and let us know what you have to send and have our agreement to its being sent before posting."

■**S & I WILLIAMS POWER PIX**, Castle Lodge, Wenvoe, Cardiff CF5 6AD Wales, United Kingdom. (0222) 595163. FAX: (0222)593905. President: Steven Williams. Picture library. Has 100,000 photos. Clients include ad agencies, public relations firms, audiovisual firms, businesses, book/encyclopedia publishers, magazine publishers, postcard companies, calendar companies, greeting card companies and music business, i.e. records, cassettes and CDs.

Specs: Uses 35mm, 2¼ × 2¼, 4 × 5 and 8 × 10 transparencies.

Payment & Terms: Pays 50% commission on b&w and color photos. General price range:£50-£500 (English currency). Written model release and captions are required.

Making Contact: Arrange a personal interview to show portfolio, query with resume of credits, query with samples or query with list of stock photo subjects. SASE. Reports in 1-2 weeks. Photo guidelines available for SASE. Distributes a tips sheet every 3-6 months to photographers on books.

Tips: Prefers to see "a photographer who knows his subject and has done his market research by looking at pictures used in magazines, record covers, books, etc. — bright colorful images and an eye for something just that little bit special."

*■**WORLD VIEW-FOTOTHEEK BV**, A.J. Ernststraat 1S1, Amsterdam, Holland 1083 GV. 31-20-420224. FAX: 31-20-6611355. Managing Director: Bert Blokhuis. Estab. 1985. Stock photo agency. Has 85,000 transparencies. Clients include advertising agencies, audiovisual firms, businesses, calendar companies and corporations.

Subject Needs: Wants to see "sizes bigger then 35mm, only model-released commercial subjects."

Specs: 2¼ × 2¼, 4 × 5, 8 × 10 transparencies only.

Payment & Terms: Pays 40-60% commission on transparencies. Offers one-time rights. Model release and photo captions required.

Making Contact: Query with samples. SASE. Reports in 3 weeks.

Tips: In freelancer's samples, wants to see "small amount of pictures (20 or 30) plus a list of subjects available and list of agents." Work must show quality.

WORLDWIDE PRESS AGENCY, Box 579, 1000 Buenos Aires, 1000 Bs As Argentina. 962-3182 and 48-9927. Director: Victor Polanco. Stock photo agency and picture library. Clients include ad agencies, book/encyclopedia publishers, magazine publishers, newspapers, postcard companies, calendar companies and greeting card companies.

Subject Needs: Handles picture stories, fashion photos, human interest, pets, wildlife, film and TV stars, pop and rock singers, classic musicians and conductors, sports, interior design, architectural and opera singers.

Specs: Uses b&w, 8 × 12 glossy prints; 35mm and 2¼ × 2¼ transparencies.

Payment & Terms: Pays 40% commission for b&w and color photos. General price range: "The Argentine market is very peculiar. We try to obtain the best price for each pic, sometimes we consult the photographer needs." Offers one-time rights. Prefers witten model release and photo captions.

Making Contact: Query with list of stock photo subjects. Does not return unsolicited material. Reports "as soon as possible."

■**ZEFA ZENTRALE FARBBILD AGENTUR GmbH**, SchanzenstraBe 20, 4000 Duesseldorf 11, West Germany. (211)55061. FAX: (211)55 06 29. Managing Director: Eckart Grob. Stock photo agency. Clients include ad agencies, public relations firms, audiovisual firms, industrial, businesses, book/encyclopedia publishers, magazine publishers, postcard companies, calendar companies, greeting card companies.

Subject Needs: All kinds of transparencies like geography (landscapes), people, industry, traffic, nature, botany and zoology.
Specs: Uses 35mm, 2¼×2¼, 4×5 and 8×10 transparencies.
Payment & Terms: Pays 50% on color photos. General price range from DM 150 – DM 10,000 (German currency). Model release and captions required. Offers one time rights.
Making Contact: Arrange a personal interview to show portfolio; query with samples or list of stock photo subjects; or send unsolicited photos by mail for consideration. SASE. Reports in 1 month. Photo guidelines free with SASE. Distributes tips sheet upon request.
Tips: Prefers to see "a first picture selection of approximately 150 images showing the spectrum of your photographic work."

***■ZEPHYR PICTURES**, Suites D & U, 2120 Jimmy Durante Blvd., Del Mar CA 92014. (619)755-1200. FAX: (619)755-3723. Owner: Leo Gradinger. Estab. 1982. Stock photo agency. Also commercial photo studio. Has several hundred thousands of photos. Clients include advertising agencies, public relations firms, audiovisual firms, businesses, book/encyclpedia publishers, magazine publishers, newspapers, postcard companies, calendar companies, developers, corporate, finance, education, design studios and TV stations. Previous/current clients: Crouch & Assoc., Ad agency, local S.D Scenic, Cover Annual Report; N.Y Times, *Business People*, promotional campaign for newspaper, (self); Beth Israel Hospital, depressed mother & child, Ad.
Subject Needs: "We handle everything from A to Z. We specialize in people (model-released) for advertising. New material is shot on a weekly basis. We also have lots of great material for the textbook and editorial markets.
Specs: Uses 35mm, 2¼×2¼, 4×5, 8×10, 6×7 transparencies.
Payment & Terms: Pays 50% commission. General price range: $100-5,000. Pays $175/b&w and color photo; 50-50 domestic, 40% to photographer on foreign sales. Offers one-time rights; other rights negotiable. Model release and photo captions required.
Making Contact: Arrange a personal interview to show portfolio; query with list of stock photo subjects. SASE. Reports in 2-3 weeks, according to time demands. Photo guidelines available occasionally. Tips sheet distributed twice a year to any photographers who are contracted for submissions.
Tips: "I am looking for a photographer who *specializes* in one maybe two areas of expertise. Be professional. Call or write to let us know who you are & what you specialize in. If we are interested, we ask you to send 20 to 40 of your very best images with a SASE & return postage.

Stock Photo Agencies/'90-'91 changes

The following stock photo agencies appeared in the 1990 edition of *Photographer's Market* but are not in the 1991 edition. Those firms whose presidents or directors did not respond to our request for an update of their listings may not have done so for a variety of reasons—they may be out of business, for example, or they may be overstocked with submissions.

Air Pixies (did not respond)
Allen Photographic Library, J. Catling (not reviewing work)
Bavaria Bildagentur GMBH (did not respond)
Cephas Picture Library (did not respond)
Christmas Archives International (did not respond)
Cutten Association, John H. (did not respond)
Envision (not reviewing work)
Florida Image File (not reviewing work)
Four by Five (not reviewing work)

Haas Photo Library, Robert (did not respond)
Horizon International Photography Limited (did not respond)
Hutchison Library, The (did not respond)
Images Photo Agency (did not respond)
J.S. Library International (did not respond)
Keystone Presedienst GMBH (did not respond)
Lewis Inc., Frederic (deleted)
Medichrome (did not respond)
Photo Environments Inc. (did not respond)

Photo Zone (no longer in market)
Science Photo Library Limited (did not respond)
Sefton Photo Library (did not respond)
Tropix Photographic Library (did not respond)
Uniphoto Picture Agency (not reviewing work)
Valen Photos (did not respond)
Vantage Photo Dynamics (out of business)
Visualworld (moved; no forwarding address)

Services & Opportunities

Contests

Whether you're an aspiring photographer or a working professional, getting feedback on your work is an excellent way to measure your progress and help you to sharpen your vision. Accordingly, by participating in photographic contests, you can fulfill both of these goals. Also, the publicity and the awards connected with some of the more prestigious contests can go a long way in actually helping you advance your career.

The 55 or so listings in this section cover a wide range of styles—such as fine art photography and photojournalism—and photographic media, including film and videotape. In particular, listings with various kinds of audiovisual, film or video needs have been marked with a special AV symbol—a solid, black square—before the listing's name for easier recognition.

The listings contain only the basic information needed to make contact with the sponsoring organization and a brief description of the styles or media open to consideration. It's recommended that you read through the listings first to get an idea of the ones for which your work would likely be eligible, then write to them requesting complete, up-to-date entry information.

When entering contests, be especially alert for any which require the surrender or transfer of "all rights" to images either upon entry or upon winning the contest. Protection of your copyright is one of your main responsibilities as a photographer (see Copyright article on page 26), and contests are one way in which photographers have sometimes lost, unknowingly, their copyrights to valuable images. Granting limited rights for publicity purposes is reasonable, but you should never assign rights of any kind without adequate financial compensation or without a written agreement. In your request for entry guidelines, be sure to request clear information about all such terms.

In the meantime, enter any competition and as many as you wish. And by the way, best of luck!

■AMERICAN FILM AND VIDEO FESTIVAL, Suite 152, 920 Barnsdale Road, LaGrange Park IL 60525. (708)482-4000. Festival Director: Kathryn Lamont. Sponsor: American Film and Video Association. Annual competition for film and video held in May or June in a variety of cities.

ANN ARBOR 8mm FILM & VIDEO FESTIVAL, 317 S. Division St., Ann Arbor MI 48104. (313)662-2470. Director: Douglas Grew.

ART ON THE GREEN, P.O. Box 901, Coeur d'Alene ID 83814. (208)667-9346. Secretary: Kathy Flint. Outdoor art & crafts festival including juried show.

■BACA'S ANNUAL FILM AND VIDEO FESTIVAL, 200 Eastern Pkwy., Brooklyn NY 11238. (718)783-4469. Directors: Chuck Reichenthal. For filmmakers.

■BALTIMORE ANNUAL INDEPENDENT FILM & VIDEO MAKERS' COMPETITION, % The Baltimore Film Forum, 10 Art Museum Dr., Baltimore MD 21218. (301)889-1993. Annual international competition.

BEST IN THE WEST, Suite 302, 251 Post St., San Francisco CA 94108. (415)421-6867. Vice President: Janet Kennedy. Sponsor: American Advertising Federation. Annual competition for advertising and design work.

*BEVERLY ART CENTER ART FAIR & FESTIVAL, 2153 W. 111th St., Chicago IL 60643. (312)445-3838. Chairman, Pat McGrail. Annual event for still photos and all fine art held in June in Chicago. March deadline for application.

CAMERA BUG INTERNATIONAL, Camera Bug Club Headquarters, 2106 Hoffnagle St., Philadelphia PA 19152. (215)342-1492. Contest Chairman: Nicholas M. Friedman. Annual contest open to all photographers. Provide SASE or 25¢ postage for submission guidlines.

*COMMUNICATION ARTS 1991 PHOTOGRAPHY ANNUAL, P.O. Box 10300, 410 Sherman Ave., Palo Alto CA 94303. (415)326-6040. Annual photography competition for all formats and subjects; sponsored by *Communication Arts Magazine.*

*COUNCIL ON FINE ART PHOTOGRAPHY, 5613 Johnson Avenue, Bethesda MD 20817. (301)897-0083. CEO: Lowell Anson Kenyon. Conducts talent search and exhibits work by emerging art photographers.

*■THE CREATIVITY AWARDS SHOW, 6th Fl., 10 E. 39th St., 6th Floor, New York NY 10016. (212)889-6500. Show Director: Dan Barron. Sponsor: *Art Direction* magazine. Annual show for still photos and films held in September in New York City.

*CURATORS CHOICE, 59 Tinker St., Woodstock NY 12498. (914)679-9957. Sponsored by the Center For Photography at Woodstock. Annual competition.

*■DANCE ON CAMERA FESTIVAL, Sponsored by Dance Films Association, Inc., Room 507, 1133 Broadway, New York NY 10010. (212)727-0764. Executive Director: Susan Braun. Annual festival competition for 16mm films with optical soundtrack and ¾-inch videotapes in NTSC format, on all aspects of dance.

EAST TEXAS INTERNATIONAL PHOTOGRAPHY CONTEST, Box 4104, East Texas Station, Commerce TX 75429. (214)886-5234, 5238. Advisor: Stan Godwin. Sponsor: East Texas State University Photographic Society. Eastman Kodak Co., Prof. Photo Div., and Canon, USA. Annual contest for still photos/prints.

EASTERN SHORE ANNUAL, Box 1233, Chincoteague VA 23336. (804)336-1152. Director: Lee Baade. Sponsor: Foto Galerie. Annual competition for still photos/prints.

ECLIPSE AWARDS, Thoroughbred Racing Associations, Suite 2W4, 3000 Marcus Ave., Lake Success NY 11042. (516)328-2660. Director of Service Bureau: Richard Schulhoff. Sponsor: Thoroughbred Racing Associations, Daily Racing Form and National Turf Writers Association. Annual event for photographers.

*EYE GALLERY—SELECTIONS '91, 1151 Mission St., San Francisco CA 94117. (415)567-6153. Director: Tom Ferentz. Annual juried photography exhibition for black & white and color prints, April through May. March deadline.

The asterisk before a listing indicates that the market is new in this edition. New markets are often the most receptive to freelance submissions.

SAMUEL S. FLEISHER ART MEMORIAL, 709-721 Catharine St., Philadelphia PA 19147. (215)922-3456. Gallery Coordinator: Lanny Bergner. Competition for avant-garde, fine art; no photojournalism or commercial.

■FOCUS (FILMS OF COLLEGE & UNIVERSITY STUDENTS), 10 E. 34th St., New York NY 10016. (212)779-0404. Director: Sam Katz. Sponsor: Nissan Motor Corp. in USA. Annual competition for film: live action/narrative, animation/experimental, documentary, sound achievement, film editing, cinematography, screenwriting and producing.

42nd INTERNATIONAL EXHIBITION OF PHOTOGRAPHY, 2260 Jimmy Durante Blvd., Del Mar CA 92014-2216. (619)755-1161. Sponsor: Del Mar Fair (22nd District Agricultural Association). Annual event for still photos/prints.

GALLERY MAGAZINE, 401 Park Ave. S., New York NY 10016-8802. Contest Editor: Judy Linden. Monthly event for still photos.

12TH ANNUAL GAZETTE PHOTOGRAPHY CONTEST, *Pure-Bred/American Kennel Gazette,* 51 Madison Ave., New York NY 10010. (212)696-8332. Sponsor: The American Kennel Club. Annual competition for photos (prints) of pure-bred dogs.

GOLDEN ISLES ARTS FESTIVAL, Box 673, Saint Simons Island GA 31522. (912)638-8770. Contact: Registration Chairman, Coastal Center for the Arts. Sponsor: Coastal Alliance for the Arts. Annual competition for still photos/prints; all fine art and craft.

GREATER MIDWEST INTERNATIONAL VI, Central Missouri State University, Warrensburg MO 64093-5246. (816)429-4481. Gallery Director: Billi R.S. Rothove. Sponsor: CMSU Art Center Gallery/Missouri Arts Council. Annual competition for all media.

*ILLUMINANCE, % Lubbock Fine Arts Center, 2600 Ave. P, Lubbock TX 79405. (806)767-2686. Director: Connie Gibbons. Annual competition/exhibit for artists using photographic media and processes; held each spring.

*■INDEPENDENT FILMMAKER PROGRAM, 2021 Northwestern Ave., Los Angeles CA 90027. (213)856-7787. Contact: Andrea Alsberg. Funding for narrative, animation, documentary and experimental projects on 16mm, 35mm or broadcast quality videotape.

INTERNATIONAL DIAPORAMA FESTIVAL, Auwegemvaart 79, 2800 Mechelen, Belgium. President: J. Denis. Sponsor: Koninklijke Mechelse Fotokring. Competition held every other year (even years) for slide/sound sequences.

*■THE INTERNATIONAL MARINE PHOTO & VIDEO CONTEST, 1141 NE 142 St., N. Miami FL 33161. (305)891-6095. Executive Director: Susan Payette. Annual competition for underwater and above water subjects shot on slides, prints and videotape.

INTERNATIONAL WILDLIFE PHOTO COMPETITION, EVST, University of Montana, Missoula MT 59812. (406)243-2477. Chairman: Mike Bashkin. Sponsor: 13th International Wildlife Film Festival. Annual competition for still photos/prints and slides. Held April 1991 in Missoula, Montana. March deadline.

*JURIED PHOTOGRAPHY EXHIBITION, 5601 South Braeswood, Houston TX 77096. (713)729-3200. Cultural Arts Director: Marilyn Hassid. Sponsor: Jewish Community Center of Houston. Competition held every other year for still photos/prints (slide entry format) in the spring in conjunction with Houston Fotofest.

*ROBERT F. KENNEDY JOURNALISM AWARDS, 1031 31st St. NW, Washington DC 20007. (202)333-1880. Contact: Linda Semans. For photojournalists.

■ *The solid, black square before a listing indicates that the market uses various types of audiovisual materials, such as slides, film or videotape.*

■THE "MOBIUS'"™ AWARDS, 841 N. Addison Ave., Elmhurst IL 60126-1291. (708)834-7773. FAX: (708)834-5565. Chairman: J.W. Anderson. Executive Director: Patricia Meyer. Sponsor: The United States Festivals Association. Annual festival for TV and Radio Commericals submitted on 16mm film and ¾-inch videotape.

MYSTIC ART ASSOCIATION, P.O. Box 259, 9 Water St., Mystic CT 06355. (203)536-7601. Executive Director: Marjorie Ciminera. Annual juried show held each April to May in Fine Arts Gallery.

■NATIONAL EDUCATIONAL FILM AND VIDEO FESTIVAL, 314 East Tenth St., Oakland CA 94606. (415)465-6885. Director: Sue Davies. Annual festival for film, videotape and filmstrips.

*NATURE IMAGES, INC., P.O. Box 2037, West Palm Beach FL 33402. (407)586-7332. Director: Helen Longest-Slaughter. Conducts 3 nature photo contests per year with prize money, ribbons and exhibitions.

*NEW MEXICO PHOTOGRAPHER CONTEST, Box 2582–ENMU, Portales NM 88130. (505)562-2253. Contact: Wendel Sloan, publisher of *New Mexico Photographer* magazine. Offers semi-annual contest for black and white photography; publishes winners in summer and winter issues of *NMP*.

NEW YORK STATE YOUTH MEDIA ARTS SHOWS, Bureau of Arts and Music Education, The State Education Department, Room 681 EBA, Albany NY 12234. (518)474-8773. Funded by the State Legislature and administered by the New York State Education Department. Annual exhibition and competition for still photos, film, videotape, creative sound, computer arts and holography.

1991 PHOTOGRAPHY ANNUAL, 410 Sherman, Box 10300, Palo Alto CA 94303. (415)326-6040. Executive Editor: Jean A. Coyne. Sponsor: *Communication Arts* magazine. Annual competition for still photos/prints. March deadline.

*■NORTH AMERICAN OUTDOOR FILM/VIDEO AWARDS, Suite 101, 2017 Cato Ave., State College PA 16801. (814)234-1011. Sponsor: Outdoor Writers Association of America. Annual competition for films/videos on conservation and outdoor recreation subjects.

*■NORTHWEST FILM & VIDEO FESTIVAL, Northwest Film and Video Center, Oregon Art Institute, 1219 SW Park Ave., Portland OR 97205. (503)221-1156. Festival Director: Bill Foster. Sponsor: Northwest Film and Video Center. Annual competition for film and videotape.

NORTHWEST INTERNATIONAL EXHIBITION OF PHOTOGRAPHY, Box 430, Puyallup WA 98371. (206)845-1771. Superintendent: Bonnie E. Nettnin. Sponsor: Western Washington Fair and approved by Photographic Society of America. Annual event for still photos and slides.

*PHOTO REVIEW 7TH ANNUAL COMPETITION, 301 Hill Ave., Langhorne PA 19047. (215)757-8921. Editor, Stephen Perloff. National annual photo competition; all winners reproduced in summer issue of *Photo Review* magazine.

PHOTOGRAPHER'S FORUM-COLLEGE CONTEST AND SPRING CONTEST, 614 Santa Barbara St., Santa Barbara CA 93101. (805)963-0439. Contact: Margie Middleton. Sponsor: *Photographer's Forum Magazine*. Competition for college level and amateur level.

PHOTOGRAPHERS' FUND, 59A Tinker St., Woodstock NY 12498. (914)679-9957. Sponsor: Center For Photography at Woodstock. Annual competition for still photos/prints, still imagery incorporating photo derived portions.

PHOTOGRAPHIC COMPETITION ASSOCIATION QUARTERLY CONTEST, Box 53550-B, Philadelphia PA 19105. (215)279-2193. Contact: Competition Committee. Sponsor: Photographic Competition Association (PCAA). Quarterly competition for still photos/prints.

■PRSA FILM/VIDEO FESTIVAL, 33 Irving Pl., New York NY 10003. (212)995-2230. Contact: Jackie Hunter. Sponsor: Public Relations Society of America. Annual festival for film and videotape.

PRO FOOTBALL HALL OF FAME PHOTO CONTEST, 2121 George Halas Dr. NW, Canton OH 44708. (216)456-8207. Vice President/Public Relations: Donald R. Smith. Sponsor: Canon USA, Inc. Annual event for still photos.

PULITZER PRIZES, 702 Journalism, Columbia University, New York NY 10027. (212)854-3841 or 3842. Administrator: Robert C. Christopher. Annual competition for still photos/prints published in American newspapers.

SALON INTERNACIONAL DE ARTE FOTOGRAFICO, Foto Club Buenos Aires, Box 5377, 1000 Buenos Aires, Argentina. Salon Chairman: Mirta Cavallero. Annual competition for still photography: monochrome and color prints; photojournalism prints and pictorial, nature and photojournalism slides.

SCHOLASTIC PHOTOGRAPHY AWARDS, Scholastic, Inc., 730 Broadway, New York NY 10003. For photographers. Purpose is to provide scholarship grants to college-bound high school seniors.

*■SINKING CREEK FILM/VIDEO FESTIVAL, Creekside Farm, 1250 Old Shiloh Rd., Greeneville TN 37743. (615)638-6524. Director: Mary Jane Coleman. Offers workshops in film & video production, media analysis. Screening of winners from its National film/video competition. Festival held in June at Vanderbilt University, Nashville, Tn. Annual competition for 16mm film and ¾" videotape. April deadline.

SPRINGFIELD INTERNATIONAL COLOR SLIDE EXHIBIT, Box 255, Wilbraham MA 01095. Sponsor: Springfield Photographic Society. Annual event for 35mm color slides.

■TEN BEST OF THE WEST, Box 4034, Long Beach CA 90804. Executive Secretary: George Cushman. Annual competition in its 35th year for film and videotape. September deadline.

*30TH ANNUAL NAVAL AND MARITIME PHOTO CONTEST, U.S. Naval Institute, Annapolis MD 21402. (301)268-6110, ext 252. Director, Library/Photography: Mrs. Patty M. Maddocks. Sponsors: United States Naval Insitute and the Government Systems Division, Eastman Kodak Company. Annual competition for still photos/prints, and 35mm slides. December deadline.

■THREE RIVERS ARTS FESTIVAL, 207 Sweetbriar St., Pittsburgh PA 15211. (412)481-7040. Assistant Director, PR: Beth C. Dell. Annual competition for still photos/prints, film and videotape. Early spring deadline.

U.S. INDUSTRIAL FILM AND VIDEO FESTIVAL, 841 N. Addison Ave., Elmhurst IL 60126-1291. (708)834-7773. FAX: (708)834-5565. Chairman: J.W. Anderson. Executive Director: Patricia Meyer. Sponsor: The United States Festivals Association. Annual festival for film and video.

*■VISIONS OF U.S. HOME VIDEO COMPETITION, 2021 North Western Ave., Los Angeles CA 90027. (213)856-7787. Contact: Kimberly Wright. Annual competition for home videos shot on 8mm video, Beta or VHS.

■VISIONS OF U.S., 2021 North Western Ave., Los Angeles CA 90027. (213)856-7787. Contact: Kimberly Wright. Sponsored by Sony and administered by the American Film Institute. Competition accepts VHS, Beta, or 8mm. Deadline: June 15.

*WESTERN HERITAGE AWARDS, 1700 NE 63rd St., Oklahoma City OK 73111. (405)478-2250. Public Relations Director: Dana Sullivant. Sponsor: National Cowboy Hall of Fame. Annual competition for film and videotape held the 2nd week of March in Oklahoma City.

With so many photographic markets today looking for photographers with fresh, imaginative visual styles, photographers are increasingly realizing their full creative potential by taking part in workshops. The workshop experience can be whatever the photographer wishes it to be—a holiday from his working routine, or an exciting introduction to new skills and perspectives on the craft. Some photographers who start out by attending someone else's workshops come away so inspired that sooner or later they end up establishing their own.

The 80 listings in this section cover a wide range of styles of photography and techniques. Conventional photography is still the primary focus of most of these programs. However, there is increasing interest from photographers in film and video, too. Accordingly, workshops which offer programs relating to film, video or other audiovisual skills have been marked with a special AV symbol—a solid, black square—before the listing's name for easier recognition.

In addition, if you are looking into workshops for the first time or are thinking of branching out and trying something different, the Close-up interview in this section provides some further insight into the nature of the workshop experience. The interview features Roger Fremier and Gail Pierce of the Photographic Center of Monterey Peninsula in Carmel, California.

These workshop listings contain only the basic information needed to make contact with the sponsor and a brief description of the styles or media covered in the programs. Read through all the listings first to see which ones offer the programs that best fit your needs and interests. Then send a request for complete, up-to-date application information.

*ADVENTURE PHOTOGRAPHY WORKSHOPS,1317 Knob Hill Road, San Marcos CA 92069. (619)739-9504. Director: J. Thomas Young. Offers photo workshops in unique locations including: Bali, New Guinea, Indonesia, Micronesia, Africa.

AMERICAN PHOTOGRAPHY INSTITUTE, Department of Photography, Tisch School of the Arts, New York University, 8th Floor, 721 Broadway, New York NY 10003. (212)998-1930. Dept. Chair: Thomas Drysdale. Inst. Director: Cheryl Younger. Offers courses and workshops at all levels of b&w, color and nonsilver processes, including history/criticism, studio, editorial, documentary, career options and master photographer workshops.

*AMERICAN SOUTHWEST PHOTOGRAPHY WORKSHOP, P.O. Box 220450, El Paso TX 79913. (915)581-7959. Director: Geo. B. Drennan. Offers intense field workshops for the serious black and white photographer.

AMPRO PHOTO WORKSHOPS, 636 E. Broadway, Vancouver BC V5T 1X6 Canada. (604)876-5501. FAX: (604)876-5502. Approved trade school. Offers a part time and fulltime career courses in commercial photographer and photofinishing technician work.

 The asterisk before a listing indicates that the market is new in this edition. New markets are often the most receptive to freelance submissions.

*ANCHELL PHOTOGRAPHY WORKSHOPS, 1411 N. Catalina St., Los Angeles CA 90027. (213)465-8777. Director: Steve Anchell. Offers workshops in fine arts photography and landscapes techniques.

ANDERSON RANCH ARTS CENTER, Box 5598, Snowmass Village CO 81615. (303)923-3181. Photography Coordinator: James Baker. Offers workshops in photography, ceramics, painting, printmaking, woodworking and other visual arts media.

*ARROWMONT SCHOOL OF ARTS AND CRAFTS, P.O. Box 567, Gatlinburg TN 37738. (615)436-5860. PR Head: Cynthia Huff, Offers one-week summer workshops in various techniques.

*BIXEMINARS, P.O. Box 6513, Canton OH 44706-6513. (216-455-0135. Founder/Instructor: R.C. Bixler. Offers three-day, weekend seminars for beginners through advanced amateurs. Usually held third weekend of February, June and October. Covers composition, lighting, location work and macro.

*BODIE FINE ART WORKSHOP SERIES/GLOBAL PRESERVATION PROJECTS, P.O. Box 30866, Santa Barbara CA 93105. (805) 682-3398. Director: Thomas I. Morse. Offers workshops promoting the preservation of the ghost town of Bodie.

HOWARD BOND WEEKEND WORKSHOPS, 1095 Harold Circle, Ann Arbor MI 48103. (313)665-6597. Owner: Howard Bond. Offers two types of 2-day workshops: Zone System For All Formats and Refinements in B&W Printing.

*MATT BRADLEY PHOTOGRAPHY WORKSHOPS, 15 Butterfield Lane, Little Rock AR 72212. (501)224-0692. Owner/Photographer: Matt Bradley. Offers 3 workshops in scenic Arkansas. "The Creative Image" is a thorough review of basics and the other two are for avid intermediate to advanced students.

THE BROOKFIELD/SONO PHOTOGRAPHIC WORKSHOP, Brookfield Alley at 127 Washington St., South Norwalk CT (203)853-6155. Offers school, gallery and open workshop, classes for beginners as well as visiting artists Master level workshops.

*NANCY BROWN HANDS-ON WORKSHOPS, 6 W. 20 St., New York NY 10011. (212)924-9105. Contact: Nancy Brown, or studio manager of Windy City Studio. Offers three one-week long workshops in New York City studio; workshops held one week each month in July, August and September.

*CAMDEN PHOTOGRAPHIC WORKSHOPS, 59 Wolcott Hill Rd., Camden NY 13316. (315)245-3614. Workshop Director: Gary Allen VanRiper. Offers one-day and weekend workshops in nature-related subjects.

*CANADIAN PACIFIC WEST COAST WORKSHOPS, 2035 W41 Ave., Vancouver, BC V6M 1Y7 Canada. (604)261-7211. Manager, Sharron Milstein. Offers week-long instructional workshops offered in Long Beach, Gulf Islands and Whistler Mountain.

*CANYONLANDS FIELD INSTITUTE PHOTO WORKSHOPS, P.O. Box 68, Moab UT 84532. (801)259-7750. Program Coordinator: David Williams. Offers programs in landscape photography in Canyonlands & Arches National Parks.

■CENTER FOR PHOTOGRAPHY, 59 Tinker St., Woodstock NY 12498. (914)679-9957. Director: Kathleen Kenyon. Coordinator of Woodstock Photography Workshops summer program. Summer weekend workshops; includes film/video series.

*CREATIVE VISION WORKSHOPS IN COLORADO HIGH COUNTRY, 317 E. Winter Ave., Danville IL 61832-1857. (217)442-3075. Director: Orvil Stokes. Offers workshops in the color Zone system, previsualization and contrast control.

*CRESTED BUTTE NATURE WORKSHOPS, 2650 S. Zuni Street, Englewood CO 80110. (303)935-0900. Director John Fielder. Conducts nature photography workshop.

CUMMINGTON COMMUNITY OF THE ARTS, Cummington Community of the Arts, RR#1, Box 145, Cummington MA 01026. (413)634-2172. Contact: Executive Director. Residences for artists of all disciplines from 1-3 months.

*DEERFIELD AT STONINGTON, 701 Elm Street, Essexville MI 48732. (517)893-6402. Director Chuck McMartin. Offers wildlife photo workshops in the Hiawatha National Forest in Michigan's upper pennisula.

*DILLMAN'S CREATIVE PHOTOGRAPHY WORKSHOPS, P.O. Box 98, 3305 Sand Lake Lodge Ln., Lac du Flambeau WI 54538. (715)588-3143. Workshop Coordinator: Amber Weldon. Offers 13 photography workshops this season—all types of photography.

*FRANCES DORRIS PHOTOGRAPHY AND HOUSING CO-OPERATIVES, P.O. Box 120691 Nashville TN 37212, (615)292-6993. Owner/Director Frances Dorris. Offers workshops in photo instruction, technique and design, Great Smoky Mountains National Park, Texas, Rio Grande Corridor, New Mexico. (Low student/teacher ratio.)

THE DOUGLIS VISUAL WORKSHOPS, Saturday Safari Seminars (Dept PM), 212 S. Chester Rd., Swarthmore PA 19081. (215)544-7977. Director: Phil Douglis. Offers one-day Saturday Safari Seminars in 11 cities.

EGYPTIAN EYE, Box 2868, San Diego CA 92112. (303)595-0245. Tour Organizer: Pam Pettee. Offers travel photography, composition and lighting challenges. Workshops held November and February. Includes 2 week tour of Egypt.

■FILM IN THE CITIES/LIGHTWORKS, 2388 University Ave., St. Paul MN 55114. (612)646-6104. Director: Ruth Williams. Offers basic through advanced level courses in photography, film/video production and studies, screenwriting, computer graphics and electronic sound composition.

■FILM/VIDEO ARTS, INC., 817 Broadway, New York NY 10003. (212)673-9361. Contact: Media Training Coordinator. Offers instruction in all aspects of film and video production. Minority scholarships available.

*FRIENDS OF ARIZONA HIGHWAYS PHOTO ADVENTURES, P.O. Box 6106, Phoenix AZ 85005-6106. (602)271-5904. Sales Supervisor: Shannon Rosenblatt. Offers photo adventures to Arizona's spectacular locations with photographers like Jerry Jacka and Jack Dykinga and P.K. Weis, whose work routinely appears in Arizona Highways.

FRIENDS OF PHOTOGRAPHY, 250 Fourth St., San Francisco CA 94103. (415)495-7000. Curator of Education: Margaret Moulton. Short-term workshops in documentary and architectural work to landscape and portraiture.

*GOLDEN GATE SCHOOL OF PROFESSIONAL PHOTOGRAPHY, P.O. Box 187, Fairfield CA 94533. (707)422-0319. Director: Jim Inks. Offers short courses in photography annually; six-day program, June 2-7, 1991.

*GREAT SMOKY MOUNTAINS PHOTOGRAPHY WORKSHOPS, 205 Wayah Road, Franklin NC 28734. (704)369-6044. Instructors: Tim Black/Bill Lea. Offers programs which emphasize the use of natural light in creating quality scenic, wildflower and wildlife images.

*JOHN M. HALL WORKSHOPS, P.O. Box 839, Nassawadox VA 23413. (804)442-3049. Contact: Secretary. Offers workshops for and on the Nature Conservancy Preserves in United States.

INTERNATIONAL CENTER OF PHOTOGRAPHY, 1130 5th Ave. at 94th St., New York NY 10128. (212)860-1776. Contact: Education Department. Offers programs in b&w photography, non-silver printing processes, color photography, still life, photographing people, large format, studio, color printing, editorial concepts in photography, Zone system, the freelance photographer, etc.

INTERNATIONAL PHOTO TOURS (VOYAGERS INTERNATIONAL), (formerly East Africa Photo Workshops), Box 915, Ithaca NY 14851. (607)257-3091. Managing Director: David Blanton. Emphasizes techniques of nature photography.

■ *The solid, black square before a listing indicates that the market uses various types of audiovisual materials, such as slides, film or videotape.*

*IRISH PHOTOGRAPHIC WORKSHOP, Voyagers, P.O. Box 915, Ithaca NY 14851. (607)257-3091. Director: Dave Blanton. Offers two-week workshop in the West of Ireland.

ART KANE PHOTO WORKSHOP INC., 1511 New York Ave., Cape May NJ 08204. (609)884-7117. Contact: Bill Deering. Offers fashion, photojournalism, portrait and fine art-photography. Also offers training in studio lighting and printing.

■THE MacDOWELL COLONY, Peterborough NH 03458. (603)924-3886 or (212)966-4860. Offers studio space to writers, composers, painters, sculptors, printmakers, photographers and filmmakers competitively, based on talent.

*JOE McDONALD'S WILDLIFE PHOTOGRAPHY WORKSHOPS AND TOURS, 116 7th St., Whitehall PA 18052. (215)433-7025. Owner: Joe McDonald. Offers small groups, quality instruction with emphasis on wildlife.

*MACROTOURS PHOTO WORKSHOPS, P.O. Box 460041 San Francisco CA 94114. (415)826-1096. Director Bert Banks(. Offers travel workshops for wildflowers, scenics, wildlife to Alaska, Southwest and Western National Parks.

THE MAINE PHOTOGRAPHIC WORKSHOPS, Rockport ME 04856. (207)236-8581. Director: David H. Lyman. Offers more than 200 one-week workshops for professionals and serious amateurs in photography, film and television.

*MESSANA PHOTO. WORKSHOP, 22500 Rio Vista, St. Clair Shores MI 48081. (313)773-5815. Joseph P. Messana. On location photographic workshops—architecture, nature, scenics, models and sculpture. Fall color trip in October; Spring trip to city.

NATIONAL INSTITUTE FOR EXPLORATION, 307 W. University Ave., Champaign IL 61820. (217)352-3667. Director: Dr. Barry W. Barker. Offers opportunities for photographers of all skill levels to become published in magazines and travel adventure books.

*NATIONAL PARK PHOTO ADVENTURE SERIES WORKSHOPS, 302 Astor Court, Delmar NY 12054. (518)439-8347. President: Peter Finger. Offers over 20 photo workshops, held in various National Parks. Also offers 15 photo workshops throughout the Northeast.

*NATURE IMAGES, INC., P.O. Box 2037, West Palm Beach FL 33402. (407)586-7332. Director: Helen Longest-Slaughter. Week and weekend photo workshops offered in Everglades National Park, Coastal NC, WV, Yellowstone National Park and Maine.

*NATURE PHOTOGRAPHY WORKSHOPS, 8410 Madeline Drive, St. Louis, MO 63114. (314)427-6311. Instructors: Ed or Lee Mason. Offers customized workshops for one, three or five days, and for 3 weeks at your location.

*NEVER SINK PHOTO WORKSHOP, P.O. Box 641, Woodbourne NY 12788. (212)929-0008; (914)434-0575. Owner: Louis Jawitz. Offers weekend workshops in scenic, travel, location and stock photography from late July through early September in Catskill Mountains.

*NEW ENGLAND SCHOOL OF PHOTOGRAPHY, 537 Commonwealth Ave., Boston MA 02215. (617)437-1868. Administrative Director: Peter Forrest. Instruction in professional and creative photography.

*NORTH LIGHT WORKSHOPS, 1416 Farmington Ave., Farmington CT 06032. (203)673-7179. Owner: Mark G. Harutunian. Offers workshops on black and white Zone System Photography.

NORTHERN KENTUCKY UNIVERSITY SUMMER PHOTO WORKSHOP, Highland Heights KY 41076. (606)572-5648. Professor of Art: Barry Andersen. Offers programs by a series of visiting photographers.

*NORTHERN NEW MEXICO PHOTOGRAPHY WORKSHOPS, 1303 E. Brockton Avenue #A, Redlands CA 92374. (714)793-8257. Director, Owner: Andrew Shumaker. Offers small workshops in high-quality black and white landscape techniques.

Close-up

Roger Fremier
Executive Director
Gail Pierce
Associate Director/Gallery Manager
The Photographic Center of Monterey Peninsula
Carmel, California

The Monterey Peninsula area has long been a mecca to photographers spellbound by the striking "wildness" of the rocky beaches and the variety of local architectural scenes to preserve on film. This tradition was begun by such notable photographers as Ansel Adams and Edward Weston and is being continued, says Gail Pierce, through The Photographic Center of Monterey Peninsula. According to Associate Director Pierce and Director Roger Fremier, the purpose of the Center is to provide a meeting ground for photographers of all levels to learn and improve their photographic skills.

"One message we hope students can take away is that photography is a way of communicating their view of life," Pierce emphasizes. "Our goal is to help develop this growth in our students. Photographers are always in search of a better image; a good workshop is a blend of both the technical and aesthetic concerns." All that workshop participants need to bring, she adds, "is a willingness to participate and explore new ideas."

The varied selection of weekend and five-day classes, offered year round, includes Location Photography Sessions throughout Monterey Peninsula and at Garrapata Beach (a favorite spot of many master photographers): "Fog, Sun, and Sea," Richard Garrod and Brad Cole; "Figure in the Landscape," Edna Bullock; "Travel Workshops to Mono Lake," Jeff Nixon; "Death Valley," Henry Gilpin; and "Fall in the Gold Country," Evelyn Z. Miller. Technically-oriented classes include: "Printing Formulas of the Masters," Richard Garrod; "Advanced Black and White Printing," five instructors; "Black and White Darkroom Techniques," Richard Garrod and Brad Cole; "Sensitometry: Beyond The Zone

System," Phil Davis, Bob Routh; and "Platinum/Palladium," Dick Arentz.

Fremier, who has more than 30 years experience as a commercial and fine-art photographer, says: "We hire instructors with both a working background and seasoned teaching experience in photography." The staff includes: Cole Weston, Douglas Madeley, Huntington Witherill, Josephus Daniels and others listed above.

The directors believe that the wide range of knowledge, technical tips, philosophical discussions, artistic direction and aesthetic concerns are not only shared in workshops but also continued in publications aimed at expanding the growth and understanding of photography. "We do this," says Fremier, "by offering a wealth of benefits both to members and non-members such as the workshops; lectures; members' publications such as newsletters and a magazine; exhibit openings; videos; booklets; and folios."

All in all, Fremier remarks that "artistic spirit flourishes when communication is free and clear among its practitioners." Noting the unexpected joys of the workshop experience, Pierce quickly adds that "photographers of any level can benefit, especially when an exchange of new and old ideas fosters personal photographic growth."

— Connie Eidenier

"The Monterey Peninsula has long been a mecca for photography," Gail Pierce says. Her photo, which provides an alternate view of Garrapata Beach, is testimony to the compelling attraction this area has for photographers.

This photo of Garrapata Beach by Photo Center Director Roger Fremier shows one of the many landmarks of the Monterey Peninsula which has inspired numerous celebrated photographers.

THE OGUNQUIT PHOTOGRAPHY SCHOOL, Box 2234, Ogunquit ME 03907. (207)646-7055. Director: Stuart Nudelman. Offers programs in photographic sensitivity, marketing photos and photodocumentation, creative workshops with guest instructors, AV symposiums for educators and traveling workshops.

ON LOCATION PHOTOGRAPHY TOURS, Suite #1, 12964 Moorpark St., Studio City CA 91604. (818)789-3760. Offers tours for people with a serious interest in travel photography.

*OZARK PHOTOGRAPHY WORKSHOP FIELDTRIP, 40 Kyle Street, Batesville AR 72501. (501)793-4552. Conductor: Barney Sellers. Offers opportunities for all day outdoor subject shooting.

THE PALO ALTO PHOTOGRAPHIC WORKSHOPS, 854 Rorke Way Palo Alto CA 94303. (415)424-0105. Co-Directors: Douglas Peck and Stacy Geiken. Offers classes in beginning photography, nature photography and 4×5 view camera.

PETERS VALLEY CRAFT CENTER, Layton NJ 07851. (201)948-5200. Offers summer workshops for all skill levels in specific techniques.

*PHOTO FOCUS/COUPEVILLE ARTS CENTER, P.O. Box 171 MP, Coupeville WA 98239. (206)678-3396. Director: Judy Lynn. Offers variety of workshops with nationally recognized instructors.

PHOTO TOURS: IN FOCUS WITH MICHELE BURGESS, 20741 Catamaran Lane, Huntington Beach, CA 92646. (714)536-6104. President: Michele Burgess. Offers overseas tours to photogenic areas with expert photography consultation, at a leisurely pace and in small groups (maximum group size 20).

THE PHOTOGRAPHIC CENTER OF MONTEREY PENINSULA, Box 1100, Carmel CA 93921. (408)625-5181. Directors: Roger Fremier and Gail Pierce. "Workshop topics are diverse, from basic instruction to advanced printing and the Zone system to creativity and business."

PRATT MANHATTAN, 295 Lafayette Ave., New York NY 10012. (212)925-8481. Director of Continuing Education: Karen Miletsky. Offers programs on photography; such as nature photography in the city.

SIERRA PHOTOGRAPHIC WORKSHOPS, Box 33, El Portal CA 95318. (209)379-2828/2841. Contact: Sierra Photographic Workshops. Offers "personalized instruction in outdoor photography, technical knowledge useful in learning to develop a personal style, learning to convey ideas through photographs, marketing nature photography."

*SINKING CREEK FILM FESTIVAL, 1250 Old Shiloh Road, Greeneville TN 37743. (615)638-6524. Director: Mary Jane Coleman. Offers workshops in film and video production and media analysis.

*SOUTH FLORIDA PHOTOGRAPHIC WORKSHOPS/IRIS GALLERY, P.O. Box 3018, Boca Raton FL 33431. (407)997-9879. Director: Anita Starkoff. Offers number of photographic workships and exhibits of photography.

SOUTHEASTERN CENTER FOR THE ARTS, INC., (SCA), 1935 Cliff Valley Way, Atlanta GA 30329. (404)633-1990. Co-Directors: Jeanne and Neil Chaput de Saintonge. Professional career program; adult education classes; national/international photography workshops and a summer intensive professional career program in Montana.

*SOUTHERN MAGNOLIA PHOTOGRAPHIC WORKSHOP, 1615 Fifth Avenue East, Tuscaloosa AL 35401. (205)752-8591. Director: M. Wayne Stanton. Offers programs in large format, fine art and b&w.

SOUTHWEST PHOTOGRAPHIC WORKSHOPS, P.O. Box 19272, Houston TX 77224. (713)496-2905. Contact: Jay Forrest. On location photographic workshops in Texas and New Mexico.

SPLIT ROCK ARTS PROGRAM, University of Minnesota, 306 Wesbrook Hall, 77 Pleasant St. SE, Minneapolis MN 55455. (612)624-6800. Registrar: Vivien Oja. One-week, intensive summer residential workshops; nature and documentary photography as well as other arts. Duluth campus on Lake Superior.

TOUCH OF SUCCESS PHOTO SEMINARS, Box 194, Lowell FL 32663. (904)867-0463. Director: Bill Thomas. Offers workshops on nature scenics, plants, wildlife, stalking, building rapport and communication, composition, subject selection, lighting, marketing and business management."

*TRAVEL PHOTOGRAPHY WORKSHOP, Box 2847, Santa Fe NM 87504-2847. (505)982-4979. Founder/instructor: Lisl Dennis, Offers one-week workshops in July and September. Instruction is given in 35mm color photography.

*TRINITY ALPS PHOTOGRAPHY WORKSHOPS, 216 Marquis Place, Santa Maria CA 93454. (805)928-3386. Director: Mary Ellen Schultz. Offers number of workshops on wildlife and nature photography; domestic and international locations include East and West coasts of U.S., Colorado, Alaska, Canada, Africa and the Far East.

*TWIN FALLS NATURE PHOTOGRAPHY WORKSHOPS, Twin Falls State Park P.O. Box 1023, Mullens WV 25882. (304)294-4000. Park Superintendent: Scott Durham. Offers spring and fall nature workshops.

*UNIVERSITY OF CALIFORNIA EXTENSION PHOTOGRAPHY WORKSHOPS, 740 Front Street, Suite 155, Santa Cruz CA 95060. (408)427-6620. Contact: Photography Program. Ongoing program of workshops in photography throughout California, also international study tours in photography.

UNIVERSITY OF NEVADA, "On Assignment Freelance Photojournalism," Reynolds School of Journalism, Reno NV 89557-0040. (702)784-4198. Director: Phillip M. Padellford. Emphasizes techniques and procedures needed to become a consistently published freelancer. Work is assigned and critiqued by panel of experts.

UNIVERSITY OF NEVADA, "On Location Freelance Photojournalism" (Mammoth Lakes,CA), Reynolds School of Journalism, Reno NV 89557-0040. (702)784-4198. Director: Phillip M. Padellford. Emphasizes producing marketable scenics, sports and outdoor subjects. Staff members from top magazines are faculty; for advanced amateurs or pros.

*VISIONQUEST PHOTOGRAPHIC ADVENTURES, Box 572, Duncan, B.C. V9L-3X9 Canada. (604)746-4341. Owner: Paul Fletcher. Offers weekend/weeklong photo workshops on Vancouver Islands' West Coast and on the Queen Charlotte Islands.

*MARK WARNER NATURE PHOTO WORKSHOPS, Box 142, Ledyard CT 06339. (203)572-8748. Offers 1-4 day workshops on nature and wildlife photography by nationally published photographer and writer at various East Coast locations.

*"A WEEKEND WITH RON SANFORD", P.O. Box 248, Gridley CA 95948. (916)846-4687. Contact: Ron Sanford. Offers programs in marketing, travel and wildlife photography. Write or call for details.

WILD HORIZONS, INC., Box 5118-PM, Tucson AZ 85703. (602)622-0672. President: Thomas A. Wiewandt. Offers workshops in field techniques in nature/travel photography at vacation destinations in the American Southwest selected for their outstanding natural beauty and wealth of photographic opportunities.

*WILDERNESS PHOTOGRAPHY EXPEDITIONS, 402 So. 5th, Livingston MT 59047. (406)222-2302. President: Tom Murphy. Offers programs in wildlife and landscape photography in Yellowstone Park.

WOODSTOCK PHOTOGRAPHY WORKSHOPS, 59 Tinker, Woodstock NY 12498. (914)679-9957. Offers workshops in fine art photography.

YELLOWSTONE INSTITUTE, Box 117, Yellowstone National Park WY 82190. (307)344-7381, ext. 2384. Registrar: Jeanne Peterman. Offers nature; wildlife close-up and children's photography.

*JOSEPH ZAIA PHOTOVISION WORKSHOPS, 275 Maybury Avenue, Staten Island NY 10308. (718)356-8968. Director/Instructor: Joseph J. Zaia. Offers personalized instruction for individuals or small groups; locally or on location.

ZONE VI WORKSHOP, % Fred Picker, Director, Putney VT 05346. (802)257-5161. Administrator: Lil Farber. "The Zone VI workshops are for the serious individual who wants to improve his technical and visual skills and probe the emotional and intellectual underpinnings of the medium.

———— Recommended Books & Publications

Photographer's Market recommends the following additional reading material to stay informed of market trends as well as to find additional names and addresses of photo buyers. Most are available either in a library or bookstore or from the publisher. To insure accuracy of information, use copies of these resources that are no older than a year.

ADVERTISING AGE, *740 Rush St., Chicago IL 60611. Weekly advertising and marketing tabloid.*

ADWEEK, *A/S/M Communications, Inc., 49 E. 21st St., New York NY 10010. Weekly advertising and marketing magazine.*

AMERICAN PHOTO, *43rd Floor, 1633 Broadway, New York NY 10019. Monthly magazine, formerly* American Photographer, *now emphasizing the craft and philosophy of photography.*

ART BUSINESS NEWS, *Myers Publishing Co., 60 Ridgeway Plaza, Stamford CT 06905. Monthly tabloid covering art supplies and industry trends.*

ART CALENDAR, *Rt. 2, Box 273-C, Sterling VA 22170. Monthly magazine listing galleries reviewing portfolios, juried shows, percent-for-art programs, scholarships and art colonies, among other art-related topics.*

ART DIRECTION, *6th Fl., 10 E. 39th St., New York NY 10016-0199. Monthly magazine featuring art directors' views on advertising and photography.*

ART DIRECTORS ANNUAL, *Art Directors Club, 250 Park Ave. South, New York NY 10003. Annual showcase of work selected by the organization.*

THE ARTIST'S FRIENDLY LEGAL GUIDE, *North Light Publishing, 1507 Dana Ave., Cincinnati OH 45207. Comprehensive guide to copyright, contracts, moral rights and taxes. Includes contracts to be copied and used.*

ASMP BULLETIN, *monthly newsletter of the American Society of Magazine Photographers, 419 Park Ave. South, New York NY 10016. Subscription comes with membership in ASMP.*

AUDIO VIDEO MARKET PLACE, *R.R. Bowker Company, 245 W. 17th St., New York NY 10011. Directory listing audiovisual and film companies.*

COMMUNICATION ARTS, *410 Sherman Ave., Box 10300, Palo Alto CA 94303. Magazine covering design, illustration and photography. Published 8 times a year.*

THE DESIGN FIRM DIRECTORY, *Wefler & Associates, Inc., Box 1591, Evanston IL 60204. Annual directory of design firms.*

EDITOR & PUBLISHER, *The Editor & Publisher Co., Inc., 11 W. 19th St., New York NY 10011. Weekly magazine covering latest developments in journalism and newspaper production. Publishes an annual directory issue listing syndicates and another directory listing newspapers.*

ENCYCLOPEDIA OF ASSOCIATIONS, *Gale Research Co., Penobscot Building, Detroit MI 48226. Annual directory listing active organizations.*

FOLIO, *Box 4949, Stamford CT 06907-0949. Monthly magazine featuring trends in magazine circulation, production and editorial.*

GEBBIE PRESS ALL-IN-ONE DIRECTORY, *Gebbie Press, Inc., Box 1000, New Paltz NY 12561. Annual directory listing newspapers, consumer and trade magazines, radio and television stations and syndicates.*

GREETINGS MAGAZINE, *MacKay Publishing Corp., 309 Fifth Ave., New York NY 10016. Monthly magazine featuring updates on the greeting card and stationery industry.*

HOW TO MAKE MONEY IN NEWSPAPER SYNDICATION, *(by Susan Lane), Newspaper Syndication Specialists, Suite 326, Box 19654, Irvine CA 92720. Complete guide to marketing cartoons and features to syndicates and to syndicating your own work.*

INTERNATIONAL DIRECTORY OF LITTLE MAGAZINES AND SMALL PRESSES, *Dustbooks, Box 100, Paradise CA 95969. Annual directory listing small, independent magazines, presses and papers.*

LEGAL GUIDE FOR THE VISUAL ARTIST, *by Tad Crawford, North Light Publishing, 1507 Dana Ave., Cincinnati OH 45207. Guide to art law covering copyright and contracts.*

LITERARY MARKET PLACE, *R.R. Bowker Company, 245 W. 17th St., New York NY 10011. Annual directory listing book publishers.*

MADISON AVENUE HANDBOOK, *Peter Glenn Publications, 17 E. 48th St., New York NY 10017. Annual directory listing advertising agencies, audiovisual firms and design studios in the New York area.*

NEGOTIATING STOCK PHOTO PRICES, *by Jim Pickerell. Hardbound book which offers pricing guidelines for selling photos through stock photo agencies. Available through American Society of Magazine Photographers. See ASMP Bulletin for contact information.*

NEWSLETTERS IN PRINT, *Gale Research Co., Penobscot Building, Detroit MI 48226. Annual directory listing newsletters.*

O'DWYER DIRECTORY OF PUBLIC RELATIONS FIRMS, *J.R. O'Dwyer Company, Inc., 271 Madison Ave., New York NY 10016. Annual directory listing public relations firms, indexed by specialties.*

OUTDOOR PHOTOGRAPHER, *Suite 800, 16000 Ventura Blvd., Encino CA 91436. Monthly magazine emphasizing equipment and techniques for shooting in outdoor conditions.*

PETERSEN'S PHOTOGRAPHIC MAGAZINE, *8490 Sunset Blvd., Los Angeles CA 90069. Monthly magazine for beginning and semi-professional photographers in all phases of still photography.*

PHOTO/DESIGN, *One Park Ave., New York NY 10016. Monthly magazine emphasizing photography in the advertising/design fields.*

PHOTO DISTRICT NEWS, *49 East 21st St., New York NY 10010. Monthly trade magazine for the photography industry.*

PHOTOGRAPHER'S GUIDE TO MARKETING AND SELF-PROMOTION, *by Maria Piscopo, published by Writer's Digest Books, 1507 Dana Ave., Cincinnati, Ohio 45207.*

POPULAR PHOTOGRAPHY, *43rd Floor, 1633 Broadway, New York NY 10019. Monthly magazine emphasizing wide range of equipment and techniques for general photography audience. Now incorporates the previously separate magazine, Modern Photography.*

PRINT, *Ninth Fl., 104 Fifth Ave., New York NY 10011. Bimonthly magazine focusing on creative trends and technological advances in illustration, design, photography and printing.*

PROFESSIONAL PHOTOGRAPHER, *published by Professional Photographers of America (PPA), 1090 Executive Way, Des Plaines IL 60018. Monthly magazine, emphasizing technique and equipment for working photographers.*

PUBLISHERS WEEKLY, *205 W. 42nd St., New York NY 10017. Weekly magazine covering industry trends and news in book publishing, book reviews and interviews.*

PUBLISHING NEWS, *Hanson Publishing Group, Box 4949, Stamford CT 06907-0949. Bimonthly newsmagazine of the publishing industry.*

STANDARD DIRECTORY OF ADVERTISING AGENCIES, *National Register Publishing Co., Inc., 3004 Glenview Rd., Wilmette IL 60091. Annual directory listing advertising agencies.*

STANDARD PERIODICAL DIRECTORY, *Oxbridge Communications, Inc., Room 301, 150 Fifth Ave., New York NY 10011. Biannual directory listing magazines, journals, newsletters, directories and association publications.*

STANDARD RATE AND DATA SERVICE, *3004 Glenview Rd., Wilmette IL 60091. Annual directory listing magazines, plus their advertising rates.*

STOCK PHOTOGRAPHY HANDBOOK, *by Michal Heron, published by American Society of Magazine Photographers, 419 Park Ave. South, New York NY 10016.*

THE STOCK WORKBOOK, *published by Scott & Daughters Publishing, Inc., 940 N. Highland Ave., Los Angeles CA 90038. Annual directory of stock photo agencies.*

WRITER'S MARKET, *Writer's Digest Books, 1507 Dana Ave., Cincinnati OH 45207. Annual directory listing markets for freelance writers. Lists names, addresses, contact people and marketing information for book publishers, magazines, greeting card companies and syndicates. Many listings also list photo needs and payment rates.*

Professional Organizations

The organizations in the following list can be valuable to photographers who are seeking to broaden their knowledge and contacts within the photography industry. Typically, such organizations have regional or local chapters and offer regular activities and/or publications for their members. To learn about a particular organization and what it can offer to you, call or write for more information.

Advertising Photographers of America (APA)
578 Broadway, New York NY 10012. (212)807-0399.

American Film Institute (AFI)
John F. Kennedy Center for the Performing Arts, Washington DC 20566. (202)828-4000.

American Society of Magazine Photographers (ASMP)
205 Lexington Ave., New York NY 10016. (212)889-9144.

American Society of Photographers (ASP)
Box 52836, Tulsa OK 74158. (918)743-2122.

American Society of Picture Professionals (ASPP)
% Comstock, Inc., 30 Irving Pl., New York NY 10003

Association for Multi-Image International (AMI)
Suite 401, 8019 North Himes Ave., Tampa FL 33614. (813)932-1692.

International Fire Photographers Association (FFPA)
P.O. Box 8337, Rolling Meadows IL 60008. (708)394-5835.

National Press Photographers Association (NPPA)
Suite 306, 3200 Cross daile Dr., Durham NC 27705. (919)383-7246.

Picture Agency Agency Council of America (PACA)
% H. Armstrong Roberts, Inc., 4203 Locust St., Philadelphis PA 19104. (215)386-6300.

Professional Photographers of America, Inc. (PPA)
1090 Executive Way, Des Plaines IL 60018. (312)299-8161.

Society of Photographers' and Artists' Representatives (SPAR)
Room 914, 1123 Broadway, New York NY 10010. (212)924-6023.

Society of Professional Videographers (SPV)
P.O. Box 1933, Huntsville AL 35807. (205)534-9722.

University Film and Video Association (UFVA)
% George Wehbi, School of Cinema Television, University of Southern California, University Park, MC2212, Los Angeles CA 90089.

Acceptance (payment on). The buyer pays for certain rights to publish a picture at the time he accepts it, prior to its publication.

Agent. A person who calls upon potential buyers to present and sell existing work or obtain assignments for his client. A commission is usually charged. Such a person may also be called a *photographer's rep.*

All rights. A form of rights often confused with work for hire. Identical to a buyout, this typically applies when the client buys all rights or claim to ownership of copyright, usually for a lump sum payment. This entitles the client to unlimited, exclusive usage and usually with no further compensation to the creator. Unlike work for hire, the transfer of copyright is not permanent. A time limit can be negotiated, or the copyright ownership can run to the maximum of 35 years. Also see Copyright and Work for Hire article, in the Business of Photography section.

All reproduction rights. See all rights.

All subsidiary rights. See all rights.

ASMP member pricing survey. These statistics are the result of a national survey of the American Society of Magazine Photographer's (ASMP) compiled to give an overview of various specialties comprising the photography market. Though erroneously referred to as "ASMP rates", this survey is not intended to suggest rates or to establish minimum or maximum fees.

Assignment. A definite OK to take photos for a specific client with mutual understanding as to the provisions and terms involved.

Assignment of copyright, rights. The photographer transfers claim to ownership of copyright over to another party in a written contract signed by both parties. Terms are almost always exclusive, but can be negotiated for a limited time period or as a permanent transfer. Also see Copyright and Work for Hire article, in the Business of Photography section.

Assign (designated recipient). A third-party person or business to which a client assigns or designates ownership of copyrights that the client purchased originally from a creator, such as a photographer.

Audiovisual. Materials such as filmstrips, motion pictures and overhead transparencies which use audio backup for visual material.

Automatic renewal clause. In contracts with stock photo agencies, this clause works on the concept that every time the photographer delivers an image, the contract is automatically renewed for a specified number of years. The drawback is that a photographer can be bound by the contract terms beyond the contract's termination and be blocked from marketing the same images to other clients for an extended period of time.

AV. See Audiovisual.

Betacam. A videotape mastering format typically used for documentary/location work. Because of its compact equipment design allowing mobility and its extremely high-quality for its size, it has become an accepted standard among TV stations for news coverage.

Bimonthly. Every two months.

Biweekly. Every two weeks.

Bleed. In a mounted photograph it refers to an image that extends to the boundaries of the board.

Blurb. Written material appearing on a magazine's cover describing its contents.

Body copy. Text used in a printed ad.

Bounce light. Light that is directed away from the subject toward a reflective surface.

Bracket. To make a number of different exposures of the same subject in the same lighting conditions.

Buyout. A form of work for hire where the client buys all rights or claim to ownership of copyright, usually for a lump sum payment. Also see All rights, Work for hire.

Caption. The words printed with a photo (usually directly beneath it) describing the scene or action. Synonymous with *cutline.*

Cibachrome. A direct process that yields fade-resistant color prints directly from color slides.

Clips. See Tearsheets.

Commission. The fee (usually a percentage of the total price received for a picture) charged by a photo agency or agent for finding a buyer and attending to the details of billing, collecting, etc.

Composition. The visual arrangement of all elements in a photograph.

Copyright. The exclusive legal right to reproduce, publish and sell the matter and form of a literary or artistic work.

C-print. Any enlargement printed from a negative. Any enlargement from a transparency is called an R-print.

Credit line. The byline of a photographer or organization that appears below or beside published photos.

Crop. To omit unnecessary parts of an image when making a print or copy negative in order to focus attention on the important part of the image.

Cutline. See Caption.

Day rate. A minimum fee which many photographers charge for a day's work, whether a full day is spent on a shoot or not. Some photographer's offer a half-day rate for projects involving up to a half-day of work. This rate typically includes mark-up but not additional expenses, which are usually billed to the customer.

Demo(s). A sample reel of film or sample videocassette which includes excerpts of a filmmaker's or videographer's production work for clients.

Disclaimer. A denial of legal claim used in ads and on products.

Dry mounting. A method of mounting prints on cardboard or similar materials by means of heat, pressure, and tissue impregnated with shellac.

EFP. Abbreviation for Electronic Field Processing equipment. Trade jargon in the news/video production industry for a video recording system that is several steps above ENG in quality. Typically, this is employed when film-like sharpness and color saturation are desirable in a video format. It requires a high degree of lighting, set-up and post-production. Also see ENG.

ENG. Abbreviation for Electronic News Gathering equipment. Trade jargon in the news/video production industry for professional-quality video news cameras which can record images on videotape or transmit them by microwave to a TV station's receiver.

Exclusive property rights. A type of exclusive rights in which the client owns the physical image, such as a print, slide, film reel or videotape. A good example is when a portrait which is shot for a person to keep, while the photographer retains the copyright.

Exclusive rights. A type of rights in which the client purchases exclusive usage of the image for a negotiated time period, such as one, three or five years. Can also be permanent. Also see All rights and Work for Hire.

Fee-plus basis. An arrangement whereby a photographer is given a certain fee for an assignment— plus reimbursement for travel costs, model fees, props and other related expenses incurred in filling the assignment.

First rights. The photographer gives the purchaser the right to reproduce the work for the first time. The photographer agrees not to permit any prior publication of the work elsewhere for a specified amount of time.

Format. The size, shape and other traits giving identity to a periodical.

Gaffer. In motion pictures, the person who is responsible for positioning and operating lighting equipment, including generators and electrical cables.

Grip. A member of a motion picture camera crew who is responsible for transporting, setting up, operating, and removing support equipment for the camera and related activities.

Holography. Recording on a photographic material the interference pattern between a direct coherent light beam and one reflected or transmitted by the subject. The resulting hologram gives the appearance of three dimensions, and, within limits, changing the viewpoint from which a hologram is observed shows the subject as seen from different angles.

In perpetuity. A term used in business contracts which means that once a photographer has sold his copyrights to a client, the client has claim to ownership of the image or images forever. Also see All rights, Work for hire.

Internegative. An intermediate image used to convert a color transparency to a black-and-white print.

IRC. Abbreviation for International Reply Coupon. IRCs are used instead of stamps when submitting material to foreign buyers.

Leasing. A term used in reference to the repeated selling of one-time rights to a photo; also known as *renting*.

Logo. The distinctive nameplate of a publication which appears on its cover.

Model release. Written permission to use a person's photo in publications or for commercial use.

Ms, mss. Manuscript and manuscripts, respectively. Their abbreviations are used in *Photographer's Market* listings.

Multi-image. A type of slide show which uses more than one projector to create greater visual impact with the subject. In more sophisticated multi-image shows, the projectors can be programmed to run by computer for split-second timing and animated effects.

Multimedia. A generic term used by advertising, public relations and audiovisual firms to describe productions using more than one medium together—such as slides and full-motion, color video— to create a variety of visual effects. Usually such productions are used in sales meetings and similar kinds of public events.

News Release. See Press release.

No right of reversion. A term in business contracts which specifies once a photographer sells his copyrights to an image or images, he has surrendered his claim to ownership. This may be unenforceable, though, in light of the 1989 Supreme Court decision on copyright law. Also see All rights, Work for hire. Also see Copyright and Work for Hire article, in the Business of Photography section.

Offset. A printing process using flat plates. The plate is treated to accept ink in image areas and to reject it in nonimage areas. The inking is transferred to a rubber roller and then to the paper.

One-time rights. The photographer sells the right to use a photo one time only in any medium. The rights transfer back to the photographer on his request after the photo's use.

On spec. Abbreviation for "on speculation." Also see Speculation, Assignment.

Page rate. An arrangement in which a photographer is paid at a standard rate per page. A page consists of both illustrations and text.

Panoramic Format. A camera format which creates the impression of peripheral vision for the viewer. It was first developed for use in motion pictures and later adapted to still formats. In still work, this format requires a very specialized camera and lens system.

Pans. See Panoramic format.

Point-of-purchase, point-of-sale. A generic term used in the advertising industry to describe in-store marketing displays which promote a product. Typically, these colorful and highly-illustrated displays are placed near check out lanes or counters, and offer tear-off discount coupons or trial samples of the product.

P-O-P, P-O-S. See Point-of-purchase.

Portfolio. A group of photographs assembled to demonstrate a photographer's talent and abilities, often presented to buyers.

Press Release. A form of publicity announcement which public relations agencies and corporate communications staff people send out to newspapers and TV stations to generate news coverage. Usually this is sent in typewritten form with accompanying photos or videotape materials. Also see Video News Release.

Property release. Written permission to use a photo of private property and public or government facilities in publications or commercial use.

Publication (payment on). The buyer does not pay for rights to publish a photo until it is actually published, as opposed to payment on acceptance.

Release. See Model release, Property release.

Rep. Trade jargon for sales representative. Also see Agent.

Query. A letter of inquiry to an editor or potential buyer soliciting his interest in a possible photo assignment or photos that the photographer may already have.

Resume. A short written account of one's career, qualifications and accomplishments.

Royalty. A percentage payment made to a photographer/filmmaker for each copy of his work sold.

R-print. Any enlargement made from a transparency. Any enlargement from a negative is called a C-print.

SAE. Self-addressed envelope. Rather than requesting a self-addressed, stamped envelope, market listings may advise sending a SAE with the proper amount of postage to guarantee safe return of sample copies.

SASE. Abbreviation for self-addressed stamped envelope. Most buyers require SASE if a photographer wishes unused photos returned to him, especially unsolicited materials.

Self-assignment. Any photography project which a photographer shoots to show his abilities to prospective clients. This can be used by beginning photographers who want to build a portfolio or by photographers wanting to make a transition into a new market.

Self-promotion piece. A printed piece which photographers use for advertising and promoting their businesses. These pieces usually use one or more examples of the photographers' best work, and are professionally designed and printed to make the best impression.

Semigloss. A paper surface with a texture between glossy and matte, but closer to glossy.

Semimonthly. Twice a month.

Serial rights. The photographer sells the right to use a photo in a periodical. Rights usually transfer back to the photographer on his request after the photo's use.

Simultaneous submissions. Submission of the same photo or group of photos to more than one potential buyer at the same time.

Speculation. The photographer takes photos on his own with no assurance that the buyer will either purchase them or reimburse his expenses in any way, as opposed to taking photos on assignment.

Stock photo agency. A business that maintains a large collection of photos which it makes available to a variety of clients such as advertising agencies, calendar firms, and periodicals. Agencies usually retain 40-60 percent of the sales price they collect, and remit the balance to the photographers whose photo rights they've sold.

Stock Photography. Primarily the selling of reprint rights to existing photographs rather than shooting on assignment for a client. Some stock photos are sold outright, but most are rented for a limited time period. Individuals can market and sell stock images to individual clients from their personal inventory, or stock photo agencies can market a photographer's work for them. Many stock agencies hire photographers to shoot new work on assignment which then becomes the inventory of the stock agency.

Stringer. A freelancer who works part-time for a newspaper, handling spot news and assignments in his area.

SVHS. Abbreviation for Super VHS. A videotape equipment format utilizing standard VHS format tape but which is a step above consumer quality in resolution. The camera system separates the elements of the video signal into two main components of sharpness and color which can be further enhanced in post-production and used for TV broadcast.

Table-top. Still-life photography; also the use of miniature props or models constructed to simulate reality.

Tabloid. A newspaper that is about half the page size of an ordinary newspaper, and which contains many photos and news in condensed form.

Tearsheet. An actual sample of a published work from a publication.

Trade journal. A publication devoted strictly to the interests of readers involved in a specific trade or profession, such as doctors, writers, or druggists, and generally available only by subscription.

Transparency. A color film with positive image, also referred to as a slide.

Tungsten light. Artificial illumination as opposed to daylight.

U-Matic. A trade name for a particular videotape format produced by the Sony Corporation.

Unlimited use. A type of rights in which the client has total control over both how and how many times an image will be used. Also see All rights, Exclusive rights, Work for hire.

VHS. Abbreviation for Video Home System. A standard videotape format for recording consumer-quality videotape. This is the format most commonly used in home videocassette recording and portable camcorders.

Video news release. A videocassette recording containing a brief news segment specially prepared for broadcast on TV new programs. Usually, public relations firms hire AV firms or filmmaker/videographers to shoot and produce these recordings for publicity purposes of their clients.

Videotape. Magnetic recording tape similar to that used for recording sound but which also records moving images, especially for broadcast on television.

Videowall. An elaborate installation of computer-controlled television screens in which several screens create a much larger moving image. For example, with 8 screens, each of the screens may hold a portion of a larger scene, or two images can be shown side by side, or one image can be set in the middle of a surrounding image.

VNR. See Video news release.

Work for hire, Work made for hire. Any work that is assigned by an employer and the employer becomes the owner of the copyright. Copyright law clearly defines the types of photography which come under the work-for-hire definition. An employer can claim ownership to the copyright only in cases where the photographer is a fulltime staff person for the employer or in special cases where the photographer negotiates and assigns ownership of the copyright in writing to the employer for a limited time period. Stock images cannot be purchased under work-for-hire terms. Also see Copyright and Work for Hire article, in the Business of Photography section.

World rights. A type of rights in which the client buys usage of an image in the international marketplace.

Worldwide exclusive rights. A form of world rights in which the client buys exclusive usage of an image in the international marketplace.

Zone System. A system of exposure which allows the photographer to previsualize the print, based on a gray scale containing nine zones. Many workshops offer classes in Zone System.

Zoom lens. A type of lens with a range of various focal lengths.

First Markets Index

The following index lists some 200 markets which are especially good for freelancers breaking into photography or wanting to build up their portfolios in a new category. Typically, these markets provide little or no payment for photos but do offer exposure, photocredits and tearsheets or extra contributor's copies as compensation. Refer to the General Index for the page number of each market.

Agri-Times Northwest
Alabama Literary Review
Alabama Municipal Journal
Alabamian, The
Alaska Fisherman's Journal
American Bee Journal
American Fire Journal
American Fitness Magazine
American Museum of Natural History Library,
    Photographic Collection
Arizona Business Gazette
Arjuna Library Press
Arkansas Farm and Country
Army Reserve Magazine
Back Home in Kentucky
Baja Times
Biology Digest
Bionics
Bird Talk
Book Author's Newsletter
Bowling Magazine
Butter Fat Magazine
Capilano Review, The
Capper's
Car Collector & Car Classics
Career Woman
Ceramics Monthly
Child & Family Services of New Hampshire
Child Life
Children's Playmate
Citizen Newspaper Group
Citröen Car Club News
City & Country Club Life Magazine
Clearvue, Inc.
Clearwater
Conservationist Magazine
Covenant Companion, The
Cranberries
Cycling: BC
Daily Shipping News
Dairy Goat Journal
Davidson & Associates
Dayton Ballet
Distributor
Diver, The
Epstein & Walker Associates
Fighting Woman News
Financial Independence Money Management
    Magazine
Fire Chief Magazine
Flooring
Florida Grower and Rancher

Forerunner, The
Golden Years
Gospel Herald
Greetwell
Guardian Newsweekly
Hampden-Sydney College
Hartford Woman
Headwaters
Helicopter International
Horse World USA
Horses Magazine
ICF Bugle, The
Independent Living
Instrumentalist, The
Intensive Caring Unlimited
International Gymnast
International Photo News
Jazz Times
Kroloff, Marshall & Associates, Ltd.
Let's Live
Live Steam Magazine
Louisville Magazine
Manitoba Teacher, The
Midwest Talent
Military Collector's News
Minnesota Opera, The
Modern Liturgy
Multinational Monitor
Music Educators Journal
National Bus Trader
National Masters News
Nevada Farm Bureau Agriculture and Livestock
    Journal
New Mexico Photographer
News Herald
Northern Logger & Timber Processor
Numismatic News
Olson & Co., C.
Pennsylvania Game News
Pentecostal Messenger, The
Pet Business
Pizza Today
Police Times/Chief of Police
Polled Hereford World
Population Bulletin
Premier Film, Video & Recording
Produce News, The
Quick Frozen Foods International
Quilt World
Recommend Worldwide
Salome: A Journal for the Performing Arts
San Jose State University

Scott Enterprises, Liz
Sentinel, The
Service Reporter
Snowmobile West
Soccer America
Sources: The Journal of Underwater Education
Southern Lumberman
Sunshine Artists USA
T-Jaye Record Company
Tennis Week
Third World
Tourist Attractions & Parks
Townships Sun, The
Tropical Fish Hobbyist Magazine

University of New Haven
Utility and Telephone Fleets
Utility Construction and Maintenance
Ventura County & Coast Reporter
Voice of South Marion
Voyager International
WDS Forum
Wines & Vines
Wisconsin Restaurateur, The
Woman Engineer
Womenwise
Wyoming Rural Electric News
Yachtsman

If the specific market you are looking for is not listed in the following General Index, check the '90-'91 Changes at the end of the appropriate section. Any listings which have had a name change will be cross-referenced in this index.

A

A.D. Book Co. 120
a.k.a. Skylight Gallery 175
A.V. Media Craftsman, Inc. 89
AAA Michigan Living 378
AAA World 378
A&A Creations 228
ABA Banking Journal 434
Aboard Magazine 247
Academe: Bulletin of the AAUP 378
Accent on Living 247
Access Control 434
Ace Photo Agency 519
Across the Board Magazine 435
Acting Company, The 154
Adams Memorial Gallery 175
Adams Picture Library 519
Adamson Advertising 75
Adirondack Life 247
Adler, Schwartz, Inc. 79
Advanced Graphics 228
Adventure Photo 519
Adventure Photography Workshops 578
Adventure Road 378
Africa Card Co., Inc. 228
Africa Report 248
After Five Magazine 248
Afterimage (see TSW/Afterimage 568)
Afterimage Photograph Gallery, The 175
AG Alert 378
AGA Gas, Inc. 154
Agent Andy 229
Agri Finance Magazine 435
Agrichemical Age 435
Agri-Times Northwest 435
AGS & R Communications 61
AI Magazine 379
Aipe Facilities Management Operations and
     Engineering 436
Air & Space/Smithsonian 248
Air Conditioning, Heating & Refrigeration
     News 436
Air Line Pilot 379
Airline Film & TV Promotions 39
Airport Services Magazine 436
Alabama Game & Fish (see Game & Fish Publi-
     cations 291)
Alabama Literary Review 248
Alabama Municipal Journal 379
Alabamian, The 379
Alamo Ad Center, Inc. 108
Alaska 249
Alaska Fisherman's Journal 202
Alaska Geographic 250

Alaska Wild Images 229
Alcalde Magazine 382
Alden Group-Public Relations Division 88
Alfa Owner 382
Alias Gallery 175
Alive Now! Magazine 250
Allied Publishing 202
Allright Corporation 154
Allsport Photography USA, Inc. 520
Aloha, The Magazine of Hawaii 250
Alphabeat 501
Alternative Energy Retailer 436
Alumi-News 437
AM Corp Video Productions 79
AM Magazine 251
Amateur Softball Association 154
Ambassador 251
Amber Lotus Designs 230
Ambergris 251
Amelia Magazine 251
America West Airlines Magazine 252
American Advertising 57
American Agriculturist 437
American Arbitration Association 121
American Arts & Graphics, Inc. 230
American Bar Association Journal 382
American Bee Journal 437
American Birds 382
American Bookseller 437
American Cage-Bird Magazine 252
American City & County Magazine 438
American Craft 383
American Dane Magazine 252
American Demographics 438
American Dental Hygienists' Association 154
American Farriers Journal 438
American Film 252
American Film and Video Festival 573
American Fire Journal 438
American Fitness 383
American Fitness Magazine 439
American Forests Magazine 383
American Hockey Magazine/U.S.A. Hockey 155
American Horticulturist 253
American Hunter 383
American Libraries 384
American Metal Market 202
American Motorcyclist 384
American Museum of Natural History Library,
     Photographic Collection 155
American Music Co. and Cuca Record & Cas-
     sette Manufacturing Co. 501
American Oil & Gas Reporter 439
American Photography Institute 578
American Power Boat Association 155
American Red Cross 155

American Society for the Prevention of Cruelty to Animals 156
American Society of Artists, Inc. 175
American Southwest Photography Workshop 578
American Sports Network 202
American Squaredance 439
American Stage Festival 156
American Stock Photography Inc. 520
American Survival Guide 253
Americana Magazine 253
Américas 253
Amiga Plus Magazine 254
Ampro Photo Workshops 578
Amwest Picture Agency 520
Anchell Photography Workshops 579
Anchor News 384
Anchorage Daily News 202
Ancient Art & Architecture Collection, The 520
And Books 121
Anderson Communications 56
Anderson Ranch Arts Center 579
Anderson/Rothstein, Inc. 47
Andes Press Agency 521
Angus Journal 384
Animal Kingdom (see Wildlife Conservation 371)
Animals 385
Animals Animals/Earth Scenes 521
Ann Arbor 8mm Film & Video Festival 573
Annual Report Group, Inc. 83
Anthro—Photo File 521
Antone's Records 501
APA Monitor 385
Aperture 385
Apon Record Company, Inc. 501
Appalachia 385
Appalachian Trailway News 386
AppaLight 521
Appaloosa Journal 386
Apparel Industry Magazine 439
Aquarium Fish Magazine 254
Archaeology Magazine 386
Architectural & Engineering Systems Magazine 439
Architectural Digest 254
Architecture California 386
ARCsoft Publishers 121
Ardrey Inc. 80
Arizona Business Gazette 254
Arjuna Library Press 121
Arkansas Farm & Country 386
Arkansas Sportsman (see Game & Fish Publications 291)
Army Reserve Magazine 387
Arnold & Associates Productions, Inc. 47
Arpel Graphics 230
Arrowmont School of Arts and Crafts 579
Art Center of Battle Creek 176
Art Direction (Colorado) 48

Art Direction (New York) 440
Art Direction Book Co. 122
Art Museum of Southeast Texas 176
Art on the Green 573
Art Resources International Ltd. 231
Artbanque 176
Artemisia Gallery 176
Asbestos Issues 91 440
Ascherman Gallery/Cleveland Photographic Workshop 177
Ashley Books, Inc. 122
Assembly Engineering 440
Associated Picture Service 522
A-Stock Photo Finder (ASPF) 522
Atlanta Chamber of Commerce 387
Atlanta Jewish Times 254
Atlanta Stock Associates 522
Atlantic City Magazine 255
Atlantic Salmon Journal 440
Audubon Magazine 255
Augsburg Fortress, Publishers 122
Austin Associates 39
Auto Trim News 387
Automated Builder 441
AV Design 50
A.V. Media Craftsman, Inc. 89
AVC 441
Ave Maria Press 122
AVID, Inc. 53
Aviso, Inc. 39
Avon Books 123
AVSC News 203
AVW Audio Visual, Inc. 108
Ayer, Inc., N.W. 46

B

B.C. Professional Engineer, The 387
Baby Times Magazine 255
Baca's Annual Film and Video Festival 573
Back Home in Kentucky 255
Baja Times 203
Balloon Life 255
Baltimore Annual Independent Film & Video Makers' Competition 574
Baltimore Museum of Art, The 177
Banjo Newsletter Inc. 203
Bankers Life & Casualty Co. 156
Barkus Company, Inc., Ted 102
Barnaby's Picture Library 522
Barnett Productions Inc. 501
Barney & Patrick Inc. 35
Baron Advertising, Inc. 96
Barrett Advertising 69
Baseball Cards 256
Basinger Company, The 57
Basketball Digest 256
Bassin' 256
BC Outdoors 256

Can't find a listing? Check at the end of each market section for the " '90-'91 Changes" lists. These lists include any market listings from the '90 edition which were either not verified or deleted in this edition.

BC Space 177
BC Woman to Woman 257
Beals Advertising Agency 101
Bean Publishing, Ltd., Carolyn 231
Bear Advertising 46
Bear Creek Direct 101
Beautiful America Publishing Company 123
Beautyway 231
Beckerman Group, The 80
Beef 441
Beef Today 441
Behrman House Inc. 123
Bennett, Aleon, and Associates 39
Berg & Associates 523
Berkshire Public Theatre, The 157
Berlin Publications, Inc. 231
Bernsen's International Press Service Ltd. 523
Besser Museum, Jesse 177
Best in the West 574
Best Wishes, Expecting 257
Beverage Dynamics 441
Beverage World 442
Beverly Art Center Art Fair & Festival 574
Bicycle USA 388
Bicycling 257
Bike Report 388
Bilans 388
Bildagentur Mauritius GMBH 523
Billiards Digest 257
Bing Advertising, Ralph 39
Biological Photo Service 524
Biology Digest 258
Bionics 388
Biopharm Manufacturing 442
Bird Talk 258
Bird Watcher's Digest 258
Bird-In-Hand Gallery 180
Birdsall-Voss & Associates, Inc. 116
Bitton Advertising Agency 57
Bixeminars 579
Black Collegian, The 258
Black Star Publishing Co., Inc. 524
Black Writer, The 388
Blackwood, Martin, and Associates 38
Blade Magazine 258
Blake Picture Library, John 524
Blate Associates, Samuel R. 69
Blount, Inc. 157
Blue Bird Publishing 123
Blue Ridge Country 259
B'Nai B'Rith International Jewish Monthly, The 259
Boat Journal 259
Boat Pennsylvania 259
Boat/U.S. Reports 389
Bodie Fine Art Workshop Series/Global Preservation Projects 579
Bodyboarding Magazine 260
Boeberitz Design, Bob 95
Bokmon Dong Communications 232
Bond Weekend Workshops, Howard 579
Bonus Book, Inc. 124
Boody Fine Arts, Inc. 180
Book Author's Newsletter 203
Borgmeyer & Musen Advertising, Inc. 76
Boston Magazine 260
Bostonia Magazine 260
Bosustow Video 40

Bouquet-Orchid Enterprises 502
Bow & Arrow 260
Bowbender 261
Bowhunter 261
Bowhunting World 262
Bowker, R.R. 124
Bowlers Journal 262
Bowling Digest 262
Bowling Magazine 389
Bradley Photography Workshops, Matt 579
Bragaw Public Relations Services 57
Brake & Front End 442
Brandt and Associates, Robert 58
Brazen Images Inc. 232
Brent Gallery 180
Brentwood Music, Inc. 502
Bridal Fair Magazine 262
Brigade Leader 262
Bright Light Productions 96
Bright of America 232
British Heritage 263
Britt & Britt Creative Services 61
Broken Diamond, The 180
Brookfield/Sono Photographic Workshop, The 579
Brookings Gallery, J.J. 180
Brooks Associates, Anita Helen 89
Brooks/Cole Publishing Company 124
Brown Advertising Agency, E.H. 61
Brown Co. Publishers, William C. 124
Brown Hands-On Workshops, Nancy 579
Bryant Stock Photography, D. Donne 525
Builder/Dealer Magazine 442
Building Supply Home Centers 442
Bulloch & Haggard Advertising Inc. 49
Burnap Advertising Agency, Inc., David K. 97
Business Atlanta 443
Business Facilities 443
Business View 443
Butler Advertising 46
Butter Fat Magazine 443
Butwin & Associates Advertising, Inc. 74
BUZZWORM: The Environmental Journal 263

C

C.E.P.A. 181
C.L. & B. Advertising, Inc. 83
Cable Publishing Group 443
Caldwell-Van Riper 65
California Angler 263
California Builder & Engineer 444
California Farmer 444
California Game & Fish (see Game & Fish Publications 291)
California Labor Federation 389
California Lawyer 389
California Magazine 263
California Monthly 390
California Museum of Photography 180
California Nurse 390
California Redwood Association 157
California School Employee 204
California Views/Pat Hathaway Collection 525
Calypso Log 390
Cambridge Career Products 116

Cambridge Multicultural Arts Center Gallery 181
Cambridge University Press 124
Camden Photographic Workshops 579
Camera Bug International 574
Camera Obscura Gallery, The 181
Camera Press Ltd. 525
Camerique Stock Photography 526
Cameron Advertising, Walter F. 83
Camex Inc. 502
Campus Life 263
Campus Voice 264
Canada Lutheran 390
Canadian Biker Magazine 264
Canadian Building Owner and Property Manager 444
Canadian Fiction Magazine 264
Canadian Pacific West Coast Workshops 579
Canoe 264
Canton Art Institute, The 181
Canyonlands Field Institute Photo Workshops 579
Cape Cod Home and Garden 265
Cape Rock, The 265
Capener Company, The 40
Capilano Review, The 265
Capital, The 204
Capper's 204
Car Collector & Car Classics 266
Car Craft Magazine 266
Carden & Cherry Advertising Agency 107
Career Woman 266
Careers & The Handicapped, Equal Opportunity Publications, Inc. 266
Caribbean Travel and Life Magazine 267
Carlton Communications Inc. 115
Carmichael-Lynch, Inc. 74
Carolina Biological Supply Company 157
Carolina Quarterly 267
Caroline Records Inc. 502
Cassandra Press 125
Cat Fancy 267
Catch America, Inc. 233
Catechist 444
Catholic Digest 268
Catholic Health World 204
Catholic Near East Magazine 268
Catholic News Service 526
Catholic World, The 269
Cats Magazine 269
Catskill Center for Photography 181
CD Review 269
CDA Journal 391
CDA Update 205
Center for Photography 579
Ceramics Monthly 444
CFO Magazine 445
Changing Men 269
Charisma Magazine 270
Charta Records/Delux Records 502

Chattanooga Life & Leisure 270
Chesapeake Bay Magazine, The 270
Chess Life 391
Chevy Outdoors 391
Chicago Computer & Light, Inc. 158
Chicago Parent News Magazine 270
Chicago Tribune Magazine, The 205
Chickadee Magazine 271
Child and Family Services of New Hampshire 158
Child Life 271
Childhood Education 391
Children's Playmate 271
Chisholm Film Productions Ltd., Jack 117
Christian Board of Publication 271
Christian Century, The 271
Christian Herald 272
Christian Home & School 391
Christian Ministry, The 445
Chronicle Guidance Publications, Inc. 125
Chronicle of Philanthropy, The 445
Chronicle of the Horse, The 272
Church Herald, The 272
Circle K Magazine 272
Circle Track Magazine 273
Citizen Newspaper Group 205
Citroën Car Club News 392
City & Country Club Life Magazine 273
City of Los Angeles Photography Centers 182
Civitan Magazine 392
Class Act Magazine 273
Class Publications, Inc. 233
Classroom Computer Learning 445
Clavier 446
Cleaning Consultant Services 125
Clearvue, Inc. 62
Clearwaters 393
Cleland, Ward, Smith & Associates 95
Coal Voice 393
Cobblestone: The History Magazine for Young People 273
Cohen, Steven 83
Colee Sartory 54
Coleman, Inc., Bruce 526
Collector Editions 274
Collector's Choice Gallery 182
Collegiate Career Woman (see Career Woman 266)
Collision 446
Colonial Homes Magazine 274
Columbus Monthly 274
Comesana-Agencia De Prensa, Eduardo 526
Commercial Carrier Journal 446
Commercial Investment Real Estate Journal 393
Commercial Property News 205
Communication Arts 1991 Photography Annual 574
Communication World 393
Communications 446
Communications Week 446

Can't find a listing? Check at the end of each market section for the " '90-'91 Changes" lists. These lists include any market listings from the '90 edition which were either not verified or deleted in this edition.

Communicators, Inc., The 70
Company 393
Compressed Air Magazine 447
Computer Magazine 394
Computers in Healthcare Magazine 447
Comstock, Inc. 527
Confident Living 394
Connecticut Magazine 274
ConnStruction Magazine 447
Conservationist Magazine 275
Conservatory of American Letters 125
Construction News 447
Construction Specifier, The 394
Construction Today 205
Contact Lens Forum (see Opthamology Management 472)
Contact Magazine 394
Contemporary Arts Center, The 182
Contemporary Christian Music 275
Contemporary Perspectives 126
Contractors Guide 447
Cook Advertising, Wm. 54
Cook Publishing Co., David C. 127, 275
Cook's Magazine 275
Cope Magazine 448
Coping Magazine 276
Cornerstone 276
Corp Video Center 50
Corporate Cashflow 448
Cosmotone Records 502
Council on Fine Art Photography 574
Country Journal 276
Country Magazine 276
Country Woman 277
Covalt Advertising Agency 54
Covenant College 158
Covenant Companion, The 277
Cox Advertising 89
CPI 127
Craftsman Book Company 127
Crain's Cleveland Business 206
Crain's Detroit Business 206
Cranberries 448
Creative Associates 80
Creative Company 101
Creative House Advertising, Inc. 72
Creative Photography Gallery 183
Creative Productions, Inc. 80
Creative Resources, Inc. 54
Creative Vision Workshops in Colorado High Country 579
Creativity Awards Show, The 574
Crested Butte Nature Workshops 579
Crosby Communications 70
Crosscurrents 277
Crow Advertising Agency, John 58
Cruise Travel 277
Cruising World Magazine 279
CS&A Advertising 58
Cummington Community of the Arts 579
Curators Choice 574
Current Affairs 50
Current Health 1 279
Current Health 2 279
Currents 394
Cushman and Associates, Inc., Aaron D. 76
Custom Medical Stock Photo 527
Custom Studios, Inc. 159

Cycle News 206
Cycle World Magazine 279
Cycling BC 395
Cycling U.S.A. 206
CYR Color Photo Agency 528

D

Daily Shipping News 206
Daily Word 279
Dairy Goat Journal 448
Dairy Herd Management 449
Dairy Today 449
Dakota Game & Fish (see Game & Fish Publications 291)
Dallas Life Magazine, Dallas Morning News 280
Dance Magazine 280
Dance on Camera Festival 574
Darkroom & Creative Camera Techniques 449
Darkroom Photography Magazine 280
Das Photo 528
Data Command Inc. 58
Data Communications Magazine 449
Datamation Magazine 450
Davidson & Associates 78
Davis Advertising Group, Susan 52
Davis Travel Photography, James 528
Dayton Ballet 159
De Palma & Hogan Advertising 84
De Wys Inc., Leo 528
Dealer Progress Magazine 395
Deer and Deer Hunting 280
Deerfield at Stonington 580
Defenders 395
Defense Science Magazine 450
DeKalb Daily Chronicle 207
Delmar Publishers Inc. 127
Delta Design Group, Inc. 128
Dental Economics 450
Dentist 450
Design & Cost Data 451
Design for People 451
Design Photographers International, Inc., (DPI) 529
Devaney Stock Photos 529
Diegnan & Associates 80
Dillman's Creative Photography Workshops 580
Dillon Press, Inc. 128
Dimensions In Health Service 396
Direct Marketing Magazine 451
Discoveries (see Middler Teacher 317)
Discovery Magazine 396
Discovery Productions (Connecticut) 51
Discovery Productions (New York) 89
Distributor 451
Ditzel Productions, William 97
Diver Magazine 281
Diver, The 280
Dixie Contractor 451
DMI Photo Agency 530
Documentary Films 40
Dog Fancy 281
Dolls—The Collector's Magazine 281
Dolphin Log, The 396
Domestic Engineering Magazine 452
Donning Co., The/Publishers, Inc. 128
Donohue Associates, Inc., Jody 90

Dorris Photography Workshop and Housing Co-operatives, Frances 580
Dorsey Advertising/PR. 108
Dort and Co., Dallas C. 72
Douglis Visual Workshops, The 580
Down Beat Magazine 281
Down East Magazine 282
Doyle Assoc., Inc., Richard L. 90
DPR Company 101
Drexel University 159
Driggs Collection, Frank 530
DRK Photo 530
Drycleaners News 452
Ducks Unlimited 396
Duff Advertising Agency, Charles 36
Duke Unlimited 69
Dykeman Associates, Inc. 108
Dynamic Graphics Inc., Clipper & Print Media Service 530

E

Eaglevision, Inc. 51
E&B Marine Inc. 159
Earnshaw's Review 452
Earth Images 530
Earwig Music Company, Inc. 503
East Texas International Photography Contest 574
Eastern Shore Annual 574
Easyriders Magazine 282
Eclipse Awards 574
Edelman Gallery, Catherine 183
Edelman, Inc., Daniel J. 62
Edelstein Advertising, Charles 102
Edelstein Gallery, Paul 183
Education Week 452
Educational Audio Visual Inc. 84
Educational Filmstrips 109
Educational Images Ltd. 84
Educational Programs, Inc. 282
Educational Theatre Association 397
Educational Video Network 109
EGD & Associates, Inc. 58
Egyptian Eye 580
Eisen Public Relations Co., Inc., Alan G. 84
EKM-Nepenthe 531
El Dorado News Times 207
Elbert Advertising Agency, Inc. 71
ELCIC Sunday Bulletins 397
Eldercards, Inc. 233
Electrical Apparatus 452
Electrical Contractor 397
Electronic Business 453
Elite Photography, Inc. 531
Elks Magazine, The 397
Ellis Wildlife Collection 532
EMC Publishing 128

Emergency, The Journal of Emergency Services 453
Employee Assistance 453
Engineered Systems 454
Enigma Entertainment 503
Enslow Publishers 128
Entrepreneur 282
Entry Publishing, Inc. 129
Environment 282
Epstein & Walker Associates 90
Equal Opportunity 283
Equinox Magazine 283
Erie & Chautauqua Magazine 283
Etherton/Stern Gallery 183
Europe Magazine 454
Evangelical Beacon, The 284
Evangelizing Today's Child 284
Evans Advertising Agency Inc. 117
Evans Photo Library, Greg 532
Evans/Kraft Advertising, Alaska Division 36
Evans/Salt Lake 114
Event 284
Everett, Brandt & Bernauer, Inc. 76
Excavating Contractor 455
Exchange & Commissary News 207
Executive Female 398
Executive Travel 284
Expecting Magazine 285
Export Today Magazine 455
Exposition Phoenix Press, Inc. 129
Expotacular Displays Div. 72
Eye Gallery—Selections '91 574
Eyecare Business 207

F

Faces: The Magazine About People 285
Falk Associates, Richard 90
Family Motor Coaching 398
Farm & Ranch Living 285
Farm Chemicals 455
Farm Industry News 455
Farm Journal, Inc. 455
Farm Store Merchandising 456
Farmer, The/The Dakota Farmer 456
Farnam Companies, Inc. 36
Fashions in Stock 532
Fell Publishers, Inc. 129
Fellowship 398
Fellowship of Christian Athletes 160
Fenton Associates, Inc., H.T. 81
Ferguson Publishing Co., J.G. 129
Field Advertising Agency, Rich 54
Field & Stream 286
Fighting Woman News 286
Film in the Cities/Lightworks 580
Film I 71
Film/Video Arts, Inc. 580

Can't find a listing? Check at the end of each market section for the " '90-'91 Changes" lists. These lists include any market listings from the '90 edition which were either not verified or deleted in this edition.

Financial Independence Money Management Magazine 286
Financial Services Week 207
Fine Homebuilding 287
Fine Press Syndicate 532
Finescale Modeler 287
Finger Lakes Magazine 287
Fire Chief Magazine 456
Fire Journal/Fire Command 398
Firehouse Magazine 456
First Light Associated Photographers 533
Firsthand Magazine, Guys, Manscape 287
Fishing and Hunting News 207
Fishing Facts Magazine 288
Fishing World 288
Flashcards, Inc. 233
Flatt and Assoc. Ltd., Joanie L. 36
Fleisher Art Memorial, Samuel S. 575
Flooring 456
Flores Publications, J. 129
Florida Foliage Magazine 398
Florida Game & Fish (see Game & Fish Publications 291)
Florida Grower and Rancher 208
Florida Specifier, The 458
Florida Underwriter 458
Florida Wildlife 399
Fly Fisherman 288
Flyfisher 399
Flying 288
Focal Point Gallery 184
Focus 399
Focus (Films of College & University Students) 575
Focus Stock Photo 533
Focus—Stock Fotografico 533
Food & Wine 288
Ford New Holland News 458
Ford Times 399
Forerunner, The 289
Formula Magazine 289
Fort Lauderdale Magazine 289
Fortune 289
Forty-Second International Exhibition of Photography 575
Fotheringham & Associates 114
Foto Expression International 534
Fotoconcept Inc. 534
Foto-Press Timmerman 534
Fotos International 534
Four Wheeler Magazine 289
Four Winds Record Productions Inc. 503
Fox Farm Recording 503
Fox Magazine (see Gallery Magazine 291)
Fox, Sweeney & True 49
FPG International Corp. 534
France Today Newsletter 208
Franklin Photo Agency 535
Franson & Associates, Inc. 40
Fraser Advertising 56
Frazier Irby Snyder, Inc. 38
Freedom Greetings 233
Freedom Magazine 290
Freeway 290
Freezeframe Greeting Card Co. 233
French & Partners, Inc., Paul 56
Fridholm Fine Arts 184
Friedentag Photographics 49

Friedman Publishing Group, Inc., Michael 130
Friendly Exchange Magazine 290
Friends of Arizona Highways Photo Adventures 580
Friends of Photography 580
Friendship Press 130
Frozen Images, Inc. 535
Fun in the Sun 290
Fundamental Photographs 535
Fun/West 290
Futures Magazine 459
Futurific Magazine 291
Futurist, The 400

G

Gallery East, The Art Institute of Boston 184
Gallery Magazine 291, 575
Gallery of Art, University of Northern Iowa 184
Gallery 614 184
Gallery, The 184
Game & Fish Publications 291
Gamma/Liaison 535
Gamut 291
Gannon Communications, Inc. 59
Garden 291
Garden Design 292
Garden Supply Retailer 459
Gardens West 292
Garfield-Linn & Company 62
Garrett Communications 56
Gartman Agency, Inc., Marilyn 536
Gary Plastic Packaging Corp. 160
Gazette Photography Contest, 12th Annual 575
Gelfond Associates, Inc., Gordon 46
General Learning Corp. 292
Gent 292
Georgia Sportsman Magazine 293
Georgia Straight 293
Geoscience Features Picture Library 536
Geoslides 536
Gift and Stationery Business 208
Glencoe Publishing 130
Glencoe/McGraw Hill 130
Global Pacific Records 503
Globe 208
Globe Photos, Inc. 536
Goes Lithographing Co. 234
Gold Gallery, Fay 185
Golden Gate School of Professional Photography 580
Golden Isles Arts Festival 575
Golden Years 293
Goldsholl Design and Film 59
Golf Course Management 400
Golf Digest 293
Golf Industry 459
Golf Journal 296
Golf Magazine 296
Golf Shop Operations 459
Good and Associates, G.R. 115
Good Housekeeping 296
Goodwick Associates, Inc. 51
Goose Lane Editions Ltd. 131
Gordon Photography, Joel 537
Go-Records 504
Gospel Herald 296

Graham Gallery, W.A. 186
Grain Journal 459
Grain Matters 208
Gramavision Records 504
Grand Canyon Natural History Association 131
Grand Rapids Calendar Co. 234
Grand Rapids Magazine 297
Graphic Arts Center Publishing Company 131
Gray's Sporting Journal 297
Great Lakes Fisherman 297
Great Smoky Mountains Photography Workshops 580
Greater Midwest International VI 575
Green Mountain Power 160
Greenhaven Press, Inc. 131
Greetwell 234
Greyhound Review, The 400
Griswold Inc. 97
Grit 210
Grocery Distribution 460
Ground Water Age 460
Group 400 Advertising 109
Group Magazine 460
Growing Edge, The 460
Growth Magazine 400
Guardian Newsweekly 210
Guernsey Breeder's Journal 400
Guide Magazine 297
Guideposts Associates, Inc. 298
Gulf Coast Golfer 211
Gulf Mariner 298
Gun World 298
Guns & Ammo Magazine 298

H

H.P. Books 132
Hackmeister Advertising & Public Relations, Inc. 55
Hadassah Magazine 298
Hall Workshops, John M. 580
Hallmark Cards, Inc. 234
Halsted Gallery Inc., The 186
Hampden-Sydney College 160
Hampton Photography, Inc./Travel Stock, Wally 537
Handmade Accents: The Buyer's Guide to American Artisans 299
Handy Co., Drucilla 62
Hard Hat Records & Cassettes 504
Harding Productions 97
Harmony House Publishers 132
Harrington Associates Inc. 85
Harris & Love, Inc. 114
Harris Works of Art, O.K. 186
Harrison House Publishers 132
Harrowsmith (Canada) 299
Harrowsmith Country Life 299

Harrowsmith (Vermont) (see Harrowsmith Country Life 299)
Hart/Conway Co., Inc. 85
Hartford Woman 299
Harvard Magazine 401
Hawaii Review 300
Hawaii-Gateway to the Pacific 300
Hawbaker Communications, Inc. 102
Hawkins Gallery, G. Ray 186
Hayes Publishing Co., Inc. 97
Headwaters 401
Health Magazine 300
Healthcare Executive 401
Hearth & Home 461
Heavy Duty Trucking 461
Heavy Truck Salesman 461
Helicopter International 461
Helriegel-Keenan Advertising 103
Heminger Advertising 65
Hepworth Advertising Co. 109
Herb Quarterly, The 300
Here's Life Publishers 132
Hicall 401
Hideaways Guide 300
High School Sports 300
High Volume Printing 461
Higher Octave Music 504
Hillmann & Carr Inc. 53
Hillsdale College 160
Hillstrom Stock Photo, Inc. 537
Historic Preservation 401
Historical Pictures Service, Inc. 537
Hitchcock's Mystery Magazine, Alfred 301
Hitchins Company, The 40
Hobie Hotline 402
Hockey Digest 301
Hockey Illustrated 301
Hodes Advertising, Bernard 41
Hog Farm Management 462
Hogs Today 462
Holland Advertising 98
Holt, Rinehart and Winston 132
Holt Studios Ltd. 538
Home 301
Home & Away Magazine 402
Home Center Magazine (see Home Improvement Center 462)
Home Education Magazine 301
Home Healthcare Nurse 462
Home Improvement Center 462
Home Plan Magazines 302
Home Planners, Inc. 133
Homestead Publishing 133
Hoof Beats 402
Horse & Rider Magazine 302
Horse Illustrated 302
Horse World USA 303
Horseplay Magazine 303
Horses Magazine 303
Hospital Physician 402

Can't find a listing? Check at the end of each market section for the " '90-'91 Changes" lists. These lists include any market listings from the '90 edition which were either not verified or deleted in this edition.

Hospital Practice 462
Hospital Trustee 403
Hot Rod Magazine 303
Hot Shots Stock Shots, Inc. 538
Houlgate Enterprises, Deke 41
Housewares 211
Houston Magazine 403
HR Magazine 403
Hubbard Milling Company 161
Hudson Valley Magazine 304
Huey, Bullock & Cook, Advertising, Inc., Barry 35
Hughes Fine Arts Center 186
Human Kinetics Pub. 133
Humm's Guide to the Florida Keys 304
Hush Productions 504
Hybrid Records 505

I

Icart Vendor Graphics 161
ICF Bugle, The 403
Ideals Magazine 304
IEEE Software 463
Ignatius Press 134
ILR Press 134
Illinois Game & Fish (see Game & Fish Publications 291)
Illinois Legal Times 463
Illinois Magazine 304
Illuminance 575
Image Associates 95
Image Bank, The 538
Image Bank/West, The 539
Image Broker 539
Image Finders Photo Agency, Inc. 539
Image Innovations, Inc. 81
Image Quest Inc. 539
Image Works, The 540
Imagery Unlimited 540
Images 186
Images Press Service Corp. 540
Images Unlimited 541
Impact Visuals Photo & Graphic, Inc. 541
"In The Fast Lane" 404
In The Wind 305
Independent Filmmaker Program 575
Independent Living 305
Independent Senior, The 305
Index Stock International Inc. 541
Indiana Game & Fish (see Game & Fish Publications 291)
Indianapolis Monthly 305
Industrial Photography 463
Industrial Safety and Hygiene News 463
Information Week 464
Innovative Design & Graphics 161
In-Plant Printer and Electronic Publisher 464
Inside Magazine 306
Inside Texas Running 211
Insight 306
Insight Associates 81
Instant and Small Commercial Printer 464
Instock Picture Agency 541
Instrumentalist, The 464
Insurance Week 465
Intensive Caring Unlimited 211

Intercontinental Greetings 235
Inter-Image, Inc. 118
Interlit 465
International Center of Photography 187, 580
International Color Stock, Inc. 542
International Diaporama Festival 575
International Family Planning Perspectives 465
International Gymnast 306
International Marine Photo & Video Contest, The 575
International Marine Publishing Company 134
International Media Services, Inc. 81
International Photo News 542
International Photo Tours (Voyagers International) 580
International Photographer 306
International Research & Education 161
International Video Network 41
International Wildlife 306
International Wildlife Photo Competition 575
Interpress of London and New York 542
Invasion Records 505
Iowa Game & Fish (see Game & Fish Publications 291)
Iowan Magazine, The 307
Irish Photographic Workshop 581
Island Grower, The 307

J

Jacoby/Storm Productions, Inc. 51
Jamestown Publishers 134
Janapa Photography Gallery Ltd. 187
January Productions 82
Jaycees Magazine 404
Jazz Times 211
Jazziz Magazine 307
Jeb Gallery, Inc. 187
Jems 465
Jeroboam, Inc. 542
Jerryend Communications Inc. 103
Jewish Exponent 212
JLI Records 505
Jobber Retailer Magazine 465
Jody Record Inc. 505
Johnson Advertising, George 76
Johnston Group, The 90
Jones Agency, The 41
Jones, Anastasi, Corbett, Lennon Advertising, Inc. (see Jones, Anastasi, Lennon Advertising, Inc. 98)
Jones, Anastasi, Lennon Advertising, Inc. 98
Jordan Associates Advertising & Communications 101
Jordan, McGrath, Case and Taylor 91
Journal of Extension 466
Journal of Family Practice, The 466
Journal of Light Construction, The 212
Journal of Ophthalmic Nursing & Technology 466
Journal of Physical Education, Recreation & Dance 404
Journal of Psychoactive Drugs 466
Journal of Psychosocial Nursing 466
Journal of Soil and Water Conservation 404
Journal of the National Medical Association 404

Journal of the National Technical Association 405
Journalism Services 543
Judicature 405
Junior Scholastic 307
Juried Photography Exhibition 575
Just Us Books, Inc. 134

K

Kahn Group, Al 162
Kane County Chronicle 212
Kane Photo Workshop Inc., Art 581
Kansas 308
Kansas Game & Fish (see Game & Fish Publications 291)
Kaplan Co., Inc., Arthur A. 235
Karate/Kung Fu Illustrated 308
Karr Productions, Paul S. 37
Karr Productions, Utah Division, Paul S. 114
Kashrus Magazine 308
Katz, Inc. 59
Keepin' Track of Vettes 308
Keller Crescent Company 65
Kennedy Journalism Awards, Robert F. 575
Kennedy/Lee, Inc. 103
Kent State University School of Art Gallery 187
Kentucky Game & Fish (see Game & Fish Publications 291)
Keroff & Rosenberg Advertising 62
Keyboard 308
KidsStock America 543
Kimbo Educational 505
Kirkland Art Center 187
Kite Lines 309
Kiwanis Magazine 405
K-Larrco Satellite Radio & T.V. 506
Klein Gallery, Robert 187
Kleiner Enterprises, Sid 506
Koehler Iversen Advertising 91
Kogle Cards, Inc. 235
Kopf, Zimmermann, Schultheis 85
Koslow Gallery 188
Kostov and Associates 115
Kramer and Associates, Inc., Joan 543
Kranzler, Kingsley Communications Ltd. 96
Kranzler, Saueressig Inc. (see Kranzler, Kingsley Communications Ltd. 96)
Kresge Art Museum 188
Kroloff, Marshall & Associates, Ltd. 53
Kurian Reference Books, George 135

L

L.A. West 309
L.R.J. Records 506
La Colotheque S.P.R.L. 543

La Crosse Area Convention & Visitor Bureau 162
Lacma Physician 405
Ladies Home Journal 309
Laguna Beach Gallery of Photography 188
Lake Superior Magazine 310
Lakeland Boating Magazine 310
Lambert Studios, Inc., Harold M. 544
Landmark Calendars 235
Landmark Communications Group 506
Landscape Architecture 406
Lane Pictures, Inc., Don 91
Lavidge and Associates 107
Law Practice Management 406
Lawrence & Schiller 107
Layla Production Inc. 135
Le Duc Video 42
Leadership 406
Lebhar-Friedman 135
Ledel Gallery 188
Leedy-Voulkos Gallery 190
Legal Economics (see Law Practice Management 406)
LeGasse Associates 79
Lehr Inc., Lewis 190
Lehr Photographs, Inc., Janet 190
Leisure Ontario (see Leisure World 310)
Leisure World 310
Lemon Square Productions 506
Leon Company, Inc., S.R. 85
Leslie Advertising Agency 106
Let's Live 310
Letters 312
Levenson & Hill 112
Levitt Assoc. Inc., Ronald 55
Lewis Advertising, Inc., J.H. 35
Lewis & Associates, Richard Bond 42
LGI Photo Agency 544
Liberty Publishing Company, Inc. 135
Liberty Report, The 212
Life 312
Lifestyle 312
Liggett Stashower Advertising, Inc. 98
Light Factory Photographic Arts Center, The 190
Light Images, Inc. 544
Light Impressions Spectrum Gallery 190
Light Productions 72
Lights and Shadows 312
Lightwave 544
Like It Is 238
Lindhult & Jones, Inc., Advertising 103
Lin's Lines 506
Lion Publishing 136
Lion, The 406
Liquid and Gas Chromatography 466
Little, Brown & Co. 136
Live Steam Magazine 312
Llewellyn Publications 136
Lodestar Productions 42

Can't find a listing? Check at the end of each market section for the " '90-'91 Changes" lists. These lists include any market listings from the '90 edition which were either not verified or deleted in this edition.

Lohre & Associates Inc. 98
Lookout, The 313, 406
Los Angeles Magazine 313
Louisiana Game & Fish (see Game & Fish Publications 291)
Louisiana Life Magazine 313
Louisville Magazine 313
Love Greeting Cards, Inc. 238
Loyola Magazine 407
Lucent Books 136
Lucifer Records, Inc. 507
Lukeman-Blocker Productions 112
Lutheran Forum 314
Lutheran, The 407
Lynch Enterprises, Jack 507
Lyons Marketing Communications 52

M

Mac User Magazine 314
McAndrew Advertising Co. 85
McCue Advertising & PR Inc. 86
McDonald Davis & Associates 116
McDonald's Wildlife Photography Workshops & Tours, Joe 581
McDougal, Littell and Company 136
MacDowell Colony, The 581
McGuire Associates 162
McGraw-Hill 137
Macintosh Communications, Inc., Rob 162
Maclean's Magazine 314
McMullen Design & Marketing 42
MacroTours Photo Workshops 581
Magic Moments Greeting Cards Publishing Co. 238
Magical Blend 314
Magid, Lee 507
Magnum Photos 544
Maine Photographic Workshops, The 581
Mainsheet 407
Mainstream—Animal Protection Institute of America 407
Maler, Inc., Roger 82
Management Accounting 408
Manhattan Video Productions, Inc. 91
Manitoba Teacher, The 408
Manufacturing Engineering 467
Map International 408
Marble House Gallery 191
Maricao Records/Hard Hat Records 507
Marken Communications 42
Marketaide, Inc. 68
Marriage Partnership 314
Marsden 91
Martial Arts Training 315
Martin Assoc. Inc., Peter 92
Martin Co., Inc., R.J. 82
Martinez & Associates 112
Martin-Williams Advertising Inc. 74
Maryland and Delaware Game & Fish (see Game & Fish Publications 291)
Maryland Farmer, Virginia Farmer, Georgia Farmer, and Alabama Farmer 212
Master of Life 315
Matthew-Lawrence Advertising & Sales Promotion Inc. 92
Matthews Assoc. Inc. 115

Mature Years 409
MBKA 137
MD Magazine 467
MDA Newsmagazine 409
MDK Allied 71
Media Forum International, Ltd. 115
Mediawerks 74
Mediaworks 82
Medical Economics Magazine 467
Medical Tribune 213
Medical World News 467
Meeting Manager, The 409
Mega Productions, Inc. 545
Mennonite Brethren Herald 410
Mennonite Publishing House 315
Men's Health 315
Mercury, The 213
Meriwether, Inc., Arthur 60
Meriwether Publishing Ltd. 50
Merrill Publishing Company 137
Messana Photo. Workshop 581
Metal Edge 316
Metamorphous Press 138
Metro 213
Metro Marketing Group 65
Michigan Business Magazine 467
Michigan Natural Resources Magazine 316
Michigan Out-of-Doors 316
Michigan Sportsman 316
Mid America Designs, Inc. 163
Mid-Atlantic Country 317
Middler Teacher 317
Midwest Motorist, The 410
Midwest Talent/Creative Talent 98
Milady Publishing Corporation 138
Military Collectors News 317
Milkweed Editions 138
Mill Gallery (see The Gallery 184)
Miller Gallery, Peter 191
Miller Communications, Inc. 71
Miller Comstock Inc. 545
Miller Films, Warren 43
Millers Inc., Barney 68
Milliken Publishing Company 138
Minnesota Opera, The 163
Minnesota Sportsman 317
Minority Engineer 317
Miracle of Aloe 163
Mississippi Publishers, Inc. 213
Missouri Game & Fish (see Game & Fish Publications 291)
Missouri Repertory Theatre 163
Missouri Ruralist 468
"Mobius"™ Awards, The 576
Modern Baking 468
Modern Drummer Magazine 318
Modern Liturgy 318
Modern Maturity 410
Modern Office Technology 468
Modern Plastics 468
Modern Steel Construction 410
Modern Tire Dealer Magazine 213
Mom Guess What Newspaper 214
Moment 318
Money Maker Magazine 318
Monitor Syndication 545
Monitoring Times 319
Montana Magazine 319

Monterey Peninsula Museum of Art 191
Moon Publications, Inc. 138
Moreton Agency, The 51
Morgan Horse, The 410
Morris Media 43
Morrison Associates, Ruth 92
Morton Productions, Inc., Jack 53
Moss & Company, Inc. 92
Mother Earth News 319
Mothering Magazine 319
Motivation Media, Inc. 60
Motor Boating & Sailing Magazine 319
Motorbooks International 139
Motorhome 320
Motorland Magazine 411
MSD Agvet 164
Muir Cornelius Moore 92
Muller, Jordan, Weiss, Inc. 93
Multinational Monitor 320
Muscle Mag International 320
Museum of Contemporary Photography of Columbia College 191
Music Educators Journal 468
Music Sales Corp. 139
Muzzle Blasts 411
Myers, Myers & Adams Advertising, Inc. 55
Myriad Productions 47
Mystic Art Association 576

N

N.E.B. Stock Photo Agency 545
N.S. Conservation 414
NACLA Report on the Americas 411
Naiad Press, Inc., The 139
Narada Productions 507
National Association of Evangelicals 164
National Association of Legal Secretaries 164
National Baseball Library 546
National Black Child Development Institute 164
National Bus Trader 469
National Cattlemen 411
National Duckpin Bowling Congress 164
National Educational Film and Video Festival 576
National Engineer 411
National Examiner 214
National Fisherman 469
National Gardening 412
National Guard 469
National Institute for Exploration 581
National Law Journal 469
National Masters News 214
National News Bureau 214, 546
National Park Photo Adventure Series Workshops 581
National Parks Magazine 320
National Racquetball 321
National Rural Letter Carrier 412

National Television News, Inc. 43
National Wildlife 321
Nation's Business 469
Nationwide Advertising, Inc. 100
Natural History Magazine 321
Natural History Photographic Agency 546
Natural Life Magazine 322
Natural Science Photos 546
Nature Conservancy Magazine, The 412
Nature Images, Inc. 576, 581
Nature Photography Workshops 581
Nawrocki Stock Photo 547
Nebraska Game & Fish (see Game & Fish Publications 291)
Neikrug Photographica Ltd. 191
Neiman Group, The 104
Nelson Productions, Inc. 117
Nelson-Hall Publishers 139
Nelson/Ralston/Robb Communications, Inc. 37
Network 413, 470
Neuger & Associates, Edwin 75
Nevada Farm Bureau Agriculture and Livestock Journal 413
Nevada Magazine 322
Never Sink Photo Workshop 581
New Age Journal 322
New Biotech 470
New Cleveland Woman Journal 322
New Dominion Magazine 322
New England Bride 323
New England Game & Fish (see Game & Fish Publications 291)
New England Monthly 323
New England Photographic Workshop Photo Gallery 191
New England School of Photography 581
New England Stock Photo 547
New Exposure—A Catalog of Fine Art Photography 165
New Hampshire Profiles 323
New Heights 238
New Home 323
New Image Stock Photo Agency Inc., The 548
New Jersey Game & Fish (see Game & Fish Publications 291)
New Leaf Press, Inc. 140
New Methods 470
New Mexico Magazine 324
New Mexico Photographer 324
New Mexico Photographer Contest 576
New Orleans Musuem of Art 192
New Realities 324
New Woman 324
New World Outlook 413
New York Alive 324
New York Game & Fish (see Game & Fish Publications 291)
New York Habitat 325
New York Magazine 325
New York State Youth Media Arts Shows 576

Can't find a listing? Check at the end of each market section for the " '90-'91 Changes" lists. These lists include any market listings from the '90 edition which were either not verified or deleted in this edition.

New York Times Magazine 214
Newmarks Advertising Agency 93
News Flash International, Inc. 549
News Herald, The 215
News Photographer 413
News-Gazette 215
Newspapers & Technology 470
Nighthawk Records 507
911 Magazine 471
1991 Photography Annual 576
Nitech Research Corporation 140
Noble & Associates 63
Normaily Marketing Systems 238
Norman Beerger Productions 78
North American Outdoor Film/Video Awards 576
North American Whitetail Magazine 414
North Carolina Game & Fish (see Game & Fish Publications 291)
North Light Workshops 581
North Shore Magazine 325
Northern Illinois University Art Museum 192
Northern Kentucky University Summer Photo Workshop 581
Northern Logger & Timber Processor, The 471
Northern New Mexico Photography Workshops 581
Northern Ohio Live 325
Northlich, Stolley, La Warre; Northlich, Stolley, Inc. 100
Northwest Film & Video Festival 576
Northwest International Entertainment 508
Northwest International Exhibition of Photography 576
Northwest Living 326
Northwest Magazine/The Oregonian 215
Norton and Company, W.W. 140
Norton-Wood PR Services 43
Nostradamus Advertising 93
NTC Publishing Group 140
Nucleus Records 508
Nugget 326
Numismatic News 216
Nursing Management 471

O

Oak Ridge Boys "Tour Book" and Fan Club Newsletter 414
Occupational Hazards 471
Ocean Navigator 326
Oceanus 471
Ocular Surgery News 472
Offshore, The Boating Magazine of New England, New York and New Jersey 326
Ogunquit Photography School, The 584
OH&S Canada 472
Ohio Business 472
Ohio Game & Fish (see Game & Fish Publications 291)
Ohio Magazine 326
Okapia K.G. 549
Oklahoma Game & Fish (see Game & Fish Publications 291)
Oklahoma Today 414
Old Cars Weekly 216
Old West 327

Olson, C.L. 140
Omega News Group/USA 549
Omni Communications 68
Omni Enterprises 60
On Location Photography Tours 584
On the Line 327
On Track 216
1001 Home Ideas 327
On-Q Productions Inc. 43
Ontario Motorcoach Review 472
Ontario Technologist, The 415
Open Space Arts Society 192
Open Wheel Magazine 327
Opera News 328
Ophthalmology Management 472
Optometric Management (see Opthalmology Management 472)
Orange Coast Magazine 328
Oregon Business Magazine 473
Oregon Coast Magazine 328
Organic Gardening 328
Original New England Guide, The 328
Orinda Records 508
Orlando Gallery 192
Orlie, Hill & Cundall, Inc. 44
Other Side, The 329
Our Animals 329
Our Family 329
Outdoor America 415
Outdoor Canada 330
Outdoor Empire Publshing, Inc. 141
Outdoor Life Magazine 330
Outdoor Photographer 330
Outline Press Syndicate Inc. 550
Outlook 473
Overseas! 330
Oxford Scientific Films 550
Oxford University Press 141
Ozark Photography Workshop/Fieldtrip 584

P

P.S. Greetings, Inc. D/B/A Fantus Paper Products 239
Pacific Discovery 415
Pacific Stock 550
Pacific Union Recorder 416
Padre Productions 141
Paint Horse Journal 330
Palm Beach Life 331
Palm Springs Desert Resort Convention and Visitors Bureau 165
Palm Springs Life Magazine 331
Palo Alto Photographic Workshops, The 584
Panoramic Stock Images 550
Paper Peddler, Inc. 239
Paper Sales 473
Parc Records, Inc. 508
Parents & Teenagers Magazine 331
Parents' Choice, A Review of Children's Media 216
Parker & Son Publications, Inc. 141
Parker Group, Inc. 76
Parker's Gateways Inst., Jonathan 44
Paton Public Relations 68
Patriot Ledger, The 216
PC Week 217

Peanut Butter Publishing 142
Pediatric Annals 473
Peebles Photography, Douglas 551
Pelican Publishing Co., Inc. 142
Pemberton & Oakes 240
Pennsylvania 334
Pennsylvania Angler 416
Pennsylvania Game & Fish (see Game & Fish Publications 291)
Pennsylvania Game News 334
Pennsylvania Heritage 416
Pennsylvania Sportsman 334
Pentecostal Messenger, The 416
People Magazine 334
Perceptive Marketers Agency, Ltd. 104
Personal Investor 335
Pet Business 473
Peters Valley Craft Center 584
Petersen's Hunting Magazine 335
Petersen's Photographic Magazine 335
Petroleum Independent 474
Pets Magazine 335
PGA Magazine 474
PGA of America 165
Pharmaceutical Technology 474
Phi Delta Kappan 165, 417
Phoenix Magazine 336
Photec 44
Photo Communication Services, Inc. 73
Photo Focus/Coupeville Arts Center 584
Photo Gallery at Portland School of Art, The 192
Photo Gems 551
Photo Library International 551
Photo Life 336
Photo Network 551
Photo Researchers, Inc. 552
Photo Review 7th Annual Competition 576
Photo Tours: In Focus With Michelle Burgess 584
Photobank 552
Photo/Chronicles, Ltd. 240
Photoedit 552
Photographer's Forum-College Contest and Spring Contest 576
Photographers' Fund 576
Photographer's Market 336
Photographic Arts Center, Ltd., The 142
Photographic Center of Monterey Peninsula, The 192, 584
Photographic Competition Association Quarterly Contest 576
Photographic Game, The 552
Photographic Resource Center 193
Photography at Oregon Gallery 193
Photography Etc. (see Curator's Choice 574)
Photomethods 474
Photophile 553
Photoreporters, Inc. 553
Phototake 553

Photri Inc. 553
Physician and Sportsmedicine, The 474
Pictor International, Ltd. 554
Pictorial Parade, Inc. 554
Picture Cube Inc., The 554
Picture Gold 240
Picture Group, Inc. 554
Picture That, Inc. 555
Picturesque Stock Photos 555
Pilot's Log, The 417
Pinne/Herbers Advertising Inc. 48
Pipeline and Utilities Construction 475
Pizza Today 475
Plane & Pilot 336
Planet Earth Pictures/Seaphot Ltd. 555
Planning 417
Plant 475
Plastics Technology 475
Plattsburgh State Art Galleries (see SUNY Plattsburgh Art Museum 196)
Playback Records/Gallery II Records, Inc. 508
Playboy Magazine 337
Players Press Inc. 142
Pleasure Boating 337
Plessner International 555
Plymouth, Inc. 240
Pneumatic Packaging 417
Pocket Books 143
Pocketfox Magazine (see Gallery Magazine 291)
Podiatry Management 337
Police Magazine 476
Police Times/Chief of Police 476
Pollaro Media Advertising & Productions 112
Polled Hereford World 476
Polo Magazine 337
Pool & Spa Magazine 337
Popular Electronics 338
Popular Photography 338
Popular Science 338
Population Bulletin 418
Portal Publications 241
Portland-The University of Portland Magazine 166
Posey School of Dance, Inc. 166
Powder Magazine 338
PR Associates, Inc. 73
Prakapas Gallery 193
Pratt Manhattan 584
Praxis Media, Inc. 51
Praying 339
Preacher's Magazine, The 476
Premier Film, Video and Recording 77
Prescription Co., The 508
Preservation News 418
Prevention Magazine 339
Princeton Alumni Weekly 418
Principal Magazine 418
Print Club, The 193
Pro Files West 555
Pro Football Hall of Fame Photo Contest 576

Can't find a listing? Check at the end of each market section for the " '90-'91 Changes" lists. These lists include any market listings from the '90 edition which were either not verified or deleted in this edition.

Pro Sound News 476
Problems of Communism 339
Proceedings/Naval History 418
Pro/Creatives 86, 509
Produce News, The 217
Product Centre-S.W. Inc., The Texas Postcard Co. 241
Professional Agent 476
Professional Builder 477
Professional Photographer 477
Progressive Architecture 477
Progressive, The 339
PRSA Film/Video Festival 576
Pruitt, Humphress, Powers & Munroe Advertising Agency, Inc. 55
Psychiatric Annals 477
PTA Today 419
Public Citizen 419
Public Employee Magazine, The 419
Public I Publicity Services 509
Public Works Magazine 478
Publications International, Ltd. 143
Pulitzer Prizes 577
Purdom Public Relations 48
Pure–Bred Dogs/American Kennel Gazette 419

Q

Quadriga Art, Inc. 241
Quality Digest 478
Qually & Company, Inc. 63
Quarasan Group, Inc., The 166
Quarter Horse Journal, The 340
Queens Tribune 217
Quick Frozen Foods International 478
Quilt World, Quick & Easy Quilting, Stitch 'N Sew Quilts 341

R

R.D.R. Productions, Inc. 556
Radiance, The Magazine for Large Women 341
Radio-Electronics Magazine 478
Ragsdale Assoc., Inc., Carl 113
Railroad Model Craftsman 341
Rainbow 556
Raintree Publishers 143
Ranch & Coast Magazine 341
Rand McNally Road Atlas 341
Randall Productions 509
Randolph Street Gallery 194
Random Records/Random Image Music 509
Ranger Rick 342
Rapp Productions 509
Rase Productions, Inc., Bill 44
RDH, The National Magazine for Dental Hygiene Professionals 478
Real Art Ways 194
Real Estate Finance Today 420
Real Estate Times (see Commercial Property News 205)
Register Citizen 217
Recommend Worldwide 479
Recreation World Services, Inc. 167
Recreational Equipment, Inc. 167
Recycled Paper Products, Inc. 241

Recycling Today 479
Reedproductions 241
Referee 479
Reflections 194
Regards 420
Registered Representative 479
Relativity Records, Inc. 512
Relax 342
Relix Magazine 342
Remodeling 479
Repertory Dance Theatre 167
Reptile & Amphibian Magazine 342
Rescue Magazine 480
Resource Publications, Inc. 143
Resource Recycling 480
Restaurant Hospitality 480
Restaurant Row Magazine 343
Restaurant/Hotel Design International 480
Retired Officer Magazine, The 420
Retirement Lifestyles 420
Review Publications 217
Richmond Surroundings Magazine 343
Rider 343
Ripon College 167
Ripsaw Record Co. 512
River Runner Magazine 343
RN Magazine 481
Road King Magazine 344
Roadrunner Records 512
Roanoker, The 344
Robb Report, The 344
Robbins Records, Inc. 512
Roberts Represents, Chris 556
Rock & Ice 344
Rock City Records 513
Rockshots, Inc. 242
Rockwell Records 513
Rocky Mountain Game & Fish (see Game & Fish Publications 291)
Roffman Associates, Richard H. 93
Rogers & Cowan, Inc. 47
Rogers Associates, Peter 93
Roggen Advertising and Public Relations, Ted 113
Roll Call Newspaper 220
Roll On Records® 513
Rolling Stone 344
Ronan, Howard, Associates, Inc. 86
Roofer Magazine 481
Rosen-Coren Agency Inc. 104
Roska Direct Marketing 104
Ross Assoc., Holly 194
Rotarian, The 421
Rothholz Associates, Inc., Peter 94
Roy, Inc., Ross 73
RSVP Marketing 166
Rubber and Plastics News 220
Ruder Finn 63
Runner's World 345
Running Heads Inc. 143
Rural Heritage 345
Rushwin Productions 513
Ryan Communications 102
Rynd Fine Arts, C.E. 167
Rytex Co., The 242

S

Sackett Executive Consultants, Richard 69
Sacramento Magazine 345
Saddle & Bridle Magazine 345
Sadlier, Inc., William H. 144
Safari Magazine 421
Sailing 346
Sailing World 346
St. Louis Magazine 346
St. Remy Press 144
Saint Vincent College 167
Salome A Journal Salome: A Journal for the Performing Arts 481
Salon Internacional De Arte Fotografico 577
Salt Water Sportsman 346
San Francisco Conservatory of Music 168
San Francisco Opera Center 168
San Jose State University 169
Sander Allen Advertising, Inc. 63
Sanders, Wingo, Galvin & Morton Advertising 113
Sandford Gallery 194
Sandhill Crane Press, Inc. 145
Sandpiper Publishing 242
Santa Barbara Magazine 347
Sarver & Witzerman Advertising 45
Saturday Evening Post Society, The 347
Save the Children 52
Scafa-Tornabene Pbg. Co. 242
Scenic Photo Imagery 557
Scepter Group, Inc. 104
Schecterson Associates, Jack 86
Scholastic Photography Awards 577
Schomburg Center for Research in Black Culture 194
School Shop 481
Schorr and Howard Company 94
Schuettge & Carleton 145
Science of Mind Magazine 347
Science Stock America 557
Science Teacher, The 421
Scientist, The 482
Scoopix Photo Library 557
Score, Canada's Golf Magazine 347
Scott Enterprises, Liz 104
Scott Productions, Tamara 45
Scottsdale Center for the Arts 195
Scrap Processing 421
Scuba Times Magazine 348
Sea Cliff Photograph Co. 195
Sea Frontiers 422
Sea, The Magazine of Western Boating 348
Seacoast Life Magazine 348
Seafood Leader 482
Seattle Business (see Sound Business 424)
Second Impressions 482
Security Dealer 482
Self 349
Self-Counsel Press 145

Senior Magazine 349
Seniors Advocate (see Independent Senior 305)
Sentinel, The (Connecticut) 422
Sentinel, The (Florida) 220
Service Reporter 220
Service Station Management 482
Services 422
Shadow Light Productions 94
Shape 349
Sheep Magazine 482
Shelter Sense 483
Shooting Sports USA 422
Shooting Star International Photo Agency 558
Sierra 422
Sierra Club Books 243
Sierra Photographic Workshops 584
Sierra Press, Inc. 145
Sight & Sound, Inc. 77
Signcraft Magazine 483
Signpost Magazine 423
Silkini Records 514
Silver Circle 349
Silver Image Gallery, The 195
Silver Image Photo Agency, Inc. 558
Singer Media Corp., Inc. 220
Single Parent, The 423
Singlelife Milwaukee 349
Sinking Creek Film Festival 584
Sinking Creek Film/Video Festival 577
Sioux City Art Center 195
Sirkis Publishers Ltd., R. 146
Sirr Rodd Record & Publishing Co. 514
Skate Magazine 349
Ski 350
Ski Canada 350
Ski Racing Magazine 350
Skies America 483
Skiing Magazine 350
Skiing Trade News 220
Skin Diver 351
Sky 351
Skydiving 221
Slide File, The 558
Slideing Board, The 105
Small Boat Journal (see Boat Journal 259)
Small World 483
Smiley Visual Productions, Inc., Ron 105
Smiley/Hanchulak, Inc. 100
Smith & Associates, Inc. 96
Smith Company, Inc., Marc 70
Smith, J. Greg 77
Smithsonian (Books) Institution 146
Snack World 423
Snow Week 351
Snowmobile Magazine 351
Snowmobile West 352
Soap Opera Digest 352
Soaring 424
Soccer America 221
Social Policy 484

Can't find a listing? Check at the end of each market section for the " '90-'91 Changes" lists. These lists include any market listings from the '90 edition which were either not verified or deleted in this edition.

Society 352
Society for Visual Education, Inc. 63
Society of American Florists, The 169
Solar Records 514
Soldier of Fortune Magazine 352
Somerstown Gallery 195
Sonic Wave Records 514
Sorin Productions, Inc. 82
Sormani Calendars 243
Sound Achievement Group, The 514
Sound Business 424
Sound Choice 484
Soundings 353
Soundings Trade Only 484
Sounds of Winchester 515
Soundycards 243
Sources—The Journal of Underwater Education 424
South American Explorer 424
South Carolina Film Office 107
South Carolina Game & Fish (see Game & Fish Publications 291)
South Florida Photographic Workshops/Iris Gallery 584
South Shore Art Center, Inc. 195
Southeastern Center for the Arts, Inc. 584
Southern Accents 353
Southern Beverage Journal 484
Southern California Business 425
Southern Exposure 353
Southern Light 195
Southern Lumberman 484
Southern Magnolia Photographic Workshop 584
Southern Motoracing 221
Southern Stock Photos 559
Southwest Photographic Workshops 584
South-Western Publishing Company 146
Souvenirs & Novelties Magazine 485
Soybean Digest 486
Sparrow Corporation, The 515
Spectroscopy 486
Spectrum 425
Speech Bin Inc., The 146
Spencer Productions, Inc. 94
Sphemusations 515
Spiritual Life 425
Spiritus Gallery, Susan 196
Spizel Advertising and Public Relations, Edgar S. 48
Split Rock Arts Program 584
Sport Fishing 353
Sport Magazine 353
Sport Scene: Focus on Youth Programs 425
Sporting Goods Dealer, The 486
Sporting News, The 221
Sporting Pictures (UK), Ltd. 559
Sports Afield 354
Sports Car 425
Sports Car International 486
Sports Illustrated 354
Sportslight Photo 559
Spottswood Video/Vilm Studio 35
Springfield International Color Slide Exhibit 577
Spur 354
Stack & Associates, Tom 559
Standard Educational Corp. 146
Star Publishing Company 147

State Government News 426
State, The 354
Step-by-Step Graphics 486
Stephan Advertising Agency, Inc. 68
Stewart Inc., E.J. 105
Stewart, Tabori & Chang 147
Stillpoint International 79
Stills 560
Stock Boston Inc. 560
Stock Car Racing Magazine 354
Stock Market, The 562
Stock Options 562
Stock Photos 562
Stock Pile, Inc. 563
Stock Shop, The 563
Stock Solution, The 563
Stockhouse, Inc., The 564
Stockphotos Inc. 564
Stone & Adler, Inc. 64
Stone and Associates, Morton B. 64
Stone Wall Press 147
Storyville Records AB 515
Straight 355
Strain, The 355
Street & Smith's College Prep Basketball 355
Street & Smith's Pro Basketball 356
Stremmel & Co., David H. 64
Student Lawyer 426
Success Magazine 356
Successful Farming 487
Successful Meetings 487
Summit 356
Summit Photofile 564
Sun 222
Sun, The 356
Sunday (see Chicago Tribune Magazine 205)
Sunflower, The 426
Sunprint Cafe & Gallery 196
Sunshine Artists USA 487
Sunshine: The Magazine of South Florida 222
SUNY Plattsburgh Art Museum 196
Suomen Kuvapalvelu Oy 565
Supermarket News 487
Superstock Inc./Superstock Catalog 565
Surfing Magazine/Bodyboarding Magazine 356
Surgical Technologist, The 426
Swain Productions, Inc., Hack 55
Swanson, Russell and Associates 78
Symmes Systems 147
Symphony 427
Syracuse Cultural Workers 243

T

Take Stock Inc. 565
Talco Productions 94
Tampa Bay Magazine 357
Tank Incorporated 565
Tank Talk 427
Tansky Advertising Co., Ron 45
Tattoo Advocate Journal 357
Taurus Photos Inc. 566
Tavern Sports International 357
Teaching Today 488
Team Magazine 427
Teens Today 357
Tel–Air Interests, Inc. 56

Telecommunications 488
Telegraph Colour Library 566
Telephoto 566
Tele-Press Associates, Inc. 95
Tempe Records 515
Ten Best of the West 577
Tennesse Sportsman (see Game & Fish Publications 291)
Tennis Industry 488
Tennis Magazine 357
Tennis Week 358
Terraphotographics/BPS 566
Test & Measurement World 488
Texas Fish & Game 358
Texas Fisherman Magazine 358
Texas Game & Fish (see Game & Fish Publications 291)
Texas Gardener 358
Texas Highways 359
Textile Rental Magazine 427
Thanatos 359
Theosophical Publishing House 148
Thiel College 169
Thinking Families Magazine 359
Third Coast Stock Source 567
Third World 359
30th Annual Naval and Maritime Photo Contest 577
Thomas, Inc., Martin 106
Thompson & Associates, Inc., Pierce 75
Thompson USA, J. Walter 57
Thorndike Press 148
Thoroughbred Record 488
Thoroughbred Times 489
Three Rivers Arts Festival 577
THT Inc. Marketing & Advertising 75
Thunder Bay Magazine 360
Tide Mark Press 243
Tidepool Gallery 196
Timeless Records 516
Times Journal 222
Tinory Productions, Rik 516
T-Jaye Record Co. 516
Tobol Group, Inc. 86
Today's Trucking 489
Top Producer 490
Tops News 169
Touch of Success Photo Seminars 585
Touchstone Gallery 196
Tourist Attractions and Parks 490
Tow-Age 490
Towing & Recovery Trade News 490
Townships Sun, The 222
TQ 360
TR Productions 71
Track and Field News 360
Tradeswoman Magazine 490
Trailblazer Magazine 428
Trailer Boats Magazine 361
Trailer Life 361

Trails-A-Way 361
Training: The Magazine of Human Resources Development 491
Trains Magazine 361
Transitions Abroad 362
Transportation Trails 148
Transtar Productions, Inc. 50
Travel & Leisure 362
Travel Image, The 567
Travel Photo International 567
Travel Photography Workshop 585
Travel/Holiday 363
Treasure 363
Treasure Chest 491
Treasure Search/Found 363
Tri Video Teleproduction—Lake Tahoe 78
Triathlete Magazine 364
Trinity Alps Photography Workshops 585
Trinity Foundation, The 148
Triple X Management 516
Tropical Fish Hobbyist Magazine 364
Trot 428
Trout 428
Truckers News 491
Truckstop World 491
True West 364
Trumpet Club, The/Bantam/Doubleday/Dell 148
T-Shirt Gallery Ltd. 169
TSW/Afterimage, Inc. 568
Tucker Wayne/Luckie & Co. 57
Turkey Call 429
Turn-Ons, Turn-On Letters, Uncensored Letters, Options, Beau 364
TV Guide 364
Twin Falls Nature Photography Workshops 585
Twins Magazine 365
2M Communications Ltd. 149
Tyndale House Publishers 149

U

Ultra Magazine 365
Unicorn Stock Photo Library 568
UNIMAR 64
Union Institute 171
Unisource 87
United Arts 492
United Evangelical Action 429
U.S. Industrial Film and Video Festival 577
U.S. Naval Institute Proceedings 491
U.S. Souvenir & Novelty Company 171
Unity 365
Univelt, Inc. 149
Univercity 223
Universal Training Systems Co. 60
University of Arizona 196
University of California Extension Photography Workshops 585

Can't find a listing? Check at the end of each market section for the " '90-'91 Changes" lists. These lists include any market listings from the '90 edition which were either not verified or deleted in this edition.

University of Nevada 585
University of New Haven 171
University of Redlands 171
University of Tampa 171
Up Here 365
Upham Gallery 197
Upstate Magazine 223
USL Union Art Galley 197
Utah Holiday Magazine 366
Utility and Telephone Fleets 492
Utility Construction and Maintenance 492
Utne Reader 366

V

V.F.W. Magazine 429
Vacarro Productions Inc., Mike 516
Vac-U-Max 172
Vagabond Creations, Inc. 244
Vail Magazine 366
Van Enck Design Limited, Walter 172
Van Leer Associates International, G.W. 64
Van Sant, Dugdale & Company, Inc. 70
Varitel Video 48
Vegetarian Times 366
VeloNews 223
Ventura County & Coast Reporter 223
Venture 366
Vermont Business Magazine 492
Vermont Life 366
Vermont Magazine 367
Veterinary Learning Systems 492
Victimology: An International Journal 367
Victimology, Inc. 149
Video I-D, Inc. 61
Video Imagery 45
Video International Publishers, Inc. 77
Video Software 493
Videosmith, Inc. 105
Virginia Wildlife 429
Virginian Magazine, The 367
Viridian Gallery 197
Virtue Magazine 368
Vision Gallery Inc. 198
Vision Magazine 368
VisionQuest Photographic Adventures 585
Visions of U.S. 577
Visions of U.S. Home Video Competition 577
Visions Photo, Inc. 568
Visual Horizons 87
Visual Images West, Inc. 568
Visual Studies Workshop Gallery 198
Visuals 569
Visuals Unlimited 569
VM & SD (Visual Merchandising and Store Design) 493
Voice of South Marion 368
Volk Company, The John 64
Volkswagen's World 430
Volleyball Monthly 368
Voyager International 223

W

Waldbillig & Besteman, Inc. 117
Walker Agency 37

Wallack & Wallack Advertising Inc. 87
Wallcoverings Magazine 493
Waller, Cook & Misamore Advertising & Public Relations 73
Walls & Ceilings Magazine 493
Wang in the News 493
War Cry, The 430
Ward Gallery, A. Montgomery 199
Ward's Auto World 494
Warne Marketing & Communications 117
Warner Advertising, Inc., Harold 87
Warner Books 150
Warner Nature Photo Workshops, Mark 585
Warner Press, Inc. 244
Washington Blade, The 224
Washington Post Magazine 369
Washington, The Evergreen State Magazine 369
Washingtonian 369
Washington-Oregon Game & Fish (see Game & Fish Publications 291)
Waste Age Magazine 430
Water Scooter 369
Water Skier, The 430
Water Well Journal 494
Waterway Guide 369
Watt, Roop & Co. 100
WDS Forum 224
Weatherstock 569
Weekend with Ron Sanford, A 585
Weight Watchers 370
Weiser, Inc., Samuel 150
West Stock, Inc. 570
West Virginia Game & Fish (see Game & Fish Publications 291)
Westart 224
Western and English Fashions 494
Western Flyer 224
Western Heritage Awards 577
Western Horseman 370
Western Outdoors 370
Western Producer Prairie Books 150
Western Producer, The 225
Western Sportsman 370
Westlight 570
Westways 371
WFCD Communicator 430
Wheelings 371
Wheetley Company, Inc., The 150
Where Magazine 371
White Advertising, Roger 88
White Productions, Inc., Dana 46
Wichita Eagle, The 225
Widdicombe, Derek G. 570
Wieser & Wieser, Inc. 150
Wild Horizons, Inc. 585
Wilderness Photography Expeditions 585
Wildlife Conservation Magazine 371
Wildlife Photography 431
John Wiley & Sons, Inc. 151
Williams Power Pix, S & I 571
Williams/McIntosh & Associates, Inc. 38
Williamson, Alix B. 516
Wilson Library Bulletin 494
Windham Hill Productions, Inc. 517
Windsor This Month 371
Wine Tidings 372
Wines & Vines 495
Wings West 495

Winning! 372
Wire Technology International 495
Wisconsin 225
Wisconsin Restaurateur, The 495
Wisconsin Sportsman 372
Wisconsin Trails 244, 372
Wisconsin Trails Books 151
With 373
Witkin Gallery, Inc., The 199
Wolf, Blumberg, Krody 100
Wolf Mansfield Bolling Advertising Inc. 88
Wolff Associates 88
Woman Bowler 431
Woman Engineer 373
Woman's World 373
Women's Sports and Fitness Magazine 374
Womenwise 431
Woodall Publishing, Company 151
Woodenboat Magazine 375
Woodmen of the World 431
Woodshop News 496
Woodstock Gallery of Art 199
Woodstock Photography Workshops 585
Worcester Center for Crafts 199
Worcester Polytechnic Institute 172
Word Publishing 151
Work Boat, The 496
Workbench Magazine 375
Working Gallery, The 199
World Encounter 433
World of Wheels Magazine 375
World View-Fototheek BV 571
World Wide Pictures 75
World Wildlife Fund/The Conservation Foundation 172
Worldwide Press Agency 571

Worldwide Television News (WTN) 53
Wrestling World 375
Writer's Digest/Writer's Yearbook 496
Writers Publishing Service Co. 152
Wustum Museum of Fine Arts, Charles A. 200
Wyatt Advertising and Public Relations, Evans 113
Wyoming Rural Electric News 433
Wyse Advertising 100

Y

Yachtsman 225
Yankee Publishing, Inc. 375
Yearbook Associates 173
Yellow Jersey Publications 376
Yellow Silk: Journal of Erotic Arts 376
Yellowstone Institute 585
YM 376
Young Children 433
Young Fashions Magazine 496
Your Health 376
Your Health & Fitness 497
Your Home 376

Z

Zachry Associates, Inc. 113
Zaia Photovision Workshops, Joseph 585
Zefa Zentrale Farbbild Agentur Gmbh 571
Zelman Studios, Ltd. 88
Zephyr Pictures 572
Zoetrope Productions, Dudley 105
Zone VI Workshop 585

Can't find a listing? Check at the end of each market section for the " '90-'91 Changes" lists. These lists include any market listings from the '90 edition which were either not verified or deleted in this edition.

OTHER PHOTOGRAPHY BOOKS
TO HELP YOU TAKE &
SELL YOUR PHOTOS

Lighting Secrets for the
Professional Photographer
Alan Brown, Tim Grondin, & Joe Braun
Create more dynamic photographs when you use this "problem/solution" approac
to special lighting tricks and techniques. 144 pages/300 color illus./$22.95, paperbac

How to Shoot
Stock Photos that Sell
Michal Heron
Features 25 specific and unique stock photo assignments to help photographe
shoot what the market needs most. Plus advice on production techniques, marketin
negotiating and many more tips to help you become a success. 160 pages/30 b&
photos/$16.95, paperback

How to Sell Your Photographs
& Illustrations
Elliott & Barbara Gordon
Photographers and illustrators can increase their freelance income with the prove
techniques, procedures and formulas this book offers. 128 pages/24 b&w photo
$16.95, paperback

The Photographer's Guide
to Marketing & Self-Promotion
Maria Piscopo
Here's everything you need to know to plan and execute your own personalized sel
promotion campaign and sell more of your photos. 128 pages/29 color, 12 b&w ph
tos/$16.95, paperback

Sell & Re-Sell Your Photos
Rohn Engh
Takes you step by step through the process of selling your photos by mail, using th
right technique for each market. Plus advice on taxes, recordkeeping and marketin
368 pages/40 b&w photos/$16.95

Developing the Creative Edge in Photography
Bert Eifer
Turn average pictures into stunning photographs with Eifer's step-by-step techniques, including how to *see* photographically and create mood and emotion. 233 pages/45 color, 34 b&w photos/$16.95, paperback

How to Shoot & Sell Animal Photos
Walter Chandoha
Top animal photographer reveals his secrets for achieving irresistible results when working with animal models. 144 pages/65 color, 85 b&w photos/$15.95, paperback

Annual Market Books

Artist's Market, edited by Lauri Miller $21.95
Children's Writer's & Illustrator's Market, edited by Lisa Carpenter $15.95, paperback
Humor & Cartoon Markets, edited by Bob Staake $15.95, paperback
Novel & Short Story Writer's Market, edited by Robin Gee $18.95, paperback
Poet's Market, by Judson Jerome $19.95
Songwriter's Market, edited by Mark Garvey $19.95
Writer's Market, edited by Glenda Tennant Neff $24.95

To order books directly from the publisher, include $3.00 postage and handling for one book, $1.00 for each additional book. Allow 30 days for delivery. Send to: Writer's Digest Books, 1507 Dana Avenue, Cincinnati, Ohio 45207. Credit card orders call TOLL-FREE 1-800-289-0963. Prices subject to change without notice.

Copyright Law & Work for Hire

Photographers should know that under the Copyright Act of 1976, section 101, a "work for hire" is defined as:

1) **a work prepared by an employee within the scope of his or her employment; or**

2) **a work . . .**
   - **specially ordered or commissioned for use as a contribution to a collective work***
   - **as part of a motion picture or audiovisual work***
   - **as a translation**
   - **as a supplementary work***
   - **as a compilation**
   - **as an instructional text**
   - **as a test**
   - **as answer material for a test**
   - **as an atlas**

. . . if the parties expressly agree in a written instrument signed by them that the work shall be considered a work made for hire.

NOTE: The asterisk (*) denotes categories within the Copyright Law which apply to photography.